Clinical Neuroscience

Clinical Neuroscience

Psychopathology and the Brain

SECOND EDITION

KELLY G. LAMBERT
Randolph–Macon College

CRAIG H. KINSLEY
University of Richmond

NEW YORK   OXFORD
OXFORD UNIVERSITY PRESS
2011

Oxford University Press, Inc., publishes works that further Oxford University's objective of excellence in research, scholarship, and education.

Oxford New York
Auckland Cape Town Dar es Salaam Hong Kong Karachi
Kuala Lumpur Madrid Melbourne Mexico City Nairobi
New Delhi Shanghai Taipei Toronto

With offices in
Argentina Austria Brazil Chile Czech Republic France Greece
Guatemala Hungary Italy Japan Poland Portugal Singapore
South Korea Switzerland Thailand Turkey Ukraine Vietnam

For titles covered by Section 112 of the U.S. Higher Education Opportunity Act, please visit www.oup.com/us/he for the latest information about pricing and alternate formats.

Published by Oxford University Press, Inc.
198 Madison Avenue, New York, NY 10016
http://www.oup.com

Library of Congress Cataloging-in-Publication Data

Lambert, Kelly.
  Clinical neuroscience/Kelly Lambert, Craig Kinsley.—2nd ed.
    p. ; cm.
  Includes bibliographical references and indexes.
  ISBN 978-0-19-973705-5 (paper : alk. paper) 1.
Neuropsychiatry, 2. Neurobiology. 3. Neurosciences. 4. Clinical
neuropsychology. I. Kinsley, Craig H. II. Title.
  [DNLM: 1. Mental Disorders—physiopathology. 2. Brain—
physiopathology. 3. Neurosciences—methods. WM 140 L222c
2011]
Rc341.L34 2011
616.8—dc22   2010021455

Printing number: 9 8 7 6 5 4 3 2 1

Printed in the United States of America
on acid-free paper

KGL: *For my mother, Glenda Arnold Pitts (1942–1996), whose valiant fight against a terminal illness inspired me to learn more about the resilience of the human mind.*

CHK: *To my family, past and present, for molding me and for defining joy for me*

Brief Contents

Contents

PART IV

Maintaining Homeostasis

Preface

THE NEED FOR CLINICAL NEUROSCIENCE

A major challenge for neuroscientists today is the translation of basic research findings, such as those that begin as presentations at the *Society for Neuroscience* meeting and then move through peer review to publication, into applied clinical approaches to treating brain disorders and mental illness. At the same time, however, mental-health practitioners—those on the front lines of mental health delivery—must acquire broad-based knowledge of neurobiology, behavior, and environment if they hope to understand the difference between adaptive and maladaptive neural functions. Molecular outcomes of drugs with equal clinical efficacy, for example, sometimes employ very different modes of action, depending on the underlying systems affected.

Another question practitioners struggle with is the value of the mental health diagnostic categories that are presented in this text. For instance, it may be more parsimonious to treat symptoms rather than mental illness labels, especially, as you'll learn in Chapter 1, when there is considerable overlap in the symptoms for two completely different diagnostic categories.

Although considerable progress has been made in laboratories across the world, significant challenges face practitioners and scientists working in the field of clinical neuroscience. To address these challenges, the National Institute of Mental Health (NIMH) awards translational research grants to encourage collaboration between neuroscientists and mental health professionals. Such collaborations facilitate the construction of a "clinical neuroscience" that converts data into treatments more rapidly for in-need patients.

By 2025, depression is forecast to become the second leading illness in the United States (McEwen & Lashley, 2002). A meta-analysis published in *Psychological Science in the Public Interest* explored the response rates of depressed patients to various treatment modalities. Consider the treatment implications of these results. Interpersonal therapy rates are equally as effective as antidepressant drugs in reducing typical symptoms associated with depression. Further, 30 percent of respondents who received a placebo treatment reported improvement; see Figure 1.1 on page 5 (Hollon, Thase, & Markowitz, 2002).

Research emphasizing methodological challenges in antidepressant research had little impact on the public's trust in these drugs as the number of Americans taking antidepressants doubled from 1996 to 2005 (increasing from 13.3 million to 27 million consumers). A recent article in *Newsweek* magazine echoed the findings of several researchers suggesting that antidepressants are no more effective than placebos. Science writer Sharon Begley ended the article with the discouraging realization that the scientific evidence supporting treatments such as antidepressants just isn't that important to most people (Begley, 2010).

Thus, in addition to the importance of clinical neuroscience research to address the unmet needs of individuals suffering from various mental illnesses, education about the importance of empirically-based mental health therapies is necessary to educate the public about the most effective treatment strategies. The clinical neuroscience course is a first-step toward addressing these important mental health issues—motivating students to conduct relevant research in the area of clinical neuroscience and reinforcing the value of empirically-based approaches to future mental health practitioners and consumers. Recent attention directed toward former Playboy model and MTV celebrity Jenny McCarthy for authoritative advice on the causes and treatments for autism certainly support the notion that empirical evidence is less important than personal experiences when it comes to selecting the most effective therapies for mental illnesses. As you'll read in Chapter 1, as treatment strategies stray from methodologically sound experimental studies providing solid empirical evidence, the results can be disastrous.

THE GENESIS OF THIS BOOK

We designed a new course called Clinical Neuroscience for our students, before we found a book for the course. We managed to find several impressive general interest books and edited volumes, but we found no suitable single textbook that integrated neurobiological mechanisms of mental health into the coverage of disorders that was readable, affordable, and comprehensive. We decided to write that textbook. We sincerely hope it satisfies the need.

We have conducted extensive reviews of all the subject matter in this book and include novel interpretations and explanations. *Clinical Neuroscience* is a resource for anyone interested in an integrative, empirically based approach to mental health and for anyone who seeks to draw connections among courses offered in departments of psychology, biology, and neuroscience—the intersection of a modern psychology.

Initially, we envisioned the courses that we were designing within a psychology curriculum, specifically for upper-level undergraduates who had a prerequisite in basic biological psychology. Fittingly, practice informed our theory: In teaching the course we discovered that students benefited from a unit on neurobiology and neurochemistry, and we have added that unit as Part II of the book. With this addition, a biological psychology prerequisite is not necessary, but it may be complementary and certainly useful. Because of the text's inclusion of more basic neurobiological information, this book may also be used in a nontraditional biology or psychology course.

AND THE AUDIENCE

Clinical Neuroscience will be of value to upper-level undergraduate courses in clinical and counseling psychology, as well as elective courses focusing on topics related to the neurobiology of mental illness in psychology and biology major courses. Momentum gathers to prepare clinicians for the possibility of gaining prescription privileges (a practice already approved in New Mexico and Louisiana and likely to spread to other states); here, Clinical

Neuroscience's value is clear. Further, the chasm separating psychology from biology—especially as it relates to brain regulation of mental activity—is growing smaller. The current volume will introduce even the most diehard dualist to evidence that the brain must be considered in all discussions of clinical treatments.

This text represents the culmination of decades'-long conversations with our neuroscientist colleagues at conferences, extensive reading of the neurobiology literature, and our own personal research. Since writing the first edition of this text, we are now more convinced than ever that clinical neuroscience is emerging not just as a course, but as a burgeoning field. Reviewers have elucidated the need for both separate courses and advanced seminars in clinical neuroscience. We believe this book will benefit neuroscience students as a reference as they navigate through their coursework and can also help them to keep an eye on applications—how neuroscience can benefit its subjects—thereby increasing the likelihood of translating the basic research into positive real-world outcomes.

As another example of accelerating treatments from lab to clinic, the medical student will also benefit from the book's integrative, medical-model approach to mental health. That avenue is appropriate for post-graduate audiences (such as internship-level faculty) as they prepare to move into mental health careers. By allowing instructors to draw connections between basic neuroscience and mental health applications, *Clinical Neuroscience* is equally appropriate for neuroscience students. Building bridges between and among formerly disparate sub-disciplines will hasten beneficial applications.

CHANGES TO THE NEW EDITION

- A new chapter on traumatic and chronic brain injury that emphasizes traditionally viewed neurobiological disorders such as TBI and Parkinson's Disease

- Existing content has been updated with hundreds of new references

- New color insert gives students a better sense of the visual complexity of the brain and related issues in the text

FORMAT OF TEXT

Because clinical approaches are an emerging area within the broad field of neuroscience, we put considerable thought into the identification, organization, and categorization of the topics covered in the text. Although diagnostic criteria from the *Diagnostic and Statistical Manual* (DSM) *IV-TR* (and its newer variant) were included as a reference for students for some conditions, we do not always follow the DSM categorizations (in part, due to their inherent vagueness and hand-waving imprecision). The structure of the text is as follows:

PART I: Foundations of Clinical Neuroscience

Chapter   1   Emergence of Clinical Neuroscience

Chapter   2   Research, Treatment, and Points of View: Historical Perspectives

The introductory chapters include historical and contemporary overviews of theories and therapies in the mental health field. They establish a need for the more integrative, empirically based discipline of clinical neuroscience, emphasizing the scientific method. Various disciplines (e.g., psychology, psychiatry, neurology, chemistry, basic research) and their unique perspectives are also addressed; it becomes increasingly apparent that their once unique boundaries are becoming less distinct. Finally, a description of these many perspectives, or levels of analysis, in *Clinical Neuroscience* sets the stage for the multifaceted approach in the text.

PART II: Fundamentals: Establishing Homeostasis

Many students may already have some experience with the basics of neural structure and function. These early chapters, then, will allow for a brief review for those students and for initial exposure to the basics of nervous function for the uninitiated. The inclusion of pedagogical components that relate directly to the field of clinical neuroscience will enable students to see direct connections between the basic information about the underlying "wet" tissue, and its regulation and dysregulation in the manifestation of the human's so-called "mental health and life." For example, neurodegenerative and cognitive processing disorders (such as Alzheimer's and attention deficit hyperactivity disorder) are included in the neurodevelopment chapter to show a direct link between basic mechanisms and the overt conditions they produce.

PART III: Disruptions of Homeostasis: Representative Clinical Disorders

In this text, mental disorders are viewed as disruptions of homeostasis/ allostasis, departures from endogenous averages and predisposed physiological coping strategies. As the internal milieu is disrupted, the teeter totters when it should not, the nervous system's attempt to compensate sometimes leads to extreme conditions that are classified as mental disorders. We have included traumatic brain injury and Parkinson's disease in Chapter 7 (a new chapter in this edition!), obsessive-compulsive disorder and Tourette syndrome in Chapter 8 (Disorders of Anxiety); major depression and bipolar disorder in Chapter 9 (Mood Disorders); and, as implied, schizophrenia and addiction are the sole disorders for Chapters 10 and 11, respectively. Although other disorders fit in these categories, a decision was made to include in-depth coverage of representative disorders within the categories rather than skim over every disorder included in the DSM. As mentioned, other disorders are presented in various chapters; for example, phobias are discussed in Chapter 1 and posttraumatic stress disorder (PTSD) is covered in Chapter 12. If instructors want to include disorders not covered in this text, supplemental readings can be used or, as we do in our classes, these disorders can be assigned for student papers and presentations.

PART IV: Maintaining Homeostasis

Chapter 12   Stress and Coping

Chapter 13   Psychoneuroimmunology

Chapter 14   Eating Regulation and Associated Disorders

Just as national conversations currently debate the most effective approaches for dispensing health services to the public, we place an emphasis in *Clinical Neuroscience* on the most effective strategies for maintaining mental health, so-called mental health homeostasis. There is overwhelming evidence that stress is a major factor in many mental disorders, prompting us to include stress and coping as a separate chapter (12) in this section. Terms such as *psychoneuroimmunology*, the topic of Chapter 13, convey the interdisciplinary relationship inherent in psychological processes, neurobiology, and immunology. It is important for students to understand this network and its web-like interactions early in their academic careers. That the nervous system intermingles with the immune system provides compelling evidence that the immune system may play a critical role in mental health. Finally, the body's various foods serve as the brain's fuel and as the source of its raw materials; consequently, eating practices as well as the food we ingest are also intertwined with physical and mental health. We therefore cover the neurobiological mechanisms of hunger motivation and regulation, and their disruption, in Chapter 14. Such material is substrate for a discussion of potential causes and treatments of obesity (although not usually considered a mental disorder) and eating disorders.

Epilogue

The explosion in neuroscience data and information has presented scientists and practitioners with challenging ethical questions and moral dilemmas. For example, should embryonic stem cells be used to repair the faulty mechanisms that regulate such neurodegenerative diseases as Parkinson's disease? Should society treat criminals differently if (or when) neuroscience finds that underlying brain mechanisms for such behavior are malfunctioning? How should information from the human genome project be used to develop treatments for various mental illnesses? Although therapeutic progress is being made within clinical neuroscience-related disciplines, many issues remain controversial; accordingly, this chapter should stimulate necessary discussion about the future use of the data arising from the study of the brain. The field is far from definitive answers on these ethical conundrums, but we must begin to think about and address them: the neurobiology of human behavior is becoming clearer, with all of its implications. Students today, the professionals of tomorrow, must be equipped to make the right decisions about the issues raised here and in other contexts. We are hopeful that *Clinical Neuroscience* is one such aid.

CENTRAL THEMES IN THE TEXT

Empirical, scientific rigor. As you read this text we hope that it is apparent that only valid and empirical information is considered as conclusions about mechanisms and treatments for mental illnesses are evaluated. That is, observable, replicable data from largely well-designed experiments and legitimate, peer-reviewed sources are described so that informed decisions can be made about the meaningfulness of such data. Although the field of mental health is rich with introspective approaches that are not amenable to scientific rigor, such approaches are not considered in this text. Throughout *Clinical Neuroscience,* the efficacy of putative and speculative treatments are critically analyzed based on the strength of their empirical evidence. In this regard, claims concerning mechanisms or treatment of certain disorders are held to the same scientific standard as any other neurobiological topic.

Multiple perspectives. The field of mental health has been dominated by the view that pharmaceutical intervention and talking therapies are the most effective modes of treatment (since the beginning of the 20th century, that is). Other approaches are discussed in this text as being relevant for understanding and treating the many mental disorders that plague our society (as they both affect the brain). Psychotherapy (e.g., interpersonal therapy), behavioral therapy, brain stimulation, developmental intervention, immunomodulation, and dietary modifications are among the various treatment approaches that are considered in this text, with their plusses and minuses. Causes and treatments are also considered from an evolutionary perspective, as our present is dictated by our ever-more-distant past. We believe that there are multiple inroads to understanding the brain; it is likely that these paths can be best traveled by practitioners schooled in and familiar with various treatment strategies.

A mind/brain–body balance. By including the section on maintaining homeostatic processes (Chapters 12, 13, and 14), we emphasize our observations that the boundaries between the brain and other areas of the body are becoming less distinctive. We include a chapter on psychoneuroimmunology to indicate the intimate relationship between the nervous and immune systems and how disruptions of this communication may lead to a host of illnesses ranging from the flu to depression. Our pattern of eating also influences many aspects of our mental and emotional lives and should be a variable in any mental health equation. Reactive stress responses represent extensive cross talk between the brain and the body and play an essential role in maintaining overall homeostasis. Further, the observation that 30% of patients respond to a placebo treatment provides additional support for the importance of serious examination of the mind/brain–body relationship in mental health training.

Animal models and clinical trials. Because humans are so complex and difficult to study in many domains, animal models are a valuable tool for learning about the brain. When conducted appropriately, the use of animal models serves as a critical step to other species, including humans. Such models provide insights into the human condition (and ironically, into the animals that are subjects, improving their care as well). For these reasons, appropriate animal models are discussed in *Clinical Neuroscience*. When available and well done, clinical trials with humans are certainly discussed to give students a thorough understanding of the research that has been conducted in those areas, but the foundation of clinical neuroscience, its history and future, still depends strongly on animal neuroscience models.

No easy solutions. The field of clinical neuroscience is awash in data. Although it is tempting to skip through all the meaningful research so that we can present only simplistic answers to complex questions, it is a disservice to the millions of individuals who have or will suffer from some of the conditions described herein. The complexity of these issues demands complex and thoughtful answers. Accordingly, we have attempted to provide representative responses to the difficult and, in many cases, controversial questions posed throughout this text. Thus, various facets and nuances of the issues are discussed, leaving the reader with the impression that few clear answers exist concerning many aspects of mental health neuroscience (but also gives students the chance to make up their own minds about them). Unanswered and difficult questions (scientific and ethical) are characteristic of a field such as clinical neuroscience, which is amassing immense stockpiles of information but is slow to use the information to solve real-world human problems. A goal of this text is to inspire talented and curious students to go into research areas that may one day enable them to uncover and deliver some of the desperately needed mental health solutions of clinical neuroscience to the individuals so in need of them.

PEDAGOGICAL ELEMENTS

Although we both have an insatiable curiosity about the neurobiology of behavior that keeps us busy in our laboratories with our students, being professors at liberal arts institutions for the last twenty years means also that we are passionate about effectively teaching these exciting topics to our students. We are, therefore, committed to providing effective pedagogical elements for this material. The narrative running throughout the text is presented in a story-like fashion, building from the classic studies marking the conception of various research areas to the latest research on each topic. Which reminds us of a story ourselves: the author of an introductory psychology text writes that he was approached by a waitress while working on his book. Upon finding out that her customer was writing a book, she asked if he was writing a book with a story, or the "other kind." The author replied that he was writing the other kind, and she said simply "oh," and quickly walked away, displaying a lack of curiosity in such obviously dull material (Fernald, 1997). We are hopeful that by presenting information in an engaging manner (including many well-developed analogy frameworks), we can facilitate interest in and retention of the substantive material for the clinical neuroscience student. These stories are not devoid of pertinent content, however. Each chapter is peppered with the most meaningful, relevant research that, from our perspective, represents the past and current status of the field.

In sum, it is our hope that *Clinical Neuroscience* will be a solid and "other kind" of text for interested students.

Pedagogical elements include an opening vignette, called *Connections,* for each chapter that highlights connections between a clinical or applied observation and a related program of basic research. Additionally, chapters include case studies, titled *A Case in Point,* to help students associate human faces with the disorders covered. Students will be able to follow diagnostic and treatment paths of patients that result in varying rates of success.

Other topics of interest are referred to as *Brain Matters*. Although we are careful not to distract the students from the text, we feel that it is important to provide related, though not integral, subjects to introduce students to the breadth of the clinical neuroscience field. Some examples include the role of religion in early mental illness perceptions; areas of the brain involved in laughter; eating and stress; increasing evidence linking football injuries to brain damage; and the relationship between baseball rituals and obsessive-compulsive disorder.

Finally, to enhance learning of key information, important terms are presented in **bold type** and defined in the margins for the reader. A glossary of these terms appears at the end of the text. A summary of key points is included at the end of each chapter as well as a listing of the key terms and their page numbers. A section titled *For Further Consideration* is a summary of recommended readings and accompanying brief descriptions for students who wish to pursue particular topics further.

SUPPLEMENTS

As instructors, we know the importance of good supplements complementary to the text and its material. We are pleased to be able to offer the following material to assist you in your teaching of *Clinical Neuroscience.*

Instructor's Resources and Test Bank *by Joe Morrissey and R. Adam Franssen, State University of New York-Binghamton.* The *Instructor's Resources* feature chapter-by-chapter topic overviews and learning objectives, thorough chapter summaries, in-class demonstrations and activities, suggested topics to launch class discussions, ideas for research and term paper projects, homework assignments and exercises, and a list of additional reading material for students looking to enhance their knowledge of the topics covered in each chapter.

The comprehensive test bank contains more than 800 multiple-choice, true/false, fill-in, and essay questions. The questions include a wide variety of applied, conceptual, and factual questions. Each question is ranked according to difficulty and keyed to the topic and page in the text where the source information appears. The test bank files are also available in Microsoft Word (on request).

ACKNOWLEDGMENTS

The content of any textbook is enhanced by the careful eyes of colleagues and critics, who offer valuable suggestions for improvements and clarifications of material; in the end, however, any and all errors are the responsibility of the authors. We are very grateful to the following reviewers for their expertise, input, and willingness to help with this edition:

Jennifer Harned Adams,
University of Colorado at Denver

Greg Crosby,
Maryhurst University

Alan Kim Johnson,
University of Iowa

David Pittman,
Wofford College

Gretchen Dahl Reeves,
Eastern Michigan University

Daniel G. Webster,
Georgia Southern University

We would also like to acknowledge the reviewers of the first edition:

Theresa Barber,
Dickinson College

Elizabeth Byrnes,
Tufts University School of Veterinary Medicine

Bryan Castelda,
Binghamton University

Judith Horowitz,
Medaille College

Craig Johnson,
Towson University

Sabra Klein,
Johns Hopkins University

Phyllis Mann,
Tufts University School of Veterinary Medicine

William McDaniel,
Georgia College and State University

Tibor Palfai,
Syracuse University

Beth Powell,
Smith College

Lawrence Ryan,
Oregon State University

Don Stein,
Emory University

Elayne Thompson,
William Rainey Harper College

Nutan Vaidya,
The Rosalind Franklin University of Medicine and Science

Sara White,
Binghamton University

In addition, we interviewed many scientists and laypeople alike to round out our coverage of the diverse topics in *Clinical Neuroscience* and to add stories and human faces to the conditions we describe. We are grateful to the following people for taking the time to speak with us, either in person or electronically, sharing personal stories as well as professional triumphs and disappointments.

The scientists:

Robert Ader,
University of Rochester

Russell Barkley,
Medical University of South Carolina

Keith Black,
Cedars Sinai Medical Center, California

Robert Bridges,
Tufts University School of Veterinary Medicine

Kelly Brownell,
Yale University

Patrick Brunden,
Lund University

Sue Carter,
University of Illinois at Chicago

Sonia Cavigelli,
Pennsylvania State University

Maribeth Champoux,
National Institutes of Health

Anna Rose Childress,
University of Pennsylvania

Michael Davis,
Emory University

Courtney DeVries,
Ohio State University

Mort Doran,
Canada

Casimer Fornal,
Princeton University

Eberhard Fuchs,
German Primate Center

Kim Huhman,
Georgia State University

Thomas Insel,
National Institute of Mental Health

Barry Jacobs,
Princeton University

Kay Redfield Jamison,
Washington DC

Hendree Jones,
Johns Hopkins University

Eric Kandel,
Columbia University

Sabra Klein,
Johns Hopkins University

Paul MacLean,
National Institute of Mental Health

Phyllis Mann,
Tufts University School of Veterinary Medicine

Paul McHugh,
Johns Hopkins University

Kenneth Pilgreen,
Louisiana State

Stephen Porges,
University of Illinois at Chicago

Judith Rapoport,
National Institute of Mental Health

Paul Rozin,
University of Pennsylvania

Ronald Ruden,
Yaffe Ruden and Associates, New York

Oliver Sacks,
New York

Jeffrey Schwartz,
UCLA

Robert Sapolsky,
Stanford University

Elaine Walker,
Emory University

Daniel Weinberger,
National Institute of Mental Health

The true pioneers in Clinical Neuroscience who shared their personal stories with us:

Deb Bahr, Nadean Cool, Joseph Dee, Sara Hunicutt, Evan Handler, Caroline Kettlewell, Brett Nielsen, Augusto Odone, Karyn Seroussi, Katherine Sherwood, Andrew Solomon, Davis and Carol Bailey "Andy," our interviewee with schizophrenia.

The authors would like to thank the professionals at Oxford University Press who tended the second edition of the book: our initial acquiring editor, Patrick Lynch; our current acquisitions editor, Jane Potter; Barbara Mathieu, our production editor; assistant editor, Adam Tyrrell; our art director, Paula Schlosser, and designer, Dan Niver.

Of course, the authors would also like to thank the professionals at Worth Publishers for their work on the first edition of the book: our initial acquistions editor, Jessica Bayne, our editor Laura Pople; Barbara Brooks, our developmental editor; Tracey Kuehn, our associate managing editor; Danielle Storm, assistant editor; Danielle Pucci, media and supplements

Editor; Patricia Marx, photo research manager; Meg Kuhta, former photo editor; Nigel Assam, photo researcher; Babs Reingold, design director; Lissi Sigillo, designer and layout editor; Bill Page, senior illustration coordinator; Matthew Holt, illustrator; Sarah Segal, production manager, and Penny Hull, production editor.

Of course, in no way could we have begun and completed this project without the inspiration of our colleagues, students, and especially our families. Thank you, thank you, thank you.

Kelly Lambert would like to personally thank:

My husband, Gary Lambert, and two daughters, Lara and Skylar, for their patience and loving support throughout this project.

My brother, Doug Gurley, for both support and professional biomedical advice on topics in the book.

My colleagues in the Department of Psychology at Randolph-Macon College (R-MC) for their frequent discussions and feedback on the topics included in the book.

My extended R-MC family—Barbara Wirth, for administrative support; the R-MC reference librarians for their assistance accessing more research articles than one can imagine; Lily Zhang for technical support; and my impressive students who have provided encouragement for this project during challenging times.

Craig Kinsley would like to personally thank:

Nancy, my wife and best friend, and our lovely children, Devon and David. They understand and inspire.

My family in California: Parents Dorothy and Howard, and sisters Cathy and Carla.

My family in Northern Virginia: Shelly and Margery Lustig.

My students who have helped with many facets and details for the book, especially: Margaret Banks, Lillian Flores-Stevens, Jessica Gatewood, Abbe Hoffman-Macbeth, Kate Karelina, Rebecca Klatzkin, Lisa Madonia-Lomas, Ilan McNamara, Elizabeth Amory-Meyers, Melissa Morgan, Angela Orthmeyer, Emily Pytlik, Brandi Rima, Jennifer Wartella, Naomi Wightman.

Colleagues, friends and associates who have helped along the way: the University of Richmond, for providing an atmosphere of challenge and encouragement; my colleagues in psychology, for making me think; Martha C. Beitner, for her constant assistance and hard work; Michael M. Koller, dear friend, writer, and thinker; and Fred J. Kozub, for a decade and a half of incisive comments.

Last, the authors would like to thank each other. For the many years it has taken to assemble this book, there have been many challenging moments, stretches of frustration, and many highs and lows—to be sure, more of the former, however. Not once, though, did we lose sight of our goal of producing a work that was worthy of our coworkers' and students' faith in us. Throughout, a strong friendship grew even deeper. If fulfillment is to be found in the journey and not the destination, then these years have been a highlight of our professional lives.

About the Authors

Kelly G. Lambert received her B.S. in psychology and biology from Samford University and her M.S. and Ph.D. in biopsychology from the University of Georgia. She is currently the Macon and Joan Brock Professor and Chair of Psychology at Randolph-Macon College in Ashland, Virginia. She is the recipient of the 2001 State Council of Higher Education in Virginia's Outstanding Faculty Award and the 2008 Virginia Professor of the Year [awarded by the Council for Advancement and Support of Education (CASE) and the Carnegie Foundation for the Advancement of Teaching]. Her research focuses generally on the topic of behavior-induced neuroplasticity and more specifically on the areas of brain/behavior responses to chronic stress and the multifaceted neurobiological effects of maternal and paternal experience. Reports of her research have been published in journals such as *Stress, Nature, Behavioral Neuroscience,* and *Physiology and Behavior.* Her most recent book *The Lab Rat Chronicles: A neuroscientist reveals life lessons from the planet's most successful mammals* (Perigee; 2011) celebrates the value of animal models in the fields of clinical and behavioral neuroscience. She lives in Mechanicsville, Virginia, with her husband, Gary Lambert (an industrial/organizational psychologist), her two daughters, Lara and Skylar, and a menagerie of pets.

Craig H. Kinsley is MacEldin Trawick Professor of Neuroscience in the Department of Psychology and Center for Neuroscience at the University of Richmond, where he is surrounded by outstanding colleagues and smart, committed students. His B.A. in psychology is from the California State University, Sonoma. His Ph.D., from the University at Albany, State University of New York, is in behavioral endocrinology. After receiving his Ph.D., he was a postdoctoral fellow and instructor in neuroscience and neuroendocrinology in the Department of Cellular Biology, Laboratory of Human Reproduction and Reproductive Biology, Harvard Medical School. His research, published in such journals as *Behavioral Neuroscience, Brain Research Bulletin, Developmental Psychobiology, Hormones and Behavior,* and *Nature,* focuses on the manifest changes that occur in the maternal brain and dictate that most important of mammalian behaviors, parental care. He is happily married to Nancy, and they have two children, Devon Alyse and David William. His hobbies include his family, fishing, and music and stereo equipment.

Chapter One

Emergence of Clinical Neuroscience

Connections

Mara: Seeking Therapy

One Friday evening, Mara, Tess, Antonio, and Josh gathered at their usual table at their favorite restaurant a couple of blocks from the university. After several minutes of lighthearted banter, the conversation got serious as Mara described her recent feelings of depression. Once a confident, competent student, Mara was now experiencing self-doubt about her ability to do well on her final exams. She also said that it was an effort even to make it to class in the morning and that it had been very difficult for her to actually show up that evening—a weekly ritual that was normally the highlight of her week.

Pointing to the gyro sandwich that had just arrived, she mentioned that she didn't have a desire to eat much anymore either. Mara had read enough about the symptoms of depression to know that she was probably suffering from this condition, but all her reading had not made it clear how to choose the best treatment. Mara was desperate for advice from her trusted friends.

Josh spoke up first, mentioning the attention antidepressants like Prozac have received and suggesting that if so many people were talking about Prozac it must work. In fact, because he knew that his family physician had prescribed antidepressants for his aunt, he suggested that Mara simply visit her family physician so that she could start taking Prozac.

Tess, a psychology student, voiced her concern that, while general medical practitioners were certainly able to prescribe medication for mental illness, they received little training for the diagnosis, maintenance, and treatment of the vast majority of mental illnesses. She had been taught that antidepressants alter neurochemical processing in the brain and that everyone should approach these drugs with extreme caution.

As the son of a clinical psychologist, Antonio agreed that Mara should be cautious before taking brain-altering drugs. Because of the controversial scientific literature related to the effectiveness of antidepressant drugs, he suggested that Mara talk to his dad about cognitive therapy. Antonio said that his dad tried to coach his clients into changing their cognitive perspective and to give them strategies to develop a new approach to life's challenges—such as Mara's upcoming finals.

Mara had been reading about some of the "talk" therapies used by psychiatrists. Some still used notions introduced by Freud in their therapeutic approach. Mara's buddies agreed that the psychodynamic, or Freudian, approach was probably past its prime on the treatment scene. Josh, the aspiring physician, spoke up again, declaring that since depression was known as a brain disease, it would be best to go to a doctor specializing in the brain—a neurologist.

Mara said, "See what I mean? It's hard to know which treatment strategy is best." The scientific literature on depression she had perused consisted mainly of research in an entirely different discipline—behavioral neuroscience. But although the behavioral neuroscientists seemed to have a lot of ideas to offer concerning the treatment of mental illnesses, they were not practitioners, so they in fact were not even a treatment option.

Mara and her friends were struck by how difficult it was for patients experiencing depression to sift through all the information to select the most appropriate treatment.

Jasmine: Seeking a Profession

Jasmine, a senior premed student, found herself visiting the campus career center more often than any of her friends. Ever since she was 5 years old and her older brother experienced a brain injury after falling off his bicycle, she had been fascinated with the relationship existing among the brain, behavior, and thoughts. She wanted to spend her career pursuing this interest, but she was having difficulty identifying the most appropriate career path.

Although she had befriended the clinical psychologist who worked with her brother for so many years, she was learning that most clinical psychology curricula have few course requirements that relate behavior to the brain. After a little research, she was discovering that psychiatry wasn't too different; she could conceivably complete medical school and her specialty training with no guarantee of being a well-versed student of the brain. Thus, her desire to incorporate neuroscientific principles into a psychiatric practice seemed unlikely.

Neurology was certainly an option; completing this curriculum would ensure that Jasmine would thoroughly know the brain. However, neurology seemed to focus on patients who had suffered damage to the brain. Although this aspect fascinated Jasmine, she was interested in the healthy brain as well and in preventing some of the mental disorders (for example, depression, schizophrenia, Alzheimer's disease) haunting our society today.

After taking several neuroscience courses, Jasmine considered a graduate program in neuroscience. But she had immediate doubts about this option because of the limited opportunities to actually work with patients. Jasmine persevered as she searched for an interdisciplinary graduate program that would provide training in both the basic and applied areas of neuroscience.

Alex: Seeking Support

Alex was exhausted after battling insurance agents on the phone. His 67-year old father had been in a horrible automobile accident 9 months earlier, and now, though his wounds and broken bones had healed, his father was haunted by the memory of his accident. Alex had taken his father to his family physician, and the doctor confirmed Alex's fears that his father was suffering from posttraumatic stress disorder (PTSD).

Alex immediately started gathering information about obtaining the best care for his father, who had received excellent insurance benefits for the physical injuries suffered in the accident. Optimistic after reading about legislation approving insurance coverage for mental health conditions, Alex quickly found out that securing coverage for his dad was going to be a difficult task. To his dismay, his father's insurance company required higher deductibles for mental illnesses such as PTSD; further, his father's company did not have enough employees to benefit from the recently approved legislation extending equitable coverage for both mental and physical illnesses. Ultimately, his dad's insurance company would not approve treatment for PTSD.

Alex explained that his father was experiencing physical symptoms (increased heart rate and insomnia) and asked why the symptoms were not considered medical. Alex asked repeatedly why problems with the brain's functioning were not considered as "medical" as those associated with the rest of the body. Why, he asked, is there such a dichotomy between mental illness and physical illness? Bewildered, confused, and angry, Alex wondered what he could do to help his father.

We are defined by our brains more than any other organ in our body. The brain offers endless possibilities; when it malfunctions, however, an individual may face an unwelcome disorder, in many cases, a live-in guest for life.

The number of people suffering from mental illnesses varies; whereas schizophrenia affects about 1% of the population, the lifetime risk for depression approximates 15%, a rate similar to Alzheimer's disease in people over 65. The billions of dollars spent on mental illnesses worldwide cost our society more than any other class of disease, including cancer and cardiovascular disease (Andreasen, 2001). In fact, of the top 10 causes of disability across the world, five (major depression, alcohol use, self-inflicted injuries, manic–depressive disorder, and schizophrenia) are related to mental illness (the remaining causes are tuberculosis, road traffic accidents, war, violence, and iron-deficiency anemia) (Andreasen & Black, 2001). Although exciting research is currently being conducted in neuroscience laboratories all over the world, a cure for mental illness is still elusive.

The mental health field is dominated by unanswered questions like the ones faced by the students portrayed at the beginning of this chapter (see Connections). Patients already in compromised health wade through a sea of disjointed recommendations from diverse fields. Students find themselves unable to distinguish among the various mental health professions. Too many patients and their caregivers experience anguish beyond that imposed by the mental illness as they struggle to identify financial support to cover treatment expenses.

How can informed research scientists and practitioners devise or acquire successful treatments for mental illness? How can they work together to promote mental health? More and more, mental health professionals are viewing the brain's functioning from as many perspectives as possible, using research methodology appropriate to each point of view. Neuroscience research is revealing multiple inroads to the brain, and it is likely that the same paths can be traveled by various treatment strategies.

The purpose of this book is to focus on perspectives that have emerged from a systematic, empirical base of knowledge. First, we introduce the characters in the mental health drama—psychotherapists, neurosurgeons, neurologists, neuropsychologists, neuroscientists, behavioral scientists, and psychiatrists. These characters play various roles and contribute a diverse array of treatment strategies. Once you peel back all the layers, however, the lead actor in the mental health drama is the **empirical evidence**, scientific research that conveys objectively how specific variables influence brain function and how the brain and body interact.

Exploring how these variables—genetic, environmental, neurobiological, developmental, evolutionary, and cultural—influence our mental functioning and mental health serves as the basic approach of *Clinical Neuroscience*. It is not until we integrate these views that a true picture of mental illness, and of mental health, begins to emerge.

empirical evidence Evidence that can be confirmed by systematic observations. This evidence should play a critical role in a researcher's or practitioner's opinion of causes and treatments for certain disorders.

STATUS REPORTS ON PSYCHIATRY AND CLINICAL PSYCHOLOGY

Typically, as students consider careers in the mental health field, two professional paths emerge as possible choices: clinical psychology and psychiatry. Currently, the educational journeys to these career destinations diverge

psychotropic (psychoactive) drug Medication that influences psychological processes.

biomedical model Therapeutic approach using mostly medical diagnoses and drug prescriptions.

psychosocial model Therapeutic approach emphasizing the relationship between client, or patient, and therapist while using therapies such as behavioral therapy, interpersonal therapy, classical psychoanalysis, or group therapy.

sharply. Psychologists, for example, receive a PhD in clinical psychology and psychiatrists receive an MD and then specialize in psychiatry.

Until 2002, another defining difference in the practices of clinical psychology and psychiatry in the United States was the ability of psychiatrists to prescribe medication—a privilege not extended to clinical psychologists. This distinction, however, is changing. Bills were passed during New Mexico's legislative hearings in 2002 and in Louisiana in 2004 authorizing adequately trained psychologists (the appropriate criteria for this distinction are yet to be defined) to prescribe **psychotropic (psychoactive) drugs**, medications that influence psychological processes (American Psychological Association, 2002). Further, in 2007, bills to extend prescription privileges in nine additional states were not passed; thus, although changes have been made concerning prescribing drugs for mental health, they are progressing at an extremely slow pace (PsychCentral, 2007).

Psychiatrists and clinical psychologists are closely watching several other states in which bills calling for extending prescription privileges to clinical psychologists are pending, and they expect specific training standards for psychologists to be set by New Mexico and Louisiana. As the distinctive lines between these two disciplines grow increasingly fuzzy, each faces a distinct set of challenges: maintaining a separate identity and offering effective treatment options.

Psychiatrists determining treatment options for patients, for example, face increasing pressures from insurance companies (Hobson & Leonard, 2001). Some psychiatrists have adopted a **biomedical model**, emphasizing medical diagnoses and drug therapy. Others focus more on a **psychosocial model**, involving such treatments as behavioral therapy, cognitive-behavioral therapy, individual psychotherapy (classical psychoanalysis, interpersonal psychotherapy), group therapy, and social skills therapy. The psychosocial therapist typically directs patients toward appropriate social services and follows up on the status of each patient (Andreasen & Black, 2001).

But researchers are discovering that the biomedical model isn't necessarily more "biological" than the psychosocial approach. Investigators are just beginning to understand how strategies used in the psychosocial model actually change the brain, enabling the patient to function more normally (Andreasen & Black, 2001). The psychosocial approach is more labor-intensive however, and health-maintenance organizations (HMOs) are reluctant to reimburse the cost of hour-long sessions with each patient; they rarely cover more than 20-minute appointments, and they prefer the more cost-effective treatment option of psychotropic medication. Consequently, the more time-intensive psychosocial therapies are being conducted by less expensive psychologists, counselors, and social workers. Overriding all these developments is the fact that today most prescriptions for mental conditions are written by general practitioners, MDs who have little formal training in diagnosing and treating mental illness (Hobson & Leonard, 2001).

Dr. Judith Rapoport, chief of Child Psychiatry at the National Institute of Mental Health, reported that she is hesitant to recommend a psychiatric

Using biofeedback techniques, individuals can determine how certain thoughts influence various physiological systems. Such integration provides strong support for the intimate relationship between physiological and psychological processes.

© LEONARD LESSIN/PETER ARNOLD, INC.

residency to medical students because of this emphasis on prescription writing. In fact, American medical students are shunning psychiatry, filling fewer than one-third of the 1,200 positions for psychiatric residents in the United States in 2001. With restricted treatment options, it is becoming increasingly more difficult to attract talented students to the psychiatry specialty (Hobson & Leonard, 2001).

Adding to the turmoil within psychiatry is the looming prospect of clinical psychologists gaining prescription privileges. Psychiatrists may soon be faced with distinguishing themselves from clinical psychologists in ways other than prescription writing. Even if they maintain their monopoly on prescription privileges, research is already suggesting that drugs don't always offer the best relief for patients suffering from mental illness. In fact, a **meta-analysis** exploring the response rates of depressed patients responding to various forms of psychotherapy and drug therapy (Hollon, Thase, & Markowitz, 2002) suggests that interpersonal therapy can be just as effective as antidepressants at reducing typical symptoms associated with depression (Figure 1.1). Additionally, in his recent book *The Emperor's New Drugs: Exploding the Myth of Antidepressants*, clinical psychologist Irving Kirsch describes meta-analytic studies indicating very small differences between antidepressant and placebo control groups. In fact, after an extensive analysis of the existing antidepressant literature, he states "Now, considering all of the data together, I have come to believe that the chemical-imbalance theory is completely implausible" (Kirsch, 2010, p. 80). Kirsch's views are controversial at this point (more about depression and neurochemicals will be discussed in Chapter 9); however, if confidence in the chemical-imbalance theory of depression erodes, this may have a strong impact on the meaningful tools available to psychiatrists.

If drugs were the undisputed clear choice of treatment for mental illness, then the movement of psychiatry away from psychosocial therapies toward the prescriptive therapies would be understandable and desirable. However, as suggested, the verdict is still out on many popular drugs. The presence of side effects presents additional challenges for the advocacy of antidepressants. Depressed individuals taking Prozac, one of the most heavily prescribed drugs for depression, report multiple side effects including headaches, diarrhea, nausea, constipation, and, in 40% of users, sexual dysfunction (Hobson & Leonard, 2001; Rothschild, 2000). Ironically, patients on antidepressants such as Prozac may need to take them chronically because the long list of side effects is enough to make them even more depressed.

Research–Treatment Disconnect

Whereas psychiatric services struggle to attract American medical students, clinical psychology programs reel in about 20 applicants per position, most from the best undergraduate schools in the country. Making the argument even stronger for selecting clinical psychologists as therapists is the fact that their services cost half of psychiatrists' services.

To any serious student of psychology, the thought of professional clinical and counseling psychologists applying their scientific knowledge of behavior and mental processes to

meta-analysis A study that includes the results of several published reports to investigate a certain hypothesis.

Figure 1.1
This figure depicts the effectiveness of several different approaches used to treat depression. As indicated, pharmacological treatments have similar outcomes to interpersonal and cognitive-behavioral therapies.
FROM HOLLON, THASE, & MARKOWITZ, 2002

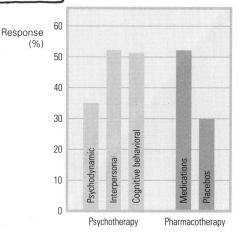

mental illness sounds perfectly reasonable and desirable. Indeed, at the end of World War II, when returning soldiers were seeking treatment at Veterans Administration hospitals that did not have enough psychiatrists, enlisting the help of research psychologists seemed like an ideal solution. But since that era, the emphasis on research methodology in clinical psychology has dwindled. In 1971, the American Psychological Association (APA) approved a new clinical program leading to the degree Doctor of Psychology (PsyD). As opposed to the traditional PhD received by most psychologists who conduct their own research projects, the PsyD degree's emphasis is on practical training and does not require as much research experience as the PhD because of the APA's conclusion that understanding research methodology is unrelated to the effectiveness of psychotherapy. Thus, clinical and counseling psychology has wandered far from its once strong research-based origins (Dawes, 1994).

In a recent scathing report, the field of clinical psychology received a harsh, but timely, reality check (Baker, McFall, & Shoham, 2008). At a time when the number of people in the United States receiving mental health care has doubled over 20 years, clinical psychologists are being "crowded out" of the practitioner role by an increasing presence of primary-care physicians and lower-cost mental health professionals such as social workers. Considering that clinical psychologists receive more training than these other two professions, these results are disturbing for the field of clinical psychology. Contributing to the current demise of clinical psychology are increasing numbers of PsyD programs and students, reports of clinical psychologists confirming that personal experience is more valuable than empirical evidence, and the continued use of assessment and treatment practices with little empirical support. Stating that the field is similar to prescientific medicine at the turn of the twentieth century, these authors call for a new rigorous accreditation system, sponsored by the Association for Psychological Science rather than the APA, that will assure science-centered educational programs.

Regardless of the graduate training (clinical psychology, PsyD, psychiatry), students who are pursuing a mental health career do both their future patients/clients and themselves a disservice if they do not take the appropriate coursework in methodology. When a new treatment is introduced, it is the responsibility of a therapist to determine its value. This determination cannot be adequately established, however, without a requisite understanding of research design. If the therapist cannot evaluate a published manuscript on the effectiveness of a new therapy, it is impossible for him or her to make an informed decision about its effectiveness.

Among the intriguing therapies recently introduced are the following:

- Eye movement desensitization reprogramming (EMDR), a treatment involving the rapid movement of the eyes to relieve severe anxiety
- Use of the herb St. John's wort to treat depression
- Drilling a hole in a person's skull to achieve a psychologically healthy "blood/brain volume"
- Performing surgery on obese individuals to reduce the capacity of the stomach to the size of a human thumb

- Transcranial magnetic stimulation (TMS), the treatment of depression with very strong magnets

- Taking reproductive hormones to increase chances of survival following traumatic brain injury

Some or all may be effective therapies, but each must undergo rigorous testing and evaluation before patients are subjected to them. (You'll learn which ones from this list are effective as you progress through the text.) The best way to discern the validity of any of these proposed treatments is to carefully and critically review the research published in peer-reviewed journals. Such an inspection of the literature requires the therapist to be informed about the primary components of research design and statistics. Of course, a conspicuous absence of published studies on a particular new treatment should be a warning sign that the treatment has yet to be supported in an empirical fashion; proceeding with such a new therapy is the therapeutic equivalent of diving into unknown waters.

It can be argued that the psychosocial model does not require psychologists to be well versed in statistics and research design; they just need to be good listeners with clinical intuition to deliver adequate psychotherapy to patients and clients. An experience described by Robyn Dawes (1994) in the early days of his clinical career suggests that clinicians run the risk of making devastatingly harmful decisions when statistical methods are ignored in diagnostic decisions.

In 1960, a 16-year-old girl was presented to Dawes as a patient because she was dating a man 10 years older. He did what most therapists did at that time: He administered the Rorschach test. This test consists of a series of cards containing inkblots that are ambiguous in form (Figure 1.2). The patient is asked to describe what he or she sees in the blot. The response is used as a "window" to the patient's mind because the patient is presumed to be projecting personal experiences onto the blot. Although this sounds like a perfectly reasonable technique to use as a **psychometric test** (or psychological measurement test), it has since been extensively reviewed and found to lack validity (Lilienfield, Wood, & Garb, 2000).

The patient, who scored at the 95th percentile on an intelligence test (126 IQ score), offered 40 reasonable responses on her Rorschach test except for card 8, which she said looked like a bear (it did not). At a subsequent staff meeting when Dawes was presenting the outcome of her tests, the head psychologist suggested that the girl must be hallucinating because card 8 did not look like a bear. When Dawes emphasized the point that the number of her good responses was higher than that of most normally functioning people, he was told that understanding statistics was not as important as understanding people and that statistics do not apply to the individual. The staff agreed that the young woman should be admitted to the mental hospital if she returned to the clinic. Dawes is not sure what happened with this client because, in frustration at the lack of methodology used in the clinical staff's decision making, he quit his career as a clinical psychologist.

psychometric test Paper-and-pencil test typically used by psychologists for diagnostic purposes. These tests need to pass reliability, validity, and standardization assessment before use with patients and clients.

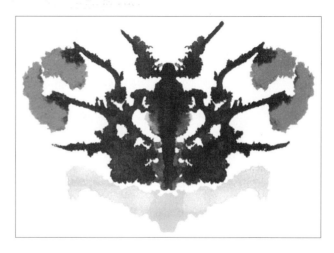

Figure 1.2
This image is similar to that used in the Rorschach inkblot test. The ambiguity of the figures is intentional, to prompt divergent responses from patients or clients.

Even today, Paul McHugh (personal communication, 2001), chair of the Department of Psychiatry and Behavioral Sciences at Johns Hopkins University, reluctantly admits that "a professional that relies on [statistical] data to treat his patients is tarred as one who cares little about his patient." McHugh, an advocate of more empirically based therapies, believes that the rigorous pursuit of neuroscience "will dignify the field of psychiatry."

It's difficult to predict the future of psychiatry and clinical psychology. As information about the brain's involvement in mental illness and mental health becomes more available, it is likely that stronger ties to the neurosciences will strengthen the foundation of each area, as McHugh suggests. Even though a criminal investigator might be very good at evaluating personal motives in determining the likelihood of guilt of a suspect, it would be shortsighted to ignore the availability of DNA screening in determining his or her guilt. Just as top-notch investigative reporting involves impressive deductive abilities, keen interviewing skills, cutting-edge forensic technology, and a persistence in identifying and finding the truth, the most effective mental health investigators use all available resources. They draw from the existing biomedical and psychosocial approaches to make informed decisions about the origins and treatment of the "suspects" of mental illness.

Classifying Mental Disorders

Psychiatrists and psychologists both refer to the same manual to diagnose and categorize mental illnesses, the American Psychiatric Association's *Diagnostic and Statistical Manual* (DSM). Now in its fourth edition, the DSM has been revised and is currently known as the DSM-IV-TR (the IV means it is the fourth edition; TR stands for Text Revision). A new version, the DSM-V, is scheduled to be published in 2012 (American Psychiatric Association, 2009). The number of disorders was a modest 60 in the first edition of this manual (1952); the current DSM has ballooned to over 400 disorders. In addition to disorder inflation, McGuire and Troisi (1998) describe the "shifting sands" of purely psychological diagnostic criteria, using borderline personality disorder as an example.

The DSM-IV-TR entry for borderline personality disorder has nine criteria, with only five of the nine required for a diagnosis (Table 1.1). This summative strategy (using the number of symptoms as a diagnostic criterion) lacks precision. For instance, two individuals may each have five of the nine overall criteria but share only a single criterion. If two people in a restaurant each order the special of the day and the waitress brings one customer a chicken plate and the other a roast beef plate, each with a salad, the customers will be confused; except for the salad the entrees seem like two very different meals. Similarly, a diagnosis that is identical for two people who differ in four of five symptoms is far from precise.

Additionally, although conditions are included in the DSM according to the four criteria of suffering, statistical variance, tissue pathology, and functional impairment, the decision to include a condition as a disorder remains subjective and may, as the numbers of both clinical practitioners and disorders increase, reflect the growth of the number of therapists rather than a real need for more disorder categories. The fact that the decisions for labeling disorders in the DSM are subjective can be easily discerned from the changes in disorders from edition to edition. For example, whereas

Table 1.1 DSM-IV-TR Diagnostic Criteria for Borderline Personality Disorder

A pervasive pattern of instability of interpersonal relationships, self-image, and affects and marked impulsivity beginning by early adulthood and present in a variety of contexts, as indicated by five (or more) of the following:

(1) frantic efforts to avoid real or imagined abandonment. **Note:** Do not include suicidal or self-mutilating behavior, covered in criterion 5.

(2) a pattern of unstable and intense interpersonal relationships characterized by alternating between extremes of idealization and devaluation

(3) identity disturbance: markedly and persistently unstable self-image or sense of self

(4) impulsivity in at least two areas that are potentially self-damaging (e.g., spending, sex, substance abuse, reckless driving, binge eating). **Note:** Do not include suicidal or self-mutilating behavior, covered in criterion 5.

(5) recurrent suicidal behavior, gestures, threats, or self-mutilating behavior

(6) affective instability due to a marked reactivity of mood (e.g., frequent displays of temper, constant anger, recurrent physical fights)

(7) chronic feelings of emptiness

(8) inappropriate, intense anger or difficulty controlling anger (e.g., frequent displays of temper, constant anger, recurrent physical fights)

(9) transient, stress-related paranoid ideation or severe dissociative symptoms

American Psychiatric Association (2000), p. 710.

homosexuality was considered a disorder in DSM-II, published in 1968, it was removed entirely from DSM-IV (American Psychiatric Association, 1994). These shifting diagnoses can exact a tremendous toll on people who spend years burdened by and being treated for a supposed disorder, only to be told, "Never mind; it's not a mental illness." It will be interesting to see if the new DSM will include status changes for existing mental illnesses.

Paula Caplan, a clinical and research psychologist, corroborates the subjectivity of the DSM. In her book *They Say You're Crazy: How the World's Most Powerful Psychiatrists Decide Who's Normal*, Caplan (1996) writes that decisions are made about the inclusion of disorders and criteria for disorders in a subjective manner, too often lacking an adequate empirical basis. Despite the controversy, we reproduce the DSM diagnostic criteria verbatim in this text because they serve as the definitive criteria for mental disorders in practice and they reveal the difficulty of defining mental states or traits with precision. Moreover, it is valuable to read the criteria exactly as they are presented to therapists and practitioners; therefore, no summaries or paraphrases are used.

Lessons Learned from the Multiple Personality Disorder Diagnosis

One problematic effect of deemphasizing empirical research in the diagnosis and treatment of mental illness is the likely occurrence of psychological fads. A tragic example of such a fad was dissociative identity disorder (DID). Table 1.2 reproduces the DSM diagnostic criteria for DID, formerly known as "multiple personality disorder" (MPD). The public became aware of this disorder, in which a person's personality is fragmented into several "alters," after the publication of books on two famous cases: Eve White (currently

Chris Sizemore) in C. H. Thigpen's *The Three Faces of Eve* in 1957 and Sybil Dorsett in F. R. Schreiber's *Sybil in 1973.*

Before *Sybil* was published, DID was one of the rarest mental disorders; about 76 cases were identified up until 1944. After the book was published, however, it was estimated that 40,000 cases were presented between 1985 and 1995 alone. In addition to case inflation, it has been reported that the number of "alters," or personalities, has grown—to over 100 in some cases (Acocella, 1998).

The literature contains a plethora of case studies of patients suffering from DID. Currently, case studies are invaluable methodological tools in areas of specific neuropsychological interest, such as identifying cognitive functions of specific brain areas in patients suffering from brain lesions (Banich, 1997). However, although case studies serve as valuable *starting* points for many research endeavors, they are rarely suitable *ending* points for making informed decisions about the efficacy of certain therapies (Myers & Hansen, 1997). (For a review of how Oliver Sacks cleverly uses case studies as a starting point for gathering more information about the interaction of the brain's physical and mental functioning, see Box 1.2.) Also, because many case studies involve retrospective data, it is important to verify the accuracy of reported events. Many patients tell their therapists that they experienced some form of abuse as children, but these claims are seldom confirmed with appropriate background checks.

The case study can also be problematic because the single case may not be representative of others. Stanovich (1998) writes about the case study as the "person-who" school of evidence gathering ("I knew a person who had DID and he . . ."). Person-who statistics make for interesting conversation but do not approach the scrutiny of acceptable research methodology for determining important factors and treatments related to mental health.

Aside from the anecdotal evidence, neuroscience research offers a few clues about DID. Electroencephalographs have provided limited knowledge about the activity of large populations of neurons in DID patients; scant evidence has indicated left-hemisphere dysfunction in some DID patients (Rosenstein, 1994), and visual anomalies have been reported in DID individuals (Shepard & Braun, 1995, cited in Miller, Blackburn, Scholes, White, & Mamalis, 1991; Miller, 1989). There is also evidence from groups of case studies that the anticonvulsant carbamazepine may be effective for

Table 1.2 **DSM-IV-TR Diagnostic Criteria for Dissociative Identity Disorder**

A. The presence of two or more distinct identities or personality states (each with its own relatively enduring pattern of perceiving, relating to, and thinking about the environment and self).

B. At least two of these identities or personality states recurrently take control of the person's behavior.

C. Inability to recall important personal information that is too extensive to be explained by ordinary forgetfulness.

D. The disturbance is not due to the direct physiological effects of a substance (e.g., blackouts or chaotic behavior during alcohol intoxication) or a general medical condition (e.g., complex partial seizures). **Note:** In children, the symptoms are not attributable to imaginary playmates or other fantasy play.

American Psychiatric Association (2000), p. 529.

DID patients (Coons, 1992). Again, the excessive use of case studies and the absence of proper controls make these conclusions highly suspect. Such methodological sloppiness can have devastating effects on the patient. It is interesting that a recent study conducted at the University of Zurich using patients diagnosed with DID with confirmed trauma in their childhoods displayed normal hippocampal and amygdala volumes and cognitive skills compared to control subjects. Alternatively, those diagnosed with posttraumatic stress disorder (PTSD) in the same study exhibited reduced volumes in these brain areas, as well as impaired cognitive abilities (Weniger, Lange, Sachsse, & Irle, 2008).

Although concerns related to the validity of certain aspects of DID have been presented, it is likely that many questions persist in your mind. If, as the empirical evidence suggests, it is uncertain that so many patients developed so many personalities, how could so many mental health professionals have found themselves both diagnosing and treating this questionable disease? And how could so many patients find themselves believing they possess dozens of personalities?

The DID patients, mostly women distraught with unmanageable anxiety, were frequently given strong medications such as alprazolam (Xanax), diazepam (Valium), and triazolam (Halcion). Many were subjected to hypnosis, during which memories related to horrifying childhoods, filled with tragedies such as sexual abuse and cult rituals, were recalled. Many psychotherapists believed that hypnosis-prompted memories were more accurate than nonhypnotic memories. Thus, the mental capacity of patients was greatly altered by heavy drug use and hypnosis, and unknowing therapists were able to plant ideas of personalities in the patients' malleable neuronal soil.

The well-known memory researcher Elizabeth Loftus points out that some therapists were unaware of the innate suggestibility of their patients and how they were reinforcing delusions and unknowingly implanting memories that corroborated the diagnosis of DID resulting from childhood sexual abuse (Loftus & Ketcham, 1994). In a sense, the patients and therapists were part of a dance—patients searching for relief from anxiety in their lives were easily influenced by the musical score introduced by the therapist.

In an alarming way, the therapist ultimately influenced the dance of the patient much as a puppeteer influences the movement of a puppet. In the background, the media (principally movies and talk shows) fueled the DID phenomenon by increasing public awareness and fascination with the topic. For example, the nature of DID began to change following the movie *Sybil* in 1977: Victims were frequently found to have more "alters" and were increasingly likely to have suffered from childhood sexual abuse after the movie was released.

But what may be an interesting plot device does not make a true mental disorder. The building wave of DID started to evaporate in the early 1990s. As women began to sue therapists for the damage this diagnosis brought to their lives (for example, multiple hospitalizations, accusations of family members, time taken away from their normal family and work lives), society became less fascinated with the topic. Paul McHugh (in Acocella, 1998) stated, "Close the dissociation services and disperse the patients to general psychiatric units. Ignore the alters. Stop talking to them, taking notes on them, and discussing them in staff conferences." Around this time, the American Psychiatric Association changed the name of the disorder from MPD to DID.

In 1993, *Time* magazine ran a cover story entitled "Lies of the Mind," emphasizing the danger of a diagnosis of repressed memories and MPD.

Thus, the tide has turned and there are fewer and fewer cases of women possessing dozens of personalities resulting from horrendous childhoods filled with satanic family rituals and chronic sexual abuse. Psychiatrists still discuss dissociative disorders, and certainly both women and men may suffer tremendous emotional despair following childhood abuse of any nature; but mental health professionals are more aware of the suggestibility of their patients as they attempt to discern the roots of certain emotional problems. Even though progress is being made, it is important for students of mental health to be reminded how easy it is to go down the wrong path when detours are taken from the empirical highways of mental health (see Box 1.1 for a case study of a tragic detour). With this concern in mind, Loftus dedicated her book, which chronicles the pain suffered by patients at the hands of unskilled therapists, to "the principles of science, which demand that any claim to 'truth' be accompanied by proof" (Loftus & Ketcham, 1994).

EXPLORING VARIOUS WINDOWS OF MENTAL HEALTH

Exploring mental illness from multiple perspectives is like viewing a house through multiple windows. Peering through each window gives you a valuable but limited view inside. Before a house is built, only the architect with the detailed plan of the structure, akin to one's genetic blueprint, can visualize the finished building. Of course, the original blueprint can be modified as the house develops—a wall can be added between the kitchen and the family room, a deck can be added, an extra window can be placed in the kitchen. Modifications can similarly be made to someone's original genetic profile—genes can mutate or be damaged by exposure to a toxic substance or other threat.

Building a house requires planning at many levels. In addition to prescribing the construction of the overall structure and the specific rooms, architectural plans lay out house functions (electrical wiring and plumbing) and make provisions for fuel lines for cooking and heating. In the same way, genetic blueprints guide our neurobiology—*neuroanatomy*, the construction of primary brain components; *neurophysiology*, how the brain functions; and *neurochemistry*, the chemical reactions that fuel its many workings.

Should the roof supports be constructed improperly or the wiring misrouted, the house will not function in the way it was designed. Life in an otherwise wonderful home can come to a halt when the furnace breaks down. In the same way, any breakdown in neuroanatomy, neurophysiology, or neurochemistry can devastate brain development and mental capacities.

Focusing on any approach in isolation—the blueprints, the construction, or peering through a window to view a single room—provides only limited information, far less than an integrated perspective. But even the most integrative information cannot replicate the experiences of the person actually living day to day with his or her particular brain in his or her particular environment. In fact, the only true sense of the house may come from living in it day to day, experiencing its creaks, the patterns of light as the sun rises, and the drafts of air that flow through the halls in the cool winter evenings. These are like

Box 1.1

A Case in Point

Diagnoses of Nadean Cool

In the early 1990s, Nadean Cool, a homemaker in Wisconsin, saw a psychiatrist for treatment of depression following an assault on her teenage daughter. Initially, she was diagnosed with posttraumatic stress disorder; but following about 7 months of extensive hypnosis and use of psychotropic drugs, Cool was given the diagnosis of multiple personality disorder (MPD). She was told she was the victim of childhood abuse that included satanic rituals involving the murder and cannibalism of babies. Further, Cool's psychiatrist told her that her father was the leader of the cult and that she had repressed her memories until they were unveiled with his clinical techniques.

Near the end of her 6-year treatment, Cool was told that she was possessed by 126 personalities—including those of a heroin addict, a teenage boy, the bride of Satan, and a duck. She was placed on a variety of drugs (up to 13 at one point), including methadone (a drug used to treat heroin addiction). Her psychiatrist prescribed the methadone because he believed, according to Cool, that since one of her personalities was a heroin addict, "the methadone would help me get in touch with additional memories" (personal communication, 2001). No mention was made of what this treatment would do to the remaining personalities (or to the duck). Further, the potential interaction of the many drugs Cool was taking was not discussed, nor were the drugs administered in any systematic way to determine if any particular drug was therapeutically beneficial for her symptoms.

During one of her repeated hospitalizations, Cool's psychiatrist performed an exorcism on her. Following protocol described in the book *Hostage to the Devil*, 1992, the psychiatrist brought a fire extinguisher to her hospital room in case she spontaneously combusted as the demon departed from her body during her exorcism. Where were sober reflection, objectivity, and skepticism in this mix of folly and trial and error?

Conveniently, Cool's therapy persisted as long as her insurance company was willing to cover her expenses; she says that her psychiatrist repeatedly told her how fortunate she was to have such wonderful insurance coverage. However, Cool's husband, once trusting that his wife's psychiatrist was using standard therapy that

Nadean Cool testifies in Outagamie County Circuit Court on February 12, 1997, in Appleton, Wisconsin
SHARON CEKADA, *THE APPLETON POST-CRESCENT*/AP PHOTO.

would ultimately lead to her recovery, realized that her therapy was making her worse. He finally convinced Cool that her therapy was problematic, and Cool realized that her psychiatrist had exacerbated her existing problems while creating new ones. Not only was she absent from her children during their teenage years because of 38 hospitalizations but her relationship with her father was also damaged. Told that her father was the leader of the satanic cult and was responsible for making her eat dead babies, she confronted her father with these accusations. He didn't respond; a week later he died. Subsequently, Cool filed a malpractice lawsuit against her former doctor and won a $2.4 million settlement. During her trial other women who had been patients of the same psychiatrist were shocked to learn that Cool's story was remarkably similar to their experiences.

Although Cool occasionally suffers from bouts of mild depression today, she is healthy once again and in control of her life. She is still haunted by the possibility that she contributed to her father's death, but she is learning to deal with that pain as well. In an attempt to protect others from the damage incurred by both herself and her loved ones at the hands of her psychiatrist, she has spoken out publicly about her situation, appearing on several news shows. Interestingly, her psychiatrist did not lose his medical license; he moved to a different state and continues practicing psychiatry.

Cool is currently an advocate for therapies derived from peer-reviewed empirical investigations. She made it clear during our interview that she wants to tell her story to students training to work in the mental health profession. Although MPD horror stories are on the decline, there is no guarantee that patients' lives won't be traumatized by other therapies looming in the mental health future.

environmental influences on people during their development. The homeowner may choose hardwood floors, striped wallpaper, and antique furniture; we may furnish our mental lives with classic novels, rap music, tennis practice, or the pursuit of a particular major, career, religion, or ethical cause.

For the serious observer of houses, valuable social and historical information is available. In any neighborhood a particular style of residence may predominate, and this style of house will be built more often than novel styles. Contractors like to stick with houses that have proved successful. Particularly striking or successful home designs can endure for centuries.

Similarly, through the *evolutionary window*, psychologists view humans as a species through history. How have humans adapted biologically to their environments? What are the biological effects when, for example, certain genes are selected and passed on from generation to generation? And how does geographical location influence evolution? Families in Africa prefer homes that are very different from homes in the American Midwest. Thus, one's *culture* also influences one's mental health—some cultures promote more social contact, others more active coping styles, and so on.

The brain, like the house, benefits from the best raw materials to build with and the best environment in which to develop. In the following sections we take a closer look at each window on mental health (Table 1.3). In the chapters that follow we consider all these perspectives as means to treat and/or to prevent mental illness.

Windows on Neurobiology

Neurobiologists study brain structure and function. For example, a neurochemical profile can be created by conducting medical tests or by observing a person's response to drugs. Information about neuroanatomy can be gained

Table 1.3 **Perspectives Emphasized in the Field of Clinical Neuroscience**

Perspective	Focus
Genetic	Role of genetics in expression of mental functioning
Neuroanatomical	Specific neuroanatomical structure(s) underlying mental functions
Neurochemical	Specific neurochemicals (e.g., neurotransmitters) underlying mental functions
Neurophysiological	Exact neural functioning accompanying mental functions (e.g., slowed action potentials in neurons)
Developmental	Specific critical windows of neuronal development and plasticity in contributing to mental functioning
Environmental	Environmental stimuli that may contribute to mental illness or mental health
Cultural	Cultural aspects that may contribute to the formation and perception of mental disorders
Evolutionary	Biological relevance of factors as they fit into the evolutionary context for particular behaviors related to mental health and mental illness

by impressive neuroimaging techniques. A person's functioning capacity, or neurophysiology, can be assessed by tests ranging from brain scans that measure how cells metabolize glucose to basic neuropsychological tests such as recalling lists of items.

Neuroanatomy. Perhaps the most famous case that points up the intimate relationship between neuroanatomy and mental health is that of Phineas Gage. On September 13, 1848, while working as the foreman of a construction gang laying the bed for an Irish railroad, Gage was tamping, or packing, explosives into solid rock when a horrible accident occurred. His tamping rod set off an explosion, shot into the air, and passed completely through Gage's head (Figure 1.3a). The tamping rod was quite large, measuring 3 feet, 7 inches long and 1.25 inches in diameter at its widest point (Figure 1.3b). Although Gage survived, his neuroanatomy was forever altered, resulting in severe psychological disturbances and differences from his former self.

Where did the damage occur? As seen in Figure 1.3a, the tamping iron entered through Gage's cheek and exited from the top of his skull (for more precise information about the entry and exit points, see Damasio, 1994), damaging his left frontal and temporal lobes as well as other areas. From a psychological standpoint, Gage reportedly suffered a partial impairment of his intellectual properties and a marked change in personality in the sense that he was more impulsive and irreverent than before and seemed to lack the social skills that he possessed prior to the accident (Macmillan, 2000). As you will read in the epilogue, Antonio Damasio has used the Gage case as an impetus for a clever line of research illuminating the role of the frontal cortex in ethical and other higher-order decision making (Damasio, 1994).

The Gage case marks the beginning of the burgeoning evidence indicating how devastating the destruction of certain neuroanatomical areas is to mental health. For example, today researchers know that the mental deterioration associated with Alzheimer's disease is accompanied by damaged or tangled clusters of neurons. Further, behavioral impairments such as tremors and difficulty moving one's limbs are observed in Parkinson's disease, a disorder accompanied by the destruction of a key area of the brain that is involved in movement. Finally, as was the case with Jasmine's older brother in the chapter-opening Connections, **traumatic brain injury (TBI)** is a major threat to the developing brains of children and the number one killer and cause of disability in children and teens in the United States (Stein, Brailowsky, & Will, 1995). The knowledge researchers and practitioners have gained from the numerous cases of TBI serves as little comfort to the 80,000 Americans reportedly experiencing long-term disability each year following complications related to brain injuries (Brain Injury Association, 2002).

In addition to describing how brain damage can lead to mental deficiencies, one goal of this book is to consider how neuroanatomical modifications might be used as a form of therapy for mental illness. For example, can we induce **neurogenesis** (the birth of new neurons) by exposure to certain

traumatic brain injury (TBI) Injury to a person's brain usually resulting from an accident.

neurogenesis Creation of new neurons. It was once thought that developed brains no longer produce new neurons, but research has confirmed the production of new neurons across the life span. Little is known, however, about the functional consequences of the new neurons.

Figure 1.3
Phineas Gage died in 1861, and his skull was later exhumed. (a) This computer graphic is based on measurements of Gage's skull and on brain imaging techniques used to reconstruct the accident. Portions of both hemispheres appear to have been damaged. (b) To gain perspective on Gage's accident, the actual tamping iron that pierced his brain is displayed here alongside his skull.

LEFT: DEPARTMENT OF NEUROLOGY AND IMAGE ANALYSIS FACILITY, UNIVERSITY OF IOWA. RIGHT: COUNTWAY LIBRARY, WARREN ANATOMICAL MUSEUM, HARVARD UNIVERSITY.

(b)

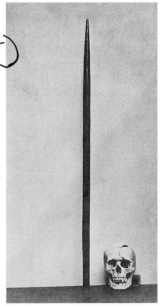

(a)

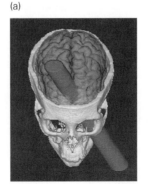

enriched environments or to chemicals called **neurotrophic factors** that are related to the production and growth of neural processes?

Of course, one essential element to understanding neuroanatomy is neuroimaging. Imaging techniques enable scientists to view both postmortem and living brain tissue. Focusing on the living brain, the **computerized tomography (CT)** scanner was the first imaging instrument to enable scientists and practitioners to observe the gross structures of a person's brain (much like an X-ray of the brain). Today, **magnetic resonance imaging (MRI)** enables researchers to observe the three-dimensional brain in all planes, also yielding a high-resolution image. Most recently, **diffusion tensor imaging** has allowed scientists to visualize fiber tracts in the brain by imaging the movement of water molecules. Adding to MRI technology, the tendency for water molecules to diffuse along the axons has provided a unique opportunity for scientists to visualize axons in living brains (Le Bihan et al., 2001). As depicted in Figure 1.4, these detailed images have opened up new neuroanatomical views of the brains of patients living with mental illness. Altered fiber tracts, for example, have been identified in patients diagnosed with schizophrenia (Camchong, MacDonald, Bell, Mueller, & Lim, 2009).

In addition to establishing consistencies between brain areas and accompanying functions, advanced neuroimaging techniques have revealed substantial differences among brains of individuals of the same species (Figure 1.4). These individual differences, though interesting, present special challenges for scientists and practitioners attempting to establish strong and inevitable relationships between neuroanatomical structures and functions or malfunctions.

Neurochemistry. Recall from the beginning of the chapter that as Mara searched for relief from depression, she found the reported success of drugs in treating psychological disorders hard to deny. Although researchers don't always know the exact mechanisms, they know that psychoactive drugs that modify chemical systems in the brain do influence mental health. Identifying a drug that offers relief from a certain disorder provides researchers a window of opportunity to explore exactly where and how the drug functions. This information, if discovered, leads to more insightful ways to treat disorders.

As you will learn in Chapter 5, multiple neurochemicals with multiple receptors all interact with one another in the brain. Scientists have identified functional families of neurochemicals, but the story is complex and far from complete. The well-known biopsychologist Elliot Valenstein, professor of psychology and neuroscience at the University of Michigan, has spent more than 40 years investigating how neurochemicals such as hormones and drugs influence behavior.

Figure 1.4

(a) Diagram of the left hemisphere of the human brain. (b) Magnetic resonance scans of six different people. Each brain shows variability in the cortical surface as well as in shape and size. Such individual differences present special challenges to practitioners and researchers when trying to determine specific locations in the brain.

(B) COURTESY OF NANCY C. ANDREASEN, MD, PHD, ANDREW H. WOODS CHAIR OF PSYCHIATRY, THE ROY J. AND LUCILLE A. CARVER COLLEGE OF MEDICINE, THE UNIVERSITY OF IOWA.

(a)

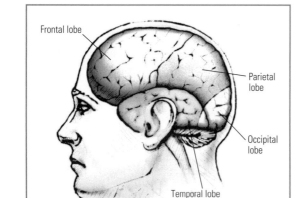

Frontal lobe
Parietal lobe
Occipital lobe
Temporal lobe

(b)

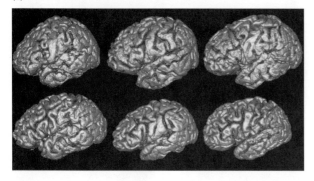

In his book *Blaming the Brain* (1998), Valenstein points out that virtually all current psychiatry department chairpersons endorse a biochemical approach to mental illness and many physicians inform patients that they are experiencing certain psychological disturbances because of a chemical imbalance. Yet no overwhelming evidence demonstrates that a majority of mental patients actually have a chemical imbalance! This contradiction does not prove that neurochemicals are not important to mental functioning; on the contrary, from the success rates of many drugs, they most probably are involved in some way, but perhaps it is a more indirect involvement than originally envisioned. The contradictions suggest that we are far from understanding the exact consequences of the psychopharmacological treatment of mental illness.

Valenstein points out that, while he certainly believes in the importance of biological factors in mental health, he also believes that "the way all biological factors are expressed in behavior and mental states depends equally on social and psychological variables" (p. 6). Who could argue with his statement? What is troubling is that these variables are frequently dismissed in a patient's treatment regime as practitioners focus only on the type and dose of drug being administered to the patient. Valenstein wants practitioners to look through more than just the neurochemical window when assessing a person's mental capacity and functioning.

Of additional concern with the neurochemical view is the direct-to-consumer advertising for various selective serotonin reuptake inhibitors (SSRIs) that has gained popularity over the past several decades. Concerns about these simplistic and ambiguous advertising campaigns to make patients, as opposed to physicians and therapists, aware of the advantages of these psychoactive drugs have been raised by Jeffrey LaCasse and Jonathan Leo. LaCasse and Leo (2005, p. 1215) indicate that the "incongruence between the scientific literature and the claims made in FDA-regulated SSRI advertisements is remarkable, and possibly unparalleled." More information about the role of antidepressants in the treatment of depression is provided in Chapter 9.

Neurophysiology. The ultimate goal of gaining information about neuroanatomy and neurochemistry is to understand exactly how the brain carries out its functions. Just knowing all the parts of an engine and the fuel it uses does not reveal how all the components interact to make the

neurotrophic factors
Neurochemicals such as brain-derived neurotrophic factor that promote the growth and complexity of neurons.

computerized tomography (CT) Neuroimaging technique developed in the 1960s that is the equivalent of taking an X-ray of the brain.

magnetic resonance imaging Technique that provides pictures of the brain by sending a magnetic field through a person's head so that the scanners can absorb radiation from hydrogen ions and a three-dimensional, high-resolution picture of brain tissue is generated.

diffusion tensor imaging. Brain-imaging technique utilizing radio frequency and magnetic field pulses to track water molecules to provide an image of fiber tracts in the living brain.

Figure 1.5
Examples of neuroimaging techniques—computerized tomography, positron emission tomography, and magnetic resonance imaging—contrasted to a photograph of a dissected human brain. A, anterior; P, posterior.

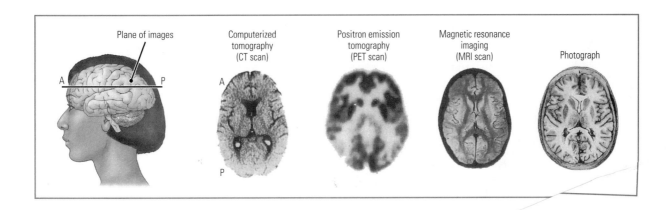

Plane of images

Computerized tomography (CT scan)

Positron emission tomography (PET scan)

Magnetic resonance imaging (MRI scan)

Photograph

electroencephalography (EEG) One of the earliest methods of recording activity of the living brain; involves placing electrodes on an individual's scalp and recording the activity of large populations of neurons. This technique has been valuable in diagnosing epilepsy and in delineating the various stages of sleep.

positron emission tomography (PET) Functional neuroimaging technique that involves injecting the patient with radioactively tagged glucose and quantifying the patient's metabolization of the radioactive glucose when the patient is presented with an experimental challenge (e.g., a cognitive task or a certain stimulus).

functional magnetic resonance imaging (fMRI) MRI that provides information about activity of the brain by quantifying cerebral blood flow during a cognitive challenge.

phenotype External expression of certain genetic influences. The phenotype for one genetic assortment may be long fingers; for another the phenotype may be brown hair.

car move. Among the exciting tools that exist today to assess neurophysiology (Figure 1.5), one of the earliest to measure activity in the living brain was **electroencephalography (EEG)**. EEG measures and records electrical activity in large populations of neurons. More advanced imaging techniques such as **positron emission tomography (PET)** and **functional magnetic resonance imaging (fMRI)** enable scientists to assess glucose metabolism and cerebral blood flow, respectively. A plethora of more specific neuroscientific techniques to explore brain tissue functions range from single-cell recording to a neuron's production of new receptors in response to a certain stimulus.

Although the current technology enables researchers to conduct fascinating experiments related to neurophysiology, adequate interpretations lag behind the technology. It has been extremely difficult to form overarching hypotheses about neurophysiological observations, especially considering that techniques such as fMRI reveal more about averages of activity rather than specific individual differences (Robinson, 2004). Among these lingering questions, does more activity in a certain area reflect the brain's enhanced ability to respond to a challenge? Or does it reflect on this particular brain area having to work harder than others (for example, employ more neurons)? An anecdote illustrates this dilemma.

Edward Peck, a neuropsychologist from Richmond, Virginia, tells the story of an experiment conducted by one of his mentors, Cesare Lombroso, a well-known pediatric neurologist at Harvard University. At the beginning of Lombroso's career, he received a grant to study EEGs of people identified as "geniuses." Lombroso had the unique opportunity to examine Albert Einstein, and he had a set of complex math problems prepared for Einstein to solve while he was hooked up to the EEG.

The story goes that Einstein was solving the problems at a rapid pace and was exhibiting a rather relaxed brain wave (alpha) when Lombroso was startled by a sudden shift in the waveform pattern to a more active waveform (beta). Excitedly, Lombroso interrupted Einstein to ask exactly what he was thinking when the shift occurred. Einstein replied, "I think I left the water on at home."

At least in some cases, more accurate thinking requires less brain activation than does uncertainty. A more recent study conducted by a team of researchers at Stanford University confirms that subjects who answered math problems correctly showed significantly less brain activation than those who provided inaccurate answers (Menon et al., 2000).

Genetics Perspective

The Human Genome Project has generated the potential for new treatments of all illnesses, even mental illness. We have certainly come a long way since the Austrian monk Gregor Mendel started crossing pea plants with different characteristics in 1860 and noted predictable patterns in the offspring. Although Mendel had no clue how peas acquire traits such as smooth or wrinkled skin, he knew that a pattern exists in the persistence of certain traits depending on the existence of these traits in the parent plants.

We now refer to the physical characteristics described by Mendel as the organism's **phenotype**. We also know that the consistencies in transmission of traits are due to the genes located in the nucleus of each of our cells.

Genetic blueprints for the development of humans are a lot more complicated than those for peas. With the exception of rare disorders such as the neurodegenerative Huntington's disease, probably very few mental illnesses are caused by one single gene. As you will learn as we focus on the description of various mental illnesses, they consist of multiple symptoms most likely caused by multiple genes.

As more is learned about genetic involvement in mental disorders, the way those disorders are viewed may change or even become confused. For example, if 30 genes are identified with schizophrenia and a person has 26 of these genes, how do we categorize this person's mental health? A popular article in *Newsweek* several years ago suggested that most people are walking around with genes identified as contributing to mental illness. Robert Sapolsky, a neuroscientist at Stanford University, suggests the notion of a "mental health continuum…a middling genetic load [of mental illness genes] gives you a personality disorder, a lighter one gives you a personality quirk and a still lighter one gives you mainstream America" (Begley, 1998, p. 53). Thus, your friend who is a very successful investment banker and spends hours cleaning her apartment each week may have a "lite" version of obsessive–compulsive disorder (OCD); your uncle who is the "life of the party" each holiday may be a little manic. According to this article, as the specific genetic elements underlying mental illness are disentangled and superimposed on a bell curve, it is likely that we will all be considered a bit crazy.

As you will learn in Chapters 7–11 and the epilogue, although we are still far from developing cures for mental disorders from genetic information, we have learned a lot about how genes might contribute to a particular disorder. Using identical twins, who are genetic clones, as subjects, **concordance rates** are calculated to determine how likely it is for both individuals to suffer from the same mental illness. Higher concordance rates point to a stronger genetic influence.

As Table 1.4 shows, concordance rates differ for various mental disorders. What has fascinated researchers is the fact that identical twins can have exactly the same genes, yet one may develop schizophrenia while the other never develops the disease. Such observations have led neuroscientists to consider genetic structure in its environmental context.

We think of our genes as unmodifiable, but neuroscientists now know, for example, that **immediate early genes** (genes that produce proteins enabling the brain to respond quickly to a changing environment) are constantly being turned on and off in our bodies in response to stimuli in the environment. This class of genes stimulates the production of particular **proteins**, the complex organic chemicals that constitute essential building materials of living cells. Using techniques to study the protein c-fos, for example, enables neuroscientists in effect to look into an animal's brain to see which cells were active in the last hour. As shown in Figure 1.6, immediate early genes have been turned on in an area involved in the stress/fear response after the animal was exposed to predator odors. When the threat subsides, the genes turn off.

concordance rate Frequency with which two individuals express the same condition. For example, the rate at which identical twins both develop schizophrenia is the concordance rate for schizophrenia.

immediate early genes Class of genes that exhibit rapid responses to certain extracellular stimuli by producing proteins that prompt the release of such neurotransmitters as c-fos, which is involved in the stress response.

proteins Complex organic chemicals that are the essential building materials of living cells.

Table 1.4 Concordance Rates for Mental Illness in Twins

Type of Illness	Identical Twins (%)	Fraternal Twins (%)
Autism	60	5
Schizophrenia	40	10
Depression	50	15
Bipolar disorder	40	10

Adapted from Andreasen (2001), p. 33.

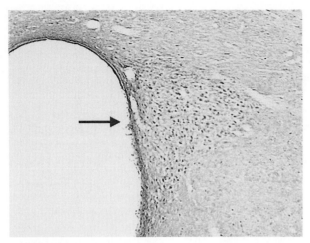

Figure 1.6
The protein c-fos produced by immediate early genes upon the presentation of a predator odor to a rat. The triangular area peppered with immunoreactive c-fos cells (arrow) represents the paraventricular hypothalamus, an area important for sending messages to prompt the release of stress hormones.

PHOTOMICROGRAPH COURTESY TOM CAMPBELL, RMC BEHAVIORAL LABORATORY

Developmental Perspective

Sunlight influences the views through the windows of a house. Looking into a room when the morning sun is bright is very different from looking at the room in evening twilight. Viewing the brain and mental functions at different developmental stages of life yields different perspectives as well. For example, the brain's neurons make connections at a surprisingly fast pace from birth to 24 months of age (see Chapter 6). Depriving children of proper stimulation during this time can devastate cognitive and motor development as well as the development of neurobiological responses to stress.

Some children experience tremendous loss of brain tissue yet develop into normal adolescents and adults. In his book *Half a Brain Is Enough* (2000), Dr. Antonio Battro, a neuroscientist in Argentina, describes his introduction to 5-year-old Nico, who, because of untreatable epileptic seizures, endured a hemispherectomy (one hemisphere of his brain was surgically removed) when he was 3 years old. Following extensive rehabilitation, including sophisticated computer instruction, Nico recovered amazingly well—he learned to enjoy swimming, tennis, computers, and music and developed excellent language skills. He did not learn to draw well however.

Extensive research has been conducted on two prominent developmental disorders, attention-deficit/hyperactivity disorder (ADHD) and autism; and brain damage has not been identified as a significant underlying cause of either condition (see Chapter 6). Rather, it is likely that altered neurochemistry affects individuals diagnosed as hyperactive or autistic. The notion that a seemingly intact brain with altered chemical functioning can lead to more severe impairment in some cases than can the removal of half the brain puzzles neuroscientists (Battro, 2000).

Another developmental interest for neuroscientists is the strong predisposition of the human brain for certain functions. For example, humans certainly seem to be "hardwired" for language, so much so that the inability to speak fails to get in the way of language development. Laura Ann Petito, at Dartmouth University, has found that deaf children babble just as hearing children do. Hearing children learn to babble by listening to sounds they make, and deaf children who are being taught sign language learn to babble by watching the movements of their hands. Although the brain must relegate different parts of the body to carry out communication in deaf children, the basic language function is not impaired (Restak, 2001).

In virtually every issue central to clinical neuroscience, development is critical to forming an integrated perspective. In the chapter-opening Connections, Jasmine's brother, who experienced brain trauma at a young age, would probably recover considerably more under the supervision of a competent neuropsychologist than would an adolescent or adult with the same injury and treatment. However, the story is not grim for older adults. Research described in Chapter 6 suggests that rat brains continue to sprout new connections in old age. Being in an enriched environment is

critical for this burst of neuronal connections in the twilight of life (Black, Greenough, & Anderson, 1987).

Environmental Perspective

In the early 1960s, an interdisciplinary team of researchers published arguably one of the most important papers
in the field of behavioral neuroscience and the future field
of clinical neuroscience. The beauty of their research is
the simplicity of its design—expose rats to an enriched
environment for less than 3 months and determine
whether this environmental exposure alters the face of the
brain in any way.

The research team, Edward Bennett, Marian Diamond,
David Krech, and Mark Rosenzweig (1964), housed a
group of rats in a large cage with lots of toys and activities
(Figure 1.7). At the end of the exposure time, the researchers compared the rats with a control group and found the
following:

- Increased levels of an enzyme that breaks down a neurotransmitter essential for learning (acetylcholine)

- Heavier cerebral cortices (a variable thought to be very
  stable)

- Larger cell bodies in cortical neurons

- Increased neuronal connections and branching

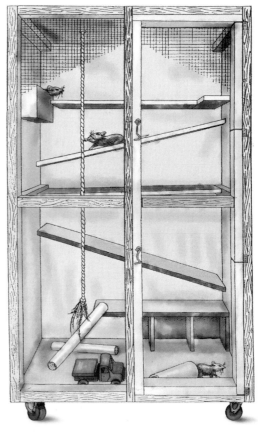

Figure 1.7
Rats placed in an enriched
environment—a large cage with
other animals and toys—display
enhanced brain functioning.

Does an enriched environment translate to enhanced
brain functioning for humans as well? As described in
Chapter 6, David Snowden's (2001) work with nuns suggests that their physically and cognitively active lifestyle, coupled with low-risk behavior and
considerable social support, leads to longer and healthier lives and protection
against neurodegenerative diseases such as Alzheimer's disease.

Experience, however, can be a blunt and indiscriminate instrument,
exerting damage as readily as benefits. The brain can be molded by negative as well as positive experiences. Impoverishing experiences can lead to
maldeveloped brains. Hubel and Wiesel (1965) have shown that depriving a
kitten's eye of light can inhibit the number of neurons responding to visual
impulses from that eye. Similarly, some forms of mental illness may be a
direct result of a person's environment (social, physical, and so on). As you
will read in Chapters 9 and 12, exposure to stress early on may alter the
brain's response to stressful stimuli and lead to future problems with depression or anxiety (Heim & Nemeroff, 2001).

If certain environments are related to mental illness, it is only logical to
conclude that therapeutic strategies that incorporate environmental variables
have potential for successful treatments. One undisputable success in this
area is with **simple (specific) phobias**. As you can see in Table 1.5, in some
people a specific stimulus provokes extreme fear that disrupts their ability
to function day to day without an ever-present anxiety about avoiding the
feared stimulus.

simple (specific) phobia
Disorder that involves an
intense fear of a particular
object (e.g., heights, spiders,
germs) that disrupts a person's normal functioning as
he or she attempts to avoid
the feared stimuli.

Conservative estimates suggest that up to 11% of Americans will experience a simple phobia in their lifetimes, according to the DSM-IV-TR. This statistic may be low because so many people are hesitant to have their phobias diagnosed. Fear is a strong emotion, and phobias have among the highest prevalence rates of all mental disorders.

Think about it: Virtually any stimulus may be associated with fear in some specific situation. A child shuts his hand in a car door and experiences severe pain as he watches the neighbor's dog run toward him to investigate. The association among pain and fear and dogs may be permanently etched in his emotional memory and may haunt him for the rest of his life. Most of us are familiar with *acrophobia* (fear of heights), *agoraphobia* (fear of leaving the safety of one's home), and *claustrophobia* (fear of enclosed spaces). The less well-known *alektorophobia*, a fear of chickens, and *arachibutyrophobia*, a fear of having peanut butter stuck to the roof of the mouth, are among the 500 phobias listed on the Web site phobialist. com (Kluger, 2001).

As detailed in Chapter 7, environmental therapies focusing on behavioral and cognitive learning approaches to overcoming anxiety have been extremely successful. As indicated by Park et al. (2001), both solo and clinician-accompanied exposure therapy (a prescribed strategy for systematic exposure to the feared stimulus in the context of a relaxing environment) for 14 weeks resulted in the subjects' relief from anxiety. Even more impressive, the subjects continued to be symptom-free 2 years later.

Obvious benefits to such cognitive and behavioral treatments include brevity, low cost, and absence of the side effects typically observed in drug-treatment regimes. Another benefit is that a person may not even need a therapist for such a treatment; a well-disciplined patient may be able to construct a self-administered therapy based on reputable literature. The use of virtual-reality computer programs to simulate the stressful stimulus exposure is becoming increasingly popular.

Evolutionary Perspective

proximate causation
Doctrine stating that the most direct cause of an event is the most important factor. In evolutionary theory, proximate questions are most often questions of mechanism and development of certain behaviors.

ultimate causation Doctrine stating that the more long-term causes of a behavior are important for a thorough understanding of the behavior. In evolutionary theory, ultimate causation questions are related to how and why certain behaviors evolve.

sexual selection Choosing a mate or competing for a mate.

Windows may offer the viewer a direct, realistic view. But a lens allows a more distant perspective. Grounded in the history of the human species, the evolutionary perspective is as much a lens as it is a window on mental health. Here, principles of natural selection formulated by Charles Darwin and associates and followers are applied to issues such as **proximate causation**, or direct causes of behavior; **ultimate causation**, or long-term evolutionary causes of behavior; **sexual selection** (the choosing of a mate); trait variation; and environment (McGuire & Troisi, 1998).

In their book *Why We Get Sick*, Randolph Neese and George Williams (1994b), discuss mental illness seen through an evolutionary lens. Neese and Williams suggest that mental illness may be an adaptation to the environment rather than a disease, a view that is very different from the traditional medical model; just as we get a fever when our immune system is working effectively to fight off infection, we may suffer from anxiety because our emotions are reacting as they should to threatening stimuli or circumstances, that is, to stress. Few of us welcome feelings of anxiety, but it may be an important emotion for evolutionary fitness.

Table 1.5 DSM-IV-TR Diagnostic Criteria for Specific Phobia

A. Marked and persistent fear that is excessive or unreasonable, cued by the presence or anticipation of a specific object or situation (e.g., flying, heights, animals, receiving an injection, seeing blood).

B. Exposure to the phobic stimulus almost invariably provokes an immediate anxiety response, which may take the form of a situationally bound or situationally predisposed panic attack. **Note:** In children, the anxiety may be expressed by crying, tantrums, freezing, or clinging.

C. The person recognizes that the fear is excessive or unreasonable. **Note:** In children, this feature may be absent.

D. The phobic situation(s) is avoided or else is endured with intense anxiety or distress.

E. The avoidance, anxious anticipation, or distress in the feared situation(s) interferes significantly with the person's normal routine, occupational (or academic) functioning, or social activities or relationships; or there is marked distress about having the phobia.

F. In individuals under age 18 years, the duration is at least 6 months.

G. The anxiety, panic attacks, or phobic avoidance associated with the specific object or situation are not better accounted for by another mental disorder, such as obsessive–compulsive disorder (e.g., fear of dirt in someone with an obsession about contamination), posttraumatic stress disorder (e.g., avoidance of stimuli associated with a severe stressor), separation anxiety disorder (e.g., avoidance of school), social phobia (e.g., avoidance of social situations because of fear of embarrassment), panic disorder with agoraphobia, or agoraphobia without history of panic disorder.

Specify type:

Animal type

Natural environmental type (e.g., heights, storms, water)

Blood-injection-injury type

Situational type (e.g, airplanes, elevators, enclosed places)

Other type (e.g., fear of choking, vomiting, or contracting an illness; in children, fear of loud sounds or costumed characters)

American Psychiatric Association (2000), p. 450.

One study categorized guppies into timid (high-anxiety), normal, and bold temperament types and then placed them in a tank with a predator bass—an obvious threat to their genetic fitness (the ability to pass genes on to offspring). After 60 hours, 40% of the timid guppies remained, whereas only 15% of the "normal" guppies and 0% of the bold guppies survived (Neese & Williams, 1994b). It is easy to see how an absence of anxiety may prevent us from hastily escaping from a wild animal—resulting in injury or death and, thus, decreased genetic fitness. The presence of anxiety may also keep a man from impulsively having an affair and leaving his wife and young children (possibly resulting in decreased genetic fitness because he can no longer provide for his children) or from engaging in risky behavior that may lead to death or injury.

Just as it is important to identify the source of a persistent fever, Neese and Williams argue that it is important to identify the source of persistent anxiety. If some forms of anxiety are adaptive for our species, then as more and more people attempt to reduce their anxiety with antidepressants and other antianxiety medications, we may be conducting an interesting experiment on ourselves.

Thus, aside from offering a long-term perspective about why certain "mental illnesses" persist in the human population, the evolutionary perspective explores the adaptive nature of mental phenotypes that seem far from being adaptive for our species today. The evolutionary researcher seeks to explain how the genes that contribute to a condition like schizophrenia—where multiple genes are activated by certain environmental experiences—might, in another combination of genes and experience, lead to some survival advantage.

Andreasen (2001) suggests that the genes that contribute to schizophrenia may also enable a person to see the world in unusual ways—ways not unrelated to creativity and genius. Albert Einstein was a genius, but his son suffered from schizophrenia. Isaac Newton, who first described the physical laws Einstein studied, reportedly lived an eccentric and solitary life and experienced at least one psychotic episode. Einstein and Newton appear to have possessed or passed on some combination of genes that contribute to schizophrenia-like symptoms. Could some combination of the key genes in schizophrenia be related to cognitive genius? Kay Redfield Jamison, whose book *Touched with Fire* (1993) describes large proportions of creative geniuses who suffered from bipolar episodes of mania and depression (William Blake, John Keats, Vincent van Gogh, to name a few), further corroborates this evolutionary view.

It is important to remember, however, that an adequate understanding of the adaptive benefits of our emotions requires a thorough understanding of their normal functioning, just as an understanding of internal medicine requires a fundamental knowledge of human physiology. Psychiatric training programs, however, do not systematically offer courses on topics such as evolutionary psychology or the psychology of emotions (Neese & Williams, 1994).

Window Provided by Culture

A past *New York Times Magazine* article (Osborne, 2001) addressed the influence of culture in the etiology of mental illness. The highlight of this article is the story of a 59-year-old woman named Dibuk ak Suut who lives in the Malaysian jungle. When her husband claps his hands unexpectedly, Dibuk jumps to her feet, appears to enter a glassy-eyed trance, and starts shouting, "Grasshopper! Grasshopper!" When her husband begins a comical dance, Dibuk does the same, as if she is suddenly her husband's puppet. In the midst of her trance, she sweats and laughs excessively. Dibuk's husband breaks the trance by tapping her firmly on the shoulder. After a few moments, a cat jumps in at the window and the trance begins again.

Even with our ubiquitous media coverage in the United States of virtually every conceivable mental disorder, you probably are not familiar with Dibuk's symptoms. In Malaysia, Dibuk is thought to be *latah*; in the West, her condition is known as hyperstartle syndrome. Why is latah much more common in Malaysia than hyperstartle syndrome is in the United States? Researchers chalk it up to cultural differences.

The list of cultural influences is long. Ever wonder why anorexia is far more prevalent in the United States than in other industrialized countries? Or why women are more likely to suffer from anorexia than men? In Nigeria, students who are overwhelmed by fatigue are known to suffer from "brain fag," and back in Malaysia some people suffer from "koro," a sudden fear of the genitalia receding into the body and causing death. If your own perspective prompts you to regard such conditions more as fiction than reality, you'll be surprised to learn that since 1994 the American Psychiatric Association has included 25 such intriguing disorders in an appendix to the DSM dedicated to **culture-bound syndromes.**

The fact that the prevalence of some disorders differs among various cultures gives even more weight to the role of the environment and culture in the etiology of mental illnesses. Lynn Payer (1996) suggests that cultural norms affect how medical practitioners tend to diagnose disorders. For example, in Germany mental illness is considered incurable. American practitioners, by contrast, emphasize treatment and prevention of mental illness.

culture-bound syndrome
Condition that appears to be culture-specific, for example, anorexia (United States), latah (Malaysia), koro (Malaysia), and brain fag (Nigeria). The DSM categorizes these disorders in this broad classification.

homeostasis Internal balance and regulation of physiological systems in an organism.

WHAT LIES AHEAD

Understanding the neurobiological foundations of mental health provides students like you, who are interested in the interactions among mental health, the brain, and the environment, with powerful tools to investigate critical mental health issues. The empirical, multifaceted approach emphasized in this text offers hope for the emergence of promising therapies for society's mental maladies.

Multiple Perspectives

This chapter and the next lay a foundation for studying clinical neuroscience. In this chapter we've introduced the many perspectives and methods of neuroscience, and in Chapter 2 we explore how these perspectives developed and how the base of empirical evidence continues to grow and evolve. The remaining chapters approach neurobiology and clinical disorders as aspects of **homeostasis**. We recognize that the term *homeostasis* is considered a bit old-fashioned in neuroscience circles and agree that the more contemporary term *allostasis*, which refers to the importance of responding to altered environments through effective change, is also valuable (and is discussed in Chapter 12). Even so, we continue to recognize the value of the term *homeostasis* and have included it in the organizational scheme of the book. In this context, homeostatic ranges (e.g., appropriate ranges for one's heart rate, temperature, or stress hormone levels) represent a more relevant approach than the more classic notions of specific set points. This approach allows a serious examination of the brain–body relationship in the quest for mental health. Although an emphasis is placed on the integration of the mind, brain, and body in upcoming chapters, we continue to use established terminology such as *psychological factors* and *physiological factors* for clarity, although in the not-so-distant future such dichotomous terms may no longer be appropriate. The epilogue addresses the future of clinical neuroscience, including ethical debates about the influence of brain trauma on asocial or criminal behavior, the harvesting of embryonic stem cells to treat disorders such as Parkinson's disease, and the potential effectiveness of self-directed neuroplasticity in maintaining mental health.

To bridge the gaps between common beliefs and actual research and between clinical practice and more traditional neuroscience perspectives, each chapter

Box 1.2

Oliver Sacks

Educating the Public About Clinical Neuroscience: The Contributions of Oliver Sacks

Oliver Sacks was born in London and enjoyed a childhood rich in scientific and intellectual stimulation. Both his parents were trained as neurologists but decided that more traditional medicine offered more exciting interactions with patients. Consequently, his house was full of medical stories—preparing Sacks to engage in clinical storytelling from a very young age.

At the beginning of World War II, Sacks was one of around 3 million English children sent away from the cities to families or boarding schools in the countryside for safety. The extended separation from his parents was difficult for him. As a child, Sacks endured migraines, which he was assured were simply a benign dysfunction of the brain. He was fascinated, though, by the visual patterns and configurations that accompanied these headaches. His early passion was for chemistry; he did not fall in love with medicine until the advanced age of 32 years, when he obtained his medical degree at Oxford.

Sacks then moved to the United States, and in 1966 he began practicing at Beth Abraham Hospital in New York, where he encountered a group of patients that would forever change his life. These patients suffered from a form of encephalitis that left them frozen like statues for decades. Sacks became obsessed with these patients and moved into an apartment close to the hospital so he could observe them up to 15 hours per day.

After learning about a new pharmacological treatment for Parkinson's disease, Sacks began to wonder if his patients' malady could be viewed as an extreme case of Parkinson's disease and that, therefore, they might benefit from a new drug known as l-dopa. He acquired the necessary license and arranged double-blind trials with the drug and a placebo. Sacks will never forget the excitement that permeated the summer of 1969 as he watched the encephalitis patients respond to the l-dopa. As depicted in the movie *Awakenings* (based on his 1973 book), the patients experienced a wonderful awakening from decades of being frozen. Sacks kept meticulous notes and photographs of his patients. But, devastatingly, the miracle shut down as the patients started to develop a sensitivity to the l-dopa. In most cases, the pharmacological window started to close when the patients experienced uncontrollable movements in response to the drug.

Although the world knows Sacks as a prolific and celebrated writer, he encountered rejection by the scientific community when he attempted to publish his observations of the effects of l-dopa on his encephalitis patients. At a time when there was much hope for l-dopa in reducing the symptoms of Parkinson's disease, the last news anyone wanted to hear was that it might be a false hope. This negative experience with traditional scientific writing reinforced Sacks's love for clinical storytelling. Following the path of the prominent Russian psychologist Dr. Aleksandr R. Luria (who wrote *The Mind of a Mnemonist* [1968] and *The Man with a Shattered World* [1972]), whom he admired greatly, Sacks decided that the best way to convey information about his patients was to do so by telling clinical stories, or neurographies, about his fascinating patients.

The seeds for this "romantic science" had been planted in Sacks's childhood as he listened to his parents' medical tales. Sacks observed every detail of his patients' lives in order to recreate the context of their existence. After nine books, it is an established fact that Sacks has chosen an appropriate venue to tell his stories and has consequently become the world's best-known neurologist.

Although they contain neurographies of many of his patients, Sacks's books also provide a sort of neurography of his own mental experiences. His early fascination

begins with Connections, a feature that connects two or more observations on the chapter topic. These research reviews often showcase the impressive accomplishments of undergraduate and graduate students in clinical neuroscience.

Within the chapters, A Case in Point boxes put a human face on research related to a special topic by describing the real-life experiences of individuals suffering from various disruptions of mental homeostasis. Brain Matters

with his migraines prompted him to write *Migraine* (1999), his transformation after observing the encephalitis patients served as the impetus for *Awakenings*, his encounter with a bull and the subsequent accident that caused severe damage to his leg brought forth *A Leg to Stand On* (1984), his early childhood fascination with chemistry served as the basis for his book *Uncle Tungsten: Memories of a Chemical Boyhood* (2001), and his passion for music and its connection with brain disorders provided the literary score for *Musicophilia* (2007). Most prominent is his continued fascination with the resourcefulness with which his patients respond to their neurological challenges—inspiring the writing of *The Man Who Mistook His Wife for a Hat* (1985), *Seeing Voices* (1990), *The Island of the Colorblind* (1997), and *An Anthropologist on Mars* (1995).

Oliver Sacks
COURTESY OF DR. OLIVER SACKS,
PHOTO © NANCY CRAMPTON.

More recently, Sacks's thoughts have been directed toward Tourette syndrome, which he finds "endlessly fascinating." Although he is painfully aware of the challenges Tourette patients encounter every day, he suggests that "a little holiday from our frontal lobes" may be a nice experience from time to time (personal communication, 2001).

He also muses about consciousness and the mind's refusal to present any sign of disconnection. His fascination with vision and photography prompts a visual example, that of the blind spot, to support this claim. We all have an area on the retina that, because of the exit point of our optic nerves, does not have the appropriate sensory receptors to receive light. But no one actually sees a black hole in the visual field: The mind seems to fill it in. Similarly, our memories are so intertwined with our identities that they are resistant to disruptions: Young children, when asked about events that occurred when they were too young to have formed memories—or the language to describe them—typically construct elaborate stories to convey their past.

Sacks is an astute observer of both the mental and behavioral functions of his patients. His elegant accounts of how his neurologically impaired patients learn to exist in their surroundings reinforce the value of one's environment in mental health. In fact, Sacks prefers to observe his patients in their own homes to get an accurate sense of their functioning capacity.

Sacks's writings have made the general public aware of the consequences of brain disorders and how, with compassionate respect, we can learn enough from patients with brain disorders to develop treatments or to enable the patients to live optimally with their alternative style of mental functioning. Why does Sacks write for such a broad audience? He believes that without a public awareness of the critical role of the brain in our mental functions and a general interest in trying to learn more about the brain, federal funds and public policies supporting the continuation of neuroscience research would dwindle away.

When asked about being interviewed for this book, Sacks replied that he wasn't sure whether his "idiosyncratic approach would be appropriate in a sober textbook on clinical neuroscience" (personal communication, December 2000). On the contrary, his approach, equally emphasizing the brain, environment, and mental functioning, could be viewed as a basis for the emerging field of clinical neuroscience. Along with other respected and accomplished investigators profiled in this book, Oliver Sacks is a true pioneer in this field, turning the general public away from an obsession with the unconscious toward an appreciation of the complexity as well as the vulnerability of our brains.

boxes provide an occasional opportunity to delve deeper into selected topics.

To assist your study, throughout each chapter, bold key terms are defined in the margins; they are also compiled in a glossary at the end of the book. A chapter summary is presented at the end of each chapter, followed by a list of selected readings called For Further Consideration.

A Brain–Body Balance

More than ever before, research is revealing a seamless interaction between the nervous system and the rest of the body. For example, the biological mechanisms underlying the stress response represent extensive cross talk between body and brain. Overwhelming evidence points directly to chronic stress as a contributing factor in many mental and physical disorders. The individual's reaction to stress plays an essential role in maintaining neurobiological homeostasis and avoiding allostatic load (a new concept you will become familiar with in Chapter 12). Similarly, research on how the nervous system interacts with and is intimately related to the immune system provides compelling evidence that a healthy immune system is as critical to mental health as it is to physical health.

In the chapters at the heart of this book, we view mental functioning as it affects homeostasis in three important ways:

■ *Establishing homeostasis* Chapters 3–6 link basic neural mechanisms at the anatomical, neurochemical, and developmental levels to overt conditions. For example, neurodegenerative and cognitive processing disorders such as Alzheimer's disease and attention-deficit/hyperactivity disorder are included in Chapter 6 on neurodevelopment. These chapters also address the role of neurobiological homeostasis in mental health, review how body and brain respond to stress, and introduce the intimate connections between the nervous and immune systems and physical and mental health.

■ *Disruptions of homeostasis* As the internal milieu is disrupted by stress or illness, the nervous system attempts to compensate. These attempts sometimes lead to extreme conditions that we classify as mental disorders. Among the representative clinical disorders addressed in Chapters 7–11 are the latest findings related to anxiety disorders (specifically, OCD and Tourette syndrome), mood disorders (major depression, bipolar disorder), schizophrenia, addiction, and neurological disorders such as TBI and Parkinson's disease.

■ *Maintaining homeostasis* In Chapters 12–14 we address the relationship among psychological processes, neurobiology, and immunology in maintaining mental health. For example, disruptions in communication between the nervous and immune systems may lead to a host of illnesses ranging from the flu to depression. Our patterns of eating also influence broad aspects of mental and emotional well-being. Developing an ability to cope with stress—to moderate the stress response and maintain mental and physical homeostasis—is proving vital to well-being.

Summary

Status Reports on Clinical Practitioners and Mental Illness

Although the fields of psychiatry and psychology share the common goal of treating mental illness, both face challenges to offering the most effective therapies in the most informed ways. These challenges derive in part from the diverse array of clinical practitioners (psychiatrists, psychologists, neurologists, clinical social workers), a diverse array of therapeutic perspectives, and changing insurance coverage and prescription privileges.

By focusing on the brain, empirical evidence can help to discern causal factors and effective treatment approaches for mental illness. The case of Nadean Cool, a patient diagnosed with dissociative identity disorder, reveals how ineffective, and sometimes harmful, diagnoses and treatments can be when practitioners fail to rely on empirical evidence.

Exploring Various Windows of Mental Health

Valuable information about mental illness and mental health can be acquired using a range of approaches, including the neurobiological (encompassing neuroanatomy, neurochemistry, and neurophysiology), genetic, evolutionary, environmental, developmental, and cultural perspectives. Focusing on only one approach harshly limits information about the mental condition.

Evolutionary and cultural perspectives are frequently left out of the causal model for mental disorders. As described throughout this text, both these approaches offer insights into the origins of mental illness.

What Lies Ahead

Understanding the neurobiological foundations of mental health yields insights about how the brain and body interact. After describing the mechanisms that establish neurobiological homeostasis in Chapters 3–6, we consider how disruptions of homeostasis lead to various mental and brain disorders in Chapters 7–11. Ultimately, a goal of mental health is to prevent such disruptions from occurring, and maintaining homeostasis is the emphasis in Chapters 12–14.

Key Terms

empirical evidence (3)

psychotropic (psychoactive) drug (4)

biomedical model (4)

psychosocial model (4)

meta-analysis (5)

psychometric test (7)

traumatic brain injury (TBI) (15)

neurogenesis (15)

neurotrophic factors (16)

computerized tomography (CT) (16)

magnetic resonance imaging (MRI) (16)

diffusion tensor imaging (16)

electroencephalography (EEG) (18)

positron emission tomography (PET) (18)

functional magnetic resonance imaging (fMRI) (18)

phenotype (18)

concordance rate (19)

immediate early genes (19)

proteins (19)

simple (specific) phobia (21)

proximate causation (22)

ultimate causation (22)

sexual selection (22)

culture-bound syndrome (25)

homeostasis (25)

For Further Consideration

Andreasen, A. (2001). *Brave new brain.* New York: Oxford University Press. Andreasen noted the trend of clinical practice merging with the field of neuroscience when she published *The Broken Brain* in 1988. She continues to advocate the incorporation of behavioral and neuroscientific knowledge into the fields of psychiatry and clinical psychology. Especially emphasized in this book are the burgeoning areas of neuroimaging and genetic research; she feels that these areas will soon change both our understanding of and treatment approaches for many disorders. Andreasen is able to present the need for this modified version of psychiatry so effectively that the reader is left with little doubt that a more neuroscientific version of psychiatry is going to be the only psychiatry of the future.

Hobson, J. A., & Leonard, J. A. (2001). *Out of its mind: Psychiatry in crisis.* Cambridge, MA: Perseus Publishing. In this book Hobson, a psychiatrist who has conducted a great deal of research on sleeping and dreaming, reports on the current state of psychiatry. Torn between practitioners who treat patients solely by pharmacological means and a dwindling few still endorsing psychoanalysis, the authors call for a restructuring of the field. They present the term *neurodynamic* to refer to the exciting field of brain science and the many possibilities of this new area of research for clinical practice in the field of mental health.

Valenstein, E. S. (2000). *Blaming the brain: The truth about drugs and mental health.* New York: Free Press. Pharmacological treatments are standard fare in psychiatric treatment, yet there is no clear evidence that people suffering from disorders such as depression actually have a chemical imbalance that can be corrected with drugs. This observation reinforces the idea that factors other than neurotransmitters are involved in the expression of mental illness. Valenstein reminds us that a brain, as complex and wonderful as it is, does not exist without an environment that provides nourishment and stimulation.

Vincent, N. (2008). *Voluntary madness.* New York: Viking. Following a "mental breakdown" after writing her first book, immersion journalist Norah Vincent reports on being a patient in three different types of mental hospitals/treatment centers, ranging from an urban hospital to a private clinic. Winding her way through excessive pharmaceutical regimes, confusing regulations, and dreadful conditions, she reports from a patient's perspective in this interesting book. Her experiences caused her to doubt the efficacy of the many drugs prescribed for mental illness; however, after experiencing cognitive behavioral therapy, she endorsed the efficacy of this type of treatment. Students interested in a personal account of someone experiencing contemporary mental health therapies will be fascinated by this courageous book.

Chapter Two

Research, Treatment, and Points of View: Historical Perspectives

Connections

Barbers and Neurosurgeons

The sixteenth-century physician Ambroise Paré began his career as a barber-surgeon. He didn't let the lack of a university degree or knowledge of Latin or the dictates of the Church keep him from conducting brain surgery. Without formal training, Paré nonetheless contributed valuable knowledge related to the removal of bone fragments from the brain and used elaborate drilling instruments to open the skull. In 1564, Paré was approached by a man who thought his brain was rotten. This man asked Paré to open his skull, remove his rotting brain, and replace it with another one. There is no evidence that Paré actually attempted this brain transplant, although he did write that he attempted to restore the man's brain.

Ironically, an etching of Paré portrays him standing next to a jar with a fetus in it. The irony lies in the fact that over 400 years later successful brain tissue transplants would occur with the use of fetal brain tissue. Is there a connection between Paré's thoughts about giving his patient a brain transplant and the fetus located next to him in the etching? Regardless of what Paré was thinking in the sixteenth century, the current pioneers of clinical neuroscience are conducting exciting research that has considerable therapeutic value for patients suffering from neurodegenerative disorders such as Parkinson's disease.

You may be thinking that the idea of transplanting even a small portion of the brain is the stuff of science fiction novels, not textbooks. The contemporary story of brain transplants, however, is far from fiction

Ambroise Paré (1510–1590)

for Dr. Patrik Brundin, who currently directs the neuronal survival group at Lund University in Sweden. When he was just 17 years old, Brundin began doing research with experimental models of Parkinson's disease. He was passionate to learn more about

Parkinson's disease because his father had been diagnosed with this debilitating condition.

After conducting his initial research project, Brundin started medical school at Lund. During his days as a medical student, he continued to monitor the current literature on Parkinson's disease. Then, one day while riding in an elevator, Brundin had a chance meeting with some special rats that had surgical clips on their heads. When he asked the technician about the clips, he was told that the rats had an experimental form of Parkinson's disease and had received brain tissue transplants in an attempt to improve their condition. Brundin had to know more about this exciting research, and his questions led him to the scientist conducting the research, Dr. Anders Björklund, a leading authority in the field of brain tissue grafting.

Within a few months, Brundin was working as a junior science student in Björklund's laboratory. For the next several years, Brundin juggled his research and medical school careers so that he could get closer to his dream—replacing dead nerve cells, creating new brain circuitry, and restoring lost motor functions in human Parkinson's patients. In 1988, about the time he was finishing his doctoral thesis, he participated in the first human clinical trials in which Parkinson's patients received fetal brain tissue transplants. The results of the initial trials were disappointing, but the team persevered. In 1990, their first report documenting clear beneficial effects of nerve cell transplants in human Parkinson's patients was published in the prestigious journal *Science*. In fact, more than a decade after his surgery, one patient was doing remarkably well at 72 years of age—showing far fewer signs of the disease than would be expected without neurotransplantation. Since those early days, the team at Lund University has performed neural cell transplants on 19 patients, and about 350 transplant surgeries have been done worldwide.

The neural transplant research has successfully restored motor functions to many Parkinson's patients, but more research is needed to increase the actual number of transplanted cells that survive and grow in the host's brain. In addition to trying to increase the graft survival rate, transplant laboratories are working to find ways to enable neural tissue from other species (like pigs) to successfully live in the human brain. They are also trying to understand more about how the patient's own stem cells taken from other parts of the body may be prompted to develop into neurons when injected into the brain.

And what about Brundin's research today? Unfortunately, his father passed away before benefiting from his work, but Brundin continues to try to improve the survival rate of transplanted tissue in Parkinson's patients and, more currently, in patients suffering from Huntington's chorea, another disabling movement disorder. He has not forgotten the professors who gave him a once-in-a-lifetime opportunity to participate in research when he was a young student. Continuing the collaborative research that he values, Brundin currently works with a team of research professors, postdoctoral assistants, graduate students, and technicians. The team's goal is to maximize the survival rate of transplanted nerve cells by identifying the perfect nurturing neurochemical environment. He also works diligently to push toward a cure for Parkinson's disease; he recently began a biotechnology company, ParkCell, to conduct research on restorative therapies for patients suffering from Parkinson's disease.

Clinical neuroscience is an old idea but a young research discipline. It's impossible to know when the first human speculated on why others behave the way they do. People probably wondered about the brain's influence on our behavior, emotions, and thinking well before the advent of civilizations and written records; we take up the story with early Greek history and end our journey in the present (see the timeline depicted in Figure 2.1). Because of the fast pace of events and discoveries in the last two centuries, most of the neuroscience pioneers presented in this chapter come from this period.

The chapter is not exhaustive: Every significant individual or event in the history of such a broad field cannot be covered here. Perhaps the most exciting aspect of clinical neuroscience is the fact that the story is not yet complete.

EMERGENCE OF THE BRAIN AS THE CONTROLLING CENTER OF BEHAVIOR, EMOTIONS, AND THOUGHT

For thousands of years of recorded human history, producing convincing theories and supporting evidence for claims about the functions of the brain proved a monumental challenge for researchers. Eventually, progress was made toward this goal and scientists began to understand the true impact of this 3-pound (1,400-g) gel-like organ on human thought and behavior. Equally fascinating as those first glimmerings of the workings of the brain are the impressive stories of how talented researchers unraveled the secrets of the once mysterious nervous system and its connections to the brain and body.

Head, Heart, and Mind–Body Problem

It's difficult to imagine a time when the brain was thought to be of no more importance than any other organ in the body. As the pioneers in this section were entering the scene, the concept that the brain plays a critical role in controlling behavior challenged the wisdom of the times.

Hippocrates: Heart of mental functions. Hippocrates (c. 460–370 BCE) is known as the father of medicine, but he also contributed to the field of neuroscience. Most of Hippocrates' contemporaries believed that the heart controls the body's functions. Hippocrates, on the contrary, felt that the brain was the controlling center. He was not sure how the brain influenced behavior, but he was convinced that it was important:

> Men ought to know that from nothing else but the brain come joys, delights, laughter and sports, and sorrows, griefs, despondency, and lamentations. And by this, in an especial manner, we acquire wisdom and knowledge, and see and hear and know what are foul and what are fair, what are bad and what are good, mad and delirious, and fears and terrors assail us.... All these things we endure from the brain.... In these ways I am of the opinion that the brain exercises the greatest power in the man. (quoted in Finger, 2000, p. 69)

At the time, most mental illness was explained as demonic possession or a falling out of favor with the gods, but Hippocrates viewed conditions such as epilepsy to be a natural brain disease. Most of Hippocrates' treatments of the damaged or diseased brain attempted to restore order in this essential organ. In perhaps the earliest advocacy of a homeostatic theory of mental health, Hippocratic physicians promoted a **humoral theory** as an explanation of the body's functions. It was thought that four humors, or body fluids (yellow bile, black bile, phlegm, and blood), needed to be balanced for a person to be healthy.

humoral theory Early physical theory of mental illness proposed by Hippocrates. Four humors, or liquids, were thought to contribute to mental illness when they became unbalanced.

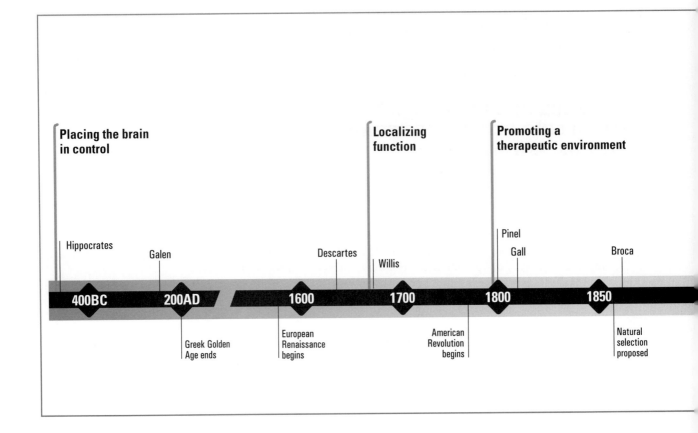

Figure 2.1
Pioneers and major research approaches in the evolution of clinical neuroscience. This timeline anchors the topics of the chapter's main sections at the point each of these ongoing approaches gained prominence. Selected historical events and scientific breakthroughs listed below the timeline serve as reference points. Individual research pioneers are listed at the point of their major contributions to forming and defining clinical neuroscience.

craniotomy Early physical therapy in which a section of a patient's skull was removed in an attempt to restore balance to the four humors, leading to recovery from mental illness.

According to the humoral theory, many illnesses could be treated simply by restoring the balance of the humors. Excessive flushing (being red in the face), for example, was a symptom of having too much blood and was treated by bloodletting (a method of draining blood from the body). The humoral theory spilled over to thoughts about the brain. A closed-head injury may have disrupted the balance of the humors as well; these injuries were often treated by performing a **craniotomy**—that is, removal of a section of the skull, exposing the brain so that excessive levels of a particular humor (blood, for example) could be drained to restore their balance. Obviously, the meaning of the term *brain drain* today is quite different from the literal one the Hippocratic physicians had in mind!

Hippocrates' accomplishments are even more impressive considering that he never performed dissections on human brains. At that time, it was thought that the human soul would be harmed if the body were manipulated before being put to rest. Additionally, there's no evidence that Hippocrates even dissected animal brains. It seems that his observations of the brain were limited to seeing patients who had brain disease or injuries—anyone whose injuries resulted in exposed brain tissue.

Galen: Spirit of mental functions. Galen (c. 129–200 CE) was born in Pergamon, a Roman territory. Galen's father felt that the medical god intended his son to be a physician, and he did everything possible to make

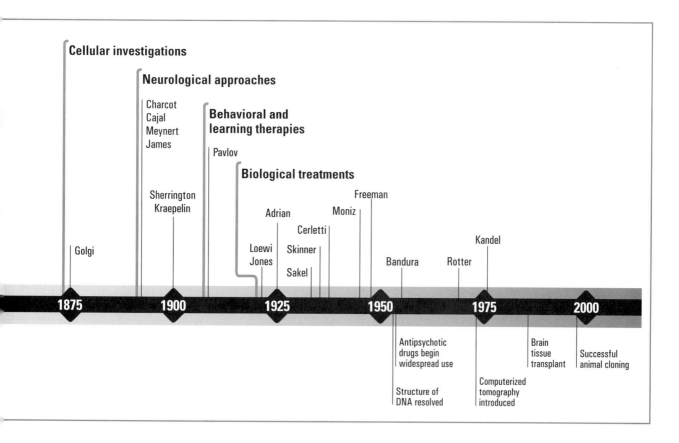

sure Galen had the best possible medical training. During his training, Galen was attracted to the notion of medicine based on anatomy and physiology.

Unfortunately for Galen, as in Hippocrates' time, the Roman Empire did not allow human autopsies. He had an occasional encounter with a wounded gladiator, but these encounters did not satisfy Galen's desire for firsthand observations of the brain. At this point, he turned to the next best thing—animals. He did not know about the existence of the great apes of Africa, but he did focus on the Barbary ape because of its "human" qualities. Galen's curiosity did not end with these primates. He went on to conduct many dissections of a diverse array of species, including pigs, oxen, and dogs.

Galen was an advocate of Aristotle's notions of empirical observation, and in trying to understand the connections and functions of various cranial and spinal nerves, he conducted actual **experiments** on the brain to test his ideas. He is well known for his squealing pig demonstration in which he sectioned the laryngeal nerves to demonstrate that the nerves from the brain, not the heart, controlled the pig's vocalization. Upon the completion of these dissections he commented "Now if the heart were the source of the nerves, as some think who know nothing of what is to be seen in dissection, it would readily move the laryngeal muscles by sending nerves directly into them....Actually...every nerve obviously takes origin from the brain or spinal cord..." (Gross, 2009, p. 42).

experiment Research technique in which variables are purposively manipulated in a systematic way to test or establish a hypothesis.

ventricles Internal capsules in the medial part of the brain that contain cerebrospinal fluid.

reflex Most basic form of behavior that involves an automatic response to an environmental event or stimulus, for example, sucking or blinking.

Galen's work extended beyond identifying the functions of nerves. He presented one of the earliest theories of brain function. Galen proposed that animal spirits inhabited the mind. These spirits were transformed from the heart's vital spirits in the brain's rete mirabile (miraculous net), a network of arteries surrounding the pituitary gland. The brain could also generate these animal spirits itself in the vascular linings of the **ventricles**, the fluid-filled cavities of the brain.

Regardless of their origin, Galen theorized that these animal spirits were stored in the brain's ventricles and, when needed, could perform amazing feats, such as moving muscles or transmitting sensory information from the body to the brain. Galen also appreciated the importance of the brain tissue surrounding the ventricles: He believed that brain tissue is involved in our highest mental functions.

Galen was both a medical practitioner and a brain researcher. This may qualify him as the first clinical neuroscientist. The field, however, was off to a slow start: Productive research related to the brain would not be conducted for more than a millennium. In fact, it wasn't until the European Renaissance that scientists resumed Galen's practice of dissecting and experimenting with brain tissue. Commenting on this time, Princeton University neuroscientist and historian Charles Gross recently wrote, "At about the time of Galen's death, classical science and medicine die. People prefer to believe rather than to discuss, critical faculty gives way to dogma, interest in this world declines in favor of the world to come, and worldly remedies are replaced by prayer and exorcism" (Gross, 2009, p. 45).

René Descartes: Body meets mind. René Descartes (1596–1650) lived in France during the post-Renaissance period. The mystique surrounding the brain at that time centered on function rather than structure. Descartes was a philosopher and did not look solely to brain dissections to understand the brain. Instead, he chose logic as the primary means to understand how the brain actually triggers behavior.

Descartes is not remembered for his neuroanatomical dissections, but he did conduct dissections as he developed his theories about brain function. Descartes, like Galen, believed that animal spirits were manufactured in the brain and that these spirits were formed in the pineal gland instead of the rete mirabile. The pineal gland was thought to release animal spirits into small valves in the ventricles, where they would travel through the nerves to the muscles. In fact, according to Descartes, the pineal gland gently tilted toward the directional flow of the animal spirits. This tilting increased the pressure with which the spirits traveled through the ventricles and nerves. On stimulation of these nerves, delicate filaments that attach to the valves of the ventricles were pulled open so that the animal spirits could travel to the muscle. During sleep, the tension of the nerve fibers relaxed, minimizing the likelihood of responding to external stimuli such as noise.

Descartes postulated this theory to explain basic automatic behaviors, such as **reflexes**, observed in both humans and other animals. However, he felt that more advanced reasoning ability was unique to humans and required a more complex explanation. Descartes proposed that thinking is driven by a rational soul that is not necessarily restricted to the confines of flesh and blood. Descartes was faced with the delicate issue of explaining how the immaterial mind could interact with the material substance of the body or brain. This philosophical question is known as the **mind–body**

problem. Descartes proposed that the immaterial soul resides in the pineal gland, where it monitors the actions of the animal spirits and consequently influences the machinery of the body.

It may seem a bit odd that, in spite of a 3-pound brain, Descartes centered his theories of both involuntary movement and reasoning ability on just one small structure—the pineal gland. Why was his focus so narrow? He wrote that the pineal gland (which is now known to be involved with physiological rhythms and biological timekeeping) is one of the few singular structures in the brain, a characteristic necessary to integrate information from the sets of sensory organs (two eyes, two ears, and so on). Also, after proposing his theory of movement, the pineal gland was familiar territory for Descartes.

You may wonder why Descartes did not choose another obvious singular structure in the brain, namely, the pituitary gland, which dangles off the base of the brain. As it happens, the pituitary gland had a bad reputation at this time. We now refer to the pituitary as the master endocrine (or hormonal) gland, but it was then thought to be the gland that drained the brain's waste (or phlegm). In fact, the well-known neuroanatomist Thomas Willis (discussed in the following section) would later refer to it as the "brain's sink." Descartes probably did not want to compromise his flashy new theory with a brain structure that held such negative connotations. Because the function of the pineal gland was unknown, however, the gland was fertile ground for fresh new ideas.

Descartes' theory that the mind and the brain interacted in the pineal gland became known as "interactionism," or Cartesian **dualism**. This theory, however, was not warmly welcomed by the more astute scientists and physicians of the time. Evidence of humans who seemed to have perfectly fine minds but damaged pineal glands cast great doubt on the validity of Descartes' theory. Also, his ideas about animal spirits were hardly new and innovative. Perhaps the most valuable result of his theory was related to the thoughts it generated in other scientists and physicians. In addition to being skeptical about the role of the pineal gland and animal spirits, many people doubted Descartes' clear distinctions between humans and other animals (or "brutes," as he called them). Obviously, Descartes did not have the benefit of the writings of Charles Darwin concerning evolution and a continuum between humans and other animals.

Descartes' fascination with the separation of the mind and body was reflected even in his death. He accepted an offer from Queen Christina of Sweden to tutor her in philosophy, but his frail body was no match for the cold, drafty conditions of the queen's house. He quickly contracted pneumonia and died a few months later. Because he was too tall for his casket, his head was detached from his body so that he could be buried.

Localizing Functions in the Brain

By the seventeenth century, it was becoming well established that the brain controls the body's functions, but a compelling question remained: Does the brain work as a totality, or do certain structures within the brain have specific functions? This idea of relating structure to function in the brain is known as **localization of function**. The scientists and physicians highlighted in this section provided convincing evidence that localized areas of the brain are involved in specific functions.

mind–body problem
Philosophical question posed to determine the nature, either mental or physical, of the mind.

dualism Philosophical position taken on the mind–body problem suggesting that the mind and body/brain are separate entities; Descartes proposed interactionism in which the two entities interacted in the physical brain, specifically in the pineal gland.

localization of function Notion that specific functions are localized in specific brain areas, as suggested by the eighteenth-century theory of phrenology.

Box 2.1

Brain Matters

Mental Illness Loses Its Religion

The Dark Ages in Europe (roughly the fourth through the fourteenth centuries) were characterized by a regression in virtually every area of knowledge. Unfortunately, the field of mental illness did not escape the stagnating consequences of this unenlightened era. The Church ruled with a firm hand, and abnormal behavior became associated with the supernatural. The only cure for mental illness would not come from physicians or scientists but from God. As had often been the case in ancient Greece, the Church taught that abnormal behavior was a result of the person consorting with or being possessed by the Devil. According to the Old Testament, consorting with the Devil was the worst crime a person could commit and the consequences were deadly.

The inhumanity of this demonic perspective of mental illness is epitomized in the 1484 publication *Malleus maleficarum* (*Hammer of the Witches*). Written by two Dominican monks, Heinrich Kraemer and Johann Sprenger, the goal of this document was to convince the world that people displaying abnormal behavior or thoughts were socializing with the Devil. This bizarre behavior was observed mostly in women, and these women were referred to as "witches"; in many cases, they were tortured and then burned to death.

In addition to being cruel and uninformed, the book is perverse in places: Kraemer and Sprenger describe in vivid detail the way witches copulate with devils. Additionally, they recommend that witches be tried in the nude, often with their pubic hair shaved because demons might hide there. Subsequently, the accused were tortured until they confessed; and with a confession, their murder was justified.

The legendary Joan of Arc, who led the French army to victory when she was only 17 years of age, was later burned as a witch after it became known that she experienced hallucinations. More than 200 years after the publication of the book, in the presumably intellectual community of Salem, Massachusetts, 19 women were hanged as witches. One brave defender of the women, Giles Corey, was put to death for supporting their innocence.

Today, it seems unimaginable that *Malleus maleficarum* went through 30 editions between 1484 and 1669. Even more unimaginable is the fact that hundreds of thousands of innocent men and women were tortured to death because of these unenlightened beliefs. As you can discern from this chapter, very little scientific knowledge was contributed to the field of clinical neuroscience during this mystical era. Ambroise Paré, introduced in Connections at the beginning of this chapter, was one of the few individuals courageous enough to challenge the deadly publication. The memory of this horrifying book should serve as a reminder that only empirically based perspectives, as opposed to mere opinions of individuals, should be accepted as actual explanations of mental illness or abnormal behavior.

Thomas Willis: Pioneer of brain functions. Thomas Willis (1621–1675) was born only 25 years after Descartes, but their ideas diverge so widely that they may as well have lived in two different eras. Willis was part of a new breed of medical physiologist that broke from the tradition of the humoral theory and other ancient philosophical notions and came to rely more heavily on clinical and scientific observations and experiments.

After receiving his medical training at Oxford, Willis immediately started building a private practice. He became interested in the brain when he met a group of natural philosophers at Oxford who were interested in neuroanatomy and neurophysiology. These men, who in a *Da Vinci*-like code called themselves "the Virtuosi," had a powerful impact on Willis's career. In 1660, Willis was offered a professorship at Oxford; he used this position to investigate the senses and the nervous system. Willis's collaboration with the Virtuosi was an early demonstration of the advantages of collaboration among talented scientists. In fact, working with this productive team, Willis published the impressive work known as *Cerebri anatome* (*Cerebral Anatomy*) in 1664.

Unlike Descartes, Willis saw a continuum in the mental lives of humans and other animals. He observed that animals exhibit evidence of perception, memory, and cognition, as humans do; animals just experience these phenomena on a more rudimentary level. Willis thus saw value in investigating both human and animal brains. His exploration of the nervous system contributed many terms that neuroscientists still use—*neurology*, *psychology*, *lobe*, *hemisphere*, and *reflexion* (reflex)—though some of these terms had slightly different meanings then.

Through astute observations and dissections, Willis started to discover the true functions of some of the structures of the brain. For example, his work deemphasized the importance of the ventricles in higher functions and pointed toward the influence of the cerebral hemispheres. He also described the corpus striatum for the first time, correctly proposing this structure's role in movement, and suggested that the lower brain stem area is involved in the most basic functions, such as respiration.

On the clinical side, Willis described a relationship between mania and melancholia (depression), suggested that impaired intelligence may be inherited, described epilepsy as a "natural" brain disease rather than a result of demonic possession, and observed that consuming too much wine may lead to mental impairment (as observed in chronic alcoholics with *Korsakoff's syndrome*, a neurodegenerative disease caused by alcoholism-induced thiamin [vitamin B1] deficiency). Willis's impressive work elevated the brain sciences to a higher plane during the latter part of the seventeenth century. His dual interests in neuroanatomy and mental illness establish his legacy as a true pioneer in the field of clinical neuroscience.

Franz Joseph Gall: Rise and fall of phrenology The next character in our cast of early neuroscientists interested in localization of brain function lived in Vienna. Whereas Willis identified more general functions with particular areas of the brain, Franz Joseph Gall (1758–1828) devoted his energy to discerning where more specific functions—certain personality characteristics—are housed in the brain.

After completing his medical degree, Gall quickly built a reputation as one of the most outstanding physicians in all of Austria. A trend of the day was to associate certain physical characteristics, such as facial structure, with personality characteristics (individuals with beady little eyes, for example, were thought to be sinister—a correlation that still seems to be alive in comic strips). Gall agreed that variations in physical structures reflected variations in function, but he wasn't interested in facial or other bodily characteristics; he was solely interested in the brain.

Gall wrote that his fascination with the relationship between brain structure and personality characteristics began when he was only 9 years old. He noticed that certain boys in his class were excellent memorizers, a skill that did not come very readily to Gall. He observed that these supermemorizers had bulging eyes (he called them "ox eyes") and proposed that their eyes protruded because of an overly developed cortical (or higher brain) area that controlled verbal memory. Building on these observations, Gall later postulated that all personality characteristics (or "faculties," as he called them) were controlled by specialized organs woven into the fabric of the **cerebral cortex**, the wrinkled, outermost layer of the brain.

cerebral cortex Most recently evolved part of the brain that envelops the midbrain; also associated with complex cognitive functions.

correlation Statistical technique used to determine how strongly two variables are related; two variables may change in a similar pattern (positive correlation) or a different pattern (negative correlation).

phrenology Term popularized to describe Gall's theory of localization of function. In this theory, bumps on the surface of the skull were deemed to predict certain mental capabilities.

Figure 2.2
(a) Location of faculties according to Spurzheim.
(b) Contemporary phrenology bust showing modified faculties that may be appropriate for the twenty-first century.
(B) BUST MADE BY ACCOUTREMENTS, SEATTLE, WASHINGTON. PHOTO COURTESY OF KELLY LAMBERT, RANDOLPH-MACON COLLEGE BEHAVIORAL NEUROSCIENCE LABORATORY

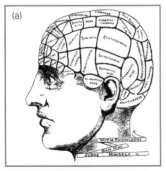

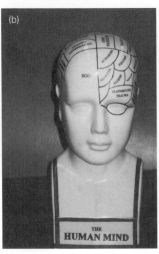
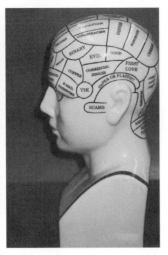

Gall set out to establish relationships, or **correlations**, between cortical structures and the intensity of the various faculties. Since he felt that variations in the brain's cortex would be represented by variations in one's overlying skull, he devised a protocol requiring actually palpating the skulls of many individuals to establish relationships between skull bumps and certain personality characteristics. In the end, Gall settled for 27 faculties, 19 of which were shared with animals (for example, reproductive instinct, sense of place) and eight of which were distinctly human (for example, wisdom, poetic talent, religious sentiment, and satire). It is important to note that Gall's idea that the skull represented the delicate bumps of the cortex was not due to a lack of knowledge of the brain. On the contrary, Gall was a gifted neuroanatomist and discovered several neural pathways of the brain.

Although Gall's new theory could be easily criticized for methodological reasons (Do skulls actually have bumps?), his first obstacle was the philosophical criticism of the conservative Catholic authorities in Austria. They felt that Gall's theory reduced the intellect and soul to the materialistic brain and warned Gall that people would lose their heads over this doctrine—literally! When Gall was 47 years old, he had no choice but to leave Austria if he wanted to pursue his interest in the localization of brain function.

Subsequently, Gall started traveling around Europe, giving lectures and performing dissections of the brain in the major cities and universities. Before leaving Austria, Gall made the acquaintance of Johann Spurzheim, who would become his assistant for the next 9 years. Although Gall seemed very impressed with Spurzheim early in their relationship, the two men parted ways in 1813 because Spurzheim began advocating a craniological system that differed from Gall's (2.2a).

Spurzheim introduced new faculties to Gall's list and espoused ideas that organs could be modified with training or learning, an idea with which Gall vehemently disagreed. Additionally, Spurzheim removed the more evil faculties from the list, enabling him to describe humans in a more optimistic light. Spurzheim was not the first person to use the term **phrenology** (from *phren*, "mind," and *logos*, "discourse"), but he was the person who popularized the term associated with Gall's theory of brain localization. (Actually, Gall never used the word *phrenology*; he felt that the term *organology* more clearly conveyed his emphasis on the brain.)

Once Spurzheim was on his own, he completed a medical degree and then became wildly popular in England, Ireland, and Scotland. In the United States, the *American Journal of Phrenology* was established. By 1840, however, phrenology was no longer perceived as a science: It existed only as a source of parlor humor.

Most scientists criticized Gall for using only selective, subjective data to support his theory. One scientist, Marie-Jean-Pierre Flourens, a French experimentalist, attacked Gall's theory with a vengeance. Flourens used acceptable methodological techniques (for example, experimentation with animals) to determine the importance of various cortical areas in several different animals. He failed to find any evidence to support Gall's claims and publicly ridiculed Gall's methods and theory.

Most scientists and physicians who were contemporaries of Gall would have chosen to simply forget about him, but he is worth remembering for several reasons. In addition to his impeccable skills as a neuroanatomist, he was passionate about understanding the role of the brain in certain higher functions. In fact, in just a few decades, evidence would be presented to support the notion of localization of function within the cerebral hemispheres. Ironically, Flourens, who used solid methodology, was subsequently wrong when he concluded that cortical localization of higher functions did not exist. As you can see in Figure 2.2b, a recent phrenological bust with more contemporary faculties (playground trauma, zipper location, dot.com faculties) is evidence that the notions of phrenology remain part of our culture even today.

Paul Broca: Localization of language. Gall's organology was widely ridiculed, but not all physicians and scientists were ready to throw out the idea of cortical localization along with phrenology. Dr. Jean-Baptiste Bouillaud, a French physician interested in brain functions, and his son-in-law, Simon Alexandre Ernest Aubertin, believed that language is localized in the anterior lobes of the cerebral cortex. Their theory was based on clinical observations of people with brain damage in this area. All they lacked was a case of obvious language difficulties linked with a confirmation of cortical damage on the patient's autopsy. It happened that one person attending Aubertin's lectures about the localization of language abilities was Paul Broca (1824–1880).

Whereas Bouillaud and Aubertin had been unable to find the landmark case that would provide overwhelming evidence supporting the idea of cerebral localization of language, Broca, who practiced at the Bicêtre Hospital, discovered a 51-year-old patient named Leborgne who had suffered from epilepsy since childhood and had not been able to speak for 20 years. By the time Leborgne became Broca's patient, he was suffering from severe *cellulitis* (an infection of the skin and subcutaneous tissue) with gangrene and was not expected to live long.

Broca immediately saw the potential in this case and invited Aubertin to witness his examination of this man who could not speak. After the patient died about a week later, an autopsy confirmed Bouillard's and Aubertin's predictions about anterior cortical areas being involved in speech, and it provided even more specificity: The damaged area was in the third convolution of the frontal cortex of the left hemisphere.

In 1861, Broca presented and published this landmark case study of the patient who would become known as Tan because this was about the only sound the man could make (Figure 2.3). Where Gall's ideas of cerebral localization were considered blasphemous half a century earlier, Broca's observations were met with enthusiasm. Finally, convincing evidence of cerebral localization had been presented. In the next several years, Broca encountered more cases that confirmed the existence of the language center. He was intrigued by the fact that the damage in all these cases was in the left hemisphere and later proposed that the language center is located there, suggesting a cerebral dominance of the left hemisphere in language abilities.

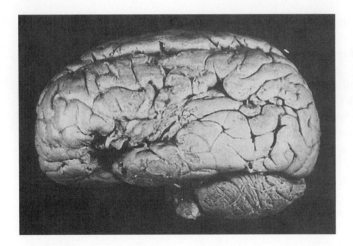

Figure 2.3
The brain of Tan, believed by some researchers to be the most famous brain in all of neuroscience, reveals a lesion around the third convolution of the left hemisphere. Contemporary neuroanatomists call this "Broca's area."
MUSEE DUPUYTREN; COURTESY OF ASSISTANCE PUBLIQUE, HOPITAUX DE PARIS

Whereas Willis had elegantly shown the existence of the localization of more general functions, Broca was the first to demonstrate the localization of higher functions—the beginning of understanding the specificity of the structures within the brain.

Pioneers of Cellular Investigations in the Brain: The Architects

In the mid-nineteenth century, when researchers were beginning to understand that various structures in the brain are related to specific functions, interest was also brewing about the makeup of these brain structures. Because adequate stains for brain tissue and high-powered microscopes had not yet been invented, not much was known about the fundamental units of the nervous system. Preliminary work by Jan Evangelista Purkyne a few decades earlier had suggested that cells with branches populate the nervous system. It was also thought that these cells formed a continuous neural network so that messages, or impulses, could travel as quickly as possible. This picture of the nervous system was about to change however.

Nerve cells couldn't be understood until advances were made in **histology**, the process of studying biological tissue. Once methods were established to visualize the cells of the nervous system, the cells had to be identified, catalogued, and documented much like new species in an exotic new land. Once stains were developed so that nerve cells could be visualized, it quickly became obvious that these tiny cells were more elaborate than anyone had ever suspected.

Camillo Golgi: Revealing neuronal structure with the perfect stain. Camillo Golgi (1843–1926) was raised in the Lombardy region of Italy and educated at the University of Pavia. His passion for research enabled him to make a histological breakthrough. Working by candlelight in the evenings, Golgi attempted to impregnate nerve cells with a silver stain so that he could visualize their structure. He immersed the tissue in silver nitrate for a day or so, then bathed it in a series of alcohol and oil solutions. Much to Golgi's delight, this process produced a picture, or blueprint, of the neuron: beautiful black nerve cells against a yellowish background (Figure 2.4). For some unknown reason, only about 3% of the nerve cells actually stained. This partial staining is significant because if all the nerve cells stained, the tissue would look like a black smudge under the microscope.

In 1873, Golgi published his first paper, in which he described the detailed structure of nerve cells. A few years later, he accepted a faculty position so that he could spend his time using his silver stain to understand the fine structure of the nervous system. A more accurate picture of the nerve cells was emerging, but Golgi continued to endorse the **nerve net theory** that suggested the nervous system is made up of continuous extensions of nerve

histology Systematic preparation of brain or other physiological tissue for microscopic study to be used for experimental and diagnostic purposes.

nerve net theory Early theory of the nature of the nervous system implying that the nervous system is made up of continuous extensions of nervous tissue.

cells (as opposed to individual nerve cell units). This theory, however, would soon be challenged.

Santiago Ramón y Cajal: Providing evidence for the neuron doctrine.

Santiago Ramón y Cajal (1852–1934) worked over 100 years ago in Spain, and his representations of the nerve cells, or **neurons**, still appear to be accurate. His research was the first to cast significant doubt on the nerve net theory.

In his autobiography, entitled *Recollections of My Life* (1917), he wrote that his first love was art but that his father, who was a physician, felt such a career was worthless and embarked on a campaign to persuade his son to become a physician. Ironically, Ramón y Cajal's interest in anatomy was born in a graveyard. In 1868, his father took him to graveyards to examine human remains that had been exhumed because the leased burial plots had not been renewed. Once Ramón y Cajal started sketching the bones from these exhumed bodies, he realized that he wanted to learn more about anatomy. His first step toward this goal was obtaining a medical degree.

While visiting Madrid to take an examination for a professorship, Ramón y Cajal had the opportunity to look through a microscope. The images he saw so entranced him that he decided to pursue a career in microscopy. He used his own money to purchase a microscope and started to build a modest lab. Once he was introduced to Golgi's silver stain, he modified the protocol to produce the best images of neurons. Reading his words today, one sees the love and fascination he had for the object of his affection, the neuron.

Ramón y Cajal found that neurons surrounded by fatty myelin tissue failed to produce clear staining, so he searched for less fatty cells and discovered that birds and young animals produced high-quality stains. Armed with his passion and talent for art, Ramón y Cajal then easily transferred these images to his sketchpad (Figure 2.5).

Ramón y Cajal's troubles did not disappear once he perfected the Golgi staining technique. He was producing very interesting data at a rapid pace, but his isolation in Spain and in the Spanish language prohibited the dissemination of his findings. Investing his own money once again, Ramón y Cajal founded a journal entitled *Trimonthly Review of Normal and Pathological Histology* so that he would have a place to rapidly publish his findings. He subsequently sent copies to leading anatomists across Europe. Unfortunately, the other anatomists did not understand Spanish.

Frustrated, Ramón y Cajal feared that his important findings suggesting that the nerve cells were not fused or connected, as dictated by the prevailing nerve net theory, were never going to be accepted by respected colleagues. This led him to have his works translated into French. He then took his papers, slides, and microscope to the German Anatomical Society in 1889. Ramón y Cajal's exhibit caught the attention of influential anatomists. During his conversations with fellow researchers, Ramón y Cajal described how he had failed

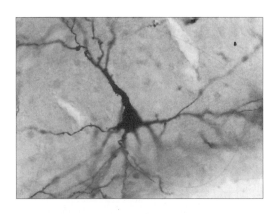

Figure 2.4
Golgi-stained pyramidal neuron in the CA1 area of the hippocampus, an area of the brain involved in learning and memory.
COURTESY OF KELLY LAMBERT, RANDOLPH-MACON COLLEGE BEHAVIORAL NEUROSCIENCE LABORATORY

neuron Fundamental unit, or cell, of the nervous system.

Figure 2.5
Neurons from the visual cortex of a several-day-old human infant as sketched by Santiago Ramón y Cajal.

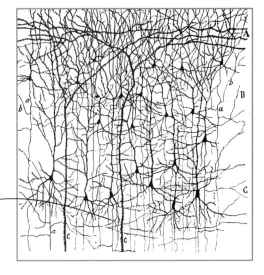

neuron doctrine Theory that separate units, or neurons, as opposed to continuous units, make up the nervous system.

synapse Tiny gap that separates two neurons and is the location of communication between the two cells.

to find any evidence of the nerve net theory in his observations of the nerve cells. He went on to suggest that neurons were independent structures.

The significance of Ramón y Cajal's work was recognized in 1906 when he was awarded the Nobel Prize for Physiology or Medicine, an award he shared with Camillo Golgi. The architecture of the individual neuron was established, but a lot of uncertainty remained about the interconnections among the neurons.

Charles Scott Sherrington: Describing the synapse. English scientist Charles Scott Sherrington (1857–1952) published his first scientific paper when he was a medical student. After graduating from medical school, he became interested in immunology, pathology, and the anatomical changes that accompany damage to the motor cortex. Sherrington became more and more enamored with the nervous system and started investigating the mechanisms of the motor reflex, specifically, the knee jerk.

Even before Ramón y Cajal's work suggested the existence of individual neurons, Sherrington was already leaning in that theoretical direction. His own research suggested that cortical lesions resulted in specific, not diffuse, damage. In 1894, when Ramón y Cajal was lecturing in London, he stayed in Sherrington's home and the two men discussed the likelihood of the nerve cells existing as individual units. This notion, which directly opposed the neural net theory, was later known as the **neuron doctrine**.

Sherrington went a step further a few years after his conversations with Ramón y Cajal and introduced the notion of a functional junction that probably existed between neurons. Initially, he used the term *synapsis* (from the Greek word meaning "to clasp") for this neuronal gap. Today, it's called the **synapse**. Sherrington's hypothesis remained theoretical until more high-powered microscopes permitted researchers to detect this tiny junction.

Pioneers of Cellular Investigations in the Brain: The Chemical Engineers

The blueprints for the nervous system were becoming more and more established, but what was the microstructure of the nerve cells? If Ramón y Cajal and Sherrington were correct about the neuron doctrine, how did separate neurons communicate with one another?

Toward the end of the nineteenth century, the prevailing thought was that neuronal communication was electrical in nature. Waves of electrical charges would shoot down the neurons and then jump across the tiny synaptic gaps. In 1877, Emil Du Bois-Reymond, a German physiologist, proposed that an alternate method might also be employed in neuronal communication. In addition to electrical stimulation, Du Bois-Reymond proposed that chemicals may be released from the endings of neurons. This chemical hypothesis was pretty much ignored until Otto Loewi entered the scene.

Otto Loewi: Dreaming of chemical communication. For his doctoral thesis, Otto Loewi (1873–1961) conducted research in pharmacology, a discipline that investigates the effect of drugs on physiological systems. Scientists and the emerging pharmaceutical industry were eager to learn just how chemicals could alter physiological functioning throughout the body, such as increasing heart rate or decreasing blood pressure. Researchers were speculating that the neurons may actually work via such chemical transmission, but no convincing evidence supported such a claim.

The answer to this neuronal communication mystery turns out literally to be the stuff that dreams are made of, and indeed this was the case for Loewi. According to scientific folklore, Loewi reported that in 1921 he awoke from a dream in the middle of the night with an outline for a creative experiment that would prove that neurons communicate via chemicals.

Loewi's dream was based on the simple observation that if you expose a frog's heart and stimulate one of the major cranial nerves that is involved in basic functions such as heart rate, you can see the heart slow down. Loewi's dream suggested that a chemical was released from the nerve endings onto the muscle of the heart and, if you collected the chemical surrounding the slowed heart and simply poured it around a second frog's heart, then—voilà—the second frog's heart would slow down as well. The story goes that Loewi took notes on his dream right away so that he could actually conduct the experiment the next day. Unfortunately, the next morning he could not read his scribbles and had forgotten the dream.

Frustrated, Loewi tried to remember the experiment throughout the next day. When he woke up after having the same dream that night, he decided not to take any chances. He quickly got up and went to the laboratory to conduct the experiment while it was fresh in his mind. In addition to slowing down the frog's heart, Loewi went a step further and stimulated the "accelerator" nerve. He saw the same general effect: The heart of the first frog accelerated, and when the fluid surrounding the heart of the stimulated frog was poured onto the second frog's heart, an increase was also observed in the heart rate of the second frog. Loewi now had convincing evidence of chemical transmission in the nervous system.

Following Loewi's significant studies, researchers speculated that the drugs, such as acetylcholine, that lower blood pressure may also work as natural substances within the nervous system. The acetylcholine used by the drug companies was isolated from a particular fungus, but it was thought that the body might produce this substance as well. This idea was speculative, though, until someone could actually extract the substance from animal tissue.

The respected neurophysiologist Henry Dale (1875–1968) felt up to the challenge. In 1929, he visited a slaughterhouse and harvested spleens from the horses and oxen that were just killed. He processed the tissue and was ecstatic when 70 pounds of horse spleen produced less than a gram of a neurochemical that was identical to the active substance in the drugs. Now the researchers could be sure that the drug known as acetylcholine, extracted from a fungus, was exactly the same as the substance in the spleens of the horses. This was just the beginning of the identification of numerous natural chemicals, or **neurotransmitters**, in the nervous system. The significance of the contributions of both Loewi and Dale was recognized in 1936 when the two men shared the Nobel Prize for their "discoveries relating to chemical transmission of nerve impulses."

Edgar D. Adrian: Amplifying the electrical language of the neuron. About the same time that some scientists were trying to understand how neurons communicate, other scientists were busy trying to understand

neurotransmitter Chemical, such as dopamine or serotonin, in the brain that is essential for communication between two neurons.

nerve impulse (action potential) Physiological basis of communication in the nervous system triggered by the exchange of certain ions across the nerve cell membrane.

all-or-none law Observation that, once the threshold is reached, all action potentials are the same size regardless of the intensity of the original stimulation.

transduction Conversion of physical energy, such as light, to energy that can be used in the nervous system.

how information was coded in individual neurons: How was energy conducted within a single neuron so that it could subsequently communicate with a second neuron? Edgar D. Adrian (1889–1977), an English physiologist, made great strides in elucidating this process.

Adrian's first substantial discovery was that neurons react, or "fire," in an all-or-none fashion. Adrian's clever set of experiments suggested that once a neuron is stimulated, it does not matter whether the original stimulus was just minimal or very intense: The strength of the **nerve impulse** (or **action potential**, as it was named by Du Bois-Reymond) consistently shot down the nerve at full strength. Just as a mousetrap snaps with the same intensity regardless of whether the cheese is gently or aggressively removed from the spring, the action potential, once triggered, proceeds down the neuron with amazing consistency.

Adrian's work with the **all-or-none law** was impressive, but he wanted to learn more about the intricacies of nerve cell communication. Unfortunately, the existing technology wasn't up to the task. Equipment that would amplify the electrical messages without distorting their natural characteristics had to be invented before more progress could be made. Eventually, the necessary amplifiers were introduced, and Adrian went on to record from individual neurons and to conduct further research related to the coding of sensory stimulation, such as visual or auditory input. He was investigating **transduction**, how the environmental energy of light and sound are converted into neural energy used by the visual and auditory sensory neurons.

Neuroscience researchers had identified the basic structure of the individual nerve cells and discovered important information about coding and communication of information within the nervous system. The ground was now fertile for many discoveries that would shed light on the nature of how the brain is involved in mental health.

NEUROLOGICAL APPROACHES TO MENTAL ILLNESS

In this section, the focus shifts from the story of how the once mysterious nervous system came to be understood to the true nature of clinical neuroscience—how neuroscience research was applied to mental illness. Could knowledge about the structure and functioning of the nervous system translate into therapeutic benefits for the mentally ill?

Mental Illness Meets the Microscope

Looking at neurons through a microscope to gain information that could lead to therapies for mental illness was an alien notion in the mid- to late nineteenth century. Still, a few bold scientists started to build the bridge between neuroanatomy and clinical symptoms. Theodor Meynert (1833–1892) was one of the first of the modern wave of clinical neuroscientists. After studying medicine in Vienna, he specialized in neuropathology. He also had an interest in psychiatry and subsequently acquired a faculty position in psychiatry. In this position, Meynert did what came naturally to him—he examined brain tissue under a microscope. He developed stains and spent countless hours searching for pathological lesions in the nerve tissue. (It is interesting

Box 2.2

Eric Kandel

From Studying the History of Neuroscience to Becoming the History of Neuroscience

When Austrian-born Eric Kandel (1929–present) graduated from Harvard College in 1952, he knew exactly what he wanted to do: attend medical school so that he could become a Park Avenue psychoanalyst. In preparation for his dream career, Kandel received a medical degree from New York University School of Medicine so that he could follow in the footsteps of a fellow Austrian-born physician, Sigmund Freud. Following graduation, Kandel worked as a research associate in the Laboratory of Neurophysiology at the National Institute of Mental Health. This research experience convinced him that he wanted to spend his career in the laboratory, not on Park Avenue.

In the early 1960s, Kandel made the bold decision to conduct research on an unlikely animal, the large sea snail, *Aplysia californica.* Kandel found this invertebrate attractive for neuroscience research because it has fewer and larger neurons than more traditional laboratory animals. This simple neural system would subsequently serve as an invaluable model for understanding the cellular and molecular basis of learning. Armed with endless research questions about the neurobiology of simple conditioning in *Aplysia*, Kandel decided to set up his laboratory at Columbia University, where he remains to this day.

Throughout his career, Kandel has also been a student of the history of neuroscience. In 2000 he wrote (with Larry Squire) an article in *Science* entitled "Neuroscience: Breaking Down Scientific Barriers to the Study of Brain and Mind." In addition to Ramón y Cajal's description of the neuron at the turn of the twentieth century (which led to the neuron doctrine), Kandel credits the work of Alan Hodgkin, Andrew Huxley, and Bernard Katz, who described the movement of ions across the neuronal membrane 40 years later, as seminal research in the history of neuroscience. According to Kandel, Ramón y Cajal's cellular approach and Hodgkin and colleagues' molecular approach provided

Eric Kandel

the basic floor plans of the nervous system and the basis for thousands of valuable research programs in the future (including his own work identifying cellular mechanisms accompanying events such as habituation and sensitization in *Aplysia*).

Kandel's fascination with the "giants" of neuroscience, as he calls them, became ironic when Kandel himself became a part of the history of neuroscience: He was awarded the Nobel Prize in Physiology or Medicine in 2000 (shared with Paul Greengard and Arvid Carlsson). Concerning the future of the field, Kandel reports:

> For neuroscience to address the most challenging problems confronting the behavioral and biological sciences, we will need to continue to search for new molecular and cellular approaches and use them in conjunction with systems neuroscience and psychological science. In this way, we will best be able to relate molecular events and specific changes within neuronal circuits to mental processes such as perception, memory, thought, and possibly consciousness itself. (Kandel & Squire, 2000, p. 1120)

Kandel's groundbreaking research has attempted to merge basic neuroscience with the more advanced behavior of learning. Consequently, the field has already made progress toward solving the neurobiological puzzle of learning behavior.

to note that one of Meynert's students, Sigmund Freud, would later become famous for psychoanalysis, a very different approach to treating mental illness.)

Unfortunately, Meynert was unable to identify significant disease-related pathology other than lesions in advanced syphilis patients. Perhaps his greatest contribution was his vision about the relationship between the nervous system and mental illness. In 1890, he wrote: "The more that psychiatry seeks, and finds, its scientific bases in a deep and finely grained understanding of the anatomical structure [of the brain], the more it elevates itself to the status of a science that deals with causes" (quoted in Shorter, 1997, p. 77). Meynert's sentiment is as important today as in his time.

At the same time that Meynert was making his prophetic statement about psychiatry and neuroscience, Emil Kraepelin (1856–1926) was awarded a professorship at the university psychiatric clinic in Heidelberg. Kraepelin was unable to study brain tissue through the microscope because of eye problems, but that did not stop him from contributing to the cause in an indirect way. He organized an impressive group of neuroscientists in his laboratory to help unravel the relationship between the brain and mental illness. Among his collaborators was Franz Nissl (1860–1919), a well-known neurohistologist who described six distinct layers within the cerebral cortex. Another neuroscientist Kraepelin hired was Alois Alzheimer (1864–1915), who in 1906 discovered the neuropathology consistent with a type of **dementia** (mental deterioration) that would later be named after him.

One barrier that existed for these early clinical neuroscientists was the absence of a systematic method of categorizing different forms of mental illness. Kraepelin made major contributions toward categorization by collecting and organizing extensive data on a wide variety of patients. His data cards on patients and their illnesses enabled him, first, to suggest that illnesses seemed to fall into particular categories and, second, to document the developmental course of the various disorders. For example, after reviewing both his data and the work of others, he wrote about patients suffering from manic–depressive illness. Also, he wrote about dementia praecox (premature mental deterioration) to describe the disorder that would later, in 1908, be referred to as **schizophrenia** by one of Kraepelin's followers, Eugen Bleuler (1857–1939).

In spite of these scientists who fought the battle against mental illness armed with microscopes, a substantial divide remained between looking at neurons and actually treating the symptoms of mental illness. Certainly, the bridge between behavioral symptoms and the structure of the nervous system needed to be more complete before real progress could be made.

Jean-Martin Charcot: Birth of Neurology

In the mid-nineteenth century, Jean-Martin Charcot (1825–1893) was appointed to the coveted position of senior physician at the Salpêtrière Hospital, a famous Parisian hospice for sick and elderly women. At the time of this appointment, the Salpêtrière, however, was not in its best condition. Charcot found many buildings in ruins, and the 5,000 patients seemed to be housed together at random.

Like Kraepelin, Charcot saw a great need to describe and categorize the symptoms and diseases suffered by the patients at Salpêtrière. He set out to find some method to the madness in this asylum of misery. One strategy he employed was to meet with and examine the women, document their symptoms, and then, after they died, conduct autopsies on their brains to determine if their condition could be related to some brain pathology.

Charcot gained a reputation as an astute observer of the behavioral symptoms of his patients. It was reported that his typical session involved

dementia Progressive loss of mental functioning atypical of normal aging processes.

schizophrenia Mental illness characterized by hallucinations, delusions, social withdrawal, and cognitive deterioration. Certain brain modifications such as a smaller hippocampus and disarrayed neurons have been observed to accompany this condition.

sitting next to the undressed patient and watching her as she made particular movements. He would also ask the patient to speak and then would test various reflexes and sensory responses. Charcot's observations, coupled with knowledge of a detailed clinical history, enabled him to determine the origin of the patient's neurological problem.

During his career, Charcot was instrumental in describing multiple sclerosis, Parkinson's disease, amyotrophic lateral sclerosis, and Tourette syndrome. He also became interested in cerebral localization and even tried to help Broca with his research by sending him some patients with compromised speech abilities. Charcot observed that some patients had what looked like a behavioral problem but no brain pathology. For example, the patient might have been *aphasic* (could not speak), yet no frontal lobe lesion could be found on autopsy.

During the final stage of Charcot's career at Salpêtrière, he concentrated on cases where the patients displayed significant symptoms, yet no accompanying pathology could be identified. These women were said to be suffering from **hysteria**, from the Greek word for "uterus." Charcot studied these cases in order to differentiate them from epilepsy cases. For some reason, he began to stray from his usual employment of empirical strategies (strategies based on observable, verifiable evidence) for accurately describing the disorders of the nervous system. For example, without any known convincing reason, he endorsed the notion that only hysterical patients could be hypnotized.

In an interesting sidebar to Charcot's story, a young Sigmund Freud (1856–1939) was seated in the audience for one of Charcot's famous weekly lectures (pictured in Figure 2.6). Freud was intrigued by the notion that mental events could set off a cascade of symptoms. In fact, Charcot probably provided Freud with the foundation for what would become his theory of psychoanalysis.

Thus, Charcot, who had been so dependent on objective clinical science to categorize a host of neurological and mental diseases, gave Freud the bricks and mortar to build his subjective theory. In many ways, **psychoanalysis**, based on speculations and theories about unconscious motives that drive behavior, was the antithesis to an empirical approach to understanding mental and nervous system diseases. Based on Charcot's introduction of hysteria as a disorder of women, Freud's psychoanalytical theories also focused on women. Because of the rise of the Nazi regime, though, psychoanalysis, which had become a mainstay of German and Austrian psychiatry, all but disappeared in Europe in the 1930s but was resurrected in the United States, where it flourished for the next three decades. In the United States, a few adaptations were made to this form of psychiatry; mainly, the focus shifted from the more debilitating disorders (psychoses) to problems of everyday life (neuroses). Psychoanalysis was still used by some to treat psychosis but without success.

Whereas Charcot studied hysterical women in the famous Salpêtrière asylum, psychoanalysts in the United States migrated to private practices located in large cities. Edward Shorter (1997), a historian of medicine, wrote that these modifications resulted in a "scientific stagnation" in the field of psychiatry during the mid-twentieth

hysteria Early characterization of mental disturbance described in women who had no known accompanying brain damage. Charcot thought that only hysterical women could be hypnotized.

psychoanalysis Therapeutic approach to mental illness developed by Freud. In this subjective theory, unconscious motives were thought to direct behavior and thoughts.

Figure 2.6
A century ago, Jean Martin Charcot concluded that the symptoms of "hysteria" could not be explained by what was then known about the brain. The susceptibility of his patients to hypnosis helped Charcot to convince others, including Sigmund Freud, that these states could be suggested and were therefore functional only and unrelated to neurobiology.
CORBIS-BETTMAN

century. In fairness to the psychoanalysts of the time, there was one attempt to validate the therapeutic value of psychoanalysis. Lawrence Kubie, president of the New York Psychoanalytic Society, convened a group to collect data about the efficacy of psychoanalytic treatment. Because the statistics were questionable, the committee decided to keep the report confidential. To make matters worse, the 3,000 reports sent to IBM for data analysis were lost.

Needless to say, the validation fiasco did not go very far in convincing the scientific community that the psychoanalytic strategy was an effective one. In many ways, the furor around psychoanalysis was the great distraction from a valid neuroscientific or neurological approach to treatment for mental illness. Because of Charcot's indirect influence in the development of this perspective after contributing so much valid information to the field of neurology, it is probably fair to say that, in the grand scheme of the history of clinical neuroscience, he giveth and then taketh away!

BIOLOGICAL THERAPIES FOR MENTAL ILLNESS

The therapies described in this section may seem crude, but they helped show the way to real possibilities for treating mental disorders. For example, some of the earliest biological treatments involved inducing fevers or comas to relieve psychotic symptoms. Some of the subsequently developed biological therapies (electroconvulsive shock therapy, psychopharmacology, and psychosurgery) also seem extreme but, because of their success, continue to exist in some form today.

Early Biological Treatments

The likelihood of finding effective treatments for the mentally ill was pretty dismal in the first half of the twentieth century. Even so, bright, motivated scientists and psychiatrists still kept trying to find a therapeutic path. At last, a few potential treatments were discovered. The initial treatments, though, were far from elegant and sometimes resulted in side effects that rivaled the symptoms of the original disorder. Even with these limitations, the new treatments were an incredible advance for clinical neuroscience. They provided indisputable evidence that at least some mental disorders could be treated with biological therapies.

In the later part of the nineteenth century, an Austrian psychiatrist named Julius Wagner-Jauregg (1857–1940) was working at the Vienna asylum. There, he observed a woman suffering from psychosis who experienced relief from her symptoms when she contracted an infection and accompanying fever. This prompted Wagner-Jauregg to speculate on the potential of inducing fevers to treat other forms of psychosis, such as neurosyphilis, a functional disorder that affected many of the patients who resided in asylums.

Wagner-Jauregg later infected patients with malaria so that they would develop a fever high enough to kill the heat-sensitive syphilis spirochetes that caused the neurosyphilis. (Malaria could be treated with quinine, so the risk associated with contracting this disease did not seem to him excessive.) In 1919, Wagner-Jauregg wrote a report heralding the successful treatment of this new neurosyphilis cure. This biological therapy helped treat one form of psychosis, so other clinical neuroscientists started to wonder if the so-called fever cure would help to alleviate other forms of psychosis. Unfortunately, it did not and, in fact, generated a set of severe side effects, leading to a dead end for the fever cure. Still, other scientists and physicians set out to find more biological therapies for mental illness, preferably without the obvious accompanying side effects. By the mid-1940s, penicillin had successfully treated neurosyphilis.

In the 1930s, Manfred Sakel (1900–1957), an Austrian physician, started to notice that some of his patients who were experiencing morphine withdrawal or agitation for other reasons enjoyed a bit of a remission following an insulin coma (hypoglycemia triggered by insulin). Consequently, he later decided to induce an insulin coma in schizophrenia patients. Amazingly, Sakel reported full recovery in 50% of the patients. At last there seemed to be some hope for schizophrenia patients.

Although Sakel was later ridiculed for this unorthodox therapy, it began to be used by British psychiatrists as a treatment for chronic depression, and then the use of **coma therapy** spread like wildfire. In fact, in the early 1960s, there were more than 100 insulin units in American hospitals. But the popularity of insulin therapy would soon be overshadowed.

Electroconvulsive Therapy

During the 1930s, doctors often used some form of shock therapy (in these early cases, shock was induced by the delivery of certain drugs, such as insulin) for patients suffering from psychotic symptoms. One researcher working in Budapest, Ladislas von Meduna (1896–1964), found that the drug metrazol produced seizures in his patients without inducing the coma produced by insulin therapy. Meduna noted significant improvements in his psychiatric patients. He later tested another drug, camphor, on schizophrenia, after noting a relationship between epilepsy and schizophrenia, and reported success. These drugs brought great hope to those suffering from psychiatric disorders, but problems such as severe anxiety and nausea led to a dead end for these shock-inducing drugs.

During this time, Ugo Cerletti (1877–1963), a psychiatry professor in Rome, was inducing epileptic seizures in dogs so that they could be used as animal models for epileptic patients. The seizures were induced by placing electrodes in an animal's mouth and anus. About this time, with all the enthusiasm surrounding the then current physical therapies in psychiatry, Cerletti decided to use the experimental approach to determine the most effective physical therapy for epilepsy.

Cerletti assigned to his laboratory assistants the investigation of insulin coma, the seizure-inducing drug cardiazol, and the possible value of using the electrode experiment as a model for epilepsy. They quickly discovered that electrical current could be delivered by placing electrodes simply on an animal's head. With this observation, Cerletti's group went to the slaughterhouse to experiment with the proper placement of electrodes.

In 1938, Cerletti attempted to deliver electrical current to a human patient suffering from schizophrenia. Systematically increasing the amount of current, the patient finally exhibited a classic seizure. The patient's psychiatric symptoms showed significant improvement. Subsequently, **electroconvulsive therapy (ECT)** became a popular treatment for mental illness. In fact, by 1959, ECT had become the treatment of choice for depression.

coma therapy Physical therapy in which an insulin coma was induced to treat mental illness in a patient. After the 1960s the use of this therapy decreased because of rising popularity of electroconvulsive therapy and psychoactive drugs.

electroconvulsive therapy (ECT) Physical therapy used for mental illnesses such as major depression and schizophrenia; involves the delivery of electrical current to an anesthetized patient in an attempt to reconfigure neural functions for normal mental functioning.

The Drug Revolution

The grueling nature of some therapies for mental illness made the thought of taking a mere drug very appealing. In the early 1800s, laxatives were considered as a cathartic, literally a release, for psychotic patients. Opium treatment also has a long history, especially for problems with anxiety and sleep; in the early 1800s, the drug morphine was isolated from opium and either taken orally or injected into the bloodstream to calm patients. Other drugs that acted as sedatives were developed throughout the nineteenth century.

Essentially, the asylum treatment approach consisted simply of the delivery of sedatives to temporarily calm agitated patients. In 1832, chloral hydrate was manufactured by Bayer Pharmaceuticals; this drug was used extensively for sedative purposes in many asylums, as well as by middle-class patients who did not want to enter the asylums.

The element bromine was isolated in 1826 from seaweed ashes and used for a variety of illnesses, such as hysterical epilepsy. In 1897, Neil Macleod, a graduate of Edinburgh Medical School, gave a rather large dose of a bromide drug to a woman suffering from a nervous breakdown; after sleeping for several days, the woman woke up symptom-free. Macleod went on to use this drug to cure other patients. Bromide-induced sleep gave scientists the idea that some psychoses may be cured with a particular drug, but it was later determined that bromine was too toxic for safe use with patients.

At the turn of the twentieth century, a new class of sedatives, **barbiturates** (named after the inventor's girlfriend, Barbara), hit the therapeutic scene. The barbiturates had the added benefit of enabling patients to wake up feeling refreshed after 8 hours of sleep, so it had wide appeal. Deep-sleep therapy was used with various combinations of barbiturates and seemed to offer modest benefits for patients suffering from mood disorders. The fate of sleep therapy acquired an interesting twist in mid-century when a Canadian psychiatrist named Ewen Cameron started exposing his patients to taped messages (he referred to it as "brainwashing") during the prolonged sleep. To make matters worse, he exposed patients without their consent to ECT to "depattern" previous brain circuits that might have led to the psychotic behavior. By 1960, sleep therapy was tainted; and with the rise of other more promising therapies on the horizon, it fell by the wayside.

The 1950s marked a veritable explosion in the field of **psychopharmacology**. Neuroscientists were beginning to understand the nature and functions of various neurotransmitters, and specific drug treatments were developed for specific disorders. Later chapters discuss the development of chlorpromazine for schizophrenia, lithium for bipolar disorder, and the various tricyclics for depression and anxiety.

Psychosurgery

Around the middle of the sixteenth century, some elaborate instruments were constructed to facilitate the craniotomy procedure initiated in ancient Greece. John Verano, a biological anthropologist at Tulane University, suggests that the first cases of **trepanning** (from the Greek word *trepanon*, "borer") were found along the south coast of Peru and date back to about 400 BCE. But discoveries of trepanned skulls that date back to prehistoric times show that the practice of intervening with the brain in order to

barbiturates Group of highly addictive depressant drugs used as anticonvulsants and tranquilizers.

psychopharmacology Discipline that explores the relationship between certain psychoactive drugs and behavior and/or mental processes.

trepanning Medical process of drilling a hole in the skull in an attempt to correct a problem associated with the brain (for example, a buildup of pressure on the brain).

relieve symptoms has been around even longer (Figure 2.7).

The modern story of removing frontal lobe and/or surrounding tissue to restore peace and sanity to those suffering from various forms of mental illness begins with a Lisbon neurologist, Egas Moniz (1874–1955). After being nominated for the Nobel Prize twice but not winning it, Moniz seemed to be looking for a discovery that would seal his chances for the elusive prize. In 1935, he attended the Second International Congress of Neurology, held in London. At this conference, Moniz attended a full-day symposium on the frontal lobes of the brain that was headed by Carlyle Jacobsen and John Fulton, both from Yale University. In the talks, these researchers described the emotional changes that were observed in a chimp after the frontal lobes were damaged. Moniz was particularly interested in a case in which the chimp went from being prone to having tantrums to being downright cheery.

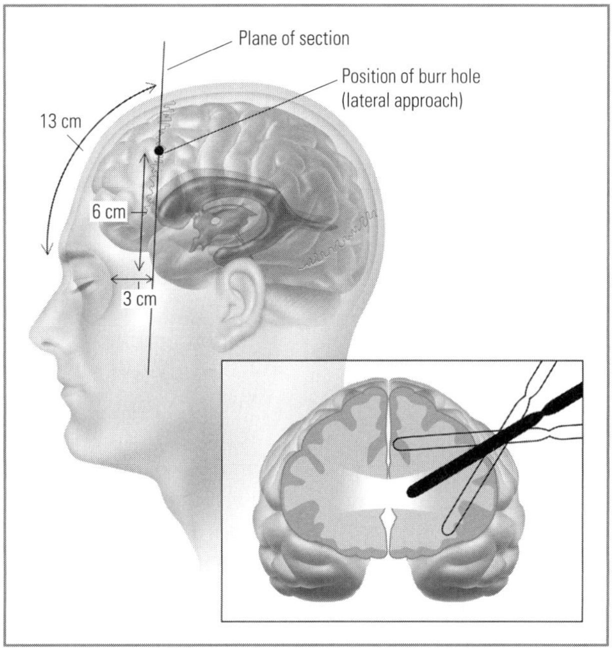

Figure 2.7
A schematic of the lobotomy procedure in which a leucotome is inserted into a 6 mm burr hole and whisked back and forth. Watts later changed his technique to a procedure in which he entered the brain through the eye socket.
ADAPTED FROM FULTON, 1951, P. 107.

After hearing these preliminary reports, Moniz stood and asked if such effects might also be observed in humans. Obviously, no one had the answer to this question. The data presented at this conference, however, became the inspiration for a new endeavor, namely, removing parts of the frontal lobes in psychotic patients to release them from their agitated symptoms. Moniz recruited a neurosurgeon, Almeida Lima, to actually perform the neurosurgery. The technique, which Moniz called *prefrontal leucotomy*, consisted of boring two holes in the top of the cranium and inserting a whisk-like instrument called a leucotome through the holes to cut the white matter in the center of the brain's frontal lobes. Moniz did not divulge a lot of details to support his claims of success, but his initial reports indicated successful outcomes.

Back in the United States, the neurologist Walter Freeman (1895–1972) and the neurosurgeon James Watts (1904–1994) became interested in the procedure, which they referred to as **lobotomy**. In 1946, they modified Moniz's technique to that of a *transorbital lobotomy* (Figure 2.7), in which they entered the brain via the orbital cavity (eye socket). In his *History of Psychiatry* (1997), Shorter recounts a conversation between two doctors at the Georgia State Sanatorium. The conversation captures the casual brutality of this technique.

> **Dr. Hatcher:** *Peter, I'm doing transorbital lobotomies this morning. Come watch me.*
>
> **Dr. Cranford:** *If I saw one, you'd have to do the next one on me.*
>
> **Dr. Hatcher:** *Nothing to it. I take a sort of medical icepick, hold it like this, bop it through the bones just above the eyeball, push it up into the brain, swiggle it around, cut the brain fibers like this, and that's it. The patient doesn't feel a thing.*

lobotomy Faddish operation to treat mental illness used in the 1930s and 1940s. The procedure involved separating sections of the frontal lobe from the rest of the brain.

> **Dr. Cranford:** *And neither do you. I was going to breakfast but I've changed my mind.*
>
> **Dr. Hatcher:** *You can change your mind, but not like I can change it.*
> *(quoted in Shorter, 1997, p. 228)*

After Freeman started conducting the procedures outside of his office, Watts started to feel uncomfortable with the relaxed nature of the surgery and ceased working with Freeman in 1947. Freeman proceeded to travel around administering transorbital lobotomies. Because he carried all his equipment in his car, some people referred to his automobile as the "lobotomobile."

In his 1951 book entitled *Frontal Lobotomy and Affective Behavior*, John Fulton estimated that about 20,000 human patients had been subjected to some form of lobotomy. He also recounted an interesting observation by the well-known physiologist David Ferrier of King's College Hospital in London. Ferrier made significant contributions in the field of cortical localization by finding areas involved with voluntary control as well as different sensory systems. More relevant to the discussion at hand, he ablated, or lesioned, part of the frontal lobe in monkeys and made the following statement in a public lecture:

> The experiments show conclusively that an animal deprived of its frontal lobes retains all its powers of voluntary motion unimpaired, and that it continues to see, hear, smell and taste, and to perceive and localize tactile impressions as before...and yet the facts seem to warrant the conclusion that a decided change is produced in the animal's character and disposition. For this operation I selected the most active, lively, and intelligent animals which I could obtain....They seemed to me, after having studied their character carefully before and after the operation, to have undergone a great change...instead of being actively interested in their surroundings, they ceased to exhibit any interest in their environment beyond their own immediate sensations, paid no attention to, or looked vacantly and indifferently at, what formerly would have excited intense curiosity, sat stupidly quiet or went to sleep...and generally appeared to have lost the faculty of intelligent and attentive observation. (quoted in Fulton, 1951, p. 21)

You may be thinking how wonderful it would have been if these observations had been made prior to subjecting humans to a similar procedure. Well, Ferrier's observations were made in 1875! The dangers of lobotomy were later reported by the famous experimental psychologist Harry Harlow in 1948. Essentially, Harlow exposed lobotomized monkeys to a battery of different learning tasks and concluded his study by suggesting that the animals showed deficits in several of the learning tasks.

Apparently, studies that cast doubt on the value of the lobotomy did not compromise Moniz's chances for winning the Nobel Prize that had escaped him before. In 1949, one year after the publication of Harlow's findings, Moniz was awarded the coveted honor because the technique seemed to be more effective than sedatives when used on schizophrenia patients. Shortly after this time, however, frontal lobotomies stopped being so freely used. As you will read in Chapter 8 a more refined lobotomy (a smaller lesion in an anesthetized patient in the context of a fully operational surgical facility) is currently used as a last resort for treating obsessive–compulsive disorder.

IMPORTANCE OF A THERAPEUTIC ENVIRONMENT

A great deal of interesting research linked the brain with mental illness. The observation that biological therapies could be used to treat patients suffering from various forms of mental illness validated the use of biological therapy. Still, the field of clinical neuroscience is an interdisciplinary endeavor. This section addresses the role of the environment in therapy for mental illness.

Philippe Pinel and the Fall of the Asylum

One of the first physicians to write about the importance of environment to mentally ill patients was the French psychiatrist Philippe Pinel (1745–1826). In 1793, Pinel was asked to direct the operations of the Bicêtre hospice. He became famous the same year when he asked to have the chains removed from the patients. Two years later Pinel became the director of the Salpêtrière (hospital where Charcot studied hysterical women) and ordered the removal of the chains from those patients as well. He went on to publish a textbook in 1801 in which he advocated the asylum as a place where a therapeutic environment could be used to strengthen patients' faculties so that they could be returned to society. Pinel was observed to put his words into practice; he is said to have been endearing with his patients—calming them with warm baths and organizing interesting activities to fill the many idle hours of the day. Because of his practices, Pinel is considered the father of modern psychiatry by many in the field.

Pinel and others envisioned the asylum as a place that would offer a healing environment for patients suffering from mental illness, but this goal was not met. Asylums became larger and larger. By the time of World War I, asylums had become vast warehouses for patients suffering from mental illness. Back in 1800, the number of beds in the more well-known asylums, such as Bedlam in England (named after the Bethlem Royal Hospital), was limited to hundreds. A hundred years later, there were 150,000 patients in mental hospitals in the United States alone. In a mere century's time, the confinement of psychiatric patients to an asylum or mental hospital went from being an unusual tactic done as a last resort to society's initial response when confronted with the slightest hint of psychotic illness. This problem is epitomized by the Georgia State Sanatorium in Milledgeville, Georgia. Its 10,000 beds made it the largest mental hospital in existence in 1950. As charted in Figure 2.8, the number of patients in mental hospitals in the United States has drastically decreased since the mid-1950s.

Behaviorism: A Different Type of Therapeutic Environment

The notion of providing a therapeutic environment in mental hospitals did not survive through the twentieth century. A different twist on environmental manipulation began to emerge as the asylums were becoming a hopeless

placebo effect Term used to describe a therapeutic effect resulting from the consumption of a physiologically inactive substance (for example, a sugar pill or some other un-related treatment); used as evidence for mind–body communications.

Box 2.3

A Case in Point

The Couple Who Needed Each Other Like a Hole in the Head

In 1965, Joe Mellen, a London publisher and art dealer, had a life-changing conversation with Bart Huges, a research librarian who lived in Amsterdam. The topic of this conversation was Huges's idea that there is an intimate relationship between consciousness and the volume of blood in the brain, or "blood-brain volume," as he called it. Similar to the trepanning described in this chapter, Huges actually drilled a hole in his own skull. He felt more relaxed after the trepanation, which led him to write a book entitled *Trepanation: The Cure for Psychosis*. As discussed in his book, trepanations enable us to go back to the time of infancy when the soft spot, or fontanel, in the skull led to a greater blood-brain volume. Once the skull hardens, according to this book, the pulsation decreases, robbing the brain of the appropriate amount of blood.

Because he felt that "life as an adult was rather flat, dull, and uphill," Huges's friend Joe Mellen was also eager to expand his mind by trepanning. As recounted in his book *Bore Hole*, Mellen's trepanation experience was nothing short of a fiasco. After consuming a dose of LSD and making the incision in his scalp, he could not cut through his skull. Following several subsequent botched attempts, Mellen finally tried an electric surgical drill and was at long last able to drill a hole through his skull. He reported feeling more energy and less self-consciousness just a few hours after his trepanation.

After seeing the benefits in Mellen, Mellen's companion, Amanda Fielding, decided that she wanted the procedure as well. Because she was unable to find a doctor to perform a trepanation, she decided to do it herself. Mellen was at her side during the procedure, filming every gory detail of her experience for a video documentary that would later be entitled *Heartbeat in the Brain* (definitely not a film for the faint of heart).

Wearing a white robe, Amanda drills a hole in her skull and then wraps her head with a bandage, eerily smiling at the camera through the whole experience. She also reported psychological benefits shortly after the trepanation; she went out to eat and then to a party that very evening. Giving new meaning to the notion of holy matrimony, Mellen and Fielding stayed together for several years. They ran an art gallery in London and had two sons (neither of whom wants a trepanation). Several years later the couple split up, and Fielding married Lord James Neidpath, a former professor at Oxford. After their marriage, Neidpath traveled to Cairo where he found a surgeon willing to cut open his head for $2,000. He, too, reports that the effects of the trepanation have been beneficial.

Just in case you are thinking that there may be something to this "hole" story, it is important to look at the procedure from another perspective. Although trepanning has been around for thousands of years, the artifacts suggest that, like now, this procedure was typically done to relieve pressure in a swelling or injured brain. Neurosurgeons agree that this process could result in blood clots, injuries, and infections that could easily lead to death. Scientists tell us that blood flow, not volume, is critical for the brain's functioning and that trepanation in a normal brain would fail to affect blood flow.

But what about the positive effects reported? Any student who has had a course in research methodology would recognize that Mellen and friends were most likely experiencing a *placebo effect*. They believed that the procedure would work, and consequently, they experienced some benefit. (The information in this article is from Colton, 1998.)

---

classical conditioning Basic form of associative learning originally studied by Ivan Pavlov; involves pairing a neutral stimulus with an unconditioned stimulus known to automatically evoke a response so that, eventually, the neutral stimulus will lead to the behavior originally produced by the unconditioned stimulus.

dead end. The landmark **classical conditioning** studies of the Russian physiologist Ivan Pavlov (1849–1936) in the early twentieth century marked the beginning of this new therapeutic approach (Figure 2.9).

Everyone knows that a dog will salivate in response to food being presented to it. Pavlov took this very simple observation and designed an elegant study that would literally change the face of psychology. He simply presented the dogs with a neutral stimulus, such as a tone or the proverbial bell, before presenting the food to the dogs. His dogs formed an association between the tone (the conditioned stimulus) and the food (the unconditioned stimulus), so eventually the dogs would salivate on hearing the tone.

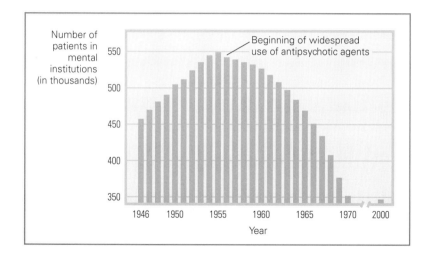

Figure 2.8

At its peak, the resident population in U.S. public mental hospitals exceeded half a million patients. The steep decline in patient populations since the mid-1950s is attributed to a growing reliance on the use of antipsychotic medications.

Figure 2.9

The interlocking arms of physiologist Ivan Pavlov, who first described classical conditioning, and Harvard medical researcher Walter Cannon, who coined the term *fight or flight* for the body's response to stress, preview interactions to come. Today, clinical neuroscience embraces brain–body interrelationships. Hobson (1999) recounts the scientists' meeting, pictured here, as Pavlov arrived in Boston after a harrowing journey from New York.

COLLECTION OF J. A. HOBSON

Pavlov's work gave the field of experimental psychology, which was desperately looking for an empirical approach to understanding mental events, new hope for becoming a respectable science of the mind. Following the establishment of one of the first psychological laboratories in Leipzig, Germany, around 1879 by Wilhelm Wundt, another psychology pioneer, the Harvard professor William James wrote a textbook of psychology, published in 1890. The work of Wundt and James played a significant role in the establishment of experimental psychology in the United States.

The field of psychology, though, quickly wandered from its intended experimental roots, and Pavlov's work was viewed as a means to return to the desired experimental rigor. J. B. Watson (1878–1958), a southern-educated, charismatic, emerging leader in the discipline of psychology, took special interest in Pavlov's work. In a famous speech entitled "Psychology as the Behaviorist Views It" in 1913, Watson suggested that the entire field of psychology needed to focus on the empirical manipulation of environmental stimuli and observable responses, or **behaviorism**, as modeled by the great Dr. Pavlov.

What does this trip down the memory lane of behaviorism have to do with mental illness? Toward the end of Pavlov's career, he experimented

behaviorism Theory advocated by J. B. Watson calling for a shift of emphasis in the field of psychology from unconscious processes to the empirical manipulation of environmental stimuli and observable responses.

with presenting his dogs with ambiguous stimuli. Animals that had been trained to associate a circle with a food reward and an ellipse with a mild shock, for example, became extremely agitated (a condition Pavlov called "experimental neurosis") when presented with an ambiguous oval stimulus, intermediate between the circle and the ellipse.

Pavlov's classical conditioning procedure is adaptive for animals and humans in that different conditioned stimuli enable us to predict the occurrence of other stimuli in our environments (for example, lightning usually presages thunder). Emotional problems can arise when an animal or person loses the sense of control over environmental stimuli, as was the case with the dogs and the ambiguous stimuli. In another application of classical conditioning to mental illness, Watson conducted a study in which he prompted a toddler (the famous Little Albert) to associate a harmless white rat with a loud noise, creating an intense fear, or phobia, of white rats in the little boy. In this study, which is considered unethical today, Watson provided evidence that emotions such as anxiety can be learned through the environment.

Perhaps the most relevant of the observations that environmental changes may have some therapeutic value for the mentally ill were contributed by Mary Cover Jones (1896–1987) in 1920. Jones had worked with Watson and became interested in developing a strategy to use the environment to treat fears and phobias instead of creating them. In her most famous case, a little boy, Peter, came to her with an intense fear of rabbits. She reduced this fear by encouraging him to engage in relaxing, enjoyable activities, while she slowly introduced a rabbit into the environmental setting. Jones was desensitizing little Peter to the presence of the rabbit: His fear in the presence of rabbits was slowly being replaced with feelings of relaxation and pleasure in the presence of rabbits. This early application of behavior modification would become a powerful tool in treating various symptoms in patients suffering from mental illnesses such as phobias (Schultz & Schultz, 2000).

Beyond Behaviorism: Rethinking the Role of Mental Processes in Mental Health

With behaviorism, psychology changed from its original emphasis on conscious processes to an emphasis on observable events in the environment. In 1963, 50 years after the publication of the landmark article by J. B. Watson calling for a change toward behaviorism, Harvard behaviorist B. F. Skinner, a pioneer in operant conditioning, wrote an article describing how behaviorism had contributed to tremendous progress in the field of psychology (Skinner, 1963). In a sense, psychology had lost its mind in this transformation, a change many psychologists considered good. As you may suspect, though, not all psychologists were willing to completely dismiss the importance of mental functions.

Albert Bandura (1925–present) was one disgruntled psychologist who was not willing to throw out the pursuit of mental abilities. Although he valued the inclusion of observable behavioral and environmental events, he was not comfortable ignoring the influence these events had on thought processes such as beliefs and expectations. After conducting a classic series of studies showing that young children learn to be aggressive simply by observing an aggressive model, Bandura had empirical support for his theory that learning could occur without an individual receiving direct reinforcement from the environment. Bandura later introduced the term **social learning theory** to emphasize how learning occurs following the observation of models in social situations. Consequently, models have become a component of behavior-modification therapy: Individuals are exposed to models demonstrating desired behavioral responses to certain stimuli (snake, bully, or dog).

Later, Bandura continued his emphasis on more cognitive factors and introduced the term **self-efficacy** into the psychology literature. Extensive work has been conducted on the self-efficacy measure; relevant to this text, individuals high in self-efficacy measures have better physical and mental health than their lower self-efficacy counterparts (Bandura, 1997).

Another psychologist who was not comfortable with radical behaviorism was Julian Rotter (1916–present). Rotter's world changed drastically in his early teens when his well-to-do father lost his business at the beginning of the 1929 Depression. He later wrote that this environmental event "began in me a lifelong concern with social injustice and provided me with a powerful lesson on how personality and behavior were affected by situational conditions" (Rotter, 1993, p. 274).

Rotter went on to become an accomplished psychologist. Like Bandura, he accepted certain aspects of behaviorism but disagreed with the total exclusion of mental, or cognitive, processes. Like the radical behaviorists, he believed that behavior was determined by external stimuli and by reinforcement. But Rotter maintained that the ultimate influence these factors have on behavior is actually determined by a person's cognitive processes. For example, we place different values on reinforcers—you may place considerable value on a chocolate reinforcer, but this form of reward is not powerful for your friend who is allergic to chocolate or who just doesn't like sweets.

Rotter also emphasized that our beliefs about the source of reinforcers play a powerful role in our behavior. People who believe that reinforcement depends on their own behavior are described as having an **internal locus of control**, whereas those who believe that reinforcement depends on environmental, or outside, forces, such as fate or other people, are described as having an **external locus of control**. Accordingly, a student who responds to a bad grade on an exam by modifying his or her study strategy has an internal locus of control. A student who responds to the bad grade by claiming that his or her performance on the next test depends on whether the professor gives a "fair" test is operating with an external locus of control. Subsequent research has shown that individuals with an internal locus of control are at less risk for heart attacks and have less anxiety and depression than their external locus of control counterparts (Schultz & Schultz, 2000).

Self-efficacy and locus of control may be unexpected topics in a neuroscience text, but they illustrate beautifully the need for integrated approaches to mental health. Rotter's and Bandura's work helps us understand how mental functions influence the brain's functions and alter our homeostasis to either reduce or increase toxic symptoms that may lead to illnesses, such as cardiovascular disease and depression. Obviously, identifying mental strategies that alter neurobiological functioning and subsequently mental and physiological health further supports the integrated brain–body approach to mental health.

social learning theory
Theory proposed by Albert Bandura emphasizing the importance of observations of models in social situations and how observations can lead to learning without direct exposure to a reinforcer.

self-efficacy Term proposed by Albert Bandura to describe a person's assessment of his or her competence in dealing with life's problems.

internal/external locus of control Components of a theory proposed by Julian Rotter that emphasized the importance of one's perception of his or her source of control in life— either within the individual or in the environment.

PROFILING THE PIONEERS OF CLINICAL NEUROSCIENCE

Let's take a step back and look at the personal characteristics of the impressive scientists and physicians we've discussed. Are there any common denominators among the complex lives of the great contributors to this field? In his book entitled *Minds Behind the Brain* (2000), Stanley Finger, a historian of neuroscience, asks that very question. He conducted an informal analysis of some of the historical figures (including Galen, Santiago Ramón y Cajal, Camillo Golgi, Paul Broca, Charles Scott Sherrington, and Otto Loewi) and found some interesting similarities.

Educationally, the giants of clinical neuroscience had cultured parents who sought the best educational opportunities for their children. The neuroscientists did not conclude their education on graduation; in fact, the end of formal education marked the true beginning of their learning. They settled in cities that provided environments full of cultural and educational opportunities and embarked on lifelong journeys of discovery. Perhaps this lifelong love of discovery was the most important characteristic the scientists shared.

As you think about the lives of these individuals, you may envision the stereotypical "nerdy" scientist who shows little interest in anything outside the laboratory; but the scientists Finger describes are far from stereotypical. They were likely to be married and to have children and were even actively engaged in the fine arts. For example, Sherrington loved the poetry of Keats, Ramón y Cajal was an artist, and Loewi wanted to study art history. Charcot, who was a painter himself, was a fan of the French Impressionists and loved to listen to the music of Mozart and Beethoven. He even looked to Shakespeare as the unrivaled master of understanding the complex mental lives of humans.

Perhaps the most obvious similarity among the individuals included in this chapter is their gender. Aside from the behaviorist Mary Cover Jones, all of the researchers introduced here were men. Admittedly, male bias has influenced past scientific and medical research. Women are better represented in clinical neuroscience today, poised to contribute to research advances in a new century.

Summary

Emergence of the Brain as the Controlling Center of Behavior, Emotions, and Thought

The ancient Greeks had long believed that the heart was the controlling center of the body when Hippocrates introduced the notion that the brain controls behavior. His theory that mental illness could be treated by restoring balance to the four humors of the body constituted one of the earliest biological theories of mental functioning.

Galen dissected numerous animal brains and proposed that animal spirits in the brain enable the body to transmit sensations and to move. Descartes went on to suggest that these animal spirits are housed in the pineal gland, traveling through ventricles and nerves to initiate movement in the muscles.

Once it was established that the brain plays a role in orchestrating the functions of the body and mind, researchers tried to find out whether specific areas of the brain have specific functions (localization of function). Willis's initial work with animal brains suggested that the cerebral hemispheres are involved in higher functions, the corpus striatum is involved in movement, and the lower brain stem is involved in basic physiological functions such as respiration. Gall's phrenology stimulated further interest in the localization of function. Paul Broca, for example, discovered that an area in the left frontal lobe was involved in the production of speech.

Before the nervous system could be fully understood, the nature of the individual units, or neurons, had to be identified and described. Golgi's discovery of a silver stain for the neuron enabled researchers such as Ramón y Cajal to describe the structure of different types of neurons. Ramón y Cajal's work also provided evidence that each neuron is an individual unit, thus casting doubt on the existing nerve net theory. Sherrington's description of the junction between neurons, the synapse, also supported the neuronal doctrine.

Using frogs, Loewi discovered that the neurons communicate with one another via the release and reception of specific chemicals. Research conducted by investigators like Dale subsequently showed that certain drugs that influence the nervous system do so by acting similar to the nervous system's natural chemicals, or neurotransmitters. This research set the stage for the field of psychopharmacology.

Finally, Adrian's all-or-none law provided information about how neurochemicals stimulate the neurons and how neurons, once stimulated, transmit information to the next neuron.

Neurological Approaches to Mental Illness

In an attempt to integrate neuroscience and psychiatry, Kraepelin organized an impressive group of neuroscientists, including Alzheimer, who discovered the neuropathology of the dementia that bears his name, and Nissl, a histologist who described the six layers of the cortex. Kraepelin went on to categorize mental illnesses so that they could be studied more efficiently.

Charcot also attempted to describe the various neurological conditions by observing patients and conducting autopsies of brains. His work led to findings that contributed to understanding mental disorders such as Parkinson's disease and Tourette syndrome. In the later part of his career, Charcot focused on patients exhibiting "hysterical" symptoms that had no obvious physical cause.

Biological Therapies for Mental Illness

In the later part of the nineteenth century, findings suggested that biological therapies might have significant value in treating mental illness. Encouraging results from induced fevers and insulin coma fueled research to identify less dangerous biological interventions. Ultimately, electroconvulsive shock therapy, psychosurgery (especially lobotomy), and certain drugs showed promise as biological therapies.

Importance of a Therapeutic Environment

Pinel emphasized the importance of a therapeutic environment for the treatment of patients suffering from mental illness. Attempts to humanize the conditions in asylums as well as to incorporate classical conditioning techniques led to the development of treatments such as behavioral modification. More recently, cognitive approaches (for example, determination of locus of control and self-efficacy) have been incorporated into behavioral therapies.

Profiling the Pioneers of Clinical Neuroscience

Focusing on the lives of the significant figures featured in this chapter, a few common denominators can be found among their professional and personal lives. Many loved the arts and humanities as well as being passionate about neuroscience.

Key Terms

humoral theory (33)
craniotomy (34)
experiment (35)
ventricles (36)
reflex (36)
mind–body problem (37)
dualism (37)
localization of function (37)
cerebral cortex (39)
correlation (40)
phrenology (40)
histology (42)
nerve net theory (42)

neuron (43)
neuron doctrine (44)
synapse (44)
neurotransmitter (46)
nerve impulse (action potential) (46)
all-or-none law (46)
transduction (46)
dementia (48)
schizophrenia (48)
hysteria (49)
psychoanalysis (49)
coma therapy (51)

electroconvulsive therapy (ECT) (51)
barbiturates (52)
psychopharmacology (52)
trepanning (52)
lobotomy (53)
placebo effect (55)
classical conditioning (56)
behaviorism (57)
social learning theory (59)
self-efficacy (59)
internal locus of control (59)
external locus of control (59)

For Further Consideration

Unlike research included in other chapters in this text, many original historical sources are unavailable or difficult to obtain; for this reason, we were fortunate to have access to many wonderful contemporary accounts of the intriguing stories that are included in this chapter such as the ones recommended below.

Finger, S. (2000). *Minds behind the brain.* New York: Oxford University Press. Finger tells the life stories of 19 key figures in the history of neuroscience. The idea for this book came from the interest that Dr. Finger's students had in the behind-the-scenes details surrounding the landmark discoveries in neuroscience. Finger tells us that Descartes, who spoke of animals as beast machines, actually had a dog named Monsieur Grat (Mr. Scratch) and that David Ferrier, a groundbreaking neuroscientist who located certain motor and sensory functions in the cerebral cortex during the 1870s, was arrested after being accused of animal abuse by militant animal-rights activists. Additionally, Finger describes the personal characteristics of the pioneers of neuroscience that helped them to persevere with their new theories at a time when other leading authorities in the field were advocating opposing theories.

Finger, S. (1994). *Origins of neuroscience: A history of explorations into brain function.* New York: Oxford University Press. Finger documents the history of neuroscience from the ancient Egyptians, Greeks, and Romans to the twentieth century. Covering topics such as sensory systems, motor systems, intellect and memory, cerebral dominance, and treatments and therapies, Finger reports the details of the discoveries of the brain. More than 350 illustrations help to bring the history of neuroscience to life.

Gross, C. G. (2009). *A hole in the head: More tales in the history of neuroscience.* Cambridge, MA: MIT Press. Gross includes meticulous details as he describes both well-known and unknown stories about the history of neuroscience. Related specifically to clinical neuroscience, chapters emphasizing the history of trepanation, Galen's heroic attempts to demonstrate that behavior is based in the brain, the discovery of the motor cortex, and John Altman's persistent attempts to refute the "no new neuron" dogma that characterized the field until recently will be of particular interest to readers.

Kandel, E. R., & Squire, L. R. (2000). Neuroscience: Breaking down scientific barriers to the study of brain and mind. *Science, 290,* 1113–1120. This is a wonderful brief overview of the history of brain science. It does an especially good job of placing the cellular and molecular discoveries into the context of the broader brain sciences. A timeline with pictures of the history-making scientists is a valuable tool for students of the history of neuroscience.

Shorter, E. (1997). *A history of psychiatry.* New York: Wiley. Shorter is a historian, and he covers the changing perspectives in the field of psychiatry from a sociological and historical point of view. Shorter's thorough coverage of the influential figures in the field of brain science, psychiatry, and psychology paints a vivid picture of the many views and explanations of mental illness that have been introduced over the past three centuries.

Chapter Three ■ Macroanatomy and the Dynamic Brain

Connections

Brain Plasticity in *Evolutionary* and in *Real* Time

A major theme throughout this text is the dynamic, adaptive nature, or **plasticity**, of the brain. In Chapter 1 you learned that enriched environments lead to a thicker cortex and increased neural connections. Research currently being conducted by Leah Krubitzer at the University of California at Davis shows clearly that the functional areas of the cortex have assumed many different shapes, sizes, and positions throughout their evolution.

Committed to unlocking nature's grand design for cortical development, Krubitzer and her students are using histological analyses and neurophysiological recording to map the functional and neuroanatomical cortical areas of a vast array of mammals including hedgehogs, mice, squirrels, flying foxes, sheep, rhesus monkeys, marmosets, and yes, even humans (Larsen & Krubitzer, 2008). It seems a daunting task to try to understand how the cortex changed from such a small size in the earliest mammals to its generous size in humans. But Krubitzer is taking creative approaches to manipulate cortical development in mammals to try to understand the different developmental paths taken as successive species climbed the phylogenetic tree.

Krubitzer's laboratory is interested in the evolution of our ability to explore and manipulate the world around us with our hands. In addition to the involvement of the motor cortex in the fine control of hand movement, other specialized areas of the cortex must contribute sensory information about tactile, positional, and visual information to gain such impressive control over an individual's hands (Padberg et al., 2007).

It probably comes as no surprise that the cortex has the ability to change over millions, thousands, even hundreds of years. But from a therapeutic point of view, you may be thinking that it's more important to know how plastic the brain is in "real" time, or over the course of an individual's life.

The case of 45-year-old Australian Brett Nielsen suggests that considerable cortical reorganization is possible within an individual's lifetime. Brett's behaviors—smoking a cigarette, drinking coffee, playing with his hair, and patting his dog Tara—are by no means atypical; however, considering that he does all this with his toes suggests considerable restructuring of his motor cortex. Brett was the first Australian baby born with the effects of thalidomide, a drug withdrawn from use 40 years ago due to its role in causing several birth defects—in Brett's case, being born with no arms. Due to his persistence to engage in "normal" behaviors, Brett can carry out an impressive array of tasks. He taught himself to play the piano with his feet at age 12. Currently, he is a successful composer, recording artist, and film-maker and has his own music production company named Big Toe Productions. And when he's out of the studio, he's busy being a parent to two children, mentor for children with no arms, a backhoe operator, and a motivational speaker (personal communication, 2004).

Where is the empirical evidence for real-time cortical reorganization observed in cases such as Brett's? Currently, we don't have neuroimaging data to support observations of reorganized cortices. However, it happens that Dr. Krubitzer's former mentor at Vanderbilt University, Dr. Jon Kaas, has investigated this very question in the squirrel monkey. Following therapeutic amputation of the forearm, the deprived cortex is stimulated to determine the surgery's effects. Interestingly, areas of the body adjacent to the amputated limb (for example, shoulder, stump, trunk) all move, providing evidence of neuroanatomical reorganization. Thus, the area of the cortex once assigned to the movement of the arm is capable of moving other body parts following forearm removal (Wu & Kaas, 1999, 2002).

Brett Neilsen at work in his studio.
BRETT NEILSEN

Thus, there is overwhelming evidence that the cortex is a dynamic brain structure that doesn't get too comfortable in any evolutionary position, always leaving the door open for adaptations to changing circumstances. Ongoing research illuminating more secrets about cortical reorganization offers hope for the many individuals suffering from impaired nervous systems and/or bodies. If science can facilitate this reorganization, the possibilities for recovery of function are staggering.

The brain is a benevolent tyrant. Its subjects are the entire extent and breadth of the body, virtually every cell. Still, the brain itself is an amalgam of interacting structures that regulate behavior. This neural concert has served us well, sweeping up in its breadth both the minutiae and magnitude of our existence. There is control of internal activities together with simultaneous observance of external sensory stimuli. There is coordination of maintenance activities necessary for existence and the rapid response to an ever-changing world. And there is recognition of the role of the past in shaping behaviors yet to be performed. From millisecond to millisecond, hour to hour, day to day, the brain processes its sensory input and makes decisions that become its motor output, that is, behavior.

How does the brain maintain its own level of activity and that of the body? How does it monitor and regulate internal processes while simultaneously tracking the external environment? By understanding the architecture of the nervous system, we can begin to address a full range of behaviors and how disruptions in the nervous system lead to clinical disorders. Whether the information in this chapter is new to you or just a refresher on the brain's macroanatomy, it will serve as a reference later as you explore the clinical disorders presented throughout the book.

plasticity Inherent flexibility of the brain in responding to environmental changes; for example, by learning or to compensate for loss of function to damaged areas.

central nervous system (CNS) One of the two main divisions of the human nervous system, consisting of the brain and spinal cord; the main coordinating and controlling center of the body that processes information to and from the peripheral nervous system.

peripheral nervous system (PNS) One of the two divisions of the human nervous system, consisting of the sensory and motor nerves outside of the brain and spinal cord (12 pairs of cranial nerves and 31 pairs of spinal nerves).

GROSS STRUCTURE AND FUNCTION OF THE NERVOUS SYSTEM

The two primary divisions of the nervous system in the mammal are the **central nervous system (CNS)**, comprising the brain and the spinal cord, and the **peripheral nervous system (PNS)**, all the rest of the nervous tissue outside the CNS. The CNS largely regulates the PNS. The PNS does not per se regulate CNS activity; rather, it transmits sensorimotor information (Figure 3.1). Data about sensory stimuli coming from the periphery toward the brain is called **afferent** (to carry toward) **information**; motor information moving from the CNS to the periphery is referred to as **efferent** (to carry away from) **information**.

Neurons are the building blocks, of the nervous system. Clusters of neurons, observed through a variety of staining techniques, form functional units within the brain called **nuclei**, in which the communication is largely local or regional. As we detail in Chapters 4 and 5, projecting fibers (*axons*) link neurons, or collections of neurons, into communication networks, like houses on streets or neighborhoods linking to major roadways. Bundles of these fibers, called **tracts** or **fiber pathways**, run like the cables from your stereo to your loudspeakers within the CNS. Tracts outside the CNS are termed **nerves**. As you read this text, your optic nerve, for instance, is carrying information about changes in light patterns to the back of your brain, where the information is decoded into meaningful images.

Organization of the Peripheral Nervous System

Anatomists subdivide the PNS into a voluntary component, the **somatic nervous system**, and an involuntary component, the **autonomic nervous system (ANS)**, as shown in Figure 3.1. The somatic component includes sensory nerve projections, which transmit information from the skin to the CNS (the skin is the largest human information sensor—in square feet—covering, as it does, the entire body), and motor nerves, which control the movement of the skeletal muscles. The ANS is involuntary because it largely regulates and maintains internal activities and organs beyond the ken or control of the person (Figure 3.2). Its

afferent information
Information carried inward toward the brain.

efferent information
Information carried outward from the CNS to the periphery.

nuclei Functional collections of neurons in specific brain regions; can be identified by histological techniques.

tract (also called **fiber pathway**) Bundle of axons within the CNS that forms a path as it connects one specific area of the brain with another specific area.

nerve Cord-like collection of nerve fibers outside the brain and spinal cord; conveys information to and from the CNS and the periphery.

somatic nervous system
Voluntary part of the peripheral nervous system that controls the movement of skeletal muscles or transmits somatosensory information to the central nervous system.

autonomic nervous system (ANS) Maintenance component of the nervous system, composed of sympathetic and parasympathetic divisions.

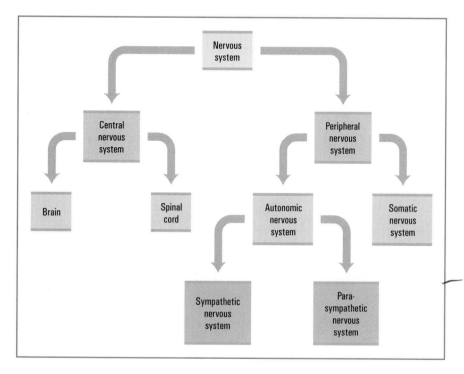

Figure 3.1
The human nervous system is organized and subdivided into efficient modules that can respond and attend to the flow of external and internal information.

sympathetic nervous system Arousing component of the autonomic nervous system.

parasympathetic nervous system Maintenance component of the autonomic nervous system.

innervation of the endocrine glands and of the gastrointestinal and vascular organs, and their accompanying sensations, make the ANS integral to activities that are considered *vegetative*, necessary to the organism's survival.

Imagine for a minute how overwhelming it would be to have to monitor your heart rate, blood pressure, immune function, or digestive processes. It is not important to "know" and monitor each item, and their control is critical to your survival. Hence, the ANS, which typically operates without overt control but is sensitive to the demands of facing and overcoming a challenge, is capable of rapid sensitivity and on-the-fly responsiveness.

ANS and Homeostasis/Allostasis

The ANS epitomizes the principle of homeostasis (or its updated version, allostasis), or physiological balance and regulation, within our bodies. This balance must be struck between the perpetual demand for reparative and restorative activities that maintain the body and the ability to effectively manage an immediate threat to survival. The balance is struck between the two subdivisions of the ANS shown in Figure 3.2, the **sympathetic nervous system**, which regulates arousal, and the **parasympathetic nervous system**, which maintains internal homeostasis via feedback and

Figure 3.2
The sympathetic and parasympathetic divisions of the autonomic nervous system largely innervate the same structures and organs, though they control very different forms of activity. The sympathetic system arouses the body to defend itself against a threat; the parasympathetic system calms the body post-threat and maintains homeostatic functioning during nonthreatening times.

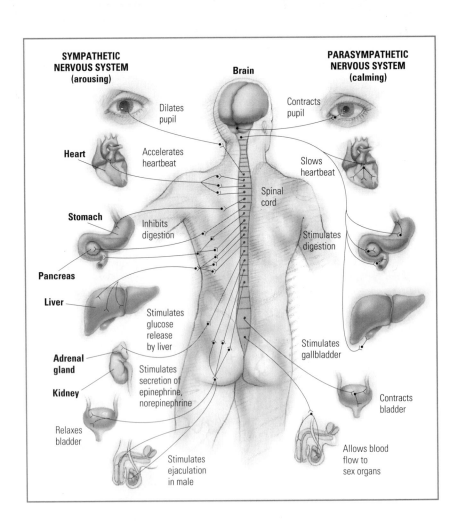

control processes within the nervous and endocrine systems. Following is an illustration of how these complementary systems work.

Imagine that you are driving down the road one afternoon, relaxed, enjoying the scenery and the song on your iPod. Under these conditions you are utilizing the somatic nervous system to take in the sensory world and control the steering wheel, the stereo, and the gas and brake pedals. Because of your relaxed demeanor, the parasympathetic nervous system is regulating your visceral functions—maintaining your heart rate, glandular secretions, and even the digestion of that sesame-seed bagel you ate for breakfast.

You decide to check a text message you just received on your cell and, as you look up, you realize that the car in front of you has slammed on its brakes. For a fearful moment, you are sure you will crash. Within milliseconds, your sympathetic nervous system is activated—increasing cardiovascular output, converting stored energy into a usable form, and inhibiting the diversion of resources toward long-term investments such as digestion, growth, and reproduction (Habib, Gold, & Chrousos, 2001). You then, sharply and reflexively, glance over your shoulder and turn the steering wheel, barely avoiding the slowing car. And, though it takes a while to wear off, a duration different for every individual, eventually you start to calm down and focus once again on driving, hopefully with the cell phone tucked neatly out of sight. At this point, the parasympathetic nervous system reestablishes physiological homeostasis. The transition occurs smoothly, like a car downshifting, and the system resets.

The stress response described in this example comes closest to being a common denominator or at least a shared, contributing circumstance in virtually every disorder in this text. For example, stressful stimuli are associated with a neural fear circuit in anxiety disorders (Chapter 8); mood disorders are characterized by an altered stress response, and environmental stressors may modulate these disorders (Chapter 9); stressful situations may trigger schizophrenia (Chapter 10); and stress can exacerbate the onset and reinstatement of a brain circuit that influences addictive behaviors (Chapter 11). Thus, it appears that stress, a normal and necessary part of life, may act like the volume knob on a preamplifier, ramping-up neural dysfunctions, from a whisper to a shout.

Strategies for maintaining homeostasis in the face of stress, which are critical to physical and psychological well-being, are discussed in Chapters 12–13. It is a knife's edge on which the organism is perched, for falling too far to the sympathetic nervous system side depletes necessary energy stores, whereas remaining in parasympathetic nervous system stasis in the face of a threat tempts disaster. Each side needs the other, as teeter needs totter. Among the topics in Part IV are the role of the sympathetic nervous system in stress responsiveness and in coping styles and strategies, the intimate relationship between stress and the immune and digestive systems, and how the stress response is linked to one's susceptibility to disease. In all, what becomes apparent is the paradoxical relationship that we organisms have with stress: We ignore it at our peril and attend to it perilously.

Development of the CNS

The brain and spinal cord are striking in their complexity and elegance, as are the simple care and protection afforded them by the skull and backbone. The skull is light yet durable, inert but alive. Under microscopic examination

meninges Three connective tissue membranes (arachnoid, dura, pia mater) that protect and enclose the brain and spinal cord.

cerebrospinal fluid (CSF) Normally clear, salty liquid produced in the ventricles, filling them and circulating around the brain in the subarachnoid layer of the meninges and central canal to nourish and protect the brain and spinal cord.

the bone appears as a series of spidery arches, interwoven with geometrically intricate openings that, like a series of arches, provide enhanced structural support and protection.

The skull and backbone absorb a lifetime of insults directed at the soft masses that lie beneath them, blows that would otherwise exact a steep price in mental and physical function. Despite its sturdy protection, however, the CNS today is at the mercy of our technology, which long ago outstripped our evolutionary progress. The brain and spinal cord and their protective and recuperative systems evolved over millions of years and have yet to—and probably never will—catch up with our contemporary ability to damage them.

Consider the limitless ways propulsive or accelerative damage can be inflicted. Bullets, explosives, fast cars, and contact sports are examples of the dangers posed by modern society. Just as our progenitors could never have envisioned today's technological innovations, so too evolution could not prepare the CNS and its associated protective devices for the dangers introduced by technological advancement. We must rely on the awareness and avoidance of such potential damage rather than on recovery from it.

Layers of protection. The skull and backbone, formidable barriers to many forms of injury and infection, are but the first line of defense for the CNS. A triple layer of connective tissue, the **meninges**, further protects and encloses the brain and spinal cord (Figure 3.3).

The tough, light gray outer layer of the meninges, the dura mater ("hard mother"), resembles a vein-covered shower cap. It covers the brain and spinal cord and provides a spongy, cushioning protection. The middle layer of the meninges, the arachnoid ("spider") mater, is a thin sheet of tissue that adheres to the bottom of the dura mater, whose network of thin filaments (filled with cerebrospinal fluid) is reminiscent of a spider's web. This fluid-filled space is called the "subdural space." The inner layer, the pia mater ("gentle mother"), is a relatively thin, nearly clear membrane that covers the surface of the brain and spinal cord and insinuates itself into every cerebral crevice. This slender, clingy tissue is tenacious and is obvious to the pathologist examining the brain's surface.

The subarachnoid space, between the arachnoid mater and the pia mater, is filled with a salty, seawater-like concoction called **cerebrospinal fluid (CSF)**. CSF is produced in the ventricles (described in the following section,

Figure 3.3
The meninges are literally a skullcap, shielding, protecting, and infusing with blood the fragile tissue underneath.

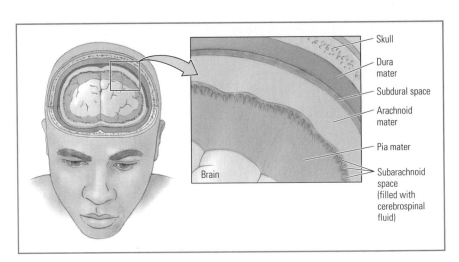

Skull

Dura mater

Subdural space

Arachnoid mater

Pia mater

Brain

Subarachnoid space (filled with cerebrospinal fluid)

Ventricular System) and circulates around the brain and spinal cord, bathing them and buffering them from external concussion, much like the water-filled barriers that one sees near highway embankments to absorb collisions. The CSF simultaneously floats the brain and reduces its weight.

CSF resembles blood plasma in its salinity (~0.9%) and mineral makeup, and it is a source of chemical information about the brain's metabolic and infection status. Close to 130 ml of CSF (nearly half the size of a 12 oz soda) circulates in the closed system of the CNS each day. Should fluid pressure build, as following a concussion, the resulting force pushes against the soft tissue of the brain and the inner surface of the bone of the skull. The resulting tissue deflection, like a swollen limb, is problematical. The engorgement of CSF depresses the brain's soft facade, damaging its delicate surface cortical tissues. In this scenario, the developing brain is at risk and a condition known as "hydrocephalus" ensues. An artificial opening or shunt must be made to remove the built-up pressure, or serious and potentially long-lasting damage may follow. Having too little CSF can be harmful as well, as anyone who has ever undergone a spinal tap can attest. Its removal can leave a fluid void that produces a spectacular headache in the patient.

Ventricular system. Literally "holes" in your head, the four ventricles in the brain are as integral to its activities as the aqueducts were to Roman society. Without them embryonic and fetal brain development would not occur, and adult activity would be severely curtailed. Further, the ventricles are an internal irrigation system capable of venting wastes and metabolic by-products.

The human body is essentially a long tube surrounded by tissues of varying complexity. The developing nervous system follows similar engineering principles. Early in our development the cells that go on to become the different parts of the nervous system proliferate, cell after cell. They fold over and around each other using the basic fluid-filled neural tube as a guide, utilizing the outward negative pressure. The cells grow around the ventricles, following a preprogrammed set of genetic instructions. Like a spelunker's dream, the ventricles eventually become enclosed and differentiate into separate, moderately sized caverns, connected to one another by a series of small-diameter channels (Figure 3.4).

The two lateral ventricles near the top of the brain spread into each of its two roughly symmetrical cerebral hemispheres. Beneath the lateral ventricles and connected by two thin, open vertical rivulets is the third ventricle, which divides the brain into roughly symmetrical right and left halves. The third ventricle is continuous with the fourth by means of a thin conduit called the **cerebral aqueduct**.

The fourth ventricle shunts the CSF along in its circulation down through the spinal or **central canal** to the spinal cord, where it reenters the circulation. In fact, the ventricles operate like an astronaut's spacesuit, another closed, liquid-circulating system in which all wastes are excreted and subsequently recycled. From the ventricles, CSF is eventually absorbed by the bloodstream, filtered, recycled, and returned as metabolic constituents to the brain by means of its blood supply.

Geography of the developing brain. Just 3–4 weeks into its development (detailed in Chapter 6), the embryonic brain can be anatomically subdivided into the three main sectors shown in Figure 3.5a: the **prosencephalon** (forebrain), the **mesencephalon** (midbrain), and the

cerebral aqueduct Narrow tube interconnecting the third and fourth ventricles of the brain, located in the center of the mesencephalon.

central canal (also spinal canal) Pathway through the vertebral column for CSF and the vertebral arteries.

prosencephalon Forebrain controlling sensation, perception, emotion, learning, thinking, and other intellectual functions; includes the olfactory bulb and tracts, cerebral hemispheres, basal ganglia, thalamus, optic tracts, and hypothalamus.

mesencephalon Midbrain joining the brain stem and forebrain and serving as a passageway for impulses to higher brain centers.

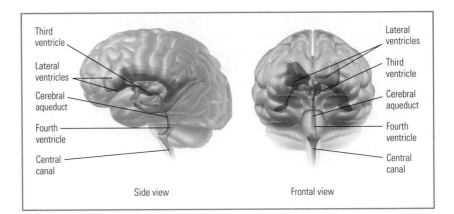

Figure 3.4
The ventricular system is like the brain's irrigation system, both providing the organ with nutrients and removing waste products.

rhombencephalon (hindbrain). Each division is defined by its order of embryonic development in relation to the ventricles.

By 7 weeks (as shown in Figure 3.5b) the forebrain has begun to differentiate into the **telencephalon** (endbrain) and the **diencephalon** (between brain). The diencephalon elaborates around the third ventricle into the structures that synthesize sensory information and regulate motivated behaviors, including the thalamus and hypothalamus. But what the average person conceives of as the human brain, the general image that comes to mind when the phrase "gray matter" is uttered, is what neuroanatomists call the "telencephalon." It is also the organizing term for the subcortical structures that surround the lateral ventricles, and it is the most recent evolutionary addition to our brains, arguably adding what is unabashedly human to the otherwise brutish neural foundation. These telencephalic regions regulate such higher-order responses as cognition and forethought, the hallmarks of consciousness.

As the forebrain grows, the hindbrain also develops further into the metencephalon (across brain) and the myelencephalon (spinal brain) (see Figure 3.5b). The hindbrain, or brain stem, controls overall movement, balance, and some vegetative functions. The midbrain (mesencephalon) is a small area separating the endbrain from the brain stem. Functionally, this middle brain area is involved in some sensory processing and basic attention and arousal processes. As we explore brain structure and function in the next section, we move from the evolutionarily older structures and more basic functions of the brain stem and midbrain to the newer components and higher-order activities of the human forebrain as diagrammed in Figure 3.5c.

CNS STRUCTURE AND FUNCTION

To navigate around the brain, our first task is to orient ourselves (Figure 3.6). When locating structures in the nervous system, the term *neuraxis* (neural axis) describes a line from the spinal cord to the front of the brain. The orientation of the neuraxis depends on whether the animal in question walks upright on two legs, as do humans, or on all fours, like the rat. In the human, the brain and spinal cord are at right angles, as is the neuraxis. The rat's neuraxis is straight.

The top or front of the neuraxis is the *rostral* (like nose), or *anterior*, end. The bottom of this imaginary line is the *caudal* (tail), or *posterior*, end. The

rhombencephalon
Hindbrain, or brain stem, that surrounds the fourth ventricle.

telencephalon "Endbrain" portion of the forebrain that includes the cerebral hemispheres, basal ganglia, olfactory bulb, and olfactory tracts.

diencephalon "Between" area of the forebrain that surrounds the third ventricle; includes the thalamus, hypothalamus, and pineal gland, structures that synthesize sensory information and regulate motivated behaviors.

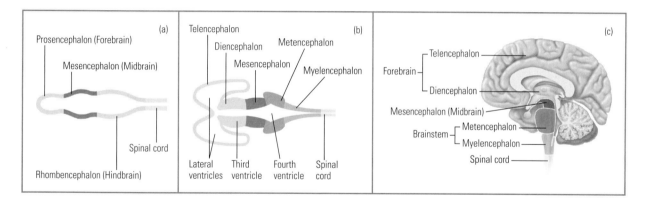

front of the human body, the face, stomach, knees, and chin, is *ventral* to the neuraxis. The back is the *dorsal* region (like the dorsal fin on a shark). Compare these orientations in humans and rats in Figure 3.6. Areas close to the middle of the body are *medial*, whereas those toward the periphery are *lateral*. Your nose and belly button are medial, your ears and love handles lateral, as are the rat's.

These anatomical terms orient an observer toward the body or brain structure of interest by its location on these three planes of reference. The names of numerous brain structures suggest their location relative to the neuraxis (for example, ventromedial hypothalamus, basolateral amygdala). Bear in mind, though, that neuroscientists differ on how they organize the brain and may fail to agree on which structures are part of which subdivision. Further, new staining and imaging techniques are developed all the time. The information they reveal can actually shift structures into different regions. Thus, it seems that the brain's nomenclature is nearly as dynamic as its functions.

Brain Stem

Ever wonder where clichés are born? On September 10, 1945, Lloyd Olsen of Fruita, Colorado, went out to kill a chicken for dinner. After singling out his victim, he strategically positioned the ax high up at the back of the chicken's skull—the better to please his visiting mother-in-law, who savored eating the neck. Once the ax fell, just slightly missing its mark, the 5-month-old Wyandotte chicken lost its head but entered neuroscientific lore. It scampered around a while, typical of freshly beheaded chickens (hence the phrase "running around like a chicken with its head cut off"). Eerily, however, the chicken kept on walking around long after it should have expired. Hours later, the hungry Mr. Olsen observed the bird sleeping with its now phantom head tucked under its wing, like a fowl demon version of Ichabod Crane. Olsen decided that if the chicken had such a will to live, he would face down his disappointed mother-in-law and help it along.

He discovered that he could feed the bird with an eyedropper—placing feed and water directly in its esophagus—and took it to the University of Utah to be examined (not to have its head examined however). The scientists there determined that, because of the placement of the ax's blow, most of the bird's brain stem remained intact. The blow missed the jugular vein, and a fortuitous blood clot had formed at just the right moment to keep the chicken

Figure 3.5
The brain's growth functions by incorporating early structures into the more complex organ it becomes.

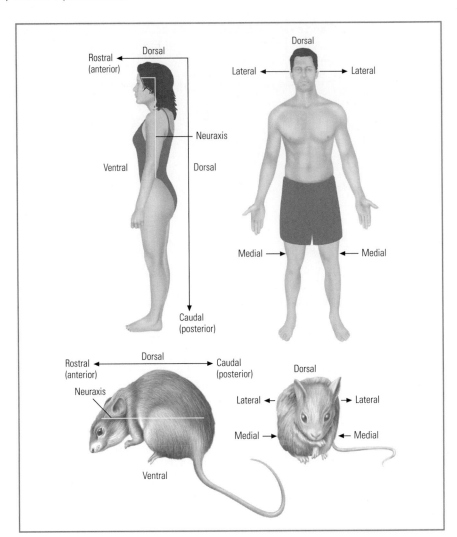

Figure 3.6
The terms for the anatomical and neuroanatomical orientation in humans (two-legged mammals) and rats (four-legged mammals) are dependent on the normal orientations of the body to the ground.

from bleeding to death. Now forever known as "Mike, the Headless Chicken," the pullet went from rotisserie to notoriety. The Olsens soon realized that the chicken's misfortune could be their windfall: Many people wanted to see this headless wonder and would pay for the privilege. So they took the chicken on (and, presumably, across) the road. Mike traveled to New York, Atlantic City, Los Angeles, and San Diego, where people paid 25 cents apiece to see it. At the height of his fame, Mike was valued at $10,000 and actually highlighted in *Life Magazine* (Headless Chicken, 1999; Quirk Fowl Play, 1945).

By all accounts, he seemed to thrive after losing his head—he gained 2.5 more pounds and lived 18 more months. He died while traveling in Arizona, choking on a kernel of corn. But Mike is not forgotten. Over a half-century later, people still gather in his hometown every third weekend of May for "Mike the Headless Chicken Day." They celebrate Mike's will to live by eating chicken salad, playing pin-the-head-on-the-chicken, and participating in a clucking contest.

Mike's story celebrates the power and persistence of the brain stem (Figure 3.7). At the base of the head, the brain stem begins where the spinal cord enters the skull and extends into the mesencephalon. The brains of fish, frogs, and lizards are the basic equivalent of the brain stem and midbrain, and little else, in mammals.

Medulla and basic survival. The **medulla oblongata** is a major regulatory site for basic vegetative or maintenance activities and the primary component of the myencephalon. Nuclei in the medulla regulate respiration and cardiovascular functions (for example, heartbeat and blood pressure) and control muscle tone. Whereas damage to other brain stem structures is serious and of grave concern for the regulation of various behaviors, damage to the medulla is nearly always fatal.

The medulla sits at the lowest, or most caudal, portion of the brain stem and appears as a tiny bulge at the upper end of the spinal cord. It is a rich neural structure with multiple types of neurons and neurochemicals. Via its multiple fiber pathways for nerve impulses entering and leaving the brain, the medulla directly controls signals to and from more rostral brain areas and the periphery of the body.

Cerebellum and motor control. The cerebellum (little brain) is among the most compact and complex brain structures. The cerebellum does for movement what the rest of the brain does for other behaviors: It monitors and controls and creates a variety of gross and fine movements. With the exception of olfactory impulses, the cerebellum must regulate a steady stream of cacophonous sensory information and respond with less-than-split-second motor commands.

Coordination among fine and gross muscles must be tightly regulated. For example, imagine the sensorimotor requirements that underscore a violinist's solo. The proper placement of the fingers on the strings; the tension on the bow; the immediate reactivity to the notes being played, with minor corrections; the feedback to the cerebellum; and the proper integration of all the stimuli must be processed rapidly. Further, the integration of the information must be fluid when combined with internal stimuli about memory of the movements and the sounds desired and in anticipation of the next flood of ever-changing information.

Consider the requirements of even simple movement—touching your right index finger to your left ear, for instance. The finger, hand, arm, and shoulder motions must all be integrated and coordinated, distances calculated, and speeds maintained before digit and ear meet, whereupon the sensory inputs from both finger and ear are fed to the cerebellum, prompting the cessation of the movement. Mini-mission accomplished.

medulla oblongata Lowest part of the brain stem; an extension into the skull of the upper end of the spinal cord; regulates basic vegetative functioning.

cerebellum Hindbrain structure concerned with the coordination and control of voluntary muscular activity and movement.

Mike, the headless chicken. Most of the regulatory functions and basic behaviors of chickens are controlled by the brain stem.
BOB LANDRY/TIME LIFE PICTURES/GETTY IMAGES

Figure 3.7
Structures of the brain stem and midbrain, relative to other "higher" structures in humans. The brain stem and midbrain play pivotal roles in vital biological functions.

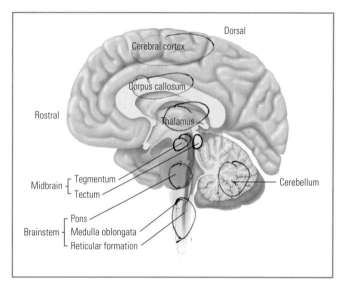

pons Large bulge in the brain stem immediately ventral to the cerebellum; relays information from the cerebral cortex to the cerebellum and contains a portion of the reticular formation, nuclei that appear to be important for sleep and arousal.

reticular formation Collection of nuclei and fiber pathways traversing the brain stem from midbrain to medulla; plays a primary role in arousal, attention, and sleep and wakefulness.

tectum Dorsal part of the midbrain; made up of the inferior and superior colliculi, control centers for auditory and visual stimuli.

tegmentum Ventral part of the midbrain, composed of various nuclei related to movement and to species-typical behaviors.

superior colliculi Nuclei in the mesencephalon that take part in controlling the body's reflexes to visual stimuli.

inferior colliculi Nuclei in the mesencephalon that take part in localizing sounds, integrating hearing reflexes, and orienting the body toward auditory stimuli.

The cerebellum does all this and more from its perch at the base of the brain (see Figure 3.7). When damaged, whether through trauma, stroke, or alcohol abuse, movement ceases to be the well-regulated phenomenon we have come to expect. Depending on the damage, movement reverts to the infantile, the dyscoordinated, where eye and hand are just beginning to work together, haltingly. In fact, police commonly use simple motor coordination tasks, such as asking suspects to close their eyes and touch their noses, to determine whether a driver is intoxicated. Motor coordination is among the first of the skills to deteriorate.

Pons and information transfer. The pons is a large bulge in the hindbrain immediately ventral to the cerebellum that relays information from the cerebellum to the cerebral cortex and regulates arousal. The pons contains a portion of the **reticular formation**, a staggering variety of nuclei and fiber pathways that play a primary role in arousal, attention, and sleep and wakefulness. The reticular formation extends from the medulla into the forebrain and coordinates information regarding the organism's baseline responses to the environment.

The spinal motor inhibition that occurs during rapid eye movement (REM) sleep does not prevent the brain from moving in its reverie: The pons is active, guiding the dreamer through these hallucinatory movements. Though the body is slumbering, the brain works away as if waking and sleeping were but a matter of semantics (Hobson, 2003). This interesting disconnect between outward somnolence and inner frenzy is also called "paradoxical sleep."

Together the cerebellum and the pons make up the metencephalon. The name *pons* derives from the Latin word for bridge, and unlike many other structures identified by anatomists, it is named for its function rather than its appearance. A major site for the crossing of fibers from the right side of the body up to the left side of the brain, and vice versa, the pons bridges the divide between the cerebral hemispheres. Where the connections cross, called the "pyramidal decussation," contributes to the characteristic right-hemisphere regulation of the left side of the body and complementary left-hemisphere regulation of the right side of the body.

The number of neural connections between and within the pons and other structures in the brain suggests that the pons is a very important regulator of sensorimotor activities and a hub of information transfer. In fact, it is because of the enormous number of entering and crossing tracts that, like stitches in a thick rug, the pons bulges as it does.

Midbrain

Shown in Figure 3.7 at the tip of the brain stem, the midbrain is among the least well-defined brain areas in terms of boundaries and nuclei, but its importance in mediating autonomic and orienting behaviors is unquestionable. The two main subcomponents of the midbrain are the **tectum**, the "roof" of the third ventricle, and the **tegmentum**, its "floor," an agglomeration of nuclei that surround the cerebral aqueduct (Figure 3.8).

The tectum in the dorsal midbrain is a control center for visual and auditory stimuli, primarily comprising two sets of nuclei. The **superior colliculi** take part in controlling bodily reflexes to visual stimuli, and the **inferior colliculi** take part in localizing sounds, integrating hearing reflexes, and orienting the body toward auditory stimuli. The tectum is at work when you turn your head to see where a sound is coming from, for example, when the whisper of your name draws your attention to its source.

The reticular formation passes from the brain stem through the tegmentum, which is itself composed of various nuclei related to eye movement, limb movement (red nuclei), and initiating movement (substantia nigra). The **substantia nigra** (literally, black substance), the largest neuronal collection in the midbrain, is rife with neurotransmitters that play major regulatory roles in initiating and inhibiting movement. For example, the loss or degeneration of the dopamine-generating neurons of the substantia nigra contributes to the symptoms of Parkinson's disease, the terrible lack of well-articulated voluntary movement. Its projections to distant brain sites that are involved in movement underscores the pervasive role that the substantia nigra plays in motor events.

The agglomeration of nuclei in the tegmentum gives rise to the **periaqueductal gray (PAG)** region, which separates the tegmentum from the tectum. The PAG is involved in the perception of pain. Its nuclei are sensitive to opioid-like neurochemicals, and a fiber pathway descending from the PAG into the spinal cord appears to be capable of terminating painful sensations, thereby mediating the individual's response to a variety of noxious stimuli.

substantia nigra Nucleus of the tegmentum; communicates with the caudate nucleus and putamen in the basal ganglia to initiate movement.

periaqueductal gray (PAG) Region of the midbrain surrounding the cerebral aqueduct; contains neural circuits involved in species-typical behaviors and pain perception.

Figure 3.8
Midbrain structures are involved in very important motor activities, the loss or compromise of which can be devastating.

Forebrain

The anatomical divisions of the forebrain (prosencephalon) are the telencephalon and the diencephalon (see Figure 3.5c). Streams of sensory input travel to specific sites within the forebrain for simple, early deconstruction and processing and subsequently to other sites for richer evaluation and resolution. When subsequently reassembled, the information has much more meaning attached to it because it has been connected to and associated with other sensory data and memory.

For example, the letters *D*, *O*, and *G* are merely combinations of lines and curves when first scanned by the visual system. These stimuli give way to recognition as symbols, or letters, and we see the word *DOG*. As this perception reverberates around the brain, utilizing ever more circuits and building layer upon layer of connections, the simple is transformed into the complex. Thus, a single word can conjure up images of thousands of kinds of dogs, their sounds and smells and other characteristics, together with particular emotional memories one may have for a dog—all accomplished in a moment.

Owing to the rich associations spun off from the original perception, we build layer after layer of personally compelling information. In fact, our realities are a construct of the brain; what we

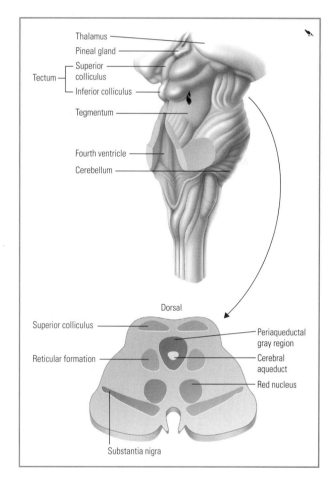

Figure 3.9
Shown here are the diencephalon, the pituitary gland, and the hormones released from the anterior portion of the pituitary. Note the rich supply of blood vessels in and around the pituitary, which allows for rapid and complete conveyance of allied chemical and hormonal signals from the diencephalon.

perceive as the external world is in actuality the disassembly and reassembly of the sensory stimulation being fed to our brains. Every thought and every memory is a reconstruction, association, and recombination of its neuronal elements. In the sections that follow we review the workings of the evolutionarily newer brain structures that enable such sophisticated information processing to occur.

Diencephalon: Regulating social and survival behaviors. Sitting like an overlord, rostral to the brain stem, the diencephalon is a major nuclear complex whose small size belies the necessary and varied activities it regulates. We will focus on the thalamus and hypothalamus, its two major components, and the pituitary gland (Figure 3.9).

The diencephalon represents only ~2% of the CNS, but its contacts with other regions of the brain, not its absolute size, imbue it with its unique

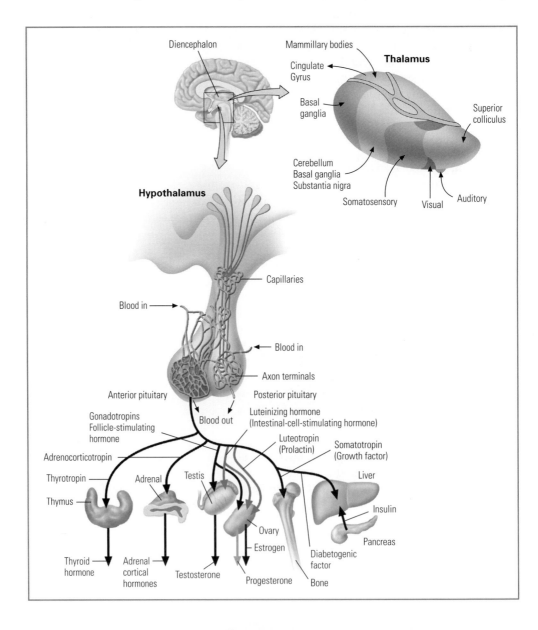

characteristics. Because the diencephalon regulates a host of complementary social behaviors (aggression, sexual behavior, maternal behavior, and the like) in a variety of diverse species, it has been a focal point of much behavioral research.

Sensory information exists in the world in the form of physical stimuli: sights, smells, sounds, tastes, and touch and balance information. Photoreceptors in the eyes transduce light into visual sensations. The nose has olfactory receptors that bind odor molecules, causing neural impulses to course back to the brain. The tongue has taste buds that transform food-embedded chemicals into taste sensations. The skin possesses a variety of sensory receptors that respond to touch or pressure and heat or cold with unique patterns of firing. Nerve cells in the joints and muscles and the inner ear fire a constant stream of information back to the brain, informing it about its location and any imbalance.

This perpetual flow of sensory information must be regulated, synthesized, and evaluated before proper action can be taken. Imagine a major hub airport with hundreds of incoming and connecting flights. Air traffic flow must be effectively and efficiently regulated and directed to the various destination sites. Once there, each "package" (mail, passengers, or information) affects the site in a unique way.

The **thalamus** is the main hub for sensory input to the cerebral cortex (see Figure 3.9). It operates like an airport hub: Incoming sensory information is routed to the thalamus (with the exception of smells, which are carried directly into the olfactory bulbs at the base of the frontal cortex and sent to the amygdala for processing). Once sensory stimuli arrive in the thalamus, the afferent, sensory projections move the data along to local routing via visual, auditory, somatosensory, and so on, nuclei. These local sites then project to specified regions of the cortex, thereby allowing information to be processed quickly and specifically. Subsequently, the sensory information is summed and collated along with cognitive information from other sites.

The complexity of the thalamic nuclei is a wonder to behold (Carpenter & Sutin, 1983). But, like a successful business, one of its defining features is the efficient division of labor and the delegation of responsibilities. What the thalamus does is vitally important to the survival of the organism. The information that the thalamus processes is coin of the realm for the brain: sensory inputs that allow for contact with, evaluation of, and action about the external world.

The **hypothalamus**, located directly under (*hypo*) the thalamus, contains about a teaspoon's worth of tissue. It regulates motivated behaviors that maintain the individual both proximally and ultimately: minute by minute, day by day, and year by year. It motivates the organism to obtain food and water, to rest, and to find, defend, and mate with partners. In essence, the hypothalamus unites those two principles that bond us to virtually every other organism on this planet: energy acquisition maintenance and reproduction. Or, eating and sex. Like the thalamus, the hypothalamus is a masterwork of overlapping and related subnuclei, neural catacombs that can be collected functionally under the umbrella of "motivated behaviors." For instance, as detailed in Chapter 14, two subnuclei in the hypothalamus play at least an indirect role in regulating feeding (in concert with other CNS and PNS structures) and may also govern bodily growth (Nakazato et al., 2001).

thalamus Structure of the forebrain; main source of input to the cerebral cortex.

hypothalamus Brain nuclei that control the endocrine system and regulate motivated behavior.

pituitary gland Master endocrine gland at the base of the hypothalamus; releases a variety of hormones that influence the activity of other glands throughout the body.

cortex (neocortex) Phylogenetically the newest cortex, the outermost layer of cerebral gray matter, including the sensorimotor and association cortices.

Figure 3.10
Should humans be considered atop the phylogenetic scale? Based on the complexity and size of the brain, maybe not. A glance at the dolphin brain portrayed here should make us wonder.

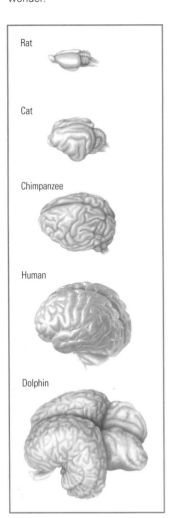

Rat

Cat

Chimpanzee

Human

Dolphin

In addition to its other activities, the hypothalamus regulates the **pituitary gland**, the body's so-called master endocrine gland (see Figure 3.9). The anterior pituitary receives information about hormone release from chemical messages that travel from the hypothalamus through the hypothalamic–pituitary circulatory system (connecting the pituitary to the hypothalamus). Additionally, neurons in the hypothalamus have processes that extend to the posterior pituitary which, when activated, release two neuropeptides (discussed in Chapter 5). Though the hypothalamus regulates their release, pituitary hormones exert themselves at very distant sites in the body through circulatory system distribution.

The pea-sized pituitary, under hypothalamic control (another small structure), regulates the body's most important and fundamental physiological processes, including the autonomic response to stress. When a stimulus is perceived as threatening, the hypothalamus responds by sending hormones through the hypothalamic–pituitary circulatory system. As we will see in Chapter 5, the CNS has engineered two regulatory processes: fast-acting, fast-duration chemical events via neurotransmitters and slow-acting, long-duration effects via hormones. The hypothalamus controls both processes.

Telencephalon and higher-order behaviors. *Telencephalon* is the organizing term for the cerebral cortex and subcortical structures that surround the lateral ventricles (see Figure 3.4). Relative to the deeper structures we have considered so far, these are the brain's most recent evolutionary additions. When viewed in the context of behavioral complexity, the telencephalic regions regulate mental processes such as cognition (thinking about dogs, for example) and forethought (planning to adopt a particular breed of dog, its needs, wants, your requirements, etc.).

The anatomical term *cortex* (from the Latin word for the bark of a tree) refers to any outer layer of cells. The kidneys, adrenal glands, even hair all have a cortex. But to neuroscientists, **cortex** (also *neocortex*) refers to the outermost layer of the brain. This thin, layered sheet of neurons, about the size and thickness of a fine linen napkin, ranges in thickness from about 1 to 5 mm, both among individuals and in different brain regions (Fischl & Dale, 2000). The cortex is so densely packed with neurons, a piece the size of a large match head contains tens of thousands of neurons and millions of their connections (Crick, 1994).

Different mammals have cortices of varying complexities and sizes, but the human has one of the most wrinkly, or convoluted (Figure 3.10). As the anthropologist Helen Fisher (1982) and others have speculated, these convolutions may be anatomical evidence of our evolution from small-brained mammals to large-brained social beings. Imagine that you want to put that aforementioned linen napkin into your pocket, an enclosure that will not accommodate the cloth in its whole, original shape. What do you do? You might lightly compress the napkin and crumple it, maintaining its surface area while reducing its overall size. It now fits into a more compact area, but you have lost none of its volume. More important, you have lost none of its function. Some researchers speculate that the folding is due to a specific gene protein and may allow for more surface area in a constrained space (Chenn & Walsh, 2002). If so, this may be a hallmark of human evolution.

The brain, especially the cortex, grew bigger as it evolved; and as complex social interaction became the norm, this larger brain both created and was capable of responding to ever-new social and environmental challenges. Some authors, among them Wyles, Kunkel, and Wilson (1983), believe that natural selection operated on these social innovations and produced more rapid change. The acceleration of anatomical evolution, fueled by social interactions, therefore might have enhanced forebrain size relative to other neural structures. To fit the newly supersized cortex into the regular-sized skull, folding and crimping were required.

Eventually, there was a constraint on the rapid evolution of the brain: the size of the skull and, more important, the uterus and birth canal in and through which the skull must develop and pass (Montagu, 1965). A large brain contained in a bulky skull would be more likely to lodge itself in the birth canal during birth. A birth canal wide enough to accommodate such a skull would be anatomically difficult to develop in the upright and bipedal human female. Ironically, absolute human brain size, therefore, is limited by the human vessel designed to carry it. The evolutionary end run around this problem was a brain that was folded in on itself, a larger gift stuffed into a smaller package.

Structures and functions of the cortex. The structure of the cortex is generally bilaterally symmetrical—two hemispheres of roughly the same size, if not activity. That is, structures and functions are not exactly mirrored in the right and left hemispheres. Functionally, for most of us, the left hemisphere is more involved in logical reasoning and language, whereas the right hemisphere regulates spatial manipulation, musical ability, emotional processing, and facial recognition. Anatomically, for example, the area of the temporal lobe that generally controls language comprehension is considerably larger in the left hemisphere than the right, whereas the area located just above it is much smaller in the left hemisphere compared to the right (Kandel, Schwartz, & Jessell, 2000). Recent data are showing the distinctions—as well as the overlap—between human language development and that of our closest relatives (Konopka et al., 2009) and those not-so-close relatives (Enard et al., 2009) in the *FOXP2* gene system. The importance of this gene and its fortuitous expression during the human evolutionary past, as well as the influence it may have had on brain development, may have been a strong force in the rise of language and social development.

Each hemisphere is divided functionally into four lobes (Figure 3.11). Moving ventral to dorsal and summarizing very simply:

- **Frontal lobe** regions, which are detailed throughout the text, regulate movement of the skeletal muscles, integrate memory and emotional activities with real-time events, and control planning and executable (realistic) strategies. The frontal cortex also imbues the human with personality, including such characteristics as sympathy, judgment, and empathy. (Recall from Chapter 1 the story of Phineas Gage.)

- The **temporal lobe** responds to auditory inputs and contains areas related to language production and recognition. Its underlying areas regulate and maintain memory and emotional processes.

- The **parietal lobe** interprets somatosensory information and spatial relationships.

- The **occipital lobe** is primarily responsive to visual sensory inputs and associations.

frontal lobe Part of the cerebral cortex in either hemisphere of the brain found directly behind the forehead; helps to control voluntary movement and is associated with the higher mental activities and with personality.

temporal lobe Division of the cerebral cortex lying at each side within the temple of the skull that responds to auditory inputs and contains areas related to language production and recognition; underlying areas regulate and maintain memory and emotional processes.

parietal lobe Main division of each hemisphere of the cerebral cortex, located beneath the crown of the skull; interprets somatosensory information and spatial relationships.

occipital lobe Region of the cerebral cortex lying at the very back of the brain, caudal to the parietal and temporal lobes; site of the primary visual cortex.

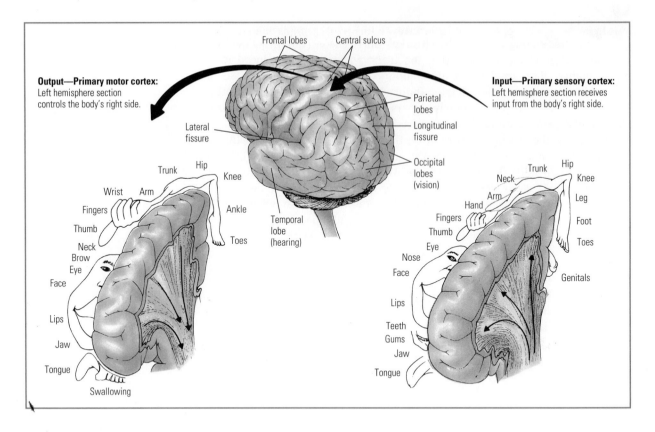

Figure 3.11
Interestingly, the external world is represented topographically on the surface of the brain. Note how more sensitive areas of the body (lips, tongue, and fingertips, for instance) occupy more neural "real estate."

association cortex Areas of the cortex that integrate information to produce cognition.

gyri (sing. gyrus)
Convolutions of the surface of the brain, caused by infolding of the cerebral cortex.

sulci (sing. sulcus) Small grooves or mounds on the surface of an organ.

This functional arrangement, a serial and parallel processing machine analogous to a computer that existed tens of thousands of years before a silicon chip, creates significant processing abilities and attaches a richness of detail to even the simplest sensation. It is not surprising, then, that the brain became too big for its skull as more and more cognitive abilities developed and were added. Two main divisions of labor in the cortex reflect the sensory and motor information the brain regulates. Recall too from the chapter-opening case of Brett Neilsen that these motor and sensory areas can be quite plastic. Cortical functions are by no means carved in stone—or flesh.

A third activity, information integration, is performed by the ubiquitous **association cortex**, which functions to integrate multiple aspects of information, leading to enhanced cognition. A seemingly uncomplicated external event becomes subtly involving and full because of its associations. First, the sensory information is processed ("What is this?"). Next, association areas compare the sensory input to stored information and evaluate it for a response ("What does it mean, and how should I respond?"). Finally, the information flow moves to motor areas for a reaction and response ("This is what will happen."). Depending on the initial sensory inputs, this simple example could involve a large proportion of neural tissue throughout the cortex, which should dispel the myth that we use but 10% of our brains.

The wrinkled surface of the cortex, the result of all that brain compaction, forms peaks and valleys, or mounds and grooves, which are called, respectively, **gyri** (gyrus, singular) and **sulci** (sulcus, singular). Sulci that extend deep into the brain and actually indent the ventricles are called **fissures**. The **longitudinal fissure**, for example, separates the left and right cerebral hemispheres, and the **lateral fissure** separates the temporal lobe from the frontal and parietal lobes. At the top of the brain, the **central sulcus** divides the parietal and frontal lobes and primary sensory and motor functions (see Figure 3.11).

Subcortical circuits: Limbic system and basal ganglia.

Deep within the forebrain lie two interconnected complexes that link forebrain and brain stem functions. The structures of the basal ganglia that are located beneath the rostral extent of the lateral ventricles coordinate body movements. The basal ganglia link to a functional grouping, the **limbic system**, which controls emotional (affective) behaviors and certain forms of memory infused with emotion by a grouping of basal nuclei called the **amygdala** (almond; named for its appearance and general size). Anatomically, the amygdala forms the tail end of the basal ganglia within the rostral temporal lobe; functionally, it is classified as a limbic structure because the amygdala regulates both the perception and production of emotions, especially fear. Without a fully functioning amygdala, navigating a social world in which the inhabitants present with a wide array of emotional facades can mean, at best, awkwardness and, at worst, shunning and ostracism. It is like being a stranger in a strange land with no hope of ever learning the language.

The basal ganglia form a circuit with the cortex and connect to the thalamus and midbrain (Figure 3.12). Together, the *caudate nucleus*, the input nuclei involved with control of voluntary movement, and the *putamen*, a nucleus that also controls body movement, comprise the **striatum**, the terminal site for all afferent fiber pathways forming the basal ganglia. One of the ways this important anatomical alliance regulates is by inhibition; that is, the striatum limits the activity of downstream, or efferent, structures. This inhibition of movement, however, is just as important as the initiation of movement. Dysfunction in the striatum, along with other regions that may also be involved, contributes to the uncontrollable movements and tics observed in obsessive–compulsive disorder and Tourette syndrome, as detailed in Chapter 8.

The striatum is especially affected in the debilitating hereditary condition **Huntington's chorea**, in which patients endure slow, inexorable

fissures Deep grooves covering the outer surface of the brain.

longitudinal fissure Deep groove that separates the left and right cerebral hemispheres of the brain.

lateral fissure Prominent groove that separates the temporal lobe from the frontal and parietal lobes.

central sulcus Deep sulcus that separates the frontal lobe (motor cortex) from the parietal lobe (sensory cortex).

basal ganglia Subcortical cluster of nuclei in the telencephalon that forms a circuit with the cortex, thalamus, and midbrain to coordinate body movements and links to the limbic system via the amygdala.

limbic system Collection of brain regions (amygdala, mammillary bodies, hippocampus, fornix, and cingulate gyrus) that collectively produce, respond to, and regulate emotional responses.

amygdala Almond-shaped structure at the tail end of the basal ganglia within the temporal lobe; functions as part of the limbic system involved in regulation of emotion and sexual urges.

striatum Terminal for all afferent fiber pathways forming the basal ganglia; dysfunction in this motor system is believed to be involved in obsessive–compulsive disorder and Tourette syndrome.

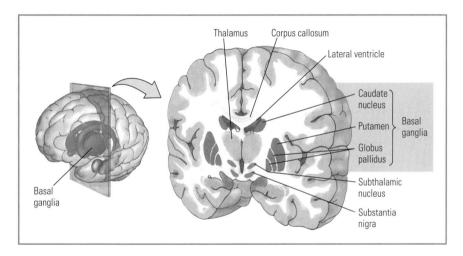

Figure 3.12
The basal ganglia comprise a group of structures that regulate movement and that have closely allied projections to inhibitory activities.

Huntington's chorea Hereditary neurodegenerative disorder of motor control characterized by ongoing involuntary jerky movements and progressive dementia; associated with hyperactivity of the dopaminergic system.

dyskinesias Abnormal involuntary motor movements and difficulty in carrying out voluntary movements.

nucleus accumbens Limbic component of the striatum, sometimes referred to as the "pleasure center" of the brain; involved in motivating behavior and reinforcing survival responses; linked to disorders ranging from anxiety and depression to addiction.

hippocampus Arching limbic structure within the temporal lobe important in learning, memory, and navigating the environment.

Figure 3.13
The limbic system, shown here, is believed to be an evolutionarily ancient collection of structures that cohere to regulate rapid responses to environmental events and the recollections of their past dangers.

degeneration of motor control, which eventually slides into constant, uncontrollable movements (choreas) and the herky-jerky shakes of a marionette on a string. People with Huntington's have some hope though: a transplant of fetal brain tissue or stem cells (Bachoud-Levi et al., 2000). If the transplant takes, partial or even full reversal may occur, though long-term success awaits longitudinal evaluation. (The epilogue expands on how research into this vitally important area and others of similar value has made advances but may be compromised by societal and political influences.)

Complementary to the striatum's inhibitory control, the globus pallidus initiates voluntary movement through regulation of its inhibitory output. Diseases of this segment of the basal ganglia usually involve abnormal and involuntary motor movements called **dyskinesias** and an overall loss of muscle tone. Typical of the movement disorders are *ballism* (a sudden forceful movement involving the shoulder), *tremor* (shaking involving primarily limbs, digits, and the lips), tics such as the head twitches one sees in Tourette syndrome, and the choreas. Treatment of these basal ganglia motor diseases has met with little success to date, but the search for effective treatments and cures continues. As is the case for most clinical issues, basic research holds much promise, but its applications—the translation of data into treatment—may be many decades down the line.

The limbic system encircles the brain stem, lining the inner border (*limbus*, Latin for border) of the cortex at an area called the *cingulate cortex*, a structure that serves as a conduit between the frontal cortex and the limbic circuit (Figure 3.13). Limbic structures are both primitive—from an evolutionary standpoint, they have been around in one form or another for a long time—and primal in service of the organism's survival—again, demonstrating survival without "frills." In Box 3.1, you will discover how Paul MacLean played an instrumental role in naming and emphasizing the importance of this emotional circuit.

Collectively, limbic structures regulate appropriate physiological and behavioral responses to social and environmental stimuli, such as stress and fear. For example, the **nucleus accumbens** is a limbic component involved in motivation and in translating environmental stimuli into the appropriate behavioral response, which is convenient because anatomically the nucleus accumbens is also part of the striatum. Neurons in the tegmentum project into the nucleus accumbens—sometimes referred to as the "pleasure center" of the brain—reinforcing behaviors critical for survival, such as hunger and sex, as well as another pleasurable activity, laughter (Box 3.2). Chapters 8, 9, and 11 detail how the functioning of the nucleus accumbens, cingulate cortex, and other limbic areas has been implicated in disorders such as anxiety, depression, and addiction.

Lying beneath the medial temporal cortex and merging into the cingulate, the **hippocampus** ("seahorse") plays a major role in memory formation and spatial navigation. The hippocampus is a large, arching limbic structure that has a prominent anterior–posterior extension, as well

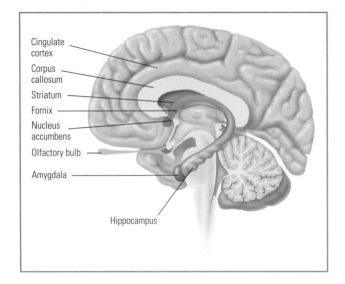

Cingulate cortex
Corpus callosum
Striatum
Fornix
Nucleus accumbens
Olfactory bulb
Amygdala
Hippocampus

as a medial–lateral extension (see Figure 3.13). It plays a prominent role in spatial maneuvering, attending to environmental cues and place signals that can aid in movement from one point to another and back again. Neurons in the hippocampus called "place cells" respond to specific locations in space (Wilson & McNaughton, 1993). Place cells provide rapid feedback about the location of the organism in its environment (the original backseat drivers), and they appear to be reactivated during dreaming, or REM sleep (Wilson & McNaughton, 1994).

The hippocampus plays a primary role in the formation of temporal as well as spatial memories, particularly those involving autobiographic events, or **episodic memory**. Many studies demonstrate that when the hippocampus is damaged, a person will suffer from a condition known as **anterograde amnesia**, in which no memories from the time of the damage to the present can be remembered easily, if at all. Older memories are spared however (Kandel et al., 2000). A major figure in the study of the hippocampus's role in memory was H. M., a patient who suffered significant damage to his hippocampus. H. M. recently died, and even as we write these words, his brain is being sliced, catalogued, and digitized for future generations of neuroscientists and the curious (Buchen, 2009).

These data suggest that the hippocampus regulates new learning and the forming of new memories. Memory researcher Daniel Schacter (1996) and others suggest that the hippocampus, which fuses with the cingulate, assembles memories from constituent associations, like a puzzle with interchangeable pieces with slightly different colors, items, etc. Each time a memory is recalled, then, there are slight differences from the previous recollection. Memory is fluid, not static, and can be influenced, subtly or otherwise. For example, excessive levels of stress hormones can compromise hippocampal structure and functioning (see Chapters 9 and 12). The hippocampus may play a role even in false memories (Schacter, 1996, 1997). Recall the case of Nadean Cool in Chapter 1, demonstrating how memories can be prejudiced, and even created, by a well-intentioned but misguided clinician.

Located at the tip of the basal ganglia, just rostral to the hippocampus, the amygdala, noted earlier, is another main functional component of the limbic system. Damage to the amygdala renders an individual incapable either of registering or of expressing the appropriate emotion and interferes with the perception and regulation of fear. Disruption of social interaction is one consequence of damage to this site as the amygdala-damaged person meets the relating of a sad story with amusement or other inappropriate responses (Adolphs, Baron-Cohen, & Tranel, 2002; Adolphs, Tranel, & Damasio, 1998; Adolphs, Tranel, Damasio, & Damasio, 1994). Further, subtle modifications in its activity through hormonal exposure or developmental insults may subtly alter the person's expressed emotions.

Rhinencephalon: Smell and the brain. The olfactory system in humans is an ancient, active, and influential sense. In many species, smell has primacy in governing behavior. In humans, olfactory afferents project to the amygdala for immediate processing of odors. The anatomical arrangement of the olfactory system, indicative of its ancient status, makes it the part of brain that is closest to the outside world. In fact, the sensory receptors

episodic memory
Autobiographic memory for personal experiences (episodes) pinpointed to specific place and time contexts.

anterograde amnesia Ability to recall long-ago events but not recent events, and a general inability to incorporate recent events into memory.

Box 3.1

Paul MacLean

Neural Investigator Paul MacLean's Pursuit of the Brain's Circuits

Paul MacLean, the third son of a Presbyterian minister, was born in Phipps, New York, in 1913. His first thoughts about the power of impulsive, emotional behavior—thoughts that would become the crux of his fascinating research—occurred when young MacLean was about 4 years old. He was seated in his father's congregation when he became captivated by a young girl who was looking at the ceiling and giggling uncontrollably.

Impulsively, MacLean climbed over the partition in the pew, a behavior that prompted his father to yell "PAUL!" from the pulpit. Before the service was over, the guilt-ridden young boy had jumped on his tricycle and run away from home. He was later located by his older brothers and delivered into the welcoming arms of his parents. During this episode, MacLean recalls thinking about why people do things that can get them into trouble even when they know better.

Toward the end of his undergraduate education in English literature at Yale University, MacLean found himself increasingly interested in philosophy. His interest turned to medicine, however, after observing a local physician diagnosing and successfully treating MacLean's ailing mother and realizing how rewarding it would be to help people in this manner. MacLean later attended Yale Medical School, completed an internship at prestigious Johns Hopkins University, and served in the Medical Corps in World War II. He had the opportunity to learn more about the brain during his military service when he was placed in charge of the psychiatric ward.

Because he was fascinated by the brain, MacLean accepted a U.S. Public Health Fellowship in 1947 working under Stanley Cobb, founder of the Department of Psychiatry at Massachusetts General Hospital. MacLean soon became intrigued by psychomotor epilepsy, seizures that were not accompanied by convulsions. Additionally, these seizures produced a modified sense of self, a kind of exaggerated feeling of what is real and important.

Upon investigation, MacLean learned that the epileptic focus of these seizures occurred in the anterior temporal region. At the heart of this region was the hippocampus, a brain area known at the time to be involved with olfaction; in other words, it was a *rhinencephalic*, or olfactory brain, structure. Puzzled by the question of why a brain area supposedly involved in smell might be involved in these pure emotional experiences in epileptic patients, MacLean turned to the literature for answers. He stumbled across an article written by Dr. James Papez in 1937, entitled "A Proposed Mechanism of Emotion." In this article, Papez pointed out that the hippocampus is connected to the hypothalamus, a structure thought at the time to be involved with emotional expression. Knowing that he was onto something meaningful, MacLean traveled to Cornell to meet with Papez, whom he referred to as "the Odyssean navigator of the brain" (MacLean, 1998, p. 258).

In 1949, MacLean published his landmark article entitled "Psychosomatic Disease and the 'Visceral' Brain," in which he emphasized that, although we have

of olfactory neurons that are embedded in the nasal mucosa are separated by mere millimeters of bone and a single short synapse from the olfactory bulb itself (Figure 3.14).

The olfactory bulb in the human mammal is small (*microsmatic*) relative to the rest of the brain (see Figure 3.13). A *macrosmatic* animal, like the rat, has a highly evolved sense of smell. The rat's olfactory bulb is large relative to the rest of its brain, whereas the human has a pair of olfactory bulbs the size and shape of shoelaces. Still, size does not matter. The intimacy of smell harks back to a time when olfaction was explicitly important in human social interactions and in navigating the environment. But even today smell has a most powerful effect upon the human, subtly altering

Dr. Paul MacLean in his sunroom.

KELLY LAMBERT, RANDOLPH-MACON COLLEGE BEHAVIORIAL NEUROSCIENCE LABORATORY

a highly developed cortex, our emotional behavior continues to be influenced by more primitive parts of the brain. In his later writings, MacLean changed the term *visceral*, which was confused with internal organs, to *limbic*, a term used earlier by Paul Broca to describe the circular structure of the cingulate cortex.

In essence, MacLean wrote that we have an ancient reptilian brain component that contains hardwired neurological programs for very basic, specific behaviors, such as those involved in aggression and sexual displays. The limbic lobe, or the paleomammalian system, is involved with play behavior, parental behavior, and the separation cry of infants. Finally, the neomammalian brain, or the neocortex, has evolved to integrate the more basic functions with the environment. In an attempt to convey how all three components interact in the human to produce behavior, MacLean introduced the term *triune* (from the Greek word meaning "three in one") brain. In 1990, MacLean published *The Triune Brain in Evolution: Role in Paleocerebral Functions*, a book that captures his life's work in this area.

In this day of reductionistic neuroanatomy, MacLean's more global view of the brain as a collection of circuits is refreshing. It enabled him to consider some very "big" questions, such as "Why, in a time when there is so much suffering, do humans continue to have children?" The answer, he wrote, lies in the limbic structures and their relationship with the newly evolved neocortex. That is, the parental and social bonds that form because of the activity of the limbic lobe influence the neocortex. Consequently, the neocortex is involved in anticipation, planning, empathy, and altruism; and it probably promotes an awareness of the well-being of family members and other acquaintances. In a sense, the neocortex might play a crucial role in promoting the welfare and proliferation of the species.

Throughout MacLean's life, he continued to be a brain investigator, traveling weekly to the National Institute of Mental Health to work on a project that he jokingly referred to as the "5,000-year project." Keenly aware of his race against time as he entered his nineties, he continued to pursue his interest in learning more about the circuits of the brain. Always a student of neuroanatomy, MacLean likened his continued adventures in the microscopic world of brain anatomy to "walking into a cathedral." He warned young investigators not to let a day go by without communing with neuroanatomical nature—"if you don't observe the brain on a daily basis, you won't hear the music" (personal communication). Indeed, the intricate and delicate connections of the circuits of the brain were like a symphony to his temporal, or emotional, cortex.

perceptions of the world—and the people who inhabit it—and influencing our behavior.

Also, airborne chemicals guide social behaviors in ways that operate just under our level of awareness. Research has demonstrated the existence of receptors for pheromones in the human and their subtle effects on behavior (Whitten, 2000). Pheromones act as chemical signals among animals of the same species. When a pheromone is released by one individual, it creates a specific behavioral response in the individuals who perceive it. Likewise, very subtle odors outside our awareness can influence our physiology and, hence, our behavior. There is a tendency for us to think that we are so far evolved, so different and removed from the forces that shaped us, that we are impervious to such crass biological influences. Research suggests, however,

Box 3.2

Brain Matters

Joking Around in the Laboratory

Question: What do engineers use for birth control?

Answer: Their personalities!

Did you laugh at this joke? If you did, why did you laugh? Was your laughter voluntary, or did it seem out of your control? Although you're probably thinking that these questions take the fun out of a joke, they are the questions researchers ask in the attempt to understand the neuroanatomical underpinnings of laughter.

A few researchers suggest an evolutionary role. Ramachandran (1998) suggests that laughter is the result of being led down one cognitive path, expecting an answer of a particular nature, and then having the old cognitive-expectation "switcheroo" pulled on you. Because there's a deflation of expectation for the initial cognitive journey, a loud explosive sound is employed to warn others that the expectation is a false alarm.

This theory is supported by several studies reporting more laughter occurring in social groups than in isolated individuals. In his book *Laughter* (2000), Provine reports several interesting social twists on laughter. Women laugh more at men than men do at women (sorry, guys), speakers laugh more than listeners, and, believe it or not, laughter is more rarely a response to jokes than it is to "It was nice to meet you" social interactions. Indeed, laughter seems to be an attempt by humans to ingratiate themselves with others. Next time you're observing people introduce themselves observe how often they start moving their shoulders up and down in laughter, even though you're certain no jokes are being told.

What about the brain structures involved in this mysterious behavior? Working in London's Institute of Neurology in Queens Square, Vinod Goel and Raymond Dolan (2001) collected functional magnetic resonance imaging (fMRI) scans of individuals listening to two types of jokes: semantic jokes (*Why don't sharks bite lawyers? It's a matter of professional courtesy*) and phonological jokes, or puns (*Why did the golfer wear two pants? He had a hole in one*). Believe it or not, they found separate neural circuitries for these two types of jokes. The semantic joke route includes bilateral temporal lobe activity, and the pun activates Broca's area in the temporal lobe, where language is processed, and the floor area of the cortex known as the insula. When jokes were funny, the medial ventral prefrontal cortex around the area of the pleasure center, or the nucleus accumbens, was activated (Dunn, 2001).

In another clever study, researchers separated the time in which subjects were "getting" the joke from the time they were "laughing" at the jokes. The subjects viewed a *Seinfeld* episode. For the duration of the episode, experimenters collected fMRI scans time-locked with the laugh track (mirthful experience—laughter) and for the moment directly preceding the laugh track (getting the joke experience). As subjects were just getting the joke, their scans showed activation of the left dorsal and inferior frontal cortex and bilateral activation of the temporal lobes. During the laughter moments, the insula of the cortex was activated, as was the amygdala (Kelley et al., 2002).

Interestingly, the insula controls autonomic functions such as breathing, and most people display altered breathing patterns as they verbalize their mirthful feelings (laugh). By exposing their subjects to visual comics during positron emission tomographic (PET) scans, Iwase et al. (2002) found bilateral activation (increased blood flow) of the supplementary motor area of the cortex and left putamen as well as visual association areas, left temporal, orbitofrontal, and medial prefrontal cortices. Alternatively, when subjects were asked to force a smile, the only areas activated

---

that the role olfaction played millions of years ago is still being played out today, dictating how we act and react (Doty, Ford, Preti, & Huggins, 1975; Jacobs, McClintock, Zelano, & Ober, 2002; McClintock, 1998).

Spinal Cord

The nervous system enables split-second decisions that ensure the organism's survival. The consequences are rapid and unforgiving: The field mouse that takes a few extra seconds to detect an approaching cat becomes a tasty feline hors d'oeuvre. Recall that the nervous system is made up of tracts

were in the primary and supplementary motor cortices. Fried, Wilson, MacDonald, and Behnke (1998) reported producing laughter through electrical stimulation of a small, 2 cm² area of the motor cortex during surgery to treat a 16-year-old girl's epilepsy. This supplementary motor area may be part of a larger circuit that regulates emotional output.

We can understand more about laughter through the use of animal models. Panksepp (2000) reported a type of laughter in his laboratory rats. When the rats were tickled, they emitted a high-frequency chirping response. In natural social interactions, the animals emitted similar responses during social play. The tickling seems to be rewarding—as is the case in humans—because the rats would seek out the hand that previously tickled it.

Panksepp contends that this animal model may be valuable in learning more about positive emotional responses such as joy. Regardless of the philosophical question of whether you can actually tickle a rat—as a comedian might ask—what is this behavior all about? How can it be that if you run your fingers up your own rib cage you have no response but if someone else does it you withdraw, assume a fetal position, and begin a series of hearty belly laughs?

Scientists think the cerebellum may play a role in this mysterious dichotomy of responses to tactile stimulation. If you are tickling yourself, the cerebellum, involved in motor coordination, seems to predict the tactile stimulation and promptly sends a message to disregard the meaningless sensation. But the cerebellum cannot predict the exact movement of an external "tickling" stimulus and send the appropriate messages to ignore the sensation; laughter results when the stimulus is determined to be nonthreatening (Blakemore, Wolpert, & Frith, 1998).

Did you ever imagine that having the giggles could evoke so many scientific questions? Brain researchers

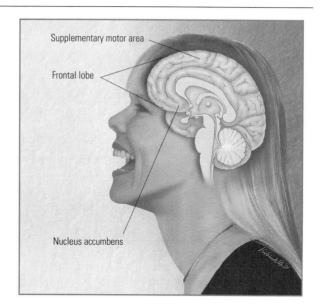

Laughter incorporates several areas of the brain including the supplementary motor area, frontal cortices, and nucleus accumbens.
LYDIA KIBUIK

continue to ponder whether laughter serves some specific evolutionary function or is just a cognitive juxtaposition (Goel & Dolan, 2001) and what areas of the brain are activated in different types of humor. But as you'll read in Chapter 13, health researchers have already discovered that laughter appears to be good medicine due to connections with the immune system. Another medicinal application that has been suggested is the potential use of nitrous oxide, or laughing gas, instead of electroconvulsive shock therapy to treat depression. As you'll learn in Chapter 9, depression is no laughing matter, but chemical-induced laughing may provide some relief—it will be interesting to see what further research in this area reveals (Milen, 2009).

designated as efferent (outgoing) or afferent (incoming) transports for neural messages. Afferent information is sensory as it goes from the body to the brain for processing. Once the information is processed, it goes from brain to periphery in efferent motor impulses. Orderly regulation of this sensorimotor information is vitally important for the control of behavior.

The CNS structure that facilitates efficient brain–body communication is the **spinal cord**, a delicate, cylindrical tube of nervous tissue about the diameter and consistency of a large stalk of tender asparagus. It is encased within the **vertebral column** (backbone), which is composed of individual

spinal cord Tube of CNS tissue extending from the base of the brain through the central canal to the upper part of the lumbar spine; conducts sensorimotor impulses between the brain and the body and is a site of reflex activity.

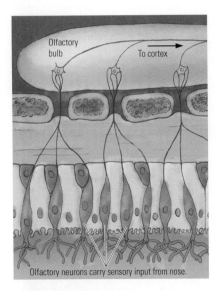

Olfactory bulb
To cortex

Olfactory neurons carry sensory input from nose.

Figure 3.14
The nose and olfactory system have an anatomically intimate relationship with the brain.

vertebral column Firm, flexible bony column extending from the base of the skull to the coccyx; longitudinal axis and chief supporting structure of the human body.

interneurons Nerve cells that associate sensory and motor activity in the CNS.

cranial nerves Twelve pairs of nerves, each pair having sensory and/or motor functions, extending to and from the brain without passing through the spinal cord.

vagus nerve (cranial nerve 10) Mixed cranial nerve pair; sensory portion transmits sensations of pain and nausea from the viscera, motor component exerts parasympathetic control of cardiovascular and abdominal function, as well as controlling the muscles of the throat.

bony vertebrae separated by cartilaginous, cushiony disks running the length of the neck and back. From the base of the brain stem, from which it is pinched off and continuous, the spinal cord runs down to the small of the back, just above the buttocks, where it terminates in a cluster of tiny and delicate rootlets called the "cauda equina,".

The vertebral column provides flexibility and mobile protection for the spinal cord during the range of movements and contortions required of or inflicted on the individual. It also displays a fascinating sex difference, allowing for the rapidly expanding pregnant female to accommodate the fetal load by stabilizing the center of mass above the hips (Whitcome, Shapiro & Lieberman, 2007). The spinal cord, as protected as it is, is still fragile tissue. It traverses the spinal column's bony vertebrae, neck to tail, in three main segments—cervical, thoracic, and lumbar—and two minor, fused segments—sacrum and coccyx, or tailbone (Figure 3.15).

Ascending sensory impulses move up the spinal cord toward the brain via the vertebrae's dorsal columns or horns. Descending, efferent motor impulses are transmitted via the ventral columns/horns.

The sensory and motor pathways are joined together in 31 pairs of ascending (sensory) and descending (motor nerve) bundles called the "dorsal" and "ventral roots," respectively, which innervate the periphery of the body with the means of commerce with the brain (Figure 3.15 inset).

The dorsal and ventral roots are joined by a mass of nerve tissue, the intermediate zone, where association cells called **interneurons** project to the motor neurons; these in turn project to the muscles. Here, we see some similarity in the activity of the spinal cord and the brain, with input, processing, and output of information best exemplified by the simplest of behaviors, the spinal reflex.

When a shard of glass, a tack, a hot surface, or some other potential threat is sensed, say, by foot or finger, the afferent sensory information en route to the brain also undergoes some initial processing in the intermediate zone that results in the limb rapidly being pulled away. That is, rather than traversing the distance between the spinal cord and the brain's sensory regions and then descending before any action or motor response, the spinal cord initiates the reflex. Having this "local" say over the withdrawal of the damaged appendage is much more efficient than awaiting central contact and decision, with their inherently lengthy time span. Spinal reflexes protect sensitive tissues from additional damage by automatically and rapidly pulling away from a threat.

Should the spinal cord be damaged or, worse, severed, motor paralysis and lack of sensation ensue. The route of entrance to the brain is near the rostral end of the spinal cord, so the higher the damage occurs, the more functions are impaired. As you will read in the epilogue, much ongoing research is aimed at treating spinal cord injuries. The hope is that basic research can develop a treatment for reassembling the neurons and the axons that have been sundered. Promising treatments include the use of stem cells and attempts to differentiate these cells into spinal neurons or axons. To date, however, the preliminary successes that have been optimistically reported in various animal models have yet to be applied to humans. Time will tell, but the basic research continues.

CRANIAL NERVES
AND BLOOD SUPPLY

The spinal cord is the main conduit for information transfer between the brain and the periphery of the body. In addition, a specialized set of **cranial nerves** emanate from nuclei in the brain stem and cortical areas to regulate information flowing to and from the internal organs and the specialized sensory systems and muscles in the head and neck. Twelve pairs of cranial nerves transmit sensory and motor impulses to and from the face, neck, and head and to the gut (Figure 3.16). Each pair has a different function, although there is much complementarity.

Some cranial nerves are sensory, some are motor, and some are mixed, that is, nerve pairs that convey both afferent and efferent information. The **vagus nerve**, for example, is a mixed nerve that regulates activities further afield than the other cranial pairs. The sensory portion of the vagus transmits sensations of pain and nausea from the viscera, whereas the motor component exerts parasympathetic control of cardiovascular and abdominal function, as well as controlling the muscles of the throat.

It is imperative for an animal to respond to the changing features of the environment, and humans are no exception. Porges (2002) argues that certain components of the vagal–peripheral nervous circuit enable the animal to maintain homeostasis during these changes. Porges's work is challenging neuroscientists' views regarding exactly which nervous system is running the behavioral show. After all, the ANS includes brain stem structures that monitor the physiological state of the internal organs, so technically it is not completely separated from the CNS. Although their research is still in an early stage, the Porges team is providing further evidence that the boundaries between the brain and the body are even less distinct than once thought.

The brain is occupied every second of our lives, a resource-heavy load. Brain activity consumes approximately 20% of the oxygen available in the body at any time (Vogel, 1992). To maintain this level of activity requires a large and steady supply of blood (Figure 3.17). The circulatory system provides an efficient answer and adaptation to the demands of the nervous system.

The brain requires about the same amount of blood that a large, hardworking muscle receives and produces an equivalent amount of heat. More specifically, although the brain constitutes only 2% of the body's weight, it

Figure 3.15
The spinal cord is a delicate collection of long axons, conveying afferent (sensory) information to the brain and efferent (motor) impulses away from it.

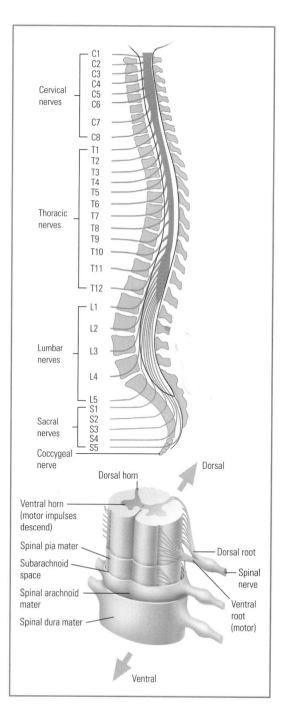

stroke Loss of brain tissue caused by blockade of a blood vessel and resultant loss of blood and, hence, oxygen; can result in sudden loss of consciousness, sensation, and voluntary movement.

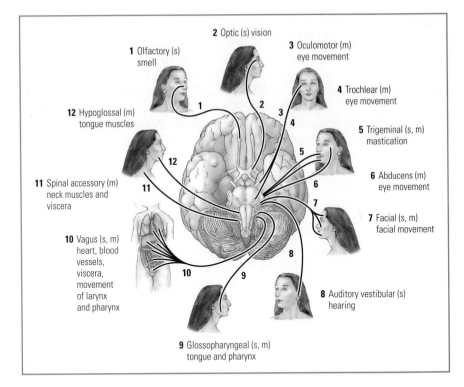

Figure 3.16
Functional anatomy of the cranial nerves. The letters *s* and *m* refer to sensory and motor functions, respectively, of the nerve.

consumes up to 20% of the body's blood supply. The blood circulation also regulates brain temperature within critical limits. A temperature just a few degrees above normal (*hyperthermia*) poses a dangerous risk of damage or death, and if the temperature drops too low (*hypothermia*), brain activity will begin to slow and shut down.

This reliance on a fine network of blood vessels can be delicate. A disruption of blood flow in any portion of a large vessel, like a cerebral artery, such as a rupture or clot, poses equally serious consequences such as a **stroke.** A stroke, can result in a sudden loss of consciousness, sensation, and voluntary movement. Deprived of oxygen, nerve cells in the affected part of the brain begin to die. Box 3.3 describes how the road to recovery is often difficult, but in some cases patients are able to make remarkable advances from the stroke-induced injury.

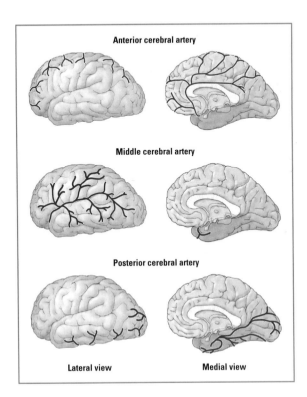

Figure 3.17
Arteries in the brain supply necessary fuels and nutrients; veins remove the wastes that result from the brain's many activities.

Box 3.3

A Case in Point

Katherine Sherwood

At the age of 44, Katherine Sherwood had everything going for her. She enjoyed a successful career as an artist on the faculty of the University of California at Berkeley. On the personal side, she was married to an artist and had a 5-year-old daughter. One afternoon in May 1997, however, within a matter of 2 minutes, her world changed forever.

After experiencing a severe headache, Sherwood collapsed. When she awoke in the hospital, the right side of her body was paralyzed. She could no longer speak or read or paint. Sherwood had experienced a stroke in the left cerebral hemisphere. Doctors told her that the hemorrhage had realigned her brain's circuitry, probably impairing the ability of the left hemisphere to seek explanations, order, and reason. For a lawyer, this realignment could result in the end of a career; but for an artist, it might enhance creativity.

After about 4 months, Sherwood was able to speak once again, and she gained enough motility in her right leg to be able to walk. She hoped that she would regain movement in her right arm and hand, but that never happened. Understandably, Sherwood became depressed. She experienced an epiphany, however, when she was in her radiologist's office having a carotid angiogram to determine whether any further bleeding was occurring in her brain.

Although she was still groggy from the anesthetics, she caught a glimpse of the blood vessels in her brain on the computer screen. The image of the wandering vessels reminded her of a favorite 1,000-year-old painting of a Chinese landscape. Suddenly, she felt that she had to have these images and asked the technician for them. Although confused, her neurologist obliged, and Sherwood went home with the X-ray images of her brain's vascular landscape.

Inspired by the pictures of her own brain, Sherwood wanted to incorporate the images into her art. She also felt compelled to incorporate into her work seventeenth-century symbols of healing purportedly created originally by King Solomon. From a symbolic point of view, she knew that the contrast between the clinical, scientific images of her brain and the ancient emblems from a sorcery handbook would be compelling. Artistically, the angiograms and mystical symbols share a curving linearity. The juxtaposition of these disparate images reminds the viewer of the multiple dimensions of our identity.

Although inspired to commence her painting once again, Sherwood still faced the challenge of learning to use her left arm, controlled primarily by her right cerebral hemisphere, to paint. Slowly, she found that she could paint with her left hand. Although fine movements were limited, she discovered that her left hand painted with a more creative flow, allowing her to work with less of the creative angst that frequently had accompanied her right-handed painting.

Today, Sherwood's work is better than ever. She has received more awards and recognition following the stroke than she received prior to it. She is also teaching a course focusing on healing and art, a natural endeavor considering how her art transformed her from a depressed stroke patient to a thriving artist.

Summary

Gross Structure and Function of the Nervous System

The central and peripheral nervous systems and the activities they regulate bring sensory/afferent information to the brain and take motor/efferent information away from it. This efficient arrangement regulates rapid and appropriate responses to internal and external events.

The skull is a light and tough encasement that provides excellent protection from physical insult. The three layers of the meninges also provide cushioning and support to the brain.

The ventricular system manufactures and circulates cerebrospinal fluid throughout the brain. This system provides a mechanism for the circulation of the major extracellular fluid involved in the movement of metabolites and nutrients to and through the brain, as well as providing protection and developmental structural benefits.

The brain is divided into three main sections, owing to anatomical and developmental relationships. These are the prosencephalon (forebrain), the mesencephalon (midbrain), and the rhombencephalon (hindbrain).

CNS Structure and Function

Brain stem structures are associated with vegetative and basic physiological regulatory processes and represent the fundamental mechanisms of life.

The midbrain structures, such as the tectum and tegmentum, control optical, auditory, and attentional activities.

The forebrain has as its main structures the cortex, which is responsible for the majority of an organism's higher cognitive activities, and the thalamus and hypothalamus. Respectively, they regulate sensory routing and motivated responses.

The spinal cord, a thin and delicate collection of axons, is the major contact between the brain and peripheral nervous system, conveying afferent and efferent data.

Cranial Nerves and Blood Supply

The cranial nerves are a set of 12 pairs of contacts transmitting sensory and motor information to and from the brain.

The blood supply to the brain is rich and complex and enables this most demanding of organs to have an adequate amount of oxygen, nutrients, and waste removal to accommodate the second-to-second activities it controls for a lifetime.

Key Terms

plasticity (64)

central nervous system (CNS) (64)

peripheral nervous system (PNS) (64)

afferent information (65)

efferent information (65)

nuclei (65)

tract (65)

nerve (65)

somatic nervous system (SNS) (65)

autonomic nervous system (ANS) (65)

sympathetic nervous system (66)

parasympathetic nervous system (66)

meninges (66)

cerebrospinal fluid (CSF) (68)

cerebral aqueduct (69)

central canal (69)

prosencephalon (69)

mesencephalon (69)

rhombencephalon (70)

telencephalon (70)

diencephalon (70)

medulla oblongata (73)

cerebellum (73)

pons (74)

reticular formation (74)

tectum (74)

tegmentum (74)

superior colliculi (74)

inferior colliculi (74)

substantia nigra (75)

periaqueductal gray (PAG) (75)

thalamus (77)

hypothalamus (77)

pituitary gland (78)

cortex (neocortex) (78)

frontal lobe (79)

temporal lobe (79)

parietal lobe (79)

occipital lobe (79)

association cortex (80)

gyri (80)

sulci (80)

fissures (81)

longitudinal fissure (81)

lateral fissure (81)

central sulcus (81)

basal ganglia (81)

limbic system (81)

amygdala (81)

striatum (81)

Huntington's chorea (82)

dyskinesias (82)

nucleus accumbens (82)

hippocampus (82)

episodic memory (83)

anterograde amnesia (83)

spinal cord (87)

vertebral column (88)

interneurons (88)

cranial nerves (88)

vagus nerve (88)

stroke (90)

For Further Consideration

Ramón y Cajal, S. (1995). *Histology of the nervous system of man and vertebrates* (N. Swanson & L. W. Swanson, Trans.). New York: Oxford University Press. Santiago Ramón y Cajal was a man ahead of his time. It makes one wonder what he could have accomplished had he had access to the tools available to the average neuroscientist today. His intricate and highly accurate drawings, made from detailed and painstaking observations of the nervous system of a variety of species, are absolutely beautiful. And they are as valuable today as they were when he first penned them. The Swansons have done a wonderful job of translating the text. Ramón y Cajal's descriptions are as fresh as ever. This two-volume set is a must-have for the artwork alone—over 1,000 meticulous images grace the pages of this magnum opus. Ramón y Cajal's love for his work, and it is prodigious, comes through in his writings as well. This book represents the pinnacle of a man's life's work. It is a love story disguised as a scientific treatise.

Freedman, D. J., Riesenhuber, M., Poggio, T., & Miller, E. K. (2001). Categorical representation of visual stimuli in the primate prefrontal cortex. *Science, 291,* 312–315. The flood of information with which the brain is inundated minute by minute is determined by the sensory system. In the brain, the information is disseminated and categorized. The latter operation is critical to the efficient processing of information by the brain. In this article, the authors examine the neural correlates of categorization in the nonhuman primate. The article demonstrates how the process occurs. The authors trained monkeys to group animals such as cats and dogs in categories that reflected the "catness" versus the "dogness" of the forms they learned. By recording the activity of specific neurons in the prefrontal cortex (PFC) and presenting the monkeys with ambiguous forms (a morphing combination of a dog and cat), they demonstrated activation of a specific set of PFC neurons in response to the category, either dog or cat, to which the stimulus belonged. The data show that the brain has robust categories into which the world is distributed and from which the brain can draw conclusions about its sensory world.

Tramo, M. J. (2001). Music of the hemispheres. *Science, 291,* 54–56. The adage that music is the universal language may be truer than ever before. Research is showing that music, in a variety of forms, is practiced and perceived by humans and other animals. Gray and colleagues discuss the use of music by a variety of species, humans included, and conclude that "the roots of music lie closer to our ancient lizard brain than to our more recent reasoning cortex" (p. 54). Therefore, music, perhaps by the rhythms inherent to its production, unites humans and other animals with a beat whose reverberations can be traced to our very origins.

Tramo's piece focuses on the human (brain's) capacity for and fascination with music. According to this analysis, our brains are wired to respond to music, with specific sites (for example, auditory cortex [superior temporal lobe], thalamus, hypothalamus, cerebellum) showing some form of activation. The article suggests that a single piece of music has the ability to involve in unison many disparate brain regions. Therefore, perhaps music brings us closer to other animals as well as closer to ourselves.

Keenan, J. P., Nelson, A., O'Connor, M. & Pascual-Leone, A. (2001). Self-recognition and the right hemisphere. *Nature, 409,* 305. Have you ever wondered how you recognize your face when you see it as a reflection in a mirror or a pool of water? That is, by what processes are you able to perform self-recognition? Keenan and colleagues examined that question in a sample of human patients in whom one or the other cerebral hemisphere was inactivated by means of intracarotid anesthesia administration (the so-called Wada test). With the right hemisphere deadened by the anesthesia, the patients were unable to recognize their own faces shown to them in photographs. In another set of patients, photographs of their own faces or those of celebrities were shown. There was greater activity in the right hemisphere when viewing pictures of their own faces. The interesting speculation is raised that self-awareness, a hallmark of consciousness and hence being human, derives from such right-hemisphere activity.

McEwen, B. S. (1998). *The hostage brain.* New York: Rockefeller University Press. This underpromoted book is an excellent general text on neuroscience and neurobiology. It is particularly notable for its illustrations. Clear, colorful, detailed, and complementing the text extremely well, the drawings are as valuable as the text in providing the reader with insight into the neuron's and the brain's functions. McEwen, who is past president of the Society for Neuroscience, is a concise writer with a lot to say. The information is presented clearly and accurately, and his passion for the field shines throughout. This fine book requires more attention from both lay and academic audiences.

Panksepp, J. (1998). *Affective neuroscience: The foundations of human and animal emotions.* New York: Oxford University Press. This volume describes the complex and difficult-to-define field of affective research—studies of emotion. If one thing is clear after reading this book, it is that what we call emotion in the human and in other animals is clearly a brain-derived phenomenon. When the brain works properly, emotion is regulated normally; when something goes awry, look out. With a particular focus on the neurochemistry of emotion, Panksepp makes the brain skeptic a fundamental believer in the biochemistry of affective responses.

Chapter Four

Microanatomy and Neurotransmission

Connections

Human and Mouse Genius

Do you remember the classmate who never studied but always got the best grades? Why do some people seem to learn so easily whereas others have to sweat for every grade? What causes such variability in learning ability?

Philosophers and psychologists have contemplated the constituents of genius for centuries. James Mill, a nineteenth-century Scottish philosopher, decided to sculpt the intellectual capacities of his son, John Stuart Mill, to make sure that John developed into a genius. To test his particular theory of mind, the elder Mill provided an enriched environment and proceeded to make his son into a regular reasoning machine.

By age 3 the younger Mill was studying Greek, and by age 8 he was studying Latin. By the time he was 10 years old he had read many classic works in these languages, and by age 12 he had written a book-length manuscript on the history of the Roman government. He later became a well-known British philosopher and eventually played a critical role in shaping the history of psychology. In his 1843 book *A System of Logic*, Mill argued for a "science of human nature" at a time when many thought that a science of the mind was a preposterous idea (Benjamin, 1993).

The enriched environment probably contributed greatly to the development of John Stuart Mill's genius, but environment alone does not explain why one individual learns better or more quickly than another. Meet Greg Smith, a latter-day J. S. Mill who began his college experience at Randolph-Macon College when he was just 10 years old. Although Greg was born to two intelligent, nurturing parents, it was not their intent to provide an environment fit for a genius. No Mozart sonatas played softly while Greg was in the womb, nor were flashcards introduced in the crib. Nevertheless, young Greg started flexing his cognitive muscles in infancy. He said his first words when he was 3 months old, and he was speaking in complete sentences and reciting entire books from memory before his first birthday. (In the average child, these events do not occur until the second or third year.) He was solving math problems by 14 months of age and was reading about dinosaurs by his second birthday.

Greg's parents fostered his intellectual development by always encouraging him to ask questions and to seek the most informed answers. This precocious child began school by spending 2 weeks in the second grade, then skipping to the fourth; and by the spring of the same year, he was flourishing in a sixth-grade honors course. At the age of 8, Greg commenced high school and went to college just 2 years later. With an undergraduate degree in math, Greg then went on to earn his master's degree in mathematics at the University of Virginia at the age of 16 with plans for several PhDs following that to prepare him for a diverse array of careers (mathematical research, biomedical applications, and international politics are current favorites in the career category).

How might neurobiology contribute to the genius Greg Smith displays? Dr. Joseph Tsien's work at Princeton University may point to an answer. Tsien became interested in a classic theory proposed by the Canadian psychologist Donald O. Hebb that is believed to be the cellular basis for learning and eventually memory. As we will see in this chapter and the next, the basis for genius may involve changes in the very basic interactions between and among neurons.

More than half a century after Hebb proposed his theory, Tsien and his group focused on the relationship between a chemical the brain produces and the sites that the chemical targets. This neurotransmitter–receptor coupling (involving glutamate, the major central nervous system excitatory neurotransmitter, and its specific receptor, *N*-methyl-d-aspartate [NMDA], both described in Chapter 5) seems to follow Hebb's proposed learning rule that requires simultaneous neuron activation and a consequent change in the interaction between two or more neurons in a circuit. Essentially, there is a difference between the biochemical activity of "learned" and "ignorant" neurons.

Tsien and his associates genetically engineered some mice that were able to make increased amounts of certain types of NMDA receptors and then tested them in a variety of learning situations (Tsien, 2000). Interestingly, the mice with enhanced NMDA receptors, dubbed "Doogie" mice after the child doctor on a TV show in the 1980s, outperformed the control animals. Tsien's work became quite popular; Doogie mice even became the topic of one of David Letterman's top 10 lists! Now at the Medical College of Georgia, Tsien recently launched the Brain Decoding Initiative to further understand the organizing principles of the brain's memory system.

Despite Tsien's efforts, neuroscientists still do not know how generalizable his findings are to human memory. Even so, it is instructive to think about possible neuronal mechanisms of enhanced and impaired learning abilities.

To look into the brain is to see living tissue and wonder. The late Francis Crick (1994), microbiologist and Nobel Prize winner, noted that everything we do and everything we think is regulated by the complex actions and interactions of wet tissue, of neurons and glia. Joseph LeDoux (2002), a well-known neuroscientist interested in the fear response and other emotions, maintains that the *synapse*, the point of communication between two neurons, is the defining element of the human being. There is nothing mystical here, nothing cosmic, just basic biochemistry available for study and explication. The phenomenon of thought, of being, begins and ends with essential, basic biological processes.

Communication between and among neurons underlies consciousness. Such neurotransmission is accomplished by elegant, understandable, and very describable electrochemical events open to study by neuroscientists. Keep in mind (that is, in your own firing neurons) that what we are describing may be infinitely complex, but it is subject to exploration and study—unlike subjective models of mind that are incapable of defining the variables they purport to study (see Chapter 1). Understanding how neurons maintain and generate their activities forms the foundation for understanding how neurons communicate. This is the objective of this chapter. Knowing this basis of neuronal communication prepares you to understand its disruption, what may go wrong in the mental disorders discussed throughout the text.

sensory neurons Refers to the specialized cells that transmit, input, and interpret physical stimuli (light, sound, touch, etc.) from the external world and translate it into neuronal impulses.

motor neurons Broad phrase referring either to the output neurons carrying out the commands from sensory and interneurons or to neurons at the interface of glands, muscles, and blood vessels.

cell membrane Membrane that retains the cell's shape and contains the cytoplasm, nucleus, and assorted organelles. The membrane is a bimolecular leaflet with semipermeable properties.

MICROANATOMY OF THE NEURON

In many respects, the neuron is similar to every other cell in the body. For example, neurons react to a variety of chemical and physical agents with some internal and, subsequently, some external modification. Whereas skin cells respond to continuous rubbing by forming a blister and then a callus, a neuron, according to the electrical and chemical inputs it receives, modifies its activity, accelerating or decelerating its interaction with other cells. This ebb and flow of neuronal activity governs and defines nervous system activity.

Two major features separate neurons from other cells and represent major evolutionary adaptations. First and most important, neurons can transmit the information they receive to other neurons and to tissues, including muscles, glands, and blood vessels; this feature enables rapid signaling and communication throughout the body. Second, neurons function collectively as circuits—the nuclei, fiber pathways, and nerves described in Chapter 3—moving information quickly and efficiently from inception to conclusion, adding to its richness en route to consciousness and behavior. We describe neural circuitry, including the neuroanatomy of stress, in Chapter 5.

Another functional peculiarity of neurons that adds somewhat to their uniqueness is their collective inability to recover naturally from damage. Although there is evidence that neurons are produced throughout the lifetime of an individual, in a phenomenon known as *neurogenesis*, the cells do not regenerate and regain function as simply as other cells in the body. If you fall down and scrape the skin off your knee, those cells grow back. Scrape your brain, damaging neurons, and they die, taking with them whatever information they may have been storing, like a trunk going down when the ship sinks. The neurons contain biological information stored as proteins: When the neurons go, they take those proteins with them.

Information begins its journey from neuron to brain in the form of sensory stimulation, signals that are unreadable by the central nervous system (CNS) in their raw, physical state. Their capture involves **sensory neurons**, specialized cellular receptors that reside at the beginning of the chain of peripheral nervous system (PNS) transmission. Sensory neurons transduce physical energy into neural impulses (propagated action potentials). That is, they convert stimuli—sound waves (hearing), photons (light/dark and color), chemicals (taste and olfactory), pressure (touch), and gravity/spatial stimuli (proprioceptive)—into electrochemical signals recognizable by the CNS. The simplest spinal reflexes, discussed in Chapter 3, are accomplished by the coordination of sensory neurons (information getting into the nervous system), interneuron activity (association, processing, and decision making); and **motor neurons** (output or action). What we call "behavior" is the net result of electrochemical neurotransmission; consciousness, our awareness of some of the brain's activity, is merely one point along this continuous loop of neural transmission.

External Structure and Function of the Neuron

How does all this highly complex activity come about? The answer, not so simply, is through the activity of the neuron, the basic unit of the nervous system. Sophisticated imaging and neurophysiological techniques utilizing single active neurons have provided a wealth of new data about the neuron, its structure and function, its chemistry and electrical activity. These data demonstrate how groups of neurons dictate brain function and flexibility. Plasticity is inherent to the brain; the brain can respond to nearly every exigency for which evolution has prepared it.

Neurons take on a nearly infinite number of shapes, lengths, branching patterns, activity levels, and interactions with other neurons and CNS structures (Figure 4.1). Neurons of all types, however, share similar characteristics and functions. For example, during neurotransmission information travels from an input signal delivered through the cell membrane to a trigger zone near the cell body and is conducted via the axon to output through the terminal buttons (Figure 4.2). Like links in a highly specialized and dynamic chain, each neuron has the capacity to receive, process, and transmit information. But because neurons are forceful and fluid structures, defining their beginning and end is subjective. Like stepping into a rapidly flowing river, we arbitrarily define "upstream" and "downstream."

Cell membrane and its gateways. The neuron's three-dimensional structure is maintained and defined by the cell membrane, the enclosure that surrounds the neuron and all other animal cells. The double-layered cell

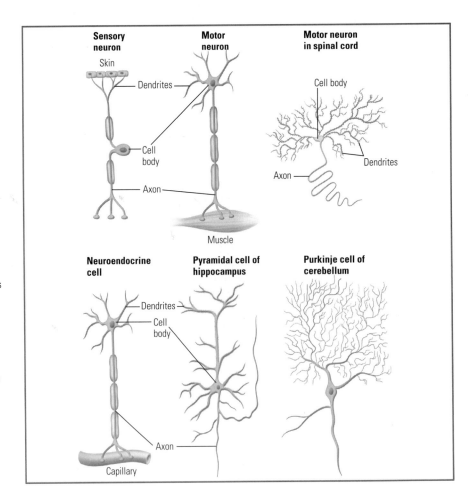

Figure 4.1
Types of neurons. The nervous system is rife with variety in shape, activity, and function in its basic unit, the neuron. Though the three general components—dendrites, cell body or soma, and axon—are present in each neuron, neurons can take on a spectacular array of shapes, sizes, and lengths, any of which may be plastic and responsive to the surrounding environment throughout the course of the organism's life.
ADAPTED FROM KANDEL, SCHWARTZ, & JESSEL, 1995, FIGURE 2.8

membrane acts as a flexible boundary between the intracellular and extracellular environments and encloses the internal structures that regulate cellular function. The cell membrane is semipermeable, functioning simultaneously as barrier and gateway to regulate the flow of chemicals (mostly water and dissolved salts) into and out of the neuron according to its activity state.

If too much water enters a cell, for example, it will burst; with too little water, it will shrivel. Likewise, the chemical balance between the inside and the outside of the cell must be regulated for the neuron to function properly. Water and dissolved salts play prominent roles in cellular function. Like the seawater that surrounded the earliest living cells billions of years ago, the fluid outside our cells is in the main a solution of dissolved sodium chloride (that's right: table salt!). The extracellular fluid is relatively more positive in electrical charge and the intracellular space slightly negative in charge due to the differing concentrations of dissolved ions (charged atoms) inside and outside the cell. Sodium (Na^+) and chloride (Cl^-) ions are prominent, along with many other dissolved salts, including potassium (K^+) and calcium chloride ($CaCl_2$).

The barrier portion of the cell membrane is made up of a dual, complementary set of phosphate and fat (lipid) molecules, arranged head to leg to form a **phospholipid bilayer** (Figure 4.3). The phosphate-containing head of the molecule is permeable to water (*hydrophilic*), and the fatty hydrocarbon leg portion is repellent to water (*hydrophobic*).

Whereas the fatty legs are electrically neutral, the phosphate heads are polar. That is, like water, phosphate carries a slight positive charge in one area and a slight negative charge in another. As shown in Figure 4.3, the heads are in contact with water inside and outside the cell, while the legs form the sheltered inner layer of the membrane. This "oil and water" arrangement acts as an effective barrier to the free passage of materials into and out of the neuron.

Charged atoms, particularly Na^+ and K^+, do leach through the cell membrane via embedded proteins that form its permeable portions. In fact, the membrane is peppered with proteins that act as **ion channels** for substances entering and leaving the cell and as **receptors**, or binding locations, for neurochemicals. These protein mechanisms selectively allow substances to cross the cell membrane to accommodate neural activity and intercourse with the extracellular space—in short, to enable neural communication.

Proteins can do all this because they have the ability to change shape when chemicals bind to them or when triggered by other chemical or electrical changes. Channels of differing sizes and shapes allow the passage or block the passage of specific substances; for example, channels allow potassium ions free entry and exit into and out of the cell (Figure 4.4a). Gated

phospholipid bilayer Basis of neuron cell membranes. Each molecule has a water-soluble head (a protein compatible with water) and a water-rejecting tail (consisting of a lipid). The head faces a watery solution (cytoplasm or extracellular fluid between cells), while the lipid tail faces another lipid tail in the interior of the cell membrane.

ion channels Membrane-spanning proteins that form a pore that allows passage of ions from one side of the membrane to the other. The process results in either depolarization or hyperpolarization of the cell.

receptors Areas on a neuron specialized to be highly sensitive to a specific type of stimulation or chemical.

Figure 4.2
Functional areas of the neuron. The neuron's functional areas operate together to generate an action potential or to remain at rest. The action potential travels from an input zone on the cell membrane (the dendrites are a major input zone) to a trigger component near the cell body, where information is integrated and a biochemical decision is made to fire or not; a conductile zone (the axon) that carries the action potential down the length of axon; and an output of neurotransmitter at the axon terminal.

ADAPTED FROM KANDEL, SCHWARTZ, & JESSEL, 1995, FIGURE 2.8

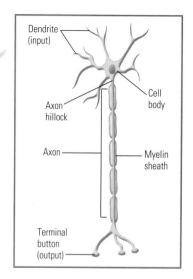

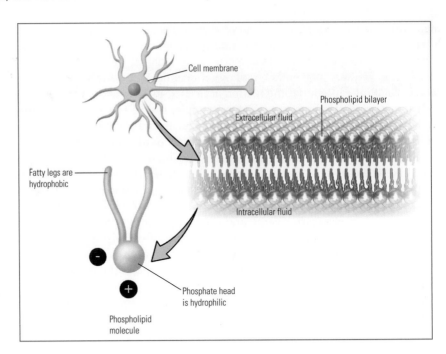

Figure 4.3
Structure of the cell membrane. The primary feature of the cell membrane is its semipermeable nature. When the neuron is at rest, the ionic balance between intracellular and extracellular space is tilted slightly toward negative inside the neuron. When an action potential is signaled, the membrane selectively allows ions to enter or leave the neuron through the pores or channels that permeate its surface, thereby briefly modifying the electrical properties of the membrane.

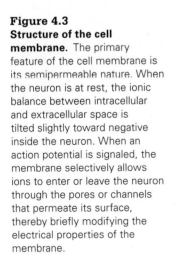

Figure 4.4
Types of ion channels in the cell membrane. (a) Ions can pass through appropriately shaped channels in the cell membrane. (b) When a gated channel is open, substances can pass through; but when the gates are closed, the substances are prevented from crossing the membrane. (c) Pumps change shape to ferry material across the cell membrane and are active most of the time, using a tremendous amount of cellular fuels.

ADAPTED FROM KOLB & WHISHAW, 2004

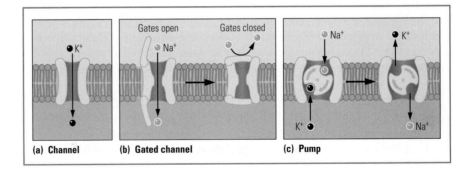

channels allow the passage of substances when open but block passage when closed (Figure 4.4b). Protein pumps change shape to ferry materials across the cell membrane (Figure 4.4c).

The cell membrane thus constitutes a mosaic of structures that defines the activity of dendrite, cell body, and axon. It becomes very apparent that the life and activity of the neuron depend in large part on the cell membrane, without whose constraints neural activity would be difficult to sustain.

Dendrites: Extending the neuron's reach. The dendrites, pinched and elongated sections of the cell body, gather information for the neuron by extending the cell membrane's surface area. Imagine a surgical glove filled with water, where the palm and back of the hand is the cell body and

dendrites Thin, widely branching fibers that emanate from the cell body of a neuron and "collect" information from adjacent neurons and other cells.

the fingers are the dendrites. The word *dendrite* is derived from the Greek *dendron*, meaning "tree." A glance at a leafless tree in wintertime is nothing so much as the image of a neuron.

Indeed, the diversity of branching patterns that dendrites display (*dendritic arborization*) is the major contributor to the anatomical complexity of neurons. The arborization can take many shapes, numbers, and ramifying directions (see Figure 4.1), as well as play a role in the diversity of interactions among neurons (through influences on the sheer number of synapses). The dendrite allows a neuron to probe well beyond its geographical location (defined as where the cell body sits) to establish synapses with more distant neurons and body tissues. This probing extends the reach of the neuron, the informational net that any one neuron casts. For instance, as shown in Figure 4.1, dendrites from **Purkinje neurons** (neurons found only in the cerebellum) have an elaborate branching network, with intricate, expansive trails going in every direction, like a bird's nest. Next to a neuron from the hippocampus, whose dendritic branching is sedate by comparison, the cerebellar neuron is notable for the amount of information processing of which it and its associated cells are capable. Thus, we have an example of a unifying principle that is repeated throughout the brain: Form follows function.

As dendrites extend the surface area of the neuron well beyond its otherwise limited radius, tiny, thorn-like projections called **dendritic spines** extend the surface area of some neurons even farther. Increased surface area enables dendrites to establish more connections with ever more neurons. Dendritic spines can number in the thousands per neuron, depending on the brain region and concentration per unit of length of the dendrite. Each spine affords the neuron an additional site for communicating with additional neurons, thereby enabling the neuron to increase its information inputs. It is here, too, that memory formation may begin.

More or longer spines give this structural latticework the capability of actively responding to stimuli and actively seeking out new connections, and this neuronal plasticity can substantially alter the information-processing capabilities of any one neuron (Engert & Bonhoeffer, 1999; Maletic-Savatic, Malinow, & Svoboda, 1999). Indeed, changes in dendritic spines, in addition to other manipulations that modify neuronal transmission (such as the altered glutamate receptors observed in the Doogie mice discussed in the chapter opening Connections), may contribute significantly to the brain's capacity to learn throughout life. The numbers of dendritic spines can fluctuate, depending on data load (the activity levels of the neuron), local chemoenvironmental conditions, and the type of neuron, and form distinct neuronal networks, as first suggested by Hebb (1949). That such anatomical features wax and wane in the face of alterations in stimulation suggests an efficient adaptation to the demands of input, processing, and output of information.

Cell Body and Organelles: A Cellular Factory

The **cell body**, or **soma**, is the site where the neuron assembles proteins, generates energy, and maintains metabolism (Figure 4.5). *Soma* is both the Greek word for "body" and the Sanskrit word for an intoxicating Vedic religious ceremonial drink. In Aldous Huxley's *Brave New World*, a tale that

Purkinje neurons Neurons in the cerebellum that are responsible for all the output from the cerebellar cortex to cerebellar nuclei.

dendritic spines Short, plastic outgrowths along the dendrites that increase surface area and where the majority of synapses are found.

cell body (or **soma**) Structure of the cell that contains the nucleus, cytoplasm, and various organelles used in cell metabolism.

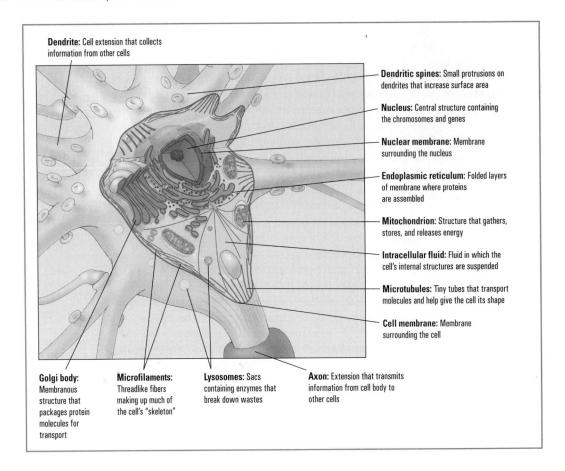

Dendrite: Cell extension that collects information from other cells

Dendritic spines: Small protrusions on dendrites that increase surface area

Nucleus: Central structure containing the chromosomes and genes

Nuclear membrane: Membrane surrounding the nucleus

Endoplasmic reticulum: Folded layers of membrane where proteins are assembled

Mitochondrion: Structure that gathers, stores, and releases energy

Intracellular fluid: Fluid in which the cell's internal structures are suspended

Microtubules: Tiny tubes that transport molecules and help give the cell its shape

Cell membrane: Membrane surrounding the cell

Golgi body: Membranous structure that packages protein molecules for transport

Microfilaments: Threadlike fibers making up much of the cell's "skeleton"

Lysosomes: Sacs containing enzymes that break down wastes

Axon: Extension that transmits information from cell body to other cells

Figure 4.5

Cell body and organelles. Many of the neuron's internal structures and organelles reside in the dendrites and axon as well as in the cell body, which is illustrated in detail here. These organelles and features collaborate to render the neuron capable of plasticity and rapid and long-lasting responsiveness to its environment.

ADAPTED FROM KOLB & WHISHAW, 2004

organelles "Organlike" structures in the cytoplasm of the cell membrane that help in the maintenance and metabolism of the cell.

nucleus Structure within the cell that contains the chromosomes.

presaged the current search for wonder neurochemicals (it was published in 1932), a substance called "soma" was ingested for correcting one's brain.

The shape of the soma can range from a tiny round body in, for example, the anterior hypothalamus to an enormous ovoid shape in spinal neurons and to the striking triangular shape characteristic of pyramidal neurons in the hippocampus. Within the cell, individual subcomponents, the **organelles**, carry out the protein production and metabolic regulation functions. Like a thriving factory, neuron function depends on the coordination of specialized organelles under the control of the genetic instructions that are encoded and transmitted to them.

Collectively, the organelles interact within the cell, but each is a discrete unit defined and enclosed by its own semipermeable membrane. The differences that abound among organelles have led many scientists to conclude that during the early stages of evolution formerly independent subcellular components banded together because it was advantageous to do so: the democracy of the cell. The resulting give and take of exchanging functions ensured survival of the cell and, eventually, the neuron (Edelman, 1993; Woese, 2002). It is an interesting scenario to ponder—and one whose likelihood increases with better understanding of the various activities of the different organelles.

Nucleus and executive function. Nucleus is derived from the Latin word for "nut." Like many anatomical descriptions that are based on what the object resembles in the namer's experience, the image of the nut, or nucleus, located roughly centrally within the "shell," or soma, probably explains its moniker.

The nucleus has as its main occupants delicately beautiful molecules of double-stranded **deoxyribonucleic acid (DNA)**. Each strand of DNA is composed of *chromosomes*, long strands of genes which are the repository of the organism's heredity. Each gene carries a set of instructions for synthesizing a specific protein necessary to the neuron's structure or function.

Protein synthesis begins with the formation of a complex of molecules called **messenger ribonucleic acid (mRNA)**. The "message" is composed of a string of nucleotides that give rise to **amino acids**, organic molecules that are the constituents of proteins derived from a specific gene on the DNA, and metaphorically is like copying a note and giving it to a person to deliver to someone else. The process of copying the DNA onto a quantity of mRNA is called **transcription**. The transcript, the bit of extruded mRNA, leaves the nucleus by means of pores in the nuclear membrane.

Endoplasmic reticulum, ribosomes, and protein synthesis. The **endoplasmic reticulum (ER)** resembles stacks of folded sheets, one on top of the other, and forms a continuous membrane with the nucleus. Such continuity and contiguity enable efficient transfer of instructions from the genome for the synthesis of proteins.

Structurally, the rough ER resembles its name: The membrane possesses groups of associated bulbous structures that resemble irregularly shaped BBs or pellets. These structures, called **ribosomes**, are the primary destination for mRNA and the location of translation and assembly of proteins in the neuron. The ribosomes come in several varieties, each of which performs some specific form of protein synthesis within the neuron. In clusters, as viewed in electron photomicrographs, they resemble tiny, round footprints, like those of a cat.

Ribosomes can be attached to the rough ER, they can be floating free in the cytoplasm, and several free ribosomes can be attached to each other by means of a thin strand of mRNA (see Figure 4.5). The mRNA transcripts arrive at these sites, amino acids are recruited in a set sequence for each protein, and synthesis ensues as determined by the codons. The messenger has taken the message, and it has arrived at its destination; it is ready to be "read." The means whereby an mRNA transcript is read and directs the formation of proteins is called **translation**.

The smooth ER lacks the number of ribosomes observed on the rough ER and, though continuous with the rough ER, synthesizes different proteins. The major difference between the smooth ER and the rough ER is the eventual destination for the proteins that each produces. The smooth ER produces proteins destined for use inside the cell. **Enzymes**, for example, are proteins that facilitate chemical reactions and are intimately involved in the regulation of activity inside the neuron. The rough ER produces proteins that migrate to the cell membrane to act as channels, gates, or pumps or outside the neuron for extracellular purposes. Neurotransmitters, for example, are produced for use outside the neuron.

Mitochondria and metabolism. As the neuron's energy center, the mitochondria are the site of cellular metabolism. Here, the precursors (foundational ingredients) of cellular fuels (fats, sugars, and proteins from food) react with

deoxyribonucleic acid (DNA) Molecule that composes the chromosomes.

messenger ribonucleic acid (mRNA) RNA molecule transcribed from DNA and translated into the amino acid sequence of a polypeptide.

amino acids The so-called building blocks of proteins, composed of an amino group (NH2) and a carboxylic acid (COOH). These are essential components of proteins and the basis for organic life.

transcription The process by which DNA is "copied" and transferred to mRNA for subsequent protein synthesis.

endoplasmic reticulum Network of thin tubes within a cell that transport newly synthesized proteins to other locations.

ribosomes Bulbous structures in the nucleus that are the primary destination for mRNA and the location of translation and assembly of proteins

translation The process by which mRNA is "read" by ribosomes in the neuron and protein synthesis is initiated.

enzymes Proteins that facilitate chemical reactions and are intimately involved in the regulation of activity inside the neuron.

mitochondria (sing. **mitochondrion)** Structures in the cell that perform the metabolic activities that provide energy.

precursors Constituent and elemental substances that serve as the initial components in a chain of chemicals. For instance, fats and sugars combine with oxygen to form cellular fuels.

adenosine triphosphate (ATP) Chemical the body uses as its primary way of delivering energy where it is needed; also used as a neurotransmitter.

Golgi apparatus Set of membranes in the cytoplasm that wraps around chemicals released by secretory cells. In neurons this structure manufactures the synaptic vesicles.

vesicle Tiny, nearly spherical packet at the axon terminal filled with the neurotransmitter.

lysosomes Neuronal organelles that engage in cellular cleansing and similar "housecleaning" activities to maintain neuronal function.

neurofilaments Neuronal structural proteins involved in membrane protein transport.

oxygen to produce **adenosine triphosphate (ATP)**. This cycle, first proposed by the German–British chemist Hans Krebs, now bears his name.

ATP is the essential metabolic fuel used by the neuron to power its myriad activities. Chief among these metabolically expensive activities is maintaining the neuron's resting internal electrical charge as negative relative to the slightly more positive extracellular fluid. This fundamental charge, found in the simplest battery, underlies neurotransmission, the basis of thought and consciousness.

Golgi apparatus and lysosomes: Packaging and recycling centers. The **Golgi apparatus** resembles and is actually a variation of the ER. Lying farther away from the nucleus than the ER, the Golgi apparatus is involved in the posttranslational sorting and packaging of proteins for transport. Many proteins are enveloped in a thin sac or membrane called a **vesicle** before they are routed to other specific regions within the neuron, the representative examples of which are neurotransmitter-filled vesicles awaiting release into the synapse.

Contrasting with these constructive activities are the activities of the **lysosomes**, mild acid-containing vesicles that permit cells literally to digest and assimilate targeted material. These organelles are very effective at clearing the neuron of the residue of neuronal activity. And since neurons are incapable of replication and substantial self-repair, the lysosomes provide the neuron with an efficient system for recovering and reusing proteins and amino acids that are the by-products of cellular activity and for removing troublesome proteins that may enter the neuron.

Neuronal Cytoskeleton: Structure and Transport

Figure 4.6 Cytoskeleton. The cytoskeleton is the scaffold on which the neuron "hangs." It is composed of different forms of fibril structures that provide the neuron with shape, support, and a variety of trafficking functions. (a) The neurofilaments (also neurofibrils) are rope-like or cable-like strands of proteins wound together in a sinewy length of filament that extends throughout the axon. (b) As the name implies, the microtubules are tiny tubular structures. (c) The microfilaments are extremely thin strands of actin that provide structural support for the neuron.

The neuron is a three-dimensional structure that requires support so that the three dimensions do not sag and collapse into two. The neuron also is capable of subtle movements, shifting back into place as the brain is propelled through space or stops suddenly after such propulsion, as in the case of a concussion. The neuron's significant internal distances pose a delivery problem for the proteins and nutrients it synthesizes, stores, and releases. The cytoskeleton is an ingenious evolutionary solution to these problems. Made up of three different systems, the cytoskeleton functions as both flexible scaffold and transport system, bending to the waves that buffet the neuron but allowing for uninterrupted commerce from site to site inside the cell. The three components of the cytoskeleton we will discuss here are the neurofilaments, the microfilaments, and the microtubules (Figure 4.6).

Resembling a chain of squat, fingerlike appendages stacked one on top of another, the **neurofilaments** are similar to structural proteins found in other cells in the body and are involved in the control and transport of membrane proteins (Kandel, Schwartz, & Jessell, 2000). Data derived from

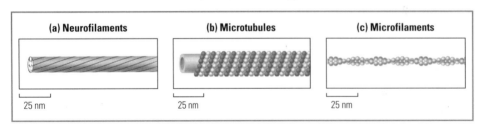

| (a) Neurofilaments | (b) Microtubules | (c) Microfilaments |

25 nm   25 nm   25 nm

Table 4.1 Inner Transport System of the Neuron

	Speed	Rate of Flow	Function	Motor Protein Used	Enzyme Used	Type of Cytoskeletal Component Involved
Anterograde transport (carried away from cell body)	Fast	Up to 400 mm/day	Carries synaptic vesicles to and throughout axon	Kinesin	ATPase	Microtubules
	Slow (slow axonal or axoplasmic flow)	0.2–2.5 (slow) and 0.4–5.0 (less slow) mm/day	Carries cytosolic proteins as well as intraneuronal "housekeeping" enzymes to and throughout cytoskeleton	Not currently known	Not currently known	Microtubules and neuro-filaments
Retrograde transport (carried toward cell body)	Fast	Up to 300 mm/day	Recycles used synaptic vesicles; works in conjunction with lysosomes	Dynein	ATPase	Microtubules

live cell imaging (Wang, Ho, Sun, Liem, & Brown, 2000) suggest that proteins move along the neurofilaments by means of "sprints, not a marathon" (Brady, 2000, p. E-43). What this means is that in addition to structural support, the neurofilaments participate in the transfer of neuronal products within the cytoplasm through an intermittent process of stop/start down their lengths. What happens when these fibrillary elements age is another matter. The data suggest that damage to or breakdowns in the neurofilaments may contribute to the neurofibrillary tangles characteristic of Alzheimer's disease and described in Chapter 6 (Arendt, 2001; Ashford & Jarvik, 1985; Ashford, Mattson, & Kumar, 1998; Ashford & Schmitt, 2001; Ashford, Soultanian, Zhang, & Geddes, 1998; Mesulam, 2000). Thus, like an elderly man unable to carry the same weights the same distance he could when he was younger, so too the aged neuron may be incapable of such once-formidable feats.

The second cytoskeletal component is the **microfilaments**, found in abundance in dendrites and axons and believed to provide structural support for them (Kandel et al., 2000). They are membrane-associated proteins attached by means of fibrous connections to the intracellular portion of the cell membrane. Numerous microscopic examinations have demonstrated that microfilaments are a rather dynamic set of cytoskeletal elements because they provide scaffold-like support for the neuron's movement, including the changing structure of its neurites (dendrites and axon) in response to a host of external stimuli (Peters, Palay, & Webster, 1991). They also act like micro-muscles, flexing and bowing and allowing contractions within the neuron to compensate for the external movements of head and body.

Microtubules are twice the size of neurofilaments and, as their name implies, are very small tubes. They run the length of the dendrites and axon. Microtubules play a role in the transfer and movement of various substances and organelles throughout the cytoplasm to intracellular locations. In particular, together with the neurofilaments, the microtubules make possible the processes of fast and slow axoplasmic transport.

microfilaments Intraneuronal flexible supporting elements associated with membranes

microtubules Proteins in the cell bodies and axons of neurons that transport nutrients within the cell, especially from the cell nucleus out to the axon and down to the terminal buttons.

axon Fiberlike outgrowth from the cell body of a neuron that is cylindrical until the very end, when it breaks into numerous small branches; the "sending" fiber of the neuron, it carries the nerve impulse.

axon hillock Swelling of the soma of the neuron, the point where the axon begins and an action potential "firing decision" is made.

Fast axoplasmic (anterograde) transport, which moves in the same direction as the action potential, refers to the movement of proteins, primarily synaptic vesicles and their internal products and precursor proteins (that may require integration into existing complexes). These materials move from the soma down the length of the axon to the terminal buttons at a rate of up to 400 mm per day—an enormous distance in cellular terms. The movement of substances is probably accomplished by means of the transport molecule kinesin, which resembles cilia or molecular feet on the body of the microtubules. The kinesin literally walks the proteins to and fro along the microtubule.

Slow axoplasmic (retrograde) transport, on the other hand, shuffles proteins around the soma, usually from axon to soma (perhaps to alert the soma to alterations in metabolic requirements). Whereas kinesin is the legs for fast axonal transport, for slow axonal transport the transport molecule is dynein (which acts similarly to kinesin). Overall, the movement of proteins, organelles, and substances around the neuron, including those to be used inside the neuron for cellular maintenance and structural integrity and those to be released for neuronal communication, is accomplished efficiently by means of these transport assemblies.

Dynamic Elements of Neuronal Communication, Connection, and the Synapse

Axon: Information conductor. The neural membrane is drawn out into radiating processes, like a piece of taffy stretched in different directions. These processes encompass the neuron's information-gathering apparatus— the dendrites and branches—and the axon, the information-conducting apparatus that transmits the action potential.

The axon is a long, threadlike structure with smooth contours and a cylindrical shape that resembles a thin peninsula off the soma; it ramifies by branching at obtuse angles. Its initial segment, as it leaves the soma and begins its meandering, is the **axon hillock**, the trigger zone where the action potential is initiated (see Figure 4.2). Where the axon branches, the divisions are generally the same diameter, demonstrating the principle of neuronal segregation of function (e.g., segregation of the actions of the axons and the actions of the dendrite). The diameter of the axon ranges in size, depending on species and type of neuron, from less than 1 μm (micrometer, 0.000001 meter) to 25 μm (in the human) to over 1 mm (and viewable with the naked eye) in the giant squid. The axon may also extend at great distances from the soma, traveling for meters in some individuals (e.g., into the PNS). Basketball players Shaquille O'Neal and Dwight Howard have very long axons.

In fact, neurons can be classified by the length of their axons. A projection neuron is one in which the axon is long, extending from one part of the brain to another, for example. A neuron with a short axon has mainly narrow effects within a local circuit. The filamentous nature of the axon belies its ruggedness as an amazing regenerating station for the conduction of the action potential and the propagation of a nerve impulse from one neuron to the next. The axon transmits the nervous signals around the brain and from the brain to distant sites in the body.

Terminal buttons: Getting the message across. As the axon snakes its way to the neurons on which it synapses, it reaches its terminus, which may involve many smaller branches from a single axon, reminiscent of Medusa standing on her head. **At the end of these multiple axonal end points are the terminal buttons,** or *boutons*. (*Bouton* is the French word for "button." *Bouton* also bears some relation to the French term *boutade*, a sudden fit of temper, which conjures up an interesting metaphor when one imagines the events taking place at the synapse: It is not difficult to envision a tiny explosion as neurotransmitter is propelled across the synapse.) **The terminal button takes many shapes, but generally it is a bulbous outgrowth from the axon tip that increases the surface area for the release of neurotransmitter toward the postsynaptic neuron or organ** (Figure 4.7).

Synapse **is a general term referring to the way in which one neuron connects to another or to a target organ,** depending on the system with which it is associated. In general, there are only two types of synapses, excitatory and inhibitory; both involve the release, action, reuptake, and degradation of the released substances. But the way in which the regulation of pre- and postsynaptic events occurs and the multiplicity of targets on which neurons synapse are testaments to the variety of nervous regulation. But all is maintained by this simple digital on–off system. Add to this the self-regulation that some neurons have by means of recurrent axonal collaterals (self-synapsing connections that are largely inhibitory), and it is apparent that a neuron is an impressive complex of activity, vigilance, and control.

NEUROGLIA

Neuroscientists believe that neurons are wondrous structures. (Ironically, it is our neurons telling us this.) Perhaps less amazing but more mysterious are the **glia** (or *neuroglia*, literally, "nerve glue"), or glial cells, additional objects in the nervous system that insulate neurons, provide support and nutrition, and remove waste products. Glia are a class of brain cell whose contributions to brain function and maintenance are just beginning to be understood and whose potentially novel role in brain activities, formerly attributed to neurons alone, is coming to light. In some brain areas, neuroglia outnumber neurons by a ratio of 50:1 (Kandel et al., 2000), indicating a vast reservoir for potential neural exploration and insight. Figure 4.8 illustrates some different classes of neuroglia.

terminal buttons At the tip of an axon, the points from which the axon releases chemicals (neurotransmitters).

glia (or **glial cells**) Nonneuronal cells in the nervous system that provide, among other things, support for neuronal structures and insulation of neuronal messages.

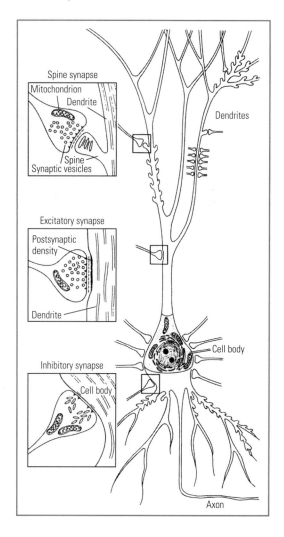

Figure 4.7

Synapses. The neuron is like the movie star at a Hollywood premier. All manner of external activity impinges on it to attract its attention. The neuron, however, is contacted by synapses that are laid on it at every level. Axodendritic (axon to dendrite) synapses, the prototypical neuronal connection, involve dendritic spines. The majority of such synapses are excitatory in nature. Axosomatic (axon to cell body) synapses are largely inhibitory. Axoaxonic (axon to axon) synapses are also largely inhibitory. Axon collaterals are synapses that arise from the neuron's own axon; they, too, are primarily inhibitory.

ADAPTED FROM THOMPSON, 2000

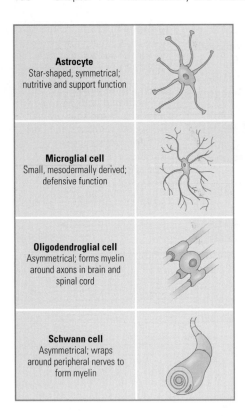

Astrocyte Star-shaped, symmetrical; nutritive and support function	
Microglial cell Small, mesodermally derived; defensive function	
Oligodendroglial cell Asymmetrical; forms myelin around axons in brain and spinal cord	
Schwann cell Asymmetrical; wraps around peripheral nerves to form myelin	

Figure 4.8
Types of neuroglia. The ubiquitous glial cell is shedding its image as a caretaker of neurons; its role as a mediator of neurotransmission is broadening and deepening as new techniques demonstrate the glial cell's importance to nervous function. The glial cell takes on many forms throughout the CNS.
ADAPTED FROM KOLB & WHISHAW, 2004

In the mid-nineteenth century, Rudolf Virchow examined neuroglia in the spinal cord and the ventricle walls of the brain. He named the cells "nerve glue" because they surround the neurons and bind them in place in the three-dimensional space of the brain. Virchow reported that the neuroglia are interposed between neurons and the blood supply and appear to act as a barrier between the two, a **blood–brain barrier** that prevents unwanted substances in the blood supply from entering the brain (Figure 4.9).

Virchow's observation presaged the role ascribed to the glia thereafter, that of neuronal support and maintenance. Peters et al. (1991) classify neuroglia as *macroglia* (including astrocytes and oligodendrocytes, on which we will focus), and *microglia* (macrophage-like scavenger cells in the CNS). Their classification system—one of many for glia—uses data largely derived from electron microscopic studies, which may differ in many ways from what is observed using other techniques and stains.

The **astrocyte**, which has a stellate or star shape, is the most numerous cell type in the brain. The astrocytes are inserted between the neuron and the blood vessels, like punctuation, where they act as a metabolic intermediary transferring nourishing glucose to the neuron from the blood supply and regulating glutamate production and neurotransmission, thereby maintaining a balance between intracellular and extracellular stores of neuronal synaptic resources. Further, the astrocytes' end-feet, the terminal portions of the glial cell that resemble the neurites of neurons, function as a capillary boundary that contributes to the functional blood–brain barrier that protects the brain from bloodborne pathogens and chemicals.

Astrocytes "harvest" excess ions from the extracellular fluid, thereby maintaining the delicate balance of chemical concentrations necessary to neurotransmission and nervous activity. Also, should a neuron die or become morbid, the astrocytes and macrophages function as scavengers, moving quickly to eliminate (by ingesting the remains) and in some cases kill off damaged neurons in a process referred to as *phagocytosis*, described in Chapter 13 (Kandel et al., 2000). Further, at these times, the astrocytes can also reorganize some of the synaptic relationships, playing a role in the plasticity of the neuronal substrate. Therefore, the astrocytes, together with the microglia, perform a valuable set of services to ensure that necrosis and neuronal littering, which could interfere with the efficient processing of electrochemical signals, are minimized and compensated for.

The oligodendrocyte complements the astrocyte. Whereas astrocytes nurture and police the neurons, the oligodendrocytes add support, particularly

blood–brain barrier Protective environment formed by tightly packed capillaries and neuroglia that prevents passage into the brain of most substances circulating in the blood.

astrocyte Relatively large, star-shaped glial cell found in the CNS.

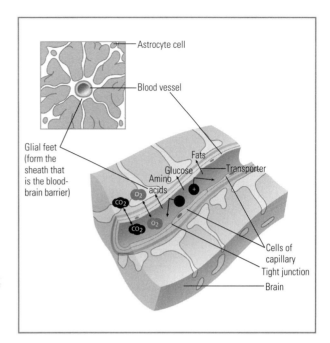

Figure 4.9
Blood–brain barrier. Cells that form capillaries in the brain have tight junctions and are blanketed by the glial feet of astrocytes, properties that prevent substances from moving in and out easily. Oxygen and carbon dioxide can flow freely across this blood–brain barrier. Substances such as fats, glucose, and amino acids can be transported across it; but most large, ionic molecules cannot cross.

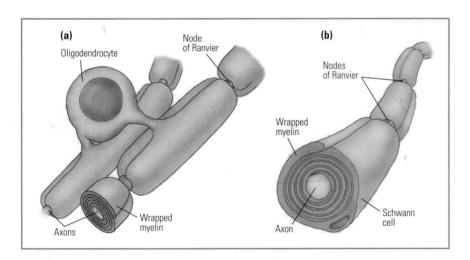

Figure 4.10
Myelination.
(a) Oligodendrocytes myelinate axons in the CNS. (b) Schwann cells myelinate axons in the PNS. Unmyelinated gaps between the glial cells are called "nodes of Ranvier." These nodes play an important role in the propagation of the action potential as they allow the electrical signal to "jump" across the gap, where the signal strength of the action potential is revivified.

ADAPTED FROM KOLB & WHISHAW, 2004

during development, and an engineering adaptation to neurons in the form of a lipid:protein (~80:20) axonal wrapping known as the **myelin sheath**. This myelin sheath increases the efficiency of the neural impulses in the CNS as they fire along axons (Figure 4.10). The oligodendrocytes produce segments of myelin during early brain development.

The PNS counterpart to the oligodendrocyte is the Schwann cell. Both gently embrace naked axons, whereupon layer after layer of the myelin is deposited from the inside out. The result is an axon wrapped in a lipid-protein covering that serves as both a protective coating and a functional enhancement for the electrochemical activities of the neuron.

myelin sheath Insulating material that covers many vertebrate axons.

depolarization The actual change in the resting charge of the neuron, from slightly negative (polarized) to less negative/more positive (i.e., less polarized).

resting (or membrane) potential Electrical potential across a membrane when a neuron is at rest.

action potential Physical basis of the nerve impulse; the depolarization of an axon produced by a stimulation beyond threshold potential.

GENERATING AN ACTION POTENTIAL

Ultimately, what we do, who we are, and what we aspire to are no more than the sum of the parts of neurotransmission. Action potentials are the foot soldiers of neurotransmission, marching along an individual neuron to the incipient roar of **depolarization** (reduction in electrical charge across a membrane) to presynaptic electrochemical volleys and the firing of postsynaptic impulses that follow. Thought arises from this electrochemical activity (Figure 4.11).

Electrochemical Activity at the Cell Membrane

The fluids on either side of the cell membrane differ in charge because of their basic ionic compositions. Recall from your grade-school science classes that like electrical charges repel, whereas opposite charges attract. Thus, a natural affinity exists between *anions* (negatively charged ions) and *cations* (positively charged ions), whereas like charges (+/+, cation/cation, and –/–, anion/anion) repel one another. Na^+ attracts Cl^-, whereas Na^+ and K^+ repel each other.

The predominant ions inside and outside the neuron are K^+, Na^+, and Cl^-; but their concentrations on either side of the cell membrane differ. Na^+ and Cl^- are in high concentration outside; K^+ and negatively charged (anionic) protein molecules (A^-) are highly concentrated inside the cell (Figure 4.12a). The semipermeable cell membrane must consume energy to maintain the separation and largely prevent the intracellular and extracellular components from coming into contact.

The difference in electrical charge between the intracellular state of the neuron (which is relatively more negative) and the extracellular surround (which is, conversely, relatively more positive) creates a charge, the **resting** (or **membrane**) **potential**, across the cell membrane of an unstimulated neuron. The difference between the two sides is approximately 65–70 mV (millivolt, = 0.001 volt; a single AA battery, by comparison, holds a charge equivalent to 1.5 volts, or 1,500 mV). In other words, the interior fluid of the cell is –70 mV relative to the fluid outside (Figure 4.12b).

Thus, the cell membrane at rest is polarized and holds the potential to change. The most extreme change from its resting state is the **action potential**, a lightning quick combination of chemical and electrical activity inside and outside the neuron that

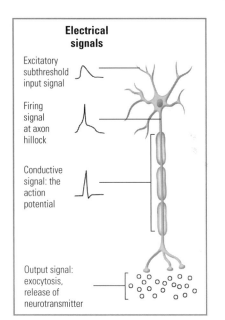

Electrical signals

Excitatory subthreshold input signal

Firing signal at axon hillock

Conductive signal: the action potential

Output signal: exocytosis, release of neurotransmitter

Figure 4.11
Path of neurotransmission. Stimulation from excitatory and inhibitory synaptic activities generates electrical signals within the neuron. As a result of integrating these signals, the neuron may maintain its slightly negative (resting) charge or may fire a signal that generates an action potential. Each functional area introduced in Figure 4.2 produces a characteristic electrical signal. At the cell membrane input zone, the neuron remains at rest, stimulated by excitatory and inhibitory (subthreshold) signals. Above-threshold stimulation at the cell membrane results in a firing signal at the trigger zone, that is, the axon hillock. The action potential signal is conducted down the axon, resulting in an output signal, represented in the release of neurotransmitter.

ADAPTED FROM KANDEL, SCHWARTZ, & JESSEL, 1995, FIGURE 2.8

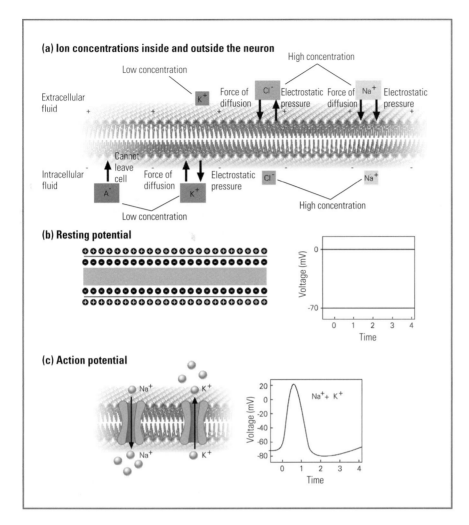

(a) Ion concentrations inside and outside the neuron

(b) Resting potential

(c) Action potential

Figure 4.12
Electrochemical activity at the cell membrane. (a) At rest, the neuron is an electrical spring waiting to be sprung. The ion concentrations are a balance between positive ions (cations) and negative ions (anions), with the balance tipped slightly in the direction of anions because of the intracellular charge. (b) The resting membrane potential is depicted here as a relative difference in intracellular and extracellular ionic charges. The cell membrane acts as a barrier to the two forces (electrostatic and diffusion pressures), attempting to bring the internal and external environments into equilibrium. (c) As the action potential is conveyed along the axon, voltage-gated channels open, allowing cations and anions to briefly exchange position, thereby changing the electrical properties of the membrane. As the channels reset, sodium–potassium pumps circulate the ions to exchange cations for anions. The neuron then readies itself for the subsequent action potential and the infinite number of ones to follow. The entire process occurs in milliseconds.
ADAPTED FROM CARLSON, 2009

actually reverses the polarity of the axon's cell membrane. For about 1 msec (millisecond, = 0.001 second), the intracellular fluid acquires a positive charge relative to the extracellular fluid (Figure 4.12c).

Two processes basic to physics operate to maintain the resting potential and to set the stage for the action potential. The first is **electrostatic pressure**, the force exerted by the attraction or repulsion of electrical charges. The complementary force is **diffusion**: If no barrier were to separate them, cations and anions would diffuse and spread evenly within a given volume. Eventually, the positive and negative charges would be evenly distributed. For example, when regular table salt (NaCl) is dissolved in a glassful of room-temperature water (H_2O), its chemical bond is broken, and the Na^+ and Cl^- ions diffuse into the surrounding fluid.

The force governing the breakup and movement of salt ions is a **concentration gradient**, the attraction of a region of high concentration for one of low concentration. Imagine a chain-link fence with thousands of music fans milling around on one side, pressing against the fence, and their favorite

electrostatic pressure
Electrical attraction and repulsion (+/– and +/+, –/–, respectively); complement to diffusion.

diffusion Tendency for dissolved ions or molecules to move from areas of high concentration to areas of low concentration.

concentration gradient In diffusion, the attraction of a region of high concentration for one of low concentration.

threshold potential The electrochemical point at which a neuron will respond to incoming stimulation with an action potential.

graded potential Series of incoming electrical signals that have little or no effect on the neuron depolarizing or firing.

band on the other. If that fence, a barrier to equilibration, were not there, the fans in high concentration on the outside would move to the area where their concentration is low on the other side of the fence. This same irresistible force drives ions to equilibrate within a space unimpeded by barriers such as a cell membrane. For example, as the concentration of Na^+ ions increases, it moves toward the region in which sodium concentration (and positive charge) is lowest, thereby establishing equilibrium, or *homeostasis*, of both sodium and the positive charges within that medium. (Because ions carry an electrical charge, the equivalent term *voltage gradient* is also used.)

The neuron has a **threshold potential** below which any stimulation results in little or no change in the membrane potential. A subthreshold voltage change, or **graded potential**, is a passive signal that degrades over time and distance, like waves breaking on the shore (Figure 4.13). As a way to visualize the neuron under different polarization events (polarized, depolarized, or hyperpolarized), imagine a couple on a dance floor, getting ready to tango. Before the music begins, they are standing apart, separated from each other by an arm's length (I———I): They are polarized. As the music begins, they move toward each other, thereby decreasing the distance (I—I) and becoming, if you will, depolarized. As the music rises in pitch, leading to a crescendo, the couple detaches and spins in the throes of a dancing fury, ending up farther apart than when they began (I———I): They are now hyperpolarized. The electromolecular tango within neurons that is occurring second by second is not unlike this pirouetting couple.

**Figure 4.13
Subthreshold
potentials.** Graded potentials are ultralocalized voltage changes that increase or decrease membrane voltage. (a) Hyperpolarization results when the extracellular fluid becomes more positive because of either an efflux of potassium ions or an influx of chloride ions. Hyperpolarization increases membrane voltage, making the membrane more negatively charged. (b) Depolarization results from an influx of sodium ions, decreasing membrane voltage and making the membrane more positively charged.

ADAPTED FROM KOLB & WHISHAW, 2004

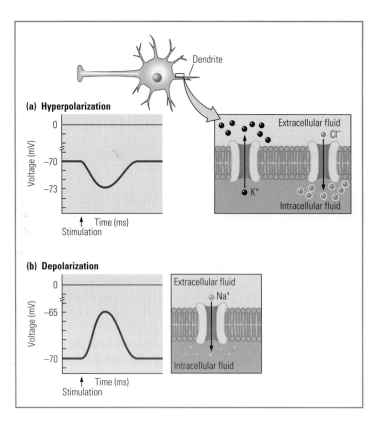

Membrane Activity as Trigger of the Action Potential

Think of the action potential as the pulling of a trigger. If the neuron receives a series of subthreshold graded potentials, they degrade easily, like a gentle, but only partial, pulling back on a pistol's trigger, taking up the slack in the trigger but resulting in no overt event. This resembles a subthreshold stimulus that is accompanied by the opening of some ion channels but not enough to reach the threshold of excitation: They quickly and quietly dissipate as the signal degrades due to the cable and resistive properties of the membrane. If, however, the signal received exceeds the threshold for excitation, like the trigger being pulled far enough back, past the point of no return, the ion channels open and the neuron fires—with everything the membrane has (Figure 4.14).

Embedded in the phospholipid bilayer of the cell membrane is a collection of proteins, a mosaic of channels and gates that both maintains the resting membrane potential and facilitates the action potential. Ion channels selectively permit Na^+, K^+, Cl^- and other cations and anions to travel between the intracellular and extracellular spaces. These ion channels, however, are closed to Na^+ when the neuron is at rest. In combination with channels selective for K^+ and Cl^-, they maintain the difference between intracellular and extracellular electrical charges. They are capable of being opened or closed by variations present in the local environment of the membrane (that semipermeable barrier separating the audience from the band above). Hence, the channels are referred to as "gated."

The relative concentration of extracellular Na^+ is very high. Na^+ is a cation and is attracted to the slightly more negative intracellular space; further, it is attracted to the lower intracellular concentration of Na^+. The pressure to bring Na^+ into the neuron, therefore, is very high, propelled

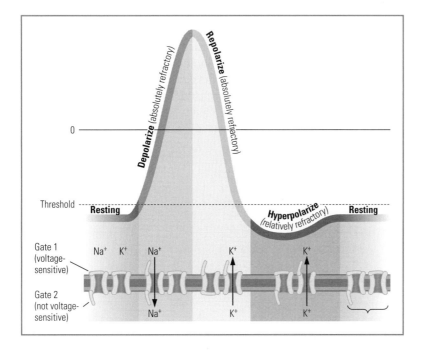

Figure 4.14
Phases of an action potential. The depolarizing neuron resembles a roller coaster. It has a resting, a rising, and a falling phase. The process begins (1) with the opening of sodium channels, which allow for the rapid influx of sodium, propelled by the forces of diffusion and electrostatic pressure. These are followed by the closing of the sodium channels (2) and the opening of the potassium channels (3). Finally, the neuron overshoots its resting potential (so-called hyperpolarization) and, with the activity of the sodium-potassium pumps in full force, restores the neuron to its resting state (4).
ADAPTED FROM KOLB & WHISHAW, 2004

voltage-gated channels Passageways for ions through a neuron's cell membrane that are opened or closed in response to changes of the membrane potential.

by the forces of both diffusion and electrostatic pressure. K^+ ions are present in higher concentration in the intracellular space than in the relatively positive extracellular space. This difference sets up a concentration gradient whose difference in charge is maintained by the neuron's cell membrane. So, the neuron at rest strains to correct these natural imbalances.

The electrical charge of the action potential changes the shape and size of the **voltage-gated channels**, opening the "gates" and allowing the specific ions to move freely across the barrier. When the action potential finally happens and the membrane is depolarized beyond threshold, momentary equilibrium is reached inside and outside the neuron and polarity is eventually reversed.

The voltage-gated Na^+ channels open quickly, allowing the Na^+ ions to rush in. As Na^+ streams into the neuron through the opened channels, the voltage of the membrane, the membrane potential, rises to $+40$ mV or more. This is known as "sodium influx," and it is rapid. The neuron responds by opening up its sodium channels, holding nothing back, and cannot quickly return to its former state until all internal mechanisms have been reset—like pulling back the hammer of the pistol once again, recocking it.

The membrane charge changes rapidly, and the conductance of the signal moving from negative to positive causes a second set of voltage-gated channels, the K^+ channels, to open. The K^+ channels lag behind the Na^+ channels; they are less sensitive to the fluctuating charge and require a greater level of depolarization.

The K^+ channels allow K^+ to leave the intracellular space (potassium efflux), propelled by the force of electrostatic pressure (Figures 4.14 and 4.15). The movement of K^+ ions through the voltage-gated K^+ channels begins to change the membrane potential back to its more negative resting state, following the influx of Na^+. After about 1 msec, the opening of the K^+ channels initiates the resetting of (i.e., it rectifies) the membrane potential and begins to shut down the Na^+ channels, preventing any more Na^+ channels from opening.

Propagating the action potential. Recall that myelin is an important player in the movement of the action potential down the axon. Intermittent gaps in the segments of myelin (the nodes of Ranvier) are packed with Na^+ channels, significantly more concentrated there than anywhere else on the

Figure 4.15
Saltatory conduction. Normal gaps in the myelin sheath, called "nodes of Ranvier," are important for the repropagation of the voltage that propels the action potential. At these nodes is an increased concentration of voltage-gated sodium channels. As the action potential fires along the axonal segment, it loses its voltage slightly because of the cable properties and associated resistance in the axon. At the nodes, the sodium channels open and cause a rush of sodium into the neuron and an invigoration of the voltage. Hence, the action potential moves onto the next axonal segment, having lost none of its vigor.

ADAPTED FROM KOLB & WHISHAW, 2004

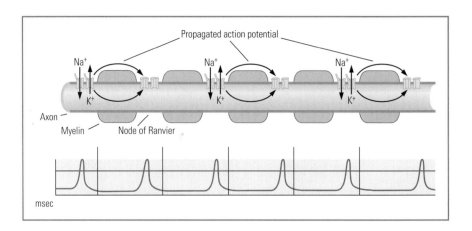

axon. Something interesting happens to the action potential at these denuded spots: The propagated action potential, or neural impulse, skips and leaps over the gaps, like the sparks of static electricity you unwittingly receive on cold, dry days (see Figure 4.15). In this saltatory conduction (a nod to the Latin word for "dance" or "jump": *saltare*), the impulse is regenerated at the node and facilitates the movement of same-voltage signals down the length of the axon. Myelin facilitates the impulse flow from node to node and refers the signal to the next segment in the chain much faster than it could traverse a naked axon. The myelin and its associated nodes are intimately involved in the propagation of the action potential.

Any variation in the many mechanisms of neural transmission, from modulation of receptors in Doogie mice to altered nerve impulse speed and blocked transport of ions such as sodium and potassium, may result in significant psychological and physical change. Some changes, enhanced intelligence, for instance, are for the better; some are for the worse, as discussed in Box 4.1.

Refractory periods: The neuron recharges. The neuron is returning to its resting membrane potential, but it still has a way to go. The K^+ channels are open and functioning, letting K^+ efflux persist. As more K^+ leaves the intracellular space, the neuron approaches its resting membrane potential. Driven by both electrostatic and diffusion pressures (at this time, the intracellular space is more positive and there is less extracellular K^+), heavy forces are operating on K^+. Following the movement back to the resting state, the K^+ channels start to close.

But an interesting phenomenon occurs. The neuron becomes **hyperpolarized**: It achieves an even greater negative charge relative to the extracellular space. As the K^+ is forced out of the neuron, it accumulates around the cell membrane, making the membrane more positive. Until the K^+ diffuses away, which it does slowly through diffusion and electrostatic pressure, and K^+ harvesting (to which the neuroglia, especially astrocytes, contribute), the neuron cannot respond to another normal action potential: The ionic "dancers" are separated by a greater expanse of dance floor.

This total inability to respond is the **absolute refractory period**. (The neuron may, however, respond to a more insistent depolarizing signal, a series of rapid, staccato impulses or ones with a greater depolarizing charge, a *relative refractory period*.) The neuron must in principle return to its resting potential, resetting like the cocking of the pistol's trigger, before it can fire again. In general, a neuron can fire at a rate of 500 Hz, or 500 times per second. Thus, each action potential takes about 2 msec. Imagine, therefore, the totality of neuronal activity and energy stores activated throughout the brain at any given point.

As effective as the cell membrane is, it is leaky. It is a difficult and vigorous process to maintain the resting membrane potential. Another important event involved in restoring the neuron to its resting state concerns active membrane-embedded protein mechanisms called **sodium–potassium pumps**, which work—very hard and continuously—to ensure that Na^+ remains in high concentration extracellularly and that K^+ remains in high concentration intracellularly. The pumps are metabolically expensive, using the majority of the ATP the neuron produces (and up to 40% of the neuron's overall energy production). As the action potential dissipates, these pumps, densely packed along the cell membrane, are integral to the removal of the Na^+ and the influx of the K^+ required

saltatory conduction The electrical movement or jumping of the action potential across gaps (called nodes of Ranvier) in the myelin sheath.

hyperpolarization A shift in the membrane potential to more negative (i.e., more polarized and farther apart). Neurons are inhibited from firing and must receive more insistent electrochemical signals to be undone.

absolute refractory period A point during the action potential, while the cell is returning to its resting potential, when the neuron cannot respond to another action potential.

sodium–potassium pumps Mechanisms that actively transport sodium ions out of the cell while simultaneously drawing potassium ions in.

Box 4.1

A Case in Point

Lorenzo Odone's Battle with Adrenoleukodystrophy

Until he was 4 years old, Lorenzo Odone's brain seemed to be working beautifully. The son of Augusto, an economist, and Michaela, a linguist, Lorenzo already spoke three languages and enjoyed listening to opera. The family had just returned home from a posting with Augusto's employer, World Bank, in the Comoro Islands off the southeastern coast of Africa when Augusto and Michaela noticed changes in young Lorenzo's behavior (Concar, 2002).

His speech became slurred, he frequently lost his balance, he initiated behavioral outbursts at school, and one evening, when his mother was reading to him, he asked if she could talk louder because he couldn't hear her. After visiting many doctors, the Odones received the devastating news that Lorenzo was suffering from a rare genetic neurological disorder known as adreno-leukodystrophy (ALD).

What exactly happens to the brain in ALD patients? The disease is the result of an X-linked male-predominant metabolic disruption that leads to loss of the myelin sheath that insulates nerve fibers and to the progressive degeneration of the adrenal glands. Because females have the protection of two X chromosomes, males (with one X chromosome) are more severely affected. ALD affects one in 45,000 births and in the classic childhood form leads to disruption of an individual's ability to metabolize long chains of fatty acids. The fatty deposits eventually build up in the myelin and in the adrenal gland, rendering both ineffectual. As the destruction of myelin progresses throughout the nervous system, the patient is incapacitated and inevitably dies.

ALD is the nervous system's equivalent of having the power lines cut. The horror of ALD is that the power cannot be reconnected. The elegant process of neurotransmission works only when the myelin insulation so important to neurotransmission is intact and functioning. Once the myelin becomes compromised, the neural circuitry grinds to a halt. Young patients, typically between 4 and 10 years of age, diagnosed with the early-onset variety of ALD usually die within 2 years.

The Odones were devastated. They quickly became very knowledgeable in the science of ALD, devouring the literature, convening the world's leading scientists to share ideas, and considering every possible treatment. After learning of a connection between certain oils in food and the fatty acid chains, Michaela tracked down a supply of pure oleic oil, which began to decrease Lorenzo's fatty acid levels but failed to bring them to baseline levels. Augusto focused on animal experiments and discerned that a second ingredient, erucic acid, a substance toxic to animals but tolerated in humans, should be added to the oleic oil. The result, called "Lorenzo's oil," was successful.

---

to restore the resting potential and ready the neuron for the next action potential. When examined in its totality, the enormous resources devoted to maintaining the resting membrane potential make perfect sense: How else could the neuron ready itself for an immediate response? Vigilance has its price.

Understanding the mechanisms that maintain neural transmission is no easy feat—and if you have come this far, you now realize it. But painful as it is to attempt to understand these complex physiological systems and relationships, it is important to remember how very important every element is to human survival. In subsequent chapters, you will see how certain drugs and other chemicals modify components of neural transmission; they have strong influences on psychological functions. And speaking of pain, those of you familiar with dentists and the inherent pain of dental procedures know that Novocain reduces the pain. You can thank your Na^+ and K^+ channels for the relief. Specifically, one way that Novocain exerts its anesthetic effects

Lorenzo, however, was not out of the woods. By the time he started showing symptoms of ALD, the therapeutic window was already closing. Lorenzo's oil halted the degeneration, but now the challenge was finding a way to rebuild Lorenzo's deteriorated myelin so that he could regain function. The Odones founded the Myelin Project, a foundation that funds promising research that may lead to a way to promote myelin regrowth. The Odones' story may be familiar to you: It's recounted in the award-winning 1992 movie *Lorenzo's Oil*.

Since featuring Lorenzo's story in the first edition of this text, we regret that Lorenzo recently passed away one day after his thirtieth birthday. As the typical life expectancy for children with this disease is closer to 2 years following diagnosis, Lorenzo's parents' achievements extended his life for more than two decades longer than expected. After years by her son's bedside, Michaela passed away in 2000. His father, Augusto, however, was by his side for the duration of his life. During this time Lorenzo's abilities were severely limited—he could not see or speak. However, Augusto reported that his mind was functioning as he responded to being read to, listening to music, or being placed in a swimming pool.

And how has the scientific community responded to Lorenzo's oil? With a healthy or, according to Augusto, an unhealthy dose of skepticism. Augusto remains troubled by the resistance of scientists to accept the effectiveness of Lorenzo's oil as an ALD treatment (see van Geel et al., 1999, for a skeptical scientific report). In 2002, Dr. Hugo Moser, a leading ALD scientist at Johns Hopkins, however, released the results of a 10-year study suggesting that Lorenzo's oil decreases the onset of ALD by approximately 70%, a finding prompting Augusto to say "I told you so" to many doubting scientists. Moser admits that his study lacked strenuous controls, so the results remain controversial.

Even with the skepticism surrounding the efficacy of Lorenzo's oil (Lerner, 2009), many parents of sons with ALD report that taking this oil every day (at a cost of about $440 for a 2-week treatment) has kept their sons from losing their nervous tissue to this crippling disease. The Myelin Project (www.myelin.org) is still in full force, and parents of ALD sons all over the world hold high hopes that current investigations will provide efficacious treatments for ALD. For example, Schwann cells, which make up the myelin sheath in the peripheral nervous system of multiple sclerosis (MS) patients, are currently being harvested from the ankle region of MS patients and transplanted into their brains. MS is also the result of deterioration of the myelin sheath, and although the causes of these two diseases are different, the treatments for MS may be applicable to ALD.

Lorenzo's case provides a powerful lesson about the importance of mastering basic neuroscience information before progress can be made in the treatment of clinical conditions such as ALD—a perfect example of the bridges that are necessary for successful clinical neuroscience.

is by altering the lipid layers of the affected cell membrane and blocking the Na^+ and K^+ channels. The pain messages, therefore, cannot be transmitted (Feldman & Quenzer, 1984).

Integrating Information at the Cell Membrane

The nerve impulse races down the axon to the terminal buttons, all the while rapidly opening and closing ion channels like a flautist's fingers on a flute. As we discussed, the neuron is continually engaged in the synthesis and distribution of various proteins. Included among these proteins are neurotransmitters, which are packaged and stored by Golgi bodies in a collection of vesicles moved by microtubules to congregate at the terminal ends of the axon. The vesicles cluster near the presynaptic membrane, awaiting an action potential, their attachment to intracellular membrane sites, and subsequent extracellular release.

exocytosis Fusion of vesicles with the plasma membrane, thereby opening the contents of the vesicles to the synaptic space, leading to the forcible release of neurotransmitter into the synapse.

Activity at the Synapse

Some of the vesicles "dock" with the terminal membrane and attach to it. The docking is accomplished by aligning proteins embedded in the membrane of the vesicle with proteins in the cell membrane. Docked and undocked vesicles both are present. The undocked vesicles will soon attach themselves to the membrane.

Once the action potential reaches the terminal buttons, it stimulates voltage-gated calcium (Ca^{2+}) channels, causing them to open. The open Ca^{2+} channels trigger a rapid influx of Ca^{2+}, which is found in high concentration in the extracellular spaces around the axon terminals and is attracted by the relatively negative charge inside the neuron. As is the case with Na^+ ions, electrostatic and diffusion pressure forces Ca^{2+} through specific Ca^{2+} channels. Once Ca^{2+} arrives, it stimulates the fusion of the docked vesicles with the membrane, producing a structure that momentarily resembles the Greek letter omega, Ω. As its shape demonstrates, the formerly enclosed vesicle is now open to the extracellular space. It then releases the packed molecules of neurotransmitter into the synapse.

This release, called **exocytosis**, is the process by which the membrane of a fused vesicle releases its contents (Figure 4.16). This release may be of a quantal nature (i.e., each vesicle contains roughly the same amount of neurotransmitter), so a single vesicle can release enough neurotransmitter to effect some graded postsynaptic potential. The number of vesicles involved and the number of times fusion-and-release occur represent another expensive metabolic proposition for the neuron. A form of recycling (endocytosis) goes on in the neuron. Used membrane is brought back to the soma and transferred to the Golgi apparatus, where it is incorporated into it and becomes membrane for the later generations of vesicles that will work their way down to the terminal buttons for fusion and release. This ballet of movement, release, and recycling occurs countless times per second in the tens of millions of neurons required for a specific behavior.

There are, however, some data that may modify the thinking about the traditional exocytosis model. Gaining acceptance is a relatively new phenomenon referred to as "kiss and run" (Aravanis, Pyle, & Tsien, 2003; Ghandi & Stevens, 2003). In this model, the vesicle only transiently binds to the membrane (creating a small fusion pore) and is open only long enough to release its contents. It then closes and thereafter binds transiently with another portion of the membrane, again loosing into the synapse molecules of neurotransmitter. The process is repeated until the vesicle's contents are exhausted. With decreased turnover of the vesicle and its membrane, the process would represent an obvious economical advantage to the neurons that employ it. Both vesicular fusing and kiss-and-run exocytosis may occur, depending on brain site. Recent data have provided support for the phenomenon (Zhang, Li & Tsien, 2009), although differences in fluorescence-tagging methodologies (quantum dots vs. pH-sensitive green fluorescent protein molecules [pHluorins]) have come to produce some debate

Figure 4.16
Exocytosis. The process by which neurotransmitter release is realized is exocytosis. It involves the fusion of a synaptic vesicle, a membranous container filled with molecules of neurotransmitter. As calcium rushes into the neuron's terminal buttons, these vesicles fuse with the cell membrane to create a fusion pore and an egress to the synapse. The vesicle membrane then is recycled—or, in a new model of exocytosis, the vesicle only "flickers" open momentarily, releasing neurotransmitter before closing up and moving to another portion of the terminal button.

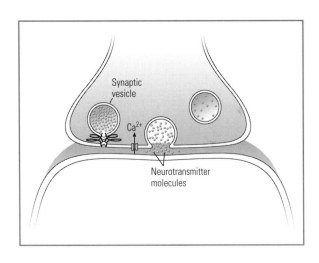

Synaptic vesicle

Ca^{2+}

Neurotransmitter molecules

regarding the generalizability of the model (Granseth, Odermatt, Royle & Lagnado, 2009).

The descriptions provided here are of the chemical synapse, the predominant type found in the mammalian nervous system. In the invertebrate nervous system (e.g., insects), electrical synapses are much more common. Electrical synapses involve a gap that is only 2–4 nm (nanometer, = 1 billionth of a meter) compared with the 20–30 nm of a typical chemical synapse. Further, these electrical synapses possess the *gap junction*, a point where the membranes of the pre- and postsynaptic neurons are continuous, allowing for very rapid signaling between pre- and postsynaptic neurons. The main functional feature of such synapses is their rapid rate of firing, an advantage for the sites where they are frequently found: regions associated with escape behaviors in invertebrates and the control of eye movements in vertebrates (including mammals).

Postsynaptic Potentials

Now that the neurotransmitter has been released into the synapse, it binds to specialized receptors on the postsynaptic membrane. Like a specific-value coin in a candy-machine slot, the neurotransmitter binds tightly with the receptor and produces one of three effects:

1. **Excitatory postsynaptic potential (EPSP):** Excitation of the postsynaptic neuron, causing a depolarization and, should the signal be strong enough (i.e., should enough ion channels be involved), subsequent propagation of the action potential in the postsynaptic membrane.

2. **Inhibitory postsynaptic potential (IPSP):** Inhibition of the postsynaptic membrane by hyperpolarization.

3. No effect, with neither active excitation nor active inhibition occurring in the postsynaptic membrane.

Effects 1 and 2 each depend on the ion channels to which the respective neurotransmitter binds.

Whether an EPSP or IPSP occurs depends on the relative strength and type of the postsynaptic stimulation. An influx of Na^+ will probably trigger an EPSP, whereas an influx of Cl^- or an efflux of K^+ will result in an IPSP. Subthreshold stimulation (graded potentials) brought about by inadequate amounts of neurotransmitter result in postsynaptic indifference to the presynaptic neurons' signals that is neither strongly excitatory nor inhibitory.

Because most postsynaptic membranes require a change of about 15 mV to achieve threshold changes in membrane potential and most single postsynaptic potentials result in only a 1 mV change in membrane potential, the neuron needs a specific strategy to assure that threshold is actually reached. Two types of neuronal signal summation take into account the quanta released by the presynaptic neuron and the graded or other potentials they subsequently produce: temporal summation and spatial summation. The first, **temporal summation**, takes advantage of the graded potentials that dissipate back to resting membrane potential following hyperpolarization or hypopolarization. As the membrane potential is moving toward resting, quick successions of nerve impulses in the postsynaptic axon result in the accumulation of membrane changes that eventually reach suprathreshold

excitatory postsynaptic potential (EPSP) Graded depolarization of a neuron.

inhibitory postsynaptic potential (IPSP) Temporary hyperpolarization of a membrane.

temporal summation Additive effects of a single neuron firing in rapid succession onto a postsynaptic membrane. Each new depolarization builds on the dissipating graded postsynaptic potential to eventually result in the appropriate hyperpolarization or hypopolarization threshold.

spatial summation
Summation of excitatory or inhibitory synaptic effects on a postsynaptic membrane resulting from the simultaneous action of several synapses at one time on one local area of the cell.

ionotropic receptors
Receptors with a binding site for neurotransmitter and a pore that regulates ion flow.

or subthreshold levels. Eventually, this additivity of a series of postsynaptic potentials results in a stair-step type of change in membrane potential comparable to the threshold for an action potential. Therefore, the number of synapses received per unit of time can affect the neuron's decision to fire or not. The second, **spatial summation**, refers to the accumulation of EPSPs or IPSPs simultaneously activating the postsynaptic membrane in a particular local area. For example, 15 EPSPs coming from 15 different neurons may sum to the 15 mV change in threshold necessary to trigger an action potential.

Together, the signals received and the graded membrane potentials they produce via the two media, one next to and the other on top of the other, are figuratively weighed. A biochemical "decision" is made to fire or not, or to be inhibited or not. Thus, the two major forces of the outer universe, space and time, are brought to bear on the most elegant of biological interactions of the inner universe, the relationship between two neurons.

A postsynaptic neuron is peppered with excitatory and inhibitory synapses. It often receives conflicting chemical information and must determine a course of action or inaction. Being presented with information about the timing (temporal) and location (spatial) of the various synaptic signals and their consequences (supra- or subthreshold) regulates the action. (See Box 4.2 for a description of action potentials that are uncontrolled. The normal synchrony inherent to neuron-to-neuron communication degenerates in epileptic seizures to become the neural equivalent of a wildfire, with devastating consequences for those afflicted.)

Activity at the Receptor

When a molecule of neurotransmitter binds to a receptor, ion channels are set in motion; the result may initiate an action potential. Two effects, direct or indirect, can be initiated postsynaptically, depending on the transmitter, the neuron, and the receptor to which the neurotransmitter is binding. As we show in more detail in Chapter 5, whatever chemical is used and whatever effect is observed will involve some combination of ionotropic and metabotropic receptors.

Ionotropic receptors produce direct effects as the direct binding of neurotransmitter to ion channels governs them (Figure 4.17). They are the much simpler type of receptor, require less energy from the neuron, occur more quickly, and last for a shorter period. Ionotropic receptor binding results in direct opening of a specific ion channel. It happens like this: The molecule of neurotransmitter moves across the synapse and binds directly to receptors on the ion channel on the postsynaptic membrane, causing that channel to open and begin the flux of ions that initiates the postsynaptic potential. The ionotropic receptor is not unlike a mousetrap, simply and swiftly springing open at the touch of the switch—namely, the binding of neurotransmitter to receptor.

Figure 4.17
Ionotropic receptor. Ionotropic receptors have direct effects: The ion channels, like a mousetrap, open when a molecule of neurotransmitter binds to the receptor. These effects are generally rapid and short-acting.
ADAPTED FROM KOLB & WHISHAW, 2004

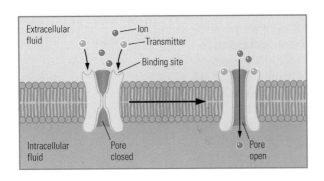

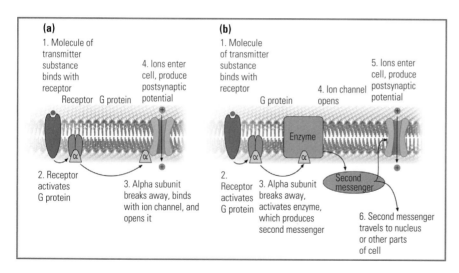

(a)

1. Molecule of transmitter substance binds with receptor

Receptor   G protein

4. Ions enter cell, produce postsynaptic potential

2. Receptor activates G protein

3. Alpha subunit breaks away, binds with ion channel, and opens it

(b)

1. Molecule of transmitter substance binds with receptor

G protein

4. Ion channel opens

5. Ions enter cell, produce postsynaptic potential

Enzyme

2. Receptor activates G protein

3. Alpha subunit breaks away, activates enzyme, which produces second messenger

Second messenger

6. Second messenger travels to nucleus or other parts of cell

Figure 4.18 Metabotropic receptors. Metabotropic receptors activate G proteins to produce effects indirectly on the opening of ion channels and to exert influences on other parts of the neuron, especially the nucleus. These effects are generally slow to start and long-lasting. (a) A receptor is bound by a molecule of neurotransmitter and begins a cascade that results in a signal to the α-subunit, binding intracellularly to ion channels to open them. (b) The α-subunit activates an enzyme that produces a second messenger that both binds to and opens an ion channel and may have effects in other regions of the neuron, prolonging the neurotransmitter's or neuromodulator's effects on the neuron.

AFTER CARLSON, 2009

The effects produced by **metabotropic receptors**, as the name suggests (*metabolic* and *tropic*, for "change-promoting"), require an expenditure of energy by the neuron and may bring about long-lasting alterations in its metabolism. These receptors utilize the cellular fuel ATP. Metabotropic receptors produce indirect effects because they take longer to happen and involve a complex series of postsynaptic intracellular activities.

The receptor-mediated effects involve intracellular events that engage a substance called **G protein** (guanosine nucleotide-binding protein), a class of intraneuronal coupling proteins that can modify the neuron's internal state and, hence, its activities. A model of metabotropic receptors hypothesizes that, as the neurotransmitter binds to the receptor, the G protein that is associated with the receptor is activated. A portion of the G protein called the α-subunit peels off and is transported through the intracellular space to the ion channel, where it binds to an intracellular portion of the receptor (Figure 4.18a). The binding of the α-subunit then opens the ion channel. This is a more complex and energy-utilizing act that takes longer to bring about, and the effects are more extensive than the ionotropic transmitter–gated reception.

A second form of metabotropic response also involves the binding of neurotransmitter to the postsynaptic receptor, activation of the G protein, and the splitting off of the α-subunit. It is called the **second messenger system**, and it shares similarities with the just-described version. In the second messenger system, however, the α-subunit activates an effector enzyme, typically adenyl cyclase, in a common form of reaction (Figure 4.18b). In addition to binding to intracellular ion channels and causing them to open, it initiates changes in proteins inside the neuron. Hence, the effects of this type of reaction (e.g., hormonal effects on neurons) last longer. Overall, therefore, the nervous system has evolved a flexible scheme to address nature's exigencies: the capacity to respond quickly and to have the response dissipate quickly (ionotropic), the facility to take longer to respond and to have the response take longer to end (metabotropic), and the ability to take longer to activate and longer for the effects to dissipate (second messenger).

metabotropic receptors Receptors that, when stimulated, produce a relatively slow but long-lasting effect through metabolic reactions.

G proteins Membrane-bound proteins that bind GTP when activated by a membrane receptor. Active G proteins can stimulate or inhibit other membrane-bound proteins.

second messenger systems A multiple-step and complex signal amplification process that occurs in the neuron that translates, for example, hormonal signals into long-lasting cellular events.

Box 4.2

Brain Matters

Epilepsy: Continued Intrigue and Lessons Learned

In Robin Cook's medical thriller *Seizure*, a zealous southern senator convinces a cutting-edge neuroscientist to implant stem cells (prompted to become dopaminergic cells) into his substantia nigra to cure his Parkinson disease. Following a minor accident resulting in movement of the surgical apparatus (necessary to guide the cannula placement to the exact area in the substantia nigra), the cells intended to go toward the dopamine-producing substantia nigra went to the temporal cortex—the seat of the limbic system. Within a short period, the politician was experiencing an interesting smell, that of pig feces. Subsequently, an intense seizure occurred, accompanied by the immediate contraction of many muscles, as well as bizarre behavior ranging from identifying with Jesus Christ (here, the stem cells were derived from blood samples obtained from the Shroud of Turin) to rude outbursts. It turned out that the stem cells were growing and activating the temporal lobe, leading to increasingly intense emotional outbursts that eventually led to the senator's demise. The fact that this contemporary medical thriller is about temporal lobe epilepsy confirms the intrigue that this condition has held for neuroscientists and medical practitioners for the past several centuries.

The famed neurologist Wilder Penfield writes that epilepsy is older than humans, evidenced by its appearance in other mammals. Further, trephined skulls (i.e., those with holes drilled in them) excavated from the caves of the Neolithic period are probable evidence of early humans' attempt to release the demons thought to be responsible for epilepsy (Penfield, 1941). Neurologist John Hughlings Jackson formally defined the condition of epilepsy about 150 years ago. He stated that epilepsy was a condition characterized by sudden, excessive local discharges within the brain's gray matter. The actual term *epilepsy* was derived from the Greek word *epilepsia*, which means to seize as grabbing with one's hand (Beatty, 2001).

Without initiation and propagation of the action potential, there would be no communication in the nervous system—in other words, there would be no functional nervous system. In the case of epilepsy, these well-timed action potentials get out of control, leading to a storm of discordant activity in the brain. Because of this salient feature, the EEG examination is the most important laboratory test for the diagnosis of epilepsy (Avoli & Gloor, 1987). Epileptic seizures are categorized as either more *diffuse generalized seizures* or more localized *partial seizures*. Given that *auras*, a preview or transient sensory event typically preceding seizures, include certain movements or sensations, the pig feces olfactory aura experienced by the fictional senator is certainly plausible. But what about the senator's religious experience during the temporal lobe, or complex partial, seizure? Research conducted by Vilayanur Ramachandran and his colleagues at University of California at San Diego, reported at the Society for Neuroscience annual meeting in 1997, suggested that patients suffering from a specific form of temporal lobe epilepsy experienced more intense religious beliefs. In response to this research, the media dubbed this area of the temporal lobe that triggered these religious beliefs the "god module" (Holtz, 1997).

Whether the topic of epilepsy is the focus of fact or fiction, it remains of immense interest among the medical and research communities. This condition, which affects 0.5%–2.0% of the general population, is not considered a disease because it has no single cause. A host of causes including genetic factors, environmental conditions, CNS infections, CNS tumors, and metabolic disorders have been known to cause seizures

(Avoli & Gloor, 1987). As researchers have tried to identify mitigating factors for epileptic patients, much has been learned about seizure-inducing factors. Among the more interesting discoveries have been the reports that certain video games and their accompanying flashing lights and visual patterns can be epileptogenic. A study in the Netherlands reported that the video game *Mario World* played on a 50 Hz television was more provocative than playing the game on a 100 Hz television. Thus, patients with photosensitive epilepsy should be careful about spending extended time in front of certain TV or computer visual presentations (Fylan, Harding, Edson, & Webb, 1999; Kasteleijn-Nolst Trenite et al., 2002). This line of research supports the notion that epilepsy can be triggered solely by environmental stimuli; thus, reflexive epilepsy is the most common form of epilepsy (Singh, Bhalla, Lehl, & Sachdev, 2001).

Because of the variety of causes of epilepsy, it's no surprise that there is no single treatment for this condition. The initial treatment regime involves antiseizure medication. In the past decade, 10 new anticonvulsant drugs have been introduced as researchers and clinicians search for more efficacious drugs with fewer negative side effects (Bazil, 2002). Many of the current antiepileptic drugs enhance GABA-facilitated inhibition (e.g., benzodiazepines, barbiturates). Other mechanisms of antiseizure medications include increasing the speed of repolarizing K^+ currents and reducing depolarizing currents (Avoli & Gloor, 1987). Another approach to altering the neuron's biochemistry is through one's diet; consequently, the ketogenic diet, a high-fat, adequate-protein, low-carbohydrate diet, has been a treatment option for the past 80 years (Stafstrom, & Bough, 2003). It is thought that this diet, which alters glucose and ketone metabolites, may reestablish brain energy homeostasis (Greene, Todorova, & Seyfried, 2003).

For patients who find themselves unresponsive to pharmacotherapy and dietary restriction, surgery is a viable option. Beginning in the nineteenth century, surgeons tried to remove the specific focal area of seizure activity in epileptic patients. Surgical techniques have ranged from the removal of specific brain areas, disconnection by commissurotomy (transecting the corpus callosum), and, as you will read in Chapter 6, removal of the entire or partial hemisphere in which the seizure activity originates (Kolb & Whishaw, 1996). Some clinicians argue that surgery should be used more often in drug-resistant patients due to the high success rates, up to 70%, for all surgical treatments (Ryvlin, 2003). Vagal nerve stimulation is an alternative surgical procedure that has recently been developed. This technique involves implanting electrodes to produce afferent stimulation of the vagus nerve and shows promise for temporal lobe epilepsy (Andrews, 2003; Kuba, Brazdil, Novak, Chrastina, & Rektor, 2003).

Although epilepsy has been an unfortunate clinical condition for the patients suffering from seizures, it has presented a valuable window into the workings of the brain. As described in Chapter 3, temporal lobe epilepsy prompted Paul MacLean to begin thinking about the role of the temporal lobe in emotional processing. Canadian neurologist Penfield investigated cortical specificity while conducting surgeries on his epileptic patients, determining that specific areas provoked specific sensations, movements, and cognitions. Roger Sperry won the Nobel Prize in 1981 for his work investigating the functions of the right and left hemispheres in patients receiving commissurotomies to relieve seizures (Pinel, 2000). More recently, forensic psychologist Anneliese Pontius has proposed that certain random violent acts committed by otherwise mild-mannered individuals could be the result of limbic seizures (LoPiccolo, 1996). Thus, although a priority in epilepsy research is the identification of mechanisms and successful treatment strategies, a host of researchers ranging from philosophers to neuroscientists continue to learn from these epileptic patients as their brain activity provides glimpses into such profound questions as the origin and characteristics of thought.

Summary

Microanatomy of the Neuron

The neuron is described in terms of its external and internal characteristics. External characteristics include the shape of the neuron and the major structures that produce its unique activities, including the cell membrane (or plasma membrane), the dendrites, the cell body (or soma), the axon, and the presynaptic terminal buttons. Internal structures of the neuron include the nucleus, the mitochondria, the endoplasmic reticulum, the ribosomes, the lysomes, the Golgi apparatus, and the cytoskeleton.

The functions of the many intracellular components of the neuron demonstrate that the neuron is in actuality a complex of interacting and interdependent structures, each operating on its own; the sum of the activities produces overall neuronal function. The shape and function of the neuroglia, the ubiquitous and essential partners to the neurons, complement the activities of the neurons and may perform some functions formerly assigned exclusively to neurons.

Generating an Action Potential

The action potential is the behavior of neurons that best exemplifies neural activity. It is the commerce of the brain, moving from individual neuron to individual neuron and, thence, from region to region, culminating in thought and action. It is a basic biochemical event with fundamental chemical processes that define it and make it available for study. The neuron at rest possesses what is called a resting membrane potential. When the neuron fires, the resting potential changes and the cell becomes depolarized, moving down the axon to the terminal buttons, where neurotransmitter is released into the adjacent extracellular space or synapse.

The release of neurotransmitter across the synapse has effects only when it binds to specific receptors on the postsynaptic neuron. These digital or on/off events, called excitatory postsynaptic potentials and inhibitory postsynaptic potentials, are the result of the action potential. Their action is spread to the postsynaptic neuron with an effect that is repeated billions of times per second across the brain.

Key Terms

sensory neurons (97)

motor neurons (97)

cell membrane (97)

phospholipid bilayer (99)

ion channels (99)

receptors (99)

dendrites (100)

Purkinje neurons (101)

dendritic spines (101)

cell body (101)

organelles (102)

nucleus (102)

deoxyribonucleic acid (DNA) (103)

messenger RNA (mRNA) (103)

amino acids (103)

transcription (103)

endoplasmic reticulum (103)

ribosomes (103)

translation (103)

enzymes (103)

mitochondria (103)

precursors (103)

adenosine triphosphate (ATP) (104)

Golgi apparatus (104)

vesicle (104)

lysosomes (104)

neurofilaments (104)

microfilaments (105)

microtubules (105)

axon (106)

axon hillock (106)

terminal buttons (107)

glia (107)

blood–brain barrier (108)

astrocyte (108)

myelin sheath (108)

depolarization (110)

resting potential (110)

action potential (110)

electrostatic pressure (111)

diffusion (111)

concentration gradient (111)

threshold potential (112)

graded potential (112)

voltage-gated channels (114)

saltatory conduction (115)

hyperpolarization (115)

absolute refractory period (115)

sodium–potassium pumps (115)

exocytosis (118)

excitatory postsynaptic potential (EPSP) (119)

inhibitory postsynaptic potential (IPSP) (119)

temporal summation (119)

spatial summation (120)

ionotropic receptors (120)

metabotropic receptors (121)

G protein (121)

second messenger systems (121)

For Further Consideration

Cowan, W. M., Sudhof, T. C., & Stevens, C. F. (Eds.) (2000). *Synapses.* Baltimore: Johns Hopkins University Press. This book, in a sense, combines the information contained in the two books on dendrites and the axon listed next. In *Synapses*, the editors draw together a wealth of information from some of the major names in the area (themselves included). A crystal-clear picture emerges of brain activity and regulation from the standpoint of the interaction between one neuron and another. The book is of great value because of the synthesized nature of the material the authors and editors provide and the fact that brain activity is the product of the firing of countless synapses and their coordination. *Synapses* is thorough, detailed, and readable.

DeFelipe, J. (2010). *Cajal's Butterflies of the Soul.* New York: Oxford University Press. Prior to the existence of advanced neuroimaging capabilities found in contemporary neuroscience laboratories, details about the microscopic cells of the nervous system were provided by scientists who had the artistic ability to recreate the cells they viewed in the early microscopes on their drawing pads. This beautiful book showcases the nineteenth-century drawings of the nervous system. As science merges with art, you'll be amazed by how realistic these drawings are. Although approximately 100 scientists are included, an emphasis is placed on Santiago Ramón y Cajal.

Gross, C. (2000). Neurogenesis in the adult brain: Death of a dogma. *Nature Reviews Neuroscience, 1,* 67–73. For most of the last century, dogma dictated that the brain was born with its allotment of neurons, that organisms lost them through means both natural and unnatural but no longer had the capacity to generate new ones. This view held sway in laboratories and in theories until recent years. Now, the dogma is slowly being revised, overturned, and revisited. Gross reviews the data for the last century, focusing on the most recent work and all its implications. It now appears that the production of new neurons, called *neurogenesis*, goes on throughout life. This process has implications for a host of behaviors, ranging from learning and memory to depression. These data point out again the seemingly limitless capacity for the characteristic plasticity of the brain.

Kandel, E. R. (2006). *In search of memory: The emergence of a new science of mind.* New York: Norton. The irony of an autobiography by a Nobel Prize–winning scientist who spent his career studying memory is an exquisite one. Here, Kandel shares with the reader his life and his development as a neuroscientist. He makes clear the incisive mind that he fostered early on in his life and the hard work and persistence that led to his groundbreaking discoveries regarding memory formation and its cellular basis. That he accomplished much of his research utilizing what some would consider an unattractive creature with an even more unattractive name, the sea slug, demonstrates for certain the adage "Love is in the eye of the beholder." (A lovely little poem written by his then 7-year-old daughter, Minouche, captures the family's fascination and facility for nature and for observation.) Overall, this is a fine foray into the scientific creative process by a pillar of the field.

Kandel, E. R., Schwartz, J. H., & Jessell, T. M. (2000). *Principles of neural science* (4th ed.), New York: McGraw-Hill. The bible of neuroscience and the singular source for all things brain. It is 1,500 pages of facts, information, data, and theory and on a level of scholarship that is unparalleled. Ever since its first edition came out in the early 1980s, this book has set the standard for erudition in the sciences and is probably on the bookshelf of almost every neuroscientist in the world—right alongside Ramón y Cajal (1989). It is not for the faint of heart, however; and it can be dense, like the field it covers. But as a reference it cannot be equaled. (Kandel, by the way, won the 2002 Nobel Prize in Physiology or Medicine for his pathbreaking studies on the molecular neurobiology of learning and memory.

Stuart, G., Spruston, N., & Hausser, M. (Eds.) (1999). *Dendrites.* New York: Oxford University Press. *Dendrites* compiles much of the information on the subject and presents it in a logical fashion, from structural to functional phenomena. The book contains and presents exhaustive detail on the dendrite, but at the end, the reader is not inundated so much as fascinated by these members of the neuron's anatomy. The dendrite is a much richer and more complex entity than one could ever imagine. Given the number of dendrites and their extent throughout the brain, the information-processing capacity of these delicate anatomical features staggers the imagination.

Young, D., Lawlor, P., Leone, P., Dragunow, M., & During, M. (1999). Environmental enrichment inhibits spontaneous apoptosis, prevents seizures and is neuroprotective. *Nature Medicine, 5,* 448–453. Your parents always told you that they knew what was best for you. "Read; don't watch TV," they exhorted. "Go outside and play," they cajoled. Had you listened, you might feel better about their advice as you mature. It turns out, according to Young and colleagues, that an enriching environment—an environment that stimulates the brain by providing it with an assortment of new challenges in context-appropriate and evolutionarily appropriate ways—has an effect on the brain not unlike the way exercise affects a muscle. Apoptosis, or programmed cell death, in which neurons commit a form of cellular suicide, also appears to be reduced. Overall, the effects on the brain are cumulative and beneficial. Now, go call your mother and apologize.

Chapter Five

Neurochemistry and Psychopharmacology

Connections

Coffee: Changing Our Culture and Our Nervous Systems

According to Ethiopian legend, the discovery of coffee can be traced to a goatherd named Kaldi, who enjoyed playing his pipe as he followed the goats across the mountainside. One afternoon, the goats didn't respond to their usual musical cue to return home, and a puzzled Kaldi eventually found them bleating with excitement, dancing on their hind legs, running around, and butting one another. Kaldi thought his goats were bewitched, until he observed them eating red berries from an unfamiliar tree. As if lingering at the first forest coffeehouse, they remained for hours before returning home.

Intrigued, the next day Kaldi joined the goats in consuming the leaves and berries from this mystery tree. Feeling a tingle moving from his tongue to his stomach and a subsequent newfound energy, he spread the word of his "coffee experience" and coffee became part of the Ethiopian culture. This event, or one like it, probably preceded the first printed description of coffee by an Arabian physician in the tenth century (Pendergrast, 1999).

We have come a long way from chewing leaves and coffee beans to achieve our morning jolt; the preparation of coffee has evolved into a ritualistic roasting and grinding of choice coffee beans and the careful addition of nearly boiling water to create a wonderful, aromatic brew. As observed by author Mark Pendergrast in his book *Uncommon Grounds* (1999), caffeine has become the world's most popular psychoactive drug. In coffee and other food and drink, including chocolate and soft drinks, an estimated 120,000 tons of caffeine are consumed across the world each year. In the United States, about 90% of the population regularly indulges in some form of caffeine consumption.

Of particular interest to clinical neuroscience is the actual neurobiological effect of caffeine. At various times throughout history, coffee has been touted as a nerve tonic, aphrodisiac, enema, and extender of life. In 1679, French doctors, afraid that coffee consumption was threatening the rate of wine consumption, claimed that coffee dried up the brain's cerebrospinal fluid, leaving the person suffering from paralysis, exhaustion, and impotence. Just 30 years later, however, a Paris physician recommended coffee to his patients to freshen their complexion and improve lower bowel function. French food is one thing, a coffee colonic quite another!

Aside from these diverse medical claims, coffee's incorporation into the social lives of various cultures was affected by the impression that it served as an intellectual stimulant. Coffeehouses emerged across the world where people gathered for lively conversation, poetry readings, and entertainment. Today, Starbucks and similar coffee establishments are immensely popular; in fact, the satirical publication and Web site *The Onion* parodied this near-addiction to coffee and places to drink it with the headline "New Starbucks Opens in Restroom of Existing Starbucks."

Research has shown caffeine to affect synaptic sites of the neurotransmitter adenosine (a central nervous system neuromodulator at inhibitory synapses) throughout the brain, especially in the reticular formation area of the brain stem. Caffeine's effects throughout the body include increased heart rate, enhanced breathing, constricted blood vessels, and more efficient muscle contraction. In 1911, when Coca-Cola was being pushed to remove caffeine from their sodas, they hired two psychologists, Harry and Leta Hollingworth, to conduct the first laboratory tests of caffeine's influences on humans. The reason there is still caffeine in that Coca-Cola you may be drinking is because, in general, the Hollingworths found caffeine to produce mild improvement in motor skills and reaction times with no other serious effects (Benjamin, Rogers, & Rosenbaum, 1991; Pendergrast, 1999).

Habitual caffeine consumption has been associated with enhanced long-term memory, faster locomotor speed, and, in rats, reduced neurochemical response to stress (Hamaleers et al., 2000; Yamato et al., 2002). Research focusing on neurons indicates that caffeine administration leads to increased growth of dendritic spines, an effect that could be an important mechanism of enhanced memory (Korkotian & Segal, 1999). In a study conducted on U.S. Navy SEALs, caffeine mitigated many of the adverse effects of 72 hours of sleep deprivation and repeated stress exposure. The caffeine subjects were observed to have improved choice reaction time, alertness, and visual vigilance and less fatigue and sleepiness, especially 1 hour after administration (Lieberman, Tharion, Shukitt-Hale, Speckman, & Tulley, 2002). On the other hand, Keith Corodimas and his students at Lynchburg College found evidence that acute caffeine exposure may interfere with certain forms of hippocampus-dependent learning in rats (Corodimas, Pruitt, & Steig, 2000).

Research reports also suggest that caffeine may provide neuroprotective effects against certain neurodegenerative diseases. In a study following the health of 8,000 Japanese-American men for 30 years in Hawaii, higher coffee intake was associated with significantly lower rates of Parkinson's disease (Ross et al., 2000). Looking more closely at the mechanism of such neuroprotection, caffeine was administered at doses comparable with human consumption levels in a mouse model of Parkinson's disease. Caffeine, along with other specific adenosine antagonists, served a protective role against the development of Parkinson-like symptoms in these mice (Chen et al., 2001). Accordingly, adenosine antagonists have been evaluated and are entering clinical trials to determine their therapeutic potential in Parkinson's disease (Ross & Petrovitch, 2001; Schwarzschild, Chen, & Ascerio, 2002; Pinna, Tronci, Schintu, Volpini, Pontis, Cristalli, & Morelli, 2010. After standing in line with dozens of other folks at the local Starbucks to get your morning "fix," you might guess that caffeine has addictive qualities; the empirical evidence, however, does not clearly suggest that caffeine is addictive. Whereas Solinas and his colleagues (2002) found increased levels of dopamine in the nucleus accumbens shell (known to be involved in addictive behaviors) in free-moving rats following behaviorally relevant doses of caffeine, Acquas, Tanda, and DiChiara (2002) found no increase in dopamine in the nucleus accumbens of rats following caffeine administration. Accordingly, evidence of physical addiction is variable across individuals but is apparent when people take themselves off caffeine. Withdrawal effects of headaches, fatigue, and muscle pain typically result. Thus, concerning the question of addiction, the jury is still out, making it a prime topic for discussion—likely over coffee.

The evidence provided by legendary goats, contemporary rats, mice, Navy SEALs, and legions of faithful customers of coffeehouses across the world suggests that there is no denying that caffeine has some attractive effect on our brains. Future research may uncover additional medicinal uses of this pervasive natural, psychoactive drug.

At each moment of each day we are perched on the brink of a chemical precipice. On one side are the depths that characterize the relative lack of essential neurotransmission; on the other are the effects that occur when too much of a natural chemical is present. Both states disrupt neurochemical homeostasis and may lead to mental illness, transient or chronic. The natural balance of neurochemistry maintains this knife's edge. It can be disrupted through diet, substance abuse, damage, or stress. When the tilt happens, we see the emergence of depression, violence, irritability, improper responses to stimuli, lethargy—the whole gamut of behavioral disorders.

In this chapter we consider neurochemistry, the currency, or means of exchange, between and among neurons. As you learned in Chapter 2, Otto Loewi's 1921 insightful dreams led to the realization that neurons spoke to one another via chemical means. As introduced in Chapter 4, we now know that neurotransmitters are released by activated neurons, travel across the synapse, and activate specific receptors on the receiving neuron.

Here, we discuss selected neurotransmitters that have received considerable attention from researchers. Each is involved in diverse behavioral and mental functions, each works alone or in combination with sets of other neurochemicals, and all have profound effects. Then, given the role of challenges to the physiological knife's edge and unique responses to them, we explain the neurochemistry of the stress response and how prolonged exposure can influence the brain. We conclude with an introduction to fundamental information characterizing the important field of psychopharmacology.

NEUROCHEMICALS

Currently, a few dozen neurotransmitters have been formally identified. But more and more neurochemicals are being identified all the time, leading neuroscientists to believe that the actual number may exceed 100.

The more recently discovered neurotransmitters are actually peptides, or small proteins, and are known as **neuropeptides** (for example, endogenous opioids). **Neurohormones** are yet another form of neurochemical that falls in an intermediate position between neurotransmitters and the hormones of the endocrine systems that are discussed in Chapter 6. Neurohormones (for example, oxytocin and vasopressin) are released by neurons, but instead of traveling across a synapse to receptors on the receiving neuron, they travel through the blood to a target organ, where they exert their effects.

Another descriptive label that is frequently used for certain neurochemicals is **neuromodulator**. Neuromodulators are chemicals that influence ongoing synaptic activity—either enhancing or impeding neuronal transmission, as seen in the effects of caffeine on neurotransmission (see Connections; Cooper, Roth, & Bloom, 1996; Julien, 2007). Similar to a brain, an MP3 player detects certain wavelength frequencies and transmits that information in the form of, say, music or video. But many factors may modulate (modify) the intensity of the transmitted message. You may change the song, increase the sampling rate of the tune so that the reception is of a higher fidelity, or turn down the volume altogether so that the message is not as loud. Continuing with the analogy, a thunderstorm may rage, an external event that can interfere with the signal. Although none of these factors is critical for the player to be able to actually function, they all have the ability to modulate the images or music that you actually hear. This comparison characterizes the function of chemical neuromodulators; they neither activate nor deactivate an existing

neuropeptides Proteins that are released by neurons and act as intercellular messengers.

neurohormones Brain substances that act like hormones and are released by neurons into the circulatory system.

neuromodulator A substance that modifies or regulates the effect of a neurotransmitter.

neurochemical system—they use a variety of strategies to enhance or diminish the existing neurochemical actions and relationships.

Although these neurochemical categories exist to simplify our understanding about how the chemicals of the nervous system function, their boundaries are sometimes fuzzier than one might desire. Further, as seen in Table 5.1, the categories are not mutually exclusive.

All these chemical substances are united in a delicate balance that regulates responses to the environment. Brain-derived compounds have evolved to undertake specific behavioral and physiological activities by joining the electrochemistry we discussed in Chapter 4. We cannot hope to cover the vast array of neurochemicals that the brain synthesizes, so we will focus on a primary set of substances that are both ubiquitous and exemplary of the other substances and their principles.

As we discuss, the neurochemistry of the brain is in exquisite balance. Timed, synchronous, and multilayered, neurochemicals flow in infinite whorls and eddies, controlled by the neurons that regulate their release.

Thought arises from the brain, and the brain arises from the conjoint activities of its many neurochemicals. As we gain understanding concerning the brain's infinite chemical interactions, we come closer to treating the many disruptions of neurochemical homeostasis that haunt so many individuals.

Before exploring the neurochemicals of the nervous system, it is important to be familiar with some of the staple terms of the neurochemical language. Now that you have mastered the concept of synaptic transmission covered in the last chapter, your own neurochemical landscapes are seeded and ready to understand these related terms, summarized in Table 5.2.

Table 5.3 at the end of this section about neurochemicals streamlines the essential information contained in the section, summarizing the receptor types and functions of each of the neurochemicals discussed.

Small-Molecule Neurotransmitters

The earliest neurotransmitters that were identified were small-molecule transmitters. These neurotransmitters are abundant in the brain and are involved in many behavioral, emotional, and cognitive functions. In the

Table 5.1 Neurochemical Categorizations

Neurochemical Categorization	General Description	Examples*
Neurotransmitter	Synthesized in neurons, released across synaptic cleft, received by specific receptors in receiving neuron	ACh, NE, DA, 5-HT, GABA, Glu
Neuropeptide	Similar properties as small-molecule neurotransmitter	Endorphins, oxytocin, AVP
Hormone	Released by endocrine gland, travels through circulation to target organ, where it has an effect	Estrogen, testosterone, cortisol, insulin, thyroxin
Neurohormone	Released by neuron into circulation and travels to target organ, where it is received by specific receptors	Oxytocin, AVP
Neuromodulator	Neurochemical that modifies an exixting synaptic circuit in some way	DA and 5-HT serve as modulators for the obsessive–compulsive disorder neural circuit (Chapter 8)

* Some neurochemicals fall into more than one category.
ACh, acetylcholine; NE, norepinephrine; DA, dopamine; 5-HT, 5-hydroxy tryptamine; 6ABA, gamma-amino butryic acid; Glu, glutamate; AVP, arginine vasopressin

Table 5.2 Terms Associated with the Neurochemical Nature of the Brain and Psychological Processes

Term	Definition
Drug	Chemical compound that affects living organisms in some way and is usually intended for the diagnosis, cure, or prevention of a disease; psychoactive drugs influence behavioral, emotional, or cognitive processes
Agonist	Drug that attaches to a certain neurochemical receptor and mimics or modulates the activity of the endogenous neurochemical
Antagonist	Drug that attaches to a certain neurochemical receptor and blocks or hinders the action of the endogenous neurochemical
Autoreceptor	Receptor located in the membrane of the presynaptic neuron that is sensitive to the neurochemical being released by the neuron so that it can monitor the neurochemical activity of the neuron
Synthesis	Formation of a particular neurochemical—typically occurs after the introduction of several enzymatic steps
Ligand	Substance that binds to a postsynaptic receptor or an ion channel (e.g., transmitter, hormone, drug)
Receptor	Binding location for neurochemicals so that they can exert their effect on specific neurons; most are specific, genetically encoded, specialized proteins
Precursor	Substance that, on entering the CNS, serves as a foundational ingredient for the subsequent formation of a neurochemical. Tryptophan, found in bananas, turkey, and milk, crosses the blood-brain barrier, interacts with certain enzymes, and results in the formation of the neurotransmitter serotonin.
Deactivating enzyme	Enzyme that alters the formation of a certain neurochemical that is activating a receptor so that the activation is terminated and the cell can regain homeostatic levels of activity to respond to the next important ligand
Metabotropic receptor	When a neurochemical binds to this type of receptor, a conformational change occurs in the receptor that binds to and activates G proteins that ultimately trigger a series of enzymatic steps necessary to produce the desired response of the neurochemical. These effects typically have a slower onset and longer duration.
Ionotropic receptor	When a neurochemical binds to this type of receptor, this large multi-subunit complex undergoes a series of conformational changes that trigger the opening of the ion channel so that the desired result of the neurochemical can be obtained. These effects are typically very rapid and short-lived.
Reuptake	Reabsorption of a neurochemical that is activating a receptor into the cell that secreted it, usually so that it can be repackaged and used again

Table 5.3 Summary of Neurochemicals, Receptors, and Associated Functions

Neurochemical	Receptors	Function
Acetylcholine (ACh)	Muscarinic (M_1–M_5); nicotinic (N_N and N_M)	Sensory functions, memory, motor coordination, neurotransmission at neuromuscular junction, ANS and PNS function
Norepinephrine (NE)	Alpha$_1$ and alpha$_2$; beta$_1$, beta$_2$, and beta$_3$	CNS sensory processing, sleep, mood, memory, learning, anxiety, SANS, cerebellar function
Dopamine (DA)	D_1–D_5 in both D_1 family and D_2 family	Movement, olfaction, reinforcement, mood, concentration, hormone control
Serotonin (5-HT)	18 receptors identified existing as part of 8 families designated $5HT_1$–$5HT_8$	Mood, appetite, sleep, emotional processing, pain processing, hallucinations, reflex regulation
Glutamate (Glu)	NMDA, AMPA, quisqualate, and kainate	Major excitatory function in the CNS and PNS, long-term potentiation, memory
Gamma-aminobutyric acid (GABA)	GABA$_A$, GABA$_B$	Major inhibitory neurotransmitter in the CNS
Glycine (Gly)		Major inhibitory function in the spinal cord
Oxytocin		Uterine contractions during childbirth, milk letdown, stress reduction, learning, social facilitation
Vasopressin (AVP, or antidiuretic hormone [ADH])		Fluid conservation, social recognition, aversive learning

ANS, autonomic nervous system; PNS, peripheral nervous system; CNS, central nervous system; SANS, sympathetic nervous system
Adapted from Julien, 2004, p. 67.

acetylcholine (ACh)
Neurotransmitter in the somatic and parasympathetic nervous systems involved in cognition and at the neuromuscular junction.

Figure 5.1
Synthesis of ACh.
Acetylcholine (ACh) was among the earliest neurotransmitters to be examined and to have its metabolic pathways elucidated. It is considered a "classical" neurotransmitter because its synthesis, release, and reuptake properties demonstrated the principles for other neurotransmitters to follow. CoA, coenzyme A; ChAT, choline acetyltransferase.
AFTER ZIGMOND ET AL., 1999, P. 217

current chapter we introduce the neurotransmitters in a broad sense. In the rest of this text, you will learn how specific neurotransmitters are involved in specific mental illnesses.

Acetylcholine. Relative to some of the other substances in this section, **acetylcholine (ACh)** has roles both within the central nervous system (CNS) and in the periphery: In short, it gets around. First identified as a substance with central and peripheral activity (neuromuscular junctions) in the early twentieth century and as a neurotransmitter in the early 1920s, ACh has been shown to play many roles in the regulation of physiology and behavior. In fact, ACh is thought of as an exemplary neurotransmitter in the sense that it serves as a model of classical neurotransmitter activity. The interaction of the ACh ligand with its receptor—the key and the lock, respectively—and the ease with which this interaction can be observed and measured enabled the early neurophysiologists you read about in Chapter 2 to conduct the necessary research and to confirm one another's observations.

The neuronal synthesis of ACh is straightforward when compared with that of the other neurochemicals (Figure 5.1). Generally, the chemical precursor choline, found in high amounts in lipids (fat-like substances) and compiled by a choline transporter, and the cation (positive ion) acetate, which is bonded to the molecule acetyl coenzyme A (acetyl CoA), are combined. Specifically, when the enzyme choline acetyltransferase (ChAT), which is synthesized in the cell body and then translocated to the terminal end of the axon, catalyzes the reaction by transferring a molecule of acetate from CoA to the choline molecule, a molecule of ACh is produced.

The cytosolic ACh product is then stored in vesicles until its docking and release into the synapse. Once in the synapse, ACh binds to specialized receptors, referred to as "nicotinic" or "muscarinic" receptors, located on both the pre- and postsynaptic membranes, and more important for this discussion, on the postsynaptic neuron (the presynaptic ones are autoreceptors). Although both nicotinic and muscarinic receptors are responsive to ACh, they are differentially responsive to specific drugs. As indicated by their names, the nicotinic receptors were experimentally demonstrated to be activated by nicotine and the muscarinic receptors are activated by muscarine, a chemical found in the mushroom *Amanita muscaria* (Feldman & Quenzer, 1984).

Following its release, the ACh molecules still occupying the synapse are brought back into the presynaptic neuron by specific choline transporters for recycling and

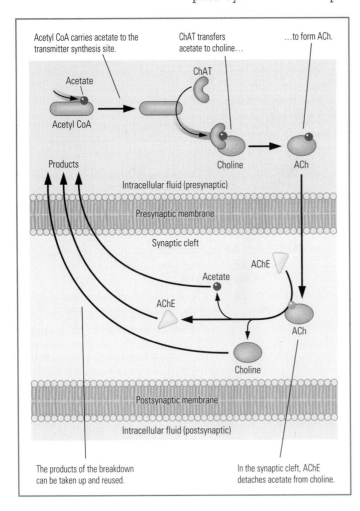

Acetyl CoA carries acetate to the transmitter synthesis site.

ChAT transfers acetate to choline...

...to form ACh.

Acetate

ChAT

Acetyl CoA

Choline

ACh

Products

Intracellular fluid (presynaptic)

Presynaptic membrane

Synaptic cleft

AChE

Acetate

AChE

ACh

Choline

Postsynaptic membrane

Intracellular fluid (postsynaptic)

The products of the breakdown can be taken up and reused.

In the synaptic cleft, AChE detaches acetate from choline.

repackaging (also known as "reuptake"). Any ACh that is left over from the act of neurotransmission is then scavenged by the deactivating enzyme acetylcholine esterase (AChE), which fractures the ACh molecule and returns it to its constituent materials, acetyl and choline. The process is repeated thousands of times per second.

ACh then binds to its specialized receptors, either muscarinic (which are metabotropic receptors) or nicotinic (which are ionotropic). From there it exerts its peripheral effects on diverse neuromuscular junctions such as heart, lungs, and muscles and its central effects on cognition and sleeping/dreaming. ACh has been studied intensively for decades; and contributing to its significance and ubiquity, the neurotransmitter is released at every neuromuscular junction affecting the skeletal musculature throughout the body, and its mediation of cognition is becoming clearer (Burnstock, 2009).

The biosynthesis, storage, and release of any neurotransmitter involve a multiplicity of steps. At any point along that long metabolic pathway, an **agonist** (which mimics or facilitates the action of the endogenous neurotransmitter it targets) can act to promote the natural neurotransmitters actions or an **antagonist** (which blocks or interferes with its neurotransmitter) can act to block the actions. For example, ACh antagonist compounds such as botulinum toxin, which inhibits the release of ACh from axon terminals, and curare, which occupies postsynaptic receptors, both block the action of ACh, thereby causing peripheral muscle paralysis. An agonist drug such as physostigmine, which inactivates the synaptic cleft enzyme AChE, therefore causes accumulation of ACh in the synapse. Depending on dosage, it can be toxic, causing choking and blurred vision, or clinically useful, causing electroencephalographic (EEG) desynchronization (a characteristic brain-wave pattern observed in both wakefulness and rapid eye movement [REM] sleep).

As mentioned, ACh is also widely distributed throughout the brain (Figure 5.2). The cholinergic cell bodies located in the basal forebrain (septal nuclei and nucleus basalis) and their projections are directed to the forebrain (hippocampus and cortex). The cholinergic cell bodies located in the midbrain project to the basal ganglia, thalamus, diencephalon, pons, cerebellum, cranial nerve nuclei, and reticular formation. It should come as no surprise, then, given the diverse ACh projections throughout the brain, that ACh is involved in many brain activities that require adaptability and flexibility.

Among ACh's many activities uncovered through its long history of discovery involves cognitive function, particularly learning and memory (Burnstock, 2009); this neurotransmitter, however, has also been implicated in attention, mood, sleep's REM cycle, and other activities. Research focusing on learning and memory has shown that drugs that increase the activity of ACh enhance memory, whereas any disruptions of CNS ACh neurotransmission impair memory (Gold, 2003). (A painful example of the devastating effects of ACh disruption occurs in the neurodegenerative condition Alzheimer's disease.)

Cells in the basal forebrain are among the first ones to perish as Alzheimer's disease begins its early progressive ravages. As discussed in Chapter 6, in the race to minimize age-related cognitive deficits in our aging society, many researchers are exploring neurochemicals and drugs that may slow down the memory decline

agonist A drug that mimics the endogenous actions of the targeted neurotransmitter.

antagonist A drug that blocks the actions of an endogenous neurotransmitter.

**Figure 5.2
Distribution of ACh neurons.** Acetylcholine is found throughout the brain, but it is localized primarily in cognitively important sites such as the basal forebrain and cortex.

AFTER BEAR, CONNORS, & PARADISO, 1996, P. 518

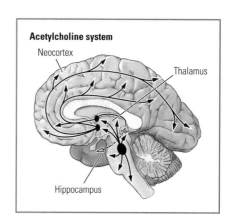

Acetylcholine system
Neocortex
Thalamus
Hippocampus

often observed in aging brains (although finding ways to enhance ACh and other endogenous cognition-promoting neurochemicals in otherwise normal and healthy people is ongoing as well [Greely et al., 2008]). Estrogen, the female gonadal steroid hormone responsible for maintaining reproduction-related structures, behavior, and activity, reduces the production of AChE, which would be expected to increase ACh-related activities, such as cognition (Daniel & Dohanich, 2001; Kadish & Van Groen, 2002).

Recently, it has been reported that estrogen, similar to other drugs that enhance ACh functioning, can provide some benefit to sufferers of Alzheimer's disease (Cholerton, Gleason, Baker, & Asthana, 2002; Hosoda, Nakajima, & Honjo, 2001; Schonknecht et al., 2001; Silva, Mor, & Naftolin, 2001; Zec & Travedi, 2002). Perhaps there is an estrogen–ACh link worth investigating. Another neurosteroid, pregnenolone, a substance that enhances ACh release in the amygdala, hippocampus, and cortex, is related to enhanced cognitive performance in aging rats (Mayo et al., 2003).

You may be thinking that another way to increase ACh in the brain might be through the simple act of eating choline in anticipation of it being synthesized into more ACh in the cholinergic cell bodies. This idea, though theoretically sound, has not been met with empirical success, perhaps because the brain synthesizes what it needs from existing provisions but does not stockpile superfluous stores. Enhanced choline consumption has not been found to increase brain ACh levels under normal conditions. Past research, however, suggests that choline supplements protect against various drug-induced cholinergic challenges, serving a neuroprotective role. Perhaps such a dietary manipulation might protect against the ACh deficits associated with the late stages of Alzheimer's disease (Wecker, 1986).

It is also of some interest that the ACh system and the activities it regulates appear to be similar across a large number of species. This preservation of function in so many different animals suggests an evolutionarily conserved ligand–receptor relationship with broad value (Aldrich, Dionne, Hawrot, & Stevens, 1985). For example, Wright and Huddart (2002) have explored ACh receptors in the pest slug *Deroceras reticulatum*. In other words, that ACh exists and works in such phylogenetically diverse species shows that it is an effective and efficient neurotransmitter that has been extant for a very long time. In fact, its existence in very simple organisms is evidence that it may have evolved very early in this planet's life. Evolution, life's sculptor, therefore, has been working on refining its activities for many millennia.

Catecholamines. The **catecholamines** include **dopamine (DA)**, **norepinephrine (NE)**—also known as noradrenaline—and **epinephrine (Epi)**—also known as adrenaline. (Given Epi's limited distribution in the brain—mainly it is a peripheral nervous system constituent involved in sympathetic responses—its discussion here will be limited.) The catecholamines are very closely related, sharing a catechol nucleus (the omnipresent benzene ring, together with its adjacent hydroxyl substituents). They also share a common biosynthetic pathway that involves many different enzymes acting on each step of the process to convert the previous molecule into the next transmitter product. That is, depending on the neuronal type (DA, NE, or Epi), additional enzymes further refine and shape the raw materials to produce the required neurotransmitter, an example of neurobiological economy.

catecholamines A group of three different amine neurotransmitters that contain catechol. These three neurotransmitters are dopamine, norepinephrine, and epinephrine (also called adrenaline).

dopamine (DA) The resulting neurotransmitter when dopa reacts with the enzyme dopa decarboxylase. This is an important neurotransmitter involved in movement and brain reward systems.

norepinephrine An amine neurotransmitter that contains tyrosine hydroxylase, dopa decarboxylase, and the enzyme dopamine B-hydroxylase (DBH). DBH is responsible for converting dopamine into norepinephrine.

epinephrine One of the three catecholamine neurotransmitters that is also called adrenaline, epinephrine neurons contain phenylethanolamine N-methyltransferase (PNMT). PNMT is the enzyme that converts norepinephrine to epinephrine.

The study of DA has a history that goes back only to the middle part of the twentieth century, but the discoveries associated with it touch many aspects of our lives. Originally believed to be an antecedent to the catecholamine NE, experimental verification revealed that there were distinct populations of DA- and NE-containing neurons throughout the brain, with the amount of DA constituting the vast majority of the catecholamine content of the brain. Much of what we now know of the distribution of DA was discovered by Swedish investigators including Hokfelt, Fuxe, and Dahlstrom, whose pioneering methodologies, which included fluorescence and immunocytochemical visualization of the catecholamines, demonstrated the distribution and localization of DA systems (Cooper et al., 1996).

The metabolic assembly is a multilayered process that, like an assembly line, involves the movement of a precursor chemical through a series of steps that modifies the molecule until the proper neurochemical is formed (Figure 5.3). Beginning with intraneuronal stores of the precursor amino acid tyrosine, the enzyme **tyrosine hydroxylase (TH)** converts the amino acid into 1-dihydroxyphenylalanine, which is subsequently modified by dopa decarboxylase into DA. The production of DA is part of the overall synthesis of the catecholamines. In the neurons in which DA is the final neurotransmitter product, once the DA is formed, the synthesis is complete; no additional enzymatic activity is required. In other catecholamine-containing neurons, such as NE and Epi, DA is transformed into NE by the enzyme DA hydroxylase and further transformed into Epi by phenylethanolamine *N*-methyltransferase (PNMT).

Therefore, as seen in Figure 5.3, an Epi-containing neuron would use four enzymes to produce its store of transmitter substance. In an NE-containing neuron, the process would involve only three, and two enzymes are required to produce DA from tyrosine (Bear, Connors, & Paradiso, 2007). Obviously, many potential targets exist for the pharmaceutical companies; interrupting any of these enzymatic steps in the synthesis of these neurotransmitters would drastically alter catecholaminergic functioning.

Following the synthesis of DA, the transmitter substances are stored in vesicles in the terminal buttons, waiting to be released into the synaptic cleft. For NE, there is an additional twist to its synthesis and storage. The enzyme dopamine β-hydroxylase (DBH), which converts DA to NE, is found mainly in the vesicles in the neuron terminals. Therefore, DA must be driven into vesicles and into contact with DBH for the enzyme to be effective. There is a transport mechanism, akin to a molecular border collie, called vesicular monoamine transporter (VMAT), that herds cytosolic DA into the vesicles, where it then is converted by DBH into NE. You will learn more about how VMAT may be manipulated to treat addiction in Chapter 11.

In general, neurotransmission of catecholaminergic neurons is virtually identical to the processes described for other transmitter systems: receipt of the depolarizing signal; influx of Ca^{2+}; docking of vesicles; and *exocytosis*, or release of transmitter molecules into the synapse. There are, however, some notable additions. Catecholamine release also can be evoked

tyrosine hydroxylase (TH) An enzyme found in all catecholaminergic neurons. TH is a catalyst in the conversion of tyrosine to dopa, which is the first step in catecholamine synthesis.

Figure 5.3 Cathecholamine synthesis. There is an economy to the production of the catecholamines, with intermediate enzymatic steps converting a previous neurotransmitter into another neuroactive substance.
AFTER ZIGMOND ET AL., 1999, P. 199

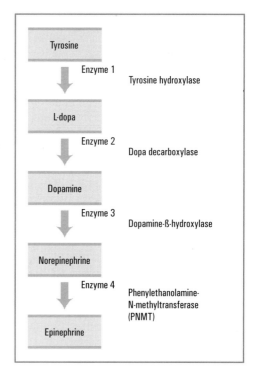

reuptake The return of spent neurotransmitter from the synapse to the presynaptic neuron by means of specialized receptors.

through a reversal of VMAT, in which case the movement of the transmitter into the vesicle is outward instead of inward. Another intriguing avenue does not even involve the axon. Data show that DA can be released from the dendrite in a nonexocytotic pattern. These examples further complicate our understanding of the catecholamine system (and explain why thousands of papers that relate to this system are presented at the Society for Neuroscience annual meetings) while simultaneously increasing our respect for the complexity of the brain and its regulation (Deutch & Roth, 1999).

Once the transmitter is released, it can produce either the excitatory postsynaptic potentials (EPSPs) or inhibitory postsynaptic potentials (IPSPs) discussed in Chapter 4, depending on the form of the receptor to which it binds. The regulation of DA and NE activity is rich and diverse, with the presence of the presynaptic receptors, or autoreceptors, playing a major role in the control of their release. These autoreceptors control the catecholamine chain from synthesis through release. By modulating molecular feedback to the neuron regarding the levels of the neurotransmitter, there is an effective governor at work to modulate all levels of neurotransmitter activity (Feldman & Quenzer, 1984; Julien, 2007).

Once the catecholamine is released and has acted on the postsynaptic neuron, its rapid removal and deactivation is critical. Overstimulation of the postsynaptic neuron is undesirable since the signal would cause deleterious downstream behavioral events (some of which are described later). Thus, there are several mechanisms by which the transmitter is rendered inactive.

The process of **reuptake** is foremost among the strategies employed. In the catecholamine neuron, reuptake—the process by which the cell that secretes a neurotransmitter reabsorbs it—is an efficient means of removing the spent neurotransmitter. This process allows the intracellular enzymatic events to break down the neurochemical and the extracellular mechanisms to focus on a smaller concentration of the neurochemical. Two transporters utilized in the reuptake process for catecholamine neurons are the DA transporter and the NE transporter. These proteins are efficient at removing the catecholamines from the synapse.

The reuptake transporters are complemented by other mechanisms that also are effective at removing the synaptic catecholamine from the cleft, among them the simplest of all, diffusion. Diffusion allows the excess transmitter to move to extracellular areas of lower concentration, thereby diluting it to noneffective levels. In other cases, deactivation of the excess catecholamine is accomplished by enzymes such as monoamine oxidase (MAO) and catechol O-methyltransferase (COMT). MAO inhibitors (MAOIs) have been used successfully in the treatment of depression; their clinical value, however, has been limited due to potential toxicity when consumed along with foods containing tyramine (such as aged cheese) and serious side effects including high blood pressure, insomnia, dizziness, sexual dysfunction, and weight gain. A newer MAOI, moclobemide, does not interact with tyramine but may interact with certain medications. Thus, MAOIs may still have clinical value but are best used only after other front-line treatments have been explored (see Chapter 9 for a full discussion of antidepressants) (Berman, Belanoff, Charney, & Schatzberg, 1999).

The distribution of catecholamine neurons is widespread. As seen in Figure 5.4, the DA neurons project from two sources (ventral tegmental and substantia nigra) to many forebrain areas, for example, the striatum (including the nucleus accumbens and the caudate), as well as cortical regions such as the prefrontal cortex. Moreover, the limbic system also receives substantial DA inputs to the amygdala, hippocampus, and septum. There are also DA cell bodies in the hypothalamus, with projections from that site moving outward as far afield as the spinal cord, and in the olfactory bulb and retina. A diversity of locations is evidence of a multiplicity of mediation and effects.

In the case of NE, cell bodies have been found in the brain stem, mainly the medulla and the pons. The influence of these cells, belying their small number, goes well beyond the brain stem. Projections ascend to the thalamus, hypothalamus, limbic system, and cortex.

Some major agonists for DA—and those with which too many individuals are familiar, at a staggering cost to society—are cocaine or its derivatives, crack, and amphetamines. As discussed in Chapter 11, cocaine hydrochloride/crack and amphetamines are considered to be CNS stimulants or psychostimulants. They act on the DA system as agonists by promoting and exacerbating the normal effects of DA or DA receptor binding. In Chapter 10 you will learn about the value of DA antagonists in the treatment of schizophrenia.

Now that we've covered the characterization and pharmacology of the catecholamines, let us consider the functions associated with these transmitter substances. As just mentioned, DA may regulate the psychological symptoms associated with schizophrenia (Chapter 10), and DA transporters have been implicated in attention-deficit/hyperactivity disorder (Chapter 6). Dopaminergic cell bodies in the substantia nigra, however, control movement, with their disruption leading to Parkinson's disease and related symptoms (discussed further in Chapter 6). Finally, DA pathways involving the nucleus accumbens and linked areas manage the brain's reward circuit (Chapter 11), reinforcing behavior that may be good or bad for the individual.

Functions of the NE system include attention, orienting, reward, analgesia, hunger, thirst, and other motivations (Julien, 2007). In subsequent chapters you will learn that disruptions of this system may be involved in stress-related disorders, such as posttraumatic stress disorder, as well as other disorders like depression (Cooper et al., 1996; Feldman & Quenzer, 1984; Julien, 2007).

Serotonin. The study of **serotonin** (or **5-hydroxytryptamine** [5-HT]) stretches back further than the study of some of the other substances discussed. In the 1950s, serotonin was synthesized from the stomach and identified as 5-HT. Preparations made from the gut yielded a concoction that had the ability to stimulate gastric secretions such as mucus while suppressing gastric acids, complementing observations of similar nervous effects of endogenous release of serotonin from the duodenum.

At first, the peripheral substance was given the name "enteramine," and the substance derived from blood platelets (the original source of this mysterious substance for experimentation) was called "serotonin." As analytical

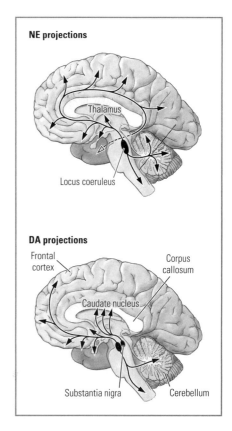

Figure 5.4
NE projections. The preponderance of norepinephrine (NE) and dopamine (DA) projections suggests tight regulation of both behavior and thought (cognition).
AFTER ZIGMOND ET AL., 1999, P. 208

serotonin (or 5-hydroxytryptamine [5-HT]) A major neurotransmitter involved in mood, aggression, and appetite regulation.

tryptophan The amino acid from which the neurotransmitter serotonin is derived. The availability of tryptophan in the extracellular fluid of neurons regulates the synthesis of serotonin.

5-hydroxyindole acetic acid (5-HIAA) A metabolic breakdown product of serotonin (5-HT). Found in the cerebrospinal fluid, 5-HIAA is the main metabolite of serotonin.

apparatus improved, chemists realized that enteramine and serotonin were one and the same, 5-HT. Adding to the data from the gut were observations wherein metabolism of serotonin was identified in the rat brain. Thus, serotonin was recognized as a potential neurotransmitter substance with diverse functions.

Serotonin shares with the catecholamines a relatively simple series of metabolic steps that leads to its synthesis. Because serotonin cannot easily cross the blood–brain barrier, CNS neurons possess the capacity to manufacture it readily, depending on the adequate and timely supply of its basic amino acid, **tryptophan.** The process begins with the entry of diet-derived tryptophan into the neuron. (Because the system is very sensitive to levels of tryptophan, diet—especially foods rich in tryptophan such as milk, bananas, and turkey—can have significant effects on the production of serotonin. You think what you eat.)

In the process of manufacturing serotonin, after the serotonergic cells collect tryptophan from the CNS circulatory system, it is transformed by the enzyme tryptophan hydroxylase into 5-hydroxytryptophan (5-HTP). A second enzyme, aromatic amino acid decarboxylase (AADC), metabolizes 5-HTP into the final product, serotonin. Again, any interruption of these enzymatic reactions alters the brain's serotonin levels.

Once synthesized, serotonin resembles the ideal or classical neurotransmitter: It follows many of the same principles for neurotransmitters in general. It is moved about and stored in the vesicles by means of a serotonin transporter that is similar to the one utilized in the catecholamine neuron. The vesicles reside in the terminal portion of the axon near their docking and release sites on the inner perimeter of the presynaptic membrane. There, they await the depolarizing signal and the consequent docking and exocytosis of the stored serotonin. The release of serotonin is also under the marked control of autoreceptors which, being intimately responsive to feedback, modulate its production and release. Such regulation produces a delicately balanced system that is extremely sensitive to changes and that may contribute to the labile nature of some serotonin-regulated responses.

To date, at least 18 serotonin receptors have been identified in eight subtype families, designated 5-HT_1–5-HT_8, and with further subtypes A–D; and this remains an active area of research. One receptor subtype, the 5-HT_{1A} receptor, acts as both postsynaptic receptor and presynaptic autoreceptor, governing serotonin release. The 5-HT_3 receptor subtype is ionotropic, whereas the remaining ones are metabotropic, utilizing G proteins to effect their postsynaptic potentials. Serotonin's effects on postsynaptic neurons are mainly inhibitory, as are the accumulated effects of serotonin-like drugs. The differentiation of receptor subtypes and their stimulation have ramifications for the therapeutic value of any serotonin analog.

Following its discharge and receptor binding, two primary mechanisms, reuptake and enzymatic degradation, inactivate any excess serotonin. Again, these events are similar to those for the catecholamines. The surplus serotonin is removed from the synapse by a specific transporter located on the presynaptic neuronal membrane called the "serotonin transporter" (SERT). This molecular 18-wheeler conveys the serotonin back into the presynaptic neuron. Once there, the serotonin undergoes enzymatic degradation by means of the enzyme MAO. The catabolic reaction eventually produces **5-hydroxyindole acetic acid (5-HIAA)**, which is often used as an after-the-fact marker for serotonin activity in neuroscience studies.

Focusing on 5-HT distribution in the brain, there is a great concentration of serotonin-containing cell bodies in the brain stem area known as the "raphe nuclei." These neurons send extensive projections to many other parts of the brain, including the forebrain, hippocampus, thalamus, hypothalamus, cerebellum, and midbrain (substantia nigra and ventral tegmental area). There are large concentrations of cell bodies in the pons and medulla that send long axonal tendrils to the dorsal horn of the spinal cord. The brain receives multiple serotonin inputs, mediating CNS activities and outputs (Figure 5.5).

Serotonin influences many different behaviors. In general, reports have it mediating the following activities: body temperature, respiration, blood pressure, hormone release (growth hormone, adrenocorticotropic hormone [ACTH], prolactin, luteinizing hormone), uterine activities, arousal and attention, food intake, mood, aggression, nociception, and sleep and dreaming (Cooper et al., 1996; Hardman, Limbird, & Gilman, 2001; Julien, 2007). Several physiological effects of serotonin alterations can be seen in the sometimes fatal 3,4-methylenedioxymethamphetamine (MDMA, or Ecstasy)–induced serotonin syndrome described in Box 5.1.

The wide number of serotonin agonists and antagonists is impressive and growing all the time as new receptor subtypes are uncovered. We will discuss only a few of each. One of the most popular agonists is the antidepressant fluoxetine, also known as Prozac. It is a selective serotonin reuptake inhibitor (SSRI). As the name describes, it disables the reuptake mechanisms, thereby allowing serotonin to remain in the synapse for longer (similar to what cocaine does to the DA transporter; Figure 5.6). As you will see in Chapter 9, these SSRIs have revolutionized the treatment of conditions such as depression (although, as we will see, based on a paucity of hard data). Also, because serotonin is a monoamine along with NE and DA,

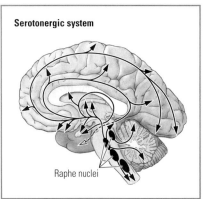

Figure 5.5
Serotonergic projections.
With cell bodies embedded in deep neural structures and long axonal projections emanating outward, serotonin exerts strong regulation over the brain's activities.

AFTER ZIGMOND ET AL., 1999, P. 211

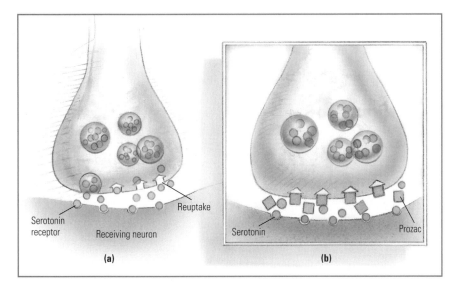

(a)   (b)

Figure 5.6
SSRI mechanism. Certain antidepressants operate through a selective serotonin reuptake inhibition (SSRI) mechanism. In this example showing fluoxetine (Prozac), serotonin is being released into the synapse and its reuptake is slowed by the drug having blocked sites into the presynaptic neuron, thereby prolonging the effects of the synapse-bound neurotransmitter.

Box 5.1

Brain Matters

MDMA: Ecstasy or Agony for the Brain?

Beginning in the 1970s, some psychiatrists used MDMA (3,4-methylenedioxymethamphetamine) as a legal adjunctive, or supplemental, therapy for psychoanalysis because it induces an altered state of consciousness accompanied by enhanced sensual overtones. Eventually, MDMA became available as a recreational drug known as Ecstasy. Although this later became a controlled substance (illegal for recreational purposes), in 1988 Ecstasy continued to be used as a recreational substance (Valentine, 2002). In 2001, 9.2% of high school seniors reported using Ecstasy, and over 4,000 Ecstasy-related emergency room visits were reported in 2000 (National Institute of Drug Abuse, 2001).

What is the appeal of Ecstasy? An oral dose of about 100 mg is known to produce heightened pleasure and a boost in self-confidence that may lead to extroversion and a feeling of excitement. These effects typically peak about 15–30 minutes following administration of the dose with a duration of about 3–4 hours (Valentine, 2002).

But the effects are not all pleasurable. Ecstasy also causes hyperactivity and hyperthermia in some users and, in extreme cases, death (Gore, 1999). The increased use of this drug at warm, overcrowded parties and dance clubs can lead to an exacerbation of the drug-related effects sometimes known as the "serotonin syndrome" (characterized by restlessness, tremors, and altered mental status). Other side effects include confusion, depression, anxiety, paranoia, sleep disruptions, muscle tension, nausea, involuntary teeth clenching, rapid eye movement, chills, and sweating.

Known as a hallucinogenic amphetamine, MDMA doesn't regularly induce hallucinations and it is not a strong psychostimulant as are other amphetamine drugs. Psychopharmacologically, the direct effect of MDMA is difficult to pinpoint because of its lack of neurochemical specificity. For example, Ecstasy increases synaptic serotonin levels and then leads to prolonged serotonin depletion due to the blocking of serotonin reuptake. To a lesser extent, MDMA also promotes dopamine release and subsequent decreases in reuptake. And making the picture even more complicated, MDMA has a high affinity for certain noradrenergic transporters. Knowing the involvement of these three different neurotransmitters, it is likely that serotonergic alterations lead to symptoms related to altered anxiety, sleep, and temperature modifications; dopamine influences may lead to increased confidence, pleasure, and excitement, and noradrenergic alterations may lead to the symptoms seen in sympathetic arousal (Hatzidimitrious, McCann, & Ricaurte, 1999; Valentine, 2002).

Scientists have debated whether acute or chronic use of MDMA leads to long-term brain effects. MDMA use has been associated with serotonergic neurotoxicity, shown by shorter processes in animals. Amazingly, even 7 years after being given a 4-day dosing regimen of MDMA, primates continued to show serotonergic neuronal deficits (Hatzidimitrious et al., 1999).

In human Ecstasy users, memory deficit is a common effect (Parrott, Lees, Garnham, Jones, & Wesnes, 1998). Additionally, using functional magnetic resonance imaging scans, MDMA users had smaller parietal and striatal cortices (Daumann et al., 2003). In a study focusing on adolescent use of MDMA, Ecstasy users had impaired attention and altered functioning in the left hippocampus (Jacobsen, Mencl, Pugh, Skudlarski, & Krystal, 2003). More recently, brain imaging of low-dose users of Ecstasy indicated lower cerebral blood flow in the globus pallidus and putamen as well as alterations in the thalamus and frontoparietal white matter (de Win et al., 2008).

In sum, although "ecstasy" is defined as intense joy, a convergence of evidence suggests that the effects of the drug on the user's brain fail to live up to its name. The rash of negative psychological and physiological side effects, accompanied by research suggesting neurotoxicity, add up to agony instead of ecstasy for the consumer's brain. Although human studies focusing on drug use are often problematic because of the polydrug-use histories of many subjects, the convergence of evidence suggests that Ecstasy likely threatens the health of the brain. Consequently, the continued high number of MDMA users (an estimated 750,000 tablets consumed in New York and New Jersey each weekend) are engaging in a very risky neuroscientific experiment until there is further clarification of the effects of this drug on brain functioning (Valentine, 2002).

MAOIs affect this neurotransmitter as well. As previously mentioned, MAO degrades serotonin, DA, and NE and its effect is reversed by MAOIs.

The number of antagonists available for serotonin is equally impressive. The main ones are exemplified by lysergic acid diethylamide (LSD). Evidence exists that LSD blocks specific serotonin receptors (5-HT$_1$ and 5-HT$_2$), preventing serotonin from binding. (There is also evidence that LSD is a serotonin agonist, so the serotonin road must be traveled with great caution.) The vivid hallucinations LSD produces have been suggested to mimic the hallucinations we have all experienced under more licit conditions: the dreams of the average sleeper (though differences abound). The hallucinations that occur with LSD overlap with those experienced by the schizophrenic patient. Hence, serotonin involvement in that disease has been intensively studied.

Amino Acid Transmitters

Although the "traditional" neurotransmitters (ACh, DA, NE, 5-HT, and so on) are very important in regulating behavior and understanding the mechanisms of psychoactive drugs, these substances are not as prevalent in the brain as the amino acid transmitters. Small amino acid molecules serve as neurotransmitters for all the other neuron populations in the brain.

Excitatory amino acid. Although aspartate and **glutamate** (Glu) are the principal excitatory neurotransmitters in the brain, most of the research has been directed toward Glu. For that reason, we focus on Glu in this discussion. Receptors for Glu can be found on most neurons, suggesting an important regulatory role for this excitatory substance. The Glu neurons are represented by, and have been mainly studied in, cortical pyramidal neurons, where they reside in complementary GABAergic company (the inhibitor neurotransmitter described shortly). These neurons, as well as the majority found throughout the brain, are projection neurons with long and proliferated axons, indicating diverse regulation by the cortex. The study of Glu has been intense recently, and it has been implicated in a variety of clinical neuroscientific conditions.

The neurotransmitter Glu is derived from a nonessential amino acid, and it is synthesized during the body's normal utilization of the sugar glucose, adding to both the ease of the reactions involved and their ubiquity. Also, glutamate serves as the precursor for **gamma-aminobutyric acid (GABA)**; specifically, the enzyme glutamic acid decarboxylase (GAD) acts on glutamate to form GABA (Julien, 2007). The role of glial cells (astrocytes) in the synthesis and control of Glu is very strong and intertwined (literally) with neuronal synthesis. One precursor for Glu is glutamine, which is produced in large pools in the glia. The glutamine leaves the glia and travels to the terminal boutons, where it is converted by means of the enzyme glutaminase into Glu. From there it is stored in vesicles that, when depolarized, react to the influx of calcium with release of their contents.

Once released into the synapse, Glu activates one of a number of receptors that are either ionotropic or metabotropic. Each of the two types of receptors (there are subtypes as well) regulates different postsynaptic events. For example, there are three ionotropic subtypes: N-**methyl-d-aspartate** (**NMDA**), **kainate**, and **alpha-amino hydroxy-methyl-isoxazolepropionate** (**AMPA**). For the metabotropic receptors, there are two forms,

glutamate (Glu) A principal excitatory neurotransmitter that regulates cortical and subcortical functions.

gamma-aminobutyric acid (GABA) An amino acid that acts as an inhibitory neurotransmitter in the central nervous system.

N-methyl-d-aspartate (NMDA) receptors A subtype of glutamate receptor that uses both Na$^+$ and Ca^{2+} influx to mediate its effects.

kainite receptor A subgroup of glutamate receptors whose functional role is not clearly understood but which has been related to hippocampal plasticity.

alpha-amino hydroxy-methyl-isoxazolepropionate (AMPA) receptor A subtype of glutamate receptor in which Na$^+$ influx causes an excitatory postsynaptic potential (EPSP).

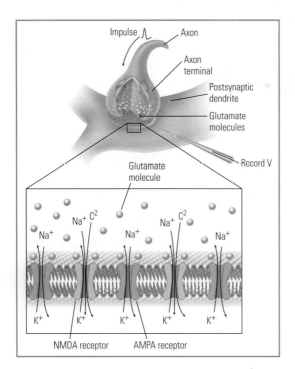

Figure 5.7
NMDA/AMPA receptors. As the excitatory neurotransmitter glutamate (Glu) is released into the synapse, it binds to so-called NMDA (Na^+ and Ca^{2+} ionic influx) and AMPA (Na^+ ionic influx)–gated channels, both of which produce excitatory postsynaptic potentials.

AFTER BEAR, CONNORS, & PARADISO, 1996, FIGURE 6.8

neurotoxicity Neural damage due to some threat presented to the nervous tissue such as toxins, low oxygen, and decreased glucose.

cleverly named metabotropic-1 and metabotropic-2 (Dr. Seuss's Thing 1 and Thing 2 spring to mind...). It is of some interest that in many sites in the brain, AMPA and NMDA receptors are co-localized (Figure 5.7). Further, NMDA receptors are distributed throughout many areas of the brain and spinal cord, especially in the cerebral cortex and hippocampus.

One of the major roles for Glu in the CNS is in the regulation of cortical and subcortical functions, particularly those associated with cognitive activities. There is significant Glu regulation in the hippocampus, with the aforementioned AMPA and NMDA receptors implicated in brain plasticity and learning and memory processes (as discussed in Connections). Accordingly, the large neuroscience product firm Cortex Pharmaceuticals has developed Ampakine to improve cognitive impairment seen in conditions such as Alzheimer's disease. As the name implies, this drug purportedly enhances AMPA receptor activity.

Overexcitation of NMDA receptors is thought to lead to **neurotoxicity**, especially following brain injury such as ischemia (decreased oxygen). It is the constellation of effects regulated by Glu that has convinced neuroscientists that schizophrenia, especially the cognitive complications of the disorder, may involve a glutamatergic facet. Of the agonistic drugs known to affect Glu regulation, the barbiturates bind to AMPA-type receptors, whereas the volatile gas nitrous oxide and the drug phencyclidine (PCP) have antagonist effects at the NMDA receptor. Other effects mediated by the Glu system include those associated with food allergies. For instance, some individuals with a taste for Chinese or other Asian foods find themselves in gustatory heaven (as a result of the actions on the taste buds of foods laced with monosodium glutamate [MSG]), only to experience the aftereffects of dizziness and swelling, also due to the (allergic) effects of the MSG (Julien, 2007).

Inhibitory amino acids. Whereas Glu is the principal excitatory neurotransmitter, GABA is considered the principal inhibitory CNS transmitter. Although opposite in function, the production of both amino acid neurotransmitters is similar: GABA is actually formed from Glu. Initially, one of the features that intrigued scientists working with GABA was its wide and apparently diverse distribution across regions and sites in the mammalian brain. This widespread scattering of GABA neurons and regulation is due, in part, to its intraneuronal and extraneuronal synthesis, which involves glucose metabolism.

Like other neurotransmitters, GABA is stored in vesicles at the terminal end of the axon, awaiting docking and release following the receipt of the action potential. Once it is released into the synapse, it binds to several different postsynaptic receptors. The primary GABA receptor is the GABA$_A$ receptor, which is associated with the chloride (Cl^-) ion channels. When a molecule of GABA binds to this receptor, the Cl^- channels open and there is an influx of Cl^- into the intracellular space. The rapid influx of this negative ion causes hyperpolarization of the postsynaptic neuron (the poles, negative and positive, get farther apart), and the neuron is made significantly more negative. It is consequently harder to get it to fire. Hence, GABA is inhibitory. Autoreception and regulation of neuronal activity are accomplished by means of the $GABA_B$ receptor, found on axon terminals. The presence of autoreceptors for GABA ensures the rapid regulation of GABA release from the presynaptic neuron; that is, a reduction in the amount of GABA that is released.

The exocytosed (released into the synapse) GABA bound neither to postsynaptic receptors nor to the autoreceptors on the presynaptic neuron undergoes removal from the synaptic cleft by an interesting mechanism. It has been documented that the released GABA is taken up by contiguous neurons and glia, mainly astrocytes. Further, the recycling and utilization of the expended GABA (given its glucose antecedents) provide raw materials for the manufacture of additional glial and neuronal products. As glucose usage is the foundation on which neuronal activity is based, glia that harvest glucose from expended transmitters seem to be engaged in an efficient and necessary strategy.

Following the release of GABA, the main mechanism by which the neurotransmitter is inactivated is through reuptake back into the presynaptic neuron. The reentry is accomplished through multiple GABA transporters (GATs), the different versions of which may be due to their distribution on various neurites and on glia. There is also enzymatic degradation of GABA accomplished by means of the enzyme GABA-oxoglutarate transaminase (GABA-T).

GABA is inhibitory in many preparations and under a variety of experimental conditions. The concentration of GABAergic neurons is very high in the cortex, the most recently evolved area of the brain, which reinforces the persistence of inhibitory functions throughout the evolution of the brain. Recent work discusses the presence of long axonal GABAergic projections from the cortex to other, distant regions of the brain such as the hippocampus, striatum, and thalamus, literally demonstrating the "reach" of GABA and its involvement in such events as stress, learning, and anxiety (Leuner & Gould, 2010).

Another arena in which the GABA system and its regulation have been implicated is seizure and epileptic activity. As this activity represents misfiring of the electrical activity of the brain, with outwardly spreading neural waves, the seizure moves rapidly from its initial localized site to incorporate other areas of the brain. It is usually a chronic and maddeningly intermittent condition that occurs with a rapid commencement and from which the sufferer has little respite. GABA has been shown to regulate some seizure activity, and its augmentation in regions such as the amygdala and the hippocampus can ameliorate seizure activity.

Drugs that affect GABA are also those that have myriad significant effects in humans, causing well-known and well-described behavioral events. For instance, **benzodiazepines** and **barbiturates** are significant GABA agonists, leading to relaxation and sedation (Cooper et al., 1996).

Perhaps the most popular drug that interacts with GABA is alcohol. This drug, as ubiquitous as it is abused, has an affinity for both GABA and glutamate receptors. Focusing on the former for now, alcohol augments the inhibitory effects of GABA by increasing the influx of Cl^- ions in neurons.

benzodiazepines A class of drugs (usually of the tranquilizer variety) that increases the frequency of Cl^- channel openings in the presence of GABA.

barbiturates Psychoactive drugs that act as CNS depressants, producing a wide array of effects ranging from relaxation to coma.

glycine (Gly) An excitatory amino acid that mediates most CNS synapses along with glutamate and GABA.

In essence, alcohol adds more inhibition to an inhibitory system. Hence, the characteristic effects of alcohol consumption include dampening of cognitive and motor skills, sedation, and motor relaxation. And following excessive consumption, there is a failure to recognize that these impairments exist because the intoxicated individual's judgment is significantly impaired (evidenced by the overwhelming number of alcohol-related car accidents in the United States).

Whereas GABA is the primary inhibitory neurotransmitter for the brain (cortex and subcortical structures), **glycine (Gly)** is the major inhibitory neurotransmitter for the brain stem, spinal cord, and retina. Of interest because of its wide distribution in bodily fluids, Gly plays a vital but circumscribed role in CNS activity compared with GABA. Because of its limited CNS activity and the fact that it is found exclusively in vertebrates, Gly has been difficult to characterize experimentally.

A clear role for Gly in neurotransmission was slow in coming, and information is still being marshaled about the activities of this substance. Werman, Davidoff, and Aprison (1968) demonstrated a strong inhibitory effect of Gly in cat spinal neurons (in particular, interneurons and the regulation of their associated motor neurons). Radioactive localization studies have placed Gly in the terminal boutons of spinal interneurons, where it exerts its downstream hyperpolarization effects. These effects, like those for GABA, involve the rapid influx of Cl⁻ into the intracellular space through activation of the Cl⁻ channel. The fate of Gly once released into the synapse—whether set on by enzymes or drawn back into the presynaptic neuron by means of specific channels or whatever—is not clear. Therefore, even though not much is known about Gly relative to the other neurotransmitters, its inhibitory actions and regions/site of action are clear. The potent poison strychnine, a culprit in many a murder mystery novel, is a potent Gly antagonist. So is the tetanus bacterium, which works by long-term blockade of the receptors for Gly. Anyone acquainted with this affliction, known as "lockjaw," will attest to the graphic appropriateness of the term: Blockade of the actions of Gly results in hyperstimulation of the motor neuron junction and a *tetanic* effect, that is, the inability of the muscles to relax. The muscles of the face, especially of the mouth, lock in a closed grimace. Still, the grotesque and deadly ramifications of infection of the Gly system, ironically, shed some light on the function of this amino acid neurotransmitter.

Neuropeptides and Neurohormones

As mentioned earlier, novel neuropeptides are being identified each year, and it is becoming increasingly difficult to keep up with their names and functions. Obviously, we cannot cover them all in this chapter, but we want to introduce a few key neuropeptides that have demonstrable functional significance for mental health: endogenous opioids, oxytocin, and vasopressin. As you read through this section, you will notice that each chemical is also considered a neurohormone since all are secreted by neuronal tissue into the circulatory system. Corticotropin-releasing hormone, a neuropeptide that is also categorized as a neurohormone, is described in the neurochemical stress response section.

Endogenous opioids. Humans, ever the curious sort, seem to have exploited nature's chemical gifts for as long as there has been nature. For instance, the curative and other properties of opium and its relatives, which are synthesized from an extract of opium poppies, have been known for millennia. The Greeks celebrated it in literature that endures today: In Homer's *Odyssey* (not a *Simpsons* episode), an inconsolable Odysseus imbibes an opium-laced tankard offered him by a daughter of Zeus. The Greeks appreciated the real-life effects of opiates, too, as references to them appeared in medical writings like those of the Greek philosopher Theophrastus (circa third century BCE). Notwithstanding such use, whereas opiate products (opium, morphine, codeine, heroin, and so on) have caused misery to many who have abused them, there are positives to sober opium use. Opium was used for centuries as a treatment for dysentery and other maladies, and the development of the morphine derivatives has proved to be a boon to the patient or soldier suffering intractable pain. Ironically, the opiates and their effects have been around for thousands of years, yet the research to understand and control them is a relatively new venture.

Collectively referred to as the **endogenous opioids**, the term merits some discussion. Given the long history of human familiarity with opiate drugs and the many effects attributed to them, it was clear that they worked on the brain—but how? The drugs had very powerful properties, suggesting that the brain had some inherent sensitivity or even receptors for these plant alkaloids (derived from the poppy, which raises some fascinating questions regarding our origins). It was not clear, however, that the brain manufactured an endogenous substance that matched the receptors for the exogenous variety of opiate drugs. It was like having a teeming key ring containing a wide array of diversely shaped keys but not knowing which one fit which locks or how. There was an effect and a cause, but everything in between was a mystery. Not until the early 1970s were the receptors and their brain-manufactured ligand elucidated, a set of discoveries that revolutionized the neurosciences and the pharmacological industry. Actually solving this mystery took the work and dedication of many talented scientists, primary among them Solomon Snyder and Candace Pert, and earned their discoverers the prestigious Albert Lasker Basic Medical Research Award. Within a pretty short time frame in the early 1970s, natural opiate receptors were identified and characterized. This discovery led to the identification of a natural endorphin substance that is involved in pain and emotional processing (Bear et al., 1996).

There are three families of opioid peptides, the **endorphins** (endogenous morphines), the enkephalins, and the dynorphins. All are derived from a different long-chain amino acid precursor: pro-opiomelanocortin (POMC), proenkephalin, and prodynorphin, respectively. Unlike the situation for classical neurotransmitters, the neuropeptides are neither synthesized using direct enzymatic oversight nor synthesized locally, at the terminal ends of the axon. Instead, the gene product, the prohormone, is the precursor to the individual neuropeptide that is being manufactured, and the final product is moved by slow axonal transport down to the bouton. As discussed earlier, neurotransmitters act quickly, and their effects dissipate quickly. For neuropeptides, the effects take longer to occur and they last longer. For the neurons that contain and release neuropeptides, the process to increase production of the substance requires genomic involvement (increase in expression) and the slow transport outlined earlier. Again, this requires time.

endogenous opioids Naturally occurring neurotransmitter-like substances found in the brain that produce analgesic and euphoric effects similar to heroin and morphine.

endorphin An opioid-like substance produced in the hypothalamus and elsewhere that is related to pain reduction and reward but also facilitates the release of epinephrine from the adrenal medulla during the stress response.

oxytocin A posterior pituitary neuropeptide involved in complementary activities such as bonding, sexual behavior, and childbirth.

Figure 5.8
Pituitary releasing oxytocin and vasopressin. The posterior pituitary is a repository for neuropeptides, such as oxytocin and vasopressin, that are produced in the hypothalamus. The posterior pituitary then regulates the release of these substances following receipt of releasing signals from the hypothalamus.

AFTER ROSENZWEIG, BREEDLOVE & LEIMAN, 2002

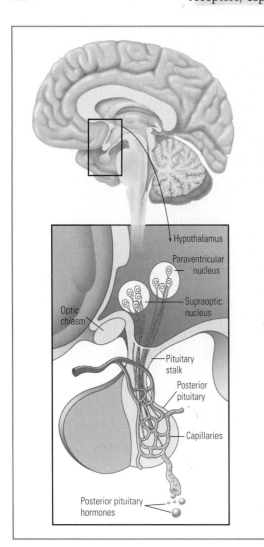

A variety of receptors and receptor subtypes have been identified for the opioids, each regulating slightly different responses. The various opioids may bind to different receptors with different affinities, bringing about a Rubik's Cube of different effects and behaviors. For instance, the opiate agonist morphine binds to mu receptors with very high affinity and to kappa receptors with less affinity but to neither delta nor sigma receptors. The opioid antagonist naloxone, a highly effective treatment for opiate (heroin and others) overdose, for example, has a high affinity for the mu receptor, where it not only blocks an opiate's effects but actively displaces the opiate from the receptor, thereby preventing further deleterious opiate receptor activation.

Once the opioid has been released and recovery from the synaptic event is under way, there is little evidence that traditional reuptake mechanisms are in place to inactivate the opioids. The major sources of inactivation of levels of synaptic opioids include enzymatic degradation and the passive process of diffusion.

There are numerous agonists for the opioids. For instance, morphine, codeine, heroin, and meperidine (Demerol) are strong agonists for the various receptors, especially mu and kappa. The effects generated by these agonists are many. At the mu receptor, the effects brought about include analgesia, euphoria, and respiratory depression (a common cause of death in cases of overdose). At the kappa receptor, the effects are analgesia, *dysphoria* (emotional lows), and respiratory depression. Recent work has established that more complex behaviors may be under the regulation of endogenous opioid systems. Research conducted by Robert Bridges and his colleagues has revealed that the display of maternal behavior is under regulation by the endogenous opioid system (Byrnes & Bridges, 2000; Byrnes, Rigero, & Bridges, 2000; Gulledge, Mann, Bridges, Bialos, & Hammer, 2000; Mann, Foltz, Rigero, & Bridges, 1999). As you will read in Box 5.2, opioid-like substances have been found in the urine of children suffering from autism and may play a causal role in some of the autistic symptoms.

Oxytocin. The famous British physician Sir Henry Dale spearheaded the study of **oxytocin** in the modern era (the last 100 years or so). His studies on posterior pituitary lobe function were difficult to perform. Because of its physical location—tucked away in a small bony enclave at the base of the brain—the pituitary gland is hard to get to for experimental purposes. In the process of studying feline uterine contractions, however, Dale chanced on the observation that posterior pituitary extracts could cause striking contractions of the uterus. He reasoned that the posterior pituitary manufactured/released some substance involved in uterine contractions and expulsion of the fetus. Thus, he discovered one of oxytocin's major peripheral effects.

The fact that oxytocin is released by hypothalamic neurons that extend to the posterior pituitary makes this substance a neurohormone. Specifically, exocytosis of oxytocin into the capillaries of the posterior pituitary occurs when

Labels in figure:
Hypothalamus
Paraventricular nucleus
Supraoptic nucleus
Optic chiasm
Pituitary stalk
Posterior pituitary
Capillaries
Posterior pituitary hormones

an action potential arrives at the terminal bouton of the oxytocin neuron. The expressed oxytocin then travels from the posterior pituitary area (Figure 5.8) into the extensive vascular and blood supply that surrounds the pituitary. From there it traverses the entire body, binding to receptors on the membranes of target organs or neural sites, for example, the uterus, mammary glands, and some selective brain regions like the hippocampus. Once oxytocin is released, something akin to a refractory period occurs, during which replenishment of oxytocin stores happens as the system resets itself. The postrelease consequences of oxytocin as it diffuses through the body serve to terminate its actions.

Oxytocin targets a fascinating array of regions, ranging from basic motivations to more complex behaviors and systems. It affects the reproductive organs, like the uterus and mammary glands, where contraction leads, respectively, to expulsion of the term infant (on average) and milk ejection. Oxytocin also stimulates orgasm in the female (by effecting vaginal contractions) and orgasm and ejaculation in the male, again through its effects on contracting muscles. Other research has implicated oxytocin in social bonding. Oxytocin receptors are more numerous in species that demonstrate pair-bonds—such as the prairie vole—than in those that do not. Research on this theory (Bales & Carter, 2003; Ferguson, Aldag, Insel, & Young, 2001; Francis, Young, Meaney, & Insel, 2002; Insel, Gingrich, & Young, 2001) has yielded some fascinating data suggesting that oxytocin may underlie the familial and warm feelings that we all have toward our loved ones. For this reason, oxytocin has been dubbed by some the "cuddle chemical." Further, fascinating work by Tomizawa and colleagues (2003) demonstrates that the learning and memory improvements that have been reported as a function of maternal experience and parity may be attributable to oxytocin's reorganization of the neuronal structure and relationships within the hippocampus. The neurobiology of maternal affiliation, therefore, is certainly regulated by neurochemistry, and these studies are the first steps toward elucidating the neurochemical path. More about the role of oxytocin in stress reduction is discussed in Chapter 12.

Vasopressin. **Arginine vasopressin** (AVP, also known as antidiuretic hormone or ADH) is another interesting neurohormone released by the posterior pituitary. Not only is this substance released in close proximity to oxytocin, it is also very close phylogenetically to oxytocin. AVP shares seven of nine amino acids with oxytocin. Both neuropeptides are synthesized by the hypothalamus, and the products are carried to the posterior pituitary via axonal transport, where they are stored and released into the circulation by means of the aforementioned intimate vascularization that embraces the so-called master gland (see Figure 5.8). An interesting feature of the two neuropeptides is their exclusive localization in mammals. Both appear to play roles in the social aspects of mammalian behavior (Albers & Bamshad, 1998; Insel et al., 2001; Insel & Shapiro, 1992; Winslow, Hastings, Carter, Harbaugh, & Insel 1993) and hence, are necessary for the unique properties that make mammals mammals.

AVP plays multiple roles. Peripherally, it regulates the resorption of water by the distal tubules of the kidneys and controls the osmotic content (thickness) of blood. AVP acts by increasing the physiological permeability of the distal tubules to fluids. When released in greater amounts, AVP contracts arterioles and capillaries, thereby increasing blood pressure. Obviously, the peripheral functions of AVP are critical to maintaining homeostasis (of body fluids) within the body, but it is the central features of AVP that concern us

arginine vasopressin A neuropeptide that is secreted by the posterior pituitary gland and by nerve endings in the hypothalamus. It affects learning functions and water resorption in mammals.

Box 5.2

A Case in Point

Controversial Dietary Intervention for Autism: Karyn Seroussi's Struggle to Help Her Son

Karyn Seroussi's son, Miles, seemed perfectly normal for the first 15 months of his life. Then, all of a sudden, he stopped using the words he had recently acquired; started engaging in repetitive behaviors (such as filling up a cup with sand); stopped interacting with others, which included pointing and maintaining eye contact; began dragging his head across the floor; and developed a chronic case of diarrhea. Seroussi, a business owner, and her husband, a PhD chemist, were heartbroken when they were told that their son suffered from autism. Although Seroussi didn't know much about this condition at the time, she was told that her son would probably never be able to make friends, engage in social conversations, participate in a normal classroom environment, or live independently.

After the shock wore off, Seroussi started reading voraciously and became intrigued by a theory suggesting that milk consumption might be related to autism. She recalled that Miles was developing perfectly normally while he was drinking soy milk (he didn't seem to tolerate her breast milk well) but started developing autistic symptoms shortly after being switched to cow's milk. Also intriguing was the fact that he seemed to crave milk, often drinking a half-gallon per day. Seroussi soon learned of a possible theoretical connection between dairy products and autism. Jaak Panksepp,

a behavioral neuroscientist working at Bowling Green State University at the time, had previously written about how young rats chronically treated with opiates exhibited symptoms similar to those observed in autism. For example, pain insensitivity, communication deficits, and little evidence of curiosity were observed in the rats—all symptoms similar to those observed in autism (Panksepp, 1998).

After reading Panksepp's work, Seroussi learned that the urine of some children with autism contained metabolic products of the milk protein (casein) that had opioid characteristics. Could Miles's consumption of dairy products be the cause of his autistic symptoms? Could his craving for milk actually be a craving for opioids? Could milk, the substance advertised as doing "a body good," actually be causing brain damage in her son? After all, autistic children's brains had been observed to have abnormalities such as a smaller cerebellum and brain stem, a larger than normal cerebrum, and excessive small neurons in the hippocampus, perhaps due to low levels of apoptosis (Panksepp, 1998). Ever the skeptic, Seroussi decided to test this hypothesis by taking Miles off dairy products. The results were dramatic. Soon after this diet commenced, he stopped dragging his head on the floor, started interacting with the outside world by pointing and establishing eye contact, and began the long process of reacquiring language. After learning that the protein gluten, found in wheat, rye, oats, and many packaged foods, also broke down into a harmful substance, she removed it as well from Miles's diet and found that her son's motor coordination improved and his language development continued to improve. At this point, although most of the pediatricians Seroussi

here. When administered to the CNS, AVP modulates various types of learning. Avoidance learning—mainly passive avoidance—is facilitated by AVP, and AVP also interferes with the extinction of avoidance learning (Kovacs, 1987). AVP infusions into the lateral septum of rats improve the memory for the cues of a conspecific, whereas an AVP antagonist into the same region interferes with such recall (Dantzer, Koob, Bluthe, & Le Moal, 1987, 1988). AVP has evolved to provide mammals with the ability to recognize members of the same species, same social group, and perhaps same family (Landgraf, Malkinson, Veale, Lederis, & Pittman, 2003). AVP has also been linked to autism and psychiatric conditions such as depression and schizophrenia (Insel, O'Brien, & Leckman, 1999). Its roles as we ascend the phylogenetic scale are yet to be elucidated and may prove to be important and vital to our understanding of brain interactions and human social behavior.

Therefore, both oxytocin and AVP have strong influences in the development of the social behaviors that characterize mammalian behavior. Larry Young,

visited refused to acknowledge the role of diet in Miles's improvement, she persisted with the diet, becoming a self-motivated expert in the area of diet and autism.

To Seroussi's delight, Miles continued to improve, eventually to the point that the doctor removed the autism diagnosis. Subsequently, Seroussi started a newsletter and a support organization called Autism Network for Dietary Intervention (ANDI) to help other parents looking for alternative treatments for their children's autistic symptoms. In 2000 she wrote a book, *Unraveling the Mystery of Autism and Pervasive Developmental Disorder* (updated in 2002). In her book, she discusses potential roles of immune functions, gastrointestinal health, and the value of behavioral therapies in the development and treatment of autism. At the time she wrote the book, Miles was continuing to progress normally—at age 6 he was in a normal first-grade class, was reading at a fourth-grade level, had many friends, frequently engaged in imaginative play with his older sister, and had just successfully played a part in his school play. More recently, at age 9, Miles tested in the intellectually gifted range. Seroussi told us that she was reminded of how far Miles had come one day when this once socially impaired, nonexpressive child told her, "Mom, I love you more than I can express; in fact, I love you even more than even a very expressive person could express."

As fascinating as Karyn Seroussi's story is, her results are, of course, based on a single case—that of her son—hardly an acceptable objective amount of data for a scientific conclusion. But case studies are valuable starting points in the development of hypotheses. Interest in the role of dietary and neurochemical imbalances in the brains of children suffering from autism has sparked more traditional empirical investigations. Karl Reichelt and his colleagues at Stavanger University College in Norway have found opioid peptides (exorphins) in the urine of autistic patients (Reichelt & Knivsberg, 2003) and both decreased autistic symptoms in patients on gluten-free and casein-free diets and a reappearance of autistic traits upon resuming consumption of these proteins (Knivsberg, Reichelt, & Nodland, 2001; Knivsberg, Reichelt, Hoien, & Nodland, 2002; Reichelt & Knivsberg, 2009). Further, scientists at the University of Rome La Sapienza also reported worsened neurological symptoms in autistic patients following the consumption of wheat and milk and decreased symptoms after the commencement of a restricted diet. Additionally, increased antibodies for casein were observed in autistic patients compared with a control group (Lucarelli et al., 1995). The research is not clear-cut though. One study reported increased essential amino acid deficiencies and lower levels of dietary neurotransmitter precursors such as tyrosine and tryptophan in children placed on the restricted diets (Arnold, Hyman, Mooney, & Kirby, 2003). When discussing the efficacy of dietary interventions for autism, the National Institute of Mental Health reminds parents that treatments need to be subjected to randomized, double-blind trials before they are accepted as proven treatments (National Institute of Mental Health, 2004). Regardless of what the future research tells us about the efficacy of this treatment for autism, it is important to consider dietary manipulations as another therapeutic window with the potential to alter neurochemicals and mental health.

at Emory University's Department of Psychiatry, has explored the effects of genetic manipulations of these systems in animal models. He has proposed that the genes underlying these neuropeptides and their respective receptors may have potential for a genetic model of treatment for disorders characterized by social deficits such as autism and social phobias (Young, 2001).

NEUROCHEMISTRY OF THE STRESS RESPONSE

Imagine the following scenario: It is a "dark and stormy night." You approach your front door with the wind howling, trees bending to its force, as you fumble for your keys. You hear what sounds like footsteps advancing toward you, then—suddenly—silence. Out of the corner of your eye, you catch the bushes moving. Is it the wind or . . . something else? You freeze in place, focused on the bushes. In that instant, your autonomic nervous system has shifted from parasympathetic homeostasis to sympathetic arousal. Heart pounding, respiration

fight-or-flight response The sympathetic branch of the autonomic nervous system triggers this response that prepares the animal to either fight the stressor or flee from the stressor.

corticotropin-releasing hormone (CRH) A releasing hormone produced in the hypothalamus that travels to the anterior pituitary, where it triggers the release of ACTH from the anterior pituitary.

adrenocorticotropic hormone (ACTH) A hormone released by the anterior pituitary which stimulates the adrenal gland to release glucocorticoids from the adrenal cortex. ACTH is a critical component of the hypothalamic–pituitary–adrenal (HPA) axis stress response.

peaking, attention focused, you must decide: Will you stay and face your fear or run away? Choose well: Your survival hangs in the balance.

Autonomic Stress Response

Physiologist Walter Cannon first described the neuroanatomical circuit underlying the stress response in 1914. He noted that the secretion of Epi and NE from the adrenal medulla and sympathetic nerves, respectively, enables an animal to mobilize its forces to survive a threat. He called this response, mediated by the sympathetic arm of the autonomic nervous system, the **fight-or-flight response**.

At this time, Cannon viewed the autonomic nervous system as controlling the various components of the body that maintain homeostasis, including body temperature and the body's pH and oxygen levels. These pertinent critical systems are maintained within a narrow range (Cannon, 1935; Lovallo, 1997; McEwen, 2000a). Viewing stress from a homeostatic perspective is especially important in the forthcoming discussions of stress disorders and coping with stress. Although the term homeostasis is an old and accepted one, the physiological principles it describes, such as maintaining optimal levels of oxygen for various brain activities, are vital for survival. More contemporary modifications of the homeostatic perspective, however, including an emphasis on allostasis are providing more comprehensive views of the stress response.

You will recall from Chapter 3 that after being activated by the hypothalamus, sympathetic nerves exit from the spinal column and project to virtually every organ, blood vessel, and sweat gland in the body (see Figure 3.2). We have even conserved an evolutionary sympathetic memory from our ancestors that leads to the development of goose bumps during sympathetic arousal. Animals that have fur on their bodies benefit from having their hair follicles stimulated because the fur standing on end leaves them looking larger and more intimidating should they choose the fight option of the sympathetic menu.

For us humans the effect is a little less dramatic—the almost invisible hair on our bodies serves as little protection against a potential assailant. Other effects of the sympathetic nervous system, however, including increased heart rate, blood pressure, metabolism, and respiration and decreased digestive and reproductive activity, facilitate our ability to face and survive a threat. All of these physiological effects enable an animal to mobilize its internal forces within seconds to successfully fight or flee, thereby enduring (Habib et al., 2001).

The sympathetic nervous system–induced piloerection displayed in this frightened cat (in this case, the true "scaredy cat") results in the appearance of a larger body, making the animal more intimidating to an approaching threatening opponent.

FRANK SITEMAN/STOCK, BOSTON

Hypothalamic–Pituitary–Adrenal Axis Response

When a stimulus is perceived as threatening, the hypothalamus responds by releasing hormones through the hypothalamic–pituitary circulatory system. As seen in Figure 5.9, the major releasing hormone, actually a neurohormone, **corticotropin-releasing hormone (CRH)**, is primarily manufactured in the paraventricular nucleus (PVN) of the hypothalamus and subsequently triggers the release of **adrenocorticotropic hormone (ACTH)** from the anterior portion of the pituitary gland.

CRH also inhibits the neurons involved in the secretion of reproductive hormones, leading to an inhibition of reproductive processes—which makes sense: Why be concerned with reproduction if you will not live beyond the next few minutes? The pituitary, the principal endocrine gland in the body, releases ACTH, which flows through the bloodstream and triggers the release of stress hormones called **glucocorticoids**, such as **cortisol**, from the adrenal cortex. Additionally, glucocorticoids levels are monitored at each step of this **hypothalamic–pituitary–adrenal (HPA) axis** (Figure 5.9). Whereas the sympathetic response occurs within seconds, the HPA axis requires minutes to be fully activated.

In addition to CRH, the hypothalamus releases β-endorphin, which mitigates pain reduction but also stimulates the release of Epi from the adrenal medulla. Finally, AVP is also released from the PVN of the hypothalamus and seems to facilitate the release of ACTH from the anterior pituitary. As you learned in the previous section, in times of severe stress, AVP plays an important role in regulating blood pressure (for example, by conserving body fluids; Habib et al., 2001).

Other Brain Areas Involved in the Stress Response

In addition to the two neurochemical stress circuits in the brain, the hippocampus, amygdala, locus coeruleus, and neocortex appear to play an integral role in stress responsivity.

The hippocampus. The hippocampus, a component of the limbic system noted for its involvement in emotional expression and memory formation, is a central brain structure for the stress response. The hippocampus has two types of adrenal steroid receptors—type I (mineralocorticoid), and type II (glucocorticoid) receptors. Together, when these receptors are activated, an abundance of neurophysiological events (for example, excitability and plasticity) take place in hippocampal neurons. In fact, Woolley, Gould, and McEwen (1990) found that 3 weeks of glucocorticoid injections led to less elaborate neuronal branching in the hippocampus. Thus, the stress hormones appear to restrict neuronal arborization.

A few years earlier, Uno, Tarrara, Else, Suleman, and Sapolsky (1989) found hippocampal damage in vervet monkeys that had died from prolonged exposure to severe social stress. The aforementioned

glucocorticoids Compounds that belong to the family of substances called corticosteroids. They affect metabolism and have anti-inflammatory and immunosuppressive effects.

cortisol The stress hormone secreted by the adrenal cortex in primates.

hypothalamic–pituitary–adrenal axis (HPA axis) The stress response originally described by Hans Selye, in which the hypothalamus secretes a releasing factor (CRH), which travels to the anterior pituitary and triggers the release of ACTH. ACTH then travels to the adrenal cortex, where it stimulates the release of glucocorticoids. Generally an adaptive response (in short bursts), this sequence and its aftermath help the animal produce enough energy to survive the impending stressor.

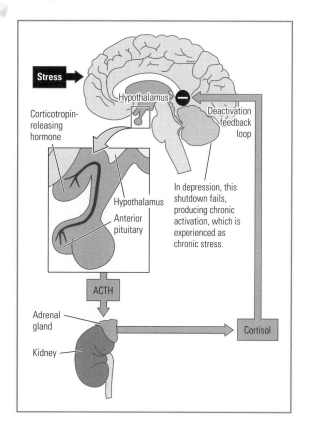

Figure 5.9
HPA axis. Everyone responds to stress differently. Once a stressful stimulus is perceived, however, the steps leading to the initiation of its response are similar for each individual because of the mechanism of the hypothalamic–pituitary–adrenal (HPA) axis. Through a series of releasing hormones (corticotropin-releasing hormone and adrenocorticotropic hormone [ACTH]) and eventual release of glucocorticoids from the adrenal cortex, there is a feedback loop onto the brain that enables regulation of (and sensitivity to) the response.

excitotoxicity An effect on cells (usually neurons) that results in damage or death due to overexcitation of the cell.

finding that just 3 weeks of chronic stress leads to neurological impairment is important as many of our human stressors exceed this duration. In reality, however, the data may be even more frightening—it may take even less time to start seeing the negative impact in the hippocampal neurons. It is important to note that not all restructuring is permanent; researchers have investigated the nature of damage that may be reversible (McEwen & Magarinos, 2001). Lambert and her colleagues (1998) observed hippocampal neural restructuring after just 6 days of chronic exposure to the activity–stress paradigm, which consists of increased activity combined with decreased availability of food.

Considerable research has been conducted to identify key neurochemicals involved in stress-induced hippocampal damage. The excitatory amino acid Glu plays a role, given the fact that an antiepileptic drug, phenytoin, which blocks Glu release, prevents the stress- and corticosterone-induced neuronal changes (Moghaddam, Boliano, Stein-Behrens, & Sapolsky, 1994). Additionally, drugs that block the Glu NMDA receptors also protect against hippocampal damage (Magarinos & McEwen, 1995; Cameron, McEwen & Gould, 1995; Watanabe, Weiland & McEwen, 1995).

Because cellular damage and death have been linked to excessive levels of Glu and overactivation of associated NMDA receptors, this process is sometimes known as **excitotoxicity**. The inhibitory neurotransmitter GABA also seems to play a role in stress-induced hippocampal damage. Benzodiazepine, a GABA agonist, blocks dendritic restructuring (Magarinos, Deslandes & McEwen, 1999). Additionally, serotonin plays a role in the demise of the hippocampal neurons during stress. An atypical antidepressant drug, tianeptine, which enhances serotonin uptake resulting in decreased extracellular levels of serotonin, has been found to reduce stress-induced dendritic shrinkage in tree shrews undergoing severe chronic stress (Czeh et al., 2001).

To date, no single mechanism has been identified as being the critical factor that leads to damaged CA3 pyramidal cells. Robert Sapolsky, of Stanford University, has written extensively about how possible actions initiated by glucocorticoids might lead to neuronal damage. He has suggested that glucocorticoid exposure leads to a metabolic vulnerability in the neurons, probably the result of an inhibition of glucose uptake. Further, it has been proposed that glucocorticoids exacerbate the damaging effects of excessive levels of Glu, oxygen radicals, and calcium mobilization. Glucocorticoids can lead to electrophysiological alterations that damage and disrupt the functions of neurotrophic (growth) factors in the hippocampus (Sapolsky, 1996; Yusim, Ajilore, Bliss, & Sapolsky, 2000). Although it is not clear if a reduction in neurogenesis might be related to hippocampal restructuring, psychosocial stress has been reported to reduce the production of new neurons in the tree shrew hippocampus (Gould, McEwen, Tanapat, Galea, & Fuchs, 1997).

Amygdala. Just as with the hippocampus, the amygdala, a second structure in the limbic system, also plays a significant role in an organism's response to stress (see Figure 3.13). Joseph LeDoux, working in the Center for Neural Science at New York University, has used a simple fear-conditioning model to identify the neural circuit underlying defensive behavior displayed by animals. As described in Chapter 8, the defensive

Robert Sapolsky

LINDA A. CICERO/STANFORD NEWS SERVICE

behaviors that interest LeDoux are innate and relatively hardwired responses to dangerous stimuli. These innate responses, however, involve the activation of several physiological systems including autonomic (for example, heart rate), endocrine (glucocorticoid release), and skeletal (freezing) systems.

According to LeDoux, the lateral amygdala is the reception area for sensory information related to fear, such as a tone consistently presented prior to a shock (LeDoux, Cicchetti, Xagoraris, & Romanski, 1990). If the lateral amygdala is temporarily inactivated, fear conditioning is disrupted. The fear-related information is subsequently routed to the central nucleus of the amygdala, which functions as the principal output station of the amygdala. Output from the amygdala will eventually activate the HPA and sympathetic neurochemical systems (Labar & LeDoux, 2001).

Locus coeruleus. The locus coeruleus is the home of the noradrenergic neurons that have been implicated in the stress response and stress-related illnesses such as posttraumatic stress disorder. As seen in Figure 5.9, an immense projection system leaves the locus coeruleus and innervates all levels of the neuraxis. Specifically, the locus coeruleus is responsible for the NE in the forebrain and hippocampus. Additionally, CRH has been identified as an influential neurotransmitter in the locus coeruleus, contributing to the nonendocrine components of the stress response. The hippocampal and forebrain activation heightens arousal and sharpens cognitive functions in the initial phase of stress—probably leading to enhanced problem-solving ability and proximal survival (Van Bockstaele, Bajic, Proudfit, & Valentino, 2001).

FOUNDATIONS OF PSYCHOPHARMACOLOGY

Now that you are aware of some of the fundamental neurochemical processes in the brain, it is easy to discern that there are nearly limitless opportunities to develop drugs that intervene with the many neurochemical metabolic pathways. Modifications of dietary precursors, critical enzymes, or transport molecules can have dramatic effects on human behavior, emotions, or thoughts. Like a spy, **psychoactive drugs** act as antagonists or agonists and actually exploit the brain's own neurochemical processes to do their work to influence these systems. As a drug's **affinity** for the natural receptor approaches that of the actual neurotransmitter it is mimicking, it becomes stronger as the **efficacy** of the drug, or its chance of activating the receptor, becomes more likely.

The development of psychoactive drugs for treatment of a particular mental illness is no easy process. During the early stages of research, investigators must establish an understanding of the drug's **pharmacokinetics**, or movement throughout the body. In accomplishing this understanding, researchers focus on four basic processes (Julien, 2007):

1. *Absorption* refers to the journey of the drug as it passes from the external world to the bloodstream. The administration route (oral, intravenous, or intranasal) has a significant impact on the absorption of a drug.

2. Once absorption is understood, researchers must follow the drug's *distribution* throughout the brain and body. This pharmacological stalking is especially important for pregnant women because a drug distributed

psychoactive drugs Drugs that produce a noticeable change in mood or perception.

affinity The strength of attraction that a neurotransmitter has for a particular type of receptor.

efficacy The capacity to produce a desired effect with a drug or treatment.

pharmacokinetics The study of the action and reaction of and to drugs in the body.

to the developing fetus could be harmful or detrimental to the new life. Many times the drug is distributed to destinations that are not the primary target—this is the root of many of the unwanted side effects of many drugs.

3. It is also important to understand how the body *metabolizes*, or breaks down, the drug so that the effect can be terminated.

4. Once metabolized, the *elimination* route is identified. Typically, metabolites are excreted in the urine, which provides an ideal "test" to determine if a person has recently consumed a particular drug.

As seen in Table 5.4, getting a drug from the idea stage to Food and Drug Administration approval is a long and tedious—and not altogether ultimately successful—process. Additionally, getting a drug from the initial laboratory investigations to the patient's bloodstream is an expensive endeavor. According to a 1993 report published by the Congressional Office of Technology Assessment, a pharmaceutical company spends over $350 million to develop a new drug. Consequently, a company such as Hoffmann-LaRoche spends about one-third of its $3 billion budget on research (Cohn, 1995). Further, marketing and sales costs for 12 months increase the price tag to $1.7 billion for the total drug-development package (Mullin, 2003). The pharmaceutical companies often invest this significant amount of money with no guarantee that the drug will ever make it to paying consumers. More recently, increased costs for clinical trials have also contributed to rising costs (Collier, 2009).

Of course, some drug consumption is not as dependent on the research, development, and marketing of pharmaceutical companies. For drugs that have desirable psychological effects, humans have been impressively creative about obtaining sufficient quantities to achieve the desired effect. These drugs have been obtained mostly from plants over the years, but individuals with a little chemistry knowledge and home-based labs have also become significant sources of "recreational" psychoactive drugs. The various effects of these substances include relaxation, increased concentration, hallucinations, and extreme excitement; some are illegal and others are sold legally

Table 5.4 Phases of Drug Development

Approx. 5 years	Discovery of the drug, development of efficient methods of synthesis, and testing with animal models
Approx. 1 year	Application to begin clinical trials and the review of basic research by government agency
Approx. 1.5 years	Phase I of human clinical trials: Screening for safety and finding the maximum safe dose
Approx. 2 years	Phase II of human clinical trials: Establishing most effective doses and schedules of treatment
Approx. 3.5 years	Phase III of human clinical trials: Clear demonstrations that the drug is therapeutic
Approx. 1.5 years	Application to begin marketing and reviews of results of clinical trials by government agency
Ongoing	Recovering development costs and continuing to monitor the safety of the drug

Adapted from Pinel, 2003, and Zivin, 2000.

every day (see Connections for information on the culturally accepted psychoactive substance caffeine). Many of these potentially addictive drugs are discussed in detail in Chapter 11 (see Table 11.3 for a summary of the neurochemical actions of representative drugs of abuse).

Summary

Neurochemicals

The brain is awash in chemicals, fueled by many types of neurochemicals including neurotransmitters, neurohormones, hormones, and neuromodulators. Ever more neuropeptide transmitters are being identified; it is clear that there are literally hundreds of functionally significant neurochemicals in our brains. If an imbalance occurs in any of these systems, it is likely that an individual may experience a significant cognitive, behavioral, or emotional effect.

Acetylcholine (ACh) is derived from the dietary precursor choline, binds to muscarinic and nicotinic receptors, and is deactivated by acetylcholine esterase. ACh neurons project from the basal forebrain to the hippocampus and cortex; other ACh neurons project to the basal ganglia, thalamus, pons, and cerebellum. ACh is involved in learning and memory; Alzheimer's patients have decreased cholinergic levels. ACh is also present at all neuromuscular junctions; consequently, interruptions lead to paralysis.

Dopamine (DA) and norepinephrine (NE) are catecholamines, synthesized from the dietary protein tyrosine. DA pathways project to forebrain and limbic areas. DA cell bodies in the substantia nigra control movement; damage to this area is linked to Parkinson's disease. Other functions of DA include pleasure and cognitive processing. NE cell bodies are located in the brain stem and project to the thalamus, hypothalamus, limbic system, and cortex. NE is involved in attention, reward, and other motivational systems.

Serotonin, or 5-hydroxytryptamine (5-HT), is synthesized from dietary tryptophan and is received by at least 18 receptor types. 5-HT cell bodies are located in the medulla, and their projections extend to the forebrain, hippocampus, thalamus, hypothalamus, cerebellum, and midbrain. Drugs such as fluoxetine increase synaptic 5-HT levels by inhibiting reuptake. 5-HT regulates several functions, such as temperature control, mood, aggression, sleep, and hunger. The deactivating enzyme monoamine oxidase degrades both the catecholamine and 5-HT synaptic molecules.

Glutamate (Glu) and gamma-aminobutyric acid (GABA) are two amino acid neurotransmitters. Glu is the principal excitatory neurotransmitter in the central nervous system, and its receptors are found on most neurons. The N-methyl-d-aspartate Glu receptor has been implicated in cognitive functions; disruptions lead to neurotoxicity and schizophrenic symptoms. GABA is the principal inhibitory neurotransmitter, and most of its cell bodies are located in the cortex. GABA agonists such as benzodiazepines lead to hallucinations, amnesia, insomnia, and anesthesia; alcohol is perhaps the most popular GABA-affecting drug.

We now know that the brain has receptors for exogenous opioids because it produces its own form of endogenous opioids. Three families of opioid peptides exist, as do three main receptor classes. Generally, the endogenous opioids produce effects such as analgesia, euphoria, and respiratory depression; recent research implicates opioid involvement in more complex systems such as maternal behavior and social communication.

Oxytocin and vasopressin are neurohormones released by the posterior pituitary. Oxytocin is involved in orgasm, ejaculation, uterine contractions, lactation, and social bonding. Arginine vasopressin influences the osmotic content of the blood and blood pressure, as well as social recognition. Both neuropeptides have been implicated in learning and may play a role in mental illnesses characterized by disrupted social behavior.

Neurochemistry of the Stress Response

A stressful event triggers the sympathetic nervous system to secrete NE to recruit immediate energy necessary to survive the threat; additionally, the hypothalamic-pituitary-adrenal axis is activated to provide subsequent energy to maintain the battle against the stressor. When the HPA axis is stimulated, corticotropin-releasing hormone is released into the pituitary portal system leading to the release of adrenocorticotropic hormone from the anterior pituitary, which travels to the adrenal cortex and triggers the release of glucocorticoids.

In the face of chronic stress, long-term health projects are sometimes compromised; additionally, brain areas full of glucocorticoid receptors, such as the hippocampus, become compromised after days to weeks of elevated stress hormone levels. Other brain areas involved in maintaining stress hormone release include the amygdala and locus coeruleus.

Foundations of Psychopharmacology

An exogenous substance that activates a receptor in the brain is said to have an "affinity" for the receptor. The closer the match to the brain's endogenous, naturally produced substance, the stronger the efficacy of the substance. As a drug is being evaluated for efficacy and safety, considerable time and money are required to conduct the necessary research. Among other things, researchers are interested in the pharmacokinetics of a drug: its absorption, distribution, and metabolic and elimination characteristics.

Key Terms

neuropeptides (129)

neurohormones (129)

neuromodulator (129)

acetylcholine (ACh) (132)

agonist (133)

antagonist (133)

catecholamines (134)

dopamine (134)

norepinephrine (NE) (134)

epinephrine (134)

tyrosine hydroxylase (TH) (135)

reuptake (136)

serotonin (5-HT) (137)

tryptophan (138)

5-hydroxyindole acetic acid (5-HIAA) (138)

glutamate (Glu) (141)

gamma-aminobutyric acid (GABA) (141)

N-methyl-d-aspartate (NMDA) (141)

kainite receptor (141)

alpha-amino hydroxy-methyl-isoxazolepropionate (AMPA) (141)

neurotoxicity (142)

benzodiazepines (143)

barbiturates (143)

glycine (Gly) (144)

endogenous opioids (145)

endorphins (145)

oxytocin (146)

arginine vasopressin (AVP) (147)

fight-or-flight response (150)

corticotropin-releasing factor (150)

adrenocorticotropic hormone (ACTH) (150)

glucocorticoids (151)

cortisol (151)

hypothalamic–pituitary–adrenal (HPA) axis (151)

excitotoxicity (152)

psychoactive drugs (153)

affinity (153)

efficacy (153)

pharmacokinetics (153)

For Further Consideration

Brock, P. (2008). *Charlatan: America's most dangerous huckster, the man who pursued him, and the age of flim-flam.* New York: Three Rivers Press. To paraphrase H. L. Mencken, no one ever went broke underestimating the gullibility of the American public. This fascinating little book tells the story of Dr. John R. Brinkley, who made a career of "fleecing" both his goats and his patients. Or, more precisely, by playing on the inherent fears of (usually) men wanting a bulwark against aging and eventual sexual demise, Brinkley devised a form of a behavioral endocrinological treatment that involved the implantation of animal testes into the human, thereby, theoretically, transferring the rejuvenating properties of the lopped-off testicular agents to the clueless recipient. Despite evidence to the contrary and the many risks of such a surgery—high-pitched bleating aside—this charade went on for quite a while. Brock chronicles other fads that proved to be absurd and downright lethal (drinking radium-laced water, the many uses of electricity as curative). Mencken also plays a role in this volume, bringing his satirical eye to the events surrounding Brinkley's (and others') dubious works and having contact with the latter's biggest critic, one Dr. Morris Fishbein. Overall, this book shows the damage that one person can do when critical thinking and objectivity give way to profiteering and the exploitation of ignorance.

Goodman, L. S., Limbird, L., & Hardman, J. G. (2001). *Goodman and Gilman's The pharmacological basis of therapeutics*, 10th ed. New York: McGraw-Hill. This is one of the authoritative volumes in pharmacology. If this book does not have it, it has not been invented or developed or discovered yet. *Goodman and Gilman* (as it is called) has the best descriptions of the body's chemistry and a wealth of information on the brain as well. From the standpoint of finding a quick and detailed description of an agonist or an antagonist or understanding possible interactions and their medical relevance, *Goodman and Gilman* has been a reliable resource for decades.

Julien, R. M. (2007). *A primer of drug action: A concise, nontechnical guide to the actions, uses, and side effects of psychoactive drugs*, 10th ed. New York: Freeman. This is a fine introduction to the area of drugs and the brain. Its coverage of neurotransmitters, interactions among neurons, and the sledgehammer-like effect that drugs have when they slam into the brain are all well documented and discussed. How the brain responds to the smallest drink of beer or the biggest line of cocaine (and the ensuing seizure and death) is described for the reader to consider. The brain is like the wilds of Alaska, pure, pristine and unsullied; a drug introduced into that kind of an environment, like an oil spill, can have untold and untoward consequences.

Chapter Six

Neurodevelopment Over the Life Span

Connections

Fate of the Aging Brain: Popular and Scientific Perspectives

Have you ever heard someone forget something and declare that they are experiencing a "senior moment"? That statement conveys how our society feels about an aging brain—that it is compromised, past its prime, and on an inexorable decline toward dementia. Movies generally portray the elderly as vulnerable, confused, and in need of constant supervision. But does cognitive decline automatically occur in the aged? We all know that a child's brain is fertile territory for neuronal growth, but what about the aging brain? Do new connections and/or neurons continue to form well into old age?

A scientific exploration of these questions provides data that challenge the stereotypes of the aging brain. We now know that Alzheimer's disease or some other form of dementia is not a natural, automatic progression of the aging process; many people live full, long lives with very little cognitive decline in their final years. And research suggests that individuals can do more than merely maintain their level of cognitive functioning into old age; on the contrary, evidence suggests that the brain has the ability to make new connections and to manufacture new neurons throughout our lives.

Working at the University of Illinois, William Greenough and his colleagues (Greenough, Larson, & Withers, 1985) reported that adult rats have the ability to form new neuronal connections, not unlike their preadolescent counterparts. Similar to the traditional enriched environment work conducted in the 1960s by Mark Rosenzweig and colleagues (1999), Greenough exposed his adult rats to a form of rat playground, with toys to manipulate and ladders and tubes to explore. Middle-aged adult rats develop about five times more neuronal branching in the occipital cortex following this 45-day playful romp compared to rats that do not experience the enriched environment (Green, Greenough, & Schlumpf, 1983). Additionally, exposing the rats to the rodent equivalent of a jungle gym produces increased cerebellar synapses in the acrobatic rats compared with voluntary exercise animals (Kleim et al., 1998). Certainly, these data from Greenough's lab demonstrate that the adult brain is anything but static when exposed to an appropriately stimulating environment. (They also raise the question, in rats, of whether a lab-raised animal, whose life consists of exposure to the four dreary walls of a plastic cage, is, in fact, a deprived animal.) But what of humans?

David Snowden (2001), working at the University of Kentucky Medical Center, has investigated this question using a unique subject population. As an epidemiologist, he is interested in the factors related to the mystery of aging; and on hearing a graduate student recount her experiences living as a nun, he decided that nuns might provide some clues to the mystery of healthy aging. As opposed to other human populations, most nuns live vigorous lives filled with many cognitive and physical activities, healthy diets, social support and interaction, and, importantly, a sense of control in stressful or trying times—in other words, enriched lives. Also, from an epidemiological standpoint, there are meticulous records kept of every member of the community throughout their lives. Snowden recounts nervously asking Minnesota's School Sisters of Notre Dame to allow him to study them, and they agreed, welcoming him into their convent. Later, when Snowden decided that the nuns might provide meaningful information about the aging brain's biggest threat—Alzheimer's disease—a group of 678 agreed to donate their brains following their death. Snowden has collected several hundred brains, and he and neuropathologist William Markesbery have to date reported several interesting bits of information about the susceptibility and progression of Alzheimer's disease. Living a healthy, stimulating life is related not only to longevity but also to a delay in age-related cognitive decline and accompanying signs of an Alzheimer's brain (which occurs in roughly 45% of people 85 years and older). Interestingly, factors such as idea density (richness of one's thought processes) and the expression of positive emotions in essays written when the nuns were in their early twenties are related to a reduced risk for Alzheimer's disease in their eighties, nineties, and hundreds. One of the nuns, Sister Esther, at 106 years old, was able to live an independent, healthy life, riding an exercise bike for 10 minutes each day and frequently completing various crafts.

Whereas lifestyle does not always protect against the onset and development of Alzheimer's disease, it seems to buffer against its effects. Snowden and Markesbery have found a few brains of perfectly cognitively competent sisters that were nevertheless riddled with the neural plaques and tangles characteristic of Alzheimer's disease. In other cases, brains of nuns with no visible cognitive impairment were found to be considerably smaller than their sister counterparts' brains, suggesting that their enriched cognitive and physical lives created a buffer against the neurodegeneration of their brains, a greater "cognitive reservoir," allowing them to live symptom-free for longer. The Nun Study is far from over, and it is likely that other variables contribute to a slowing of the aging process. Such factors will be identified as the brains of more of these generous nuns are added to the study.

E pluribus unum, the dictum on our coins, is Latin for "From many, one." It is an apt metaphor when referring to the brain as well, for arising from the enormous number of neurons and their connections in a single brain comes the raw materials from which the unique characteristics of the human mind emerge. How you got to the point in your life at which you are sitting where you are, reading these words, and interpreting them in your own unique fashion owes more to the movement and interaction of countless developing neural cells and their eventual destinations than anything else. Imagine trillions of cells and connections, the equivalent of a microscopic universe in your head, all whirling and tumbling and aimless. Without the active guidance of this mass of newborn cells—which are being created at an alarming rate during nervous-system development—the democracy of the brain would, instead, become neural anarchy.

PRENATAL BRAIN DEVELOPMENT

Many authors divide development of the brain and nervous system into a chronology of six to eight overlapping stages (Bloom et al., 2001; Lemke, 2009; Rosenzweig et al., 1999; Sanes, Reh & Harris, 2005): induction, proliferation, migration, aggregation, differentiation, circuit formation, programmed cell

Figure 6.1
Building a brain The nervous system requires many interrelated steps (parts of which are ill-defined and overlap) in order to develop. Essentially, neurons and glial cells must be born (neurogenesis), move to their sites of eventual activity (migration), associate with similar cells (aggregation), have their activity and function become more finely tuned (differentiation), establish connections and circuits with complementary neurons (synaptogenesis and circuit formation), have excess neurons and circuits pruned away (apoptosis), and have the final pathways refined and established (synapse rearrangement).
AFTER ROSENZWEIG, BREEDLOVE, & LEIMAN, 1999, P. 160

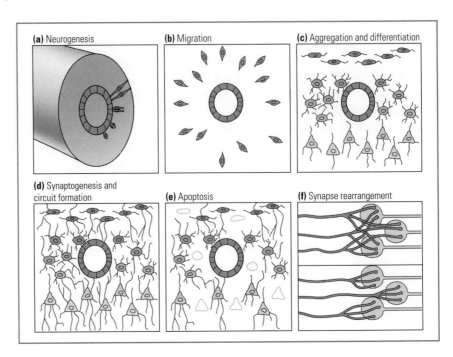

apoptosis Programmed cell death initiated by nuclear signals associated with age or other health-related variables of the cell; serves as a form of neuronal sculpting in the developing brain.

pluripotent The potential of a single stem cell to develop into many types of cells in the body.

stem cells Cells that, when nurtured in the appropriate chemical culture, have the ability to divide and develop into specialized cells for an indefinite time period.

death or apoptosis, and synapse rearrangement. During induction, a portion of the ectoderm, one of three layers of the developing embryo, becomes the nervous system, whereas other cells become hair and fingernails (Hall, 2009). As seen in Figure 6.1, the proliferative stage is, as the name implies, a time of immense cellular division, also known as "neurogenesis": Migration involves the movement of newly minted cells to various places in the forming brain. Aggregation is the process whereby similar neurons associate to become specific neuronal populations. Differentiation involves finer delineation of cells into specific neurotransmitter/neurochemical types and the like and occurs early as well as later on in development. Synaptogenesis leads to circuit formation, which comprises two elements, axonal and synaptic growth and regulation, and concerns the segregation of groups of neurons into discrete pathways and connections with logical precision. **Apoptosis**, or programmed cell death, renders the tremendous overproduction of neurons into a cleanly operating collection by selectively pruning synapses and eliminating inefficient or redundant pathways. Finally, following the death of certain neurons, synapse rearrangement occurs as neural connections reestablish synaptic arrangements with neurons that did not fall victim to apoptosis.

Emergence and Journey of the Brain's Neurons

In the human, late in the first month of life, the developing nervous system begins to take shape and the processes of induction and differentiation are initiated. As we describe this process, keep in mind that the genes are the primary influence guiding development: They dictate the number, size, and rate of cell division as well as the qualities of the cells being born and their potentials, at this time and later on during brain formation. For example, the genes involved in the construction of a neuron as a neuron, creating its dendrites versus its axon, are many and varied and interact with similar external (i.e., extracellular) cues from adjacent and nearby neurons (Barnes & Polleux, 2009). Aside from the obvious complexity inherent to building a human being (or other organism) from scratch, the principles are rather straightforward. As one layer of cells is created, using chemical signals that are thus far indistinct, it makes way for another and another and so on. Layer is placed upon layer, as with bricks or phyllo dough, and symmetrically and asymmetrically, which leads to, for example, similar hemispheres but with differences in structure size (temporal lobe versus frontal) until later on when differentiation of cell types occurs. Until then, cells are **pluripotent**, able to become many different things, from skin to neurons. These are the so-called **stem cells** that, as discussed later in the chapter, have evoked such excitement and passion from scientists and doctors and such fear from the moralists and ethicists who envision their misuse or the lengths to which some will go to obtain and study them.

Working backward from the adult peripheral and central nervous systems (CNS), how does all this orchestrated chaos happen? Late in the third week of the human's life, following fertilization and implantation of the egg, a thickened layer of cells forms from the ventral surface of the dividing egg (it is derived from the former initial group of cells called the "inner cell mass"). This cellular carpet is called the **ectoderm**. It is accompanied by the **mesoderm** and then the **endoderm**, and together they form the three layers on which the human is built (Hall, 2009). These plates of cells, formed very early in the development of the nervous system, with the most dorsal, the ectoderm, giving rise to the **neural plate**, are very active and programmed to proliferate at varying rates (Figure 6.2). For example, the rate of cell division at the ends of the neural plate exceeds the rate in the medial section, which leads to a thickening at the ends and a thinning in the middle, called the **neural groove**. As the neural groove deepens, the continued thickening creates the **neural fold**. When viewed from the side, the neural fold appears like two waves approaching and then enveloping each other. The resulting space in the middle, formed when the two sides of the neural fold meet, results in a fluid-filled cavity called the **neural tube**. The neural tube is bounded on its dorsal surface by a layer of cells resembling a cape about the shoulders of the neural tube. This is called the **neural crest**, and eventually it splits, both halves moving to the dorsomedial region of the neural tube (Hall, 2009). There, they become incorporated into the yet-to-be-formed spinal cord, forming the portion of the cord that relays sensory information to the brain.

At either end of the neural tube, prior to closure of the margins of the neural plate, lie two openings that are conduits to the amniotic fluid that swirls around the developing embryo. These openings are called the anterior and posterior **neuropores**. As further development commences, the anterior neuropore undergoes specific and increased cell division, which begins to create the premature brain. It is from these three main vesicles, or enlargements, that the developing brain begins to elaborate and form. Cellular division at this time (proliferation) occurs at a rate that staggers the imagination. At its peak, given the enormous capacity of the geometric progression of cell division, tens of thousands of neurons can be produced per minute (Hall, 2009); each of these then, literally, must distinguish top from bottom, head from toe, as intra- and intercellular activities guide their development

ectoderm The outer layer of the fertilized egg, or zygote, that eventually gives rise to the skin, nerve cells, and most of the neuroglia.

mesoderm The middle layer of the fertilized egg, or zygote, that eventually gives rise to many muscles, the skin, skeleton, and connective tissue.

endoderm The innermost layer of the fertilized egg, or zygote, that eventually gives rise to the developing fetus's internal organs.

neural plate A group of cells derived from the embryonic ectoderm that subsequently develop into the neural groove and neural tube, the origins of the mature nervous system.

neural groove The groove found between the neural folds in the developing embryo; once the neural folds join, the neural groove becomes the neural tube.

neural folds A portion of the ectoderm of the embryo develops into folds that form around the neural tube; eventually, these folds will give rise to the entire nervous system.

neural tube An early form of the nervous system observed during prenatal development: The rostral section develops into the brain and the caudal section eventually develops into the spinal cord.

neural crest The tissue that starts to develop on each side of the neural tube that later becomes the peripheral nervous system.

neuropores Openings at each end of the neural canal that eventually give rise to the brain and spinal cord.

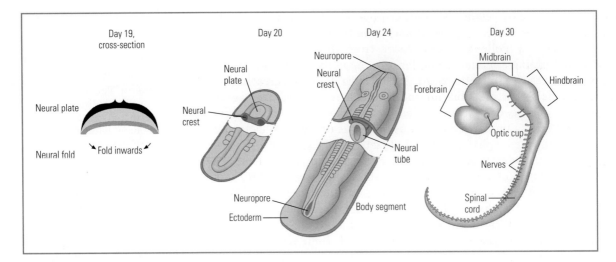

Day 19, cross-section

Neural plate

Neural fold

Fold inwards

Day 20

Neural plate

Neural crest

Neuropore

Ectoderm

Day 24

Neuropore

Neural crest

Neural tube

Neuropore

Body segment

Day 30

Midbrain

Hindbrain

Forebrain

Optic cup

Nerves

Spinal cord

Figure 6.2
The embryonic nervous system The head versus body orientation is represented here by the neuropore, openings at either end, rostral and caudal, of the embryonic neural canal.

AFTER BLOOM, NELSON, LAZERSON, 2001, P. 62

(Barnes & Polleux, 2009). Fittingly, these neurons go on to become organized and integrated into an organ capable of pondering the intricacy of its own genesis.

Cell division continues apace. By the fourth week of life the embryonic nervous system, including the nascent brain, begins to resemble its mature version, cells have begun moving from sites of creation to sites of eventual integration (migration), and the neural tube nears closure. Spatial arrangement of the structures is in place, but the size, density, and activity are all vastly different from what they will become in the fully formed nervous system. The three vesicles that form prior to closure of the neural tube are the basis for the three main divisions of the brain that we discuss in Chapter 3: forebrain, midbrain, and hindbrain. These structures elaborate to assume the characteristic shape of the mature brain, and the more caudal elements of the now closed neural tube thin, elongate, and branch out to become the spinal cord (see Figure 6.2).

Following closure of the anterior neuropore and the beginnings of the three main divisions/vesicles, the aggregation stage commences, in which cells with similar structure and function accumulate geographically. The three vesicles at this stage are fluid-filled, the precursors to the eventual ventricular system. The negative pressure exerted by these fluid-filled cavities contributes to maintaining the shape of the developing brain and the compartmentalization into specific brain regions; still, there is much cell proliferation and the formation of connections and **neuropil** that ultimately dictate the final shape of the structure under construction. The form and function, too, are regulated in large measure by the external events that swirl around the developing nervous system. Though much more prevalent after birth, these external events contribute to the formation and maintenance of the connections that arise during this time.

By 12 weeks or so, the immature brain becomes brain-like: It begins to assume the shape it will have in the mature person (Figure 6.3a), and it begins to work like a nervous system. The fundamental pattern of the ventricles and their distinctive shape are apparent in the 8-week-old embryo, already assuming the characteristics of its adult counterpart. The ventricles become integrated into the adult form not by any kind of migration or movement but rather by their function as hydraulic casks around which the proliferating brain is forming. By 12 weeks of age, the embryonic brain has

neuropil The intricate network of interwoven glial and neuronal processes that lie between axons.

the appearance of all five subdivisions discussed in Chapter 3: telencephalon, diencephalon, mesencephalon, metencephalon, and myelencephalon (Figure 6.3b). An interesting feature of the newly formed brain is the exclusive but interrelated forms it assumes. Though the regions are separate, each establishes discrete connections with the other regions, near and distant connections that are formed early and under a variety of conditions but that remain with the organism for the rest of its life.

If one stops to consider the fate of the newborn nervous system, it is apparent that these immature cells are at the beginning of a figurative and literal lifelong journey. Among the steps involved with neuronal birth and connectivity are the definition of the fresh neuron into its own major subdivisions, dendrite and axon, with the polarity or input/output facets of the cell being paramount (Barnes & Polleux, 2009). The processes inherent to this cellular event demonstrate the fundamental requirement that the neuron be able to regulate how information works its way into and then out of the cell, en route to the next neuron in the chain. Once that initial problem is resolved, putting them all together becomes necessary. There is much left to do to sculpt the mature brain out of the new and raw materials of neurons, glia, neurotransmitters, neuropeptides, and so on. As wondrous as it sounds, each neuron can establish tens of thousands of connections with other neurons, and the proper establishment of these connections is essential for proper functioning. The process whereby this assembly occurs is multifaceted and intricate. Further, it is susceptible to the many internal and external forces that roil the waters of development, from the initial directives of the genes and their subtle messages through diet, hormones, environmental toxins, trauma, and the mass of sensory stimuli that flood the new brain with novel and compelling information about its unfamiliar world. That it happens as effectively, and with as few problems, as it does—given the huge number of normal mammals walking around—is truly amazing.

Figure 6.3
Embryonic and fetal brain development (a) Spreading upward and outward, the developing human brain demonstrates the ever-increasing facets that accompany maturation of the nervous system and, early on, resembles its adult counterpart. (b) In more detail, it is apparent that the brain regions that are present early as the nervous system develops remain and grow ever more convoluted and larger as the nervous system continues to develop.

(A) AFTER COWAN, 1979, P. 116; (B) AFTER BLOOM ET AL., 2001, P. 63

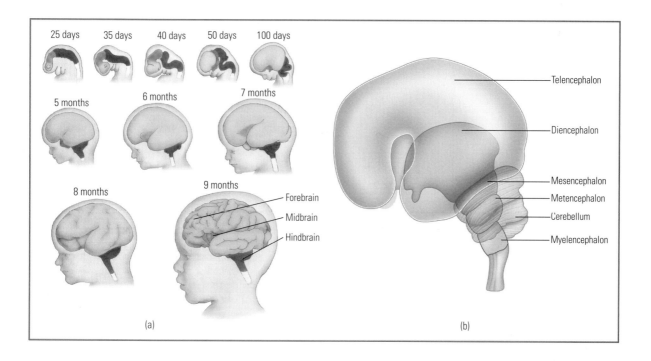

25 days   35 days   40 days   50 days   100 days

5 months   6 months   7 months

8 months   9 months

Forebrain
Midbrain
Hindbrain

Telencephalon
Diencephalon
Mesencephalon
Metencephalon
Cerebellum
Myelencephalon

(a)

(b)

filopodia An extremely fine tube-shaped extension that emerges from the neuron's growth cone.

Establishing and Fine-Tuning the Brain's Circuits

The process of circuit formation forges the ultimate relationships among neurons, stamping them with the markers of chemistry and function. Together with the local connections, or intranuclear associations, there are distant, region-to-region connections that are established, fostering the eventual transfer of more and more involved information for additional processing (Restak, 2003; Lemke, 2009).

The processes involved in forming the circuits of the brain bear some further discussion. The neurons that have moved into position following their migratory travels are in the process of establishing final synapses with the adjoining cells in the vicinity. They send out probes that undulate and snake toward their neighbors, searching out connections, like travelers on a defined but circuitous path. There is a scene in the final moments of the classic movie *Field of Dreams* in which the camera pulls away from a nighttime view to reveal what looks like thousands of cars moving toward the farm where much of the film takes place. It is an apt visual symbol for the way in which neuronal circuits are established in the early brain. A catch phrase from that movie is similarly apropos of brain development: "If you build it, they will come." In essence, the circuits that arise at this time are constructed and constricted by active processes such as internal neurochemistry and commands and as much by external stimulation as by the sensory load being processed by these new cells and circuits. Sensory stimulation can direct connections.

Circuits are formed in the new brain by a combination of seeker neurons and target neurons and their interaction. As the new neurons are born, they move through the three-dimensional space literally by feel, using the end plate of the axon called the "growth cone." At the extreme ends of the growth cone are delicate digit-like projections called **filopodia** (Figure 6.4). Like toes tentatively dropped into a hot bath to test the water, the filopodia inch along the forming neuropil in search of connections. They follow a chemical gradient that is a further example of the digital nature of the nervous system. The filopodia depend just as much on chemical signals (*chemosignals*) that

Figure 6.4
Filopodia The developing brain is represented by millions of migrating neurons, moving great distances to establish contact with complementary cells by means of chemical attractants and repellants. Filopodia, the vital tips of migrating neurons, are like a hand reaching up to feel around an unknown surface, searching for an object or direction in the dark.
COURTESY DENNIS BRAY

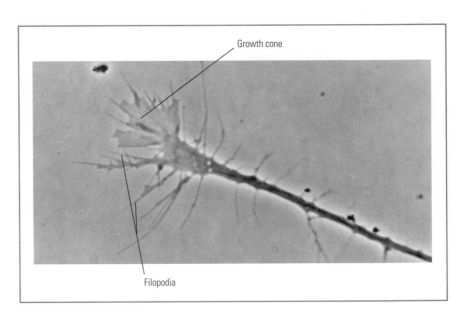

Growth cone

Filopodia

repel them as on signals that attract. Some examples of these signals are the **neurotrophins** or neurotrophic factors, chemicals such as **brain-derived neurotrophic factor (BDNF)**, **nerve growth factor (NGF)**, and **cell adhesion molecules (CAMs)**; other signals are present in various amounts and locations at these critical stages of development. Together, there are four possible ways in which synapses are formed by axons—*chemoattraction* and *chemorepulsion* (whereby the filopodia are affected distantly by the chemicals) and *contact attraction* and *contact repulsion* (in which the axon literally bounces off a neuron on which a connection was sought but is chemically inappropriate). These chemoattractants and chemorepellants (one neuron's attractant may be another's repellant) work in tandem, like molecular tugboats, to navigate an axon into place or shove it away from its docking site, establishing pre- and postsynaptic connections that may last a lifetime. Once the synapse is complete, there is a burst of activity that follows, reinforcing the fresh connection.

With this process writ large—billions of times once the brain has nearly reached the end of its early development (with its approximately 100 billion neurons)—the connections that are in place are difficult, but not impossible, to dislodge (see Chapter 7 for graphic evidence of the fragility of these neuronal connections). In fact, the brain has a built-in process akin to natural selection that ensures that only the best and most efficient connections remain. It can be thought of as "neural Darwinism" (the title of a 1987 book by Nobel Prize winner Gerald Edelman). That is, there is a dramatic cellular struggle that takes place once the brain has begun to slow down its production of new cells and connections, a synaptic competition of the most severe sort, with the victorious neurons and connections remaining to exert influences on virtually every facet of brain activity thereafter and the losers consigned to reabsorption.

The loss of existing neurons and connections is regulated by multiple factors, among them the access to neurotrophic factors, the interaction with the postsynaptic elements (target organ/muscle, neuron), and interestingly, the sensory information that floods into the new nervous system. All of these sources represent feedback to the neurons that the connection is a working one. Like the atrophy that occurs when a muscle is not worked, neurons cease to be connected if the connection is shown to be unnecessary or redundant. One reason that physical rehabilitation is attempted so soon after an injury is that the feedback provided to the brain by means of the muscle helps to maintain the neural regulation of the muscle. It prevents having to rehabilitate both ends of the connection.

Among the neurons and their synapses lost in development are the ones that are purged through apoptosis, or programmed cell death. This phenomenon was first reported by Dale Purves and Jeff W. Lichtman (1980), causing much interest in the reasons for the event. This process, which naturally rids the newly formed brain of redundant, unnecessary, or inefficient synapses, produces a lean and functional organ with inherent speed and capabilities. When a gardener prunes trees in the spring, he or she is guiding the development of the branches and promoting efficient growth. Subsequently, the pruned tree is usually healthier and better functioning. Like the pruned tree, the shape that the brain takes is intended to produce an efficient, elegant final product. As discussed, though, getting to that point may be accomplished in basic, brutal, Darwinian fashion as neurons and their synapses compete.

neurotrophins
Neurochemicals secreted in an activity-dependent fashion that are thought to be involved in the restructuring of synaptic connections.

brain-derived neurotrophic factor (BDNF) A stimulating factor localized in the CNS that promotes the growth and survival of neurons.

nerve growth factor (NGF) A neurochemical secreted by the postsynaptic neuron during the formation of synaptic connections between neurons; it is considered a trophic factor because it stimulates the growth of the presynaptic neuron's axon.

cell adhesion molecules (CAMs) Glycoproteins located on the cell surface that play a role in guiding growing axons as they move toward their final destinations in the brain.

The brain manufactures neurons at an astonishing rate. At that pace, it begins its existence with a significantly greater number of neurons than it requires or that will be there upon maturity; estimates place the excess at more than 50% and in some regions at more than 80% (Gilbert, 2000; Kandel et al., 2000). That is, the brain is overproducing neurons in massive amounts, resulting in a shapeless blob of vital cells with little functionality that must be reduced in size and density—it must be brought under control. Apoptosis, then, can be likened to a sculptor who starts out with a mass of marble or other material and slowly and meticulously shapes it into a final object, a vision realized. But in the case of a brain, the process begins with a large number of functioning neurons.

The production of too many neurons and their connections, however, creates a situation that is both advantageous and maladaptive. If too many neurons are produced and kept, the speed and efficiency of neural transfer of information are imperiled; furthermore, dependence on faulty connections increases the likelihood of loss of function in a "weak-link" scenario. The large number produced, however, sets the stage for tremendous competition among the neurons, ensuring that only the best will survive to establish themselves in neural circuits. It is a process that is designed to winnow the wheat from the chaff, producing a neural substrate that will work well for a long time.

Recently, much attention has been focused on apoptosis. There may be a genetic cue to the onset of apoptosis that is linked to the number of cell divisions that the neurons undergo. With accumulated activity associated with each cell division, programmed cell death may be set into motion by genes that lead to overexpression of various proteins so that subsequently divided neurons are marked for death. Other cellular dynamics, such as the removal of neurotrophic factors, may contribute to apoptosis. Neurotrophins are like rainwater for neurons: They contribute to their growth and elaboration and maintenance—their survival. Removing their influence would have the effect that a drought would have on a garden. For instance, one mechanism that NGF may mediate is suppression of an apoptotic program that is set to operate in neurons. The presence of NGF may keep the program from turning on in the neuron, keeping that neuron in the circuit.

Last, another mechanism that ensures survival of neurons and their connections and circuits is the feedback provided by the target to the neuron. The reciprocal signaling is prima facie evidence that the connection is a fully functioning one. Thus, maintaining a feedback loop between pre- and postsynaptic neurons holds the apoptotic processes at bay. This signaling process may operate through stimulation of neurotrophic factors or suppression of internal apoptotic programs, but it exemplifies the importance of maintaining and exercising the existing links between neurons. There are a couple of adages that apply to brain and circuit formation, and they apply here in relation to apoptosis: (1) neurons that fire together wire together and (2) use it or lose it. Like the pioneering work by Hubel and Wiesel (e.g., 1970) that demonstrates loss of innervation and complexity of visual cortex if that portion of brain is deprived of sensory (visual) stimulation, circuits and connections depend on regular activity and the traffic moving through them.

The cells that survive the apoptotic phase of development must adapt yet again by establishing connections with the surviving neurons. Connections

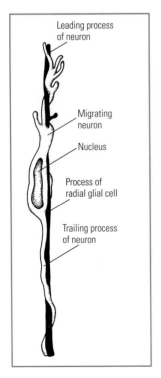

Figure 6.5
Radial glia and development The most abundant cells in the brain, the glia, play a major role in the assignment of neurons to brain regions. Here, we see a radial glial cell being used as a scaffold over which a migrating neuron is moving en route to its destination.

FROM BLOOM & LAZERSON, 1988, P. 62

Leading process of neuron

Migrating neuron

Nucleus

Process of radial glial cell

Trailing process of neuron

formed with previously existing neurons are rerouted to existing neurons so that an optimal synaptic web forms for each neuron to maximize potential for adaptive functioning.

We have focused on neuron-to-neuron and neuron-to-target interactions, but keep in mind that there are other cells in the brain that also establish connections and are involved in the facilitation of neuronal organization. As discussed in Chapter 4, these cells, the glia, play an integral role in the formation of the brain, in its maintenance and protection, and in the arrangement of the neurons (Kriegstein & Alvarez-Buylla, 2009). During the process of migration, for instance, **radial glia**, formed prior to the migration of newly minted neurons, extend long fibers that can reach for many millimeters. New neurons attach themselves by means of their growth cone and move up the radial glial fiber as if they were climbing a rope, using the fiber as a kind of scaffold on which to achieve purchase, orientation, and direction (Figure 6.5). Thus, glia are integral to the migration of new neurons and in the development of distant brain sites (distant, that is, from the area where the population of neurons is born). Recently, the divisions between glia and neurons became less distinct when researchers found that radial glial cells serve another function as neural stem cells, cells that have the potential of unlimited neural repairs (Kriegstein & Alvarez-Buylla, 2009).

radial glia Neuroglial cells characterized by very long branches that serve as a physical guide or road map for developing neuroblast cells as they migrate toward their final destinations; following the development of the brain, it is thought that these cells develop into astrocytes.

POSTNATAL BRAIN DEVELOPMENT

The neonatal brain resembles the adult brain in the same way that a stripped-down Mini Cooper resembles a fully loaded Mercedes 500 SEL: All the basic parts are there, and you can do some of things with the Mini that you can do with the Mercedes (such as getting from point A to point B), but the Mercedes is much more massive and complex—and expensive—than the Mini. Unlike the Mini, however, the neonatal brain will grow to become the equivalent of the Mercedes with all of its bells and whistles. The process by which this development occurs relies heavily on the external world and its many sensory and experiential forces. The brain at birth is a cavernous labyrinth that swallows up whatever sensory information is near its entrance. One consequence of this unyielding stream of sensory information is a dramatic alteration in the neuronal relationships within the brain. The brain changes to accommodate this flood of information, much as a library adds folders, then binders, then shelves and stacks, then rooms, and then new wings and buildings (or nowadays just hard-drive space!) to hold the information that comes into it. The brain changes, adding new storage space to the various regions charged with recording, or memorizing, the new information. The exact manner in which the information storage is accomplished remains a mystery, although recent forays into the neurobiology of memory formation suggest that both new neurons and modifications of existing ones play major roles (Gage et al., 2007; Kempermann, 2005; Segal, 2005).

Infancy and Childhood

Figure 6.6 shows the dramatic growth and development of the brain between birth and 6 years of age. What is apparent is that the brain is becoming more detailed with age, a reflection of the relentless stream of new information it must process to stay alive and adapt. *Adaptation*, or learning, is the response

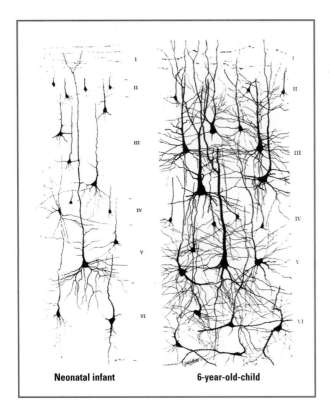

Neonatal infant

6-year-old-child

Figure 6.6
Early brain development and stimulation It is apparent that the brain grows dramatically between conception and birth. It grows even larger and more complex during the extended and critical postnatal period, during which the infant is fast soaking up the information that stimulates new neurons and, mainly, the new connections among those and existing neurons.

AFTER CONEL, 1939–1967

to the world that the brain makes in the face of change. Learning is the brain's hedge against extinction, and the brain accommodates learning by making more and more space for it. Moreover, in addition to the space that is created, new connections are established between disparate bits of neuronal information, formerly disconnected pieces of data that, when combined, represent a wholly novel way of looking at the information—in other words, new connections, new ways of making sense of or *thinking about* information.

The brain accomplishes these amazing cognitive processing feats by changing physically. At birth, the brain has capacity, awaiting information to stimulate it. But it is shrunken, emaciated compared with what it looks like about age 6. The greatest difference does not appear to be in the number of neurons; rather, it is the myriad connections among the neurons. And no wonder! A child masters hand–eye coordination, walking, social recognition and communication, love, laughter, and a sense of self-awareness (virtually everything defining the human) during this important developmental window, so it is obvious that dramatic increases in neuronal elaboration are necessary. The area that has experienced the most growth in the human 6-year-old is the cortex; in fact, the cortex is the area of the brain that truly differentiates us from other animals. Although the macaque monkey is a fellow primate, its cortex is only 10% the size of the human cortex. And although most of the neuroscience research is conducted on rats, the human cortex is 1,000 times larger than the modest rodent cortex (Restak, 2003). As impressive as the cortex is, however, our views are quickly changing about the number of neurons occupying this area. Whereas past research suggested that up to 70% of the brain's neurons were found in the cortex, recent research suggests that the percentage of neurons in the cortex is closer to 19% (even though the cortex comprises up to 82% of the brain's mass), while the cerebellum contains closer to 80% of the brain's neurons (Herculano-Houzel, 2009).

A body of elegant work has shown experimentally the effects of experience on the brain. As mentioned in Chapter 1 and in the Connections of this chapter, Greenough and his colleagues have demonstrated how neurons respond to stimulation. For instance, Greenough et al. (1985) investigated the effects of experience on the sensorimotor forelimb cortex of rats. Rats were trained to reach into a tube to retrieve a food reward with their preferred paw (rats, like humans, are right- or left-handed). The rats were then trained to use their nonpreferred paw to grasp the food. After training to use the nonpreferred paw, the rats' cortices were examined for changes in neuronal structure—in particular, changes in oblique branches from pyramidal neurons. The training caused increased branching of the dendrites with accompanying (but implied) increases in synapses, and overall it magnified the dimensions of the neurons' dendritic fields. Other examples of neural responsiveness to behavioral demands are discussed in the epilogue; these behavior-induced brain changes are akin to going from a whisper to a shout as the range of neuronal influence spreads outward farther and wider.

The postnatal production of new neurons, or **neurogenesis**, accompanies the increasing brain volume in the developing child. The brain needs to add neurons to the more developed infrastructure in order to add new computing power. Fred Gage and his colleagues at the Salk Institute in La Jolla, California, have shown that rich environments can stimulate neurogenesis much as the novel environment of the neonate probably stimulates similar processes (everything is novel to a baby) (Kempermann, Kuhn, & Gage, 1997). There are more neurons in the neuropil of an older child, but the biggest differences are in the branching patterns of the existing neurons. Therefore, the tremendous growth that is apparent in brain size between the two ages is attributable primarily to expansion of existing neurons. By making these patterns more elaborate, adding to their structure the equivalent of more library space, the vast amount of information with which the child must contend is seamlessly integrated into what was integrated before and the brain is ready to accommodate new information that awaits the child. The plasticity of the nervous system into childhood is seen in children from whom, because of persistent epilepsy, an entire hemisphere has been removed. As discussed in Chapter 1 and in Box 6.1, children have an astonishing capacity to recover lost function by increasing the structure and functions of the remaining hemisphere.

neurogenesis Mitotic division of cells to produce new neuronal cells.

Adolescence and Attention-Deficit/ Hyperactivity Disorder

It is interesting how the development of the brain occurs in repetitive motions, much like waves washing on the shore—slowly building up momentum and then washing away the excess as the wave reaches its destination on the shore. After experiencing massive proliferation followed by apoptosis during neonatal and infant development, it was once thought that the brain was fully developed by the end of childhood, needing only fine-tuning in the upcoming adolescent and adult years. More recent research suggests, however, that the brain does not reach full maturity, characterized by fullest circuit completion, until one's early to mid-twenties—and it happens earlier in females than in males [Lenroot et al., 2007]). And once again, the rhythm of proliferating and pruning must occur to produce the optimally functioning adult brain. This second wave of apoptotic pruning occurs during adolescence.

Jay Giedd, a neuroscientist at the National Institute of Mental Health in Bethesda, Maryland, examined normal children and adolescents with magnetic resonance image (MRI) scans to investigate brain changes that might underlie behavioral changes during adolescence. His findings suggest that, although brain volume stays roughly the same, specific areas undergo dynamic changes (Giedd et al., 1999). For example, the gray matter increases in preadolescence and decreases prior to adulthood, whereas the white matter increases with age without the downward spiral (Durston et al., 2001). The heightened flexibility of the brain during adolescence reinforces the importance of this developmental stage in the formation of the brain's hoped-for final product—a massively complex, yet efficient processing machine.

**attention-deficit/
hyperactivity disorder
(ADHD)** A condition
observed in children and
adults characterized by
inattention, hyperactivity, and
impulsivity.

**frontostriatal
circuitry** Neuroanatomical
connections between the
basal ganglia and frontal
cortical areas that mediate
many behavioral responses.

The final area of the brain to mature is the executive portion, or the frontal lobes. Considering that the development of this rational component of the brain lags behind the maturation of limbic areas involved in sexual and aggressive behaviors, it becomes easy to see why adolescence is such a turbulent time in development—the brain is literally trying to keep up with the emerging emotional and motivational behavior. Just as the mice will play while the cat's away, the mature limbic lobes will play while frontal lobe completion is delayed.

An increasingly common developmental disorder, **attention-deficit/ hyperactivity disorder (ADHD)**, is characterized by an inability to sustain one's attention for an appropriate amount of time, accompanied by frequent inappropriate impulsive behavior (Table 6.1 gives diagnostic criteria). With a worldwide prevalence of 3%–10% (depending on the criteria used), this is the most prevalent neurobiological condition treated in children and adolescents (Cherkasova & Hechtman, 2009; Farone, Sergeant, Gillberg, & Biederman, 2003). It presents special challenges for preadolescents and adolescents as they encounter the whirlwind of neuroanatomical changes that accompany these developmental periods (Dopheide & Pliszka, 2009; Wilens, Biederman & Spencer, 2002). Of considerable concern for adolescents with ADHD is the observation that they are about twice as likely to abuse drugs during this volatile phase of development. Some turn to drugs as an attempt to calm the feelings of restlessness and anxiety produced by the disorder; others seek stimulants to enhance their ability to focus (such as the psychostimulant methylphenidate [Ritalin]; Restak, 2003; August, 2006).

Although there are no obvious (that is, no easily in vivo observable) brain deficits in ADHD individuals, subtle yet significant changes have been observed. A study conducted at the National Institute of Mental Health found that ADHD children had significantly smaller brain volumes (approximately 3%), specifically around the cerebrum and cerebellum (Castellanos et al., 2002). In general, the neuroimaging studies conducted on ADHD subjects have pointed to the **frontostriatal circuitry** as the chief dysfunctional brain area in this disorder (Cherkasova & Hechtman, 2009). A meta-analysis of 16 neuroimaging studies of ADHD patients reported significant patterns of hypoactivity in the frontal regions, known for their roles in executive functions (Dickstein, Bannon, Castellanos, & Milham, 2006). The basal ganglia, relevant in in movement and potentially associated with impulsivity and hyperactivity, have also been frequently investigated. For example, positron emission tomographic (PET) scans reveal lower metabolic rates in basal ganglia and the frontal cortex (Pary, Lewis, Matuschka, & Lippmann, 2002) in subjects diagnosed with ADHD.

Interestingly, the investigation of ADHD symptoms related to executive functions such as response inhibition has prompted researchers to focus on the frontal cortex. When researchers have investigated brain areas associated with other prevalent symptoms, however, alterations in additional relevant areas have been identified. As mentioned above, altered cerebellar volumes have been identified. Symptoms such as temporal information processing and movement sequencing and planning represent functions associated with the cerebellum. Sarah Durston and her colleagues at Cornell University have assessed errors and cerebellar activity in adolescents with ADHD (Durston et al., 2007). Their investigations indicate that, compared with age-matched control subjects, children and adolescents diagnosed with ADHD exhibited

Table 6.1 Diagnostic Criteria for Attention-Deficit/Hyperactivity Disorder

A. Either (1) or (2):

    (1) six (or more) of the following symptoms of **inattention** have persisted for at least 6 months to a degree that is maladaptive and inconsistent with developmental level:

    Inattention

        (a) often fails to give close attention to details or makes careless mistakes in schoolwork, work, or other activities

        (b) often has difficulty sustaining attention in tasks or play activities

        (c) often does not seem to listen when spoken to directly

        (d) often does not follow through on instructions and fails to finish schoolwork, chores, or duties in the workplace (not due to oppositional behavior or failure to understand instructions)

        (e) often has difficulty organizing tasks and activities

        (f) often avoids, dislikes, or is reluctant to engage in tasks that require sustained mental effort (e.g., schoolwork or homework)

        (g) often loses things necessary for tasks or activities (e.g., toys, school assignments, pencils, books, or tools)

        (h) is often easily distracted by extraneous stimuli

        (i) is often forgetful in daily activities

    (2) six or more of the following symptoms of **hyperactivity–impulsivity** have persisted for at least 6 months to a degree that is maladaptive and inconsistent with developmental level:

    Hyperactivity

        (a) often fidgets with hands or feet or squirms in seat

        (b) often leaves seat in classroom or in other situations in which remaining seated is expected

        (c) often runs about or climbs excessively in situations in which it is inappropriate (in adolescents or adults, may be limited to subjective feelings of restlessness)

        (d) often has difficulty playing or engaging in leisure activities quietly

        (e) is often "on the go" or often acts as if "driven by a motor"

        (f) often talks excessively

    Impulsivity

        (g) often blurts out answers before questions have been completed

        (h) often has difficulty awaiting turn

        (i) often interrupts or intrudes on others (e.g., butts into conversations or games)

B. Some hyperactive–impulsive or inattentive symptoms that caused impairment were present before age 7 years

C. Some impairment from the symptoms is present in two or more settings (e.g., at school [or work] and at home)

D. There must be clear evidence of clinically significant impairment in social, academic, or occupational functioning

E. The symptoms do not occur exclusively during the course of a pervasive developmental disorder, schizophrenia, or other psychotic disorder and are not better accounted for by another mental disorder (e.g., mood disorder, anxiety disorder, dissociative disorder, or a personality disorder)

American Psychiatric Association, 2000, pp. 92–93.

decreased cerebellar activity when expected stimuli were presented at an unexpected time. Because cerebellar inputs into the prefrontal cortical areas are involved in the prediction of events, it has been hypothesized that the frontocerebellar circuits may be compromised in children with ADHD (Cherdasov et al (2009). Additionally, the parietal lobes, involved with integrating relevant sensory information related to the body, are involved with attentional functions and have been found to have smaller volumes than their non-ADHD counterparts. Thus, the multiple symptoms of ADHD have

Box 6.1

A Case in Point

Relieving Ashlee's Seizure-Induced Wiggles

March 23, 1993, is a date forever etched in Deb Bahr's mind. On this day, Terry and Deb's 1-year-old daughter, Ashlee, experienced her first seizure and was rushed to the hospital. After having another seizure the next morning, Ashlee was placed on anticonvulsant medication. Unfortunately, the seizures continued; at one point, when she was experiencing 30–50 seizures per day, Ashlee's parents and doctors became desperate to find a way to decrease their frequency. They decided to place Ashlee in a coma to slow down the seizures while possible treatment solutions were considered. Unfortunately, an effective treatment was not identified; and for the next 3 years, Deb Bahr took little Ashlee to occupational and physical therapy each week. During this time, a neurologist at UCLA offered a diagnosis of cortical dysplasia, a condition in which disorganized gray matter induces seizures.

By November 1995, it was becoming obvious that Ashlee was not responding to anticonvulsant medications. Consequently, Ashlee visited neurologists at UCLA and was evaluated for an alternative treatment strategy. However, it was determined that Ashlee was not a good candidate for surgical therapy at this point. Four years and nine anticonvulsant medications later, Ashlee's parents took her once again to UCLA for another round of evaluations. Deb and Terry had been reading about treatment options especially for medically intractable seizure patients such as Ashlee. Their reading led them to the conclusion that surgery—a form of *hemispherectomy* (removal of the hemisphere in which the seizures originate)—was probably the best option for Ashlee.

A critical step in determining whether surgery was the best option was capturing a seizure with electroencephalographic (EEG) telemetry. So, at 8 years of age, Ashlee entered UCLA once again and was fitted with an electrode cap with leads to a computerized video camera so that her next seizure would be recorded for a more detailed analysis. Much to everyone's dismay, Ashlee, who had been experiencing frequent seizures, went an astounding 30 days with no seizures—a record for any epileptic patient being tracked with EEG telemetry. Convinced that her head needed a rest, the doctors sent Ashlee home, where, after a few days, she had a seizure. After another failed attempt to record a seizure in the hospital, Ashlee was sent home with a portable telemetry unit and once again defied the odds by going 7 weeks without a seizure. And just 2 days after removing her electrode cap, Ashlee experienced a seizure. It is interesting to speculate why Ashlee didn't experience seizures while she had her electrode cap on—perhaps the electrodes altered the electrical fields or activity of the neurons involved in the genesis of the seizures.

Desperate to take action, Terry Bahr convinced the neurosurgeons that they knew enough about the origin of the seizures to go forward with the surgery. They observed Ashlee time and time again as she experienced seizures and knew that the left side of the body was the first to be affected during seizures, indicating that the right hemisphere was damaged. Additionally, Ashlee was experiencing physical disabilities with her left hand and foot, indicating that the repeated seizures had further damaged the right hemisphere. The panel of surgeons at UCLA were convinced by Terry's astute observations and agreed to perform surgery to fix Ashlee's seizure-induced "wiggles" on August 17, 2000. Because complications—namely, leakage of blood into the resection cavity—had been observed in some patients with a complete hemisphere removed, a *functional hemispherectomy* was performed, in which tissue from the frontal and occipital poles was left in the cavity with the existing blood supplies intact but all nerve connections were severed.

Although approval for the surgery was the answer to the Bahrs' prayers, the hemispherectomy was still a very scary endeavor. Following a hat party at which Ashlee's

been associated with several brain areas including the prefrontal cortex, basal ganglia, parietal cortex and cerebellum (Cherdasov et al., 2009).

Focusing on neurochemical factors, researchers have found that the dopamine transporter (DAT) may be altered in ADHD patients (Krause, Dresel, Krause, la Fougere, & Ackenheil, 2003). Consequently, the most popular treatment for ADHD is the use of psychostimulants (e.g., Ritalin), drugs that activate the catecholamine neurotransmitter system. About two thirds

Ashlee, age 12

friends and family gave her 53 hats and 14 scarves for her soon-to-be shaved head, Ashlee was admitted to the hospital for surgery. Fearful but hopeful, Terry and Deb waited patiently during the 12-hour procedure and were elated when they were told that everything had gone smoothly and that their daughter was expected to be fine. During this stressful day, the Bahrs agreed to allow the Discovery Channel to follow Ashlee's progress throughout the day in an attempt to share Ashlee's story with the public. Even with successful surgery, recovery was a challenge. First came a 10-day bout of depression and frequent headaches. However, after about 12 days, Ashlee was walking and, after nearly 3 weeks, she was given a day pass to go to Disneyland. She was released from the hospital just a few days later.

Six months after Ashlee's surgery, the whole family traveled to Disneyworld in Orlando, Florida, a trip given to the Bahr family from the Starlight Wish Foundation. Nearly 4 years after her surgery, 12-year-old Ashlee was thriving—and had not had a single seizure since the removal of her right hemisphere. Her language improved immediately following surgery: The frequent seizures had interrupted processing prior to the hemispherectomy. Because the motor cortex that controlled her left body was removed, Ashlee is still striving to gain control of the left side of her body. She wears a brace on her left leg but is able to walk with a slight limp, she can move her left shoulder and arm but is still working to gain control over her left fingers, and she has an impaired visual field. Ashlee and her family agree that, although challenging, these surgery-related effects are small costs to pay for the removal of the frequent seizures that were interrupting her life every day. Following her surgery, Ashlee was placed in a special school class with fewer students to facilitate her recovery as she worked to make up lost school time and to catch up with her age-matched peers. As a preventative measure, Ashlee still takes a mild dose of an antiseizure medication to ensure that seizures will not begin in her left, seizure-free, hemisphere.

From a psychological perspective, we were interested in Ashlee's personality—did the removal of nearly half her brain interrupt the essence of her personality—her sense of humor, interactive style, optimism, and so on? Deb told us that prior to Ashlee's surgery she was a bit demanding, asking for a drink of orange juice, something she could not have as she was about to undergo anesthesia and prolonged surgery. When Ashlee returned to the intensive care unit and finally woke up, after 12 hours of anesthesia and having nearly half her brain removed, her parents were relieved at the first words out of her mouth: "Mom, I want that orange juice NOW." From not knowing if Ashlee would be able to speak, it turned out that her language was fine, her memory was perfect (even electroconvulsive therapy disrupts immediate memories), and, to her parents' delight, their little girl was just as determined as ever—her personality was definitely intact. It is reasonable to assume that Ashlee's strong sense of determination has facilitated her recovery and will continue to enable her to live a seizure-free life. Her case is a testament to the plasticity of the human brain (personal communication, 2003).

of patients with ADHD improve after pharmacological treatment (Oades et al., 2005). It has been suggested that these drugs influence dopaminergic or noradrenergic functions. More specifically, impairments in reinforcement learning and working memory have been related to low striatal dopamine levels and noradrenergic deficits have been associated with other cognitive deficits (Ellison-Wright, Ellison-Wright, & Bullmore, E., 2008). Even so, surprisingly little information is known about the actual underlying neural mechanisms associated with the cognitive and behavioral effects of these drugs (Berridge et al., 2006). Drug-related improvements, however, may be associated with side effects including loss of appetite, sleeping problems, and more rarely, movement tics and flat-affect. Concerns have recently been raised about unexplained sudden death resulting in adolescents taking methylphenidate (Dopheide & Pliszka, 2009).

In a chapter titled "Attention Deficit: The Brain Syndrome of Our Era," neuropsychiatrist and author Richard Restak (2002) implicates our contemporary fast-paced environment in changing attention spans. He suggests that our society may be selecting brains that can process several pieces of information at one time as opposed to being able to sustain uninterrupted focus on a single problem. Thus, some researchers view attention deficits as a cognitive style that is actually an adaptive response to our fast-paced world filled with text messages, cell phones that never stop ringing, and split-screen TVs with scrolling headlines so that we don't have to choose to devote our attention to just one source of information. Still other clinicians are concerned about possible overdiagnosis of ADHD (Thapar & Thapar, 2003).

The role of the environment in ADHD, however, is controversial. Many researchers, such as Russell Barkley, a clinical psychologist at the State University of New York (SUNY) emphasize the important roles of genetics and neurology in the genesis of ADHD. Barkley argues that ADHD is not a problem related to input; rather, it is a problem with the organization of the output of the brain. In support of this hypothesis, he has found that children diagnosed with ADHD pay attention appropriately in the immediate context but have difficulties responding in an effective manner, suggesting that ADHD may be more aptly described as a problem with *intention*—the ability to plan the most appropriate response to incoming stimuli. For example, in an interesting simulated driving study, subjects with ADHD routinely performed worse than their non-ADHD counterparts (Barkley et al., 2002; Barkley et al., 2005). Occasionally, upon encountering an invasive approaching stimulus (such as an oncoming car), these ADHD subjects would rather steer toward a sidewalk filled with pedestrians and accelerate, compared to control subjects, who were more likely to apply the brakes and/or steer away from the imminent danger on both sides (i.e., the oncoming car and the pedestrians) (R. Barkley, personal communication, April 2001).

THE AGING BRAIN

As discussed in Connections, it is obvious that brain and cognitive decline need not be the defining events of the last decades of life. Understanding the neurobiology of the aging brain is vital to knowing what events lie behind normal brain maturation. Further, comparing normal with abnormal aging of the brain and pathological with nonpathological conditions provides insights into what goes wrong and how to treat the conditions.

Normal Aging Processes

Though plastic, adaptable, and expansive, the brain is still subject to the wear and tear of a lifetime of use. Like other organs, the brain endures the cumulative effects of major and minor insults that take a toll on structure and function, inexorably wearing down both structure and function (see Chapter 7). Ironically, although the brain knows a lot and possesses an overwhelming store of information (the neural components of wisdom), the aging brain becomes less and less effective at retrieving and processing it all. Cognitive activity in the older brain is more susceptible to disruption and damage from a host of small and large threats, any one of which can dramatically and permanently reduce the utility of the brain.

Early histological analyses suggested that aging was accompanied by significant neuronal loss; however, more recent accurate **stereological analysis** has not supported the earlier claims (Long, Mouton, Jucker, & Ingram, 1999). When researchers compared the cortical areas of 20-year-olds and 90-year-olds, the number of neurons was fewer by only 10% in the older subjects; significant reductions were not observed in cortical glial cells either. There were some significant changes however. The length of myelinated axons and number of synapses decreased (Pakkenberg et al., 2003), and in rodents neurogenesis declines in the hippocampus (Bizon & Gallagher, 2003). Also seen in the aging brain is a reduction in dendritic expansion. Although the healthy 70-year-old brain is able to compensate for subtle cellular loss by developing more enhanced dendritic connections, this ability declines in the normal 90-year-old brain—and much earlier in those with Alzheimer's disease (Restak, 2003).

Complicating the picture is a disparity often found between brain condition and cognitive function. Some research, such as Snowden's nun aging project and certain hemispherectomy case studies, suggests that it is difficult to make direct connections between function and neuronal density. Supporting this notion in research on aging, researchers have found that old tree shrews (squirrel-like primates) demonstrated impairment in a working memory task; there was, however, no discernible difference in the young and aged hippocampal areas (Keuker, de Biurrun, Luiten, & Fuchs, 2004).

As described in Connections, the studies indicating continued brain growth into old age are perhaps the most encouraging of all research on aging. In one study, the neurotrophic factor BDNF increased in elderly rats (22 months) following the simple regime of daily swimming exercise; increased BDNF was also observed following antidepressant administration (Garza, Ha, Garcia, Chen, & Russo-Neustadt, 2004). Thus, not only are some aging brains able to hold their own until an advanced age but many are able to continue to display growth and elaboration until the very end.

Neurodegenerative Decline: Alzheimer's Disease

Unfortunately, many neurobiological conditions accelerate the normal pace of the aging brain. Brayne (2007) makes the argument that the ill health that accompanies old age is different between the sexes, with these differences becoming more pronounced the older one gets. To sum up: Whatever the proportion of life that remains can be expected to be lived in much different health states than at present. In other words, we can all expect a slow but inexorable decline. Aging is accompanied by pressure on the brain and nervous system; any form of brain damage caused by stroke, tumors, or traumatic brain injury will lead to compromised functioning; and that will lead to signs of cognitive aging (Mattson & Magnus, 2006). Other conditions, known as **neurodegenerative diseases**, have a slower onset but ultimately lead to severe behavioral and cognitive impairment (Knott, Perkins, Schwarzenbacher Bossy-Wetzel, 2008). Although several neurodegenerative diseases threaten the mental health of aging adults, there are other very good discussions of these conditions; consequently, we will only discuss

stereological analysis
Unbiased optical method of counting cells by randomly sampling various areas and depths within neural tissue.

neurodegenerative diseases Conditions that are sometimes inherited or acquired due to some sporadic condition that result in the progressive deterioration of some portion of the nervous system.

Alzheimer's disease in this chapter. Another neurodegenerative disease, Parkinson's disease, will be discussed in Chapter 7.

The main features of Alzheimer's disease seem to be the plaques and neurofibrillary tangles that are present in the brain. These neuronal features are anything but normal and are reminiscent of the underbrush that clutters an otherwise clear forest. Like neural kudzu, the plaques (deposits of the otherwise necessary neuronal protein β-amyloid) and tangles gum up and interfere with the normal processing of action potentials. Further, these deposits hamper interneuronal associations, packing the adjacent neuropil with clutter. As neurons become more and more encumbered and choked off, they begin to die; formerly useful pathways, some in use since infancy, lose efficacy. Dendritic arbors, the span of a neuron and its range of influence, also show changes, though these are region-specific and may reflect compensatory mechanisms on the part of affected neurons or nuclei. Although much research is currently being conducted on this debilitating disease, especially research related to declining levels of acetylcholine (ACh) observed in Alzheimer patients, a cure still eludes the medical community. Efforts have focused on some of the intraneuronal pool of proteins that seem to go awry, including β-amyloid, the cholesterol carrier, apolipoprotein (Bu, 2009), tau (Ballatore, Lee & Trojanowski, 2007), and α-synuclein (also affected in Parkinson's sufferers [Goedert, 2001]). A recent compilation (Mucke, 2009) highlights the work being done on therapies for those with Alzheimer's disease, and provides a glimmer of hope for patients. Among the promising treatments (see Table 1 in Mucke, 2009), for which various clinical stage trials are ongoing, are immunizations against β-amyloid, in essence vaccinating against Alzheimer's disease, together with treatments that affect immunoglobulins, also targeting β-amyloid removal from brain. Finally, therapies that focus on the mitochondria, the canaries in the coal mine of neural degeneration, also present a hopeful approach to preventing or slowing down the onslaught of Alzheimer's disease progression (Knott et al., 2008).

DEVELOPMENT OF KEY NEUROHORMONAL CIRCUITS

Once the brain is formed, it continues to influence the many neurobiological systems that shape the organism's future. Because it is rare for just one brain area to be involved in certain behavioral responses, we speak of "neurobiological circuits" to describe a collection of areas that communicate with one another to assure the most effective responses. As you learned in Chapter 5, neurochemicals such as neurotransmitters and hormones greatly facilitate the communication among various brain and body structures. In this section we discuss two *neurohormonal circuits*—these pathways integrate appropriate brain and body areas through specific hormonal signals that significantly influence important response systems, namely, sexual differentiation and the development of the stress response. As we discuss these systems, two among many such circuits, the importance of hormones in maintaining appropriate functions becomes apparent. Although the sexual and stress hormones are emphasized here, most of the influential hormones, all important in the orchestration of development and maintenance of important physiological functions, are presented in Table 6.2 and the structures that release these hormones are shown in Figure 6.7.

Table 6.2 Major Hormones Influencing Development in the Body

Source	Hormone	Primary Function(s)
Hypothalamus	Hypothalamic releasing hormones (e.g., corticotropin-releasing hormone [CRH], gonadotropin-releasing hormone [GnRH])	Stimulates or inhibits the release of pituitary hormones
Anterior pituitary	Luteinizing hormone (LH)	Stimulates the production of testosterone (in men) and progesterone (in women); promotes ovulation
	Follicle-stimulating hormone (FSH)	Promotes spermatogenesis in men; stimulates estrogen secretion and maturation of the ovum (in women)
	Growth hormone (GH) (also known as somatotropin)	Promotes protein synthesis and body growth
	Adrenocorticotropic hormone (ACTH)	Promotes glucocorticoid secretion
	Thyrotropin/thyroid stimulating hormone (TSH)	Promotes thyroxin secretion and increases metabolic rate and growth
Posterior pituitary	Arginine vasopressin/antidiuretic hormone (AVP/ADH)	Promotes water reabsorption in kidneys; involved with social interactions
	Oxytocin (OT)	Promotes milk letdown and uterine contractions during the birth process; involved in social interactions such as maternal and sexual behavior
Pineal gland	Melatonin	Influences biological rhythms (e.g., sleep/wake cycles) and reproductive functions
Parathyroid gland	Parathyroid hormone (PTH)	Increases calcium levels in the blood
Thyroid gland	Thyroxine	Increases metabolic rate and growth
Adrenal cortex	Glucocorticoids (cortisol, corticosterone)	Elevate blood sugar levels in liver; increase protein and fat metabolism (typically during stress)
Adrenal medulla	Epinephrine, norepinephrine	Promote increased blood pressure and other responses characteristic of sympathetic arousal
Pancreas	Insulin	Facilitates storage of glucose in cells; promotes storage of fats
Ovary	Estrogens	Promote female sexual maturation; regulate sexual behavior
	Progesterone	Promotes uterine and mammary gland development; maintains pregnancy
Testis	Testosterone	Promotes male sexual maturation; spermatogenesis

Adapted from Kalat, 2001

Sexual Differentiation and Brain Development

In mammals, the developing organism receives an X chromosome–bearing gamete (the egg) from the mother and a Y chromosome–bearing or an X chromosome–bearing gamete (the sperm) from the father. If the offspring receives two X chromosomes, the child will be a genetic female; if the child receives both an X and a Y chromosome, the child will be a genetic male. At the foundation of the respective sexes lies a brain that is shaped by these genetic forces to become male or to become female—an effect that will color virtually everything the individual person is capable of doing.

From the standpoint of the brain, what does it mean to be male or female? How is the dichotomy accomplished? The genes set into motion a cascade of events that culminates in the differential exposure of the developing brain

Box 6.2

Brain Matters

The Maternal Brain

"'M' is for the many things she does" is a variation of the venerable old paean to mother. Have you ever stopped to notice the behavior of a typical mom? Carrying a child on one hip while preparing dinner with the other hand and holding the phone under her chin, at the same time calling spelling words out to an older child at the kitchen table. Every mother, whether human or rat, does a vast number of things for her offspring to ensure their survival, growth, and development. In the process and underlying her motivations, she protects her own priceless genetic investment. Of the systems that are affected as a result of pregnancy and that regulate the many behavioral changes characteristic of the maternal female, the brain experiences striking modifications.

We (the authors) have been examining the changes in the mother rat that mark her transition from virgin to pregnant to postpartum female. The experiences combine to fundamentally change structural, neural, glial, and behavioral facets of the female's pup-related repertoire—all designed to protect the female's large genetic and metabolic investment in her offspring. Interestingly, we are finding a kind of symbiosis in the postpartum period: The mother helps her offspring, but the offspring seem to help their mother as well. We have observed improvements in learning and memory and, more recently, reductions in neural and behavioral indices of anxiety, stress responsiveness, and propensity to addiction in maternal rats. Further, we have found that the offspring themselves may directly— through sensory stimulation of their mothers—contribute to both their and their mother's development. In

short, pregnancy and the resulting offspring stimulation characteristic of the postpartum period may represent a type of enriching environment to the mothers, which may produce ancillary effects that extend far beyond the maternal–infant interaction.

Among the brain changes we have observed in the maternal rat are increased cell size in the hypothalamus (medial preoptic area), more dendritic spines in the hippocampus, and less stress-induced c-fos activation in the amygdala and hippocampus. Additionally, these effects appear to be long-lasting or permanent. Senescent females who have had one or two litters maintain learning and memory performance on some tasks that far exceeds that of their age-matched nulliparous counterparts when tested at 6, 12, 18, and 24 months of age. Further, the levels of a protein that presages neurodegeneration (for example, Alzheimer's disease), amyloid precursor protein (APP), are significantly higher in the brains of old (24 months) rats that have had no maternal experience.

Together, these data paint an interesting picture of offspring-induced changes in the female that supports the hypothesis that the effects on the mother may extend far beyond the postpartum period and into neurobiology and behavior associated with, but not directly controlling, infant care and protection. Furthermore, the offspring may play a much more active role in their own survival and care through sensory cue–induced modifications of their mother's (or caregiver's) neurobiology. The mother and pup relationship may be much more of a symbiosis than the current, generally held unidirectional (mother to young) model. The reproductive changes we and others are observing may represent a wholesale alteration of brain and behavior that reaches into many more facets of the female's life, and for significantly longer, than currently realized (Kinsley et al., 1999; Kinsley & Lambert, 2006, 2008; Wartella et al., 2003).

to gonadal steroid hormones. The hormones direct the development of brain regions (and gross body anatomy) that eventually respond to the activating actions of male versus female hormones during puberty and thereafter. For the female, additional hormonal fluctuations that are attributable to the menstrual cycle, pregnancy, and lactation contribute to a brain that is vastly different from the male's brain (Box 6.2). In general, nature produces male and female brains that are similar, but hormones push the brains toward different ends of a continuum that produces nearly as many differences as similarities.

During prenatal development, once the respective gonads are established, the stage is set for sexual differentiation, the process whereby males become male and females, female. The ovaries of the female and the testes of the male come into play as the embryo becomes the fetus. From the standpoint of the male's tissues, including the brain, it is the presence of **testosterone** that marks him as a male. Possessing the XY genotype is no guarantee that the fetus will be male in the ways in which it is idiomatically understood: Phenotypically, a male acts male-like, engaging in sex-specific/stereotypical aggressive, parental, and sexual behaviors. Only through the stimulation of the brain by male hormones does the male become what the average person thinks is male. For the female, exposure to male-like levels of testosterone would masculinize her and in high enough levels could render her sterile—which raises interesting questions about how to define the terms *male* and *female*.

Males and females are born and shaped into their respective neurobiological roles through a succession of hormone–neuron interactions. Males have two complementary processes that male hormones initiate. One is called *defeminization*, the process by which inherent female characteristics and behaviors are suppressed by exposure to male hormones. The complementary process to defeminization is *masculinization*, in which male-like behaviors and characters are promoted. The effects of both processes are played out in the standard repertoire of male behaviors. For the female, the processes required for development include behavioral mechanisms that ensure female-like behavior and physiological systems. The female, therefore, undergoes a process of *feminization*, in which female-characteristic behaviors are developed, and *demasculinization*, in which any male-like tendencies are suppressed. Together, male and female development depends on the proper timing and levels of exposure to the requisite hormonal states. For males, testosterone is required; for females, the lack of testosterone is important and necessary. Deviations from these basic structures may result in alterations, or variation, in sexual differentiation. Again, this raises the issue of how gender is defined: Genetically? Neurally? Behaviorally? Based on superficial characteristics such as wardrobe or musical tastes? In fairness, it is obvious that nature approaches sexual/gender roles simply, as merely avenues of normal variability. Both are dictated by the wiring that the brain undergoes following hormone exposure.

The steroid hormones released by the testes, primarily testosterone, interact with the brain to guide development, similar to the way in which neurotransmitters interact with neurons to influence action potentials. The hormones circulating in the bloodstream (or hormones produced directly by the brain, called *neurohormones*) are lipophilic substances, able to gain easy access to and through fatty membranes like the cell and nuclear membranes. Some hormones, like testosterone, bind to specific receptors either on the membrane of neurons or, once inside the neuron, to receptors in the cytosol or on the nuclear membrane. Once bound to the receptor, the hormone is actively transported to the nucleus via intracellular proteins (in the case of cell membrane or cytosolic receptors). Once the hormone molecules gain

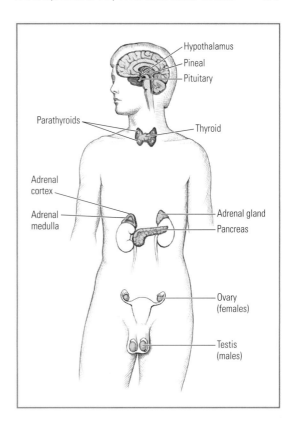

Figure 6.7
Endocrine system Shown here are the major endocrine glands that release hormones throughout the body.
AFTER STRAUB, 2002, P. 94

testosterone A steroid hormone produced by the testes that is important in the differentiation of the male brain and body.

sexually dimorphic nucleus of the preoptic area (SDN-POA) Region of the anterior hypothalamic preoptic area that has a larger volume in male rats than in female rats.

access to the nucleus, they have the capacity to alter the genomic modulation of intraneuronal activities. They can speed up or slow down or otherwise change what the neuron is designed to do. They can alter the protein synthesis within the neuron, affecting the shape, size, and function of the cell. They add to the enormous capacity for neuroplasticity inherent to the brain. In essence, hormones are modulators, prodding the activity of neurons in specific directions (Figure 6.8). They are like the volume knob on a preamplifier, turning up or down the signal until it is tuned properly.

Testosterone makes changes in the brain that alter structure and function. Its presence increases the size of various nuclei in the male's brain, for instance, in a well-described structure called the **sexually dimorphic nucleus of the preoptic area (SDN-POA)**. The male nucleus is significantly larger than the female's, an effect that disappears if the newborn male is deprived of testosterone (i.e., demasculinized). Conversely, a female treated with testosterone displays a male-like SDN-POA. At puberty, the ebbs and flows of hormones cascade and wash over the organizational infrastructure of the brain to enact so-called activational effects (e.g., body hair growth, sexual behavior, antlers [in deer and related species]). That is, the hormones characteristic of puberty—testosterone in the male, estrogen and progesterone in the female—feed back to the brain, again binding to and occupying receptors on the neurons and contributing to further development of the brain.

Sex hormones produce brain differences beyond the SDN-POA. Generally, male brains are larger and more asymmetrical than female brains (Kovalev, Kruggel, & von Cramon, 2003). A plethora of more microanatomical sex differences persist as well, but they are too numerous to discuss in the constraints of this chapter. It is important to know, however, that such brain sex differences exist. Sex differences in the brain, referred to as "organizational" because of their early and apparently permanent effects, dictate the ways in which neurons act individually or in combination and the many ways in which the neurons establish synapses with each other. Certainly, hormonal and neuroanatomical differences contribute to well-described sex differences in mental health.

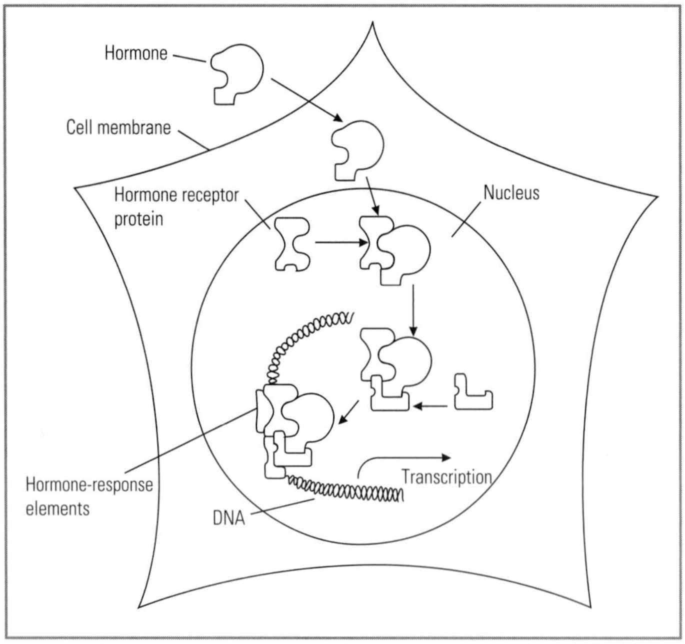

Figure 6.8
Hormone–neuron interactions The hormones that exert such striking effects on the brain and behavior begin by exerting their effects on the neuron. By binding to receptors on the surface of the neuronal membrane or by being absorbed into the neuron, the hormone travels to the nucleus. There, it interacts with the DNA to modify its inherent program of neuronal regulation.
AFTER MCEWEN, P. 69

Development of the Stress Response

Although Hans Selye advocated the generalized adaptation syndrome (GAS), in which different stressors led to standard stress responses, ever more research demonstrates that significant individual differences exist in responding to stress (see Chapter 12 for more on Selye's work). For example, a student in one of our labs undertook the simple task of exposing young adult laboratory rats to fox urine, a predator odor. The student reported that the rats had very different responses to the urine-saturated cotton ball. Some fled to the opposite sides of the cages and remained frozen for several minutes. Some approached the cotton balls, picked them up, stuffed them in the cage tops above, and proceeded to move around the cages, digging and moving the bedding. Still others approached the cotton balls and proceeded to shred them to pieces. Why should a major stressor—that of a threatening predator—evoke such diverse responses? Could it be related to the variance inherent to behavior, leading to beneficial and adaptive outcomes depending on unique environmental situations that exist at that moment?

Keep in mind that the rats are practically genetic clones of one another and had been exposed to very similar environments up to that point. What could account for such differing behavioral responses to this stressful stimulus? Research on parental involvement, aging, and sex differences suggests reasons for these differing responses.

Mom's impact on the developing stress response. Those of you who embrace Freud's ideas—but only briefly and gently, it is hoped—will be interested to discover that an animal's infancy and relationship with its mother play a critical role in the subsequent development of the stress response. Seymour Levine, who worked at the University of California–Davis in the last years of his career, conducted extensive research on a period during postnatal days 4–14 known as the "stress hyporesponsive period," in which young rats do not show the normal stress response that you learned about in Chapter 5. Specifically, Levine and others have shown that maternal factors play an integral role in suppressing the ACh and glucocorticoid responses to most stressful stimuli. Tactile stimulation (for example, grooming), feeding, and passive contact all contribute to the suppressed hypothalamic–pituitary–adrenal (HPA) axis activation (Levine, 2001).

Although there is no specific evidence of such a rigid time of hyporesponsiveness in human infants, research by Megan Gunnar and her colleagues at the University of Minnesota's Institute of Child Development suggests that striking parallels exist in human children. She has observed a suppressed HPA response in infants with healthy relationships with their caregivers. These infants mature into children who respond to novel situations with lower cortisol responses than their counterparts who experienced weaker attachments with their caregivers during this critical time (Gunnar, 1998). Experience dictates subsequent responsiveness: The child is father of the man.

Genetics may not be the only way for the inheritance of traits to be passed on. Michael Meaney and colleagues at McGill University have shown that maternal contact has a prominent impact on the development of a rat's stress response (Meaney, Aitken, & Sapolsky, 1991). His team was interested in findings reporting that when pups were separated from their mothers for about 15 minutes each day for the first 2 weeks of postnatal life—a process known as "handling" or "maternal separation," the rats develop a more efficient stress response, persisting through adulthood, protecting it from the damaging effects of a hyperresponsive HPA axis. When the handled offspring are tested in adulthood, they show increased binding capacity at the glucocorticoid receptors but not the mineralocorticoid receptors in the hippocampus. More glucocorticoid receptor sites lead to a more efficient negative feedback system in the hippocampus, resulting in lower levels of glucocorticoids than in nonhandled controls (Meaney et al., 1985).

Specifically, handling increases glucocorticoid-receptor binding capacity in the frontal cortex and hippocampus but interestingly not in the amygdala, septum, hypothalamus, or pituitary. The net effect of the handling seems to be an enhanced negative feedback system that results in approximately a 50% reduction in stress hormone production for the entire life of the rat (Caldji et al., 2001; Meaney et al., 1991).

Meaney's investigations into the mechanisms involved in this effect have revealed that it is the mother's increased attention, not lack of attention, which is critical. When Meaney and his colleagues observed the mother–pup interactions in handled animals, they found that the mothers of handled pups spent significantly more time manipulating (for example, licking, as seen in Figure 6.9) their offspring than did mothers of nonhandled pups (Francis & Meaney, 1999).

In an article titled "Like Mother, Like Daughter" Champagne and Meaney (2001) describe how the maternal strategy, defined by variations in licking, grooming, and arched back nursing, is passed on to the next generation—or from mothers to daughters. This intergenerational transmission, however, is not based on genetics. When rat pups from a low-contact mother were raised by a high-contact foster mother, the grown rat exhibited maternal behavior similar to the high-contact mother, suggesting a behavioral, or nongenomic, transmission of maternal behavior (Francis, Diorio, Liu, & Meaney, 1999). More recent work (McGowan et al., 2009) verified the effect of maternal care influences on glucocorticoid-receptor expression and extended it to humans. The effect in the hippocampus suggests some interesting and long-lasting regulation of memory in the human, the implications of which may extend into many facets of social interaction.

Stress and aging. Life is stressful. This paradoxical axiom (i.e., a simple but discouraging observation) is, considering the detrimental role the stress hormone cortisol or corticosterone has on the hippocampus, accurate. As described in Chapter 5, as we age, the stress time of the hippocampus accumulates, resulting in increased vulnerability to upcoming challenges. According to Sapolsky (1996), in addition to reduced dendritic processes, hippocampal cells exposed to excessive levels of glucocorticoids are likely to undergo reduced synaptic plasticity, inhibited neurogenesis, and finally, when the neurons cannot respond to the usual neuronal insults, cell death.

Any method of reducing glucocorticoid levels or its effects, such as Meaney's modest handling technique, leads to increased survival of these important neurons. In a more drastic attempt to remove glucocorticoids in rats, adrenalectomies (the removal of the glucocorticoid-secreting adrenal gland) have been conducted. Six to nine months after removing the primary source of glucocorticoids, the animals had fewer signs of hippocampal aging (measured by assessing pyramidal neuronal density and astrocyte reactivity) than their same-age adrenal-intact counterparts (Landfield, 1987; Landfield, Baskin, & Pitler, 1981).

A dramatic demonstration of the importance of glucocorticoid levels in successful aging was reported by Sonia Cavigelli and Martha McClintock at the University of Chicago (2003). Juvenile male rats were divided into either exploratory (neophilic) or inhibited (neophobic) behavioral dispositions according to their exploration of a novel environment. When tested in novel environments across the life span, the shy rats remained shy—showing hesitancy to explore the environment accompanied by a

Figure 6.9
Maternal–offspring interaction Maternal–offspring interaction is the foundation of the development of the social life of the mammal. The subtle interactions that occur between mother and young set the stage for the offspring's reaction to, and survival in, the world to come. Here, a mother rat is shown licking one of her pups, an intimate and reciprocal behavior that can modify the pup's responsiveness and can contribute to the mother's enhanced maternal behavior.

COURTESY OF DOUG BUERLEIN, R-MC BEHAVIORAL NEUROSCIENCE LABORATORY

long-lasting elevation of stress hormones—whereas the bolder animals continued to be exploratory in the novel environment across their lifetime and showed a more transient rise in glucocorticoid levels and a faster return to baseline. Additionally, the shy rats' total life span was reduced by 20%. The two brothers in Figure 6.10 are the same elderly age of 27 months but, because of differential stress responses, vary greatly in health status. It was hypothesized that a lifetime of more efficient stress responses and uninhibited responses led to a healthier brain (especially hippocampus) and body in the bolder rat.

Figure 6.10
Coping These two brothers are 27 months of age, although the one on the left looks considerably older than his sibling. They were raised in identical environments, but they each displayed different coping strategies from their juvenile days. The rat on the right was bolder and exhibited lower corticosteroid levels than its shy brother.
COURTESY OF SONIA A. CAVIGELLI

Sex differences in the stress response. As discussed earlier in this chapter, different reproductive hormonal landscapes characterize males and females. It should come as no surprise, then, that there are sex differences in the stress response. When male and female rats are observed in different stressful tests, sex differences are often observed in both physiological and behavioral responses. For example, in the exploratory open field test, females are more active, suggesting that they are less emotional than males (Heinsbroek, van Haaren, & van de Poll, 1988). On the physiological side, however, females typically show higher baseline and stress-induced levels of glucocorticoids, suggesting that they may be more emotionally reactive in stressful situations (Michaelis et al., 2001). Thus, it appears that levels of glucocorticoids are not always a reflection of the degree of "emotionality" observed in the animal's behavior. This should not be surprising given the multifaceted stress response.

Turning to research on humans, some findings suggest that, whereas women may be more susceptible to stress-related mental illness, men may be more susceptible to stress-related cardiovascular illness. In one study, men and women were asked to perform stressful mental arithmetic and public speaking and were monitored throughout the stress and recovery periods. Compared with the women, the men had higher blood pressure during this task (Matthews, Gump, & Owens, 2001).

In another interesting study, married couples were brought in to the laboratory and asked to discuss a topic on which they disagreed. Generally, men were more likely to demonstrate increased blood pressure and anger, accompanied by a more hostile interpersonal style (Matthews et al., 2001). Such stress-related effects in men might explain their increased vulnerability to cardiovascular disease in midlife (McEwen, 1998). On the other hand, most epidemiological studies suggest that women are more likely to develop psychiatric disorders, such as depression, as a by-product of stress. In Chapter 12 we discuss more research related to the development of the stress response and, more important, effective coping strategies for stress-induced illness.

SCIENTIFIC INTERVENTIONS WITH DEVELOPMENTAL NEUROBIOLOGY

Thus far, we have discussed nature's developmental path toward the final destination of brain development. Scientists have learned much about CNS development; in fact, so much has been learned that researchers now have

embryonic stem (ES) cells Undifferentiated cells derived from the embryo that have the potential to develop into a wide variety of cell types.

blastocyst The 150-cell preimplantation embryo comprising an outer layer, a fluid-filled cavity, and a cluster of interior cells.

the ability to intervene at certain developmental stages in an attempt to aid a disabled brain. In the following, we discuss two examples of advanced technologies and their implications for psychobiological disorders.

Stem Cells

When we first wrote this section, the study of **embryonic stem (ES) cells** was in the grip of a hard political hand—not where a developing science, ironically, in its own embryonic stages, would likely be successful. Thus, such research has been slowed by political and ethical issues secondary to the vast promise of such therapies. Still, some progress was made despite the restrictions on federal funding for such research.

The developing brain is a fount of potential. Among the sources of this enormous potential are the ES cells (Figure 6.11). These cells are pluripotent: They can differentiate into virtually any type of cell in the body, from fingernail to neuron. They are derived from the inner cell mass of the **blastocyst**, the early ball of preembryonic tissue, where they can be harvested as undifferentiated cells and maintained as such theoretically forever. The strength of these cells lies in their pluripotency: They can be chemically coaxed into becoming whatever type of cell is needed. Thus, they represent, theoretically at least, a singular opportunity for repair of the human body.

The promise of ES cells is vast, but thus far it is just that: promise. There is a tremendous amount of research devoted to their study, slowed because of the aforementioned concerns, and practical uses for the cells remain years

Figure 6.11
Stem cell differentiation The promise and peril of renewing the nervous system are exemplified by the use of embryonic stem cells. Such cells are theoretically infinitely adaptable, possessing the capacity to become or replace any cell in the body. Here, embryonic stem cells are depicted as differentiating into neurons and glia. Other tissues and organs, too, may be the beneficiaries of the embryonic stem cell's chameleonic properties. As much more basic research is required before the applications and limits of stem cells are known, political and moral obstacles must be addressed. The accompanying dilemmas must be adjudicated; otherwise, progress or alternatives—and the human lives involved—will be hindered.

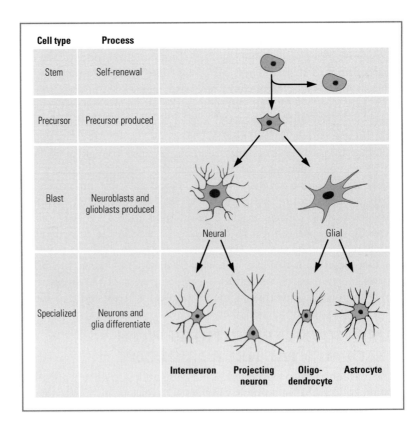

away. The cells generate such high hopes because of their two major properties. First, they are virtually immortal. That is, in the proper media and with adequate stimulation, they can generate copies of themselves indefinitely. Among the questions about stem cells is that of chromosomal integrity: Is the millionth copy of the ES cell identical to the original?

Further, the cells are undifferentiated—unassigned, as it were—and require a signal or series of delicate, subtly timed signals that sets them on their path to a lifetime of function. The chemosignals, derived nominally from adjacent tissues and environments, regulate the cells and direct their genomes to alter the production of specific proteins. The shape and activity—indeed, the cell itself—are altered. The cell becomes what it is instructed to become. Thus, an unlimited supply of stem cells can be produced and maintained following their harvest. This supply of ES cells can then be made to augment or replace the dead and dying or absent cells that are the result of disease or damage—in theory.

Recent work has suggested that ES cells are capable of treating Parkinson's disease (Kim et al., 2002). In a mouse model of the disease, the authors were able to produce ES cells by expressing a protein that is a transcription factor that regulates the differentiation of ES cells into neurons that express dopamine (DA). As mentioned in chapter 5 (and will be discussed in chapter 7), the loss of DA from midbrain neurons is the cause of Parkinson's disease. Hence, the cells that Kim and colleagues (2002) produced and subsequently transplanted in the 6-hydroxy-DA (6-OH-DA)–lesioned midbrains of rats led to both electrophysiological and behavioral recovery. That is, these cells behaved just like the animals' own normal cells. Extending this promising work to humans will mean an effective treatment for a debilitating neurological disease caused, usually, by aging.

Parkinson's disease has several characteristics that make it a primary target for ES cells. First, the site of the damage that underlies parkinsonian symptoms is very constrained. Unlike other conditions, the neural damage that produces the disease is localized to the substantia nigra in the midbrain of the patient, making it a discrete lesion whose regional inputs and outputs have been well characterized. Second, Parkinson's disease has been shown to be the result of a loss of specific neurotransmitter activity. The damage that produces Parkinson's disease is limited to a set of cells that produces the neurotransmitter DA. Augmenting DA levels or replacing the malfunctioning or absent DA neurons restores DA levels to normal and halts the neurodegenerative decline.

Researchers at Johns Hopkins University explored the therapeutic value of ES cells in an animal model of paralysis. Rats were injected with a virus that targeted the motor neurons in the spinal cord, resulting in paralysis of their hindquarters. ES cells derived from human embryonic germ cells were administered to the animals via the cerebrospinal fluid and navigated their way through the spinal fluid, appearing to have developed into mature motor neurons. The final outcome of the cells, however, remains a question. It is possible that trophic (growth) factors in the ES cocktail stimulated the new growth of the virus-infected cells (Kerr et al., 2003). It is easy to see how such results would provide hope for the many humans suffering from neuromuscular impairment.

Other conditions, such as Alzheimer's disease, diabetes, spinal cord injuries, and arthritis, may also one day be treatable by means of ES cell therapy.

adult stem cells
Undifferentiated cells located in a currently differentiated tissue; these cells have the ability to renew themselves and differentiate, within certain limits, to various specialized cell types characteristic of the tissue from which they were derived.

The ES cells derived from human embryos have, however, been embroiled in controversy almost from the moment that scientists first identified them (see Connections in the epilogue). Another type of stem cell, **adult stem cells**, might be less controversial. These are undifferentiated cells that are taken from differentiated cells in a developed organism. These cells give rise to mature cells that have specific characteristics and functions. For example, stem cells that develop into blood cells are found in the bone marrow. The primary difference between ES cells and adult stem cells is their origin. It is thought that adult stem cells exist in several types of tissue in the human body and are quite rare. ES cells have been shown to develop in tissue culture following their derivation from the inner cell mass of the developing embryo. Further, adult stem cells do not seem to have the pluripotency of ES cells that allows for differentiation into a vast number of cell lineages; this threshold limits their use. Overall, their flexibility and promise are not as great as those of ES cells, but they evoke fewer moral dilemmas than their contentious ES counterparts (National Institutes of Health, 2009). Recent work has reinforced the value—and limitations—of adult stem cells (National Institutes of Health, 2009); but our life sciences community is nothing if not innovative, and it is likely that with continued support, important and valuable discoveries will be made.

Mammalian Cloning

In a famous scene in the 1946 Disney movie *Fantasia*, Mickey Mouse, as the sorcerer's apprentice, is confronted by the scores of brooms he has inadvertently created. Starting with one, he ends up with rooms full of brooms full of swishing activity, but none behaving as he had anticipated. The image that ensues is a disastrous slapstick of chaos and confusion. Today, it symbolizes the average person's fears about the idea of cloning, the marriage of technology and the immaturity of the forces that would control it, like a child waving a loaded gun. Could Mickey's tribulations be a metaphor for the perception of chaos that may result from cloning technology?

The promise and specter of artificially creating identical copies of an organism have been around for decades. Though nature performs cloning in a variety of ways, many of which we have come to take for granted, having the means and motive to do it ourselves raises the process to another level. Inbreeding does (more or less) naturally what cloning does but with a large difference: The descendents are nearly genetically identical (sharing more than 99% of genes), but they are not copies of one another. A parthenogenetic (asexual) organism such as the diploid Colorado checkered whiptail (*Cnemidophorus tesselatus*), in which nearly all the offspring are female and reproduction takes place in the male's absence, is closer to the idea of a clone. But this organism has a different chromosomal set and a vastly different natural history from a mammal.

In the cloned sheep Dolly, researchers removed the DNA of an adult sheep from well-defined somatic cells and injected it into an egg whose genome had been removed, thereby replacing the resident DNA with the adult's version. The resulting "offspring," born on July 5, 1996, was the first true clone. What made Dolly different was that she contained the DNA from just a single parent, the donor, following a process referred to as "somatic cell nuclear transfer." In essence, she was a deferred twin of the donor animal (Wilmut, Schnieke, McWhir, Kind, & Campbell, 1997).

It had been theoretically possible to take an adult organism, remove a portion of the DNA—its genetic "blueprint"—and then "grow" the DNA as an identical copy of the organism. In fact, research into this very technique had been going on since the 1960s. The creation of Dolly confirmed the theories, but the work by Ian Wilmut's group added features to the theory. For instance, removing the genome of an established adult cell, then finding that its function could be reestablished in a blastocyst had not been known. Further, the work demonstrated that the implanted DNA was capable of full activity, though the host was a mature cell. The steps leading to Dolly's creation, a delayed copy of an existing adult, were almost as significant as the act itself.

The notion of the word "copy," however, causes the rub. A clone will be a genetic replica, sharing the superficial and silent characteristics of the donor; but the resemblance is, nearly literally, only skin deep. And, it has been demonstrated, not even that: Dolly, who died sooner than expected, evinced some marked phenotypical differences from her parent. In Figure 6.12 you'll see a kitten (named "CC" for "Copy Cat") cloned from the cat beside it (Rainbow)—their fur patterns are not even similar. Because of variations in environmental pressures, not only is their appearance very different but also the researchers at Texas A&M report that CC is much more playful than the reserved Rainbow. Thus, this clone is far from a phenotypical copy (cat). That is, the donor and the clone share the nature portion of the nature-nurture equation, but a shared or even a remotely similar environment is impossible to duplicate. We have to remember that clones have been among us for as long as women have been having children. The "natural" clones are identical twins. Even when two individuals who are genetic clones are raised in the same home by the same parents at the same time, many individual differences can exist between twins. Unless the twins are conjoined, their environments will be vastly different; even if conjoined, literally attached at the hip, small differences in the way in which they are facing or looking could produce variation in their respective sensory environments.

In the case of cloning an organism from an adult, the unique experiences that shaped the brain of the organism cannot be recreated in its clone. They are lost. Consequently, those who promote cloning of mammals—themselves, their friends and loved ones, and (expensively) their pets as a way of preserving the loved qualities of the donors—fundamentally miss the point: How does one recreate in the clone those personal memories that make up the personality of the donor individual when the memories are exclusive and irreproducible?

On hearing the word "clone," the average person conjures up a science fiction image of cell scrapings morphing into identical copies of the original—the sorcerer's apprentice's brooms. This type of cloning is referred to as "reproductive cloning," and it bears the brunt of the ethical criticisms related to cloning. Another type of cloning, therapeutic cloning, is less likely to evoke the stiff resistance that has met the announcement of cloning technology. Similar to reproductive cloning, therapeutic, or research, cloning also includes the replacement of the donor egg nucleus with DNA from an adult cell. But unlike reproductive cloning, the cell is not transplanted to a surrogate uterus so that it can develop into an organism. In therapeutic cloning protocols, after a few

Figure 6.12
Cloning The kitten is a clone of the cat, but, as evident in the picture, genetic clones do not always develop identical phenotypes.
COURTESY OF TEXAS A&M UNIVERSITY, COLLEGE OF VETERINARY MEDICINE

days of dividing, ES cells are harvested. It is thought that these cells may be prodded into the development of specific cells to replace degenerating cells, such as a replacement liver or pancreas or the degenerating substantia nigra cells in patients with Parkinson's disease. Thus, therapeutic cloning offers hope for those suffering from neurodegenerative disease.

Summary

Prenatal Brain Development

Following fertilization, the emerging nervous system goes through a whirlwind of changes on its journey to becoming the organ we recognize as a brain. Following the pattern of induction, proliferation, migration, aggregation, differentiation, circuit formation, apoptosis, and synapse rearrangement, a brain and associated nervous system spring to life. Prior to differentiation, these pluripotent cells have the potential to become various types of cells, ranging from skin to neurons. During the developmental process, the layer of cells known as the ectoderm gives rise to the neural plate, leading to the eventual emergence of the neural tube, from which the rostral opening becomes the premature brain. During this intense time of development, tens of thousands of neurons can be produced per minute. By just 12 weeks of prenatal age, the human brain assumes the shape it will have in the mature individual. At this point, neurotrophins and radial glia play an important role in establishing the many important connections among the immature neurons. Unnecessary neurons are pruned away to make room for the essential neurons necessary to form the brain's many circuits.

Postnatal Brain Development

The postnatal brain is further influenced by the many sensory and experiential forces that the newborn encounters throughout its development. Research suggests that exposure to more enriching environments leads to enhanced complexity of cortical neurons. During this continued development, neurogenesis, or the production of new neurons, continues to accommodate increasing brain volume. The final areas of the brain to mature are the executive frontal lobes, which typically mature during adolescence. Altered brain development may result in conditions such as attention-deficit/hyperactivity disorder.

The Aging Brain

As the brain ages, about 10% of its neurons are lost; however, the brain maintains its capacity for neural plasticity. In some cases, neurodegenerative diseases such Alzheimer's disease result in accelerated loss of brain tissue and accompanying function.

Development of Key Neurohormonal Circuits

Differentiated neural areas that communicate with one another comprise the neurobiological circuits essential for efficient brain processing. Further, neurohormonal circuits exist to integrate appropriate brain areas with important hormonal signals. One such circuit oversees sexual differentiation. In the genetic male, testosterone plays a critical role in leading to masculinization of the animal. One well-known sexually dimorphic brain structure is the preoptic area of the hypothalamus, which is larger in males than in females. After influencing the organizational infrastructure of the brain, neurohormonal circuits continue to play critical developmental roles by triggering activational effects, such as body hair growth, as the animal matures. Another critical neurohormonal circuit is the stress response. There is evidence that some animals undergo a stress hyporesponsive period early in postnatal development that may play a critical role in CNS maturation. Alterations of stress hormones early in an animal's life have been shown to influence stress responsiveness across the life span. Animals experiencing elevated stress hormone secretion across their lifetimes are susceptible to hippocampal damage and other health risks later in life.

Scientific Interventions with Developmental Neurobiology

As scientists have learned more about how the CNS develops and technological breakthroughs have been made, practitioners and researchers have been able to intervene with the developing brain. Stem cells are the topic of intense discussion as scientists consider ways to guide their development into cells that may be damaged in an individual's brain, such as the substantia nigra in a patient suffering from Parkinson's disease. Therapeutic cloning is also being considered as a possible mechanism to replace failing nervous system structures. These techniques, however, are controversial and must satisfy both scientific and public concerns before being used for therapeutic purposes.

Key Terms

apoptosis (160)

pluripotent (160)

stem cells (161)

ectoderm (161)

mesoderm (161)

endoderm (161)

neural plate (161)

neural groove (161)

neural folds (161)

neural tube (161)

neural crest (161)

neuropores (161)

neuropil (162)

filopodia (164)

neurotrophins (165)

brain-derived neurotrophic factor (BDNF) (165)

nerve growth factor (NGF) (165)

cell adhesion molecules (CAMs) (165)

radial glia (167)

neurogenesis (167)

attention-deficit/hyperactivity disorder (170)

frontostriatal circuitry (170)

stereological analysis (175)

neurodegenerative diseases (175)

testosterone (178)

sexually dimorphic nucleus of the preoptic area (SDN-POA) (180)

embryonic stem (ES) cells (184)

blastocyst (184)

adult stem cells (186)

For Further Consideration

Bainbridge, D. (2001). *Making babies: The science of pregnancy.* Cambridge, MA: Harvard University Press. This book could be subtitled "Everything you always wanted to know about pregnancy but didn't know how to ask." The author explains a multidetermined process in a very entertaining fashion. A good writer, Bainbridge is able to convey the wonder he feels about the entire process together with the science that is at the heart of his descriptions.

Colapinto, J. (2001). *As nature made him: The boy who was raised as a girl.* New York: Harper Perennial. Twin infant boys are taken to a hospital to be circumcised. In one circumcision, the cauterizing device goes awry, reducing the infant's penis to an ashen stalk. The parents, faced with an awful decision, and getting the then "best-guess" medical advice, choose to raise their son as their daughter. The decision in this case would prove to be a bad one. Although the parents made every attempt to turn the boy into a girl, his life was rife with self-doubt and confusion, and he never felt comfortable with the fiction surrounding him. When, in his middle teens, he decided to abandon the charade and came to grips with the fact that he was a male, the process was wrenching and eventually fatal. The book emphasizes the important influences of prenatal and early postnatal gonadal hormone exposure.

Purves, D. (1994). *Neural activity and the growth of the brain.* Cambridge, UK: Cambridge University Press. This small volume is packed with very interesting information on the formation of the brain, embryo to adult. The book begins with an examination of the steps involved in nervous system development and follows with the layer-upon-layer maturation that gives rise to the mature brain. The images in the text, drawings and photomicrographs, also capture the diverse and rich steps involved in the formation of the brain and nervous system. Purves, a stalwart in the field of developmental neuroscience, has managed to produce a book that is free of unnecessary clutter, focused like a lens on the myriad biochemical interactions that define the developing brain.

Raisman, G., & Field, P. M. (1971). Sexual dimorphism in the preoptic area of the rat. *Science, 173,* 731–733. Before this pioneering study was undertaken and reported, the question of physical differences between the sexes—that males and females look different—was little contested. Behavioral sex differences, the subtle and not so subtle palette of activities undertaken by males and females and usually viewed in terms of deficiencies on the part of one sex or the other, were more grudgingly accepted. The possibility that the brains of males and females were different, though obvious now, was viewed with tremendous skepticism 30 years ago. Using electron microscopy, Raisman and Field examined the hypothalami of males and females. They studied the synaptic input to neurons from that region, reporting that females had a greater number of synapses than did males on a comparable set of hypothalamic neurons. These data were provocative because they were among the first set to document with great clarity what many scientists and the general public already believed: that the brains of males and females were different, leading to behavioral differences. These data set into motion a field that today is finding remarkable effects of hormones on a variety of neural systems.

Singh, I. (2008). *Beyond polemics: science and ethics of ADHD. Nature Reviews Neuroscience,* 9, 957–964. This in-depth review examines the benefits and applications that accrue to a multidisciplinary approach to the study and treatment of individuals with ADHD. The review encourages relationships that depend not on one particular approach, but on the synergy that results from close attention to the data from complementary fields—particularly as they are applied to ADHD. As neuroscience has the best hope of understanding the underpinnings of ADHD, it stands to inform the other fields deeply, but cannot be done in a vacuum or without, in the parlance of NIH, translational contexts. Only then, that author states, can they best "establish an empirical evidence base from which to assess the risks and benefits of psychotropic drugs for children" (p. 963). Currently, those children with ADHD, and pediatric psychiatry, in general, deserve better than they receive now.

Zhou, J. N., Hofman, M. A., Gooren, L. J., & Swaab, D. F. (1995). A sex difference in the human brain and its relation to transsexuality. *Nature, 378,* 68–70. Sexual preference is only one aspect of a person's sexuality. Gender identity, the feeling that one is male or female, may be regulated by brain structures and influenced by developmental forces such as hormones. For instance, homosexual males are male, they "think" of themselves as male, but they are attracted to males. Male-to-female transsexuals, on the other hand, feel that they are *females* and are attracted to males—an important distinction. Zhou and colleagues examine the volume of a structure called the bed nucleus of the stria terminalis, central subdivision (BNSTc) in postmortem heterosexual males and females, homosexual males, and male-to-female transsexuals. The BNSTc was shown to be virtually identical in heterosexual and homosexual males and significantly larger than those of the heterosexual females. In the male-to-female transsexuals, however, the BNSTc was very similar to that of heterosexual females. These data suggest strongly that this brain region may play a role in self-identification with the gender toward which one is fated to orient.

Multiple Perspectives of Clinical Neuroscience

In this insert, multiple neurobiological perspectives are presented to reinforce the Windows of Clinical Neuroscience presented in Chapter 1. As we gather information about the brain's complex functions, in most cases, the most informed views will emerge from a convergence of relevant evidence. As students of Clinical Neuroscience, it is imperative that we continue to consider multiple perspectives as we draw conclusions about the brain's functions in the maintenance of mental health.

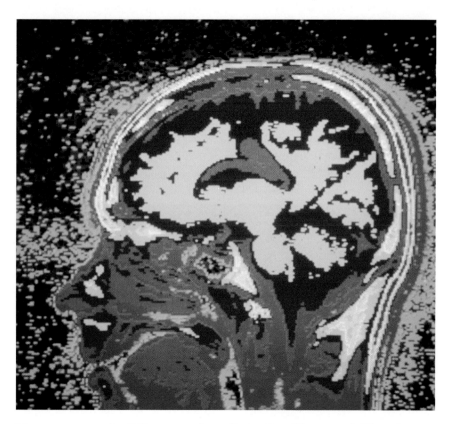

Neuroanatomical Perspective: Complex Neuronal Circuits

In this computer-generated image, we're reminded of the immense interconnections among the various structures of the brain. Like a person standing on an enormous beach holding a tiny handful of sand, our knowledge of the brain is modest but growing. As more information is revealed about the brain's structure, we gain the ability to understand and, hopefully, treat those situations where the "wiring diagram" goes slightly awry.

Computer screen with image of brain scan © Richard Pasley/Doctor Stock/Science Faction/Corbis.

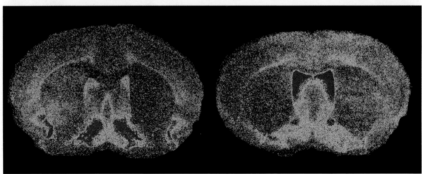

Neurochemical Perspective:
Is "Love" or "Chemistry" for Real?

The prairie vole (pictured above) has received attention for its monogamous mating strategy. Larry Young (Emory University) has found that the neuropeptide vasopressin plays an integral role in these animals' pair-bonding and behavior.

Pictured below the prairie voles are photomicrographs of brains from the monogamous prairie vole (left) and the polygamous montane vole (right); the red areas indicate dense patches of concentrated vasopressin receptors. In the prairie vole the receptors are clustered around the brain's so-called reward center, the ventral pallidum and nucleus accumbens (McGraw & Young, 2009). Hence, it can be argued that complex behaviors such as pair-bonding and monogamy are neurochemically-regulated.

Above: Courtesy of Dr. Todd H. Ahern. Below: Courtesy of Dr. Larry Y. Young.

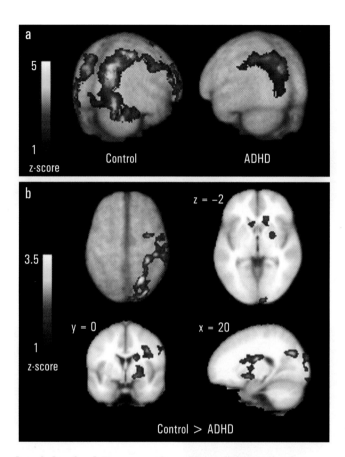

Neurophysiological Perspective: The ADHD Brain

These images depict fMRI scans of the brains of two groups of 8–12 year old boys: a group diagnosed with ADHD and a control group. When asked to perform a mental rotation task, the response times and accuracy rates were similar, but the brain activation patterns were very different. As seen in both images, the control brains have more activity (depicted in red) in the parietal and occipital lobes when compared to the children diagnosed with ADHD. Thus, these fMRI images suggest that the neurophysiology is different between control and ADHD males (Vance, Silk, Casey, Rinehart, Bradshaw, Bellgrove, et al., 2007).

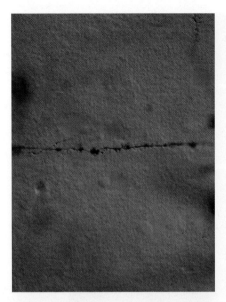

Neurodevelopment Perspective: Neuronal Changes Continue Throughout Life

A segment of a neuron's dendrite taken from the hippocampus of a virgin female rat is pictured above left, showing the paucity of dendritic spines, which increase the surface area of a neuron and are involved in synaptic communication. Above right, a similar hippocampal neuronal dendritic segment, this time from a lactating female rat. Note the marked difference in the quality and quantity of the dendritic spines. Such anatomical differences may account for the striking behavioral differences and capacities of maternal females compared to their virgin counterparts, including enhanced spatial memory and predatory behavior.

Below: Courtesy of J-L. Klein and M-L. Hubert/Photo Researchers, Inc.

Environmental Perspective: The Importance of Environmental Complexity

A rat in the wild inhabits and experiences a vastly different world than the same animal in the lab. Pictured below, a rat is housed in a laboratory version of an enriched environment, scooting through a tunnel placed in its cage. Such environments have been shown to produce a more complex brain. Wild rats, as shown above, inhabit the natural equivalent of the plastic tunnel pictured below. Increasingly, the use of more ethologically relevant habitats has become a priority for behavioral neuroscientists.

Above: Courtesy of GDelpho Gdelpho/Photo Researchers, Inc. Below: Courtesy of Dmitry Maslov at iStockphoto.

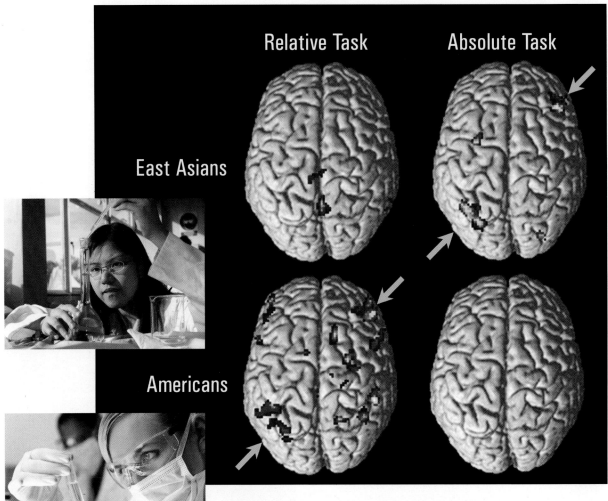

Relative Task

Absolute Task

East Asians

Americans

Cultural Perspective : Eastern and Western Cultures Differentially Shape the Brain

Noting that Americans were known for emphasizing the independence of objects, whereas the East Asians emphasized the interdependence of objects with their context, MIT researchers designed a perceptual task requiring relative judgments about the stimuli (object interdependence), and others requiring absolute judgments (object independence). In the fMRI images above, the red areas depict areas that are active when a task is demanding, requiring attention to complete. As shown, the Americans found the relative task more difficult than the absolute task whereas the opposite was observed in the East Asian subjects. These results confirm that cultural differences in lifestyles influence neural response strategies. (Hedden, Ketay, Aron, Markus, & Gabrieli, 2008).

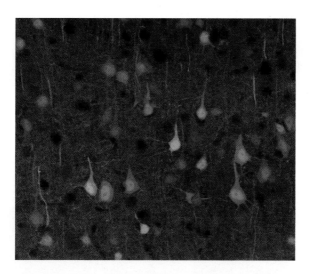

Genetic Perspective: Methodological Approaches

This image shows a portion of cortex from a "Brainbow" transgenic mouse. Its neurons were labeled with combinations of proteins tagged with fluorescent dyes that are expressed as particular genes are expressed. Far from Golgi's black reaction limited to staining a small percentage of the brain's neurons, this technique provides more representative images of the neural geography of the brain.

Courtesy of Dr. Jean Livet.

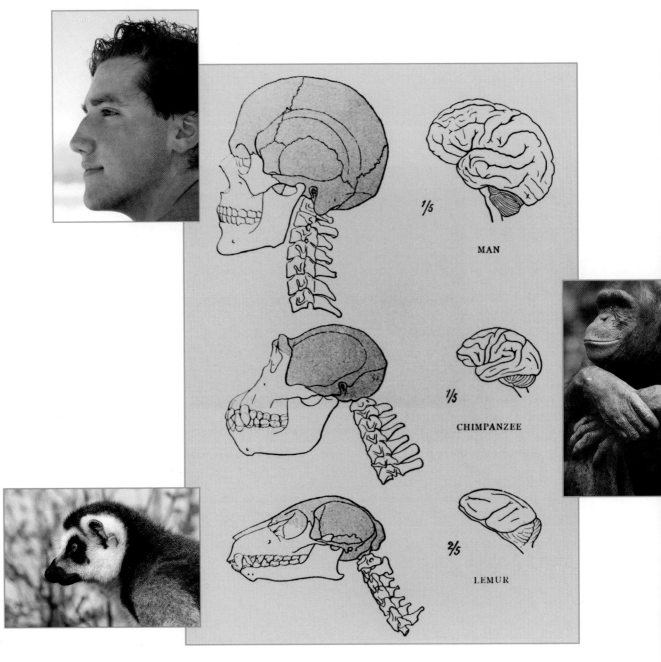

Evolution Perspective:
Species Differences in Primate Brains

Although anatomical similarities exist among human and nonhuman primate species, a striking difference is seen in the complexity of the cortex, a feature that leads to impressive cognitive abilities in humans. Accompanying the vast expansion of the brain's territory, however, is the increased risk of maladaptive development, as discussed throughout the pages of this text.

Chapter Seven

Traumatic and Chronic Brain Damage

Connections

Educated Minds, Neural Reserves, and Recovery from Brain Injury

When ABC news reporter Bob Woodruff suffered a traumatic brain injury on January 29, 2006, his future as a news reporter was grim. While covering the war in Iraq, embedded with the military, Woodruff was injured by an improvised explosive device while on assignment in Taji, Iraq. The crude roadside bomb had been packed with rocks and stones to magnify the impact when it was detonated. The left side of Woodruff's head and upper body were hit, with hundreds of pieces of rock shrapnel lodged in his face, neck, and back. The force of the blast was so intense that it blew his helmet off his head and sent it flying through the air to land several yards from Woodruff's body. Additionally, the blast crushed the bone over the left temporal lobe of his brain, the area known to be integrally involved with language—a priceless bit of brain real estate for anyone, especially a news reporter.

As his wife, Lee, learned of her husband's injuries, doctors warned her that he may never regain the ability to walk or talk, or even much cognitive function. Although Woodruff did not experience any penetrating damage to the brain, the impact of the explosion and the subsequent force with which the brain was jolted from its safe, secure environment within an intact skull had likely damaged millions of neurons. Woodruff's neurosurgeon, Rocco Armonda, explained to Lee that her husband would need to have tubes inserted to drain fluid from his ventricles

and that the swelling would have to subside, and his strength increase, before the 14 cm opening in his skull could be replaced with an acrylic composite (Woodruff, 2009).

In the midst of hearing all the terrifying news about her husband's prospects for recovery, Lee Woodruff was comforted by some words of encouragement conveyed by Rocco Armonda:

> If you are a person like Bob Woodruff, who is forty-four and has made great use of his brain in his life, speaks multiple languages, has an intellectual curiosity and abundant life experiences, you have a better shot at how well those neurons are going to reconnect. Think of those neurons as a road—I-95, for example. If the only way your brain knows how to get from New York to Washington is along I-95, and a giant jackknifed truck closes all lanes of the highway, you are in trouble....But if you are Bob Woodruff and you know alternate routes, you can take back roads or board Amtrak or hop on the shuttle flight at Reagan National. If you are a person who can come up with other solutions, who has really used your brainpower, you have more chances to develop alternate pathways for cognitive function and reasoning and putting all those neurons back together again. (Woodruff & Woodruff, 2007, p. 92)

Armonda's prediction that Woodruff would have an advantage in recovery due to his enriched brain appeared to be correct. On March 6, 2006, Bob finally regained consciousness, in a memorable moment, he opened his eyes, sat up in his bed, and when his wife entered his hospital room that morning, smiled and extended his arms toward her as he calmly asked, "Hey sweetie, where've you been?" His emotions, memory, and personality were intact; the most prevalent symptom related to his language was *aphasia*, an inability to recall or delay in recalling appropriate words. After months of cognitive rehabilitation to regain basic cognitive abilities such as speed of processing, vocabulary, and other areas of "executive function," his cognitive and language abilities continued to improve. In fact, his recovery was so impressive that just 13 months later he returned to ABC News with a report about his fascinating personal journey.

neural reserve Complexity and redundancy of neural networks that may provide a buffer against loss of function following traumatic brain injury.

Does research support the notion that level of education or enrichment prior to an injury increases the probability of a recovery? Australian researchers investigated whether one's **neural reserve**, defined as the brain's capacity based on the formation of neural processes and complex connections influenced by prior experiences, is influenced by preinjury behavior that both diminishes and enhances neural health. The researchers found that the strongest factors predicting recovery from posttraumatic amnesia following mild traumatic brain injury (TBI) were higher levels of intelligence and education (also known as "cognitive reserves"). Thus, building neural reserves may serve as a form of neural insurance in the unfortunate event of brain injury (Dawson, Batchelor, Meares, Chapman, & Marosszeky, 2007). In another study investigating variables related to more positive outcomes 5 years after TBI, researchers found that preinjury education level and employment were both important in more positive outcomes (Connelly, Chell, Tennant, Rigby, & Airey, 2006).

Thus, research appears to reinforce the words of wisdom that Rocco Armonda gave Lee Woodruff early in her husband's recovery process. It is very likely that the neural reserves Woodruff accumulated as he earned his undergraduate and law degrees, supplemented by his ability to speak multiple languages and his being engaged in a career that required constant learning of new information, may have indeed given him a distinct advantage in his journey to recovery. Additional information about the role of engaging and enriched environments in the postinjury time period will be

Figure 7.1
Journalist Bob Woodruff's recovery from TBI After being injured by an improvised explosive device while on assignment in Iraq, Woodruff's skull over his left temporal lobe was crushed, as seen just 2 days after awaking from a coma (left). Following surgery and rehabilitation, Woodruff has made remarkable progress, as depicted in the picture with his family (right).

(A) WOODRUFF FAMILY, (B) DIMITRIOS KAMBOURIS, © GETTY IMAGES

discussed in this chapter. His recovery gives a cheerful face to an aphorism from Shakespeare's *Othello*: "The robbed that smiles steals something from the thief."

OVERVIEW OF CHAPTER

In many of the disorders we have discussed in *Clinical Neuroscience* thus far, the exact location and extent of brain damage remain elusive; however, in many unfortunate circumstances leading to a diagnosis of TBI, significant tissue damage is easily detected by various brain-imaging techniques (described in Chapter 1). Brain tissue damage may result from an exogenous force such as falling on a hard surface or from an endogenous event such as a stroke; additionally, it may be sudden as in an automobile accident or slowly building as observed in conditions such as Parkinson's disease. Technically, the term *TBI* is reserved for brain injuries caused by an external physical source (Jain, 2008). Regardless of the source of damage (e.g., TBI, stroke, or degenerative disease), however, loss of critical neuronal circuits threatens the existence of the most integral components of our identities—our memories, our problem-solving abilities, our passions. Researchers have made great strides in identifying the pattern of neuronal destruction so that critical interventions can be made to alleviate the ultimate damage. Just as important, preventative measures have become integrated in our society in the form of laws and warning signs that have been extremely effective in reducing TBI. With the goal of reducing the extent of both traumatic and chronic forms of brain injuries, predictive factors have been investigated to alert health officials to the most vulnerable brains so that they can be protected in various ways before the onset of life-altering damage. Though resisted by some as intrusive, safety regulations such as seat-belt laws, helmet laws for bikes and motorcycles, and other reasonable measures to prevent even minor but permanent loss of brain function are viewed as a small price to pay for protection and "peace," as opposed to "pieces," of mind.

As you begin this chapter, it will be beneficial to revisit the notion of "neuroplasticity," a term discussed often in this book. The discovery that the brain indeed has the ability to adapt to changing demands throughout our lifetimes offers individuals with brain injuries hope for recovered function. This view, however, has not always been embraced in the field of neuroscience. In his interesting book *The Brain that Changes Itself*, psychiatrist Norman Doidge (2007) discusses one of the earliest pioneers in the area of neuroplasticity, Paul Bach-y-Rita, whose ideas about the "plastic" nature of the brain changed dramatically after his father suffered a disabling stroke. Prior to this event, Bach-y-Rita was already demonstrating that he had unique views of the flexibility of the brain, evidenced by his work suggesting that cortical areas traditionally viewed as localized for a specific function were "plastic processors, connected to each other and capable of processing an unexpected variety of input" (Doidge, 2007, p. 25). After showing that the cat's visual cortex responded to other sensory stimuli such as touch and sound, he introduced the notion of the "polysensory" nature of the brain.

Bach-y-Rita's convictions regarding brain plasticity were strengthened after watching his 65-year-old father recover from a stroke that initially paralyzed the left side of his body, leaving him unable to speak. After his father failed to improve following the standard 1 month of rehabilitation,

Bach-y-Rita's brother thought he could help his father by following the same pattern of development used when he was an infant—crawl, then stand, then walk. Similar "baby steps" were taken with manual tasks and language, and within a year, the elder Bach-y-Rita had recovered enough to teach full time at City College in New York. After he eventually died, an autopsy confirmed that, despite his apparent recovery, Bach-y-Rita's father's brain damage was still severe and far-reaching, with extensive lesions in the brain stem and cortex.

After watching his father's recovery in late life, Bach-y-Rita became excited about the possibilities of recovery for others suffering from various forms of brain injury. Accordingly, he switched careers from research to the practice of neurology and rehabilitation medicine. Based on his insight and multiple contributions to the field, Bach-y-Rita is remembered as a pioneer of neuroplastic ideas in neuroscience at a time when most researchers focused on localization of function. His work reinforced the idea that humans are born with an adaptable opportunistic brain, far from the idea that there was little room for neuronal modifications in the adult brain (Doidge, 2007).

Now that we have revisited the importance of peering through the neuroplasticity window when evaluating critical issues relating to brain injuries, you are prepared for this chapter focusing on traumatic and chronic brain damage. In the first part of this chapter, TBI will be discussed. Not all brain injuries, however, have a rapid onset. Many develop slowly over the course of years or decades. Although there are many unfortunate neurological examples of chronic, slowly developing brain injuries, in the second section of this chapter, Parkinson's disease (briefly discussed in chapter 6) was chosen as an example for an in-depth analysis to compare to TBI. In addition to more typical neurological information, relevant clinical neuroscience research (e.g., discussion of a diverse array of preventative, causal, and therapeutic factors) will be considered in the coverage of both conditions.

TRAUMATIC BRAIN INJURY

Epidemiological Factors

Considering its age, the modern brain remains a marvel of engineering. The brain evolved a solid and effective protective covering, the skull and meninges; but our technological advancement has far outstripped these flimsy protections. The skull and meninges did not evolve to protect us against a car crash at 65 miles per hour, a gunshot wound to the head, or, it is turning out, too many blows to the helmeted head of a modern quarterback. We remain vulnerable to the neural chaos created by TBI.

TBI, unfortunately, is a common condition, accounting for approximately 50,000–80,000 deaths and 235,000 hospitalizations each year (Flanagan, Cantor, & Ashman, 2008; Kraus & Chu, 2005). It is also estimated that approximately 5.3 million individuals in the United States currently suffer from chronic TBI and all the accompanying physical, behavioral, emotional, and cognitive problems (Cohen et al., 2007; Thurman, Alverson, Dunn, Guerrero, & Sniezek, 1999). According to the National Health Interview survey, approximately 1.5 million head injuries occur each year (Sosin, Sniezek, & Thurman, 1996); additionally, in 1999, over 5 million Americans, approximately 2% of the U.S. population, were living with disabilities related to TBI (Thurman et al., 1999). In addition to personal costs, the financial costs associated with TBI are staggering, with the average medical and nonmedical costs being close to $150,000 each year and the costs associated with each fatal TBI case closer to $450,000 (National Institute of Neurological Disorders and Stroke, 1989).

What are the general characteristics of individuals at highest risk for TBI? Research suggests that young individuals have an increased risk of brain injury in the United States, with ages 15–24 years being the most vulnerable. Individuals over the age of 64 years also possess a high risk for TBI. Focusing on gender, males are a higher risk group than females. Accidents occurring when a person has been consuming alcohol are likely to lead to TBI; one study reported that approximately 56% of adults diagnosed with a brain injury tested positive for blood alcohol concentration, with a high percentage exceeding the legal level of 0.10% (Kraus, Morgenstern, Fife, Conroy, & Hourjah, 1989). Being in a lower socioeconomic status category is also a risk factor (Kraus & Chu, 2005); having enough money to purchase various forms of transportation, however, also places an individual in a high-risk category. Most often, brain injury is caused by automobile, motorcycle, bicycle, watercraft, and aircraft transportation (Kraus & Chu, 2005). Eventually, old age will put us all in a high-risk category for TBI as we will become more likely to experience falls and resulting head impacts.

A final epidemiological factor to consider is participation in sports. About 3% of all hospital admissions are for sports-related brain injuries, the majority of these cases being mild (NIH Consensus Development Panel on Rehabilitation of Persons with Traumatic Brain Injury 1999; Freeman, Barth, Roshek, & Plehn, 2005). Football accounts for about 65% of the reported concussions, followed by wrestling (10%) and women's basketball (5.2%). Interestingly, despite the view of rugby as a high-impact sport, rugby players experience fewer concussions than football and soccer players (Farace & Alves, 2000). This is an interesting statistic, implying as it does a form of self-regulation. That is, when we feel protected, we tend to take more risks. The fully exposed head of the rugby player may serve as a deterrent to an otherwise similarly outfitted foe.

Of course, in all sports, wearing a helmet protects against, but does not eliminate, the occurrence of TBI. In cycling, wearing a helmet can decrease the incidence of TBI by as much as 50% (Sacks, Holmgreen, & Smith, 1988). Recently, a *Consumer Reports* poll indicated that, whereas 83% of adults reported that wearing a helmet while cycling was very or extremely important, only 44% reported that they would actually wear one (Consumer Reports, 2009). Wearing a helmet is, of course, a small price to pay to reduce the likelihood of a debilitating brain injury.

Hypothesized Events Associated With the Aftermath of TBI

Early observations of patients following brain injury who appeared unaffected initially yet later deteriorated or, worse, died, suggested that brain injuries result in various waves of potential damage. As when a hurricane hits, with its immediate and obvious structural damage—downed trees and power lines, collapsed roofs—there follow the delayed effects: toxic chemical spills, contaminated water, no electricity, etc. An analogous situation

axon shearing Diffuse damage to neuronal axons following traumatic brain injury that leads to neuronal damage and compromised neural networks.

subdural hematoma Collection of blood under the surface of the dura mater that may follow a brain injury.

epidural hematoma Collection of blood between the skull and dura mater following a head injury.

contusion A bruise in the brain due to brain trauma.

occurs in the case of TBI. The primary effects, experienced at the moment of injury (e.g., impact of head on hard surface, sheared axons resulting from acceleration injuries), are distinguished from secondary or delayed effects (e.g., sustained restriction of oxygen to brain site, excessive release of various neurochemicals, glial reactions) (Gennarelli & Graham, 2005).

Primary effects. Brain lesions occur when an object penetrates the skull and brain in some manner. Tissue damage also occurs due to acceleration/deceleration from unrestricted movement; in these cases, unrestricted movement of the head results in the shearing of brain tissue (known as **axon shearing**), often leading to **subdural hematoma** (a localized collection of clotted blood and accompanying increased pressure in the brain) when widespread damage of blood vessels and axons occurs. Another type of hematoma, known as an **epidural hematoma**, results from the collection of blood between the dura mater and the skull. Generally, more focal pathologies are observed following contact injuries, whereas more diffuse pathologies are observed following acceleration/deceleration injuries.

More severe brain injuries are typically associated with a greater extent of skull fractures. These fractures, however, are not always indicative of underlying tissue damage. Even if the fractures are severe enough for them to become depressed into the brain tissue, patients often suffer only brief loss of consciousness and brain function generally remains intact. On the other hand, the absence of a skull fracture does not guarantee the absence of a brain injury as 20% of fatal cases of TBI reveal no skull fractures (Gennarelli & Graham, 2005).

Contusions, defined generally as closed-head injuries resulting in damage to the brain's circulatory system such as hematomas, are typically viewed as the hallmark of brain damage following a brain injury. In approximately 96% of fatal brain injury cases, contusions and lacerations on the surface of the brain have been observed. These injuries likely result

Figure 7.2
Axonal shearing When brain injuries occur due to accelerating or decelerating motion, axonal processes are often injured. If the myelin sheath is damaged, as seen in the middle neuron, both the processing ability and health of the neuron are compromised, often leading to neuronal death.

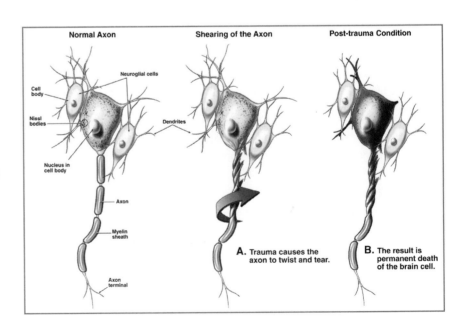

in bleeding into the subarachnoid space and brain swelling, potentially acting as a large lesion in the brain and leading to eventual death. Many cases in which patients seem perfectly fine at first but then deteriorate are likely due to some form of intracranial hematoma (Bullock & Teasdale, 1990). The bleeding begins at the time of injury, but it takes time for the blood collection to interrupt functioning; thus, a person may appear absolutely fine following a fall yet lose consciousness a few hours later, often never recovering.

Recently, the tragic case of award-winning actress Natasha Richardson followed this typical time trajectory of symptoms. While skiing at a Canadian resort, Richardson fell on a beginner's slope, showing no initial signs of injury; in fact, witnesses reported that she was even joking about the incident. Within a few hours, however, her condition worsened, and she was rushed to the hospital, where she was classified as brain-dead. Her death was caused by an epidural hematoma that took over the functions of critical brain areas (Maron, 2009).

In the absence of the formation of hematomas, brain injuries may also result in more diffuse axonal injury in which some aspect of the axons are sheared or, after a bit of time, swell so that connections to critical resources (e.g., blood vessels) or communication with other neurons is disrupted. Patients with diffuse axonal injury may be comatose at the time of injury with no significant recovery (Gennarelli & Graham, 2005).

Figure 7.3
Actress Natasha Richardson Richardson suffered an epidural hematoma following a recent skiing accident; her essential brain functions were compromised, leading to her death hours later.
STEPHEN SHUGERMAN, © GETTY IMAGES

After the impact: Secondary factors related to sustained brain injuries.

Animal models of TBI indicate metabolic disruption following a concussion. Of primary significance is a reduction in cerebral blood flow (and the glucose and oxygen it delivers to the cells). The duration of this disruption is predictive of final outcome (Hovda et al., 1999). Additional neurobiological effects that follow TBI in animal models include the general condition known as **ionic flux**, specifically associated with altered intracellular concentrations of several ions such as decreased magnesium and potassium and increased calcium. Neurons in ionic flux require energy to maintain homeostatic functioning or death will be imminent. Optimally, ionic flux triggers a process known as **hyperglycolysis**, an excessive breakdown of existing glucose into energy sources, so that homeostatic levels can be achieved once again (Hovda et al., 1999). If baseline levels are not achieved, then an energy crisis (or an allostatic overload) emerges as the cells in the area encounter a decrease in blood and glucose availability (Giza & Hovda, 2001). If further injuries do not occur, the disrupted cellular metabolism may last up to 10 days, even longer in immature rodent models (Hovda et al., 1999; Freeman et al., 2005).

Another significant metabolic effect is an increase in the extracellular excitatory amino acids (EAAs) glutamate and aspartate (Jenkins et al., 1988; Katayama, Becker, Tamura, & Hovda, 1990; Gennarelli & Graham, 2005), which can lead to cell death and the continued release of excitotoxic molecules (Jain, 2008). Excessive levels of extracellular glutamate often observed following TBI may also contribute to ionic flux (Jain, 2008). The mechanism of EAA death likely involves intracellular sodium accumulation and subsequent swelling and delayed calcium influx (Gennarelli & Graham, 2005). In an interesting study with human TBI patients, researchers assessed cerebral acid-base homeostasis in individuals following their injury. In the patients

ionic flux Altered movement of ions that influence cellular homeostatic processes across the cell membrane following a traumatic brain injury.

hyperglycolysis Increased glucose utilization following traumatic brain injury; occurs both locally and globally across the brain in response to the injured brain's altered chemical environment.

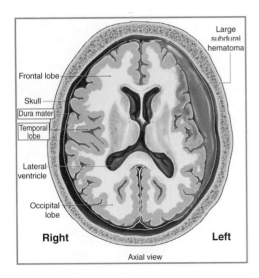

Figure 7.4

Subdural hematomas Certain brain injuries produce intracranial hemorrhages, known as subdural hematomas, beneath the layer of the dura mater and the skull. Increased bleeding in these cases leads to increased pressure on the brain, interrupting essential neural processing and brain functions.

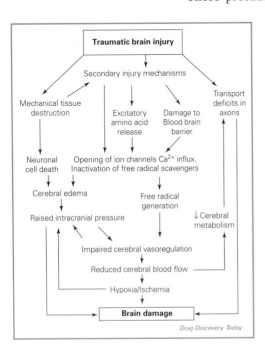

Figure 7.5

Primary and secondary brain injury cascades Once the initial impact occurs, both direct and indirect effects have significant effects on the brain's eventual recovery from the injury.

who had a poor outcome (i.e., death or persistent vegetative state) the brain tissue pH was significantly lower than that observed in patients with better outcomes. The pH changes persist for about a day following the trauma. Thus, the brain's ability to maintain homeostasis—and all of its accompanying mechanisms—is a critical factor for a positive outcome (Clausen et al., 2005).

Focusing on more structural delayed effects of TBI, axonal damage that is not necessarily the direct result of the TBI but rather, the result of delayed cytoskeletal changes, may lead to the collapse or impairment of the transport system in the axon. The massive release of various neurotransmitters following the insult may alter the sensitivity of the receptors throughout the brain; this hypersensitivity may lead to further insult. Finally, the blood–brain barrier (BBB) may become impaired following severe TBI. Specifically, enhanced permeability of the BBB is often observed, creating even more neurophysiological disruptions throughout the brain (Jain, 2008).

As we leave this section, it is important to review Figure 7.5, which incorporates the many immediate and delayed events following a TBI. This knowledge is critical for many reasons. First, it is important to know that the damaging effects persist long after the actual injury. A child who has a mild concussion following a tackle in football practice, for example, should not be encouraged to reenter practice that afternoon for several reasons. First, he should be evaluated to make sure there are no delayed effects. Second, even if he appears to be fine, the neurochemical disruptions can persist for at least 24 hours, and if the child gets tackled a second time that afternoon, his brain is much less likely to achieve a homeostatic state. These precautionary measures are important for any situation in which there is some question about delayed effects due to a head injury (see Box 7.1 for a discussion of long-term effects on cognition and brain health in professional football players). Although in some cases a seizure or impairment in consciousness provides strong clues that a TBI has been experienced, there is no existing definitive diagnostic test to determine the extent of the damage. Until such a test is created, informed vigilance is the best tool for determining if the patient needs further observation or medical intervention. Once the decision that a TBI has been experienced, another wave of questions arise related to the best treatment for the existing trauma. The next section will explore both traditional and innovative approaches to minimizing the damage induced by the TBI.

Box 7.1

Brain Matters

The Perils of Using Your Head in the National Football League

In 2003, Ann McKee, a neuropathologist at Boston University School of Medicine, made an interesting observation when she was examining the brain of a 72-year-old man who had suffered from dementia for 15 years prior to his death. Fully expecting to see a brain riddled with evidence of Alzheimer's disease, containing evidence of both β-amyloid and tau, she was caught off guard when she only saw staining for tau, a toxic protein, with no evidence of the traditionally observed β-amyloid plaques. Instead of Alzheimer's disease, this patient's brain conveyed to McKee that he suffered from **chronic traumatic encephalopathy** (CTE), a progressive neurological disease observed in individuals with a prior history of brain trauma. In addition to the abnormal presence of tau in CTE brains, atrophy is found in several areas including the medial temporal lobe, cerebral hemispheres, thalamus, and brain stem. This patient had suffered brain damage previously in his life—he was a boxer. After this initial case, McKee turned her interest to football players. She subsequently found that, regardless of their age or cause of death, deceased National Football League (NFL) players exhibited evidence of tau. Most of the players she has examined were linemen or linebackers. Depending on their age, the expression of associated symptoms accompanying CTE include cognitive impairment, depression, and impulsivity (Gladwell, 2009; Omalu et al., 2006).

Bennet Omalu, a forensic neuropathologist, has also examined the brains of former NFL players and, in each case, has confirmed the existence of CTE. The only autopsy of a former NFL player that didn't reveal this neurodegenerative condition was that of a 24-year-old running back who had played for only 2 years prior to his death. An autopsied brain of an 18-year-old who had played football for a couple of years, however, showed evidence of abnormally high levels of tau—thus, even young brains are at risk for this disorder (Gladwell, 2009).

Recently, a survey conducted by the University of Michigan's Institute for Social Research (at the request of the NFL) provided further evidence of dementia-like brain disruptions in NFL players. The survey was completed by 1,063 retired NFL players. The results indicated that 6.1% of players aged 50 or older had been diagnosed with a dementia-related condition, a value which is fivefold greater than the national average of 1.2%. Younger players (30–49 years old) had a rate of 1.9%, a number which is 19 times that of the national average of 0.1% (Schwarz, 2009).

The presence of these neurodegenerative markers so early in the life of these athletes appears to be due to repeated concussions. Additionally, even subconcussive trauma is probably traumatic to the brain, especially when it is repetitive. Interestingly, the University of North Carolina's football team works with the university's Concussion Research Program, which places special sensors into the players' helmets so that the head hits can be tracked. Focusing on one player, it was determined that in just one day he was hit in the head 31 times. This cumulative trauma could produce significant damage to the brain.

Given the love affair the United States has with football, these findings are producing uncertainty about how to resolve these issues. Better helmets, complete with shock absorbers, may help; but there is likely no piece of equipment that is going to make this game of physical contact safe for vulnerable brains (Gladwell, 2009; McKee et al., 2009).

Treatment and Recovery

The initial step in the treatment of TBI is to determine the extent of the damage. Early in the treatment process, a standard scale, the **Glasgow Coma Scale** (GCS), is frequently used as a clinical prognostic indicator for the assessment of injury severity. As seen in Table 7.1, various scores are assigned to functions following the injury, and the scores at various times from the time of the injury become a critical component of the patient's medical record, providing important information about chances for recovery. If a patient scores between 13 and 15, the diagnosis of mild TBI is assigned to

chronic traumatic encephalopathy Potential permanent brain damage due to recurrent concussions.

Glasgow Coma Scale A neurological scale designed to provide a reliable assessment of consciousness following brain trauma.

Box 7.2

A Case in Point

Surviving a Life-Threatening Automobile Accident

As I (K. G. L.) was thinking about a case study for this chapter, I decided to look to my own community for someone who had experienced TBI recently. As would be the case for most of us, I did not have to look far to find someone whose life had been profoundly affected by a brain injury. Davis Bailey, a son of one of the staff members in our Residence Life office on campus, was in a tragic car accident a few weeks prior to his twenty-first birthday. He suffered from multiple basilar skull fractures, a small subarachnoid hemorrhage, and disruption of his maxillary sinuses. After being in a medically induced coma for 3 weeks, Davis finally awoke, blurting out "F...you" to the nurse. His mom was thrilled that he could speak but horrified by his choice of words. As more conversational language emerged, it was clear that his language was generally intact, even though he had initial trouble remembering the names for various items. "Foxhorn" became the stand-in word for all items that could not be recalled. His family and friends, however, declared that they had never heard Davis use this word before.

As Davis sat in my office more than 2 years after that horrible January evening, I commented on my inability to detect any verbal or cognitive deficits.

He recalled that following the accident he had lost his memory for events that occurred prior to the accident—family vacations, his first date, buying his truck, and other memorable life events. He had a very clear memory, however, of three types of material that he had been exposed to prior to the accident: words to songs, details of movies, and details and statistics for basketball games he had watched on television (Davis is a huge basketball fan). This seemingly odd compartmentalization of memories confirms the fascinating and intriguing nature of human memory and raises questions about why some memories are wiped out and others are protected following TBI. In Davis's case, it seemed that his most resilient memories were those of events in which he played a more passive role—listening to music, watching movies, watching games; in essence, his *spectator* memories were more resilient than his personal memories. In some cases, he may have "rehearsed" these events more than his personal life events. Davis expressed confusion about why he could not remember important life events but he could remember every word to the sitcom theme song from *The Fresh Prince of Bel-Air* that he watched as a kid. As I listened to Davis and his mother recount their story, I noted on three different occasions that Davis corrected his mother's memory. Clearly, Davis's memory of events occurring postinjury was just fine, perhaps even better than his mother's.

Once Davis worked with an occupational therapist it was obvious that he retained basic cognitive skills to

---

the case. Patients who appear lethargic and score between 9 and 13 are given a moderate TBI diagnosis, whereas patients who are comatose (i.e., unable to open eyes or follow commands) and have a score lower than 9 are considered to have suffered a severe TBI (Kraus & Chu, 2005).

As soon as possible, TBI patients undergo more extensive neurotrauma evaluations to identify the severity of the initial damage with a goal of preventing secondary damage. Symptoms such as nausea, headaches, seizures, pupillary asymmetry, and lethargy are interpreted as signs of degeneration; and a head computerized tomographic (CT) scan is typically ordered to confirm the damage (Hartl & Ghajar, 2005).

Injuries necessitating surgical interventions. After reviewing the GCS score, CT scan findings, and other relevant neurological factors, a decision about the necessity of surgery is made. Table 2 below provides three examples of traumatic brain injuries that typically require surgery (Hartl & Ghajar, 2005).

Davis Bailey's truck The sudden impact of Davis's truck led to severe deceleration injuries and a lengthy recovery process.

enable him to carry out routine daily activities related to living on his own such as getting dressed and taking his medication. His medical reports still indicated various cognitive deficits, especially in the areas of auditory and visual memory and attention span. These deficits were understandable given that, following the accident, Davis was blind in his right eye and partially deaf in his left ear.

When asked about the differences he perceived between his mental functions pre- and postinjury, Davis was not able to identify any obvious differences at this point, 2 years after the accident. He commented that his vision with one eye even seems "normal" and that he could not remember what it was like to see with two eyes. Obviously, his brain had adapted efficiently following his accident.

What about Davis's future? Well, clear differences were observed between the cases of Bob Woodruff described in the Connections section and Davis. Woodruff received ample financial support from his employer, and fans and supporters across the country expressed their sympathy and hopes for recovery. Most TBI patients do not have the full support of a major television network, and this was certainly the case with Davis. His insurance was dropped early in the process, forcing him to join an experimental study to receive the minimal amount of rehabilitative therapy (fitting, in light of the ongoing debate regarding universal health care). His medical restrictions from driving and continued cognitive deficits impeded his ability to work away from home in any capacity, forcing him to be a prisoner in his home. Being labeled "disabled" is also an important piece of his recovery puzzle. In order to receive minimal funds to live on, Davis and other TBI patients are encouraged to remain disabled until they are absolutely certain that they are ready to join the workforce. This added pressure makes it even more difficult for patients to trust their recovery enough to move on to full-time employment. In this case, the "system" seems to discourage the full recovery of TBI patients in a timely fashion. Prior to the accident, Davis had enjoyed working in the heating and cooling industry, and once he regains the ability to drive, he looks forward to working in this area once again. The challenges associated with problem solving in various forms of work may be the most valuable therapy for TBI patients, so it is important to get patients into challenging work environments as soon as it is safe to do so. We wish Davis the best of luck in his recovery journey.

Informed decisions about the appropriate treatment for patients have led to a significant reduction in mortality in TBI cases in the past several decades. Today, mortality rates in severe TBI patients range 15%–25%, a marked improvement from rates exceeding 50% in the 1970s and 1980s. See Table 7.2 for a description of typical surgeries to evacuate potentially damaging collections of blood.

Pharmacological interventions. As patients recover from the initial trauma associated with the brain injury, many complaints may arise. In order to assess the damage more thoroughly, neuropsychiatric evaluations aimed at monitoring changes in cognitive, emotional, behavioral, and physical functioning are conducted. Days following the injury, many TBI patients complain of headaches, dizziness, memory disturbances, decreased attention, and slowed information processing (McLean, Temkin, Dikmen, & Wyler, 1983). Fortunately, most of these symptoms subside in 1–6 months in most patients; however, a subgroup of patients continue to experience difficulties with information processing, reasoning, memory, vigilance, attention, anxiety, and depression (Arlinghaus, Shoaib, & Price, 2005).

These delayed symptoms are sometimes treated with various pharmacological approaches. Because few controlled clinical trials have assessed the effects of medications in TBI patients, caution should be taken when each patient is placed on medication. Three neurotransmitter systems have received the most research and clinical attention. Addressing various forms of cognitive impairment, dopamine and acetylcholine have been investigated. For patients suffering from emotional symptoms including depression, the serotonergic neurotransmitter system has been targeted.

Dopamine-active agents such as methylphenidate (given to children for attention-deficit/hyperactivity disorder) likely increase the release of both dopamine and norepinephrine, ultimately activating the ascending reticular activating system as well as other cortical–subcortical circuits. Such effects may enhance arousal, attention, and speed of processing (Silver, Arciniegas, & Yudofsky, 2005). One study used a design in which 11 patients were taken on and off methylphenidate and reported that, although one patient did not tolerate the drug well, the drug improved attention, assessed by digit span and symbol search tasks, and was associated with improved Disability Rating Scale scores (Kaelin, Cifu, & Matthies, 1996).

A subsequent study, however, used a randomized, double-blind, placebo-controlled, repeated crossover design (a Cadillac of such studies) and failed to find that methylphenidate significantly improved any aspect of attention, although the drug did improve speed of processing (Whyte et al., 1997). Thus, psychostimulants may improve speed of processing information, which may or may not lead to substantial cognitive improvement.

Because acetylcholine has been associated with memory processes and both short- and long-term alterations in memory processes have been observed in TBI patients, pharmacological

Table 7.1 Diagnostic Criteria Included in the Glasgow Coma Scale

Criteria	Scores
Eye opening (E)	
Spontaneous	4
To speech	3
To pain	2
Nil	1
Best motor response (M)	
Obeys	6
Localizes	5
Withdrawn	4
Abnormal flexion	3
Extensor response	2
Nil	1
Verbal response (V)	
Oriented	5
Confused conversation	4
Inappropriate words	3
Incomprehensible sounds	2
Nil	1
Coma score (E + M + V) = 3–15	

Adapted from Kraus & Chu (2005).

Table 7.2 Brain Injuries that Typically Require Surgery

Diagnosis	Incidence in TBI Patients	Symptoms and Treatment Strategies
Epidural hematomas	3%	Typically, about one-third to one-half of patients with this injury are comatose upon admission to the hospital. Typical causes include falls, traffic accidents, and assaults. Although many variables factor into the decision to operate, if the mass is larger than 30 cc, the decision to surgically evacuate the mass is typically made.
Acute subdural hematomas	12%–29%	These injuries are characterized by a collection of blood under the dura mater covering the brain (see Figure 7.4). As observed with epidural hematomas, typical causes include motor vehicle accidents, falls, and assaults. If the clot thickness exceeds 10 mm, surgical evacuation is typically conducted.
Depressed skull fractures	6%	This diagnosis is made when the impact to the head fractures the skull. These fractures are common following forceful encounters with blunt objects such as rocks. If the skull becomes depressed below the thickness of the skull, surgery is typically recommended.

agents that influence this neurotransmitter have been explored. One drug that has been assessed is physostigmine, a cholinesterase inhibitor that produces longer-duration cholinergic receptor stimulation. One study used a double-blind, placebo-controlled design and reported that physostigmine enhanced sustained attention on a continuous-performance test (Levin et al., 1986). Unfortunately, the potentially toxic side effects of this drug limit its use as a treatment; consequently, other cholinesterase inhibitors have been assessed (Silver et al., 2005). A second-generation cholinesterase inhibitor, donepezil, improved memory impairment during the 3 weeks the patients were on it (Taverni, Seliger, & Lichtman, 1998). In a less controlled study in which the patients knew they were taking the drug, researchers reported improvements in intelligence as assessed by the Wechsler Adult Intelligence Scale (Whelan, Walker, & Schultz, 2000). Even a year and a half following the injury, another study, using a very small sample size of seven patients, reported memory improvements following a 6-month trial of donepezil (Morey, Cilom, Berry, & Cusick, 2003).

Don Stein in his laboratory at Emory University.

TBI patients suffering from depression respond to selective serotonin reuptake inhibitors (SSRIs). In an 8-week nonrandomized, placebo-controlled, single-blind study, the SSRI sertraline (Zoloft) was assessed in 15 patients suffering from mild TBI and experiencing symptoms of depression. Eighty-seven percent of the subjects experienced reduced depressive symptoms, some even achieving remission. Possibly due to serotonin's pervasive effects in the brain, improvements were also observed with anger, aggression, and psychological distress (Fann, Uomoto, & Katon, 2000). Further, in an 8-month open label study, Horsfield and colleagues (2002) assessed the effects of fluoxetine (Prozac) on five patients with TBI and related depression. Improvements were observed in both mood and cognitive measures such as working memory, attention, and processing speed. Still other symptoms related to aggression and irritability were observed to decrease following TBI in patients receiving sertraline; in this case, the drug influenced these symptoms more than depressive symptoms (Kant, Smith-Seemiller, & Zeiler, 1998). Thus, there is some evidence that SSRIs, especially sertraline, may benefit patients following TBI. As described, these studies have had small numbers of subjects; consequently, more research should be conducted in this area before decisions are made about the true efficacy of these types of drugs. Another concern about the SSRI fluoxetine was raised when the drug seemed to have lowered the posttrauma threshold for seizures (observed in some patients following TBI) (Wroblewski, Guidos, Leary, & Joseph, 1992).

In addition to medicinal avenues targeting neurotransmitters, steroid hormones have been investigated. Initial enthusiasm was directed toward administration of the stress hormone glucocorticoid following TBI, to reduce edema; more recent research, however, has failed to indicate clear benefits of this type of therapy (Alderson & Roberts, 1997). More recently, attention has focused on the role of a major reproductive steroid hormone, progesterone, and its ability to minimize the negative effects of TBI. The interesting research revealing the benefits of progesterone therapy is described in the next section.

Discovering the impact of progesterone on TBI: A story of hard knocks. When Don Stein was a young researcher lesioning areas of rat brains to document the effects on their behavior in the 1960s, he got side-tracked. His diversion was related to the observation that females seemed to recover from their injuries more readily than their male counterparts. How could this be? Stein's supervisors told him to ignore this observation and stick to his more traditional brain lesion research. Throughout his 40-year career as a university administrator and brain researcher, he just could not stop thinking about this interesting sex effect in the area of brain recovery. Could it be that the existing neuroscience dogma exalted by Nobel Prize–winning neuroscientist Santiago Ramón y Cajal (1928) claiming that neural pathways were fixed and could not regenerate was wrong after all?

Stein kept plugging along with his research, often without funding or adequate lab space. After ruling out the neuroprotective effects of estrogen in his studies, he turned to progesterone, a reproductive hormone that exerts multiple effects to maintain healthy pregnancies. Although typically associated with females (as it is produced in the ovaries and corpus luteum), it is also produced in the adrenal glands of males (Cekic, Sayeed, & Stein, 2009). Focusing on different phases of the female rat's menstrual cycle, Stein noted that the females in phases of higher progesterone seemed to recover faster. Thinking that he had made a significant discovery, Stein hit another wall because the medical establishment was not excited about finding that a natural substance, one that was already marketed generically for infertility, offered medicinal value. Money could be made only if the discovery would lead to the patent of a new drug. He persevered, conducting research indicating that not only did brain-impaired female rats perform better in mazes following progesterone injections but males did as well. In 1991 his team showed that progesterone led to less brain swelling than control rats. Still, it was difficult for Stein and his team to receive funding to support his research.

In 1995, Stein accepted a position as dean of the graduate school at Emory University in Atlanta, Georgia. He received no formal lab space with this position, but that did not stop him from securing a moldy double-wide trailer in a nearby parking lot. Seemingly fitting at the time, he placed pink flamingos around his parking lot laboratory. By 2000, his research was receiving the attention it deserved. Even though things were looking up in his rodent laboratory, he knew that there was an essential next step for this research; that is, taking his findings from the rodent laboratory to human trials.

The initial human trial study focused on 100 TBI patients who were admitted to the emergency room at Grady Memorial Hospital in downtown Atlanta. According to protocol, some patients received intravenous progesterone at levels that were three times those of the highest levels occurring naturally at the end of pregnancy, while others received a placebo. Both the groups received state-of-the-art treatment currently administered to TBI patients. When Stein received a call one Saturday morning reporting the results of this first critical human trial, he was thrilled to hear that patients receiving the progesterone treatment had a lower death rate of 13%, whereas the standard treatment group had a death rate of 30%. In fact, he was so excited that he had to pull over and let his wife drive. In an interview in the *Wall Street Journal* about this moment, he stated, "Most bench scientists work for years to discover a truth about nature. Very few of us ever get to have a major impact on people's lives. How can you not be excited?" (Burton, 2007, p. A1).

Stein and other researchers continue to explore the effects of progesterone on TBI. In addition to lower mortality rates, moderate TBI groups exhibit better functional outcomes and no adverse side effects. Also important for clinical trials, there is a large therapeutic window, meaning that the positive effects are still observed when the progesterone is administered several hours following the brain damage. Research focusing on the nonreproductive functions of progesterone has provided several potential mechanisms of its neuroprotective effects, including modulation of several neurotransmitter receptors such as nicotinic acetylcholine, *N*-methyl-d-aspartate (NMDA), and γ-aminobutyric acid (GABA); promotion of myelinating glial cells in the central nervous system (i.e., oligodendrocytes) and peripheral nervous system (i.e., Schwann cells); regulation of channel proteins involved in water homeostasis; maintenance of mitochondrial functions; reduction of lipid peroxidation; and increased trophic factors such as brain-derived neurotrophic factor (BDNF) and nerve growth factor (NGF) (Cekic et al., 2009; Schumacher, Guennoun, Stein, & De Nicola, 2007). Although this research suggests that human females may be protected from the most severe effects of TBI, research has yet to confirm these claims (Bazarian, Blyth, Mookerjee, He, & McDermott, 2009). Although inconclusive, the multiple mechanisms and effects of progesterone likely lead to its impact on recovery from brain trauma.

Cognitive rehabilitation. *Cognitive rehabilitation* is generally defined as therapy directed toward helping patients develop skills and strategies to compensate for cognitive deficits following TBI. Similar terms include *cognitive remediation* and *cognitive retraining*. Generally, a clinical neuropsychologist delivers the cognitive rehabilitation therapy; however, in some cases larger teams including speech pathologists and occupational therapists will assist the neuropsychologist (Gordon & Hibbard, 2005). Using this therapy, a patient with a problem writing complete sentences may be taught to read the written sentences aloud in order to listen for omitted words; once competent with this step, the patient is instructed to read the sentences silently to identify omitted words. Hence, a form of cognitive scaffolding is used in this type of therapy as patients are taken through various steps to compensate for the lingering cognitive impairments following TBI.

Early work with cognitive rehabilitation was conducted by Yeshuda Ben-Yishay, who traveled from Israel in the 1950s to the New School for Social Research in New York. Once establishing that patients suffering from a stroke or other brain injury exhibited a general framework of learning styles that were similar to individuals without a brain injury, he went on to develop cognitive remediation programs (Butler & Namerow, 1988). These programs became quite popular. By the 1990s, 95% of TBI rehabilitation programs included some form of cognitive remediation or rehabilitation (Mazmanian, Kreutzer, Devany, & Martin, 1993). Deficits in memory, attention, executive functions, visual perception, and language abilities have been common targets in cognitive rehabilitation programs (Gordon & Hibbard, 2005). Do these programs work? Two large reviews aimed at answering that question have been published. In one meta-analysis, 32 studies investigating the efficacy of cognitive rehabilitation were assessed. After reviewing these studies, the authors concluded that the strategies improved cognitive functioning of the patients (Carney et al., 1999). A similar review was conducted with

171 published studies and found support for program efficacy for the following deficits: visual perceptual problems following stroke, language deficits following stroke, and attention, memory, and executive deficits following TBI (Cicerone et al., 2000). It is important to point out that a thorough neuropsychological evaluation should be given to the patient prior to the commencement of any cognitive rehabilitation program so that progress can be documented in an accurate fashion. In addition to the diagnostic information, these evaluations will typically include a plan for relevant intervention (Gordon & Hibbard, 2005). Further, it is recommended that, once progress has been achieved through this type of therapy, booster treatments are important for the maintenance of acquired cognitive skills and techniques, especially when significant changes such as job changes or the loss of a loved one occur in the patient's life.

Ben-Yishay also developed a more comprehensive program for patients with TBI known as the "holistic neuropsychological rehabilitation program," consisting of both individual and group therapies as well as a combination of cognitive remediation and psychotherapeutic interventions. Vocational rehabilitation is also included in these programs. The time commitment is substantial as most comprehensive programs meet up to five times a week for several hours each day and the patients may continue to participate for several months to years (Gordon & Hibbard, 2005). Research assessing the efficacy of these programs suggests that, in a 1-year follow-up, 50% of the participants had returned to work (Ben-Yishay et al., 1985). Similarly, another study indicated that a comprehensive day-treatment program increased the return to active military duty of participants suffering severe TBI (Salazar et al., 2000). Generally, these programs are perceived to reduce disability and improve neuropsychological functions (Gordon & Hibbard, 2005).

A Unique Behavioral Approach

Although there are several types of behavioral therapies that appear to benefit patients with TBI, one unique approach, **constraint-induced (CI) movement therapy**, presents a creative approach from the perspective of neuroplasticity endorsed by Bach-y-Rita. Different from the cognitive rehabilitation approaches, the goal of CI therapy is to reduce incapacitating *motor* deficits in the upper limbs of patients in order to increase independence in the real world. This is accomplished by restricting the use of the unaffected limb, forcing the patient to use the more affected limb. Because researchers had seen success with this type of therapy in patients suffering from stroke, Edward Taub and his team at the University of Alabama in Birmingham wondered if they would see similar results in patients following TBI. Consequently, they asked patients to participate in a 2-week therapy intervention program, including 6 hours each weekday during which patients would engage in repetitive practice of various tasks. Patients were closely supervised by experimenters during this time, dispensing verbal feedback including information about progress and positive comments about task performance. To keep the patients from using the less affected arm and hand, they wore a protective safety mitt 90% of the time (and were encouraged to continue to wear the mitt outside of the laboratory). Patients signed a contract confirming that they would restrain from using their "good" hands outside of the laboratory. The results were exciting; just 2 weeks of therapy

constraint-induced (CI) movement therapy Type of rehabilitation therapy requiring an individual to constrain his or her "good arm" to stimulate use of the "bad" arm.

Box 7.3

Brain Matters

Gourmand Syndrome: TBI and Fine Dining

A small percentage of TBI and stroke victims experience postinjury symptoms that they do not mind; in fact, they like the symptoms so much that they crave them. These patients find themselves thinking about fine food, even though their eating habits were quite mundane prior to the neural insult. For example, after experiencing a hemorrhagic infarction around the right middle cerebral artery (i.e., a stroke), one patient experienced motor deficits in the left side of his body, as well as specific memory impairments. Prior to the incident, the patient was mostly occupied with thoughts of his career as a political journalist and was not overly concerned with food, experiencing no real food preferences. After the incident, however, he reported that the hospital food was awful and the only thing on his mind was delicious food served in a fine restaurant. More specifically, he wrote

> ...sex I start to really miss, and it is time for a real hearty dinner, e.g., a good sausage with hash browns or some spaghetti Bolognese, or risotto and a breaded cutlet, nicely decorated or a scallop of game in cream sauce with spatzle (a German specialty)...What a

connoisseur I am, and now I am dried up here, just like in the desert. Where is the next oasis? With date trees and lamb-roast or couscous and mint tea, the Moroccan way, real fresh. (Regard & Landis, 1997, p. 1186)

This patient abandoned his career in political journalism and began to write columns about eating.

A review of this novel condition was conducted by Marianne Regard and Theodor Landis in Zurich, Switzerland. Following an analysis of 723 patients who reported suffering from a lesion in the brain, 34 instances of gourmand syndrome were identified, each of the 34 patients typically having suffered damage to the right frontal region. More specifically, most patients reporting these symptoms experienced unilateral damage in the right-hemisphere lesion, primarily involving anterior corticolimbic regions. Interestingly, even though the gourmet cravings persist, there is no strong evidence that these patients become overweight. And, interestingly, there are many individual differences concerning what constitutes fine cuisine, and there are no clear preferences for sweet or salty or other distinct tastes (Raloff, 1997).

Although the establishment of this condition as an actual syndrome is controversial, this information about food-related symptoms associated with specific right-hemisphere damage provides some palatable food for thought about brain damage.

(albeit intense therapy) resulted in significantly improved movement of the affected limb. As expected, patients reporting more adherence to the strict rules of the program had more improvement than the less adherent patients. These results provide further support for the neuroplasticity of not only the healthy brain but also the injured brain. Taub and colleagues attribute these improvements to changes in brain organization that have been documented in previous studies assessing CI as well as the valuable lesson of overcoming the learned nonuse of the affected limb (Shaw et al., 2005).

Environmental Enrichment and Recovery from

TBI. The dramatic effects of environmental enrichment were introduced in the very first chapter of this text. In review, when rats are housed in an environment with other rats and several stimuli designed to stimulate motor, sensory, and cognitive neural systems, the animals exhibit enhanced cognitive abilities and associated neurobiological modifications. Interestingly, the *original* enriched environment study was conducted in the home of experimental psychologist Donald Hebb, who took a few rats home to play with his children and noticed that, compared to rats housed in standard laboratory

Figure 7.6
Pediatric constraint-induced therapy The stronger hand is restrained so that patients are forced to use the weaker hand to regain diminished function.
COURTESY OF ACQUIREC THERAPY (PEDIATRIC CI), BIRMINGHAM, AL

environments, they had enhanced learning abilities. A more scientific version of the enriched environment, however, emerged from the landmark studies of Mark Rosenzweig, Ed Bennett, David Krech, and Marian Diamond at the University of California at Berkeley. The laboratory version of enriched environments typically involves housing multiple animals in large cages filled with objects that they can interact with in various ways. These stimuli are changed on a regular basis during the enrichment, which typically last at least 1 month. Relevant to this chapter, an abundance of research has focused on the effects of an enriched environment on recovery from TBI.

In an early study focusing on the effects of enriched environments on recovery from TBI, 1-day-old rats received bilateral posterior cortical lesions and were subsequently raised in a complex environment until early adulthood. Exposure to the enriched environments facilitated recovery of function so efficiently that the rats with cortical lesions made fewer errors in a learning task than nonlesioned rats that were housed in a standard laboratory environment (Schwartz, 1964). Since that report of the dramatic effects of enriched environments, additional research has been conducted over the past five decades focusing on specific aspects of this global effect. Generally, the effect has held up, but researchers saw potential methodological challenges early in the research. The enriched environment manipulation is methodologically messy in the sense that it taps into many different systems. As researchers have attempted to design more sophisticated studies to identify the most salient features of the enriched environment, it has become clear that the rats were exposed not only to changing physical stimuli but also to social cues from their cagemates, were more physically active as they ran in activity wheels, and had more opportunities for learning or training experiences as they attempted to teach themselves how to climb ladders or traverse ropes. In an interesting review of this literature, Mark Rosenzweig and his colleagues examined three aspects that should be explored as potential therapeutic strategies when thinking about translating the work to human rehabilitation: (1) environmental enrichment (generally speaking), (2) physical exercise, and (3) specific formal training (Will, Galani, Kelche, & Rosenzweig, 2004). Interestingly, they compared the neurobiological effects of these manipulations based on rodent work. A summary of the many effects of these three environmentally enriched strategies is included in Table 7.3.

As seen, a long list of seemingly positive neurobiological effects accompanies each of these manipulations. If forced to choose just one option, the standard enriched environment appears to be the most engaging for the brain, leading to increased synaptogenesis rates that are not observed in the exercise group manipulation. Additionally, neither the exercise nor the training manipulations increased neuroprotection; in fact, at certain times each may exacerbate symptoms (Will et al., 2004).

In one case, these three manipulations were compared in a single study. Specifically, the social component of the enriched environment was associated with increases in the expression of NGF mRNA in several regions of the cortex as well as the hippocampus. Recovery of motor function following middle cerebral artery occlusions was better in the socially enriched rats than the isolated enriched environments. Additionally, the results suggested that, even when focusing on motor performance, tasks that involve learning offer increased value over repetitive exercise (Dahlqvist et al., 2003). Concerning neurogenesis, exercise appears to be the most influential factor

Table 7.3 Neurobiological Benefits of Various Forms of Enriched Environments

Environmental Strategy	Neurobiological Effects
Enriched environment	Heavier cerebral cortices, especially occipital; increased glial cells, especially oligodendrocytes; larger neuronal cell bodies; increased dendritic arborizations and age-related increases in spine density; larger synapses; denser packing of synaptic vesicles in synapses; increased cholinergic activity; increased neurogenesis but not cell proliferation in general; protection against TBI-induced impairments (e.g., lesion area, apoptosis); increased cellular activation (i.e., fos-positive cells) during training; enhanced production of growth factors such as NGF, BDNF, NT-3, GDNF
Physical exercise	Increased thickness of motor cortex; increased expression of neurotrophic factors (BDNF, NGF, and FGF); enhanced angiogenesis in cerebellar and motor cortical areas; increased serotonergic and cholinergic neurotransmission; upregulation of genes related to the glutamatergic system; downregulation of GABA-related genes; enhanced neurogenesis in the hippocampus
Formal motor training	Increased gliogenesis; increased thickness of motor cortex; increased volume of the cerebellar paramedian lobule when motor training is used; increased hippocampal area when spatial learning is utilized; enhanced synaptogenesis in the hippocampus or cerebellum with spatial and motor training, respectively; increased angiogenesis due to increased neuropil volume (as opposed to increased metabolic demands as seen in physical activity); some evidence that neurogenesis is increased; increased expression of BDNF

TBI, traumatic brain injury; NGF, nerve growth factor; BDNF, brain-derived growth factor; NT-3, neurotrophin-3; GDNF, glial cell–derived neurotrophic factor; FGF, fibroblast growth factor; GABA, γ-aminobutyric acid.

Adapted from Will et al. (2004).

enhancing the general proliferation of cells, whereas both enriched environments and exercise promote the survival of newborn cells. Concerning synaptogenesis, both enriched environments and training lead to increases, although timing of training is important (Greenough, Cohen, & Juraska, 1999; Will et al., 2004).

In sum, Rosenzweig and his colleagues concluded that the combined components of enriched environments are a powerful "therapeutic tool" that lead to neuroprotective effects including the reduction of secondary damage and facilitated compensatory responses following reorganization of the intact neural systems. Also worth mentioning is the fact that there are few risks associated with this form of therapy, especially when compared to more traditional neurobiological treatment approaches such as neurosurgery or pharmacological manipulation. In order for enriched environments to be used as therapies for various neurological insults, additional research is needed to determine more about efficacy rates or the most beneficial time to administer treatment following the injury. Confirming the complexity of the efficacy of these types of therapies, one study reported that recovery may be task-specific when enriched environments are utilized (Hoffman et al., 2008). Additionally, research suggests that recovery may differ between males and females (Wagner et al., 2002).

As we leave this section, it is worth pausing and looking once again at Table 7.3. Imagine how exciting it would be if a drug offered all the effects that an enriched environment offers. Pharmaceutical companies would be racing to get patents and Food and Drug Administration approval because these drugs would no doubt be considered revolutionary with hopes of becoming best-sellers, especially if there was not the traditional long list of negative side effects. It is encouraging to consider that these therapeutic effects already lie in our grasp in the sense that, for the most part, we control the complexity of our environments.

Prevention of TBI: Impact of Safety Regulations and Legal Policies

As efforts are made to improve the probability of recovery of function following TBI, attention has been directed toward keeping individuals from experiencing TBI in the first place. Effective research in this area moves beyond trophic factors and damage-minimizing drugs to another recurring theme in this text—behavior. As already mentioned, TBI is pervasive in our society, more prevalent than better-known conditions including spinal cord injury, multiple sclerosis, breast cancer, and acquired immunodeficiency disorder syndrome. As depicted in Figure 7.7, the annual incidence of TBI greatly surpasses all of these health threats. Because TBIs often occur in young individuals, the cost to both the individual and society is immense. Considering the enormous amount of suffering and economic hardship, it is important to remind ourselves that these catastrophic events are often preventable.

Two general approaches are used to promote the prevention of injury: passive and active preventative measures. The last time you drove your car, several passive strategies were in place including air bags and road barriers to reduce your speed. Thus, passive strategies require no effort on the part of the "host" and, consequently, have the potential to affect a larger percentage of the population. Active strategies are also beneficial but require cooperation of the host. Using seat belts; avoiding driving when sleepy, intoxicated, or texting; wearing helmets when driving motorcycles; strapping young ones into car seats; and playing more chess and less football are all active strategies for TBI prevention.

How do we enhance compliance with active prevention strategies? Education, such as what is happening as you are reading this chapter, is one component. However, education is most effective with appropriate incentives. Early public-service announcements about the danger of driving without a seat belt were ineffective in the 1970s prior to the existence of seat-belt laws. When the laws were passed in 1984, the rates of use were still only 15%, probably because the laws were not properly enforced. The rates increased to 62% in 1992 when secondary enforcement laws were enacted (i.e., citations were written if the driver was pulled over for another driving

Figure 7.7
Leading injuries/diseases vs. brain injuries A comparison of traumatic brain injury and leading injuries or diseases: annual incidence. AIDS, acquired immunodeficiency syndrome; HIV, human immunodeficiency virus.

ADAPTED FROM ELOVIC & ZAFONTE, 2005, P. 728

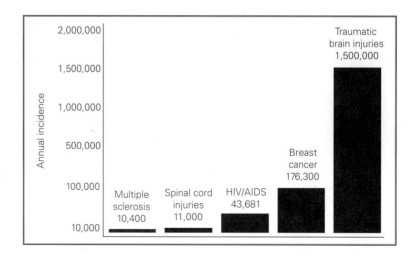

offense), and usage increased to nearly 80% when primary enforcement was practiced (i.e., a ticket could be written when seat-belt noncompliance was the only offense). Thus, active prevention strategies are enhanced with an approach that combines education, legislation, and enforcement.

Although it is still imperative to identify the most effective treatment strategies to minimize damage following TBI, the best solution is to prevent the damage from ever happening. Wearing protective gear while participating in sports, practicing all the active strategies related to driving (and benefiting from the passive strategies), and providing safe environments for our children and elderly are more powerful strategies than any drug or surgical technique (Elovic & Zafonte, 2005).

PARKINSON'S DISEASE

TBI makes its impact, figuratively and literally, by shredding the brain's connections in an instant, creating damage that is instantaneous. Other damage to the brain occurs over decades, slowly, but with just as devastating a set of consequences. Among these chronic conditions is Parkinson's disease.

Identification of Relevant Brain Damage

In 1817, James Parkinson wrote a monograph entitled "An Essay on the Shaking Palsy," in which he described the clinical symptoms of the disorder that would later bear his name. Today, the hallmark features of Parkinson's disease include a resting tremor, gait disturbance, bradykinesia, rigidity, and postural instability. Parkinson's disease is currently the second most common neurodegenerative disease, typically expressing itself around 60 years of age (0.3% overall prevalence that increases to 2% of the population over 60 years of age) (Olanow, Stern, & Sethi, 2009). Approximately 1 million individuals have been diagnosed with Parkinson's disease in the United States and Europe, with approximately 5 million people across the world.

Although scientists are still not sure of the specific initial cause of Parkinson's disease, the characteristic pathology associated with it is the degeneration of dopaminergic neurons in the midbrain's substantia nigra (see Figure 7.8). Other neurotransmitters, however, have also been implicated, including acetylcholine, serotonin, and norepinephrine, in various areas throughout the brain (Forno, 1996). Additionally, research suggests that nondopaminergic pathology in the olfactory and dorsal motor regions may precede the characteristic dopaminergic pathology in the substantia nigra (Braak et al,, 2003). Thus, although dopamine has received the majority of attention in Parkinson's disease, research suggests that parallel deficits or modifications in complementary neurotransmitter systems may precede and exacerbate the parkinsonian pathologies.

Treatment Strategies

In the history of attempts to treat Parkinson's disease, surgery was used to mitigate tremors. Initially, lesioning of the corticospinal tracts was observed to successfully calm the tremors, but it came with the cost of inhibiting voluntary movement. In the 1940s, the globus pallidus became a target of lesioning; however, the close proximity to the internal capsule sometimes

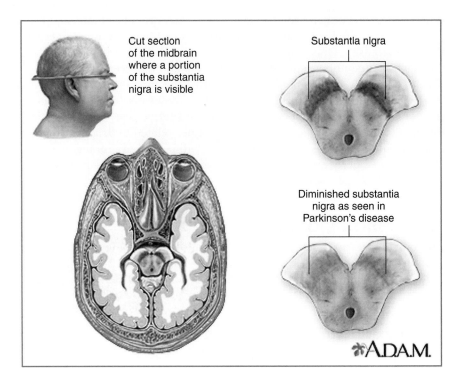

Figure 7.8
Diminished substantia nigra in Parkinson's disease.

thalamotomy Neurosurgery involving the precise destruction of portions of the thalamus in order to diminish negative side effects accompanying Parkinson's disease.

pallidotomy Neurosurgery in which a small portion of the globus pallidus is destroyed to reduce brain activity, leading to Parkinson symptoms such as tremors and unwanted involuntary movements.

levodopa (l-dopa) A dopamine agonist that has served as a gold standard pharmaceutical treatment for Parkinson's disease for years.

decarboxylase inhibitor A type of drug that blocks the conversion of l-dopa to dopamine in the peripheral nervous system, diminishing l-dopa-induced side effects, in patients taking l-dopa for Parkinson symptoms.

led to cognitive impairment. After a surgical intervention in which the anterior choroidal artery was accidentally ligated during a surgery in the 1950s, resulting in damage to the thalamus and a surprising improvement in parkinsonian symptoms, **thalamotomy** became more popular than **pallidotomy**. In the 1960s, however, with the discovery of the drug **levodopa** (l-dopa), attention shifted from invasive surgical procedures to pharmacological interventions. The agonist l-dopa, the gold standard treatment for Parkinson's disease, is a precursor for the neurotransmitter dopamine. l-Dopa crosses the BBB after being taken by patients, increases the intracellular pool of dopamine, and subsequently enhances dopaminergic functioning in the brain. This provides benefits to most patients with Parkinson's disease, allowing them to continue to work and engage in their normal daily activities. With chronic use, however, adverse effects develop, including psychiatric complications, motor fluctuations, nausea, and low blood pressure resulting from sudden shifts in body position (or orthostatic hypotension). If l-dopa is taken with a **decarboxylase inhibitor**, which prevents the conversion to dopamine in the peripheral nervous system, these negative side effects are largely mitigated (Olanow et al., 2009). Considering the noninvasive nature along with the high efficacy rate of l-dopa, researchers continued to utilize this powerful drug and learned more about pharmacological interventions on the progressive nature of parkinsonian symptoms.

In an attempt to identify drugs that retain the high efficacy rates of l-dopa without the adverse side effects, many pharmacological strategies have been developed. Because of their therapeutic success, dopamine agonists, which act on the dopaminergic postsynaptic receptors in the striatum, are still prescribed for Parkinson's disease. Anticholinergic drugs have also been evaluated due to the observation that acetylcholine becomes overactive in patients with Parkinson's disease. Finally, NMDA receptor blockers appear to increase dopamine reuptake and potentially have anticholinergic functions (Hristova & Koller, 2000). Even with the onslaught of new pharmacological treatments for Parkinson's disease, l-dopa remains the gold standard against which all new drugs have to be tested (Olanow et al., 2009).

The 1990s saw a resurgence in surgical procedures for patients exhibiting symptoms of advanced Parkinson's disease. Although still invasive, safety advances, significant progress in neuroimaging techniques to pinpoint targeted brain areas, and continued evidence that some of these surgeries are effective have contributed to a rise in neurosurgeries for Parkinson's disease. Although these surgeries have been developed to target several motor-related structures throughout the brain, two early approaches (thalamotomy and pallidotomy) continue to successfully treat essential tremor and advanced parkinsonian symptoms. Additionally, high-frequency **deep brain stimulation** (DBS) offers benefits without introducing destructive lesions. This treatment involves implanting electrodes that stimulate four target sites. Typical targets include the ventral intermediate nucleus of the thalamus, globus pallidus, subthalamic nucleus, and putamen. As depicted in Figure 7.9, a mild pulse generator is connected to an electrode and placed subcutaneously in the chest. The stimulation settings can be adjusted to achieve maximal effects and decrease side effects, but the batteries are the weak link: They have to be replaced, typically every 1–3 years, requiring surgical intervention and general anesthesia (Olanow et al., 2009; Hristova & Koller, 2000).

An additional form of surgical intervention that emerged in the 1990s involved the transplantation of dopaminergic neurons in an attempt to restore dopaminergic function. This therapeutic strategy was the product of one of the most interesting detective stories in the field of clinical neuroscience. In the early 1980s, doctors in northern California saw something they had never seen before: a *young* man with the symptoms of Parkinson's disease. This one anomalous patient was followed by several others in rapid succession, and the cluster raised the possibility of some type of new and powerful infection or poison. Several related items were of interest in the group. First, the patients were displaying symptoms of Parkinson's disease. Second, they were all young, much younger than the age at which the symptoms would be expected to manifest themselves. Third, they all had a history of drug abuse with a home-made potion that was marketed to them as a heroin facsimile. This drug, with the composition 1-methyl-4-phenyl-1,2,3,6-tetrahydrapyridine (MPTP), eventually attracted the attention of affiliated scientists. Animal studies confirmed what the doctors originally had surmised, that the drug somehow targeted the substantia nigra with devastating precision. Ironically, after causing so much misery, studying this drug has helped many people by encouraging research into the mechanics of Parkinson's disease through the use of these MPTP animal models (Brownell et al., 2003).

Initially, transplanted dopaminergic fetal cells were found to survive in the striatum of rodents and primates, which sparked hope for human clinical trials. Controversy, however, has surrounded this therapeutic approach due to a host of

deep brain stimulation
Surgical treatment for Parkinson's disease in which a neurostimulator is implanted below the collarbone that delivers mild stimulation to electrodes implanted in various areas of the brain such as the thalamus.

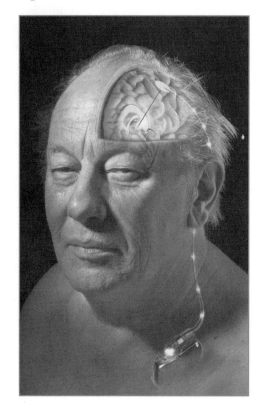

Figure 7.9
Deep brain stimulation for Parkinson's disease This treatment strategy involves implanting a pacemaker in the chest area that sends an excitatory signal to electrodes implanted in various areas of the brain.

TIM VERNON, LTH NHS TRUST/PHOTO RESEARCHERS, INC.

methodological challenges, the ethical issues related to the use of human tissue for this purpose (see Chapter 6), and confusing results in clinical trials (Olanow et al., 2009). Patrick Brundin, mentioned in Chapter 2, and his team at the University of Lund continue to explore various ways to promote the differentiation of embryonic stem cells into the dopaminergic neurons necessary for this type of therapeutic surgery (Correia, Anisimov, Li, & Brundin, 2008). Embryonic stem cell lines can be maintained using cell culture protocols and do not require fetal cell transplants, as was the case for the earliest transplants. Recently, researchers at Advanced Cell Technology showed that they could remove single blastomeres without embryo destruction (Chung et al., 2008). As additional research produces protocols that minimize the controversial nature of this therapeutic approach, it will be interesting to see how successful cell-based therapies will be in the future.

Perhaps the most exciting research associated with Parkinson's disease is focusing on neuroprotection (Olanow et al., 2009). If researchers could establish exactly when the slow demise of neurons in the substantia nigra begins, heroic measures may be taken to slow the degeneration or, even better, stop it before the symptoms of Parkinson's disease commence. Interestingly, presymptomatic markers have been identified. The ability to identify odors decreases in a majority of patients prior to the onset of motor symptoms (Getchell, Doty, & Bartochik, 1991). Additionally, diminished capacity in skilled hand tasks, such as writing, as well as in skilled motor tasks, such as language, have been identified as preclinical markers for Parkinson's disease (Tetrud, 1991; Hecker, 1988; Critchley, 1981; Hristova & Koller, 2000). Biochemical markers are also being evaluated. Brains from patients with Parkinson's disease, for example, have more antibodies for dopaminergic neurons in the substantia nigra than tissue from age-matched control subjects (Carvey et al., 1991), suggesting that a form of autoimmune attack may be playing a role in the region's deterioration. Of course, once clear preclinical markers are determined, researchers need to know more about the nature of neuronal destruction in Parkinson's disease before effective interventions can be implemented.

Regardless of the nature of the therapeutic approach, most researchers seek the latest information related to effective therapies from a single source. Ironically, this critical source of information was created by a passionate celebrity, Michael J. Fox, who publicly announced his parkinsonism in 1998 after secretly living with the disease for 7 years. In an interview published in the *New York Times*, Fox said that at first he did not want to become the "PD poster boy" but later realized that his celebrity might be important in identifying a cure for the disease. Like other celebrities before him, Fox established a foundation, The Michael J. Fox Foundation, for which he serves as both chairperson and inspired leader. Unlike other foundations, however, the Fox Foundation has created a different method for funding research, demanding more sharing of information and more frequent reports of results so that timely decisions can be made about abandoning seemingly dead-end research and commencing on more promising ideas. Although these strategies differ from those of other funding institutions, they appear to be successful as the Fox Foundation has become the most credible source of information on Parkinson's disease research. Thus, although not planned, Michael J. Fox was transformed from light-hearted situation comedy star to a serious force in both the political and scientific circles related to Parkinson's disease. It will be exciting to follow the future of the Fox Foundation and this new "business plan" for conducting science (Nocera, 2008).

Box 7.4

Brain Matters

Striatal Neurons Hit the Dance Floor

Researchers from the Washington University School of Medicine have recently investigated a very novel therapeutic approach to combat the aversive symptoms of Parkinson's disease. After reviewing the effectiveness of several exercise programs that currently exist, such as Fit 'N Fun and Motivating Moves, they decided that they were interested in exploring the most effective movement therapy for parkinsonian symptoms. After learning of a presentation at the Society for Neuroscience suggesting that Argentine tango lessons offered impressive gains for elderly dance students, the Washington University researchers set out to design their own study (Jacobson, McKinley, Leroux, & Rainville, 2005). Over a course of 13 weeks, 19 patients diagnosed with Parkinson's disease participated in either 20 1-hour tango classes or a comparable number of exercise classes. Interestingly, the subjects participating in the dance class demonstrated better scores on various movement measures than their exercising counterparts (Hackney, Kantorovich, Levin, & Earhart, 2007). In a follow-up study with 58 subjects diagnosed with Parkinson's disease, the efficacy of the Argentine tango was compared to that of American ballroom dances including the waltz and fox trot. Although both dance groups improved in the areas of balance, gait, and backward stride strength compared to nondancing controls, it appeared that the tango group experienced more improvements than the waltz/fox trot groups (Hackney & Earhart, 2009).

Why should the tango improve parkinsonian symptoms? While dancing, participants are involved in a multitasking activity requiring shifts in balance, timing, and various forms of movement. This dance could be considered a movement obstacle course of sorts, requiring vigilance and training in many aspects of motor coordination, initiation, and execution. The tango includes an important social aspect as dancers must be in perfect synchrony with their partners, it is progressive as it requires the dancers to build on existing skills in a continuous learning process, and it presents a situation in which the movement is triggered by the external cue of music, which may be of clinical importance. Thus, the rhythmic, measured movements characteristic of tango dancing may selectively activate basal ganglia neurons. Of course, these demands are seen in many styles of dance. Of therapeutic importance is that patients may be more compliant to dancing programs than other therapeutic strategies such as more mundane physical therapy or exercise classes. This enhanced motivation was confirmed by observations of subjects continuing dance lessons after the study ended (Hackney & Earhart, 2009; Hackney et al., 2007). Although the research has not been done, it would also be interesting to discern if dancing offers neuroprotective benefits against Parkinson's disease, the effects of TBI, or other neurodegenerative disorders.

Summary

Overview of Chapter

After reading this section, you may want to sit down and enfold your head in bubble-wrap. It is apparent that the brain is a fragile organ: Indeed, the spirit is willing, but the flesh is very weak—especially against the dangers of the twenty-first century. The brain has evolved strategies to protect itself in the event of injury; it is a self-repairing machine. But these mechanisms evolved under states that are, at best, a dim atavistic memory, taxing the brain's recovery following mild concussions, small penetrating injuries, hypoxia, etc. Too extreme and the brain is overwhelmed, unable to fix itself. In this chapter we have highlighted the sorts of damage, traumatic and chronic, that we face every day. In fact, sadly, some of you reading these words will become victims of the very types of conditions we have highlighted herein. Basic research, with its translational applications, represents the best hope for understanding, preventing, and treating brain damage of every sort. Let us hope that there are more of you who decide to go on to research careers and make the fundamental discoveries to help everybody else.

Traumatic Brain Injury

Although the brain suffers from injuries from both external and internal sources, the term *traumatic brain injury* (TBI) is most often associated with damage resulting from an external physical source. Optimism related to recovery from TBI can be found in the neuroplasticity literature. The knowledge that neuronal circuits continue to adapt to changing demands throughout our lives offers an opportunity for recovery for TBI patients.

TBI is a prevalent condition, leading to approximately 80,000 deaths and 235,000 hospitalizations each year, as well as accompanying personal and financial costs. Individuals between the ages of 15 and 25 years and those older than 64 years are the most vulnerable for TBI. Other risk factors include being male, consuming alcohol, and being in a low socioeconomic status category. Focusing on participation in sports, football injuries comprise the majority of reported concussions, whereas, interestingly, rugby players experience much lower numbers of concussions.

Once an injury is experienced, the effects are generally thought to occur in two distinctly different phases. The term *primary effects* refers to the damage from the physical insult including, but not limited to, sheared axons or various types of hematomas, whereas *secondary effects* result from more long-term effects of the compromised tissue and neural circuits. Surviving neurons may suffer additional damage due to homeostatic fluctuations such as decreased potassium and increased calcium. At times a vicious circle of cellular damage exists as extracellular excitatory amino acids (EAAs) such as glutamate contribute to cell death and subsequent EAAs release from the dying neurons, contributing to further neuronal decline. As the effects of the primary damage are processed throughout the brain, further structural damage may develop as the axonal transport systems are impaired. These observations have important implications for the care of individuals suffering from TBI; specifically, caution should always be taken when a concussion is observed—sending a child back into a game following an initial concussion, even though everything seems to be fine, may enhance secondary damage or the ability to recover from a second impact to the head should one occur.

Once the extent of damage is determined, typically via use of the Glasgow Coma Scale and an image of the brain tissue, a decision is made about the necessity of surgical intervention. As hematomas are identified, the size of the hemorrhage determines whether or not surgery will follow. Skull fractures may also require surgical intervention, especially if the skull is depressed onto the surface of the brain. As patients enter the recovery phase, various pharmacological interventions may be utilized. Dopaminergically active agents (e.g., methylphenidate) have been found to enhance arousal, attention, and speed of processing. Sustained attention may be enhanced with cholinesterase inhibitors, especially second-generation cholinesterase inhibitors that have fewer side effects. Finally, SSRIs have been found to help with depression symptoms, as well as anger, psychological distress, and cognitive impairments.

The persistent work of Donald Stein has indicated that the steroid hormone progesterone increases survival in patients suffering from TBI. Patients receiving the hormone up to several hours following the injury benefit from the its effects. It is thought that variations in neurotransmitter systems such as acetylcholine, NMDA, and GABA, as well as alterations in glial activity and other metabolic and neurotrophic activities, may be related to progesterone's effects on TBI.

Cognitive rehabilitation programs have been found to improve cognitive functioning following TBI. One such program, the Holistic Neuropsychological Rehabilitation program, consists of a combination of individual and group therapies, as well as cognitive and psychotherapeutic interventions and vocational rehabilitation. Patients participating in this program are more likely to return to work 1 year following the injury than patients who have not been exposed to the program.

Constraint-induced movement therapy is used to recover from motor deficits. Patients are encouraged to use their impaired hand by restraining (typically with an oven mitt) their functional hand. Intense training with this method has produced significant gains in movement in just 2 weeks. Environmental enrichment, assessed in animal models, has also been seen to lead to significant recovery of function following TBI. Enriched environments, physical exercise, and formal motor training lead to enhancements in multiple measures of neuroplasticity.

Behavioral interventions can reduce TBI in the general population by implementing various safety regulations. These regulations are viewed as passive (e.g., speed bumps to force you to slow down) or active (e.g., wearing a seatbelt in the car). With appropriate education and incentives, compliance with these regulations leads to prevention of TBI and related injuries.

Parkinson's Disease

Unlike the case with TBI, some brain damage is the result of slowly degenerating tissue. Parkinson's disease is associated with degeneration of the brain's substantia nigra, resulting in reduced levels of dopamine throughout the brain's movement centers. Various drugs (e.g., l-dopa) and surgeries (e.g., thalamotomy) have been used as therapeutic strategies through the years. Currently, deep brain stimulation is receiving much attention as a therapeutic option. As more scientists are able to conduct research with fetal cells, more information will be gleaned concerning the value of transplantations in Parkinson's disease patients.

Key Terms

neural reserve (192)

axon shearing (196)

subdural hematoma (196)

epidural hematoma (196)

contusion (196)

ionic flux (197)

hyperglycolysis (197)

chronic traumatic encephalopathy (199)

Glasgow Coma Scale (199)

constraint-induced (CI) movement therapy (206)

thalamotomy (212)

pallidotomy (212)

levodopa (l-dopa) (212)

decarboxylase inhibitor (212)

deep brain stimulation (213)

For Further Consideration

Doidge, N. (2007). *The brain that changes itself.* New York: Penguin Press. Students who enjoy reading about the "stories" of clinical neuroscience will enjoy reading this fascinating book. Doidge invested a considerable amount of time interviewing both researchers and patients in the field, and their stories confirm the undeniable plasticity of the brain. These observations offer hope for those experiencing challenges related to brain functions, not only TBI patients but also patients born with challenges that compromise their ability to function in their day-to-day living. The brain continues to adapt to changing demands in its environment throughout an individual's life; consequently, patients of all ages will benefit from learning about the research described in this book.

Gladwell, M. (2009, October 19). Offensive play: How different are dogfighting and football? *The New Yorker.* Malcolm Gladwell is an excellent storyteller, and he presents a disturbing account of the impact of repeated concussions on professional football players in this *New Yorker* article. Key neuropathologists who have done relevant and pioneering research on this topic are interviewed. Gladwell even compares the damage associated with football injuries to dogfighting, a sport that our society has deemed illegal due to the health risks for its players—in this case, dogs. As the emerging data suggest that NFL players experience both cognitive decline and associated brain damage very early in their lives, our society will likely be forced to reevaluate the risk for football players—even if it is a favorite sport in the United States.

Silver, J. M., McAllister, T. W., & Yudofsky, S. C. (Eds.). (2005). *Textbook of traumatic brain injury.* Washington DC: American Psychiatric Publishing. This is a must-read for the serious scholar in the field of TBI. In this approximately 800-page edited volume, 40 chapters, covering essential areas ranging from epidemiology to functional imaging of brain damage to effective treatments, are written by the most active scholars in the field. The contributing authors represent a nice array of researchers and practitioners; thus, this book is helpful for students interested in either research or applied aspects of TBI.

Stein, D. G., Brailowsky, S., & Will, B. (1995). *Brain repair.* New York: Oxford University Press. Although a bit dated at this point, this book is a classic in the field of neuroplasticity. After a nice summary of historical achievements that have informed the scientific community about the brain's ability to repair itself following injury, important contemporary topics are covered, such as key events that occur following brain damage, the pharmacology of brain repair, the role of environment in brain repair, and a consideration of neural tissue transplants. As you will learn in the book, researchers in this area have come a long way from Ramón y Cajal's statement that the brain was fixed and immutable.

Woodruff, L., & Woodruff, R. (2007). *In an instant: A family's journey of love and healing.* New York: Random House. This personal account of Bob Woodruff's recovery from his TBI suffered while on assignment in Iraq is successfully told by both Bob and his wife, Lee. This book conveys the realities of recovery from brain damage as the couple works with the medical community to learn about the best types of therapies. Unlike many other TBI realities, this book has a happy ending as it conveys Woodruff's successful recovery.

Chapter Eight

Disorders of Anxiety: Obsessive–Compulsive Disorder and Tourette Syndrome

Connections

Common Denominators in Real-Life and Laboratory-Induced Compulsions?

Caroline Kettlewell is a woman with a secret: She compulsively cut herself for two decades to relieve anxiety. Caroline grew up at a boy's boarding school where her parents were on the faculty. As she entered puberty in this environment, Caroline experienced insurmountable anxiety: She felt that she was "on display" for all the older male students. Finding no refuge in family and friends at the time, she searched for alternative ways to calm herself. Her cutting compulsion started when she was 12 years old.

Intrigued with dissections and the symbolism of blood, Caroline found solace in cutting herself, in controlling the most important substrate of her existence. After being caught in the seventh grade trying to carve her arm with a Swiss army knife, she perfected her technique with razor blades. Caroline kept her self-mutilating obsession a secret as she continued to carve her hips and shoulders through middle school, high school, and college and into adulthood. Although her skin still bears witness to her emotional scars, Caroline eventually settled into a successful marriage, gave birth to a son, and learned to cope with her anxiety in constructive ways. In an attempt to provide encouragement for the estimated 2–3 million Americans who compulsively hurt themselves, she also wrote *Skin Game: A Cutter's Memoir*, a book she describes as a "coming of age memoir with an edge."

Just north of the city where Caroline Kettlewell lives, undergraduate student researchers at Randolph-

After being exposed to the activity-stress paradigm, the rat is actively trying to open the access door to the wheel—demonstrating a strong motivation to run.

COURTESY OF KELLY LAMBERT, RANDOLPH-MACON COLLEGE BEHAVIORAL NEUROSCIENCE LABORATORY

Macon College have investigated why rats, when housed in activity wheels and fed for only 1 hour per day, voluntarily increase their running levels to about 7 miles per day. Similar to compulsive cutting, this compulsive running seems to represent a maladaptive response strategy. Why would an animal with restricted food resources expend so much energy running? What brain mechanisms accompany this compulsive behavior?

The student researchers' data suggest that increased activity in a brain area involved in reward, the nucleus accumbens, accompanies the rats' increased running. Closing the access door to the wheel creates something akin to withdrawal. The animals experience changes in two components of the brain reward circuit—a drop in nucleus accumbens activity and reduced levels of dopaminergic immunoreactivity (Aurentz et al., 1999; Glasper et al., 2000; Lin et al., 2001).

Compulsions, like personalities, take different forms. In both cases described here, the subjects were faced with anxiety—for Caroline, produced by excessive self-consciousness brought on by entering puberty on an all-male campus; for the rats, brought on by restriction of valuable resources. Caroline's cutting compulsion was very different from the rats' running compulsion, but it is possible that both relieved anxiety—at least momentarily—and both were reinforcing, probably incorporating the brain's reward mechanisms. Thus, learning the common denominators of the diverse compulsions observed across individuals and species will help us understand their genesis and discover the most effective modes of treatment.

The range of topics covered in this chapter on anxiety disorders strays a bit from the traditional categorization used in the *Diagnostic and Statistical Manual of Mental Disorders* (DSM). We limit our discussion to generalized anxiety disorder and panic disorder in the overview section and then focus the bulk of the chapter on roots and remedies for obsessive–compulsive disorder (OCD) and Tourette syndrome. Recall that phobias, also classified as anxiety disorders, were presented in Chapter 1 in the context of behavioral interventions in mental disorders. Posttraumatic stress disorder (PTSD), which is triggered by an actual stressful event or the memory of an experienced stressful event, is discussed in Chapter 12.

The onset of Tourette syndrome typically occurs during childhood, and the syndrome is presented within the category of childhood disorders in the DSM. But the building evidence of **comorbidity** (the presence of two or more health problems in the same individual) of OCD and Tourette syndrome and of shared familial risk and brain mechanisms suggest an alternative categorization. Tourette syndrome has an affinity with other anxiety disorders, especially OCD (Johannes et al., 2003; Leckman et al., 2003; Muller et al., 2003). The characteristic responses vary in OCD and Tourette syndrome, but anxiety appears to be the genesis of both disorders. Both involve excessive responding. OCD may defend against the anxiety provoked by perceived threats; the involuntary, repetitive movements and verbal responding observed in tourettic **tics** are highly sensitive to the person's anxiety levels.

ANXIETY DISORDERS: AN OVERVIEW

Our highly adaptive stress response has evolved to help us deal with challenges we encounter throughout our lives. Approached by someone with a weapon, for example, our sympathetic nervous system is activated so that we will engage in the "fight or flight" necessary to survive the situation (see Figure 3.2). There is no denying that sympathetic activation and subsequent hypothalamic–pituitary–adrenal axis activity (see Figure 5.9) enable organisms to mobilize their physiological forces and survive threatening situations.

A problem emerges, however, if aspects of emotional and physiological arousal creep into our lives when immediate doom is not obvious. Harboring feelings of intense fear when viewing the latest horror film is perfectly normal even though our cognitions tell us the movie is not real, but actually experiencing these symptoms when no threat stimulus is present can become problematic and is the crux of anxiety disorders.

comorbidity Presence of two or more health problems in the same individual.

tics Rapid, repetitive, stereotyped movements or vocalizations; characteristic symptom of Tourette syndrome.

generalized anxiety disorder (GAD) Vague sense of anxiety not directly related to an anxiety-provoking event.

panic disorder Intense anxiety-stress response, typically without an actual fear stimulus present. Physical components, including chest pain, shortness of breath, and nausea, resemble the symptoms of a heart attack.

obsessive–compulsive disorder (OCD) Chronic condition characterized by recurring upsetting thoughts (obsessions) and subsequent ritualistic acts (compulsions).

obsessions Recurring, upsetting thoughts typically observed in OCD patients; typically related to contamination, doubts, order, aggression, and sexual imagery.

compulsions Ritualistic acts that accompany obsessions in OCD patients; typically include hand washing, checking, repeating actions, ordering, praying, and counting.

The first diagnostic category of anxiety disorders was identified in 1871 when DaCosta published an article describing a condition he referred to as "irritable heart" in the *American Journal of Medical Sciences*. DaCosta attributed the primary symptoms of this disorder (dizziness, chest pain, and palpitations) to an overactive nervous system. Freud later emphasized the psychological rather than physiological aspects of anxiety as he introduced the term *anxiety neurosis* (Andreasen & Black, 2001). Today, if you look at the DSM, several conditions are categorized as anxiety disorders, including (but not limited to) generalized anxiety disorder, panic disorder, OCD, PTSD, and certain phobias.

In a sense, our "anxiety response" exists on a continuum ranging from fear of a very specific event in our environment (for example, exposure to spiders) to a nonspecific sense that something is just not right in our lives (for example, chronic worrying). When the response becomes less specific and more and more ubiquitous, the typical diagnosis is **generalized anxiety disorder (GAD)**, a vague sense of anxiety that isn't directly related to an anxiety-provoking event. Individuals suffering from chronic generalized anxiety (about 4%–7% incidence rate in the general population) worry excessively about single or multiple aspects of their lives—finances, romantic relationships, health—without tangible reasons for worrying.

Although an actual threat does not exist, the body responds as it does in other threatening situations, and the person experiences restlessness, sleep complications, and impaired concentration. As detailed in Box 8.1, acute episodes of anxiety are observed in **panic disorder**, an intense anxiety-stress response typically without an actual fear stimulus present. Physical components include chest pain, shortness of breath, and nausea. Observed in about 3% of women and half as frequently in men, the panic response is so severe that early attacks frequently lead people to the emergency room fearing they are suffering from a heart attack (Andreasen & Black, 2001).

OBSESSIVE–COMPULSIVE DISORDER

Obsessive–compulsive disorder (OCD) is a chronic condition characterized by **obsessions** (recurring upsetting thoughts) and **compulsions** (subsequent ritualistic acts). The most prevalent obsessions include repeated thoughts about contamination, doubts, order, aggression, and sexual imagery (American Psychiatric Association, 1994). Frequently observed compulsions include excessive hand washing and repeated checking, ordering, praying, and counting.

Patients report that they feel driven to perform these ritualistic behaviors in an attempt to mitigate the anxiety produced by unsettling obsessive thoughts. For example, patients experiencing contamination obsessions may try to reduce their anxiety by repeatedly washing their hands until the skin is actually raw. For the most part, OCD involves thoughts and behaviors that are appropriate for normal functioning—who doesn't wash their hands, make sure they turned off the oven before leaving on a trip, or check a few times to confirm that an essential step in a recipe was not omitted? The problem is that these appropriate responses are taken to an extreme level, a level that is not a logical means to protect the person against the invading obsession (Table 8.1).

OCD affects about 2%–3% of the population. It is the fourth most common psychiatric disorder after phobias, substance abuse, and major depression (Jenike, Rauch, Cummings, Savage, & Goodman, 1996; Bear, Fitzgerald, Rosenfeld & Bittar, 2010). The typical age at onset is late adolescence or early twenties; men typically develop the disease at 17.5 years of age, whereas the

Table 8.1 Diagnostic Criteria for Obsessive-Compulsive Disorder

A. Either obsessions or compulsions:

Obsessions as defined by (1), (2), (3), and (4):

(1) recurrent and persistent thoughts, impulses, or images that are experienced, at some time during the disturbance, as intrusive and inappropriate and that cause marked anxiety or distress

(2) the thoughts, impulses, or images are not simply excessive worries about real-life problems

(3) the person attempts to ignore or suppress such thoughts, impulses, or images or to neutralize them with some other thought or action

(4) the person recognizes that the obsessional thoughts, impulses, or images are a product of his or her own mind (not imposed from without as in thought insertion)

Compulsions as defined by (1) and (2):

(1) repetitive behaviors (for example, hand washing, ordering, checking) or mental acts (for example, praying, counting, repeating words silently) that the person feels driven to perform in response to an obsession, or according to rules that must be applied rigidly

(2) the behaviors or mental acts are aimed at prevention or reducing distress or preventing some dreaded event or situation: however, these behaviors or mental acts either are not connected in a realistic way with what they are designed to neutralize or prevent or are clearly excessive

B. At some point during the course of the disorder, the person has recognized that the obsessions or compulsions are excessive or unreasonable. Note: This does not apply to children.

C. The obsessions or compulsions cause marked distress, are time consuming (take more than 1 hour a day), or significantly interfere with the person's normal routine, occupational (or academic) functioning, or usual social activities or relationships.

D. If another Axis I disorder is present, the content of the obsessions or compulsions is not restricted to it (for example, preoccupation with food in the presence of an eating disorder; hair pulling in the presence of trichotillomania; concern with appearance in the presence of body dysmorphic disorder; preoccupation with drugs in the presence of a substance use disorder; preoccupation with having a serious illness in the presence of hypochondriasis; preoccupation with sexual urges or fantasies in the presence of a paraphilia; or guilty ruminations in the presence of major depressive disorder).

The disturbance is not due to the direct physiological effects of a substance (e.g., a drug of abuse, a medication) or a general medical condition.

American Psychiatric Association, (2000, pp. 462–463).

average age at onset in women is a bit later—19.8 years (Rasmussen & Eisen, 1990). Box 8.2 describes a man who developed the disorder in childhood. Overall, OCD is found in equal numbers of men and women. Early-onset cases, however, are most frequently observed in males and are accompanied by motor tics such as head twitches and shrugging shoulders (Miguel, Rauch, & Jenike, 1997). Researchers have not yet discovered the reasons for these sex differences.

There is evidence of a genetic basis for OCD. Studies conducted on twins report concordance rates in monozygotic (identical) twins that range from 53% to 87%. Concordance rates observed in dizygotic (fraternal) twins range from 22% to 47% (Miguel et al., 1997; Rasmussen, 1993). Statistics also suggest that if a person in your nuclear family suffers from OCD, then there is a 23% chance (nearly 1 in 4) that you will develop the disorder (Rasmussen & Eisen, 1990). But a person's genetic profile is not the sole contributing factor to OCD susceptibility. Because the concordance rate for monozygotic twins is less than 100%, environmental factors also influence the development of this disease.

In a recent autobiographical memoir, comedian Howie Mandel provided evidence of the importance of meaningful environmental experiences in the development of OCD when he wrote about his fear of germs and his other OCD symptoms. Interestingly, he described a childhood incident in which sand flies bit him during a Miami vacation and laid eggs under his skin in several places. When he scratched the irritated skin, the larvae would literally move or crawl under his skin. This was very scary for a 6-year-old child and enhanced his vigilance about germs being on or under his skin. Such

Box 8.1

Brain Matters

Panic Disorder: A Faulty Brain Stem Surveillance System?

We usually take it for granted, but a breath of fresh air is the most critical fuel for our existence. Perhaps you have had a nightmare about the walls closing in, being trapped in a car submerged in water, or being buried under dirt or debris. If ever our bodies needed an alarm system, it is in a situation like this because death will inevitably follow the depletion or restriction of life-giving air.

As discussed in Chapter 3, the brain stem controls the basic autonomic response of breathing. We currently don't know exactly how the neurons can detect vital signs such as blood levels of carbon dioxide and oxygen (Feldman, Mitchell, & Nattie, 2003), but these mechanisms may operate in panic disorder. The symptoms—increased heart rate, shortness of breath, chest pain, dizziness, fear of dying, chills—are similar to the

symptoms experienced by someone suffering a heart attack or suffocation.

If we use the U.S. Department of Homeland Security's alert system as an analogy, a person's normal stress response—for example, to giving an impromptu talk to a group of strangers (a common stressor used in experiments)—may fall in the middle yellow category or even register in the orange category. Orange alert represents a significant event that requires the body's undivided attention, but a panic attack represents the most severe category of threat—the red alert. When the brain interprets the situation as leading to suffocation and death, a full-blown stress response is the body's best chance at mobilizing the person to find air.

But panic disorder rarely involves an actual incident of restricted air. On the contrary, a person may simply be sitting in class and suddenly experience a panic attack for no apparent reason. In fact, some researchers propose that this kind of panic attack may be the product of a false alarm emitted by the brain stem.

---

an incident, presented to a child with a certain temperament predisposed toward anxiety, could result in obsessions and compulsions throughout the child's development. Although a successful comedian and game show host, Mandel never shakes hands in public (he is known for his "fist bump") and wears a surgical mask when traveling on a plane (Mandel, 2009).

Research suggests remarkably consistent prevalence rates for OCD across the world. OCD is found in both developed and developing countries, which suggests little or no influence of culture. In fact, even the types of obsessions are strikingly consistent across countries. The most common obsessions appear to be related to contamination, followed by those related to aggression, body issues, religion, and sex (Table 8.2).

Table 8.2 Percent of Sample (*n*) Reporting Obsessions in Six Countries

| Country (*n*) | Obsession | | | | |
	Dirt/ Contamination	Harm/ Aggression	Somatic	Religious	Sexual
United States (425)	38%	24%	7%	6%	6%
India (410)	32%	20%	14%	5%	6%
United Kingdom (86)	47%	27%	N/A	5%	10%
Japan (61)	39%	12%	13%	N/A	5%
Denmark (61)	34%	23%	18%	8%	6%
Israel (34)	50%	20%	3%	9%	6%

N/A, not available.
Adapted from Sasson et al. (1997).

Researchers have investigated the sensitivity of patients suffering from panic disorder to levels of carbon dioxide and oxygen. A popular model is the infusion of sodium lactate, a natural salt and metabolic by-product of lactic acid that the brain interprets as indicating low oxygen levels (hypoxia). Patients suffering from panic disorder exhibit more pronounced cardiovagal responses to the lactate infusion than do control subjects (Yeragani, Srinivasan, Balon, Ramesh, & Berchou, 1994). And when subjects are exposed to hyperventilation challenge tests (taking about 30 breaths per minute for 4 minutes), patients with a panic disorder diagnosis are more responsive (for example, have higher heart rates) than normal subjects (Nardi, Valenca, Nascimento, & Zin, 2001).

Because the brain's reaction to hypoxia is an exaggeration of the stress response, factors that exacerbate or mitigate this response can be influential in the development and maintenance of panic disorder. Early life events such as childhood physical and sexual abuse have been linked with panic attacks (Friedman et al.,

2002), and various therapies aimed at reducing anxiety or stress have been beneficial in the treatment of panic attacks.

Antidepressant medication (which also influences levels of anxiety, a telltale sign of depression), anti-anxiety drugs such as the benzodiazepines, and drugs such as β-adrenergic blockers that interfere with autonomic arousal have all been used with success. Behavioral strategies that encourage avoiding stimulants such as caffeine are also recommended. And any cognitive-behavioral therapy that may either distract a patient during an attack or help the patient make a more accurate cognitive appraisal of the actual trigger (autonomic response, not real restriction of oxygen) may be helpful (Andreasen & Black, 1991). In sum, evidence is building that taking mom's advice to sit down and take deep breaths may actually reestablish homeostatic processing in the brain stem's cells that survey levels of carbon dioxide, oxygen, and lactate and prevent the onset of an approaching panic attack.

Tracing the Neurobiological Roots of OCD

As neuroscientific technology advances, it is becoming increasingly evident that specific brain structures contribute to OCD and certain neurochemicals modulate the responses observed in OCD patients. In this section, we discuss the involvement of neurotransmitters such as serotonin, dopamine, glutamate, and γ-aminobutyric acid (GABA) in OCD symptoms. Finally, the involvement of the neuropeptide oxytocin will be discussed. Generally, the brain systems involved with threat assessment, anxiety, movement, and reward have been implicated.

OCD neuroanatomical circuit. On February 3, 1967, Jean Talairach and his colleagues at a Parisian hospital accidentally identified one of the components of the OCD circuit (Talairach et al., 1973). In an attempt to localize the foci, or origins, of seizures in epileptic patients, these doctors stimulated various areas of the patients' brains. When the cingulum of one of the patients was stimulated, this patient could not suppress the urge to engage in repetitive behaviors. The **cingulum** (Latin for "belt") is a principal association tract located directly above the corpus callosum in the cingulate gyrus. The cingulum projects to the **entorhinal cortex**, a cortical area proximal to the amygdala that is rich in interconnections with the hippocampus and other limbic structures (Carpenter & Sutin, 1983).

A subsequent study of 52 epileptic patients confirmed the suggestion of the initial findings that the cingulum is involved with complex repetitive movements such as rubbing fingers and pinching skin. Subsequently, neuroanatomical investigations of OCD provided evidence that the cingulum is interconnected with other brain areas implicated in OCD, specifically, the

cingulum An association tract located in the cingulate gyrus that projects to the entorhinal cortex; stimulation of this area results in a desire to engage in repetitive behaviors.

entorhinal cortex Cortical structure on the medial surface of the temporal lobe that surrounds limbic structures such as the amygdala and has rich interconnections with the hippocampal formation.

Box 8.2

A Case in Point

Joseph Dee's Life with OCD

Joseph Dee cannot remember a time in his life that didn't include OCD symptoms. As a young boy, meals with his family became a source of anxiety invaded by one of his earliest obsessions—making the sign of the cross in a perfect motion during grace—and then repeating the motion until, as he described it, his head told him he had done it right. If he failed this task, he was certain he would go to hell. So he kept making the sign, sometimes having to go to the restroom to complete the ritual.

The number 8 had a special significance because there were eight people in Dee's family. Failure to engage in his rituals eight times would, according to his obsessive thoughts, result in the death of a family member. When he watched TV and happened to look over his shoulder, another obsession compelled Joseph to look over each shoulder eight times. At school, when a friend brushed up against him, he was compelled to lick his finger and touch the "offended" area eight times.

Even as a young child, Dee had an eerie feeling that he was not sane. When he was 10 years old, he watched an afternoon television special about an insane person being thrown into a mental institution and decided that he had to hide his condition—even from his parents—to avoid a similar fate. It's difficult to imagine having such overwhelming anxiety as a child—fears of being responsible for a family member's death, fears that his own soul might burn in hell, and fear that he must keep his rituals a secret to avoid being committed to a mental institution. Although it may seem obvious to you that Dee was suffering from OCD during his childhood, he didn't know about such a condition, nor did anyone close to him. Thus, on top of all his anxiety, he lived with the fear that he was different from everyone else in the world.

Dee's problems continued in adolescence. Driving brought about a whole new set of obsessions and compulsions. Every bump evoked obsessions about running over someone, requiring Joseph to engage in the compulsion of looking excessively in the rearview mirror, stopping the car, and looking around for bodies. The anxiety got so unbearable he turned to alcohol and drugs for relief. Alcohol calmed his OCD, but the other drugs usually exacerbated the symptoms.

OCD loop Brain structures thought to be involved in the maintenance of OCD; loop includes the orbitofrontal cortex, cingulate gyrus and embedded cingulum, caudate, thalamus, and amygdala.

orbitofrontal cortex (OFC) Anterior area of the prefrontal cortex, involved in more advanced cognitions and associations.

limbic system and the striatum (Marino & Cosgrove, 1997). Recall from Chapter 3 that limbic structures regulate emotional responses and that the striatum, a motor structure comprising the caudate nucleus, putamen, and globus pallidus, is the terminal for all afferent pathways that form the basal ganglia.

In a more elaborate neural-circuit model, Jack Modell and his colleagues (Modell, Mountz, Curtus, & Greden, 1989) at the University of Michigan Medical Center proposed the existence of an **OCD loop** comprising specific components of the orbitofrontal cortex, striatum, and thalamus (Figure 8.1). The **orbitofrontal cortex (OFC)** is an anterior area of the frontal cortex, the cortical area involved in advanced cognition and associations. Research has suggested that the frontal lobes and cingulate cortex project, or send neural messages, to the caudate component of the striatum, which in turn projects inhibitory impulses to the thalamus. The thalamus completes the circuit by feeding back into the cortex. In support of this neuroanatomical circuit, neurosurgical interruption of the OFC area or the thalamus is associated with improvement of OCD symptoms.

Adequate functioning of this neuroanatomical circuit depends on appropriate information being transmitted from the thalamus to the frontal cortex. Just like an air-conditioning system with a faulty thermostat (that, for example, registers that the air is warmer than it really is), the OCD system may continue to run excessively. A person whose neural circuit is

One day Dee decided to quit his chemical habits, including smoking. He succeeded, but this new goal became prime territory for a new set of obsessions and compulsions. He feared that everything he touched might contain alcohol that would be absorbed into his body and lead to a relapse—he could never be sure that the pizza or the chicken or the salad served him wasn't contaminated with alcohol or other drugs. The new obsessions led to more anxiety, but the OCD enabled him to be extremely vigilant about avoiding drugs.

After being sober for a year and a half, Dee started seeing a psychiatrist, who, after hearing about his life, recommended a book entitled *The Boy Who Couldn't Stop Washing* (1990) written by Judith Rapoport. This book provided Joseph, at age 24, the first evidence that he wasn't completely alone with his bizarre behavior; other children had lived similar lives. This revelation was so powerful that just reading the book—and his subsequent cognitive reappraisal of his symptoms as a brain disorder experienced by other people—resulted in significant improvement.

The next year Dee moved from New York City to Los Angeles, where he eventually ended up in the care of Jeffrey Schwartz at UCLA. Schwartz's cognitive-behavioral program, which we discuss in the Therapies for OCD section of this chapter, proved priceless in helping Dee live a successful life with OCD. When Dee felt an obsession coming on, he pulled a sheet of paper from his pocket with the words "caudate nucleus" written on it to remind him that his obsessions were the result of the misfiring of his brain, not a real threat. He subsequently refocused his attention to another task.

Because of the severity of his symptoms, Dee has opted for a multifaceted approach to treatment. Ten years later, he continues to participate in Schwartz's group sessions and has made prayer and meditation priorities in his life. He has struggled to identify the best pharmaceutical treatment, taking various doses of many antidepressants; but he has suffered seizures and unwelcome side effects.

Dee's cognitive therapy has taught him to avoid giving in to the obsessions in his head—fearing a downward OCD spiral much as an alcoholic fears falling off the wagon as a result of one drink. On all counts, Dee has learned to live a functional life with his OCD, feeling that he has "rewired" his OCD brain. He has written two screenplays and a novel and is currently writing a thriller in which the main character suffers from—you guessed it—OCD.

not responding to feedback from the thalamus may engage excessively in a particular behavior.

Why might the striatum and related limbic structures be involved in the excessive responding observed in OCD? After all, the striatum is known for its involvement in movement, not emotional processing. Some researchers suggest that the striatum is involved with very basic learning processes—and it enables us to carry out automatic behaviors (grooming, for example) without having to consciously focus on every step (Rauch & Savage, 1997). For example, many people find it difficult to avoid self-grooming (playing with hair, pulling on beards, picking dried, peeling skin), although they try to suppress it in public. Recall that when the anterior cingulate gyrus, with its projections to the striatum, was stimulated in the studies on epileptic patients, they exhibited simple, repetitive, automatic behaviors such as rubbing and touching.

Further evidence of the "automatic" nature of striatum-induced behavior is our ability to perform simple movements while concentrating on something more complex—doodling while concentrating on a challenging lecture, typing while carrying on a deep discussion with a friend, or tapping your pencil to the beat of your favorite CD while you read this text. Thinking in terms of computers, the striatal area allows us to multitask, that is, to run one program (carrying on a phone conversation with a friend) while another

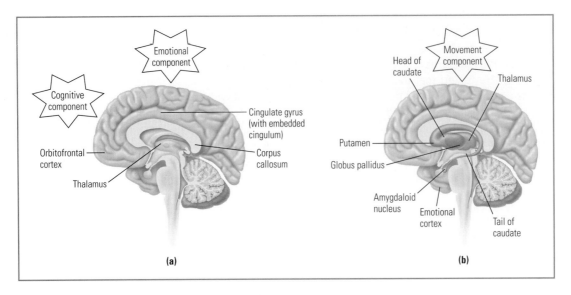

Figure 8.1
OCD loop. The vast interconnections among the components of the proposed neuroanatomical circuitry of OCD enable the circuit to engage at multiple sites to activate OCD responses. **(a)** Thoughts generated in the orbitofrontal cortex (cognitive/ obsessive component) may send neural messages to the cingulate gyrus and embedded cingulum (emotional/integrative component) that activate the caudate nucleus (movement/ compulsion component) shown in (b). Likewise, a movement that activates the caudate may activate the cingulum and then the orbitofrontal cortex. **(b)** Projecting laterally from thalamus to temporal cortex, the amygdala, located in close proximity to the entorhinal cortex, also contributes to the emotional component of OCD, for example, as it relays information about fear stimuli.

(folding clothes) runs in the background. It seems adaptive for us, as it is efficient for a computer, to carry out these simple behaviors without devoting all our attention to them.

Our preparedness to engage in automatic behaviors may be easily nudged to excessive responding because these movements, which often are related to survival, are reinforcing—and rightly so, to assure that animals will perform them. In fact, rather than being classified as an anxiety disorder, OCD may be more accurately classified as a point on a continuum of movement disorders that results from altered striatal activity (Chiocca & Martuza, 1990). Recently, a specific component of the striatum, the putamen (also known for its role in cognitive and motor control), was found to be larger in children diagnosed with OCD than in non-OCD control subjects. Research focusing on children with OCD symptoms provides a valuable opportunity for important clues about this disorder as 80% of the cases are reported to have a pediatric onset (Szesko et al., 2008). Using magnetic resonance imaging (MRI), researchers reported that adult patients with OCD had less developed folding in the anterior cingulate cortex (described above as a component of the OCD circuit), a finding suggesting that alterations in the OCD neurocircuitry resulted from subtle deviations in the neurodevelopment of the structure, occurring around the second and third trimesters of gestation (Shim et al., 2009). Once again, these data demonstrate that, although typically manifested in late adolescence, the foundation for OCD likely exists much earlier in a person's life.

If OCD is characterized by disruptions of movement, why is it typically classified as an anxiety disorder? Recall that a major component of the proposed OCD loop, the cingulate gyrus, is part of the limbic system. Another component of the OCD circuit, the OFC, is activated during threatening situations, suggesting that this area is also involved in processing anxiety-related information. Convincing research also suggests the involvement of another limbic structure, the amygdala.

Joseph LeDoux, at the Center for Neural Sciences at New York University, examined the role of the amygdala in the threat response. As illustrated in Figure 8.2a, his research shows that information about a threatening stimulus (for example, an overflowing garbage can and its associated germs) is processed, and the impulses sent to the visual component of the thalamus, where it is projected to the visual cortex. In some situations, very preliminary information about the stimulus is sent directly from the thalamus to the amygdala to prime the amygdala for interpreting the impending threat.

Once the visual stimulus is actually decoded as a garbage can, projections quickly activate the amygdala, which is intimately involved in evaluating the *emotional significance* of certain stimuli (for example, should you be fearful of the germs?). The OFC receives information from the amygdala and projects it back to the lateral amygdala. The fact that the amygdala is activated by a lower brain area (the thalamus) ultimately saves time in dangerous situations because if you had to wait to receive a message from the frontal cortex about your cognitive assessment of the situation, it might be too late!

Of course, with our advanced cortex, we humans need not actually encounter a stressful or fearful stimulus; we can simply remember or imagine such stimuli (Figure 8.2b). David Zald and SuckWon Kim (1996a, 1996b) at the University of Minnesota have proposed that the ability of the OFC to maintain mental images of fear-related stimuli in our working memory (for example, remembering that you just played with the dog, so you need to wash your hands before eating) may simply go into overdrive

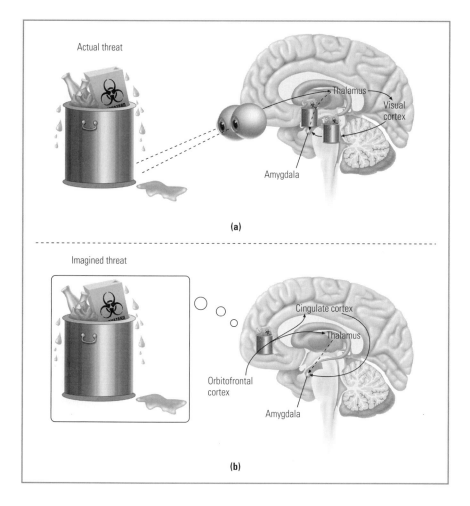

Figure 8.2
Threat response. Real and imaginary fears can activate the same neural circuits. **(a)** The *actual threat* scenario depicts the activation of the emotional circuit described by LeDoux (1994). The visual stimulus (germs associated with the garbage can) is processed through the visual component of the thalamus and then projected to visual cortex, where the information is decoded and subsequently activates the amygdala. Occasionally, preliminary information about the threatening stimulus (dashed line) is sent directly from thalamus to amygdala for quicker evaluation. **(b)** In the *imagined threat* scenario, the mere thought of garbage and germs activates the cingulate cortex, thalamus, and amygdala (as described by Zald & Kim, 1996). Consequently, equivalent emotional responses are experienced following exposure to both real and imagined threat stimuli.

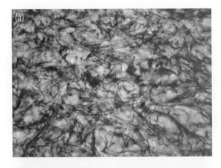

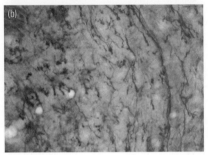

Figure 8.3
Activity-stress pathways.
The stained processes in
each photomicrograph depict
pathways that are actively
utilizing the neurotransmitter
dopamine in the area of the
amygdala in **(a)** an activity-
stressed rat and **(b)** a pair-fed
control rat.

COURTESY OF KELLY LAMBERT, RANDOLPH-
MACON COLLEGE BEHAVIORAL NEUROSCIENCE
LABORATORY

in OCD patients (Goldman-Rakic, 1987). This excessive responding of the OFC results in a patient's failure to inhibit thoughts about the anxiety-provoking stimuli (dog slobber and accompanying germs in this case). Rebecca Elliott, a neuroscientist at Manchester University, and her colleagues have proposed specific functions within the OFC; specifically, based on neuroimaging evidence, they proposed that the medial OFC monitors stimuli in a changing environmental context whereas the lateral OFC contributes to the interruption of behavioral sequences based on previous rewarding responses. Thus, if a patient with OCD had previously experienced a strong sense of reward or pleasure following repeated behaviors to calm a specific anxiety, the lateral OFC may be reluctant to interrupt a behavioral sequence due to its rewarding payoff upon its completion (Elliott, Dolan, & Frith, 2000; Szesko et al., 2008).

In the OCD patient's constant state of awareness of environmental conditions, the information becomes "locked online." The desire to wash one's hands, for example, to avoid being contaminated by dog germs takes primary importance over other cognitive or behavioral events. In support of this interesting theory, when OCD patients were exposed to contaminants, activity in the more general OFC area was positively correlated with the intensity of the patients' desire to start cleaning (McGuire, Bench, & Frith, 1994). Perhaps the increased orbitofrontal activity observed in these OCD patients increased the chances of developing a hand-washing obsession.

Additional evidence from neuroimaging studies. Using MRI, Michael Jenike, Hans Breiter, and their colleagues at Massachusetts General Hospital and Harvard Medical School (1996) found that female OCD patients had less white matter volume than control subjects. Additionally, these patients had significantly greater *opercular cortex* volumes. (This area in the frontal cortex lies adjacent to the banks of the lateral sulcus and covers the internal area of the insula.) Severity of OCD symptoms positively correlates with opercular volume. Therefore, patients with heavier opercular cortex volumes were more likely to experience OCD symptoms than patients with lighter volumes. Focusing on caudate morphology, at least two studies report reduced caudate volumes in OCD patients (Luxenberg et al., 1988; Robinson et al., 1995).

Using the technique of voxel-based morphometry (Ashburner & Friston, 2000), researchers have also found significantly more gray matter in the OFC of children diagnosed with OCD than in age-matched healthy subjects (Szesko et al., 2008). Together with the aforementioned studies in adults, it appears that cortical activity in key areas is associated with heightened symptoms of OCD. Accordingly, some forms of pharmacological treatment (as discussed later in the chapter) are correlated with decreases in OFC activity (Swedo et al., 1992).

Whereas functional brain image studies have consistently pointed to the involvement of certain brain structures in OCD, structural neuroimaging results have been less consistent. The volume of the caudate nucleus, for example, has been found to be smaller than, larger than, and, in some cases, not different from that of control subjects (Luxenberg et al., 1988; Scarone et al., 1992; Bartha et al., 1998). Researchers in the Netherlands wondered if the varied nature of symptoms that patients experience with OCD contributed to the heterogeneity of these findings. Using voxel-based morphometry for 55 nonmedicated patients with OCD and 50 age-matched controls, these researchers found specific neuroanatomical areas associated with specific symptom dimensions. More specifically, the symmetry/ordering dimension was associated with smaller global white and gray matter volumes and, focusing on more regional areas, smaller gray matter volume in the right motor cortex, left parietal cortex, and left insula and larger temporal lobe volume. Scores on the contamination/washing dimension were associated with smaller bilateral caudate nucleus gray matter volume as well as smaller right parietal white matter than the control subjects. Further, the harm/checking dimension was associated with smaller temporal lobes. Hence, it appears that the cause of OCD is heterogenous due to the multiple brain areas affected by specific symptom dimensions. A patient exhibiting excessive washing and concerns about contamination may have a different profile of regional brain volume sizes from a patient exhibiting excessive concerns about the symmetry and order of various objects in the environment (Van den Heuvel et al., 2009).

These observed differences in the volume of certain brain structures also prompt some researchers to hypothesize that OCD may be due to delayed maturation of the frontostriatal circuitry, or components comprising the frontal cortex, striatum, or integrating circuits. Further evidence of the *delayed-maturation theory* of OCD is found in a study in which cingulate volume was measured in pediatric OCD patients and control subjects. Whereas a significant correlation between age and cingulate volume was found in the control subjects, no such relationship was found in the OCD children. Thus, this study suggests that the maturation of the cingulate may be delayed or even arrested in OCD patients (Rosenberg & Keshavan, 1998).

Neuroimaging provides the most influential data supporting the proposed OCD circuit. In addition to suggesting that the structures in the circuit have different shapes and volumes in OCD compared to non-OCD patients, neuroimaging studies enable researchers to look at the level of activity (using a positron emission tomographic [PET] scan) in each critical area while the patients engage in various activities or thought processes. For example, when OCD patients are asked to engage in the simple activity of resting quietly, researchers observe more neural activity in the OFC, anterior cingulate cortex, and striatum than they do in the same structures of non-OCD subjects at rest.

Thus, the baseline neuronal activation levels in the various structures of the OCD loop are higher in OCD patients than in control subjects. Following therapy, the baseline hyperactivity subsides. These areas are still quite functional, however, because once the patient is actually shown the object of his or her prior obsessions (germs, for example), activity in the OCD circuit increases once again (Miguel et al., 1997).

Some studies even suggest **lateralization** (hemisphere dominance) of neural activation in OCD. In one PET study, OCD symptoms were provoked by exposing patients to either a dirty glove or a sterile glove. In the dirty-glove trials, activation was observed in the OFC in both hemispheres, whereas activation of the anterior cingulate cortex and caudate nucleus was observed only in the right hemisphere of OCD patients (Rauch et al., 1994).

When interpreting these neuroimaging studies, however, it's best to be mindful of the many characteristics of the subject population, which

lateralization The observation that different functions have been assigned, or lateralized, to each hemisphere of the brain.

behavioral addiction Notion that a human or other animal may develop a physiological addiction (similar to drug addiction) to engaging in certain behaviors such as compulsions.

activity-stress paradigm Animal model of chronic stress and compulsive behavior in which rats are housed in activity wheels and exposed to restricted food resources. Rats typically increase running and exhibit multiple signs of stress-induced illness when faced with these conditions.

complicate any conclusions. For example, when a study failed to find structural abnormalities or altered metabolic rates in the caudate of OCD patients, the authors subsequently suggested that the heterogenous nature of this disorder (OCD with and without tics in this case) might contribute to some of the inconsistencies found in the literature, a problem typical of research in the field of mental illness (Aylward et al., 1996; Trivedi, 1996).

Neurochemistry of OCD. If you envision OCD as an addiction to specific cognitive-behavioral rituals, then the addiction literature might be useful in understanding this disorder (see also Chapter 11). Recall that the nucleus accumbens is the limbic component of the striatum, sometimes referred to as the "pleasure center" of the brain (see Figure 3.13). Substantial research suggests that dopaminergic activity in the nucleus accumbens plays an integral role in the rewarding properties of psychotropic drugs such as cocaine and amphetamine (Koob & Nestler, 1997a, 1997b). One distinctive difference, however, between substance abuse and OCD is that an exogenous substance (one originating outside the body) is continuously introduced into the central nervous system in substance abuse, an event that does not occur in OCD.

Could the nucleus accumbens be involved in a **behavioral addiction**? This is the idea that a human or other animal can develop a physiological addiction to engaging in certain behaviors. Looking back at the model of rat behavior described in the chapter-opening Connections might provide a clue. Recall that the rats are fed for 1 hour per day and housed with activity wheels. The rats increase their running to such excessive levels that they die of stress-related symptoms if the experimenter does not intervene (Lambert, 1993; Lambert et al., 1998).

These animals have increased cellular activity in the nucleus accumbens, as well as increased dopaminergic activity (the neurotransmitter involved in addiction) throughout the extended amygdala, as shown in Figure 8.3 (Aurentz et al., 1999). The effect is so pronounced that researchers have suggested this **activity-stress paradigm** as a valid model of OCD. In fact, one study found that antidepressants, a sometimes successful treatment for OCD, are also effective for the compulsive running observed in this paradigm (Altemus, Glowa, & Murphy, 1993). Thus, it appears that rats engaging in such a severe behavioral compulsion fit the same neurobiological profile of animals addicted to cocaine. These findings begin to convey just how intense the desire to engage in certain behaviors is in OCD patients (Figure 8.4).

Drugs that enhance serotonergic (5-hydroxytryptamine [5-HT]) activity, namely the selective serotonin reuptake inhibitors (SSRIs) discussed in Chapter 5, are somewhat effective in treating OCD; specifically, these drugs are effective in 40%–60% of cases (Math and Janardhan Reddy, 2007; Jenike, Rauche, et al., 1996). It is therefore easy to conclude that OCD is caused by lowered or modified serotonin levels. Research, however, does not support this conclusion.

Isolated findings of 5-HT abnormalities have been reported (Insel, Mueller, Alterman, Linnoila, & Murphy, 1985), but no consistent serotonin abnormalities have been identified (Rapoport & Fiske, 1998). In fact, among the transmitters associated with the proposed OCD loop, two additional neurochemicals stand out: glutamate activity between the OFC and the caudate nucleus (part of the striatum) and GABA, the principal transmitter among the components of the striatum. Cerebrospinal fluid (CSF) samples

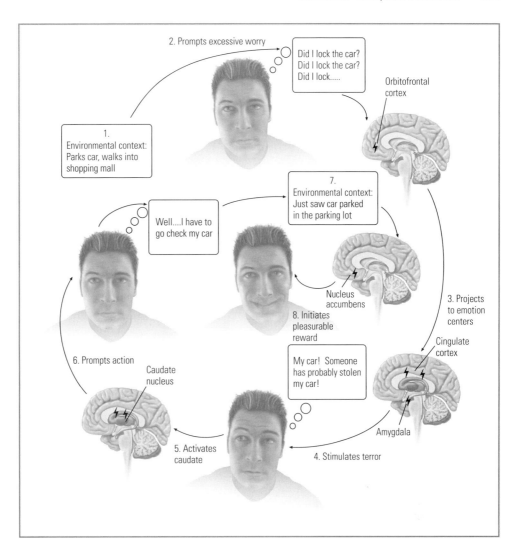

of patients with OCD had higher glutamate levels than those of control subjects, suggesting glutamatergic excess in the pathophysiology of OCD (Chakrabarty, Bhattacharyya, Christopher, & Khanna, 2005). So where does serotonin come into play? It has been suggested that serotonin, in addition to dopamine, serves as a *neuromodulator*, a neurotransmitter that increases or decreases the activity of other neurotransmitters (see Chapter 5).

As depicted in Figure 8.5, dopamine may modulate a specific aspect of the OCD circuitry (the caudate nucleus), whereas serotonin modulates another component (the globus pallidus). The brain needs glutamate and GABA to receive and transmit messages in the OCD circuitry, yet the volume and clarity of reception may be adjusted in the presence of neuromodulators such as dopamine and serotonin.

The indirect involvement of serotonin in the OCD circuitry may account for the variability observed in studies in which OCD patients are given serotonergic reuptake inhibitors (SRIs). Focusing on a potential indirect role of dopamine, dopaminergic receptor subtype-2 (D_2) antagonists are effective

Figure 8.4
Spiraling behavior pattern. A simple trip to the shopping mall can trigger a complex series of responses for a person with OCD. Environmental context, cognition, neural activity, and behavior all intersect in a spiraling pattern.

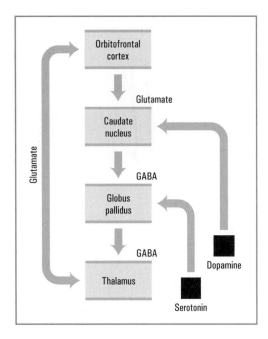

Figure 8.5
Neurochemistry of the OCD loop. Glutamate pathways are necessary for communication between the OFC and caudate nucleus and between the thalamus and OFC. GABA pathways are found between the caudate and globus pallidus and the globus pallidus and thalamus. Although not specifically part of the transmitter communication among the circuit structures, dopamine acts as a neuromodulator in the caudate and serotonin in the globus pallidus.

ADAPTED FROM JENIKE, RAUCH, ET AL., 1996.

fixed action pattern (FAP) Motor program that seems to develop automatically in particular species of animals (e.g., the courting displays of many birds); once triggered, these rigid, consistent, and predictable responses are continued to completion.

for motor tics, providing more evidence that dopamine may be a modulator involved in the behavioral compulsions observed in OCD.

Pregnant animals, including humans, change their behavior around the time of giving birth—building a nest or nursery, checking the surroundings, cleaning up. At least in humans, this behavior often is exacerbated by obsessional thoughts about the delivery or being a competent parent. Neill Epperson and her colleagues at Yale University had the fertile idea that the compulsions and obsessions observed in these "glowing" women might offer a clue to what may be going on in OCD.

The researchers focused their attention on oxytocin, a neuropeptide released by the posterior pituitary and involved in uterine contractions and milk ejection, as well as in social bonding (see Chapter 5). From a behavioral perspective, oxytocin seems to enhance the expression of grooming, reproductive, and affiliative behaviors in animals (Epperson, McDougle, & Price, 1996). Interestingly, some women with preexisting OCD report worsening of symptoms during pregnancy. Although this oxytocin hypothesis is extremely interesting, the jury is still out about its actual role in OCD or OCD-like behavior (Epperson et al., 1996; Leckman et al., 1994).

Evolutionary Perspectives: Fixed Action Patterns and Ritualistic Behavior

Evolutionary biologists and psychologists refer to behavioral responses that are rigid, consistent, and predictable as **fixed action patterns (FAPs)**. In most cases, these seemingly inherent behaviors serve some function related to survival. A young bird opens and closes its mouth to initiate feeding from its parent. A frog flicks its tongue to catch flies.

Because FAPs are important to survival, animals are biologically prepared to make the patterned response. From an evolutionary viewpoint, then, people with OCD clean to avoid contamination and sickness. They check and count to confirm the safety of family and friends. They repeatedly order items in their environment in an attempt to protect their resources.

It is easy to conceive many of these rituals as closely related to FAPs (Turbott, 1997). Most of the ritualistic behaviors associated with OCD—avoiding contamination, purifying the body, vigilance for environmental threats, observing social rules or religious rituals, checking to make sure an important task has been completed—are related to survival in some manner (Rapoport & Fiske, 1998). Recall also that the ritualistic behaviors of OCD are consistent across cultures. Given this cross-cultural consistency, OCD rituals can be likened to more elaborate FAPs observed in nonhuman animals.

A personal experience illustrates how behaviors critical for survival can escalate into compulsions. When my youngest daughter was about 14 months old, I (K. G. L.) dropped her off at her babysitter's one rainy morning. When I got out of the van, I accidentally hit the lock button, leaving my keys inside;

by the time I ran around to get my daughter from her car seat I realized that I couldn't get to her. I stood next to her window for 30 minutes in the pouring rain trying to make reassuring faces as she was reaching out for me and screaming in fear.

This experience created a heavy dose of maternal anxiety. Years later, I continue to check to make sure I have my keys at least twice every time I get out of my vehicle—regardless of whether my children (now old enough to unlock the doors) are in the car. This compulsive checking behavior began with the need to protect my daughter—who, in evolutionary terms, represents a significant genetic investment.

Animal models. FAPs also seem to be ballistic in the sense that once they are triggered by the appropriate stimulus they are difficult to suppress. If you've ever been around cats, you are familiar with the stereotypical behavior they demonstrate after they use the litter box—digging and covering, digging and covering. In the cat's natural environment this behavior is perfectly reasonable, to keep unwanted visitors from knowing that the cat had eliminated in the area.

Have you also observed a cat's behavior when it defecates on a bare floor? The cat still goes through all the motions of burying even though the burying response makes no sense when there is nothing to move over its feces. In this situation, the cat seems unable to respond to the environment and spends the same amount of time moving air over the soiled area.

This behavior may be similar to that of humans, who wash their hands to remove dirt that is not there or check locks they have checked dozens of times. Seksel and Lindeman (1998) investigated the effectiveness of the antidepressant clomipramine on compulsive behaviors of the cat, such as urine spraying, overgrooming, and excessive vocalization. The drug was well tolerated in the feline patients and, when combined with behavior modification, effective at ameliorating the annoying behaviors in 100% of the cases!

Further evidence that OCD may be related to FAPs can be seen in raccoons. In its natural habitat, the raccoon spends lots of time along the riverbank, running its sensitive fingers through the shallow water looking for food. In captivity, these animals are known for compulsive-like food washing—dropping the food in the water, losing it, picking it up, dropping it again. It is likely that the raccoons are interested not in cleaning the food but in hunting for it; it is more plausible that these behaviors are caused by their inability to hunt for their food in captivity. FAPs are difficult to suppress even when they are not necessary for a specific animal's survival.

Human models: Baseball rituals. Watching a baseball game after studying this chapter may inspire armchair diagnostics of some players. For example, you may observe a pitcher who always adjusts his hat, hits his glove, twists his ankle counterclockwise, and spits over his left arm before delivering a pitch. Like an FAP, once initiated, the pitcher always goes through the entire sequence before ending the behavior. Similar to behaviors observed in OCD, the pitcher engages in the behavior excessively and, if asked why, says he feels—irrationally—that something bad will happen if the compulsion is not expressed to completion.

Could it be that these talented, disciplined, physically fit men all have a specific form of baseball-induced OCD? After all, some of these behaviors seem anything but rational. Former Red Sox player Wade Boggs ate chicken

superstitious behavior
Response resulting from random reinforcement; thought to explain some ritualistic behavior.

before every single game of his professional career (and he had many other rituals); and Dennis Martinez, former pitcher for the Orioles, drank a small cup of water after each inning and placed each cup under the bench upside down. Interestingly, most ritualistic behaviors are associated with hitting and pitching, where more variables are perceived to be out of the players' control, than playing the field (Gmelch, 1992). Although these behaviors meet some of the criteria for OCD, it is important to note that players don't typically engage in these rituals off the field, they don't perceive their compulsions as excessive, and they don't feel that the compulsions interfere with success on the field. On the contrary, many players feel that their specific rituals are necessary for their success. And who could argue that someone who has a career playing his or her favorite game and is receiving a seven-digit salary is not successful?

In most cases, the ritualistic behavior observed in athletes is considered **superstitious behavior**, that is, responses that result from random reinforcement. For example, if a pigeon receives a pellet of food every minute regardless of whether or not it engages in a specific behavior, many times the pigeon will form an association between its last behavior and the food reward. Before long, the animal is repeatedly engaging in the random behavior (for example, turning in a semicircle) to prompt the delivery of the food. After a baseball player wears a red undershirt and eats pineapple-flavored jelly beans before a game in which he goes four for four and hits a home run, the distinctive cues of the T-shirt and jelly beans become linked in his mind to his success in the game. From that point on the player is likely to engage in these behaviors repeatedly in an attempt to repeat the initial success. It is important to point out that the rituals typically emerge from exceptionally good performances and are the product of the player not attributing the exceptional play to his or her skill but to a noticeable event or stimulus in the environment (Gmelch, 1992).

The next time you wear your lucky socks to an exam, you may want to analyze your reasons. Is the behavior truly related to the consequences? Well, if it makes you feel more confident, it probably won't do any harm as long as you continue to realize that studying is the most important behavior for producing the consequences of the good grade you desire. Although superstitious behaviors can lead to dysfunctional responding, they may serve as confidence boosters in certain situations, leading to reduced anxiety and more successful responding.

Therapies for OCD

Various forms of treatment benefit OCD patients: pharmaceutical therapy, cognitive-behavioral therapy, neurosurgical treatment, and brain stimulation. Pharmaceutical therapy attempts to reestablish more normal baseline neurochemistry in the brain. Five drugs currently have Food and Drug Administration approval for the treatment of OCD. Unfortunately, pharmaceutical therapy does not suppress symptoms in all OCD patients. Some patients experience improvement with certain behavioral and/or cognitive therapy; others, out of desperation, turn to neurosurgery or, more recently, to deep brain stimulation.

Psychopharmacological therapy. Recall that, although no prevailing serotonergic abnormalities have been observed in OCD patients, drugs that alter 5-HT functioning (SRIs and SSRIs) improve the symptoms of many OCD patients. These observations suggest that serotonin may have an indirect effect on OCD. However, with the more sophisticated assays of the serotonergic system currently available, differences in 5-HT systems may become apparent in the near future. For example, decreased platelet 5-HT levels in adolescent OCD patients have been correlated with clinical improvement (Flament, Rapoport, Murphy, Lake, & Berg, 1987). Further, focusing on 5-HT metabolites might yield interesting information; for example, increased levels of 5-hydroxyindoleacetic acid (5-HIAA, a 5-HT metabolite more easily detected in CSF than 5-HT) have been observed in OCD patients (Insel et al., 1985).

Although the specific explanation for the success of SRIs is yet to be uncovered, it hasn't prevented the prescription of such drugs for OCD. After all, OCD patients are more interested in the successful outcome of a treatment than a scientific explanation for the treatment's effectiveness. Let's look at some of the drugs that successfully treat OCD symptoms.

Clomipramine (Anafranil), originally introduced as an antidepressant in Europe in 1966, was the first serotonergic treatment that proved effective for some cases of OCD (Kobak, Greist, Jefferson, Katzelnick, & Henk, 1998). Clomipramine blocks 5-HT and norepinephrine (as well as having some dopamine receptor–blocking properties) and is considered a more global SRI than the contemporary SSRIs (McDougle, 1999). Although effective at treating OCD symptoms, clomipramine induces side effects such as sedation, constipation, insomnia, nervousness, and male impotence (Ackerman, Greenland, Bystritsky, & Datz, 1996) and can be lethal in overdoses (Kobak et al., 1998).

Fewer side effects attend the prescribed SSRIs, which include fluoxetine (Prozac), sertraline (Zoloft), paroxetine (Paxil), and fluvoxamine (Luvox). The SSRIs, however, are not free from side effects; some produce nausea, headaches, and sleep disturbances. In many cases, however, SSRI side effects wane after several months. Generally, OCD patients require higher doses than those given to depressed patients (Math & Janardhan Reddy, 2007). In the case of all pharmacological treatments, it seems to take as long as 3 months before OCD patients notice an initial response and up to 6 months for a maximal effect (Dolberg, Iancu, Sasson, & Zohar, 1996). (See Chapter 9 for more information on SSRIs.)

How effective are these pharmacological therapies? This is a difficult question to answer because much of the data do not come from controlled studies and many patients are placed on more than one treatment protocol. Treatment "packages" for OCD patients might consist of multiple pharmacological interventions along with behavioral and/or cognitive therapy. The exact choice of SRI is typically determined by potential side effects (Math & Reddy, 2007). There also appears to be a considerable placebo response when treating OCD pharmacologically—as high as 50%, although up to 20% report getting worse (Zohar, Judge, & OCD Paroxetine Study Investigators, 1996).

Despite these complications, it is reported that drug therapies have a success rate that ranges about 40%–70% (Dolberg et al., 1996; Fineberg & Gale, 2005). This recovery rate is impressive, but relapse rates are high when patients cease taking their medication (Dolberg et al., 1996). Additionally, other drugs may be prescribed to augment recovery. For example, D_2 antagonists may be used for prevalent tics (Jenike, Rauch, et al., 1996) and

clomipramine SRI that prevents the reuptake of serotonin and norepinephrine from the synapse, ultimately increasing the availability of serotonin; similar in structure to imipramine, a tricyclic antidepressant; used as therapy for OCD.

anxiolytics Drugs such as the benzodiazepines that work to reduce anxiety.

stereotaxic apparatus Scientific device that enables the experimenter or surgeon to access any three-dimensional point in the brain; used for placement of electrodes and various forms of neurosurgery.

anxiolytics, or anxiety-reducing agents (for example, benzodiazepines), may help to reduce anxiety associated with OCD (Miguel et al., 1997).

Neurosurgical treatment. Neurosurgery is sometimes used in the most extreme OCD cases, when patients treated with drugs fail to improve or, once improved, find themselves relapsing (Mindus & Jenike, 1992). In this case, *neurosurgical treatment*, a more contemporary term than *psychosurgery*, introduced in Chapter 2, may be defined as "a destruction of histologically normal brain tissue with the objective of alleviating severe symptoms of chronic psychiatric disorders" (Mindus & Jenike, 1992, p. 922). Why perform the extreme act of cutting into an OCD patient's brain? Is there sufficient evidence that neurosurgical treatment works? Let us start with a little history.

In the 1930s, accumulating evidence suggested that the frontal lobe and connections might be involved in anxiety-related disorders (Fulton & Jacobsen, 1935; MacLean, 1954; Papez, 1937). Following the introduction of the **stereotaxic apparatus** in 1947, surgeons could enter the brain and manipulate structures with great precision (Figure 8.6). In 1947, Talairach and other surgeons attempted to treat patients suffering from anxiety neurosis by interrupting the frontal–thalamic connections. Because the side effects on personality were not as severe as those observed in the more traditional frontal lobotomies, an increase in stereotaxic surgeries occurred for a variety of psychiatric illnesses (Bingley, Lekskell, Meyerson, & Rylander, 1977; Chiocca & Martuza, 1990). The most successful results, however, were observed in OCD patients (Fodstad, Strandman, Karlsson, & West, 1982).

Currently, four surgical protocols show the greatest potential as effective treatments for OCD patients: anterior capsulotomy, anterior cingulotomy, subcaudate tractotomy, and limbic leukotomy (Chiocca & Martuza, 1990). Most of these procedures require local anesthesia accompanied by mild sedation or light general anesthesia. The surgery itself has been described as painless, inducing little stress in the patient, although individual cases vary (Marino & Cosgrove, 1997). Generally, improvement takes anywhere from weeks to months after the surgery (Mindus & Jenike, 1992).

As you read the descriptions and accompanying success rates for each surgery, keep in mind that these observations are far from scientific perfection. Obviously, no control groups are included—it would not be ethical to conduct a sham surgery on OCD patients. Additionally, the follow-ups are generally only for the first couple of years, so long-term data are not available for most of the studies. For these reasons, countries such as the Russian Republic and Japan prohibit neurosurgical intervention to treat intractable or persistent OCD (Mindus & Jenike, 1992). The following neurosurgical procedures are summarized in Table 8.3:

■ *Anterior capsulotomy* Introduced by Leksell in the 1950s (Herner, 1961), this procedure involves placing bilateral lesions in the anterior part of the internal capsule. This band of nerve fibers projects from the brain stem to the frontal lobe; the anterior portion separates the caudate from the putamen (see Figure 8.1 to review anatomical directions). This procedure successfully suppressed symptoms in up to 70% of the patients, but disturbing side effects related to impulse control and other personality changes were observed in some patients.

■ *Anterior cingulotomy* Originally performed by Whitty in 1952, the anterior portion of the cingulate gyrus is excised (Whitty, Duffield, & Tow, 1952). Overall, this surgery has a success rate of about 50% and a very low complication rate. A long-term follow-up has reported a more conservative success rate of 30% (Jenike et al., 1991). Interestingly, anterior cingulotomy appears to have no effect on the patient's intellectual, behavioral, or emotional capacities, making it the most prevalent among the neurosurgical protocols for OCD (Marino & Cosgrove, 1997). It has been speculated that this surgery improves symptoms by diminishing the anxiety component rather than the compulsion component of the disease. For example, if an individual consistently engaged in compulsive hand washing when she felt anxious, the compulsions would decrease if, following this surgery, she were less likely to feel anxious. Nonetheless, when faced with final exams or another significant stressful event, compulsive rituals would probably reemerge for the duration of the anxiety.

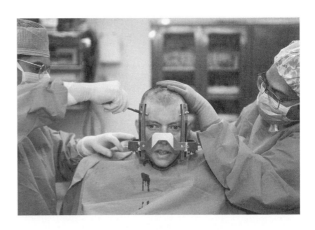

Figure 8.6
Stereotaxic apparatus. A fearful patient is fitted into a stereotaxic apparatus, or calibrated frame, so that the neurosurgeon can maneuver through the brain with great precision (accurate to the millimeter) to cut particular nerve fibers. In the case of intractable OCD, the lesions, or cuts, generally separate some of the pathways of the frontal cortex from the emotional circuit of the limbic system.
JOE MCNALLY

■ *Subcaudate tractotomy* This procedure, in which lesions are made in the orbital cortex (positioned ventral to the head of the caudate nucleus), was introduced by Knight in 1969. Although research on this procedure is minimal, researchers suggest that clinical improvement was seen in about 50% of patients with minor rates of adverse personality traits, an outcome not observed with anterior cingulotomy (Goktepe, Young, & Bridges, 1975).

■ *Limbic leukotomy* Introduced in 1973 by Kelly, Richardson, and Mitchell-Heggs, this procedure consists of bilateral lesions of the lower medial portion of the orbitofrontal areas plus bilateral lesions of the anterior cingulate bundle area. The disruption of both areas influences connections among the thalamic and limbic pathways. Not surprisingly, this more extensive surgery seems to be more successful than the aforementioned procedures, with success rates as high as 84% and no long-term side effects. Consequently, there is considerable enthusiasm for the limbic technique (Perse, 1988).

Given this information, how should an intractable OCD patient who has not responded to pharmacological or cognitive-behavioral therapies be treated? Because of the low side effect rate and modest tissue damage, it is often recommended that the surgeon start with cingulotomy. If this surgery fails to lead to a satisfactory recovery, then the surgeon can reenter the brain and create a lesion in the orbitomedial frontal areas, making the procedure a limbic leukotomy or anterior capsulotomy (Chiocca & Martuza, 1990).

Even with all the information on these techniques, it is important to remember that surgical therapy is still in its infancy. It is hoped that more sophisticated neuroimaging techniques will help to identify more specific areas critical for understanding OCD. The identification of such areas will lead to interventions requiring the least possible neurological damage (Mindus & Jenike, 1992).

exposure and response prevention (ERP) Behavioral therapy for OCD; patients are encouraged to remain in contact with a feared stimulus while simultaneously suppressing the rituals they typically use to decrease anxiety.

Deep brain stimulation. Another technique used to manipulate the brains of patients with OCD is deep brain stimulation (DBS). This technique was discussed in Chapter 7 as a therapy for Parkinson's disease and will also be discussed in Chapter 9. As applied to OCD, this technique involves the stereotaxic placement of electrodes in key areas of the brain thought to be involved with obsessions and compulsions. The battery-operated neurostimulator is implanted subcutaneously in the subclavicular area, allowing for continual stimulation of the brain. The first successful use of DBS for treatment-resistant OCD was accomplished in the late 1990s (Nuttin & Cosyns, 1999). Typically, the electrodes have been placed in the anterior limb of the internal capsule; however, more recently, German researchers have investigated the efficacy of placing electrodes in the right hemisphere's nucleus accumbens. In this double-blind, sham-controlled, crossover study (i.e., patients received 3 months of DBS followed by 3 months of sham stimulation or vice versa), 50% of patients exhibited at least a 25% decrease in symptoms (Huff et al., 2009). Due to the limited number of patients who have received this therapy, however, DBS should be considered as an experimental therapeutic approach (Denys & Mantione, 2009).

Cognitive-behavioral therapy. Behavioral therapy was used to treat OCD as early as 1900. Unfortunately, behaviorism was suppressed by Freud's psychoanalytic movement, which explored the meaning of obsessions and compulsions rather than treatment for them (Miguel et al., 1997). A second wave of behavior therapy, **exposure and response prevention (ERP)**, surfaced in the early 1970s and proved to be the first empirically validated successful treatment for OCD (Kobak et al., 1998). Research suggests that about 50%–70% of patients improve as a result of ERP, an improvement rate similar to pharmacological therapies (Dolberg et al., 1996). In fact, a few studies have indicated that behavioral therapy is slightly more effective than individual medications for OCD (Marks, 1997).

Patients undergoing ERP are instructed to expose themselves to feared stimuli and encouraged to stay in contact with the stimuli through the subsequent anxiety. During this exposure, patients are instructed to actively suppress the usual rituals (response) used to minimize anxiety. For example, a patient with a germ obsession might have to come into contact with the most feared germs and refrain from cleaning or avoiding the germs. Patients

Table 8.3 Summary of Neurosurgical Procedures for Severe OCD

Type of Surgery	Manipulation	Success Rate	Side Effects
Anterior capsulotomy	Bilateral lesions of anterior internal capsule	Approx. 70%	Impulse-control problems and personality changes
Anterior cingulotomy	Excision of anterior cingulate gyrus	Approx. 30%–50%	Hemiplegia and medication controlled epilepsy in <1% of patients
Subcaudate tractotomy	Lesions of rostral orbital cortex (ventral to head of caudate)	Approx. 50% (minimal research)	Minor personality alterations such as overeating and extravagance in some patients
Limbic leukotomy	Bilateral lesions of lower medial quadrant of orbitofrontal areas and anterior cingulate bundle	Approx. 84%	No long-term side effects observed

are assigned these tasks as homework, to be carried out on the patient's own for 1 hour daily.

The average therapy time is 10 hours for outpatients and 20 hours for more difficult cases (typically inpatients). ERP was initially thought to be most useful for treating ritual behaviors but is now used for obsessions as well. The patient is instructed to think anxiogenic (anxiety-producing) thoughts and then suppress the mental rituals or neutralizing thoughts that usually accompany the anxiety (Marks, 1997).

Because ERP involves contact with the OCD patient's most feared situations, it comes close to the patient's worst nightmare. The anticipated fear and anxiety make some patients reluctant to proceed, and some drop out of therapy early (Marks, 1997). One recent innovation, *virtual-reality ERP*, in which a person interacts with a fearful stimulus through interactive video, may reduce their trepidation (Clark, Kirdby, Daniels, & Marks, 1998). For the more cautious OCD patient, vicarious computer-aided techniques in which a patient merely watches another patient encounter fearful stimuli on a computer screen lead to significant improvement, although not as much as actual ERP (see Epilogue for more about virtual-reality treatment). ERP can be uncomfortable for patients, but it can eliminate fear and anxiety, often without pharmacological aids. As described in Chapter 1, this behavioral therapy is also used successfully to treat phobias.

Perhaps the most promising form of behavioral therapy is ERP used in combination with cognitive therapy. In an innovative study, Jeffrey Schwartz and his colleagues at the University of California in Los Angeles (Schwartz, Stoessel, Baxter, Martin, & Phelps, 1996) demonstrated the interactions among behavioral therapy, cognitive therapy, and neuroscience. (Schwartz was discussed earlier in Box 7.2.) Schwartz's team had patients meet once or twice a week with a therapist to review individualized ERP assignments. Patients were further instructed to keep diaries to help them self-monitor their progress.

The cognitive component consisted of the *four Rs* (Schwartz et al., 1996):

- *Relabeling* the unwanted thoughts as mere obsessions and compulsions

- *Reattributing* the origin of the thoughts to a physiochemical disorder of the brain and not a danger that exists in reality

- *Refocusing* during the unwanted thoughts so that the patient can quickly substitute more comfortable thoughts for the anxiety-provoking thoughts

- *Revaluing* so that the patient realizes that the unwanted thoughts are merely worthless distractions and should be ignored

The PET scan in Figure 8.7a compares the energy being used in the brains of a control subject and a person with OCD. PET scans of patients who responded to the treatment show significant decreases in caudate glucose metabolic rates, an effect that was not observed in the poor responders (Figure 8.7b). Prior to treatment, high activation of the orbital gyri, the head of the caudate nucleus, and the thalamus (especially in the right hemisphere) was observed. After treatment, this activity was minimized in both hemispheres. These data demonstrate that an effective cognitive therapy changes the patient's neurobiology. These findings provide further support of the existence of the OCD loop, consisting of the OFC, striatum, and thalamic components

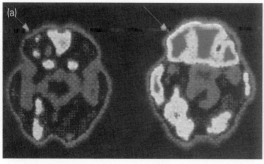
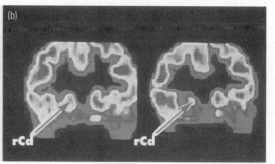

Normal control   Obsessive-compulsive   Pretreatment   Posttreatment

Figure 8.7
PET scans of relative energy use in OCD. (a) The level of cellular activation (denoted by lighter-colored areas) is higher in the OCD patient on the right compared with the control subject on the left. (b) Right caudate (rCd) activity in the patient's brain post-self-treatment is less than it was pretreatment.

SCHWARTZ & BEYETTE, 1996. COURTESY OF JEFFERY SCHWARTZ, M.D., AND LEWIS R. BAXTER, JR., M.D.

(see Figure 8.1). According to Schwartz & Beyette (1997), this circuit "locks" the brain in gear, inducing the repetitive obsessions and compulsions.

These data confirm what cognitive-behavioral therapists have thought for some time—that this form of ERP therapy can modify the brain in ways similar to pharmacological or surgical therapies. The idea of brain changes being self-generated and not dependent on pharmacological intervention makes ERP very attractive. It should be noted, however, that medication is used at times during cognitive-behavioral therapy. The use of drugs early in the treatment, as patients begin to expose themselves to their worst fears, has been likened to children's use of water wings to reduce the anxiety that accompanies many early encounters with water (Schwartz et al., 1997). Just as most children grow out of that anxiety and learn to float or swim without aids, patients are removed from pharmacological interventions following the early stages of treatment (Schwartz et al., 1997). The bottom line is that any clinical improvement must be accompanied by neurobiological alterations in the brain.

TOURETTE SYNDROME

Have you ever developed a hacking cough that persisted through an important lecture? Been at an interview when your stomach started growling voraciously? Gotten the hiccups while trying to give an oral presentation in class? The fact that your body is making disruptive noises is very distracting as you muster all your energy to try to suppress the coughing, growling, or hiccupping. These experiences offer only a partial insight to the constant dread many Tourette syndrome patients experience as they try to suppress their vocal and motor tics in public. For deeper insight, read Box 8.3.

Similar to other clinical disorders addressed in this text, **Tourette syndrome** is multifaceted. Like OCD, it involves excessive responding, in this case, involuntary movement along with vocal outbursts of sounds such as barking or words, often scatological. Just as in the obsessions we discussed in the OCD section, many patients report that their symptoms become more intense in times of anxiety, emotional stress, or excitement.

Tracing the Neurobiological Roots of Tourette Syndrome

Tourette syndrome A neurological condition characterized by involuntary "tic" movements and vocalizations.

In 1825, it was reported that a French noblewoman, the Marquise de Damplerre, developed body tics, made barking sounds, and frequently uttered obscenities. Much to her dismay, all these responses were involuntary. In

Box 8.3

A Case in Point

Living with Tourette Syndrome

Growing up in Galashiels, Scotland, John Davidson faced the typical challenges encountered by other teenagers and more. At an age when most people were trying to fit in, John really stood out in the crowd. Even today, his thoughts are constantly focused on suppressing embarrassing language, movement, and gestures. "It's hard to explain—when I feel like I'm going to say something I feel like I *have* to say it." His involuntary vocal tics, the result of Tourette syndrome, make Davidson feel as if the words are being forced out of him.

As a documentary film crew follows Davidson and his mother through the grocery store, he holds his lip in an attempt to keep the words from erupting from his mouth. Even so, he repeatedly chirps, "F...off." At times, the vocal tics seem to be related to the environment; for example, Davidson is more likely to emit tics of a sexual nature when he is in the presence of young females. At times, they are directed to individuals: "Slut, Mom, you're a slut," he says as he shops with his mother. Displaying admirable tolerance and understanding of her son's condition, Davidson's mother is not distracted by such outbursts and continues her shopping journey through the grocery store.

As you might imagine, Tourette syndrome is especially difficult to tolerate in the quietness of the classroom. Some of Davidson's teachers were impatient with his tics, making it difficult to continue his education in mainstream classrooms. He ultimately focused on more specific vocational training and settled on horticulture. In another arena the simple task of having dinner was incredibly stressful for Davidson and his family because of his most invasive tic, spitting. His father chose not to eat with the family because of this behavior. The rest of the family joined Davidson at mealtimes, but dishes were strategically covered to protect the food from his saliva.

It is interesting that Davidson's facial tics, barks, spitting, head jerks, and obscenities seem prompted by anxiety associated with being in the presence of others. As he fishes along a tranquil river in solitude, there is no evidence of his disorder. He also feels more relaxed when he plays basketball. His motor and vocal tics are less conspicuous in the midst of all the loud sounds and movements inherent to the game. In agreement with anecdotal evidence that Tourette patients are skilled musicians and athletes, Davidson is an impressive basketball player.

Davidson's situation has improved in the years following the BBC documentary on his condition, filmed when he was 15 years old. "It was a total transformation overnight and life became so much easier...I started to make friends...It was like I had proved to people that I wasn't a freak" (Geoghegan, 2009).

Unfortunately, aside from fishing and sports, John is one of those patients who does not find relief from this disorder through drug or behavioral therapy. Although he still lives with the fear of approaching an attractive woman and then spitting on her or offending her with vile language, he has found some peace by learning to live with his mental illness and organizing an annual summer camp for children living with Tourette syndrome.

1885, Georges Gilles de la Tourette, a French physician, became interested in patients such as the marquise. Eventually, this collection of symptoms became known as "Tourette syndrome" (Singer & Walkup, 1991).

Today, multiple motor tics and one or more vocal tics are considered the essential diagnostic features of Tourette syndrome (Table 8.4). Tourettic tics may be simple or complex. Eye blinks and head twitches are considered simple motor tics; touching patterns, facial movements, and obscene gestures are considered complex motor tics. Clearing one's throat or making barking noises is a simple vocal tic; multiple syllables or words are more complex vocal tics (for example, saying "no, no" or "oh, boy"). In addition to tics, many patients frequently express symptoms indicative of attention-deficit/hyperactivity disorder (see Chapter 6) and/or OCD (Singer & Walkup, 1991).

Table 8.4 Diagnostic Criteria for Tourette Disorder

A. Both multiple motor and one or more vocal tics have been present at some time during the illness, although not necessarily concurrently. (A *tic* is a sudden, rapid, recurrent, nonrhythmic, stereotyped motor movement or vocalization.)

B. The tics occur many times a day (usually in bouts) nearly every day or intermittently throughout a period of more than 1 year, and during this period there was never a tic-free period of more than 3 consecutive months.

C. The disturbance causes marked distress or significant impairment in social, occupational, or other important areas of functioning.

D. The onset is before age 18 years.

E. The disturbance is not due to the direct physiological effects of a substance (e.g., stimulants) or a general medical condition (e.g., Huntington disease or postviral encephalitis).

American Psychiatric Association (2000, p. 114).

Boys are more likely to be diagnosed with Tourette syndrome than girls; prevalence rates are approximately 1:2,000 for boys and 1:10,000 for girls (Barr & Sandor, 1998). Onset may occur as early as 2 years of age, but the typical age at onset is 7 years. The duration of the disorder is typically life-long; some patients, however, may experience remission periods lasting from weeks to years (American Psychiatric Association, 1994).

Research suggests a genetic basis for Tourette syndrome. Focusing on evidence provided by twin studies, concordance rates range about 50%–90% for monozygotic twins compared with 8%–25% for dizygotic pairs (Price, Kidd, Cohen, Pauls, & Leckman, 1985; Walkup et al., 1988). Although strong, the concordance rates of less than 100% in monozygotic twins open the door for environmental factors that may influence the development of this disorder. Interestingly, in monozygotic twins who are not concordant for Tourette syndrome, the twin with the lower birth weight is more likely to be the tourettic one (Leckman et al., 1987).

Role of the basal ganglia and associated neurochemistry. The bizarre behavior and sounds prompted early therapists to think that Tourette syndrome had emotional or psychiatric roots. Today, these psychogenic theories have been replaced with theories related to neurotransmission within certain neuroanatomical areas (Singer & Walkup, 1991).

The basal ganglia have received considerable attention in neuroscientific studies of Tourette syndrome. One neuroimaging study reported a reduction in the size of certain areas of the basal ganglia in the left hemisphere (Peterson et al., 1993). Confirming its involvement, one study investigated five sets of monozygotic twins who both had Tourette syndrome but differed in the severity of symptoms (Wolf et al., 1996). These researchers delivered a potent dopamine receptor antagonist (D_2 subtype) in different regions of the striatum. Binding of this antagonist was greatest in the caudate nucleus, a specific area within the basal ganglia, in each of the more severely affected twins (Robertson, 1996). These findings suggest that the more severely affected twins had more D_2 receptors in the striatum—possibly leading to more activation of this motor area, that is, frequent tics.

In addition to the basal ganglia, neuroimaging studies have reported alterations in the cortex and thalamus; consequently, it has been proposed that Tourette syndrome is the result of modified synaptic transmission in the

cortical–striatal–thalamic–cortical circuit of the brain (Ludolph et al., 2006). Voxel-based morphometry has indicated increased volumes in the putamen (which along with the basal ganglia comprises the striatum) and decreased hippocampal volumes (Ludolph et al., 2006). The neuroimaging studies, however, need to be approached with caution as many studies fail to control for medication and use small sample sizes. In contrast to these findings, a study conducted in Germany using a larger number of subjects (38 nonmedicated boys with Tourette syndrome and 38 healthy age-matched controls) reported no structural differences between the two groups; of course, a lack of structural differences does not infer a lack of functional differences. Future research with adequate controls will elucidate the confusion in the existing literature concerning alterations in brain development (Roessner et al., 2009).

The observation that dopamine receptor antagonists decrease motor and vocal tics in tourettic patients provides additional evidence that some dysfunction of the dopaminergic system, either directly or indirectly, is central to the disorder (Singer & Walkup, 1991). Endogenous opiates have also been implicated. Decreased responses of dynorphin A (a specific endogenous opioid) were observed in the fibers projecting to the globus pallidus in one patient. And increased levels of this opiate have been observed in the CSF of tourettic patients (Haber, Kowall, Vonsattel, Bird, & Richardson, 1986; Leckman et al., 1988). Recently, the glutamate neurotransmitter system has been targeted for potential therapy. Glutamate, the primary excitatory neurotransmitter for approximately 60% of the brain, plays a significant role in the striatum, cortex, and thalamus, all areas implicated in tourettic symptoms (Singer, Morris, & Grados, 2009). Other neurotransmitter systems have been implicated, including GABA, serotonin, and noradrenaline; but more research is necessary to fully illuminate the role these substances play in the disorder.

Possible environmental factors. Some researchers maintain that infectious processes may play an integral role, at least in some Tourette cases. The observation of a few children who developed Tourette syndrome following streptococcal infection was the initial evidence that an infection may be involved. These children did not respond to the standard dopaminergic treatment but did respond to prednisone, a drug that suppresses immune reactivity.

These observations suggest that, in some cases, Tourette syndrome is an autoimmune disorder that manifests itself in the basal ganglia (Kurlan, 1998). The research prompted the American Psychiatric Association to create a new category of Tourette syndrome called **PANDAS** (pediatric autoimmune neuropsychiatric disorders associated with streptococcal infection). Higher levels of antibody titers for intracellular infectious agents such as chlamydia have been found in individuals diagnosed with Tourette syndrome (Krause et al., 2010). See Chapter 13 for a full discussion of the role of the immune system in mental health.

PANDAS Pediatric autoimmune neuropsychiatric disorders associated with streptococcal infection; thought to be the cause of Tourette syndrome in some children.

Treatment for Tourette Syndrome

Tourette syndrome presents a fascinating combination of symptoms. The sudden movements have no meaning in some contexts but are directly

haloperidol Neuroleptic drug that blocks dopaminergic activity; used in the treatment of schizophrenia and Tourette syndrome.

related to the surrounding environment in others. Vocal tics range from meaningless gibberish to verbal tirades of the most bizarre, obscene nature. The repertoire of exhaustive tics may disappear in a calming or engaging environment, only to reappear when the environmental context becomes more stressful. Thus far, a combination of pharmacological and behavioral therapies represents the most typical approach to treat Tourette syndrome; however, recent research has reported that thalamic DBS may also show promise (Porta et al., 2009).

Psychopharmacological therapy. Drugs that interrupt dopaminergic transmission are the most effective pharmacological defense against tourettic symptoms. **Haloperidol** (Haldol), a dopamine blocker widely used to treat schizophrenia, is effective at suppressing tics in about 80% of Tourette syndrome cases; but it leaves the patient with debilitating side effects such as sedation, depression, phobias, and even more movement abnormalities. Fewer side effects are seen with other dopamine-interfering drugs such as pimozide (Orap) and fluphenazine (Prolixin) (Singer & Walkup, 1991).

Clonidine (Catapres), a drug that interferes with presynaptic norepinephrine release, may prove helpful in patients with milder symptoms (Singer & Walkup, 1991). The original success rate of about 70%, however, has not been confirmed by other researchers (Goetz et al., 1987). Even so, the side effects are modest, consisting mostly of transient sedation. The glutamate antagonist riluzole has shown promise as an effective therapy for OCD symptoms; however, the results are preliminary at this point (Singer et al., 2009).

Paul Sanberg and his colleagues at the University of South Florida are conducting research that may lead to a new therapeutic approach. In the late 1980s Sanberg conducted research in rats suggesting that nicotine enhances the effects of neuroleptic drugs such as haloperidol that alleviate psychotic symptoms, especially psychomotor activity, whereas nicotine delivered by itself had no effect on movement in the study. When tourettic children were given nicotine gum as an adjunctive treatment, about 80% showed improvement. Unpleasant side effects (such as bitter taste and nausea), however, prompted most of the children to discontinue the gum (Sanberg et al., 1989).

Mort Doran

In another study, these researchers showed that the gum even had some therapeutic value by itself but only while it was actually being chewed (McConville et al., 1991). Using a nicotine patch instead of gum, they found a reduction in symptoms in patients ranging from 9 to 15 years old who were not on other neuroleptic therapy (Silver, Shytle, Philipp, & Sanberg, 1996).

The researchers initially thought that the nicotine enhanced the effects of haloperidol because it acted as a nicotine acetylcholine receptor agonist—as it does in smoking. They now believe, however, that the low doses of nicotine actually desensitize the receptor, acting more like a cholinergic antagonist instead of an agonist, that is, blocking instead of facilitating cholinergic activity. Additionally, researchers in London have shown that a single dose of nicotine excites motor cortex inhibitory circuits in tourettic patients (Orth, Amann, Robertson, & Rothwell, 2005).

Continuing with their investigations of the nicotinic/cholinergic factor in Tourette syndrome, Sanberg and colleagues tested the cholinergic receptor antagonist **mecamylamine** (Inversene) and found that in initial trials this medication reduces symptoms in Tourette syndrome patients. The drug offers most benefit, however, when used as an adjunctive therapy with haloperidol (Silver et al., 2001; Shytle, Silver, & Sanberg, 2000). If a drug such as this becomes an accepted adjunctive therapy for Tourette syndrome, it is likely to have far-reaching effects for other disorders influenced by the dopaminergic system, including OCD, attention-deficit/hyperactivity disorder, and schizophrenia.

mecamylamine Drug that acts as a cholinergic receptor antagonist; currently being tested for use with tourettic symptoms.

Behavioral and cognitive strategies. A case presented by Oliver Sacks (see Box 1.2) is perhaps most representative of the contrasts that exist in this disorder. In *An Anthropologist on Mars* (1995) Sacks describes a Tourette syndrome patient, Mort Doran (in the book, the pseudonym "Carl Bennett" is used), who is a surgeon—and a pilot!

Doran is certainly a study in contrasts. At one point during the day he may be having a conversation with his colleagues during which he is in distorted positions and repeatedly tapping them on the shoulders with his toes as he discusses a relevant surgical case. The following hour, he strides confidently into the operating room and performs highly skilled, life-saving, 2-hour surgery, exhibiting no evidence of tics. The minute the operation is over, Doran returns to his ritualistic touching (tapping various objects and people), coupled with his obsession with symmetry (touching things in a particular symmetrical pattern).

Doran is now semiretired from his career in surgery. Each winter he enjoys teaching classes in anatomy and surgery at the University of Arizona Medical School. Although the pace of his career has slowed down, Doran reports that his tics are as active as ever; the distracting thoughts, however, have decreased.

Doran calms himself each morning by pedaling furiously on a stationary bike while smoking a pipe and reading a pathology book. He displays no tics and no compulsions during this time. Research suggests that symptoms of Tourette syndrome are exacerbated during sympathetic arousal; specifically, when patients are taught to relax, resulting in lower levels of recorded physiological arousal, symptoms diminish (Nagai, Cavanna, & Critchley, 2009). It is easy to look at Doran's calming behavior and apply some of the knowledge presented in this chapter and other areas of this book to hypothesize why this seemingly bizarre coping response may be effective.

Exercise is related to endogenous opioid release; the rhythmic circular motion and repeated pedaling may be related to increased serotonergic release and a subsequent reduction in anxiety (more on this in Chapter 9). Nicotine in the pipe tobacco may potentiate the effect of other medication or at least alter the cholinergic receptors in a way that calms the tics, and the pathology text provides a cognitive activity that directs Doran's thoughts away from the impending tics. We cannot prove that any of these proposed therapeutic mechanisms work, but theoretically this surgeon's self-prescribed treatment may be just what the doctor ordered!

Summary

Anxiety Disorders: An Overview

Although most of us try to avoid it, anxiety plays an important role in our lives: It directs our attention toward potentially harmful stimuli. Some of us direct our attention toward stimuli that do not pose a reasonable threat, and the anxiety response becomes more of a danger to mental health than the initial perceived threat. At times this kind of anxiety is directed toward a specific threatening stimulus, as in phobias, and at times it is difficult for individuals to pinpoint the source of their debilitating anxiety, as in generalized anxiety disorder. Severe acute attacks of anxiety are observed in individuals experiencing panic attacks as they fear they are suffocating and frantically attempt to reestablish physiological homeostasis.

Obsessive–Compulsive Disorder

OCD is multifaceted, consisting of recurring, upsetting thoughts (obsessions) and ritualistic behaviors (compulsions). Areas of the brain involved in anxiety, movement, and reward are probably involved in OCD. The proposed OCD neuroanatomical loop is composed of primarily the orbitofrontal cortex, the cingulate cortex, the thalamus, and the caudate nucleus. Other areas, such as the amygdala and nucleus accumbens, may also play a role. Glutamate and GABA are the principal neurotransmitters that directly communicate among the components of the OCD circuit. Dopamine and serotonin act as neuromodulators for the synaptic activity within the OCD loop.

The consistency of many compulsions observed in OCD patients (e.g., checking, cleaning, grooming) and in animal models coupled with the relationship of these rituals to survival or fitness suggest that animals are biologically predisposed toward OCD-like responding. Adaptive responding transforms into excessive responding when humans or other animals find themselves experiencing threatening or disrupting stimuli and/or environments. Some of the compulsions observed in OCD have been compared with species-specific behaviors in animals known as "fixed action patterns" (FAPs). The involvement of the striatum in both FAPs and compulsions provides further evidence that compulsions may be remnants of speciesspecific behaviors that at one time had significant relevance for our survival.

Therapies aimed at modifying neurochemicals, neuroanatomy, and behavior and/or cognitions have all been moderately successful for OCD patients. Antidepressant drugs that enhance the activation of the serotonergic synapse (SSRIs, for example) are effective at suppressing OCD symptoms in some patients. In severe cases, neurosurgical techniques that disrupt various components of the OCD loop have proved effective. Cognitive-behavioral therapies such as exposure and response prevention yield success rates that rival pharmacological rates, with fewer side effects. Clinicians must consider all relevant components of OCD to create an optimal treatment regime for each patient.

Tourette Syndrome

Patients suffering from Tourette syndrome exhibit both motor and vocal tics. The basal ganglia constitute the most likely neuroanatomical area involved in the activation of the tic response. Excessive dopaminergic activity seems to be a causal agent; dopamine antagonists provide relief of tics in some patients. In addition, mecamylamine, a cholinergic receptor antagonist, is currently being investigated for efficacy as an adjunctive treatment. Environmental factors such as streptococcal infection may also cause some cases of Tourette syndrome. It is possible that several cognitive-behavioral strategies may also benefit an individual, for example, by altering neurochemicals through exercise, diverted attention, and relaxation techniques.

Key Terms

comorbidity (219)

tics (219)

generalized anxiety disorder (GAD) (220)

panic disorder (220)

obsessive–compulsive disorder (OCD) (220)

obsessions (220)

compulsions (220)

cingulum (223)

entorhinal cortex (223)

OCD loop (224)

orbitofrontal cortex (OFC) (224)

lateralization (229)

behavioral addiction (230)

activity-stress paradigm (230)

fixed action pattern (FAP) (232)

superstitious behavior (234)

clomipramine (235)

anxiolytics (236)

stereotaxic instrument (236)

exposure and response prevention (ERP) (238)

Tourette syndrome (241)

PANDAS (243)

haloperidol (244)

mecamylamine (245)

For Further Consideration

Mandel, H. (with Young, J.). (2009). *Here's the deal: Don't touch me.* New York: Bantam. If you want to read about living with OCD while at the same time experiencing a few chuckles, this is an entertaining and informative book. Comedian Howie Mandel discloses details associated with his many fears, anxieties, and related obsessions and compulsions in this autobiographical memoir.

Marks, I. (1997). Behaviour therapy for obsessive-compulsive disorder: A decade of progress. *Canadian Journal of Psychiatry, 42*, 1021–1027. Although a bit dated, this article is a wonderful review of the studies that have tested the effectiveness of exposure and ritual prevention (ERP). Many issues are reviewed, including the long-term effects, value as an adjunctive therapy with antidepressant medication, and cost-effectiveness of behavioral therapy.

Rapaport, J. L. (1991). *The boy who couldn't stop washing: The experience and treatment of obsessive–compulsive disorder.* New York: Signet. This book, written for a popular audience, is a comprehensive introduction to the world of OCD. Rapaport's descriptions of her fascinating patients give this disorder a human face.

Sacks, O. (1995). *An anthropologist on Mars.* New York: Knopf. Sacks is unmatched in his ability to describe the adventures of the human mind and its underlying neural mechanisms. In the chapter "A Surgeon's Life," you are exposed to the daily activities and challenges faced by someone with Tourette syndrome. The fact that this patient is a surgeon makes the chapter unforgettable.

Schwartz, J. M. (with Beyette, B.) (1996). *Brain lock: Free yourself from obsessive–compulsive behavior.* New York: HarperCollins. After convincing his readers that OCD is a brain disorder, Schwartz presents persuasive cases and evidence that cognition and behavior can influence the OCD neurocircuitry. His step-by-step cognitive-behavioral therapy has proven to be quite successful for some patients.

van den Heuvel, O. A., Remijnse, P. L., Mataix-Cols, D., Vrenken, H., Groenewegen, H. J., Uylings, H. B. M., van Balkom, A. J. L. M., & Veltman, D. J. (2009). The major symptom dimensions of obsessive-compulsive disorder are mediated by partially distinct neural systems. *Brain, 132*, 853–868. This article takes a different approach to understanding the key brain areas associated with OCD by identifying separate symptom dimensions and exploring neural systems associated with each symptom profile.

Chapter Nine

Mood Disorders

Connections

Foods and Moods

After a particularly bad day, do you turn to food to help relieve your anxiety and make you feel better? Growing up in the south (for K.G.L.), grandmother's homemade vegetable soup, chicken and dumplings, and peach cobbler were dietary artillery against the blues. You'll probably agree that going home after a stressful exam and eating your favorite food does wonders for your mood.

The relationship between food and mood is a popular notion in today's society. After collecting uplifting life stories of dozens of people, Jack Canfield and Mark Hansen, both motivational speakers, thought long and hard about the best title for their optimistic anthology. It is no great surprise that they likened the ability of their heartwarming stories to—what else?—the most famous "comfort" food, chicken soup. By 2003, The *Chicken Soup for the Soul* series had sold over 50 million copies and won numerous awards. It seems that the connection between food and an elevated mood is a natural association easily understood by the book-consuming public. Speaking more directly to the effectiveness of food as regulators of our mood are books such as Jack Challem's *The Food-Mood Solution* (2008).

The notion that a favorite, familiar food warms the soul and heals emotional pain sounds reasonable, but is there empirical evidence to support such a claim? In the 1950s, it was discovered that drugs leading to depleted levels of monoamines (serotonin, norepinephrine, and dopamine) caused depression-like symptoms, whereas drugs leading to increases in these neurotransmitters produced antidepressant effects in patients. In 1974, Fernstrom and Wurtman demonstrated that the consumption of foods rich in tryptophan (a dietary amino acid that is a precursor to serotonin in the brain), such as bananas, milk, and turkey, increases levels of serotonin in the brain. Because carbohydrate consumption is necessary for the brain's utilization of serotonin, it is troubling to consider the effect the low-carbohydrate Atkins diet is having on millions of dieters in the United States and Europe. According to Judith Wurtman, director of the Program in Women's Health at the MIT Clinical Research Center, "Carbohydrates are essential for effective dieting and good mood, and filling up on fatty foods like bacon and cheese makes you tired, lethargic, and apathetic—an emotional zombie" (MIT News Office, 2004).

If you have ever fallen asleep after a hefty turkey dinner at Thanksgiving, you can attest to tryptophan's effect. Further, this finding gave credence to the old saying that drinking milk before going to bed facilitates relaxation and sleep. Since Fernstrom and Wurtman's seminal findings, some doctors have recommended that their patients take a nutritional supplement, 5-hydroxytryptophan (5-HTP), a compound naturally produced by tryptophan in the body, because it has a significant boosting effect on serotonergic levels in the central nervous system (Murray, 1998).

In an interesting line of research at the National Institutes of Health, Joseph Hibbeln and Maribeth

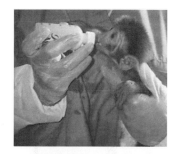

Working at the National Institutes of Mental Health, scientist Maribeth Champoux feeds a young rhesus monkey a special diet to determine the importance of docosahexaenoic acid on development.

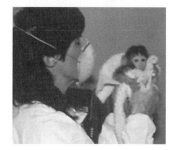

She gently assesses the infant for motor capabilities and emotional responsiveness.
COURTESY OF MARTIN F. KRIETE

Champoux investigated a different type of connection between foods and moods. They were interested in the impact of removing docosahexaenoic acid (DHA), an omega-3 fatty acid that is highly concentrated in the central nervous system, from the diets of infants. DHA is present in all mammalian (including human) breast milk, but because of negative marketing factors such as a short shelf-life, it has only recently been included in commercially available infant formulas in the United States (Austad et al., 2003). The removal of such a product from the diet may have had a significant impact on mental health: Research has suggested that rates of depression are higher in populations that consume low levels of omega-3 fatty acids.

Are individuals who received a diet devoid of DHA susceptible to depression later on? Hibbeln and Champoux examined this question by manipulating the formula fed to infant rhesus monkeys. Most recently, they found greater motor deficits in the DHA-deprived animals than in the supplemented-formula group. Anxiety and temperament scores, however, were not affected by the diet. Further research will verify the influence of DHA consumption on human infants by determining any long-lasting effects of DHA deprivation in bottle-fed babies (Champoux et al., 2002). Focusing even earlier during prenatal development, Hibbeln and his colleagues have found that low maternal consumption of fish during pregnancy was associated with less than optimal emotional, cognitive, and motor responses in offspring (Hibbeln et al., 2007).

Many connections exist between food and moods (see Chapter 14 for more on this topic). Neurochemistry is altered by our diets, and we certainly learn to associate certain feelings with the consumption of certain foods. Thus, through cognitive expectations and neurochemistry, we may be able to temporarily curb the blues with a generous helping of our favorite comfort food.

We begin this chapter by discussing the diverse variables that may contribute to a person's susceptibility to mood disorders. No single, logical, neat, or simplistic explanation exists; but it is this very fact that makes the quest for understanding the mood disorders so compelling. Because humans evolved in an ever-changing environment, it seems adaptive that our moods (temporary emotional states) evolved to help us interact effectively with the environment's changing demands. For example, the pleasurable moods associated with food consumption lead to foraging, and the anxiety produced by being in proximity to a larger, more aggressive animal may lead to avoidance of aggression and physical harm. To be effective, this must be a plastic system influenced by multiple internal and external factors—neurobiological, social, and environmental.

Problems arise when mood does not fluctuate in synchrony with environmental demands. Symptoms associated with mood disorders involve neuroanatomical areas from the brain stem to the prefrontal cortex. Although serotonin has been considered the primary contributing neurochemical in

mood (affective) disorders
Disturbances of mood typically accompanied by inappropriate expression of pleasure or misery; some people experience vigorous swings between the two extremes.

major depressive disorder One of the most common psychiatric illnesses, occurring in about 17% of the population, with females suffering at about twice the rate of males and characterized by one or more major depressive episodes of at least 2 weeks and at least four additional symptoms of depression (for example, sleep disturbances, loss of concentration, decreased energy, guilt).

bipolar disorder Mood disorder characterized by episodes of mania interspersed with episodes of depression. This disorder occurs in about 1%–1.6% of the population and is sometimes referred to as "manic depression."

depression Mood disorder characterized by feelings of sadness, diminished pleasure, alterations in sleep, fatigue, difficulty concentrating, and feelings of worthlessness; several variations exist (for example, major depression, dysthymic disorder).

producing depressive symptoms, several leading researchers suggest that this system may be secondary to dopaminergic modulation or to other neurophysiological events, such as neurogenesis.

With so many contributing paths leading to depression, it is not surprising that multiple roads to treatment exist. Although a single drug therapy that is equally efficacious for everyone suffering from depression would be more than welcome, current research suggests that finding such a single treatment is as unlikely as finding one size of shoe that fits everyone. Cognitive-behavioral therapy or conjunctive therapies that involve more than one approach may offer more long-term potential as they probably modulate more of the complex neurobiological system underlying mood expression than selected neurochemicals.

MOOD DISORDERS: AN OVERVIEW

Most of the time we are able to shift moods effortlessly, and our oscillating moods contribute to the rich tapestry of our emotional lives. We laugh when our friends tell us jokes, we cry when we lose a loved one. In fact, we would be considered abnormal if we failed to respond to these situations with the appropriate emotions. We sometimes engage in behaviors for the sole purpose of temporarily changing our moods: We may pay money to sit through a sad movie or attend a comedian's performance. Although these temporary shifts in mood probably have little meaning for the ongoing reality of our lives, it may be reinforcing just to experience a shift in mood.

Mood, or **affective**, **disorders** emerge when one experiences difficulty in changing or controlling mood states. In some ways, mood disorders are like a car transmission that is stuck in one gear. Different moods help us respond to and evaluate our lives at any given moment. These moods, however, lose their value if they do not correspond appropriately to the demands of life. If our mood gets stuck in one position, we are unable to function effectively.

Although we are focusing in this chapter only on **major depressive disorder** (characterized by more than one episode of severe depression) and **bipolar disorder** (characterized by mood swings from mania, or euphoric states, to depression), they are but two variations on the diverse menu of mood diagnoses. Table 9.1 lists brief descriptions of the range of mood disorders included in the *Diagnostic and Statistical Manual of Mental Disorders*, fourth edition, text revision (DSM-IV-TR). This range, however, has not always been recognized. According to the early work of Emil Kraepelin (the pioneer clinical neuroscientist introduced in Chapter 2), a century ago, any disruption of mood states was diagnosed as manic—depressive insanity (Healy, 1997).

The most prominent signs of **depression** are a profound sadness and a drastic reduction in one's activity levels. As originally described by Kraepelin in 1921, mood disorders differ from disorders such as schizophrenia because, rather than taking a continuous, progressively worsening course, they follow an intermittent pattern, fluctuating, for example, between bouts of mania and bouts of depression (Post & Weiss, 1999). Even without treatment, a person suffering from depression usually enters a recovery phase after about 4 months (American Psychiatric Association, 2000). (See Table 9.2 for diagnostic material on major depression.)

Table 9.1 DSM-IV-TR Range of Mood Disorder Diagnoses

Major depressive disorder is characterized by one or more major depressive episodes (i.e., at least 2 weeks of depressed mood or loss of interest accompanied by at least four additional symptoms of depression).

Dysthymic disorder is characterized by at least 2 years of depressed mood for more days than not, accompanied by additional depressive symptoms that do not meet criteria for a major depressive episode.

Depressive disorder not otherwise specified is included for coding disorders with depressive features that do not meet criteria for major depressive disorder, dysthymic disorder, adjustment disorder with depressed mood, or adjustment disorder with mixed anxiety and depressed mood (or depressive symptoms about which there is inadequate or contradictory information).

Bipolar I disorder is characterized by one or more manic or mixed episodes, usually accompanied by major depressive episodes.

Bipolar II disorder is characterized by one or more major depressive episodes accompanied by at least one hypomanic episode.

Cyclothymic disorder is characterized by at least 2 years of numerous periods of hypomanic symptoms that do not meet criteria for a manic episode and numerous periods of depressive symptoms that do not meet criteria for a major depressive episode.

Bipolar disorder not otherwise specified is included for coding disorders with bipolar features that do not meet criteria for any of the specific bipolar disorders defined in this section (or bipolar symptoms about which there is inadequate or contradictory information).

Mood disorder due to a general medical condition is characterized by a prominent and persistent disturbance in mood that is judged to be a direct physiological consequence of a general medical condition.

Substance-induced mood disorder is characterized by a prominent and persistent disturbance in mood that is judged to be a direct physiological consequence of a drug of abuse, a medication, another somatic treatment for depression, or toxin exposure.

Mood disorder not otherwise specified is included for coding disorders with mood symptoms that do not meet the criteria for any specific Mood Disorder and in which it is difficult to choose between **depressive disorder not otherwise specified** and **bipolar disorder not otherwise specified** (e.g., acute agitation).

American Psychiatric Association (2000, pp. 345–346).

Table 9.2 DSM-IV-TR Criteria for Major Depressive Episode

A. Five (or more) of the following symptoms have been present during the same 2-week period and represent a change from previous functioning; at least one of the symptoms is either (1) depressed mood or (2) loss of interest or pleasure

   Note: Do not include symptoms that are clearly due to a general medical condition, or mood-incongruent delusions or hallucinations.

   (1) Depressed mood most of the day, nearly every day, as indicated by either subjective report (e.g., feels sad or empty) or observation made by others (e.g., appears tearful). Note: In children and adolescents, can be irritable mood.

   (2) Markedly diminished interest or pleasure in all, or almost all, activities most of the day, nearly every day (as indicated by either subjective account or observation made by others).

   (3) Significant weight loss when not dieting or weight gain (e.g., a change of more than 5% of body weight in a month), or decrease or increase in appetite nearly every day. Note: In children, consider failure to make expected weight gains.

   (4) Insomnia or hypersomnia nearly every day.

   (5) Psychomotor agitation or retardation nearly every day (observable by others, not merely subjective feelings of restlessness or being slowed down).

   (6) Fatigue or loss of energy nearly every day.

   (7) Feelings of worthlessness or excessive or inappropriate guilt (which may be delusional) nearly every day (not merely self-reproach or guilt about being sick).

   (8) Diminished ability to think or concentrate, or indecisiveness, nearly every day (either by subjective account or as observed by others).

   (9) Recurrent thoughts of death (not just fear of dying), recurrent suicidal ideation without a specific plan, or a suicide attempt or a specific plan for committing suicide.

B. The symptoms do not meet criteria for a mixed episode.

C. The symptoms cause clinically significant distress or impairment in social, occupational, or other important areas of functioning.

D. The symptoms are not due to the direct physiological effects of a substance (e.g., a drug of abuse, a medication) or a general medical condition (e.g., hypothyroidism).

E. The symptoms are not better accounted for by bereavement, i.e., after the loss of a loved one, the symptoms persist for longer than 2 months or are characterized by marked functional impairment, morbid preoccupation with worthlessness, suicidal ideation, psychotic symptoms, or psychomotor retardation.

American Psychiatric Association (2000, p. 356).

MAJOR DEPRESSION IN CONTEXT

Research has uncovered interesting individual differences, from population and cultural factors to genetics and environmental exposures, related to susceptibility to mood disorders. Examining possible evolutionary explanations for changes in moods and how they might relate to evolved survival strategies has helped researchers understand individual differences.

Sex Differences and Sociocultural Influences

Major depressive disorder is perhaps the most common mental illness, with a lifetime prevalence of about 17% in the U.S. population (Fava & Kendler, 2000). One interesting feature of depressive illnesses is the disproportionate rate of this disorder in women. Specifically, it has been estimated that 21% of women will experience an episode of depression in their lifetimes compared to a lifetime incidence of 13% in men (Yonkers, Kando, Hamilton, & Halbreich, 2000). Further, women experience depressive episodes about twice as frequently as men (American Psychiatric Association, 2000).

The underlying causes for this discrepancy between the sexes remain unclear but likely involve mechanisms described in Chapter 6. Current research on the potential mechanisms underlying this gender variation emphasizes differences in stress responsivity, and it may offer some answers in the near future (Cousino-Klein & Corwin, 2002). Further, now that researchers know that sex differences exist in the brain's metabolic rates of utilizing some antidepressant drugs—in addition to differential rates of the disorder in males and females—all new drugs are tested on both sexes. Originally, only males were examined, to sidestep testing women whose fluctuations in reproductive hormones during their childbearing years complicate research.

Although depression can be observed in virtually every culture, Joseph Hibbeln and Norman Salem of the National Institute of Alcohol Abuse and Alcoholism (1995) have presented a fascinating hypothesis that attempts to explain some differences in the rates of depression across cultures. Their theory centers on the dietary consumption of fish. Obviously, it is not likely that a condition as complex as depression is regulated solely by the amount of fish we eat; but this intriguing hypothesis has value in explaining some of the cultural differences that exist in rates of depression, so let's explore it a bit further.

Hibbeln and Salem (1995) argue that humans evolved on a diet that consisted of fewer saturated fats (fats that are solid at room temperature, like butter) and more polyunsaturated fats (liquid at room temperature, like olive oil) than Americans currently consume. Of the polyunsaturated fats we do consume, we eat more n-6 polyunsaturates than n-3 polyunsaturates; n-3 polyunsaturates, which are found in the meat of wild and free-ranging animals, were also a bigger part of our ancestors' diets than they are of ours. In fact, Hibbeln and Salem argue that societies that consume more fish, which have high levels of n-3 polyunsaturates, are less likely to experience depression than non-fish-consuming societies (see also Freeman et al., 2006).

In one study, rates of depression for North Americans and Europeans were 10 times higher than those for a Taiwanese population that consumed more fish. Rates in the United States were about five times higher than rates in Hong Kong, where fish is consumed more than in the United States. In Japan, where fish consumption is high, low rates of depression have been observed; among the elderly in one Japanese fishing village, the depression rate was observed to be 0% (Hibbeln, Umhau, George, & Salem, 1997). In a related study, a community in Finland was surveyed for depression and consumption of fish (Tanskanen & Hibbeln, 2001). The researchers found that the residents of the community who consumed more fish were less likely to experience depression and less likely to have suicidal thoughts.

Another factor influencing the occurrence of depression in a particular population is related to the level of anxiety its members experience. For example, the literature suggests that the sick and the aged are at higher risk for depression (Schwartz, Gunzelmann, Hinz, & Brahler, 2001). Theo Sandfort and his colleagues at Utrecht University in the Netherlands have been investigating rates of depression in homosexual populations, who are likely to experience high levels of anxiety resulting from increased social isolation (Sandfort, de Graaf, Bijl, & Schnabel, 2001). In a study of more than 7,000 subjects, these researchers reported that homosexual men are more likely to experience depression than heterosexual men and that homosexual women are more likely to develop addiction disorders than heterosexual women. In an interview conducted by Andrew Solomon (2001), Sandfort described additional research suggesting that rates of depression are higher for closeted homosexuals than for those who are more open about their orientation.

Genetic Influences and Evolutionary Factors

Studies conducted with identical and fraternal twins certainly indicate a strong genetic contribution in mood disorders. Concordance rates for mood disorders in identical twins have been reported to be as high as 60%–70% compared with rates of 20% for fraternal twins (Sanders, Detera-Wadleigh, & Gershon, 1999).

The search for a single depression gene is an ongoing endeavor. It is looking more and more likely that a whole set of "blue" genes contributes to depression (Stahl, 2000). The serotonin transporter gene has received a lot of attention lately, as this gene has been associated with increased risk of depression (Caspi et al., 2003; Beevers & Schyner, 2009),. Although there is convincing evidence that individuals inherit a susceptibility for mood disorders, the concordance rate is well under 100%, so the environment appears to be a significant contributor—even the ultimate trigger—for the manifestation of depressive disorders.

Evolutionary explanations for moods offer clues about how environmental factors contribute to mood disorders. Is it adaptive that so many people suffer from depression? Or is depression a pathological condition not related to a specific adaptive function? It appears that Charles Darwin struggled with these questions well over a century ago: "Pain or suffering of any kind, if long continued, causes depression and lessens the power of action; yet it is well adapted to make a creature guard itself against any great or sudden evil" (Carroll, p. 431).

Evolutionary theories are intriguing and offer possible explanations of depression-like behaviors, but they must be approached with caution. Obviously, once an evolutionary change has occurred, it is extremely challenging to secure empirical evidence to support such proposed evolutionary theories. Randolph Neese (2000) of the Institute for Social Research at the University of Michigan has long pondered the evolutionary adaptiveness of many conditions, including depression. He is intrigued by the observation that depression-like behaviors, or low moods, may have evolved in social animals as a means to obtain help from others—such as a baby crying to get the attention of the mother to provide nourishment and protection. But it is not clear that the passive withdrawal that so often characterizes severe adult depression consistently results in help being offered.

Thinking more about the adaptiveness of low moods, Neese contends that they probably evolved to steer animals away from sources of threat that might result in bodily harm and thus compromise their viability and subsequent reproductive fitness. For example, though a deer may be starving, in conditions of extremely low temperatures and deep snow it is adaptive to depress the urge to forage because the deer will save vital energy by sitting motionless until the conditions for foraging become more favorable. In Chapter 13, we offer evidence indicating that low moods might be adaptive to the extent that they keep sick people at rest when their bodies are extremely vulnerable because of a challenged immune system. In another line of thinking about the adaptive nature of depression, it has been proposed that the mind becomes more analytical and focused during bouts of depression and these cognitive strategies are useful for solving complex problems when they arise (Andrews & Thomson, 2009).

Thus, moods may serve to upregulate our motivation when a payoff is predicted and downregulate our motivation when the behavior will likely lead to a greater cost than gain. Neese is quick to point out that, although low moods and a degree of depression may be adaptive in some contexts, we should not let this distract us from the reality that major depression is one of the most serious medical problems facing Americans today.

In a book edited by Leon Sloman and Paul Gilbert (2000), the role of subordination and defeat in the evolution of depressive disorders is considered. As complex social behaviors evolved hundreds of millions of years ago, submissive behaviors such as defeat, flight, infantile appeals, and submissive displays coevolved to facilitate the social dynamics of aggression and affiliation. Although humans and other animals exhibiting submissive behavior are often viewed as weak and extremely vulnerable, expressing submissive behavior may also be viewed as a strategic defense that will prolong life. According to Paul MacLean (1990), the featured investigator in Chapter 3, "a passive response (a submissive display) to an aggressive display may make it possible under most circumstances to avoid unnecessary, and sometimes mortal, conflict. Hence it could be argued that the submissive display is the most important of all displays because without it numerous individuals might not survive" (p. 235).

If you were a late bloomer (physically speaking), frequently bullied by more aggressive students in your school, you might have prolonged your life (or at least maintained the composition of your facial features) by demonstrating submissive rather than aggressive behavior. The submissive episodes might not have contributed to high self-esteem, but, in keeping with Neese's and MacLean's views, as a strategy they probably kept you from bodily harm. Sloman and Gilbert argue, however, that once individuals pass adolescence and enter adulthood, where it is more difficult to either fight or flee in complex social relationships, they sometimes switch from active submission to depressive demobilization, a condition characterized by a feeling of being trapped, spiraling into more depressive symptoms.

TRACING THE NEUROBIOLOGICAL ROOTS OF DEPRESSION

Once mental health researchers established that drugs effectively treat some forms of depression, they placed emphasis on the neurochemistry of the disorder. Now that neuroimaging technology allows researchers to glimpse the depressed brain, the neuroanatomical circuits involved are also being identified and mapped out. It is becoming increasingly apparent that the brain's plasticity—its ability to restructure itself—may also underlie a person's susceptibility to depression. Finally, an individual's cognitive responses to environmental changes may also contribute to the onset of a depressed mental state.

Depression's Neuroanatomical Circuit

Before the introduction of neuroimaging technology, neuroanatomical research was restricted to postmortem analysis of volumetric measures of specific brain structures or numbers of neurons, glial cells, or specific receptors in an area of interest. Although these studies are still valuable, we can now use neuroimaging to observe the activity of the brain in real time. The convergence of research suggests a depression circuit in the brain (Figure 9.1).

Prefrontal cortex. Both postmortem and neuroimaging data support the involvement of the **prefrontal cortex (PFC)** in major depression. Postmortem studies indicate both cellular atrophy and cellular loss in this area of the frontal cortex that is involved in higher cognitive functions

prefrontal cortex (PFC) Area of the frontal cortex involved in many higher functions. Evidence suggests that atrophy of neurons or compromised activity in this area may lead to symptoms of depression.

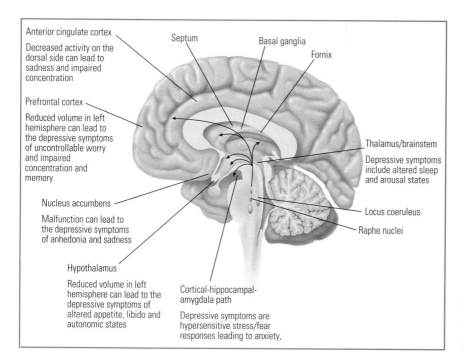

Figure 9.1

Neuroanatomical circuit of depression

NEMEROFF (1998), ADAPTED FROM RESSLER & NEMEROFF (2000)

(Rajkowska, 2000). Focusing on the living brain, especially the dorsolateral PFC (DLPFC) thought to exert control over emotional experiences, decreased blood flow and metabolism have been found in depressed patients when compared with healthy controls (Gotlib & Hamilton, 2009)

The PFC and its surround are a prime association area of the cortex, meaning that it receives information from a number of brain areas, enabling this advanced brain structure to associate many different types of information in arriving at a solution or conclusion to some query. In fact, the PFC has been described as the "crucial convergence zone" because of its two very important roles: sustaining attention to the animal's external world and receiving important information from the limbic cortical pathways that convey information about internal states such as mood and immune functioning (Liotti & Mayberg, 2001). Rajkowska (2000) describes the PFC as the common site of neuropathology in major and bipolar depression.

Just to give you a taste of how complicated neuroimaging data can be, when scientists control for the reduced PFC size in the left hemisphere, positron emission tomographic (PET) data show that metabolic rates are actually increased (Drevets, 2000). This finding makes sense when we consider that some antidepressants ultimately result in decreased PFC metabolic activity (Drevets, 1999). In fact, one study looked at the effects of five different antidepressant medications on PFC activity and observed decreases in just 48 hours. Interestingly, no decrease in PFC activity was observed in patients who failed to experience therapeutic recovery from using the antidepressants (Cook & Leuchter, 2001). Further, it was reported that cognitive-behavioral therapy leading to clinical improvement was accompanied by decreased PFC activity. The authors noted the contrast between this outcome and the effect of the antidepressant paroxetine (Paxil), another clinically effective treatment, on depression. In this case, the antidepressant increased PFC activity (Goldapple et al., 2004). Thus, the PFC seems to play a critical role in depression, although the specific nature of this role has yet to be clearly defined.

Hippocampus and amygdala. The PFC has well-established reciprocal connections with the hippocampus, as well as other areas in the limbic system. Recall from Chapter 5 that chronic stress leads to decreased hippocampal volume, (Eitan & Lerer, 2009), suggesting its integral role in the stress response. Accordingly, magnetic resonance imaging (MRI) studies of depressed patients who have been in remission for at least 4 months have shown reductions in hippocampal volume, with the larger reduction consistently occurring in the left hemisphere (Bremner et al., 2000; Sheline, Wang, Gado, Csernansky, & Vannier, 1996).

A multitude of theories have been proposed to explain both stress- and depression-induced atrophy including neurotoxicity, glial cell loss, and inhibited neurogenesis (Sheline, 2000). The hippocampal volume reduction observed in depression, however, does not seem to be an immediate effect. Younger depressed patients, in their thirties and forties, do not show the atrophy that their depressed counterparts in their late sixties show in MRI scans (Vakili et al., 2000). Thus, if the hippocampus is indeed grossly altered following chronic depression, it is very likely that communication with the PFC is also disrupted, leading to altered neuronal functioning in this circuit.

The hippocampus and amygdala are actually continuous structures, so it is difficult to imagine that a significant disruption in hippocampal functioning

Box 9.1

A Case in Point

Andrew Solomon's Noonday Demon

An observer of Andrew Solomon's childhood in the 1960s probably would not predict that life-threatening depressive breakdowns lay ahead. Although Solomon received support from his parents and brother at home, he endured bantering from other kids in elementary and middle school because he had no real athletic ability. However, he managed to graduate from high school with many friends and an increased sense of self-confidence. He attended Yale University, where he studied hard and played hard and made many lifelong friends. Following graduation, he went to London to acquire a master's degree and then, uneventfully, commenced a career as a writer.

You may wish your life had been so "all-American" in young adulthood. Solomon's life, unfortunately, subsequently took a turn for the worse as he experienced the torturous symptoms of major depression. Although looking back Solomon vividly remembers several times during his childhood and adolescence in which he experienced acute anxiety, at the time of his first depressive breakdown he was totally unprepared for a battle with depression for the rest of his life. In fact, the depression didn't invade Solomon's emotional life until after he had experienced several emotional challenges. The most traumatic challenge occurred with the death of his mother, who suffered from ovarian cancer. He appeared to work through this tremendous loss, bought a new house, and was writing for *The New Yorker*.

In 1994, Solomon published his first novel, entitled *A Stone Boat*. Although the book received praise and was a runner-up for the LA Times First Fiction Prize, Solomon was unaffected by these exciting events. He kept going through the motions of life but was undoubtedly heading for what would be the first of three depression-related breakdowns. Already emotionally vulnerable since the death of his mother, the physical event of kidney stones, which led to severe pain, might have been a triggering event for his subsequent descent into emotional turmoil. He wrote of this time, "It is not pleasant to experience decay, to find yourself exposed to the ravages of an almost daily rain, and to know that you are turning into something feeble, that more and more of you will blow off with the first strong wind, making you less and less" (Solomon, 2001, p. 17).

After establishing an emotional balance with antidepressant medication and psychotherapy, Solomon regretfully decided to cease his medication—cold turkey. The sudden disruption of neurochemicals precipitated a second breakdown, which was so severe that he decided to try to acquire AIDS by having unprotected sex with strangers so that his body would be as sick as he felt his mind was at the time. Fortunately, Solomon's strategic attempt at prolonged suicide failed. His third breakdown occurred in 1999 following the breakup of a relationship and, once again, acute pain related to a dislocated shoulder. With the proper mix of medication, rest, social support, and psychotherapy, he was able to bounce back from this breakdown sooner than from the earlier ones.

Solomon's depression left such a mark on his emotional life that he decided to write a comprehensive book chronicling his experience and those of other individuals suffering from depression. *The Noonday Demon: An Atlas of Depression* (Solomon, 2001) has been described as a "definitive" work on depression. Solomon spent 5 years writing the book, and now he is trying to make a difference in the lives of those suffering from this disease by increasing awareness in other ways.

Solomon strongly believes that more financial assistance and/or insurance coverage should be provided for the treatment of mental illness, reporting that his first breakdown cost him 5 months of work, $4,000 worth of visits to the psychopharmacologist, $10,000 for psychotherapy, and $3,500 for medication. It currently costs him about $20,000 a year to maintain his mental health with an antidepressant cocktail consisting of Effexor, Wellbutrin, BuSpar, and Zyprexa, as well as other prophylactics such as talk therapy and exercise. As he pointed out in his book, only a limited segment of the population can afford to defend themselves against depression.

(as observed in chronic stress and depression) would not affect the amygdala or vice versa. Indeed, a few studies also show an effect of major depression on the amygdala: not a decrease but an increase in volume (Bremner et al., 2000). It is not clear how depression leads to a larger amygdala. Bremner suggests that, because of the amygdala's role in emotional processing, the demands on its cells may be increased, thereby leading to an increased

anterior cingulate cortex
Front portion of the older lobe of the cerebral cortex that surrounds the corpus callosum. Decreased activity in this area has been found to accompany profound sadness; thus, this area has been implicated in the symptoms of depression.

volume. Additionally, PET scans indicate increased aymgdala activity in depressed individuals responding to personal negative stimuili (Hamilton & Gotlib, 2008). Whereas investigating the neural inputs and outputs of the amygdala is important, it is also worthwhile to document information transfer with another limbic structure, the hypothalamus. The hypothalamus plays a role in triggering the release of stress hormones that contribute to the damage to the hippocampus just described.

The PFC and amygdala areas share extensive connections with the mediodorsal nucleus of the thalamus and ventral striatum (the ventromedial caudate and the nucleus accumbens). Neuroimaging and postmortem studies show that thalamic and ventral striatum volumes are significantly decreased in patients suffering from major depression (Baumann et al., 1999; Krishnan et al., 1992). Further, metabolic rates are reduced in the caudate of depressed patients, and blood flow is decreased in depressive relapse when patients are subjected to tryptophan depletion (Drevets, 2000).

Cingulate cortex. One brain area that relays information from the limbic areas to the PFC is the **anterior cingulate cortex**, the front portion of the older lobe of the cerebral cortex that surrounds the corpus callosum, introduced in Chapter 8. The anterior cingulate cortex is involved in attentional processing in healthy individuals (Liotti & Mayberg, 2001). But research focusing on the involvement of this area in depression has pointed to decreased activity in the dorsal anterior cingulate.

Mario Liotti at the University of Texas in San Antonio and Helen Mayberg at the University of Toronto describe some interesting methodologies for further exploring the role of the cingulate cortex in depression (Liotti & Mayberg, 2001). Because a hallmark symptom of depression is profound sadness, one way to focus on the brain areas involved is to simply induce sadness by having subjects read rehearsed autobiographical scripts intended to elicit either a sad or a neutral mood.

In accordance with neuroimaging studies with depressed patients, a decrease in activity was observed in both the dorsal anterior cingulate and the PFC. When these researchers focused on the ventral anterior cingulate, however, a different response was observed: Induced sadness activates this area. Thus, extreme sadness induces a reciprocal pattern of responses—deactivation of the PFC and dorsal anterior cingulate and activation in the ventral anterior cingulate and related limbic structures.

In a second exploration, these researchers attempted to tease apart sadness from anxiety by using autobiographical scripts to induce sadness, anxiety, or a neutral mood. Whereas sadness was accompanied by deactivation of the right PFC and parietal cortex, anxiety was accompanied by activation in areas of the PFC such as the orbitofrontal cortex and deactivation of the parahippocampal gyri and inferior temporal cortex (cortical areas surrounding the hippocampal area).

Hence, sadness seems to be characterized by selective dorsal cortical deactivations, whereas ventral cortical deactivations are observed in anxiety (Liotti, Mayberg, et al., 2000). Providing further evidence of the functional differences of the dorsal and ventral corticolimbic streams, Pizzagalli and colleagues (2001) have found that patients who respond to antidepressants with more activation in the ventral area of the anterior cingulate demonstrate a better response to drug treatment several months later. Confirming this finding, more recent research shows that patients who respond to negative stimuli with greater anterior cingulate activity demonstrate the most robust improvement with antidepressant therapy (venlafaxine) (Davidson, Irwin, Anderle, & Kalin, 2003).

These findings help to explain why depressed patients experiencing profound sadness may have difficulty focusing their attention and concentrating on tasks. If structures in the brain—for example, the PFC and associated areas—that are typically involved in sustaining attention are deactivated, it is easy to see that the person is going to experience difficulties in focusing attention. In a clever series of studies, Liotti, Woldorff, Perez, and Mayberg (2000) explored further this notion of deactivation of attentional circuits during depression or induced sadness. In the Stroop test of perception, the name of a color, such as green, is typed in a different color, for example, purple. Subjects are instructed to report the color, not the word. In this challenging task the brain has to suppress information—the actual word—so that it can report another bit of information—the actual color. Research on humans who have experienced damage to the anterior cingulate cortex suggests that this area is important in monitoring the competing pieces of information and inhibiting the inappropriate response. Interestingly, Stroop performance is impaired in depressed individuals (Liotti, Woldorff, et al., 2000; Pardo, Pardo, Janer, & Raichle, 1990).

Another area of the anterior cingulate, namely the midline subgenual anterior cingulate cortex, has been implicated in depression. Specifically, neuroimaging studies indicate small reductions in this area; additionally, as you will read in the treatment section of this chapter, stimulation of this area reduces depressive symptoms (Mayberg et al., 2005).

Nucleus accumbens. Essentially the relay between limbic and basal ganglia structures, the nucleus accumbens, which is involved in reinforcement and pleasure, mediates the interface of emotional and motor responses (see Chapter 8). Naranjo, Trembley, and Busto (2001) reasoned that, because depression is characterized by **anhedonia** (loss of pleasure) and deeply entrenched feelings of sadness, it makes sense to focus research on the nucleus accumbens. In fact, if the nucleus accumbens processes information about our environment so that we may respond in an appropriate, adaptive manner, then this structure can be viewed as regulating an animal's learning to adapt to a changing environment. Depression has been equated to the experimental model known as **learned helplessness**. In this paradigm, an animal or person fails to respond appropriately to his or her environment and that condition might result from a malfunctioning nucleus accumbens (Naranjo et al., 2001).

To test the involvement of the brain's reward system in depression, depressed subjects were given an injection of d-amphetamine to stimulate the brain's reward system. This drug, which works via the dopaminergic system, has a powerful ability to promote feelings of reward and pleasure. Naranjo and colleagues call this administration of d-amphetamine a "probe test"; it activates the reward center in the subjects' brains. Once subjects receive the pharmacological probe, their feelings of depression are measured using the Hamilton Depression Scale, a paper-and-pencil test of depression. Compared to nondepressed subjects, depressed subjects have greater drug-induced rewarding effects.

anhedonia Lack of desire or pleasure. Drugs that interfere with the mesolimbic dopaminergic system produce this state.

learned helplessness Usually resulting from several bouts with failure, the acquired belief that no effort can remove an individual from a stressful environment. Seligman suggests that this phenomenon may be a basis for clinical depression.

You may be thinking that this is just the opposite of Naranjo et al.'s hypothesis, but let's thoroughly consider these results. If a person was experiencing less dopaminergic activity in the nucleus accumbens, it is very likely that the brain would produce more sensitive dopaminergic receptors in an attempt to compensate for the reduction so that the person could maximize the response to existing low levels of dopamine. When, with more sensitive receptors (for example, upregulation or higher affinity for ligand), this person receives a dose of d-amphetamine, a dopaminergic agonist, the receptors will probably respond in a wildly active manner due to their increased sensitivity to dopamine.

Even if this explanation is not correct, the fact that differences are observed between depressed and nondepressed subjects provides substantial evidence that the brain's reward system is somehow affected in depression. For that reason, this sensitivity may be used as a biological marker for depression and may give some insight about the patient's response to treatment. If this is the case, then the dopaminergic–nucleus accumbens area may have potential as a therapeutic target area for pharmaceutical development.

Because of the close communication among the nucleus accumbens, striatum, and prefrontal cortex, it has been hypothesized that this circuit may be critical for sustaining motivated behaviors. Further, due to the striatum's prevalent role in this circuit and the striatum's role in physical movement, it is thought that the brains' rewards are especially salient when they follow physical effort. Tasting a delicious meal that you have planned and spent time cooking, for example, likely engages these key brain areas more than simply ordering take-out food. Consequently, it has been argued that **effort-driven rewards** may be important for mental health and that the rise in depression occurring around the mid-twentieth century may have accompanied the introduction and reliance on energy-saving devices (e.g., dishwashers, vacuum cleaners) that invaded the lives of those living in western cultures (Klerman, 1985; Lambert, 2006; Lambert, 2008a; Lambert, 2008b).

Providing further support for the role of physical effort in the prevention of depression, Edward McAuley (2009) and his colleagues at the University of Illinois found that patients with a chronic illness such as multiple sclerosis were more protected against the emergence of depression if they engaged in physical activity and had a heightened sense of self-efficacy (a perception that one can accomplish their goals, as discussed in chapter 2); hence, having a perception of mastery over various challenges in the environment was an antidepressant in this vulnerable population.

Brain stem tracts. The brain stem is another critical brain area that communicates with the PFC. Two neurochemical circuits critical to depression and anxiety, serotonin and noradrenaline, are produced by nuclei in the brain stem. The dorsal raphe nucleus is the brain stem area that houses the serotonergic (5-hydroxytryptamine [5-HT]) neurons that project to the PFC (as well as to a host of other areas in the brain; see Figure 5.5).

Bligh-Glover and colleagues (2000) reported that suicide victims with major depression have significantly increased serotonin transporters throughout the dorsal raphe nucleus. Additionally, an increase in the number and density of 5-HT neurons in the dorsal raphe nucleus of depressed suicide victims has been reported (Underwood et al., 1999). Generally, it is thought that these effects are due to a suppression of the serotonergic system in the brain stem.

The second brain stem area contributing to the massive cellular communications with the cortex is the locus coeruleus (LC), which contributes over 70% of the forebrain's norepinephrine (NE) innervation by projecting to the cortex and the subcortical and limbic structures (Ressler & Nemeroff, 2000) (see Figure 5.4). Utilizing a variety of measures, NE activity is enhanced or increased in depression (Ressler & Nemeroff, 2000).

The LC fires fastest when an animal is alert and responding to its environment. For example, when a rat is grooming, a behavior in which there is low NE activation, the LC neurons suddenly become active if a loud noise occurs, prompting the rat to cease grooming and orient toward the sound. In fact, while the animal is grooming, which is a more internal, homeostatic behavior, serotonin firing increases. Hence, according to Ressler and Nemeroff (2000) of Emory University, the serotonergic activity in the dorsal raphe nucleus maintains more homeostatic behavior whereas the LC noradrenergic system maintains the animal's vigilant responses to the environment.

White matter. Now that we have established the brain circuits involved in depression, it is also relevant to explore the integrity of its communication pathways. Would disrupted communication among all these sites lead to negative effects? Working with a team of scientists at the Erasmus University Medical School in the Netherlands, Jan de Groot explored this question (2000). They conducted MRIs on a sample of over 1,000 nondepressed elderly subjects to assess the number of lesions in the subcortical white matter.

The white matter is also known as the communication matter because it comprises primarily the myelinated axons of neurons (see Chapter 4). Subjects with severe white matter lesions were more likely to experience symptoms of depression than subjects who did not display lesions. These authors propose that white matter lesions, often due to cerebrovascular events such as stroke, may be a factor in late-onset depression (occurring after the age of 40 years).

Neurochemistry of Depression

Finding a single brain area or a single type of damage that leads to a depression syndrome seems less and less likely as neuroscientists uncover new and complex information related to the disorder. As suggested by Ressler and Nemeroff (2000), depression may be thought of more accurately in terms of balances between internal homeostatic processes and vigilant processing of our external worlds.

If monitoring systems get out of balance, too great a focus may fall on internal processes monitored by the serotonergic system or on external processes monitored by the NE system. This homeostatic imbalance is then reflected in an unbalanced expression of moods. Beginning in the 1950s, a whirlwind of research activity took aim at identifying the role of specific neurotransmitters in depression. (See Table 9.3 for a description of these neurotransmitters.)

Serotonin (5-HT). Since the 1950s, substantial evidence has supported the hypothesis that a dysfunctional serotonergic system may play a role in

Table 9.3 Summary of Evidence Supporting Neurochemical Involvement in Depression

Neurotransmitter	Supporting Evidence
Norepinephrine	Norepinephrine-deficient diet promotes symptoms of depression in patients on norepinephrine uptake blockers; efficacy of norepinephrine uptake blockers
Serotonin	Low levels of 5-HIAA in CSF of depressed patients; reduced platelet serotonin transport sites in depressed patients; serotonin-depletion diets promote depressive symptoms in patients currently taking SSRIs; efficacy of SSRIs; SSRI-induced alterations in specific serotonergic receptor sensitivity
Corticosteroids	Increased levels of corticosteroids in depressed patients; reduced CRH-binding sites in suicidal victims; insensitivity of depressed patients to dexamethasone test; preliminary efficacy of anti-CRH antidepressants
Combination of monoamines	Efficacy rates of tricyclic antidepressants; current preliminary efficacy rates of SNUBs

depression. If drugs that increase levels of serotonin help treat the symptoms of depression, it seems obvious that depression must be caused by low levels of serotonin. We have to proceed with caution, however, with this line of reasoning. It is a bit like assuming that because a rash on your foot improves after placing steroid cream on it, the rash is caused by a steroid deficiency (Delgado & Moreno, 2000).

Nonetheless, indirect evidence does support the serotonin-depletion hypothesis. For example, lower levels of one breakdown, or metabolic, product of serotonin, known as 5-hydroxyindoleacetic acid (5-HIAA), have been found in the cerebrospinal fluid of depressed patients (Cheetham, Katona, & Horton, 1991). Further, fewer serotonin transporter sites are found on the platelets of depressed patients before they are placed on antidepressants (Healy & Leonard, 1987).

The serotonin-depletion theory is not clear-cut, however, because several studies have failed to find evidence of reduced serotonergic functioning in depressed patients (Gjerris, 1988). In a fascinating study, Pedro Delgado (2000) at the University of Arizona's Department of Psychiatry hypothesized that if a depletion of serotonin leads to depression, then a diet low in tryptophan, the precursor of serotonin, would lead to a return to symptoms of depression in patients being treated with antidepressants. Indeed, two-thirds of the subjects experienced a relapse of depressive symptoms within a mere 5–7 hours of dietary tryptophan depletion.

But when Delgado placed depressed patients who were not on antidepressant medication on the tryptophan-free diet, he saw a minimal change on the first day and only a few patients got worse on the second day (see this chapter's Connections for more about dietary tryptophan). These patients did not seem to be as sensitive to fluctuations in serotonin as the patients on antidepressant medication. Even more interesting, when healthy subjects were placed on the tryptophan-free diet, minimal evidence of depression emerged in those with no family history of depression, whereas symptoms occurred in about one-third of the subjects with a family history of affective disorders.

This research suggests that the onset of depressive symptoms may depend less on actual levels of circulating serotonin and more on the sensitivity of the postsynaptic neurons that respond to this neurotransmitter (Figure 9.2). This probably explains the observations in the depressed patients on

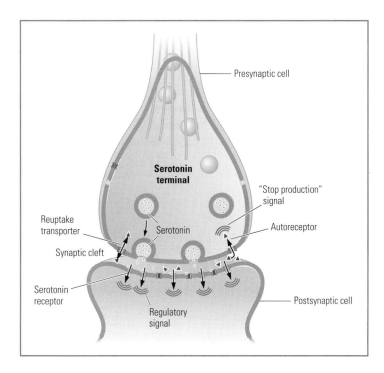

Figure 9.2
The serotonergic synapse Serotonin is released from the presynaptic cell and travels across the synaptic cleft to the postsynaptic cell, where it attaches to specialized receptors. Autoreceptors on the presynaptic cell help to regulate the amount of serotonin released, and reuptake transporters facilitate the reuptake of released serotonin into the presynaptic cell.

antidepressants. These subjects had been on their medications long enough for the receptors to change in sensitivity to the newly increased levels of serotonin. As a result, they responded immediately (or within hours, in this case) to a diet devoid of the essential elements for the production of serotonin.

These findings also address one of the most puzzling questions concerning the serotonin-depletion hypothesis of depression. Antidepressant drugs increase serotonergic activity within a matter of days, but their therapeutic action depends on chronic administration for several weeks. One explanation for this delay is that the autoreceptors on the serotonergic neurons that monitor the amount of serotonin released by its own cell quickly adapt to the increased levels of serotonin induced by the antidepressant medication (see Figure 9.2). Activation of these autoreceptors results in a decreased firing rate for the monoaminergic neurons to compensate for the increased levels of circulating monoamines.

But remember, to see therapeutic improvement, increased levels of serotonin, or monoamines, are desirable. Researchers have observed, however, that the compensatory increase in the autoreceptor activation and subsequent inhibition of the firing of the 5-HT neuron diminishes over time—interestingly, about the time of the observed clinical improvement (Blier & Montigny, 1994; Duman, 1999). In fact, most of the current research focusing on the serotonergic system is providing evidence that the activity of the serotonergic receptors that detect the presence of serotonin in the synapse, rather than absolute levels of circulating serotonin, is an integral piece of the serotonin hypothesis of depression.

In addition to the autoreceptor, other receptors on the presynaptic and postsynaptic surfaces have been investigated. Research suggests that chronic administration of some antidepressant medications leads to an increase

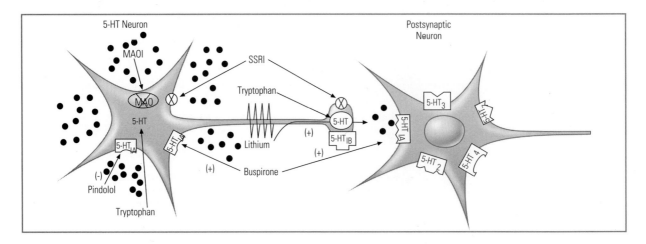

Figure 9.3
Drug mechanisms that influence serotonergic functioning 5-HT_{1A} and 5-HT_{1B} autoreceptors inhibit 5-HT neuronal firing and release of transmitter. Plus signs indicate activation, whereas minus signs indicate antagonism of a particular function. Circles on the 5-HT neuron represent the reuptake transporters; if they contain an X, they are inhibited. Small dots represent the concentration of the 5-HT transmitter, which is twice as dense around the 5-HT cell bodies compared with postsynaptic structures.
BLIER & ABBOTT (2001, P. 39)

in sensitivity to the 5-HT_{1A} receptors located on the post-synaptic surface (Duman, 1999) Research on the 5-HT_{1A} receptor is far from conclusive, however, and depends on the type of antidepressant and the area of the brain being investigated. For example, Fujita and his colleagues have found decreased receptor sensitivity in presynaptic 5-HT_{1A} receptors in depressed subjects (Fujita, Charney, & Innis, 2000). (See Figure 9.3 for an illustration of 5-HT_{1A} and 5-HT_{1B} receptors on the serotonin neurons.)

A group of researchers in the Department of Psychiatry at Oxford University explored the role of a different serotonergic receptor, the 5-HT_{1D} receptor found on both the presynaptic and postsynaptic surfaces of the serotonergic neurons. After recruiting men and women suffering from major depression, the Oxford researchers gave the patients a drug known as zolmi-triptan, a 5-HT_{1D} receptor agonist. After manipulating this receptor system, they went on to assess the patients' responses to antidepressant treatment—which increases levels of serotonin. The Oxford researchers found that, prior to treatment with the agonist, patients had an impaired sensitivity of the postsynaptic 5-HT_{1D} receptor. Following antidepressant treatment, a further reduction in 5-HT_{1D} sensitivity was observed, probably resulting from a compensatory response to increased levels of synaptic 5-HT (Whale, Clifford, Bhagwagar, & Cowan, 2001).

As the name *receptor* implies, these structures receive and respond to the presence of serotonin in the synapse; ultimately, receptors pass on their information to intracellular structures for further processing. Accordingly, researchers are interested in the effects of antidepressants on cellular processes such as the second-messenger signal-transduction pathways discussed in Chapter 4 (Duman & Nestler, 1995).

A behavioral study conducted by Patrick Ronan and his colleagues at the Department of Veterans Affairs Medical Center in Dallas, Texas, also demonstrates that the absolute levels of serotonin are less critical than the nature of the activity induced by serotonin (Ronan, Steciuk, Kramer, Kram, & Petty, 2000). These researchers exposed rats to shock while they were in restraint tubes and unable to escape the aversive stimulus. On the second day the animals were shocked and given an opportunity to escape the shock by running across the shuttlebox. Subsequently, the rats were required to run across twice to terminate the shock. Interestingly, about half the animals worked to turn off the aversive stimulus of shock while the other half did not attempt to escape it. Box 9.2 describes the previously mentioned phenomenon known as learned helplessness as well as other paradigms used to study depression.

Following this behavioral testing, microdialysis probes were placed in the animals' lateral septum (a limbic structure) so that levels of serotonin and its breakdown product 5-HIAA, as well as other monoamines, could be assessed. The only neurochemical difference detected between the helpless and nonhelpless rats was an increase in 5-HIAA in the nonhelpless rats. These results suggest that increased metabolism of serotonin might play a role in protecting the organism against stress, a condition that often precipitates depression.

Norepinephrine. In 1965, Joseph Schildkraut of Harvard University introduced the catecholamine hypothesis, in which he stated that depression results from a deficiency of NE whereas mania results from an abundance of NE (Schildkraut, 1965). Although the discovery in the 1980s of the clinical effectiveness of selective serotonin reuptake inhibitors (SSRIs) elevated serotonin as the preeminent neurotransmitter influencing depression, other research has supported the theory that NE is influential (Nemeroff, 1998; Jeannotte, McCarthy & Sidhu, 2009).

As reviewed by Delgado and Moreno (2000), NE-depletion studies initially brought researchers back to the NE hypothesis of depression. In these depletion studies, alpha-methyl-paratyrosine (AMPT, an inhibitor of tyrosine hydroxylase, an enzyme that is important in the production of catecholamine transmitters) was used to decrease the amount of NE in subjects. Researchers found that depressed patients given an antidepressant medication (desipramine) that selectively increases NE instead of serotonin suffered a relapse when given AMPT to reduce NE. AMPT had no effect on the continued effectiveness of antidepressant drugs that manipulate the serotonergic system.

As mentioned in the serotonin section, similar depletion studies suggest that subjects who respond positively to drugs that increase serotonin suffer relapses when placed on a serotonin-deficient diet but fail to be affected by an NE-deficient diet. This dichotomy of responses to specific neurotransmitter-depletion diets provides evidence that NE is probably a legitimate player in the depression game.

Working in the clinical physiology and neuroscience departments at Sahlgrenska University in Sweden, Gavin Lambert and his colleagues conducted an interesting study that provided evidence of the involvement of NE in depression (Lambert, Hohansson, Agren, & Friberg, 2000). They brought patients into the lab who either were suffering from depression or were healthy. Internal jugular venous catheters were placed in the subjects so that blood from the brain could be collected for analysis for the presence of the monoaminergic transmitters.

Blood samples indicated that depressed patients had significantly lower plasma concentrations of NE and other principal central nervous system metabolites (Figure 9.4). Administration of the NE transporter blocker desipramine resulted in a significant reduction in NE turnover, or use, in depressed patients. Interestingly, these researchers found that turnover rates in dopamine, not in NE, seemed to be a stronger predictor of the severity of depression.

Figure 9.4
Norepinephrine levels and depression Levels of norepinephrine (NE) and metabolites (3,4-dihydroxyphenylglycol [DHPG], 3-methoxy-4-hydroxyphenylglycol [MHPG], and homovanillic acid [HVA]) were significantly reduced in depressed patients. No statistical difference was found between serotonergic levels (5-hydroxyindoleacetic acid [5-HIAA]) in healthy and depressed patients.
LAMBERT ET AL. (2000, P. 791)

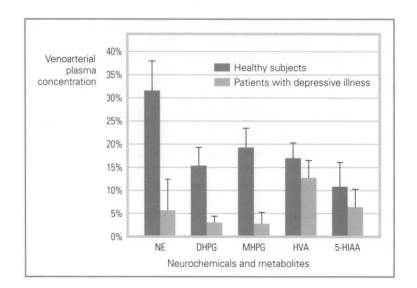

The results obtained by Lambert and his colleagues provide strong support for the role of NE in depression but do not rule out the involvement of other monoamines (dopamine and serotonin). In support of the ubiquitous involvement of the monoamines in depression, Ressler and Nemeroff (2000) suggest that depression is probably due not to specific malfunctions in the NE or serotonergic system but to the role of the systems in modulating other neurobiological systems that mediate the symptoms of depression.

Corticosteroids. In a research review, Glorian Holsboer (2000) of the Max Planck Institute of Psychiatry in Munich, Germany, proposed that four convincing lines of evidence support the involvement of corticosteroids, the stress hormones, in depression:

1. Secretory impulses of adrenocorticotropic hormone (ACTH), which stimulate the release of **corticosteroids** from the adrenal cortex, and cortisol are increased in depressed patients. These increased impulses are reflected in increased cortisol levels in the depressed patients' urine (Rubin, Poland, Lesser, Winston, & Blodgett, 1987).

2. Levels of corticotropin-releasing hormone (CRH), the neurochemical that stimulates the release of ACTH from the pituitary, are elevated in depressed patients (Nemeroff et al., 1984).

3. The number of neurons that secrete CRH is increased in limbic regions of the brain such as the hypothalamus (Raadsheer, Hoogendijk, Stam, Tilders, & Swaab, 1994).

4. When looking at the brains of depressed patients who committed suicide, reduced CRH-binding sites were observed in the frontal cortex, a likely compensatory reaction to the increased CRH found in depressed patients (Nemeroff, Owens, Bissette, Andorn, & Stanley, 1988).

Also implicating the hypothalamic–pituitary–adrenal (HPA) axis in depression is the administration of the synthetic glucocorticoid dexamethasone in the dexamethasone-suppression test (DST). In healthy patients, natural levels of cortisol should decrease in response to the administration of a cortisol-like substance. Depressed patients, however, fail to experience the

corticosteroids Hormones secreted by the adrenal cortex during stress. These neurochemicals influence the brain and are thought to be a trigger for depressive symptoms. Some drugs targeted at reducing corticosteroids reduce symptoms of depression.

suppression of cortisol after receiving the DST (Carroll, 1982). Researchers are focusing on mouse breeds in which pertinent genes necessary for the regulation of the HPA axis are inactivated (making it difficult for the animals to maintain HPA homeostasis) so that a clearer picture of the role of HPA functioning in anxiety and depression-like behavior can be investigated (Holsboer, 2000). In general, recent knowledge related to the role of the HPA axis has emphasized the importance of understanding more about how the functional normalization of the axis can be used in the successful treatment of depressive symptoms (Lopez-Munoz & Alamo, 2009).

As discussed in Chapter 5, there are dozens and dozens of neurotransmitters, and it is likely that many play either direct or indirect roles in major depression. In addition to the monoamines and corticosteroids, researchers have investigated the role of vasopressin, oxytocin, glutamate, substance P, thyroid hormones, and growth factors in depressive disorders (Zelena, 2009; Lopez-Munoz & Alamo, 2009). In the next section, we discuss how altered neurochemistry within the neuroanatomical circuit of depression (and elsewhere) may converge to produce mutations in the brain. When neuroplasticity is interrupted, the brain may become vulnerable to depression.

Brain Plasticity

Recent research on the role of brain plasticity in the etiology of depression proves how quickly the field of clinical neuroscience changes. It hasn't been too much longer than a decade ago that we were just learning that neurons continue to be generated throughout a human's life; now we're finding out that the production of new neurons, as well as the expansion of existing neurons, may contribute to depression (Eriksson et al., 1998). Glial cells have also been found to be significantly decreased in limbic regions in depressed patients (Rajkowska & Miguel-Hidalgo, 2007). In a short time, some convincing evidence of the involvement of brain plasticity in depression has been published, making this one of the most exciting new research areas in depression. As stated by Fred Gage (2000), former president of the Society for Neuroscience and a researcher at the Salk Institute, "Clearly, this is an exciting field of study, and the evidence supporting structural changes in major depression is likely to have significant impact on diagnosis, treatment, and therapy" (p. 714).

Brain structure and neurogenesis. As discussed in Chapter 3, the hippocampus is involved in learning and memory, a most important function as animals constantly process new information about their environments. Focusing on the rat and mouse hippocampus, the granule cell layer of the hippocampus contains about 1–2 million cells. Every day, however, 1,000–3,000 new cells are produced. These new cells may play an important role in processing current information (Jacobs, van Praag, & Gage, 2000).

It is likely that these baseline neurogenesis rates are influenced by external factors such as stressful stimuli in the environment. Indeed, studies suggest that exposure to a stressor such as fox odor suppresses neurogenesis in the dentate gyrus of the rat (Galea, Tanapat, & Gould, 1996). Additionally, chronic psychosocial stress has led to reduced neurogenesis in tree shrews (Gould et al., 1997).

What about humans? As we've discussed, the hippocampus can shrink in chronically stressed and/or depressed subjects. Temporal lobe epilepsy affects the brain area containing the hippocampus and is associated with extensive cell loss in various structures surrounding the hippocampus. People with

Box 9.2

Brain Matters

Animal Models of Depression

Presented here are a few of the more popular animal models used to investigate depression-like behavior. Brief summaries are provided for each model, but it is important to note that each paradigm has strengths and weaknesses; a thorough investigation should always be performed prior to making a decision about the appropriateness of a particular model. Information about these models was taken from several sources (Holsboer, 1999; Redei et al., 2001; Seligman & Beagley, 1975; Suomi, 1983; Weiss & Kilts, 1995; Willner, Muscat, & Papp, 1992).

Learned helplessness. In this paradigm, animals are presented with a stressor such as a shock and not allowed to escape. Researchers subsequently test for deficits in escaping from this task; when animals exhibit behavioral deficits, they are thought to demonstrate learned helplessness. Animals that are allowed to turn off the shocks are less likely to exhibit behavioral deficits. Hence, perception of control seems to be pertinent in this paradigm. In the diagram, the avoidance rats are able to turn off the stressor whereas the yoked animal has no escape from the stressor. Antidepressants reduce behavioral deficits in some cases.

Social defeat. When an intruder animal is placed in the home cage of another animal, the resident is likely to aggressively attack the intruder (some animals

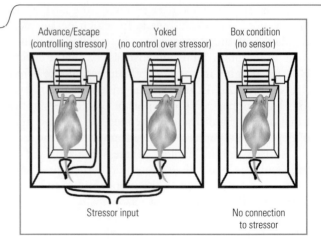

Learned helplessness

need to be trained to reliably defeat intruders). This single episode appears to trigger a cascade of effects leading to defeated animals exhibiting depression-like behavior for around a week. Because of their aggressive tendencies, hamsters are a popular animal used in this paradigm.

Forced swim test. In this paradigm, rats or mice are placed in a cylinder or tank that is half-filled with water, as shown in the figure. Variables such as latency to swim, latency to float, number of dives, and number of attempts to escape up the wall are recorded. Some researchers view floating in this paradigm as "behavioral despair." This paradigm has been used as a test for antidepressants with the notion that effective antidepressants should prolong the latency to float. It

---

temporal lobe epilepsy are more likely to experience depression than patients suffering from any other form of epilepsy (Perini et al., 1996).

We also discussed the role of the PFC in depression. Recent postmortem studies suggest significant reduction in the number of glial cells in the PFC of depressed patients. Additionally, the neuronal cell bodies are smaller than those in nondepressed counterparts (Rajkowska, 2000).

It is difficult to assess the parameters and existence of new cells in living depressed patients. One way to determine whether alterations of brain plasticity play a role in human depression is to verify whether therapies that are successful for depressed humans also influence plasticity in animal models. When electroconvulsive therapy (ECT) is administered to rats repeatedly—that is, five times over 10 days—the number of 5-HT fibers sprouting off the axon doubles. Additionally, increased levels of 5-HIAA have been observed (Madhav, Pei, Grahame-Smith, & Zetterstrom, 2000).

One study investigated the effect of either single or multiple ECT seizures on neurogenesis in the dentate gyrus of the rat hippocampus (Madsen et al.,

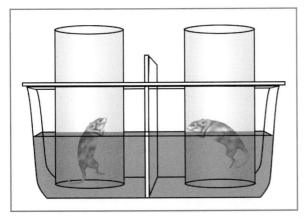

Forced swim test

stimuli that range from very mild stressors, such as tilted cages, to more intense stressors, such as exposure to predator odors. After about 2 weeks in such a paradigm, some animals develop *anhedonia*, or a reduction in their motivation to obtain rewards such as sucrose solution or to carry out such maintenance behaviors such as nest building (see photo). This model is useful because its unpredictable nature closely simulates chronic human stress.

Stress-sensitive rats. Selective breeding for particular traits related to depression (e.g., anxiety, lack of activity) has also been used to produce an animal model of depression. The Maudsley reactive rats have been selected for their emotionality (e.g., freezing in place) in the open field test; these rats also show depression-like behaviors in other paradigms. Additionally, the Wistar Kyoto (WKY) rat is thought to be a valuable animal model for endogenous (internally driven) depression. These animals show increased anxious and depressive behaviors in several behavioral tests and respond to antidepressants.

may be adaptive, however, for rodents that have had previous experience with this inescapable task to float sooner to conserve energy.

Early life stressors. Recall from Chapter 6 that when infant monkeys are separated from their mothers they respond with agitation, vocalizations, and sleep disturbances. Interesting individual differences, however, contribute to the severity of this response. Steve Suomi, who is currently at the National Institutes of Mental Health, is interested in why some primates are more vulnerable to the effects of separation stress and respond with "despair" whereas others seem to take it in stride.

Chronic unpredictable stress. This model involves exposure of animals to various stressors in an unpredictable pattern. The paradigm includes

Nest building
California deer mouse building a nest.
COURTESY OF KELLY LAMBERT

2000). Just one ECT seizure significantly increased newborn cells, and a series of seizures increased neurogenesis in a dose-dependent fashion. The authors concluded that ECT may be an effective therapy for depression because of the generation of new neurons. Also supporting the role of neurogenesis in depression are multiple findings that other treatment strategies for depression (e.g., taking various antidepressants such as SSRIs, tricyclics, and monoamine inhibitors) alter neurogenesis in rodent models (Eitan & Lerer, 2009).

Role of BDNF in depression. Antidepressant drugs have been shown to influence brain plasticity via increased production of a major growth factor in the brain, brain-derived neurotrophic factor (BDNF). As you learned in Chapter 6, BDNF contributes to the maintenance and growth of neuronal systems. When rats are given antidepressant medications, an upregulation of BDNF mRNA is found in the hippocampus and cortex (Nibuya, Morinobu, & Duman, 1995).

Depressed patients also report relief from depression following exercise, and physical activity is known to upregulate BDNF mRNA (Hill, Storandt, & Malley, 1993). In an interesting extension of the antidepressant and exercise studies, Russo-Neustadt, Beard, Huang, and Cotman (2000), working at the University of California, Santa Barbara, investigated the combined effects of exercise and antidepressant medication. They found that this combination increased levels of BDNF mRNA more than the treatments used in isolation. In fact, this laboratory has confirmed that BDNF mRNA expression is related to an animal model of depression. When rats were placed in an unescapable water tank, increased swimming, which is interpreted by many as the more adaptive, nondepressed response, was correlated with increased BDNF mRNA levels (Russo-Neustadt, Ha, Ramirez, & Kesslak, 2001).

A certain strain of rats known as the Flinders sensitive line (FLS) expresses several depressive symptoms such as reduced activity, learning disturbances, anhedonia, and abnormal circadian rhythms, all of which are diminished by antidepressants. To assess baseline levels of growth factors including BDNF in these depressed rats, researchers working at the Karolinska Institute in Stockholm, Sweden, and the Institute of Neurobiology in Rome, Italy, focused on the hypothalamus, hippocampus, striatum, and frontal cortex. Expecting to find that the rats had lower baseline growth factor levels, they were surprised that the FLS rats had higher BDNF and nerve growth factor (NGF) levels in some brain regions than the nondepressed strain of rats. Additionally, females had significantly less NGF than males. These findings are important because they show that there are indeed altered levels of neurotrophins in an animal model of depression. Because antidepressants are known to increase neurotrophins, the unexpected increase in BDNF and NGF levels might reflect the brain's attempt to reverse the altered cellular or glial alterations. If so, it's likely that BDNF and NGF changes are not the fundamental causes of depression but rather a compensatory mechanism used by the brain to bring structural and functional processing back to an acceptable baseline level (Angelucci, Aloe, Vasquez, & Mathe, 2000). Further, researchers have suggested that neurotrophins such as BDNF are necessary for the adaptation of neuronal networks to changing environmental situations (Castren & Rantamaki, 2010).

In accordance with this study, Vollmayr, Faust, Lewicka, and Henn (2001), working at the University of Heidelberg, assessed BDNF in the hippocampus of another strain of rat, a congenital helpless strain, bred for its intensity of depressive symptoms. This strain has lost behavioral plasticity in response to antidepressants. As found by Angelucci and colleagues (2000), the hippocampus of the congenital helpless strain had higher levels of BDNF in response to shock stress (in the learned helplessness paradigm) than did the control animals. These findings reinforce the fact that more research is needed to clarify the exact nature of BDNF in depression. Currently, it is not clear whether compromised neuronal growth is the cause of depression or if the depressed brain, which has compromised structural complexity, compensates by producing higher levels of some of the growth factors.

STRESS AND DEPRESSION

No one can deny that internal events vary in response to environmental conditions. Anyone who has experienced a tragic loss can verify that a single external event can instantaneously throw a healthy, optimistic person into a prolonged state of severe depression. Prolonged stress can also trigger depression, as can the changing of the seasons.

Life's Losses

Episodes of depression due to a profound life loss constitute an expected reaction that subsides with time. But there is evidence that losses encountered early in life may alter a person's susceptibility to depression later in life. Rat pups that are separated from their mothers for up to 6 hours per day for the first 3 weeks of their lives have increased levels of stress hormones when subjected to stress as adults (Ladd, Owens, & Nemeroff, 1996). On the contrary, as previously mentioned, rat pups that are stimulated by being handled by humans for 15 minutes per day for the first 3 weeks of life develop a reduced stress reaction as adults (Plotsky & Meaney, 1993). Rhesus monkeys that are raised individually in isolated nurseries from the time they are 8 weeks old exhibit increased symptoms of anxiety and depression such as reduced social interaction and impaired cognitive function as adults (Sanchez, Hearn, Do, Rilling, Herndon, 1998). Thus, animal models suggest that early stress conditions, such as the loss of essential early contact, can alter the stress response of the adult, leading to an increased susceptibility to depression (Kaufman, Plotsky, Nemeroff, & Charney, 2000).

Sexual Abuse in Childhood

Childhood sexual abuse makes humans more susceptible to adult-onset depression. This finding might shed light on the gender difference in depression. As stated earlier, women are much more likely to suffer from depression than men. Likewise, childhood sexual abuse of girls is much more common than that of boys (Weiss, Longhurst, & Mazure, 1999).

Christine Heim, working with colleagues at Emory University, conducted a study with three groups of women: women with a history of early childhood abuse with no current symptoms of depression, women with a history of childhood abuse with current depression, and women with depression who suffered no childhood abuse (Heim, Newport, Bonsall, Miller, & Nemeroff, 2001). The researchers measured the responses of each group to the administration of the stress hormones, CRH, and ACTH.

The women suffering depression with no history of sexual abuse exhibited a blunted response to CRH and the abused women with no signs of depression exhibited an exaggerated response to CRH compared with the control group. These findings suggest that women who had suffered childhood abuse but were currently experiencing no depression had an altered pituitary and adrenal response to the administration of stress hormones. Because of continuous homeostatic processes in the brain, these alterations could lead to a downregulation of CRH receptors and the future expression of anxiety and depression. That the brain continued to be modified 20 years after a stressful event is testament to both the impact of the abuse and the brain's resilience.

Seasonal Changes in Light

Seasonal changes influence moods in some of us. People who experience depressive symptoms during the winter in high latitudes, when the days are short, suffer from **seasonal affective disorder (SAD)**. A common therapy for this "winter depression" is mere exposure to bright light.

seasonal affective disorder (SAD) Form of depression that occurs in winter months when the duration of natural light decreases.

Locations with extended darkness are especially likely to induce SAD in vulnerable people. For example, in the northern Russian village of Lovozero, at 10:00 a.m. in the winter it looks more like midnight. Actually, if artificial light was no longer available, it might be adaptive to experience lower activity levels at a time when it would be difficult to maneuver around a dark environment. In fact, although disturbed sleep is one of the most prominent symptoms of depression, evidenced by longer sleep latencies, more nighttime wakefulness, and earlier awakenings in the morning, SAD patients are more likely to sleep longer than their control counterparts (Soldatos & Bergiannaki, 1999).

In places such as Lovozero, light therapy begins early to reestablish hormonal balances; in young children, the light seems to be necessary for bone growth; as they grow older, light therapy may be used to alter moods (Achenbach, 2001). Interestingly, a SAD patient who responds successfully to just an hour of light therapy is likely to respond successfully to pharmacological therapy as well (Sher et al., 2001).

TREATMENT FOR DEPRESSION

With so much information relating to causes of depression, you might think that researchers are close to finding an effective treatment for this condition. Although impressive research is being conducted, a miracle cure is certainly not within our grasp. Given the multifaceted nature of depression, it is no surprise that treatment strategies are diverse. Pharmacotherapy, electroconvulsive shock therapy, transcranial magnetic stimulation, and cognitive-behavioral therapies all are enlisted in the fight against depression, as is the herbal remedy St. John's wort, described in Box 9.3.

Pharmacotherapy

In the 1950s, **iproniazid**, a compound developed as an antibacterial agent, was serendipitously found to improve the moods of patients taking the drug to treat tuberculosis. This prompted the American psychiatrist Nathan Kline to carry out clinical trials of iproniazid's behavioral effects, which showed that it was an effective antidepressant. Although it was widely used at the end of the 1950s, the mechanism of action was not known.

In the next few years, it became apparent that iproniazid inhibited monoamine oxidase (MAO), an enzyme described in Chapter 5 that participates in inactivating the monoamine transmitters: serotonin, NE, and dopamine. Thus, iproniazid seemed to work because it increases the duration of synaptic activation of some combination of the three monoamines. This drug was the first of the **monoamine oxidase inhibitors (MAOIs)**.

Another drug, **imipramine**, was originally synthesized by the Swiss pharmaceutical company Geigy as a potential antipsychotic drug to be used with schizophrenic patients. After finding that it was not an effective antipsychotic, Roland Kuhn, a Swiss psychiatrist, observed that it had antidepressant properties. The acceptance of imipramine as an antidepressant quickly spread, and it became the first in a long series of drugs known as **tricyclic antidepressants**, drugs that increase the activity of serotonin in the synapse by blocking its reuptake back into the presynaptic neuron.

Once again, clinical efficacy was determined before there was any idea of the mechanism of the drug. In a few years, however, researchers discovered

iproniazid Drug developed in the 1950s as an antibacterial agent but later found to have antidepressant effects in patients. Researchers later showed that this drug was a monoamine oxidase inhibitor, which prolonged the presence of monoamines in the synapse.

monoamine oxidase inhibitors (MAOIs) Class of drugs that deactivate monoamine oxidase in the synaptic area so that the monoamines have a prolonged period of activity.

imipramine Synthesized originally for treatment of schizophrenic patients, this drug was observed to have antidepressant qualities. Researchers found that it influenced the synapse by blocking the reuptake of monoamine transmitters back into the terminal.

tricyclic antidepressants Drugs such as imipramine that increase the activity of serotonin (along with other monoamines) in the synapse by blocking its reuptake into the presynaptic neuronal terminal.

Box 9.3

Brain Matters

St. John's Wort

St. John's wort (*Hypericum perforatum*) is a small shrub with bright yellow flowers that appear in midsummer. It is thought that the shrub received its name because the flowers bloom about the time of St. John the Baptist's birthday. In the seventh century, this wildflower was found to be a useful treatment against worms, madness, and melancholy (Field, Monti, Greeson, & Kunkel, 2000). Today, worms are less a threat to our health, and interest in the plant's ability to treat depression is at an all-time high. In 1998, sales of this herbal remedy approached $400 million in the United States, which was modest compared with the $6 billion spent on St. John's wort in Europe. In Germany, St. John's wort is the leading treatment for depression—it is prescribed 20 times more often than fluoxetine (Prozac) (DiCarlo, Borrelli, Ernst, & Izzo, 2001; Greeson, Sanford, & Monti, 2001).

Because St. John's wort is considered a natural remedy for depression, it might be more attractive than other antidepressants prescribed by a physician. It is difficult, however, to differentiate between natural remedies and synthesized drugs concerning actions in the brain; it's not always the case that a "natural" remedy is milder or less harmful than a prescribed medication. Even if a product can be easily bought in any health food store, it is always important to check the empirical literature to investigate clinical efficacy, toxicity, and side effects before using it. Although a few European studies suggest that St. John's wort is more effective for the treatment of mild to moderate than severe depression, a recent multisite, randomized, double-blind, placebo-controlled study found no significant improvement compared with placebo in patients diagnosed with major depression. It is interesting to note that the approved antidepressant sertraline (Zoloft) also failed to differentiate itself from placebo in the two primary outcome measures (Kupfer & Frank, 2002).

Fewer adverse side effects have been noted with St. John's wort than with synthetic antidepressants, but some users report tiredness, dizziness, dry mouth, gastrointestinal irritation, headaches, and restlessness. High doses might lead to photosensitization (resulting in skin irritations on exposure to ultraviolet light) in fair-skinned people (DiCarlo et al., 2001). The mode of action of St. John's wort is still a bit of a mystery. A considerable amount of research suggests a complex array of effects. Primarily, like other antidepressants, it inhibits reuptake of monoamines—noradrenaline, dopamine, and serotonin—with equal efficacy. Unlike other antidepressants, St. John's wort also inhibits the reuptake of GABA and glutamate.

Because of the number of transmitters affected by this medicinal herb, it is considered a nonselective reuptake blocker. St. John's wort achieves its reuptake ability by elevating sodium ion concentrations. This treatment has similar effects on the regulation of certain receptor types of the monoamine transmitters as do antidepressants (Nathan, 2001). In a more "radical" line of research, St. John's wort has been observed to be a potent inhibitor of oxygen free radicals (at low doses) that inhabit the nervous system and cause damage with their high reactivity levels. If this finding holds true, this herb might also have therapeutic potential in protecting against neurodegenerative diseases in the elderly (Hunt, Lester, Lester, & Tackett, 2001). Obviously, more scientific digging is required to determine the efficacy of this flowering weed (Shelton, 2009).

---

that, like iproniazid, imipramine alters the amine transmitters. Julius Axelrod, a biochemist, found that imipramine worked by blocking reuptake of the monoamine transmitters. In 1970, he won the Nobel Prize for this important work elucidating the biosynthesis and subsequent degradation of the monoamine transmitters.

Are you surprised at the lack of insight that attended the discovery of the early antidepressant drugs? Clearly, it would have been preferable to have had a plan and then conduct studies to confirm the hypotheses, but like so many important events in science, the discoveries happened quite by accident. The important aspect of this story is that the scientists were

fluoxetine Selective serotonin reuptake inhibitor (SSRI) produced by Eli Lilly pharmaceutical company in 1985; this drug had the specific effect of blocking the reuptake of serotonin.

clever enough to identify something important and further develop that line of research.

The process became a little more organized at the point when Axelrod went on to establish that specific proteins could be used to selectively transport NE, dopamine, or serotonin. Although attention was first directed toward the selective reuptake of NE and dopamine, research eventually shifted toward the selective reuptake of serotonin—the SSRIs discussed in Chapter 8 as a treatment for obsessive–compulsive disorder. As you are probably aware, the SSRI fluoxetine (Prozac) has enjoyed enormous popularity. It is interesting to note that it is not more effective than its antecedent imipramine; it just has fewer side effects (Barondes, 1993).

Although we will now discuss the antidepressant drugs in terms of the relevant neurotransmitters, some general aspects of the antidepressants need to be clarified. As previously discussed, antidepressants alter the synapse of a particular neurotransmitter system in a number of hours or days. Their clinical effects, however, are not experienced for weeks.

Although more questions than answers remain concerning the mechanisms of antidepressants, their administration is the front line of defense for most practitioners. In many cases, antidepressants are prescribed in combination with some form of supportive psychotherapy (Richelson, 2001). The following discussion considers antidepressant drugs in the following six categories: MAOIs, SSRIs, NE transport blockers, dopamine transport blockers, 5-HT$_{2A}$ receptor blockers, and CRH blockers (Table 9.4).

Serotonergic manipulation. As described in Chapter 8, the earlier MAOIs are unpopular in practice today because of side effects including elevations in blood pressure (if the patient ingests food containing tyramine, such as cheese and beer), headaches, nausea, and sweating. A newer MAOI, moclobemide, does not interact with diet, but it is currently not available in the United States (Tiller, 1993).

In the midst of a flurry of activity springing from scientists in various labs working on versions of more general and specific reuptake inhibitors, on May 8, 1972, David Wong and his colleagues at the Eli Lilly pharmaceutical company produced **fluoxetine**. Eventually, research started to suggest that the SSRIs might have an antidepressant effect, and in 1985, clinical trial evidence suggested that the drug might be helpful in humans. Fluoxetine was licensed in the United States in 1987 (Richelson, 2001).

Although researchers knew they had produced an SSRI, they were not clear about how the drug might be useful. Because serotonin was known to be so widely and diffusely dispersed across the brain, it was doubtful that a drug that increased the synaptic availability of 5-HT would have the specific effect of treating depression. Long-term administration of SSRIs to animals results in desensitization and downregulation of

Table 9.4 Various Antidepressants and Their Associated Functions

Function	Antidepressant
Monoamine oxidase inhibitor	Isocarboxazid
	Phenelzine
	Tranylcypromine
Norepinephrine transport blocker	Amoxapine
	Desipramine
	Doxepin
	Maprotiline
	Nortriptyline
	Protriptyline
	Reboxetine
Serotonin transport blocker	Amitriptyline
	Citalopram
	Clomipramine
	Fluoxetine
	Fluvoxamine
	Imipramine
	Paroxetine
	Sertraline
	Trimipramine
	Venlafaxine
Dopamine transport blocker	Bupropion
Serotonin 5-HT$_{2A}$ receptor blocker	Mirtazapine
	Nefazodone
	Trazodone
Corticotropin-releasing hormone blocker	Antalarmin

Adapted from Richelson (2001, p. 513).

serotonergic autoreceptors. These effects result in increased firing rates in the raphe neurons, increased manufacturing of serotonin, and an enhanced release of serotonin (Richelson, 2001).

These specific effects in experimental animals, however, have not been confirmed in humans. In addition to the research on $5HT_{1A}$, $5HT_{1B}$, and $5HT_{1D}$ receptors, there is conflicting evidence of both downregulation in $5\text{-}HT_{2A}$ receptors in depressed patients and antidepressant-induced upregulation of these receptors (Massou et al., 1997; Yatham et al., 1999). Even more confusing, in the studies that reported downregulation due to antidepressant treatment, the downregulation of $5\text{-}HT_{2A}$ receptors was not due to a clinical effect of the drug; both responders (who were experiencing less depression) and nonresponders (whose condition had not changed) demonstrated reduced receptor numbers.

Nevertheless, certain antidepressants specifically antagonize the $5\text{-}HT_{2A}$ receptors (examples are amoxapine, nefazodone, and mirtazapine). Research suggests that these antidepressants might be superior to SSRIs since they are less likely to induce sexual side effects. In fact, these drugs may be used in combination with SSRIs in patients who have intolerable sexual side effects due to SSRI administration (for example, lack of arousal and difficulty achieving orgasm) (Richelson, 2001).

Helen Mayberg, currently at Emory University, and her colleagues found a metabolic effect in the brain specific to an SSRI-induced clinical effect (Mayberg et al., 2000). Using PET scans, these researchers looked at the changes in brain glucose metabolism in depressed men being treated with fluoxetine. The patients were tested following both 1 week and 6 weeks of pharmacological treatment.

Whereas the glucose metabolic patterns were similar for the nonresponders and responders at the 1-week examination, differences were observed after 6 weeks. Specifically, clinical improvement was associated with decreases in glucose metabolism in the limbic and striatal areas (for example, the cingulate and hippocampal areas) and increases in the brain stem and dorsal cortical areas (for example, the prefrontal, parietal, and cingulate cortices). Similar findings were reported when depressed patients were given a different SSRI, paroxetine. Following successful therapy, increased metabolic rates were observed in the prefrontal areas and decreased rates in the hippocampal area (Kennedy et al., 2001). Thus, according to these studies, it seems that a reciprocal, as opposed to a unidirectional, pattern of glucose metabolism is important for treatment success.

Another recent study suggests that the effects of SSRIs are quite complicated. In this investigation, Eberhart Fuchs and his colleagues at the German Primate Center in Göttingen gave the European drug tianeptine to tree shrews (small primates) undergoing social stress (Czeh et al., 2001). Whereas animals typically respond to this paradigm with a shrinkage in the hippocampal area (also observed in chronic depression), this drug blocked the effect. The interesting and counterintuitive part of this study is that tianeptine is not an SSRI but an *SSRE*, specific serotonin reuptake enhancer; instead of inhibiting reuptake, it enhances reuptake. Certainly, more research needs to be done on this drug before we understand its effect and potential therapeutic value.

In sum, although the SSRIs are the most popular pharmacological treatment for depression, we are just beginning to determine the complexity of their effects in the brain. Recall that SSRIs have been implicated in

reboxetine Relatively new drug that selectively inhibits the reuptake of noradrenaline in the synapse. Used as an antidepressant, this drug is thought to be more effective than other antidepressants at restoring social functioning in depressed patients.

antalarmin New drug that inhibits the release of corticotropin-releasing hormone and has been found in animal models to reduce anxiety-like behaviors in animals. Researchers are hopeful that this drug may be used as an antidepressant in humans in the future.

neurogenesis, suggesting that these drugs mitigate depressive symptoms because of this effect. A major concern surrounding SSRIs is their side effects. Up to 75% of patients experience sexual disturbances; other side effects include gastrointestinal problems and motor effects (Richelson, 2001). Finally, some have proposed that the evidence supporting the clear superiority of SSRIs over placebos in clinical trials is not sufficient.

Using a meta-analysis to investigate the influence of SSRIs over a placebo, Kirsch and Sapirstein (1998) conclude that inactive placebos contribute to 75% of the effect of this class of drug. As you might guess, this article is controversial, as shown in the editor's explanatory disclaimer, which appears at the bottom of the title page. Such a disclaimer is rarely included in research articles, suggesting that, for better or for worse, this research question about the clinical efficacy of Prozac has become much more than a simple research question but rather a question complicated by ethics, politics, and profits (Kirsch & Antonuccio, 2002).

Noradrenergic manipulation. In an attempt to identify an antidepressant that is superior to the older tricyclics, drugs are also targeted toward the noradrenergic system. Recall that the noradrenergic system is involved in vigilance and drive—two factors involved in depression—and that the effects of all three monoamines involve mood, emotion, and cognition. Serotonin and dopamine also influence appetite and sex, which might be related to some side effects of the SSRIs.

Noradrenaline, however, influences social functioning but has no effect on sex and appetite. Perhaps a drug that influenced only the noradrenergic system would have fewer side effects and an added benefit of restoring social function (a symptom listed in the DSM diagnostic criteria for major depression). That is exactly what is observed with the new selective noradrenergic reuptake inhibitor **reboxetine**. In addition to restoring social functioning, this drug increases the latency for patients to enter rapid eye movement (REM) sleep. Additionally, when patients who are not responding to fluoxetine are switched to reboxetine, positive results have been observed with manageable side effects (Fava, McGrath, & Sheu, 2003). Although reboxetine is not currently approved for use in the United States, it has been approved in 21 countries, including the United Kingdom, Italy, and Germany. It will be interesting to follow its effects and success if and when it is introduced in the United States (Dencker, 2000).

Inhibiting CRH. As you know, the stress response is an integral component of the symptoms of depression. Consequently, researchers are beginning to think about drugs that might influence the HPA axis. One such anti-CRH drug, **antalarmin**, was recently tested with rhesus macaques. Monkeys were exposed to intense social stress consisting of placing two unfamiliar males in cages adjacent to their home cage. Antalarmin reduced anxiety-like or stress responses such as grimacing, body tremors, teeth gnashing, urination, and defecation while increasing exploratory and sexual behaviors. Further tests confirmed that this drug diminished the increases in CRH in the cerebrospinal fluid (Habib et al., 2000). Based on such results, it is likely that we will hear more about anti-CRH drugs in the near future (Zoumakis, Rice, Gold, & Chrousos, 2006).

In sum, whereas SSRIs still enjoy successful sales, many new types of drugs have been introduced. New attention is being focused on noradrenaline manipulation, specific serotonergic receptors, and anti-CRH drugs. Whereas dopaminergic reuptake blockers such as bupropion (Zyban) have been used, it is suspected that this drug (also marketed as Wellbutrin) also influences noradrenergic systems (Ascher et al., 1995).

Additionally, pharmaceutical companies are seeking drugs that block both NE and serotonergic transporters (double-action drugs such as venlafaxine and milnacipran) or that block the transport of NE, serotonin, and dopamine. These drugs are known as SNRIs (serotonin and neorepinephrine reuptake inhibitors) and **SNUBs (super neurotransmitter uptake blockers)** (Montgomery, 2000; Richelson, 2001).

You may be thinking that the new drugs are simply new versions of the original tricyclics that blocked the reuptake of all of the monoamines. In a sense that is correct, but the new generation of antidepressants is weaker than the original tricyclic compounds. This weaker inhibition of reuptake should minimize the adverse side effects that plagued the original tricyclics (Richelson, 2001; Koenig & Thase, 2009). The push for new forms of antidepressant drugs is fueled by the many controversial issues raised about the current drugs. In addition to the unwanted side-effects, these drugs only affect about half of the patients diagnosed with depression, typically after several weeks of agonizing symptoms (Koenig & Thase, 2009).

Electroconvulsive Therapy

ECT involves using electrical stimulation in anesthetized patients to induce a series of seizures to help patients combat the symptoms of depression (Krystal et al., 2000). As mentioned in Chapter 2, ECT is one of the oldest neurobiological treatments for mental illness. As psychopharmacology became a more appealing method of treatment in the 1960s, the use of ECT decreased dramatically. During the past 20 years, however, its popularity has once again increased.

It is no surprise that ECT is back in favor: It is one of the most effective treatments for depression. The efficacy rate falls between 60% and 80%, a higher success rate than that of any other somatic treatment (Abrams, 1992). Because of the intensity of this treatment strategy and its fairly characteristic side effects (including transient disorientation and memory impairment), ECT is not a front-line therapy. Generally, ECT is offered as a second- or third-line defense against depression following unsuccessful attempts with antidepressants and cognitive-behavioral therapies.

Since the resurrection of ECT, research has been conducted on parameters such as optimal electrical dose, electrode placement, and treatment schedules. Optimal electrical doses are determined by the degree to which the dose exceeds the individual's seizure threshold. Bilateral electrode placement therapies are more effective than unilateral placements. And although a schedule of three sessions per week is associated with the most rapid recovery from depression, it carries the cost of significant side effects such as memory loss. Consequently, this treatment schedule is used only in drastic cases such as when patients are refusing to eat; in most cases, two treatments per week are administered (Nobler, Sackheim, & Devanand, 2000).

Although ECT sounds draconian, it is effective at reducing depression symptoms. Research suggests that ECT does not create any new brain damage in the patient. For example, Zachrisson and colleagues at Goteborg University investigated the effect of ECT on cerebral structure and function

SNUBs (super neurotransmitter uptake blockers) Drugs that are designed to block the reuptake of more than one monoamine transmitter. These drugs differ from the original tricyclics in their weaker nature and consequently fewer side effects.

repetitive transcranial magnetic stimulation (rTMS) Relatively new antidepressant treatment that involves placing a powerful electromagnet or coil on the scalp. The magnet produces depolarization in the underlying neurons in the brain.

by measuring markers of degeneration in neurons and glial cells found in the cerebrospinal fluid. Following six ECT treatments over a 2-week period, all nine patients were significantly improved (less depressed), demonstrating the clinical efficacy of this treatment. Interestingly, ECT did not significantly alter levels of the markers; further, the integrity of the blood–brain barrier was found to be unaltered by the treatment (Zachrisson et al., 2000).

Perhaps the most curious aspect is the fact that, after all these years of using ECT, researchers are still unsure about exactly how it works to reduce depression. Recently, however, several studies have identified ECT effects that provide clues concerning its clinical efficacy. In one study, patients who responded successfully to ECT demonstrated increases in regional cerebral blood flow (rCBF) that approached the rCBF of nondepressed patients (Milo et al., 2001). Additionally, as previously mentioned, ECT leads to enhanced neurogenesis in rats. Another study conducted on rats found that ECT, along with antidepressants, decreases spontaneous firing in the locus coeruleus, which reacts to environmental events (Grant & Weiss, 2001). Yet another study reported that ECT results in lower glucose metabolism in the areas of the frontal and parietal cortex, left temporal cortex, and cingulate gyrus (Nobler et al., 2001). Perhaps, in some cases, part of the recovery mechanism of ECT involves decreased activity around certain perseverating cognitive/emotional brain circuits.

In sum, although ECT is controversial, recent research has provided guidelines for its administration that result in fewer cognitive side effects and increased clinical efficacy. The acceptance of this treatment, however, remains highly variable across the spectrum of mental health practitioners.

Repetitive Transcranial Magnetic Stimulation

Although the overwhelming treatment emphasis for depression has been on antidepressant drugs since the 1950s and 1960s, a different somatic treatment strategy introduced in 1985 involves the use of powerful electromagnets (Barker, Jalinous, & Freeston, 1985; George, Nahas, et al., 1999). Because electricity and magnetism are interdependent, **repetitive transcranial magnetic stimulation (rTMS)** works by placing a powerful electromagnet on the scalp (Figure 9.5). The magnet emits high-intensity currents in a rapid on/off succession that depolarize the underlying neurons. The rTMS magnetic field is about 1,000 times the strength of a refrigerator magnet (enough to wrench a paper clip from grasp) and lasts about 100–200 microseconds.

Conveniently, rTMS treatments can be administered in outpatient settings. Unlike ECT, this treatment neither causes seizures nor requires anesthesia (George et al., 2000). Although rTMS is a new technique that requires further research, the side effects currently seem to be fewer and less severe than those related to ECT. Typically, patients report mild to severe headaches and discomfort at the stimulation sites; these effects usually respond to acetaminophen.

It is important to distinguish rTMS from the questionable new-age technique of placing low-intensity magnets on the

Figure 9.5
Transcranial magnetic stimulation Transcranial magnetic stimulation involves situating a strong magnet on the scalp. Changes in the magnetic field influence action potentials in neural tissue and have been found to have clinical efficacy in depression patients.

GEORGE RUHE/THE NEW YORK TIMES

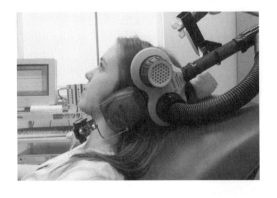

body. These magnets are weaker, are not necessarily placed on the brain, and are constantly on—and there is no empirical evidence concerning their effectiveness. rTMS treatments, on the other hand, have been subjected to clinical trials. George et al. (2000) delivered daily rTMS to the left prefrontal cortical area for 2 weeks and found this treatment to reduce the depressive symptoms in significantly more depressed patients than the sham treatment (50% of patients in the treatment group improved, whereas 0% in the sham group improved). In this study, about 6% of the sessions resulted in mild headaches and no seizures or memory deficits were observed.

As is the case with ECT, researchers are still not certain how rTMS works, but a few studies suggest some possible mechanisms. Functional neuroimaging studies of healthy, nondepressed adults indicate that prefrontal rTMS results in subsequent activation in the cingulate gyrus, amygdala, and other areas that have been implicated in the maintenance of mood (George, Stallings et al., 1999). In another study, conducted on rats bred for either high or low anxiety–related behavior, rTMS had an effect on coping behavior in the high-anxiety animals. When placed in the forced swimming test, the high-anxiety animals actively struggled more to escape the tank and floated less. The high-anxiety rats receiving rTMS had lower corticosterone levels than the nontreated high-anxiety animals (Keck et al., 2001).

Similar to the effects observed with antidepressants, rTMS exerts an effect on depressed human patients while having no effect on nondepressed individuals (Keck et al., 2001). Another rat study found that, similar to antidepressants, rTMS results in decreased sensitivity of the 5-HT_{1A} and 5-HT_{1B} autoreceptors. Thus, it is possible that rTMS and antidepressant drugs may share some common mechanisms of action (Gur, Lerer, Dremencov, & Newman, 2000).

rTMS is still in its preliminary stages of testing, but the current research suggests that it exerts at least short-term effects on depressive symptoms. Although we don't know the true duration of the benefits of rTMS, this strategy may be used as an alternative to ECT in treatment-resistant patients. Additionally, rTMS could potentially be used to relieve the symptoms of depression until the clinical effects of the drugs are apparent (George, Nahas, et al., 1999).

Deep Brain Stimulation (DBS)

Recently, a more specific version of brain stimulation has been assessed in patients who have not responded to traditional treatments. Helen Mayberg and her colleagues, then at the University of Toronto, published a report in 2005 indicating that the surgical placement of electrodes into the subgenual cingulate gyrus (described earlier in this chapter) offered promise in the treatment of depressive symptoms. The implanted electrodes' ability to chronically stimulate areas around the subgenual cingulate gyrus significantly decreased symptoms in four of six patients. Subsequent PET scans revealed decreased blood flow in limbic and cortical brain areas (Mayberg et al., 2005). This procedure is currently being assessed in larger scale clinical trials in the US.

In an article entitled *Happiness is a warm electrode* published in *Popular Science*, the case of one of the patients receiving DBS therapy was discussed (Mone, 2007). Diane Hire had been depressed for 20 years and had

cognitive-behavioral therapy (CBT) Therapy developed in the 1960s that involves the therapist working with the depressed patient to educate him or her about the disorder so that they can eventually alter behaviors and cognitions to reduce the symptoms of depression.

failed to respond to years of therapy, ten different forms of antidepressants, and six rounds of ECT. After voluntecring for a clinical trial assessing DBS, her head was shaved so that two holes could be drilled enabling the neurosurgeon to insert electrodes into the subgenual cingulate area of her brain. The electrodes were plugged into two small battery packs implanted in her chest. When the first current was tested, enough to power a wristwatch, Diane's initial response was that she felt warm, then she reported that the room looked brighter and, for the first time in two decades, she told the neurosurgeon that she felt happy. As you'll recall, this treatment has been approved for severe cases of OCD. Obviously this controversial treatment strategy requires continued research to firmly establish its efficacy rate.

Cognitive-Behavioral Therapy

The most popular form of **cognitive-behavioral therapy (CBT)** was established by Aaron Beck and his team in the 1960s and was tested for clinical efficacy in 1977. Since that time, Beck's CBT has received extensive support in both group and individual formats and in both inpatient and outpatient settings. Generally, CBT involves (1) educating the patient about how cognitions influence emotions, (2) discussing how patients can serve as their own cotherapists and change their behavior and cognitions to alter depression, and (3) treatment sessions in which the patient and therapist construct and work through an agenda in which role playing and imaging serve as tools for restructuring the patients' cognitions and behaviors (Deckersbach, Gershuny, & Otto, 2000).

When compared to antidepressants, CBT offers approximately equal clinical efficacy. In one study, treatment outcomes for a 12-week session of either CBT or imipramine were compared. Following treatment, 62% of the patients receiving CBT demonstrated significant improvement, whereas 56% of the imipramine patients responded favorably (Hollon et al., 1992). Consistent with this finding, a review of 58 studies conducted between 1976 and 1986 investigating the effectiveness of CBT found that, generally, CBT was equally as effective as antidepressants (Robinson, Berman, & Neimeyer, 1990).

Some researchers have attempted to combine pharmacotherapy and CBT to augment the success rate. Although response rates are a bit higher than for either treatment in isolation, the differences have failed to reach statistical significance (Deckersbach et al., 2000). In T. M. Luhrmann's book *Of Two Minds: The Growing Disorder in American Psychiatry* (2000), a case is made for the combination of talk therapy and pharmacotherapy, citing evidence of a compromised psychological treatment system resulting from drastic financial cuts for talk therapy with patients. Based on the effectiveness of both pharmacotherapy and CBT, Deckersbach and colleagues have proposed that pharmacotherapy be used for severe cases and CBT for low to moderate depression.

One advantage CBT appears to have over pharmacotherapy is its long-term protection against the hauntingly high relapse rate of 80% observed following pharmacotherapeutic approaches (Jarrett et al., 2001). Relapse rates are lower following CBT than following antidepressant therapy. For example, in one interesting study, 121 depressed patients were assigned to groups receiving CBT, relaxation therapy, nondirective psychotherapy, or pharmacotherapy. Two years following treatment, 64% of the CBT patients remained significantly improved compared with 28% of the pharmacotherapy patients (psychotherapy and relaxation treatments resulted in 36% and 26% sustained recovery rates, respectively) (MacLean & Hakstian, 1990).

Because of the long-term effects of cognitive therapy, Martin Seligman and his colleagues at the University of Pennsylvania investigated the effectiveness of exposing at-risk individuals to an 8-week prevention workshop (Seligman, Schulman, & DeRubeis, 1999). This workshop decreased the number of subsequent moderate depressive episodes but had no effect on severe depressive episodes. Certainly, the establishment of therapies that might prevent subsequent depression in vulnerable individuals deserves further study.

Of course, other behavioral and cognitive therapies have been effective. Behavioral Activation is a form of therapy that focuses on the patient's interactions with the environment, identifying any avoidance behaviors that may be keeping the person from achieving goals (Martell, Addis, & Jacobsen, 2001). For example, a person may report feeling depressed because he or she doesn't have a job. A therapist utilizing Behavioral Activation analyzes the behavior that will increase the probability of finding a job, emphasizing the problems associated with any form of avoidance behavior (i.e., not looking for a job because you don't feel that anyone would want to hire you). Sona Dimidjian (2006) at the University of Washington and her colleagues compared the efficacy of behavioral activation therapy and found that this type of therapy was more effective than SSRI therapy, cognitive therapy, and placebo groups in the most severely depressed patients. Also important from a clinical perspective was the observation that the patients were more compliant with the behavioral and cognitive therapies than for the SSRI treatment.

As mentioned previously, physical exercise relieves depressive symptoms in humans (Hill et al., 1993). In a rat model, exercise, used in combination with antidepressants, was found to increase BDNF, a neurotrophic factor discussed earlier that has been implicated in depression (Russo-Neustadt et al., 2001).

BIPOLAR DISORDER

As observed in Table 9.1, mood disorders consist of more than one variation of mood extremes. In addition to experiencing depressed emotions and activity, some people experience abnormally elevated moods. These elevated moods are typically described as **manic episodes**. About 1%–1.5% of the population experience symptoms of both depression and mania and are diagnosed with bipolar disorder (National Institute of Mental Health, 2001; Strakowski, DelBello, Adler, Cecil, & Sax, 2000). See Table 9.5 for diagnostic criteria.

Typically, the onset of mania occurs abruptly and lasts from a few days to a few weeks. The manic episodes are usually briefer than the depressive episodes. Unfortunately, manic episodes often are followed by depressive episodes, placing the patient on an emotional roller coaster.

Although some patients report that the exhilaration experienced when manic can be rewarding and pleasurable at times, these episodes typically come with great personal cost. They affect patients' marriages, businesses, finances, and health; and they lead to exhaustion, occasional drug use, and other risk-taking behaviors that place the patient in frequent danger. At the

manic episodes
Hyperactivity characterized by euphoria and impaired judgment; exists with depression in bipolar disorder.

Table 9.5 Diagnostic Criteria for Manic Episode

A. A distinct period of persistently elevated, expansive, or irritable mood, lasting at least 1 week (or any duration if hospitalization is necessary).

B. During the period of mood disturbance, three (or more) of the following symptoms have persisted (four if the mood is only irritable) and have been present to a significant degree:

    (1) inflated self-esteem or grandiosity

    (2) decreased need for sleep (e.g., feels rested after only 3 hours of sleep)

    (3) more talkative than usual or pressure to keep talking

    (4) flight of ideas or subjective experience that thoughts are racing

    (5) distractibility (i.e., attention too easily drawn to unimportant or irrelevant external stimuli)

    (6) increase in goal-directed activity (either socially, at work or school, or sexually) or psychomotor agitation

    (7) excessive involvement in pleasurable activities that have a high potential for painful consequences (e.g., engaging in unrestrained buying sprees, sexual indiscretions, or foolish business investments)

C. The symptoms do not meet criteria for a mixed episode.

D. The mood disturbance is sufficiently severe to cause marked impairment in occupational functioning or in usual social activities or relationships with others or to necessitate hospitalization to prevent harm to self or others, or there are psychotic features. The symptoms are not due to the direct physiological effects of a substance (e.g., a drug of abuse, a medication, or other treatment) or a general medical condition (e.g., hyperthyroidism).

Note: Maniclike episodes that are clearly caused by somatic antidepressant treatment (e.g., medication, electroconvulsive therapy, light therapy) should not count toward a diagnosis of bipolar I disorder.

American Psychiatric Association (2000, p. 368).

extreme, the manic patient is at an increased risk for death due to cardiac complications and has an increased tendency toward suicide in the transition from mania to depression, when patients realize the inappropriateness of their behavior (Andreasen & Black, 2001). Box 9.4 focuses on Kay Redfield Jamison's experience with bipolar disorder.

Tracing the Neurobiological Roots of Bipolar Disorder

A review of the literature by Baumann and Bogerts (2001) suggests that the brains of patients suffering from bipolar disorder differ significantly from those of patients who are not suffering from mood disorders. Specifically, the basal ganglia are somewhat smaller in both bipolar and depressive patients; the most drastic reductions are found in the nucleus accumbens, that key structure in the translation from environmental stimuli to motivation of response. Structural deficits are also found in the dorsal raphe nucleus, a site for serotonin production.

In another review of the neuroimaging literature, abnormalities were observed in the striatum, amygdala, and PFC. This review supports the notion of frontal–subcortical circuits being involved in bipolar disorder (Strakowski et al., 2000). Additionally, decreased cerebellar size has been observed (Stoll, Renshaw, Yurgelun-Todd, & Cohen, 2000).

The most common finding of MRI studies is the presence of white matter hyperintensities at higher rates than expected. *White matter hyperintensities* are small areas characterized by a higher signal intensity than that of

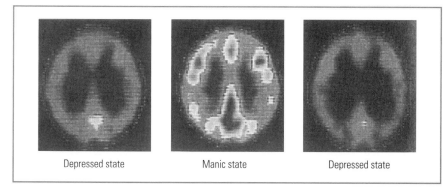

Depressed state   Manic state   Depressed state

Figure 9.6
Brain activity and bipolar disorder This positron emission tomographic (PET) scan shows a dramatic increase in the brain's metabolization of glucose when the patient goes from a depressed to a manic state.
COURTESY OF DRS. LEWIS BAXTER AND MICHAEL E. PHELPS, UCLA SCHOOL OF MEDICINE

the surrounding tissue. These hyperintensities are most commonly found in aging patients and patients suffering from cardiovascular events. Also, processes such as demyelination, *astrogliosis* (formation of new or growth of existing astrocytes), and axonal loss may lead to the formation of white matter hyperintensities.

Although these anomalies are observed in bipolar patients at a higher rate than expected, the observation that most bipolar patients do not have the hyperintensities suggests that they may play a minimal causal role in this disorder. Thus, it is more likely that they form because of the lifestyle that is characteristic of manic patients (higher rates of substance abuse and cardiovascular risk) than because of a patient's susceptibility to bipolar disorder. However, further research is needed to clarify the role of white matter hyperintensities in bipolar disorder (Stoll et al., 2000).

Lower whole-brain glucose metabolic activity has been observed across the brains of bipolar patients experiencing bipolar depression than in patients experiencing bipolar mania (Baxter et al., 1985). Although one study has shown higher whole-brain blood flow during mania (Rush, Schlesser, Stokely, Bonte, & Altshuller, 1982), many have failed to show blood-flow differences in bipolar mania or depression compared with healthy controls (Strakowski et al., 2000) (see Figure 9.6).

Treatment for Bipolar Disorder

Pharmacotherapy has been quite successful in treating bipolar disorder. Although the chemical element **lithium** was recognized over 150 years ago as having some potential for treating affective disorders, its potential efficacy as a treatment for bipolar disorder did not surface until the work of John Cade (1949). Cade, an Australian psychiatrist who reportedly had little research training, was working in a small hospital with minimal equipment when he became convinced that a toxic substance was contributing to the mood swings observed in mania and depression. Specifically, the presence of this hypothesized toxic substance contributed to mania and the absence of this substance contributed to the symptoms of depression.

To test his idea, Cade took the urine from his manic patients (he thought the urine might contain this toxic substance) and injected it into guinea pigs. All urine is toxic to guinea pigs, and Cade initially observed that the urine from the manic patients killed the animals at a faster rate—only about one-third of the typical lethal dose of urine from nonmanic patients was needed. At this point, Cade knew he was onto something. After elegantly separating

lithium Chemical element approved in the 1970s as a drug for treatment of bipolar disorder. Although the specific biological mechanism is unknown, lithium is known to share ionic properties with some of the important ions maintaining neural functions such as magnesium and calcium.

Box 9.4

A Case in Point

Kay Redfield Jamison

Kay Redfield Jamison has written four successful books on mental illness/health, and in November 2001, she was awarded the prestigious MacArthur Genius Grant. Jamison's first book, *An Unquiet Mind: A Memoir of Moods and Madness* (1996), carefully documents the highs and lows of her emotional struggles with bipolar disorder. Her first feeling of emotional despair occurred at the vulnerable age of 15, when her father, an Air Force meteorologist and pilot, moved the family from their familiar home in Washington, D.C., to California. Being a military kid in a school where most of the students' parents worked in the film industry was a bit overwhelming.

Although she began to make friends over the next couple of years, Jamison also became aware that she had intensive levels of energy that seemed to exhaust the people around her. During her first battle with mania, she felt a bit seduced by the seemingly positive symptoms of pleasure, promise, and a decreased need for sleep. But these periodic highs were followed by depressed phases in which she was preoccupied with the notion of death.

As an undergraduate at UCLA, Jamison struggled with managing classes around her diverse mood swings. She found some solace when the professor of her personality theory class asked her to assist in his research. She loved the independence and flexibility in her work schedule that accompanied the research. During her junior year, she opted to escape from her tumultuous life at UCLA by going to study and conduct research at the University of St. Andrews in Scotland. Her brother, who was studying abroad, encouraged her to venture out of the United States; that and her admiration of the Scottish music and poetry that she associated with her Scottish ancestry contributed to her decision to make the trip.

During that year Jamison worked with a prominent neurophysiologist, making electrophysiological recordings of locust auditory nerves. She found this research challenging, and she found the atmosphere in Scotland healing for the emotional wounds she had developed with her mental illness. On returning to UCLA, Jamison decided to pursue a career in psychology; she was especially interested in individual differences in emotional capacity. A reprieve in her illness enabled her to successfully complete graduate school, where she trained to become a clinician. Although she had been battling the highs and lows of bipolar

the chemical components of the urine from the manic patients, he found that urea was the toxic substance leading to the faster death of the guinea pigs. When he injected only urea, the guinea pigs responded as if they had received a urine injection. The other components of urine, uric acid and creatinine, failed to produce any toxic effects; but uric acid mildly enhanced the toxicity of urea.

Cade wanted to investigate further the finding that uric acid facilitated toxicity but ran into a hurdle trying to dissolve the uric acid crystals in water for the injections. To address the insolubility problem, he simply chose the most soluble urate, lithium, to combine with urea for injections. Subsequently, Cade injected a few guinea pigs with the urea that was saturated with lithium urate and waited to observe the toxic effects. He was very surprised to see that, instead of killing the guinea pigs, the urea's toxicity was reduced. Cade shifted his emphasis to the potential protective qualities of the lithium.

But how could lithium, which is found in nature in only small quantities compared with chemicals such as sodium, magnesium, potassium, and calcium, have such a striking effect? The answer was not clear, but Cade trusted his data and pursued his research. He switched from the lithium ion to lithium carbonate because it produced fewer troublesome side effects.

disorder for years, she did not recognize herself as a manic–depressive even after studying mental illness in graduate school.

On earning her doctorate, Jamison was hired in the Department of Psychiatry at UCLA, where she enthusiastically set out in her new career. She felt madness approaching during her first summer as a professor; her mania had progressed to behavior that raised suspicions in her colleagues and led to the demise of her first marriage. When she started to hallucinate, Jamison knew she had to get professional help.

Jamison was then introduced to lithium and was able to focus on her career once again. She wrote in *An Unquiet Mind*, "My work and professional life flowed. But nowhere did this, or my upbringing, or my intellect, or my character, prepare me for insanity" (1996, p. 81). Through this time, her psychiatrist recommended aggressive pharmacotherapy and psychoanalysis. Not wanting to surrender to the idea that she needed lithium to maintain a normal existence, she decided to stop taking her medication just 6 months after beginning it. She continued an on-again, off-again pattern of lithium use and active illness, which led to a suicide attempt. Ironically, Jamison took an overdose of the very drug that was saving her life—lithium. Her suicide attempt was unsuccessful, but it left her comatose. On recovering, Jamison learned to ride with her emotions and accomplished enough professionally to get tenure at UCLA.

After receiving tenure, Jamison was devastated when the man she was seeing died of a heart attack. Jamison decided to take a year's sabbatical in England, where she could focus on moods—mourning her friend and studying the relationship between mood disorders and eminent British writers and artists. This work later became the book *Touched with Fire* (1993).

Although many people with bipolar disorder struggle their entire lives and are unable to maximize their career potential, Kay Redfield Jamison has certainly thrived. She shared her mental illness with the world when she published *An Unquiet Mind*. Subsequently, she wrote a book on suicide entitled *Night Falls Fast* (1999), followed by *Exuberance: The Passion for Life* (2004) and, after her husband Richard Wyatt died, *Nothing Was the Same* (2009). After moving back to Washington, D.C., she accepted an appointment in the Psychiatry Department at Johns Hopkins University. She still takes lithium to protect against drastic mood fluctuation, but her maintenance doses are lower than the doses she started taking years ago.

Again, he found that lithium carbonate decreased the urea-induced mortality by 50%. And when Cade injected only lithium carbonate into the guinea pigs, he also observed interesting effects. Following injections, when he placed the guinea pigs on their backs, instead of the typical frantic attempts to return to their normal upright position, they just lay back and gazed at the experimenter.

Cade had seen enough to take his laboratory efforts to the clinic; he decided to try the lithium carbonate on manic patients. Following the old medical maxim *Primum non nocere* (First do no harm), he decided to be the first person to take the lithium pills. After observing no ill effects, he gave lithium pills to 10 manic patients. The results seemed miraculous; patients who had been institutionalized were released from their manic episodes and given an opportunity to live outside the hospital. In 1949, Cade published his findings in the *Medical Journal of Australia*.

Cade's exercise in cool logic is one of the best examples of serendipity that can be found in the literature. No theory current at the time suggested that lithium was beneficial in manic episodes, and it is unlikely that any scientist would have encountered its effectiveness in treating mania if Cade had not stumbled across it trying simply to find a salt that is more soluble than uric acid. Fortunately, Cade was informed enough to follow the intriguing findings he was reporting in this line of research and was able to improve

valproate Anticonvulsant drug that shows promise as an effective treatment for bipolar disorder.

the quality of life of hundreds of thousands of people suffering from manic episodes (Restak, 1994). Interestingly, Cade did not go on to research fame. He went back to his patients and never conducted research again.

Although Cade made his discovery in the 1940s, lithium was not approved in the United States until the early 1970s; until recently, it was the only drug available for treating bipolar disorder. Before reviewing the more recent drugs, let's take a look at the possible effects of lithium. At the outset, it is important to note that researchers still do not know the biological basis for its therapeutic efficacy. On a general level, the fact that lithium shares ionic properties known to regulate the nervous system with some of the heavy-hitting ions, such as sodium, magnesium, and calcium, may be very important. Its chemical similarity with these ions allows lithium easy access into cells, where it probably exerts an impact on a host of intracellular processes.

It is conceivable that the nonspecific aspect of lithium uptake in multiple types of cells may affect both poles of bipolar disorder. Additional studies suggest that lithium may influence protein kinase C, a ubiquitous enzyme in the brain that regulates both presynaptic and postsynaptic components of neural transmission (see Chapter 4). Research suggests that shortterm lithium exposure enhances protein kinase C–related effects and long-term exposure attenuates these responses.

Overall, lithium seems to enhance presynaptic activity in the serotonergic system, although this effect depends on the duration of treatment and the neuroanatomical site being tested. It has been suggested that the widespread nature of its effects leads to the reestablishment of homeostatic processing among the structures of the limbic system and its associated areas (this research was reviewed in Manji, McNamara, & Lenox, 2000).

Lithium's many unwanted side effects (including tremors, weight gain, gastrointestinal disturbances, frequent urination, memory problems, sedation, and decreased levels of thyroid hormones) have led researchers to search for less harmful pharmacological treatments (Strakowski et al., 2000). In fact, as delineated in the Jamison case study discussed earlier, if dosages are not closely monitored, lithium toxicity can lead to a host of devastating effects such as seizures, coma, and death.

During the past several years, it has become evident that anticonvulsant medications are also effective for the treatment of bipolar disorder. Ariprazole, a partial dopamine and serotonin agonist , as well as an antagonist for certain serotonin receptors, has been used to treat bipolar disorder (Manning & McElroy, 2009). The anticonvulsant **valproate** also looks very promising for bipolar patients. In addition to being as effective as lithium in the treatment of acute mania valproate has recently been shown to have neuroprotective functions (Monti, Polazzi, & Contestabile, 2009). Lithium also seems to offer some antidepressant effects for some bipolar patients, and this effect has not been observed with valproate. On a positive note, valproate produces fewer side effects, and a wider therapeutic margin, or range of doses, can be given without toxic side effects. Although lithium remains the tried and true treatment for bipolar disorder, substances such as valproate may offer significant benefits to patients who do not respond to lithium or to those whose disorder is characterized by rapid cycling.

Summary

Mood Disorders: An Overview

The mood-related disorders, all with different intensities, durations, and patterns, differ from many clinical disorders: They follow an intermittent pattern instead of a progressively worsening course. Major depression is among the most common mental illnesses, affecting approximately 17% of the population. Several factors seem to influence susceptibility to mood disorders, including gender, diet, stress, and certain genetic predispositions.

Evolutionary psychologists hypothesize that moods evolved to facilitate successful responses to an ever-changing environment, with more positive moods attracting us toward stimuli associated with increased survival (for example, food) and more negative moods repelling us from stimuli associated with decreased survival (for example, predator attacks). Problems arise when mood does not modulate in response to the appropriate stimuli in the environment.

Tracing the Neurobiological Roots of Depression

An elaborate neuroanatomical circuit has been proposed to underlie the symptoms of depression. The PFC lies at the heart of the circuit (multiple forms of data indicate a general atrophy of the PFC in depressed patients). The PFC has intimate connections with other brain areas implicated in depression, such as the hippocampus, amygdala, anterior cingulate cortex, thalamus, and nucleus accumbens. Collectively, these neuroanatomical sites contribute to commonly observed symptoms such as profound sadness, fear, anxiety, anhedonia, and difficulty in cognitive tasks. This circuit is modulated by two brain stem systems: serotonin secreted by the raphe nuclei and norepinephrine secreted by the locus ceruleus.

The serotonin-depletion hypothesis suggests that, because drugs that increase serotonergic functions in the synapse are successful in the treatment of depressive symptoms, depressed patients have low levels of serotonin. Although decreased serotonergic functions in depressed patients have been observed, other evidence suggests that alterations in serotonergic activity fail to influence depressive symptoms. The convergence of evidence, however, suggests that alterations in the sensitivity of serotonergic receptors play the biggest role in reducing symptoms of depression.

The catecholamine hypothesis proposed in the 1960s suggests that depression is caused by decreased levels of norepinephrine whereas mania is caused by excessive levels of norepinephrine. This theory became less popular with the introduction of the serotonin-depletion theory, but nonetheless it remains viable. When patients who are taking drugs that increase norepinephrine in the synapse are placed on a norepinephrine-deficient diet, their symptoms reemerge, as seen when patients taking SSRIs are placed on a serotonin-deficient diet. It is currently thought that norepinephrine, like other monoamines, has a modulating role on the systems involved with depression: Any manipulation of these systems can conceivably influence depression symptoms.

Corticosteroids, released during the stress response, are present in high levels in depressed patients. For this reason, researchers are investigating the role of these hormones in depression as well as the potential value of drugs that block their release.

An exciting area of research suggests that depression may result from decreased brain plasticity. Successful depression therapies such as ECT and SSRIs have been shown to influence brain plasticity; specifically, ECT results in an increased production of new brain cells and SSRIs increase the production of the neurotrophic factor BDNF.

Stress and Depression

Environmental stressors play a significant role in the etiology of depression. An interrupted parental bond (separation or abuse) early in an animal's life can disrupt the stress response system and lead to an increased susceptibility to depression. Additionally, disruptions in environmental variables such as seasonal changes in light seem to increase susceptibility to depression.

Treatment for Depression

Although MAOIs and tricyclic antidepressants were the first pharmacological therapies for depression, SSRIs have generally replaced these drugs. SSRIs aren't necessarily more effective than the earlier drugs, but they have fewer threatening side effects. Because SSRIs are not free from side effects, new antidepressants are being investigated. New drugs such as reboxetine (a norepinephrine uptake blocker), anti-corticotropin-releasing hormone drugs, and various SNUBs are being introduced as pharmacological therapies.

ECT is a long-standing somatic therapy for depression. Because this therapy requires the patient to be anesthetized and frequently results in memory loss, it is used only as a last resort. A newer somatic therapy, rTMS, involves placing a magnet on the scalp to alter the conductivity of underlying neurons. Preliminary evidence suggests that this therapy may be as effective as ECT without the dangerous side effects, but more research is necessary before informed conclusions can be made. Additionally, studies are currently being conducted to determine the efficacy of deep brain stimulation on brain areas such as the subgenual cingulate gyrus.

Cognitive-behavioral therapy—therapist-guided discussions about depression and how to cognitively and behaviorally respond to life situations to alter the likelihood of depressive episodes—often results in efficacy rates similar to antidepressants. Similar results have been observed with behavioral therapies such as behavioral activation therapy. Advantages to various forms of cognitive-behavioral therapy include higher compliance rates and is a reduced relapse rate compared to pharmacotherapy.

Bipolar Disorder

Approximately 1%–1.5% of the population suffers from bipolar disorder, in which episodes of depression are interspersed with episodes of mania. Neuroanatomical studies suggest that the neurobiological components are similar to those seen in depression with the additional involvement of the basal ganglia. Hyperintensities of the white matter have also been observed in bipolar patients; more research is required, however, to determine whether hyperintensities are a cause or an effect of bipolar disorder.

Although the specific mechanisms remain unknown, the most successful treatment for bipolar disorder is the drug lithium. Other drugs, such as valproate, an anticonvulsant, are currently being explored as alternative pharmacological treatments for patients who are not able to take lithium because of severe side effects.

Key Terms

mood (affective) disorders (250)

major depressive disorder (250)

bipolar disorder (250)

depression (250)

prefrontal cortex (PFC) (255)

anterior cingulate cortex (258)

anhedonia (259)

learned helplessness (259)

corticosteroids (266)

seasonal affective disorder (SAD) (271)

iproniazid (272)

monoamine oxidase inhibitors (MAOIs) (272)

imipramine (272)

tricyclic antidepressants (272)

fluoxetine (274)

reboxetine (276)

antalarmin (276)

SNUBs (super neurotransmitter uptake blockers) (277)

repetitive transcranial magnetic stimulation (rTMS) (278)

cognitive behavioral therapy (CBT) (280)

manic episodes (281)

lithium (283)

valproate (286)

For Further Consideration

Jacobs, B. L., van Praag, H., & Gage, F. H. (2000). Adult brain neurogenesis and psychiatry: A novel theory of depression. *Molecular Psychiatry, 5,* 262–269. Just when we thought that we had a pretty good understanding of the role of certain neurochemicals such as serotonin in depression, these authors propose that brain plasticity plays a significant role in depression. They specifically point to neurogenesis in the hippocampus as an important contributing variable in depression.

Jamison, K. R. (1996). *An unquiet mind: A memoir of moods and madness.* New York: Vintage Books. This book is written by a psychologist who has bipolar disorder. Jamison describes the highs and lows of her personal life with the unique perspective of a psychologist. She conveys the lure of the manic phases in the earlier stages of her disorder and how exhausting the disorder became at later stages. By disclosing the personal details of her life, she gives the reader a clear picture of what it is like to live with bipolar disorder.

Kirsch, I. (2010). *The Emperor's New Drugs.* New York: Basic Books. Considering the crude and nonspecific therapies that have been historically available for depression, the thought of a pill acting as an effective agent against the tumultuous symptoms of this disease was appealing to everyone in the mental health industry. But, as Irving Kirsch points out in this book, there is considerable controversy in the scientific literature over the efficacy of antidepressants. Although the antidepressant industry is a multi-billion dollar industry, depression rates continue to rise. He conveys that it is not likely that such a complex array of symptoms would be effectively treated by a pharmacological agent impacting a single neurotransmitter out of the context of real life. Of particular interest is Krisch's analysis of the placebo effect in the antidepressant research.

Lambert, K.G. (2008). Depressingly Easy. *Scientific American Mind*, August/September.

In this article, the neurobiological effects of the sedentary lifestyle that has become characteristic of Western cultures is discussed. About the time that energy (human energy, that is) saving appliances were introduced to our culture, depression rates started to rise; accordingly the author suggests that more sedentary lifestyles fail to activate the brain as much as physical effort directed toward specific goals and can lead to depressive symptoms.

Ressler, K. J., & Nemeroff, C. B. (2000). Role of serotonergic and noradrenergic systems in the pathophysiology of depression and anxiety disorders. *Depression and Anxiety, 12,* 2–19. This is a wonderful review of both serotonin and noradrenaline in depression and anxiety. Although drugs that are effective in treating depression generally increase serotonergic function and generally decrease noradrenaline, these authors suggest that there is more to the depression-neurochemical story. They suggest that serotonin and noradrenaline modulate some unknown system. This article also explores the specific brain areas responsible for specific symptoms observed in depression.

Richelson, E. (2001). Pharmacology of antidepressants. *Mayo Clinic Proceedings, 76,* 511–127. This article is a thorough review of depression and the specific efficacy and underlying pharmacology for each of the drugs currently used in the battle against this disorder. In addition to the efficacy of each drug, relevant issues are specific neurophysiological effect, adverse side effects, and interactions with other drug or neurochemical systems. A discussion of possible new antidepressants is included in the last section of the article.

Solomon, A. (2001). *The noonday demon.* New York: Scribner. Andrew Solomon is a journalist, not a scientist; but his investigative skills enable him to approach depression from several different angles. In addition to including interviews with scientists and individuals suffering from depression, he provides a painful analysis of his own bout with depression. Because of Solomon's skill in storytelling, the reader can begin to feel the misery associated with this dreaded disorder. This book helps the reader to view depression from the multiple perspectives endorsed in this textbook.

■ Chapter Ten ■ **Schizophrenia**

Connections

Home Movies, Childhood Behavior, and Schizophrenia

One of the greatest challenges for scientists interested in schizophrenia is the observation that, on the surface, a child seems perfectly fine throughout childhood only to experience a drastic alteration in late adolescence or early adulthood that leads to a diagnosis of schizophrenia. How could a seemingly healthy child, a child perhaps excelling at school, be so suddenly taken hostage by a schizophrenic brain? Elaine Walker, working at Emory University, is investigating this question with an unlikely source of data. Walker is using family photographs and home movies to determine facial and motor abnormalities that may have been present in children who would subsequently be diagnosed with schizophrenia (Walker, Lewine, & Neumann, 1996; Walker, Grimes, Davis, & Smith, 1993; Walker, Savoie, & Davis, 1994; (Personal Communication, Tuesday, 13 January, 2004).

While collecting photographs through the parent network of the National Alliance of the Mentally Ill, one of the parents suggested that Walker might

Walker's examination of home movies of children prior to their diagnosis of schizophrenia suggests early motor patterns such as atypical hand movements shown in this picture.
COURTESY OF ELAINE WALKER

want to look at home movies of the children. Walker immediately realized the richness of this source of data—home movies are filmed at times of emotional relevance such as birthday parties and holidays, and the occasions provide a wonderful backdrop for assessing the appropriateness of facial expressions/movements (e.g., smiles). Additionally, home movies are filmed at developmental landmarks in the child's life, such as the first time a child rolls over, sits up, and walks, and thus provide valuable data related to motor development.

Walker and her students proceeded to collect a sufficient number of home movies of preschizophrenic children and devised a strategy to systematically code the videotapes for any physical/motor, social behavior, or facial expression anomalies. Researchers scoring the tapes were blinded to whether they were assessing a preschizophrenic child or a nonschizophrenic sibling. Subtle neuromotor abnormalities were evident in the first 2 years of preschizophrenic children. For example, these children engaged in more abnormal involuntary hand movements than their nonschizophrenic siblings.

The studies have revealed differences in the expression of emotions as well; specifically, preschizophrenic children exhibited more negative facial emotions, such as crying, during their first year of life than did nonschizophrenic children. These findings have been associated with abnormal development of certain brain structures. When magnetic resonance imaging was conducted on schizophrenic patients,

Elaine Walker (second from left) and her team of researchers
COURTESY OF ELAINE WALKER

Walker found that neuromotor deficits and negative affect in early childhood were associated with larger ventricle size in the subsequently developed brain of the adult.

Walker is also working with her colleagues on an investigation of the development of *schizotypal* adolescents, a condition closely related to schizophrenia. Additionally, they are exploring developmental markers in other forms of mental illness. For example, they are studying the behavioral and psychological responses to stress in infants of depressed mothers.

Walker's data suggest that certain behavioral and affective anomalies exist in children who eventually will probably manifest the symptoms of schizophrenia. Learning of such early markers provides little relief to parents of children who have increased risk of developing schizophrenia until there is some therapeutic intervention associated with early identification. This research is still in its infancy; however, Walker and her colleagues would like to identify therapeutic interventions in the future. In the meantime, clarifying exactly when the brain is experiencing alterations will probably contribute valuable information to the existing knowledge of this devastating disease.

Schizophrenia represents a brain divided. Although schizophrenia has likely existed since the dawn of humankind, it has been objectively described and studied only for a century or so. In that time, treatment has moved from mere institutionalization and hopelessness to dramatic reversal of symptoms by a variety of strong pharmacological agents. What began the revolution in treating schizophrenia was the recognition that it is a brain disorder, the result of malformation of structure and function. Like gazing at the stars but never being able to travel there, however, curing schizophrenia remains elusive yet tantalizingly within our grasp. Neuroscience is this century's best hope for conquering it.

The climb up the mountain of diagnoses, data, and subjectivity that make up the field of research into schizophrenia is arduous. This chapter begins with a general overview of the vast symptomology that characterizes the disorder, a word salad that can, at times, rival that of the patient him- or herself in terms of its vagueness and generality. Next, we present the neurobiology of schizophrenia, intertwined with theories of its etiology and potential causes. We conclude with an overview of treatments for schizophrenia, including pharmacological, psychosocial, and cognitive therapies.

OVERVIEW OF SCHIZOPHRENIA

A (portion of a) recent editorial in the prestigious science periodical *Nature* (2010) encapsulates the peril and hope that is the field of schizophrenia:

> Schizophrenia—a combination of delusions, reduced motivation and diminished cognitive functions—exemplifies many of the research challenges posed by psychiatric disorders as a whole. The extreme behaviours covered by the media are far from typical. Population studies indicate that the lifetime prevalence of all psychotic disorders (whose sufferers experience some sort of misperception of reality) is as much as 3%. Schizophrenia is controllable by medication

and cognitive therapy, with a significant chance (a few tens of per cent) of beneficial positive outcomes.

Frustratingly, the effectiveness of medications has stalled. Nobody understands the links between the symptoms of schizophrenia and the crude physiological pathologies that have so far been documented: a decrease in white brain matter, for example, and altered function of the neurotransmitter dopamine. The medications, which are often aimed at the dopamine systems associated with delusions, have advanced over the decades not in their efficacy but in a reduction of their debilitating side effects.

Both diagnosis and drugs primarily address a late stage in the development of schizophrenia—the presentation of delusions. The earlier stages are much less defined and ambiguous in that, as currently characterized, they could lead to a number of alternative conditions. Here, above all, is where progress is needed in the form of reliable biomarkers to identify those at risk and to allow biomedical or cognitive interventions to prevent or mitigate the development of the disorders. Early intervention would lead to better outcomes.

A deeper understanding of the underlying biology is essential to improve diagnoses and therapies. New techniques—genomewide association studies, imaging and the optical manipulation of neural circuits—are ushering in an era in which the neural circuitry underlying cognitive dysfunctions, for example, will be delineated. Tantalizingly, work in genetics is indicating how non-specific some genes are for schizophrenia, having associations in common with bipolar disorder and with autism. This suggests that the earlier stages of psychiatric disorders are multivalent, reinforcing the hope that early detection, coupled with a clearer understanding of the environmental factors, may allow prevention. (p. 9)

Prevalence rates for schizophrenia have been reported to range from 0.5% to 1.5% of the adult population, with similar occurrence in all ethnic groups, worldwide. The disorder is generally diagnosed between the ages of 15 and 35 years and is estimated to afflict over 24 million people worldwide (about 19% of the 450 million estimated to suffer from some mental health condition). Of these millions, more than 90% live in developing countries and fewer than 50% are receiving care and treatment (American Psychiatric Association, 2000; World Health Organization, 2003). In the United States, schizophrenia is an equal-opportunity condition. It appears to afflict both men and women equally, although males experience an earlier onset. Symptoms such as hallucinations and delusions are usually observed between the ages of 16 and 30 (with mean onset ages of 27 years for women and 21 years for men), with the likelihood of becoming schizophrenic decreasing dramatically after age 45 (Mueser & McGurk, 2004). It is rare to observe schizophrenia in children, but, as described in the Connections of this chapter, symptoms or predictors of childhood-onset schizophrenia are increasing (Masi, Mucci & Pari, 2006). Teenagers are another story: So many confounds are extant in the teen's life—lability in friendships, fluctuations in scholastic performance, irritability, moodiness, sleep issues, etc.—that reliably diagnosing schizophrenia or its antecedents is fraught with problems. On the other hand, some predictors do exist. Social isolation from friends and family, suspicious thoughts, and bizarre ideation combined with a family history of psychosis can all increase the likelihood of developing schizophrenia later on (Cannon et al., 2008).

Causes associated with cultural differences in this disorder are unknown. Higher prevalence is reported in areas of Sweden, Croatia, and Ireland and among the Tamils of southern India and Canadian Catholics. Lower rates are observed in the American Amish and the aboriginal tribes of Taiwan and Ghana (Andreasen & Black, 2001). The numbers affected, the age at onset (defining the length of time one would suffer from schizophrenia), and the debilitating mental nature of the condition conspire to make this disease a major problem facing the world's population.

Further, although the worldwide incidence rate is low, the chronic conditions of individuals receiving no or inadequate care lead to a significant cost to the individuals and surrounding community; hence, schizophrenia represents a prevalent cost to society. More important, however, is the cost to individuals diagnosed with schizophrenia: Statistics suggest that they are less likely to marry and have children, are more likely to be in low social classes, exhibit high rates of violent behavior (probably due to impaired thoughts and hallucinations), and are high risks for suicide (33% attempt, 10% are successful) (Andreasen & Black, 2001).

History, Descriptions, and Definitions

The beginning of modern (keep in mind this is a relative term) schizophrenia research can be traced to Emil Kraepelin a century ago (see Chapter 2 for a fuller discussion of Kraepelin's contributions). Kraepelin, a psychiatrist and researcher, was among the first to attempt to distinguish different forms of mental distress. From among the many mental patients Kraepelin and his colleagues treated, there emerged a group with a cluster of partially overlapping symptoms:

1. Auditory and visual **hallucinations**

2. Motor tics

3. Poor regulation of speech or disordered thought

4. **Catatonia**, an absence of movement often observed in the schizophrenic patient, coupled with **hebephrenia**, an inappropriate and uncontrollable form of laughter

Kraepelin termed this constellation of behaviors, observed in the thousands of patients he had treated, **dementia praecox** (early dementia), with an emphasis on the relatively early onset he and others had observed among their patients.

As noted in Chapter 2, Kraepelin advanced the field by distinguishing between patients who got better, such as those with depression, and those who moved inexorably toward dementia, as he observed in his schizophrenic patients. He was among the first to recognize the existence of dementia praecox, the precursor to schizophrenia. He saw something that others did not or had merely hinted at. Like the first paleontologist to interpret the shape of a newly uncovered bone as indicative of a new species of dinosaur, though, Kraepelin realized that he was seeing two separable phenomena.

With this basic observation in hand, Kraepelin set out to describe and catalog schizophrenia with the naturalist's eye. His rich descriptions are still consulted as much for their completeness as for their objectivity.

hallucination An internal perception of a realistic sensory event in the absence of any external stimuli.

catatonia Absence of movement; often observed in the schizophrenic patient.

hebephrenia Inappropriate and uncontrollable form of laughter.

dementia praecox Older term for schizophrenia, describing what was believed to be a progressive and incurable deterioration of mental functioning that typically began in adolescence.

Eugen Bleuler, a Swiss psychiatrist, then built on Kraepelin's observational foundation.

Contemporary Views of Schizophrenia

Bleuler renamed Kraepelin's dementia praecox **schizophrenia**, to more accurately reflect the fracture among various psychological activities. This new name was derived from the Greek words *schizo*, meaning "splitting," and *phrene*, meaning "psychic functions." Bleuler intended this new term to emphasize the splitting of normal psychological processes: The emotional and cognitive processes were not operating in a logical and synchronized fashion. Bleuler found no evidence that patients' abilities deteriorate, and he thought the emphasis on the splitting of normal processes would convey this observation. He had no intention of describing the even rarer or dubious "split personality" associated with dissociative identity disorder, formerly called "multiple personality disorder" (Andreasen & Black, 2001; Green, 2001; see Chapter 1).

Bleuler categorized the symptoms associated with schizophrenia into fundamental and accessory symptoms. The fundamental, or core, symptoms included ambivalence, affective disturbances, and alterations in association. Accessory symptoms were the product of the fundamental symptoms and included hallucinations, delusions, and speech and behavioral abnormalities.

Interestingly, for most of the twentieth century, the accessory symptoms, not the fundamental symptoms, received most of the clinical attention. According to Green (2001), the accessory hallucinations and delusions became the "elephant in the middle of the room," demanding all the attention of the clinical experts. Other symptoms began to be considered in the 1980s. Today, statistical procedures such as factor analysis have enabled the *Diagnostic and Statistical Manual of Mental Disorders* (DSM) to provide not two but three broad categories of schizophrenic symptoms (Table 10.1). This three-part categorization is especially valuable today as researchers and clinicians interpret the differential success of psychoactive drugs on each category of symptoms.

1. Hallucinations and delusions are **positive symptoms**, in the sense of adding a new symptom to the repertoire.

2. Behaviors that are "taken away" from the patient's normal functioning (e.g., a lack of appropriate emotional expression, reductions of speech and thoughts, and a decreased desire for social interactions) are referred to as **negative symptoms**. It is easy to see how negative symptoms of schizophrenia might be confused with symptoms of depression; such social withdrawal, however (Bleuler's core fundamental symptoms), might very well contribute to the more distinctive positive (accessory) symptoms.

3. **Disorganized symptoms** (for example, disorganized speech and thought patterns) are Bleuler's "alterations in association," which he considered a core symptom (Green, 2001).

Views of a Schizophrenic Mind

One way to understand how the symptoms of schizophrenia are expressed is to talk with a patient. Following is a short conversation with a man who was diagnosed with chronic schizophrenia in his early twenties. An outpatient at a Richmond, Virginia, area clinic, "Andy" has been following a regimen of antipsychotic medication for the last decade.

schizophrenia Mental disorder characterized by disordered thoughts, delusions, hallucinations, and other bizarre behaviors.

positive symptoms Characteristics or attributes that are added to a schizophrenic patient's nature, such as hallucinations.

negative symptoms Characteristics or attributes that are absent from the nature of a person with schizophrenia, such as reduced desire for social interaction.

disorganized symptoms Symptoms in a schizophrenic patient such as nonlogical thoughts and speech.

Table 10.1 Diagnostic Criteria for Schizophrenia

A. *Characteristic symptoms*: Two (or more) of the following, each present for a significant portion of time during a 1-month period (or less if successfully treated):

(1) delusions

(2) hallucinations

(3) disorganized speech (e.g., frequent derailment or incoherence)

(4) grossly disorganized or catatonic behavior

(5) negative symptoms, i.e., affective flattering,alogia, or avolition

Note: Only one criterion A symptom is required if delusions are bizarre or hallucinations consist of a voice keeping up a running commentary on the person's behavior or thoughts or two or more voices conversing with each other.

B. *Social/occupational dysfunction*: For a significant portion of the time since the onset of the disturbance, one or more major areas of functioning such as work, interpersonal relations, or self-care are markedly below the level achieved prior to the onset (or when the onset is in childhood or adolescence, failure to achieve expected level of interpersonal, academic, or occupational achievement).

C. *Duration*: Continuous signs of the disturbance persist for at least 6 months. This 6-month period must include at least 1 month of symptoms (or less if successfully treated) that meet criterion A (i.e., active-phase symptoms) and may include periods of prodromal or residual symptoms. During these prodromal or residual periods, the signs of the disturbance may be manifested by only negative symptoms or two or more symptoms listed in criterion A present in an attenuated form (e.g., odd beliefs, unusual perceptual experiences).

D. *Schizoaffective and mood disorder exclusion*: Schizoaffective disorder and mood disorder with psychotic features have been ruled out because either (1) no major depressive, manic, or mixed episodes have occurred concurrently with the active-phase symptoms or (2) if mood episodes have occurred during active-phase symptoms, their total duration has been brief relative to the duration of the active and residual periods.

E. *Substance/general medical condition exclusion*: The disturbance is not due to the direct physiological effects of a substance (e.g., a drug of abuse, a medication) or a general medical condition.

F. *Relationship to a pervasive developmental disorder*: If there is a history of autistic disorder or another pervasive developmental disorder, the additional diagnosis of schizophrenia is made only if prominent delusions or hallucinations are also present for at least a month (or less if successfully treated).

Classification of longitudinal course (can be applied only after at least 1 year has elapsed since the initial onset of active-phase symptoms):

Episodic with Interepisode Residual Symptoms (episodes are defined by the reemergence of prominent psychotic symptoms); *also specify if*:

With Prominent Negative Symptoms

Episodic with No Interepisode Residual Symptoms

Continuous (prominent psychotic symptoms are present throughout the period of observation); *also specify if*:

With Prominent Negative Symptoms

Single Episode in Partial Remission; *also specify if*: **With Prominent Negative Symptoms**

Single Episode in Full Remission

Other or Unspecified Pattern

American Psychiatric Association (1994, pp. 285–286).

Reportedly a happy and active child, he was smart, effusive (his word), and curious. As a teenager, he played the piano and loved to write music. On the day of the interview at the clinic, he had not yet taken his medication. Note especially the instant familiarity, as if he were practiced in talking about his schizophrenia; note also the sensual nature and focus of some of his descriptions and, perhaps most obvious, the interplay of lucidity and fantasy, as if his imagination is controlling his speech.

Interviewer: Tell me a little about your day.

Patient: I wake up and see the moons in the face of my mother. She loves me and God loves me and I have cereal for breakfast. I like to eat Cheerios sometimes because they remind me of the wheels on the road by my house. The cars and trucks go fast and they make me forget about my pains.

Interviewer: What does it feel like when you are having your pains?

Patient: I don't like it much. My head gets tight and I hear the cars talking and they tell me that I am going too fast and that I need to watch over the smells. I smell dogs and dog poop and I have to smoke the trucks that drive by my house.

Interviewer: *What do you dream about at night?*

Patient: *The night scares me. The devil comes sometimes and I can smell him and I can smell the smoke that sticks to him from hell. I drink my Coke and my hamburger and I wait to fall asleep with the walls that cover me.*

Interviewer: *What do you want to do in the future?*

Patient: *I want to think and to fly and have the devil go away. The pills I take help me and they keep the devil's talking away, and I can see my mom, so I can fly in my room.*

(C. Kinsley, personal communication, 2004)

In a mere 12 sentences, a vast array of schizophrenic symptoms are apparent. Auditory hallucinations are conveyed in his reports of hearing cars and the devil talking; disorganized thinking is apparent in sentences such as the ones about having to smoke the trucks going by his house and perceiving that walls, blanket-like, cover him. "Andy" also reports olfactory hallucinations of smelling the devil and "dog poop." Thus, the positive and disorganized symptoms are easily seen in this conversation.

Negative symptoms are more difficult to detect in a conversation, but social withdrawal and inappropriate emotional expression are vividly portrayed in the movie *A Beautiful Mind*, based on the life of Nobel Prize–winning mathematician John Nash (Nasar, 1999). As described in Box 10.1, social isolation was one of the earliest symptoms the Nash family noticed. Nevertheless, it is clear that "Andy" suffers from a significant disruption of his mental life, one that removes him from the social network of fellow human beings and, at present, consigns him to a future both cold and lonely.

NEUROBIOLOGY OF SCHIZOPHRENIA

From animal models and brain scans using functional magnetic resonance imaging (fMRI) to detailed genetic analyses, including newly acquired data from the Human Genome Project, we now have the means to examine schizophrenia comprehensively and with respect to its complexity. We are a long way from a cure or even a treatment free from significant drawbacks, but hope abounds. The neurobiological direction in which schizophrenia research is moving is the best hope for this condition and promises to yield a clearer understanding of the disease, its etiology, and most effective treatment options.

Genetic Factors

The observations of Franz Kallmann in the 1920s and 1930s suggested a possible role for heredity in the transmission, incidence, and severity of schizophrenia. After losing his university position in Berlin in 1935, Kallmann, a Jew in the wrong place at the wrong time, emigrated to New York, where he conducted an elaborate study of the relative roles of heritability and environmental influences in schizophrenia. Using an archival methodological strategy, he examined the medical records of New York State mental hospitals to assess the heritability of schizophrenia. Kallmann's initial data recorded a concordance rate of 86% in identical twins and 15% in fraternal twins.

More recent work has demonstrated that schizophrenia appears to cluster in families. Although the condition appears in about 1% of the general population, it is overrepresented in those families with a parent, sister, or brother (that is, a first-degree relative) with schizophrenia; those family members with grandparents, aunts, uncles, and cousins (i.e., second-degree relatives) with schizophrenia are also more likely to develop it (Cardno & Gottesman, 2000).

Seymour Kety, Irving Gottesman, and others have refined the genetic approach introduced by Kallmann to reliably demonstrate a high likelihood of inherited biological factors as the major contribution to developing schizophrenia (Gottesman, 1991; Suddath, Christison, Torrey, Casanova, & Weinberger, 1990). Adoption studies in which data for twins reared apart are compared also provide compelling evidence for the genetic contribution to the expression of schizophrenia. If one identical twin has schizophrenia, the other is much more likely to develop it.

Today, no one questions the link between schizophrenia and genetics, although the likelihood that a single gene is responsible is extremely low given the rate of mutations reported in such individuals and the mere fact that any behavior or brain event(s) is multiply determined (Harrison & Weinberger, 2005). As seen in Figure 10.1, however, some studies report lower concordance rates in monozygotic (identical) twins (i.e., a range of 41%–65%, with most reporting an average of about 48%) than originally reported by Kallmann (Barondes, 1993; Cardno & Gottesman, 2000; Torrey, Bowler, Taylor, & Gottesman, 1994). These fluctuating numbers reflect a

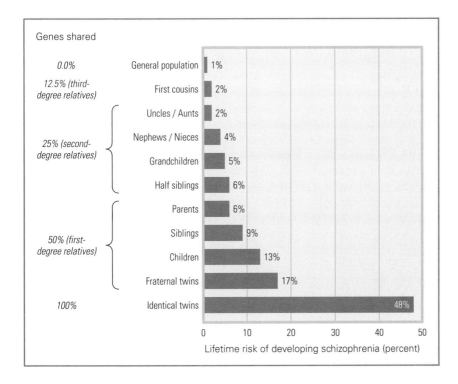

Figure 10.1
Heritability in schizophrenia.
The genetic contribution in schizophrenia is determined by investigating concordance rates in relatives with varying degrees of genetic similarity.

Box 10.1

A Case in Point

The Transformations of John Nash's Schizophrenic Mind

As a child, John Nash was bright and curious but introverted. He preferred to stay inside and read rather than play with the other neighborhood children. In retrospect, there were signs that are now identifiable as evidence of the mental turmoil that would wrack the adult Nash's life. Elaine Walker's research, described in the chapter-opening Connections, suggests that signs of motor difficulties may presage the development of schizophrenia. Nash gripped his pencil like a stick, and his handwriting was illegible. Although he preferred his left hand, his father insisted that he use his right hand. A picture of Nash sitting among his high school peers shows a child with his eyes rolled back in his head, appearing bored. He was the recipient of endless teasing for his many social mishaps and nonsocial, weird behaviors.

Even his hopeful mother, Virginia, thought her son was a mere bookworm; and she was passionate about providing a stimulating, educational environment for him. Although labeled as a bit of a social misfit, he managed to find his niche in academe as he excelled in mathematics. In 1945 he commenced his college education at the Carnegie Institute of Technology in Pittsburgh with the goal of becoming a chemical engineer, and he found success in his studies. His achievements in the classroom did not, however, transfer to his social life. He continued to appear immature to his friends; additionally, after making a clumsy pass at a male friend, he was teased for this homosexual-oriented behavior.

In 1948, Nash began graduate studies in mathematics at Princeton University. By this time, he had assumed a cocky, arrogant persona, frequently boasting of his mathematical accomplishments. As evidence of his extreme self-confidence, he once visited Einstein and suggested some new ideas for amending quantum theory. In 1950, he proposed *Nash's equilibrium*, an idea suggesting that the outcome of a game depends on the strategies of all the players. Nash went on to accept his first teaching position at the Massachusetts Institute of Technology (MIT).

On the personal side, Nash fathered a baby out of wedlock in 1953. As might be predicted by his social immaturity and arrogance, he refused to support the baby's mother; and his first son, John David, spent some time in foster care. In 1956, he met Alicia Larde, an MIT coed and aspiring physicist, who would have an intense influence in his life. After having him as a professor in her advanced calculus class, Alicia was smitten with the handsome and intellectual Nash. They were married in 1957 and had one son, John Charles.

In the spring of 1959, Nash's world started to change in dramatic ways. At 30 years of age and on the brink of becoming a full professor, he became increasingly convinced that he was being followed. Among other things, he claimed that he was able to decipher encrypted messages from aliens that were printed in various newspapers. After having a confusing conversation with a colleague, he was committed to McLean Hospital for treatment.

When later asked how such a logical mathematician could believe that extraterrestrial beings were sending him messages trying to recruit him to save the world, he replied, "Because the ideas I had about supernatural beings came to me the same way that my mathematical ideas did. So I took them seriously" (Nasar, 2001 p. 11). After this first episode of paranoid schizophrenia, Nash became obsessed with numerology and religious prophecy and symbols, believing that he was an important religious figure.

This schizophrenic episode was the starting point of a tumultuous relationship with a devastating mental illness. For the next 30 years, Nash would flee to Europe several times, be hospitalized involuntarily about six times, and, sadly, become a phantom of the arrogant and brilliant Nash of Princeton University. Throughout his sickness he encountered a wide variety of treatments. During his first hospitalization, Nash was given an initial dose of Thorazine to calm him down. Subsequently, due in part to the prevailing influence of Freud, Nash was exposed to extensive psychoanalysis, curiously leading to (because of a breakdown coincident with Alicia's pregnancy) a diagnosis of "fetus envy" (Nasar, 1999).

Additionally, his repressed homosexuality was thought to be a culprit causing him to suffer from "homosexual panic." Although his second hospitalization was in a unit known for aggressive electroconvulsive therapy, there is no documentation that Nash received this type of treatment. When the family's money began to dwindle, Nash was forced to enter Trenton State Hospital (which is near Princeton) in 1961. At the time, Trenton had 2,500 patients, 10 times more than the private hospitals he had previously been in.

While at Trenton, Nash was transferred to the "elite" insulin unit, and for 6 weeks he received daily insulin treatments. After early-morning insulin injections, Nash's blood sugar would drop drastically, causing him to experience drowsiness followed by delirium. By about 9:30 a.m., Nash would become comatose as his body became rigid and his fingers curled. A nurse would then place a rubber hose in his nose and esophagus through which a glucose solution was administered. Nash would slowly and agonizingly awake around 11:00. Each afternoon, he would attend occupational therapy.

Nash described the insulin therapy, first introduced by Manfred Sakel (see Chapter 2), as "torture" (Nasar, 1999). Just as radiation treatments are administered to cancer patients in an attempt to kill the unhealthy tumor cells, insulin treatment was thought to kill the marginally functioning neurons. We now know that there is no empirical evidence to support such a claim, and insulin use has fallen into disfavor.

Nash managed to pull his life together. In the mid-1960s, he was offered a faculty position at Princeton, but he couldn't escape the crushing waves of schizophrenia long enough to rebuild his reputation as one of the country's most brilliant mathematicians. He was placed on antipsychotics while he was hospitalized, but because he didn't like the side effects, he didn't take the drugs following his release.

Nash just couldn't maintain a functional life—his marriage ended in divorce, he had no consistent relationship with his sons, and he wasn't able to keep his job at Princeton. In 1967, he retreated to his hometown of Roanoke, Virginia, to live with his mother, where he remained for 3 years.

In the 1970s Nash migrated back to Princeton, not as a professor but more as an eccentric fixture. Wearing high-top tennis shoes, he would write his "problems" on numerous blackboards throughout the department. Ironically, this intense cognitive effort and the neural resources devoted to stating these problems may have contributed to the eventual remission of his schizophrenia. Around 1990, glimpses of rationality started to be seen in Nash as he began asking insightful questions at some of the departmental seminars.

When Nash later described his remarkable transition from delusions to remission, he stated, "I emerged from irrational thinking ultimately without medicine other than the natural hormonal changes of aging" (Nasar, 1999, p. 353). In support of the cognitive training discussed later in this chapter, he credits willpower for his remission. He believes his intense cognitive activity may have played a role in his recovery.

To those who have seen the movie *A Beautiful Mind*, the dramatic ending to Nash's story is well known. In 1994, Nash was awarded the Nobel Prize in Economics for his game theory. Not knowing how he would endure the stress of travel and the excitement of receiving the award, Nash was perceived as a risk to receive the award. The ceremony, however, went well, and the award has had a powerful and positive effect on his life.

Nash currently has an office at Princeton, where he continues to spend many of his days. He has since reconciled with Alicia, and together they take care of their son. John Charles, who received a PhD in mathematics from Rutgers University, is presently incapacitated with schizophrenia. Nash has received a considerable amount of media attention because of the release of the Academy Award-–winning film featuring his life's story. When Nash met Russell Crowe, the actor who portrayed him in the movie, he warned him, "You're going to have to go through all these transformations!"—an apt term to describe Nash's life with schizophrenia.

combination of the imprecision inherent to gene expression and penetrance, as well as the murky diagnostic criteria, idiosyncratic behavioral expression, and unique environmental interactions that summate to produce the schizophrenic symptom set (Walsh et al., 2008).

Perhaps the most dramatic evidence of familial contributions to schizophrenia is the case of identical sisters, known as the Genain quadruplets, all of whom were diagnosed with schizophrenia. The environment, however, may also have played a role, for the girls varied in the severity of schizophrenic symptoms. The variability in the expression of symptoms could have resulted from varied effects of early brain injury, low birth weights, and harsh punitive treatment as children.

As seen in Figure 10.2, the girls looked healthy and happy as young children; this changed, however, as they matured. They were diagnosed with schizophrenic symptoms between the ages of 22 and 24 years and have been repeatedly evaluated at the National Institute of Mental Health since the 1950s (Barondes, 1993). Most recently, at the 39-year follow-up examinations, at 66 years of age, the women were reported to exhibit improved cognition compared with previous tests, a finding supporting the notion that the cognitive impairment observed in schizophrenia is not due to degenerative processes (Mirsky et al., 1984, 2000).

The concordance rate for identical twins approaches only 50%, so environmental influences are very important in the expression of schizophrenia. Studies have indicated that the most significant life differences in identical twins are birth complications; the twin suffering from birth complications is more likely to develop schizophrenia. It seems, though, that discordant twins carry the same genetic susceptibility for schizophrenia. Researchers find the same rates of schizophrenia in the families of discordant pairs of twins as observed in concordant pairs. Thus, if a twin is spared schizophrenia, the same risk of schizophrenia is found in his or her offspring as in the family of the twin who developed schizophrenia (Torrey et al., 1994).

In what ways do the genetic factors express themselves? How does the brain go from normality to the depths of madness following the exquisitely timed orchestrations of genes being expressed, of turning on and off, as the brain plays the tune and the mind moves to it? It is a question as tangled as the neural organization of the schizophrenic brain.

At this time, no single gene has been identified as the "disease" gene for schizophrenia; rather, research suggests a growing list of genetic contenders that contribute moderate effects to the expression of the disease (McDonald & Murphy, 2003; Pulver, 2000). These genetic links are believed to reside on chromosomes 1, 6, 8, 10, 13, 15, 18, and 22 and the X chromosome (Bassett, 1989; Dawson & Robin, 1996; Heinrichs, 2001; Hyman & Nestler, 1993). The exact contribution of these genes in the healthy brain is still being determined through painstaking quantitative analyses and through application of the data from the Human Genome Project (whose promise so far is much greater than the data in hand). Initial insights into the function of some of these genes are beginning to come to light; these functions at a few chromosomal locations are highlighted in Table 10.2.

Figure 10.2
Genain quadruplets
EDNA MORLOK

Recently, Ken Kendler at Virginia Commonwealth University and his colleagues have reported that an interesting feature of the many candidate genes for schizophrenia is a potential connection with dysfunction in glutamatergic neurotransmission (Riley & Kendler, 2006).

Neuroscience research is a long way from understanding what goes wrong in the application pathways of these genes. Regardless, the genes are providing instructions, translating their commands into action by means of protein production. Whatever alterations might be present in the genetic code that leads to schizophrenia are manifested in the collection of proteins and subsequent structures and activities that are coded for. Recently, gene promoters for the GABAergic system operating throughout the development of the prefrontal cortex were implicated in the neurobiology of schizophrenia (Huang et al., 2007). In a neural domino effect, the net result may be deficits in higher-order brain regions and processing, and its promise as a diagnostic tool is high.

Neuroanatomy

The exact etiology of schizophrenia is unknown. Though the existence of significant neuroanatomical alterations in the schizophrenic brain is undisputed, under what conditions or through what interactions these alterations occur are research questions of the greatest interest. The alterations reported in the neural architecture of the schizophrenic brain are large and obvious (Walsh et al., 2008).

Tuning in to the neural substrates of auditory hallucinations.

Some think that they might find a conversation with a disembodied deity both fascinating and affirming, but the reality is unnerving. Nicole Gilbert's experience with "voices" began when she had difficulty reading, reporting that whatever she was reading was about her. The voices frequently suggested that Nicole was Jesus, only then to tell her that they were joking, suggesting that she was stupid to believe such comments. Now, significantly recovered, Nicole reports that she could not believe it when friends told her that the voices she had been hearing were, in fact, not real (Goode, 2003).

Neuroimaging techniques afford a look into the workings of the schizophrenic brain that not even the most imaginative early schizophrenia researchers could have envisioned. One window into the schizophrenic brain was cracked by Silbersweig and colleagues (1995) when they examined, in real time, the brains of schizophrenics who were simultaneously experiencing auditory hallucinations.

Table 10.2 Location of Putative Genes Involved in Schizophrenia

Chromosome	Function
1	G-protein regulation (important in synaptic functioning)
6	Protein associated with synaptic structure
8	Growth factor involved in formation of synaptic structure
13	Modulates NMDA glutamate transmission
15	Modulates acetylcholine transmission
22	Modulates dopamine transmission

Adapted from Freedman (2003).

The belief—the surety—of those affected with schizophrenia that they hear the voice of God, the CIA, their neighbor's dog, or some otherworldly figure authoritatively speaking directly, personally, threateningly to them is a positive symptom synonymous with schizophrenia. Although bizarre, as are many psychotic symptoms, auditory hallucinations represent an extreme form of a behavior observed in many individuals. For example, as a child, did you ever talk to an imaginary friend? Did your friend talk back? Shortly after her best friend moves away, a child may acquire a new, imaginary friend. In this case, hearing the voice of this imaginary friend provides comfort for her through the stressful time of losing her actual best friend.

Voices associated with imaginary friends can be quite adaptive as they reduce levels of stress in certain situations; and who among us has not talked to him- or herself at some point, berating or praising or questioning something? In contrast, the voices characterizing the auditory hallucinations of schizophrenia command and compel the recipients, with unceasing regularity and force, to commit acts against their will. Those of us not so afflicted take for granted the thin curtain that separates our mind from our mind's voice; we *know* when we are having an internal dialogue and when we are simply talking to ourselves; this distinction is less obvious for people suffering from schizophrenia. The consequences can be frightening.

It is clear that, unlike the voice of an imaginary friend, the voices and commands conjured up out of the imagination of the schizophrenic brain constitute a severe liability. That these voices do not actually exist is irrelevant: They are real to the individual suffering from schizophrenia. Imagine the many unwanted thoughts that you have in any given day transforming themselves into commands.

From where do the voices come? How are they produced? Some compelling findings using fMRI imaging show excess neural activity in the temporal lobes of the individual experiencing auditory hallucinations (Silbersweig et al., 1995). The researchers recruited a number of chronic schizophrenic patients, placed them in an fMRI apparatus, and asked them to signal when they were experiencing vocal hallucinations. The subjects' responses were compared to controls in whom the internal voices were silent. The data demonstrate significantly more activity in the thalamus, striatum, and hippocampus and in the cingulate, orbitofrontal, and auditory cortices during auditory hallucinations (Copolov et al., 2003; Silbersweig et al., 1995). Researchers are currently exploring the role of Broca's area in the production of auditory hallucinations (Goode, 2003; Hoffman et al., 2003). With such extensive brain involvement in the production of auditory hallucinations, it is easy to understand how difficult it may be for the individual to differentiate between brain activation resulting from external voices and brain activation resulting from internal voices (Figure 10.3).

It is important to remember that to process any sounds, including real voices, physical stimuli must be transduced into neural impulses by those same brain areas. Thus, the final pathway for the voice is in the brain. In the schizophrenic brain, the initial steps are absent, but the illusion of the voice is produced nonetheless. For example, activation in the thalamic nuclei, where audition is initially processed, is particularly interesting: perception without sensation. Therefore, the circuitry and its active engagement in these regions (including both afferents and efferents) must be very different in the schizophrenic brain relative to normally functioning brains. History abounds with prophets and fakers, each claiming to hear the voice of a god, each acting according to its wishes. To what extent such auditory stimulation is evoked in similar fashion to that of the schizophrenic patient is a topic as sensitive as it is fascinating. Following is a discussion of some of the general cellular and structural alterations observed in schizophrenic brains associated with disordered thought.

Cellular disorganization and alterations.

Several observed effects in the brains of patients diagnosed with schizophrenia suggest disruptions in early brain wiring. Developmentally, their brains show marked neural disorganization, like a neural landslide. During development, the nascent brain cells in one region are destined to mature and grow and populate another, and thus they require the ability to migrate to their destination using a combination of chemical and glial paths. If these delicate migratory patterns are disrupted, the neurons fail to arrive at and align into precisely their correct locations. Like a heavy wind that arises during a flock's travels south during the winter, the neurons of the schizophrenic brain appear to get blown off course and arrive neither at their proper destination nor in the proper orientation.

As to the causes of the disrupted neural migratory patterns, some speculation centers on viral infection (discussed later in this chapter) and interference with the genetic instructions guiding the neuron-by-neuron assembly of the fetal brain. Regardless of the cause, since the event occurs at a crucial time, when the very base of the brain is being built, the result can be disastrous for neuronal communication.

One area characterized by misaligned neurons is the hippocampus. Abnormal orientation of pyramidal cells in the hippocampus, as shown in Figure 10.4, is prevalent, where the displacement of the normal "north–south" orientation is a feature of schizophrenia reported by many different researchers (Kovelman & Scheibel, 1984; Bunney & Bunney, 1999). Research has also indicated cytoarchitectural alterations in the entorhinal cortex, the cortex surrounding the hippocampal area. Specifically, some patients have differential densities of neuronal populations across the layers of the cortex (Bunney & Bunney, 1999). Though the awry patterning has been reported most often in postmortem analyses of the cortex and hippocampus, where the neurons are rotated, like a hand waving from side to side, there may be other areas with poor neural organization and function.

Selemon and his colleagues at the Yale University School of Medicine found increased density of neurons in the prefrontal and occipital cortex of individuals with schizophrenia, yet the neuropil, or neuronal space that contains the axon and dendrites, was smaller compared with normal controls

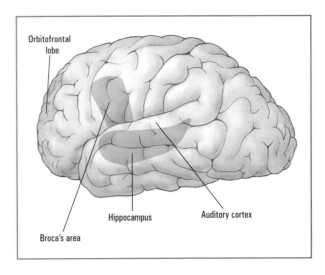

Orbitofrontal lobe

Hippocampus

Auditory cortex

Broca's area

**Figure 10.3
Investigating neuroanatomical areas contributing to auditory hallucinations.** Current fMRI research suggests that orbitofrontal, temporal/auditory, and cingulate cortices, as well as limbic and striatal structures are activated during auditory hallucinations. (Striatal structures not shown; see Chapter Three.) Currently, research is focused on the role of Broca's area in auditory hallucinations.

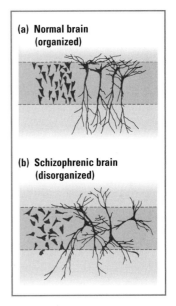

(a) **Normal brain (organized)**

(b) **Schizophrenic brain (disorganized)**

**Figure 10.4
Cellular organization in the schizophrenic brain.** Orientation of pyramidal cells in the hippocampus is organized in the normal brain (a) and disorganized in the schizophrenic brain (b).

(Selemon, Rajkowska, & Goldman-Rakic, 1995). This study reminds us that a study focusing on just one piece of the neuroanatomy can be incomplete; the increased neuronal density was misleading until the decreased volume and neuropil in the cortical area were also identified.

Such effects, where the proper "populating" of a site with its quota of neurons is distorted, can result in poor or problematic transfer of information. Excessive numbers of neurons or connections may lead to ineffective information processing, overprocessed and/or prematurely rerouted, whereas decreased numbers and/or connections may lead to alterations in the normal augmentation of neuronal signals as they move from neuron to neuron or region to region.

A groundbreaking study conducted by Judith Rapoport and her colleagues at the National Institute of Mental Health identified early-onset schizophrenic patients (patients who met DSM criteria by the age of 13) and followed their neuronal loss over the next 5 years (Thompson et al., 2001). Each patient, along with normal controls and nonmedicated controls, was subjected to three MRI scans over the course of the study. As seen in Figure 10.5, the developmental trajectory of gray matter loss in these patients spread progressively from the parietal cortices to the temporal and finally frontal regions of the cerebral cortex.

In individuals diagnosed with early-onset schizophrenia, gray matter loss occurred at about 5% per year in the areas of the frontal eye fields and the parietal, temporal, and supplementary motor cortices in both hemispheres. Normal adolescents experienced subtle losses of about 1% per year, confirming that at least a low level of neuronal pruning exists through adolescence. To answer the question of whether the medication administered to the patients suffering from schizophrenia was the significant contributor to the neuronal loss, a group of patients who exhibited schizophrenia-like symptoms but were never diagnosed with schizophrenia were used as medication-matched control subjects. These individuals received similar medications for their symptoms (for example, for control of aggressive outbursts) even though they were not as impaired as the schizophrenic patients.

Neuronal loss in this important control group fell between the normal controls and early-onset schizophrenic subjects. The medication-matched subjects experienced about half the loss of the schizophrenic patients, suggesting that, whereas the medication might contribute to neuronal loss, it was not the sole contributor. Finally, the extent of neuronal loss was significantly associated with the severity of both positive and negative schizophrenic symptoms. A significant departure from normality in the nature or number of the brain's connections would be expected to result in aberrant neurotransmission and, hence, abnormal behavior.

Reports demonstrate that the neurons are smaller in the schizophrenic hippocampus (Arnold et al., 1995). A reduction in the size of the neuron, whether it is cell body, dendritic arbor, or length of the axon, may have a detrimental impact on its function, relative to a normal-sized neuron. Literally smaller and shorter, this effect suggests underactivity and/or understimulation in the neuron; consequently, the reach of the neuron is wanting. Additionally, alterations in the myelin surrounding the axons has been reported, an effect that could confound the signal being transmitted (Casanova & Lindzen, 2003; Davis et al., 2003).

Because we tend to contemplate the brain as a complex structure made up of enormous nests of neurons and connections, effects of the size or structure of a relative handful of neurons seem trivial. When placed in the context of the region where the effects have been reported in the schizophrenic brain (hippocampus, frontal lobes) and of the activities regulated there, such small alterations in neuronal size and number take on greater significance.

Focusing on the more microscopic neural landscape, the number of connections may also be compromised. One attempt to address this question is the assessment of synaptophysin, an abundant presynaptic vesicle-associated protein that plays a key role in neurotransmitter transmission. Schizophrenic patients have less synaptophysin-immunoreactive tissue in the prefrontal cortex than do control subjects (Eastwood & Harrison, 1995; Glantz & Lewis, 1997), suggesting synaptic transmission deficits in addition to the scores of problems already discussed.

Single neurons are capable of influencing thousands of other, downstream neurons and thus can exert effects out of proportion to their absolute number. A neural signal is only as resonant as the last neuron(s) that carries it. As the Chinese proverb has it, the thousand-mile journey begins with a single step, and that neural signal must move from groups of neurons made up of individual neurons to other neurons in the circuit.

In the schizophrenic brain, misfiring or malfunctioning neurons (due to number, organization, size, neurotransmission problems, etc.) can produce a distorted and problematic signal. The net result is information that is "recognizable" neither by other malfunctioning neurons nor by unaffected ones. Thus hallucinations, distorted thinking, and paranoia—the challenging symptom constellation of schizophrenia—occur because of the inability of the individual and collective processing units, the neurons, to operate properly.

Structural alterations in schizophrenic brains. One of the earliest discoveries suggesting structural alterations in brains afflicted with schizophrenia was that the ventricles are larger than those of normal brains (Andreasen & Black, 2001). Recall from Chapter 3 that the ventricles are well-defined, fluid-filled cavities in the brain where cerebrospinal fluid is made as part of an intrabrain circulatory system. In particular, the third and lateral ventricles are expanded, which suggests the other side of the expansion of the volume of the ventricles: compression or loss of existing nervous tissue (Figure 10.6).

In a study using identical twins, one of whom who developed schizophrenia while the other was unaffected, Suddath and colleagues (1990) showed that ventricular enlargement might be considered a reliable factor in the diagnosis of schizophrenia. Although it is difficult to ascribe a cause to the enlarged ventricles, despite corresponding loss of gray matter, the correlational effect is a persistent one, reported in many studies on schizophrenia (Bunney & Bunney, 1999).

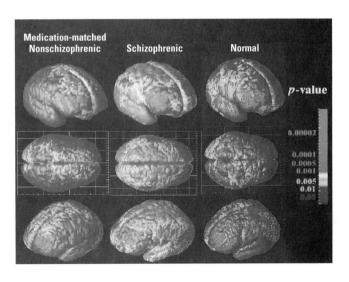

Figure 10.5
Mapping neuronal loss in the schizophrenic brain. These MRI scans indicate higher neuronal loss (indicated by brighter areas) in the schizophrenia brains. Because the medication-matched subjects had more bright areas, indicating cell loss, than the normal controls, it was concluded that medication taken for schizophrenia contributes modestly to neuronal loss.
THOMPSON ET AL., 2000, PNAS

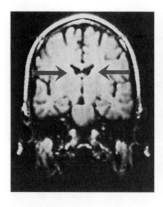

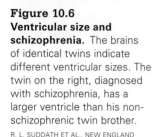

Figure 10.6
Ventricular size and schizophrenia. The brains of identical twins indicate different ventricular sizes. The twin on the right, diagnosed with schizophrenia, has a larger ventricle than his non-schizophrenic twin brother.

R. L. SUDDATH ET AL., NEW ENGLAND JOURNAL OF MEDICINE 322 (1990): 789–94

The ventricles play a role in the development of the anatomical relationships of the brain. The ventricles form a kind of template or guide around which the nascent brain develops (see Chapter 6). From the outset, the proliferating cells pour onto each other and into areas around the ventricles, using them as a pressure-filled field of resistance. The new and migratory neurons inch their way along these spaces. It is interesting to speculate about deficits that might occur in areas such as the hippocampus and the temporal lobe in general as a result of disruptions of cellular migration patterns.

Although ventricular enlargement is the most commonly reported neuroanatomical alteration, other consistent differences have been observed in schizophrenic brains. The sulci that make up the convolutions of the immense cerebral cortex are enlarged (Andreasen & Black, 2001). Lower in the brain, the total volume of the mid-portion of the cerebellum is smaller in individuals diagnosed with schizophrenia (Okugawa, Sedvall, & Agartz, 2003).

A growing body of evidence suggests frontal lobe involvement in the development and expression of schizophrenia, including neuronal loss in the frontal lobes as described earlier. The overlapping symptom array includes apathy, inattention, motor deficiencies, lack of spontaneity, and a reduction in general motivation. Also, interesting parallels exist between patients with frontal lobe damage and patients with schizophrenia, suggesting a commonality of regulation of overlapping cognitive deficits.

There are indications that executive function, the oversight of brain and behavioral activity that is accorded frontal lobe regulation, is impaired in schizophrenic patients. Deficits have been observed in the Wisconsin Card Sorting Test and the Controlled Oral Word Association task, both reliable indices of frontal lobe activity (Heinrichs, 2001; Heinrichs & Zakzanis, 1998). Additionally, the Stroop Test, which gauges impulsivity by asking patients to recite color names printed on different-colored backgrounds, presents greater problems for schizophrenic patients (Heinrichs & Zakzanis, 1998) as their impulsivity forces too rapid responses. When combined with complementary anatomical and brain activation evidence that supports the behavioral testing, there is a further suggestion of frontal lobe deficits in the schizophrenic individual (Andreasen et al., 1986, 1994, 1997; Goldman-Rakic, 1999).

In an interesting study aimed at identifying structural areas underlying cognitive alterations in schizophrenia, Nancy Andreasen and her colleagues compared blood-flow patterns associated with random episodic silent thought in schizophrenic patients and healthy volunteers (Andreasen & Black, 2001; Kemether et al., 2003). In the former, blood-flow abnormalities were found throughout the frontal cortex and temporal cortex, as well as in the cerebellar and thalamic areas. The thalamus is smaller in schizophrenic patients. Thalamic involvement is especially interesting since it may be thought of as a sensory relay station—the brain's O'Hare Airport—that could easily play a role in the accuracy with which sensory messages are routed to the cortex.

In summary, although a single salient structure or circuit has not emerged as the indicative substrate of schizophrenia, the literature suggests the involvement of several structures in the frontal and temporal cortex, hippocampus, cerebellum, and thalamus. The structural abnormalities characteristic of the schizophrenic brain appear to be robust and cumulative, but any individual effect may be small. Heinrichs (2001) has examined the effect size of studies reporting neuronal effects. He states, "If the postmortem studies from both hippocampal and frontal cortex are considered together, it is evident that no findings are large and consistent enough to argue for a *single* cytoarchitectural anomaly in schizophrenia.... No neurological 'smoking gun' has been found so far" (p. 201).

It is true that no "smoking gun" has been found, but there are certainly plenty of fingerprints all over the "gun" that is there. What the data do demonstrate is that the schizophrenic brain is clearly and reliably different, anatomically and functionally, from a nonschizophrenic brain. The difficulty lies in defining and documenting the finer-level responses of such myriad brain events in the human and in accounting for the extraneous variables and confounds that are lurking about.

Before we leave the discussion of neuroanatomical alterations in the schizophrenic brain, it is important to remember that the long-term neuroanatomical effects on the brains of schizophrenic patients who have taken a lifetime of powerful antipsychotic drugs can only be guessed. Further, recent work has begun to focus on the effects of the multiple pharmacological approach to schizophrenia (so-called polypharmacy), both the benefits (crude though they may be) and the pitfalls of treatments (Zink, Englisch & Meyer-Lindenberg, 2010). Some advantages to the approach may be, theoretically, apparent; but the unanticipated interactions between and among drug combinations, dosages, internal state of the patient, etc., all indicate that critical thinking based on empiricism, caution, and good old-fashioned *primum non nocere* be the creed of those doing the helping. The effects of these powerful drugs on the neuronal machinery bring us to an examination of the neurochemistry of schizophrenia.

Neurochemistry

It seems self-evident now that the neurochemistry of the schizophrenic brain is different from that of a normal brain. But the discovery of a concomitant neurochemical abnormality came about, if not by accident, by chance. As is true of so many clinical disorders, early treatment with some drugs was found to be effective without much being known about their action within the brain.

Dopamine hypothesis of schizophrenia. Working backward from the encouraging results in schizophrenic patients who were dosed with these early drugs subsequently led to examinations of the drugs' neurochemical bases. Thus, observations that the powerful antihistamine drug chlorpromazine (Thorazine) could mollify delusional patients led to widespread treatment of schizophrenics with different forms of these phenothiazines. Only after establishing that these drugs were effective did research commence into why, in a counterintuitive "ready!-fire!-aim!" sequence. The finding that they affect a specific neurotransmitter (dopamine [DA]) system gave rise to a better understanding of the neurochemistry of schizophrenia, directing the bright light of research onto changes in a specific neurotransmitter.

A key finding that drove this new DA hypothesis of schizophrenia was the observation that the clinical efficacy of the early drugs correlated with their ability to block DA in vitro, as opposed to in vivo (or a whole living human being) (Byne, Kemether, Jones, Haroutunian, & Davis, 1999). Because of this seemingly powerful relationship between mitigation of positive symptoms of schizophrenia and a drug's ability to block DA, even more attention was concentrated on DA. It was hypothesized that in schizophrenia DA present in the synapse, or excess DA, could not be cleared adequately or quickly enough, resulting in additional receptor stimulation and firings/per unit of time of the downstream neurons. Although aspects of this theory are correlational in nature and subject to cause-and-effect conflation, the DA hypothesis has driven much research into brain–mental illness relationships.

The mesocortical and the mesolimbic DA systems play a role, at least indirectly, in schizophrenic symptomology. The mesolimbic system arises from cell bodies in the ventral tegmental area (VTA) with projections that run into many limbic structures. The mesocortical system, like the mesolimbic, also arises from cell bodies in the VTA; but the projections run to the neocortex (the frontal lobes, in particular). Given the especially higher cognitive functions assigned to the areas innervated by mesolimbic and mesocortical DA projections, activities that are diminished and modified in the schizophrenic patient, attention has been devoted to DA regulation in general and to those regions in particular.

Also supporting the DA hypothesis of schizophrenia was the observation that drugs that resulted in temporarily excessive levels of DA led to schizophrenic symptomology. For example, an individual experiencing a cocaine-induced high reacts neurophysiologically to the drug's action blocking the DA transporter, thereby inhibiting reuptake and leading to exacerbation of DA-receptor activation. Similarly, a person under the influence of amphetamine, another DA agonist, experiences psychotic ideations that include schizophrenia-like hallucinations and paranoia. Even seemingly benign substances, such as the Parkinson disease treatment l-dopa, can produce schizophrenia-related behaviors in a nonschizophrenic person. These data demonstrate that increasing DA levels through manipulations that rescue endogenous DA from degradation or amplify its release leads to the appearance of schizophrenic symptoms (Barondes, 1993), thereby strengthening the DA–schizophrenia link.

Further support for the notion that the DA system is involved in the production of schizophrenic symptoms lies in research investigating binding densities of DA receptors. The effects on endogenous levels of DA work in combination with the receptor systems to which the DA binds. Six types of DA receptors have been identified and described. For instance, the D_2 receptor subtype is inhibitory in the second-messenger cascade. It inhibits adenylyl cyclase, which, as we learned in Chapter 5, normally catalyses adenosine triphosphate (ATP) to cyclic adenosine monophosphate (cAMP). The D_1 receptor, on the other hand, does the opposite: It activates adenylyl cyclase, thereby facilitating the production of cAMP. Abi-Dargham and coworkers (2000) found increased receptor-binding densities for D_1 DA receptors in the dorsolateral prefrontal cortex of schizophrenic patients with poorer cognitive function in working memory tasks. They hypothesized, however, that the increased receptors may be a compensatory effect for cognitive impairments; the compensatory mechanism did not significantly improve cognition.

Understanding more about the distribution of the DA receptors may help to elucidate the aforementioned receptor-binding density study. In schizophrenia, some symptoms involve altered functioning of areas regulated by brain regions that contain specific DA receptor subtypes, implicating a DA regulation. For example, rich concentrations of D_2 receptors populate the nucleus accumbens, caudate, and putamen as well as the cortex, hippocampus, and amygdala—areas that receive DA projections from the mesolimbic DA system. Surprising, though, is the high concentration of D_1 receptors in the caudate, cortex, and hippocampus—areas that receive DA projections from the mesocortical and mesolimbic DA systems. The sprinkling of D_2 and D_1 receptors in regions associated with emotion, memory, and cognition provides dopaminergic dominion over those processes. Hence, when considering the functions associated with areas of the brain involved in dopaminergic transmission, the DA hypothesis received further confirmation.

As compelling as the DA hypothesis is, however, additional research has highlighted inconsistencies in this theory. Consider the following conflicting evidence described by Robert Freedman (2003) of the University of Colorado:

1. When DA transmission is blocked, the symptoms of schizophrenia are not fully alleviated. The suggestion is that DA may interact with yet another neurotransmitter or neuromodulator, with its effects being primary and DA's, secondary.

2. The reduction in positive symptoms that is observed following antipsychotic medications is not accompanied by observed reductions in levels of DA receptors and metabolites—both of which remain in the range of normal values, indicating little effect on the DA system therein.

3. The role of DA is extremely complex in the brain and not likely to simply serve as a switch for the activation of psychotic symptoms. Yet, too simplistic a focus on DA alone leads to not a proper focus but rather a myopia in the requisite research.

4. The new antipsychotics discussed in the treatment section do not solely target DA receptors in the way that the earliest drugs did (they also target other neurotransmitters, such as serotonin and glutamate), yet they are successful at treating schizophrenic symptoms. The net result is a too complex set of interactions and subtle modulation that indicate multilevel control of basic cognition by the brain's neurochemistry has gone awry. A too simple obsession with a single neurotransmitter is detrimental to a finer understanding of these multiple subtleties.

So where does this evidence leave us? After spending a considerable amount of time learning about the potential role of DA in schizophrenia, do we just abandon the theory after considering the refuting evidence or refine it? The latter is clearly the best way to approach the problem empirically: hypothesize–test–reevaluate. Contemporary schizophrenia researchers have responded to the dilemma of partial confirmatory evidence with two research strategies. First, as suggested by Kenneth Davis and coworkers of the Mt. Sinai School of Medicine in New York (Davis, Kahn, Ko, & Davidson, 1991), the original hypothesis that schizophrenic symptoms were due to excessive levels of DA is being reconceptualized to suggest that decreased DA activity exists in the prefrontal cortex (perhaps leading to negative effects) and increased DA activity exists in the mesolimbic system (perhaps leading to positive symptoms). Second, increased attention is being placed on other neurochemicals that may be involved in the production of both positive and negative schizophrenic symptoms. Serotonin, glutamate, and acetylcholine are all being considered as potential neurochemical players in schizophrenia. Thus, whereas DA has not been abandoned as a neurochemical target of schizophrenia, the investigation has extended beyond it to include other neurochemicals and their interactions. It is becoming increasingly clear that the DA theory of schizophrenia is much more complicated than originally thought—no surprise, really, given the manifest and striking symptoms characteristic of the condition.

Nondopaminergic neurochemical involvement in schizophrenia. Serotonin may influence the neurochemical balance of schizophrenia. Theoretically, the "serotonin hypothesis" has merit: Serotonin regulates the hallucinogenic effects of psychedelic drugs such as lysergic acid diethylamide (LSD). Although such drugs typically induce mainly (but not exclusively) visual as opposed to auditory hallucinations, given serotonin's ubiquity, researchers still perceive a role for this neurotransmitter in the positive symptoms of schizophrenia (Aghajanian & Marek, 2000).

For example, serotonin is intimately linked to DA transmission. Specifically, serotonin largely inhibits dopaminergic function in both the midbrain and forebrain areas. Thus, drugs that antagonize serotonin ultimately release DA from inhibition, an effect that may be particularly helpful in the forebrain where DA activity appears to be low. As discussed in the next section, drugs such as clozapine have focused on the interaction between serotonin and DA (Kapur & Remington, 1996).

Another drug, phenylcyclohexylpiperidine (also known as PCP), has led researchers to focus on yet another neurotransmitter system. As is the case with many drugs developed for one purpose and ultimately abandoned for another, PCP was originally developed as an anesthetic but later forsaken when it was discovered that patients being so treated experienced adverse and unusual effects. At high dosages, PCP mimics much of the symptomology of schizophrenia, including delusions, hallucinations, and disordered thinking. PCP operates as a glutamate receptor antagonist, thereby leading to research on a role for glutamate in schizophrenic symptoms. Generally, levels of glutamate are lower in the cortex of schizophrenic patients, but interestingly, increased numbers of glutamatergic-positive axons have been observed, suggesting a reservoir of glutamate (Byne et al., 1999). Decreased levels of a glutamatergic enzyme were observed in postmortem analyses of dorsolateral prefrontal cortical tissue samples of postmortem schizophrenic patients. Subsequent analysis indicated increased expression of message for this particular enzyme (Ghose et al., 2004) in the latter, indicating genetic upregulation of cell signaling. Therefore, whereas glutamate seems to be altered in schizophrenia, the direction of this finding—not quite cause, not quite effect—remains unclear.

Finally, a drug with which schizophrenic patients have much voluntary experience and otherwise causes significant health problems, may provide another, albeit ironic, clue to the neurochemistry of schizophrenia. About 80% of individuals diagnosed with schizophrenia reportedly smoke cigarettes—lots of cigarettes. Two behaviors characteristic of schizophrenia, sensory-gating deficits (discussed later) and deficient smooth pursuit eye movements, are corrected by the nicotine emanating from the cigarettes (McEvoy & Allen, 2002). Thus, smoking may provide transient improvement for schizophrenic patients; it may be viewed as a form of self-medication (Freedman et al., 1994). Because brain nicotinic receptors are activated by the neurotransmitter acetylcholine, research has focused on its role in schizophrenia. The atypical antipsychotic clozapine interacts with another cholinergic receptor, the muscarinic receptor, thereby providing further evidence for the role of acetylcholine in the regulation of schizophrenia (Raedler et al., 2003). So, the patient diagnosed with schizophrenia is faced with a good news–bad news paradox: the Faustian option of impermanent relief from the fog of the condition versus further deterioration of basic health and well-being.

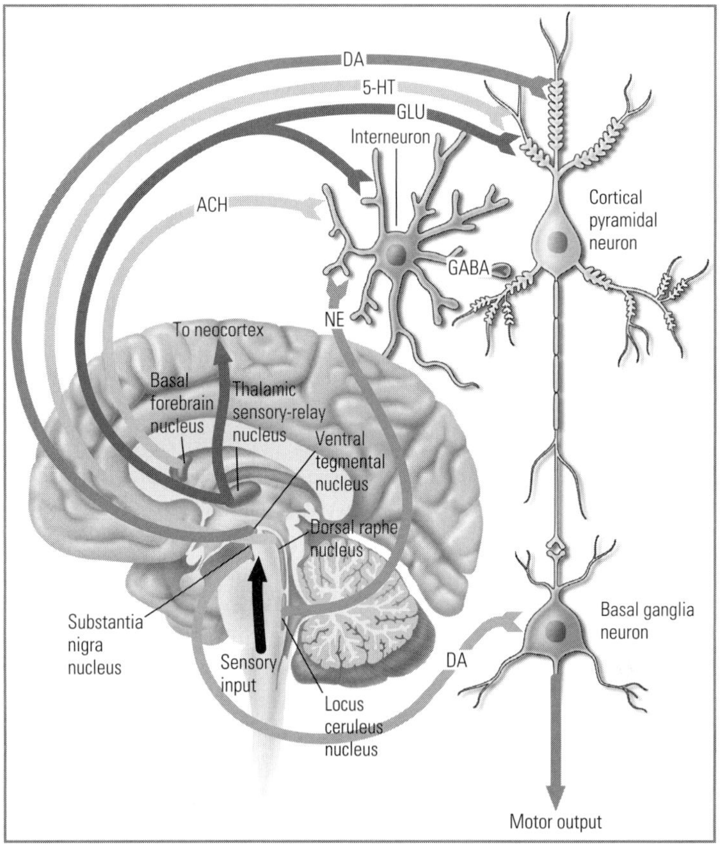

In sum, the once simplistic DA theory of schizophrenia is becoming increasingly complex as we now entertain the reconceptualized theory of schizophrenia. It has become increasingly apparent over the past several decades that several neurotransmitter systems are likely involved in schizophrenia. As seen in Figure 10.7, all four neurochemical candidates (DA, serotonin, glutamate, and acetylcholine) ultimately reach cortical pyramidal neurons, a region that is significantly altered—neurochemically, structurally, functionally—in schizophrenia.

DEVELOPMENTAL MARKERS OF SCHIZOPHRENIA

Thus far we have discussed neuroanatomical and neurochemical aspects of schizophrenia. To gain insight into the onset and developmental trajectory of this multifaceted brain disease, we now consider clues to schizophrenia's triggering stimuli and broader organization. We evaluate contributing factors from physical development, sensory-gating deficits, stress, and the controversial viral theories as they relate to the onset and development of schizophrenia.

Figure 10.7
Proposed neural circuits of schizophrenia. Cortical pyramidal neurons, seemingly so important in the development of schizophrenia, receive neurochemical input from ventral tegmental nucleus (DA), dorsal raphe nucleus (serotonin) and thalamic (Glutamate) afferents. Additionally, interneurons in the cerebral cortex receives ACh input from the basal forebrain nucleus, NE input from the locus coeruleus, and glutamatergic input from the thalamus. These interneurons influence the cortical pyramidal neurons via GABA release. The cortical pyramidal neurons, along with additional DA input from the substantia nigra nucleus, influence the basal ganglion neurons involved in motor output.

AFTER FREEDMAN, 2003

minor physical anomalies (MPAs) Minor structural abnormalities located in various areas of the body; they are typically investigated in accessible areas of the body including the head, mouth, ears, eyes, hands, and feet.

sensory-gating deficits The inability of schizophrenic patients to habituate the startle response to somewhat expected stimuli.

Evidence from Minor Physical Anomalies

Recall from this chapter's Connections that early motor and anomalous emotional signs are apparent in preschizophrenic children. In addition, some scientists report that subtle and not so subtle physical deformities—**minor physical anomalies (MPAs)**—are part of the makeup of the schizotypal individual. We all have small, minor neurodevelopmental mishaps—perhaps our ears are not perfectly aligned, our eyes are a bit too far apart, our hairline starts too far back, we have fewer neurons in some parts of our brains than we would like—that make us unique. Usually, these all too human conditions are nothing to be alarmed about, but as is evident in Down syndrome, numerous MPAs may represent significant misalignment in development, both external and internal.

Some research indicates that MPAs characteristic of schizophrenia shed visible light on disruption of the development of the brain (Green, 2001; Green, Satz, Ganzell, & Vaclav, 1992). For example, as we learn from our earliest exposure to media detectives, our fingerprints are unique; but such distinctive skin designs may be as valuable to clinical neuroscientists as criminologists: They may be telling indices of neurodevelopmental anomalies. In the human, the whorls and lines of our fingerprints are established between the fourteenth and twenty-second weeks of gestation. Thus, any aberrations in these prints may indicate a concomitant developmental disturbance. Some reports suggest that schizophrenic patients manifest fingerprint abnormalities, including atypical ridges. This observation may shed light on the variability that underlies the differences in schizophrenic incidence between identical twins. The fingerprints in Figure 10.8 show that the twin with schizophrenia has roughly half the ridge count of the normal twin (Bracha, Torrey, Bigelow, Lohr, & Linington, 1991; Bracha, Torrey, Gottesman, Bigelow, & Cunniff, 1992; Green, 2001). Though an interesting correlation, this "digital" marker tells a silent story of prenatal factors gone awry.

Hand preference, too, may provide additional confirmation of a disruption in neurodevelopment. Schizophrenic patients seem to shift away from an established handedness to a more ambiguous hand preference or ambidexterity. They switch hands depending on task and, when asked to repeat a task, may switch hands to perform the same task. The normal population displays no such parallel facility: Only about 2% of individuals adopt such atypical handedness, whereas in the schizophrenic population about 20% do (Green, 2001; Satz & Green, 1999).

Figure 10.8
Fingerprint patterns in schizophrenia. The total finger ridge count is almost twice as high in the healthy twin (left) as compared with the twin with schizophrenia.

BRACH, ET AL., AMERICAN JOURNAL OF PSYCHIATRY, 1992

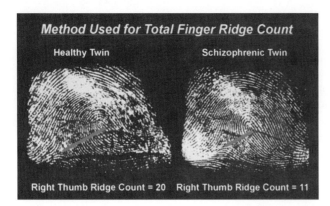

Sensory-Gating Deficits as a Common Denominator

If someone told you, "Now, get ready: After you hear this sound I am going to try scare you," what would happen? Not much, right? You will have anticipated the stimulus, and its effects would be muted. In a sense, you were able to *gate* this sensory stimulus in a way that diverted it from fear. Individuals with schizophrenia, however, find it difficult to show such habituation to auditory stimuli, a phenomenon known as "**sensory-gating deficit**."

Research on sensory gating examines the unexpected presentation of a loud auditory stimulus typically followed by a startle response in the subject. This startle response is accompanied by an easily identifiable response, like an eye-blink. In the next phase, a less threatening tone is presented prior to the loud noise, kind of a brief preview. Normally, the startle response is diminished by the presentation of the less threatening tone; in individuals with schizophrenia, though, the startle response rarely diminishes. They cannot suppress their startle response to the auditory stimulus even though they are aware that the stimulus poses no threat (Green, 2001). Another version of this laboratory test can be done with electroencephalographic patterns in which the P50 brain-wave response is assessed following the auditory stimuli. Again, unlike schizophrenics, normal subjects display a suppressed P50 wave following the repeated presentation of the auditory stimulus (Adler, Freedman, Ross, Olincy, & Waldo, 1999).

Sensory-gating deficits are very interesting when we consider the current knowledge about alterations to the thalamus in schizophrenia. Because the thalamus routes sensory information to the cortex for interpretation, it is easy to speculate that this structure may play a role in sensory-gating deficits, in much the same way that providing someone with bad directions delays or confuses the person. The inability to "filter" out irrelevant stimuli can easily be viewed as a simple model of what is going on in the brain of the patient with schizophrenia. The inability to filter out irrelevant auditory stimuli, past memories, or inner voices may be the result of sensory-gating deficits.

This effect also has interesting heritability as it is found not only in patients with schizophrenia but also in first-degree relatives with no such symptomology. Freedman and colleagues (1997) identified a gene on chromosome 15 that is associated with both sensory-gating deficits and the cholinergic nicotinic receptor. As we describe in Box 10.2, this relationship is important in schizophrenia research using animal models.

Stress and Developmental Predisposition

Why does it take so long for schizophrenia to develop if the conditions are extant before birth or in childhood? Are these early states, involving brisk and sensitive neuronal development, imaginary friends, sensory worlds alive with distracting stimuli, somehow more persistent or susceptible to bending to the whim of preschizophrenic events? Strong theoretical evidence points to stress, broadly defined, as a significant variable at work in the expression of schizophrenia. Researchers suggest that stress may, for example, play a role in the physical anomalies linked to the disorder. Koenig, Kirkpatrick, and Lee (2002) report that adrenal hormones, particularly the glucocorticoids, may interfere with normal development. The additional strain of these chemical events may lead to deleterious changes in the delicate developing brain. This **neural diathesis–stress model** of schizophrenia assumes, first, that individuals possess a certain predisposition (a diathesis) toward schizophrenia and, second, that a subsequent significant stressor can foster later expression of schizophrenic symptoms. This is due to an interaction: Either alone may be inconsequential; together, they facilitate schizophrenia.

In their work on schizotypal factors described at the beginning of this chapter, Elaine Walker and colleagues suggest that adolescence—a time of

neural diathesis–stress model of schizophrenia
Updated adaptation of the classic diathesis–stress model that emphasizes the role of alterations in steroidal hormones in the expression and severity of schizophrenic symptoms. Because of the dramatic changes in these hormones at puberty, Elaine Walker and colleagues have proposed that adolescence should be considered a critical phase in the development of schizophrenia.

Box 10.2

Brain Matters

Animal Models of Schizophrenia

Like thieves, diseases that affect the mind rob a piece of humanity from the afflicted person, be it thought, consciousness, or self-control. As detailed in Chapter 9, animal models of disease or of treatment have accelerated the pace of research on mental disorders, particularly in the development of drug treatments. For schizophrenia, serendipity played a large role, but the real progress in antidopaminergic medications and other antipsychotics was pioneered in animal models.

The evidence that disturbances in the prefrontal cortex were a significant part of the cognitive deterioration of schizophrenia was confirmed in nonhuman primates. And future neurobiological therapies and treatments will be tested for efficacy in animals en route to their application to the schizophrenic brain.

El-Khodor and Boksa (2001) have extended in rats an interesting association observed in schizophrenia.

Schizophrenia is correlated with increased birth complications (which affects mesolimbic dopamine levels), and stress has been shown to mediate schizophrenic symptoms. In the rat, cesarean birth alters adult levels of dopamine (DA) D_1 receptors and the stress-induced regulation of brain D_3 and D_4 receptors as well. The authors conclude that "interactions between an individual's experience of stress at adulthood, together with other environmental events in their history, such as birth complications, can be important determinants of brain DA receptor levels" (p. 423). The data are intriguing because of the link between the role of DA and its receptors and early experiences in the expression of schizophrenia.

One application for schizophrenia comes from the research on knockout mice, which lack a variety of substances known to be involved in schizophrenia. Gainetdinov, Mohn, and Caron (2001) advocate and support the use of transgenic knockout mice lacking, respectively, for example, the DA transporter and the NMDA receptor (which binds glutamate, the brain's major excitatory neurotransmitter). In general, they make the point that selective knockout mice make powerful animal models for the study of

stress for both child and parent—is a critical developmental phase for schizophrenia precisely because of the altered processing of steroid hormones (e.g., gonadal and hypothalamic–pituitary–adrenal [HPA] axis hormones). Adrenal steroid hormones enhance DA functioning—an effect that, given the DA data and connections we have discussed, could easily influence schizophrenia (Walker & Diforio, 1997; Walker, Logan, & Walder, 1999). Corticosterone increases DA synthesis across the brain, and HPA activation alters DA receptors—effects that are more prevalent in adulthood (Walker & Diforio, 1997; Henry et al., 1995), suggesting a developmental interaction.

In a past review of the relevant stress literature, Norman and Malla (1993a, 1993b) found little evidence supporting the observation that schizophrenic patients experienced more severe postnatal stressors than did nonschizophrenic individuals, but they reported a correlation between stressful events and the severity of schizophrenic symptoms. Others have reported that increased stressful life events are more likely to occur in the months preceding relapse (Walker & Diforio, 1997).

Read, Perry, Moskowitz, and Connolly (2001) examined the hypothesis that stress of another and later form—childhood abuse and harm—may play a role in the multidetermination of schizophrenia. They report that many observations of the home life of schizophrenic patients document a history of abuse. They argue that developmental exposure to such difficult conditions may hypersensitize sensory and stress-responsive systems in the adult, thereby contributing to the eventual display of schizophrenic symptoms. It is difficult

schizophrenia and its treatment, especially its neuro-chemical underpinnings.

Another research direction of interest and one that represents overlap between humans with schizophrenia and animal models is prepulse inhibition (PPI). The presentation of a signaling stimulus has the usual effect of diminishing a response to a larger, subsequently presented stimulus, much like an immunization creates a buffer against the subsequent disease. As described in this chapter, hearing a briefly presented tone reduces a startle response to another sound presented more loudly milliseconds later. Schizophrenic patients display a reduced PPI, suggesting a significant sensory-gating deficit (Parwani et al., 2000). In other words, more data can intrude on their brains.

Modeling this sensorimotor-gating phenomenon in animals, Black, Selk, Hitchcock, Wettstein, and Sorensen (1999) implicate the gaseous neurotransmitter nitric oxide (NO) in the development of schizophrenia and effects on PPI. They treated young rats with the NO antagonist l-nitroarginine, which depletes NO by acting on its enzyme, NO synthase. They report that in adulthood treated males showed hypersensitivity to DA agonists and deficits in PPI and that females showed a similar effect for phencyclidine (PCP) but not PPI. The effects on the neurochemical systems are interesting, as is the report of the sex difference, both of which bear on observations made in humans with schizophrenia.

The use of PPI as a bridge between humans and other animals has been investigated further. Paylor and Crawley (1997) reported on the feasibility of using inbred mice for the modeling of schizophrenic symptoms and treatments, especially sensorimotor gating and PPI responses. Their detailed parametric work paved the way for many animal studies investigating the link between a well-observed phenomenon in human schizophrenics and an empirical and replicable behavioral response in animals, that of PPI. Crawley and coworkers (1997) also demonstrate that certain inbred strains may provide useful animal models for many psychiatric or neurobiological conditions, such as anxiety, drug abuse, aggression, and social behaviors. Therefore, the use of animal models can go a long way to providing the necessary "neuroscience" that eventually unites to the "clinical," thereby speeding the delivery of treatments and cures to those afflicted with a variety of disorders.

to disentangle, too, the possibility that aberrant behavioral patterns may have invited scorn or unwanted attention to the borderline or developing preschizophrenic, thereby contributing to or exacerbating the onset of the condition.

In a detailed study of German schizophrenic patients and their families, Holzinger, Kilian, Lindenbach, Petscheleit, and Angermeyer (2003) report that psychosocial stress is regularly observed in the background of adults with schizophrenia. These correlations suggesting exacerbating properties of stress are thought-provoking, but they require additional empirical confirmation. Additionally, it is important to consider that many schizophrenic patients report no such significant stressors in their childhood.

Viral Theory Controversy

The schizophrenic brain is wired differently and, consequently, malfunctions accordingly. How might such effects come about? One novel explanation with some empirical support suggests that the fetus is exposed to a virus during a critical stage of prenatal development (Karlsson et al., 2001). Support for this idea started, like many areas of science, with the observation of an intriguing correlation. The city of Helsinki, Finland, fell victim to a pandemic of influenza in the late 1950s, infecting scores of pregnant women in their last two trimesters. The offspring of these flu-exposed mothers were significantly more likely to display schizophrenic symptoms per 1,000 live births compared with the rates in the city of Helsinki at other time periods before or after the pandemic.

Other, less confounded explanations for the data have been suggested, and the evidence that the subjects were actually infected with the flu is indirect (no cultures were taken and then saved for subsequent analyses, for example); but the association is compelling. Subsequent work investigating the viral theory produced mixed results (Mednick, Machon, Huttunen, & Bonett 1988), but a 2003 investigation of the effects of influenza was conducted on nearly 1,000 adults with schizophrenia (Limosin, Rouillon, Payan, Cohen, & Strub, 2003). When compared with nonschizophrenic siblings, those with schizophrenia were more likely to have been exposed to influenza, especially during the fifth month of the mother's pregnancy.

These data point to a critical prenatal period during which the fetal brain may be especially susceptible to viral insults, of the sort that might disrupt the fragile processes of neurogenesis and migration, described in Chapter 6. Nevertheless, it may be the temporal aspects, not the infection per se, that derails brain development and predisposes the infant to dementia down the line. At a time when the brain is actively developing, literally dividing itself over and over again, the virus, with its own DNA-altering machinery and ramifications, may redirect brain structure and function. During the latter months of fetal growth, brain development occurs swiftly. In fact, the brain begins to resemble the human version, with its wrinkly and multilayered complexity, involutions, and characteristic appearance, only during the last few months of gestation. This is plenty of time for the viral monkey-wrench-in-the-works to wreak neural havoc.

TREATMENTS FOR SCHIZOPHRENIA

Therapy for schizophrenic symptoms exists in multiple forms. Several different types of antipsychotics exist, and awareness of the importance of psychosocial intervention and neurocognitive training is increasing. Now that researchers are gaining a more accurate picture of the neuroanatomical, neurophysiological, and neurochemical alterations in the schizophrenic brain, alternative treatments with enhanced success and limited side effects are sure to emerge. Currently, about 40% of patients diagnosed with schizophrenia show improvement over time. Although encouraging to physicians and researchers, this number is discouraging for the millions of individuals coping with this unwelcome neuronal "poltergeist" (Green, 2001).

Contemporary treatment regimens include a miscellaneous array of pharmacological agents that change continually as we map their diverse underlying chemical currents and eddies. Additionally, as the concept of the plasticity of the brain across the life span is increasingly accepted, neurocognitive training programs are becoming more prevalent. Certain psychosocial approaches benefit the schizophrenic patient through training and by modifying behaviors that enable the individual to fit into society. These programs emphasize the importance of attention from many valuable sources such as family, peers, and medical practitioners.

Somatic Therapies

In Chapter 2 we described some historic—and drastic—treatments of schizophrenia, such as insulin comas, frontal lobotomies, and the most prevalent form of therapy for schizophrenia during the first half of the twentieth century, hydrotherapy. Here, patients were placed in a hammock, submerged in a frigid tub, and exposed to either wet packs or continuous baths. A sheet was placed over the top of the tub with only the patient's head showing, mummy-like. Treatments could last up to several hours, an interminable amount of time for the "dunkee."

Doctors who administered this treatment, with little empirical support, saw hydrotherapy as an authentic strategy that influenced the brain via the avenue of the body; the damp and shriveled patients, however, were not as enthusiastic. It was perceived as torturous by some, especially when extreme water temperatures were used (Green, 2001). Here, like so much else in the checkered treatment history of this condition, some familiarity with empirical assessment would have shown these otherwise intelligent physicians what a foolhardy approach this was.

A recent treatment, repetitive transcranial magnetic stimulation (rTMS), discussed in Chapter 9, appears to suppress auditory hallucinations in medication-resistant patients, with the effects lasting for months (Hoffman et al., 2003). Although still in its infancy, rTMS is viewed as a milder form of electroconvulsive therapy (ECT), which also influences the firing patterns of large populations of neurons within the brain. Today, though its mechanism is unknown, ECT is viewed as a treatment option for schizophrenic patients who have not responded to the standard therapies described in this section— cold-immersion baths notwithstanding. Additionally, ECT is successful for catatonic schizophrenic patients (Chanpattana & Kramer, 2003; Suzuki, Awata, & Matsuoka, 2003). Nevertheless, shocking the delicate tissues of the brain seems a crude way to effect change.

Pharmacological Therapy

A cornucopia of drugs represents the peril and the hope of the biological treatment of schizophrenia. Treating deficiencies using a chemical strategy that focuses on dopaminergic transmission has been effective at restoring the schizophrenic patient to society, albeit incompletely and with a separate set of problems or side effects brought on by the very drugs that are supposed to help. For example, like a pharmacological oil spill, the drug effects spread farther and wider and into regions in which the fragile balance of neuron and transmitter is working properly, thereby creating a problem where there was none previously. Although schizophrenia is becoming better understood, the practical drug treatment regimen lags behind the theorizing and data that support its use.

Drugs do work, but they merely manage the symptoms of schizophrenia; they do not cure the disease. Like the diabetes for those patients who require a daily regimen of insulin, without medication, the disease will overtake the patient. Drug therapy generally does wonders for some forms of schizophrenia, but side effects can be horrendous and intrusive and force the patient (or the doctor) to decide between two evils: the degradation of the disease or the debilitating effects of the pharmaceuticals designed to treat it. In some cases, the cure is worse than the disease.

The several classes of drugs we describe all share one insidious feature: They act all over the brain, including regions that are not deficient, and interfere with perfectly normal neurochemical activity, the oil-spill metaphor. In particular, as mentioned earlier, are the extrapyramidal effects, in which

antipsychotics Psychoactive drugs that reduce psychotic symptoms but have long-term side effects resembling symptoms of neurological diseases.

the antidopaminergic actions of the drugs cause a range of motor/movement problems. In addition to doing what is intended, inadvertent effects create parallel problems, reducing the patient's motivation to continue taking the drugs. The vicious cycle of symptoms/drug/side effects is a condition from which today's patient cannot, as yet, be rescued. The drugs do much good, but they do harm as well.

Interestingly, certain drugs affect certain categories of schizophrenic symptoms. Recall that positive symptoms are symptoms that are displayed by the schizophrenic patient but not observed in normal individuals (Andreasen, 2001). These symptoms include delusions, irrational beliefs, and hallucinations, most of which interact to create vivid internal storms and frightful external symptoms. Negative symptoms are behaviors displayed by nonschizophrenic individuals but not typically observed in schizophrenic patients (Andreasen, 2001). For example, a flattening of affect results in decreased emotional communication and is displayed by schizophrenic patients as they stare relentlessly outward, disconnected, failing to respond to others or to the environment.

Four major groups of drugs known as **antipsychotics** are used to treat schizophrenia. Three of the groups are further characterized as *typical antipsychotics*—these groups are older and, hence, called "typical" or "classic"—and one as *atypical antipsychotics*. Typical antipsychotic drug groups include the butyrophenones (haloperidol), the phenothiazines (chlorpromazine), and the thioxanthenes and are generally more effective against positive symptoms. The atypical antipsychotics include the drugs clozapine, olanzapine, and risperidone and are generally more effective against negative symptoms.

The first drug shown to have a significant positive effect on the schizophrenic patient—quite inadvertently—was chlorpromazine (Thorazine). Originally developed as an antihistamine and later used as a tranquilizer to mollify postsurgical patients, chlorpromazine was extended from the surgical ward to the psychiatric clinic by observant and innovative physicians who realized its potential. Heinrichs (2001) presents a brief and interesting history of this first antipsychotic, which demonstrates that serendipity is sometimes as valuable as deduction.

The cascade of bizarre behaviors that categorizes schizophrenia—the auditory and visual hallucinations, the staccato word salad, the disordered thought patterns—is becalmed by chlorpromazine (Thorazine). This calming effect gives rise to an undesirable symptom, a motor condition in which the patient slowly and haltingly skates along an imaginary track from point to point, giving this side effect its derisive and well-known nickname, the "Thorazine shuffle."

Following the success of Thorazine and the discovery of its DA-antagonistic properties, new drugs with an increased ability to antagonize DA receptors were developed. Haloperidol (Haldol), for example, was 100 times more potent than chlorpromazine. The increase in potency came with its own neurochemical baggage: an increase in side effects. The enhanced DA blockage in the basal ganglia led to Parkinson-like symptoms, including the development of the haunting, uncontrollable facial and tongue movements of *tardive dyskinesia*.

Today, these earlier medications are known as first-generation antipsychotic agents. Generally, only about 20% of patients experience a complete remission following treatment with these drugs. Most patients, however, experience a reduction in symptoms. These drugs also significantly decrease relapse rates: Roughly 30% experience relapse compared with an 80% relapse rate in nonmedicated patients.

As mentioned previously, the first-generation antipsychotics produced many unwelcome side effects. In addition to the involuntary extrapyramidal effects (namely, tardive dyskinesia and tremor), these agents produced symptoms such as severe restlessness, decreased voluntary movement, and core temperature dysregulation. Consequently, a second generation of antipsychotic drugs was later introduced in an attempt to decrease the side effects associated with the earlier ones. Additionally, enhancing efficacy was a priority in the development of these drugs.

Clozapine (Clozaril) was the first drug introduced in the second wave of antipsychotics. Clozapine was considered an atypical antipsychotic because it possessed more efficacious antipsychotic effects with minimal movement effects. This drug was not perfect—it introduced the new, dangerous side effect *agranulocytosis*, an acute diminution in infection-fighting white blood cells (leukocytes). Because this condition was observed in 0.39% of users, it is important that all patients taking this medication have their white blood cell counts closely monitored by a physician. Interestingly, clozapine successfully treated schizophrenic symptoms in about 30% of the patients who did not respond to the other pharmacological treatments.

How do the mechanisms of the first atypical antipsychotic drug differ from those of the typical antipsychotics? Clozapine results in antagonist effects at a more diverse array of DA receptors, including D_1, D_2, and D_4 receptors. Additionally, the drug antagonizes serotonin and noradrenaline receptors. Finally, clozapine increases the amount of acetylcholine released at the synapse, which is interesting considering that patients who had been heavy smokers prior to medication reduce smoking once clozapine treatment commences.

The differential D_2 DA receptor binding can be seen in Figure 10.9. Notice that the brain to the left, which is a nonmedicated brain, has an abundance of activity in the basal ganglia. In contrast, the middle brain is medicated with haloperidol and consequently shows no available D_2 receptors. The third brain is medicated with clozapine and shows a moderate amount of D_2 DA receptor availability (Barondes, 1993). Therefore, the various interactions of drug with DA-system components are evident.

With the success of clozapine, additional second-generation agents were introduced. These newer drugs, including risperidone (Risperdal), olanzapine (Zyprexa), quetiapine (Seroquel), and ziprasidone (Geodon), capitalized

Figure 10.9 Dopaminergic Receptor Activity in Medicated Schizophrenia Patients. PET scans of these brains indicate D_2DA receptor binding and are used to learn more about the activity of successful schizophrenia medications. As seen in the unmedicated brain on the left, extensive binding in the basal ganglia is observed in the absence of pharmacological interventions. The brain medicated with haloperidol (in middle), a D_2DA ligand, exhibits no binding due to receptor sites already occupied by the drug. The brain on the right is medicated with clozapine and exhibits moderate D_2 receptor binding.

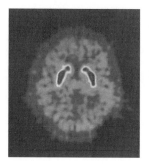 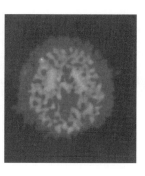 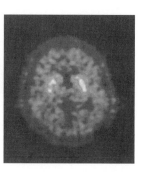

on the dual serotonergic/dopaminergic action of clozapine. Generally, these second-generation antipsychotics are as successful as or more successful than the first-generation drugs at treating the symptoms of schizophrenia with fewer motor side effects, including decreased occurrences of the hellish tardive dyskinesia.

Whereas the first-generation antipsychotics effectively treated the positive symptoms, the newer drugs also successfully treated negative symptoms. Regarding the disadvantages, the second-generation drugs can cause significant weight gain, as well as diabetes mellitus (Freedman, 2003; Tamminga, 1999). See Table 10.3 for a summary of popular antipsychotic drug effects and their physiological effects.

Because the perfect antipsychotic has yet to be introduced, the search for more effective medications continues. Treating schizophrenia with agents that mark the neurotransmitter glutamate is being explored. Blockade of the N-methyl-d-aspartate (NMDA) receptor for glutamate in control subjects can produce clinical symptoms very similar to those of schizophrenia (Krystal et al., 1994; Malhotra et al., 1996). Further, NMDA agents such as d-cycloserine and d-serine, taken in combination with existing antipsychotics, have been shown to ameliorate schizophrenic symptoms (Goff, Tsai, Manoach, & Coyle, 1995; Tsai, Yang, Chung, Lange, & Coyle, 1998). Finally, a few of the newer antipsychotics are focusing strictly on the dopaminergic receptor again—but to varying degrees in different receptors. For example, amisulpride (Solian) antagonizes D_2 and D_3 DA receptors in the cortex but not in the basal ganglia, and aripiprazole (Abilify) facilitates only low-level DA receptor stimulation (Freedman, 2003).

In sum, antipsychotic drugs were—and remain—a boon to the treatment of schizophrenia. Before their introduction, patients were a mass of symptoms. The trade-off between cognitive improvement and significant side effects was in favor of the patient, who showed marked progress. The shortcoming of the antipsychotic drugs is that they treat only the symptoms of schizophrenia, not the cause. Like taking aspirin for a headache caused by a fractured skull, once the drug's effects wear off, the system remains unchanged. Furthermore, after the assault on the existing malfunctioning

Table 10.3 Antipsychotic Drugs and Their Mechanisms

Pharmacological Target	Drug	Physiological Result
D_2 DA antagonist	Haloperidol	Blocks DA-facilitated pyramidal neuron activation
D_2 DA and serotonin$_{2A}$ antagonism	Olanzapine, resiperidone, quetiapine, ziprasidone	Blocks DA-facilitated pyramidal neuron activation as well as serotonin facilitation of glutamate secretion
Diverse actions	Clozapine	DA and serotonergic antagonism resulting in decreased pyramidal neuronal activation; increased ACh release, norepinephrine antagonism resulting in increased interneuron communication with pyramidal neurons
Dopamine agonism/antagonism	Aripiprazole	Activates low-level stimulation of DA receptors; suppresses high-level stimulation
DA D_2 and D_3 antagonism	Amisulpride	Blocks cortical DA receptors with no effect on basal ganglia

DA, dopamine; ACh, acetylcholine.
Adapted from Freedman (2003).

neurochemistry, the inundation by these powerful drugs further alters the chemistry of the brain, making a formerly sensitive system increasingly resistant, thereby increasing the dosage required to achieve the same effect, or stimulating interactions in otherwise normally functioning neural regions.

This reciprocity demonstrates the delicate balance that is steamrolled by the aggressive antipsychotic chemicals used in the medical treatment of schizophrenia. Thus, although these pharmacological agents provide a priceless respite from the voices and cognitive derailments associated with schizophrenia, they should be used with extreme caution under the close supervision of an appropriate, cautious, and empirical practitioner. In fact, it is usually recommended that pharmacological treatment accompany other forms of treatment such as neurocognitive training and psychosocial therapy, which can reinforce the effects of the drugs.

Neurocognitive Training

Therapeutic interest has recently turned to attempts to enhance the cognitive abilities of schizophrenic patients. When a person suffers an accident and loses the ability to move, a physical therapist exercises the afflicted muscles to restore their flexibility, mobility, and strength. Mental health researchers have begun to wonder if cognitive exercises could act similarly, restoring full cognitive function to schizophrenic patients.

Though in its infancy, the research is promising, suggesting that schizophrenic patients do show improvement in cognition after intense and focused cognitive training. For example, gains have been observed in card sorting and vigilance, frontal lobe–mediated tasks often abridged in those individuals (Green, 1993; Green et al., 1992; Medalia, Aluma, Tryon, & Merriam, 1998). More research is necessary to determine the most effective modes of cognitive training, the required duration, and the modes of action. According to Andreasen (2001), cognitive training programs are "designed to help patients learn to focus attention more precisely, to solve problems more efficiently or more rapidly, to monitor ideas and speech more effectively, and to improve both motor and mental coordination" (p. 214). These goals and objectives summate to focus on areas that define the problem set of schizophrenia.

Recently, Michael Merzenich and his colleagues have investigated the effects of neuroplasticity-based cognitive therapy on global cognitive effects in patients with schizophrenia. In one study, clinically stable patients diagnosed with schizophrenia were exposed to either 50 hours of auditory training software or the same amount of time interacting with computer games. Following assessment, significant improvements in verbal cognitive processes were observed in the neuroplasticity-based auditory training group (Fisher, Holland, Merzenich, & Vinogradov, 2009). In another study, patients with schizophrenia received either targeted cognitive training (via software) or a computer game control condition. Even at a 6-month follow-up assessment, the cognitive training (targeting auditory, visual, and cognitive control functions) led to improvements in verbal learning/memory and cognitive control. In a group of patients exposed to a "dose" of 100 hours of cognitive training exposure, improvements in processing speed and global cognition were observed (Fisher, Holland, Subramaniam, & Vinogradov, 2009). Although requiring additional objective verification and testing, the work holds some promise.

Psychosocial Therapy

In the book *Of Two Minds*, Luhrmann (2000) makes the point that a large divide separates therapists who would treat the schizophrenic patient and those who would treat the schizophrenic brain. Reinforcing the notion that a multifaceted approach is effective, though with clearly an emphasis on the latter, a strategy that combines the cognitive/social and the biochemical approaches appears to be preferable to a single approach alone. Variations of the psychotherapy approach recognize that schizophrenia is a disease that has inputs (stressors, intrusive thoughts, and so on) from many different areas of the patient's life. Emphasizing the layers that contribute to the totality of the schizophrenic patient's thoughts and actions, the therapeutic approaches utilized by the clinic focus many forces on the patient's recovery.

Multitiered approaches are able to combine different aspects of the individual treatments available to the patient. For instance, outpatient facilities are available for schizophrenic patients; these services allow for the observation and treatment of the person in times of crisis and help and support at other times. The interaction with other clinic inpatients adds support and shared experiences to the cognitive load of the patient. This treatment plan, though more challenging to quantify and assess than more narrow treatment approaches, is reported to be efficacious (Cozolino, Goldstein, Nuechterlein, West, & Snyder, 1988; Heinrichs, 2001).

The outpatient clinic also has the advantage of having medical intervention close by, if needed, and access to more complete psychiatric services. Further, the structure afforded by the regimentation of the hospital environment may be beneficial to the schizophrenic patient on an as-needed basis for brief periods (weekends, for instance). The individual in these clinics is less a patient and more a person; greater attention has benefits that translate into success rates for the schizophrenic patient.

When combined with support from family members and friends outside the clinic (who themselves require some education, and stress-reduction training, in how to live and interact with an individual diagnosed with schizophrenia), there is marked reduction in recurrence and severity rates (Lenroot, Bustillo, Lauriello, & Keith, 2003). Again, the familial and personal resources brought to bear on combating the illness ensure that the patient will benefit from one or more of the tacks being offered. In short, the social support systems work by extending the clinic to the home. There, the patient can be exposed to a "best of both worlds" combination of family/friend support and professional guidance.

Summary

Overview of Schizophrenia

Bleuler chose *schizophrenia* as the name for the cluster of symptoms consisting of social withdrawal, delusions, hallucinations, and disorganized cognition because he felt that the cognitive abilities were "splitting" from the normal functions of the mind. Today, positive, negative, and disorganized symptoms are associated with this disorder.

Neurobiology of Schizophrenia

The strong genetic relationship in schizophrenia is revealed by a concordance rate of nearly 50% in identical twins reared apart. It is well established that schizophrenia is associated with significant neural architectural anomalies, including malformations in the arrangement of neurons in the cortex and hippocampus, together with gross effects such as enlargement of the ventricles and consequent loss of gray matter.

Schizophrenia has classically been defined, neurochemically, by dysregulation of dopamine. The so-called dopamine hypothesis states that an excess of dopamine interferes with normal neurotransmission. This is a simplistic picture of a complex condition, akin to attributing depression to deficit of serotonin. Today, however, other neurochemicals such as glutamate, serotonin, and acetylcholine have been associated with schizophrenic symptoms.

Developmental Markers of Schizophrenia

Several developmental theories have been proposed to help us understand the initial trigger and trajectory of the expression of schizophrenic symptoms. Certain minor physical anomalies in individuals who develop schizophrenia suggest that neuronal misalignment occurs in the earliest stages of development of the schizophrenic patient. Impairment observed in schizophrenic patients' ability to habituate to certain tones suggests that an ineffective processing of nonthreatening stimuli may be a common

denominator in the schizophrenic brain. Other research suggests that stress may trigger the schizophrenic cascade in predisposed individuals. Finally, immunological challenges such as virus exposure may also serve as a trigger for the development of schizophrenia.

Treatments for Schizophrenia

Pharmacotherapy is currently the most pervasive form of therapy for schizophrenia. The first generation of drugs used to combat schizophrenic symptoms targeted the dopaminergic system. More recently, second-generation drugs have targeted other neurochemicals such as serotonin, glutamate, and various dopamine receptors. With attention focused on neuroplasticity, it is now thought that certain forms of cognitive training may benefit the disorganized cognitive symptoms associated with schizophrenia. Finally, attention is also focused on integrative psychosocial treatment approaches in which life-functioning strategies, the support of family and friends, and outpatient medical services are all considered significant components of the treatment strategy.

Key Terms

hallucinations (293)

catatonia (293)

hebephrenia (293)

dementia praecox (293)

schizophrenia (294)

positive symptoms (294)

negative symptoms (294)

disorganized symptoms (294)

minor physical anomalies (MPAs) (312)

sensory-gating deficits (312)

neural diathesis–stress model of schizophrenia (313)

antipsychotics (318)

For Further Consideration

Andreasen, N. C. (2001). *Brave new brain: Conquering mental illness in the era of the genome.* New York: Oxford University Press. Andreasen set out to produce a book that captures the excitement of neuroscientists who are looking toward the future when "mental illness" will move into the realm of serious cures. She succeeds. Furthermore, this volume captures the anticipation of the forthcoming results from the nascent Human Genome Project. One thing to remember, however, is that promise is one thing but results are quite another. Unfortunately, we have a long way to go.

Freedman, R. (2003). Schizophrenia. *New England Journal of Medicine, 349,* 1738–1749. If you are interested in a review of the past and present drugs used to treat schizophrenia, this article will take you on a journey through the development of the typical and atypical antipsychotics. Freedman subsequently presents an argument against the traditional dopaminergic theory of schizophrenia. Additionally, current research investigating several different neurotransmitter systems such as glutamate, serotonin, and acetylcholine is discussed with an emphasis placed on the emerging apparent importance of glutamate involvement in schizophrenia. Readers will walk away from this well-written article with a healthy appreciation of the complex nature of the neurochemistry underlying schizophrenic symptoms.

Green, M. F. (2001). *Schizophrenia revealed: From neurons to social interactions.* New York: Norton. Green is a professor in the UCLA Department of Psychiatry and Biobehavioral Sciences and is chief of the treatment unit of the Department of Veterans Affairs Mental Illness Research clinical center. Therefore, Green writes from the double perspective of clinician and researcher and is able to present a full, multifaceted perspective of schizophrenia and potential treatments. This book is written for the layperson, so there is more breadth than depth in his narrative. The book includes many recent references, however, that interested readers can consult.

Heinrichs, R. W. (2001). *In search of madness: Schizophrenia and neuroscience.* New York: Oxford University Press. As the title suggests, this book focuses on the place that neuroscience can and will hold in understanding and treating schizophrenia. Heinrichs plays the skeptic throughout, critically examining and evaluating the multifaceted study of this terrible disease. It is not an easy task or read, but his use of meta-analyses and his application of effect sizes keep the data in perspective for the reader. One is less likely to be wowed by grandiose claims about new treatments and effects when one sees that the difference between experimental and control groups is marginally significant. He keeps the field grounded and tied to its critical roots. Psychiatry would do well to pay attention to the cautious and empirical approach displayed in Heinrichs's book.

Karlsson, H., Bachmann, S., Schröder, J., McArthur, J., Torrey, E. F., & Yolken, R. H. (2001). Retroviral RNA identified in the cerebrospinal fluids and brains of individuals with schizophrenia. *Proceedings of the National Academy of Sciences USA, 98,* 4634–4639. In this very detailed and technologically advanced study, the authors investigate the hypothesis that retroviruses play a significant role in the pathogenesis of schizophrenia. In 29% of recent-onset schizophrenic or schizoaffective disorder patients, the authors found evidence of retroviral genes (human endogenous retroviral, HERV-W family) in the sampled cerebrospinal fluid (CSF); 5% of chronic schizophrenics' CSF contained virus. Further, evidence of the virus was found in the frontal cortex in the schizophrenics. In contrast, no evidence of the retroviruses was observed in control patients (those with noninflammatory neurological disease or nonpsychiatric subjects). The authors conclude that "the transcriptional activation of certain retroviral elements within the central nervous system may be associated with the development of schizophrenia in at least some individuals. Correlation does not infer causation, but these data strongly support the virus theory of schizophrenia development."

Silbersweig, D. A., Stern, E., Frith, C., Cahill, C., Holmes, A., Grootoonk, S., et al. (1995). A functional neuroanatomy of hallucinations in schizophrenia. *Nature, 378,* 176–179. This is a seminal paper. It shows for the first time the inner workings of the schizophrenic brain, shedding a sober scientific light on a mental illness. Furthermore, it goes a long way to removing the stigma of schizophrenia and should reduce any argument any skeptic has that schizophrenia is not a brain/biological malady.

Thompson, P. M., Vidal, C., Giedd, J. N., Gochman, P., Blumenthal, J., Nicolson, R., et al. (2001). Mapping adolescent brain change reveals dynamic wave of accelerated gray matter loss in very early-onset schizophrenia. *Proceedings of the National Academy of Sciences USA, 98,* 11650–11655. This paper attempts to reconcile the nature-versus-nurture debate that surrounds the study of schizophrenia—as Updike called it, the "inheritance and circumstance" of life (John Updike, "A Soft Spring Night in Shillington," 1989). The authors applied a clever brain-mapping technique that utilizes fMRI technology in a population of early-onset schizophrenics. The patients were scanned every 2 years for a period of 6 years. The data showed a shifting pattern of tissue loss in schizophrenia that was correlated with a variety of symptom sets (for example, a mirroring "of the neuromotor, auditory, visual search, and frontal executive impairments in the disease," p. 11650, and subsequent loss of gray matter). For the first time, as if watching a time-lapse video of an event unfolding, the neuroscientists were able to observe the progression of this disorder in the brains of the subjects.

Connections

Vulnerability to Addiction: Threatened Territories in North America and in the Laboratory

Chief Joseph and his Nez Percé tribe were ordered off lands in the Pacific Northwest by the U.S. government in 1873. Joseph's refusal to relinquish his land prompted a series of battles between his tribe and U.S. Army troops. Eventually, Joseph and 750 Nez Percé tribal members were forced to retreat toward Canada. Just outside the Canadian border, U.S. troops surrounded Joseph and his people, forcing the chief to surrender. The bold leader seemed helpless and defeated as he made his famous speech: "Hear me, my chiefs! I am tired; my heart is sick and sad. From where the sun now stands I will fight no more forever."

Chief Joseph's story is one among countless examples (the Cherokees' Trail of Tears is another) of the severe, chronic stress suffered by the Native Americans as their familiar worlds and ways of life were stripped from them. Today, compared with Americans of all other races and ethnicities, Native Americans die more often from suicide, homicide, and accidents—most related to alcohol addiction. In fact, epidemiological data suggest epidemic levels of alcohol-related deaths, especially motor vehicle crash fatalities, among Native Americans (Campos-Outcalt, Prybylski, Watkins, Rothfus, & Dellapenna, 1997; Chang, Lapham, & Barton, 1996; Christian, Dufour, & Bertolucci, 1989; Lamarine, 1988).

More than a century after Chief Joseph was forced toward Canada to escape the threat of the U.S. Army, Canadian Suzane Erb, then a doctoral student at Concordia University, investigated the relationship between chronic stress and relapse in the addiction syndrome. To explore the relationship, she trained rats to press a lever for cocaine administration.

Once the rats were addicted to cocaine, the drug was removed from the lever. After a while, the rats caught on and stopped trying to self-administer the nonexistent drug. When the rats were later exposed to stress in their home cages, however, they would run back to the lever, suggesting that the stress prompted a craving response. In an elegant series of experiments, Erb showed that the stress neurochemicals corticotropin-releasing hormone and noradrenaline contribute to stress-induced relapse (Erb, Salmaso, Rodaros, & Stewart, 2001).

Could the chronic stress experienced by the Native Americans be connected to their high rates of addiction? Are other populations faced with such powerlessness and hopelessness at risk for high rates of addiction? Is stress a valuable issue to address when treating addiction patients? Do any therapies incorporate stress reduction into their treatment regime? These questions—and many more—are addressed in this chapter.

drug addiction Strong desire to consume a drug accompanied by diminishing capacity to limit the intake of the drug.

addiction syndrome Vast array of variables, sometimes difficult to tease apart, typically associated with drug addiction, including one's predisposition to consume drugs, the development of tolerance to a drug, withdrawal symptoms on the removal of a drug, craving for a drug, and the likelihood of relapse after ceasing consumption of a drug.

tolerance Characteristic of drug addiction in which the individual becomes increasingly less sensitive to the drug, requiring higher doses to obtain the initial effect of the drug.

withdrawal Defining feature of drug addiction in which the individual experiences either physiological or psychological symptoms after ceasing the consumption of a particular drug.

negative reinforcement Cessation of an aversive stimulus on the presentation of a particular response. Relapse into drug use is reinforced because it reduces the negative experience of withdrawal.

dependence Development of tolerance and withdrawal following chronic use of a drug; physical and psychological problems arise upon cessation of drug use.

"Gotta have it" is the driving thought of an addict. A drink, a drag, a hit, a line, a pill, another piece of chocolate. "Gotta have it." Getting it is all that matters. Scrounging in the garbage for cigarette butts, stealing pills from a friend's medicine chest, driving into a dangerous neighborhood at night to meet a drug dealer, wiping out a child's bank account. Nothing is more important than smoking, swallowing, snorting, shooting, somehow securing and consuming it, and feeling its effects, *now*. Not health or physical safety. Not love or work or sex or money or relationships or responsibility. Not commitment or common sense or self-respect. Not the law or the truth. This urgent inner demand overrides all others, undermines reason, resolve, and will. It is relentless. It does not stop until it is satisfied. And then, it starts again. "Gotta have it!" What drives this madness? (Ruden, 1997, pp. 1–2)

What does drive the madness of drug addiction? In this chapter we discuss the general nature of this syndrome and the influences of variables such as sex, culture, and genetic profile. We also address the question of how such a seemingly maladaptive behavior evolved.

Although specific drugs of abuse are introduced, the chapter focuses on drug addiction in a more general sense—supposing common predispositions, symptoms, and causes for most forms of addiction, whether cocaine addiction or alcoholism. Once we consider the neuroanatomical and neurochemical mechanisms related to addiction and subsequent craving, we consider the potential role of environmental context by focusing on stress in the addiction syndrome. Finally, we review various therapies, old and new, for addiction.

DRUG ADDICTION IN CONTEXT

Drug addiction is generally defined as an uncontrollable desire to take a drug accompanied by diminished control in limiting intake and the emergence of an unpleasant emotional state (Koob & Nestler, 1997a, 1997b; Koob & LeMoal, 2008). Because of the multiple factors related to addiction (e.g., predisposition, acquisition, craving, withdrawal, relapse), we sometimes use the term **addiction syndrome** to convey the expansive nature of this condition. Considering the prevalence of drug addiction and the threats it poses to our society, drug addiction, as opposed to other behavioral addictions or compulsions (as emphasized in Chapter 8), is the focus of this chapter.

The maladaptive pattern of drug use often leads to the individual desiring more and more of the drug to recreate the first encounter. Reduced responsiveness, or **tolerance**, to a drug may result from several mechanisms, such as the body's and brain's increased efficiency at breaking down the drug.

Addicts also experience **withdrawal** during times of abstinence (when the drug is not being consumed). Many times the patient is motivated to resume taking drugs to avoid aversive symptoms, an elegant example of **negative reinforcement**. As the individual's life becomes increasingly consumed with searching for and obtaining a particular drug, other important aspects of a fully rounded existence, such as those related to health, family, friends, and work, are usually compromised.

Once tolerance and withdrawal are experienced, the person is generally thought to be dependent on the drug. **Dependence** can be viewed as either *physiological*, as demonstrated by modifications in the individual's physiology due to repeated use of the drug, or *psychological*, as shown by a person's perception that he or she requires the drug to function normally or to just get through the day. The different types of dependence may occur simultaneously or individually; regardless, each can be a powerful, motivating pull toward acquiring a drug. See Table 11.1 for diagnostic criteria for substance dependence and Table 11.2 for diagnostic criteria for substance abuse.

Table 11.1 DSM Criteria for Substance Dependence

A maladaptive pattern of substance use, leading to clinically significant impairment or distress, as manifested by three (or more) of the following, occurring at any time in the same 12-month period:

(1) tolerance, as defined by either of the following:

    (a) a need for markedly increased amounts of the substance to achieve intoxication or desired effect

    (b) markedly diminished effect with continued use of the same amount of the substance

(2) withdrawal, as manifested by either of the following:

    (a) the characteristic withdrawal syndrome for the substance (refer to criteria A and B of the criteria sets for withdrawal from the specific substances)

    (b) the same (or a closely related) substance is taken to relieve or avoid withdrawal symptoms

(3) the substance is often taken in larger amounts or over a longer period than was intended

(4) there is a persistent desire or unsuccessful efforts to cut down or control substance use

(5) a great deal of time is spent in activities necessary to obtain the substance (e.g., visiting multiple doctors or driving long distances), use the substance (e.g., chain-smoking), or recover from its effects

(6) important social, occupational, or recreational activities are given up or reduced because of substance use

(7) the substance use is continued despite knowledge of having a persistent or recurrent physical or psychological problem that is likely to have been caused or exacerbated by the substance (e.g., current cocaine use despite recognition of cocaine-induced depression or continued drinking despite recognition that an ulcer was made worse by alcohol consumption)

Specify if:

With Physiological Dependence: evidence of tolerance or withdrawal (i.e., either item 1 or 2 is present)

Without Physiological Dependence: no evidence of tolerance or withdrawal (i.e., neither item 1 nor 2 is present)

American Psychiatric Association (2000, p. 197).

Table 11.2 DSM Criteria for Substance Abuse

A. A maladaptive pattern of substance use leading to clinically significant impairment or distress, as manifested by one (or more) of the following, occurring within a 12-month period:

    (1) recurrent substance use resulting in a failure to fulfill major role obligations at work, school, or home (e.g., repeated absences or poor work performance related to substance use; substance-related absences, suspensions, or expulsions from school; neglect of children or household)

    (2) recurrent substance use in situations in which it is physically hazardous (e.g., driving an automobile or operating a machine when impaired by substance use)

    (3) recurrent substance-related legal problems (e.g., arrests for substance-related disorderly conduct)

    (4) continued substance use despite having persistent or recurrent social or interpersonal problems caused or exacerbated by the effects of the substance (e.g., arguments with spouse about consequences of intoxication, physical fights)

B. The symptoms have never met the criteria for substance dependence for this class of substance

American Psychiatric Association (2000, p. 199).

Prevalence of Addiction

Addiction can afflict anyone who is capable of consuming a drug. In a report compiled by the Substance Abuse and Mental Health Services Administration (2008), a profile of drug use in the United States for 2007 presented few differences from trends observed in 2006. Focusing on illicit drugs in general (i.e., marijuana, cocaine, heroin, hallucinogens, prescription medications used for nonmedical reasons), it was reported that nearly 20 million Americans (8%) over the age of 12 years consumed these drugs within the past month. Of these drugs, marijuana is the most frequently used, whereas hallucinogens (Ecstasy in about half the cases) are reported to be used at the lowest rates. About 50% of, or 127 million, American adults consume alcohol, with about 23% participating in binge drinking (i.e., consuming five consecutive drinks). These rates are much higher in young adults 18–25 years of age, of whom nearly 42% report binge drinking. Focusing on tobacco consumption, approximately 71 million Americans (27%) report tobacco product use; more specifically, 24% of Americans 12 years and older smoke cigarettes and, most disturbing, 16% of pregnant women also report that they smoke cigarettes (Substance Abuse and Mental Health Services Administration, 2008).

Addiction is found in both men and women, but it is more prevalent in men than in women (American Psychiatric Association, 2000). For example, in a comprehensive study that investigated sex differences in alcohol consumption across several cultures, men were more likely to identify themselves as current drinkers and reported more frequent heavy-drinking episodes. Focusing on Canada, Israel, the Czech Republic, and the United States, in most cases, men were more than twice as likely to be identified as "drinkers," whereas women were more likely to be lifetime abstainers (Wilsnack, Vogeltanz, Wilsnack, & Harris, 2000).

As these statistics suggest, it is important to remember that drug abuse does not exclude children and adolescents. In 1998, 10% of adolescents in one study reported illicit drug use sometime during the past month (Comerci & Schwebel, 2000); similar rates were observed in 2008. Even more daunting are data from a survey of 45,000 high school students. Of the students, who were tenth-graders in the year 2000 in this study, 45% reported using an illicit drug; specifically, 40% reported using marijuana, 7% reported using cocaine, and 55% reported smoking cigarettes in their lifetime. Additionally, 23% reported being drunk in the month prior to the survey (National Institute on Drug Abuse, 2001).

One drug that is on the rise in adolescent circles is MDMA, or Ecstasy (see Box 5.1), a drug that has both stimulant and hallucinogenic properties and is at this writing one of the most popular "club drug" for teens. In fact, the 18- to 25-year-old age group is the heaviest using group of Ecstasy (National Institute on Drug Abuse, 2001). Thus, drug addiction can begin as early as 12 or 13 years of age (and earlier in some cases) and persist as long as the drugs are available for consumption.

As with any disorder, there are costs associated with addiction. In the United States alone, the total cost associated with drug abuse is estimated at $67 billion per year (National Institute on Drug Abuse, 2001). This figure includes both social and medical costs associated with the drugs of abuse and does not include nicotine-related costs. The social cost is high—more than half of the cost accrues to drug-related crime. Not only does drug abuse cost society but it affects the economic status of individual users as well—it is estimated that Americans spent $57.3 billion on drugs between 1988 and 1995, $38 billion going to cocaine (National Institute on Drug Abuse, 2001).

Addiction Across Cultures

Addiction is found virtually everywhere. It is impossible, however, to compare and contrast rates of addiction across cultures because of the vast range of perspectives about what actually constitutes an addiction. For example, within the United States, different religious affiliations vary in their acceptance of alcohol consumption; some condemn its use in any context, and others celebrate its use in various religious ceremonies.

Stepping outside the United States, the issue becomes terribly complex. If you are sitting down to dinner in Greece, little attention is paid to the amount of alcohol consumed; but drinking alcohol during meals is not considered normal in India (Gureje, Vazquez-Barquero, & Janca, 1996). One common perspective observed across cultures, however, is that most people are more accepting of alcohol than other addictive substances. For example, in most cultures, a person classified as suffering from a drug-use problem typically exhibits less impairment than that required for a diagnosis of an alcohol-use problem. This distinction is probably related to the illegal status of most drugs compared with the legal status of alcohol (Gureje et al., 1996).

Hereditary Influences on Addiction

Evidence amassed from alcoholism research suggests that addiction has a significant genetic component (American Psychiatric Association, 2000). For example, boys and girls who are adopted have a greater risk of being an alcohol user if their biological parents are alcoholics. Alcohol abuse in the adoptive parents has no real predictive value for determining alcoholism in their adoptive children; only low occupational status (a likely stressor) of the adoptive father seems to put the child at risk for becoming an alcohol abuser (Bohman, Cloninger, Sigvardsson, & von Knorring, 1987).

Research with rodents provides further support for the role of genetics in predisposing an individual for drug abuse. Certain strains of rats and mice have been bred for susceptibility to drug abuse and/or preference for certain drugs. When two different strains of rats are raised in the same environment, they exhibit differences in the amount of drugs consumed in a particular amount of time. Because differences in drug consumption cannot be explained by differences in the environment, the drug-preferring strains of rodents offer powerful evidence that genetics provide a meaningful piece of the addiction puzzle. Another confusing piece in this puzzle is the notion that a behavior that is so devastating to the species can have such a strong genetic component. Understanding more about the potential evolutionary role of the neurobiological system underlying addiction brings some clarity to this confusion.

Considering Addiction in the Context of Evolution

The rules of the evolution game have always focused on one important goal—*survival*. Our neuroanatomy was established hundreds of millions of years ago as nature was designing a hardwired system that would drive the organism to survive—to eat, drink, and copulate. The neurobiology that underlies addiction evolved in the brain long before the "mind" emerged. This older part of our brain—the part we have in common with other animals such as rodents—is the extended limbic system (see Figure 3.13). Our brain ensures that we engage in the appropriate behaviors, such as sex and eating at the appropriate time, to ensure survival of the species (Ruden, 2000).

Have you ever felt as if you would do anything for your favorite dessert? Bart Hoebel at Princeton University has demonstrated that it is possible to become "addicted" to certain foods. Hoebel has shown that rats (as well as humans) feel that way about sugar. Knowing what we do about the value of a strong initial "high" in the addiction syndrome, he designed the study so that the rats would initially binge on sugar. Each day he deprived them of food and then presented them with an appealing glucose drink. The animals quickly consumed the sweet drink each day for a week. When the glucose was removed, the rats showed signs of withdrawal such as chattering their teeth, fanning their paws, and shaking their heads.

It appears that this natural reward system can lead to addictions to certain foods that were of prime importance during the evolution of the mammalian species. Hoebel's research lends a certain amount of validity to our cravings for sugar (the proverbial sweet tooth) and salt (not being able to eat just one potato chip), which makes sense considering the important roles of glucose and sodium in physiology and neurological processing (Hoebel, Rada, Mark, & Pothos, 1999).

Humans, however, have learned to bend the rules a bit in this survival game. By introducing external substances—drugs of abuse—that stimulate reward, we have devised a system in which we experience a handsome perceived payoff without engaging in the necessary behavior. Once you are aware of how the system evolved, it is easy to see how quickly a person can slip from a normal level of motivation to an intense desire when consuming psychoactive drugs. This is why simple recreational use of the drug develops into a more serious condition—addiction or compulsive drug seeking (Wise, 1999).

Most of our knowledge about the neurobiology of addiction has come from animal models, but true addiction seems to be unique to humans. Animals become addicted only when humans help out a bit (as with the bingeing program designed by Hoebel). Animal models encompass some characteristics of the addiction syndrome, but they do not represent the true condition of human addiction (Wise, 1999). Some of the key ammunition against the war on drugs, such as commercials in which celebrities tell us that drugs kill, cannot be tested on an animal model. The influence of peer pressure is also a challenge to evaluate with animal models. Addiction seems to be driven by basic animal processes, but the highly evolved cortex of humans makes the addiction puzzle more complex.

In an attempt to evaluate the role of higher cerebral functioning in survival, evolutionary theorists have introduced **evolutionary game theory**, quantitative models derived from strategies used by animals to optimize survival and reproductive fitness. When considering the survival strategies of humans, the psychological structural system *self-perceived fitness* (SPFit) has been introduced. In essence, this system suggests that human behaviors and accompanying feelings related to survival and reproductive fitness are

evolutionary game theory Quantitative models used by evolutionary theorists to understand strategies used by animals to maximize survival (e.g., mating).

saved on the motivational hard drive and habitually repeated even though the behavior may be maladaptive. For example, after consuming alcohol, many report a feeling of "power" and "sexual energy," even though alcohol severely compromises actual strength and sexual vigor. It is the perception, or feeling—which may or may not be an accurate reflection of the actual effect—that people equate with taking the drug.

According to evolutionary game theory, drugs of abuse send the deceptive message to the brain that the individual has just experienced a huge fitness benefit. This theory addresses a central paradox of substance abuse, a paradox exemplified in Box 11.1. Why do people and animals become addicted to something that harms them? The artificially inflated SPFit becomes associated with the drug that is actually contributing to the demise of the individual's nervous system (Newlin, 1999).

TRACING THE NEUROBIOLOGICAL ROOTS OF ADDICTION

In the 1950s, James Olds and Peter Milner designed a study to determine whether stimulating the reticular formation in the brain stem would influence a rat's choice to turn a different way in a maze (Olds & Milner, 1954; Reeve, 1992). Quite serendipitously, the scientists observed interesting behavior in the animals receiving electrical stimulation—they seemed to like it! Also to their surprise, on autopsy of the brains, they discovered that the electrodes were not implanted in the brain stem as desired; they were accidentally placed in the septal nucleus of the limbic system.

They designed further studies that allowed the rats to deliver their own stimulation to this limbic area, and it became apparent that the animals were activating some type of reward circuit. Animals that received electrical stimulation to a general area of the brain known as the **medial forebrain bundle**, a large collection of axons that extend from the hypothalamus to the septum, could not get enough stimulation. They would press the bar continuously, sometimes as many as 2,000 times per hour, until they passed out from exhaustion (Olds, 1958). This research was an important step toward understanding that certain brain areas are specifically involved with the phenomenon of reward.

Today, we know that the nucleus accumbens, one end point of the medial forebrain bundle, plays a key role in brain reward. For example, if the nucleus accumbens is damaged, animals no longer self-administer the rewarding drug cocaine. It is as if the animal needs a healthy, working nucleus accumbens to experience the pleasures associated with cocaine (Pettit, Ettenberg, Bloom, & Koob, 1984).

Neural Circuits Involved in Establishing Addiction

The seminal work of Olds and Milner was just the beginning of an active area of research into the role of the nucleus accumbens in addiction. A half-century later, the nucleus accumbens continues to be considered a key brain structure driving addiction. This structure doesn't work in isolation however; it communicates with other influential brain areas. One brain area interacting with the nucleus accumbens is the orbitofrontal cortex (OFC), a more recently evolved cortical structure implicated in the maintenance of

medial forebrain bundle Large collection of axons that extend from the hypothalamus to the septum, a structure in the limbic system. Animals respond continuously to receiving electrical brain stimulation in this area; consequently, it is considered the most prevalent brain reward system of the nervous system.

Box 11.1

A Case in Point

Running from Addiction

As Frank completes his leg of the 4-by-800 relay, he experiences pure joy. He feels his body cut through the air, his arms pumping his legs at a faster and faster pace, and a serene sense of pleasure. At 44, he wins the Men's National Masters Championship Relay by running at a 4:32/mile pace. Even more thrilling to Frank is that he is able to experience this pleasure by doing something he is proud of—not by the drug abuse that plagued him for years.

Frank was born to a blue-collar family in Chatham, New Jersey. His childhood days were filled with climbing trees, building forts, exploring the woods, and watching TV. He preferred reading to sports during middle school but discovered that running offered an escape from the pain and insecurity typical of the adolescent years. After his younger brother was fatally injured in an automobile accident, Frank discovered another escape from the pain—alcohol.

As Frank progressed through high school he also started smoking marijuana. He tried to moderate his marijuana and alcohol use so that he could continue to run, but moderation turned into uncontrollable addiction as he graduated from high school. Frank refused the many college scholarships offered to him and chose, instead, to stay at home and work for a landscaping company. A coworker introduced him to heroin and cocaine and all the rituals, and Frank began to love driving to New York City to buy drugs.

Two years out of high school, Frank found himself using heroin up to four times a week and decided to enroll in a methadone program to help curb his cravings. Methadone supposedly relieves the symptoms of heroin withdrawal without producing its psychological effects, but Frank quickly learned from other patients how methadone's effects can be boosted with cocaine or Valium.

Finding that he liked the high even better than heroin, Frank maintained his new methadone habit for the next 5 years. He bought methadone from other patients in his program and supported his habit by turning to crime—stealing household items and then selling them to buy more drugs. He was eventually arrested and spent 4 agonizing months in jail detoxifying the natural way, without medication.

The day he was released, Frank bought a bottle of methadone and some pills. Little did he know that his body had lost tolerance to the drugs during his drug-free stay in prison. Consequently, he overdosed and was rushed to the hospital, where he lay comatose for days. His family intervened and sent him to a therapeutic community to recover. This community emphasized strict discipline in a highly structured environment. Things started to look up for Frank. He completed the program, started running again, and was eventually offered a job as a trainee counselor.

Frank ignored recommendations to attend a social support group such as Narcotics Anonymous (NA) during this time; he felt he had the strength to maintain abstinence on his own. Then, after an impressive 10 years of sobriety, he made the mistake of having a glass of wine. When nothing catastrophic happened, it gave Frank the confidence to start experimenting with drugs once again. It wasn't long before he found himself buying methadone, taking pills, and shooting heroin.

This downward spiral prompted Frank to enroll in another rehabilitation program. He was assigned to a competent, friendly counselor and was required to attend NA meetings. He fell in love with the woman whom he would later marry but was still not able to remain clean very long. After a year, he was back in the familiar downward spiral fueled by heroin, methadone, marijuana, and pills.

At the insistence of his girlfriend, he checked himself into a detox unit at a local hospital, where he underwent medical withdrawal from the Valium. A couple of weeks later, he was discharged and referred to another methadone clinic, where he was watched closely for additional drug use. Things started to look up again for Frank, but before he could be completely sober, he had to undergo two more detox cycles.

In 1995, Frank was completely free of drugs—this time paying close attention to aftercare treatment. He attended NA meetings daily, continued with a sponsor, and started regaining his physical strength. Today, he remains sober and is building a business, enjoying spending time with his wife. He gets high only the natural way—by running very fast!

Adapted from Fernandez (1998).

craving. These two key structures, the nucleus accumbens and OFC, are discussed in the following section.

Role of the nucleus accumbens.

The nucleus accumbens is part of a larger brain circuit that determines whether a response (in this case, the consumption of a drug) is important enough to repeat. The nucleus accumbens receives messages directly from the **ventral tegmental area (VTA)** in the midbrain, where a majority of dopamine is synthesized. The nucleus accumbens receives input, or projections, from other areas in the brain including the amygdala, hippocampus, and medial prefrontal cortex, as shown in Figure 11.1 (Robbins & Everitt, 1999).

Now that the structure of the nucleus accumbens has been studied extensively, it is known to consist of a core and a shell (Figure 11.1 inset). The core has characteristics of the caudate and putamen (recall from Chapter 3 that these movement structures are collectively known as the "striatum"), and the shell seems to be an extension of the emotionally charged central amygdala (Everitt et al., 2000). Because the nucleus accumbens shell has morphological similarities with other structures, including the **bed nucleus of the stria terminalis (BNST)**, a subcortical limbic structure involved in the stress/anxiety response, and portions of the amygdala, the area diagrammed in Figure 11.1 is sometimes referred to as the **extended amygdala** (Koob & Nestler, 1997a, 1997b).

The two different components—the core and the shell—allow the nucleus accumbens a very important function in governing behavior. It serves as a mediator between the limbic structures that evaluate the emotional relevance of a particular environmental stimulus and the striatum, which can actually generate a motor response. As Hoebel suggests, the nucleus accumbens is

ventral tegmental area (VTA) Cluster of cell bodies in the midbrain that synthesize dopamine; extends to the nucleus accumbens and is involved with reward circuits of the brain.

bed nucleus of the stria terminalis (BNST) Subcortical limbic structure considered part of the extended amygdala that plays a role in the stress/anxiety response.

extended amygdala Brain structures continuous with and sharing morphological similarities with the amygdaloid nuclei, including the nucleus accumbens, BNST, and olfactory lobe.

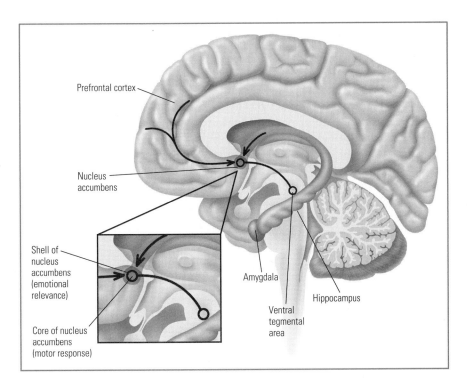

Figure 11.1
Extended amygdala The ventral tegmental area projects to the nucleus accumbens, the neuroanatomical structure that plays a central role in addictive behavior. This structure, however, does not work alone; the amygdala, hippocampus, and medial prefrontal cortex send excitatory projections to the nucleus accumbens, shown in detail in the inset.
ADAPTED FROM ROBBINS & EVERITT (1999)

the brain's sensory–motor interface, in which an environmental stimulus is processed, along with the animal's plans to respond to this stimulus (Hoebel et al., 1999). Hence, the nucleus accumbens plays a critical role in initiating and maintaining an animal's motivation toward stimuli relevant to its survival and propagation such as eating, drinking, and sex (Carelli & Deadwyler, 1994; Mermestein & Becker, 1995). If a behavior seems particularly relevant, the nucleus accumbens places the important variables associated with it in the brain's version of boldface type and then saves it to the brain's long-term memory stores so that the animal will respond similarly when faced with the same stimulus in the future.

The process of emphasizing certain variables in the environment enables the animal to become more efficient at either avoiding danger (not entering a field in which a predator lives) or gaining rewards (entering a field that contains an abundance of food). This adaptive learning system, however, can lead to behavior that is not important for survival. The phenomenon is illustrated beautifully in the case of two literature professors who became addicted to gambling after succumbing to the lure of the riverboat casinos lining the banks of the Mississippi. In their essay published in *The New Yorker*, the professors convey how every blip in the environment thrives with meaning when they are playing blackjack and the game is going either especially well or especially badly (Barthelme & Barthelme, 1999).

In the brain's reward circuitry, bad gambling attempts are processed as threatening stimuli and good attempts are processed as potential rewards. Consequently, many frivolous associations are formed during the games. For example, a certain number of ice cubes may be associated with bringing bad luck, while a particular song may relate to bringing good luck (Barthelme & Barthelme, 1999). The abundance of these strong associations in their memory stores makes it difficult for these gamblers to forget even the most trivial information. As described in this example, it is easy to see how the nucleus accumbens plays a role in forming perceptions of many cues in an addict's environment (such as money, drug paraphernalia, or certain friends) as extremely relevant.

Hans Breiter and colleagues at Massachusetts General Hospital in Boston provide evidence that the brain responds to gambling in a similar fashion to the way it responds to drugs of abuse. Using a creative protocol, Breiter had subjects participate in a game of chance in which an arrow was spun on a disk to determine whether they won or lost money. Functional magnetic resonance imaging (fMRI) scans indicated that, as the arrow was whirring around on the disk, the extended amygdala, nucleus accumbens, and hypothalamus were activated—as observed in subjects consuming cocaine. Consequently, Breiter and colleagues reported that this circuitry is fundamental for processing information about rewards and losses, an endeavor that is central to most anything we do (Breiter, Aharon, Kahneman, Dale, & Shizgal, 2001).

Although this system may sometimes lead to faulty responding, for the most part, the nucleus accumbens circuitry is an efficient executor of responses. When an appetizing food is consumed, the nucleus accumbens may register the food so that the next time it is encountered the animal will be motivated to approach and consume it. In the day-to-day living of the typical animal, it experiences small doses of nucleus accumbens–induced pleasure as it engages in these survival-related behaviors (building relationships, caring for offspring, grooming, resting). Perversely, this beautifully adaptive system makes our brains vulnerable to addictive substances found in nature (Hyman, 1999). As described in the gambling professors example, sometimes an animal discovers that a drug or activity is the emotional equivalent of robbing the nucleus accumbens pleasure bank (Elster, 1999). The following passage conveys such an experience for a rat:

> The rat rapidly acquires the lever-pressing "habit"—giving itself approximately 5,000–10,000 pleasure/reward "hits" during each one-hour daily test session. During these test sessions, the rat is totally focused on obtaining the desired electrical stimulation—lever pressing at maximum speed and ignoring other attractions within the test chamber (food, water, playthings, sexually receptive rats of the opposite sex). After several weeks, the rat suddenly faces a new and unexpected behavioral contingency. An electrified metal floor grid has been placed in the test chamber between the entrance and the wall-mounted lever. This floor grid delivers intensely painful foot-shocks. The rat enters the chamber, receives a footshock, and jumps back off the floor grid. It stands in the entrance, looking alternately at the aversive floor grid and the appealing wall-mounted lever. After some minutes of indecision, it crosses the floor grid, receiving intensely painful footshocks with every step (and flinching and squealing in pain), to reach the lever and once again self-administer the pleasurable brain stimulation. (Gardner & David, 1999, p. 94)

But, you say, this is a rat—an animal that has a cortex the size of a postage stamp. Surely, a human would not succumb to such ridiculous behavior. Well, we would all like to think that, but one look at the life of a drug-addicted person—a life in which the individual does anything to acquire a drug—suggests that humans are not too different from our rodent friends in this regard. The nineteenth-century American psychiatrist Benjamin Rush observed such addiction-driven frenzy in a chronic alcoholic who made the following statement: "Were a keg of rum in one corner of a room, and were a cannon constantly discharging balls between me and it, I could not refrain from passing before that cannon, in order to get at the rum" (cited in Elster, 1999, p. x).

Terry Robinson at the University of Michigan and Bryan Kolb at the University of Lethbridge provided even more evidence that the nucleus accumbens is intricately involved with addiction. These researchers were intrigued by the fact that chronic drug abuse seems to create long-lasting changes in brain and behavior, even after the drug is no longer being consumed. For example, when a previously addicted rat is exposed to an environment in which it once received the drug, the nucleus accumbens may become activated, accompanied by a behavioral change of hyperactivity or orientation toward the lever.

This observation prompted Robinson and Kolb (1999) to wonder if the drug may have permanently altered the structure of the neurons in the nucleus accumbens. They tested their idea by administering cocaine, amphetamine, or no drug to animals. Because these drugs result in increased levels of activity, another control group in which animals were housed with activity wheels (but received no drug) was utilized to control for the possibility that increased activity may alter the structure of accumbens neurons.

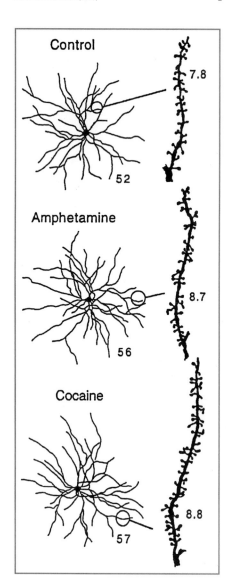

Control

7.8

52

Amphetamine

8.7

56

Cocaine

8.8

57

Following 4 weeks of injections or running wheel experience, the animals were left alone for 25 days. Animals treated with either amphetamine or cocaine had increased dendritic branches and spine density in the medium spiny neurons of the nucleus accumbens shell (Figure 11.2). These results suggest that addiction, or chronic drug use, may produce long-lasting or even permanent changes in the morphology of the brain.

Role of the OFC. It is well established that the nucleus accumbens plays an important role in acquiring an addiction, but other evidence suggests that there is more to the picture than simple pleasure. For example, an animal will still self-administer a drug after it has developed tolerance to it and at times continue to self-administer in the presence of adverse effects of the drug. Nora Volkow and Joanna Fowler at the State University of New York have proposed that a more recently evolved brain structure, the OFC, may also play a role in maintaining addictions (Volkow & Fowler, 2000).

Several lines of evidence point to the involvement of this structure, which is part of the obsessive–compulsive disorder (OCD) neuroanatomical circuit (see Figure 8.1). When rats are placed in an environment previously associated with cocaine, the OFC becomes activated, not the nucleus accumbens (Brown, Robertson, & Fibiger, 1992). Additionally, if electrodes are placed in the OFC of both rats and rhesus monkeys, they will also press the bar to deliver the stimulation to their brains (Phillips, Mora, & Rolls, 1979). As we discuss later in the chapter, orbitofrontal activation is observed when human addicts report drug craving (Volkow & Fowler, 2000).

Recall from Chapter 8 that the OFC plays a key role in maintaining the persistent thoughts and behaviors associated with OCD. Actually, it is easy to see the relationship between OCD and the drive and perseverance of behaviors typical of drug addiction (Volkow & Fowler, 2000). Neuroanatomically, the OFC is a likely accomplice to drug addiction because the nucleus accumbens projects to the OFC by way of the mediodorsal nucleus of the thalamus. To keep the lines of communication open, the OFC sends messages back to the nucleus accumbens. Finally, the OFC also receives input from limbic areas such as the amygdala and hippocampus. Thus, a picture of the OFC as an extension of the nucleus accumbens is emerging, providing researchers with an explanation of how, once an animal hits the pleasure lottery by activating the nucleus accumbens, it will continue to search for the big payoff again and again—at any cost.

More recently, discrete circuits have been proposed to mediate separate phases of the addiction cycle, including binge/intoxication, withdrawal/negative effect, and preoccupation/anticipation (craving). Specifically, nucleus accumbens shell and core, along with the dorsal striatum, mediate the binge/intoxification phase—driving the animal toward the drug and executing the necessary movement to consume the drug. Withdrawal and its negative characteristics are mediated by components of the extended amygdala, including the BNST (also involved in anxiety). Finally, cognitive preoccupations associated with craving have been associated with the conditioning functions of the basolateral amygdala, the contextual processing maintained by the hippocampus, and the executive control of the prefrontal cortex. Additionally, the orbitofrontal and anterior cingulate cortical areas and the amygdala are involved in the more subjective aspects of craving (Koob & Volkow, 2010). Distinguishing specific neuroanatomical circuits for the various phases of the addiction syndrome provides an alternate foundation that researchers can use to develop more targeted therapeutic strategies.

Neurochemistry of Addiction

Most drugs of abuse either directly or indirectly activate the dopaminergic (DA) system (Nestler, 2005), which is intimately involved with the extended amygdala. Serotonin may also play a role in addiction. Another neurochemical of the nucleus accumbens, acetylcholine, is implicated as well but in aversive rather than pleasurable behaviors.

Dopamine: Primary fuel of addiction. A technique called **microdialysis** enables experimenters to implant probes into the brains of animals and measure levels of a neurotransmitter in freely moving animals. During cocaine self-administration, microdialysis studies reveal that DA is released in the nucleus accumbens and maintained above baseline levels (Pettit & Justice, 1991). Also, if rats receive a drug that antagonizes DA, they will respond longer than nontreated animals in the self-administration task (Corrigall & Coen, 1991). One interpretation of these data is that the reinforcing property of cocaine is diminished by the antagonist, prompting the rats to work harder to receive any amount of reward (Carelli, King, Hampson, & Deadwyler, 1993).

Most researchers hypothesize that the **mesolimbic dopaminergic pathway** is the quintessential reward circuit in the brain. As you'll remember from Chapter 5, the DA pathway extends from the cell bodies containing DA in the VTA to the nucleus accumbens, prefrontal cortex, and dorsal striatum. Figure 11.3 depicts the mesolimbic DA pathway and a second, more motor-related nigrostriatal pathway projecting from the substantia nigra into the basal ganglia. Interestingly, exposing a rat to a single dose of cocaine resulted in alterations in glutamate transmission (specifically, altered long-term potentiation) in DA neurons (Ungless, Whistler, Malenka & Bonci, 2001), Further, mice that lack the DA D_1 receptor do not self-administer cocaine (Caine et al., 2007).

This DA hypothesis is strengthened by the fact that most abused substances (except for the anxiolytics called "benzodiazepines") increase DA release somewhere along the mesolimbic pathway (Betz, Mihalic, Pinto, & Raffa, 2000). Cocaine, for example, increases the availability of DA in the synapse by inhibiting the dopamine transporter (DAT), described in Chapter 5, which is responsible for absorbing the DA molecule back into the synaptic vesicle (reuptake). See Table 11.3 for effects of other commonly abused drugs.

Neuroimaging studies with humans add another interesting twist to the DA–reward story. These studies suggest that the psychological high experienced by cocaine users is more closely associated with the rate at which cocaine enters the brain and antagonizes DA transporters than with the actual amount of the drug in the brain. Reductions in the number of DA receptors in the cingulate gyrus and the OFC have been observed in cocaine

microdialysis Neurochemical technique in which the level of a neurotransmitter from a particular area of the brain is assessed. This technique is unique because the researcher can extract the neurotransmitter while the animal is engaging in a particular behavior.

mesolimbic dopamine pathway Neurons extending from the midbrain to the forebrain produce and release dopamine into the forebrain. Two pathways make up this system: (1) the mesocorticolimbic (reward circuit) system extends from the ventral tegmental area to the nucleus accumbens; (2) the nigrostriatal pathway, involved in neuromuscular functions, extends from the substantia nigra to the corpus striatum.

Figure 11.3
Two dopamine pathways in the brain The nigrostriatal pathway related to movement, originates in the substantia nigra and projects to the basal ganglia. The second pathway is critical for reward. This mesolimbic dopamine pathway originates in the ventral tegmentum area and projects to the nucleus accumbens and then to the prefrontal cortex.
ADAPTED FROM RUDEN (2000)

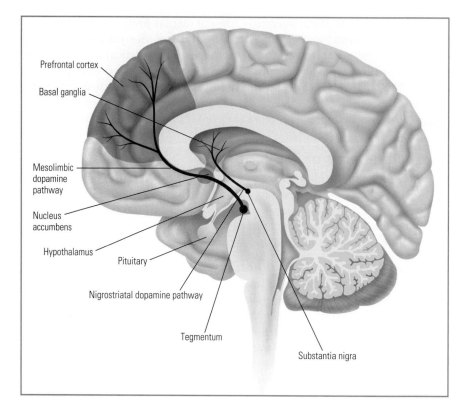

Prefrontal cortex
Basal ganglia
Mesolimbic dopamine pathway
Nucleus accumbens
Hypothalamus
Pituitary
Nigrostriatal dopamine pathway
Tegmentum
Substantia nigra

Table 11.3 Effects of Common Drugs of Abuse

Drug	Neurochemical Action	Psychological Effects
Cocaine	Inhibits dopamine transporters, resulting in increased dopamine in synapse	Pleasure; hyperactivity
Opiates	Stimulate opioid receptors; inhibit release of GABA, resulting in increase in dopamine	Relief from pain; pleasure
Amphetamines	Stimulate release of monoamines (including dopamine)	Pleasure; hyperactivity
Ethanol	Increases GABA receptor function; inhibits NMDA glutamate receptor function; increased dopamine release	Reduced anxiety; euphoria; disinhibition
Nicotine	Facilitates nicotinic acetylcholine receptors; increases release of dopamine	Relaxation; pleasure
Hallucinogens	Partially stimulate 5-HT$_{2A}$ receptors; thought to indirectly affect dopamine	Relaxation; hallucinations; pleasure
Cannabinoids	Stimulates cannabinoid receptors; triggers release of dopamine	Relaxation; mild hallucinations; pleasure
Ecstasy	Increases synaptic serotonin levels; leads to prolonged serotonin depletion due to blocked serotonin uptake; high affinity for noradrenaline receptors; promotes dopamine release and subsequent decreases in reuptake	Heightened pleasure; boost in self-confidence; feelings of extroversion

Adapted from Nestler (1999).

abusers. This reduction probably contributes to a less efficient occupancy rate of receptors and an accompanying tolerance to the psychological effects of cocaine (Volkow, Fowler, & Wang, 1999). In other words, addicts lose the previously experienced high following drug consumption.

It is unclear whether the reduced number of DA receptors in cocaine addicts is a cause or an effect of their condition. There is evidence that a person with fewer D_2 receptors is more likely to find psychostimulants reinforcing—in this case methylphenidate (Ritalin)—than individuals with higher levels of receptors (Volkow, Wang, et al., 1999). Making the DA receptor story even more complicated, increased D_3 receptor messenger RNA and binding have been observed in cocaine addicts' brains at autopsy (Staley & Mash, 1996).

If you wanted to determine the value of the DATs in the addiction syndrome, wouldn't it be interesting to "engineer" a mouse that does not have them? Recent advancements in molecular biology enable neuroscientists to systematically turn off (or "knock out") genes that perform certain functions. Rocha and colleagues (1998) at the University of North Texas looked at the effect of cocaine and amphetamine on these **knockout mice** (DAT knockouts) and reported that they did not appear to be affected by the drug because it failed to increase their activity. Due to the lack of DAT, the mice exhibited high levels of extracellular DA yet still continued to self-administer cocaine and developed a place preference for the drug, suggesting that they were somehow experiencing pleasure from the drug without the services of the DATs (Figure 11.4).

Another type of knockout mouse was developed in which the brain vesicular monoamine transporter is inactivated. This knockout mouse (VMAT2 knockout) lacks the ability to have its transmitter synaptic vesicles accumulate, or recycle, monoamines (DA and serotonin) from the cytoplasm. Such a genetic effect results in less efficient packaging of DA and may prolong its activity. The VMAT2 knockouts were less likely to develop a place preference for amphetamine than were their control mouse counterparts (Caron, 1997).

The finding that VMAT2 knockout mice did not develop a place preference suggests that serotonin may also be a neurochemical player in addiction. Cocaine decreases the reuptake of serotonin as well as DA; additionally,

knockout mice Product of a recently developed technique in behavioral neuroscience in which certain genes are eliminated ("knocked out") so that their function can be determined in the genetically modified animal.

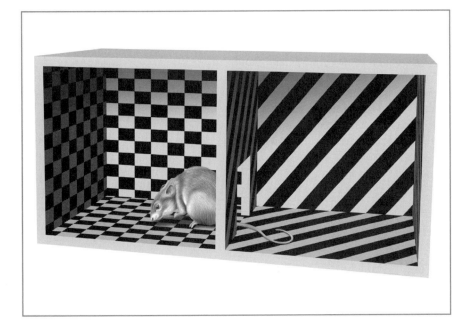

Figure 11.4
Conditioned place preference After receiving repeated injections in one distinct compartment, the drug-free rat is given a choice between it and another compartment. If place preference is established, the rat will quickly go back to the drug compartment. The observation of conditioned place preference suggests that the animal finds the drug pleasurable because it chooses an environment that is associated with administration of the drug. Addicts who repeatedly visit the same street corners or clubs in which they previously obtained drugs are also demonstrating conditioned place preference.
(ADAPTED FROM PINEL, 2000, P. 366)

serotonin neurons connect with the mesolimbic DA system. Low sero-tonin levels are related to depression, impulsive behavior, and alcoholism (Gamberino & Gold, 1999). Rats selectively bred to prefer alcohol have low levels of serotonin in the cortex, striatum, nucleus accumbens, hippocampus, and hypothalamus (Gongwer, Murphy, McBride, Lumeng, & Li, 1989). There is also evidence that some human alcoholics have low levels of serotonin in their cerebrospinal fluid (Cloninger, 1987).

What do these knockout studies mean? Do we throw the DA hypothesis out because of the place preference in the DAT knockout animals? Certainly not. We should be cautious about drawing definitive conclusions from these studies because we are not certain how this genetic manipulation influences other physiological systems.

In Dr. Seuss's book *Because a Little Bug Went Ka-Choo*, a simple sneeze sets off a cascade of subsequent rhyming events in the bug's environment. A little bug sneezing causes a seed to drop on a worm's head, which prompts the worm to kick a coconut tree, which results in a coconut falling on a turtle's back—you get the picture. The point is that events do not occur in a vacuum. If a particular gene that makes a certain protein is turned off, the animal is very likely to compensate for the loss in some way. For example, other systems may produce a substitute for the protein, or another protein may serve a similar function. Thus, although fascinating, we have to be careful about interpreting the results of the knockout studies.

Potential role of acetylcholine. Hoebel and his colleagues have proposed a provocative theory: The acetylcholine neurons that reside in the nucleus accumbens along with DA neurons might serve the opposite function of DA. Let's consider some evidence for their theory.

Normally, rats drink large quantities of water sweetened with saccharin. The rate of drinking, however, decreases when the saccharin water is paired with high levels of acetylcholine in the nucleus accumbens (Taylor, Davidson, Mark, Rada, & Hoebel, 1992). This research suggests that the structure that has become an icon in behavioral neuroscience for pleasure seeking may also be involved in aversion. The notion that acetylcholine may stop the behavior triggered by the DA mesolimbic system may help us understand why, even when a behavior (eating, drinking, having sex) feels so good, we eventually stop engaging in it.

Perhaps exogenous drug use fails to tap into the acetylcholine system and creates a situation similar to driving a car that has no brakes. Hoebel's research is important because it suggests that manipulation of acetylcholine in the nucleus accumbens may help form limits on the high rates of addictive behaviors. Just as something tells us to stop eating that third serving of pie, a brain mechanism such as the cholinergic system may reduce the number of times a drug is consumed in a particular time period. As seen in Box 11.2, some natural behavior–reward systems, such as the sexual drive of the squirrel, are difficult to restrain and appear to be in need of a boost from the cholinergic system.

Craving Response

craving response Persistent, intense desire to consume a drug.

Once an addiction is established, many individuals report a psychological **craving response**, a strong desire to experience the effects of a psychoactive drug that the user previously consumed (Diana, 1996). Cravings for specific

Box 11.2

Brain Matters

Substance Abuse and Behavioral Compulsion: Two Expressions of the Same Neurobiological System?

In the sweltering heat of the summer of 1997, Army Sergeant Gail Baker drove to a convenience store in Jasper County, South Carolina, and commenced a 7-hour binge of video poker. When Gail finally returned to her steaming car, she discovered that her 10-day-old baby, whom she had left in the car, had not survived her video-poker overdose. Her husband later argued that he did not hold her responsible for the death of their child because she had an addiction (Bragg, 1998). Is he right? Are substance-abuse addictions and behavioral compulsions tapping in to the same neurobiological systems?

The fact that Baker continued to engage in her behavioral compulsion when the consequences were so great (a child's life) suggests that gambling was highly rewarding to her. The intensity of her drive to gamble certainly resembles the drives or cravings of drug addicts who continue their habit with no regard to the consequences. We've already discussed how the mesolimbic dopaminergic system and extended amygdala are involved in motivating animals to engage in certain behaviors related to survival. Is it possible for these natural behaviors to activate the system to the degree that drugs do? When you consider the sexual behavior of the squirrel, you will probably conclude that, at least temporarily, the male squirrel is as addicted to sex as the most addicted of drug users.

John Koprowski in the Wildlife Department at the University of Arizona has been observing the sexual lives of squirrels for years. It just so happens that the female goes into heat for a mere 6 hours during breeding season—6 hours for the entire year—which occurs in the dead of winter to assure the arrival of the young squirrels in the spring. To impregnate females in this

COURTESTY JOHN KOPROWSKI

short time period, the males have to be extremely driven to engage in sexual behavior—at the cost of everything else.

Koprowski has observed females emerging from their nest with as many as 22 male callers "looking for love." At this time, the great chase begins. Males continue to chase the female to copulate, and if one is fortunate enough to have such an opportunity, other impatient males often try to displace the copulating male. When the female's 6 hours are up, the males direct their attention toward the next female in heat.

Koprowski observes that these squirrel Casanovas look very much like drug addicts. Males will continue the pattern for days—chasing females without even stopping to eat. A few times he even observed males emerge from their nest only to fall over dead—probably due to exhaustion and a depletion of resources (autopsies reveal that they don't have an ounce of body fat on them). As with drug addicts who engage in risky behavior (such as crime) to get a hit, this behavioral addiction of squirrels continues in the face of danger. As seen in the photo above, a male squirrel is continuing to copulate even though the branch has broken and he is about to plummet to the ground!

---

drugs may vary. For instance, a craving for cocaine is characterized by some of the same symptoms of actually consuming cocaine (light-headedness, chest tightness, ear ringing, generalized arousal, euphoria, and even the taste of cocaine in the back of the mouth). This suggests that craving and actual drug use may be driven by some of the same biological mechanisms (Childress et al., 1999).

Craving as a conditioned response. Craving is a key problem in the fight against addiction. Not only does craving sustain an addiction—even after a person has abstained for months or years—but it might also cause the individual to start using again, which is called *relapse*, as Frank did in Box 11.1. Craving and relapse are as maddening to the therapists working with addicts as they are to the addicts themselves, but these states are not surprising to researchers aware of conditioned responses (see Chapter 2 for a discussion of Pavlov's work).

Quickly and effortlessly, the nervous system starts to make associations between the conditioned stimuli—sight of the drug, the drug paraphernalia, even the décor of a room in which a person frequently uses—and the physiological and psychological effects of the drug. Once this predictive power is established with the conditioned stimuli, the cues can trigger a drug-related response in the individual. The response, whether aversive or inviting, is likely to lead to further drug use.

Given this information, the occurrence of relapse following a lengthy abstinence is disappointing but considered a logical step in the conditioning process (Robbins & Everitt, 1999). A rehabilitated drug user may actively avoid strong cues related to prior drug use, but it is impossible to step into a world devoid of all potential triggers. For most people, it is only a matter of time before they encounter a powerful cue and become physiologically overwhelmed, testing the strongest of wills.

Neural components of the craving response. Related to the brain areas involved in preoccupation/anticipation mentioned previously in this chapter, Anna Rose Childress and her colleagues at the University of Pennsylvania have designed clever experiments to determine the brain areas that are activated during craving. In one study, 20 men who regularly used cocaine but who reported that about 13 days had passed since last using were brought into the lab and shown a drug-related video (with all the drug triggers) and a non-drug-related video. Positron emission tomographic (PET) scans indicated that the addicts showed increased activity in the amygdala, anterior cingulate, and dorsolateral frontal cortex during the drug-related video. (Unfortunately, the nucleus accumbens is too small for adequate resolution with the PET scan.) Lifelong abstainers failed to show limbic activation in response to the drug video (Childress et al., 1999).

Other neuroimaging studies have been conducted utilizing PET, single-photon emission computerized tomography (SPECT), and fMRI on patients experiencing craving. In addition to the areas mentioned in the foregoing paragraph, the thalamus, caudate, orbital cortex, and insular cortex have been implicated in craving in humans. Except for the thalamus, all of these areas receive neural messages from DA-releasing neurons in the midbrain. Collectively, these brain areas are related to the basal ganglia–thalamocortical circuits (described in Chapter 3) that play an important role in making decisions about the appropriate behavior for a particular context (Hommer, 1999).

Focusing on rat models of craving, Barry Everitt, working with his colleagues at Cambridge University, reports that the basolateral area of the amygdala is a key component of the neural circuitry that contributes to drug craving and subsequent relapse. His research has shown that damaging this brain area switches off the rats' conditioned cravings for morphine

(Schulteis, 2000). Hence, robust evidence in both humans and rodents suggests the critical role of the amygdala in the production of cravings.

After abstaining from a drug, long-lasting changes in the DA system may also play a role in craving and relapse. Studies have shown that in rats dependent on either morphine or ethanol the mesolimbic neurons fired less often than in their nonaddicted counterparts. If a certain baseline level of firing in the mesolimbic system is necessary for normal levels of motivation, then a marked decrease in neuronal activity may lead to the dysphoric, or depressed, state sometimes typical of withdrawal. Certainly, a lack of pleasure may also lead to craving or relapse (Diana, 1996).

In withdrawal from cocaine addiction, cells in the nucleus accumbens are less responsive. This means that more stimulation than is typically required to achieve action potentials in these neurons must be encountered to elicit a response. For example, if a single-scoop ice cream cone used to make a person excited, it may take a triple-scoop cone to do the trick under these circumstances. This inactivity of the area of the brain involved in coordinating motivation and response patterns (the nucleus accumbens) may be related to withdrawal-induced **anhedonia** (lack of pleasure) and depression (Wise, 1982; Zhang, Hu, & White, 1998). The fact that these modifications in the mesolimbic DA system continue to exist even after the more physical withdrawal symptoms disappear may prompt a person to feel as if something were not quite right, making him or her more likely to return to drug use if an opportunity arises (Diana, Muntoni, Pistis, Melis, & Gessa, 1999).

Researchers also think that serotonin may play a role in craving. Many of the psychiatric symptoms associated with drug withdrawal, such as irritability/ aggression, insomnia, and depression, may be caused by altered functioning of the serotonergic system. Similar to the unpleasant feelings associated with the low DA–induced anhedonia, a disruption of the serotonergic system may also contribute to the psychological distress experienced by many patients during drug withdrawal.

Relapse is likely to occur as a person attempts to self-medicate by reintroducing the drug into the body. The former user is quite familiar with obtaining and ingesting the drug to feel better, a task that seems quicker and easier than seeking out expensive or even painful medical treatment. Further, low levels of brain serotonin have been implicated in a decrease of impulse control. Obviously, abstaining from drug use when a person encounters trigger after trigger takes a healthy amount of impulse control. Any compromise in this system is related to increased relapse rates (Ciccocioppo, 1999).

A group of researchers recently investigated potential predictive factors that may be related to an animal's vulnerability to relapse during a period of abstinence from chronic drug administration. Whereas behavioral responses to drugs or stressors failed to predict whether an animal would relapse during abstinence, the amount of the drug consumed during early drug use was influential in predicting relapse (Sutton, Karanian, & Self, 2000). This finding is interesting if you consider research conducted by Volkow, Wang, and their colleagues (1999) indicating that more than 50% of the DAT blockade is required for a person to report experiencing a "high." In other words, a significant amount of DA must be allowed to circulate through the mesolimbic system before it becomes intensely pleasurable.

Additionally, as previously mentioned, the rate at which the drugs enter the brain contributes to a more intense high (Volkow, Fowler, et al., 1999).

anhedonia Lack of desire or pleasure; drugs that interfere with the mesolimbic dopaminergic system produce this state.

Perhaps the higher amount of drug consumed by the rats leads to relapse because of the more intense high experienced during early drug use. These findings suggest that the intensity of the high experienced with the first use of the drug plays a powerful role in determining the magnitude of the subsequent craving responses.

STRESS AND ADDICTION

People faced with stress are susceptible to addiction. Research suggests that previous stress experiences might predispose an individual to becoming an addict. Further, as you learned in Connections at the beginning of this chapter, extensive research on the stress response has identified the key neurochemicals (for example, corticotropin-releasing hormone, cortisol) in the stress response that underlie drug addiction.

Two decades ago, Pier Piazza at the University of Bordeaux conducted research indicating that an animal's stress response and stress history may be important in determining whether it will self-administer (or abuse) amphetamine. Simply observing how an animal reacted to being placed in a new environment provided important clues about its predisposition to become an addict. Specifically, the more reactive the animal was in this new situation, the more likely it would be to acquire amphetamine self-administration (Piazza et al., 1990).

Further exploring the possibility that susceptibility to amphetamine self-stimulation was somehow related to a more reactive stress response, other researchers exposed animals to footshock and subsequently monitored activity in the nucleus accumbens. DA levels increased in the shell of the nucleus accumbens, the area related to reward (Kalivas & Duffy, 1995). This study is a beautiful example of how the nucleus accumbens is thrown into action when a threatening stimulus is encountered. Hence, stress and amphetamine administration both tap into the same DA system. In some cases, stress may serve as a primer for the mesolimbic DA system, making an individual more likely to self-administer psychoactive drugs in the future (Wise, 2000).

Does this research mean that stress can be pleasurable? That's difficult to answer, but the data do indicate that the same reward system is activated in both situations. Perhaps these findings explain why some people actually pay money to be stressed—to engage in behaviors such as skydiving, watching scary movies, and riding roller coasters. If the notion that the mesolimbic DA system is important in translating relevant environmental stimuli into appropriate actions is true, then it makes sense that it would be turned on during these stressful times. As expressed in John Mellencamp's song "Hurts So Good" (a song your parents may remember), it seems that, in some situations, the emotional responses of stress and reward may be blurred to some extent and may exhibit some crossover effects.

Jane Stewart of Concordia University in Montreal thinks that stress might help to answer a question that has baffled addiction researchers: Why do certain individuals who are addicts abstain for a while only to relapse during a stressful period in their lives? The relapse doesn't seem to be due to negative factors related to withdrawal because these individuals seem to be doing fine—until they encounter stress.

Stewart (1999) designed an animal model in rats to explore stress-induced relapse. In this model, rats were trained to press a lever to self-administer a drug. Once the rats were addicted, Stewart suddenly removed the drug so that pressing the bar no longer resulted in a drug hit. The rats, however, were free to keep trying to administer the drug, but after a while they tired and stopped responding to the drug lever. After approximately 6 weeks, the animals did not seem to be motivated to administer the drug, the presentation of brief footshocks sent them running to the bar—not unlike humans running to a bar when their lives become complicated!

Of course, Stewart and her team wanted to know why stress caused the animals to relapse. Their research points to corticotropin-releasing hormone (CRH), the initial step in the hypothalamic–pituitary–adrenal (HPA) axis cascade described in Chapter 5, which triggers the release of adrenocorticotropic hormone (ACTH) from the anterior pituitary gland. Just delivering CRH into the brains of rats reinstates heroin seeking; giving the animals a drug to antagonize the CRH receptors in the brain suppresses the relapse.

Where does CRH work to produce this form of relapse? CRH receptors are located in the central amygdala and the BNST, two structures involved in the limbic/reward system. Further work, however, has indicated that the BNST seems to play a more important role here than the central amygdala. Hence, this line of research suggests that stress or anxiety may trigger CRH receptors in the BNST, which activates the HPA axis. Stress hormones released by the HPA axis activation prompt the animal to search for a way (e.g., drug administration, behavioral compulsion) to reestablish hormonal homeostasis (Stewart, 1999). Further, anxiety produced by the acute withdrawal from drugs of abuse can be reversed by the administration of CRH antagonists (Koob & Le Moal, 2008).

What if researchers could conduct a study in which people were placed in a stressful situation, allowed to develop an addiction, and then promptly removed from the stressful situation? Do you think the addiction would stop on cessation of the stress? If the intensity of the addiction changed after the cessation of stress, the hypothesis that addiction is facilitated by stress and its accompanying HPA activation would be supported.

It would certainly be unethical to conduct such a study, but returning U.S. soldiers from the Vietnam War were subjected to this set of conditions. During the summer of 1971, the military began screening the urine of servicemen as they were preparing to return to the United States. Even though the soldiers knew of the drug screening, 5% of the enlisted men tested positive for drug use.

About this time the military effort was being rapidly reduced, and thousands of men were returning to the United States each month amid great concern about treating the large number of addicts and about possible criminal actions that might accompany their drug use. Consequently, a study was conducted by the White House Special Action Office for Drug Abuse Prevention to follow these men. On returning to the United States, 45% of the servicemen reported narcotic use in Vietnam and half of them perceived themselves as addicts. Once these men reestablished themselves in the United States—away from the trauma of warfare—only 7% reported being addicted to narcotics.

When you get to the therapy section of this chapter, you will not read about any therapies that have been as effective as simply taking these servicemen out of Vietnam and the chronic stress of war (Robins, Davis & Nurco, 1974; Ruden, 2000). Drug companies dream of developing drugs with

detoxification Initial step in the treatment of drug addiction that involves clearing a patient's system of the abused drug. This process can be accomplished by requiring a patient to abstain from drug use, or it may be facilitated by certain pharmacological agents.

such successful effects. Of course, one cannot rule out the fact that, with the drastic environmental change accompanying the move back to the United States, many of the drug-related cues were also changed. A reduction in these environmental triggers might have reduced the cue-induced craving and led to decreased use of the drug.

As you read in Connections, stressful situations, such as Native Americans fighting for their land or rats trying to avoid footshock, disrupt the internal milieu, or neurobiological homeostasis, of the organism. In an attempt to reduce this aversive state, new habits may be formed or old habits may be reinstated to help the animal feel physiologically balanced once again.

After reading about the influence of stress and environmental cues on craving, it is apparent that several factors are related to the production of craving that leads one to relapse into drug use. See Table 11.4 for a summary of these factors.

THERAPY FOR DRUG ADDICTION

Multiple factors influence one's predisposition and susceptibility to addiction. It should come as no surprise, then, that there is no single treatment for this complex condition. For the most part, therapy is an individual process. The clinician must find the most effective combination of therapies to effectively treat each patient.

This section introduces the process of **detoxification**, the initial step of the recovery process that involves clearing one's system of the abused drug. It would be wonderful if the problems of addiction ended with the exit of the drugs from the patient's body, but many addicts relapse after detoxification. Now that we know that relapse is due to the drug-induced changes in the brain that persist beyond the removal of the drug, focus is placed on trying to keep the detoxified user's brain from relapsing. The strategies for keeping a person clean of drugs include various medications (for example,

Table 11.4 Possible Reasons for Craving that May Lead to Relapse

Reason	Description
Drug priming	When animals are reexposed to a drug during a period of abstinence, they show interest in self-administering the drug.
Stress/anxiety	Research suggests that corticotropin-releasing hormone triggers an animal to engage in drug seeking during a period of abstinence.
Dysphoria	During drug withdrawal, some individuals report a distinct lack of pleasure that is aversive and motivates them to seek pleasure—i.e., consume the drugs once associated with a pleasurable feeling.
Physical distress	When users stop taking drugs, some experience physical discomfort such as nausea and headaches. Because these individuals are aware that these aversive feelings are due to the removal of the abused drug in their body, they self-medicate by seeking the drug.
Strong initial high	Both human and animal research indicates that the high experienced during initial drug use is a powerful factor determining whether the user will continue to seek out the drug during periods of abstinence.
Environmental triggers	Associations are formed between drugs and their related stimuli (needles, money, etc.), but the stronger these associations are, the more likely it is that a person will experience craving during periods of abstinence when these cues in the environment are encountered.

antagonists and agonists) that interrupt the drug's ability to generate the desired response in the user, cognitive-behavioral therapies (for example, acupuncture and support groups), and the newest therapy on the drug research scene, vaccination.

Initial Step: Detoxification

A primary concern when tackling the addiction syndrome is the patient's physiological dependence on the abused substance. Knowing that administration of the drug changes the individual's neurochemistry, the therapist must initially remove the drug to decrease the user's dependence on it. Detoxification can be achieved naturally by ceasing intake of the drug, or the process can be aided with various medications.

Typically, the type of drug abused determines the detoxification process. For example, the withdrawal syndrome for most cocaine addicts is far from fun, but the symptoms of fatigue and depression usually resolve themselves in a few days without the aid of other interventions. Heroin addicts, however, experience more serious symptoms typical of a bad case of the flu (sweating, nausea, cramps, diarrhea, tremors), and the detoxification phase of recovery can be made less aversive with an agonist. In this form of detoxification, an opiate agonist such as **methadone** is given to the patient. Methadone occupies the opiate receptors and decreases the negative effects of withdrawal from heroin, typically without producing the rewarding psychological effects of the drug. When used in the detoxification process, doses of methadone can be gradually decreased to help the body ease into a detoxified state. Alternatively, when detoxifying cocaine abusers, the antidepressant bupropion (marketed as Wellbutrin and Zyban), a drug that blocks the reuptake of serotonin, DA, and norepinephrine, used in combination with monetary incentives, was found to be an effective treatment (Poling et al., 2006).

In more extreme cases, rapid detoxification can be achieved by putting a person under general anesthesia and then administering an opioid antagonist such as **naloxone** or naltrexone, a drug with similar function. The patient wakes up hours later in a detoxified state. Rapid detoxification is an expensive new strategy in great need of research to identify its advantages and disadvantages. Finally, antianxiety drugs such as the benzodiazepines, discussed in Chapter 8, are used during detoxification from alcohol to decrease the sometimes life-threatening symptoms experienced during alcohol withdrawal (O'Brien, 1999).

Maintaining Abstinence

In most cases, detoxification is the simple part of the recovery process: The challenge lies in keeping the individual from consuming drugs after leaving the detoxification facility. Relapse rates vary with different drugs but can be as high as 80% during the first year (Wickelgren, 1998). This is why the addiction syndrome should be approached as a chronic, rather than acute, condition that persists beyond detoxification.

In addition to use in the detoxification process, methadone is used to maintain abstinence from opiates. Even after detoxification, methadone stabilizes opioid addicts, making them less likely to suffer from negative withdrawal symptoms and craving for heroin (Dole & Nyswander, 1965). This finding opened the door for medical approaches to prevent a previous

methadone Opiate drug that is given to heroin addicts to help wean them from opiate addiction because it minimizes withdrawal symptoms and is not thought to produce a high that is comparable to that induced by heroin or morphine.

naloxone Drug that blocks opiate receptors in the brain; counteracts drugs such as morphine. Naltrexone has a similar function.

buprenorphine Recent drug approved by the Food and Drug Administration to treat opioid addiction; works as a partial agonist for mu-opioid receptors.

sensitization Process by which an animal or person becomes increasingly responsive to a particular stimulus following repeated presentation.

user from relapsing; consequently, by 1999, 115,000 patients in the United States were being maintained on methadone to reduce their cravings for heroin (O'Brien, 1999). Concern, however, has been raised about increased rates of methadone-related deaths in heroin addicts (Paulozzi et al., 2009). Consequently, these drugs need to be monitored closely.

In the fall of 2002, the Food and Drug Administration approved the use of **buprenorphine** for people suffering from dependence on heroin, prescription painkillers, or other opioids. (It is estimated that in the United States 800,000 of these individuals are currently not receiving any treatment.) Buprenorphine is a partial agonist for mu-opioid receptors that exhibits mechanisms similar to those of pure agonists such as heroin but with only about 40% of the agonist's potency. And buprenorphine likes to occupy the mu-opioid receptors because of its high affinity for these receptors, making it impossible for a heroin addict to experience a high from another opiate agonist for an extended period of time, sometimes lasting for days. The hope was that this drug would enable clinicians to slowly wean patients off the opiate agonists without the abrupt crash observed in most detoxification procedures. This drug, however, still requires more research to establish its true value as a tool for treating addictions to various opioids (Benson, 2003).

The first medication used to prevent relapse in alcoholics was disulfiram. This drug blocks the metabolism of alcohol, resulting in a buildup of the chemical acetaldehyde. This substance is very unpleasant to those suffering from alcoholism because it nauseates them. The hope was that the patients would associate the sickness with the alcohol—transforming alcohol from a desired substance to an avoided substance—a conditioned taste aversion. The theory was sound in practice, but it has been understandably very difficult to get patients to comply and take a drug that they know will make them sick (O'Brien, 1999).

Because previous research had established a relationship between opioids and alcohol consumption, opioid therapy has also been used successfully to prevent relapse in alcoholism. Naltrexone, the previously mentioned opioid antagonist, suppresses craving for alcohol. In addition, a recently discovered drug, bremazocine, that antagonizes certain opioid receptors while serving as an agonist for others, is proving even more effective than naltrexone in animal studies (Nestby et al., 1999).

Researchers have had less success identifying a substance that will facilitate cocaine abstinence. Certain antidepressant and anticonvulsant drugs have been used with limited success (O'Brien, 1999). Research with BP897, the first D_3 receptor agonist, shows that it appears to successfully reduce drug-seeking behavior in rodents. This drug is interesting because, similar to bremazocine, it has both agonist and antagonist qualities. Of course, the drug will have to be tested on humans before it is offered as a medicinal therapy for cocaine addicts.

We have already discussed the critical role conditioning plays in the acquisition and maintenance of an addiction. One line of attack is to try to diminish the strong associations between environmental cues and drug effects. Given the role of glutamate in learning processes, researchers started to investigate the possibility of reducing craving for drugs in general by altering glutamatergic levels. In addition to its role in learning, glutamate has been shown to be critical for an animal's sensitization to amphetamine or cocaine (Wickelgren, 1998). **Sensitization** is the process by which an animal or person becomes increasingly responsive to a particular stimulus following repeated presentation.

To appreciate the behavioral ramifications of sensitization, imagine the behavior of young children on Christmas morning. As they are waiting for their parents to stumble out of bed, find their robes, and start the video camera, they find it impossible to remain still. In anticipation of the pleasure they have previously associated with opening presents, they jump up and down, run around in circles, and laugh with delight. These children are sensitized to the rewards of presents.

Similarly, rats, when placed in conditions reminiscent of receiving psychostimulants, will run around, move their heads back and forth, and engage in what appears to be purposeless behavior in anticipation of their next hit of the drug. MK-801, an antagonist for one of the glutamatergic receptors, N-methyl-D-aspartate (NMDA), inhibits cocaine self-administration in rats. Pilot data in humans demonstrate diminished withdrawal symptoms in opiate addiction (Bisaga & Popik, 2000; Wickelgren, 1998). Because of glutamate's general role in learning, it is probably involved in associations that drive most cravings for drugs. Thus, glutamatergic antagonists may help abusers of many types of drugs.

Stanley Glick and Isabelle Maisonneuve, working in the Department of Pharmacology and Neuroscience at Albany Medical College, have literally been beating the bushes for a novel medication for drug addiction. The African shrub known as *Tabernanthe iboga* has a long medicinal history: African hunters have used it for years to help them stay awake yet motionless while stalking prey. Studies in France at the turn of the century indicated that iboga has hallucinogenic and stimulant properties.

Interest in iboga as an antiaddictive substance emerged in the 1980s when patents addressing this shrub's potential antiaddiction properties started to be requested. Iboga was thought to abolish craving for drugs, an effect that supposedly lasted for months. Interestingly, animal studies corroborated these findings, but the initial reports of this miracle cure were too good to be true. It turned out that, in addition to the hallucinogenic and stimulant properties, iboga induced body tremors in rats.

Going back to the chemistry bench, researchers discovered that the antiaddiction properties of the compound could be separated from the tremor properties. Further work produced a new compound, 18-methoxycoronaridine. This compound suppressed craving for morphine, cocaine, and alcohol by reducing drug-induced DA release in the nucleus accumbens. This evidence suggests that the iboga-related alkaloid may be an effective therapy for addiction to multiple drugs (Glick & Maisonneuve, 1999.)

Vaccination: Therapeutic Shot in the Dark?

Imagine yourself in the year 2020. You take your infant to the pediatrician for vaccinations. In addition to the traditional immunizations, the doctor asks your permission to vaccinate your child against cocaine, heroin, and alcohol addiction. The scenario sounds like something out of a science fiction movie but may be closer to reality.

Research into vaccination therapy actually began in 1974 when Charles Schuster, formerly director of the National Institute on Drug Abuse and currently at Wayne State University, observed that heroin-addicted monkeys found heroin no more alluring than salty water after they were injected with a heroin-immunosensitive protein conjugate (Bonese, Wainer, Fitch, Rothberg, & Schuster, 1974). This reduction in craving, however, came at a cost. The inoculation regime was intense, causing lesions at the injection sites; and the effects were short-lived.

Nevertheless, this study was groundbreaking in that it introduced the notion of immunotherapy for addiction. The *active immunity* vaccination rationale is as follows. Injecting individuals with a specific drug fitted with a protein leads the body's immune system to make antibodies to this compound (Figure 11.5). Some time later, when our fictional child experiments with a particular drug, the antibodies rush to the drug as it enters the body, making it difficult for the drug to cross the blood–brain barrier and enter the brain (No More Kicks, 2000).

As previously described, modest success was achieved in the initial attempt to immunize animals against drugs of abuse, but the costs were considered too great to continue this line of research. More than 20 years later, scientists revisited the potential of an addiction vaccine in a desperate attempt to secure at least one victory in the grueling war on drugs. Kim Janda and his colleagues at the Scripps Research Institute in La Jolla, California, developed a refined active immunity vaccination that dramatically decreases the psychoactive effects of cocaine in rats (National Institute on Drug Abuse, 1996; No More Kicks, 2000).

In a report by Janda's team, *passive immunity* was tested (Carrera et al., 2000). The researchers tested the effect of merely injecting animals with antibodies designed to bind tightly to the drug, making it impossible for it to cross the blood–brain barrier. In passive immunity, the body plays no role in the antibody production. Thus, Janda believes that the active, or natural, immunity combined with the superstrength of the passive immunity strategy offers a double line of defense against addiction.

As impressive as these findings are, recent research has indicated a passive immunity strategy that might be even more effective. Researchers report that a catalytic antibody that facilitates the transition of cocaine to a

Figure 11.5
Vaccination therapy for drug abuse In active immunotherapy, a rat is injected with a combination of the drug, in this case cocaine, and certain immunoreactive compounds so that its immune system will actively generate antibodies to the drug, should cocaine be introduced into the body at a later time.
ADAPTED FROM NATIONAL INSTITUTE ON DRUG ABUSE (1996)

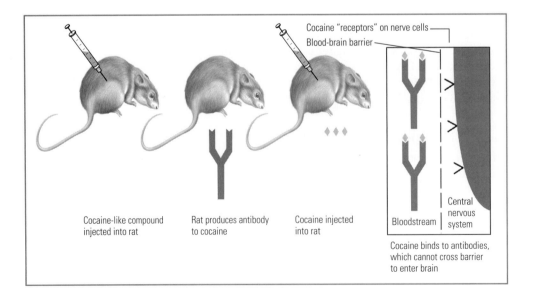

Cocaine "receptors" on nerve cells
Blood-brain barrier

Bloodstream | Central nervous system

Cocaine-like compound injected into rat

Rat produces antibody to cocaine

Cocaine injected into rat

Cocaine binds to antibodies, which cannot cross barrier to enter brain

psychologically inactive compound greatly diminishes animals' responsivity to cocaine. For example, rats injected with a catalytic antibody were protected against cocaine-induced seizures and sudden death. This protection was not observed in animals receiving a noncatalytic antibody (Mets et al., 1998).

Focusing on humans, one study investigated the efficacy of vaccinations containing anticocaine antibodies designed to increase natural antibody production: Thomas Kosten and his colleagues at Baylor College of Medicine delivered a series of five shots to current cocaine users participating in a methadone-treatment program. If effective, the vaccinations would cease the drug's ability to enter the brain. Throughout testing, 38% of the subjects developed antibody levels high enough to dull the effects of the drug; further, the antibodies stayed active for 8–10 weeks after the last injection. In this high-antibody group, about half of the subjects refrained from cocaine use in half of the urine tests compared to 23% of the subjects producing lower amounts of antibodies. Thus, immunization did not achieve abstinence in subjects, but the reduction may translate to enhanced quality of life in the patients. The authors conveyed concern, however, that the cocaine users given the vaccination attempted to increase cocaine consumption due to the blunted cocaine response they were experiencing. Although no overdoses were observed in the study, some subjects had approximately 10 times more cocaine in their systems than typically observed levels (Martell et al., 2009).

Seeing how quickly immunotherapy has advanced suggests that it is just a matter of time before it is used in some addiction-treatment regimes. More information about how the immune system is currently viewed as an integral factor in clinical neuroscience is discussed in Chapter 13.

Behavioral Therapies for Addiction

In an attempt to prevent relapse, it is typically recommended that patients see a therapist on an individual basis and/or join a support group to facilitate abstinence. We use the term *behavioral therapy* to refer to such diverse treatments as support groups, incentive programs, and acupuncture. (However, in addition to the perception that attending a support group is a behavioral therapy, this approach may be considered as *psychosocial therapy* because of the social component or *cognitive therapy* because of the attempts to change addicts' perceptions and thoughts.) Generally, behavioral therapy is recommended as an additional protection even if medicinal therapies are being used. Whereas medicinal therapy directly influences the patients' physiology, cognitive-behavioral therapy helps patients build a psychological collection of coping mechanisms (also resulting in altered physiology) to help assure a drug-free life.

Alcoholics Anonymous, a popular support group created in 1935, encourages cognitive awareness of the addiction by requiring frequent attendance at meetings. The requirement keeps this awareness in the forefront of the patients' thinking. Other types of support groups exist. Rational Recovery, a therapy based on the work of the rational–emotive psychologist Albert Ellis, encourages self-analysis as a key step to recovery. This philosophy is less religious than Alcoholics Anonymous, requires fewer meetings, and expects the patient to no longer need the therapy after 6 months to a year (Ruden, 2000). Although empirical evidence is hard to obtain, these groups probably work for some patients because they help to diminish stress, provide an environment with fewer drug-related cues, and offer cognitive strategies for responding to the constant temptations to relapse. These groups are generally more effective when combined with supervised medical treatment (O'Brien, 1999).

Researchers at the Yale University School of Medicine tried a creative behavioral therapy when faced with the difficult issue of treating patients addicted to both heroin and cocaine (Avants, Margolin, Holford, & Kosten, 2000). These patients were placed on methadone for their heroin addiction, and because there is no currently approved medical treatment for cocaine, they continued to use cocaine. The Yale researchers tested the efficacy of acupuncture by inviting the users to come in daily for 45 minutes. During this time, the experimental subjects had needles inserted into the ear, a procedure typical of traditional acupuncture, while the control subjects either had the same number of needles placed in random places along the ear or experienced a mere relaxation period. Urine screens were used to determine whether the subjects had metabolized cocaine during the testing period. The results indicated that the acupuncture group was more likely to submit cocaine-negative urine. However, a more recent study suggests that acupuncture is not effective as a stand-alone therapy and holds more potential as an ancillary treatment (Margolin et al., 2002).

Some behavioral programs have been designed to offer rewards for drug-free urine. Working under the supervision of Hendree Jones, the Johns Hopkins Center for Pregnancy and Abuse uses an incentive program to keep women from using drugs during their pregnancies. As with the acupuncture therapy, this nondrug therapy is safe for the developing fetus. Women in the Hopkins program frequently submit urine for screening to determine whether they are using drugs. Clean urine results in rewards such as vouchers for food and baby supplies. This program is successful during the time of close scrutiny of the investigators, but it is not likely to lead to long-term results unless it is combined with other therapies (Jones, personal communication, 2000). Behavioral incentives are also combined with pharmacological treatments—using methadone or buprenorphine to diminish withdrawal effects accompanying diminished drug use in pregnant women attempting to abstain from drug use (Jones, Johnson, Jasinski, & Milio, 2005).

In his book *The Craving Brain*, Ronald Ruden (2000) acknowledges the importance of the DA system in motivating an individual toward a drug and the serotonergic system in reducing the craving-related anxiety following consumption of the drug. This is the brain's natural system for survival-related rewards, so it is important for everyone to strive to balance the DA and serotonergic systems for adaptive, nonaddictive responding. Ruden encourages his patients to engage in various activities and/or pharmacological therapies to bring these systems to a healthy homeostasis. For example, the avoidance of stress may decrease DA activity in the accumbens area, and participation in a support group may reduce anxiety and result in raised serotonin levels.

Thus, according to Ruden, the craving brain is one that has either a sensitized mesolimbic DA system (leading to a prevalent drive to seek drugs) or a compromised serotonergic system (leading to a search for ways to reduce the uncomfortable feelings associated with anxiety). Empirical support for Ruden's theory can be found with the investigation of ondansetron, a drug previously used to fight nausea in cancer patients. This drug reduced the number of drinks consumed each day and increased the number of abstinent days in challenging alcoholism cases. It is believed that the drug works by regulating interactions between the DA and serotonergic systems, perhaps turning the craving brain into a homeostatically balanced brain (Johnson et al., 2000).

Ruden also advocates the use of **neurofeedback**, a biofeedback technique in which patients are trained to maintain certain electrical brain-wave rhythms to achieve relaxation and brain homeostasis. Intensive training sessions enable patients to maintain *alpha brain waves* (8–13 cycles per second, typically observed in relaxed states) and *theta brain waves* (slower, 4–7 cycles per second, typically observed during information processing or learning). Preliminary research suggests that neurofeedback results in less frequent relapses in alcoholics (Peniston & Kulkosky, 1989; Saxby & Peniston, 1995). Further research, however, is required to determine the true value of this approach.

You should be familiar enough with the brain by now to realize that it is doubtful that a person's propensity toward addiction and relapse depends on the balance of just two neurotransmitters. We have discussed several other neurotransmitters that seem to be involved in withdrawal. Thus, it is likely that the recipe for increasing a patient's resistance to relapse comprises several different ingredients. See Table 11.5 for a review of the various neurochemicals involved in this process.

neurofeedback Form of biofeedback in which patients learn to maintain certain electrical brain wave rhythms to achieve relaxation and brain homeostasis.

Ethical Questions About New Addiction Therapies

We have discussed several therapeutic approaches to help people remain free from drugs. But it is important to keep in mind that ethical considerations arise as scientists develop new treatments for addiction.

Is it ethical to immunize a child against a particular drug? Or is it a person's right to decide if drugs are worth trying? Is it ethical to make a person very ill when he or she takes a drug—a response over which many addicts say they have no control? Is it responsible to require addicts who have committed a crime to serve time in prison—an enormous economic cost—only to be released without treatment to the same environment that prompted the addiction in the first place?

Table 11.5 Neurochemicals Involved with Withdrawal Phase of Addiction Syndrome

Neurochemical	Relative Change During Withdrawal	Withdrawal Symptom
Dopamine	Decrease	Dysphoria
Opioids	Decrease	Pain, dysphoria
Serotonin	Decrease	Pain, dysphoria, depression
GABA	Decrease	Anxiety, panic attacks
Corticotropin-releasing hormone	Increase	Stress
Norepinephrine	Increase	Stress
Glutamate	Increase	Hyperexcitability

Adapted from Koob (1998).

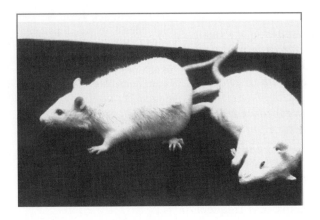

Figure 11.6
Masking effects of addiction?
These two rats had the same dose of alcohol. The one on the right is obviously passed out, while the one on the left, which was given Ro15–4513, is quite sober.

STEVEN PAUL/NATIONAL INSTITUTE OF MENTAL HEALTH

An example of the symbiotic relationship between therapy and ethics is evident in the discovery of a novel treatment introduced to the scientific community in 1986. Chemists at the Hoffmann-La Roche drug company synthesized a substance, R015–4513, that had the potential of solving the problem of drunk driving. Alcohol stimulates the γ-aminobutyric acid (GABA) receptor, and this drug blocks alcohol's ability to activate the receptor. Rats given a large dose of alcohol could be dramatically sobered up with this drug (Figure 11.6). Also, if given the drug prior to consumption, the rats could consume a toxic level of alcohol with no apparent intoxication or threat to their health (Kolata, 1986).

These findings were exciting and provided further information about the mechanisms related to alcohol intoxication, but ethical concerns thwarted the commercial development of this drug. Would such a medication encourage more drinking? If for some reason the medication did not work and the intoxicated driver caused an accident, would the blame lie with the individual, the drug company, or the establishment that served the drinks? Obviously, such decisions about the development of addiction therapies should be approached with a great deal of scrutiny and caution.

Summary

Drug Addiction in Context

Physiological components of the addiction syndrome include tolerance, withdrawal, and dependence. Views about drug use differ in various cultures, but virtually every culture is plagued by drug addiction. The aggregation of drug addiction in families and across cultures provides further evidence of common genetic and neurobiological contributions to the acquisition and maintenance of drug addiction.

It appears that the reinforcement experienced by drug users is a product of the brain area that evolved to make survival-related behaviors rewarding. In drug addiction, humans bypass these natural rewards and trigger a flood of activity in this evolutionarily old limbic brain region.

Tracing the Neurobiological Roots of the Addiction Syndrome

Brain structures surrounding and continuous with the nucleus accumbens—known as the "extended amygdala"—have been implicated in addiction. The nucleus accumbens, the brain's sensory–motor interface, is divided into two parts: the shell that is continuous with certain limbic structures such as the amygdala and the core that is continuous with the striatum. Evidence is accumulating that the orbitofrontal cortex, an area that projects to the nucleus accumbens, plays a role in maintaining addiction—perhaps related to recurring thoughts and associations related to drug use.

Dopamine, with its involvement in reward and movement, is a critical neurotransmitter in addiction; but acetylcholine, serotonin, and glutamate also influence the syndrome. Once an addiction is established, craving is typically experienced by individuals and leads to relapse. The intense emotions associated with drug use produce strong conditioning; consequently, environmental triggers often lead to craving and relapse.

Stress and Addiction

Stress has been identified as a significant factor contributing to the acquisition and maintenance of drug addiction and to relapse. Laboratory studies suggest that previously addicted animals search for drugs when stressors are introduced, even after exhibiting for an extended duration no interest in self-administration of the drug. It is thought that cortiocotropin-releasing hormone interacts with two limbic structures, the amygdala and the bed nucleus of the stria terminalis, to reinstate drug-seeking behavior at times of stress.

Therapy for Drug Addiction

Because the addiction syndrome is multifaceted, several therapeutic approaches have shown moderate success. Following detoxification, medicinal therapies may be used to maintain abstinence (for example, methadone). In addition to detoxification, behavioral/cognitive therapies include aversive conditioning, incentives, and relaxation techniques.

Psychosocial approaches are seen in support programs such as the pervasive Alcoholics Anonymous. Pharmacological therapies are also used in the battle against drug addiction to facilitate reduction in drug consumption or to reduce anxiety to minimize temptation and prevent relapse. New approaches on the therapeutic horizon include vaccinations against specific drugs.

With the advent of innovative therapies such as aversion therapies and vaccinations, questions arise concerning the ethics of imposing such approaches on addicted individuals. Trying to balance certain rights of individuals with the prospect of successful treatment is a challenge for our society.

Key Terms

drug addiction (326)
addiction syndrome (326)
tolerance (326)
withdrawal (326)
negative reinforcement (326)
dependence (326)
evolutionary game theory (330)
medial forebrain bundle (331)

ventral tegmental area (VTA) (333)
bed nucleus of the stria terminalis (BNST) (333)
extended amygdala (333)
microdialysis (337)
mesolimbic dopamine pathway (337)
knockout mice (339)

craving response (340)
anhedonia (343)
detoxification (346)
methadone (347)
naloxone (347)
buprenorphine (348)
sensitization (348)
neurofeedback (353)

For Further Consideration

Barthelme, F., & Barthelme, S. (1999, March 8). Good losers. *The New Yorker*, 46–61. If you have ever wondered how intelligent people find themselves in the throes of addiction, risking everything they have worked so hard to achieve, you will find this article fascinating. The Barthelme brothers obtained their graduate degrees from Johns Hopkins and are currently professors at the University of Mississippi. Initially attracted to the gambling casinos on the banks of the Mississippi out of sheer boredom, they quickly found themselves on an addiction ride that was controlling their lives. Although they knew the risks, these men lost their savings and their inheritance and continued to be seduced by the casino riverboats. They vividly describe their sensitivity to every event in the environment as their brains were desperately trying to make associations between environmental events and winning. After reading this article, it is easy to understand the notion that all addictions—even behavioral addictions—probably share the common denominator of mesolimbic reward.

Childress, A. R., Mozley, P. D., McElgin, W., Fitzgerald, J., Reivich, M., & O'Brien, C. P. (1999). Limbic activation during cue-induced cocaine craving. *American Journal of Psychiatry, 156*, 11–18. This research article captures the innovative research of Anna Rose Childress and her colleagues. In this study, cocaine users and naive control subjects were exposed to videos with potent cocaine-related cues while the researchers used positron emission tomography to measure their regional blood flow. During the video, the cocaine users reported that they were experiencing cravings, and the researchers found that they also displayed a pattern of increased cerebral blood flow in the limbic areas and decreased blood flow in the basal ganglia. No such patterns were observed in the control subjects. These data suggest that limbic activation accompanies psychological craving in addicted subjects.

Koob, G. F., & Volkow, N. D. (2010). Neurocircuitry of addiction. *Neuropsychopharmacology Reviews, 35*,

217–238. Written by two of the most respected researchers in the field of neuroscience of addiction, this article presents updated neurobiological data on addiction. Additionally, the authors propose a specific neurocircuitry underlying three separate phases of the addiction syndrome: binge/intoxification, withdrawal/negative effect, and preoccupation/anticipation (craving). This categorization is useful in deriving effective treatment strategies for various symptoms experienced by individuals addicted to certain substances.

Ruden, R. (2000). *The Craving Brain* (2nd ed.). New York: HarperCollins. Ron Ruden is the medical director of an addiction clinic in New York City, where he interacts with dozens of patients suffering from various forms of addiction every day. Consequently, this book gives the reader a more clinical perspective on addiction. More specifically, Ruden articulates the delicate balance between the dopaminergic and the serotonergic neurochemical systems and how a disruption in this balance can lead to cravings that ultimately result in addiction. He describes how he attempts to reduce cravings by helping patients reestablish neurochemical homeostasis. This edition discusses the intriguing field of neurofeedback and the possibility of reducing craving by teaching subjects to produce alpha and theta brain waves. Because of its interesting combination of clinical and neurochemical perspectives, this is a worthwhile book to use as a supplement to the more traditional neurobiological references.

Wise, R. A. (2000). Addiction becomes a brain disease. *Neuron, 26*, 27–33. Wise is an expert on motivation in animals and presents a nice overview of the past and present research in the field of addiction. He describes the importance of the environmental setting, neuroplasticity, and the role of genetics (assessed by numerous studies with drug-seeking strains of rats) in the addiction syndrome. Finally, the roles of stress and learning in the acquisition and maintenance of addiction are addressed. Written at the end of the 1990s, the decade of the brain, Wise identifies the challenges of the next decade as scientists continue to try to understand addiction.

Connections ■

Pacing and Prozac

Imagine that you are waiting for your best friend to arrive at your apartment after a long multistate trip. By your best estimate, he should have arrived 2 hours ago. Why hasn't your friend phoned you or answered your calls? After all, he always has a cell phone with him and is typically very responsible about letting you know if he's going to be late. You start thinking about why your friend may not have contacted you. An accident? An abduction? Gotten lost?

You feel so anxious and full of worry that you can't stop pacing back and forth in the kitchen. Finally, you think it's best if you sit down and try to relax. After a few minutes, you notice more movement. This time it's your fingers; they're tapping a pencil against a book you are holding in your lap. After making these observations, you stop to consider why it is so difficult for you to remain *motionless* as you wait anxiously for your friend to arrive. You find it difficult to explain your uncontrollable drive to *move*.

Research conducted by Barry Jacobs and Casimir Fornal at Princeton University reveals that this repetitive movement may be just what the doctor ordered for stress (Jacobs, 1994; Casimir Fornal, personal communication, 2002). More specifically, the Princeton laboratory has been looking closely at the activity of serotonergic neurons in cats. Increased serotonergic activity results in diminished depression symptoms in many patients (Chapter 9).

Generally, the research team found that the cats' serotonergic neurons exhibit the highest rates of firing when they are engaging in frequent, repetitive movement such as walking on a treadmill. Firing of the serotonergic neurons decreases during slow-wave sleep, a time when there is little, if any, body movement. Additionally, virtually no serotonergic activity is observed during rapid eye movement (REM) sleep, a time when there is no muscle tone. Further, patients suffering from depression sometimes benefit from reduced REM sleep, perhaps because of the decreased exposure to the sleep stage in which no serotonergic activity occurs.

Jacobs and Fornal have also investigated the activity of serotonergic neurons during times of fatigue. When cats have been placed on a treadmill for an extended time and become visibly fatigued, the serotonergic neurons stop firing. Thus, the convergence of evidence suggests that the serotonergic activity underlying movement may be related to mood fluctuations. When animals encounter stressful stimuli and become increasingly emotional, or stressed, it might be adaptive to engage in behavior that results in the secretion of serotonin. If this is the case, then chewing gum, riding a bicycle, jogging, and bouncing your leg up and down when you're seated may all be methods of administering the physiological equivalent of tiny doses of Prozac into your own brain!

Back to your missing friend. Once he arrives, your stress response subsides and you are able to sit perfectly still as you catch up on the last several months. At this point, there is no need for the brain or body to search for behavioral coping strategies that will reduce the amount of stress being experienced—or prepare you to respond to the impending danger associated with that stress. So what explains the fact that when your friend announces that he is getting married—a nonthreatening, happy event—you can't stop jumping up and down?

Any event that interrupts homeostasis is stressful. Typically, we consider stress to be threatening, similar to the fear you have about losing your missing friend; but the physiological waters are also roiled during happy, exciting events such as finding out your friend is getting married. The interactions among your nervous system, emotions, cognitions, and coping responses determine the neurobiological impact of these events and how you cope with stress.

Unless you've been living in a protective bubble somewhere, you have had a lot of personal experience with stress. It seems as much a part of our world as breathing, yet there is so much about this complex response that we do not know. Why do some people embrace challenges, whereas others avoid them? Why do some people survive horrendous events, whereas others seem to crumple at the first sign of trouble? How can a psychological phenomenon such as stress cause physiological damage to our bodies and brains?

Although researchers do not have all the answers to these questions, they have made considerable progress toward solving the many mysteries surrounding our ubiquitous stress response. We begin this chapter by recounting classic research on stress and reviewing the neurobiological roots of the stress response as we discussed in Chapters 5 and 6. Next, we examine factors that influence responsiveness to stress over the life span. Then, we apply this knowledge to strategies for coping with stress and mitigating the severity of the stress response. At the end of the chapter, we consider the symptoms, causes, and current treatments for posttraumatic stress disorder.

REVISITING THE STRESS RESPONSE

In 1925 Hans Selye was completing his studies in medicine at the University of Prague. After attending numerous lectures on anatomy, physiology, and biochemistry, he was thrilled to be allowed to visit patients. On that momentous day, he was introduced to several patients displaying the earliest stages of various infectious diseases. Although the patients were suffering from different forms of infection, young Selye was struck by the similarity of their symptoms—they all felt ill and complained of diffuse aches and pains in their joints and of gastrointestinal problems. He also noted that most had enlarged spleens, inflamed tonsils, and fever.

Selye thought this commonality was an important observation, but his professor did not think it noteworthy. On the contrary, the professor was more interested in the specific characteristics of the various illnesses, even though most details could not be seen until a disease was at an advanced stage. The fact that the symptoms displayed by all of the patients at the onset of an illness were general made them less valuable to the professor—nonspecific symptoms were of no use to physicians at that time. Selye agreed with his professor that identifying certain symptoms was important for prescribing the most effective drugs, yet he was struck by the fact that only a few specific symptoms are characteristic of any particular disease, whereas most general symptoms are common to many or even all diseases (Selye, 1964).

Although Selye's observations remained in the back of his mind, he didn't revisit his initial revelation concerning sickness until he was an assistant professor in the Biochemistry Department of McGill University in the midst of investigating a new hormone from cattle ovary extracts. Selye discovered that all of the ovarian extracts, regardless of their preparation, produced the exact same syndrome in the animals, a *sickness syndrome* consisting of an enlarged adrenal cortex, gastrointestinal ulcers, and atrophied, or shrunken, thymus and lymph nodes. Initially, he was discouraged that there was nothing particularly interesting about the work; then, he realized that he had produced an experimental model of the sickness syndrome that so intrigued him when he was a medical student (Selye, 1964).

Selye's discovery marked the dawn of an exciting new era in biomedical research. As he embarked on a research journey focusing on this sickness syndrome, he borrowed a term from engineering terminology, *stress*. Stress seemed to convey the idea of wear and tear on the human machinery that is a prevalent feature of our lives. It appears, however, that the physiologist Walter Cannon had used the term in the same general sense in the medical literature in the 1920s (Sapolsky, 1998).

Selye referred to the stress response as the **general adaptation syndrome**. He proposed that this syndrome consists of three stages: (1) the *alarm reaction*, in which the body mobilizes its defensive forces to respond to the stressor; (2) *resistance*, which reflects full adaptation to the stressor; and (3) *exhaustion*, which occurs when the stressor is severe and chronic and leads to depletion of energy and, if continued, death (Selye, 1936, 1976).

Selye went on to test the general nature of his stress syndrome. He exposed animals to multiple physical stressors—cold, noise, the boiler room in his building—and all of the animals developed the same symptoms observed with Selye's original ovarian extract injections. Selye likened the stress response to a home alarm system: No matter how the system is initiated, the same response occurs. Regardless of whether a threat occurs at a window or a door, the house alarm is activated and the authorities are called; accordingly, the stress alarm is activated on any type of threat to the body.

Selye was an extremely productive scientist, who made many contributions to the field of stress. Throughout this chapter, however, we will address a few questions that challenge at least two assumptions proposed in his earlier theories about stress: Does an animal have the same response to all stressors? Does an animal die from stress because of the depletion, or wearing down, of certain defenses?

Some stressors are like ships passing in the night: They come and they go, and they don't have a significant impact on our lives once they are gone. Other stressors, however, tie up to our physiological docks for an extended stay. Our bodies seem to be designed for the stress-ships-passing-in-the-night scenario—we can respond sufficiently to such threats—but our physiological systems are severely threatened when the stress is prolonged.

Acute Stress Response

Have you ever felt terrified? At what moment of your life were you most afraid? Perhaps you narrowly escaped a serious car accident when you were trying to change radio stations or you got dangerously close to a poisonous

general adaptation syndrome Syndrome originally described by Hans Selye; he felt that stressed individuals undergo three phases during the stress response; alarm, in which the individual's body registers the threat of the imposing stressor; resistance, in which the body mobilizes its forces to fight off the stressor; and if the stressor persists, exhaustion as the body runs out of energy to fight off the stressor.

snake on a camping trip or you showed up in a class realizing that the professor was distributing an exam that you knew nothing about. Sometimes just remembering such moments recreates the stressful response inside your body. Can you feel it? Your heart starts racing, your palms get sweaty, you feel a rush of energy running through your body.

As Stanford University biologist Robert Sapolsky describes so eloquently and entertainingly in his book *Why Zebras Don't Get Ulcers* (1998), this response makes perfect evolutionary sense when we think about surviving an *acute*, or short-term, stressor. Many physiological processes enable the zebra to escape the pursuit of a lion: increased focus on the task of escaping; increased breathing rate, heart rate, and blood pressure to get glucose and oxygen to the muscles so that the zebra can run faster; the rapid conversion of stored energy into usable energy for the escape response; and a temporary shutdown of reproductive, digestive, immunological, and growth processes.

Why shut down valuable physiological processes during the stress response? As described by Sapolsky, these are long-term investments of energy that mean nothing if the zebra is eaten by the lion and doesn't survive to the next day to reproduce, digest a meal, grow, or build up antibodies for the next sickness to pass across the African plains. In an apt analogy, he suggests that if you know a hurricane is about to hit your house, your time is better spent boarding up windows than hanging wallpaper in the guest bathroom.

If a wild animal is about to attack another animal, is it really smart for the prey to turn off its immune system? Maybe immunological energy directed toward surveillance of tumors or exotic diseases that may develop and kill the prey animal in the next several months is better spent contributing to escape (Sapolsky, 2000). But what if the zebra is wounded by the lion and survives the attack? It is likely to be left with a gaping wound filled with foreign antigens. Did that scenario factor into the evolution of this response?

Firdaus Dhabhar and his colleagues in the Department of Oral Biology at Ohio State University have conducted some interesting research addressing immune functioning during the stress response (Dhabhar, Satoskar, Bluethmann, David, & McEwen, 2000). This research has shown that, contrary to original thought, acute stress significantly enhances the movement of pathogen-fighting white cells from the blood to the skin—the exact place the lion's claws will invade the zebra's body. We consider the effect of stress on the specific activity of the immune system more thoroughly in Chapter 13.

A final aspect of the acute stress response is its consistency. Does an animal always have the same response upon the presentation of a stressful stimulus—as stated by Selye in his general adaptation syndrome? The best answer is probably yes and no. Yes, animals have the same general response of stress hormone release and the suppression of a few long-term, optimistic processes (growth, reproduction, and so on). But there are differences as well. For example, the stressful stimulus of social defeat in rats produces increases in mean arterial blood pressure, whereas electric footshock decreases blood pressure (Adams, Lins, & Blizard, 1987). Fear of footshock produces both immobility and *bradycardia* (slowness of heart rate) in most rats, whereas fear of a dominant rat results in half the rats demonstrating bradycardia and the other half immobility (Roozendaal, Koolhaas, & Bohus, 1990).

Given these different responses to various stressful stimuli, Robert Blanchard of the University of Hawaii argues that experimenters should be careful to use stressors that are biologically relevant across species, such as social stress that affects both rats and humans (Blanchard, McKittrick, & Blanchard, 2001). Certainly, the type of stressor should be carefully chosen and should have **ecological relevance** (likely to be found in the animal's natural environment). Some may argue that, whereas footshock and cold restraint result in a stress response, these stimuli are not **species-specific stressors** for rats. If stress responses vary, even in subtle ways, on the presentation of different stimuli, then the use of more artificial stimuli may result in a distorted picture of the stress response.

It is also interesting to consider that the same stimulus presented repeatedly can produce different stress responses (at least different in intensity) as the animal either habituates (becomes less responsive) or sensitizes to the stimulus. As children learn what the smiling nurse is really going to do with that glistening needle, their stress response heightens. On the other hand, as the sensation seeker parachutes out of the plane for the twentieth time, his or her stress response is diminished compared with the initial jump. Thus, it seems that we've come a long way from Selye's claim that the stress response is best described as *one size fits all*; conversely, as observed with other emotional responses, individual differences abound.

Chronic Stress Response

The acute stress response is well orchestrated and critical to survival. When this response is not cut off, however, our survival can be threatened by the very system designed to keep us alive. It was the chronic effects of stress that Hans Selye originally described as the general adaptation syndrome.

It's been reported that Selye was not the most skilled researcher when it came to injecting rats, and after numerous days of being handled, dropped, chased, and injected, the rats in his lab started to develop the sickness symptoms previously described—gastric ulcers, hypertrophied adrenal glands, and atrophied thymus glands (Sapolsky, 1998). And when he was trying to stress his animals, Selye exposed them to the designated stressors (boiler room noise, cold temperatures) for extended periods of time. Clearly, his rats were chronically stressed.

When the stress response cannot be turned off, the immune system is suppressed, which obviously leads to an increased vulnerability to sickness (Raison & Miller, 2001). If you've ever gotten sick immediately following a stressful week of final exams, you can relate to this observation. In addition to a higher susceptibility to disease or sickness, the cardiovascular system is threatened by chronic stress. The heightened activity of the cardiovascular system is very effective for a short period of time, but having an increased heart rate and blood pressure for extended durations simply wears out the heart muscle.

To add insult to injury, residue from the transfer of stored energy substances (sugars and fats) into available energy for a quick response starts to build up in the blood vessels after a while, leading to a condition called **atherosclerosis**. This condition is exacerbated if chronic high blood pressure produces plaques, small tears, and pits in the internal lining of the blood vessels, where the glucose and fatty acids can find a place to accumulate.

ecologically relevant Term used to describe stressors that an animal may find in its natural environment. Example: Social defeat is a more ecologically relevant stimulus for hamsters than cold or restraint.

species-specific stressor Stressor that is specific for a particular species. Example: Weasel urine is a natural stressor for rats but is not stressful for dogs.

atherosclerosis Buildup of lipid substances in lesions in the blood vessels; can eventually lead to hardened arteries and disrupted blood flow.

Finally, chronically high levels of glucocorticoids alter the body's energy resources and subsequently influence eating strategies in humans. In many people who increase their consumption of certain foods (especially high-fat and high-carbohydrate "comfort food"), fat is more readily deposited around the mid-section for energy availability (Dallman et al., 2003). See Box 12.1 for a further discussion of stress and eating.

It's easy to envision a blood vessel that is already clogged becoming smaller and smaller during an acute stress response, getting dangerously close to forming an occlusion, or blockage, in the blood vessel. Jay Kaplan, a physiologist, and his colleagues at Bowman Gray Medical School showed this effect in monkeys (Manuck, Marsland, Kaplan, & Williams, 1995). When placed in a stressful, unstable social group, the low-ranking animals—those that had little control over their environment and probably experienced more stress—were more likely to develop atherosclerotic plaques than the higher-ranking animals. In response to the question posed earlier regarding illness resulting from a worn-down stress response, it is important to note that this stress-induced heart disease is the result not of an exhausted stress response but of chronic activation of the stress response.

Stress and personality traits. In the 1960s, two cardiologists, Meyer Friedman and Ray Rosenman, conducted research exploring the relationship between certain personality profiles and cardiovascular disease (Rosenman et al., 1975). They found that subjects who were high achievers, very competitive, and always conscientious of the time were more likely to suffer cardiovascular disease than their more laid-back counterparts. Friedman and Rosenman used the labels *type A* for the competitive personality style and *type B* for the more relaxed style. Before you press your parents' phone number on your speed dial to justify your relaxed performance in some of your classes, it's important to keep reading; there's an interesting twist to this story.

This work was very influential, and a Duke University physician, Redford Williams, has attempted to replicate some of the findings of Freidman and Rosenman (Dahlstrom & Williams, 1983). Williams's work suggests that hostility is a more powerful personality predictor for cardiovascular disease than a more general type A personality. This is especially true if a person has been chronically stressed.

As described previously, the chronic stress response will often leave a person's blood vessels clogged with substances absorbed for the utilization of energy in the fight-or-flight response. This is an especially high price to pay because we really don't need the extra energy most of the time—these days many people experience crises and solve them without even getting up from their office desk. So when this person has a subsequent full-blown stress response, the constriction of the blood vessels might result in a blockage, leading to either a heart attack or a stroke.

As depicted in Figure 12.1, the outrageous fits of hostility demonstrated by the successful former basketball coach Bobby Knight may lead his team to a winning season but at significant cost to his health. Adding fuel to the fire, many hostile individuals carry their stress response around with them for longer periods of time, finding it hard to let go of their anger (Fredrickson et al., 2000). Sustaining a dangerous condition for longer periods of time also increases susceptibility to cardiovascular disease.

Box 12.1

Brain Matters

Eating and Stress

Does stress influence how you eat? Some people respond to stressful situations by heading straight to the refrigerator; others tend to avoid food during anxiety-laden times. Elissa Epel and her colleagues in the Health Psychology Program at the University of California at San Francisco recently investigated the influence of psychological and physiological variables in determining the eating response to stress (Epel, Lapidus, McEwen, & Brownell, 2001).

They found that women who responded to stress with high cortisol levels were more likely to consume more calories on the days they were exposed to stress. These high-cortisol reactors also ate more sweet food throughout the experiment. So if you find yourself eating more during stressful times, it is possible that you respond to stress with high cortisol secretions.

Stress may also influence the pattern of fat distribution in individuals. Have you ever noticed that some people seem to have a disproportionate amount of fat in their mid-section? Central body fat is an indicator of greater visceral fat, which is extremely susceptible to cortisol's influence on fat accumulation and transfer in the bloodstream. Thus, increased central body fat is a risk factor for diseases such as hypertension, diabetes, stroke, and coronary heart disease (Kissebah & Krakower, 1994).

In one study that attempted to identify the types of individuals most at risk for increased mid-section fat, women were exposed to stress sessions consisting of 45 minutes of psychological tests and challenges (e.g., speech tasks, serial arithmetic) for 3 days, followed by a day of rest. Throughout this time the women's salivary cortisol levels and coping responses were measured. When these researchers correlated cortisol level with body type, they found that women with high levels of central fat reported being more threatened by the stress tests and secreted significantly more cortisol than the women with less central body fat. Another interesting finding in this study is that lean women with central body fat were less likely to habituate to the stress tests than any other group; that is, their cortisol responses were still significantly increased on the third day of testing.

In a study focusing on healthy, nonobese adults, corticotropin-releasing hormone (CRH) was infused into the subjects at a level that was subjectively undetectable but produced robust cortisol responses. Compared to a placebo, the subjects receiving the CRH consumed more snack foods—calories and total consumption—at the peak cortisol response time (George, Khan, Briggs, & Abelson, 2010).

Why does this relationship between eating and stress exist? Perhaps the rats can tell us. Kevin Laugero (2001), at the University of California–San Francisco's School of Medicine, reported the surprising finding that mere sucrose ingestion stabilizes eating, energy balance, and CRH in rats that have received an adrenalectomy. Remember that the adrenal glands secrete glucocorticoids and adrenaline, so removal of this organ drastically alters an animal's ability to respond to stressful stimuli.

Laugero argues that the relationship between eating and the hypothalamic–pituitary–adrenal (HPA) axis response to stress makes sense when the stress response is thought of as a response to reestablish energy levels in the organism following the initial threat and subsequent sympathetic response. Laugero's argument is strengthened by the observation of the simultaneous emergence of HPA axis receptivity and adult glucose sensitivity during an organism's development (Widmaier, 1990). Thus, the HPA axis may have evolved for the more general purpose of maintaining energy levels in the body. In fact, during nonstressful times, HPA axis function follows circadian rhythms, peaking just prior to times of increased energy expenditure—namely, waking, increased activity, and foraging (Dallman et al., 2002).

Just being mindful that during times of significant stress we're going to be motivated to eat high-calorie, "comfort" foods may make us more aware of our eating patterns during these times (Dallman et al., 2003). Of course, in the short run, a candy bar makes us feel better, but repeated coping in this manner can increase mid-section fat and make us vulnerable to a host of cardiovascular and related diseases. As we will see in Chapter 14, which is on eating regulation and associated disorders, any drastic changes in eating patterns can also become a detrimental threat to our homeostasis by making us susceptible to conditions such as anorexia, bulimia, diabetes, and obesity.

peptic ulcers Lesions that occur in the stomach lining; usually caused by a bacterium but exacerbated by stress.

Figure 12.1
Toxicity of hostility Basketball coach Bobby Knight may be leading his team to victory, but his coaching style could score a real loss for his cardiovascular system.

ROD AYDELOTTE, WACO TRIBUNE HERALD/AP/ WIDE WORLD PHOTO

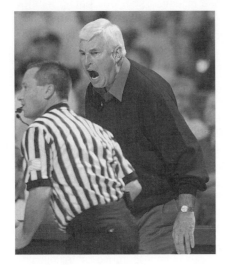

Figure 12.2
Stress ulceration A rat's stomach removed after 5 days of being housed in an activity cage and fed 1 hour per day. The necrotic tissue (black streaks) in the corpus of the stomach show the ulcerations.

KELLY LAMBERT, RANDOLPH-MACON COLLEGE BEHAVIORAL SCIENCE LABORATORY

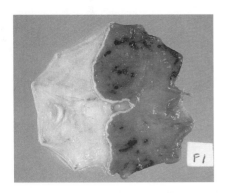

Stress ulcers. Lesions in the lining of the stomach called **peptic ulcers** are a common consequence of chronic stress. As you recall, ulceration was one of the original symptoms Selye observed in chronically stressed rats. The cause of peptic ulcers was a mystery until a revolutionary finding in the 1980s. Up until this time most people were comfortable with the belief that ulcers were caused by an excessive amount of hydrochloric acid in the stomach because, sure enough, antacid medications were a rather effective treatment. However, because the relapse rate was high, it was apparent to the clinicians in the field that antacid medication was a mere peptic Band-Aid and there was more to the story. If chronic stress led to a reduction of gastric activity—and acid secretion—how could an ulcer form? That dry mouth you develop as you try to give an oral presentation is an early sign of the decreased digestive juices secreted during stress. It appeared contradictory to our knowledge of what was happening during the stress response; if anything, it appeared that a person should be *protected* against ulceration during a stressful period.

But study after study showed that animals exposed to stress developed stress ulcers. As detailed in Chapter 8, the activity-stress paradigm, which consists of exposing animals to a restricted feeding regimen and free access to a running wheel, produced severe ulcers in just 4 days (Figure 12.2). It was thought that the mucosal lining of the stomach became compromised during the digestive acid–, glandular secretion–deficient period which leads to an ulcer as soon as the digestive acids resumed their activity. Again, though, a piece of the puzzle was missing.

A creative twist to this ulcer drama came in the 1980s when Barry Marshall, an Australian pathologist, announced at a conference that he had found a bacterium, *Helicobacter pylori*, in the stomach lining of humans suffering from peptic ulcers and gastritis (Sapolsky, 1998; Warren & Marshall, 1983). At that time, it was thought that bacteria could not survive in the acidic lining of the stomach; even more damning was the fact that numerous studies had shown a connection between stress and peptic ulcers. Consequently, Marshall's hypothesis was not warmly welcomed.

This reception prompted Marshall to take drastic measures. He actually ate some of the bacteria, waited, and documented the genesis of his very own peptic ulcer—perhaps the world's first planned and anticipated human peptic ulcer. This result was successful in attracting the interest of other researchers, who went on to confirm Marshall's findings. Even more exciting was the realization that if ulcers are caused by a bacterium, then antibiotics will be an effective treatment. This hypothesis turned out to be the case. Many patients suffering from ulcers are able to obtain longer-lasting relief from antibiotics than from antacid treatments.

After the *Helicobacter* theory of ulceration gained acceptance, it seemed for a while that the door was shut to this area of investigation in psychology (Melmed & Gelpin, 1996). But researchers could not deny the fact that stress was still an important factor since so many studies had shown that stress exposure exacerbates ulceration. After experiencing traumatic head injury, for example, patients with higher levels of cortisol were more likely to develop stress ulcers (Li, Wang, Jiang, Geng & Qiang, 2010). It appears that we might have evolved a defense mechanism that protects us against the destructive actions of the bacteria but that this defense system is compromised in some way when we have to endure chronic stress.

Today, researchers are trying to understand how stress makes an individual more vulnerable to bacteria-induced ulceration. Several possibilities exist: a compromised immune system may enliven the bacteria, a compromised mucosal lining may degrade the barrier that protects the stomach lining from the bacteria, or decreased blood flow during sympathetic arousal may create an optimal environment for the bacteria. Regardless, researchers and clinicians are once again convinced that stress plays an important role and that the bacteria are a necessary, but not sufficient, cause of ulceration.

Thus, whereas the acute stress response is a wonderful adaptation to survive an impending threat, chronic stress, whether real or imagined, is a different story. In fact, going back to the title of Sapolsky's book, this point addresses the question of *Why Zebras Don't Get Ulcers*. Once the lion gets tired of chasing the zebra and the zebra is safely out of harm's way, the zebra's stress response is terminated, so all the digestive acids start to flow again, creating a more hostile environment for the bacteria and inhibiting their ability to create ulcers.

Considering this information, you may think that it does not appear that we were designed to undergo chronic stress and, for that reason, we get sick. It almost seems like an evolutionary mistake. We are reminded that the forces guiding evolutionary pressures are quite complex. As certain bodily systems evolved, there was no guarantee that others would not be compromised. In other words, we are not always able to have our evolutionary cake and eat it too. For humans, as our neocortex became larger and larger, holding the capacity to store stressful memories, share others' pain, and generate anxiogenic thoughts and scenarios, it was inevitable that we enter the world of chronic stress. Don't close your book now in frustration—after we review the effects of nature and nurture on the stress response, we'll consider ways to cope with chronic stress.

The Brain's Stress Circuit

Not long after Cannon described the role of the sympathetic nervous system in reestablishing physiological homeostasis, as detailed in Chapter 5, Hans Selye described the sickness syndrome associated with stress. One of the general symptoms is an enlarged adrenal gland. This symptom pointed to another important stress circuit in the brain, the hypothalamic–pituitary–adrenal (HPA) axis, that isn't quite as immediate as the sympathetic response but is just as valuable.

At the heart of the HPA circuit are the glucocorticoids, or stress hormones, released by the adrenal cortex. Selye theorized that the adrenal glands were enlarged because they were pumping out so many glucocorticoids due to the chronic stress (Sternberg, 2000). Today, we know considerably more about the HPA-axis mechanisms related to the release of cortisol in humans. As Table 12.1 reveals, cortisol influences the hippocampus, an area rich with glucocorticoid receptors.

Bruce McEwen, a noted neuroscientist at Rockefeller University, has conducted considerable research delineating the effects of chronic glucocorticoid secretion on the functioning and structure of the hippocampal neurons

(a)   (b)

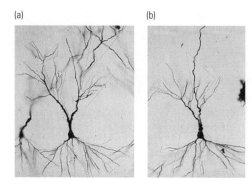

Figure 12.3
Stress-induced restructuring of hippocampal neurons CA3 pyramidal neurons from (a) a control rat and (b) a rat that received 21 days of injections of glucocorticoids. The control rat's dendritic processes both are longer and have more connections than the neuron from the animal receiving exogenous stress hormones.

BRAIN RESEARCH, 531 (1990) 225–231, ELSEVIER. COURTESY OF CATHERINE S. WOOLLEY, ET AL., LABORATORY OF NEUROENDOCRINOLOGY, THE ROCKEFELLER UNIVERSITY

excitotoxicity Process that probably occurs in CA3 neurons of the hippocampus. This effect is caused by excessive glutamate activity in the neurons, which may lead to neuronal death; prolonged exposure to stress hormones may trigger the process.

(McEwen, 2008). In 1990, McEwen and his collaborators Catherine Woolley and Elizabeth Gould examined neurons in the CA3 area following 21 days of injections of exogenous glucocorticoids (Figure 12.3) (Woolley, Gould, & McEwen, 1990). This 3-week period may be similar to many of our own chronic stress phases—worrying about an upcoming exam or a relationship or suffering from a prolonged bout with the flu.

To the researchers' surprise, significant dendritic restructuring occurred in CA3 neurons after this seemingly short duration (Figure 12.3). As you can see, the glucocorticoid-injected neuron (b) has fewer and less elaborate dendritic branching than its control counterpart (a). This finding was also confirmed in rats that were exposed to 6 hours of restraint (psychological stress) for 21 days (Watanabe, Gould, & McEwen, 1992).

To date, no single mechanism has been identified as being the chief factor that leads to the damaged CA3 pyramidal cells. Because cellular damage and death have been linked to excessive levels of glutamate and activation of associated N-methyl-D-aspartate (NMDA) receptors, this process is sometimes known as **excitotoxicity**. The inhibitory neurotransmitter γ-aminobutyric acid (GABA) also seems to play a role in stress-induced hippocampal damage. Benzodiazepine, a GABA agonist, blocks stress-induced dendritic restructuring (Magarinos et al., 1999). Additionally, serotonin may play a role in the demise of hippocampal neurons during stress. An atypical antidepressant drug, tianeptine, which enhances serotonin uptake resulting in decreased extracellular levels of serotonin, has been found to reduce stress-induced dendritic alterations in tree shrews undergoing severe chronic stress (Czeh et al., 2001).

Although it is not clear whether a reduction in neurogenesis might be related to these hippocampal effects, psychosocial stress has been reported to reduce the production of new neurons in the tree shrew hippocampus (Gould et al., 1997). What effect might reductions in hippocampal dendritic branching have on our brains and memory processes? McEwen (2000b) suggests that the structural changes are reversible following termination of HPA-axis activation. Thus, if the stress subsides before the cells atrophy (die), there is hope for their recovery. As for the effect of the altered neurons on cognitive processes, stress produces deficits in both episodic and spatial memory systems. in humans and other animals. If the stress is chronic (lasting several years), it is likely that the hippocampus will be smaller in the most severely impaired individuals and recovery will be more of a challenge than in more acute stress situations (Lupien et al., 1998; McEwen, deLeon, Lupien, & Meaney, 1999).

One measure of the value of the stress response can be assessed by the sheer number of brain areas devoted to carrying out some aspect of stress responsivity (McEwen, 2010). The sympathetic nervous system's fight-or-flight response to an impending threat such as a loud noise is one of the earliest responses observed in the stress-response cascade. The auditory stimulus associated with the loud noise will also activate the amygdala and its associated fear circuit (see Chapter 8). Neurochemicals important for sustaining the increased activity necessary to escape the stressor are triggered by the HPA axis (glucocorticoids) as well as by the locus coeruleus (noradrenaline).

The hippocampus and forebrain are also part of the brain's stress circuit as animals are required to place stressful stimuli in appropriate contexts to determine the most effective response or must problem-solve to determine possible escape routes from various stressors (Perez-Cruz, Simon, Czeh, Flugge, & Fuchs, 2009; McEwen, 2010). Later in this chapter, we'll discuss the transition from *reaction* to *action*—how an animal evaluates emotional information from the basic stress circuits in the brain and then makes voluntary decisions about how to respond. Such planned responses require the forebrain and hippocampus to a greater extent than the more basic stress responses such as freezing in place or running.

Table 12.1 Effect of Cortisol on Various Tissues in the Body

Tissues	Effect
Neuron	Increased catecholamine synthesis
Hippocampus	Enhanced memory formation
Thalamus	Increased sensitivity to incoming stimuli
Adrenoreceptors	Increased alpha and beta receptor sensitivity
Adrenal medulla	Increased synthesis of catecholamines
Immune system	Both excited and inhibited
Inflammation	Inhibited
Glucose	Increased production
Fatty acid	Increased release from energy stores
Kidney	Water diuresis and retention of sodium

After Lovallo (1997, p. 49).

STRESS RESPONSIVITY OVER THE LIFE SPAN

Although Selye advocated the generalized adaptation syndrome in which different stressors led to standard responses, increasingly the research shows that significant individual differences exist in responding to stress. In Chapter 6, for example, we noted how parental involvement, aging, and sex differences can affect a person's response to stress. Now, we expand on the relevance of developmental research in explaining differing behavioral responses.

Role of Mother–Infant Interactions

Harry Harlow's classic work investigating the effects of extended maternal separation in rhesus monkeys provided convincing evidence that mother–infant interaction is critical to the development of the stress response as well as to other aspects of development. Harlow reported that the animals were agitated in the beginning and then entered a lethargic stage for the rest of the 3-week separation (Suomi, 1983).

The hyperresponsive stress response was also seen when the motherless animals were allowed to play with other motherless infants. As seen in Figure 12.4, whereas other healthy monkeys would probably be engaging in bouts of rough-and-tumble play, these animals huddled together in a cautious, tense posture (Harlow & Harlow, 1962). Confirming Michael Meaney's findings, reported in Chapter 6, that rodent maternal attention directed toward pups plays a significant role in the development of the animal's response to challenges as adults, Harlow reported that these motherless primates were not good mothers themselves—their behavior ranged from indifference to abuse.

Of course, it would not be ethical to conduct maternal deprivation studies in humans; unfortunately, some natural circumstances provide opportunities to collect relevant data. Early studies conducted by Spitz (1946) and Bowlby (1960) suggested that human children respond to prolonged separation with

Figure 12.4
Effects of maternal separation Rhesus monkeys raised in separation from their mothers show anxious behavior when placed with same-age peers. Juvenile rhesus monkeys raised with their mothers typically engage in rough-and-tumble play when introduced to peer monkeys.

HARLOW PRIMATE LABORATORY, UNIVERSITY OF WISCONSIN

initial protest followed by a phase characterized by dejection and social withdrawal (Mineka & Suomi, 1978). More recently, economic problems and social policies in Romania during the 1980s resulted in over 65,000 children being placed in orphanages; 85% were placed in the orphanages during their first month of life.

The Romanian orphanages were grossly understaffed; child–caregiver ratios were 10:1 for infants and 20:1 for children over 3 years of age. Consequently, infants were kept in their cribs unattended for up to 20 hours per day (Ames & Carter, 1992; McMullan & Fisher, 1992). Generally, these children developed behavioral abnormalities typically seen in maternal and socially deprived primates, characterized by self-stimulatory behaviors, various motor stereotypies (a *stereotypy* is an almost mechanical repetition of posture or speech; rocking back and forth is an example), and insecure attachments (Chisholm, Carter, Ames, & Morison, 1995; Suomi, 1997). As expected, they also developed a host of physical deficits due to malnutrition (Chugani et al., 2001).

Mary Carlson and Felton Earls (1997) of Harvard University had an opportunity to measure cortisol levels in Romanian orphans who were 2–3 years old. They took advantage of an intervention program in which orphans were placed in enriched social conditions starting at an average of 6 months of age. After about 13 months of the intervention program, the cortisol levels of the children raised in the neglected conditions of the orphanage were compared with those of home-raised children.

Cortisol was assessed several times throughout the day. Overall, the home-reared children had higher cortisol levels in the morning than the intervention and orphanage-raised children, but the home-raised children had lower levels throughout the rest of the day than the other children. Cortisol levels typically peak prior to times of increased activity, so the lack of an increase in the orphanage group denotes a deficiency in the HPA axis.

As described earlier in this chapter, sustained increased levels of cortisol throughout the day can be harmful to the pyramidal cells of the hippocampus (see Figure 12.3 inset). Indeed, Carlson and Earls (1997) noted that the children with the highest cortisol levels had the lowest scores in motor and mental development. In another study, positron emission tomographic (PET) scans of adopted Romanian orphans were compared with those of normal adults and children with refractory focal epilepsy. The Romanian orphans showed decreased rates of glucose metabolism in several limbic structures including the frontal gyrus, amygdala, hippocampus, and temporal cortex (Chugani et al., 2001).

Thus, HPA-axis development in humans is vulnerable to the stress of maternal separation. Certainly, events as stressful as parental separation have a severe impact on the developing stress-response system. Research also suggests that, even when children grow up with parents, acute and chronic stressful conditions alter the stress response. One study indicated that undergraduate students who described their parents as cold and detached were four times more likely to develop chronic illness, including depression

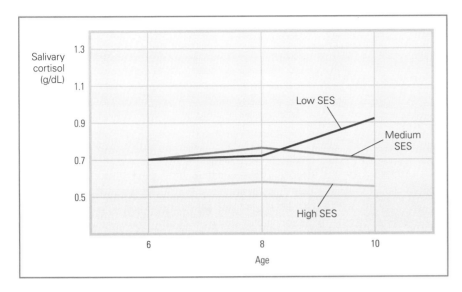

Figure 12.5
Cortisol levels and socioeconomic status (SES) Morning basal cortisol levels measured in children 6, 8, and 10 years old. Children of high SES had lower levels in each age group. Among children of low SES, the 10-year-old group recorded the highest levels.
ADAPTED FROM LUPIEN ET AL. (1998, P. 978).

and alcoholism, in midlife (Russek & Schwartz, 1997). As described in Chapter 9, girls who were sexually abused had increased cortisol responses to mild stress as adults (Heim & Nemeroff, 2002).

Socioeconomic status (SES), too, can affect HPA responsiveness in children. As seen in Figure 12.5, salivary cortisol levels taken during the first hour of school were lowest in children with high SES. The most drastic effect was seen in 10-year-old children; low-SES children had cortisol values that were twice those of the high-SES children (Lupien, King, Meaney, & McEwen, 2000).

Aging-Related Effects of Stress

Sonia Lupien of McGill University studied elderly subjects who secrete high levels of cortisol and found a 14% reduction in hippocampal volume and accompanying cognitive impairment (Figure 12.6) compared with subjects of similar age who secreted lower levels of cortisol (Lupien et al., 1998; McEwen et al., 1999). These high levels of glucocorticoids produce cognitive deficits in hippocampus-dependent learning in just a few days (McEwen & Sapolsky, 1995). These human data corroborate Meaney's findings, discussed in Chapter 6, that nonhandled rats that secrete high levels of corticosterone perform more poorly in the hippocampus-dependent swim task than the handled, stress response–efficient animals (Meaney et al., 1985, 1991).

As we age, it becomes increasingly difficult to turn off the stress response, perhaps because of the decreased number or sensitivity of receptors in the hippocampus. The resulting increases in stress hormones for longer durations can lead to aging-related pathologies (Porter, Herman, & Landfield, 2001; Sapolsky, 2000; Toth et al., 2008). Figure 12.7 diagrams the glucocorticoid hypothesis of cognitive impairment observed in elderly subjects.

Figure 12.6
Cortisol-induced hippocampal shrinkage The hippocampi in two elderly subjects are indicated by arrows in these images. The subject on the left secreted normal levels of cortisol, whereas the subject on the right secreted high levels. The hippocampus on the right is 14% smaller than the hippocampus of the normal-secreting elderly subject.
FROM EMBER (1998, P. 21)

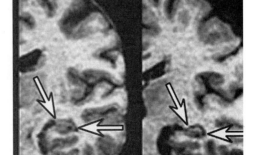

Figure 12.7
The aging hypothalamic–pituitary–adrenal axis and hippocampal neurons Healthy pyramidal neurons in the hippocampus facilitate learning and memory and provide appropriate feedback to the pituitary to moderate stress hormone secretion. After prolonged, excessive adrenocorticotropic hormone (ACTH) and glucocorticoid release, pyramidal neurons become more vulnerable to threats such as oxygen free radicals and disease.
ADAPTED FROM MCEWEN & GOODMAN (2001, P. 297)

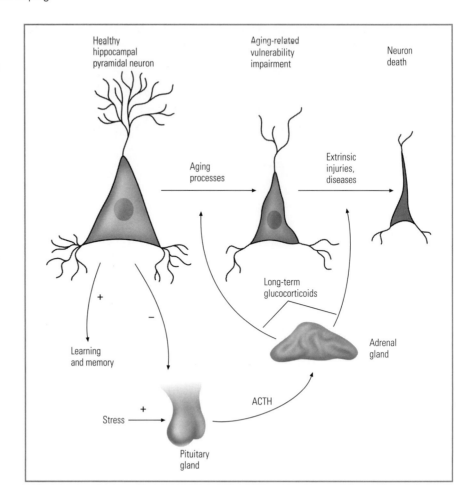

Effects of Sex Differences on Responses to Stress

William Pare and his colleagues at the Veterans Affairs Medical Center in Perry Point, Maryland, emphasize the importance of looking at both acute and chronic stress when assessing sex differences in the stress response (Pare, Blair, Kluczynski, & Tejani-Butt, 1999). When they exposed rats to either an acute session or repeated sessions (chronic condition) of restraint stress, a more complete picture of sex differences in the stress response began to emerge. Although females were more active in the open-field test after one session of stress, the sex differences disappeared after five sessions. In a test of simple learning, female rats were impaired following acute and chronic stress, whereas males were impaired only following acute stress.

Food consumption progressively decreased for female rats, whereas males regained baseline levels after 5 days. Males were more likely to develop stress ulcers than females, but females had heavier adrenal glands, suggesting more activity of the HPA axis. As shown by the varying sex effects for different variables, one must be careful when only one measure is used. Pare and colleagues concluded that female rats seem to be more vulnerable than males to the effects of chronic stress.

This conclusion sheds light on the observation suggested by most epidemiological studies that women are more likely to develop psychiatric disorders, such as depression, in which HPA-axis dysregulation is a likely causal factor (Wolf, Schommer, Hellhammer, McEwen, & Kirschbaum, 2001). When studies have focused on the age of men and women, increased HPA-axis activation is more commonly observed in older women (Seeman, Singer, Wilkinson, & McEwen, 2001). Men, however, have higher levels of salivary cortisol than women before and after placing a bet in a horse race (Franco, Paris, Wulfert, & Frye, 2010).

In addition to differences in physiological responsivity, Shelley Taylor and her colleagues at the University of California in Los Angeles have proposed an evolutionary hypothesis highlighting the adaptive significance of men and women having different behavioral response strategies (Taylor et al., 2000). They propose that the typical fight-or-flight response is actually a more representative male style and that the female stress response is more accurately described as a *tend-and-befriend* style. In particular, Taylor's team argues that the male response may be more influenced by sympathetic arousal (and fight-or-flight) and the female response more by physiological factors related to caregiving (tend-and-befriend). More empirical evidence, however, is needed before the ultimate value of this intriguing hypothesis can be determined.

COPING WITH STRESS

How do you combat the stressors in your life? Are you more likely to take charge of the situation, or do you retreat and just wait for the stressor to pass? Do you run to the support of your family and friends during stressful times, or do you prefer to be alone? The transition from a reaction to a stressor to a decision about the most appropriate voluntary action is a complex, multifaceted process.

Researchers, however, are starting to look at the nature of the behavioral stress response as well as the physiological response. The research is painting a picture in which the behavioral response that an animal makes when presented with a stressor has important implications for the physiological response and subsequent health-related consequences. Sense of control, social support, and level of activity in the behavioral stress-response strategy all offer significant ways to mitigate the dangerous effects of an unrelenting stress response.

In the film *Life Is Beautiful*, Guido instructs his son Joshua in the rules of "the game," his attempt to minimize the terror of imprisonment in a Nazi death camp.

THE EVERETT COLLECTION

Perception of Control

In the Italian film *La Vita e Bella* (*Life Is Beautiful*), the main character, Guido, is a bookseller in the Tuscan town of Arezzo during the stressful time of the German occupation of Italy in World War II. In this fable, Guido falls in love with the beautiful Dora and they have a son, Joshua. The fairy tale turns into a tragedy when the family is taken to a Nazi death camp.

A significant part of the movie recounts Guido's attempt to alter the stressful nature of this horrific experience for his precious son. He does this by convincing Joshua that the day-to-day horrors imposed

by the Nazis are part of an exciting game. He explains that three scenarios will result in losing the game—crying, asking to see his mama, and whining about being hungry. The winner of the game, Guido tells Joshua, will receive an army tank. If you've seen the movie, you know that Joshua eventually gets to ride in the tank because he was able to follow his father's rules. But more important, this story illustrates the potent effect of perceived control in stressful situations.

This award-winning film is controversial because some argue that it makes light of the terrifying conditions of the Nazi concentration camps. Political and cultural implications of the film aside, the strategy Guido chooses to cope with an almost unimaginably stressful experience is extremely adaptive. He is able to create a world for his son in which he has some sense of control—if he follows the rules, he will win a tank! Juxtaposed to the reality of being held prisoner by a group that has no concern for their welfare, Guido's scenario is certainly preferable.

Research on control. This theatrical anecdote is persuasive in demonstrating that perception of control is important in mitigating the stress response, but what does the research suggest? The empirical story of the impact of coping responses came to light with a famous study conducted by Joseph Brady in 1958. In this study, known as the "executive monkey study," Brady selected four pairs of rhesus monkeys. One of each pair he dubbed the "executive" monkey and the other was the "yoked" monkey. The paired monkeys were placed in a restraint chair and subjected to periodic bursts of unsignaled electrical shock. The executive monkey was able to postpone the shock for 20 seconds by pressing a lever. Failure to press the lever resulted in a shock for both the executive and yoked monkeys.

Thus, both monkeys received the same number of shocks but only the executive monkey had control over the shock. When the first two executive monkeys died in the apparatus, Brady examined their stomachs and discovered duodenal ulcers. The yoked animals did not develop ulcers. At this point, Brady realized that this shock-avoidance procedure was successful at producing ulcers. He continued to examine the remaining monkeys, and the remaining executive monkeys developed ulceration as well.

You may be wondering whether this is the most appropriate study to convince you that having control over stress is a good thing, given that all of the executive monkeys developed ulcers. In fact, for several years, Brady's data were interpreted to mean that being "in charge" or an "executive" may mean a larger salary but it also means more stress-associated health problems. But there is more to this monkey business.

For the next decade, researchers attempted to replicate Brady's study, but they had difficulty producing ulcers in the executive monkeys. In fact, one study reported that the only ulcers observed were in one of the yoked animals (Foltz & Millett, 1964). The emphasis continued to shift to the yoked animals in 1977 when Jay Weiss reported that rats with the ability to control shock by turning a wheel—executive rats—developed less severe gastric ulcers (as opposed to duodenal ulcers in Brady's executive monkeys) than the yoked control rats. In this experimental design, a signal was presented to all rats (including a no-shock control group) 10 seconds prior to the shock.

Weiss was very interested in why his research produced results that differed so significantly from Brady's. After conducting a series of studies, he concluded that two important aspects of Brady's study contributed to the opposing results. First, Brady selected the executive monkeys on the basis of how active the monkeys were on a preliminary task; additionally, he did not use signaled shock. Thus, Brady probably chose the most reactive of the monkeys to serve as the executives, which served as a confounding variable in a study designed to assess stress responses. The lack of a signal before the electric shock also contributed to higher rates of ulceration (Weiss, 1972, 1977).

Another famous series of experiments conducted in the 1960s emphasizes the importance of perception of control over a stimulus. Using dogs as subjects, Martin Seligman and Steven Maier, then at the University of Pennsylvania, conducted a study in which one group was exposed to footshock in an experimental compartment with no possibility of escape (Seligman, 1990). Another group experienced the shock but had an opportunity to escape.

Interestingly, when the dogs that were initially provided no escape route were subsequently exposed to shock in a compartment that had an escape route, the majority failed to attempt escape—they literally sat and accepted the stress. On the contrary, dogs that had experienced their initial shock session in the area with an escape route proceeded to escape in subsequent shock sessions. It was as if the dogs in the initial inescapable shock condition had learned that their behavioral responses had no consequences—that they had no control over the stressor. As you learned in Chapter 9, Seligman and Maier called this phenomenon "learned helplessness." This animal model has been used extensively as a model of human depression.

Since these seminal studies, subsequent research has confirmed the importance of having control—or at least the perception of control—over stressful stimuli. A chronic stress paradigm developed by Jean Kant and Sally Anderson at the Walter Reed Army Institute of Research in Maryland attempted to simulate chronic stress experienced by soldiers in combat (Anderson et al., 1996). In this paradigm, rats received signaled footshock every 5 minutes, 24 hours per day for 2 weeks. Although this program would seem extremely stressful, rats adapt easily to this design. After a few days of increased glucocorticoid production, the animals maintain their body weight and manage to obtain sleep durations comparable with controls (although in more frequent bouts), and the females' normal estrous cycle persists. The presentation of signals that predict the shock seems to decrease the magnitude of the stress response in these chronically stressed animals.

Although researchers have refrained from shocking humans to test the idea of perception of control, Carl Lejuez and Michael Zvolensky of Brown University designed a similar study to test the idea of control over a noxious stimulus (in Carpenter, 2000). In this study, subjects were given a breathing mask to wear and told that air enriched with 20% carbon dioxide would be delivered to them. Carbon dioxide is considered a noxious stimulus because it produces feelings of panic or anxiety in subjects. Half the subjects in this study were told a tone would warn them of the upcoming carbon dioxide bursts; the remaining subjects received no such warning. The researchers measured skin conductance activity and breathing patterns. All of the subjects found the stimulus stressful, but overall they preferred that its administration be preceded with the signal.

decatastrophizing Any attempt to minimize the impact of a stressor, likely to result in a decreased allostatic load. Some people may decatastrophize by gaining an increased perception of control or employing active coping strategies to minimize the negative impact.

affiliative social contact Nonthreatening social contact. This type of social contact probably increases oxytocin, which subsequently triggers a cascade of responses that maximize growth and minimize stress.

paraventricular nuclei A collection of neurons located in the hypothalamus; the processes extend into the posterior pituitary, where oxytocin and vasopressin are released.

supraoptic nuclei Hypothalamic nuclei that produce oxytocin.

Coping with lack of control. More recently, research has focused on low SES as an ecologically relevant form of chronic stress in which people have little control over their environments. Moving down the SES scale, life choices become more limited; hence, the perception of control over environment is probably lower than that of individuals with higher SES. In support of this hypothesis, low-SES children up to age 16 have increased cortisol levels compared with high-SES subjects; fortunately, though, this difference subsides during the high school years (Lupien, King, Meaney, & McEwen, 2001).

Research with rodents, dogs, and primates shows that having a sense of control offers protection against the damaging effects of chronic HPA-axis activation. Whereas Selye emphasized the dangerous effects of physical stress, the studies conducted by Weiss and others highlight the importance of psychological stress. In these studies, the amount of physical stress, or shock, was held constant between groups, yet the amount of control over the stressors, a psychological variable, determined the stress-induced pathology.

These studies also opened the door for research to focus on the value of modifying psychological variables in situations in which it is not possible immediately to remove the stressful conditions (for example, poverty, living in an unpredictable world). After being asked at a conference why a few dogs do attempt to escape after being placed in the inescapable condition, Martin Seligman focused his research attention on why some people demonstrate persistent coping responses even when they're not always reinforced. He calls this phenomenon "learned optimism." Seligman (1990) claims that psychological strategies such as attempting to minimize the impact of a stressor, or **decatastrophizing** stressful events, as Guido did in the death camp, can be a valuable weapon in our coping arsenals.

Social Support

There is an old saying that misery loves company: When you're down and out, the best strategy is to have someone experience the stressful situation with you. It's not clear that having a social partner actually reduces the stress in any way—it just seems to reduce our responsiveness to the stressor. In this section we'll address just how important **affiliative social contact** is in reducing the stress response.

Let's start in the **paraventricular nuclei** and **supraoptic nuclei** of the hypothalamus, where, as you learned in Chapter 5, the neuropeptide oxytocin is produced and transported to the posterior pituitary prior to its release into the bloodstream. In addition to being responsible for milk ejection, nursing mothers experience lowered blood pressure, decreased cortisol levels, and increased gastrointestinal hormones resulting from increased oxytocin. The neurotransmitter GABA is also increased in the mother during suckling; this inhibitory neurotransmitter decreases noradrenaline activity in the locus coeruleus (Carter, Altemus, & Chrousos, 2001; Kendrick, Keverne, Hinton & Goode 1992). Psychologically, women who are breast-feeding report being calmer than women who are not breast-feeding; the degree of calmness correlates with the oxytocin levels. Table 12.2 summarizes the stress-related benefits of nursing on the mother and the child.

Table 12.2 Neurobiological Effects of Nursing on Mother and Infant

Mother	
Physiological Effects	**Psychological Effects**
Decreased HPA responsivity	Decreased anxiety
Increased oxytocin	Decreased muscle tone
Increased GABA	Increased positive interactions with infant (e.g., smiles)
Decreased cardiovascular reactivity	Reduced vulnerability to depression
	Increased tolerance of monotony
	Decreased suspicion
	Increased socialization

Infant	
Physiological Effects	**Psychological Effects**
Increased oxytocin	Development of strong social bonds
Increased growth	Decreased vulnerability to developing depression
Decreased HPA responsivity	

HPA, hypothalamic–pituitary–adrenal axis; GABA, γ-amino butyric acid.

A subsequent exploration of the effects of lactation on personality traits was conducted by Uvnas-Moberg and her colleagues at the Swedish University of Agricultural Sciences (Sjogren, Widstrom, Edman, & Uvnas-Moberg, 2000). The researchers found that, during the first 3–6 months following childbirth, women who had been breast-feeding for at least 8 weeks had lower anxiety, muscular tension, monotony avoidance, and suspicion scores and higher scores on the socialization scale. The team concluded that pregnancy and lactation prepare women for a lifestyle that is more relaxed and tolerant of monotony (e.g., being quiet while the baby rests).

The effects of oxytocin are not limited to lactating mothers. Oxytocin is produced in both males and females, and in general, its repeated administration results in decreased sympathetic nervous system activation, lowered activity in the HPA axis, increased activity of the vagal nerve, enhanced digestive activity, and a feeling of calmness. Hence, Uvnas-Moberg (1998) argues that oxytocin has an antistress effect on both physiological and psychological processes.

You may be thinking that it would be nice to bottle oxytocin and take a healthy dose when we're feeling stressed. Well, we may be closer to that situation than you think. Although they weren't focusing on the stress, Paul Zak and his colleagues at Claremont Graduate University have demonstrated than nasal infusions of oxytocin have significant effects in human subjects. In one study, for example, humans infused with oxytocin were 80% more generous in an experimental altruism task (i.e., they gave away more money to strangers) than their saline-infused counterparts (Zak, Stanton, & Ahmadi, 2007).

While the mass production of oxytocin still hangs in the balance, the solution to self-administering this valuable neuropeptide may be as simple

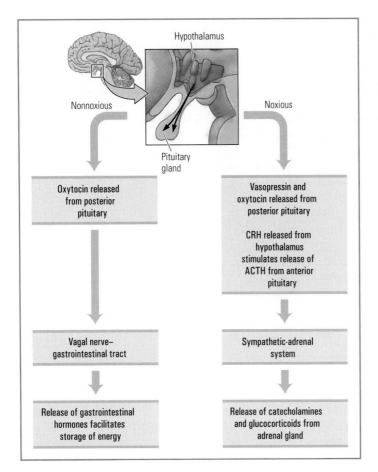

Hypothalamus

Nonnoxious

Noxious

Pituitary gland

Oxytocin released from posterior pituitary

Vasopressin and oxytocin released from posterior pituitary
CRH released from hypothalamus stimulates release of ACTH from anterior pituitary

Vagal nerve– gastrointestinal tract

Sympathetic-adrenal system

Release of gastrointestinal hormones facilitates storage of energy

Release of catecholamines and glucocorticoids from adrenal gland

Figure 12.8
Hypothalamic responses to noxious and nonnoxious stimuli During nonnoxious social stimulation (left), oxytocin is released, facilitating an antistress response pattern that conserves energy. During noxious social stimulation (right), corticotropin-releasing hormone (CRH) triggers the stress hormonal cascade that mobilizes the body to expend energy very quickly to survive the impending threat. ACTH, adrenocorticotropic hormone.
ADAPTED FROM UVNAS-MOBERG (1998, P. 25)

as reaching out and touching someone. In one study, rats were stroked, or massaged, for 5 minutes. Following this stimulation, decreases of 20 mm of mercury (Hg) in blood pressure and 60 beats per minute in heart rate were observed in the animals for up to 4 hours. The control animals that were held but received no stroking had a 20 mm Hg increase in blood pressure and an increase in heart rate of 60 beats per minute for up to 1 hour following the handling (Lund, Lundeberg, Kurosawa, & Uvnas-Moberg, 1999). In addition to touch, several forms of nonnoxious stimuli, such as vibration, warm temperature, and elec-troacupuncture, have been associated with oxytocin increases in the plasma and cerebrospinal fluid. Figure 12.8 shows the possible divergent routes of noxious and nonnoxious stimuli in the brain.

As shown in Figure 12.9, grooming may provide another form of nonnoxious stim-ulation—especially considering the relaxed posture of one of the primates. If primate grooming is calming, it is interesting to speculate why going to the hair salon is a popular endeavor for many of us. As evidence, when Andrew Solomon (2001), the journalist featured in Box 9.1, went to Cambodia to interview survivors of the horrible atrocities suffered at the hands of the Khmer Rouge, he was especially struck by the story of Phaly Nuon, a nominee for the Nobel Peace Prize. Nuon told Solomon that she had attempted to facilitate healing in Cambodian women who had suffered unspeakable atrocities by setting up something akin to a psychotherapy hut, incorporating a host of different therapies from traditional Khmer medicine to antidepressants to cognitive therapies.

Nuon was desperate to find some way to reach these debilitated women, many of whom were unable to talk or even take care of their children follow-ing their "utterly incapacitating posttraumatic stress" (Solomon, 2001, p. 36). Following some cognitive exercises to help the women forget the pain, she would try to distract them with music or knitting (perhaps releasing sero-tonin because of the repetitive movements); and finally, she attempted to reestablish their ability to form affiliative relationships, or to love. Together with the relaxing effects of social contact previously discussed, Nuon used grooming behavior to restore the social bonds of these isolated women.

And then when they have mastered work, at last, I teach them to love. I built a sort of lean-to and made it a steam bath....I take them there so that they can become clean, and I teach them how to give one another manicures and pedicures and how to take care of their fingernails, because doing that makes them feel beautiful, and they want so much to feel beautiful. It also puts them in contact with the bodies of other people and makes them give up their bodies to the care of others. It rescues them from physical isolation, which is a usual affliction for them, and that leads to the breakdown of the emotional isolation. While they are together washing and putting on nail polish, they begin to talk together, and bit by bit they learn to trust one another, and by the end of it all, they have learned how to make friends, so that they will never have to be so lonely and so alone again. Their stories, which they have told to no one but me they begin to tell those stories to one another. (Solomon, 2001, p. 36)

Figure 12.9
Grooming-induced relaxation
These Java macaques at Monkey Jungle (in Miami, Florida) spend much of the day grooming each other. Recipients typically display a range of relaxed postures, from seated positions to the totally relaxed loss of muscle tone shown here.
KELLY LAMBERT

The interplay between oxytocin and the HPA axis contributes to the formation of social bonds in the prairie vole. This mouselike rodent has serum corticosterone concentrations that are about 10 times higher than levels observed in rats. As opposed to other mammals that respond to the negative feedback of the activated HPA axis, social cues seem to be a primary factor that influences corticosterone secretion in prairie voles. Prairie voles are unique in that they are monogamous, and glucocorticoid levels drop in the pair-bonding process, suggesting that the HPA axis may contribute to this process in some way. Providing further support that oxytocin is involved in the formation of the pair-bonds in these animals, prairie voles fail to form social bonds when oxytocin is disrupted (Carter & Getz, 1993; DeVries, 2002).

Forming strong pair-bonds offers evolutionary advantages for this mammal, including enhanced pup survival and development and a buffer against the harmful effects of stress (Carter, 1998; Getz & Carter, 1992). It is not clear whether oxytocin plays a central role in human pair-bonding, but it is known that it is released during human sexual contact. Because sexual contact is neither necessary nor sufficient to maintain human pair-bonds, the role of oxytocin in human pair-bonding remains unclear. Further, the distribution of human oxytocin receptors is different from that observed in the prairie vole, so we need to be cautious before we apply the prairie vole model of pair-bonding to humans (Insel & Winslow, 1999).

It is important to note that the pair -bond doesn't have to have a sexual foundation to serve as a buffer against stress. In another monogamous species, the California deer mouse, same-sex siblings raised together since birth exhibit fewer behavioral signs of stress when tested in the *chronic unpredictable stress paradigm*. In this paradigm, animals are exposed to annoying and unpredictable stimuli such as a tilted cage, predator odors, and altered light–dark schedules. The paired deer mice exhibit fewer signs of emotionality when tested in an open field and have lower levels of corticosterone following exposure to a predator odor (Lambert et al., 2001). This social buffering effect has been observed in multiple species, ranging from guinea pigs to humans (DeVries, 2002).

Once established, though, the disruption of social bonds can be stressful. We have already discussed the consequences of prolonged durations of mother–infant separation on the developing infant. Several primate species,

social defeat paradigm
Model of chronic stress in which an animal is exposed to a larger, more aggressive animal and is defeated in a single aggressive encounter. For up to a month or longer, the defeated animal will not exhibit defensive behavior when an animal—even a smaller one—is placed in its cage.

such as titi monkeys, marmosets, and cotton-top tamarins, also exhibit increased cortisol concentrations in response to being separated from an established partner (Mendoza & Mason, 1986; Norcross & Newman, 1999; Smith, McGreer-Whitworth, & French, 1998).

Social contact can play a beneficial role in combating another form of stress: recovery from trauma, sickness, or disease. Courtney DeVries and her colleagues at Ohio State University showed the importance of social contact during recovery from experimentally induced stroke (DeVries, 2002). Male mice housed with females had less damaged brain tissue and less severe cognitive impairment than mice housed in isolation.

Research conducted by Tiffany Field (1993, 2002) at the Touch Research Institute at the University of Miami School of Medicine has shown that another form of social contact, massage, benefits premature infants. Specifically, massaged infants have lower levels of cortisol and grow at a significantly faster rate than same-age infants who do not receive a massage (the two groups did not differ in food consumption). Thus, it is likely that touch- or contact-related health benefits can be attributed to the interaction of social contact with the HPA axis. As you will learn in Chapter 13, complex interactions exist among the level of social contact, stress responsivity, health, and immune functioning.

As we leave this section on social contact, it is important to point out that the type of contact is very important when considering its impact on the stress response. When DeVries and colleagues (2001) exposed brain-injured mice to social stimuli of an aggressive nature, the contact exacerbated the brain injury. In fact, social contact, the variable that we have been describing as having a significant stress-mitigating effect, can be deleterious if the nature of the relationship is agonistic. Eberhard Fuchs and colleagues (2001), at the German Primate Laboratory in Göttingen, have demonstrated that tree shrews become so stressed being housed in another tree shrew's territory that they die—not from being attacked but from the effects of the potent psychological stressor of being housed with a more dominant, resident animal.

Research with Syrian hamsters has shown that social stress can be long-lasting. Kim Huhman and colleagues at Georgia State University use a **social defeat paradigm** in which a hamster is placed in the home cage of a larger, more aggressive hamster (Huhman, Banks, Harmon, & Jasnow, 2002; Huhman, Mougey, & Meyerhoff, 1992). Following the defeat of the intruder hamster by the resident hamster, the defeated animal will no longer attempt territorial aggression. Even when smaller hamsters are placed in their home cages, the defeated animal fails to defend its home territory. This conditioned defeat effect lasts for at least a month following the initial defeat. Because corticotropin-releasing hormone (CRH) exacerbates conditioned defeat and conversely a CRH receptor antagonist diminishes the submissive behavior, it is clear that this agonistic social encounter is intimately integrated with HPA responsivity.

Paul MacLean (1998) wrote that mammals differ from reptilian vertebrates in three distinguishing forms of behavior: audiovocal communication, parenting, and play. In most mammals, these behaviors involve social contact and/or interaction. An extreme portrayal of the human desire for contact was seen in the film *Cast Away*. The protagonist, Chuck, played by Tom Hanks, developed a close affiliative bond with a companion named Wilson after being stranded on a deserted island. If you've seen the movie, you know that Wilson was a unique companion—he was a Wilson volleyball with a blood-painted face and grassy hair. Perhaps our intense predisposition to seek out and maintain affiliative social contact explains why audiences willingly accepted the idea of developing a close friendship with a ball. Because of the evolutionary relevance of affiliative contact, it is likely that even more biologically relevant consequences of social contact will be uncovered in the future.

Active Versus Passive Coping

When confronted with the bad news that your car is going to cost thousands of dollars to repair, do you remain motionless as you contemplate what you are going to do with the car? Or do you go immediately to the nearest garbage can and give it a swift kick? As we discussed earlier in this chapter and in Chapter 6, some people develop active responses to stressful stimuli, whereas others prefer a more passive response. But what do these differences in behavioral responding really mean? Researchers are just beginning to ask this question in a systematic fashion, but the literature is far from providing definitive answers.

Whereas the physiological response to stress is well documented, many questions remain about the nature of behavioral responses to stressful stimuli. For example, increased cortisol levels are generally viewed as an index of stress in animals, but increased behavioral responsiveness is not always considered an indication of stress. In a defensive burying task, prolonged digging is generally viewed as evidence of increased anxiety or stress but increased activity in the open-field test is generally considered a sign of decreased stress or anxiety (Palanza, Gioiosa, & Parmigiani, 2001; Pinel, Mumby, Dastur, & Pinel, 1994). So it is interesting to consider whether an animal's behavioral response to a stressor is specific to that particular stressor or if animals develop certain pervasive response strategies to a diverse array of stressors.

Some research supports the notion that a general active response strategy is beneficial. Jay Weiss (1972), now at Emory University, conducted a simple experiment in which he shocked rats in their cages; one shock group was placed in their home cages with another rat in the cage, whereas the other group was placed in their home cages with no other animal. Weiss investigated the ulceration of these animals' stomachs. Interestingly, the rats that had another rat in the cage developed fewer ulcers than the isolated controls.

Weiss (1972) attributed these differences to the observation that the shocked rats would routinely and vigorously bite the other rat in the cage. Likewise, when a piece of wood was placed in the cage as an alternative biting target, less ulceration was observed. Thus, in this case, a more active response resulted in reduced stress-induced ulceration.

Jaap Koolhaas and his colleagues at the University of Groningen in the Netherlands have analyzed extensively the nature of coping styles in animals (Koolhaas et al., 1999; Koolhaas, de Boer, Buwalda, & van Reenen, 2007). They define **coping style** as a persistent, consistent collection of physiological and behavioral responses to stressful stimuli. Instead of speaking of active and passive coping styles, they prefer the terminology *proactive* and *reactive*. For example, a male rat that is consistently aggressive toward other

coping style Persistent response strategy in the presence of stressful stimuli. An animal may have an active, passive, or flexible style.

males is categorized as proactive, whereas a less aggressive rat is considered reactive because it responds only when absolutely necessary.

Generally, physiological differences exist between the proactive and reactive animals. Proactive coping styles are characterized by low HPA-axis activity (shown by low cortisol levels) and high sympathetic activity (such as high catecholamine levels). More passive reactive coping styles are characterized by higher HPA-axis reactivity and higher parasympathetic activity. These differences also persist for baseline levels of hormones; aggressive mice have low levels of corticosterone during baseline conditions compared with their nonaggressive counterparts (Koolhaas et al., 1999). The benefit of hitting a punching bag for reducing the stress response suddenly makes sense!

More evidence for divergent coping styles in animals can be gained from a visit to a farm where researchers have established a test to assess individual coping styles in pigs. This "back test" involves placing the animal on its back and keeping it in a supine position for 1 minute (Figure 12.10). When this is done, some pigs struggle to escape and are classified as "resistant," while others do not show any signs of struggle. Pigs exhibiting few escape attempts are known as "nonresistant" copers. Interestingly, pigs that are tested at a couple of weeks of age retain their coping style throughout their lives.

In keeping with the rodent data, the more active pigs are also more exploratory in an open field and have lower baseline levels of cortisol than the less active pigs (Schouten & Wiegant, 1997). The back test can even be done with hens. Two lines of hens differing in their propensity to feather-peck have been tested. When the birds are kept on their side for 8 minutes, the high-feather-pecking line was more resistant, or active, whereas the low-feather-pecking line was less resistant. Corticosterone levels were higher in the low-pecking birds and sympathetic responsivity was highest in the high-feather-pecking birds (Koolhaas et al., 1999; Korte, Beuving, Ruesink, & Blokhuis, 1997). (Neuroscientists have yet to establish whether birds of a like-feather-pecking line flock together. We'll leave that question to the social psychologists.)

Additional support for the notion that more active responding leads to a diminished stress response comes from the research conducted by Barry Jacobs's laboratory at Princeton University (Jacobs, 1994). As described in the chapter-opening Connections, the serotonergic neurons are most active during repetitive movement. Using cats as subjects, Jacobs has shown high firing rates of the serotonergic neurons in the raphe nucleus during walking and virtually no firing in REM sleep when the animal has no muscle tone.

Because most antidepressants enhance serotonergic levels, it is possible that repetitive movements such as chewing gum or pacing the floor are comparable to the effects of SSRIs (Jacobs, 1994). Even the stereotypies sometimes observed in captive animals have been reported to lower cortisol and arousal levels; if this is the case, this seemingly abnormal behavior of pacing back and forth in a cage might be quite adaptive in reducing the amount of stress responsivity experienced by the animals (Koolhaas et al., 1999).

Figure 12.10
Profiling the stress response of piglets Pigs are used as subjects at the University of Groningen to establish varying styles of behavioral coping. During the back test they are simply held on their backs and the researchers record the number of times the animal struggles to escape.

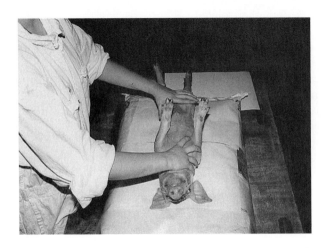

Thus, whereas more active coping strategies seem most adaptive in general, it is important to remember that specific circumstances require appropriate responses. There are certainly times when an animal frozen in movement will survive when an animal making noises in proximity to a predator will not. Do you remember the guppies described in Chapter 1? In this study, all the bold guppies became lunch for the predator bass in the tank, whereas 40% of the timid, nonresponsive guppies survived the predator.

There may also be cases when having the capacity to respond in a variety of styles proves more adaptive. A study focusing on rats' coping strategies in response to many different stressors identified three categories: low reactivity, variable reactivity, and high reactivity. Interestingly, the variable reactivity group exhibited more hypothalamic and amygdala activation in the face of stress, perhaps leading to enhanced vigilance in the animals (Campbell, Lin, DeVries & Lambert, 2003).

Extending the use of the back test to assess coping strategies in rats, passive, active, and flexible coping rodents were identified and exposed to a subsequent chronic stress paradigm. In this study, the back test was repeated twice—rodents that exhibited few responses in each test were profiled as passive copers, those that exhibited active responses in each test were profiled as active copers, and those that were passive in one assessment and active in another were profiled as flexible. In the midst of the chronic stress paradigm, all animals were exposed to swim stress and, living up to their names, the flexible rats showed more variability in their responses. Whereas all animals increased their float times from the first to the third swim tests, the flexible copers increased their float times on the second swim, a step ahead of the other coping groups. At the end of the chronic stress exposure, **neuropeptide Y (NPY)**, a pervasive neuropeptide known to be involved in resilience, was assessed via immunocytochemistry. Interestingly, higher levels of NPY immunoreactivity were observed in the flexible, or variable, copers. In another study, when NPY was infused into the amygdala of rats exposed to subsequent stressors, they exhibited less intense stressful responses (Sajdyk et al., 2008). Thus, natural levels of NPY in flexible copers may predispose them to exhibit more resilience than passive and active copers (Hawley et al., 2010).

In the human's large brain, perhaps a coping style that employs more of the brain might lead to the more adaptive response. Knowing when to react and when to be passive may also be a critical factor in adaptive coping. In support of this idea, Japanese college students who possessed more flexible coping strategies exhibited fewer signs of depression than more rigid responders (Kato, 2001).

How does one achieve flexible coping strategies? James Gross and his colleagues at Stanford University have emphasized the value of emotional regulation as a way to achieve adaptive flexibility in coping responses. According to the Stoic philosopher Seneca, "Anger, I say, has this great fault—it refuses to be ruled." If you've ever been so angry that you felt as if you had no control over your actions, you can relate to Seneca's observation. Gross and his colleagues have investigated the effectiveness of **cognitive reappraisal**, the ability to change the way we view emotional events, as a way to gain some control over toxic emotions. In one clever study, college students were exposed to an annoying laboratory protocol, including being asked to do demanding cognitive tasks, treated in a condescending manner by the

neuropeptide Y (NPY) A 36-amino acid peptide that is one of the most abundant neurotransmitters in the mammalian brain; NPY stimulates eating and reduces energy expenditure.

cognitive reappraisal A coping strategy in which an individual cognitively transforms an emotionally threatening experience into a less threatening situation.

experimenters, told that they would have to start over—you get the picture. Emotional responses were recorded during this phase of the experiment. The subjects were subsequently debriefed and told they were purposely made angry so that their emotional responses could be recorded. A week later, the subjects were invited back into the lab so that their emotional responses could be recorded as they revisited the laboratory environment that was so annoying the previous week. The subjects exhibiting the greatest decrease in negative emotions were classified as high cognitive reappraisers; those who remained angry, even after learning that it was just part of the protocol, were classified as low cognitive appraisers. The high cognitive reappraisers, possessing the ability to change an initial emotional response once valuable information has been obtained, had more adaptive cardiovascular functioning. They also exhibited milder emotional responses during the initial stressful experience (Mauss, Cook, Cheng, & Gross, 2007). Similar to the value of having the ability to maintain a poker face in order to keep from tipping off a competitor that you have a winning hand, being able to regulate your emotions has health benefits.

Allostatic Load

We have established that the stress response can be significantly modified by the coping strategy adopted by the stressed individual. Generally, incorporating social support, active behavioral responses, a sense of control over our lives, and flexible coping strategies enables us to respond to stress more effectively and efficiently. Actually, the method of minimizing the stress response is less important than the fact that it is being diminished in some way.

According to McEwen and Lashley (2002), once faced with a stressor, a person's physiological homeostasis is threatened. Fortunately, as described earlier in this chapter, we have an arsenal of responses to help us escape the stressor; these responses include activation of the HPA axis, the sympathetic nervous system, and various brain centers. McEwen and Lashley point out that responses triggered in the face of a stressful stimulus are important: They reestablish homeostatic balance.

These stress-induced responses are allostatic. The term **allostasis** is derived from the Greek root *allo*, which means "variable" and is used in this context to emphasize the point that dynamic physiological systems keep the body stable (McEwen & Lashley, 2002; Juster, McEwen, & Lupien, 2009). To maintain homeostasis, or internal balance, the body must exhibit a wide range of changes, such as varied heart rate, hormonal secretions, and energy storage. It is ironic that change (allostasis) is required to maintain balance (homeostasis) in the body.

Homeostasis thus may not be the norm for our bodies. Other than a few variables, such as body temperature, which must be maintained within a narrow range, our physiological systems—heart rate, for example—are characterized by a varied response range. Appropriate for this chapter, allostasis more accurately describes our dynamic physiological responses that are directed toward optimal responding in times of threat (McEwen & Wingfield, 2009). According to Jay Schulkin (2003), "Allostasis also highlights our ability to anticipate, adapt to, or cope with impending future events" (p. 17).

allostasis Literally, maintaining stability through change; the active process of maintaining physiological homeostasis in the face of any challenge.

If the allostatic processes have to work extensively to maintain homeostasis, the added work may contribute to wear and tear in the system—or **allostatic load**. Let's consider an analogy to make it clearer: Suppose that your car breaks down. You take it to a local mechanic for a diagnostic workup, and when you return, the mechanic describes in agonizing and uninteresting detail what the problems are. Your mind wanders—until he gets to the point of telling you what it will cost to repair. You snap to attention. On hearing the price, you have to quickly determine how you will handle it. Will it interfere with purchasing basics such as room and board, that trip you had been planning, or even paying your tuition?

Never good news and, depending on your current financial situation, car repairs can be a real hardship. In this example, though, we have created stress for both you and your car. A particular event(s) resulted in your car breaking down and was thus the stressor for your car. The repairs that the mechanic will perform (provided you can pay) will bring it back to baseline condition: This is allostasis. The allostatic load was the wear and tear on the car that led to the breakdown. Determining how to reduce your car's allostatic load (regular maintenance, oil changes, etc.) may mean less money out of pocket—which ultimately reduces your own allostatic load.

In this analogy of homeostasis and allostasis, you have to assume the responsibility of your car's allostatic load; in reality, no one can pay that cost for your body—you always have to pay the allostatic bill following every threat to homeostasis. Thus, any coping strategy, regardless of its specific nature, is effective if it reduces your allostatic load. Although journalist Terry Anderson (Box 12.2) was held hostage for 7 hellish years, he was able to employ effective coping strategies to keep his brain and body from entering terminal allostatic overload.

POSTTRAUMATIC STRESS DISORDER

Once a stressful stimulus is removed, in most cases, the stress response subsides so that it is ready for activation when the person is faced with the next stressor life has to offer. On rare occasions, however, the stress response recurs or does not diminish; it persists to the point that it interferes with day-to-day activities. In 1980, a diagnostic category was created in the third edition of the *Diagnostic and Statistical Manual of Mental Disorders* (DSM-III) for such a condition, **posttraumatic stress disorder (PTSD)**.

Generally, PTSD is defined as an anxiety disorder characterized by the reexperiencing of a traumatic event, accompanied by both enhanced arousal and avoidance of trauma-related stimuli (American Psychiatric Association, 2000). Because the traumatic trigger results in a severe stress response, we feature PTSD here in our discussion of stress and coping.

PTSD is currently thought to affect between 1% and 9% of the population (Mezey & Robbins, 2001). These rates, however, can be considerably higher under extreme conditions. A sample of Cambodian refugees in the United States was recently found to have an 86% prevalence rate (Carlson & Rosser-Hogan, 1991; Paunovic & Ost, 2001). The typical duration of PTSD varies: Whereas some victims experience relief after a year, others report persistent symptoms for much longer. For example, 19 years following combat exposure in Vietnam, 15% of male veterans suffered from PTSD (Kulka et al., 1990).

allostatic load Wear and tear on the body that results from repeated activation of the processes that maintain homeostasis.

posttraumatic stress disorder (PTSD) Disorder characterized by symptoms such as memories and dreams related to a traumatic event that recur up to months or years following the event. Individuals with this disorder feel as if they are reexperiencing the trauma and have the accompanying physiological arousal to enhance their belief of impending danger.

Box 12.2

A Case in Point

How Terry Anderson Survived as a Hostage

Early on a Saturday morning in 1985, Terry Anderson, 38, a talented journalist working for the Associated Press in Beirut, Lebanon, got up, kissed his fiancée (who was then 6 months pregnant with their child), and headed for the tennis courts to meet his colleagues. On the way back, Anderson's car was pulled over, his glasses were snatched from his face, and he was instructed to kneel down in a small space between the front and back seats, where he was hidden under a blanket. As fear spread throughout his body, his captor calmly told him, "Don't worry. It's political" (Anderson, 1993, p. 7). The date was March 16, the beginning of a 2,454-day nightmare for Terry Anderson.

Anderson's ankles were chained to a cot in a very small room with no windows and, for most of his nearly 7 years of captivity, no companionship. He was forced to wear a blindfold while guards were in his room or when he left his quarters. The food was barely fit to eat and, most humiliating for this accomplished correspondent, he was at the mercy of his young, immature, aggressive captors for the privilege of even going to the bathroom.

No music, no conversation, no outdoor scenery, nothing to read, no freedom to control any aspect of his life characterized his days. Anderson described this time as "long nights, squirrel-in-a-cage nights. Mind spinning, thoughts, emotions whirling. Anger. Frustration. Pain. Guilt" (p. 89). How does anyone cope with such stress? Is there any way for the human mind to survive such torment?

Terry Anderson took advantage of every possible factor to strengthen his chances of surviving. A basic physical need that he addressed about a month into his captivity was washing off all the filth that his body had accumulated. Smelling like a mixture of sweat and urine, his hair caked with dirt and oil, he decided to strip and bathe himself with a hose attached to a water tap on the wall during one of his short bathroom trips. A guard blasted through the door and threatened him, but Anderson knew from his military training how important hygiene is for avoiding illness and staying alive.

One of the biggest threats to Anderson's sanity was isolation. He didn't speak Arabic, so he couldn't even understand the conversations of the guards outside his door. Anderson tried ceaselessly to recall the image of his fiancée and to feel the presence of his loved ones. In the midst of such loneliness he craved any companionship. Whenever he was placed in rooms with other hostages he maximized the social exchange by having extensive conversations with his new "roommates."

Even without the company of other hostages, Anderson attempted to develop social relationships with any guards who seemed remotely sympathetic. When he knew hostages were being kept in adjacent rooms, he devised elaborate ways to communicate, such as tapping on the walls between the rooms. A mouse that made regular stops in his room during the middle of the night even became his companion, and he faithfully saved a bread crumb on his pillow each evening. During times when it might have been easier to retreat within himself, Anderson's concerted efforts to maintain social contact probably contributed greatly to his continuing sanity.

Almost impossible to tolerate was complete lack of control. Yet again, Anderson coped. He gained control whenever he could—even if it was minimal. Taking the initiative to bathe himself, even though he risked retaliation, was one great success in regaining some control over his seemingly hopeless situation. He kept track of the passing days to gain a sense of control over the passing of time. And although many hostages would have been too fearful to challenge the guards, Anderson persisted in asking for things that were critical to his sanity. He asked for books, for a radio, for his chains to be loosened when they were cutting off his circulation, and for medical care for another hostage who was very ill.

PTSD is characterized by symptoms such as recurring memories and dreams related to the traumatic event (Table 12.3). At times, people affected by the disorder feel that they are reexperiencing the trauma, and the accompanying physiological arousal enhances their belief of impending danger. As patients try to avoid stimuli that will trigger these memories, their ability to function day to day is diminished.

Terry Anderson (left) in 1985, before captivity, and (right) in 1991, 5 months prior to release.
AP/WIDE WORLD PHOTOS

Anderson also gained a sense of control by relying on religion, reciting biblical passages that he had committed to memory, asking for a Bible and reading it over and over, talking about religion when fellow hostages were present. In painfully small increments, he was able to see that some of his attempts to change his predicaments resulted in minor changes, an observation that was important for maintaining psychological health.

Another aspect of maintaining his health during this time was getting some exercise, even trying to let his muscles move. After several years, he developed an automatic pacing pattern that enabled him to make the best use of his 5-foot chains without jerking them or tripping. He asked to go to a larger space for a few minutes on some days to exercise. At one point, he used filled water jugs as free weights.

You now know enough about the brain to know that it did not evolve to exist in a sea of nothingness for 7 years. Anderson had to fight to keep his mind functioning and disciplined. Early in his captivity, he wrote a daily journal; but after a time, he realized that its mere existence made him even more vulnerable to his captors. Once he had persuaded a guard to bring him anything at all to read, he quickly reveled in these books, reading them over and over.

When others were in his room, he made games such as chess or cards out of leftover paper or played 20 questions. He designed elaborate buildings in his mind, decided what he would do if he had a million dollars, and thought about his loved ones. When he was housed with Tom Sutherland, a former professor at Colorado State University, Anderson persuaded Sutherland to go over all his lectures in all his classes. At one point he even started studying Arabic.

Although Anderson was amazingly successful at maintaining his sanity during this time, he admits to having some experiences with depression, describing it as "enormous, a thick, black blanket smothering me" (p. 179). At another point, he described losing control and beating his head against the wall until a guard stopped him. All in all, however, he survived the ordeal with his mental faculties intact. In fact, toward the end of his captivity a guard picked up his Bible, gesturing that he wanted to learn the English word for it. Anderson responded by saying "cup," and each time he picked up the Bible, he slowly said "cup" as if teaching the guard the correct word for Bible. This event actually sparked a bout of laughter among Anderson and the other hostages, another sign of mental health.

On December 4, 1991, Anderson was released to the American government. He was reunited with his fiancée and met his 6-year-old daughter for the first time. He has continued to engage in responses beneficial to his mental health. He married his fiancée and accepted a teaching position at the School of Journalism at Ohio University. He fought back at the Iranian government officials whom he suspected of sponsoring his captors by suing them as an attempt to hold them responsible for their actions. His more recent activities include working for and supporting several charities, raising and training horses on his ranch, pursuing political causes and offices, hosting a radio talk show, and owning a blues bar. If he's tapping his foot to the music, he may be assuring that his serotonergic neurons are always functioning in concert with this rhythmic movement and, as discussed in the Connections section, perhaps relieving residual anxiety.

With the increased deployment of U.S. soldiers to serve in ongoing conflicts, the PTSD diagnostic criteria have become controversial. Harvard psychologist Richard McNally recently commented in a *Scientific American* article on the topic: "PTSD is a real thing, without a doubt. But as a diagnosis, PTSD has become so flabby and overstretched, so much a part of the culture, that we are almost certainly mistaking other problems for PTSD and

Table 12.3 DSM-IV-TR Diagnostic Criteria for Postraumatic Stress Disorder

A. The person has been exposed to a traumatic event in which both of the following were present:

  (1) the person experienced, witnessed, or was confronted with an event or events that involved actual or threatened death or serious injury, or a threat to the physical integrity of self or others

  (2) the person's response involved intense fear, helplessness, or horror. Note: In children, this may be expressed instead by disorganized or agitated behavior

B. The traumatic event is persistently reexperienced in one (or more) of the following ways:

  (1) recurrent and intrusive distressing recollections of the event, including images, thoughts, or perceptions. Note: In young children, repetitive play may occur in which themes or aspects of the trauma are expressed

  (2) recurrent distressing dreams of the event. Note: In children, there may be frightening dreams without recognizable content

  (3) acting or feeling as if the traumatic event were recurring (includes a sense of reliving the experience, illusions, hallucinations, and dissociative flashback episodes, including those that occur on awakening or when intoxicated). Note: In young children, trauma-specific reenactment may occur

  (4) intense psychological distress at exposure to internal or external cues that symbolize or resemble an aspect of the traumatic event

  (5) physiological reactivity on exposure to internal or external cures that symbolize or resemble an aspect of the traumatic event

C. Persistent avoidance of stimuli associated with the trauma and numbing of general responsiveness (not present before the trauma), as indicated by three (or more) of the following:

  (1) efforts to avoid thoughts, feelings, or conversations associated with the trauma

  (2) efforts to avoid activities, places, or people that arouse recollections of the trauma

  (3) inability to recall an important aspect of the trauma

  (4) markedly diminished interest or participation in significant activities

  (5) feeling of detachment or estrangement from others

  (6) restricted range of affect (e.g., unable to have loving feelings)

  (7) sense of a foreshortened future (e.g., does not expect to have a career, marriage, children, or a normal life span)

D. Persistent symptoms of increased arousal (not present before the trauma), as indicated by two (or more) of the following:

  (1) difficulty falling or staying asleep

  (2) irritability or outbursts of anger

  (3) difficulty concentrating

  (4) hypervigilance

  (5) exaggerated startle response

E. Duration of the disturbance (symptoms in criteria B, C, and D) is more than 1 month

F. The disturbance causes clinically significant distress or impairment in social, occupational, or other important areas of functioning

Specify if:

Acute: duration of symptoms is less than 3 months

Chronic: duration of symptoms is 3 months or more

Specify if:

With delayed onset: onset of symptoms is at least 6 months

American Psychiatric Association (2000, pp. 467–468).

thus mistreating them." (Dobbs, 2009, p. 65) Thus, this disorder is currently under scrutiny in order to differentiate between adaptive and maladaptive experiences related to recovery from exposure to traumatic events.

Tracing the Neurobiological Roots of PTSD

The triggering stimulus for PTSD is obvious—a traumatic event. Less obvious is why a majority of people experience an appropriate stress response that subsides when the traumatic stimulus is removed, while, as observed in PTSD patients, others have problems suppressing the stress response for months or years following the event. As described earlier in the section on social contact, extreme stress such as that experienced by the Cambodian women results in a much higher rate of PTSD-like symptoms; thus, severity of the stressor is an important factor in determining the likelihood of PTSD. Although it appears that the PTSD patient is experiencing a heightened stress response, cortisol levels are often decreased (Metzger et al., 2008). It has been proposed that the significant trauma enhances the negative feedback components of the HPA axis (Anisman, Griffiths, Matheson, Ravindran, & Merali, 2001), making it more sensitive to lower levels of cortisol.

In one study, researchers investigated the areas of the brain that might be involved in perpetuating the PTSD symptoms (Lanius et al., 2001). The investigators conducted a functional magnetic resonance imaging (fMRI) scan of PTSD patients as they were recalling the traumatic event associated with their symptoms. The fMRI scans were compared with those of nine patients who had been exposed to a traumatic event but had not met the criteria for the diagnosis of this disorder. The results suggest that the PTSD patients had lower activity in the thalamus, medial frontal cortex, and anterior cingulate gyrus (Figure 12.11).

Disruptions in these areas may inhibit the PTSD patient's ability to interpret memories of the traumatic event as memories rather than impending dangers. This study is interesting, however, because the brain area that is most often associated with fear—the amygdala—was not found to be more active in PTSD patients. The results do suggest, however, that altered brain functions underlie traumatic recall in PTSD patients (Lanius et al., 2001). In addition to altered functions, reduced amygdala and cingulate cortex volumes have been observed in PTSD patients (Rogers et al., 2009).

Treatment for PTSD

Current treatments for PTSD include cognitive-behavioral therapies and various pharmacological treatments. Most of these therapies are associated with modest improvements; however, no cures for this disorder currently exist. As shown by the recent popularity of the novel treatment known as eye movement desensitization and reprocessing, patients and clinicians should approach new therapies with caution and skepticism.

One cognitive-behavioral therapy that may be used to treat PTSD is **exposure therapy**, where patients are encouraged to experience gradually increasing representations of the original trauma. The idea is that the strong association between actually experiencing the event and having memories of it should dissolve as the patient realizes that that memory is not predictive of the traumatic event. In another type of cognitive-behavioral therapy, the patient is taught to avoid catastrophizing following intruding memories. Patients are also encouraged to practice controlled breathing to counteract the irregular breathing that typically accompanies a recollection. The efficacy of these two therapies was recently assessed; the results suggest that both are more effective than a placebo and that the two therapies are equally effective for PTSD patients (Paunovic & Ost, 2001).

Pharmacological treatments include drugs that may reduce arousal or anxiety, such as tricyclics and selective serotonin reuptake inhibitors

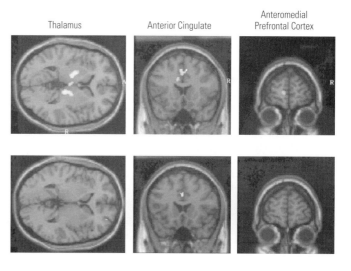

Thalamus   Anterior Cingulate   Anteromedial Prefrontal Cortex

Figure 12.11
Brain activation in posttraumatic stress disorder (PTSD) patients A comparison of functional magnetic resonance imaging scans of a non-PTSD patient (top) and a PTSD patient (bottom) reveals less activity (shown as brighter areas) in the thalamus, anterior cingulate cortex, and prefrontal cortex.

LANIUS ET AL. (2001) AMERICAN JOURNAL OF PSYCHIATRY, 158, 1920–1922. © 2001, AMERICAN PSYCHIATRIC ASSOCIATION, HTTP://AJP.PSYCHIATRYONLINE.ORG. REPRINTED BY PERMISSION

exposure therapy Type of therapy sometimes used with PTSD patients in which the facilitator exposes the patient to the stimulus/event that is most feared in an attempt to have him or her see that exposure isn't always associated with a negative outcome.

eye movement desensitization reprocessing (EMDR) Type of therapy introduced for the treatment of PTSD; consists of having the patient follow the therapist's finger back and forth for about 20-second intervals to produce a rapid and rhythmic pattern of eye movements, while thinking about the negative aspects of the trauma experience associated with the PTSD.

(SSRIs). Although there is still a need for controlled studies to test the efficacy of various drugs on PTSD symptoms, a recent double-blind, placebo controlled, long-term study that investigated the SSRI sertraline provided evidence of its value for treating PTSD. Sertraline was shown to enhance sustained improvement in symptoms and to protect patients against relapse (Davidson et al., 2001). Relapse, however, is likely to occur on termination of the pharmacological treatment, so a combination of behavioral and pharmacological therapies is likely to offer the patient the most protection against relapse.

Eye movement desensitization and reprocessing (EMDR), a novel and controversial treatment for PTSD and other anxiety disorders, was introduced by Shapiro in 1989. Using EMDR, a patient is instructed to induce rapid and rhythmic eye movements by following the therapist's finger back and forth for about 20 seconds. During this time the patient is instructed to elevate the negative emotions and cognitions associated with the trauma to the "forefront of the mind," where they can be replaced with positive emotions. According to the protocol, this procedure continues until the traumatic emotions and memories are significantly reduced (Shepherd, Stein, & Milne, 2000).

Since its inception, EMDR has increased in popularity: Over 25,000 trained clinicians regularly use this procedure. James Herbert and his colleagues at Hahnemann University in Philadelphia, Pennsylvania, warn us that we need to be cautious when evaluating the validity and efficacy of this treatment (Herbert et al., 2000). It seems that the majority of research articles suggesting that EMDR is successful consist of vivid case studies or studies lacking the appropriate control groups. In fact, Herbert and colleagues provide convincing evidence to suggest that this treatment is built on pseudoscientific techniques. Such techniques may prove helpful, but critical therapists are encouraged to wait for empirical evidence of efficacy before incorporating EMDR into their treatment regime for trauma-related anxieties.

Summary

Revisiting the Stress Response

There are generally two stress responses: (1) the sympathetic fight-or-flight response originally described by Cannon (see Chapter 5) and (2) the hypothalamic–pituitary–adrenal (HPA) axis response described by Selye. Both systems are designed to help the body mobilize adequate resources to be able to defend itself in an acute stress response. When a stress response enters the chronic phase, the body and brain face numerous health risks.

Although type A personality traits were originally associated with chronic stress–induced cardiovascular disease, research has identified hostility as a more powerful personality predictor for cardiovascular risk. Another health risk associated with chronic stress is gastric ulceration. A type of bacteria, *Helicobacter*

pylori, has a causal role in the creation of ulcers; however, chronic stress exacerbates ulceration.

The glucocorticoids released by the adrenal glands in HPA axis activation interact with the brain's stress circuit, namely, the hippocampus. Researchers have found that neuronal restructuring following chronic stress leads to a reduced hippocampal volume. Further, as the brain has evolved, the frontal cortex probably has worked with the hippocampus to interpret the context of a challenging event so that the most adaptive response will be produced.

Stress Responsivity over the Life Span

A plethora of research indicates that an animal's experiences early in life have a significant impact on the development of the stress response. For example,

Meaney's work suggests that maternal interactions result in a more efficient stress response, whereas maternal neglect, as seen in Harlow's monkeys, leads to increased anxiety when the infants mature.

As an individual ages, the brain becomes less sensitive to circulating glucocorticoid levels and becomes vulnerable to hippocampal damage and cognitive impairment. Thus, effective coping strategies throughout a lifetime enhance hippocampal and cognitive function in old age. Although both sexes experience stress, there may be subtle differences in their responses. For example, males may be more susceptible to ulceration and females to stress-related mental illness following chronic stress.

Coping with Stress

A sense of control is important when responding to stress. Research with animals suggests that having control or even the perception of control over a stressor is significantly better than having no perception of control over the stimulus.

During affiliative social contact, oxytocin is released and likely results in an "antistress" effect of lowering blood pressure. Lactating women report less stress, and anesthetized rats that received massages demonstrated lower blood pressure. Oxytocin plays a role in the establishment and maintenance of pair-bonds in the prairie vole (a rodent with very high circulating levels of glucocorticoids). Agonistic social contact,

on the other hand, can be one of nature's most potent stressors.

Generally, animals that respond to stress with more active styles have lower levels of glucocorticoids and stress-related illness. Also, repetitive movement is associated with increased activity of the serotonergic neurons in the raphe nucleus. Flexible coping strategies have also been found to be beneficial in rodent models, with accompanying changes in the resiliency neurochemical neuropeptide Y. Humans exhibiting emotional regulation through the use of cognitive reappraisal also exhibit adaptive coping responses. In general, any coping response that reduces allostatic load, the wear and tear on the body, is an effective strategy.

Posttraumatic Stress Disorder

PTSD, characterized by a persistent stress response that extends well beyond the duration of the actual stressor, sometimes develops in people who have experienced severe stress or trauma. Although a normal response initially, recurring memories and dreams make it difficult to function normally. Lower than normal levels of cortisol are typically found in PTSD patients. Antidepressants are sometimes used for treatment along with behavioral and cognitive therapies. Eye movement desensitization reprocessing is an interesting therapy but lacks empirical support for the successful treatment of PTSD.

Key Terms

general adaptation syndrome (359)	affiliative social contact (374)	allostasis (382)
ecological relevance (361)	paraventricular nuclei (374)	allostatic load (383)
species-specific stressor (361)	supraoptic nuclei (374)	posttraumatic stress disorder (PTSD) (383)
atherosclerosis (361)	social defeat paradigm (378)	
peptic ulcers (364)	coping style (379)	exposure therapy (387)
excitotoxicity (366)	neuropeptide Y (381)	eye movement desensitization reprocessing (EMDR) (388)
decatastrophizing (374)	cognitive reappraisal (381)	

For Further Consideration

Dobbs, D. (2009, April). The post-traumatic stress trap. *Scientific American, 300,* 64–69. This article includes interviews with various experts about the value of the contemporary diagnostic criteria and treatment strategies for PTSD. Never questioning the validity of the disorder itself, clinical psychologists and psychiatrists

express concern about overdiagnosis of the disorder. Specifically, it is likely that symptoms of depression may be confused for PTSD symptoms; further evidence is presented suggesting that some symptoms of PTSD can be viewed as normal coping strategies. The bottom line is that soldiers are returning with allostatic load and more research is needed to identify the most effective treatment strategies for these individuals.

Franco, C., Paris, J. J., Wulfert, E., & Frye, C. A. (2010). Male gamblers have significantly greater salivary cortisol before and after betting on a horse race than do female gamblers. *Physiology & Behavior, 99*, 225–229. This article addresses the controversies currently surrounding the PTSD diagnosis, especially whether or not the diagnosis is overused. Several key researchers are interviewed, expressing concerns that the actual PTSD rates are lower than initially thought; further, these researchers and practitioners suggest that many of the individuals diagnosed with PTSD exhibit normal, adaptive responses to trauma recovery.

Koolhaas, J. M., Kortec, S. M., DeBoer, S. F., Van Der Vegt, B. J., Van Reenen, V., Hopster, H., et al. (1999). Coping styles in animals: Current status in behavior and stress physiology. **Neuroscience and Biobehavioral Reviews, 23**, 925–935. This is a comprehensive review of behavioral and physiological responses to stressors across a wide array of species. The authors consider the validity of assuming two coping styles in animals: proactive and reactive strategies. These coping strategies are observed in both laboratory and farm animals and have predictive potential for the identification of disease susceptibility.

Korte, S. M., Koolhaas, J. M., Wingfield, J. C., & McEwen, B. S. (2005). The Darwinian concept of stress: Benefits of allostasis and costs of allostatic load and the trade-offs in health and disease. **Neuroscience and Biobehavioral Reviews, 29**, 3–38. This review article provides an evolutionary perspective concerning varying behavioral strategies used by animals to cope with stress. Using analogies of hawks and doves, the authors discuss potential neurobiological correlates of varying coping strategies as well as likely health consequences.

McEwen, B. (with Norton Lasley, E.) (2002). *The end of stress as we know it.* Washington, DC: Joseph Henry Press. In this book, Bruce McEwen suggests that we need to modify our perceptions of the stress response. Specifically, he suggests that stress is not always the uncontrollable villain in life; in fact, we can do a lot to decrease the negative effect of stress on our bodies. After covering the fundamentals of the stress response, McEwen highlights strategies to minimize allostatic load in chapters entitled "How Not to Be Stressed Out," "Positive Health," and "Where We Could Go from Here." This is an interesting, informative review of stress research.

Sapolsky, R. M. (1998). *Why zebras don't get ulcers: An updated guide to stress, stress-related diseases, and coping.* New York: Freeman. This book is a "must read" for anyone interested in the stress response. Sapolsky's expertise as a leading neuroscientist assures an informed coverage of the most influential studies in the stress literature. In addition to his expertise and knowledge, Sapolsky uses the perfect blend of wit, historical cases, personal insight, popular culture, and human interest stories to make this read more like a novel than a scientific book. Topics such as the fundamentals of the stress response, stress-related diseases, stress and memory, stress and depression, and managing stress are among the many covered in the book.

Schulkin, J. (2003). *Rethinking homeostasis: Allostatic regulation in physiology and pathology.* Cambridge, MA: MIT Press. For those of you who enjoy musing over theories, this book reviews basic theoretical approaches proposed to explain an individual's response to a threat. The accuracy of viewing homeostasis as a representative characterization of our physiological responses is questioned as the value of allostasis is considered a more accurate description of effective responding. In the context of allostasis, Schulkin focuses on the general notion of motivation, considering that motive states such as cravings are engaged to maintain the energy demands of the body.

Chapter Thirteen

Psychoneuroimmunology

Connections

Species, Scents, and Sex

In the mostly forgettable science fiction movie *Species II*, a hybrid "human" female is created from DNA obtained from a mission to Mars. This high-priority science project, named Eve, grows up in a tightly guarded laboratory. Once she reaches sexual maturity, Eve, a tall, beautiful young woman, is isolated from males and any presence of testosterone in order to suppress her sexual motivation. Of course, this gender isolation can last only so long. Later, a second American mission to Mars results in an astronaut's being infected with Martian DNA, which retroactively changes his genetic constitution (while apparently keeping his human form and personality intact).

In the film, evolution on Mars follows the same general principles as evolution on Earth (with reproductive fitness being the priority); the astronaut's altered DNA drives him to seek out human females to impregnate them with the Martian DNA. Eventually, Eve is exposed to the male space traveler with the mutated Martian DNA (similar to her own) and her sex drive develops to such intense levels that it becomes very difficult to restrain her in the laboratory.

Her enhanced sex drive, however, is very selective. When another male astronaut approaches Eve's living enclosure, she moves toward the glass wall with interest and then walks away, suggesting that she has no sexual interest in this male. At that point, the scientist in the film remarks that, since this African American man is a carrier for sickle cell anemia, Eve's DNA could not cope because it has no defense against our diseases. Consequently, because of genetic incompatibility, she had no desire to have sex with this man.

The notion that our genetic composition influences our romantic inclinations is an intriguing idea for a science fiction movie, but obviously it has no influence on our romantic preferences in real life. After all, genetic profiles are not the topics of conversation in singles bars or Internet chat rooms. Sabra Klein, a researcher in the Department of Molecular Microbiology and Immunology at the Johns Hopkins School of Public Health, has provided empirical evidence that certain immunological characteristics can indeed be sexy to certain animals.

Klein's research supports the notion that the secondary sex characteristics that we find so visually appealing (for example, enlarged biceps in males and breasts in females) may be important because they advertise our immunocompetence. Both secondary sex characteristics and immune functioning are intimately related to sex hormones. Conducting research with a little rodent known as a meadow vole, Klein has found that when given the choice between bedding with the odor of males infected with the *Trichinella spiralis* parasite or uninfected males, females prefer the scent of uninfected, or healthier, males. Additionally, when male prairie voles (which are monogamous) contract a bacterial infection, the females spend less time with them than with their noninfected counterparts. Klein's ongoing research

Sabra Klein
COURTESY OF DR. SABRA KLEIN

investigating how different aspects of the immune system influence mating strategies suggests that our immune system's ability to resist disease, probably detected through olfaction or secondary sex characteristics, is a powerful factor in the romantic lives of rodents (Klein, Gamble, & Nelson, 1999; Swonguer, Lambert, & Klein, 2003).

Rodents have extremely sensitive olfactory systems, so it is easy to understand how olfaction may play a role in their sexual attractions; but is there a connection between immune functioning and romance in humans? Could body odor possibly override dancing eyes, warm personality, or sense of humor? As mentioned previously, it is possible that physical and even behavioral characteristics in humans are related to immunocompetence and thus attraction; research also suggests that humans, like other animals, do not ignore the power of odor.

As you will discover in this chapter, humans produce chemicals with associated odors, and research suggests that when given an opportunity to sniff out smelly T-shirts, subjects prefer the T-shirts of individuals with a more diverse genetic profile to T-shirts of people with more similar genetic profiles. This reproductive choice makes adaptive sense when you consider that more diverse immunological abilities, serving as a form of insurance policy for resisting certain diseases, translate into enhanced survival in the offspring. Thus, exciting new discoveries in the field of psychoneuroimmunology are informing us that the immune system certainly influences both what we do and with whom we do it!

psychoneuroimmunology (PNI) Exploration of the relationships among the brain, behavior, and the immune system.

The emerging field of **psychoneuroimmunology (PNI)** explores the relationships among the brain, behavior, and the immune system. Although formally introduced as a field of scientific inquiry in the early 1980s, the notion that emotions influence health has been around for thousands of years.

To the ancient Greeks, the god of healing, Asclepius, along with his daughters Hygieia and Panacea, symbolized the importance of maintaining the proper balance of healthy diet, pure waters, social support, and exercise. The ancient Greeks also thought that one's emotions were critical to one's health; they advocated soothing emotions by music, sleep, and prayer. The idea that the mind was an important factor in the healing of the body was so revered that the image of Asclepius carrying a wooden staff (representing the body) with a serpent wrapped around it (representing the mind) became an established symbol of the relationship between the mind and the body. In fact, today this image, the caduceus, is the universal symbol for medicine (Sternberg, 2000).

Considering these early thoughts about the intimate relationship between body and mind, it is curious that Western medicine has focused primarily on the physiological causes and cures for diseases instead of how psychological processes may play a role in making an individual more or less susceptible to disease. In fact, the notion that a relationship exists between psyche and body has been more often seen in cartoons and jokes (for example, the cartoon depicting a tombstone that reads "See, it wasn't psychosomatic") than in medical textbooks. We are moving toward an era, however, in which health professionals can no longer deny that the ancient Greeks were on to a meaningful theory.

It has taken a few millennia, but the notion that psychological processes such as emotions influence both the brain and the immune system is being acknowledged by formal health-related disciplines once again. In fact, ancient Asian healing practices (meditation, yoga, and tai chi, for example) are now being subjected to Western-style clinical tests to establish medical validity. Comparing the efficacy of Asian healing traditions, however, with the efficacy of traditional Western medicine is no small methodological feat. The Asian emphasis on emotional, cognitive, spiritual, and cultural influences presents a challenge to researchers as they attempt to establish clinical efficacy over the placebo response, which also draws from cognitive and emotional factors (Fabrega, 2002).

After reading this chapter, you'll begin to understand how the three areas of PNI—psychological, neural, and immune factors—can work together to maintain health. Basic knowledge about how the immune system operates is critical for understanding how it interacts with the nervous system, so we describe immune functioning first. Next, we review neuroanatomical and neurochemical evidence that supports a relationship between the nervous system and immune functioning. The last section of this chapter considers research on how psychophysiological processes such as stress and sense of control influence immune functioning.

FUNDAMENTALS OF THE IMMUNE SYSTEM: THE BODY'S INTERNAL SECURITY AGENTS

Just as the primary goal of the FBI is to protect the citizenry against any form of criminal enterprise or threat, the goal of the immune system is to protect the body against any threat to its homeostatic balance. It is simultaneously sensitive, vigilant, adaptable, and effective.

The Body's Most Wanted Invaders

When an individual poses a threat to public safety, a picture of the person is distributed across the country—especially in post offices—so that he or she will be recognized when encountered. In fact, the Federal Bureau of Investigation (FBI) regularly publishes the 10 most wanted fugitives list. The body also has a most wanted list. The putative criminals of the body are infectious agents known as **pathogens** that have the ability to replicate in host cells to cause tissue damage and disease. Humans' most wanted pathogen list includes four groups: viruses, bacteria, fungi, and parasites. The monumental task assigned to the immune system is to protect against these invaders (Westermann & Exton, 1999).

The best protection against pathogens is offered by the physical barriers of the body. Just as countries have immigration checks to make sure that undesirables do not cross their boundaries, our bodies are covered with skin—two square meters of border. This physical barrier keeps the majority of potential invaders from entering our bodies. More resourceful invaders,

pathogen Microorganism (a virus or bacterium) that can cause disease.

however, seek out alternative entry points into the body, such as our respiratory, digestive, and reproductive tracts.

The pathogens that enter these tracts are not home free; they encounter a mucosal lining similar in texture to syrup in which the motility, or movement, of the pathogens is compromised (Jacobs & Schmidt, 1999). The total area covered by the mucosa-lined tracts in our bodies measures on average 400 square meters (Sompayrac, 1999). In case the physical barriers of the skin and mucosal tracts are not sufficient to ward off invaders, a host of specialized cells is stationed in and around these areas to make sure the pathogens are terminated before causing damage.

Innate Immunity: The Immune System's Front-Line Defense

If a pathogen breaches the physical barriers of the skin or mucosa, it has yet more defenders awaiting it—the cells of the **innate immune system**. These cells take immediate action at the first sign of an invasion, but although powerful and effective, they are typically one-trick ponies: They respond similarly to all pathogens.

A prominent early-response cell is the **phagocyte** ("eating cell") that can ingest foreign material that invades the body. If a pathogen manages to sneak past the physical barriers of the skin or mucosal tracts, it is likely to encounter a type of phagocyte known as a **macrophage**, or "big eater." Suppose you get a splinter in your finger; the splinter serves as a transportation system for a host of bacteria to enter your body. Once the bacteria have entered the system, the macrophages are able to detect foreign chemical messages emitted by the invading pathogen. As seen in Figure 13.1, once the macrophages are activated by the chemicals, they start reaching out to capture the bacteria. Upon contact, the macrophage moves in for the kill. It engulfs a bacterium so that it can expose the pathogen to internal **lysosomes**, specialized organelles containing chemical weapons (enzymes) that inactivate and destroy the bacterium by degrading its constituent proteins.

As the macrophage voraciously consumes the bacterium, it periodically "burps" some of the pathogen, or its remnants, back into the tissue; these poor table manners are actually beneficial because the bacterial debris alerts other immune cells to a potential battle. Also, as the macrophage is battling the bacterium, it releases a protein messenger, or *cytokine*, to other cells so that other components of the system are abreast of its activities. Once the invader has been neutralized, the macrophage goes back to its other favorite activity, being a garbage collector—that is, consuming everything it encounters (Sompayrac, 1999).

Focusing again on your sore finger, you may wonder why it typically swells and turns red. As seen in Figure 13.2, you can

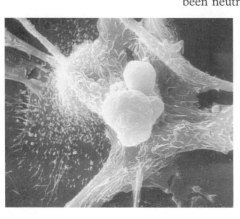

Figure 13.1
Macrophage attack This macrophage has detected the presence of a pathogen via chemical signals and is engulfing the foreign substance. The macrophage will wrap the captured bacterium in a pouch, or vesicle, and then escort the vesicle into its intracellular compartment, where the vesicle will meet with destructive chemicals, leading to its demise. This process is known as "phagocytosis."
MICROWORKS/PHOTOTAKE

thank your macrophages for that effect as well. To confine the invader to the finger, the macrophages send another chemical to constrict any outgoing blood vessels, leading to a buildup of blood in the area around the splinter. The cells in the skin of your finger also constrict, and as they do, some of the cellular fluid leaks into the tissue around the splinter. This is the cause of the swelling.

As impressive as the versatile macrophage is, the **neutrophil** may be the most important phagocyte. About 70% of the white blood cells (also called "lymphocytes" or "leukocytes") in circulation are these specialized phagocytes. Lymphocytes are characterized by their dense nucleus and small amount of cytoplasm relative to other cells.

The body manufactures on average 100 billion neutrophils each day. The life span of these cells is only a few days, so they have but a short time to conduct their sentinel activity. Interestingly, the neutrophils die by committing cellular suicide (also known as "apoptosis"; see Chapter 6) after diving into an area occupied by an invader such as a bacterium; the dying neutrophils subsequently decompose (with the help of hungry macrophages) into a mound of pus (Sompayrac, 1999). In a military analogy of the immune system, the neutrophils would be World War II kamikaze pilots. They search out a battle with a pathogen and move in, ready to kill. Most neutrophils contain lysosomes that they release at the invasion site (Abbas, Lichtman, & Pober, 2000).

A third type of cell making up the innate immune system is the **natural killer (NK) cell**. NK cells travel through the blood to the site of infection, where they can kill many types of cells, including tumor cells, parasites, fungi, bacteria, and virus-infected cells. What is the killing method these special agents use? One option is to drill a hole in the infected cell by secreting a cocktail of damaging enzymes. This cocktail is known as **perforin**, and when released, it forms a channel to the cell's vulnerable interior chamber.

neutrophil Most abundant white blood cell circulating in the blood; these cells are recruited to inflammation sites, where they utilize either phagocytosis or enzymatic digestion of pathogens.

natural killer (NK) cells Cells in bone marrow that are a component of the innate immune system. On recognizing a microbe, these cells move in for the kill, using techniques such as secreting toxic substances and creating fatal damage to the invading cell.

perforin Protein used as a weapon by killer T cells and NK cells that drills a hole in the infected cells so that other enzymes can continue the destruction of the cells.

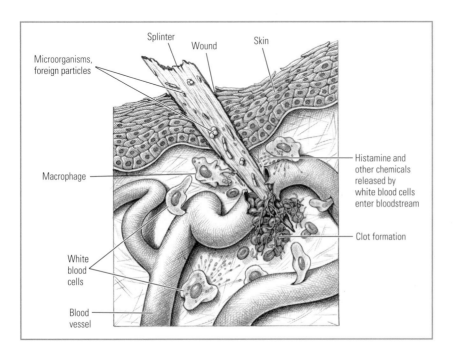

Figure 13.2
The innate immune system in action The foreign invaders, or microbes, transported into a wound by this splinter activate macrophages to approach and destroy the unwelcome pathogens. The macrophages also emit chemical signals to constrict the blood flow so that pathogens managing to survive the macrophage attacks can't escape to infect other areas of the body.

ADAPTED FROM STRAUB (2002, P. 106)

cytokines "Messenger" proteins secreted by many cells that regulate immune functions and mediate communication among the cells of the immune system; also called "immunotransmitters" or "interleukins."

complement complex Group of nonimmune proteins that combines to form an important part of the immune system, which can damage threatening cells by quick responses such as cutting holes in the pathogen cells.

acquired immune system B cells and T cells that, following exposure to infectious pathogens, are stimulated to develop a selective immunity that results in a faster response should the same type of pathogen invade the body again; also known as "adaptive immunity."

vaccination Preparation of a specific antigen that is administered to an individual to stimulate the acquired immune system to protect against actual, natural exposure to the antigen, should it occur.

Once the cell interior is exposed, the NK cells deposit enzymes that cause the cell to die. NK cells can also use another weapon: A protein is expressed on the surface of the NK cells when in contact with a protein on the target cell and triggers apoptosis—programmed cellular death—in the unwelcome cells (Sompayrac, 1999).

A fourth component of the innate immune system is the **cytokines**, low-molecular weight proteins that regulate immune functions and facilitate communication among the various cells of the immune system. Cytokines are manufactured as they are needed and stored in granules in the various innate immune cells (Jacobs & Schmidt, 1999). Cytokines are sometimes referred to as "immunotransmitters" or "interleukins" (literally, between white blood cells).

In an emergency situation, the immune system relies on a group of non-immune proteins in the blood and other organs known as the **complement complex** that can combine to damage threatening pathogens by literally boring holes in them. Similar to situations in which the FBI needs to rely on the local police because the latter can respond quickly to a crisis, a distinguishing characteristic of the complement component of the innate system is the speed at which it can respond to an intruder (Sompayrac, 1999).

Acquired Immunity: Cells That Plan for the Future

Although the innate immune system is powerful, it cannot successfully protect us from infectious pathogens such as viruses because these responses do not enable us to develop resistance. Therefore, in addition to the body's physical barriers and innate immunity, a third line of defense, the **acquired immune system**, evolved to provide further protection against these formidable invaders. The adaptive capabilities of this system were identified in the eighteenth century when Edward Jenner discovered that he could condition what would later be called the immune system to build defenses against deadly viruses.

Jenner made this discovery in 1790 when he was trying to develop a way to protect people against the deadly smallpox virus. Hundreds of thousands of people died from this disease; if they did not die, they were often horribly disfigured from the skin lesions produced by the virus. Jenner noticed that milkmaids often developed a few minor skin lesions due to a related virus, cowpox. Interestingly, the milkmaids who contracted the cowpox virus never seemed to develop smallpox. It was as if the cowpox protected the women from contracting the deadly smallpox.

This observation of the milkmaids gave Jenner an idea for an experiment. What would happen if you collected pus (dead neutrophils and virus) from cowpox lesions in the milkmaids and injected it into a person? Would that person be protected against subsequent exposure to smallpox?

Jenner injected the cowpox pus into a little boy named Phipps and then injected him with smallpox pus—not an experiment that would pass an institutional review board today. Amazingly, Phipps did not contract smallpox—he had developed immunity. Today, we would say that Phipps was vaccinated against smallpox. The word **vaccination** is derived from the Latin word *vacca*, which means "cow" (as in cowpox). Phipps, however, was able to contract measles and mumps, indicating that his acquired immunity was specific (Sompayrac, 1999).

Phipps's immune system had acquired a memory of the smallpox virus and therefore was prepared to respond immediately on a subsequent exposure to the virus. How can the immune system accomplish such an amazing feat? It depends on the actions of two specialized lymphocytes that serve as "special agents" for the acquired immune system: B cells and T cells.

Antibodies and B cells. B cells originate from undifferentiated stem cells in the bone marrow, located in the center of bones, where all blood cells are generated. While still in the bone marrow, young B cells acquire gene segments that enable them to develop specialized weapons against pathogens called "antibodies." Antibodies, or immunoglobulins (Ig), are small proteins that circulate in the blood following the invasion of a foreign substance and systematically search for specific pathogens to destroy.

Once mature, B cells become antibody factories. Although each individual B cell produces only one kind of Ig, the total collection of B cells produces enough different types of antibodies to be able to recognize virtually any organic molecule that crosses its path. And how many potential invasive molecules do the B cells need to be ready to encounter? Immunologists estimate about 100 million. This diversity is a product of an elaborate DNA-shuffling scheme that goes on as the young B cells are developing.

In general, the Igs formed by the B cells have a prototypical Y shape formed by two pairs of different proteins, a heavy chain on the inside and a light chain on the outside (Figure 13.3). This is a very effective structure designed for grabbing an **antigen** (a molecule that activates an antibody) with either "arm" and binding to another immune cell with its "feet." In fact, the feet, or the receptor-binding regions of the antibody, determine the type of cell it binds to and the class of the antibody.

A good security system such as the FBI needs weapons specially designed for various threats. For example, the FBI trains agents specifically for chemical, terrorist, computer, and espionage threats to our security. The immune system has a comparable strategy in that it evolved at least four classes of antibodies produced by the B cells. Each Ig class has a unique structure, making it well-suited to target certain antigens. See Table 13.1 for a description of classes of antibodies.

T cells. A second type of lymphocyte contributing to the acquired immune system is the T cell or T lymphocyte. T cells originate in the bone marrow but mature in the **thymus**, an organ of the immune system located near the heart—hence the name "T cell." T cells develop receptors (T-cell receptors, or TCRs) that can recognize a foreign protein, or antigen, whereas B cells

---

B cells or B lymphocytes Cells that originate in the bone marrow and migrate to lymphoid tissue, and in low numbers, the blood. These are the only immune cells with the capability of producing antibodies.

bone marrow Located in the center of the bone; serves as the site of the generation of all blood cells (e.g., lymphocytes and B cells).

antibody or immunoglobulin (Ig) Glycoprotein molecule produced by B lymphocytes that binds to specific antigens. The four types are IgA, IgE, IgG, and IgM.

antigen Molecule that binds specifically to either an antibody or a T-cell receptor.

T cells or T lymphocytes Mature in the thymus, travel in the blood, and populate secondary lymphoid tissue; make up cell-mediated immunity and function by exposing receptors that recognize foreign particles.

thymus Immune system organ (containing epithelial cells, dendritic cells, macrophages, and precursor cells) that becomes the maturation site of T lymphocytes from bone marrow–derived precursor cells.

Table 13.1 Classes of Antibodies

Antibody Class	Description
IgA	Secreted in milk; helps build resistance to stomach acid; protects the body's mucosal lining
IgE	An organism's protection against parasites; involved in allergies
IgG	Involved in blood's complement system; facilitates the ability of natural killer cells to kill; known to cross the placenta
IgM	Involved in blood's complement complex; first antibody produced in the body

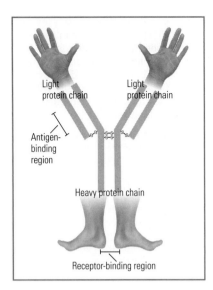

Figure 13.3

The immunoglobulin G (IgG) antibody This Y-shaped antibody molecule consists of two different proteins—a heavy chain and a light chain. The antibody is multifunctional: It can bind to antigens with its two "hands," found in the antigen-binding regions, and to various receptors on cells with its "feet" region. IgG antibodies make up approximately 75% of the blood's antibodies. The binding region of the antibody determines the type of cell it binds to and the antibody class.

ADAPTED FROM SOMPAYRAC (1999)

recognize any organic molecules such as peptides, lipids, and polysaccharides. TCRs are diverse, like the antibodies produced by the B cells; but whereas the B-cell receptors detach from the B cells and form antibodies, TCRs are permanent fixtures of T cells.

When an antigen is recognized by a TCR, a cloning process begins in which the T cell proliferates to respond to a particular antigen. This, however, takes a bit of time—the B-cell antibody response is relatively fast and the T-cell response is slower. Whereas the antibody response is analogous to purchasing more specialized weapons for existing special agents, the T-cell response is equivalent to recruiting and hiring additional special agents to capture a particular fugitive.

Although there may be more, two types of T cells have received a lot of attention. **Helper T cells** are "helpful" because they produce cytokines and help B cells produce antibodies; **killer T cells** kill pathogens. On being exposed to an antigen, the T cells send, via cytokines, communications (perhaps comparable with e-mail mass mailings) to all appropriate cells in the organs of the immune system.

Whereas the antibodies of the B cells recognize a pathogen on their own, helper T cells require a proper chemical introduction by another immune cell, an **antigen-presenting cell (APC)**. Macrophages, for example, serve as APCs. The macrophages eat the antigen, and after accompanying signals from certain "battle" cytokines, they "burp" up certain amounts of the specific antigen (as described earlier) so that it is presented on the surface of the macrophage. Once the antigen has made its way to the surface, the macrophage can present the antigen to the helper T cell, with the appropriate exchange of chemical signals. Sending a message to commit significant energy into cloning a type of T cell is serious, so the macrophages also present a second type of protein on the surface, which has to be matched in addition to the antigen–receptor match. This security system helps protect against faulty activation of the helper T-cell response.

Another APC is the **dendritic cell**, akin to an FBI undercover agent because it resides on the front lines of the immune system, such as the skin, acting like a typical phagocyte, consuming large amounts of extracellular fluids in order to monitor any intruders in the area. Along with lymphocytes, dendritic cells make up a network of **lymph nodes** through the body. Fluid derived from blood plasma, also known as "lymph," flows through these filtering "field stations." Figure 13.4 shows the locations of the lymph nodes as well as other immune structures in the body.

When an invader ends up inside the body, the dendritic cell leaves its field assignment and travels to a nearby lymph node to "deliver the goods," acting as an APC to virgin T cells (Figure 13.5). Thereafter, the T cells will be activated to respond to this particular antigen (Rabin, 1999; Schedlowski & Tewes, 1999; Sompayrac, 1999; Westermann & Exton, 1999). These

helper T cell Type of T lymphocyte that activates macrophages and stimulates the release of antibodies from B lymphocytes.

killer T cell (also known as "cytotoxic T cell") T cell that recognizes and kills virus-infected host cells; utilizes the protein perforin, which enables it to drill holes in cells, leaving them to die.

antigen-presenting cell (APC) Cell that displays fragments of protein antigens, along with MHC molecules, on its surface in order to activate T cells.

dendritic cells Serve as antigen-presenting cells for naive T cells; important for acquired immunity. Originate in the bone marrow but eventually end up in the skin and lymphoid tissue.

lymph nodes Small nodules made up of lymphocyte-rich tissue found along the lymphatic channels in the body. Location of the origin of acquired immune functioning.

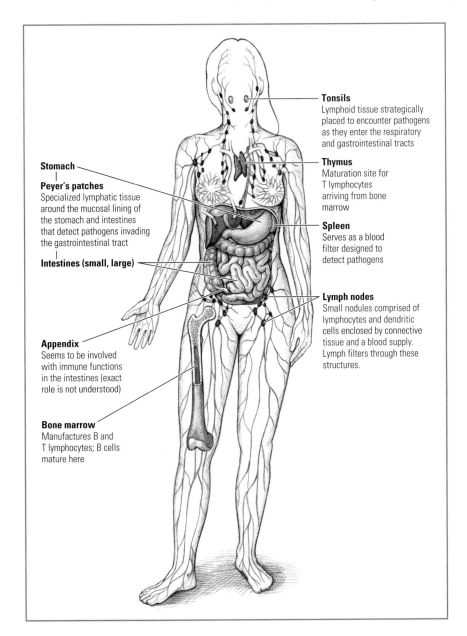

Figure 13.4
**Components of the immune
system**
ADAPTED FROM STRAUB (2002, P. 104)

Tonsils
Lymphoid tissue strategically placed to encounter pathogens as they enter the respiratory and gastrointestinal tracts

Thymus
Maturation site for T lymphocytes arriving from bone marrow

Spleen
Serves as a blood filter designed to detect pathogens

Lymph nodes
Small nodules comprised of lymphocytes and dendritic cells enclosed by connective tissue and a blood supply. Lymph filters through these structures.

Stomach

Peyer's patches
Specialized lymphatic tissue around the mucosal lining of the stomach and intestines that detect pathogens invading the gastrointestinal tract

Intestines (small, large)

Appendix
Seems to be involved with immune functions in the intestines (exact role is not understood)

Bone marrow
Manufactures B and T lymphocytes; B cells mature here

specialized functions of the dendritic cells have prompted immunologists to refer to them as the "professional" APCs (Butts & Sternberg, 2008).

Although the antibodies produced by B cells are quite successful at identifying pathogens outside the cell, how would the body's acquired immune system defend itself against a virus that has penetrated the genetic code embedded in cells and is busy making copies of itself? Killer T cells, or cytotoxic lymphocytes, are designed to handle just this type of threat to the body's homeostasis. Playing a similar role as the innate immune system's NK cells, after receiving the appropriate cytokine message, the killer T cells are primed to start manufacturing the protein perforin.

As discussed previously, perforin is like an assassin's weapon in an immunological James Bond thriller that enables killer T cells to drill a hole in and kill the virus-infected cells. Just like any well-trained secret agent, the killer

Figure 13.5
Covert operations of the dendritic cells Disguised as run-of-the-mill phagocytes, dendritic cells reside on the front lines of the immune system, monitoring intruding antigens and traveling to the lymph nodes to present the intruder to T cells, which will mount an attack against the specific antigen.
ADAPTED FROM WEISSMAN & COOPER (1993, P. 23)

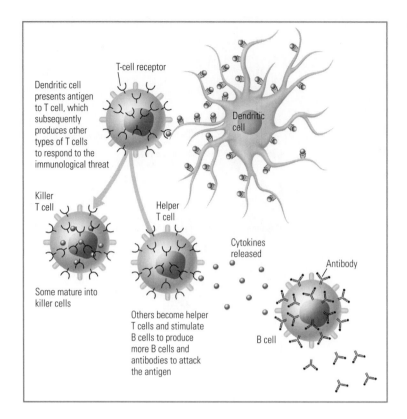

T cells have other means of destruction. They may pass off a package of enzymes to the target cell. After the target cell accepts the pouch of enzymes, it is escorted inside the cell via carrier proteins on the cell's surface. Once inside, the enzymes trigger apoptosis in the infected cell. Subsequently, the potentially damaging chemicals are stored in pouches that are systematically consumed by macrophages.

Contrasting acquired immune defense strategies. To summarize, consider the differences we have discussed between the acquired immune defense's B cells and T cells. Both types originate in the bone marrow, but B cells mature there and T cells migrate to the thymus to mature and differentiate.

B cells act as first responders to virtually any potentially threatening molecules. Once their receptors identify a pathogen, B cells become antibody factories. These antibodies are released into the bloodstream, where, like "smart" missiles, they search out specific pathogens. Because antibodies exist in the blood, the B-cell defense is known as the **humoral immune system** (*humoral* refers to the body's fluids, such as blood).

T cells take a little longer to respond to a particular antigen. They mature following programmed sets of activities designed to build effective defenses against pathogens inside as well as outside cells. Once the antigen is presented to immature T cells, the cells start cloning either helper T cells that release cytokines to stimulate the intracellular action of B cells or killer T cells that can recognize and destroy pathogens that have hijacked genetic material inside the cell to reproduce themselves (see Figure 13.5). Killer T cells operate

humoral immune system
Primarily antibodies released by B lymphocytes.

by drilling holes in the affected cells, leaving them to die. Because killer T cells actually destroy other cells, this defense is known as the **cellular immune system** (Jacobs and Schmidt, 1999; Sompayrac, 1999).

Major Histocompatibility Complex and Information Dissemination

For any security organization to be effective, it must be keenly aware of what is happening both inside and outside. Like the FBI, the immune system disseminates vital information about its ongoing activities and known invaders in the body. We can think of the cytokines as the body's immuno-chemical communications system. Another information system, the **major histocompatibility complex (MHC)**, works by displaying two groups of glycoproteins on the surface of cells. **MHC I molecules** advertise what is going on inside the cell, and **MHC II molecules** advertise what is going on outside the cell. Here's how the MHC works.

MHC I molecules serve as a kind of billboard system for displaying fragments of all the proteins being manufactured by the cell. If the cell has been invaded by a virus and is producing proteins encoded by the virus, this activity will also be displayed on the surface of the cell. Class I MHC molecules are found on virtually every cell in the body and help the immune system distinguish between its own material and something foreign. Killer T cells travel around to monitor the MHC I signals to determine whether a virus has invaded the cell's protein factories and to destroy any infected cells.

MHC II molecules are produced only by cells of the immune system because their purpose is to monitor the activity of the various immune cells and broadcast the information so that helper T cells can be recruited if danger is in the vicinity. Consequently, you need only enough cells expressing MHC II molecules to sample the environment outside the cell.

As stated in this chapter's opening Connections, the MHC may play a role in mate selection in some animals. For example, it is in the best interest of the animal to find a mate with MHC genes that are somewhat variable from its own complex to offer the offspring more diverse protection against pathogens. Variability and diversity are key characteristics of the MHC system; mice have up to 100 different alleles (or versions) at each locus, which contributes to an extreme level of heterozygosity, or genetic diversity, in MHC genes.

Wedekind and Penn (2000) at the University of Edinburgh conducted fascinating research on the role of MHC in human mating preferences. In addition to finding that humans can detect MHC variability through olfaction, they showed how such a mechanism can inhibit inbreeding. For example, they report that a study of married couples in a reproductively isolated community of Austrian-German ancestry (the American Hutterites) suggested that the married couples had a more diverse MHC genetic profile than individuals chosen by chance.

If our MHC influences our attraction to potential mates and even the immunological fitness of our offspring, then some of our more recent cultural behavior seems to go against the use of this selection system. For example, it has been reported that contraceptive pills alter women's olfactory preferences and the cologne and body hygiene industry prides itself on covering up our body odors. With this information it is easy to speculate about

cellular immune system Component of adaptive immunity composed of T cells that defend the body by either activating B-cell release or proliferating so that the T cells themselves can attack the ntigen.

major histocompatibility complex (MHC) In humans, a genetic locus on chromosome 6 that encodes the peptides recognized by T lymphocytes; additionally, this genetic code influences cytokines and antigen proteins.

MHC I molecule MHC glycoproteins found on all cells of the body that display information related to the invasion of the cells by viruses.

MHC II molecule MHC glycoprotein produced in the immune cells; shares information only with the immune cells.

the tentative nature of human marriages. Perhaps this masking of important genetic information contributes to the high divorce rate—once women stop taking their contraceptive pills and spouses stop being so vigilant about using nice-smelling products, it may become apparent that the formerly attractive odor of an individual is now unpleasant—for MHC reasons.

Humans are complex organisms, and many factors contribute to mate selection; but olfaction may be one among several significant factors. Further, a lack of MHC variability may contribute to fertility problems among couples; those experiencing problems conceiving a child may share more MHC genes than those who conceive more easily. Perhaps the Eskimos, who rub noses—and consequently engage in mutual sniffing—have a genetic advantage in mate selection over those of us in the Western world who use artificial odors and the nonsniffing version of a kiss (Furlow, 1996).

Finally, the MHC has another very important implication. If you are going to receive an organ transplant, you need to find a donor who has very similar MHC I genes so that your immune system will identify the transplant as "self" and not reject it. Researchers experimenting with transplanting tumors in mice quickly saw the results of attaching skin and tumor on an animal with a different MHC I genetic profile. It turns out that killer T cells are just waiting for foreign MHC molecules and quickly attack the cells when they encounter them. The killer cells especially like to attack the blood cells of the foreign tissue; once the blood supply is cut off, the tissue usually dies.

Immunologists started working with "inbred" strains of mice so that they would not have to worry about tissue rejection. Today, before patients receive an organ transplant, genetic screening is done to make sure the tissue is compatible and will not be rejected by the donor. Now you understand why this system is known as the major histo*compatibility* complex (Eggert & Ferstl, 1999; Sompayrac, 1999).

When Good Cells Turn Bad

Training of an individual or system is rarely perfect. For instance, despite all the effort that goes into the selection, instruction, and support of FBI agents, sometimes internal or external pressures compromise the functioning of an individual. An agent may be persuaded to work for the "other side," giving in to temptations from members of the criminal element, the very constituency the agent was trained to identify and destroy. Likewise, the immune system may become overactive at seemingly inappropriate times, as seen with allergies and arthritis. It may even contribute to self-destruction by killing healthy body tissue, as is seen in **autoimmune diseases** such as **multiple sclerosis**, in which glial cells making up the myelin sheath of the nerves are destroyed.

Another threat to the smooth functioning of the FBI is an ambitious agent who tries to sabotage the organization because of some personal designs to gain power. In a sense, this agent is analogous to cancer. Although cancer may be triggered by an external event, such as exposure to a particular pollutant or virus, it is in fact part of our own bodies, a genetic code that undergoes a mutation and then starts producing an excessive number of cells. Eventually, if not squelched by the immune system, the cancer cells lead to the body's demise.

autoimmune disease
Disease that results when the mechanisms designed to preserve self-recognition in the immune system are compromised so that the adaptive immune system responds to self-antigens in the same manner as it responds to foreign antigens, leading to cellular and tissue damage.

multiple sclerosis
Neurodegenerative autoimmune disease in which T cells are thought to destroy the myelin sheath of the neurons. Leads to nausea, vertigo, bladder dysfunction, depression, and memory deficits.

For the most part, the etiology of cancer remains a mystery. Aside from understanding that it is the product of genetic mutation, researchers have yet to identify the definitive event that causes cancer. In a creative hypothesis, Michael Ruff and Candice Pert (1984) proposed that lung cancer in cigarette smokers might be due to macrophages that have been recruited in mass numbers to clean up the tar left from the cigarette smoke. The toxins from smoking may lead to a mutation in the macrophages whereby these cells are altered and subsequently start growing and destroying the very organ they were originally sent to defend.

In support of their controversial hypothesis, Ruff and Pert found macrophage antibodies bound to the cancerous lung cells. The observation that macrophages can travel around the body with such ease offered new explanations of the rapid growth of tumors, the lack of rejection of tumor tissue, and the ease with which tumor tissue can metastasize, or spread, to other parts of the body (Pert, 1999). This idea was illustrated in a rather unlikely venue, an animated movie entitled *Osmosis Jones*, in which a "killer virus" attempts to recruit existing cells of the host to "take him down." To do this, the deadly virus travels to the armpit and throbbing ingrown toenail to persuade the immune cells to work for the "other side."

A final example of the immune system itself leading to a person's demise can be seen once an individual is infected with human immunodeficiency virus (HIV), which leads to acquired immune deficiency syndrome (AIDS). This virus attacks the individual's most important weapon in the fight against illness—the immune system. In the early, or acute, stage of infection, the immune system brings out the usual defense cells—B cells, helper T cells, and

Table 13.2 **Examples of Immunopathology: When the Immune System Malfunctions**

Disease	Symptoms	Cause
Cancer	Depend on affected organ. Although the disease may begin in a specific organ, it will metastasize if not stopped.	Mutations in normal genes of the body's own cells.
AIDS (acquired immune deficiency syndrome)	Flulike symptoms early and then symptoms associated with particular opportunistic infections that occur much later	Human immunodeficiency virus (HIV) that leads to the destruction of T cells.
Multiple sclerosis	Multiple neurological deficits involving different components of the nervous system, including brain stem dysfunction leading to nausea and vertigo, bladder dysfunction, depression, and memory deficits.	Usually thought to be a T cell–mediated autoimmune condition; evidence that it is autoimmune is based on rodent models, but it is possible that the cause may be a virus; chronic inflammation destroys the myelin sheath.
Myasthenia gravis	Muscle weakness, fatigue. This disease is life-threatening if respiratory system is involved.	T cells attack postsynaptic nicotinic receptors in the neuromuscular junction, making skeletal muscles unable to contract.
Rheumatoid arthritis	Crippling inflammation of joints, particularly hands, wrists, and knees. The patient has difficulty moving affected joints.	Autoantibodies called rheumatoid factors act against a portion of the normal self-IgG in most, but not all, cases.

Adapted from Song & Leonard (2000) and Sompayrac (1999).

killer T cells. Usually, this reaction is enough to rid the body of the virus. In the case of AIDS, the virus manages to survive the initial immunological attack and enters a chronic phase that can last 10 or more years. After a while, the helper T cells start to diminish, leading to decreased activation of important killer T-cell responses. At this point, the immune defenses become overwhelmed, leaving the AIDS patient in a state of immunosuppression and increased vulnerability to any future immunological challenges.

It probably shouldn't be a surprise that a system as multifaceted and intricate as the immune system can malfunction in response to several different mechanisms. Table 13.2 summarizes the origins and symptoms related to several examples of immunopathology, when the immune system itself leads to tissue damage or sickness.

INTEGRATIVE OPERATIONS: IMMUNE AND NERVOUS SYSTEM COMMUNICATION

As powerful and effective as the FBI is on its own, it is important that there is some integration between the FBI and other agencies such as the Central Intelligence Agency (CIA). Working together, these organizations share their expertise, making it less likely that the nation's security will be breeched. It can be argued that the nervous system is the body's CIA. We now know that the immune system and the nervous system collaborate and communicate in multiple ways.

Conditioning the Immune System: A Serendipitous Discovery

In 1974, Robert Ader was working on a conditioning study with mice at the University of Rochester. Borrowing from the behavioral techniques introduced by Pavlov (see Chapter 1), he used the drug cyclophosphamide, which nauseates rodents, as the unconditioned stimulus. Ader presented water sweetened with saccharin and then injected the drug. As is the case with all classical conditioning studies, Ader's mice quickly learned to avoid water that tasted like saccharin.

The interesting observation came when Ader stopped injecting the drug, a known immunosuppressant, but kept the sweet water in the cages: The animals started dying. Why would an animal die when the drug that influenced the immune system was no longer being used? Further, why would the animals that consumed the most saccharin be the first to die?

Ader, an observant psychologist, quickly surmised that in addition to conditioning the mice to avoid the sweet water, he had conditioned their immune systems to become suppressed whenever the animals were exposed to the saccharin water. Thus, the more times an animal came in contact with the water, the more suppressed the immune system became and the less likely it was that the immune system could defend itself from foreign pathogens. Although this observation made perfect sense to Ader, his conclusion was not readily accepted in the field of immunology because, at that time, the dogma was that there were no connections between the immune system and the nervous system. After all, an immunologist can observe immune responses in cells in a test tube in the absence of a nervous system. Ader's proposed conditioning of the immune system meant that the nervous system interpreting the presence of the sweet water was somehow communicating with the immune system.

At that point, Ader started collaborating with Nicholas Cohen, an immunologist at the University of Rochester; and using all of the proper experimental control groups, they confirmed the immunoconditioning and have been working together ever since (Ader & Cohen, 1975; Moyers, 1993). In 1981, Ader coined the term *psychoneuroimmunology* (PNI) for both a conference and a book.

A decade later, another protective response to a bodily threat, pain, was shown to have conditioning capabilities. Working at the University of Colorado at the time, Erik Wiertelak, Steven Maier, and Linda Watkins (1992) conducted a clever study indicating that morphine-induced *analgesia* (decreased perception of pain) was interrupted by the presence of conditioned safety cues—as if the analgesic response wasn't necessary if there were cues predicting the absence of the threat. Their subsequent research emphasized the role of the amygdala in maintaining conditioned analgesia (Watkins, Wiertelak, & Maier, 1993). Although different from the immune system per se, evidence of conditioning of pain responses confirms the complex interactions between the nervous system and other physiological systems dedicated to promoting health and well-being.

Although the term *PNI* was introduced only in 1981, a little digging in the literature reveals that observations suggesting possible conditioning of the immune system were made many years prior to Ader's mouse studies. For example, in 1896, Mackenzie published an article describing a case in which an allergic patient would sneeze upon the presentation of an artificial rose. It has also been reported that Russian investigators used pavlovian conditioning to pair a neutral stimulus with injections of foreign proteins, resulting in conditioned antibody production (Metal'nikov & Chorine, 1926, 1928).

These initial observations were not formally interpreted as examples of crosstalk between the immune and nervous systems until the landmark work of Ader and Cohen. Obviously, this formal introduction into the scientific literature prompted researchers to think about some exciting possibilities. If immunosuppression is possible, can one demonstrate immunoenhancement? Is immunoconditioning related to the fascinating phenomenon known as the "placebo effect"? Could results with mice generalize to humans? Since the initial reports in this field, abundant research has been conducted; but many questions concerning the boundaries and mechanisms of immunoconditioning remain (Ader & Cohen, 1991).

Additional Pieces of the Neuroimmune Puzzle

A serendipitous discovery by David Felten, also at the University of Rochester, provided evidence of a neuroanatomical link between the immune and nervous systems. One day in the 1980s, when observing spleen cells under the microscope, Felten observed nerve fibers. (The **spleen**, a filtering organ located in the abdomen and shown in Figure 13.4, plays a large role in defending the body against bloodborne antigens.) Surprised by the finding of nerve tissue in immunological tissue, Felten pursued the discovery. He and his colleagues subsequently found that not only do nerve fibers weave throughout the spleen but they extend to virtually every immune organ, laying the foundation for an extensive communication system

spleen Filtering organ, located in the abdomen, that plays a large role in defending the body against bloodborne antigens.

interleukin-1 (IL-1) Cytokine produced primarily by activated phagocytes that activates B and T cells, influences NK and macrophage activity, and induces fever.

(Felten, Ackerman, Wiegand, & Felten, 1987; Moyers, 1993; Sapolsky, Rivier, Yamamoto, Plotsky, & Vale, 1987).

In 1984, a publication by Edwin Blalock, who is currently at the University of Alabama at Birmingham, provided another interesting piece of the nervous system/immune system communication puzzle. His work pointed to the nature of the messages being sent between the nervous and immune systems. Specifically, he reported that when exposed to a viral infection, leukocytes produce endorphins and the stress hormone antecedent adrenocorticotropic hormone (ACTH). This line of research suggested that leukocytes produce numerous neuropeptides and, sealing the partnership between these systems, have receptors for most of the neuroendocrine hormones. Thus, immune tissue can both produce and receive neural messages.

Completing the picture, Sapolsky et al. (1987) demonstrated that the nervous system could also respond to cytokines, specifically **interleukin-1 (IL-1)**, a cytokine produced primarily by activated phagocytes that activates B and T cells, influences NK and macrophage activity, and induces fever. When they injected IL-1 into the veins of rats, a rise in ACTH was found, an increase that they determined was mediated by corticotropin-releasing hormone (CRH) secreted by the hypothalamus. Thus, it appears that the brain has receptors for cytokines of the immune system.

Stress: Mediator Between the Immune and Neural Agencies

As discussed in Chapters 5, 6, and 12, stressors prompt an elaborate cascade of physiological events, including immunological responses. In a sense, the stress and immunological responses are the body's key systems for warding off any event or pathogen that may threaten homeostasis. Without realizing it, you are already aware of the interaction between these two systems—when you have a nasty rash that is swollen and painful (evidence that your immune system is actively trying to oust the invading infection), you probably put a cortisone cream on the rash in an attempt to help reduce the swelling. The active ingredient in this cream is the glucocorticoid cortisol, a substance recognized as a principal neurochemical in the stress response. Cortisol treatments are also used for the inflammation associated with arthritis and for certain medical situations such as organ transplants (Rabin, 1999).

Aside from being involved in skin rashes and joint inflammation, do glucocorticoids or other neurochemical components of the stress response play a more central role in immune functioning? Esther Sternberg and Philip Gold (1997), working at the National Institute of Mental Health, have taken a serious look at the relationship between stress and the immune responses. Starting with neuroanatomy, as seen in Figure 13.6, the hypothalamic neurons that secrete CRH send fibers to the brain stem. Some of these fibers regulate the sympathetic nervous system, which ultimately innervates immunological organs such as the thymus, spleen, and lymph nodes. Other fibers in the brain stem activate the locus coeruleus, a neural circuit discussed in Chapter 5 involved in general arousal, including fear and enhanced vigilance.

Recall that the amygdala is a primary brain area involved with fear responses. The amygdala also features CRH-secreting neurons that communicate with the hypothalamus (which also secretes CRH) and the locus coeruleus. And adding even more "relations" to this immunoneuronal family, the CRH neurons are activated by the immune cells during an immune response.

Sapolsky's finding that the injection of IL-1 results in a rise in stress hormones lends further support to the notion of an immune system–CRH relationship. The relationship is beneficial because it enables the immune system to recruit the cortisol response to restrain the immune response a bit—as when you apply cortisol cream to your swollen rash. Additionally, as you will read later in the chapter, hypothalamic–pituitary–adrenal (HPA) axis activation induces behaviors that assist in helping the individual recover from the illness.

Sickness Behavior and Its Role in Maintaining Health

The heading may strike you as oxymoronic, but recall from our discussion of the protection offered from being exposed to small amounts of antigens in vaccinations that being sick can be your insurance to a prolonged life. A little background information will clarify how the immune and nervous systems interact to produce sickness behavior.

Let's start with the "sick response." Have you ever noticed that, regardless of the type of sickness you may have, you experience the same general set of symptoms? It's very likely that the last time you were sick you felt cold and feverish, you wanted to sleep all day, your joints ached when you tried to walk around, and you lost interest in food and sex. In fact, Benjamin Hart (1988), a veterinarian at the University of California at Davis, has identified over 60 common diseases that result in the same list of symptoms. Regardless of whether the animal has a respiratory or a digestive illness, the symptoms are quite similar.

The body works diligently to produce, not reduce, these behaviors (Sapolsky, 1997). Instead of being the result of an exhausted body in the midst of expending all its energy to fight off pathogens, sickness is more accurately viewed as an organized strategy that is necessary for the survival of the animal (Dantzer, 1999). To understand why the body orchestrates the multifaceted defense of sickness behavior, let's look at each general symptom a little more closely.

Fever. The key response to surviving a pathogen is the fever. Fevers, which occur even in primitive organisms, are adaptive because most of the microbial organisms flourish at temperatures comparable with the body temperature of the host (for us, 98.6°F). Once the body temperature is elevated, the pathogens are not able to reproduce and thus become compromised. Additionally, fevers enhance the immunological response to the infection. For example, white blood cells divide more quickly and phagocytes kill more

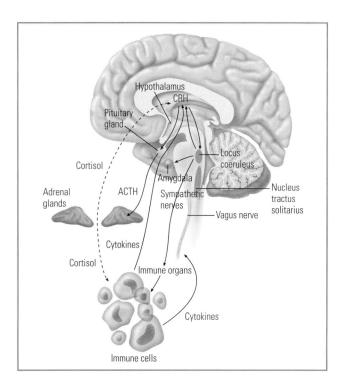

Figure 13.6
Hypothalamic–pituitary–adrenal (HPA) axis and immune functions The arrows in this diagram denote interactive pathways between the nervous and immune systems. Cytokines are produced from immune cells and activate the vagus nerve, which in turn activates various parts of the brain. The locus coeruleus in the brain stem activates the hypothalamus, which subsequently initiates the HPA axis, resulting in the release of adrenocorticotropic hormone (ACTH). The locus coeruleus also projects to the amygdala, a brain area involved in fear and vigilance responses. Ending this feedback loop, the stress hormone cortisol influences immune and hypothalamic cells. CRH, corticotropin-releasing hormone.

ADAPTED FROM STERNBERG (2000, P. 89)

efficiently at higher body temperatures (Maier & Watkins, 1998). Of course, few things come without a cost, and a fever exacts a huge metabolic cost.

For the body to increase its temperature, cytokines signal the hypothalamus to reset the body temperature *set point*, or ideal temperature for optimal functioning, resulting in an organism that feels cold because its body temperature is below the new optimal temperature. The animal conserves heat by keeping the blood flow in the central part of the body and by seeking warm places to rest. The feverish animal also tries to produce heat by shivering and increasing the metabolic rate.

Although shivering seems like a mild response, it increases the metabolism about fourfold. Recognizing the value of a fever may contradict our usual practice of "treating" a fever with *antipyretics*, or fever-reducing medications, such as acetaminophen. Some studies show that people take longer to get well when taking drugs to reduce their fever as the drugs interfere with the body's well-orchestrated responses (Nesse & Williams, 1994a).

Now that the role of the fever and its high cost to the body are understood, it is probably becoming apparent why you have a desire to sleep and are not motivated to be active or to engage in social activities when you are sick. These behaviors simply cost too much energy at a time when energy stores are critical for maintaining the fever. Achy joints may provide even more justification for taking it easy.

Loss of appetite. One behavior, anorexia, or decreased eating, does not seem to follow the logic of the other symptoms. At a time when your body has such high metabolic costs, why would you reduce your food intake? Scientists do not have the answer to this question but speculate that increased food intake may increase plasma levels of iron (which is not advantageous for a fever), that a reduced appetite decreases the possibility of the animal expending energy foraging for food, or that a sick and compromised animal out rummaging around in the environment may be extremely vulnerable to predators (Maier & Watkins, 1998).

Role of cytokines. We mentioned that cytokines play a significant role in inducing the sick response. Let's look a little closer at exactly how this happens. A group of Swiss scientists found that IL-1 was the key cytokine in inducing a fever. By injecting particles of bacteria known as "lipopolysaccharides" (LPSs) into the stomachs of mice, these researchers showed indirectly that brain IL-1 was produced (Fontana, Weber, & Dayer, 1984).

In the fashion of true FBI agents, Steven Maier and Linda Watkins (1998) of the University of Colorado have conducted a detailed analysis of the role of cytokines in behaviors related to sickness. They stress the importance of the vagus nerve (a large cranial nerve that extends into the abdominal cavity) in the cytokine-mediated communication with the brain. If the vagus nerve is cut, the sickness response does not develop.

But how does IL-1 in the periphery stimulate the vagus nerve to activate critical areas in the brain? Maier and Watkins report that the macrophages initially release IL-1 on the presentation of a pathogen and that IL-1 binds to receptors on clusters of neurons known as "paraganglia" around the vagal nerve fibers. The paraganglia release a chemical message that travels back to the brain via the vagus nerve (afferent direction). The message activates the brain stem area known as the "nucleus tractus solitarius" (NTS), which is situated near the area postrema—the area of the brain involved in another sickness behavior that helps to rid your body of unwanted particles, vomiting.

The NTS subsequently carries messages to the hypothalamus and hippocampus, triggering the secretion of IL-1 in the brain. Thus, IL-1 produced by the macrophages triggers a cascade of responses that ultimately result in the production of IL-1 in the brain. Figure 13.7 diagrams this process.

The intimate relationship between the two primary defense systems—the stress response and the immune response—helps assure an animal's survival. If a predator is approaching, the stress response helps the animal to escape; if a pathogen approaches, the immune system helps the body survive the invasion. Thinking further about these two protective systems, Maier and Watkins suggest that the fight-or-flight reaction is a recently evolved stress response that enables an animal to produce enough energy to survive a distal threat such as an approaching predator. The immune response is also a stress response to the pathogen interrupting the homeostatic balance of the body. This response requires only the animal's ability to distinguish self from nonself—even sponges contain phagocytes and can respond to this proximal stress.

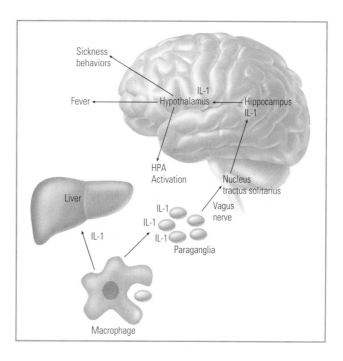

Figure 13.7
Inducing a sick response Lipopolysaccharide is consumed by a macrophage, triggering the release of interleukin-1 (IL-1), which subsequently stimulates the paraganglia of the vagus nerve. The vagus nerve stimulates the liver and the nucleus tractus solitarius, which further activates the hippocampus and the hypothalamus, ultimately resulting in hypothalamic–pituitary–adrenal (HPA) axis activation, the production of a fever, and more IL-1 release in the brain.
ADAPTED FROM MAIER & WATKINS (1998)

PUTTING THE "PSYCH" IN PSYCHONEUROIMMUNOLOGY

How might the interplay between the immune and nervous systems lead to mental illness? According to a recent study conducted by the World Health Organization, many patients with chronic diseases such as arthritis, diabetes, and asthma also suffer from depression; in fact, up to 23% of patients with a chronic physical disease also suffer from depression (Moussavi et al., 2007). Further, several researchers have pointed out the parallels between sickness behavior and depression (Leonard & Myint 2009). Depressed patients often suffer from hyperinsomnia (or other sleep-related problems) and a loss of motivation to eat or engage in sex, and as mentioned in Chapter 9, depressed patients exhibit a sustained hypersecretion of cortisol. In fact, one may view depression as an organized anxiety state as opposed to an inactive state. Depressed patients are hypervigilant about distal threats such as relationship failures or the inability to maintain a job. It may be that depression is less about a serotonin reduction and more directly influenced by a stress response that is stuck in the "on" position.

Imipramine, a drug known to help with depression symptoms, has been found to decrease CRH and HPA activity in healthy persons. The observation that patients suffering from rheumatoid arthritis, a condition brought on by an overactive immune system, develop depression at a higher rate than normally expected also provides evidence that an overactive stress response system may be involved in depression. Thus, viewing depression as an overactive vigilance system (activated by a more recently evolved component of the acquired immune system) that may be treated from an immunological perspective is drastically different from the perspectives currently used to approach this disorder.

We have spent considerable time discussing the fundamentals of the immune system and how it interacts with the nervous system. But this chapter is entitled "psychoneuroimmunology," not "neuroimmunology." If the *psycho* prefix denotes psychological processes, then how does psychology fit into the PNI domain?

We have already touched on a few psychological connections: Sexual motivation and sickness-related behaviors may be influenced by the immune system. But at the heart of the question of the role of psychological processes in PNI is the question of individual differences, a central concern of much psychological inquiry. After you and your sweetheart spend the weekend with a niece who has a cold, why do you contract a cold the next week but your significant other does not? You were both exposed to the same stimuli: Shouldn't both of you get sick? Why do you get sick after a grueling finals week and your best friend feels great? How can the immune system act so differently in two members of the same species?

The answers can be found in the variation in environments, social situations, and psychological profiles. As described in Chapter 12, when faced with a threatening stimulus, one person may express fear and aggression, another may run to the security of loved ones, and another may respond to the threat in solitude. Each of these responses has a very different influence on the immune system (Kemeny & Laudenslager, 1999). Jaak Koolhaas (2008), conducting research at the University of Groningen, has emphasized the importance of coping styles (as discussed in Chapter 12) in determining vulnerability to immune-mediated diseases. Ronald Glaser (2005), in his presidential address to the Psychoneuroimmunology Research Society, reminded its members that an understanding of behavior informs researchers and practitioners of an important "system modulator" in complex immune functions.

Accordingly, in this section we consider how varying responses to stress and social relationships, as well as various environmental elements, influence the immune response. Beware, though, as we move from examining the immune system in the Petri dish or the single organism in the lab to considering its activity in the integrated context we typically refer to as "real life," the studies become less controlled and the conclusions become a little more tentative. As discussed in Box 13.1, however, this line of research is imperative if the PNI field is going to lead to enhanced immune functioning outside the controlled laboratory setting (for example, in hospitals). Once we navigate through this interesting literature, the convergence of evidence will enable us to make some specific conclusions.

Psychological Factors Leading to Compromised Immune Function

We have already discussed the connection between the stress system and immune functioning. As a psychological factor that threatens the body's homeostasis, researchers have found that stressors have a significant impact on an animal's immune system (Kemeny, 2009).

Box 13.1

A Case in Point

Evan Handler

At the age of 24, Evan Handler seemed to be right on track with his life and his career. His girlfriend, Jackie, had just moved into his New York apartment, and he was preparing to play a leading role in the Broadway production of Neil Simon's *Biloxi Blues*. And he had scheduled a meeting with Warren Beatty to finalize his part in a movie Beatty would soon be making with Dustin Hoffman.

Handler's world fell apart when he went to the doctor to check out a rash on his feet and why he had been feeling a little sick lately. Those innocent symptoms translated into a dreaded diagnosis—leukemia. Handler never made the movie with Beatty and Hoffman, which he didn't regret too much because it turned out to be the box office flop *Ishtar*. Instead, he took on the leading role in his own life drama, the drama of surviving leukemia.

Handler checked into New York's Memorial Sloan-Kettering Cancer Center because it had a reputation as a research hospital that could offer him the latest treatments to successfully attack the leukemia. From the time Handler entered the hospital and became patient 865770, he realized that, in addition to his immune system being in turmoil, his emotional world was about to enter a downward spiral. In a procedure typical of many leading research hospitals at the time, he was herded through corridors filled with dying, moaning patients. He was also made to wait long hours in miserable waiting rooms. Worst of all, he was treated as if he should accept the fact that his odds were dismal and that he should start to get used to the idea that he might not survive the disease.

At that point Handler realized that if he was going to recover, he could not put his fate in the hands of that hospital staff; he would have to take an extremely active role in his recovery process. Handler accomplished this goal by adopting what he called a strategy of "opportunistic optimism," utilizing meditation, visualization, hypnotherapy, personal therapy, psychic sessions, nutritional therapy, massage, and aromatherapy, which are all strategies that helped him to relax as he endured his extended, tormenting hospital stay. He also attempted to remove all doubt-provoking stimuli from his life. For example, his girlfriend screened his mail

Evan Handler
CARLO ALLEGRI/GETTY IMAGES

and books so that he could focus only on the positive. Finally, Handler became keenly aware of the value of the love and support of others and turned even more frequently to the support of his girlfriend.

Handler endured many months of chemotherapy and experienced a remission. Following his three rounds of chemotherapy, Handler went on to star in two movies and got a part in Neil Simon's *Broadway Bound*. Unfortunately, the leukemia returned; at this point, he opted for a bone marrow transplant at Johns Hopkins University. He was amazed at the contrast between Hopkins and Sloan-Kettering. Hopkins's staff was extremely sensitive to the psychological needs of the patients, attempting to treat the entire person as opposed to a compartmentalized disease. The bone marrow transplant was successful, and Handler is currently back in his acting life. In addition to playing dramatic roles in films such as *Ransom* and *Natural Born Killers*, he has tried his hand at writing. In 1996, Handler wrote *Time on Fire: My Comedy of Terrors*, an autobiographical account of his journey from cancer to recovery. You might recognize Handler from one of his more recent roles as the lawyer Harry Goldenblatt in the popular television series *Sex and the City*.

Handler's story offers ample evidence that patients suffer not only from a particular disease but from a barrage of emotional experiences as well. Current research suggests that stress and anxiety rob the immune system of much needed energy. But Handler used a very active coping strategy, including exercising a sense of control over his life-threatening condition. As discussed in Chapter 12, an increased perception of control leads to reduced stress responsivity. Thus, Handler's story reminds us of the wisdom of Asclepius, mentioned earlier in this chapter—healing is about focusing on the relationship between psychological and physical factors. Ignoring either one leaves a patient more vulnerable to the disease.

Focusing on rodent models, scientists have employed a multitude of stressors including shock, forced swim, restraint, and rotational stress and have found that stress reduces lymphocyte-mediated cytotoxicity, diminishes stem graft rejection, and suppresses antibody responses (Shavit, 1991). Although these studies have produced interesting results, the stressors typically used are somewhat artificial. Most animals live in complex social structures, not individually in small territories (such as laboratory cages). Consequently, observations of animals in natural or seminatural conditions are necessary to understand how an animal might respond in a stressful situation and subsequently how the response influences the immune system.

An example of a seminaturalistic approach can be found in work done on *Antechinus stuartii*, a small insectivorous marsupial that resembles a mouse with a long pointed nose and lives in the forests of Australia. Because of stress, the males rarely live past their first breeding season (less than a year) and females may live a little longer but never past 2 years. In fact, the males seem to have the more stressful existence. They enter an intense mating period in late winter when the weather conditions are harsh—consisting of low temperatures, rain, and occasionally snow. During the frenzy and stress of mating, males lose body weight and develop enlarged adrenal glands as well as increased production of corticosteroids and androgens. To add to the animals' stress, the males become extremely aggressive during this time as they attempt to defend their territories.

Does this extreme form of stress have an effect on the immune system? Absolutely. When examined, these animals are heavily infested with endo- and ectoparasites. If brought into the lab, the male antechinus produces very low levels of antibodies to sheep red blood cells (a commonly used laboratory immune challenge). In the wild, due to compromised immune systems, the animals die shortly after copulating as a result of both gastrointestinal hemorrhage and invasion of parasites and microorganisms. Thus, with all the animals' energy directed toward sexual behavior, little is left for the immune system. The cost of this sexual encounter is enormous for the individual antechinus male—death.

Do these effects generalize to humans? Although research suggests that human males are more motivated than females to engage in sexual behavior, few would probably risk their lives for one intimate encounter. Consequently, scientists do not go to singles bars to investigate the human stress experience; instead, they turn to another situation with which you, as a student, are very familiar. Scientists believe that the stress of taking exams is a useful model of naturalistic stress in humans. Researchers have found that medical students taking exams exhibit lower lymphocyte proliferation, IL-2 production, and NK-cell activity (Guidi et al., 1999; Kiecolt-Glaser & Glaser, 1991; Glaser, 2005).

Academic stress also decreases apoptosis. It is thought that apoptosis is one mechanism that the body uses to protect against the growth of abnormal cells that may eventually result in cancer. Thus, prolonged stress may place the body in a situation where it cannot rid itself of cells containing DNA interruptions that may mutate into cancer cells (Kiecolt-Glaser and Glaser, 1999).

A troubled relationship is another stressful situation that has been explored in humans. Janice Kiecolt-Glaser and Ron Glaser of Ohio State University studied 90 newlywed couples (Kiecolt-Glaser, Glaser, Cacioppo, &

Malarkey, 1998). The couples were instructed to discuss one or more areas of disagreement for 30 minutes. As the couples were engaged in this discussion, the researchers taped and scored the behaviors that occurred during the session.

Hostile behaviors such as raising one's voice were related to higher blood pressure and neuroendocrine increases as well as NK-cell and T-cell decrements. In wives, both norepinephrine and cortisol increased as the husbands exhibited withdrawal during the encounter. The researchers also found that separated or divorced men were more distressed and reported more illnesses than their married counterparts. When tested, these men had compromised immune systems (for example, lower antibody response to herpes viruses).

Another stressful situation that has been assessed is the chronic stress and despair experienced by individuals who are caregivers for Alzheimer's patients. Glaser and his colleagues gave an influenza virus vaccination to 32 caregivers and matched controls (Glaser, Sheridan, Malarkey, MacCallum, & Kiecolt-Glaser, 2000). The caregivers had poorer antibody and activated T-cell responses. These researchers also gave a series of three hepatitis B vaccinations to medical students on the third day of 3-day exam period blocks (Glaser, Kiecolt-Glaser, Malarkey, & Sheridan, 1998). Higher antibody responses were observed in students who reported greater social support and lower levels of anxiety.

Wound healing was also assessed in women caring for a spouse with Alzheimer disease. After receiving a 3.5 mm skin punch biopsy, researchers simply observed the rate of healing for each woman's wound. Interestingly, it took the caregiver group 24% longer for the wounds to close than nonstressed subjects (Kiecolt-Glaser, Marucha, Malarkey, Mercado, & Glaser, 1995).

Thus, the stressful situations of taking medical exams, experiencing marital discord, and taking care of a loved one suffering from Alzheimer disease have all been empirically linked to compromised immune functioning. Knowing, as you do, the relationship between stress and the immune system, the finding that stress affects the immune system shouldn't come as a surprise. But in addition to pointing out factors that produce immunological deficits, researchers have worked diligently to identify factors related to immunological enhancements.

Psychological Factors Leading to Enhanced Immune Function

After reading the previous section you may be tempted to think that a person can enhance immune functioning by just avoiding any type of stress. That may be true, but life is rarely that simple. A few studies suggest that acute stress may actually result in *increased* immune system activation (Dhabhar, 2009).

At the height of the Iraqi Scud missile attacks on the cities of Israel during the 1991 Persian Gulf War, for example, Weiss and his colleagues (1996) subjected 22 male volunteers living in Jerusalem to a battery of psychological tests as well as to various immunological and neuroendocrine assays. These subjects were tested again after the end of the war. The results suggested that anxiety and anger were higher during the war than after and that NK-cell activity was significantly elevated during the war. Neuroendocrine measures such as ACTH indicated that physiological stress levels were also highest during the war—a time in which Iraq's professed goal was to reduce Israel to ashes

Some interesting work using actors as subjects confirms that negative emotions such as fear and sadness result in increases in immunological functioning. In the "actor" studies, subjects are asked to improvise a monologue that will produce either sad or happy emotions. Much to the researcher's surprise, during an intense sad state, NK cells were increased in the actor's bloodstream. As expected (and as described in Box 13.2), intense happy states also produced immunological enhancement (Futterman, Kemeny, Shapiro, & Fahey, 1994).

Recall that during times of stress the immune system is compromised because the body's energy is directed toward actions necessary for survival—the fight-or-flight response. How can it be adaptive, then, for the body to use some of its valuable energy to fuel the immune system during times of fear and stress? Firdaus Dhabhar (1998) of Ohio State University has proposed that stress may have a bidirectional effect—in certain conditions, stress may enhance immunological functioning, whereas other conditions may result in immunosuppression.

Further, acute stress may suppress certain functions while enhancing other immune actions. During an acute stress episode (for example, being attacked by a lion), it is likely that, should you survive, your body will be exposed to immediate immune challenges such as wounds. Dhabhar suggests that the body may direct blood leukocytes to migrate to certain immunological battle stations such as the skin to help the animal survive the attack and the impending immunological threat. This stress-induced enhancement is likely to occur only in acute, rather than in chronic, stress. If this theory is correct, there may be some value in trying to eliminate chronic stress in patients while periodically exposing them to acute stress to activate the immune system.

Aside from acute stress, researchers have found that social ties boost immunological protection. In one study, 276 healthy volunteers were given nasal drops that contained one or two rhinoviruses (cold viruses that invade the nasal passages). The scientists simply waited to see who developed coldlike symptoms. In the end, subjects with more types of social relationships (friends, family, coworkers, spouse) were less likely to develop coldlike symptoms (cough, runny nose). Additionally, the subjects with more social support generated less mucus with a lower viral count (Cohen, Doyle, Skoner, Rabin, & Gwaltney, 1997).

In a related study focusing on susceptibility to influenza, other researchers have provided evidence that flu infections are more likely to occur in families viewed as rigid or chaotic than in more engaged, balanced families (Clover, Abell, Becker, Crawford, & Ramsey, 1989). Thus, positive interpersonal relationships can have a strong impact on immune functioning.

In a study consisting of probably more subjects than any other experiment in this text, further evidence for health benefits of social ties was found. In Evans County, Georgia, 3,201 subjects were recruited for a study investigating lifestyle factors and longevity. In general, the researchers found that, at least in white subjects, increased mortality risk was found in those with few social ties. Additionally, they found that spending spare time in church benefited females (Schoenbach, Kaplan, Friedman, & Kleinbaum, 1986).

In another large study conducted a few years later, researchers at Duke University Medical Center collected blood samples from 1,718 subjects

Box 13.2

Brain Matters

Humor's Influence on Health:
No Laughing Matter!

Among the pioneers who helped convince health professionals that the mind is indeed involved with health was a very unlikely figure—Norman Cousins, the editor of the influential magazine *The Saturday Review*. In 1964, Cousins became extremely ill with a severe connective tissue disease, ankylosing spondylitis. Cousins was less than impressed with the standard treatment offered by the hospital, complete with tasteless food, powerful medications with debilitating side effects, and a steady stream of interruptions.

Although Cousins had no prior medical training, he took an active role in his quest for recovery. He traded his hospital room for a motel room and began a treatment regime built on megadoses of vitamin C and Charlie Chaplin. He reported that a good 10-minute belly laugh had an anesthetic effect that allowed him to have at least a couple of hours of pain-free sleep (Cousins, 1976, 1979).

Cousins worked with an open-minded physician who valued his patient's views about recovery. About a decade after recovering from the illness, Cousins publicly told his story in 1976 in an article in the *New England Journal of Medicine*, followed by a book entitled *Anatomy of an Illness*. Toward the end of his life, Cousins worked with the UCLA School of Medicine to facilitate the study of more global and compassionate perspectives in the healing profession.

Evidence of Cousins's philosophy was seen by millions of Americans in a movie titled *Patch Adams*, based on a book entitled *Gesundheit: Good Health Is a Laughing Matter*. In the film, the actor Robin Williams portrays a real-life physician, Hunter "Patch" Adams, who became disillusioned during his training for a career in medicine with the apparent lack of

compassion and attention toward a person's emotional state. In an attempt to treat the patient as well as the illness, Adams went on to incorporate laughter and compassion in his treatment strategies. He established the Gesundheit! Institute in West Virginia, where humor is regularly prescribed for patients who are offered treatment free of charge.

As you know, case studies, books, and movies are very interesting but offer a weak substitute for true empirical evidence of a particular effect. What does traditional science say about humor and the immune system? In one study (Berk, Tan, Napier, & Eby, 1989), experimental subjects watched the comedian Gallagher on a life-size screen while having their blood collected at various intervals during the hour-long video. Compared with the control subjects, the subjects exposed to the Gallagher video expressed less cortisol, epinephrine, and dopamine—or at least a metabolite of dopamine. Another study conducted by the same research group (Berk, Tan, Fry, et al., 1989) found that mirthful laughter also increased natural killer-cell activity.

In another study (Newman & Stone, 1996), subjects were asked to view a silent, stressful film. One group was instructed to write a humorous monologue for the film, whereas a second group was asked to write a serious monologue. Various measures were taken before, during, and after the film. Subjects who were instructed to generate a humorous monologue exhibited lower tension, a less negative emotional state, and less psychophysiological reactivity (heart rate, for example) than the serious monologue group.

Thus, although it is certainly not clear that laughter is the best medicine, mounting evidence demonstrates that it helps relieve stress, which many times restricts the efforts of the immune system. Akin to the humorous antics of the Gesundheit! Institute, an Australian hospital has created a laughter room in which patients augment their treatment protocol with a dose of humor (May, 1996).

---

to assess specific immune regulators such as IL-6, the proinflammatory cytokine (Koenig et al., 1997). The researchers also found a relationship, although subtle, between religious attendance and IL-6 production; specifically, attending religious services was related to decreased production of this inflammatory cytokine, which is related to aging processes. As described by Strawbridge, Cohen, Shema, and Kaplan (1997), the benefits of attending religious services may be partly explained by the lifestyle of many religious individuals, including more stable marriages, increased social contacts, and improved health practices (for example, a likelihood of decreased smoking and increased exercise).

James Pennebaker joined forces with Janice Kiecolt-Glaser and Ron Glaser (1988) to investigate another factor possibly related to enhancing one's immune defenses. In this study, 50 college students were randomly assigned to either a group instructed to write about a traumatic event or a group instructed to write about superficial topics for 20 minutes per day for 4 days. The subjects in this study agreed to have their blood drawn the day before writing, the day of the last writing session, and 6 weeks later.

During the writing phase, subjects in the traumatic event group poured out their hearts in their writing, disclosing instances of rape, suicide attempts, death, child abuse, and family conflict. Each day, the subjects writing about traumas reported feeling more upset than the group writing about superficial topics. Once the blood was collected, white blood cells were isolated and their reactions to foreign substances were assessed. The results suggested that people who wrote about traumatic events had a more heightened immune response to foreign invaders than did the superficial topics group. This effect was more pronounced on the last day of writing, but it persisted for the next 6 weeks.

Just a year later, another landmark study was published suggesting that "opening up" one's feelings or emotions may have therapeutic value for patients. David Spiegel and his colleagues at Stanford University School of Medicine (Spiegel, Bloom, Kraemer, & Gottheil, 1989), impressed with the emotional bonds that were created among cancer patients undergoing group psychotherapy, decided to look a little closer at any benefits experienced by women suffering from breast cancer who participated in this form of group therapy. They found that the life spans of the women in therapy were significantly longer than those of control subjects not participating in group therapy.

Concentrating on positive emotions, the relationship between immune factors and optimism in first-year law students was assessed by a group of researchers at the University of California in Los Angeles (Segerstrom, Taylor, Kemeney, & Fahey, 1998). During the initial months of law school, 50 students had their blood drawn and were instructed to complete questionnaires about their dispositions. The researchers found that optimism was associated with higher numbers of helper T cells and NK-cell cytotoxicity. In a different more recent study conducted by David Snowden and his colleagues (Danner, Snowdon, & Friesen, 2001), then at the University of Kentucky, nuns who expressed positive emotions (love, happiness, joy) in autobiographies written in their early twenties lived up to 10 years longer than nuns who expressed fewer positive emotions. If you're happy and you're aware of it, you just may live longer!

Additional evidence drawing relationships between disposition, or temperament, and immune responses is provided in a recent study focusing on a group of men with asymptomatic HIV infection. Following up on anecdotal observations that extroverted individuals were healthier and longer-lived than introverted AIDS patients, Naliboff and his colleagues (Cole, Kemeny, Fahey, Zack, & Naliboff, 2003) assessed personality profiles (for example, social inhibition, or shyness), stress responses, and HIV viral load and number of T cells (two immunological defenses destroyed by AIDS). The results were clear—the shy men with more reactive stress responses had higher viral loads, up to eight times higher than nonshy patients, indicating a compromised defense against HIV. These data provide perhaps the first clinical evidence that increased neural activity (for example, autonomic nervous system responsivity) is the mediating factor between psychological variables and infectious disease progression.

Finally, exercise has been associated with immune enhancement (Crist, Mackinnon, Thompson, Atterbom, & Egan, 1989; Simon, 1991). Although exercise may be viewed as a stressor because it disrupts the homeostasis of the body's physiology, it can relieve tension and promote relaxation. Focusing on immune functions, increased leukocyte, NK cell, and IL-1 levels have been found in subjects following exercise.

Now that a case has been made for the role of psychological processes in immune functions, it should be easier to see that the ancient Greeks' notion of health being a function of both the mind and the body was right on target. The ancient Greeks even wrote about the mitigating effect of specific psychological processes such as despair and hopelessness on the immune system. Thucydides, an Athenian general who wrote about a devastating plague that struck Athens in 430 BCE and who personally suffered from this dreaded plague, made some interesting observations about the disease:

> The most terrible thing of all was the despair into which people fell
> when they realized that they had caught the plague; for they would
> immediately adopt an attitude of utter hopelessness, and, by giving
> in this way, would lose their powers of resistance. (Clark, 1995)

Clearly, Thucydides was gathering anecdotal evidence on the relationship between psychological states and resistance to disease. Whether or not the hopelessness led to impaired resistance or was simply the product of the sickness behavior triggered by the activated immune system has yet to be clarified in the health arena. With the field of PNI becoming more and more visible, researchers and practitioners will extend the effort to view health as the multifaceted phenomenon that more accurately reflects its nature. As suggested by Sternberg and Gold (1997), classifying illnesses into medical and psychiatric specialties seems more and more artificial once we understand that the once demarcated boundaries between the mind and the body are themselves artificial.

Summary

The notion that one's health is influenced by a convergence of psychological, physiological, and immunological systems has been around for thousands of years. However, as Western medicine evolved, the role of psychological factors in one's susceptibility to illness took a back seat to an emphasis on physiological causes and cures for diseases. An increasing amount of literature supporting the role of psychological processes in health and the emerging field of psychoneuroimmunology are forcing researchers to once again embrace the integrative notions of the ancient Greeks and of many Asian traditions.

Fundamentals of Immune System Function: The Body's Federal Bureau of Investigation

The central threat to one's immune system is infectious agents known as "pathogens," including viruses, bacteria, fungi, and parasites. The body's initial defense against pathogens is the skin and the mucosal lining of the respiratory, digestive, and reproductive tracts. Once a pathogen breaches the barriers of the immune system, cells of the innate immune system (macrophages, neutrophils, and natural killer cells) provide a front-line defense.

The body's defense also involves an acquired immune system made up of antibody-producing B cells as well as T cells that proliferate in response to the appearance of an antigen from the organism's past. The major histocompatibility complex helps the body process the massive amounts of information related to responses to various antigens and ultimately helps the immune system distinguish between self and nonself.

The components of the immune system are distributed throughout the body and include the bone marrow, thymus, lymph nodes, spleen, tonsils, and Peyer's patches. With the massive amount of information being exchanged among the elements of the immune system, mistakes sometimes occur—pathogens sometimes slip through, and sometimes a body's own immune cells destroy healthy tissue.

Integrative Operations: Immunological and Nervous System Communication

Serendipitous studies confirming the conditioning of the immune system provided seminal empirical evidence that the nervous system communicates with the immune system. Following these studies, the field of psychoneuroimmunology was created. Subsequent to this finding, nerve fibers were observed in immunological tissue, and surprisingly, leukocytes were observed to produce neurochemicals.

The stress response mediates between the nervous and immune systems—providing further evidence of the abundance of crosstalk between these two systems. The "sick response" is a product of input from the nervous and immune systems to assure that an individual conserves energy while the body wages war against a pathogen.

Putting the "Psych" in Psychoneuroimmunology

Several so-called psychological factors have been demonstrated to influence susceptibility to illness. Chronically stressful situations such as troubled relationships, taking exams, and caring for sick loved ones may compromise immune functions, whereas positive social relationships, disclosure of painful emotions, decreased stress responsivity, humor, and exercise have all been shown to enhance immune functioning.

Key Terms

psychoneuroimmunology (PNI) (392)
pathogen (393)
innate immune system (394)
phagocyte (394)
macrophage (394)
lysosome (394)
neutrophil (395)
natural killer (NK) cells (395)
perforin (395)
cytokines (396)
complement complex (396)

acquired immune system (396)
vaccination (396)
B cells or B lymphocytes (397)
bone marrow (397)
antibody or immunoglobulin (Ig) (397)
antigen (397)
T cells or T lymphocytes (397)
thymus (397)
helper T cells (398)
killer T cell (398)
antigen-presenting cell " (APC) (398)

dendritic cells (398)
lymph nodes (398)
humoral immune system (400)
cellular immune system (401)
major histocompatibility complex (MHC) (401)
MHC I molecule (401)
MHC II molecule (401)
autoimmune disease (402)
multiple sclerosis (402)
spleen (405)
interleukin-1 (IL-1) (406)

For Further Consideration

Glaser, R. (2005). Stress-associated immune dysregulation and its importance for human health: A personal history of psychoneuroimmunology. *Brain, Behavior, and Immunity, 19,* 3–11. This article, a synopsis of Glaser's presidential address to the Psychoneuroimmunology Research Society, is a wonderful review of the important research he has conducted throughout his career.

The impact of various psychological stressors on a plethora of immune measures has confirmed the mitigating effects of chronic stress on immune functions. Throughout the article, Glaser reminds the reader of the importance of exploring psychological functions when attempting to understand the complexity of the immune system.

Handler, E. (1997). *Time on fire: My comedy of terrors.* New York: Henry Holt. This autobiographical book provides an honest, realistic view of what it is like for the immune function to be taken over by a disease—in this case, leukemia. Handler, then a young, aspiring actor, describes his emotions, desires, fears, and strategies for survival. Several MDs have declared this book required reading for health practitioners as it provides an opportunity to glimpse into the world of the patient. Now that you have become acquainted with the PNI field, you will appreciate the impact of Handler's emotional ups and downs on his fragile immune system.

Moussavi, S., Chatterji, S., Verdes, E., Tandon, A., Patel, V., & Ustun, B. (2007). Depression, chronic diseases, and decrements in health: Results from the World Health Surveys. *Lancet, 370,* 851–858. This report of the World Health Organization's survey of comorbidity between depression and other chronic illnesses confirms the interaction between depression, often thought of as a "mental disorder," and more traditionally "physical disorders" such as asthma, diabetes, and arthritis. Consequently, the authors emphasize that depression should be viewed as a public-heath priority in order to reduce disease-related disability and increase overall world health.

Nelson, R. J., Demas, G. E., Klein, S. L., & Kriegsfeld, L. J. (2002). *Seasonal patterns of stress, immune function, and disease.* Cambridge, UK: Cambridge University Press. If you enjoy considering how evolution shaped our physiological functions, this book focuses on how the natural fluctuations of seasons alter immune functioning. The question of the natural rhythms of the immune system is important and may lead to clinically relevant findings directing medical practitioners to consider how the current energy demands of the season might influence a patient's battle with a particular disease. A dramatic example of researchers assessing the functioning of the immune systems of bold individuals who live in Antarctica during the winter, enduring its –30°C daily temperatures, provides powerful evidence that seasonal fluctuations influence immune functions.

Schedlowski, M., & Tewes, U. (Eds.). (1999). *Psychoneuroimmunology: An interdisciplinary introduction.* New York: Kluwer Academic/Plenum. For those of you who want to read more original literature on the many topics in this chapter, the 27 chapters of this book are written by leading researchers on a diverse array of PNI-related topics ranging from the fundamentals of the immune system to exercise and immune functions and sleep and immune functions. The book is filled with the most relevant research in the field and many valuable illustrations.

Sternberg, E. M. (2000). *The balance within: The science connecting health and emotions.* New York: Freeman. This is a beautifully written story of how the mind/brain interacts with immune functions. It is fascinating to learn how Sternberg went from a child running around her father's laboratory in the same building as Hans Selye (the "father" of stress) to a respected researcher in the field of PNI. The book is about the science of mind–body interactions and how they influence health, but Sternberg's inclusion of real-life information makes the book read more like a novel at times—it will surely keep your interest. Serving as the director of the Molecular, Cellular, and Behavioral Integrative Neuroscience Program and chief of the Section on Neuroendocrine Immunology and Behavior at the National Institutes of Health, Dr. Sternberg has a lot to say on the matter of neural--immune interactions in health issues.

Sternberg, E. M. (2009). *Healing spaces: The science of place and well-being.* Cambridge, MA: Harvard University Press. This book considers the importance of one's environment in immune functions. The author emphasizes that the "places" we occupy are more than just a mere backdrop for our immunological functions, they integrate with the immune system in intricate ways. According to the messages conveyed in this fascinating book, we may want to include architects, travel guides, artists, landscapers, and interior designers in our university departments of immunology!

Chapter Fourteen

Eating Regulation and Associated Disorders

Connections

Increased Rates in Eating Out Accompany Increased Inches in Our Waistlines

Odds are that the fast food industry has so insidiously become part of the context of our lives that we don't notice it. As you drive across town singing along with their jingles on the radio, you will probably see several billboards advertising fast food specials; as you watch TV, you will see commercials showing lean, healthy people munching on high-fat burgers; as you walk through the children's toy departments, you think nothing of seeing McKids Adventure DVDs, drive-through play carts, or french fry backpacks. And with the sheer density of the restaurants themselves lining America's main streets, it is convenient to pull into a drive-through at a minute's notice and order the meal deal of the week.

Fast Food Nation by Eric Schlosser (2002) brings some startling facts about the fast food industry to the attention of American citizens. The industry, with roots in southern California, has swept across the nation; fast food restaurants are found not only on the highways and byways of our society but in places such as airports, schools, Wal-Marts, gas stations, cruise ships, and even hospital cafeterias. As a society, we are certainly responding to all these salient food cues: Whereas in 1970 Americans spent around $6 billion on fast food, today we spend closer to $118 billion. Obviously, fast food is big business; in 1997, Burger King launched a whopper of an advertising campaign—$70 million—to

simply promote the supremacy of their french fries over those of their competitors. It's a sobering fact that Americans now spend more on fast food than on higher education.

But it's not only fast food restaurants that are influencing our eating habits; more and more Americans are eating out at table-service restaurants as well. The event of dining out has evolved from a rare occurrence in past generations to a common practice today. Whereas Americans spent about 19% of their "food" money eating out in some type of restaurant in the 1950s, today we spend closer to 41%, including $100 billion on non-fast food restaurants and cafeterias.

Another book written for popular consumption, titled *Restaurant Confidential* by Michael F. Jacobson and Jayne Hurley (2002) of the Center for Science in the Public Interest, illuminates the effective strategies utilized by the restaurant and fast food industry. In the past several decades, both plates and portions have become bigger, resulting in our waistlines getting bigger. An extreme example of increasing portions can be seen with soda size. In the 1950s, sodas were dispensed in 8-ounce servings; today 7-Eleven sells the Big Gulp, which is a hefty 32 ounces, and if that isn't large enough, their Double Big Gulp is 64 ounces and 768 calories. As restaurants spend minimal resources making the food irresistible with extra-large portions, our fat consumption skyrockets. Seemingly unaware of the caloric consequences, Americans are slurping up 1,160-calorie vanilla triple-thick milkshakes at McDonald's and wolfing down 2,000-calorie fried onions at their favorite neighborhood restaurant.

In the documentary *Super Size Me*, Morgan Spurlock conducted an interesting experiment by placing himself on a diet consisting of only McDonald's food for 1 month and limiting his exercise to that of an average American. An expanding waistline was the least of his worries: In addition to gaining 25 pounds, he became lethargic, showed signs of depression and food addiction, significantly increased his cholesterol levels, and developed potentially serious liver problems.

Kelly Brownell, director of the Rudd Center for Food Policy and Obesity at Yale University and, along with Katherine Horgen, author of the book *Food Fight* (2004), is aware of the health consequences of our ever increasing propensity to dine out in restaurants. He and his students are also trying to make the public aware of the consequences of unhealthy eating, claiming that in the absence of high-fat food and high rates of inactivity, there would be virtually no obesity (Brownell, 2002a, 2002b). But while rates of food consumption are increasing, exercise is decreasing; the U.S. surgeon general's report recently stated that 60% of American adults fail to get enough daily exercise. Consequently, according to the National Center for Health Statistics, about 60% of Americans are overweight. Brownell and his students are painfully aware that the increased portions costing merely pennies to the food vendors will result in billions of dollars in health-related costs as our overweight society ages. Additionally, psychological costs emerge as overweight individuals find themselves the targets of discrimination. The team observed that seemingly harmless "before and after" weight-reduction advertisements promoted the perception that overweight people are lazy or lack enough self-control to look like the "after" picture in the advertisements. Constant reminders of an inability to accomplish the weight loss demonstrated by all the smiling models in these ads promote low self-esteem in overweight people (Geier, Schwartz, & Brownell, 2003).

Because obesity is very difficult to treat, Brownell feels that the current eating crisis cries out for prevention, and he is attempting to change public policy concerning the eating industry. By doing so, Brownell is moving away from the medical model, in which the individual is investigated for reasons for his or her obesity, to a public-health model that considers why our nation is obese. This public-health model has led him straight to the influence of the environment. Brownell and his colleagues and students are gearing up to fight the food industry. When asked about the daunting task of going head-to-head with such a powerful foe, Brownell explained: "Twenty years ago the same could have been said about challenging the tobacco industry—but look at how public opinion has changed about the health consequences of smoking" (Brownell, personal communication, 2003). Currently, Brownell has six policy proposals in mind: (1) enhancing opportunities for physical activity, (2) regulating food advertisements targeted to children, (3) removing fast foods and soft drinks from schools, (4) restructuring school lunch programs, (5) subsidizing the purchase of healthy foods, and (6) taxing foods that have poor nutritional value.

Although some of the topics covered in this text may be difficult for you to relate to personally, this chapter discusses a behavior that is near and dear to us all—EATING. Eating is such a common daily occurrence that most of us do it almost unconsciously—food is there, we eat it, and that is that. This behavior, however, is anything but simple; a multitude of variables contribute to the likelihood that you will eat a particular food at a certain time. As you will learn in this chapter, several neurochemicals, such as leptin and neuropeptide Y, play a role in the amount of hunger we experience at any given moment as they interact with specific areas of the brain. Further, our environment and past learning history contribute significantly to this process.

How many times have you eaten because it was the established time to eat (not because you were hungry) or because it was courteous for you to eat a meal (even if you didn't especially like the food)? Certainly, these environmental and cultural variables play a role in this important behavior. Not surprisingly, aspects of our well-established hunger-regulation system can easily malfunction, producing a disruption of homeostasis and possibly severe sickness leading to death. Malfunctions come in many varieties—eating too much, not eating enough, and eating and then purging the body of the food. In this chapter we will discuss the current findings related to eating regulation and the evolutionary context in which these behaviors developed. Why include a chapter on eating regulation in a text about mental health? As discussed in Chapters 5 and 9, food affects moods and serves as a precursor for neurochemicals. You learned in the Connections section that obesity may be related to psychological problems (such as low self-esteem), and as we will discuss throughout this chapter, unhealthy eating behavior can lead to illness and even death. Thus, it is important to understand the most salient factors related to this life-sustaining behavior.

EATING REGULATION

Before we get to the variables related to eating disorders, it is important to understand the fundamental neurobiological factors that regulate eating in healthy animals. After describing the classic Washburn and Cannon investigation of stomach factors involved in hunger (and subsequent research), neuroanatomical, neurochemical, and environmental factors will be described.

Early Hunger Research Was Difficult to Swallow

The earliest research on hunger focused on the digestive system, an expansive network of storage organs and tubules situated inside the abdominal area. Once food enters the mouth, it travels down the esophagus to the stomach and then passes through the duodenum and small and large intestines before making its exit via the anus (Figure 14.1). At many of the digestive stops along the way, enzymes are mixed with the food to aid in the process. As the food passes through the digestive system, certain substrates, such as fats, proteins, simple sugars, electrolytes, and water, are absorbed at various sites before the excess food remnants are discharged from the body.

Without fail, when students are asked how they know they are hungry, their first responses are related to the stomach in some way. They report that their stomachs growl, grumble, or just feel empty. Thus, it is not surprising that one of the earliest hunger experiments focused on the role of the activity of the stomach in initiating hunger. In this creative experiment, conducted by W. B. Cannon and A. L. Washburn in 1912, the researchers investigated the notion that the activity of the stomach dubbed "stomach pangs" constituted the hunger signal. To support this notion, Washburn swallowed a balloon that was later inflated. As can be seen in Figure 14.2, the balloon was connected to a recording device that was sensitive to any movement of air or contractions within the stomach or balloon. Additionally, Washburn was instructed to press a button each time he felt a hunger craving. Sure enough, stomach pangs coincided with the movement of air in the balloon—when the stomach contracted, a hunger pang was felt.

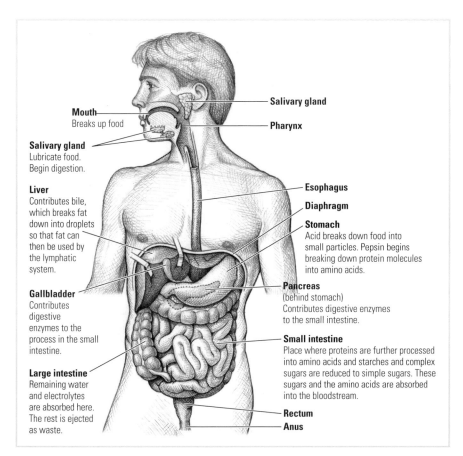

Mouth
Breaks up food

Salivary gland
Lubricate food.
Begin digestion.

Liver
Contributes bile,
which breaks fat
down into droplets
so that fat can
then be used by
the lymphatic
system.

Gallbladder
Contributes
digestive
enzymes to the
process in the small
intestine.

Large intestine
Remaining water
and electrolytes
are absorbed here.
The rest is ejected
as waste.

Salivary gland

Pharynx

Esophagus

Diaphragm

Stomach
Acid breaks down food into
small particles. Pepsin begins
breaking down protein molecules
into amino acids.

Pancreas
(behind stomach)
Contributes digestive enzymes
to the small intestine.

Small intestine
Place where proteins are further processed
into amino acids and starches and complex
sugars are reduced to simple sugars. These
sugars and the amino acids are absorbed
into the bloodstream.

Rectum

Anus

**Figure 14.1
Human digestive system**

AFTER PINEL (2000)

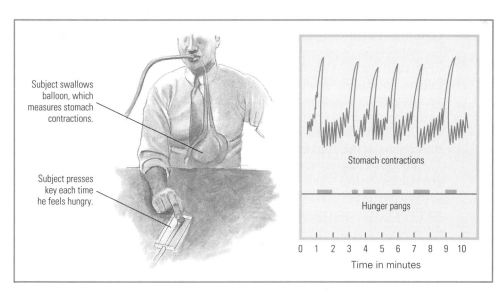

Subject swallows
balloon, which
measures stomach
contractions.

Subject presses
key each time
he feels hungry.

Stomach contractions

Hunger pangs

Time in minutes

**Figure 14.2
Hunger pangs and stomach contractions** Diagram of Washburn and Cannon's crude experiment
that involved swallowing a balloon that would be sensitive to the contractions of the stomach. As
seen on the graph, the hunger pangs coincided with stomach contractions.

AFTER MYERS (2004)

For decades researchers felt that the mystery to hunger had been solved—it was the movement of the stomach that prompted us to go to the kitchen to make ourselves a snack. But there was a small problem with these conclusions. In 1959, another team of researchers used abdominal electrodes to record the stomach's activity and found that the stomach is actually at its quietest when it is empty. Davis, Garafalo, and Kveim (1959) repeated Washburn and Cannon's experiment but replaced the step of swallowing a balloon with merely recording the movement of the stomach with electrodes positioned on the skin outside the stomach. In this situation, the stomach was found to be the least active during times of hunger or food deprivation. In retrospect, it was obvious that the movement of the stomach in Cannon and Washburn's experiment was an artifact of having a balloon placed in it- the stomach was merely trying to digest the balloon. Additional contradictory evidence was the observation that many human patients who had their stomachs removed due to medical problems continued to report feelings of hunger and satiety (Pinel, 2003). Thus, it was concluded that the activity of the stomach played a minimal role in triggering hunger.

At this point you may be a bit confused. After hearing this historical review, most of our students throw their hands in the air and report that their stomachs do indeed become active when they are hungry; after all, most everyone has experienced the embarrassment of a growling stomach during an otherwise quiet moment. This is a good point that shouldn't be overlooked. Keep reading—we'll come back to this question later in the chapter.

Neurobiology of Hunger Regulation

In the 1940s, investigations of the brain's role in hunger began. Researchers found that animals become *hyperphagic* (they eat too much) after receiving bilateral lesions in their **ventromedial hypothalamus (VMH)** (Hetherington & Ranson, 1940). After a few weeks of eating everything in sight, known as the *dynamic phase*, their eating declines a bit as they enter the *static phase* of hunger alteration. In 1951, researchers found that delivering bilateral lesions to the **lateral hypothalamus (LH)** severely restricted hunger and thirst in an animal. Unless an experimenter intervened, the animal would die of starvation (Anand & Brobeck, 1951). Subsequently, an influential article written by Stellar (1954) proposed the **dual-centers hypothesis of hunger regulation**; specifically, one nucleus of the hypothalamus was the hunger center, while another was the satiety center.

Although these roles of the VMH and LH are taught to virtually every general psychology student, it's becoming evident that the initial conclusions derived from the experiments have been a bit distorted from the actual truth. As Pinel (2003) points out, recent evidence suggests that, rather than being a satiety center, the hypothalamus plays a significant role in energy metabolism. It is now thought that the VMH-lesioned rats overate because the altered metabolism made them become obese. Specifically, the VMH lesion altered the amount of insulin levels in the blood, which increased the amount of body fat and decreased the number of usable forms of energy. Thus, the rat had to increase food consumption to maintain appropriate levels of energy. A side effect of the brain surgery, however, was increased body fat.

Additionally, a close investigation of the neuroanatomy of the hypothalamus reveals that a large fiber bundle known as the **noradrenergic bundle**

---

ventromedial hypothalamus (VMH) Brain area which, when lesioned in rats, caused the rats to become hyperphagic. Initially dubbed the "satiety center," it is now believed to be involved in energy metabolism.

lateral hypothalamus (LH) Brain area which, when lesioned in rats, caused the rats to become hypophagic and to die unless the experimenter assisted with feeding. In addition to diminishing hunger, LH lesions decrease general motivation.

dual-centers hypothesis of hunger regulation Proposed by Stellar in 1954, the VMH was considered the hunger center and the LH was the satiety center.

noradrenergic bundle Bundle of fibers originating in the locus coeruleus of the brain stem that travel to limbic and cortical structures. These noradrenergic fibers have been strongly associated with brain reward and arousal.

passes through the VMH and is probably critical to maintaining hunger levels. A neighboring nucleus of the hypothalamus, the **paraventricular nucleus (PVN)**, is currently receiving more attention as the critical nucleus of the hypothalamus involved in hunger regulation (see Figure 14.3 for the anatomical locations of the LH, VMH, and PVN). More information about the role of the PVN will be presented in the section on neurochemical factors. Current research on LH lesions suggests that there are so many deficits associated with these lesions—ranging from motor deficits to a lack of responsiveness—that concluding that the LH is specifically related to eating satiety is somewhat like suggesting that a person in a coma isn't responding due to a lack of interest.

Another classic line of research in hunger regulation was the consideration of the role of glucose in triggering the exact amount of motivation an animal should have to consume additional energy. After all, glucose is an important fuel for both the body and the brain. The brain would be particularly sensitive to declining levels of this precious fuel. In accordance with this line of thinking, Jean Mayer (1953) proposed that the delivery of glucose to the body's cells was the key factor in hunger motivation. When insulin levels were high, animals did not eat; and when they were low, animals ate. After noting that individuals with diabetes, who had high circulating levels of glucose, were constantly hungry, Mayer modified his theory to include the criterion that the glucose had to be metabolized in the cells before influencing hunger, or the **glucose utilization theory of hunger regulation** (Mayer, 1955). Once diabetics are given insulin, their glucose is utilized by their body's cells and their hunger subsides.

Neurochemical Factors

Today, the focus in hunger-regulation research is on the neurochemical and neuroendocrine signals produced by various states of hunger and satiety. In the body's periphery, the actions of glucose and cholecystokinin will be discussed. In the central nervous system, the influences of neuropeptide Y and leptin will be covered.

Glucose. Although the initial excitement about the glucostatic theory waned as a result of research suggesting that glucose levels varied little during normal life conditions (LeMagnen, 1981), more recent research suggests

paraventricular nucleus
Nucleus of the hypothalamus thought to be more intimately involved in hunger regulation than the VMH and LH.

glucose utilization theory of hunger regulation Proposed by Jean Mayer, this theory suggested that hunger was more influenced by the level of glucose metabolization in the cells than circulating levels of glucose.

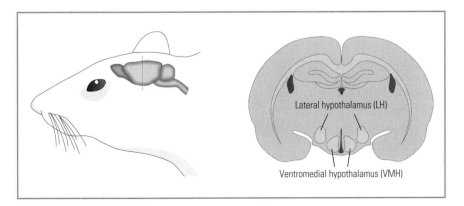

Lateral hypothalamus (LH)

Ventromedial hypothalamus (VMH)

Figure 14.3
Hypothalamic feeding centers
Coronal section of a rat brain showing the ventromedial, lateral, and paraventricular areas of the hypothalamus.
AFTER PINEL (2003)

cholecystokinin (CCK)
Gastrointestinal peptide released following ingestion of a meal in order to coordinate different functions of the digestive system.

leptin Neurochemical produced in fat cells and detected by receptors in the brain. Genetically obese mice (*ob/ob*) deficient in leptin are extremely overweight, and the obesity is diminished by exogenous injections of leptin.

that alterations in glucose may indeed be meaningful. In studies conducted by Campfield and Smith (1986, 1990), rats were housed individually in cages where they had free access to food and water. As previously described, the baseline glucose level rarely varies more than 1%–2% over long periods of time but prior to a spontaneous meal, the glucose level drops for about 12–20 minutes. Once the glucose level drops to about 12% below baseline, it starts to increase and, within a matter of minutes, the rat approaches the food bin for a meal (Figure 14.4). Providing stronger evidence for these findings, Campfield and Smith have shown that rats also eat following pharmacologically induced decreases in glucose that mimic the natural pattern of fluctuation.

Cholecystokinin. Cholecystokinin (CCK) is a gastrointestinal peptide that is released following ingestion of a meal to coordinate different functions of the digestive process. When administered to both humans and other animals, CCK reduces meal size (Leibowitz, 1992). This substance has a short half-life. In rodents, CCK needs to be administered within 2 minutes of the meal; a longer duration, say 15 minutes, will not have an effect on meal size (Gibbs, Young, & Smith, 1973). Further research suggests that the satiety effect of CCK is abolished when the vagal nerve is cut (also known as *vagal deafferentation*) but remains intact in the decerebrate rat model (the rat's cerebrum has been removed), suggesting that the CCK effect is mediated by an interaction of the vagal nerve and the brain stem. Additionally, two CCK receptors have been identified. The specific nature of CCK's effects, however, is controversial; some researchers have suggested that CCK's suppression of appetite may be due to increased nausea rather than a decrease in feelings of hunger (Baldwin, Parrott, & Ebenezer, 1998).

Leptin. Although a "satiety" signal had long been proposed, the neurochemical **leptin** seemed as if it might be the critical factor that prompts an animal to feel full and cease eating. The leptin story goes back to the 1950s when a genetic mutation occurred that resulted in very obese mice that weighed up to three times more than their normal-weight counterparts. The mutated mice were called *ob/ob* because they were homozygous recessive for

Figure 14.4
Fluctuations in glucose across feeding episodes Graph showing the time course of glucose declines in a rat and the initiation of a meal. As the glucose begins to rise following the initial drop, the animal moves to the food bin to begin a meal.
WOODS AND STRUBBE (1994, FIGURE 3, P. 148)

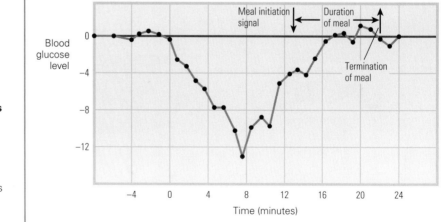

the mutant *ob* gene (pictured in Figure 14.5 are examples of obese rat models demonstrating similar principles). These overweight mice ate considerably more than their normal-weight siblings and were very efficient at converting their calories into fat. After the *ob/ob* gene was cloned, it became apparent that the fat cells produced the protein leptin, from the Greek word *lepos*, meaning "thin" (Blum, 1997; Pinel, 2003). This hormone is also produced by the stomach, mammary glands, ovarian follicles, and fetal organs such as the heart, bone, and cartilage (Austin and Marks, 2009). When leptin was merely injected into *ob/ob* animals, their weight decreased, with no apparent side effects. Thus, in the leptin-deficient mouse, the exogenous administration of leptin counters obesity. In accordance with the original dual-centers theory of hunger regulation, abundant levels of leptin receptors have been found in the VMH (Williams et al., 2001). But what about humans? Although it is true that leptin-deficient overweight patients would benefit from the administration of this fat regulator, very few such patients exist (it is estimated that about 5% of obese individuals are leptin-deficient to some degree [Sinha & Caro, 1998]. In fact, most overweight individuals are far from leptin-deficient: They have high levels of leptin. It has been suggested that these obese people have an impaired sensitivity to leptin (Blum, 1997).

In one study, 23 overweight male and female subjects agreed to participate in a strict diet program for 10 weeks. After about 4 weeks, leptin levels dropped significantly and increased only slightly for the duration of the program. If leptin works in humans as it does in the animal models, this reduction would stimulate appetite and reduce the subjects' energy expenditures, two factors that would not contribute to a successful diet. Perhaps leptin decreases are responsible for the many unsuccessful attempts people have with diets (Scholz et al., 1996). In the future, more information related to variables associated with leptin receptor sensitivity may be useful in the battle against obesity.

Neuropeptide Y. Neuropeptide Y (NPY) is a pancreatic polypeptide and an abundant neurotransmitter in the mammalian brain. Most NPY neurons are located in the **arcuate nucleus (ARC)** of the hypothalamus, which lies at the base of the third ventricle. Additionally, NPY has been found in the paraventricular area of the hypothalamus around the third ventricle, the suprachiasmatic nucleus, and the supraoptic nucleus. In addition to its involvement in functions such as memory processing and the regulation of blood pressure, NPY is known for its ability to stimulate eating and reduce an animal's expenditure of energy—the perfect formula for obesity. Just a nanomolar dose of NPY into a rat's ventricles can stimulate eating, and multiple NPY injections induce obesity. Likely candidates for NPY's role in obesity include decreased nonshivering thermogenesis and enhanced formation of triglyceride deposits (Williams et al., 2001). Adding to the complexity of NPY's role in obesity is the observation that there are six types of NPY receptors (Balasubramaniam, 1997).

It appears that the NPY neurons are sensitive to depleted energy stores. Once an animal's energy reserves drop (as seen in starvation, lactation, and insulin-dependent diabetes), the neurons become overactive, apparently initiating feeding and more efficient metabolic responses to conserve energy. For example, animals with depleted energy reserves will engage in food-seeking behavior at the cost of other behaviors that may be related to regulating

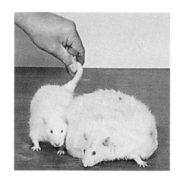

Figure 14.5
Obese *ob/ob* rat and control rat

PINEL (2003, P. 319)

neuropeptide Y (NPY)
Pancreatic polypeptide that is one of the most abundant neurotransmitters in the mammalian brain; NPY stimulates eating and reduces energy expenditure.

arcuate nucleus (ARC)
Nucleus of the hypothalamus where most of the NPY neurons are located.

fat storage, such as thermogenesis (Williams et al., 2001). The observations that NPY gene expression increases prior to food intake and that diabetes-induced hunger is reduced by anti-NPY antibody injections provide support for the stated relationship between NPY and eating (Fuxe, Tinner, Caberlotto, Bunnemann, & Agnati, 1997; Sahu, Sninsky, & Kalra, 1997). Further, doses of leptin that reduce eating have been found to reduce mRNA production in NPY neurons in the PVN and ARC (Baskin et al., 1999).

Researchers at the Institute of Experimental Medicine in Budapest, Hungary (a fitting location for eating research!), found that in the human brain the corticotropin-releasing hormone (CRH) neurons' perikarya and dendrites were coaligned with the axons of the NPY neurons in the hypothalamus (Mihaly, Fekete, Lechan, & Liposits, 2002). These data suggest that the NPY neurons are regulating CRH neurons in the human hypothalamus, implying that some of the effects of NPY on eating regulation are mediated through the CRH system. As you'll recall, additional information related to the integration of NPY in coping responses was discussed in Chapter 13.

Another study reported increased levels of NPY in diabetic women but no differences between obese women and controls (Milewicz, Mikulski, & Bidzinska, 2000). Corroborating these findings, Goldstone, Unmehopa, Bloom, and Swaab (2002) failed to find immunocytochemical evidence of altered NPY in obese autopsied subjects, suggesting that the subjects were responding appropriately to peripheral levels of NPY.

Another connection between NPY and hunger regulation is related to the interesting observation that *calorie restriction* (restricting calorie intake by 10%–40%) leads to a prolonged life span. Because calorie restriction raises NPY levels in the ARC, this neuropeptide has been proposed as a neurochemical correlate of this antiaging effect. Thus, some of the downstream effects of NPY activation accompanying a "starvation-type response," such as increased and decreased secretion of various hormones, may prompt the body to enter an adaptive mode that enhances resilience in specific ways, slowing the aging process (Minor, Chang, & Cabo, 2009). Living longer is an attractive benefit, but the cost—decades of feeling hungry—makes it an unrealistic option for most people.

Ghrelin, another hormone known as an appetite stimulant, is produced in the stomach, small intestine, brain (hypothalamus and pituitary gland), pancreas, reproductive organs, kidney, and immune cells (Austin & Marks, 2009). Recently, researchers have made an important observation about the actual trigger of this hunger hormone. Although ghrelin has been thought to accumulate before meals, triggering hunger, research suggests that food itself may be a critical trigger. Ghrelin requires an enzyme (i.e., ghrelin *O*-acyl-transferase, or GOAT) to add a fatty acid prior to activation. Interestingly, the essential fatty acids required for ghrelin activation come directly from the fat we ingest (a wonderful example of an external factor related to hunger). This new information suggests that, instead of being a hunger stimulator, ghrelin is a fat sensor in the stomach that tells the brain when calories are available, triggering the green light for energy-dependent processes such as growth (Castaneda, Tong, Datta, Culler, & Tschop, 2010). Accordingly, ghrelin is also known for its function as growth hormone–releasing hormone (Austin & Marks, 2009). When interviewed about these fascinating findings, University of Cincinnati researcher Matthias Tschop said, "When exposed to certain fatty foods, mice with more GOAT gain more fat. Mice without GOAT gain less fat since their brain does not receive the 'fats are here, store them' signal" (*Science Daily*, 2009).

Thus, several neurochemicals have been associated with eating and hunger. The utilization of glucose and the release of leptin from the fat cells of the body generally suppress eating, whereas NPY and ghrelin are generally associated with increases in eating. This chapter is by no means comprehensive in its coverage of possible neurochemical influences on hunger—other neurochemicals such as **orexins** and intestinal hormones such as oxyntomodulin are also receiving attention in the eating literature (Cai et al., 2002; Wu & Kral, 2004; Austin & Marks, 2009).

Although the neurochemicals covered here appear to be intimately involved with hunger regulation in animal models (Table 14.1), their effect on human consumption is uncertain, a real challenge to the pharmaceutical industry. This industry continues to search for the panacea drug that will enable people to control their appetites. Because of the complexity of the interactions among these neurochemicals and the strong propensity for compensation in the brain and body, such a drug will undoubtedly require an ingredient that will interact with several neurochemicals. With so many factors involved in hunger regulation, several hunger and satiety signals would likely have to be altered before a disruption of the process would occur.

> **orexins** Neuropeptides that are secreted from the lateral hypothalamic neurons and involved in eating, arousal, and other motivated behaviors. Administration of orexins to the central nervous system results in increased food intake.

Environmental Factors

In addition to levels of specific neurochemicals in the brain, factors in the environment can have a meaningful impact on hunger and satiety. In the obesity section, we will consider the importance of our contemporary lifestyles, steeped in high-fat fast food and low activity levels. As you will read, these factors play a huge role in the amount and type of food we consume. Additionally, de Castro and colleagues (2007) at Sam Houston State University have conducted some interesting research on the role of social factors on one's appetite. Their research has utilized a unique source of data collection, personal diaries that students have kept in which they report their eating behavior and associated contexts day after day. Their work generally suggests that we eat larger meals when we eat with others. The more people we eat with, the more we eat. Although students report that they eat less when they're around others (as is the case when you're on a first date), the opposite is true. Eat with a small group and you'll eat about 44% more; eat with a large group and you'll consume about 76% more food (Gauntt, 2009). Possible explanations for these findings include the notions

These Alaskan Eskimo children are enjoying a whale blubber snack.

Table 14.1 **Neurochemicals and Related Functions**

Neurochemical	General Function
Glucose	Animals tend to eat following a drop in glucose levels
Cholecystokinin	Reduces meal size; leads to satiety
Leptin	As levels decrease, eating is stimulated
Neuropeptide Y	Stimulates eating and reduces energy expenditure

that friends (1) increase arousal and therefore food intake, (2) relax our vigilant monitoring of the amount of food we're consuming as well as the duration of time we spend eating, and (3) increase competitiveness for the available food.

Do the diaries reveal other weight-reduction tips? de Castro (2007) recently reported that subjects whose intake was relatively higher in the morning ate fewer calories throughout the day. Late-night eating, on the contrary, was correlated with higher daily consumption of calories.

Prior associations influence our motivation to eat certain foods. A food always served by your grandmother as she showered you with her unconditional adoration may be appealing for the duration of your life. On the other hand, foods associated with illness are likely to be avoided throughout life (Garcia, Kimmeldorf, & Koelling, 1995). When I (K. G. L.) was a child, a neighbor made a casserole with water chestnuts in it. The crisp texture of water chestnuts in a casserole was foreign to me, so later that evening, when I got sick, I quickly attributed my sickness to the water chestnuts because they stood out so clearly in my mind. Three decades later, I'm still avoiding water chestnuts, even though I know it was a stomach flu—not the water chestnuts—that made me ill.

EVOLUTIONARY THEORIES OF HUNGER REGULATION

Now that we have covered some of the fundamentals of hunger research, in this section we will consider some of the theories concerning how eating behaviors and physiological systems evolved. As with most topics in this text, understanding the roots of the behavior may enhance our knowledge of hunger regulation.

Set-Point Theory

set-point theory of hunger regulation Theory suggesting that animals are motivated to eat when food energy levels drop below a particular level.

lipostatic theory of hunger regulation Early eating-regulation theory that proposed that some fuel or form of adipose tissue circulated throughout the blood and was interpreted by the brain so that current energy levels could be detected. If lipostatic measures were too high, it was theorized, the animal would cease eating. The defining lipostatic measure was never discovered.

The **set-point theory of hunger regulation** is one of the most widely accepted hunger/satiety theories. This theory is similar to basic supply-and-demand theories: When the food or energy level drops, the demand for food increases. Researchers have spent decades trying to find set-point signals—glucose, insulin, or some hypothesized fat metabolite, the last of which was initially proposed in Kennedy and Mayer's **lipostatic theory of hunger regulation** (Kennedy, 1953; Mayer, 1955). As we discussed in the last section, more refined players such as leptin and NPY are currently being considered. Whereas this approach seems perfectly reasonable, set-point theory has serious flaws (Pinel, Assandt, & Lehman, 2000). First, if our bodies were designed to respond to current energy supply, how do we explain the fact that over half our population is overweight? Or the fact that some individuals, such as anorexic patients, fail to respond to demand signals for increased food consumption? If there is a set-point signal, the reception seems to be more than a bit off because our society is plagued with a variety of eating disorders.

Second, if one considers the evolution of human eating, our ancestors did not have the luxury of easy food accessibility. In fact, the availability of food was quite unpredictable; consequently, to survive, it was important to consume food as it was available and to store it as fat—people never knew where the next meal would come from. The individuals who ceased eating to rub their bellies and let out their loincloths a notch once they had reached their set point would not have endured long winters or periods of drought. Warm-blooded animals require significant amounts of food to maintain thermoregulation, and it is illogical for our bodies to have evolved to respond only to deficits—once a real deficit is detected, the animal is in a critical state. A better design would be to use precautions against ever reaching the level of energy depletion.

A third weakness of set-point theory is that although it has been around for over half a century, credible evidence for it is still lacking. Yes, people are hungry after being deprived of food, but deprivation is more extreme than the normal day-to-day fluctuations of energy levels. Apparently, about half our population has an excess of fat deposits and their eating is certainly not deterred by any set point of some particular molecule.

Preparatory Response Theory

Stephen Woods (University of Washington) and Jan Strubbe (University of Groningen in the Netherlands) wrote an interesting article in 1994 proposing the **preparatory response theory of hunger regulation**. Instead of thinking about hunger and all its associated cues as a system designed to *prompt* you to eat, the more immediate purpose may be to *prepare* your body for incoming food. Let's think about this for a minute. You're sitting there reading your textbook several hours after eating lunch. Everything is probably just fine with your digestive system and energy availability; however, if you should eat a large meal (a chunk of meat, several servings of vegetables, bread, and soda), your digestive system is suddenly thrown completely out of its resting state.

If a meal is invasively large—an all too common characteristic of our eating patterns—all the changes associated with it could threaten the body's physiological homeostasis. In fact, Woods (1991) views a large meal as a drug that is delivered to the body and, in the process of digestion, disrupts many precisely monitored homeostatic processes. A solution to this sudden turmoil of the digestive system is time to prepare for it. It makes perfect sense for the body to elevate its temperature to facilitate the digestive processes and decrease blood glucose levels prior to receiving a new energy load. The Russian physiologist Ivan Pavlov (1927) was one of the first to write about anticipatory responses of the digestive system. When his canine subjects perceived a cue that was associated with food, they started salivating—their mouths were preparing for the incoming food. The increase in insulin level prior to meals has also received a lot of research attention (Teff, Mattes, & Engelman, 1991). Strong support for the importance of premeal insulin secretion is the observation that, in the absence of the response, animals eat smaller meals, suggesting that this anticipatory function is necessary for the processing of food (Inoue, Bray, & Mullen, 1978). Also in support of this notion is a study in which rats given food at a standard time each day ate more than rats that missed their standard meal and were fed several hours later. The delayed-feeding group had gone longer without food and, according to the traditional hunger theories, should have eaten more; ironically, they ate less and more slowly (Bousfield & Elliott, 1934). The fact that their

preparatory response theory of hunger regulation Theory suggesting that the feeling of hunger may be more closely related to the body's preparation to eat than any deficit of food.

positive-incentive theory of hunger regulation Theory suggesting that people eat because it is a pleasurable, rewarding experience.

bodies were not allowed to prepare for the incoming food seemed to result in less consumption.

Before we leave the preparatory response theory, let's revisit the growling stomach. If the stomach is at its quietest when it has no food to digest, then why does it rumble at eating time? When food enters the stomach, the stomach engages in *peristalsis*, or the movement of the walls of the stomach to work the food down toward the intestines. In line with the preparatory response theory, we can propose that the empty, growling stomach is merely "warming up" in preparation for its next workout. The sound is present because the stomach is unfilled and the muscle walls make a noise as they rub against one another. In support of this preparatory growling hypothesis is the notion that the stomach has been conditioned to engage in this movement at a particular time every day. You can confirm this with your own gastric "vocalizations." Try an experiment on yourself: The next time your stomach begins growling preceding a time when you usually eat a meal, just skip the meal and record your stomach's activity. If your stomachs are like ours, instead of becoming increasingly intense as mealtime passes (and your system becoming even more depleted), the growling typically subsides—until the next time you typically eat a meal. So you may feel hungry when your stomach is growling because, based on your routine, it is time to eat.

Positive Incentive Theory

How do you explain the fact that after just eating two portions of everything at the all-you-can-eat buffet at your favorite restaurant you salivate when the dessert tray comes around?

In fact, the only factor that stops your consumption is the physical discomfort you experience as you finish your dessert. The **positive incentive theory of hunger regulation**—we eat because it is a pleasurable, rewarding experience—suggests that humans and other warm-blooded animals evolved to eat to their physiological capacity.

Historically, excessive eating behavior would have been adaptive in food-replete times. In these times of readily available food, however, this food strategy has had severe effects on weight and health. For example, as we have stated repeatedly, overeating and obesity have reached epidemic levels in many wealthy societies—one recent study reports that 64.5% of the population of the United States, that is 127 million people, are overweight (Brownell & Horgen, 2004). As food has become more plentiful in our environment, the rate of obesity has grown at an alarmingly rapid pace. Not only is eating in general a pleasurable response, but particular tastes that, in nature, promote human survival seem especially pleasing (Pinel, Assanand, & Lehman, 2000). For example, humans especially like foods that taste sweet, fatty, and salty; interestingly, these foods are naturally rich in energy and essential minerals and vitamins. We do not desire many bitter substances because that taste is often naturally associated with poison.

In a society in which there is a never-ending supply of sweet, fatty, and salty foods, it is easy to see why the rates of consumption are skyrocketing. The empirical research suggests that nonhuman animals also are strongly influenced by the positive incentive of taste. Rogers and Blundell (1980) placed laboratory rats on a diet in which two palatable foods, bread and chocolate, were available. According to depletion models of eating, the rats should have maintained their consumption rates; but that was not the case. The caloric intake of the rats increased by 84%, resulting in a 50% weight gain over a period of 4 months. Alternatively, when Brandes (1977) diminished the positive incentive associated with eating by flavoring the rats' food with the bitter-tasting quinine, the rats decreased their eating and, even when made hypoglycemic with insulin injections, they continued to reduce their consumption rates. Clearly, the rats in these studies were responding not only to physiological need but to taste.

Why would nature do this to us? If the foods to which we are most attracted are rich in calories, fat, salt, and sugar, our battle of the bulge will be never-ending. It would be so nice to find foods such as carrots and broccoli irresistible—we'd be lean and loaded with lots of antioxidants for our aging brains! As previously suggested, our craving for foods such as movie popcorn and chocolate-covered raisins can be traced to our evolutionary roots. As warm-blooded animals, our ancestors needed to spend a large portion of the day making sure that they ate an adequate amount of food, especially sufficient amounts of sweet, fatty, and salty foods. Additionally, because they never knew when and where their next meal was going to be, it was adaptive for them to eat as much as they could to protect against some future food-scarce incident.

Those of us who live in times of feast as opposed to famine have ample opportunity to maximize our eating capacity. In fact, just to give you an idea about the degree of excess energy stores in contemporary humans, a lean human has enough stored energy to meet the body's energy requirements for a month, average-sized persons can store energy for up to 2 months, and overweight individuals are typically packing enough energy insurance for more than a year. Obviously, our evolutionary roots are at odds with our contemporary situation. If you are unhappy with the amount of excess weight you are carrying around, recall that obese people in today's society probably would have been the individuals most likely to survive in a more natural environment due to their ability to eat large amounts of food when it was available and to store it for further use. The restraint exercised by lean individuals probably would have prevented them from surviving the first period of low food availability.

Thus, the positive incentive theory helps to explain why, in an environment of readily available foods rich in fat and calories, our population is getting heavier and heavier. This theory also explains the findings from another study, which showed that, when faced with access to a large supply of a preferred food, 81% of the subjects typically ate until they felt ill (Assanand, Pinel, & Lehman, 1996).

Sensory-Specific Satiety

This theory addresses the types of food we consume. It is daunting to think that over the course of our eating we need to make sure that we consume all of the essential nutrients required for healthy living. Barbara Rolls of Penn State University proposed the **sensory-specific theory of satiety** to help us understand our eating habits when faced with food options (Rolls, 1986). Think about your favorite food for a moment. Is it french fries? Chocolate cake? Pizza? Filet mignon? Whale blubber? You might eat a favorite food until you felt miserable, but would you do so if you could eat only your favorite food? If you're like most people, after just a few meals of your favorite food your consumption would decrease and your motivation to find another food would increase.

sensory-specific theory of satiety Theory suggesting that animals are motivated to consume a different taste after previously eating to satiety; this hypothesis explains why animals and humans placed on a diverse cafeteria diet frequently overeat.

According to Rolls, another evolutionary pressure in eating regulation was consumption of a variety of foods to ensure the consumption of dietary nutrients required for survival. This theory helps explain why, after eating a large portion of your favorite food—to the point of refusing any more—your eyes light up when a different food is offered to you. It also explains why increased variation in food leads to enhanced consumption—to confirm this, just spend time at your local all-you-can-eat restaurant and observe the patrons' rate of consumption—and body weight.

Sensory-specific satiety seems to be influenced by the sensory properties of food rather than any gastric feedback from the food in the digestive system. Normal-weight subjects rated several commercially available foods prior to having the opportunity to eat one of these foods as a meal. After just 2 minutes of eating the food, its pleasantness rating started to decrease, whereas the pleasantness rating for the foods not being consumed remained unchanged. The pleasantness ratings were followed over the duration of an hour and the greatest decrease was 2 minutes following their consumption—when the sensory properties of the ingested food seem to diminish. Thus, in a meal, after eating a particular food for about 2 minutes, the subjects would be motivated to eat another type of food (Rolls, 1986). Perhaps this is the reason that some diets require the dieters to eat only a few types of food—or eat one type of food all day—all the grapefruit you can eat on Monday, all the pasta you can eat on Tuesday, and all the baked potatoes you want on Wednesday. After several bites, the desire—and consumption—diminishes. On the other hand, after finding that patients with amnesia would eat up to three lunches when offered intermittently throughout the lunch period, Rozin, Dow, Moscovitch, and Rajaram (1998) concluded that these patients were making decisions unrelated to gastrointestinal factors about whether or not to eat a meal because they had no memory of previously eating lunch.

DISORDERS OF EATING REGULATION

In this section we will consider three common disruptions of eating—obesity, anorexia nervosa, and bulimia nervosa. These conditions seem to be less about preexisting distortions of the neurobiological correlates of hunger/satiety than about the influence of a toxic eating environment and specific psychological variables. Hence, they might just as easily go into other chapters, such as the addiction or anxiety disorder chapters; but because they involve eating behavior, they are included in this chapter. There are no easy cures for these disruptions of eating, but we are learning more and more about them each day.

Obesity

obesity A state of being pathologically overweight due to both genetic and environmental factors. Technically one is considered obese if one's body mass index (BMI) is 30 kg/m2 or greater.

Obesity is considered a general medical condition in the *International Classification of Diseases*, but it isn't included in the *Diagnostic and Statistical Manual of Mental Disorders*, fourth edition, text revision (DSM-IV-TR), because of the lack of evidence suggesting that obesity is associated with a psychological or behavioral syndrome. Because **obesity** involves the behavior of eating too much and is often associated with feelings of insecurity and self-consciousness (psychological effects), we include this condition as an eating disorder.

Possible causes. If you type in the words "weight loss" in an Internet search engine, odds are you'll get over 150,000,000 hits. As you look through women's magazines, it is obvious that the female icon has become much slimmer than she was a half-century ago. Grocery stores are carrying many more fat-free and healthful food choices than they did a few decades ago. Fueled by a $30-billion dieting industry advocating the sales of diet books, videos, pills, and exercise devices, approximately 40% of women and 25% of men can be found to be dieting at any given time (Brownell & Rodin, 1994; Horm & Anderson, 1993; Serdula et al., 1993). So with a lot of general interest in losing weight, the social ideal of a slim physique, and many options for fat-free food, a sociologist could conclude that our society is now much leaner than it was a half-century ago. How in the world could a culture so obsessed with thinness and weight control be so—well—fat!

The psychological well-being of overweight individuals may be more vulnerable than originally thought; research is currently indicating discrimination against overweight individuals. For example, 28% of teachers conveyed that obesity was the worst thing that could happen to a person; 24% of nurses confessed to being repulsed by obese patients; and, also distressing, when grades and income variables are kept constant, parents provide less money for college for their overweight children than for their thin children (Puhl & Brownell, 2001). In addition to mental health costs, obesity is associated with a host of medical costs, including increased risk for diabetes type 2, hypertension, cardiovascular disease, and some cancers (Brownell & Rodin, 1994). Thus, we feel that there is ample reason to consider obesity as a legitimate eating disorder in this chapter.

With 34% of U.S. adults classified as obese and another 27% classified as overweight (i.e., 61% of U.S. adults overweight or obese), professionals in the field are describing the overweight condition of our society as an "epidemic" (Ogden, Yanovski, Carroll & Flegal, 2007; Brownell & Horgen, 2004). In fact, from 1900 to 1999, rates of obesity doubled (Brownell & Rodin, 1994; Flegal, Harlan, & Landis, 1988; National Center for Health Statistics, 1999). Considering the attention and resources devoted to losing weight, it is imperative that researchers determine the factors contributing to our ever-increasing

Figure 14.6
Tracking rates of adult obesity in the United States
Age-adjusted prevalence of overweight and obesity among U.S. adults, 20 years or older. The number of overweight and obese individuals is slowly rising each decade. Currently, more adults than not fall in one of these categories.

NATIONAL CENTER FOR HEALTH STATISTICS, HTTP:WWW.CDC.GOV/NCHS/PRODUCTS/PUBS/PUBD/HESTATS/OVER99FIG1.HTM, FLEGEL, CARROLL, OGDEN & CURTIN (2010)

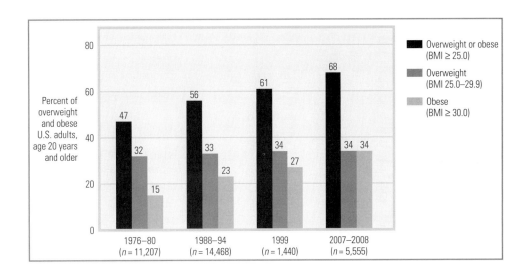

body weights. As described in the neurochemical section of this chapter, although neuropeptides such as leptin and NPY are certainly involved in hunger regulation, researchers have fallen short of identifying a neurochemical magic bullet to reduce the hunger or fat storage in overweight individuals. And although genetic mutations have produced obese rats and mice, these mutations are not the underlying cause of obesity in humans. Past research on genetic factors, for example, has indicated that 25%–40% of body-weight variability in the population can be attributed to genes that regulate factors such as metabolic rate and number of fat cells (Brownell & Horgen, 2004). However, Eric Stice (2002) of the University of Texas at Austin suggested that since obesity rates have increased from 4% to 30% in the last century and genes do not change that quickly, obesity must be behaviorally mediated. Even though genetic research may identify variables that make individuals susceptible to obesity, Fairburn and Brownell (2002) state the following:

> Searching for obesity genes in hopes of establishing cause may be akin to pursuit of a gene explaining lung cancer in smokers. True, the discovery might identify those most at risk and perhaps lead to ways to counteract the disastrous effects of tobacco, but the cause of the cancer is environmental. Removal of the toxin would eliminate most of the disease.

In keeping with the aims of this textbook we will emphasize the role of the brain in the epidemic of obesity and possible treatment and prevention of this condition. Instead of focusing on reductionist neurobiology, however, we will focus on the cognitive processing of information about eating behavior (which eventually influences neurobiological responses to food stimuli). For example, consider the following two examples of typical consumption in our fast-paced world of eating out:

Scenario A

Breakfast:	Cinnamon scone and a grande cappuccino with whole milk
Lunch:	Fast food meal with 6-ounce hamburger, large fries, and large Coke
Afternoon snack:	Cup of yogurt
Dinner:	12 buffalo wings with celery and ranch dressing as appetizer, Oriental chicken salad, 12-ounce beer
Late-night snack:	Chocolate chip cookie and 12-ounce glass of whole milk

Scenario B

Breakfast:	Cereal with reduced-fat milk, orange juice, slice of toast, fruit, caffe latte with skim milk
Lunch:	6-ounce roasted chicken breast sandwich, baked chips, diet soda
Dinner:	Minestrone soup, pasta with chicken and vegetables, two slices of bread, ice water with lemon, 8-ounce glass of white wine
Late-night snack:	Scoop of low-fat coffee fudge ice cream

As you consider each of the daily meal scenarios, it is obvious that scenario B is the lower in calories, but by how much? After all, in scenario A the person has a small breakfast, yogurt as a snack, and an appetizer and salad for dinner—that can't be too bad, can it? Well, brace yourself: There are more than twice the calories in scenario A than scenario B (scenario A has an estimated 4,830 calories, whereas scenario B has an estimated 2,300 calories). Worse, scenario A has 86% more fat than scenario B—265 grams and 38 grams of fat, respectively. It is recommended that one consume only 65 grams of fat in a 2,000-calorie diet (Jacobson & Hurley, 2002). This example shows that the toxicity of the eating environment in our society, coupled with the lack of rigorous exercise, produces a surefire recipe for obesity. Thus, changing these behaviors through education seems to be the most promising brain approach to the threat of obesity.

Treatment. As mentioned previously in this section, although several individual neurochemicals have been identified in the hunger/satiety literature, researchers have yet to develop a panacea to combat obesity. Several years ago, a drug known as fen-phen (a combination of fenfluramine and phentermine) hit the market and seemed to be a promising pharmaceutical agent against obesity. This drug increased the availability of both serotonin and noradrenaline and successfully increased weight loss, but it was withdrawn from the U.S. market in 1997 because of its association with abnormalities in the cardiac valves of adults (Jones et al., 2002; Volmar & Hutchins, 2001).

Although new neurochemicals are frequently identified in the literature as having promise for the pharmaceutical treatment of obesity, only a few drugs are currently approved for the long-term treatment of obesity. The drug sibutramine (Meridia) inhibits the reuptake of both norepinephrine and serotonin, and the drug orlistat (Xenical) blocks the enzyme lipase and increases the fecal loss of triglyceride. Clinical trials indicate that these drugs produce a 5%–10% decrease in body weight. These weight losses do not come without health costs—sibutramine has been associated with blood pressure increases, and orlistat has been associated with unappealing side effects such as wet flatulence, increased urge of bowel movement, incontinence of stool, and abdominal bloating (Bray, 2001). Other drugs, such as fluoxetine and phentermine, may be prescribed for obesity as well (Proietto, Fam, Ainslie, & Thorburn, 2000).

The behavioral interventions of reducing caloric and fat intake and increasing physical activity are additional options for treating obesity. Although early reports suggested that the effects of dieting were discouraging—only a small percentage of individuals could lose weight and keep it off (Stunkard & McLaren-Hume, 1959)—more recent studies offer more favorable results (Bjorvell & Rossner, 1992). It's probably no surprise that programs with low-calorie intake, a behavioral modification component, and an intensive education program offer very favorable long-term results (Beliard, Kirschenbaum, & Fitzgibbon, 1992; Nunn, Newton, & Faucher, 1992). As indicated by Brownell and Rodin (1994), it is important to consider the benefits of even modest success with weight-loss programs; small weight losses have been associated with medical benefits such as improved blood pressure and blood glucose control. Dieting and exercise, however, are not as easy to swallow as a pill per day, so patient enthusiasm for such programs is not exceedingly high.

liposuction Surgical technique used to extract fat from the body.

gastric bypass surgery (*also known as bariatric surgery***)** Surgery conducted in obese individuals to reduce the stomach to about 1% of its original capacity.

dumping syndrome Side effect sometimes seen in patients following gastric bypass surgery; syndrome consists of nausea or general sickness following the consumption of fat or sugar.

Drastic surgical measures are available for obese individuals. If a patient has a fat "trouble spot," the fat cells can literally be sucked out of the spot with the medical equivalent of a vacuum cleaner. This surgery, known as **liposuction**, became the most common procedure conducted by plastic surgeons (American Society of Plastic and Reconstructive Surgeons, 1990).

An even more drastic procedure, known as **gastric bypass surgery**, is becoming an attractive option for morbidly obese patients who have tried every weight-loss technique with no success. In gastric bypass surgery, the stomach is reduced to a tiny pouch about the size of a thumb (approximately 1% of the size of the preoperative stomach) and is reconnected with the intestines. As described in Box 14.1, obese patients can lose weight very quickly—generally 66% in 1–2 years—and the weight stays off in most patients (Holzwarth, Huber, Majkrzak, & Tareen, 2002). The surgery doesn't come without risks however. Box 14.1 highlights details of gastric bypass surgery, which has been called lifesaving by many health professionals.

A small group of health professionals remains cautious about submitting patients to such major surgery, especially considering some of the side effects experienced by a small percentage of patients (e.g., small-bowel obstructions, major leaks, and gallbladder disease) (Blachar, Federle, Pealer, Ikramuddin, & Schauer, 2002; Fobi et al., 2002). Further, because of the reduced number of calories consumed by gastric bypass patients and the reduced size of the stomach, the ability and opportunity for the absorption of vitamins are greatly reduced. In order to reduce the chances of micronutrient deficiencies, patients must take vitamins and supplements, especially to avoid deficiencies (Sugerman, 2001). Another annoying side effect is known as **dumping syndrome**—a feeling of nausea, vomiting, dizziness, and weakness that occurs if a bypass patient eats too much fat or sugar (Commonwealth Surgeons, 2002). But the side effects are not all bad. Gastric bypass surgery significantly improves hypertension, type 2 diabetes, and hyperlipidemia; additionally, symptoms of sleep apnea and depression often subside following surgery (Holzwarth et al., 2002). All in all, the benefits seem to outweigh the disadvantages, a fact noticed by health-insurance companies, which are covering bypass surgery at an increasing rate. It is worth noting that additional techniques such as the more recently Food and Drug Administration–approved adjustable gastric banding system (also known as "lap band") have been established to modify the volume of the gastric chamber with minimal surgical intervention (U.S. Food and Drug Administration, 2001).

Children and obesity. For an adult, losing weight is a long, involved process that involves lifelong changes in eating and rates of physical activity. Certainly, the best way to treat obesity is to prevent it from occurring in the first place. This brings us to the children of our society. If 60% of the adults are facing weight problems, does the future look better for our children? Let's consider some observations. On average, children in the United States see about 10,000 food advertisements per year, 95% of which are advertising sugared cereals, candy, soft drinks, and fast foods (Brownell, 2002b). The children's menu at most restaurants perpetuates the consumption of high-calorie, high-fat foods, such as macaroni and cheese, chicken fingers, french fries, and grilled cheese sandwiches—it is difficult to find evidence of a green vegetable on a children's menu.

A favorite icon of children is Ronald McDonald, the spokesperson for McDonald's. The McDonald's corporation currently operates about 8,000 playgrounds at its restaurants—cleverly increasing children's positive associations with the restaurant, incentives that are likely to persist throughout their adulthood as paying customers. But the cleverness doesn't stop there. The key positive incentive for kids seems to be toys. In a typical week McDonald's sells about 10 million Happy Meals; however, in April of 1997 after introducing a Teenie Beanie Baby with each purchase, Happy Meal sales skyrocketed to 100 million per week. And McDonald's is just one example; other restaurants have ways of luring kids as customers as well (Schlosser, 2002).

More distressing is what is happening in the schools. As parents, we had naively assumed that our children could purchase only the meal advertised on the school menu calendar that we keep posted on our refrigerators each month or a chef's salad. On the contrary, in our Virginia school district, students aged 5–11 make their own decisions about what they want to eat. As well as the traditional meal of a meat, vegetable, and fruit cup, children can purchase cookies, chips, Italian ice, and ice cream. A 5-year-old can choose between a traditional meal and a meal of cookies and chips. Additionally, over 5,000 schools in the United States have fast food "outlets" in their cafeterias. If the fast food isn't contracted out, many school cafeterias serve their own version of fast food—french fries, hamburgers, chicken nuggets—on a regular basis. Contracts between fast food and soft drink corporations are also appearing on the horizon. In 1993, a public school district in Colorado Springs became the first in the United States to distribute Burger King ads in the school's hallways and on the sides of school buses (Schlosser, 2002). In 1998, the Colorado Springs school district signed a multimillion-dollar contract with the Coca-Cola Company. Fearful that the students were not buying enough Coke products, a letter was sent to all principals recommending that the soft drink machines be moved to locations more accessible to the students. Teachers were also encouraged to allow Coke products in the classroom (DeGette, 1998). Sadly, our children are receiving an abundance of information about eating habits, but most of it is coming from the food-sales industry, with virtually no formal educational programs about healthy eating habits.

It should come as no surprise at this point that children are as much at risk for obesity as adults. Unhealthy eating habits, coupled with increased viewing of television and playing of computer games and decreased physical activity, lead to an unhealthy child population. As seen in Figure 14.7, increasing numbers of children are becoming overweight each year. From 1971 to 2006 the percentage of overweight children aged 6–11 increased from 4% to 17%. And these overweight children are going to become overweight adults with all of the related health risks and costs—if they don't develop these health complications as children.

The increased number of adipose cells resulting from a child's weight gain can never decrease—unless liposuctioned out. Further, the increased number of adipose cells probably leads to more difficulty when the person attempts to lose weight since there are more adipose cells to try to satisfy with fat (Logue, 1991). Even children are beginning to have gastric bypass surgery (Morgan, Tanofsky-Kraff, Wilfley, & Yanovski, 2002).

It is frightening to consider how quickly our society is becoming obese. Increased awareness and appropriate social policy concerning healthy eating

Box 14.1

Brain Matters

A Closer Look at Gastric Bypass Surgery

After trying various diets and exercise programs, Alberto Guerrero, a nurse in Miami, was at the end of his rope. His 5-feet, 9-inch frame was overburdened by the 358 pounds he was carrying around. The simple act of going to sleep was one of Alberto's biggest problems: His huge stomach would push against his diaphragm, making it difficult for him to breathe. He would go 2 or 3 nights before his body got so exhausted that he could sleep through the night. When faced with the option to have bariatric (gastric bypass) surgery, Alberto decided that it was necessary if he was ever going to live a normal life. He subsequently had the Roux-en-Y procedure, which, as seen in the illustration, reduces the stomach to about 1% of its normal size. With such a reduced stomach size, patients feel sated more rapidly and for longer durations than with their larger stomachs. In a year, Alberto lost 150 pounds. He no longer has problems going to sleep at night and has adapted to his new eating strategy of avoiding high-fat food; today, when he goes to a restaurant he splits an entrée with his wife and takes small bites. He says his new eating restrictions are worth it because he feels as if he has a whole new life (Contreras & Noonan, 2002).

More and more, we are reading about miraculous transformations following bariatric surgery; and with insurance companies paying for it more frequently, the number of surgeries will undoubtedly continue to rise. In addition to being life-altering for gastric bypass

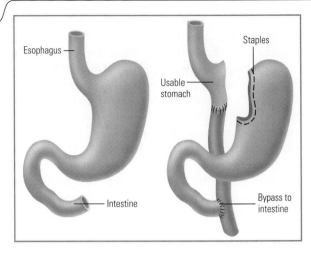

Procedure to reduce the stomach to approximately 1% of its normal size.

patients, this type of surgery provides valuable information about hunger regulation. Although the empirical results are just beginning to appear in the literature and much of our information has been retrieved in case-study scenarios, we can learn a lot from this surgery. For example, we have discussed the role of many neuropeptides such as leptin and neuropeptide Y in hunger regulation, but this surgery emphasizes a factor that falls outside the general vicinity of the brain—that is, the stomach. The primary modification in bypass patients is a reduction of the area of the stomach. With the smaller stomach, patients report feeling full after eating a very small meal. What does this tell us about the role of the stomach in hunger regulation? In this preliminary stage of sifting through the gastric bypass

and increased exercise seem to be the key to reversing the trends to more reasonable body weights.

Anorexia Nervosa

anorexia nervosa (AN) An eating disorder characterized by decreased food consumption and excessive physical activity. Although individuals with this disorder are severely underweight, they remain reluctant to eat to regain their health. If not treated, this condition may lead to the patient's death.

Eating too much is a problem for many individuals, but for a small percentage of our population, the problem is an inability to eat enough to be healthy. As seen in Table 14.2, individuals suffering from **anorexia nervosa (AN)** lose excessive amounts of weight and fear gaining it back. AN is more prevalent in industrialized societies, characterized by an abundance of food—especially societies in which thinness is considered attractive. Over 90% of cases occur in females, typically beginning in mid- to late adolescence and rarely in females older than 40 years of age (American Psychiatric Association, 2000). Familial patterns exist; in one study focusing on concordance rates

data, it appears that the fullness of the stomach, or the tautness of the lining of the stomach, may play an important role in hunger and satiety. If this is the case, obese patients may find themselves in a never-ending battle because the more they eat, the larger the stomach becomes—requiring more food to achieve a feeling of satiety.

From these initial observations, other means of decreasing the size of the stomach without undergoing traumatic bypass surgery are worth considering. Work by Allan Geliebter and his colleagues suggests that, when subjects were placed on a 600 kcal/day diet for 4 weeks, their gastric capacity decreased by about 30% (Geliebter, Schachter, Lohmann-Walter, Feldman, & Hashim, 1996). In another interesting study conducted by Geliebter and Hashim (2001), gastric capacity was measured in normal-weight, obese, and bulimic women.

In case you're wondering how gastric capacity is measured, here are the details. Subjects are asked to fast overnight and report to the hospital around 10:00 a.m. the next day. After loosening any tight clothing and sitting in a relaxed position, the subjects are asked to swallow a 10 cm portion of a condom attached to a lubricated tube. Eventually, the condom is filled with water at a rate of 100 ml/min. After each 100 ml, subjects are asked to rate their hunger, fullness, nausea, and any discomfort. Intragastric pressure is also measured throughout this process. The process ends when the subjects express discomfort. From the tolerated volume data, bulimics had significantly larger gastric capacities; when another measure, the volume required to increase intragastric pressure by 5 cm of water, was

used, the obese and bulimic groups were more likely to have larger stomach capacities than the normal-weight subjects. Hence, the bulimics may be able to tolerate the massive amounts of food consumed during binges because of a large stomach. On the other hand, if bulimics have a significantly larger stomach capacity, large amounts of foods may be necessary to produce a feeling of satiety.

Aside from reducing stomach capacity, gastric bypass surgery provides information about the importance of incentives in hunger regulation. Case-study evidence suggests that, after having surgery, bypass patients no longer crave the high-fat foods that had been such a large part of their lives prior to surgery. On one level, this is easy to understand. As mentioned in the obesity-treatment section, patients experience aversive consequences when they consume carbonated drinks, sugar, or high-fat foods. Generally, we avoid food that makes us sick, but the interesting point is that these patients don't even seem to desire eating the food. It appears that once these foods are associated with negative consequences, the patient no longer craves them. One gastric bypass patient conveyed that, after carrying a soda around with her every minute of the day for years and years, she doesn't even miss them. These preliminary observations about consequences associated with particular foods suggest that behavioral therapy may have unrealized potential.

As insurance companies are stepping up to pay for surgery in obese patients, we will undoubtedly learn more about the role of gastric capacity and incentives in the role of hunger regulation.

---

in monozygotic and dizygotic twins, the monozygotic twins had a 55% concordance rate compared to a 14% rate for the dizygotic twins (Holland, Hall, Murray, Russell, & Crisp, 1984).

Possible causes. Up until the 1960s, AN was thought to be a defense against an anxiety related to sexual maturity; in a sense, because AN induces amenorrhea (cessation of menstruation), it can delay the onset of puberty. In the 1960s, however, when thinness became fashionable, researchers made an observation about a disturbance of body image; and by 1970, it was accepted that it was a fear of fat that prompted women to starve themselves (Russell & Treasure, 1989). The association between lean fashion trends and the realization that young anorexic women seemed to be fearful of being fat has prompted researchers to consider another time during the twentieth century in which thinness was fashionable. During the 1920s, "flapper fashion"

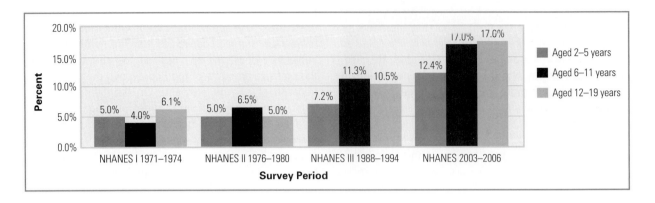

Figure 14.7
Tracking rates of childhood obesity in the United States
Prevalence of overweight among children and adolescents aged 2–19 years. According to the National Center for Health Statistics, the percentage of obese children 6–11 years of age more than quadrupled from 1963 to 2006 (4% and 17%, respectively). NHANES, National Health and Nutrition Examination Survey.

was the trend, characterized by noncurvaceous figures. Although it is hard to obtain adequate evidence, existing evidence suggests that there was a decrease in weight of college students during that time (Russell & Treasure, 1989; Silverstein, Peterson, & Perdue, 1986). Walter Kaye of the Department of Psychiatry at the University of Pittsburgh and Michael Strober of the Department of Psychiatry at UCLA (2001), in a review of the neurobiology of eating disorders, point out that although cultural attitudes about physical attractiveness constitute a relevant influence in the psychopathology of eating disorders, there seems to be more to this disorder. If dieting to look thin like the models is a primary cause of AN, then why don't more women develop AN? After all, dieting behavior is quite commonplace in our society, yet AN affects only about 0.5% of women. Further, descriptions of cases of AN have been found from the mid-nineteenth century, a time when it was not fashionable to be thin. Thus, it appears that although our thinness-crazed culture may form the backdrop for the development of AN, other factors determine who will develop this deadly disorder.

Aside from cultural influences, research suggests that AN patients have certain personality traits in common, including conformity, obsessionality, perfectionism, lack of affect and emotional expressiveness, and decreased social spontaneity. These traits do not seem to be mere correlates of the women going through the AN sickness; they persist once the AN patient has been in long-term recovery (Casper, 1990; Kaye & Strober, 2001; Strober, 1980).

It is likely that neurobiological correlates underlie these differences in personality traits. A hyperactive hypothalamic–pituitary–adrenal axis has been documented in AN patients (Putignano et al., 2001); this effect normalizes after weight restoration (Kaye & Strober, 2001). Stress responsivity is probably expressed in personality traits, especially those related to anxiety. Further, cerebrospinal fluid (CSF) β-endorphin levels are lower in underweight AN patients than in normal-weight controls (Kaye, 1992; Kaye & Strober, 2001) but become normalized following recovery. The neuropeptides of the posterior pituitary are also affected in AN patients. CSF vasopressin, which regulates fluids in the kidney, is increased in AN patients. On the other hand, the other posterior pituitary neuropeptide, oxytocin, which is involved with uterine contractions and milk letdown following the birth process, along with other influences on stress reactivity, is decreased in the CSF (Demitrack et al., 1990). Again, these abnormalities stabilize following recovery (Kaye & Strober, 2001).

Table 14.2 DSM-IV-TR Diagnostic Criteria for Anorexia Nervosa

Refusal to maintain body weight at or above a minimally normal weight for age and height (e.g., weight loss leading to maintenance of body weight less than 85% of that expected or failure to make expected weight gain during period of growth, leading to body weight less than 85% of that expected).

Intense fear of gaining weight or becoming fat, even though underweight.

Disturbance in the way in which one's body weight or shape is experienced, undue influence of body weight or shape on self-evaluation, or denial of the seriousness of the current low body weight.

In postmenarcheal females, amenorrhea, i.e., the absence of at least three consecutive menstrual cycles. (A woman is considered to have amenorrhea if her periods occur only following hormone, e.g., estrogen, administration.)

Specify Type:

Restricting Type: During the current episode of anorexia nervosa, the person has not regularly engaged in binge-eating or purging behavior (i.e., self-induced vomiting or the misuse of laxatives, diuretics, or enemas).

Binge-Eating/Purging Type: During the current episode of anorexia nervosa, the person has regularly engaged in binge-eating or purging behavior (i.e., self-induced vomiting or the misuse of laxatives, diuretics, or enemas).

American Psychiatric Association (2000).

Among the neuropeptides related to eating behavior, NPY is elevated in underweight AN patients. As discussed, NPY is a powerful stimulant of feeding behavior, so you may wonder why it doesn't promote feeding in AN patients. Researchers don't know the answer to this question but speculate that the high NPY levels may contribute to the somewhat paradoxical obsession AN patients have with food (Kaye, Berrettini, Gwirtsman, & George, 1990). CCK has also been measured, but the results are mixed. Some studies report high levels of CCK in underweight AN patients. However, this effect stabilizes at recovery. It could be theorized, if this effect is indeed robust, that high CCK levels could contribute to levels of satiety in AN patients (Geracioti, Liddle, Altemus, Demitrack, & Gold, 1992). Finally, as one would suspect, the hormone leptin is significantly decreased in AN patients, suggesting that AN patients have a normal response to starvation (Grinspoon et al., 1996). Finally, another study focused on the neuropeptide **galanin**, which stimulates appetite and fat consumption. This study investigated galanin levels in recovered AN patients and healthy control women. The results suggested that galanin levels were lower in the recovered AN patients than in the controls (Frank, Kaye, Sahu, Fernstrom, & McConaha, 2001).

Because of the established role of the monoamines in anxiety and the emotionality system, this system has been intensely studied as well. Generally, AN patients have low central and peripheral noradrenergic activity. This finding corroborates studies of normal-weight subjects undergoing a starvation regime (Pirke, 1996).

Walter Kaye at the University of Pittsburgh Medical Center has proposed a provocative theory related to serotonin levels and AN. Considering that serotonin generally is involved in mood regulation, impulse control, behavioral constraints, and obsessiveness, it is easy to contemplate the notion that serotonin may underlie the behavioral characteristics of AN. As mentioned previously, AN patients score high in obsessiveness, perfectionism, attention to detail, and/or harm avoidance—characteristics shared by the most

galanin A neuropeptide that stimulates feeding behavior, particularly fat intake, when injected into the paraventricular hypothalamus.

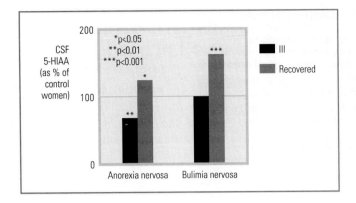

Figure 14.8
Cerebrospinal fluid (CSF)
5-hydroxyindole acetic acid
(5-HIAA) levels in sick and
recovered anorexia nervosa
(AN) and bulimia nervosa (BN)
patients As indicated in the
figure, compared with healthy
women, AN patients have
decreased 5-HIAA activity while
ill and increased levels during
recovery. BN patients have
altered (i.e., increased) 5-HIAA
levels only in recovery.
AFTER KAYE & STROBER (2001)

successful scientists! More to the point of this discussion, however, is the observation that these characteristics occur in patients who have high levels of serotonergic activity. As seen in Figure 14.8, when one metabolite of serotonin, 5-hydroxyindolacetic acid (5-HIAA), is assessed in ill and recovered AN patients, it becomes apparent that the serotonergic system is involved in AN and perhaps a spectrum of eating disorders. Underweight AN patients have significantly decreased concentrations of 5-HIAA in the CSF, and CSF levels of 5-HIAA are elevated in recovered anorexics (Kaye & Strober, 2001). The 5-HIAA levels in recovered AN patients are thought to provide a window to the condition of the system prior to the onset of the illness; it appears that AN patients had high circulating levels of this metabolite and serotonergic activity prior to the onset of AN. Again, high levels of the monoamine might lead to the perfectionist behavior, as well as to feelings of satiety.

The anxiety caused by serotonin-induced perfectionism could be diminished, or medicated, by depleting the system of dietary precursors of serotonin. As discussed in Chapter 5 on neurochemistry, tryptophan is a dietary precursor that leads to significant increases in brain levels of serotonin. Kaye and others are arguing that starvation may decrease the levels of tryptophan entering the central nervous system, resulting in lower levels of serotonin and subsequently decreasing the anxiety caused by obsessing about having the perfect body weight (Kaye, 2001; Kaye et al., 2001). Also making this an interesting story is the observation that increased serotonin leads to feelings of satiety, possibly making it easy for the potential AN patient to restrict eating in the early phases of the sickness. This finding is also supported by the finding that fluoxetine is not an effective treatment for underweight AN patients when the serotonergic system is hyporesponsive but following recovery can reduce relapse from 90% in the placebo group to just 30% in the fluoxetine group. Once recovered, levels of serotonin are reestablished and more likely to be responsive to selective serotonin reuptake inhibitors (SSRIs).

Researchers have also implicated dopamine in AN. Dopaminergic activity in the nucleus accumbens is associated with natural rewards such as eating. A group of researchers at the Istituto Scientifico Ospedale San Raffaele in Milan, Italy, have recently proposed that central dopamine function might play a role in AN. It appears that restricting their eating and engaging in excessive levels of exercise are rewarding to the AN patient. The Italian researchers found evidence of a downregulation of postsynaptic D_2 receptors and suggested that hypersecretion of dopamine was also a likely characteristic in the AN patients (Brambilla, Bellodi, Arancio, Ronchi, & Limonta, 2001). In fact, the decreased sensitivity of the D_2 receptors is probably a compensatory mechanism for the overactive dopaminergic system. In addition to being related to experiencing pleasure and rewards, dopamine suppresses the appetite, which might contribute to the ability to starve oneself. In fact, AN patients given pimozide, a D_2 receptor blocker, showed clinical improvement of AN symptoms (Chowdhury & Lask, 2001).

Table 14.3 DSM-IV-TR Diagnostic Criteria for Bulimia Nervosa

Recurrent episodes of binge-eating. An episode of binge-eating is characterized by both of the following:

> Eating in a discrete period of time (e.g., within any 2-hour period) an amount of food that is definitely larger than most people would eat during a similar period of time and under similar circumstances.

> A sense of lack of control over eating during the episode (e.g., a feeling that one cannot stop eating or control what or how much one is eating)

Recurrent inappropriate compensatory behavior in order to prevent weight gain, such as self-induced vomiting; misuse of laxatives, diuretics, enemas, or other medications; fasting; or excessive exercise.

The binge-eating and inappropriate compensatory behaviors both occur, on average, at least twice a week for 3 months.

Self-evaluation is unduly influenced by body shape and weight.

The disturbance does not occur exclusively during episodes of anorexia nervosa.

Specify Type:

Purging Type: During the current episode of bulimia nervosa, the person has regularly engaged in self-induced vomiting or the misuse of laxatives, diuretics, or enemas.

Nonpurging Type: During the current episode of bulimia nervosa, the person has used other inappropriate compensatory behaviors, such as fasting or excessive exercise, but has not regularly engaged in self-induced vomiting or the misuse of laxatives, diuretics, or enemas.

American Psychiatric Association (2000, p. 594).

Further, the decreased serotonin levels in ill AN patients may contribute to increased dopamine secretion—and the subsequent ability to exist on minimal food consumption (Brambilla, 2001).

Brambilla's proposal of dopaminergic involvement supports recent findings with the activity stress paradigm, also known as **activity-based anorexia**. As previously described, rats are housed in running wheels and fed 1 hour per day. Rats commence high running levels and fail to eat enough to remain healthy. As observed in the Chapter 5 Connections feature, these animals are very motivated to get to their wheel. Our students have observed increased c-*fos* activity in the nucleus accumbens of anorexic rats (Aurentz et al., 1999). Also, when activity-stress rats were given pimozide, the survival rate was increased by 50% (Lambert & Porter, 1992). Vandereycken and Pierloot (1982) found dopaminergic activity important in human anorexic patients after observing that patients given pimozide experienced a suppression of AN symptoms. The role of dopamine in activity-stress suggests that another cause of AN may be related to pleasure and/or control rather than trying to look like a supermodel or delaying puberty. Feeling a dopaminergic-induced "high" after restricting food consumption could be rewarding enough for the AN patient to become addicted to the restrictive behavior and excessive exercise.

What about the data from brain-imaging studies of AN patients? These studies suggest that underweight AN patients have decreased gray matter volumes that sometimes, but not always, fully reverse following recovery (Chowdhury & Lask, 2001). One study reported that the ventricles of the AN patient are still small 3 years following recovery (Katzman, Christensen,

activity-based anorexia An animal (rodent) model of anorexia nervosa in which animals that are food-restricted increase activity levels to the point that they become very ill if the experimenter does not intervene.

Young, & Zipursky, 2001). In a study using magnetic resonance imaging of the hippocampus–amygdala formation in AN and control subjects, the results of AN patients showed a smaller volume of their hippocampal amygdala formation than did the results of the control subjects (Giordano et al., 2001). Another study used single-photon emission computed tomography (SPECT) in women who were either sick or recovered AN patients. AN patients had obvious hypoperfusion of the temporal, parietal, occipital, and orbitofrontal lobes. In the recovered young women, hypoperfusion was observed in the temporoparietal and orbitofrontal regions of the brain (Rastam et al., 2001). In an interesting positron emission tomographic study conducted by Catherine Gordon and colleagues (2001), the researchers exposed AN patients to high-calorie food stimuli (bagel and cream cheese) and low-calorie food stimuli (lettuce salad with no dressing). AN patients reported elevated anxiety on exposure to the high-calorie diet compared to the responses of normal-weight subjects. Further, patients with AN responded with higher rates of elevated bilateral medial temporal lobe regional cerebral blood flow than did normal-weight controls. The elevated anxiety and activity in the temporal areas involved in the emotionality component of the brain suggest that food, a rewarding stimulus for most, elicits phobia-like responses in AN patients.

In sum, many studies have been conducted in which some neurobiological variable is assessed in either sick or recovered AN patients and healthy control subjects. As described, many interesting differences have been observed. These findings, however, should be received with caution because they do not necessarily prove that the variables are causal in any way. In every case, the altered neurobiological variable could be the result of the starvation that the subject experienced either recently or several years ago. To get a better handle on actual causes, McHugh, Moran, and Killilea (1989) have called for an emphasis on epidemiological research to identify risk factors for this disease.

Treatment. Unfortunately, progress in the treatment of AN has been slow. Frequently, patients are hospitalized for extended durations to restore weight. AN patients are hospitalized at a higher rate than patients with any psychiatric disorder other than schizophrenia and organic disorders (McKenzie & Joyce, 1992). Although this intervention is lifesaving in the short term, it falls short of offering long-term benefits. In fact, this type of treatment can be very traumatic for the AN patient—hospitalizing and force-feeding the patient so that she or he rapidly gains weight is the equivalent of throwing someone with a phobia of snakes into a snake pit. Hospital stays are expensive, and insurance companies rarely cover the recommended inpatient and outpatient treatment sessions (DeAngelis, 2002). For these reasons, traditional hospitalization does not seem to be the most effective form of treatment.

Excitement is currently building around a form of family therapy that invites the parents to participate in the patient's journey back to health. This therapy was developed by Christopher Dare and Ivan Eisler at the Maudsley Hospital in London. Although the preliminary results look promising, official endorsements of this form of therapy await the data from ongoing clinical trials (DeAngelis, 2002; Le Grange, 1999; Lock, Le Grange, Agras, & Dare, 2001). Residential treatment centers, with a more calming, relaxing, and homey environment than hospitals, also provide alternative treatments for anorexic patients (see Box 14.2 for a description of one such program). As mentioned previously, in some cases the antidepressant fluoxetine has been found to lessen AN symptoms and is often incorporated into treatment strategies (Kaye & Strober, 2001; Kaye, Weltzin, Hsu, & Bulik 1991; Kaye et al., 1997).

bulimia nervosa (BN) An eating disorder characterized by bouts of both overeating and self-induced vomiting/laxative use. Symptoms are often responsive to serotonergic treatments.

Bulimia Nervosa

Another eating disorder, **bulimia nervosa (BN)**, has also intrigued researchers and practitioners. Typically beginning during adolescence or early adulthood, BN frequently develops during a dieting episode. BN patients, often as obsessed with food as AN patients, frequently eat so much that they become uncomfortable. Because of their concern with weight, many BN patients compensate for the huge influx of calories by purging the system of food. BN patients may induce vomiting, use excessive amounts of laxatives, or exercise for extended durations to rid themselves of the calories. BN affects approximately 1%–3% of women, and similar to AN, BN is one-tenth as prevalent in males. BN patients are more difficult to identify because they are more likely than AN patients to remain at a normal body weight. BN is seen in most industrialized countries that have been studied, including the United States, Europe, Canada, Australia, New Zealand, Japan, South Africa, and the countries of Europe (American Psychiatric Association, 2000) (see Table 14.3).

Purging is related to a host of medical problems. If excessive vomiting is used, the BN patient's teeth can be damaged due to a permanent loss of dental enamel. Increased cavities are also frequently observed. The abuse of laxatives may lead to a dependence on such products to stimulate bowel movement. Purging in any form may lead to fluid and electrolyte imbalances; further, on rare occasions, severe medical complications such as cardiac arrhythmias, esophageal tears, and gastric rupture may develop (American Psychiatric Association, 2000).

Possible causes. Because the concordance rate of BN for monozygotic twins is higher than it is for dizygotic twins (50% and 35%, respectively), genetic influences for this disorder are of particular interest to researchers. There also seems to be a strong relationship between AN and BN; research suggests that the twin of a twin suffering from AN is almost three times more likely to have BN than the twin of an unaffected twin (Walters & Kendler, 1995). However, research also suggests a more general eating disorder phenotype as opposed to more specific AN and BN phenotypes. This research is confusing, though, because many individuals with eating disorders also suffer from other psychiatric symptoms such as depression and, conversely, many individuals suffering from psychiatric disorders develop eating disorders that are secondary to the primary disorder. Hence, it is difficult to differentiate between the genetic chicken and egg in these studies (Kaye & Strober, 2001).

Another possible cause of BN is related to overconcern about body shape and weight, a concern that may be related to cultural norms of body weight. Researchers find that even recovered BN patients have these concerns and continue to have abnormal eating habits and mood fluctuations. The persistence of these symptoms after recovery suggests that they were probably

Box 14.2

A Case in Point

Sara Hunnicutt's Bout with Anorexia Nervosa

A few years ago, when Sara Hunnicutt heard her stomach growling as she went to bed, it brought a smile to her face and a sense of accomplishment, knowing that she had managed to defy nature and deny herself food yet one more day. Accomplishment and achievement were very important to her; she was valedictorian of her Pennsylvania high school class, and during her sophomore year at the University of Richmond, she maintained a 3.8 grade point average. But Hunnicutt was also becoming an overachiever on the dieting front. Typical of many freshmen who find themselves selecting food from what seems like an endless list of choices in the cafeteria each day—in addition to enjoying pizza late at night with friends— Hunnicutt's weight increased from 115 to 130 pounds (on a 5-feet, 1-inch frame). She soon started a rigid diet of cereal with skim milk each morning; a cereal bar, fruit, or pretzels for lunch; and some type of pasta for dinner. Additionally, she exercised excessively. This rigor resulted in the loss of the weight she wanted to lose plus a lot more: about 40 pounds, as she dropped to a low of 90 pounds. Hunnicutt was proud of the self-discipline she used to deprive herself of food. Even though she wore a size 0 and bought some of her clothes in children's departments, she still didn't perceive herself as anorexic. In her mind, anorexics ate only lettuce and were the size of a stick, but she ate a little more. When she stopped menstruating for several months, her gynecologist knew that her massive loss of fat was the reason and recommended that Hunnicutt gain weight.

One of the intriguing questions about anorexia is how an intelligent person who has spent his or her life going from one impressive accomplishment to another can fail to engage in the one behavior necessary for survival—eating. Every young woman's story is different, but let's look at what brought Hunnicutt to this point. Primarily, while she was in high school, her father died after losing a battle with brain cancer; and although she tried to keep going, Hunnicutt was still in a lot of emotional pain as she entered college. Additionally, once she got to the University of Richmond, she was faced with not being a big fish in a little pond anymore—she was just one of a sea of valedictorians. Hence, emotional angst due to losing her father at a young age and anxiety about competing for grades at college set the stage for a drastic coping response. When she thought that she needed to lose weight, her coping response seemed obvious—gaining control over eating. As she felt more and more accomplishment with every pound she lost, she also knew that she was sending a message to her loved ones about the emotional pain she was still experiencing.

peptide YY (PYY) Peptide closely related to NPY and also implicated in hunger stimulation.

present before the development of BN; however, the development of the eating disorder probably exaggerates these symptoms—for example, concerns about thinness, symmetry, and perfectionism (Collings & King, 1994; Kaye & Strober, 2001).

As with AN, altered neuropeptide levels have been observed in BN. Similar to AN, decreased levels of CSF β-endorphin have been observed in sick BN patients, and these levels normalize following recovery (Kaye, 1992). The research with the strong cousin of NPY, **peptide YY (PYY)**, presents an interesting scenario. Although levels of PYY are normal in acutely ill BN patients, they increase about 1 month following abstinence from binge-eating and purging. It is unknown what role this postsickness increase might suggest: a compensatory response to the reduction in binge-eating, some epiphenomenon of the pathological eating in which the BN patient engaged during the sickness, or a preexisting condition that was normalized with the binge episodes (Kaye & Strober, 2001). The apparent satiety neuropeptide CCK is

Once it was recommended that Hunnicutt gain weight, she was so far into the anorexia disorder that she couldn't gain weight on her own. She decided to enter the Renfrew Center for Eating Disorders in Philadelphia, which was close to her home. This residential facility provided a warm, cozy, homelike environment for patients and provided opportunities for both group and individual counseling each day. Although food consumption was monitored closely, patients weren't force-fed in any way. For each meal they had the opportunity to select the particular entrées they wanted to eat—a task that continued to give the patients control over their eating and enabled them to become active participants in their recovery process. If they didn't finish the appropriate amount of food during the daily meal sessions, they were required to make up the missed calories by drinking Ensure at the end of the day. Loaded with fat and calories, this product was a nightmare for anorexic patients, so they were motivated to avoid that consequence. At any point during the meals or during the day, there were plenty of counselors around to talk about anxieties. Accustomed to being an obedient student, Hunnicutt always ate her meals as she was told. As an additional component of her program, she met with psychologists and psychiatrists throughout her recovery period. She also was placed on Prozac as a pharmacological aid. Sara's insurance paid for only 2 weeks of inpatient therapy, so she moved out and continued as an outpatient at the center every day from 8:00 to 5:00. She subsequently weaned

herself to 3 nights per week and then one group session per week.

After taking a year off from school to focus on her recovery, Hunnicutt was ready to go back and complete her major in sociology. Evidence of her confidence in her recovery is seen in her decision to study abroad in Scotland for her final semester—thousands of miles from her family and therapists. After graduation, Hunnicutt adopted healthy eating habits; and although she still loves to exercise, she keeps it to a reasonable amount. As she reflects on the whole ordeal with anorexia, she says that the time when she was sick seems like a blur but that her recovery has clearly been a miracle. When asked how she currently copes with anxiety, Sara admitted that she uses exercise as a coping response when she's feeling anxious—but she limits stress workouts to no longer than an hour. She also knows that it is okay to just relax and watch TV when she needs a mental break.

Thus, Hunnicutt is currently a healthy, happy, well-adjusted young woman. She has worked her way from a fragile 90-pound person who was dominated by thoughts of food to a college graduate with a career, supportive family, and boyfriend. And how much does she weigh now? She reports that her weight is in a healthy range—and that was good enough for us. It seems harmful to define her success in recovery by a number, considering that her obsession with certain weight- and food-related numbers played an important role in the development of anorexia in the first place.

also reduced in BN patients, and intravenous CCK-8 was found to suppress a binge in BN patients (Brambilla, 2001).

Among neurotransmitters, the most significant findings have been found once again with serotonin, suggesting that this neurotransmitter may be related not just to one specific eating disorder but to the spectrum of eating disorders. Looking at the right half of Figure 14.8, you'll notice that whereas 5-HIAA levels are the same as those in healthy controls during recovery, recovered levels exceed 150% of normal levels (Kaye & Strober, 2001). Thus, in both recovered AN and BN individuals, levels of CSF 5-HIAA are high, which may contribute to the obsessions with symmetry and exactness and a tendency toward perfectionism, suggesting that high 5-HIAA levels may contribute to a spectrum of behavior characterized by overcontrol (Kaye & Strober, 2001). Other evidence of serotonergic involvement was found when serotonin 2A receptor activity was measured in recovered BN patients and normal control women. Whereas the normal controls had age-related decreases in 5-HT$_{2A}$ receptors, no age-related changes were observed in the recovered BN patients (Kaye et al., 2001).

Treatment. Because altered serotonergic activity has been documented in BN patients, it is no surprise that one of the most effective pharmacological therapies is antidepressants, either tricyclic antidepressants or SSRIs (Brambilla, 2001). The pharmacologically induced benefits may fade over time however. Additionally, a recent multisite study testing the efficacy of two forms of psychotherapy reported encouraging results. Cognitive-behavioral therapy addressing the unrealistically negative thoughts related to body image that plague BN patients was compared to interpersonal psychotherapy addressing problems in current relationships. Both were effective treatments, although a more immediate effect was observed with the cognitive-behavioral therapy (Agras, Walsh, Fairburn, Wilson, & Kraemer, 2000). Most of the research indicates that cognitive-behavioral therapy is effective for about 60%–70% of BN patients, with remission rates approaching 30%–50% (Arnow, 1997).

DIGESTING THE CONFLICTING THEORIES OF EATING REGULATION

In this chapter we have taken a multifaceted approach to understanding the influential factors that determine the quantity and type of food we place in our mouths. Although we began this chapter thinking that the bulk of these factors would be the neurochemicals and neuroanatomical circuits involved with hunger regulation, an emphasis of this textbook, it quickly became obvious that two other factors—namely, human evolutionary predispositions toward certain foods and the environment in which we live—play equal, if not more significant, roles in hunger regulation.

Trying to understand the mechanisms underlying eating disorders was considered in the last part of this chapter. Because obesity affects both brain and behavioral factors, it was included with the more traditionally observed eating disorders, AN and BN. The toxic food environment characterized by huge portions, high-fat foods, and unhealthy eating strategies undoubtedly contributes to obesity. AN and BN represent extremes of control and consumption in the spectrum of eating disorders. Although extensive research has been conducted on these disorders, there are more questions than answers related to effective treatment strategies. Genetics has been implicated as being a causal factor in several eating disorders, but, as Walter Kaye suggests, genetics probably only loads the eating disorders gun; it is the environment—complete with high-fat foods, superthin models, and an abundance of stress—that actually pulls the trigger.

After an in-depth look at the historical and contemporary literature concerned with hunger regulation and related disorders, it is easy to feel confused about some of the conflicting ideas that emerge in these studies. Let us consider a few of these conundrums. If humans evolved to take advantage of eating opportunities leading to adequate intake of fat, sugar, and salt, how can certain individuals with AN override their evolutionary past and starve themselves? If the sensory-specific satiety theory is correct in suggesting that we also evolved to eat a diverse diet, why do so many parents have to fight with their children to get them to eat anything other than chicken nuggets?

And what happened to turn those children from infants who would place anything in their mouths to kids with pathologically discriminating tastes? Why is it that parents don't hesitate to vaccinate their children against chicken pox, an admittedly annoying virus that lasts about a week, but seem to resist any type of inoculation against obesity, a condition that may cause significant lifelong health and psychological problems as well as a shorter life?.

On another note, if positive incentives are related to increased consumption of certain foods, how do gastric bypass patients ignore a life's worth of positive associations related to excessive eating and lose even their desire to eat these foods after having surgery? And if gastric feedback about the contents of the stomach is so important—as indicated in the gastric bypass patients—how is it that experimental amnesic patients completely ignored the two lunches already occupying their stomachs and welcomed a third lunch? If cultural influences are so important in the development of eating disorders, why do only 0.5% of young women exposed to our cultural environment of abundant foods and thin female icons develop AN? If the stomach is mostly active during the digestion of food, why do our stomachs growl so much when we are hungry—and have no food to digest? If obesity involves disruptions of behavior (eating behavior), psychological processes (feelings of a lack of control, low self-esteem, and so on), and life functioning (possibly due to an inability to engage in certain tasks and activities because of body size and documented discrimination), why is it not recognized in DSM-IV-TR as an eating disorder? We've addressed some of these questions in the text of this chapter, but many of these conflicting theories and findings remain difficult to swallow, much less digest.

Summary

Eating Regulation

Washburn and Cannon conducted the classic study suggesting that the activity of the stomach was a critical criterion for experiencing hunger. Later studies suggested that the stomach is quietest when no food is present.

Several areas of the hypothalamus have been implicated in hunger regulation. The ventromedial hypothalamus was initially viewed as the satiety center and the lateral hypothalamus as the hunger center—both contributing to the dual-centers hypothesis of eating. Today, the paraventricular nucleus is recognized as being more heavily involved in hunger regulation.

Several neurochemicals, such as glucose, leptin, neuropeptide Y, cholecystokinin, and insulin, have been shown to contribute to hunger regulation in the controlled settings of laboratories. To have a significant impact on hunger regulation, a pharmaceutical agent would probably have to influence more than one of these important substances.

Based on certain genetic variations leading to overweight rats and mice, such as *ob/ob* mice and Zucker rats, it is obvious that genetics is a contributing factor to an individual's susceptibility to obesity. Finding examples of these genetic mutations in humans, however, is a difficult task.

Evolutionary Theories of Hunger Regulation

Several evolutionary theories have been proposed to explain the eating strategies of humans and other animals. In this chapter, the following evolutionary theories were described: set-point theory, preparatory response theory, positive incentive theory, and sensory-specific satiety.

Disorders of Eating Regulation

Obesity is on the rise and becoming a threat to the well-being of our society. Although the neurobiology of obesity is important, social policies related to consumption and environmental influences are also important pieces of the hunger-regulation puzzle. Treatments for obesity are quite drastic; for example, bariatric or gastric-bypass surgery is becoming more popular for the treatment of severe obesity. Rates of obesity in children are growing each year. It is important that children are informed about the hazards of obesity and that eating healthy foods and maintaining a healthy lifestyle are required to diminish the high rates.

Anorexia nervosa is seen in 0.5% of young women and has the highest death rate of all psychiatric disorders. Although societal values related to body ideals may set the stage for the development of these disorders, other factors such as stress, desire for control, and variations in neurochemicals such as serotonin and dopamine also contribute to susceptibility to the development of this disease.

Bulimia nervosa is slightly more prevalent than anorexia; this disorder responds to both pharmacological and cognitive-behavioral therapies.

Key Terms

ventromedial hypothalamus (VMH) (424)

lateral hypothalamus (LH) (424)

dual-centers hypothesis of hunger regulation (424)

noradrenergic bundle (424)

paraventricular nucleus (425)

glucose utilization theory of hunger regulation (425)

cholecystokinin (CCK) (426)

leptin (426)

neuropeptide Y (NPY) (427)

arcuate nucleus (ARC) (427)

orexins (429)

set-point theory of hunger regulation (430)

lipostatic theory of hunger regulation (430)

preparatory response theory of hunger regulation (431)

positive incentive theory of hunger regulation (432)

sensory-specific theory of satiety (433)

obesity (434)

liposuction (438)

gastric bypass surgery (438)

dumping syndrome (438)

anorexia nervosa (AN) (440)

galanin (443)

activity-based anorexia (445)

bulimia nervosa (BN) (447)

peptide YY (PYY) (448)

For Further Consideration

Brownell, K. D., & Horgen, K. B. (2004). *Food fight.* New York: Contemporary Books. Brownell, a respected researcher in the field of eating behavior and director of the Yale Center for Eating and Weight Disorders, takes his academic gloves off as he attempts to wage a war against the public-health policies (or lack of them) that are encouraging our society to overeat. Considering that obesity has now surpassed smoking in terms of health-care costs, Brownell fears that the food industry's free access to children may lead to the current generation of children being the first to have shorter lives than their parents, Brownell is serious about bringing these issues to the public arena. He claims that, in a society in which pets are fed better diets than our children, public indifference toward the food industry, coupled with corporate opportunism, have to be addressed in order to get our society back on a healthy track. Brownell and Horgen also present potential public-policy initiatives that may reverse the obesity trend.

Kaye, W., & Strober, M. (2001). The neurobiology of eating disorders. In D. S. Charney, E. J. Nestler, & B. S. Bunney, B. S. (Eds.), *Neurobiology of mental illness* (pp. 891–906). New York: Oxford University Press. This thorough chapter reviews the relevant empirical evidence addressing the neurobiological risk factors and clinical pathology of anorexia nervosa and bulimia nervosa. Atypicalities in numerous neurochemical systems (e.g., neuropeptide Y, B-endorphin, cholecystokinin, vasopressin, oxytocin, leptin, serotonin, norepinephrine), mood and cognitive characteristics, and medical physiology are discussed. Kaye and Strober advocate aggressive, sustained, multifaceted treatment that encompasses nutritional, behavioral, and psychological elements of the syndromes. An emphasis is placed on the pharmacological normalization of monoaminergic and neuropeptidergic functions in treating these disorders.

Pinel, J. P. J., Assanand, S., & Lehman, D. R. (2000). Hunger, eating, and ill health. *American Psychologist,*

55, 1105–1116. This article evaluates our contemporary eating habits through an evolutionary window. Existing in an environment with limited food resources, the authors argue that our ancestors evolved the ability to consume as much food as possible when it was available to protect against future starvation. The problem comes, however, when that biological system is placed in today's environment (rich with food resources); contemporary humans still experience a strong motivation to consume to excess. Ironically, these authors point out that "the individual who is most at risk in modern societies—the individual with an insatiable appetite who uses her or his energy efficiently and stores the excess—would be most suited to live in a natural environment" (p. 1112). The positive-incentive theory of food consumption is also discussed and presented as a potential explanation for anorexia nervosa with therapeutic implications.

Schlosser, E. (2002). *Fast food nation.* Perennial: New York. Schlosser acts as an investigative reporter to unearth the origins of our fascination with fast food and the immense success of this industry. Warning: If you enjoy fast food, go out and order your favorite meal before reading *Fast Food Nation* because your perception of that food will likely be permanently altered after reading this book. Among other disturbing societal changes, the author claims that the fast food industry has fueled the obesity epidemic and will continue to do so as our children are continuously bombarded with fun fast food messages through the media.

Epilogue

Connections

Superman, Stem Cells, and the Senate

Until the summer of 1995, Christopher Reeve was a successful actor, the embodiment of Superman, who he portrayed in a popular series of movies. A gifted athlete in real life, Reeve enjoyed many sports, including sailing, scuba diving, and horseback riding. His life changed, however, after an accident in a May 1995 jumping competition. When his horse balked at a jump, Reeve was pitched forward onto the ground, headfirst, severing his spinal cord at the second cervical nerve. He was paralyzed from the shoulders down.

In that split second, Reeve was transformed into, as he later described it (see Reeve, 2002), a "forty-two-year-old toddler," dependent on a ventilator for every breath and on the care of others for the most mundane daily activities. Even the most optimistic among us would find it difficult to maintain sufficient cognitive and emotional energy to recover from such an accident. Reeve quickly realized, though, that he would have to focus on many more issues than his own medical regimen to recover. He soon learned that, contrary to his doctors' proclamation that his spinal cord would never regenerate, a few scientists thought otherwise—and were working toward that very goal.

These scientists faced many obstacles—money and political support among them—for pursuing exciting new embryonic stem cell research on restoring spinal function (see Chapter 6). Christopher Reeve soon realized that fund-raising and politics were as important to his recovery as his daily rehabilitation therapy. With the energy and enthusiasm typical of his theatrical work, Reeve attacked each obstacle.

He lobbied for more funds to be directed toward the National Institutes of Health (NIH), especially for spinal cord injury projects. Next he went after the then NIH ban on funding for embryonic stem cell research by lobbying each member of the Senate as they considered the Stem Cell Research Act of 2000. Today, after a dark period where NIH-funded researchers were severely limited by government strictures on the kind of basic research that is critical to any hope of recovery for patients like Christopher Reeve, the restrictions have finally been lifted. Reeve, in words that are as relevant today as they were in 2002, wrote

> It is our responsibility to do everything possible to protect the quality of life of the present and future generations. A critical factor will be what we do with human embryonic stem cells....They have been called "the body's self-repair kit."

> No obstacle should stand in the way of responsible investigation of their possibilities....In fertility clinics, women are given a choice of what to do with unused fertilized embryos: they can be discarded, donated to research, or frozen for future use....But why has the use of discarded embryos suddenly become such an issue? Is it more ethical for a woman to donate unused embryos that will never become human beings, or to let them be tossed away as so much garbage when they could help save thousands of lives?

While we prolong the stem cell debate, millions continue to suffer. It is time to harness the power of government and go forward. (p. 96)

Reeve repeatedly took the stage, in motorized wheelchair, as an informed and passionate speaker on the topic of spinal cord recovery, addressing thousands of laypeople and neuroscientists. Once, at a Society for Neuroscience meeting in New Orleans, he spoke poignantly of the need and support for basic research, where he was the first nonscientist ever to address this august group.

Sadly, as we completed final edits for the first edition of this text, Christopher Reeve died of heart failure. Until his final, mechanized breath, Reeve was a vocal and ardent defender of stem cell research. Ironically, unable to rely on the potential promise of stem cell applications for himself for repair of the nervous system, he nevertheless sustained a rigorous physical therapy program and an intense mental focus. Five years after his injury he surprised himself and amazed his doctors and the scientific community by demonstrating movement in his fingers and arms. These accomplishments were difficult to explain, considering that the spinal cord nerves that convey motor signals and move the fingers and arms are located below the point where his spinal cord was severed. Medical textbooks have taught doctors in the past that this should be impossible; Reeve, however, seemed to enjoy rewriting the pages on spinal cord recovery. Following his untimely death, the Christopher Reeve Paralysis Foundation continues his legacy, which is to support innovative research in the area of neural regeneration.

We have now come full circle. We began this book by arguing for the value of the emerging discipline of clinical neuroscience. We covered the historical, methodological, and fundamental science behind this exciting field. We discussed the relevance and therapeutic potential for treating a representative set of clinical disorders. We considered the use of a wide array of basic neuroscience information, recognizing the value of incorporating strategies such as pharmacological and cognitive-behavioral interventions in successfully treating and preventing mental illness. In this last chapter, we consider some emerging ethical controversies that spring from clinical neuroscience research and discuss additional evidence that confirms the basic plasticity of the nervous system. Finally, we emphasize the absolute importance of going forward in a responsible, ethical, and methodologically sound manner. Good data evaluated honestly and competently will advance the field of clinical neuroscience.

ETHICS BUFFETED ON THE SEA OF NEUROSCIENCE

We have covered much information about both the fundamentals and the applications of neuroscience in this text. As the experience of Christopher Reeve and others makes clear, greater knowledge about the nervous system is accompanied by more questions and increased responsibilities concerning the morality and clinical efficacy of neuroscience findings and applications. **Neuroethics** is a convergence of disciplines as diverse as philosophy and

neuroethics Convergence of several disciplines, such as philosophy, religion, and medicine, to recognize the importance of ethical issues related to the rapidly changing field of neuroscience.

religion, medicine and psychology, to recognize and address moral issues related to the rapidly growing and changing field of neuroscience.

In May 2002, the rising tide of ethical considerations was evident at a conference entitled Neuroethics: Mapping the Field (Marcus, 2002). More than 150 neuroscientists, psychiatrists, psychologists, bioethicists, philosophers, lawyers, and journalists convened in San Francisco for this landmark event. The neurobiology of criminal behavior and morality, the medicalization of our brains, cloning, cell transplants, brain enhancement, and the role of religion in neuroscience were among the vast array of topics covered. Since then, these many formerly scientifically inaccessible and still sensitive topics have arrived at the frontiers of examination.

Neuroethics is quickly gaining recognition as a formal piece of the clinical neuroscience puzzle. Knowledge that has the potential to reduce suffering or enhance quality of life does not grow in a vacuum: Gains in knowledge must coincide with a government willing to financially and legally support the research. More than ever before, neuroscientists are required to leave their comfortable laboratory benches and ivory towers; they must speak to various political audiences and the general population about the benefits of their research. They must engage in lively interdisciplinary conversations with colleagues in fields that attempt to divine the social and economic costs and benefits of moving forward with certain lines of research. And data must be the lingua franca that frames these exchanges.

Here, we limit our coverage to two of the important controversies facing contemporary neuroscientists: (1) how neuroscience is influencing our thoughts about criminal behavior and relevant legal evidence and (2) how the hype surrounding psychopharmacology and behavioral engineering is influencing the brain.

Neuroscience and Criminal Behavior

In Chapter 1 you read about Phineas Gage, perhaps the first clinical neuroscience case study and certainly the poster boy for the brain's regulation of character. Recall that damage to Gage's frontal lobe resulted in behavioral changes (namely, loss of impulse control and judgment problems) in the absence of other general medical problems (see Figure 1.3) and raised questions regarding the manner in which disruptions of brain function exact a toll on personality. Can such disruptions actually cause criminal behavior? Could early brain damage predict a life of crime or antisocial behavior? Could a neurobiological malfunction in adulthood lead a once moral, upstanding member of the community to a life of crime? Neuroscience is heading down the path that astronomy and chemistry have taken in challenging once assured assumptions about the governance of the natural world: Human behavior is merely another consequence of natural activity. If so, how might a jury assign responsibility for a crime, mete out appropriate punishment, and ensure that justice and fairness reign?

Brain areas influencing criminal behavior: The usual suspects.
Neurologists Jeffrey Burns and Russell Swerdlow (2003), then at the University of Virginia, reported a case study suggesting that a brain tumor might explain otherwise reprehensible criminal behavior. The neurologists described a schoolteacher who, contrary to his personal history, began acting impulsively and hypersexually, soliciting prostitutes and visiting child

pornography Web sites. When his wife learned that he had made sexual advances toward children, moving from the virtual to the actual, she had him evicted from their home.

The case took a neural turn when the teacher checked himself into the hospital complaining of headaches and compulsive thoughts about raping his landlady. Magnetic resonance imaging (MRI) scans showed an egg-sized tumor in the right orbitofrontal cortex, an "executive area" known to be associated with moral decision making. When the tumor was removed, so too were the sexual, pedophiliac, and rape obsessions. Eventually, however, his heinous thoughts returned: Sure enough, MRI scans confirmed the regrowth of the tumor.

As this example strongly demonstrates, brain abnormalities such as a tumor can lead to amoral or criminal behavior, which may necessitate a reevaluation of legal terms such as *crime*, *motive*, and *punishment*. But does an assault on one's brain tissue lead to a specific effect on one's ethical thoughts and behaviors? Some "gambling" experiments have shed light on this question. Antonio Damasio, a neurologist then at the University of Iowa, College of Medicine, and his colleagues designed a program of research in which they observed subjects with frontal lobe damage playing a card game. Prior to the game, the subjects were given $2,000 in realistic-looking play money and told that the object of the game was to lose as little of it as possible. The subjects soon learned that when cards from two of the four decks on the table were turned over, they might get a decent payment or occasionally be hit with a rather large monetary penalty. The other two decks generally paid less but did not have exceptionally high surprise penalties. When subjects in this experiment were monitored for skin conductance, a measure of emotionality that assesses subtle physiological events, such as sweating, differences were observed between patients with frontal lobe damage and normal subjects.

Damasio found that, prior to turning over a card from the high-risk deck, normal subjects exhibited significantly more electrodermal, or somatic, activity than the patients with frontal lobe damage. This research appears to validate the "gut" feelings so many of us experience when we are on the brink of making an important decision. In this case, prior to making an "intuitive" decision, we experience a **somatic marker** that typically makes us step back and reassess the situation before acting.

A person without this physiological response might be more likely to engage in risky behavior. In his book *Descartes' Error*, Damasio (1994) suggests that the prefrontal cortex (PFC) is one of the few brain regions that can eavesdrop on virtually every activity occurring in our bodies and brains at a given time. Consequently, he has noticed more risk-taking and uninhibited behavior in many of his patients suffering from damage to this important brain surveillance system.

Research conducted by Adrian Raine (Abbott, 2001) of the University of Southern California in Los Angeles supports Damasio's ideas about the importance of the PFC in ethical decisions. More specifically, his work suggests that a section of the PFC, the orbitofrontal cortex (OFC), is involved in the psychopathic condition leading to criminal acts. As seen in Figure E.1, positron emission tomographic (PET) scans suggest that convicted

somatic marker Body signal, such as altered electrodermal activity, that is interpreted by the brain as an indication of a relevant impending event.

Figure E.1
OFC activity in criminal behavior Positron emission tomographic scans show that the orbitofrontal cortex activity in the prefrontal cortex (PFC) is much lower in convicted murderers than in noncriminals. This suggests an important role in ethical decision making for the PFC.

RAINE, NATURE, 410 (2001)

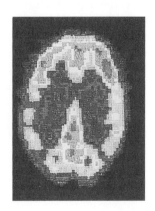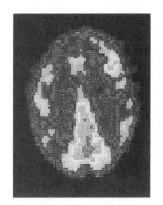

murderers have less OFC activity than noncriminal subjects. MRI scans suggest that PFC volume is reduced by 14% in men who have committed violent crimes.

In a related line of research, James Blair, currently at the National Institute of Mental Health, believes that the amygdala plays an influential role in criminal behavior (Abbott, 2001). His work has shown that this structure responds to sadness and anger in others—empathy, if you will—in normal subjects. He hypothesizes that amygdala dysfunction might lead to a lack of fear and empathy, making intrusive, aggressive social behavior more likely.

Further support for brain involvement in criminal behavior has been gathered by psychiatrist Dorothy Lewis and neurologist Jonathan Pincus. (Gladwell, 1997). They have spent considerable time performing clinical interviews on juvenile offenders in Connecticut. Overwhelmingly, both investigators conclude that most vicious criminals have experienced a combination of child abuse and brain injury. According to Lewis and Pincus, this toxic mixture results in an impediment in the individual's ability to follow the "rules" of society—a likely task for the executive function of the PFC.

Evidence of deficits in following rules is seen in a card-sorting task in which a juvenile offender has to change from using color as a sorting variable to using number—the subject simply keeps following the old rule that is no longer appropriate. Also, these subjects have difficulty when there are no structured rules. For example, when Lewis and Pincus use the word-fluency task, they ask the subject to name as many words as possible that begin with a certain letter, let's say F, in 1 minute.

People with a history of frontal lobe damage have trouble with this activity. This unstructured task requires successful subjects to make free associations as they mentally jump around from word to word. These subjects, however, get stuck on one root word—*four, fourteen, forty, forty-four*—using it over and over and not coming up with the normal number of about 14 words. If you give the same subject a more structured task—say, name 16 items in the grocery store in 1 minute—he or she will perform at the same level as subjects without frontal lobe damage (Gladwell, 1997).

So how does this line of research affect society's thoughts about criminal behavior? It is certainly easier to think that criminals are "bad" people who deserve to be punished. The thought that a malfunctioning brain might push someone to commit a crime, in a similar fashion as a malfunctioning nerve in the arm may lead to paralysis, is quite unsettling for many of us. It defies our normal reliance on right versus wrong; instead, we are faced with the difference between fixed and broken.

This leap into the neurobiological muddies the waters about personal responsibility, intent, and blame. Whereas defense lawyers already rely on researchers in the courtroom to testify on behalf of their clients who may have suffered a form of brain injury, the jury—both literally and figuratively—is still out on this line of research. It is difficult to tease out the brain injury from chronic substance abuse in many of these studies; also, most of the imaging of the violent individual's brain is conducted after the person has been sitting in a jail cell for some time, and it is difficult to discern what effect such an altered environmental experience has had on the prisoner's brain.

Many of the young offenders studied by Lewis and Pincus exhibited a lifetime of bad decisions and violent behavior, making it difficult to pinpoint a single cause of the criminal behavior. If a person suddenly starts engaging in criminal behavior following a lifetime of adhering to the rules, however, as observed in the above schoolteacher who suddenly developed an attraction to children, there may be an acute neural cause such as a brain tumor.

Another example of the brain causing an abrupt shift to a criminal act may be seen in the data collected by forensic psychiatrist Anneliese Pontius (LoPiccolo, 1996). After interviewing about 200 alleged murderers, she noticed a pattern. Of the suspects interviewed, a portion (20) were to some extent loners and very shy, experienced what seemed to be a psychotic break, and then committed a heinous crime. Many times the victim was unknown and there was no motive. After the event, each suspect was remorseful and did not hesitate to confess to the crime.

Pontius argues that the dysfunctional social behavior, years and years of loneliness and rumination about life's stresses and traumas, might lead to an eventual brain seizure in the limbic circuit. Although the specifics of these cases varied, all of the suspects reported experiencing strange hallucinations preceding the crime and no rage or feeling during the murder—acting, if you will, like an animal attacking its prey.

The perpetrators also reported certain visceral responses such as nausea, incontinence, and a racing heart during the violent act, as if responding at some level. Only afterward, when the somatic feelings and hallucinations subsided, did they report feeling overwhelming remorse over the act. This **kindled limbic seizure** proposed by Pontius is, as you can imagine, very controversial. Part of the reason lies with the virtual impossibility of gathering evidence that an actual seizure occurred while the murder was taking place (LoPiccolo, 1996).

Neuroscience and the burden of proof. In addition to providing theories about the causes of criminal behavior, the rigorous scientific methodology inherent to neuroscience is being used to identify people who have committed criminal acts. One way to ascertain guilt is to determine whether a person is lying about involvement in a crime since, throughout history, altered physiological functions such as nervousness, sweaty palms, and a dry mouth have been associated with untruths (in most people: the socio-/psychopath is loathe to show emotion). In one of the early lie-detector tests, the Chinese forced suspected liars to chew on rice powder and then spit it out. If the powder was dry (due to sympathetic arousal—see Chapter 3), the suspect was determined to be lying (Gayle, 1988). It is certainly better than seeing if they sank like the witches of old New England.

The more modern lie detector, or polygraph, measures other indices of autonomic activity—galvanic skin response (electrodermal activity), blood pressure, heart rate, and respiration. The reasoning behind polygraph testing is that a person will be selectively emotional when asked about specific information related to a particular crime. For example, a suspect would not be expected to show emotion when asked to give his or her address but should if asked to identify a murder weapon (if that person indeed committed the crime). Although this seems like a reasonable assumption, most behavioral neuroscientists could spend hours describing its shortcomings.

David Lykken, working at the University of Minnesota prior to his recent death, wrote extensively about the subjective problems with the use of polygraphs for lie detection, including inadequate equipment and training, lack

kindled limbic seizure
Temporal lobe seizure thought to be related to the accumulation of chronic stress and loneliness; may be accompanied by uncharacteristic violent behavior.

brain fingerprinting Theory suggesting that specific brain-wave activity accompanies the identification of familiar stimuli. This technology may be used in criminal investigations.

of statistical validity when analyzing the data, and perhaps most important, the ease with which the autonomic nervous system can be adjusted to fool the polygrapher. In his book *A Tremor in the Blood*, Lykken (1998) described how criminals can do things like place a tack in a shoe or generate a provocative thought to evoke what looks like an "emotional" response to many types of questions, making it impossible for the polygrapher to identify the crime-relevant emotional responses.

In fact, these concerns are so troubling that congressional action in 1988 severely limited the use of polygraph tests in employment situations (except, curiously, for certain government positions). Further, because validity studies fail to show the predictive value of the test, polygraph evidence is rarely accepted in the courtroom. Why, then, do we still hear so much about polygraph tests being used in police investigations and see it as a stalwart of the television crime drama? If a test is found to lack validity for use in employment screening and courtroom evidence, how does it have enough validity to be used in important police investigations? If a neurobiological response is involved in lying, how can we assess it in a valid way to determine the perpetrator of a crime or if someone has criminal intentions or plans to commit an act of terrorism? An approach known as **brain fingerprinting** holds promise for being the neuroscientific (and more objective, less problematical) equivalent of the polygraph. In December 2000, the television news show *60 Minutes* interviewed neuroscientist Larry Farwell, from Iowa, about this new technology that has caught the attention of the CIA and FBI (Farwell, 2000).

Essentially, Farwell's technique incorporates past research indicating that the brain responds in a certain brain-wave pattern (that is, with a peak known as a p300 wave) when it recognizes some piece of information. As Farwell and others report, the p300 wave is a reliable index of attention. In addition, p300 is a component of a large brain wave that he has identified and (painfully) named a "MERMER" (memory and encoding–related multifaceted electroencephalographic response). Farwell's test requires subjects to observe words or images on a computer screen while brain-wave activity is monitored. If a suspect fails to show the brain-wave pattern in response to critical information to which the perpetrator would have been exposed and would then remember, then the suspect would be deemed innocent (Figure E.2).

Figure E.2
Brain fingerprinting In one case study, Larry Farwell conducted a brain fingerprinting test on convicted murderer Johnny Ray Slaughter (pictured on left). To conduct the test, Farwell identified three types of stimuli to be presented while monitoring electroencephalographic (EEG) responses: target (information relevant to the crime that is known by Slaughter), irrelevant (information that may be related to a crime but has no specific relevance for the particular crime in question), and probe stimuli (information containing accurate information about the crime that the perpetrator denies knowing, such as the position of the victim's body). Slaughter's EEG record showed the typical recognition response (i.e., p300 and MERMER) for the target stimulus but did not exhibit recognition of the irrelevant and probe stimuli; thus, "information absent" was declared for Slaughter's test (at a statistical significance of 99%).
BRAIN FINGERPRINTING LABS

The CIA has given Farwell $1 million in hopes that such a technique can detect potential terrorists. The final scientific validity for such a technique remains to be seen; currently, Farwell is assessing individuals previously convicted of a crime. Although the approach is intriguing, the legal community has been slow to embrace this technology and its claims.

Other approaches have merit too. Daniel Langleben of the University of Pennsylvania, along with his colleagues, is currently using functional MRI (fMRI) technology to get to the truth about the brain areas underlying deception (Ross, 2003). The rationale is as follows. If a person is telling the truth, a certain area of the brain should be activated; but if a person is telling a lie, it is likely that the same area activated during truth telling would be activated in addition to another area that must be employed to suppress the true information and supply new, false information.

In short, telling the truth and telling a lie are two very different cognitive and neurobiological tasks. Langleben found that two areas are activated during lying—the anterior cingulate cortex and the left PFC. Specifically, when shown a playing card, more activation was observed in these areas when subjects were asked to falsely deny that they were seeing, for example, the five of clubs, than when they truthfully reported the identity of the card.

Practical applications of brain fingerprinting are still unknown, and it is not likely that police stations are all going to have fMRI scanners any time soon (though the technology does improve and get smaller/less expensive). Of course, there's the overriding ethical question that colors this discussion: Do we really want a fail-proof technique to identify lying? Be careful what you wish for. Such devices would undoubtedly create anxiety for politicians, promiscuous spouses, and spies!

In sum, basic and applied clinical neuroscience research is providing evidence that will redefine traditional ideas about right and wrong, guilt and innocence, valid evidence of truth telling and its variants. What remains for now, but will likely be the target of the continued march of neuroscience and technology, will be the rights of individuals to protect that most personal and cherished of the natural: one's own thoughts and feelings.

Designer Brains, Designer Disorders

Throughout this text we have considered a host of valid reasons for trying to change brain chemistry. This section is not about transforming a malfunctioning brain into a functional brain but, rather, brain enhancement, also known as **euneurics** or "transhumanism," characterized by the increasing use of treatments, usually drugs, to change a healthy brain into a "better" brain (as defined by the owner of the brain). One aspect of these augmentations is **cosmetic pharmacology**, the use of psychoactive drugs for personality modification or lifestyle alterations unrelated to mental illness. Think face-lift for the brain.

In the popular book *Listening to Prozac*, psychiatrist Peter Kramer (1993) describes his first patient to use fluoxetine (Prozac) to combat depression. This patient, named Tess, had a miserable childhood and early adulthood, characterized by child abuse, an alcoholic father, and the responsibility of caring for siblings and an aging mother. When Tess met with Kramer, he reported that she met the criteria for depression; and he subsequently put her on the traditional medication imipramine. After a month of taking the drug, Tess reported that she was better—she was herself again.

euneurics Movement to design "better" brains.

cosmetic pharmacology Using psychoactive drugs for personality modification or lifestyle alterations unrelated to mental illness.

Kramer wrote that after meeting with her for 15 minutes every month or two, he was not satisfied with her progress. About that time Prozac became available, and he recommended that she take the drug "to terminate her depression more thoroughly" (p. 7). The results were striking. Tess had more energy than ever before, had up to three dates a weekend, was laughing more, and had more self-confidence than ever before—what a transformation!

Eventually, Tess stopped taking Prozac. After about 8 months off the drug, Tess told Kramer that she no longer felt like herself; she was slipping back into the grip of her depression. Her company was undergoing union negotiations, which made her feel anxious and vulnerable; she turned again to Prozac. Faced with the dilemma of placing a patient on a medication for personality rather than medical reasons, Kramer wrote, "I discussed the dilemma with her, but then I did not hesitate to write the prescription. Who was I to withhold from her the bounties of science? Tess responded again as she had hoped she would, with renewed confidence, self-assurance, and social comfort" (p. 10).

More recently, the antidepressant sertraline (Zoloft) was approved for treating social anxiety disorder (essentially, severe shyness). Although documented as a disorder in the *Diagnostic and Statistical Manual of Mental Disorders*, fourth edition, text revision (DSM-IV-TR), social anxiety may be more accurately viewed as a personality trait than a mental disorder (Restak, 2003). Pfizer Corporation, the manufacturer of Zoloft, provides the following explanatory passage on its Web site:

> If you have social anxiety disorder, you often get very nervous around other people. It feels like everyone is watching you and judging you. You're afraid of making a mistake or looking like a fool. You'll do anything to keep that from happening. You might even avoid certain people, places, or social events. Social anxiety disorder affects over 16 million Americans. It's a real medical condition. Social anxiety disorder can happen to anyone. Often it starts in the mid-teen years.
>
> *Social anxiety disorder can make you fear or avoid*
>
>   —meeting new people
>
>   —talking to your boss—or anyone in charge
>
>   —speaking in front of groups
>
>   —drawing any attention to yourself
>
> *If you have to do these kinds of things, you may*
>
>   —blush
>
>   —sweat
>
>   —tremble
>
>   —have a fast heart-rate (http://www.zoloft.com/anxiety_types.aspx)

To entice the potential Zoloft user, Pfizer sponsors an advertisement in the popular press and on television simplistically depicting how serotonin floats across the synaptic gap at a lower level in the "depressed" neuron, with its unhappy, blushing face. After taking the drug, however, the neuron absorbs less serotonin, allowing more to glide across the junction, now wheedling the neuron into happiness and a more content state, as exemplified with its now happy, more confident face. As you'll recall from the discussion in Chapter 9, the physiological mechanisms of selective serotonin reuptake inhibitors (SSRIs) are a bit more complicated than depicted in this advertisement. You may also recognize the symptoms of social anxiety disorder listed on the Web site as important social autonomic functions that are acceptable, and even adaptive, under many conditions.

Social anxiety disorder is but one example of how the use of prescription drugs is moving from the treatment of severe mental dysfunctions such as major depression, obsessive–compulsive disorder, bipolar disorder, and schizophrenia to medicalizing certain perfectly normal reactions, personality styles, or lifestyles. From the perspective of pharmaceutical companies, the motivation to provide a pharmacological treatment for more people (normal people) is attractive because it drastically increases the number of potential users and profits.

Consider another example. The pharmaceutical company Cephalon sells **modafinil**, marketed as Provigil (abbreviation for "promotes vigilance"), for the treatment of **narcolepsy**, a sleeping disorder characterized by irresistible urges to fall asleep at inappropriate times, such as while driving or speaking in public. Despite the fact that narcolepsy is rare, occurring in about 1 of every 2,000 Americans (0.05%), sales in 2001 totaled a whopping $150 million. Most of the purchasers (75%) did not have narcolepsy; they were perfectly normal and were taking the drug to combat drowsiness. Researchers have also explored other uses of the drug and report that modafinil can keep healthy individuals awake for more than 2 days without showing a deficit. This effect is another example of a drug treating a lifestyle rather than a disorder (Restak, 2003).

Thus, it appears that the increasing availability of certain drugs to treat various aspects of mental health and illness has increased the number of individuals taking drugs for lifestyle alterations. Also, according to David Healy at Cardiff University in Wales, the increased availability of psychopharmacological choices may be influencing the number of individuals reported to be suffering from disorders. In his book *The Creation of Psychopharmacology*, Healy (2002) reports that in the 1950s less than 0.5% of the population was diagnosed with a depressive disease. Prevalence rates for major depressive disorder in the 1990s rose more than 20-fold to 10% of the population, and some studies have reported rates up to 25%. He states that this significant increase in depressed patients provides a huge market for antidepressants.

Using drugs to influence lifestyle and normal emotional experiences may have a drastic effect on our emotional lives, as illustrated in Box E.1. Richard Restak (2003), a neurologist and neuropsychiatrist at George Washington University Medical Center in Washington, D.C., warns that the same drugs that bring welcome relief to sufferers of severe mental illness may result in social engineering when enlisted to enhance normal functioning. He points to the example of psychiatrists frequently diagnosing people with pessimistic personalities as having dysthymic disorder.

We can all think of examples of negative situations leading to something positive—medicine, peace negotiations, a poem. What are the societal consequences of taking the edge off one's life situations, of creating a life that is the equivalent of vanilla ice cream? One letter to the editor of the *Washington Post* stated the following:

> Human development is often stimulated in response to a perceived lack or need. Drugs that mask oppressive social conditions by increasing feelings of self-worth would effectively obscure the need

modafinil Drug originally developed to keep narcoleptic patients from suddenly falling asleep. It is also being used by nonnarcoleptic patients to stay awake for extended periods of time.

narcolepsy A condition in which individuals succumb to irresistible urges to sleep, even at such inappropriate times as while driving or speaking in public.

for further social and material progress. A drug-induced euphoric haze can cloud human awareness to social realities and inure one to the inequality and inhumanity of existing world conditions. (Restak, 2003, pp. 137–138)

A satirical view of the medicalization of emotions was published in *The Onion*, a satirical tabloid of societal events that is sometimes irreverent and humorous. *The Onion*'s "Pfizer launches 'Zoloft for Everything' Ad Campaign" (*Onion*, 2003) reports that the

Zoloft for Everything campaign will employ print and TV ads to inform potential users about the "literally thousands" of new applications for Zoloft. Among the conditions the drug can be used to treat: anxiety associated with summer swimsuit season, insecurity over sexual potency and performance, feelings of shame over taking an antidepressant, and a sense of hollowness stemming from losing an online auction....Do you find yourself feeling excited or sad? No one should have to suffer through those harrowing peaks and valleys.

This fanciful account reflects how extensive the use of antidepressants has become in our society. We do not have the answers to all the questions, but you will recall from Chapter 9 that our ability to experience a rich, varied emotional life is probably very important for our mental health.

GENETICS AND CLINICAL NEUROSCIENCE: BASIC RESEARCH, BASIC APPLICATIONS

Neurogenetics, broadly defined, represents a subdiscipline in the field that is providing data, second by second it seems sometimes, that show promise for understanding the very bases of the brain as well as treatment strategies (Manolio et al., 2009). In this brief section, we will highlight the prominent place that some applications, tools, and strategies of James Watson's and Francis Crick's discovery hold in neuroscience today and in the foreseeable future. Theirs, like a huge tsunami, has burly waves that, 50 years hence, still undulate through the field of biology.

To begin, when we discuss the role that genetics plays in clinical neuroscience, we refer not to one's own genes (necessarily) but to the many ways in which genetic techniques have been brought to bear on research strategies and application in the neurosciences. For instance, techniques such as in situ hybridization, in which the scientist can measure the message coming from the nucleus of the neuron by examining, with antibodies, the specific string of messenger RNA being coded for, allows for the precise quantification of the building blocks of the proteins being called for by the cell's nuclear code. Rather than focusing on the end product (proteins themselves), which can be influenced by multiple downstream factors, this technique gets to the heart of the matter.

Together with the basic research techniques is the voluminous amount of work being done with another Nobel Prize–winning genetics technique, quantitative real-time polymerase chain reaction. Here, the scientist is able to examine the expression of specific genes as they are activated or suppressed under a variety of natural conditions. For the first time, the observer

Box E.1

A Case in Point

Richard Restak's "Ted"

This hypothetical case from Restak's *The New Brain* (2003), included here in its entirety, exemplifies the growing concern in the neuroscience community about cosmetic psychopharmacology and how it may be changing our brains.

Our subject is a 54-year-old entrepreneur. Let's call him Ted. As a result of frequent business travel, Ted's sleep pattern tends to be irregular and affected by the different time zones he finds himself in from one day to another. After traveling across several time zones, Ted typically arrives too tired to function efficiently. But Ted has recently solved that problem with modafinil…whose exact mode of action remains unknown.

Two weeks prior to the current trip, Ted's younger brother, Jim, died in a car accident. Although Ted was initially upset when hearing the news, he quickly regained his composure by taking a tranquilizer. Three days later he took another tranquilizer so that he could remain calm and composed during the funeral service. Apparently the drug worked, since Ted didn't shed a tear at his brother's funeral. Immediately after the service Ted took a cab to the airport and resumed his business trip.

Now, after two weeks of travel, Ted is starting to find himself thinking of his brother. In the airport in Dallas he suddenly burst into tears "for no reason." But Ted isn't going to give in to any "morbid" responses. Based on his reading he has correctly diagnosed himself as experiencing the onset of depression secondary to an aborted grief reaction. When he reflects briefly on whether he should have acted differently, he ends up regretting nothing. Sure, it might have been nice to cancel his business trip for a few days and make himself available to comfort Jim's widow and children, but what was there to say, really? Jim is gone and nothing is to be gained by morbidly dwelling on that fact.

Ted has in his possession some antidepressants left over from two years ago when he became, in his words, "nonfunctional" and "moped around the house" wondering what "my life was all about." The antidepressant worked and he soon stopped moping and asking himself such questions. Now Ted reasons that the antidepressant should work equally well in regard to his current "fixation" on his brother's death. Ted considers it best to "get over it" and to "move on."

If the antidepressant "works" well Ted will soon stop thinking of his brother. He will operate at his maximum efficiency, completely free of grief or any morbid inclinations to dwell on the past. When he gets to his hotel room later he'll accustom himself to the five-hour time change by taking the modafinil. At the end of his business meetings he'll return to his room and take a sleeping pill. And in the morning he'll take his antidepressant and begin his new day **without any feelings at all**. (pp. 139–140)

can determine what influence an external or environmental factor has on the genomic activity of the neuron. By understanding this chain of events, leading again eventually to proteins, scientists are able to determine normal and faulty gene-expression patterns. Mental illness is, in part, likely a result of genetic deficiencies or modifications at some level.

Related to this are a host of genetics and genomic approaches that combine to complement, verify, and extend these approaches. Western and Northern blots, DNA microarrays, transgenic animals, and gene-splicing approaches, as well as a cursory glance at the advertising in the journals *Nature* and *Science*, demonstrate the enormous diversity of basic genetics research practices available to contemporary scientists. Today's student faces a surfeit of amazing and bewildering tools at his or her disposal, all of which take advantage of the cell's basic plan. Stem cells, which we discuss in this section and throughout the book, hold the promise they do because of the potential to alter their genetic code in such a way as to promote growth and activity toward or away from the direction they were formerly headed naturally. (And research into expressing this vast promise was given new life by the stroke of a pen, as President Barack Obama signed into law the Stem Cell Executive Order on 9 March, 2009, saying, "Today...we will bring the change that so many scientists and researchers; doctors and innovators; patients and loved ones have hoped for, and fought for, these past eight years: we will lift the ban on federal funding for promising embryonic stem cell research.") Thus, as a tool, exploiting genetic and genomic activity and assembling and studying the proteome together represents a rich opportunity to understand nervous system development and repair.

There are other genetic approaches which take advantage of existing genetic alterations or are aimed at understanding the subtle genetic dynamics at play in individual or collective diseases. For example, Francis Collins, the director of the National Institutes of Health (NIH), has been a major proponent of genetic approaches to understanding the brain. He presented a major policy talk that was attended by one of the authors (KGL) at a recent Society for Neuroscience meeting, in Chicago (October 2009). In this speech he discussed the valuable role that an understanding of genomics would play in the future of clinical neuroscience. Such techniques, he said, would help us "to understand fundamental biology and to uncover the causes of specific diseases." Of the latter, conditions such as autism spectrum disorders (ASD) and their genomic contributions, in which there are greater than 50 genetic variants involved, are likely to yield results as examinations of implicated target genes, of that portion of the genome that codes for proteins important for ASD displays, begin to elucidate the very root causes of the condition. This, then, could lead to both screening and prevention.

Other conditions are exemplary of the approach that the NIH would like to take, although with more accelerated benefits (Manolio et al., 2009). Fragile X syndrome, which is the most common heritable cause of learning and other disabilities and leads to major intellectual impairment, is an example of a condition that may benefit from increased attention to its genomic makeup. A gene, *FMR1*, was identified in 1991 (Verkerk et al., 1991), a mutation in which causes a trinucleotide repeat, leading to dysregulation of RNA-binding protein. Subsequent work identified a problem with a particular receptor system, metabotropic glutamate receptor 5 (mGluR-5). Recently, clinical trials in human volunteers have begun in which a treatment utilizing an mGluR-5 antagonist is employed in the hopes that suppressing its overactivity will reverse some of the effects of fragile X. Thus, from identification of a genetic role in a condition to animal models to applications, the focus on genomics may yield a treatment for the many sufferers of this condition. Government support, in the form of grants and support of basic research in general, is crucial for continued advances.

LOOKING TO THE FUTURE THROUGH THE LENSES OF CLINICAL NEUROSCIENCE

We end this book where we began, by elaborating on two issues that we emphasized in Chapter 1: (1) the value of viewing mental health from multiple perspectives as a balance between body and brain and (2) the importance of being vigilant about using empirical methodologies and research designs.

Integrating Mental Health Perspectives

Several lenses on mental health were introduced in Chapter 1, from neurobiology and genetics to environment and evolution. Like a microscope with multiple objectives, each providing a greater magnification or a different way to view, the material of clinical neuroscience is best examined from many different perspectives. As we discuss treatment strategies throughout this text, however, you have likely noticed that the neurochemical lens is the one most frequently used in clinical neuroscience. Psychopharmacology has provided much-needed relief for some severe symptoms associated with many mental disorders; this benefit, however, has come at the cost of excessive use of drugs for medicalizing our lifestyles in addition to treating mental illnesses. As helpful as drugs can be when used appropriately and responsibly, it is also important to consider other effective treatment strategies with fewer side effects.

In our coverage of therapeutic options to maintain the homeostasis in one's mental health, we have discussed exposure therapy for phobias, transcranial magnetic stimulation for depression, neurosurgical treatment for obsessive–compulsive disorder (OCD), cognitive training for schizophrenia, and relaxation therapies for addiction. Recently, increased attention has been focused on **cognitive/behavioral therapy–induced neuroplasticity**, our phrase for those underlying changes in neurobiology that result from significant cognitive and/or behavioral training. That is, just as the simplest form of learning results in physical changes to neurons, so too must there be accompanying alterations in neuronal structure and function in those cases where a talking therapy has succeeded. We discussed one prime example in Chapter 8—Jeffrey Schwartz's cognitive-behavioral therapy (CBT) for OCD. CBT results in gross brain changes measurable by PET scans. Unlike neurosurgical treatments or psychoactive drugs that alter brain structure and functioning, CBT offers a far less invasive way to change the brain; but it changes it nevertheless.

William James, the father of American psychology, wrote nearly 120 years ago of the plasticity of the nervous system in his *Principles of Psychology* (1890). Notwithstanding, much of twentieth-century psychology was dominated by the view that the nervous system is fixed and amenable to change only at certain rigidly defined critical periods in development. Even though evidence of environmentally induced plasticity (for example, via enriched environments) was reported several times throughout the last century, neuroscientists did not begin to rethink the idea that the brain is mutable until the mid-1980s. Today, research conducted on multiple species, including humans, provides convincing evidence that the brain changes in response to the changing demands of the environment

Focusing on "normal" brains, experience—that is, learning and adaptation— has significant effects on neurobiological functions. For example, neuroscientists in the United Kingdom examined the brains of London taxi drivers. They found that the drivers' posterior hippocampus was significantly larger than that of non-taxi driver controls. Have you ever wondered how taxi drivers negotiate such tight spaces and have such good memory for directions? Perhaps, owing to the "training" these individuals receive during their many daily forays, their brains respond more sensitively and accurately to the traffic and embedded road cues (Maguire et al., 2000, 2003).

cognitive-behavioral therapy–induced neuroplasticity Changes in a person's neurobiology resulting from significant cognitive and/or behavioral training.

dyslexia Learning disability that results in slow reading and comprehension; it is thought that the exposure of affected subjects to repetitive auditory language facilitates recovery.

Additional evidence of neuroplasticity in humans abounds. Scientists in Germany report on another fascinating aspect of the brain's capacity for change, this time capitalizing on the time-honored skill of juggling. Subjects that accomplished a juggling training program saw their brains develop increased gray matter in the middle temporal area of the visual cortex and the left posterior lobe when performing at their highest skill level. But the effects go away, much like one's muscles atrophy if an exercise regimen is discontinued: After abstaining from juggling for 3 months, the jugglers' brains reverted to the equivalent of those of the control group's (Draganski et al., 2004). Recently, Quallo et al. (2009) reported that rhesus macaques showed evidence of similar neuroplasticity following intensive training with tools. The work demonstrates the plasticity of the nervous system and, further, the potential advantage accruing to such adaptation-within-adaptiveness, in that survival was much more likely in those of our ancestors who mastered tool use in their daily lives, thereby increasing their own gray matter in the process, which contributed to their survival—and here you are.

It is easy to discern that the brain changes in the normal individual to allow for more accurate or appropriate responding. The more relevant question for us, however, may involve the therapeutic value of cognitive-behavioral therapy–induced neuroplasticity for various nervous system dysfunctions. Recall Christopher Reeve's successful use of physical therapy to obtain partial movement in his fingers.

Cognitive-behavioral therapy–induced neuroplasticity is also being considered for individuals suffering from the reading disability **dyslexia**. Michael Merzenich, of the University of California at San Francisco, has investigated the potential benefits of treating dyslexic children with extensive training trials. These trials, consisting of many hours of various sound repetitions, attempt to sensitize the brain to phonological processing. Merzenich's lab then conducted fMRI scans on 20 dyslexic children, aged 8–12, during and after phonological training (Temple et al., 2003). A correlation was observed between their improvement in oral language ability and increased activation of the left temporoparietal cortex. Accordingly, Merzenich has begun the first neuroplasticity enterprise, "Fast ForWord," to train children as more efficient readers, with the accompanying benefits to brain and behavior (Holloway, 2003; Schwartz & Begley, 2002).

Overall, it appears that intensive CBT can contribute to significant and improved therapeutic outcomes for those with brain injury as a result of stroke or trauma (as discussed in Chapter 7); further, certain sensory and language impairments such as dyslexia may be amenable to similar therapies. We have already discussed the effectiveness of CBT in treating OCD, where it induces significant changes to brain activity; but what of its effectiveness for other disorders? Moreover, can cognition or thought alone lead to clinical changes?

In the book *The Brain and the Mind: Neuroplasticity and the Power of Mental Force* (2002), Jeffrey Schwartz and Sharon Begley highlight a study by Alvaro Pascual-Leone and his colleagues that provides convincing evidence for the manner in which thought exercises can indeed alter neuroanatomy and neurophysiology, analogous to how repeated physical therapy helps restore bodily function (Pascual-Leone et al., 1995). In this study, one group of subjects practiced a five-finger piano exercise; their brain's functional map was compared with a group that mentally practiced the same exercise for the same amount of time. Interestingly, both physical and mental exercises resulted in parallel alterations in motor cortex activity, a result that aligns with the experience of many a sports psychologist who may use similar imagery and technique to help bolster client-athletes' actual competition motor performance.

There is promise, too, for such techniques under more clinical conditions. In Chapter 1, for example, we discussed the effectiveness of behavioral conditioning (brain changing of another sort) in treating patients with phobias. In one study, subjects, with various degrees of arachnophobia were exposed to CBT. Subsequent and posttherapy fMRI scans in these same patients, concomitant with less subjective fear of spiders, showed less prefrontal and parahippocampal activity. The researchers state that "changes made at the 'mind' [quotation marks added by the present authors] level, within a psychotherapeutic context, are able to functionally 'rewire' the brain" (Paquette et al., 2003, p. 409). In other words, learning = brain changes.

In Chapter 9, we discussed CBT's clinical efficacy with depressed patients; but does this therapy lead to actual physical changes in the brain? Related to depression is the ability to sequester or eliminate unwanted memories. Successful repression of unwanted memories was associated with increased dorsolateral prefrontal activation, reduced hippocampal activity, and increased forgetting of the memories (Anderson et al., 2004). Recently, Schiller et al. (2009) reported a novel way to erase fearful memories: pharmacological manipulation of the neural reconsolidation process, whereby memories are brought to the fore in consciousness. It remains to be seen if such treatments have long-term efficacy, but the data showing that memories are labile and can be manipulated and that talking/cognitive therapy modifies neurons provide further support for the evidence that CBT is clinically effective in a variety of patient types.

The activity devoted to accomplishing this CBT effect requires active participation of the individual, as opposed to the merely passive nature that accompanies licit drug use. A recent study, however, reminds us that the use of psychopharmacology and CBT need not be mutually exclusive and, in fact, can positively interact. Michael Davis and his colleagues at Emory University have reported that patients with a fear of heights respond to a form of CBT known as virtual reality therapy (i.e., virtual elevator rides) in eight sessions of training. The number of sessions required to procure clinical efficacy, however, decreases to only two if the virtual therapy is combined with the n-methyl-d-aspartate (NMDA) uptake blocker d-cycloserine (a memory enhancer) (Davis, 2004).

Neuroscientists have not been comfortable with terms such as *volition*, *mental force*, and *mindfulness* because these states cannot be either easily

Figure E.3
Virtual reality therapy Virtual reality therapy, investigated by Michael Davis and colleagues, consists of working with a virtual reality tour of an elevator shaft (pictured below) to desensitize patients to their fears of heights. View (a) looks up from a glass elevator, view (b) looks out at the fifth floor, and view (c) looks down. When this therapy is combined with an NMDA reuptake blocker, the number of therapy sessions required for efficacy drops.
RESSLER ET AL. (2004)

(a)

(b)

(c)

self-directed neuroplasticity
Systematically altering one's brain via extensive mental and/or physical training.

defined or measured. With the recent and proliferating body of data showing that such "soft" activity alters neurophysiology, it is becoming increasingly difficult to ignore this therapeutic strategy. The term **self-directed neuroplasticity** has been proposed to convey the idea that focused training and mental and/or physical effort systematically alter the brain's function in a potentially therapeutic manner (Schwartz & Begley, 2002). This approach, although requiring considerable effort on the part of the patient, holds special promise because of its multifaceted nature—behavioral, cognitive, and environmental manipulations that alter psychological, neurophysiological, and neuroanatomical responses.

In sum, it appears that cognitive, or so-called mental, therapies, have the potential to produce neuroplasticity sufficient for therapeutic improvement in an impaired nervous system, at least under specified conditions. By utilizing one of the fundamental properties of neurons, that of change in response to environmental input, it should come as no surprise, therefore, that both normal and abnormal psychology should arise from the accumulation of their subtle modifications.

Cleansing Our Views with Empirical Evidence: Remembering Past Lessons

In the last section we emphasized the range of therapeutic approaches to the nervous system. As important as the range is, it is not nearly as important as making sure that the appropriate methodology is utilized to yield the most accurate, informed results. You may be on the right road to a desired destination, but if your mode of transportation isn't working, you're not going to get there.

We have discussed numerous therapeutic approaches in this text. It is probable that some will stand the test of time, yet others will be identified as faulty and misleading, methodological "lemons" that fall short of yielding accurate or reliable information. Obviously, clinicians and neuroscientists need to do everything possible to hone their critical thinking skills and to avoid making methodological or interpretational mistakes in the haste to find "magic bullet" cures for various mental illnesses that afflict the human condition. As neuroscientific techniques become more molecular and genetic, it appears that we are gaining methodological and technical power that must be balanced against high experimental and evaluative standards. We should not lose sight of the simple and terrible fact that living with a mental illness presents a significant challenge to the afflicted. They don't need the added burden of taking unnecessary detours on their therapeutic highways of life.

To add some perspective, a colleague provided us with an article from *Life Magazine*, dated March 3, 1947, and entitled "Psychosurgery: Operation to Cure Sick Minds Turns Surgeon's Blade into an Instrument of Mental Therapy" (see Psychosurgery, 1947). Like a splash of cold water, reading through this article provided a powerful reminder of why we need informed and critical students and practitioners in the field of clinical neuroscience.

Life reported that, by that point in time, over 2,000 American patients had received prefrontal lobotomies; and the article went on to celebrate the success of this then-innovative therapy, claiming particular effectiveness in depression, a mortality rate of "only" 3% ("only" 60 people out of the 2,000). The article also described the mechanisms that contributed to the success of prefrontal lobotomies. The depressed individual, the author writes, was thought to suffer from an overactive conscience (residing in the PFC) that suppresses impulses (themselves originating somehow in the brain stem), thereby disrupting judgment (apparently residing in the occipital lobe) and executive function (around the parietal cortex). In a confusing and seemingly insensitive fashion, the article discusses with false assurance topics such as the neural residence of the *superego* as if it were fact.

This misinformed article, barely a half-century old, is not describing techniques used by some ancient society, no trepanning with a sharp stone tool. No, this is Nobel Prize–winning work and a recent piece of our history. True, we are applying 20/20 hindsight to this dark period in our neuroscientific history; and further, the popularity of this technique was rather short-lived. That said, critical thinking would have saved a lot of people from this barbaric practice: Certainly, more accurate methodological techniques, including deeper analyses of the existing animal literature, more accurate preoperative assessments (with less emphasis on vague concepts), and meaningful and valid control groups, would have dampened the enthusiasm for the lobotomy technique.

In *The Trouble with Testosterone* (1997), Robert Sapolsky describes another unthinkable case of unnecessary and invasive surgery. At the turn of the nineteenth century, it was unknown why some infants died in their sleep—a condition referred to as "crib death" then but currently known as **sudden infant death syndrome (SIDS)**. Today, research suggests that SIDS is caused by a neural malfunction in the medulla, which regulates breathing. At that time, however, upon autopsy, physicians noted that the thymus gland of the SIDS infant was much larger than that of "control" infants, non-SIDS deaths. But a significant confound existed, one that our introductory research design and statistics students could easily identify.

The non-SIDS infants were typically from impoverished, stressful environments and had likely been chronically stressed prior to their unfortunate and premature deaths. Recall that chronic stress causes minor atrophy of the thymus. Thus, SIDS infants did not have abnormally large thymus glands: They were being compared to chronically stressed infants with abnormally small ones.

Again, hindsight clarifies the past. The pediatricians of a century ago were not as methodologically sophisticated as those of today and went on to hypothesize that the large thymus glands in SIDS infants pressed on the trachea while the infant was sleeping, leading to difficulty breathing and death. An inaccurate reading and evaluation of the literature led to further disaster. By the 1920s a treatment, which lasted well into the 1950s, was recommended in many pediatric textbooks for this disorder, known as *status thymicolymphaticus*. Pediatricians recommended irradiating the throats, and hence shrinking the otherwise dangerous thymus, of infants. Again, this treatment failed to help a nonexistent condition; because the thymus is adjacent to the thyroid gland (which regulates growth and metabolism), thousands of cases of thyroid cancer developed.

No one knows how many mistakes of this magnitude are being made today. What we do know is that appropriate empirical evidence is the best antidote. Working on a mental health problem from many perspectives helps to ensure against taking an unwanted detour. Informed, dedicated, clear-thinking, hard-working, and compassionate practitioners and researchers will keep us on the best therapeutic paths in the future.

sudden infant death syndrome (SIDS) Respiratory malfunction, perhaps influenced by an immature medulla, that results in an infant's death.

Summary

Ethics Buffeted on the Sea of Neuroscience

Clinical neuroscience research does not exist in a vacuum but must connect to and inform those forces delivering its applications to the ones in need. Contemporary researchers, at both the front end (experimental design and conduct) and the back (translation into applications), are concerned with the ethical considerations of new data and findings as they emerge and are integrated into the existing empirical base. For example, researchers suggest that specific neuroanatomical regions, such as the prefrontal cortex and amygdala, are involved in violent behavior. As more data pour in and are synthesized regarding the brain structures involved in criminal behavior, the legal community is forced to consider the possibility that someone may commit a crime due to an organic malfunction. The parallel to a run-of-the-mill medical condition, say asthma, in which a behavior, breathing, manifests problems due to a biological cause, constricted airways, is inescapable. Asthma is not a moral failing. Like the insanity defense, with its lowered bar of proof of regulation, how will such findings shape society's ideas about personal responsibility and conduct in the future?

Too, neuroscience information is being used to identify truth-telling versus lying in criminal investigations. Though the polygraph is legally thought to lack validity, new approaches such as brain fingerprinting and functional magnetic resonance imaging hold promise as potential lie-detecting devices.

Another important ethical issue in clinical neuroscience is the field of psychopharmacology. Brain-altering drugs have been reported to be successful in the treatment of mental disorders such as depression and schizophrenia, though with significant side effects. Additionally, drugs are being increasingly developed and prescribed for the purpose of altering personality style, rather than regaining mental health. Imagine a life without the emotional ups and downs that characterize daily activities. It is very important to consider the long-term effects of medicalizing and homogenizing personality styles.

Genetics and Clinical Neuroscience: Basic Research, Basic Applications

Now that the human genome has been completed, the search is on for genetic variants associated with various mental illnesses. Conditions such as Autism Spectrum Disorders likely involve as many as 50 genetic variants; consequently much patience is required to transition from candidate genetic variations to therapeutic interventions. Although a single gene has been associated with Fragile X syndrome, the identification of clear associations between specific genes and complex mental illnesses has been slow to emerge. It will be interesting to determine if the completion of the human and other animal genome projects will lead to tangible treatment strategies for mental illness in the future.

Looking to the Future Through the Lenses of Clinical Neuroscience

Throughout this text, many perspectives are used to examine the data, treatment, and outcomes of normal and abnormal states and conditions. These are like the objectives or lenses of a microscope, as we previously discussed. The neurochemical lens is a popular treatment approach, addressing as it does the chemical interactions among neurons; cognitive-behavioral therapies, however, are quickly gaining respect as effective therapeutic options, and both approaches work because they change the brain in some fashion. Cognitive-behavioral therapy leads to detectable brain changes and accompanying improvement in clinical outcomes. Of course, the best way to determine clinical efficacy is through the use of appropriate research methodologies and controls, critical evaluation of results, and careful application of their findings by knowledgeable clinicians. Unfortunately, the history of clinical neuroscience—indeed, of science itself—is rife with examples of misdirected therapies that, upon repeated examination, were eventually shown to be ineffective—only after the damage was done. With well-designed and interpreted research, we are less likely to subject vulnerable patients to such ineffective treatments. The future of the clinic must be informed by the rigor inherent to science and to neuroscience. Clinical neuroscience represents a valuable approach to providing effective care and treatment to the patient formerly fated to less effective diagnostic and management strategies. The student interested in psychology today will one day likely be the beneficiary of a science shaped by the future gains of clinical neuroscience.

Key Terms

neuroethics (455)

somatic marker (457)

kindled limbic seizure (459)

brain fingerprinting (460)

euneurics (461)

cosmetic pharmacology (461)

modafinil (463)

narcolepsy (463)

cognitive/behavioral-induced
   neuroplasticity (467)

dyslexia (468)

self-directed neuroplasticity
   (470)

sudden infant death syndrome
   (SIDS) (471)

For Further Consideration

Barrash, J., Tranel, D., & Anderson, S. W. (2000). Acquired personality disturbances associated with bilateral damage to the ventromedial prefrontal region. *Developmental Neuropsychology, 18,* 355–381. If a general acceptance of the idea that basic regulation of complex human behavior is accomplished by prosaic biochemical activities in the brain is going to be accepted one day, more solid studies such as this one need to be done. These researchers closely examined individuals with prefrontal damage (two types of ventromedial lesions [bilateral and unilateral]) compared to those without. They measured differences in personality related to the brain damage. They concluded that damage to the prefrontal area, especially the ventromedial portion, is responsible for the poor decision making, emotional regulation (both subjective experience and overt displays), and lack of "insight" characteristic of sociopaths. The connection between brain damage, subtle and otherwise, and a personality type associated with the worst kinds of crimes and behavior is intriguing. Other studies such as this will begin to assemble a database showing how minor brain damage or malfunction can have major consequences.

Blight, A. R. (2002). Miracles and molecules—Progress in spinal cord repair. *Nature Neuroscience, 5*(supplement), 1051–1054. As anyone who has ever witnessed the devastating aftermath of a spinal cord injury (SCI) knows, being able to find a way to reverse the damage would be a dream come true to the paralyzed individual and his family. Here, Blight reviews the hopeful advances that have been made in the area of SCI and its treatment. He discusses the strategies for treating SCI immediately afterward, to minimize further damage, and for slowing down or preventing "hemorrhagic necrosis," a progressive loss of spinal cord tissue that inevitably spirals out of control, leading to more damage. It is shameful that these and other treatments go understudied or do not get applied because their commercial value (cost:benefit ratio) is so slim. Other work covered includes techniques to regenerate axons lost, through transplantation or directly treating the spinal demyelination that occurs. A molecular biological approach that includes new understanding of the Nogo molecule and its regulatory control of myelin formation also holds promise. He ends by discussing the basis of the scientific method for this field—hypothesis, test, reformulation of hypothesis, retest, etc. It is because of and through this elegant procedure that the future holds promise for SCI.

Dennett, D. (2001). Are we explaining consciousness yet? *Cognition, 79,* 221–237. Dennett is the gadfly of current theorizing about consciousness. He buzzes around with new problems for the "wet" scientists (those who study the neurobiology of his favorite subject) to solve, creating new tasks that must be accomplished before consciousness can be satisfactorily explained or accounted for. He provides a necessary foil to the neuroscientists who are engaged in the search for the ultimate human character. In this article, he poses the idea that the cause of consciousness is different from the state of consciousness, both of which are different from the "aftermath" of consciousness, presumably one's self-awareness. It is a philosophical labyrinth best navigated carefully and with an eye out for the next, sudden turn. Dennett is a skillful polemicist, but in this article his language sometimes interferes with the points he is making. Overall, however, it makes for an important and necessary read for one interested in the larger picture about the humanness problem.

LeDoux, J. (2002). *Synaptic self: How our brains become who we are.* New York: Viking Press. A companion volume to another of LeDoux's interesting offerings (called *The Emotional Brain*), *Synaptic Self* explores some new territory and treads upon some well-worn ones. First, the premise is one that is in need of expressing widely: That human consciousness is a result of complex, but prosaic nevertheless, interactions that neurons provide. Synapses are the critical unit for LeDoux, and he does a wonderful job of making the case for them. Because of their development and expression by endogenous biological mechanisms and their sensitivity to environmental, real-world stimulation, the synapse represents the brain's window on the world and, hence, thought, self-awareness, learning, etc. LeDoux argues convincingly for these myriad plastic sites (which number Francis Crick has stated exceeds that of charged particles in the known universe). It is a book well worth having and, appropriately enough, thinking about.

Lambert, K.G., & Lilienfeld, S.O. (2007). Brainstains: Traumatic therapies can have long-lasting effects on mental health, Scientific American Mind, 46–53. In this article, the authors follow up on another patient of the psychiatrist who treated Nadean Cool (discussed in Chapter 1 of this text). Following the publication of the first edition of *Clinical Neuroscience*, another patient, Sheri Storm, contacted K.G.L. This article chronicles Sheri's harrowing story. After seeking therapy for insomnia, Sheri's psychiatrist told her she had multiple personality disorder; she was subsequently placed on an intensive regime of pharmacological and hypnotic "therapy." Following her psychiatric "treatment," Sheri emerged in a vulnerable, hyper-responsive, chronically-stressed mental condition. This case study reminds us that mental health can be compromised if evidence-based therapies are not used in appropriate ways.

McLaren, A. (Ed.). (2002). *Cloning.* Strasbourg: Council of Europe Publishing. The need for this book was not apparent 10 years ago. The cloning genie, however, is out of the bottle. This volume does a fine job of presenting the many arguments, for and against, the science of cloning. Legal, ethical, religious, and other perspectives are represented from a wide variety of thinkers, scientific and other. Background on the science of cloning, its technical wizardry and inherent difficulty, also is highlighted by those in the thick of the work. The overall effect is one of a complex topic, presented fairly, that falls firmly in the gray area between beneficial and dangerous.

Parvizi, J., & Damasio, A. (2001). Consciousness and the brainstem. *Cognition, 79,* 135–160. In the same issue as Dennett's article described earlier, these authors attempt to reconcile consciousness with what is known about the neurobiology of consciousness. It is not unlike a philosophical Tower of Babel—many different languages attempting to build an edifice. They frame their discussion of consciousness into several regions of regulation (basal, vegetative, and internal and external sensory monitors). The concept of consciousness must include all of these levels, summing as they do to produce and maintain the organism and, in the case of the human, awareness of activities. It is self-referential, but Parvizi and Damasio's arguments, and their understanding of the neural systems that underlie the activities they outline, are tight and reasoned. It is an important article to help understand how the brain leads to the mind.

Whitaker, R. (2010). *Anatomy of an Epidemic: Magic bullets, psychiatric drugs, and the astonishing rise of metnal illness in America.* **New York: Crown Publishers.** Scientific journalist Robert Whitaker investigates what he calls a medical mystery in this book. Specifically, he's interested in why, if we have improved drugs for mental illness, the rates of mentally ill patients being classified as disabled has triped over the past 20 years. The rates for children being added to government diability rolls is the most startling. As Whitaker takes the reader through the research, it becomes apparent that long-term effects of psychiatric medications has not received appropriate attention; in fact, when long-term effects are taken into consideration the efficacy of many psychiatric drugs is called into question.

Glossary

absolute refractory period. A point during the action potential, while the cell is returning to its resting potential, when the neuron cannot respond to another action potential.

acetylcholine (ACh). Neurotransmitter in the somatic and parasympathetic nervous systems involved in cognition and at the neuromuscular junction.

acquired immune system. B cells and T cells that, following exposure to infectious pathogens, are stimulated to develop a selective immunity that results in a faster response should the same type of pathogen invade the body again; also known as *adaptive immunity.*

action potential. Physical basis of the nerve impulse; the depolarization of an axon produced by a stimulation beyond threshold potential.

activity-based anorexia. An animal (rodent) model of anorexia nervosa in which animals that are food-restricted increase activity levels to the point that they become very ill if the experimenter does not intervene.

activity-stress paradigm. Animal model of chronic stress and compulsive behavior in which rats are housed in activity wheels and exposed to restricted food resources. Rats typically increase running and exhibit multiple signs of stress-induced illness when faced with these conditions.

addiction syndrome. Vast array of variables, sometimes difficult to tease apart, typically associated with drug addiction, including one's predisposition to consume drugs, the development of tolerance to a drug, withdrawal symptoms on the removal of a drug, craving for a drug, and the likelihood of relapse after ceasing consumption of a drug.

adenosine triphosphate (ATP). Chemical the body uses as its primary way of delivering energy where it is needed; also used as a neurotransmitter.

adrenocorticotropic hormone (ACTH). A hormone released by the anterior pituitary which stimulates the adrenal gland to release glucocorticoids from the adrenal cortex. ACTH is a critical component of the hypothalamic–pituitary–adrenal (HPA) axis stress response.

adult stem cells. Undifferentiated cells located in a currently differentiated tissue; these cells have the ability to renew themselves and differentiate, within certain limits, to various specialized cell types characteristic of the tissue from which they were derived.

afferent information. Information carried inward toward the brain.

affiliative social contact. Nonthreatening social contact. This type of social contact probably increases oxytocin, which subsequently triggers a cascade of responses that maximize growth and minimize stress.

affinity. The strength of attraction that a neurotransmitter has for a particular type of receptor.

agonist. A drug that mimics the endogenous actions of the targeted neurotransmitter.

all-or-none law. Observation that, once the threshold is reached, all action potentials are the same size regardless of the intensity of the original stimulation.

allostasis. Literally, maintaining stability through change; the active process of maintaining physiological homeostasis in the face of any challenge.

allostatic load. Wear and tear on the body that results from repeated activation of the processes that maintain homeostasis.

alpha-amino hydroxy-methyl-isoxazolepropionate (AMPA) receptors. A subtype of glutamate receptor in which Na^+ influx causes an excitatory postsynaptic potential (EPSP).

amino acids. The so-called building blocks of proteins, composed of an amino group (NH2) and a carboxylic acid (COOH). These are essential components of proteins and the basis for organic life.

amygdala. Almond-shaped structure at the tail end of the basal ganglia within the temporal lobe; functions as part of the limbic system involved in regulation of emotion and sexual urges.

anhedonia. Lack of desire or pleasure. Drugs that interfere with the mesolimbic dopaminergic system produce this state.

anorexia nervosa (AN). An eating disorder characterized by decreased food consumption and excessive physical activity. Although individuals with this disorder are severely underweight, they remain reluctant to eat to regain their health. If not treated, this condition may lead to the patient's death.

antagonist. A drug that blocks the actions of an endogenous neurotransmitter.

antalarmin. New drug that inhibits the release of corticotropin-releasing hormone and has been found in animal models to reduce anxietylike behaviors in animals. Researchers are hopeful that this drug may be used as an antidepressant in humans in the future.

anterior cingulate cortex. Front portion of the older lobe of the cerebral cortex that surrounds the corpus callosum. Decreased activity in this area has been found to accompany profound sadness; thus, this area has been implicated in the symptoms of depression.

anterograde amnesia. Ability to recall long-ago events but not recent events and a general inability to incorporate recent events into memory.

antibodies or immunoglobulins (Ig). Glycoprotein molecules produced by B lymphocytes that bind to specific antigens. The four types are IgA, IgE, IgG, and IgM.

antigen. Molecule that binds specifically to either an antibody or a T-cell receptor.

antigen-presenting cell (APC). Cell that displays fragments of protein antigens, along with major histocompatibility complex molecules, on its surface in order to activate T cells.

antipsychotics. Psychoactive drugs that reduce psychotic symptoms but have long-term side effects resembling symptoms of neurological diseases.

anxiolytics. Drugs such as the benzodiazepines that work to reduce anxiety.

apoptosis. Programmed cellular death characterized by fragmentation of the cell; prompted by nuclear or other related signals from within the cell or from signals outside the cell. Serves as a form of neuronal sculpting in the developing brain.

arcuate nucleus. Nucleus of the hypothalamus where most of the neuropeptide Y neurons are located.

arginine vasopressin. A neuropeptide that is secreted by the posterior pituitary gland and by nerve endings in the hypothalamus. It affects learning functions and water resorption in mammals.

association cortex. Areas of the cortex that integrate information to produce cognition.

astrocyte. Relatively large, star-shaped glial cell found in the central nervous system.

atherosclerosis. Buildup of lipid substances in lesions in the blood vessels; can eventually lead to hardened arteries and disrupted blood flow.

attention-deficit/hyperactivity disorder (ADHD). A condition observed in children and adults characterized by inattention, hyperactivity, and impulsivity.

autoimmune disease. Disease that results when the mechanisms designed to preserve self-recognition in the immune system are compromised so that the adaptive immune system responds to self-antigens in the same manner as it responds to foreign antigens—leading to cellular and tissue damage.

autonomic nervous system (ANS). Maintenance component of the nervous system, composed of sympathetic and parasympathetic divisions.

axon. Fiberlike outgrowth from the cell body of a neuron that is cylindrical until the very end, when it breaks into numerous small branches; the "sending" fiber of the neuron, it carries the nerve impulse.

axon hillock. Swelling of the soma of the neuron, the point where the axon begins and an action potential "firing decision" is made.

axon shearing. Diffuse damage to neuronal axons following traumatic brain injury that leads to neuronal damage and compromised neural networks.

B cells or B lymphocytes. Cells that originate in the bone marrow and migrate to lymphoid tissue, bone marrow, and, in low numbers, the blood. These are the only immune cells with the capability of producing antibodies.

barbiturates. Psychoactive drugs that act as central nervous system depressants, producing a wide array of effects ranging from relaxation to coma. They are highly addictive.

basal ganglia. Subcortical cluster of nuclei in the telencephalon that forms a circuit with the cortex, thalamus, and midbrain to coordinate body movements and links to the limbic system via the amygdala.

bed nucleus of the stria terminalis (BNST). Subcortical limbic structure considered part of the extended amygdala that plays a role in the stress/anxiety response.

behavioral addiction. Notion that an animal or human may develop a physiological addiction (similar to drug addiction) to engaging in certain behaviors such as compulsions.

behaviorism. Theory advocated by J. B. Watson calling for a shift of emphasis in the field of psychology from unconscious processes to the empirical manipulation of environmental stimuli and observable responses.

benzodiazepines. A class of drugs (usually of the tranquilizer variety) that increases the frequency of chloride channel openings in the presence of GABA.

biomedical model. Therapeutic approach using mostly medical diagnoses and drug prescriptions.

bipolar disorder. Mood disorder characterized by episodes of mania interspersed with episodes of depression. This disorder occurs in about 1%–1.6% of the population and is sometimes referred to as "manic depression."

blastocyst. The 150-cell preimplantation embryo comprising an outer layer, a fluid-filled cavity, and a cluster of interior cells.

blood–brain barrier. Protective environment formed by tightly packed capillaries and neutroglia that prevents passage into the brain of most substances circulating in the blood.

bone marrow. Located in the center of the bone; serves as the site of generation of all blood cells (e.g., lymphocytes and B cells).

brain-derived neurotrophic factor (BDNF). A stimulating factor localized in the central nervous system that promotes the growth and survival of neurons.

brain fingerprinting. Theory suggesting that specific brain-wave activity accompanies the identification of familiar stimuli. This technology may one day be used in criminal investigations.

bulimia nervosa. An eating disorder characterized by bouts of both overeating and self-induced vomiting/laxative use. Symptoms are often responsive to serotonergic treatments.

buprenorphine. Recent drug approved by the FDA to treat opioid addiction; works as a partial agonist for mu-opioid receptors.

catatonia. Absence of movement; often observed in the schizophrenic patient.

catecholamines. A group of three different amine neurotransmitters that contain catechol. These three neurotransmitters are dopamine, norepinephrine, and epinephrine (also called "adrenaline").

cell adhesion molecules (CAMs). Glycoproteins located on the cell surface that play a role in guiding growing axons as they move toward their final destinations in the brain.

cell body (or soma). Structure of the cell that contains the nucleus, cytoplasm, and various organelles used in cell metabolism.

cell membrane. Membrane that maintains the cell's shape and contains the cytoplasm, nucleus, and assorted organelles. The membrane is a bimolecular leaflet with semipermeable properties.

cellular immune system. Component of adaptive immunity composed of T cells that defend the body by either activating B-cell release or proliferating so that the T cells themselves can attack the antigen.

central canal (or spinal canal). Pathway through the vertebral column for cerebrospinal fluid and the vertebral arteries.

central nervous system (CNS). One of the two main divisions of the human nervous system, consisting of the brain and spinal cord; the main coordinating and controlling center of the body that processes information to and from the peripheral nervous system.

central sulcus. Deep sulcus that separates the frontal lobe (motor cortex) from the parietal lobe (sensory cortex).

cerebellum. Hindbrain structure concerned with the coordination and control of voluntary muscular activity and movement.

cerebral aqueduct. Narrow tube interconnecting the third and fourth ventricles of the brain, located in the center of the mesencephalon.

cerebral cortex. Most recently evolved part of the brain that envelops the midbrain; also associated with complex cognitive functions.

cerebrospinal fluid (CSF). Normally clear, salty liquid produced in the ventricles, filling them and circulating around the brain in the subarachnoid layer of the meninges and central canal to nourish and protect the brain and spinal cord.

cholecystokinin. Gastrointestinal peptide released following ingestion of a meal in order to coordinate different functions of the digestive system.

chronic traumatic encephalopathy. Potential permanent brain damage due to recurrent concussions.

cingulum. Latin for *belt*; an association tract located in the cingulate gyrus that projects to the entorhinal cortex; stimulation of this area results in a desire to engage in repetitive behaviors.

classical conditioning. Basic form of associative learning originally studied by Ivan Pavlov; involves pairing a neutral stimulus with an unconditioned stimulus known to automatically evoke a response so that, eventually, the neutral stimulus will lead to the behavior originally produced by the unconditioned stimulus.

clomipramine. Serotonin reuptake inhibitor that prevents the reuptake of serotonin and norepinephrine from the synapse, ultimately increasing the availability of serotonin; similar in structure to imipramine, a tricyclic antidepressant; used as therapy for obsessive–compulsive disorder.

cognitive/behavioral therapy–induced neuroplasticity. Changes in a person's neurobiology resulting from significant cognitive and/or behavioral training.

cognitive-behavioral therapy (CBT). Therapy developed in the 1960s that involves the therapist working with the depressed patient to educate him or her about the disorder so that he or she can eventually alter behaviors and cognitions to reduce the symptoms of depression.

cognitive-induced movement therapy. A form of behavioral therapy designed to restrict the use of a functioning limb such as a hand in order to force a patient to use the impaired limb.

coma therapy. Physical therapy in which an insulin coma is induced to treat mental illness in a patient. After the 1960s the use of this therapy decreased because of rising popularity of electroconvulsive therapy and psychoactive drugs.

comorbidity. Presence of two or more health problems in the same individual.

complement complex. Group of nonimmune proteins that combines to form an important part of the immune system, which can damage threatening cells by quick responses such as cutting holes in the pathogen cells.

compulsions. Ritualistic acts that accompany obsessions in obsessive–compulsive disorder patients; typically include hand washing, checking, repeating actions, ordering, praying, and counting.

computerized tomography (CT). Neuroimaging technique developed in the 1960s that is the equivalent of taking an X-ray of the brain.

concentration gradient. In diffusion, the attraction of a region of high concentration for one of low concentration.

concordance rate. Frequency with which two individuals express the same condition. For example, the rate at which identical twins both develop schizophrenia is the concordance rate for schizophrenia.

constraint-induced (CI) movement therapy. Type of rehabilitation therapy requiring an individual to constrain his or her "good arm" to stimulate use of the "bad" arm.

contusion. A bruise in the brain due to brain trauma.

coping style. Persistent response strategy in the presence of stressful stimuli. An animal may have an active, passive, or flexible style.

correlation. Statistical technique used to determine how strongly two variables are related; two variables may change in a similar pattern (*positive correlation*) or a different pattern (*negative correlation*).

cortex (neocortex). Phylogenetically the newest cortex, the outermost layer of cerebral gray matter, including the sensorimotor and association cortices.

corticosteroids. Hormones secreted by the adrenal cortex during stress. These neurochemicals influence the brain and are thought to be a trigger for depressive symptoms. Some drugs targeted at reducing corticosteroids reduce symptoms of depression.

corticotropin-releasing hormone (CRH). A releasing hormone produced in the hypothalamus that travels to the anterior pituitary, where it triggers the release of ACTH from the anterior pituitary.

cortisol. The stress hormone secreted by the adrenal cortex in primates.

cosmetic pharmacology. Using psychoactive drugs for personality modification or lifestyle alterations unrelated to mental illness.

cranial nerves. Twelve pairs of nerves, each pair having sensory and/or motor functions, extending to and from the brain without passing through the spinal cord.

craniotomy. Early physical therapy in which a section of a patient's skull was removed in an attempt to restore balance to the four humors, leading to recovery from mental illness.

craving response. Persistent, intense desire to consume a drug.

culture-bound syndrome. Condition that appears to be culture-specific, for example, anorexia (United States), latah (Malaysia), koro (Malaysia), and brain fag (Nigeria). The *Diagnostic and Statistical Manual of Mental Disorders* categorizes these disorders in this broad classification.

cytokine. "Messenger" protein secreted by many cells that regulates immune functions and mediates communication among the cells of the immune system; also called "immunotransmitter" or "interleukin."

decarboxylase inhibitor. A type of drug that blocks the conversion of L-dopa to dopamine in the peripheral nervous system, diminishing L-dopa-induced side effects, in patients taking L-dopa for Parkinson symptoms.

decatastrophizing. Any attempt to minimize the impact of a stressor, likely to result in a decreased allostatic load. Some people may decatastrophize by gaining an increased perception of control or employing active coping strategies to minimize the negative impact.

deep brain stimulation. Surgical treatment for Parkinson's disease in which a neurostimulator is implanted below the collarbone that delivers mild stimulation to electrodes implanted in various areas of the brain such as the thalamus.

dementia. Progressive loss of mental functioning atypical of normal aging processes.

dementia praecox. Older term for schizophrenia describing what was believed to be a progressive and incurable deterioration of mental functioning that typically began in adolescence.

dendrites. Thin, widely branching fibers that emanate from the cell body of a neuron and "collect" information from adjacent neurons and other cells.

dendritic cells. Serve as antigen-presenting cells for naive T cells; important for acquired immunity. Originate in the bone marrow but eventually end up in the skin and lymphoid tissue.

dendritic spines. Short, plastic outgrowths along the dendrites that increase surface area and where the majority of synapses are found.

deoxyribonucleic acid (DNA). Molecule that composes the chromosomes.

dependence. Development of tolerance and withdrawal following chronic use of a drug; physical and psychological problems arise upon cessation of drug use.

depolarization. The actual change in the resting charge of the neuron, from slightly negative (polarized) to less negative/more positive (i.e., less polarized).

depression. Mood disorder characterized by feelings of sadness, diminished pleasure, alterations in sleep, fatigue, difficulty concentrating, and feelings of worthlessness; several variations exist (e.g., major depression, dysthymic disorder).

detoxification. Initial step in the treatment of drug addiction that involves clearing a patient's system of the abused drug. This process can be accomplished by requiring a patient to abstain from drug use, or it may be facilitated by certain pharmacological agents.

diencephalon. "Between" area of the forebrain that surrounds the third ventricle; includes the thalamus, hypothalamus, and pineal gland, structures that synthesize sensory information and regulate motivated behaviors.

diffusion. Tendency for dissolved ions or molecules to move from areas of high concentration to areas of low concentration.

diffusion tensor imaging. Brain-imaging technique utilizing radio frequency and magnetic field pulses to track water molecules to provide an image of fiber tracts in the living brain.

disorganized symptoms. Symptoms in a schizophrenic patient such as nonlogical thoughts and speech.

dopamine (DA). The resulting neurotransmitter when dopa reacts with the enzyme dopa decarboxylase. This is an important neurotransmitter involved in movement and brain reward systems.

drug addiction. Strong desire to consume a drug accompanied by a diminishing capacity to limit the intake of the drug.

dual-center hypothesis of hunger regulation. Proposed by Stellar in 1954, the ventromedial hypothalamus was considered the hunger center and the lateral hypothalamus was the satiety center.

dualism. Philosophical position taken on the mind–body problem suggesting that the mind and body/brain are separate entities; Descartes proposed interactionism in which the two entities interacted in the physical brain, specifically in the pineal gland.

dumping syndrome. Side effect sometimes seen in patients following gastric bypass surgery; syndrome consists of nausea or general sickness following the consumption of fat or sugar.

dyskinesias. Abnormal involuntary motor movements and difficulty in carrying out voluntary movements.

dyslexia. Learning disability that results in slow reading and comprehension; it is thought that the exposure of affected subjects to repetitive auditory language facilitates recovery.

ecologically relevant. Term used to describe stressors that an animal may find in its natural environment. Example: Social defeat is a more ecologically relevant stimulus for hamsters than cold or restraint.

ectoderm. The outer layer of the fertilized egg, or zygote, that eventually gives rise to the skin, nerve cells, and most of the neuroglia.

efferent information. Information carried outward from the central nervous system to the periphery.

efficacy. The capacity to produce a desired effect with a drug or treatment.

electroconvulsive therapy (ECT). Physical therapy used for mental illnesses such as major depression and schizophrenia; involves the delivery of electrical current to an anesthetized patient in an attempt to reconfigure neural functions for normal mental functioning.

electroencephalography (EEG). One of the earliest methods of recording activity of the living brain; involves placing electrodes on an individual's scalp and recording the activity of large populations of neurons. This technique has been valuable in diagnosing epilepsy and in delineating the various stages of sleep.

electrostatic pressure. Electrical attraction and repulsion (+/– and +/+, –/–, respectively); complement to diffusion.

embryonic stem cells. Undifferentiated cells derived from the embryo that have the potential to develop into a wide variety of cell types.

empirical evidence. Evidence that can be confirmed by systematic observations. This evidence should play a critical role in a researcher's or practitioner's opinion of causes and treatments for certain disorders.

endoderm. The innermost layer of the fertilized egg, or zygote, that eventually gives rise to the developing fetus's internal organs.

endogenous opioids. Naturally occurring neurotransmitter-like substances found in the brain that produce analgesic and euphoric effects similar to heroin and morphine.

endoplasmic reticulum. Network of thin tubes within a cell that transport newly synthesized proteins to other locations.

endorphin. An opioid-like substance produced in the hypothalamus and elsewhere that is related to pain reduction and reward but also facilitates the release of epinephrine from the adrenal medulla during the stress response.

entorhinal cortex. Cortical structure on the medial surface of the temporal lobe that surrounds limbic structures such as the amygdala and has rich interconnections with the hippocampal formation.

enzymes. Proteins that facilitate chemical reactions and are intimately involved in the regulation of activity inside the neuron.

epidural hematoma. Collection of blood between the skull and dura mater following a head injury.

epinephrine. One of the three catecholamine neurotransmitters that is also called "adrenaline"; epinephrine neurons contain phentolamine.

episodic memory. Autobiographic memory for personal experiences (episodes) pinpointed to specific place and time contexts.

euneurics. Movement to design "better" brains.

evolutionary game theory. Quantitative models used by evolutionary theorists to understand strategies used by animals to maximize survival (e.g., mating).

excitatory postsynaptic potential (EPSP). Graded depolarization of a neuron.

excitotoxicity. Process that probably occurs in CA3 neurons of the hippocampus. This effect is caused by excessive glutamate activity in the neurons, which may lead to neuronal death; prolonged exposure to stress hormones may trigger the process.

exocytosis. Release of chemicals from cells into the extracellular fluid (release by the axon terminal of a chemical neurotransmitter into the synaptic cleft).

experiment. Research technique in which variables are purposively manipulated in a systematic way to test or establish a hypothesis.

exposure and response prevention (ERP). Behavioral therapy for obsessive–compulsive disorder; patients are encouraged to remain in contact with a feared stimulus while simultaneously suppressing the rituals they typically use to decrease anxiety.

exposure therapy. Type of therapy sometimes used with posttraumatic stress disorder patients in which the facilitator exposes the patient to the stimulus/event that is most feared in an attempt to have him or her see that exposure is not always associated with a negative outcome.

extended amygdala. Brain structures continuous with and sharing morphological similarities with the amygdaloid nuclei, including the nucleus accumbens, bed nucleus of the stria terminalis, and olfactory lobe.

external locus of control. Component of a theory proposed by Julian Rotter that emphasized the importance of one's perception of one's own source of control in life—either within the individual (internal) or in the environment (external).

eye movement desensitization reprocessing (EMDR). Type of therapy introduced for the treatment of posttraumatic stress disorder (PTSD); consists of having the patient follow the therapist's finger back and forth for about 20-second intervals to produce a rapid and rhythmic pattern of eye movements while thinking about the negative aspects of the trauma experience associated with the PTSD.

fight-or-flight response. The sympathetic branch of the autonomic nervous system triggers this response that prepares the animal to either fight the stressor or flee from the stressor.

filopodia. An extremely fine tubular extension that emerges from the neuron's growth cone.

fissures. Deep grooves covering the outer surface of the brain.

fixed action pattern (FAP). Motor program that seems to develop automatically in particular species of animals (e.g., the courting displays of many birds); once triggered, these rigid, consistent, and predictable responses are continued to completion.

fluoxetine. Selective serotonin reuptake inhibitor (SSRI) produced by Eli Lilly pharmaceutical company in 1985; this drug had the specific effect of blocking the reuptake of serotonin.

frontal lobe. Part of the cerebral cortex in either hemisphere of the brain found directly behind the forehead; helps to control voluntary movement and is associated with the higher mental activities and with personality.

functional magnetic resonance imaging (fMRI). MRI that provides information about activity of the brain by quantifying cerebral blood flow during a cognitive challenge.

G proteins. Membrane-bound proteins that bind GTP when activated by a membrane receptor. Active G proteins can stimulate or inhibit other membrane-bound proteins.

galanin. A neuropeptide that stimulates feeding behavior, particularly fat intake, when injected into the paraventricular hypothalamus.

gamma-aminobutyric acid (GABA). An amino acid that acts as an inhibitory neurotransmitter in the central nervous system.

gastric bypass surgery (also known as *bariatric surgery*). Surgery conducted in obese individuals to reduce the stomach to about 1% of its original capacity.

general adaptation syndrome. Syndrome originally described by Hans Selye; he felt that stressed individuals undergo three phases during the stress response: alarm, in which the individual's body registers the threat of the imposing stressor; resistance, in which the body mobilizes its forces to fight off the stressor; if the stressor persists, exhaustion as the body runs out of energy to fight off the stressor.

generalized anxiety disorder (GAD). Vague sense of anxiety not directly related to an anxiety-provoking event.

Glasgow Coma Scale. A neurological scale designed to provide a reliable assessment of consciousness following brain trauma.

glia (or glial cells). Nonneuronal cells in the nervous system that provide, among other things, support for neuronal structures and insulation of neuronal messages.

glucocorticoids. Compounds that belong to the family of substances called "corticosteroids." They affect metabolism and have anti-inflammatory and immunosuppressive effects.

glucose utilization theory of hunger regulation. Proposed by Jean Mayer, this theory suggested that hunger was more influenced by the level of glucose metabolization in the cells than circulating levels of glucose.

glutamate (Glu). A principal excitatory neurotransmitter that regulates cortical and subcortical functions.

glycine (Gly). An excitatory amino acid that mediates most central nervous system synapses along with glutamate and GABA.

Golgi apparatus. Set of membranes in the cytoplasm that wraps around chemicals released by secretory cells. In neurons this structure manufactures the synaptic vesicles.

graded potential. Series of incoming electrical signals that have little or no effect on the neuron depolarizing or firing.

gyri (sing. gyrus). Convolutions of the surface of the brain, caused by infolding of the cerebral cortex.

hallucination. An internal perception of a realistic sensory event in the absence of any external stimuli.

haloperidol. Neuroleptic drug that blocks dopaminergic activity; used in the treatment of schizophrenia and Tourette syndrome.

hebephrenia. Inappropriate and uncontrollable form of laughter.

helper T cells. Type of T lymphocyte that activates macrophages and stimulates the release of antibodies from B lymphocytes.

hippocampus. Arching limbic structure within the temporal lobe important in learning, memory, and navigating the environment.

histology. Systematic preparation of brain or other physiological tissue for microscopic study to be used for experimental and diagnostic purposes.

homeostasis. Internal balance and regulation of physiological systems in an organism.

humoral immune system. Primarily antibodies released by B lymphocytes.

humoral theory. Early physical theory of mental illness proposed by Hippocrates. Four humors, or liquids, were thought to contribute to mental illness when they became unbalanced.

Huntington's chorea. Hereditary neurodegenerative disorder of motor control characterized by ongoing involuntary jerky movements and progressive dementia; associated with hyperactivity of the dopaminergic system.

5-hydroxyindole acetic acid (5-HIAA). Metabolite of serotonin (5-HT), found in the cerebrospinal fluid; levels are reduced in sick anorexics and elevated in recovered anorexic patients.

hyperglycolysis. Increased glucose utilization following traumatic brain injury; occurs both locally and globally across the brain in response to the injured brain's altered chemical environment.

hyperpolarization. A shift in the membrane potential to more negative (i.e., more polarized and farther apart). Neuron is inhibited from firing and must receive more insistent electrochemical signals to be undone.

hypothalamic–pituitary–adrenal axis (HPA axis). The stress response originally described by Hans Selye, in which the hypothalamus secretes a releasing factor (corticotropin-releasing hormone) which travels to the anterior pituitary and triggers the release of adrenocorticotropic hormone (ACTH). ACTH then travels to the adrenal cortex, where it stimulates the release of glucocorticoids. Generally an adaptive response (in short bursts), this sequence and its aftermath help the animal produce enough energy to survive the impending stressor.

hypothalamus. Brain nuclei that control the endocrine system and regulate motivated behavior.

hysteria. Early characterization of mental disturbance described in women who had no known accompanying brain damage. Charcot thought that only hysterical women could be hypnotized.

imipramine. Synthesized originally for treatment of schizophrenic patients, this drug was observed to have antidepressant qualities. Researchers found that it influenced the synapse by blocking the reuptake of monoamine transmitters back into the terminal.

immediate early genes. Class of genes that exhibit rapid responses to certain extracellular stimuli by producing proteins that prompt the release of such neurotransmitters as c-*fos*, which is involved in the stress response.

inferior colliculi. Nuclei in the mesencephalon that take part in localizing sounds, integrating hearing reflexes, and orienting the body toward auditory stimuli.

inhibitory postsynaptic potential (IPSP). Temporary hyperpolarization of a membrane.

innate immune system. Components of the immune system, such as skin, phagocytic cells (e.g., macrophages), natural killer cells, the complement system, and cytokines, that exist prior to an invasion by a pathogen; also known as the "front-line defense."

interleukin-1 (IL-1). Cytokine produced primarily by activated phagocytes that activates B and T cells, influences natural killer and macrophage activity, and induces fever.

internal locus of control. Component of a theory proposed by Julian Rotter that emphasized the importance of one's perception of one's own source of control in life—either within the individual (internal) or in the environment (external).

interneurons. Nerve cells that associate sensory and motor activity in the central nervous system.

ion channels. Membrane-spanning proteins that form a pore, allowing passage of ions from one side of the membrane to the other. The process results in either depolarization or hyperpolarization of the cell.

ionic flux. Altered movement of ions that influence cellular homeostatic processes across the cell membrane following a traumatic brain injury.

ionotropic receptors. Receptors with a binding site for a neurotransmitter and a pore that regulates ion flow.

iproniazid. Drug developed in the 1950s as an antibacterial agent but later found to have antidepressant effects in patients. Researchers later showed that this drug was a monoamine oxidase inhibitor, which prolonged the presence of monoamines in the synapse.

kainate receptor. A subgroup of glutamate receptors whose functional role is not clearly understood but has been related to hippocampal plasticity.

killer T cells (also known as "cytotoxic T cells"). T cells that recognize and kills virus-infected host cells; utilize the protein perforin, which enables them to drill holes in cells, leaving them to die.

kindled limbic seizure. Temporal lobe seizure thought to be related to the accumulation of chronic stress and loneliness; may be accompanied by uncharacteristic violent behavior.

knockout mice. Product of recently developed technique in behavioral neuroscience in which certain genes are eliminated (knocked out) so that their function can be determined in the genetically modified animal. (The first knockout rat, which has its BRCA2 gene "removed," was just introduced to the research world.)

lateral fissure. Prominent groove that separates the temporal lobe from the frontal and parietal lobes.

lateral hypothalamus (LH). Brain area which, when lesioned in rats, caused the rats to become hypophagic and to die unless the experimenter assisted with feeding. In addition to diminishing hunger, LH lesions decrease general motivation.

lateralization. The observation that different functions have been assigned, or lateralized, to each hemishpere of the brain.

learned helplessness. Usually resulting from several bouts with failure, the acquired belief that no effort can remove an individual from a stressful environment. Seligman suggests that this phenomenon may be a basis for clinical depression.

leptin. Neurochemical produced in fat cells and detected by receptors in the brain. Genetically obese mice (*ob/ob*) deficient in leptin are extremely overweight and the obesity is diminished by exogenous injections of leptin.

levodopa (l-dopa). A dopamine agonist that has served as a gold standard pharmaceutical treatment for Parkinson's disease for years.

limbic system. Collection of brain regions (amygdala, mammillary bodies, hippocampus, fornix, and cingulated gyrus) that collectively produce, respond to, and regulate emotional responses.

lipostatic theory of hunger regulation. Early eating-regulation theory that proposed that some fuel or form of adipose tissue circulated throughout the blood and was interpreted by the brain so that current energy levels could be detected. If lipostatic measures were too high, it was theorized, the animal would cease eating. The defining lipostatic measure was never discovered.

liposuction. Surgical technique used to extract fat from the body.

lithium. Chemical element approved in the 1970s as a drug for treatment of bipolar disorder. Although the specific biological mechanism is unknown, lithium is known to share ionic properties with some of the important ions maintaining neural functions such as magnesium and calcium.

lobotomy. Faddish operation to treat mental illness used in the 1930s and 1940s. The procedure involved separating sections of the frontal lobe from the rest of the brain.

localization of function. Notion that specific functions are localized in specific brain areas as suggested by the eighteenth-century theory of phrenology.

longitudinal fissure. Deep groove that separates the left and right cerebral hemispheres of the brain.

lymph nodes. Small nodules made up of lymphocyte-rich tissue found along the lymphatic channels in the body. Location of the origin of acquired immune functioning.

lysosomes. Neuronal organelles that engage in cellular cleansing and similar "housecleaning" activities to maintain neuronal function by degrading proteins; these organelles also play a role in the MHC II molecule pathway.

macrophage. Phagocytotic cell of the immune system that is activated by chemicals released from foreign microorganisms and T-cell cytokines. In addition to engulfing microorganisms, they may secrete proinflammatory cytokines and serve as antigen-presenting cells.

magnetic resonance imaging. Technique that provides pictures of the brain by sending a magnetic field through a person's head so that the scanners can absorb radiation from hydrogen ions to generate a three-dimensional, high-resolution picture of brain tissue.

major depressive disorder. One of the most common psychiatric illnesses, occurring in about 17% of the population, with females suffering at about twice the rate of males and characterized by one or more major depressive episodes of at least 2 weeks and at least four additional symptoms of depression (e.g., sleep disturbances, loss of concentration, decreased energy, guilt).

major histocompatibility complex (MHC). In humans, a genetic locus on chromosome 6 that encodes the peptides recognized by T lymphocytes; additionally, this genetic code influences cytokines and antigen proteins.

manic episode. Hyperactivity characterized by euphoria and impaired judgment; exists with depression in bipolar disorder.

mecamylamine. Drug that acts as a cholinergic receptor antagonist; currently being tested for use with Tourette symptoms.

medial forebrain bundle. Large collection of axons that extends from the hypothalamus to the septum, a structure in the limbic system. Animals respond continuously to receiving electrical brain stimulation in this area; consequently, it is considered the most prevalent brain reward system of the nervous system.

medulla oblongata. Lowest part of the brain stem; an extension into the skull of the upper end of the spinal cord; regulates basic vegetative functioning.

meninges. Three connective tissue membranes (arachnoid, dura, pia mater) that protect and enclose the brain and spinal cord.

mesencephalon. Midbrain joining the brain stem and forebrain and serving as a passageway for impulses to higher brain centers.

mesoderm. The middle layer of the fertilized egg, or zygote, that eventually gives rise to many muscles, the skin, skeleton, and connective tissue.

mesolimbic dopamine pathway. Neurons extending from the midbrain to the forebrain produce and release dopamine into the forebrain. Two pathways make up this system: (1) the mesocorticolimbic (reward circuit) system extends from the ventral tegmental area to the nucleus accumbens; (2) the nigrostriatal pathway, involved in neuromuscular functions, extends from the substantia nigra to the corpus striatum.

messenger RNA (mRNA). RNA molecule transcribed from DNA and translated into the amino acid sequence of a polypeptide.

meta-analysis. A study that includes the results of several published reports to investigate a certain hypothesis.

metabotropic receptor. Receptor that, when stimulated, produces a relatively slow but long-lasting effect through metabolic reactions.

methadone. Opiate drug that is given to heroin addicts to help wean them from opiate addiction because it minimizes withdrawal symptoms and is not thought to produce a high that is comparable to that induced by heroin or morphine.

MHC I molecules. MHC glycoproteins found on all cells of the body that display information related to the invasion of the cells by viruses.

MHC II molecules. MHC glycoproteins produced in the immune cells; share information only with the immune cells.

microdialysis. Neurochemical technique in which the level of a neurotransmitter from a particular area of the brain is assessed. This technique is unique because the researcher can extract the neurotransmitter while the animal is engaging in a particular behavior.

microfilaments. Intraneuronal flexible supporting elements associated with membranes.

microtubules. Proteins in the cell bodies and axons of neurons that transport nutrients within the cell, especially from the cell nucleus out to the axon and down to the terminal buttons.

mind–body problem. Philosophical question posed to determine the nature, either mental or physical, of the mind.

minor physical anomalies (MPAs). Minor structural abnormalities located in various areas of the body; they are typically investigated in accessible areas of the body including the head, mouth, ears, eyes, hands, and feet.

mitochondria (sing. mitochondrion). Structures in the cell that perform the metabolic activities that provide energy.

modafinil. Drug originally developed to keep narcoleptic patients from suddenly falling asleep. It is also being used by nonnarcoleptic patients to stay awake for extended periods of time.

monoamine oxidase inhibitors (MAOIs). Class of drugs that deactivate monoamine oxidase in the synaptic area so that the monoamines have a prolonged period of activity.

mood (affective) disorders. Disturbances of mood typically accompanied by inappropriate expression of pleasure or misery; some people experience vigorous swings between the two extremes.

motor neurons. Broad phrase referring either to the output neurons carrying out the commands from sensory and interneurons or to neurons at the interface of glands, muscles, and blood vessels.

MPTP (1-methyl-4-phenyl-1,2,3,6-tetrahydropyridine). A neurotoxin that causes a neural disorder resembling Parkinson's disorder in primates.

multiple sclerosis. Neurodegenerative autoimmune disease in which T cells are thought to destroy the myelin sheath of the neurons. Leads to nausea, vertigo, bladder dysfunction, depression, and memory deficits.

myelin sheath. Insulating material that covers many vertebrate axons.

naloxone. Drug that blocks opiate receptors in the brain; counteracts drugs such as morphine. Naltrexone has a similar function.

narcolepsy. A condition in which individuals succumb to irresistible urges to sleep, even at such inappropriate times as while driving or speaking in public.

natural killer (NK) cells. Cells in bone marrow that are a component of the innate immune system. On recognizing a microbe, these cells move in for the kill, using techniques such as secreting toxic substances and creating fatal damage to the invading cell.

negative reinforcement. Cessation of an aversive stimulus on the presentation of a particular response. Relapse into drug use is reinforced because it reduces the negative experience of withdrawal.

negative symptoms. Characteristics or attributes that are absent from the nature of a person with schizophrenia, such as reduced desire for social interaction.

nerve. Cordlike collection of nerve fibers outside the brain and spinal cord; conveys information to and from the central nervous system and the periphery.

nerve growth factor. A neurochemical secreted by the postsynaptic neuron during the formation of synaptic connections between neurons; it is considered a trophic factor because it stimulates the growth of the presynaptic neuron's axon.

nerve impulse (action potential). Physiological basis of communication in the nervous system triggered by the exchange of certain ions across the nerve cell membrane.

nerve net theory. Early theory of the nature of the nervous system implying that the nervous system is made up of continuous extensions of nervous tissue.

neural crest. The tissue that starts to develop on each side of the neural tube that later becomes the peripheral nervous system.

neural diathesis–stress model of schizophrenia. Updated adaptation of the classic diathesis–stress model that emphasizes the role of alterations in steroidal hormones in the expression and severity of schizophrenic symptoms. Because of the dramatic changes in these hormones at puberty, Elaine Walker and colleagues have proposed that adolescence should be considered a critical phase in the development of schizophrenia.

neural folds. A portion of the ectoderm of the embryo develops into folds that form around the neural tube; eventually, these folds will give rise to the entire nervous system.

neural groove. The groove found between the neural folds in the developing embryo; once the neural folds join, the neural groove becomes the neural tube.

neural plate. A group of cells derived from the embryonic ectoderm that subsequently develop into the neural goove and neural tube, the origins of the mature nervous system.

neural reserve. Complexity and redundancy of neural networks that may provide a buffer against loss of function following traumatic brain injury.

neural tube. An early form of the nervous system observed during prenatal development. The rostral section develops into the brain and the caudal section eventually develops into the spinal cord.

neurodegenerative diseases. Conditions that are sometimes inherited or acquired due to some sporadic condition that results in the progressive deterioration of some portion of the nervous system.

neuroethics. Convergence of several disciplines, such as philosophy, religion, and medicine, to recognize the importance of ethical issues related to the rapidly changing field of neuroscience.

neurofeedback. Form of biofeedback in which patients learn to maintain certain electrical brain-wave rhythms to achieve relaxation and brain homeostasis.

neurofilaments. Neuronal structural proteins involved in membrane protein transport.

neurogenesis. Creation of new neurons through mitosis. It was once thought that developed brains could no longer produce new neurons, but research has confirmed the production of new neurons across the life span.

neurohormones. Brain substances that act like hormones and are released by neurons into the circulatory system.

neuromodulator. A substance that modifies or regulates the effect of a neurotransmitter.

neuron. Fundamental unit, or cell, of the nervous system.

neuron doctrine. Theory that separate units, or neurons, as opposed to continuous units, make up the nervous system.

neuropeptides. Proteins that are released by neurons and act as intercellular messengers.

neuropeptide Y (NPY). Pancreatic polypeptide that is one of the most abundant neurotransmitters in the mammalian brain; NPY stimulates eating and reduces energy expenditure.

neuropil. The intricate network of interwoven glial and neuronal processes that lie between axons.

neuropores. Openings at each end of the neural canal that eventually give rise to the brain and spinal cord.

neurotoxicity. Neural damage due to some threat presented to the nervous tissue, such as toxins, low oxygen, and decreased glucose.

neurotransmitter. Chemical such as dopamine and serotonin in the brain that is essential for communication between two neurons.

neurotrophic factors. Neurochemicals such as brain-derived neurotrophic factor that promote the growth and complexity of neurons. Think "fertilizer" for the brain.

neurotrophins. Neurochemicals secreted in an activity-dependent fashion that are thought to be involved in the restructuring of synaptic connections.

neutrophil. Most abundant white blood cell circulating in the blood; these cells are recruited to inflammation sites, where they utilize either phagocytosis or enzymatic digestion of pathogens.

N-methyl-d-aspartate (NMDA) receptors. A subtype of glutamate receptor that uses both Na^+ and Ca^{2+} influx to mediate its effects.

noradrenergic bundle. Bundle of fibers originating in the locus ceruleus of the brain stem that travel to limbic and cortical structures. These noradrenergic fibers have been strongly associated with brain reward and arousal.

norepinephrine. An amine neurotransmitter that contains tyrosine hydroxylase, dopa decarboxylase, and the enzyme dopamine B-hydroxylase (DBH). DBH is responsible for converting dopamine into norepinephrine.

nuclei. Functional collections of neurons in specific brain regions; can be identified by histological techniques.

nucleus. Structure within the cell that contains the chromosomes.

nucleus accumbens. Limbic component of the striatum sometimes referred to as the "pleasure center" of the brain; involved in motivating behavior and reinforcing survival responses; linked to disorders ranging from anxiety and depression to addiction.

obesity. A state of pathological overweight due to both genetic and environmental factors. Technically, one is considered obese if one's body mass index (BMI) is 30 kg/m^2 or greater.

obsessions. Recurring, upsetting thoughts typically observed in obsessive–compulsive disorder patients; typically related to contamination, doubts, order, aggression, and sexual imagery.

obsessive–compulsive disorder (OCD). Chronic condition characterized by recurring upsetting thoughts (obsessions) and subsequent ritualistic acts (compulsions).

occipital lobe. Region of the cerebral cortex lying at the very back of the brain, caudal to the parietal and temporal lobes; site of the primary visual cortex.

OCD loop. Brain structures thought to be involved in the maintenance of obsessive–compulsive disorder; loop includes the orbitofrontal cortex, cingulate gyrus and embedded cingulum, caudate, thalamus, and amygdala.

orbitofrontal cortex (OFC). Anterior area of the prefrontal cortex, involved in more advanced cognitions and associations.

orexins. Neuropeptides that are secreted from the lateral hypothalamic neurons and involved in eating, arousal, and other motivated behaviors. Administration of orexins to the central nervous system results in increased food intake.

organelles. "Organlike" structures in the cytoplasm of the cell membrane that help in the maintenance and metabolism of the cell.

oxytocin. A posterior pituitary neuropeptide involved in complementary activities such as bonding, sexual behavior, and childbirth.

pallidotomy. Neurosurgery in which a small portion of the globus pallidus is destroyed to reduce brain activity, leading to Parkinson symptoms such as tremors and unwanted involuntary movements.

PANDAS (pediatric autoimmune neuropsychiatric disorders associated with streptococcal infection). Thought to be the cause of Tourette syndrome in some children.

panic disorder. Intense anxiety-stress response, typically without an actual fear stimulus present. Physical components, including chest pain, shortness of breath, and nausea, resemble the symptoms of a heart attack.

parasympathetic nervous system. Maintenance component of the autonomic nervous system.

paraventricular nuclei. A collection of neurons located in the hypothalamus; the processes extend into the posterior pituitary, where oxytocin and vasopressin are released. Thought to be intimately involved in hunger regulation.

parietal lobe. Main division of each hemisphere of the cerebral cortex, located beneath the crown of the skull; interprets somatosensory information and spatial relationships.

pathogen. Microorganism (virus or bacterium) that can cause disease.

peptic ulcers. Lesions that occur in the stomach lining; usually caused by a bacterium, but they are exacerbated by stress.

peptide YY (PYY). Peptide closely related to NPY and implicated in hunger stimulation.

perforin. Protein used as a weapon by killer T cells and natural killer cells that drills a hole in the infected cells so that other enzymes can continue the destruction of the cells.

periaqueductal gray (PAG). Region of the midbrain surrounding the cerebral aqueduct; contains neural circuits involved in species-typical behaviors and pain perception.

peripheral nervous system (PNS). One of the two divisions of the human nervous system, consisting of the sensory and motor nerves outside of the brain and spinal cord (12 pairs of cranial nerves and 31 pairs of spinal nerves).

phagocytes. Cells, such as macrophages, that protect the body from invaders by engulfing them.

pharmacokinetics. The study of the action and reaction of and to drugs in the body.

phenotype. External expression of certain genetic influences. The phenotype for one genetic assortment may be long fingers; for another the phenotype may be brown hair.

phenylethanolamine (PNMT). PNMT is the enzyme that converts norepinephrine to epinephrine.

phospholipid bilayer. Basis of neuron cell membranes. Each molecule has a water-soluble head (a protein compatible with water) and a water-rejecting tail (consisting of a lipid). The head faces a watery solution (cytoplasm or extracellular fluid between cells), while the lipid tail faces another lipid tail in the interior of the cell membrane.

phrenology. Term popularized to describe Gall's theory of localization of function. In this theory, bumps on the surface of the skull were deemed to predict certain mental capabilities.

pituitary gland. Master endocrine gland at the base of the hypothalamus; releases a variety of hormones that influence the activity of other glands throughout the body.

placebo effect. Term used to describe a therapeutic effect resulting from the consumption of a physiologically inactive substance (e.g., a sugar pill or some other unrelated treatment); used as evidence for mind–body communication.

plasticity. Inherent flexibility of the brain in responding to environmental changes; for example, by learning or to compensate for loss of function to damaged areas.

pluripotent. The potential of a single stem cell to develop into many types of cells in the body.

pons. Large bulge in the brain stem immediately ventral to the cerebellum; relays information from the cerebral cortex to the cerebellum and contains a portion of the reticular formation, nuclei that appear to be important for sleep and arousal.

positive symptoms. Characteristics or attributes that are added to a schizophrenic patient's nature, such as hallucinations.

positive-incentive theory of hunger regulation. Theory suggesting that people eat because it is a pleasurable, rewarding experience.

positron emission tomography (PET). Functional neuroimaging technique that involves injecting the patient with radioactively tagged glucose and quantifying the patient's metabolization of the radioactive glucose when the patient is presented with an experimental challenge (e.g., a cognitive task or a certain stimulus).

posttraumatic stress disorder (PTSD). Disorder characterized by symptoms such as memories and dreams related to a traumatic event that recur up to months or years following the event. Individuals with this disorder feel as if they are reexperiencing the trauma and have the accompanying physiological arousal to enhance their belief of impending danger.

precursors. Constituent and elemental substances that serve as the initial components in a chain of chemicals. For instance, fats and sugars combine with oxygen to form cellular fuels.

prefrontal cortex (PFC). Area of the frontal cortex involved in many higher functions. Evidence suggests that atrophy of neurons or compromised activity in this area may lead to symptoms of depression.

preparatory response theory of hunger regulation. Theory suggesting that the feeling of hunger may be more closely related to the body's preparation to eat than any deficit of food.

prosencephalon. Forebrain controlling sensation, perception, emotion, learning, thinking, and other intellectual functions; includes the olfactory bulb and tracts, cerebral hemispheres, nasal ganglia, thalamus, optic tracts, and hypothalamus.

proteins. Complex organic chemicals that are the essential building materials of living cells.

proximate causation. Doctrine stating that the most direct cause of an event is the most important factor. In evolutionary theory, proximate questions are most often questions of mechanism and development of certain behaviors.

psychoactive drugs. Drugs that produce a noticeable change in mood or perception.

psychoanalysis. Therapeutic approach to mental illness developed by Freud. In this subjective theory, unconscious motives were thought to direct behavior and thoughts.

psychometric test. Paper-and-pencil test typically used by psychologists for diagnostic purposes. These tests need to pass reliability, validity, and standardization assessment before use with patients and clients.

psychoneuroimmunology (PNI). Exploration of the relationships among the brain, behavior, and the immune system.

psychopharmacology. Discipline that explores the relationship between certain psychoactive drugs and behavior and/or mental processes.

psychosocial model. Therapeutic approach emphasizing the relationship between client, or patient, and therapist while using therapies such as behavioral therapy, interpersonal therapy, classical psychoanalysis, or group therapy.

psychotropic (psychoactive) drug. Medication that influences psychological processes.

Purkinje neurons. Neurons in the cerebellum that are responsible for all the output from the cerebellar cortex to cerebellar nuclei.

radial glia. Neuroglial cells characterized by very long branches that serve as a physical guide or road map for developing neuroblast cells as they migrate toward their final destinations; following the development of the brain, it is thought that these cells develop into astrocytes.

reboxetine. Relatively new drug that selectively inhibits the reuptake of noradrenaline in the synapse. Used as an antidepressant, this drug is thought to be more effective than other antidepressants at restoring social functioning in depressed patients.

receptors. Areas on a neuron specialized to be highly sensitive to a specific type of stimulation or chemical.

reflex. Most basic form of behavior that involves an automatic response to an environmental event or stimulus, for example, sucking or blinking.

repetitive transcranial magnetic stimulation (rTMS). Relatively new antidepressant treatment that involves placing a powerful electromagnet or coil on the scalp. The magnet produces depolarization in the underlying neurons in the brain.

resting (or membrane) potential. Electrical potential across a membrane when a neuron is at rest.

reticular formation. Collection of nuclei and fiber pathways traversing the brain stem from midbrain to medulla; play a primary role in arousal, attention, and sleep and wakefulness.

reuptake. The return of spent neurotransmitter from the synapse to the presynaptic neuron by means of specialized receptors.

rhombencephalon. Hindbrain, or brain stem, that surrounds the fourth ventricle.

ribosomes. Bulbous structures in the nucleus that are the primary destination for mRNA and the location of translation and assembly of proteins.

saltatory conduction. The electrical movement or jumping of the action potential across gaps (called "nodes of Ranvier") in the myelin sheath.

schizophrenia. Mental illness characterized by hallucinations, delusions, social withdrawal, and cognitive deterioration. Certain brain modifications such as a smaller hippocampus and disarrayed neurons have been observed to accompany this condition.

seasonal affective disorder (SAD). Form of depression that occurs in winter months when the duration of natural light decreases.

second-messenger systems. A multiple-step and complex signal-amplification process that occurs in the neuron that translates, for example, hormonal signals into long-lasting cellular events.

self-directed neuroplasticity. Systematically altering one's brain via extensive mental and/or physical training.

self-efficacy. Term proposed by Albert Bandura to describe a person's assessment of his or her competence in dealing with life's problems.

sensitization. Process by which an animal or person becomes increasingly responsive to a particular stimulus following repeated presentation.

sensory-gating deficits. The inability of schizophrenic patients to habituate the startle response to somewhat expected stimuli.

sensory neurons. Refers to the specialized cells that transmit, input, and interpret physical stimuli (light, sound, touch, etc.) from the external world and translate them into neuronal impulses.

sensory-specific theory of satiety. Theory suggesting that animals are motivated to consume a different taste after previously eating to satiety; this hypothesis explains why humans and other animals placed on a diverse cafeteria diet frequently overeat.

serotonin (5-hydroxytryptamine, 5-HT). A major neurotransmitter involved in mood, aggression, and appetite regulation.

set-point theory of hunger regulation. Theory suggesting that animals are motivated to eat when food energy levels drop below a particular level.

sexual selection. Choosing a mate or competing for a mate. Usually related to some desirable physical characteristic, such as body size, attractiveness, etc.

sexually dimorphic nucleus of the preoptic area (SDN-POA). Region of the anterior hypothalamic preoptic area that has a larger volume in male rats than in female rats.

simple (specific) phobia. Disorder that involves an intense fear of a particular object (e.g., heights, spiders, germs) that disrupts a person's normal functioning as he or she attempts to avoid the feared stimuli.

SNUBs (super neurotransmitter uptake blockers). New drugs that are designed to block the reuptake of more than one monoamine transmitter. These drugs differ from the original tricyclics in their weaker nature and consequently fewer side effects.

social defeat paradigm. Animal model of chronic stress in which an animal is exposed to a larger, more aggressive animal and is defeated in a single aggressive encounter. For up to a month or longer, the defeated animal will not exhibit defensive behavior when an animal—even a smaller animal—is placed in its cage.

social learning theory. Theory proposed by Albert Bandura emphasizing the importance of observations of models in social situations and how observations can lead to learning without direct exposure to a reinforcer.

sodium–potassium pumps. Mechanisms that actively transport sodium ions out of the cell while simultaneously drawing potassium ions in.

somatic marker. Body signal, such as altered electrodermal activity, that is interpreted by the brain as an indication of a relevant impending event.

somatic nervous system. Voluntary part of the peripheral nervous system that controls the movement of skeletal muscles or transmits somatosensory information to the central nervous system.

spatial summation. Summation of excitatory or inhibitory synaptic effects on a postsynaptic membrane resulting from the simultaneous action of several synapses at one time on one local area of the cell.

species-specific stressor. Stressor that is specific for a particular species. Example: Weasel urine is a natural stressor for rats but is not stressful for dogs.

spinal cord. Tube of central nervous system tissue extending from the base of the brain through the central canal to the upper part of the lumbar spine; conducts sensorimotor impulses between the brain and the body and is a site of reflex activity.

spleen. Filtering organ, located in the abdomen, that plays a large role in defending the body against blood-borne antigens.

stem cells. Cells that, when nurtured in the appropriate chemical culture, have the ability to divide and develop into specialized cells for an indefinite time period.

stereological analysis. Unbiased optical method of counting cells by randomly sampling various areas and depths within neural tissue.

stereotaxic apparatus. Scientific device that enables the experimenter or surgeon to access any three-dimensional point in the brain; used for placement of electrodes and various forms of neurosurgery.

striatum. Terminal for all afferent fiber pathways forming the basal ganglia; dysfunction in this motor system is believed to be involved in obsessive–compulsive disorder and Tourette syndrome.

stroke. Loss of brain tissue caused by blockade of a blood vessel and resultant loss of blood and, hence, oxygen; can result in sudden loss of consciousness, sensation, and voluntary movement.

subdural hematoma. Collection of blood under the surface of the dura mater that may follow a brain injury.

substantia nigra. Nucleus of the tegmentum; communicates with the caudate nucleus and putamen in the basal ganglia to initiate movement.

sudden infant death syndrome (SIDS). Respiratory malfunction, perhaps influenced by an immature medulla, that results in an infant's death.

sulci (sing. sulcus). Small grooves or mounds on the surface of an organ.

superior colliculi. Nuclei in the mesencephalon that take part in controlling the body's reflexes to visual stimuli.

superstitious behavior. Response resulting from random reinforcement; thought to explain some ritualistic behavior.

supraoptic nuclei. Hypothalamic nuclei that produce oxytocin.

sympathetic nervous system. Arousing component of the autonomic nervous system.

synapse. Tiny gap that separates two neurons and is the location of communication between the two cells.

T cells or T lymphocytes. Cells that mature in the thymus, travel in the blood, and populate secondary lymphoid tissue; they make up cell-mediated immunity and function by exposing receptors that recognize foreign particles.

tectum. Dorsal part of the midbrain; made up of the inferior and superior colliculi, control centers for auditory and visual stimuli.

tegmentum. Ventral part of the midbrain, composed of various nuclei related to movement and to species-typical behaviors.

telencephalon. "Endbrain" portion of the forebrain that includes the cerebral hemispheres, basal ganglia, olfactory bulb, and olfactory tracts.

temporal lobe. Division of the cerebral cortex lying at each side within the temple of the skull that responds to auditory inputs and contains areas related to language production and recognition; underlying areas regulate and maintain memory and emotional processes.

temporal summation. Additive effects of a single neuron firing in rapid succession onto a postsynaptic membrane. Each new depolarization builds on the dissipating graded postsynaptic potential to eventually result in the appropriate hyperpolarization or hypopolarization threshold.

terminal buttons. At the tip of an axon, the points from which the axon releases chemicals (neurotransmitters).

testosterone. A steroid hormone produced by the testes that is important in the differentiation and maintenance of the male brain and body.

thalamotomy. Neurosurgery involving the precise destruction of portions of the thalamus in order to diminish negative side effects accompanying Parkinson's disease.

thalamus. Structure of the forebrain; main source of input to the cerebral cortex.

threshold potential. The electrochemical point at which a neuron will respond to incoming stimulation with an action potential.

thymus. Immune system organ (containing epithelial cells, dendritic cells, macrophages, and precursor cells) that becomes maturation site of T lymphocytes from bone marrow–derived precursor cells.

tics. Rapid, repetitive, stereotyped movements or vocalizations; characteristic symptom of Tourette syndrome.

tolerance. Characteristic of drug addiction in which the individual becomes increasingly less sensitive to the drug, requiring higher doses to obtain the initial effect.

Tourette syndrome. A neurological condition characterized by involuntary tic movements and vocalizations.

tract (also called "fiber pathway"). Bundle of axons within the central nervous system that traverses long distances and connects different parts of the brain (distal) or is relatively short (local) and connects close-in nuclei and groups of neurons.

transcription. The process by which DNA is "copied" and transferred to mRNA for subsequent protein synthesis.

transduction. Conversion of physical energy, such as light, to energy that can be used in the nervous system.

translation. The process by which messenger ribonucleic acid (mRNA) is "read" by ribosomes in the neuron and protein synthesis is initiated.

traumatic brain injury (TBI). Injury to a person's brain usually resulting from an accident.

trepanning. Medical process of drilling a hole in the skull in an attempt to correct a problem associated with the brain (e.g., a buildup of pressure on the brain).

tricyclic antidepressants. Drugs such as imipramine that increase the activity of serotonin (along with other monoamines) in the synapse by blocking its reuptake into the presynaptic neuronal terminal

tryptophan. The amino acid from which the neurotransmitter serotonin is derived. The availability of tryptophan in the extracellular fluid of neurons regulates the synthesis of serotonin.

tyrosine hydroxylase (TH). An enzyme found in all catecholaminergic neurons. TH is a catalyst in the conversion of tyrosine to dopa, which is the first step in catecholamine synthesis.

ultimate causation. Doctrine stating that the more long-term causes of a behavior are important for a thorough understanding of the behavior. In evolutionary theory, ultimate causation questions are related to how and why certain behaviors evolve.

vaccination. Preparation of a specific antigen that is administered to an individual to stimulate the acquired immune system to protect against actual, natural exposure to the antigen, should it occur.

vagus nerve (cranial nerve 10). Mixed cranial nerve pair; sensory portion transmits sensations of pain and nausea from the viscera, motor component exerts parasympathetic control of cardiovascular and abdominal function, as well as controlling the muscles of the throat.

valproate. Anticonvulsant drug that shows promise as an effective treatment for bipolar disorder.

ventral tegmental area (VTA). Cluster of cell bodies in the midbrain that synthesize dopamine; extends to the nucleus accumbens and is involved with reward circuits of the brain.

ventricles. Internal capsules in the medial part of the brain that contain cerebrospinal fluid.

ventromedial hypothalamus. Brain area which, when lesioned in rats, causes the rats to become hyperphagic. Initially dubbed the "satiety center," it is now believed to be involved in energy metabolism.

vertebral column. Firm, flexible bony column extending from the base of the skull to the coccyx; longitudinal axis and chief supporting structure of the human body.

vesicle. Tiny, nearly spherical packet at the axon terminal filled with the neurotransmitter.

voltage-gated channels. Passageways for ions through a neuron's cell membrane that are opened or closed in response to changes of the membrane potential.

withdrawal. Defining feature of drug addiction in which the individual experiences either physiological or psychological symptoms after ceasing the consumption of a particular drug.

References

Abbas, A. K., Lichtman, A. H., & Pober, J. S. (2000). *Cellular and molecular immunology* (4th ed.). New York: Saunders.

Abbott, A. (2001). Into the mind of a killer. *Nature, 410,* 296–298.

Abi-Dargham, A., Rodenhiser, J., Printz, D., Zea-Ponce, Y., Gil, R., Kegeles, L. S., et al. (2000). Increased baseline occupancy of D_2 receptors by dopamine in schizophrenia. *Proceedings of the National Academy of Sciences, USA, 97,* 8104–8109.

Abrams, R. (1992). *Electroconvulsive therapy.* New York: Oxford University Press.

Achenbach, J. (2001, October 1). The power of light. *National Geographic,* 3–31.

Ackerman, D. L., Greenland, S., Bystritsky, A., & Datz, R. J. (1996). Relationship between early side effects and therapeutic effects of clomipramine therapy in obsessive–compulsive disorder. *Journal of Clinical Psychopharmacology, 16*(4), 324–328.

Acocella, J. (1998, April 16). The politics of hysteria. *New Yorker,* 64–79.

Acquas, E., Tanda, G., & DiChiara, G. (2002). Differential effects of caffeine on dopamine and acetylcholine transmission in brain areas of drug-naive and caffeine-pretreated rats. *Neuropsychopharmacology, 27,* 182–193.

Adams, N., Lins, M. D., & Blizard, D. A. (1987). Contrasting effects of social stress and foot shock on acute cardiovascular response in salt-sensitive rats. *Behavioral Neural Biology, 48,* 368–381.

Ader, R., & Cohen, N. (1975). Behaviorally conditioned immunosuppression. *Pyschosomatic Medicine, 37,* 333–340.

Ader, R., & Cohen, N. (1991). The influence of conditioning on immune responses. In R. Ader, D. L. Felten, & N. Cohen (Eds.), *Psychoneuroimmunology* (2nd ed.). New York: Academic Press.

Adler, L. E., Freedman, R., Ross, R. G., Olincy, A., & Waldo, M. C. (1999). Elementary phenotypes in the neurobiological and genetic study of schizophrenia. *Biological Psychiatry, 46*(1), 8–18.

Adolphs, R., Baron-Cohen, S., & Tranel, D. (2002). Impaired recognition of social emotions following amygdala damage. *Journal of Cognitive Neuroscience, 14,* 1264–1274.

Adolphs, R., Tranel, D., & Damasio, A. R. (1998). The human amygdala in social judgment. *Nature, 393,* 470–474.

Adolphs, R., Tranel, D., Damasio, H., & Damasio, A. R. (1994). Impaired recognition of emotion in facial expressions following bilateral damage to the human amygdala. *Nature, 372,* 669–672.

Aghajanian, G. K., & Marek, G. J. (2000). Serotonin model of schizophrenia: Emerging role of glutamate mechanisms. *Brain Research: Brain Research Reviews, 31*(2–3), 302–312.

Agras, W. S., Walsh, B. T., Fairburn, C. G., Wilson, G. T., & Kraemer, H. C. (2000). A multicenter comparison of cognitive-behavioral therapy and interpersonal psychotherapy for bulimia nervosa. *Archives of General Psychiatry, 57,* 459–466.

Albers, H. E., & Bamshad, M. (1998). Role of vasopressin and oxytocin in the control of social behavior in Syrian hamsters (*Mesocricetus auratus*). *Progress in Brain Research, 119,* 395–408.

Alderson, P., & Roberts, I. (1997). Corticosteroids in acute traumatic brain injury: Systematic review of randomized contolled trials. *British Medical Journal, 314,* 1855.

Aldrich, R. W., Dionne, V. E., Hawrot, E., & Stevens, C. F. (1985). Ion transport through ligand-gated channels. In T. E. Andreoli, J. F. Hoffman, D. D. Farestil, & S. G. Schultz (Eds.), *Physiology of membrane disorders.* New York: Plenum Press.

Altemus, M., Glowa, J. R., & Murphy, D. L. (1993). Attenuation of food-restriction-induced running by chronic fluoxetine treatment. *Psychopharmacology Bulletin,* *29*(3), 397–400.

American Psychiatric Association. (1994). *Diagnostic and statistical manual of mental disorders* (4th ed.). Washington, DC: Author.

American Psychiatric Association. (2000). *Diagnostic and statistical manual of mental disorders* (DSM-IV-TR). Washington, DC: Author.

American Psychiatric Association. (2009). *DSM-IV-TR: The current manual.* Retrieved November 1, 2009, from http://www.psych.org/mainmenu/research/dsmiv/dsmivtr.aspx

American Psychological Association. (2002). New Mexico governor signs landmark law on prescription privileges for psychologists. Retrieved March 2004 from http://www.apa.org/about/division/officers/dialogue/2002/05/practice.aspx#1

American Society of Plastic and Reconstructive Surgeons. (1990). Press release retrieved from http://www.plasticsurgery.org/news_room/PST-03-05.cfmby

Ames, E. W., & Carter, M. (1992). Development of Romanian orphanage children adopted to Canada. *Canadian Psychology, 33,* 503.

Anand, B. K., & Brobeck, J. R. (1951). Hypothalamic control of food intake in rats and cats. *Yale Journal of Biology and Medicine, 24,* 123–140.

Anderson, M. C., Ochsner, K. N., Kuhl, B., Cooper, J., Robertson, E., Gabrieli, S. W., et al. (2004). Neural systems underlying the suppression of unwanted memories. *Science, 303,* 232–235.

Anderson, S. M., Saviolakis, G. A., Bauman, R. A., Chu, K. Y., Ghosh, S., & Kant, G. J. (1996). Effects of chronic stress on food acquisition, plasma hormones, and the estrous cycle of female rats. *Physiology and Behavior, 60,* 325–329.

Anderson, T. (1993). *Den of lions.* New York: Ballantine Books.

Andreasen, N. C. (2001). *Brave new brain: Conquering mental illness in the era of the genome.* New York: Oxford University Press.

Andreasen, N. C., Arndt, S., Swayze, V., Cizaldo, T., Flaum, M., O'Leary, D., et al. (1994). Thalamic abnormalities in schizophrenia visualized through magnetic resonance imaging averaging. *Science, 266,* 294–298.

Andreasen, N. C., & Black, D. W. (1991). *Introductory textbook of psychiatry* (2nd ed.). Washington, DC: American Psychiatric Association.

Andreasen, N. C., & Black, D. W. (2001). *Introductory textbook of psychiatry* (3rd ed.). Washington, DC: American Psychiatric Association.

Andreasen, N. C., Nasrallah, H. A., Dunn, V., Olson, S. C., Grove, W. M., Ehrhardt, J. C., et al. (1986). Structural abnormalities in the frontal system in schizophrenia: A magnetic resonance imaging study. *Archives of General Psychiatry, 43,* 136–144.

Andreasen, N. C., O'Leary, D., Flaum, M., Nopoulos, P., Watkins, G. L., Boles Ponto, L. L., et al. (1997). Hypofrontality in schizophrenia: Distributed dysfunctional circuits in neuroleptic-naive patients. *Lancet, 349,* 1730–1734.

Andrews, A. M. (2009). Does chronic antidepressant treatment increase extracellular serotonin? *Frontiers in Neuroscience, 3,* 246–247.

Andrews, P. W., & Thomson, J. A. (2010, January/February). Depression's evolutionary roots. *Scientific American Mind,* 57–61.

Andrews, R. J. (2003). Neuroprotection trek—the next generation: Neuromodulation I. *Annals of the New York Academy of Sciences, 993,* 1–13.

Angelucci, F., Aloe, L., Vasquez, P. J., & Mathe, A. A. (2000). Mapping the differences in the brain concentration of brain-derived neurotrophic factor (BDNF) and nerve growth factor (NGF) in an animal model of depression. *NeuroReport, 11,* 1369–1373.

Anisman, H., Griffiths, J., Matheson, K., Ravindran, A. V., & Merali, Z. (2001). Posttraumatic stress symptoms and salivary cortisol levels. *American Journal of Psychiatry, 58*(9), 1509–1511.

Aravanis, A. M., Pyle, J. L., & Tsien, R. W. (2003). Single synaptic vesicles fusing transiently and successfully without loss of identity. *Nature, 423,* 643–647.

Arendt, T. (2001). Alzheimer's disease as a disorder of mechanisms underlying structural brain self-organization. *Neuroscience, 102*(4), 723–765.

Arlinghaus, K. A., Shoaib, A. M., & Price, T. R. P. (2005). Neuropsychiatric assessment. In J. M. Silver, T. W. McAllister, & S. C. Yudofsky (Eds.), *Textbook of traumatic brain injury.* Washington, DC: American Psychiatric Publishing.

Arnold, G. L., Hyman, S. I., Mooney, R. A., & Kirby, R. S. (2003). Plasma amino acids profiles in children with autism: Potential risk of nutritional deficiencies. *Journal of Autism and Developmental Disorders, 33,* 449–454.

Arnold, S. E., Franz, B. R., Gur, R. C., Gur, R. E., Shapiro, R. M., Moberg, P. J., et al. (1995). Smaller neuron size in schizophrenia in hippocampal subfields that mediate cortical–hippocampal interactions. *American Journal of Psychiatry, 152,* 738–748.

Arnow, B. (1997). Psychotherapy of anorexia and bulimia. In W. H. Kayne & D. C. Jinerson (Eds.), *Bailliere's clinical psychiatry.* London: Bailliere, Tindall & Cox.

Ascher, J. A., Cole, J. A., Colin, J. N., Feighner, J. P., Ferris, R. M., Fibiger, H. C., et al. (1995). Bupropion: A review of its mechanisms of antidepressant activity. *Journal of Clinical Psychiatry, 56,* 395–401.

Ashburner, J., & Friston, K. J. (2000). **Voxel-based morphometry—the methods.** *NeuroImage, 11,* **805–821.**

Ashford, J. W., & Jarvik, K. L. (1985). Alzheimer's disease: Does neuron plasticity predispose to axonal neurofibrillary degeneration? *New England Journal of Medicine, 5,* 388–389.

Ashford, J. W., Mattson, M., & Kumar, V. (1998). Neurobiological systems disrupted by Alzheimer's disease and molecular biological theories of vulnerability. In V. Kumar & C. Eisdorfer (Eds.), *Advances in the diagnosis and treatment of Alzheimer's disease.* New York: Springer.

Ashford, J. W., & Schmitt, F. A. (2001). Modeling the time-course of Alzheimer dementia. *Current Psychiatry Reports, 3,* 20–28.

Ashford, J. W., Soultanian, N. S., Zhang, S. X., & Geddes, J. W. (1998). Neuropil threads are collinear with MAP2 immunostaining in neuronal dendrites of Alzheimer brain. *Journal of Neuropathology and Experimental Neurology, 57,* 972–978.

Assanand, S., Pinel, J. P. J., & Lehman, D. R. (1996). *Common misconceptions about the regulation of feeding.* Unpublished manuscript, University of British Columbia, Vancouver, Canada.

August, G. J., Winers, K. C., Realmuto, G. M., Fahnhorst, T., Botzet, A. & Lee, S. (2006). Prospective study of adolescent drug use among community samples of ADHD and non-ADHD participants. *Journal of American Academy of Child and Adolescent Psychiatry, 45,* 824–832.

Aurentz, C. A., Felts, P. T., Lowry, C. A., Wartella, J. E., Miller, S. D., Amory, E. A., et al. (1999). *Increased c-fos and tyrosine hydroxylase activity in the extended amygdala of rats displaying compulsive-like running.* Poster presented at the International Behavioral Neuroscience Society, Nancy, France.

Austad, N., Scott, D. T., Janowsky, J. S., Jacobsen, C., Carroll, R. E., Montalto, M. B., et al. (2003). Visual, cognitive, and language assessments at 39 months: A follow-up study of children fed formulas containing long-chain polyunsaturated fatty acids to 1 year of age. *Pediatrics, 112,* 177–183.

Austin, J., & Marks, D. (2009). Hormonal regulators of appetite. *International Journal of Pediatric Endocrinology,* doi: 10.1155/2009/141753.

Avants, S. K., Margolin, A., Holford, T. R., & Kosten, T. R. (2000). A randomized controlled trial of auricular acupuncture for cocaine dependence. *Archives of Internal Medicine, 160,* 2305–2312.

Avoli, M., & Gloor, P. (1987). Epilepsy. In G. Adelman (Ed.), *Encyclopedia of neuroscience.* Boston: Birkhauser.

Aylward, E. H., Harris, G. J., Hoehn-Saric, R., Barta, P. E., Machilin, S. R., & Pearlson, G. D. (1996). Normal caudate nucleus in obsessive–compulsive disorder assessed by quantitative neuroimaging. *Archives of General Psychiatry, 53,* 577–584.

Bachoud-Levi, A. C., Remy, P., Nguyen, J. P., Brugieres, P., Lefaucheur, J. P., Bourdet, C., et al. (2000). Motor and cognitive improvements in patients with Huntington's disease after neural transplantation. *Lancet, 356,* 1975–1979.

Bainbridge, D. (2001). *Making babies: The science of pregnancy.* Cambridge, MA: Harvard University Press.

Baker, T. B., McFall, R. M., and Shoham, V. (2008). Current status and future prospects of clinical psychology toward a scientifically principled approach to mental and behavioral health care. *Psychological Science in the Public Interest, 9,* 67–103.

Balasubramaniam, A. A. (1997). Neuropeptide Y family of hormones receptor subtypes and antagonists. *Peptides, 18,* 445–457.

Baldwin, B. A., Parrott, R. F., & Ebenezer, I. S. (1998). Food for thought: A critique on the hypothesis that endogenous cholecystokinin acts as a physiological satiety factor. *Progress in Neurobiology, 55*(5), 477–507.

Bales, K. L., & Carter, C. S. (2003). Developmental exposure to oxytocin facilitates partner preferences in male prairie voles (*Microtus ochrogaster*). *Biochemical Neuroscience, 117,* 854–859.

Ballatore, C., Lee, V. M.-Y., & Trojanowski, J. Q. (2007). Tau-mediated neurodegeneration in Alzheimer's disease and related disorders. *Nature Reviews Neuroscience, 8,* 663–672.

Bandura, A. (1997). *Self-efficacy: The exercise of control.* New York: Freeman.

Banich, M. T. (1997). *Neuropsychology.* Boston: Houghton Mifflin.

Barker, A. T., Jalinous, R., & Freeston, I. L. (1985). Noninvasive magnetic stimulation of the human motor cortex. *Lancet, 1,* 1106–1107.

Barkley, R. A., Murphy, K. R., DuPaul, G. J., & Bush, T. (2002). Driving in young adults with attention deficit hyperactivity disorder: Knowledge, performance, adverse outcomes, and the role of executive functioning. *Journal of the International Neuropsychological Society, 8,* 655–672.

Barkley, R. A., Murphy, K. R., O'Connell, T., & Connor, D. F. (2005). Effects of two doses of methylphenidate on simulator driving performance in adults with attention deficit hyperactivity disorder. *Journal of Safety Research, 36*, 121–131.

Barnes, A. P., & Polleux, F. (2009) Establishment of axon-dendrite polarity in developing neurons. *Annual Review of Neuroscience, 32*, 347–381.

Barondes, S. H. (1993). *Molecules and mental illness.* New York: Freeman.

Barr, C. L., & Sandor, P. (1998). Current status of genetic studies of Gilles de la Tourette syndrome. *Canadian Journal of Psychiatry, 43*, 351–357.

Bartha, R., Stein, M. B., Williamson, P. C., Drost, D. J., Neufeld, R. W. Carr, T. J., et al. (1998). A short echo 1H spectroscopy and volumetric MRI study of the corpus striatum in patients with obsessive–compulsive disorder and comparison subjects. *American Journal of Psychiatry, 155*, 1584–1591.

Barthelme, F., & Barthelme, S. (1999, March 8). Good losers. *New Yorker,* 46–61.

Baskin, D. G., Schwartz, M. S., Seeley, R. J., Woods, S. C., Porte, D., Breininger, J. F., et al. (1999). Leptin receptor long-form splice-variant protein expression in neuron cell bodies of the brain and co-localization with neurpeptide Y mRNA in the arcuate nucleus. *Journal of Histochemistry and Cytochemistry, 138*, 196–202.

Bassett, A. S. (1989). Chromosome 5 and schizophrenia: Implications for genetic linkage studies. *Schizophrenia Bulletin, 15*, 393–402.

Battro, A. M. (2000). *Half a brain is enough.* Cambridge, UK: Cambridge University Press.

Baumann, B., & Bogerts, B. (2001). Neuroanatomical studies on bipolar disorder. *British Journal of Psychiatry, 178*, 142–147.

Baumann, B., Danos, P., Krell, D., Diekmann, S., Leschinger, A., Stauch, R., et al. (1999). Reduced volume of limbic system–affiliated basal ganglia in mood disorders: Preliminary data from a post mortem study. *Journal of Neuropsychiatry and Clinical Neuroscience, 11*, 71–78.

Baxter, L. R., Phelps, M. E., Mazziotti, J. C., Schwartz, J. M., Gerner, R. H., Selin, C. E., et al. (1985). Cerebral metabolic rates for glucose in mood disorders. *Archives of General Psychiatry, 42*, 441–447.

Bazarian, J. J., Blyth, B., Mookerjee, S., He, H., & McDermott, M. (2009). Sex differences in outcome after mild traumatic brain injury. *Journal of Neurotrauma,* doi: 10.1089/neu.2009.1068.

Bazil, C. W. (2002). New antiepileptic drugs. *Neurologist, 8*, 71–81.

Bear, M. F., Connors, B. W., & Paradiso, M. A. (1996). *Neuroscience: Exploring the brain.* Philadelphia: Lippincott, Williams & Wilkins.

Bear, M. F., Connors, B. W., & Paradiso, M. (2007). *Neuroscience: Exploring the Brain* (3rd ed.). New York: Lippincott Williams & Wilkins.

Bear, R. E., Fitzgerald, P., Rosenfeld, J. V., & Bittar, R. G. (2010). Neurosurgery for obsessive–compulsive disorder: Contemporary approaches. *Journal of Clinical Neuroscience, 17*, 1–5.

Beatty, J. (2001). *The human brain.* London: Sage Publications.

Beevers, C. G., & Schnyer, D. M. (2009). Serotonin and cognitive control of emotion in depression vulnerability. *Frontiers in Neuroscience, 3*, 248–249.

Begley, S. (1998, January 26). Is everybody crazy? *Newsweek,* 53.

Begley, S. (2010, February 8). The depressing news about antidepressants. *Newsweek,* 34–41.

Beliard, D., Kirschenbaum, D. S., & Fitzgibbon, M. L. (1992). Evaluation of an intensive weight control program using a priori criteria to determine outcome. *International Journal of Obesity, 16*, 623–625.

Benjamin, L. T. (1993). *A history of letters.* Dubuque, IA: Brown & Benchmark.

Bennett, E. L., Diamond, M. L., Krech, D., & Rosenzweig, M. R. (1964). Chemical and anatomical plasticity of brain. *Science, 206*, 649–654.

Benson, E. (2003). A new treatment for addiction. *Monitor on Psychology, 3*(6), 18–20.

Ben-Yishay, Y., Rattock, J., Lakin, P., Piasetsky, E. D., Ross, B., Silver, S., et al. (1985). Neuropsychological rehabilitation: Quest for a holistic approach. *Seminars in Neurology, 5*, 252–307.

Berk, L. S., Tan, S. A., Fry, W. F., Napier, B. J., Lee, J., Hubbard, R. W., et al. (1989). Neuroendocrine and stress hormone changes during mirthful laughter. *American Journal of Medical Science, 298*, 390–396.

Berk, L. S., Tan, S. A., Napier, B. J., & Eby, W. C. (1989). Eustress of mirthful laughter modifies natural killer cell activity. *Clinical Research, 37*, 115A.

Berman, R. M., Belanoff, J. K., Charney, D. S., & Schatzberg, A. F. (1999). Principles of the pharmacotherapy of depression. In D. S. Charney, E. J. Nestler, & B. S. Bunney (Eds.), *Neurobiology of mental illness.* New York: Oxford University Press.

Berridge, C. W., Devilbiss, D. M., Andrzejewski, M. E., Arnsten, A. F., Kelley, A. E., Schmeichel, B., Hamilton, C., & Spencer, R. C. (2006). Methylphenidate preferentially increases catecholamine neurotransmission within the prefrontal cortex at low doses that enhance cognitive function. *Biological Psychiatry, 60,* 1111–1120.

Betz, C., Mihalic, D., Pinto, M. E., & Raffa, R. B. (2000). Could a common biochemical mechanism underlie addictions? *Journal of Clinical Pharmacology and Therapeutics, 25,* 11–20.

Bingley, T., Lekskell, L., Meyerson, B. A., & Rylander, G. (1977). Long-term results of stereotactic anterior capsulotomy in chronic obsessive–compulsive neurosis. In W. H. Sweet, S. Obrador, & J. G. Martin-Rodrigues (Eds.), *Neurosurgical treatment in psychiatry, pain, and epilepsy.* Baltimore: University Park Press.

Bisaga, A., & Popik, P. (2000). In search of a new pharmacological treatment for drug and alcohol addition, *N*-methyl-D-aspartate (NMDA) antagonists. *Drug and Alcohol Dependence, 59,* 1–15.

Bizon, J. L., & Gallagher, M. (2003). Production of new cells in the rat dentate gyrus over the lifespan: Relation to cognitive decline. *European Journal of Neurology, 18*(1), 215–219.

Bjorvell, H., & Rossner, S. (1992). A ten-year follow-up of weight change in severely obese subjects treated in a combined behavioural modification programme. *International Journal of Obesity, 16,* 623–625.

Blachar, A., Federle, M. P., Pealer, K. M., Ikramuddin, S., & Schauer, P. R. (2002). Gastrointestinal complications of laparoscopic Roux-en-Y gastric bypass surgery: Clinical and imaging findings. *Radiology, 223,* 625–632.

Black, J. E., Greenough, W. T., & Anderson, B. J. (1987). Environment and the aging brain. *Canadian Journal of Psychology, 41,* 111–130.

Black, M. D., Selk, D. E., Hitchcock, J. M., Wettstein, J. G., & Sorensen, S. M. (1999). On the effect of neonatal nitric oxide synthase inhibition in rats: A potential neurodevelopmental model of schizophrenia. *Neuropharmacology, 38,* 1299–1306.

Blakemore, S. J., Wolpert, D. M., & Frith, C. D. (1998). Central cancellation of self-produced tickle sensation. *Nature Neuroscience, 1,* 635–640.

Blalock, J. E. (1984). The immune system as a sensory organ. *Journal of Immunology, 132,* 1067–1070.

Blanchard, R. J., McKittrick, C. R., & Blanchard, D. C. (2001). Animal models of social stress: Effects on behavior and brain neurochemical systems. *Physiology and Behavior, 73,* 261–271.

Blier, P., & Abbott, F. V. (2001). Putative mechanisms of action of antidepressant drugs in affective and anxiety disorders and pain. *Journal of Psychiatry and Neuroscience, 26,* 37–43.

Blier, P., & Montigny, C. (1994). Current advances and trends in the treatment of depression. *Trends in Pharmacology, 15,* 220–226.

Bligh-Glover, W., Kolli, T. N., Shapiro-Kulnane, L., Dilley, G. E., Friedman, L., Balraj, E., et al. (2000). The serotonin transporter in the midbrain of suicide victims with major depression. *Biological Psychiatry, 47,* 1015–1024.

Bloom, F. E., & Lazerson, A. (1988). *Brain, mind, and behavior* (2nd ed.). New York: Freeman.

Bloom, F. E., Nelson, C. A., & Lazerson, A. (2001). *Brain, mind, and behavior* (3rd ed.). New York: Worth.

Blum, W. F. (1997). Leptin: The voice of the adipose tissue. *Hormone Research, 48,* 2–8.

Bohman, M., Cloninger, C. R., Sigvardsson, S., & von Knorring, A. L. (1987). The genetics of alcoholism and related disorders. *Journal of Psychiatric Research, 21,* 447–452.

Bonese, K. F., Wainer, B. H., Fitch, F. W., Rothberg, R. M., & Schuster, C. R. (1974). Changes in heroin self-administration by a rhesus monkey after morphine immunization. *Nature, 252,* 708–710.

Bousfield, W. A., & Elliott, M. H. (1934). The effect of fasting on the eating behavior of rats. *Journal of Genetic Psychology, 45,* 227–237.

Bowlby, J. (1960). Grief and mourning in infancy and early childhood. *Psychoanalytic Study of the Child, 15,* 9–52.

Braak, H., Del Tredici, K., Rub, U., de Vos, R. A., Jansen Steur, E. N., & Braak, E. (2003). Staging of brain pathology related to sporadic Parkinson's disease. *Neurobiological Aging, 24,* 197–211.

Bracha, H. S., Torrey, E. F., Bigelow, L. B., Lohr, J. B., & Linington, B. B. (1991). Subtle signs of prenatal maldevelopment of the hand extoderm in schizophrenia: A preliminary monozygotic twin study. *Biological Psychiatry, 30,* 719–725.

Bracha, H. S., Torrey, E. F., Gottesman, I. I., Bigelow, L. B., & Cunniff, C. (1992). Second-trimester markers of fetal size in schizophrenia: A study of monozygotic twins. *American Journal of Psychiatry, 149,* 1355–1361.

Brady, J. V. (1958). Ulcers in "executive" monkeys. *Scientific American, 199,* 95–100.

Brady, S. T. (2000). Neurofilaments run sprints, not marathons. *Nature Cell Biology, 2,* 43–45.

Bragg, R. (1998, January 22). End video poker gambling, South Carolina chief urges. *The New York Times,* p. A14.

Brain Injury Association. (2002). *The costs and causes of traumatic brain injury.* Retrieved July 15, 2003, from http://www.biausa.org

Brambilla, F. (2001). Aetiopathogenesis and pathophysiology of bulimia nervosa. *CNS Drugs, 15*, 119–136.

Brambilla, F., Bellodi, L., Arancio, C., Ronchi, P., & Limonta, D. (2001). Central dopaminergic function in anorexia and bulimia nervosa: A psychoneuroendocrine approach. *Psychoneuroendocrinology, 26*, 393–409.

Brandes, J. S. (1977). Insulin induced overeating in the rat. *Physiology and Behavior, 18*, 1095–1102.

Bray, G. A. (2001). Drug treatment of obesity. *Review of Endocrine Metabolic Disorders, 2*, 403–418.

Brayne, C. (2007). The elephant in the room—healthy brains in later life, epidemiology and public health. *Nature Reviews Neuroscience, 8*, 233–239.

Breiter, H. C., Aharon, I., Kahneman, D., Dale, A., & Shizgal, P. (2001). Functional imaging of neural responses to expectanch and experience of monetary gains and losses. *Neuron, 30*, 619–639.

Bremner, J. D., Narayan, M., Anderson, E. R., Staib, L. H., Miller, H. L., & Charney, D. S. (2000). Hippocampal volume reduction in major depression. *American Journal of Psychiatry, 157*, 115–118.

Bridge, J. A., Greenhouse, J. B., Kelleher, K. J. (2009). Reporting system for violent deaths and youth suicide—reply. *The Journal of the American Medical Association, 301*, 485–486.

Brown, E. E., Robertson, G. S., & Fibiger, H. C. (1992). Evidence for conditional neuronal activation following exposure to a cocaine-paired environment: Role of forebrain limbic structures. *Neuroscience, 12*, 4112–4121.

Brownell, A. L., Canales, K., Chen, Y. I., Jenkins, B. G., Owen, C., Livni, E., et al. (2003). Mapping of brain function after MPTP-induced neurotoxicity in a primate Parkinson's disease model. *NeuroImage, 20*(2), 1064–1075.

Brownell, K. D. (2002a). The environment and obesity. In C. G. Fairburn & K. D. Brownell (Eds.), *Eating disorders and obesity: A comprehensive handbook* (2nd ed., pp. 433–438). New York: Guilford Press.

Brownell, K. D. (2002b). Public policy and the prevention of obesity. In C. G. Fairburn & K. D. Brownell (Eds.), *Eating disorders and obesity: A comprehensive handbook* (2nd ed., pp. 619–624). New York: Guilford Press.

Brownell, K. D., & Horgen, K. B. (2004). *Food fight.* New York: Contemporary Books.

Brownell, K. D., & Rodin, J. (1994). The dieting maelstrom: Is it possible and advisable to lose weight? *American Psychologist, 49*, 781–791.

Bu, G. (2009). Apolipoprotein E and its receptors in Alzheimer's disease: pathways, pathogenesis and therapy. *Nature Reviews Neuroscience, 10*, 333–344.

Bullock, R., & Teasdale, G. (1990). Surgical management of traumatic intracranial hematomas. In R. Braakman (Ed.), *Handbook of clinical neurology: Head injury* (Vol. 15). New York: Elsevier Science.

Bunney, W. E., & Bunney, B. S. (1999). Neurodevelopmental hypothesis of schizophrenia. In D. S. Charney, E. J. Nestler, & B. S. Bunney (Eds.), *Neurobiology of mental illness* (pp. 225–235). New York: Oxford University Press.

Burns, J. M., & Swerdlow, R. H. (2003) Right orbitofrontal tumor with pedophilia symptom and constructional apraxia sign. *Archives of Neurology, 60*, 437–440.

Burnstock, G. (2009). Autonomic neurotransmission: 60 years since Sir Henry Dale. *Annual Review of Pharmacology and Toxicology, 49*, 1–30.

Burton, T. M. (2007, September 26). One doctor's lonely quest to heal brain injury. *The Wall Street Journal*, p. A1.

Butler, R. W., & Namerow, N. S. (1988). Cognitive retraining in brain-injury rehabilitation: A critical review. *Neurorehabilitation and Neural Repair, 2*, 97–101.

Butts, C. L., & Sternberg, E. M. (2008). Neuroendocrine factors alter host defense by modulating immune function. *Cellular Immunology, 252*, 7–15.

Byne, W., Kemether, E., Jones, L., Haroutunian, V., & Davis, K. (1999). The neurochemistry of schizophrenia. In D. S. Charney, E. J. Nestler, & B. S. Bunney (Eds.), *Neurobiology of mental illness* (pp. 236–257). New York: Oxford University Press.

Byrnes, E. M., & Bridges, R. S. (2000). Endogeneous opioid facilitation of maternal memory in rats. *Behavioral Neuroscience, 114*, 797–804.

Byrnes, E. M., Rigero, B. A., & Bridges, R. S. (2000). Opioid receptor antagonism during early lactation results in the increased duration of nursing bouts. *Physiology and Behavior, 70*, 211–216.

Cade, J. F. J. (1949). Lithium salts in the treatment of psychotic excitement. *Medical Journal of Australia, 36*, 349–352.

Cai, X. J., Liu, X. H., Evans, M., Clapham, J. C., Wilson, S., Arch, J. R., et al. (2002). Orexins and feeding: Special occasions or everyday occurrence? *Regulatory Peptides, 104*(1–3), 1–9.

Caine, S. B., Thomsen, M., Gabriel, K. I., Berkowitz, J. S., Gold, L. H., Koob, G. F., et al. (2007). Lack of self-administration of cocoaine in dopamine D_1 receptor knock-out mice. *Journal of Neuroscience, 27*, 13140–13150.

Caldji, C., Liu, D., Sharma, S., Diorio, J., Francis, D., Meaney, M. L., et al. (2001). Development of individual differences in behavioral and endocrine responses to stress: Role of the postnatal environment. In B. S. McEwen & H. M. Goodman (Eds.), *Coping with the environment: Neural and endocrine mechanisms* (pp. 271–292). New York: Oxford University Press.

Camchong, J., MacDonald, A. W., Bell, C., Mueller, B. A., & Lim, D. O. (2009). Altered functional and anatomical connectivity in schizophrenia. *Schizophrenia Bulletin*, doi: 10.1093/schbul/sbp131.

Cameron, H. A., McEwen, B. S., & Gould, E. (1995). Regulation of adult neurogenesis by excitatory input and NMDA receptor activation in the dentate gyrus. *The Journal of Neuroscience, 15,* 4687–4692.

Campbell, T., Lin, S., DeVries, C., & Lambert, K. (2003). Coping strategies in male and female rats exposed to multiple stressors. *Physiology and Behavior, 78,* 495–504.

Campfield, L. A., & Smith, F. J. (1986). Functional coupling between transient declines in blood glucose and feeding behavior: Temporal relationships. *Brain Research Bulletin, 17,* 427–433.

Campfield, L. A., & Smith, F. J. (1990). Transient declines in blood glucose signal meal initiation. *International Journal of Obesity, 14,* 15–33.

Campos-Outcalt, D., Prybylski, D., Watkins, A., Rothfus, G., & Dellapenna, A. (1997). Motor-vehicle crash fatalities among American Indians and non-Indians in Arizona, 1979 through 1988. *American Journal of Public Health, 87*(2), 282–285.

Canfield, J., & Hansen, M. V. (2003). *Chicken soup for the soul: Living your dreams* (10th Anniversary Special Edition). Dayfield Beach, FL: Health Communications, Inc.

Cannon, T. D., Cadenhead, K., Cornblatt, B., Woods, S. W., Addington, J., Walker, E., et al. (2008). Prediction of psychosis in high-risk youth: A multi-site longitudinal study in North America. *Archives of General Psychiatry, 65,* 28–37.

Cannon, W. B. (1935). Stresses and strains of homeostasis. *American Journal of Medical Sciences, 189,* 1–14.

Cannon, W. B., & Washburn, A. (1912). An explanation of hunger. *American Journal of Physiology, 29,* 441–454.

Caplan, P. J. (1996). *They say you're crazy: How the world's most powerful psychiatrists decide who's normal.* Reading, MA: Addison-Wesley.

Cardno, A. G., & Gottesman, I. I. (2000). Twin studies of schizophrenia: From bow-and-arrow concordances to star wars Mx and functional genomics. *American Journal of Medical Genetics, 97*(1), 12–17.

Carelli, R. M., & Deadwyler, S. A. (1994). A comparison of nucleus accumbens neuronal firing patterns during cocaine self-administration and water reinforcement in rats. *Journal of Neuroscience, 14,* 7735–7746.

Carelli, R. M., King, V. C., Hampson, R. E., & Deadwyler, S. A. (1993). Firing patterns of nucleus accumbens neurons during cocaine self-administration in rats. *Brain Research, 626,* 14–22.

Carlson, E. B., & Rosser-Hogan, R. (1991). Trauma experiences, posttraumatic stress, dissociation, and depression in Cambodian refugees. *American Journal of Psychiatry, 148,* 1548–1551.

Carlson, M., & Earls, F. (1997). Psychological and neuroendocrinological sequelae of early social deprivation in institutionalized children in Romania. In C. S. Carter, L. L. Lederhendler, & B. Kirkpatrick (Eds.), *The integrative neurobiology of affiliation.* New York: Annals of the New York Academy of Science.

Carlson, N. R. (1994). *Physiology of behavior* (5th ed.). New York: Allyn & Bacon.

Carlson, N. R. (1999). *Physiology of behavior* (6th ed.). New York: Allyn & Bacon.

Carney, N., Chesnut, R. M., Maynard, H., Mann, N. C., Patterson, P., & Helfand, M. (1999). Effect of cognitive rehabilitation on outcomes for persons with traumatic brain injury: A systematic review. *Journal of Head Trauma Rehabilitation, 14,* 277–307.

Caron, M. G. (1997). Knockout of the vesicular monoamine transporter 2 gene results in neonatal death and supersensitivity to cocaine and amphetamine. *Neuron, 19,* 1285–1296.

Carpenter, M. B., & Sutin, J. (Eds.). (1983). *Human neuroanatomy* (8th ed.). Baltimore: Lippincott, William & Wilkins.

Carpenter, S. (2000). Preferring the predictable. *Monitor on Psychology, 31,* 42–43.

Carrera, M. R., Ashley, J. A., Zhou, B., Wirsching, P., Koob, G. F., & Janda, K. D. (2000). Cocaine vaccines: Antibody protection against relapse in a rat model. *Proceedings of the National Academy of Sciences USA, 97,* 6202–6206.

Carroll, J. (1982). Clinical applications of the dexamethasome suppression test for endogenous depression. *Pharmacopsychiatry, 15,* 19–24.

Carroll, J. (Ed.). (2003). *On the origin of species.* New York: Broadview Press.

Carter, C. S. (1998). The neuroendocrinology of social attachment and love. *Psychoneuroimmunology, 23,* 779–818.

Carter, C. S., Altemus, M., & Chrousos, G. P. (2001). Neuroendocrine and emotional changes in the post-partum period. *Progress in Brain Research, 133,* 241–249.

Carter, C. S., & Getz, L. L. (1993). Monogamy and the prairie vole. *Scientific American, 268,* 100–106.

Carvey, P. M., McRae, A., Lint, T. F., Ptak, L. R., Lo, E. S., Getz, C. G., et al. (1991). The potential use of a dopamine neuron antibody and a striatal-derived neurtrophic factor as diagnostic markers in Parkinson's disease. *Neurology, 41,* 53–58.

Casanova, M. F., & Lindzen, E. C. (2003). Changes in gray-/white-matter ratios in the parahippocampal gyri of late-onset schizophrenia patients. *American Journal of Geriatric Psychiatry, 11,* 605–609.

Casper, R. C. (1990). Personality features of women with good outcome from restricting anorexia nervosa. *Psychosomatic Medicine, 52,* 156–170.

Caspi, A., Sugden, K., Moffitt, T. E., Taylor, A., Craig, I. W., Harrington, H., et al. (2003). Influence of life stress on depression: Moderation by a polymorphism in the 5-HTT gene. *Science, 301,* 386–389.

Castellanos, F. X., Lee, P. P., Sharp, W., Jeffries, N. O., Greenstein, D. K., Clasen, L. S., et al. (2002). Developmental trajectories of brain volume abnormalities in children and adolescents with attention-deficit/hyperactivity disorder. *Journal of the American Medical Association, 288*(14), 1740–1748.

Casteneda, T. R., Tong, J., Datta, R., Culler, M., & Tschop, M. H. (2010). Ghrelin in the regulation of body weight and metabolism. *Frontiers in Neuroendocrinology, 31,* 44–60.

Castren, E., & Rantamaki, T. (2010). Role of brain-derived neurotrophic factor in the aetiology of depression: implications for pharmacological treatment. *CNS Drugs,* doi: 10.2165/11530010-000000000-00000. Retrieved December 15, 2009.

Cavigelli, S. A., & McClintock, M. K. (2003). Fear of novelty in infant rats predicts adult corticosterone dynamics and an early death. *Proceedings of the National Academy of Sciences USA, 100,* 16131–16136.

Cekic, M., Sayeed, I., & Stein, D.G. (2009). Combination treatment with progesterone and vitamin D hormone may be more effective than monotherapy for nervous system injury and disease. *Frontiers in Neuroendocrinology, 30,* 158–172.

Chakrabarty, K., Bhattacharyya, S., Christopher, R., & Khanna, S. (2005). Glutamatergic dysfunction in OCD. *Neuropsychopharmacology, 30,* 1735–1740.

Challem, J. (2008). *The food-mood solution.* New York: Wiley.

Champagne, F., & Meaney, M. J. (2001). Like mother, like daughter: Evidence for non-genomic transmission of parental behavior and stress responsivity. *Progress in Brain Research, 133,* 287–302.

Champoux, M., Hibbeln, J. R., Shannon, C., Majchrzak, S., Suomi, S. J., Salem, N., et al. (2002). Fatty acid formula supplementation and neuromotor development in rhesus monkey neonates. *Pediatric Research, 51,* 273–281.

Chang, I., Lapham, S. C., & Barton, K. J. (1996). Drinking environment and sociodemographic factors among DWI offenders. *Journal of Studies on Alcohol, 57,* 659–669.

Chanpattana, W., & Kramer, B. A. (2003). Acute and maintenance ECT with flupenthixol in refractory schizophrenia: Sustained improvements in psychopathology, quality of life, and social outcomes. *Schizophrenia Research, 63,* 189–193.

Cheetham, S. C., Katona, C. L. E., & Horton, R. W. (1991). Post-mortem studies of neurotransmitter biochemistry in depression and suicide. In R. W. Horton & C. L. E. Katona (Eds.), *Biological aspects of affective disorders* (pp. 192–221). London: Academic Press.

Chen, J. F., Xu, K., Petzer, J. P., Stal, R., Xu, Y. H., Beilstein, M., et al. (2001). Neuroprotection by caffeine and α_{2a} adenosine receptor inactivation in a model of Parkinson's disease. *Journal of Neuroscience, 21,* RC143.

Chenn, A., & Walsh, C. A. (2002). Regulation of cerebral cortical size by control of cell cycle exit in neural precursors. *Science, 297,* 365–369.

Cherkasova, M. V., & Hechtman, L. (2009). Neuroimaging in attention-deficity hyperactivity disorder: Beyond the frontostriatal circuitry. *The Canadian Journal of Psychiatry, 54,* 651–664.

Childress, A. R., Mozley, D., McElgin, B. A., Fitzgerald, J., Reivich, M., & O'Brien, C. P. O. (1999). Limbic activation during cue-induced cocaine craving. *American Journal of Psychiatry, 156,* 11–18.

Childs, D., & Stark, L. (March 9, 2009). Obama reverses course, lifts stem cell ban. *ABC News.* Retrieved from http://abcnews.go.com/Health/Politics/story?id=7023990&page=1.

Chiocca, E. A., & Martuza, R. L. (1990). Neurosurgical therapy of obsessive–compulsive disorder. In M. L. Jenike, L. Baer, & L. Minichiello (Eds.), *Obsessive–compulsive disorders: Theory and management* (2nd ed., pp. 283–294). Chicago: YearBook Medical Publishers.

Chisholm, K., Carter, M. C., Ames, E. W., & Morison, S. J. (1995). Attachment security and indiscriminately friendly behavior in children adopted from Romanian orphanages. *Developmental Psychopathology, 7,* 283–294.

Cholerton, B., Gleason, C. E., Baker, L. D., & Asthana, S. (2002). Estrogen and Alzheimer's disease: The story so far. *Drugs & Aging, 19,* 405–427.

Chowdhury, U., & Lask, B. (2001). Clinical implications of brain imaging in eating disorders. *Psychiatric Clinics of North America, 24*(2), 227–234.

Christian, C. M., Dufour, M., & Bertolucci, D. (1989). Differential alcohol-related mortality among American Indian tribes in Oklahoma, 1968–1978. *Social Science and Medicine, 28,* 275–284.

Chugani, H. T., Behen, M. E., Muzik, O., Juhasz, C., Nagy, F., & Chugani, D. C. (2001). Local brain functional activity following early deprivation: A study of postinstitutionalized Romanian orphans. *NeuroImage, 14,* 1290–1301.

Chung, Y., Klimanskaya, I., Becker, S., Li, T., Maserati, M., Lu, S. J., et al. (2008). Human embryonic stem cell lines generated without embryo destruction. *Cell Stem Cell, 2,* 113–117.

Ciccocioppo, R. (1999). The role of serotonin in craving: From basic research to human studies. *Alcohol and Alcoholism, 34,* 244–253.

Cicerone, K. D., Dahlberg, C., Kalmar, K., Langenbahn, D. M., Malec, J. F., Bergquiste, T. F., et al. (2000). Evidence-based cognitive rehabilitation: Recommendations for clinical practice. *Archives of Physical Medicine and Rehabilitation, 81,* 1596–1614.

Clark, A., Kirdby, K. C., Daniels, B. A., & Marks, I. M. (1998). A pilot study of computer-aided vicarious exposure for obsessive–compulsive disorder. *Australian and New Zealand Journal of Psychiatry, 32,* 268–275.

Clark, W. (1995). *At war within: The double-edged sword of immunity.* New York: Oxford University Press.

Clausen, T., Khaldi, A., Zauner, A., Reinert, M., Doppenberg, E., Menzel, M., et al. (2005). Cerebral acid-base homeostasis after severe traumatic brain injury. *Journal of Neurosurgery, 103,* 597–607.

Cloninger, C. R. (1987). Neurogenetic adaptive mechanisms in alcoholism. *Science, 236,* 410–416.

Clover, R. P., Abell, T., Becker, L. A., Crawford, S., & Ramsey, C. N. (1989). Family functioning and stress as predictors of influenza B infection. *Journal of Family Practice, 28,* 535–539.

Cohen, B. A., Inglese, M., Rusinek, H., Babb, J. S., Grossman, R. I., & Gonen, O. (2007). Proton MR spectroscopy and MRI-volumetry in mild traumatic injury. *American Journal of Neuroradiology, 28,* 907–913.

Cohen, P. (2000). No more kicks. *New Scientist, 11*(2).

Cohen, S., Doyle, W. J., Skoner, D. P., Rabin, B. S., & Gwaltney, J. M., Jr. (1997). Social ties and susceptibility to the common cold. *Journal of the American Medical Association, 277,* 1940–1944.

Cohn, J. P. (1995). *FDA consumer special report. The beginnings: Laboratory and animal studies.* Retrieved June 1, 2004, from http://www.fda.gov/fdac/special/newdrug/begin.html

Colapinto, J. (2001). *As nature made him: The boy who was raised as a girl.* New York: Harper Perennial.

Cole, S. W., Kemeny, M. E., Fahey, J. L., Zack, J. A., & Naliboff, B. D. (2003). Psychological risk factors for HIV pathogenesis: Mediation by the autonomic nervous system. *Biological Psychiatry, 54,* 1444–1456.

Collier, R. (2009). Rapidly rising clinical trial costs worry researchers. *Canadian Medical Association Journal, 180,* 277–278.

Collings, S., & King, M. (1994). Ten-year follow-up of 50 patients with bulimia nervosa. *British Journal of Psychiatry, 164,* 80–87.

Colton, M. (1998, May 31). You need it like….a hole in the head? *The Washington Post.*

Comerci, G. G., & Schwebel, R. (2000). Substance abuse: An overview. *Adolescent Medicine, 11,* 79–101.

Commonwealth Surgeons. (2002). Surgical weight loss: Risks. Retrieved October 1, 2002, from http://www.commonwealthsurgeons.com/surgicalweightlossbenefitsandrisks.htm

Concar, D. (2002, January 26). Lessons from Lorenzo. *New Scientist.* http://www.newscientist.com/article/mg17323274.700-lessons-from-lorenzo.html

Conel, J. L. (1939–1967). *The postnatal development of the human cerebral cortex* (Vols. 1–8). Cambridge, MA: Harvard University Press.

Connelly, J., Chell, S., Tennant, A., Rigby, A. S., & Airey, C. M. (2006). Modelling 5-year functional outcome in a major traumatic injury survivor cohort. *Disability Rehabiliation, 28,* 629–636.

Consumer Reports. (2009). Retrieved July 19, 2009, from http://www.consumerreports.org/health/healthy-living/health-safety/helmets/

Contreras, J., & Noonan, D. (2002, June 10). The diet of last resort. *Newsweek, 139,* 46–47.

Cook, I. A., & Leuchter, A. F. (2001). Prefrontal changes and treatment response prediction in depression. *Seminars in Clinical Neuropsychiatry, 6,* 113–120.

Coons, P. M. (1992). The use of carbamazepine for episodic violence in multiple personality disorder and dissociative disorder not otherwise specified: Two additional case studies. *Biological Psychiatry, 32,* 717–720.

Cooper, J. R., Roth, R., & Bloom, F. E. (1996). *Biochemical basis of neuropharmacology* (6th ed.). New York: Oxford University Press.

Copolov, D. L., Seal, M. L., Maruff, P., Ulusoy, R., Wong, M. T., Tochon-Danguy, H. J., et al. (2003). Cortical activation associated with the experience of auditory hallucinations and perception of human speech in schizophrenia: A PET correlation study. *Psychiatry Research, 122*(3), 139–152.

Corodimas, K. P., Pruitt, J. C., & Steig, J. M. (2000). Acute exposure to caffeine selectively disrupts context conditioning in rats. *Psychopharmacology, 152*, 376–382.

Correia, A. S., Anisimov, S. V., Li, Y., & Brundin, P. (2008). Growth factors and feeder cells promote differentiation of human embryonic stem cells into dopaminergic neurons: A novel role for fibroblast growth factor-20. *Frontiers in Neuroscience, 2*, 26–34.

Corrigall, W. A., & Coen, K. M. (1991). Cocaine self-administration is increased by both D_1 and D_2 dopamine antagonists. *Pharmacology, Biochemistry and Behavior, 39*, 799–802.

Cousino-Klein, L., & Corwin, E. J. (2002). Seeing the unexpected: How sex differences in stress responses may provide a new perspective on the manifestation of psychiatric disorders. *Current Psychiatry Report, 4*, 441–448.

Cousins, N. (1976). Anatomy of an illness (as perceived by the patient). *New England Journal of Medicine, 295*, 1458–1463.

Cousins, N. (1979). *Anatomy of an illness.* New York: Norton.

Cowan, W. M. (1979). The development of the brain. *Scientific American, 241*, 106–117.

Cowan, W. M., Sudhof, T. C., & Stevens, C. F. (Eds.). (2000). *Synapses.* Baltimore: Johns Hopkins University Press.

Cozolino, L. J., Goldstein, M. J., Nuechterlein, K. H., West, K. L., & Snyder, K. S. (1988). The impact of education about schizophrenia on relatives of varying levels of expressed emotion. *Schizophrenia Bulletin, 14*(4), 675–687.

Crawley, J. N., Belknap, J. K., Collins, A., Crabbe, J. C., Frankel, W., Henderson, N., et al. (1997). Behavioral phenotypes of inbred mouse strains: Implications and recommendations for molecular studies. *Psychopharmacology, 132*, 107–124.

Crick, F. (1994). *The astonishing hypothesis: The scientific search for the soul.* New York: Scribner's.

Crist, D. M., Mackinnon, L. T., Thompson, R. F., Atterbom, H. A., & Egan, P. A. (1989). Physical exercise increases natural cellular-mediated tumor cytotoxicity in elderly women. *Gerontology, 35*, 66–71.

Critchley, E. M. R. (1981). Speech disorders of parkinsonism: A review. *Journal of Neurology and Neurosurgical Psychiatry, 44*, 751–758.

Czeh, B., Michaelis, T., Watanabe, T., Frahm, J., de Biurrun, G., van Kampen, M., et al. (2001). Stress-induced changes in cerebral metabolites, hippocampal volume, and cell proliferation are prevented by antidepressant treatment with tianeptine. *Proceedings of the National Academy of Sciences USA, 98*, 12796–12801.

Dahlqvist, P., Ronnback, A., Risedal, A., Nergardh, R., Johansson, I. M., Seckl, J. R., et al. (2003). Effects of postischemic environment on transcription factor and serotonin receptor expression after permanent focal cortical ischemia in rats. *Neuroscience, 119*, 643–652.

Dahlstrom, W., & Williams, R. (1983). Hostility, CHD incidence, and total mortality: A 25-year follow-up study of 255 physicians. *Psychosomatic Medicine, 45*, 59.

Dallman, M., Pecoraro, N., Akana, S., la Fleur, S., Gomez, F., Houshyar, H., et al. (2003). Chronic stress and obesity: A new view of "comfort food." *Proceedings of the National Academy of Sciences USA, 100*, 11696–11701.

Dallman, M., Viau, V., Bhatnagar, S., Gomez, F., Laugero, K. D., & Bell, M. E. (2002). Corticotropin-releasing factor (CRF), corticosteroids, stress and sugar: Energy balance, the brain, and behavior. *Hormones and Behavior, 1*, 571–632.

Damasio, A. R. (1994). *Descartes' error: Emotion, reason, and the human brain.* New York: Avon Books.

Damasio, H., Grabowski, T., Frank, R., Galaburda, A. M., & Damasio, A. R. (1994). The return of Phineas Gage: Clues about the brain from the skull of a famous patient. *Science, 264*, 1102–1105.

Daniel, J. M., & Dohanich, G. P. (2001). Acetylcholine mediates the estrogen-induced increase in NMDA receptor binding in CA1 of the hippocampus and the associated improvement in working memory. *Journal of Neuroscience, 21*, 6949–6956.

Danner, D. D., Snowden, D. A., & Friesen, W. V. (2001). Positive emotions in early life and longevity: Findings from the Nun Study. *Journal of Personality and Social Psychology, 80*, 804–813.

Dantzer, R. (1999). Sickness behavior: A neuroimmune-based response to infectious disease. In M. Schedlowski & U. Tewes (Eds.), *Psychoneuroimmunology: An interdisciplinary introduction.* New York: Kluwer Academic/Plenum.

Dantzer, R., Bluthe, R., Koob, G., & Le Moal, M. (1987). Modulation of social memory in male rats by neurohypophyseal peptides. *Psychopharmacology, 91*, 363–368.

Dantzer, R., Koob, G., Bluthe, R., & Le Moal, M. (1988). Septal vasopressin modulates social memory in male rats. *Brain Research, 457*, 143–147.

Darwin, C. (1887). *The life and letters of Charles Darwin.* New York: Appleton.

Daumann, J., Schnitker, R., Weidemann, J., Schnell, K., Thron, A., & Gouzoulis-Mayfrank, E. (2003). Neural correlates of working memory in pure and polyvalent ecstasy (MDMA) users. *NeuroReport, 14,* 1983–1987.

Davidson, J., Pearlstein, T., Londborg, P., Brady, K. T., Rothbaum, B., Bell, J., et al. (2001). Efficacy of sertraline in preventing relapse of posttraumatic stress disorder: Results of a 28-week double-blind, placebo-controlled study. *American Journal of Psychiatry, 158,* 1974–1981.

Davidson, R. J., Irwin, W., Anderle, M. J., & Kalin, N. H. (2003). The neural substrates of affective processing in depressed patients treated with venlafaxine. *American Journal of Psychiatry, 160,* 64–75.

Davis, K. L., Kahn, R. S., Ko, G., & Davidson, M. (1991). Dopamine in schizophrenia: A review and reconceptualization. *American Journal of Psychiatry, 148,* 1474–1486.

Davis, K. L., Stewart, D. G., Friedman, J. I., Buchsbaum, M., Harvey, P. D., Hof, P. R., et al. (2003). White matter changes in schizophrenia: Evidence for myelin-related dysfunction. *Archives of General Psychiatry, 60,* 443–456.

Davis, M. (2004, June 16). *Facilitation of fear extinction in rats and exposure-based psychotherapy in humans with the functional NMDA agonist d-cycloserine.* Talk presented to the International Behavioral Neuroscience Society, Key West, FL.

Davis, R. C., Garafalo, L., & Kveim, K. (1959). Conditions associated with gastrointestinal activity. *Journal of Comparative and Physiological Psychology, 52,* 466–475.

Dawes, R. (1994). *House of cards: Psychology and psychotherapy built on myth.* New York: Free Press.

Dawson, E., & Robin, M. (1996). Schizophrenia: A gene at 6p. *Current Biology, 6,* 268–271.

Dawson, K. S., Batchelor, J., Meares, S., Chapman, J., & Marosszeky, J. E. (2007). Applicability of neural reserve theory in mild traumatic brain injury. *Brain Injury, 21,* 943–949.

DeAngelis, T. (2002). Promising treatments for anorexia and bulimia. *APA Monitor, 33,* 38–41.

de Castro, J. M. (2007). The time of day and the proportions of macronutrients eaten are related to total daily food intake. *British Journal of Nutrition, 98,* 1077–1083.

de Castro, J. M., & de Castro, E. S. (1989). Spontaneous meal patterns of humans: Influence of the presence of other people. *American Journal of Clinical Nutrition, 50,* 237–247.

Deckersbach, T., Gershuny, B. S., & Otto, M. W. (2000). Cognitive-behavioral therapy for depression. *Depression, 23,* 795–809.

DeFelipe, J. (2010). *Cajal's Butterflies of the Soul.* New York: Oxford University Press.

DeGette, C. (1998, November 22). To ensure revenue: Coke is it: Schools urged to boost sales. *Denver Post,* p. B1.

de Groot, J. C., de Leeuw, F. E., Oudkerk, M., Hofman, A., Jolles, J., & Breteler, M. M. B. (2000). Cerebral white matter lesions and depressive symptoms in elderly adults. *Archives of General Psychiatry, 57,* 1071–1076.

Delgado, P. L. (2000). Depression: The case for a monoamine deficiency. *Journal of Clinical Psychiatry, 61,* 7–11.

Delgado, P. L., & Moreno, F. A. (2000). Role of norepinephrine in depression. *Journal of Clinical Psychiatry, 61,* 5–12.

Demitrack, M. A., Lesem, M. D., Listwak, S. J., Brandt, H. A., Jimerson, D. C., & Gold, P. W. (1990). CSF oxytoxin in anorexia nervosa and bulimia nervosa: Clinical and pathophysiologic considerations. *American Journal of Psychiatry, 147*(7), 882–886.

Dencker, S. J. (2000). The need for new and better antidepressants: Reboxetine a new option. *Acta Psychiatrica Scandinavica, 101,* 6–11.

Denys, D., & Mantione, M. (2009). Deep brain stimulation in obsessive–compulsive disorder. *Progress in Brain Research, 175,* 419–427.

Deutch, A. Y., & Roth, R. H. (1999). Neurotransmitters. In M. G. Zigmond, F. E. Bloom, S. C. Landis, J. L. Roberts, & L. R. Squire (Eds.), *Fundamental neuroscience* (pp. 193–234). New York: Academic Press.

DeVries, A. C. (2002). Interaction among social environment, the hypothalamic–pituitary–adrenal axis, and behavior. *Hormones and Behavior, 41*(4), 405–413.

DeVries, A. C., Joh, H. D., Bernard, O., Hattori, K., Hurn, P. D., Traystman, R. J., et al. (2001). Social stress exacerbates stroke outcome by suppressing Bcl-2 expression. *Proceedings of the National Academy of Sciences USA, 98*(20), 11824–11828.

De Win, M. M., Gooij, J. G., Neneman, L., Schilt, T., Lavini, C., Olabarriaga, S. D., et al. (2008). Sustained effects of ecstasy on the human brain: A prospective neuroimaging study in novel users. *Brain, 131,* 2936–2945.

Dhabhar, F. S. (1998). Stress-induced enhancement of cell-mediated immunity. *Annals of the New York Academy of Sciences, 840,* 359–372.

Dhabhar, F. S. (2009). Enhancing versus suppressive effects of stress on immune function: Implications for immunoprotection and immunopathology. *Neuroimmunomodulation, 16,* 300–317.

Dhabhar, F. S., Satoskar, A. R., Bluethmann, H., David, J. R., & McEwen, B. S. (2000). Stress-induced enhancement for skin immune function: A role for gamma interferon. *Proceedings of the National Academy of Sciences USA, 97,* 2846–2851.

Diana, M. (1996). Dopaminergic neurotransmission and drug withdrawal: Relevance to drug craving. In C. Ohye, M. Kimura, & J. McKenzie (Eds.), *The basal ganglia V.* New York: Plenum Press.

Diana, M., Muntoni, A. L., Pistis, M., Melis, M., & Gessa, G. L. (1999). Lasting reduction in mesolimbic dopamine neuronal activity after morphine withdrawal. *European Journal of Neuroscience, 11,* 1037–1041.

Di Carlo, G., Borrelli, F., Ernst, E., & Izzo, A. A. (2001). St. John's wort: Prozac from the plant kingdom. *Trends in Pharmacological Sciences, 22,* 292–297.

Dickstein, S. G., Bannon, K., Castellanos, F. X., & Milham, M. P. (2006). The neural correlates of attention deficit hyperactivity disorder: An ALE meta-analysis. *Journal of Child Psychology and Psychiatry, 47,* 1051–1062.

Dimidjian, S., Hollon, S. D., Dobson, K. S., Schmaling, K. B., Kohlenberg, R., Addis, M., et al. (2006). Randomized trial of behavioral activation, cognitive therapy, and antidepressant medication in the acute treatment of adults with major depression. *Journal of Consulting and Clinical Psychology, 74*(4), 658–670.

Dobbs, D. (2009, April). The post-traumatic stress trap. *Scientific American, 300,* 64–69.

Doidge, N. (2007). *The brain that changes itself.* New York: Penguin Press.

Dolberg, O. T., Iancu, I., Sasson, Y., & Zohar, J. (1996). The pathogenesis and treatment of obsessive–compulsive disorder. *Clinical Neuropharmacology, 19*(2), 129–147.

Dole, V. P., & Nyswander, M. (1965). A medical treatment for acetylmorphine (heroin) addiction: A clinical trial with methadone hydrochloride. *Journal of the American Medical Association, 193,* 80–84.

Dopheide, J. A., & Pliszka, S. R. (2009). Attention-deficit-hyperactivity disorder: An update. *Pharmacotherapy, 29,* 656–679.

Doty, R. L., Ford, M., Preti, G., & Huggins, G. R. (1975). Changes in the intensity and pleasantness of human vaginal odors during the menstrual cycle. *Science, 190,* 1316–1318.

Draganski, B., Gaser, C., Busch, V., Schuierer, G., Bogdahn, U., & May, A. (2004). Neuroplasticity: Changes in grey matter induced by training. *Nature, 427,* 311–312.

Drevets, W. C. (1999). Prefrontal cortical–amygdalar metabolism in major depression. *Annals of the New York Academy of Sciences, 877,* 614–637.

Drevets, W. C. (2000). Neuroimaging studies of mood disorders. *Biological Psychiatry, 48,* 813–829.

Duman, R. S. (1999). The neurochemistry of mood disorders. Preclinical studies. In D. S. Charney, E. J. Nestler, & B. S. Bunney (Eds.), *Neurobiology of mental illness* (pp. 333–347). New York: Oxford University Press.

Duman, R. S., & Nestler, E. J. (1995). Signal transduction pathways for catecholamine receptors. In F. E. Bloom & D. J. Kupfer (Eds.), *Psychopharmacology: The fourth generation of progress* (pp. 303–320). New York: Raven Press.

Dunn, J. R. (2001). Humor in the brain: New discoveries. *Psychology Online Journal,* Retrieved January 2004 from http://www.psychjournal.com

Durston, S., Davidson, M. C., Mulder, M.J., Spicer, J. A., Galvan, A., Tottenham, N., et al. (2007). Neural and behavioral correlates of expectancy violations in attention-deficit hyperactivity disorder. *Journal of Child Psychology and Psychiatry, 48,* 881–889.

Durston, S., Hulshoff Pol, H. E., Casey, B. J., Giedd, J. N., Buitelaar, J. K., & van Engeland, H. (2001). Anatomical MRI of the developing human brain: What have we learned? *American Journal of Child and Adolescent Psychiatry, 40,* 1012–1020.

Eastwood, S. L., & Harrison, P. J. (1995). Decreased synaptophysin in the medial temporal lobe in schizophrenia demonstrated using immunoautoradiography. *Neuroscience, 69,* 339–343.

Edelman, G. M. (1987). *Neural Darwinism: The theory of neuronal group selection.* New York: Basic Books.

Edelman, G. M. (1993). *Bright air, brilliant fire: On the matter of the mind.* New York: Basic Books.

Editorial (2009). Psychology: a reality check. *Nature, 461,* 847.

Eggert, F., & Ferstl, R. (1999). Functional relationship between the olfactory and immune systems. In M. Schedlowski & U. Tewes (Eds.), *Psychoneuroimmunology: An interdisciplinary introduction.* New York: Kluwer Academic/Plenum.

Eineberg, N. A., & Gale, T. M. (2005). Evidence-based pharmacotherapy of obsessive–compulive disorder. *International Journal of Neuropsychopharmacology, 8,* 107–129.

Eitan, R., & Lerer, B. Hippocampal neurogenesis and depression. *Frontiers in Neuroscience, 3,* **258–259.**

El-Khodor, B., & Boksa, P. (2001). Caesarean section birth produces long-term changes in dopamine D_1 receptors and in stress-induced regulation of D_3 and D_4 receptors in the rat brain. *Neuropsychopharmacology, 25,* 423–439.

Elliott, R., Dolan, R. J., & Frith, C. D. (2000). Dissociable functions in the medial and lateral orbitofrontal cortex:

Evidence from human neuroimaging studies. *Cerebral Cortex, 10*, 308–317.

Ellison-Wright, I., Ellison-Wright, Z., & Bullmore, E. (2008). Structural brain change in attention deficit hyperactivity disorder identified by meta-analysis. *BMC Psychiatry, 8:51*: doi: 10.1186/1471-244X-8-51.

Elovic, E., & Zafonte, D. O. (2005). Prevention. In J. M. Silver, T. W. McAllister, & S. C. Yudofsky (eds.), *Textbook of traumatic brain injury.* Washington, DC: American Psychiatric Publishing.

Elster, J. (1999). Introduction. In *Addiction: Entries and exits.* New York: Russell Sage Foundation.

Ember, L. R. (1998, May 25). Surviving stress. *Chemical and Engineering News, 76*, 12–24.

Enard, W., Gehre, S., Hammerschmidt, K., Holter, S. M., Blass, T., Somel, M., et al. (2009). A humanized version of Foxp2 affects cortico-basal ganglia circuits in mice. *Cell, 137*, 961–971.

Engert, F., & Bonhoeffer, T. (1999). Dendritic spine changes associated with hippocampal long-term synaptic plasticity. *Nature, 399*, 66–70.

Epel, E. S., Lapidus, R., McEwen, B., & Brownell, K. (2001). Stress may add bite to appetite in women: A laboratory study of stress-induced cortisol and eating behavior. *Psychoneuroendocrinology, 26*, 37.

Epperson, C. N., McDougle, C. J., & Price, L. H. (1996). Intranasal oxytocin in obsessive–compulsive disorder. *Biological Psychiatry, 40*, 547–549.

Erb, S., Salmaso, N., Rodaros, D., & Stewart, J. (2001). A role for the CRF-containing pathway from central nucleus of the amygdala to bed nucleus of the stria terminalis in the stress-induced reinstatement of cocaine seeking in rats. *Psychopharmacology, 158*, 360–365.

Eriksson, P. S., Perfilieva, E., Bjork-Eriksson, T., Alborn, A. M., Nordborg, C., Peterson, D. A., et al. (1998). Neurogenesis in the adult human hippocampus. *Nature Medicine, 4*(11), 1313–1317.

Everitt, B. J., Parkinson, J. A., Olmstead, M. C., Arroyo, M., Robledo, P., & Robbins, T. W. (2000). Associative processes in addition and reward: The role of amygdala–ventral striatal subsystems. *Annals of the New York Academy of Sciences, 877*, 412–438.

Fabrega, H. (2002). Medical validity in Eastern and Western traditions. *Perspectives of Biological Medicine, 45*, 395–415.

Fairburn, C. G., & Brownell, K. D. (Eds.). (2002). Eating disorders and obesity: A comprehensive handbook (2nd ed.). New York: Guilford Press.

Fann, J. R., Uomoto, J. M., & Katon, W. J. (2000). Sertraline in the treatment of major depression following mild traumatic brain injury. *Journal of Neuropsychiatry and Clinical Neuroscience, 12*, 226–232.

Farace, E., & Alves, W. M. (2000). Do women fare worse: A meta-analysis of gender differences in outcome after traumatic brain injury. *Journal of Neurosurgery, 93*, 539–545.

Faraone, S. V., Sergeant, J., Gillberg, C., & Biederman, J. (2003). The worldwide prevalence of ADHD: Is it an American condition? *World Psychiatry, 2*, 104–113.

Farwell, L. (2000, December 10). Highlights of CBS *60 Minutes* featuring brain fingerprinting [Interview with Mike Wallace]. Retrieved January 8, 2004, from http://www.brainwavescience.com/Highlights60Minutes.htm

Fatty foods—not empty stomach—fire up hunger hormone. (June 8, 2009). *Science Daily.* http://www.science-daily.com/releases/2009/06/090605151351.htm

Fava, M., & Kendler, K. S. (2000). Major depressive disorder. *Neuron, 28*, 335–341.

Fava, M., McGrath, P. J., & Sheu, W. P. (2003). Switching to reboxetine: An efficacy and safety study in patients with major depressive disorder unresponsive to fluoxetine. *Journal of Clinical Psychopharmacology, 23*, 365–369.

Feldman, J. L., Mitchell, G. S., & Nattie, E. E. (2003). Breathing: Rhythmicity, plasticity, chemosensitivity. *Annual Review of Neuroscience, 26*, 239–266.

Feldman, R. S., & Quenzer, L. F. (1984). *Fundamentals of neuropsychopharmacology.* Sunderland, MA: Sinauer.

Felten, D., Ackerman, K. D., Wiegand, S. J., & Felten, S. Y. (1987). Noradrenergic sympathetic innervation of the spleen: I. Nerve fibers associate with lymphocytes and macrophages in specific compartments of the splenic white pulp. *Journal of Neuroscience Research, 18*, 28–36.

Ferguson, J. N., Aldag, J. M., Insel, T. R., & Young, L. J. (2001). Oxytocin in the medial amygdala is essential for social recognition in the mouse. *Journal of Neuroscience, 21*, 8278–8285.

Fernandez, H. (1998). *Heroin.* Center City, MN: Hazelden.

Fernstrom, J. D., & Wurtman, F. J. (1974). Control of brain serotonin levels by the diet. *Advances in Biochemical Psychopharmacology, 11*, 133–142.

Field, H. L., Monti, D. A., Greeson, J. M., & Kunkel, E. J. S. (2000). St. John's wort. *International Journal of Psychiatry in Medicine, 30*, 203–219.

Field, T. (1993). The therapeutic effects of touch. In G. G. Brannigan & M. R. Merrens (Eds.), *The undaunted psychologist.* New York: McGraw-Hill.

Field, T. (2002). Massage therapy. *Medical Clinics of North America, 86*, 163–171.

Finger, S. (2000). *Minds behind the brain*. New York: Oxford University Press.

Fischl, B., & Dale, A. M. (2000). Measuring the thickness of the human cerebral cortex from magnetic resonance images. *Proceedings of the National Academy of Sciences, USA, 97*, 11050–11055.

Fisher, H. (1982). *The sex contract: The evolution of human behavior*. New York: William Morrow.

Fisher, M., Holland, C., Merzenich, M. M., & Vinogradov, S. (2009). Using neuroplasticity-based auditory training to improve verbal memory in schizophrenia. *American Journal of Psychiatry, 166*, 805–811.

Fisher, M., Holland, C., Subramaniam, K., & Vinogradov, S. (2009). Neuroplasticity-based cognitive training in schizophrenia: An interim report on the effects 6 months later. *Schizophrenia Bulletin*, doi: 10.1093/schbul/sbn170.

Flament, M. F., Rapoport, J. L., Murphy, D. L., Lake, C. R., & Berg, C. J. (1987). Biochemical changes during clomipramine treatment of childhood obsessive–compulsive disorder. *Archives of General Psychiatry, 44*, 219–225.

Flanagan, S. R., Cantor, J. B., & Ashman, T. A. (2008). Traumatic brain injury: Future assessment tools and treatment prospects. *Neuropsychiatric Disease and Treatment, 4*, 877–892.

Flegal, K. M., Carroll, M. D., Ogden, C. L., & Curtin, L. R. (2010). Prevalence and trends in obesity among US adults 1999–2008. *Journal of the American Medical Association, 303*, 235–241.

Flegal, K. M., Harlan, W. R., & Landis, J. R. (1988). Secular trends in body mass index and skinfold thickness with socioeconomic factors in young adult women. *American Journal of Clinical Nutrition, 48*, 535–543.

Fobi, M., Lee, H., Igwe, D., Felahy, B., James, E., Stanczyk, M., et al. (2002). Prophylactic cholecystectomy with gastric bypass operation: Incidence of gallbladder disease. *Obesity Surgery, 12*, 350–353.

Fodstad, H., Strandman, E., Karlsson, B., & West, K. A. (1982). Treatment of chronic obsessive–compulsive states with stereotactic anterior capsulotomy or cingulotomy. *Acta Neurochirurgica, 62*, 1–23.

Foltz, E. L., & Millet, F. E., Jr. (1964). Experimental psychosomatic disease states in monkeys. 1. Peptic ulcer—"executive monkeys." *Journal of Surgical Research, 26*, 445–453.

Fontana, A., Weber, W., & Dayer, J. M. (1984). Synthesis of interleukin 1/endogenous pyrogen in the brain of endotoxin-treated mice: A step in fever induction. *Journal of Immunology, 133*, 1696–1698.

Forno, L. S. (1996). Neuropathology of Parkinson's disease. *Journal of Neuropathological Experimental Neurology, 55*, 259–272.

Francis, D. D., Diorio, J., Liu, D., & Meaney, M. J. (1999). Nongenomic transmission across generations of maternal behavior and stress responses in the rat. *Science, 286*, 1155–1158.

Francis, D. D., & Meaney, M. J. (1999). Maternal care and the development of stress responses. *Current Opinion of Neurobiology, 9*(1), 128–134.

Francis, D. D., Young, L. J., Meaney, M. J., & Insel, T. R. (2002). Naturally occurring differences in maternal care are associated with the expression of oxytocin and vasopressin (V1a) receptors: gender differences. *Journal of Neuroendocrinology, 14*, 349–353.

Franco, C., Paris, J. J., Wulfert, E., & Frye, C. A. (2010). Male gamblers have significantly greater salivary cortisol before and after betting on a horse race, than do female gamblers. *Physiology & Behavior, 99*, 225–229.

Frank, G. K., Kaye, W. H., Sahu, A., Fernstrom, J., & McConaha, C. (2001). Could reduced cerebrospinal fluid (CSF) galanin contribute to restricted eating in anorexia nervosa. *Neuropsychopharmacology, 24*, 706–709.

Fredrickson, B. L., Maynard, K. E., Helms, M. J., Haney, T. L., Siegler, I. C., & Barefoot, J. C. (2000). Hostility predicts magnitude and duration of blood pressure response to anger. *Journal of Behavioral Medicine, 23*, 229–243.

Freedman, R. (2003). Schizophrenia. *New England Journal of Medicine, 349*(18), 1738–1749.

Freedman, R., Adler, L. E., Bickford, P., Byerley, W., Coon, H., Cullum, M. C., et al. (1994). Schizophrenia and nicotinic receptors. *Harvard Review of Psychiatry, 2*(4), 179–192.

Freedman, R., Coon, H., Myles-Worsley, M., Orr-Urtreger, A., Olincy, A., Davis, A., et al. (1997). Linkage of a neurophysiological deficit in schizophrenia to a chromosome 15 locus. *Proceedings of the National Academy of Sciences, USA, 94*, 587–592.

Freeman, J. R., Barth, J. T., Broshek, D. K., & Plehn, K. (2005). Sports injuries. In J.M. Silver, T.W. McAllister, & S.C. Yudofsky (Eds.), *Textbook of Traumatic Brain Injury*. Washington, DC: American Psychiatric Publishing, Inc.

Freeman, M. P., Hibbeln, J. R., Wisner, K. L., Davis, J. M., Mischoulon, D., Peet, M., et al. (2006). Omega-3 fatty acids: evidence basis for treatment and future research in psychiatry. *The Journal of Clinical Psychiatry, 67*, 1954–67.

Fried, I., Wilson, C. L., MacDonald, K. A., & Behnke, E. J. (1998). Stimulating laughter. *Nature, 391*, 650.

Friedman, R. A. (2006). Uncovering an epidemic—screening for mental illness in teens. *The New England Journal of Medicine, 355*, 2717–2719.

Friedman, S., Smith, L., Fogel, D., Paradis, C., Viswanathan, R., Ackerman, R., et al. (2002). The incidence and influence of early traumatic life events in patients with panic disorder: A comparison with other psychiatric outpatients. *Journal of Anxiety Disorders, 16,* 259–272.

Fuchs, F., Flugge, G., Ohl, F., Lucassen, P., Vollmann-Honsdorf, G. K., & Michaelis, T. (2001). Psychosocial stress, glucocorticoids, and structural alterations in the tree shree hippocampus. *Physiology and Behavior, 73,* 285–291.

Fujita, M., Charney, D. S., & Innis, R. B. (2000). Imaging serotonergic neurotransmission in depression: Hippocampal pathophysiology may mirror global brain alterations. *Biological Psychiatry, 48,* 801–812.

Fulton, J. F. (1951). *Frontal lobotomy and affective behavior.* New York: Norton.

Fulton, J. F., & Jacobsen, C. F. (1935). *Fonctions des lobes frontaux: Etude comparée chez l'homme et les singes chimpanzes.* London: International Neurological Congress.

Furlow, F. B. (1996, March/April). The smell of love. *Psychology Today,* 38–45.

Futterman, A. D., Kemeny, M. E., Shapiro, D., & Fahey, J. L. (1994). Immunological and physiological changes associated with induced positive and negative mood. *Psychosomatic Medicine, 56,* 499–511.

Fuxe, K., Tinner, B., Caberlotto, L., Bunnemann, B., & Agnati, L. F. (1997). NPY Y1 receptor-like immunoreactivity exists in a sub-population of beta-endorphin immunoreactive nerve cells in the arcuate nucleus: A double immunolabelling analysis in the rat. *Neuroscience Letters, 225,* 49–52.

Fylan, R., Harding, G. F., Edson, A. S., & Webb, R. M. (1999). Mechanisms of video-game epilepsy. *Epilepsia, 40,* 28–30.

Gage, F. H. (2000). Structural plasticity: Cause, result, or correlate of depression. *Biological Psychiatry, 48,* 713–714.

Gage, F. H., Kempermann, G., & Song, H. (Eds.) (2007). *Adult Neurogenesis.* New York: Cold Spring Harbor.

Gainetdinov, R. R., Mohn, A. R., & Caron, M. G. (2001). Genetic animal models: Focus on schizophrenia. *Trends in Neurosciences, 24,* 527–533.

Galea, L. A. M., Tanapat, P., & Gould, E. (1996). Exposure to predator odor suppresses cell proliferation in the dentate gyrus of adult rats via a cholinergic mechanism. *Society for Neuroscience Abstracts, 22,* 1196.

Gamberino, W. C., & Gold, M. S. (1999). Neurobiology of tobacco smoking and other addictive disorders. *Addictive Disorders, 22,* 301–312.

Garcia, J., Kimmeldorf, D. J., & Koelling, R. A. (1955). Conditioned aversion to saccharin resulting from exposure to gamma radiation. *Science, 122,* 157–158.

Gardner, E., & David, J. (1999). The neurobiology of chemical addiction. In J. Elster & O. Skog (Eds.), *Getting hooked: Rationality and the addictions.* Cambridge, UK: Cambridge University Press.

Garza, A. A., Ha, T. G., Garcia, C., Chen, M. J., & Russo-Neustadt, A. A. (2004). Exercise, antidepressant treatment, and BDNF mRNA expression in the aging brain. *Pharmacology, Biochemistry and Behavior, 77*(2), 209–220.

Gauntt, J. (2009). Dean offers eating tips for busy students. http://media.www.houstonianonline.com/media/storage/paper229/news/2009/12/03/CampusNews/Dean-Offers.Eating.Tips.For.Busy.Students-3844200.shtml

Gayle, A. (Ed.). (1988). *The polygraph test: Lies, truth, and science.* Newbury Park, CA: Sage.

Geier, A. B., Schwartz, M. B., & Brownell, K. D. (2003). "Before and after" diet advertisement escalate the stigma of obesity. *Eating and Weight Disorders, 8*(4), 282–288.

Geliebter, A., & Hashim, S. A. (2001). Gastric capacity in normal, obese, and bulimic women. *Physiology and Behavior, 74,* 743–746.

Geliebter, A., Schachter, S., Lohmann-Walter, C., Feldman, H., & Hashim, S. A. (1996). Reduced stomach capacity in obese subjects after dieting. *American Journal of Clinical Nutrition, 63,* 170–173.

Gennarelli, T. A., & Graham, D. I. (2005). Neuropathology. In J. M. Silver, T. W. McAllister, & S. C. Yudofsky (eds.), *Textbook of traumatic brain injury,* Washington, DC: American Psychiatric Publishing.

Geoghegan, T. (2009). What happened to the boy with Tourette's? *BBC News Magazine.* http://news.bbc.co.uk/2/hi/uk_news/magazine/8070740.stm

George, M. S., Nahas, Z., Kozel, R. A., Goldman, J., Molloy, M., & Oliver, N. (1999). Improvement of depression following transcranial magnetic stimulation. *Current Psychiatry Reports, 1,* 114–124.

George, M. S., Nahas, Z., Molloy, M., Speer, A. M., Oliver, N. C., Li., X., et al. (2000). A controlled trial of daily left prefrontal cortex TMS for treating depression. *Biological Psychiatry, 48,* 962–970.

George, M. S., Stallings, L. E., Speer, A. M., Spicer, K. M., Vincent, D. J., Bohning, D. E., et al. (1999). Prefrontal repetitive transcranial magnetic stimulation (rTMS) changes relative perfusion locally and remotely. *Human Psychopharmacology, 14,* 161–170.

George, S. A., Khan, S., Briggs, H., & Abelson, J. L. (2010). CRH-stimulated cortisol release and food intake in healthy, non-obese adults. *Psychoneuroendocrinology, 35,* 607–612.

Geracioti, T. D., Liddle, R. A., Altemus, M., Demitrack, M. A., & Gold, P. W. (1992). Regulation of appetite and cholecystokinin secretion in anorexia nervosa. *American Journal of Psychiatry, 149,* 958–961.

Getchell, T. V., Doty, R. L., & Bartochik, L. M. (Eds.) (1991). *Smell and tastes in health and disease.* New York: Raven Press.

Ghandi, S. P., & Stevens, C. F. (2003). Three modes of synaptic vesicular recycling revealed by single-vesicle imaging. *Nature, 423,* 607–613.

Ghose, S., Weickert, C. S., Colvin, S. M., Coyle, J. T., Herman, M. M., Hyde, T. M., et al. (2004). Glutamate carboxypeptidase II gene expression in the human frontal and temporal lobe in schizophrenia. *Neuropsychopharmacology, 29*(1), 117–125.

Gibbs, J., Young, R. C., & Smith, G. P. (1973). Cholecystokinin decreases food intake in rats. *Journal of Comparative and Physiological Psychology, 84,* 488–495.

Giedd, J. N., Blumenthal, J., Jeffries, N. O., Castellanos, X., Liu, H., Zijdenbos, A., et al. (1999). Brain development during childhood and adolescence: A longitudinal MRI study. *Nature Neuroscience, 2,* 861–863.

Gilbert, S. (2000). *Developmental biology.* New York: Sinauer.

Giordano, G. D., Renzetti, P., Parodi, R. C., Foppiani, L., Zandrino, F., Giordano, G., et al. (2001). Volume measurement with magnetic resonance imaging of hippocampus–amygdala formation in patients with anorexia nervosa. *Journal of Endocrinological Investment, 24,* 510–514.

Giza, C. C., & Hovda, J. J. (2001). The neurometabolic cascade of concussion. *Journal of Athletic Training, 36,* 228–235.

Gjerris, A. (1988). Baseline studies on transmitter substances in cerebrospinal fluid in depression. *Acta Psychiatrica Scandinavica, 78,* 1–36.

Gladwell, M. (1997, February 24 and March 3). Damaged. *New Yorker,* 132–147.

Gladwell, M. (2009, October 19). Offensive Play: How different are dogfighting and football? *The New Yorker.* http://www.newyorker.com/reporting/2009/10/19/091019 fa_fact_gladwell

Glantz, L. A., & Lewis, D. A. (1997). Reduction of synaptophysin immunoreactivity in the prefrontal cortex of subjects with schizophrenia: Regional and diagnostic specificity. *Archives of General Psychiatry, 54,* 943–952.

Glaser, R. (2005). Stress-associated immune dysregulation and its importance for human health: A personal history of psychoneuroimmunology. *Brain, Behavior, and Immunity, 19,* 3–11.

Glaser, R., Kiecolt-Glaser, J. K., Malarkey, W. B., & Sheridan, J. F. (1998). The influence of psychological stress on the immune response to vaccines. *Annals of the New York Academy of Science, 840,* 649–655.

Glaser, R., Sheridan, J., Malarkey, W. B., MacCallum, R. C., & Kiecolt-Glaser, J. K. (2000). Chronic stress modulates the immune response to a pneumococcal pneumonia vaccine. *Psychosomatic Medicine, 62,* 804–807.

Glasper, E. R., Lambert, K. G., Aurentz, C., Amory, E., Griffin, G., Graber, A., et al. (2000). *An investigation of the neurobiological mechanisms of withdrawal in activity-stress rats.* Poster presented at the American Psychological Society, Miami, FL.

Glick, S. D., & Maisonneuve, I. M. (1999). Development of a novel medication for drug abuse. *Annals of the New York Academy of Sciences, 909,* 88–103.

Gmelch, G. (1992). Superstition and ritual in American baseball. *Elysian Fields Quarterly, 11,* 25–36.

Goedert, M., Spillantini, M. G., Serpell, L. C., Berriman, J., Smith, M. J., Jakes, R., et al. (2001). From genetics to pathology: Tau and alpha-synuclein assemblies in neurodegenerative diseases. *Philosophical Transactions of the Royal Society of London, Series B, Biological Sciences, 356,* 213–227.

Goel, V., & Dolan, R. J. (2001). The functional anatomy of humor: Segregating cognitive and affective components. *Nature Neuroscience, 4,* 237–238.

Goetz, C. G., Tanner, C. M., Wilson, R. S., Carroll, V. S., Como, P. G., & Shannon, K. M. (1987). Clonidine and Gilles de la Tourette syndrome: Double-blind study using objective rating methods. *Annals of Neurology, 21,* 307–310.

Goff, D. C., Tsai, G., Manoach, D. S., & Coyle, J. T. (1995). Dose-finding trial of D-cycloserine added to neuroleptics for negative symptoms in schizophrenia. *American Journal of Psychiatry, 152*(8), 1213–1215.

Goktepe, E. O., Young, L. B., & Bridges, P. K. (1975). A further review of the results of stereotactic subcaudate tractotomy. *British Journal of Psychiatry, 126,* 270–280.

Gold, P. E. (2003). Acetylcholine modulation of neural systems involved in learning and memory. *Neurobiology of Learning and Memory, 80,* 194–210.

Goldapple, K., Segal, Z., Garson, C., Lau, M., Bieling, P., Kennedy, S., et al. (2004). Modulation of cortical-limbic pathways in major depression: Treatment-specific effects of cognitive behavior therapy. *Archives of General Psychiatry, 61*(1), 34–41.

Goldman-Rakic, P. S. (1987). Circuitry of primate prefrontal cortex and regulation of behavior by representational memory. In F. Plum & V. Mountcastle (Eds.), *Handbook of physiology: The nervous system* (pp. 373–417). Bethesda, MD: American Physiological Society.

Goldman-Rakic, P. S. (1999). The physiological approach: Functional architecture of working memory and disordered cognition in schizophrenia. *Biological Psychiatry, 46,* 650–661.

Goldstone, A. P., Unmehopa, U. A., Bloom, S. R., & Swaab, D. F. (2002). Hypothalamic NPY and agouti-related protein are increased in human illness but not in Prader-Willis syndrome and other obese subjects. *Journal of Clincial Endocrinological Metabolism, 87,* 927–937.

Gongwer, M. A., Murphy, J. M., McBride, W. J., Lumeng, L., & Li, T. K. (1989). Regional brain contents of serotonin, dopamine and their metabolites in the selectively bred high and low alcohol drinking line of rats. *Alcohol, 6,* 317–320.

Goode, E. (2003, May 6). Experts see mind's voices in new light. *New York Times.*

Gordon, C. M., Dougherty, D. D., Fischman, A. J., Emans, J., Grace, E., Lamm, R., et al. (2001). Neural substrates of anorexia nervosa: A behavioral challenge study with positron emission tomography. *Journal of Pediatrics, 139,* 51–57.

Gordon, W. A., & Hibbard, M. R. (2005). Cognitive rehabilitation. In: J. M. Silver, T. W. McAllister, & S. C. Yudofsky (Eds.), *Textbook of traumatic brain injury.* Washington, DC: American Psychiatric Publishing.

Gore, S. M. (1999). Fatal uncertainty: Death-rate from use of ecstacy or heroin. *Lancet, 354,* 2167.

Gotlib, I. H., & Hamilton, J. P. (2009). Neural functioning in major depressive disorder. *Frontiers in Neuroscience, 3,* 254–256.

Gottesman, I. I. (1991). *Schizophrenia genesis: The origins of madness.* New York: Freeman.

Gould, E., McEwen, B. S., Tanapat, P., Galea, L. A. M., & Fuchs, E. (1997). Neurogenesis in the dentate gyrus of the adult tree shrew is regulated by psychosocial stress and NMDA receptor activation. *Journal of Neuroscience, 17,* 2492–2498.

Granseth, B., Odermatt, B., Royle, S. J., & Lagnado, L. (2009). Comment on "The dynamic control of kiss-and-run and vesicular reuse probed with single nanoparticles." *Science, 325,* 1499.

Grant, M. M., & Weiss, J. M. (2001). Effects of chronic antidepressant drug administration and electroconvulsive shock on locus coeruleus electrophysiological activity. *Biological Psychiatry, 49,* 117–129.

Greely, H., Sahakian, B., Harris, J., Kessler, R. C., Gazzaniga, M., Campbell, P., et al. (2008). Towards responsible use of cognitive-enhancing drugs by the healthy. *Nature, 456,* 702–705.

Green, E. J., Greenough, W. T., & Schlumpf, B. E. (1983). Effects of complex or isolated environments on cortical dendrites of middle-aged rats. *Brain Research, 264,* 233–240.

Green, M. F. (1993). Cognitive remediation in schizophrenia: Is it time yet? *American Journal of Psychiatry, 150,* 178–187.

Green, M. F. (2001). *Schizophrenia revealed: From neurons to social interactions.* New York: Norton.

Green, M. F., Satz, P., Ganzell, S., & Vaclav, J. F. (1992). Wisconsin Card Sorting Test performance in schizophrenia: Remediation of a stubborn deficit. *American Journal of Psychiatry, 149,* 62–67.

Greene, A. E., Todorova, M. T., & Seyfried, T. N. (2003). Perspectives on the metabolic management of epilepsy through dietary reduction of glucose and elevation of ketone bodies. *Journal of Neurochemistry, 86,* 529–537.

Greenough, W. T., Cohen, N. J., & Juraska, J. M. (1999). New neurons in old brains: Learning to survive? *Nature Neuroscience, 2,* 203–205.

Greenough, W. T., Larson, J. R., & Withers, G. S. (1985). Effects of unilateral and bilateral training in a reaching task on dendritic branching of neurons in the rat motor-sensory forelimb cortex. *Behavioral and Neural Biology, 44,* 301–314.

Greeson, J. M., Sanford, B., & Monti, D. A. (2001). St. John's wort (*Hypericum perforatum*): A review of the current pharmacological, toxicological, and clinical literature. *Psychopharmacology, 153,* 402–414.

Grinspoon, S., Gulick, T., Askari, H., Landt, M., Lee, K., Anderson, E., et al. (1996). Serum leptin levels in women with anorexia nervosa. *Journal of Clinical Endocrinological Metabolism, 81,* 3861–3864.

Gross, C. (2000). Neurogenesis in the adult brain: Death of a dogma. *Nature Reviews Neuroscience, 1,* 67–73.

Gross, C. G. (2009). *A hole in the head: More tales in the history of neuroscience.* Cambridge, MA: MIT Press.

Guidi, L., Tricerri, A. Vangeli, M., Frasca, D., Errani, A. R., DiGiovanni, A., et al. (1999). Neuropeptide Y plasma levels and immunological changes during academic stress. *Neuropsychobiology, 40,* 188–195.

Gulledge, C. C., Mann, P. E., Bridges, R. S., Bialos, M., & Hammer, R. P., Jr. (2000). Expression of mu-opioid receptor mRNA in the medial preopdtic area of juvenile rats. *Developmental Brain Research, 119,* 269–276.

Gunnar, M. R. (1998). Quality of early care and buffering of neuroendocrine stress reactions: Potential effects on the developing human brain. *Preventive Medicine, 27*(2), 208–211.

Gur, E., Lerer, B., Dremencov, E., & Newman, M. E. (2000). Chronic repetitive transcranial magnetic stimulation induces subsensitivity of presynaptic serotonergic autoreceptor activity in rat brain. *NeuroReport, 11,* 2925–2929.

Gureje, O., Vazquez-Barquero, J. L., & Janca, A. (1996). Comparisons of alcohol and other drugs: Experience for the WHO collaborative cross-cultural applicability research (CAR) study. *Addiction, 91,* 1529–1538.

Haber, S. N., Kowall, N. W., Vonsattel, J. P., Bird, E. D., & Richardson, E. P., Jr. (1986). A postmortem neuropathological immunohistochemical study. *Journal of Neurological Sciences, 75,* 225–241.

Habib, K. E., Gold, P. W., & Chrousos, G. P. (2001). Neuroendocrinology of stress. *Neuroendocrinology, 30,* 695–728.

Habib, K. E., Weld, K. P., Rice, K. C., Pushkas, J., Champoux, M., Listwak, S., et al. (2000). Oral administration of a corticotropin-releasing hormone receptor antagonist significantly attenuates behavioral, neuroendocrine, and autonomic responses to stress in primates. *Proceedings of the National Academy of Sciences, USA, 97,* 6079–6084.

Hackney, M. E., & Earhart, G. (2009). Effects of dance on movement control in Parkinson's disease: A comparison of Argentine tango and American ballroom. *Journal of Rehabilitative Medicine, 41,* 475–481.

Hackney, M. E., Kantorovich, S., Levin, R., & Earhart, G. (2007). Effects of tango on functional mobility in Parkinson's disease: A preliminary study. *Journal of Neurologic Physical Therapy, 31,* 173–179.

Hall, B. K. (2009). *The neural crest and neural crest cells in vertebrate development and evolution* (2nd ed.). New York: Springer.

Hamaleers, P. A., Van Boxtel, M. P., Hogervorst, E., Riedel, W. J., Houx, P. J., Buntinx, F., et al. (2000). Habitual caffeine consumption and its relation to memory, attention, planning capacity and psychomotor performance across multiple age groups. *Human Psychopharmacology, 15,* 573–581.

Hamilton, J. P., & Gotlib, I. H. (2008). Neural substrates of increased memory sensitivity for negative stimuli in major depression. *Biological Psychiatry, 63,* 1155–1162.

Handler, E. (1997). *Time on fire: My comedy of terrors.* New York: Holt.

Hardman, J. G., Limbird, L. E., & Gilman, A. G. (2001). *Goodman and Gilman's The pharmacological basis of therapeutics* (10th ed.). New York: McGraw-Hill.

Harlow, H., & Harlow, M. K. (1962). Social deprivation in monkeys. *Scientific American, 207,* 136–146.

Harris, W. (2002). *Restraining rage: The ideology of anger control in classical antiquity.* Boston: Harvard University Press.

Harrison, P. J., & Weinberger, D. R. (2005). Schizophrenia genes, gene expression, and neuropathology: On the matter of their convergence. *Molecular Psychiatry, 10,* 40–68.

Hart, B. (1988). Biological basis of the behavior of sick animals. *Neuroscience and Biobehavioral Reviews, 12,* 123.

Hartl, R., & Ghajar, J. (2005). Neurosurgical interventions. In: J. M. Silver, T. W. McAllister, & S. C. Yudofsky (Eds.), *Textbook of traumatic brain injury.* Washington, DC: American Psychiatric Publishing.

Hatzidimitrious, G., McCann, U. D., & Ricaurte, G. A. (1999). Altered serotonin innervation patterns in the forebrain of monkeys treated with (±)3,4-methylene-dioxymethamphetamine seven years previously: Factors influencing abnormal recovery. *Journal of Neuroscience, 19,* 5096–5107.

Hawley, D. F., Bardi, M., McEwen, A. M., Higgins, T. J., Tu, K. M., Kinsley, C. H., et al. (2010). Neurobiological constituents of active, passive, and variable coping strategies in rats: Integration of regional brain neuropeptide Y levels and cardiovascular responses. *Stress, 13,* 172–183.

Headless chicken. (1945, October 22). *Life,* 53–54.

Headless rooster: Beheaded chicken lives normally after freak decapitation by ax. (August, 1999). *Science,* 29.

Healy, D. (1997). *The antidepressant era.* Cambridge, MA: Harvard University Press.

Healy, D. (2002). *The creation of psychopharmacology.* Cambridge, MA: Harvard University Press.

Healy, D., & Leonard, B. E. (1987). Monoamine transport in depressive: Kinetics and dynamics. *Journal of Affective Disorders, 12,* 91–103.

Hebb, D. O. (1949). *The organization of behavior.* New York: Wiley.

Hecker, M. H. (1988). *Comparative evaluation of Sinemet CR and standard Sinemet based on speech analysis. Report on a pilot study: Identifications of speech changes related to Parkinson's disease.* Menlo Park, CA: SRU International.

Hedden, T., Ketay, S., Aron, A., Markus, H. R., & Gabrieli, J. D. (2008). Cultural influences on neural substrates of attentional control. *Psychological Science, 19,* 12–17.

Heim, C., & Nemeroff, C. B. (2001). The role of childhood trauma in the neurobiology of mood and anxiety disorders. Preclinical and clinical studies. *Biological Psychiatry, 49,* 1023–1039.

Heim, C., & Nemeroff, C. B. (2002). Neurobiology of early life stress: Clinical studies. *Seminars in Clinical Neuropsychiatry, 7*(2), 147–159.

Heim, C., Newport, D. J., Bonsall, R., Miller, A. H., & Nemeroff, C. B. (2001). Altered pituitary–adrenal axis responses to provocative challenge tests in adult survivors of childhood abuse. *American Journal of Psychiatry, 158,* 575–581.

Heinrichs, R. W. (2001). *In search of madness: Schizophrenia and neuroscience.* New York: Oxford University Press.

Heinrichs, R. W., & Zakzanis, K. K. (1998). Neurocognitive deficit in schizophrenia: A quantitative review of the evidence. *Neuropsychology, 12,* 426–445.

Heinsbroek, R. P., van Haaren, F., & van de Poll, N. E. (1988). Sex differences in passive avoidance behavior of rats: Sex-dependent susceptibility to shock-induced behavioral depression. *Physiology and Behavior, 43*(2), 201–206.

Henry, S. C., Guegant, G., Cador, M., Arnauld, E., Arsaut, J., Le Moal, M., et al. (1995). Prenatal stress in rats facilitates amphetamine-induced sensitization and induces long-lasting changes in dopamine receptors in the nucleus accumbens. *Brain Research, 685,* 179–186.

Herbert, J. D., Lilienfeld, S. O., Lohr, J. M., Montgomery, R. W., O'Donohue, W. T., Rosen, G. M., et al. (2000). Science and pseudoscience in the development of eye movement desensitization and reprocessing: Implications for clinical psychology. *Clinical Psychology Review, 20,* 945–971.

Herculano-Houzel, S. (2009). The human brain in numbers: A linearly scaled-up primate brain. *Frontiers in Human Neuroscience, 3,* 31, doi: 10.3389/neuro.09.031.2009.

Herner, T. (1961). Treatment of mental disorders with frontal stereotaxic thermo-lesions: A follow-up study of 116 cases. *Acta Psychiatrica Scandinavica, 36*(Suppl. 158), 1–140.

Hetherington, A. W., & Ranson, S. W. (1940). Hypothalamic lesions and adiposity in the rat. *Anatomical Record, 78,* 149–172.

Hibbeln, J. R., Dais, J. M., Steer, C., Emmett, P., Rovers, I., Williams, C., et al. (2007). Maternal seafood consumption in pregnancy and neurodevelopment outcomes in childhood (ALSPAC study): An observational cohort study. *The Lancet, 369,* 578–585.

Hibbeln, J. R., & Salem, N. (1995). Dietary polyunsaturated fatty acids and depression: When cholesterol does not satisfy. *American Journal of Clinical Nutrition, 62,* 1–9.

Hibbeln, J. R., Umhau, J. C., George, D. T., & Salem, N. (1997). Do plasma polyunsaturates predict hostility and depression? *World Review of Nutrition and Dietetics, 82,* 175–186.

Hill, R. D., Storandt, M., & Malley, M. (1993). The impact of long-term exercise on training on psychological function in older adults. *Journal of Gerontology, 48,* 12–17.

Hobson, J. A. (1999). *Consciousness.* New York: Scientific American Library.

Hobson, J. A. (2003). *Dreaming: An introduction to the science of sleep.* New York: Oxford University Press.

Hobson, J. A., & Leonard, J. A. (2001). *Out of its mind: Psychiatry in crisis.* Cambridge, MA: Perseus.

Hoebel, B. G., Rada, P. V., Mark, G. P., & Pothos, E. N. (1999). Neural systems for reinforcement and inhibition of behavior: Relevance to eating, addiction, and depression. In D. Kahneman, E. Diener, & N. Schwarz (Eds.), *Well-being: The foundations of hedonic psychology.* New York: Russell Sage Foundation.

Hoffman, A. N., Malena, R. R., Westergom, B. P., Luthra, P., Cheng, J. P., Aslam, H. A., et al. (2008). Environmental enrichment-mediated functional improvement after experimental traumatic brain injury is contingent on task-specific neurobehavioral experience. *Neuroscience Letters, 431,* 226–230.

Hoffman, R. E., Hawkins, K. A., Gueorguieva, R., Boutros, N. N., Rachid, F., Carroll, K., et al. (2003). Transcranial magnetic stimulation of left temporoparietal cortex and medication-resistant auditory hallucinations. *Archives of General Psychiatry, 60*(1), 49–56.

Holland, A. J., Hall, A., Murray, R., Russell, G. F., & Crisp, H. H. (1984). Anorexia nervosa: A study of 34 twin pairs and one set of triplets. *British Journal of Psychiatry, 145,* 414–419.

Hollon, S. D., De Rubeis, R. J., Evans, M. D., Wiemer, M. J., Garvey, M. J., Grove, W. M., et al. (1992). Cognitive therapy and pharmacotherapy for depression: Singly and in combination. *Archives of General Psychiatry, 49,* 774–781.

Hollon, S. D., Thase, M. E., & Markowitz, J. C. (2002). Treatment and prevention of depression. *Psychological Science in the Public Interest, 3,* 39–77.

Holloway, M. (2003). The mutable brain. *Scientific American, 289,* 78–85.

Holsboer, F. (1999). Animal models of mood disorders. In D. S. Charney, E. J. Nestler, & B. S. Bunney (Eds.), *Neurobiology of mental illness* (pp. 317–322). New York: Oxford University Press.

Holsboer, F. (2000). The corticosteroid receptor hypothesis of depression. *Neuropsychopharmacology, 23,* 477–501.

Holtz, R. L. (1997). Brain's "God module" may affect religious intensity. *Los Angeles Times.*

Holzinger, A., Kilian, R., Lindenbach, I., Petscheleit, A., & Angermeyer, M. C. (2003). Patients' and their relatives' causal explanations of schizophrenia. *Society for Psychiatry and Psychiatric Epidemiolology, 38*, 155–162.

Holzwarth, R., Huber, D., Majkrzak, A., & Tareen, B. (2002). Outcome of gastric bypass patients. *Obesity Surgery, 12*, 261–264.

Hommer, D. W. (1999). Functional imaging of craving. *Alcohol Research and Health, 23*, 187–196.

Horm, J., & Anderson, K. (1993). Who in America is trying to lose weight? *Annals of Internal Medicine, 119*, 672–676.

Horsfield, S. A., Rosse, R. B., Tomasino, V., Schwartz, B. L., Mastropaola, J., & Deutsch, S. I. (2002). Fluoxetine's effects on cognitive performance in patients with traumatic injury. *International Journal of Psychiatry in Medicine, 32*, 337–344.

Hosoda, T., Nakajima, H., & Honjo, H. (2001). Estrogen protects neuronal cells from amyloid beta-induced apoptotic cell death. *NeuroReport, 12*, 1965–1970.

Hovda, D. A., Prins, M., Gecker, D., Lee, S., Bergsneider, M., & Martin, N. (1999). Neurobiology of concussion. In J. E. Bailes, M. R. Lovell, & J. C. Maroon (Eds.), *Sports related concussion*. St. Louis, MO: Quality Medical Publishing.

Hristova, A. H., & Koller, W. C. (2000). Early Parkinson's disease: What is the best approach to treatment. *Drugs and Aging, 17*, 165–181.

Huang, H. S., Matevossian, A., Whittle, C., Kim, S. Y., Schumacher, A., Baker, S. P., et al. (2007). Prefrontal dysfunction in schizophrenia involves missed-lineage leukemia 1-regulated histone methylation at GABAergic gene promoters. *Journal of Neuroscience, 27*, 11254–11262.

Hubel, D. H., & Wiesel, T. N. (1965). Binocular interaction in the striate cortex of kittens reared with artifical squint. *Journal of Neurophysiology, 28*, 1041–1059.

Hubel, D. H., & Wiesel, T. N. (1970). The period of susceptibility to the physiological effects of unilateral eye closure in kittens. *Journal of Physiology, 206*, 419–436.

Huff, W., Lenartz, D., Schormann, M., Lee, S., Kuhn, J., Koulousakis, A., et al. (2009). Unilateral deep brain stimulation of the nucleus accumbens in patients with treatment-resistant obsessive–compulsive disorder: Outcomes after one year. *Clinical Neurology and Neurosurgery*, doi: 10.1016/j.clineuro.2009.11.006.

Huhman, K. L., Banks, M. C., Harmon, A. C., & Jasnow, A. M. (2002). Acquisition and maintenance of conditioned defeat in male and female Syrian hamsters. Manuscript in preparation.

Huhman, K. L., Mougey, E. H., & Meyerhoff, J. L. (1992). Hormonal response to fighting in submissive hamsters: Separation of physical and psychological effects. *Physiology and Behavior, 51*, 1083–1086.

Hunt, E. J., Lester, C. E., Lester, E. A., & Tackett, R. L. (2001). Effect of St. John's wort on free radical production. *Life Sciences, 69*, 181–190.

Huxley, A. (1932). *Brave new world*. London/Garden City, NY: Chatto & Windus/Doubleday, Doran & Co.

Hyman, S. E. (1999). Substance abuse disorders. In D. S. Charney, E. J. Nestler, & B. S. Bunney (Eds.), *Neurobiology of mental illness*. New York: Oxford University Press.

Hyman, S. E., & Nestler, E. J. (1993). *The molecular foundations of psychiatry*. Washington, DC: American Psychiatric Press.

Inoue, S., Bray, G. A., & Mullen, Y. S. (1978). Transplantation of pancreatic B-cells prevents development of hypothalamic obesity in rats. *American Journal of Physiology Endocrinology and Metabolism, 235*, E266–E271.

Insel, T. R., Gingrich, B. S., & Young, L. J. (2001). Oxytocin: Who needs it? *Progress in Brain Research, 133*, 59–66.

Insel, T. R., Mueller, E. A., Alterman, I., Linnoila, M., & Murphy, D. L. (1985). Obsessive–compulsive disorder and serotonin: Is there a connection? *Biological Psychiatry, 20*, 1174–1188.

Insel, T. R., O'Brien, D. J., & Leckman, J. F. (1999). Oxytocin, vasopressin, and autism: Is there a connection? *Biological Psychiatry, 45*, 145–157.

Insel, T. R., & Shapiro, L. E. (1992). Oxytocin receptor distribution reflects social organization in monogamous and polygamous voles. *Proceedings of the National Academy of Sciences, USA, 89*, 5981–5985.

Insel, T. R., & Winslow, J. T. (1999). The neurobiology of social attachment. In D. S. Charney, E. J. Nestler, & B. S. Bunney (Eds.), *Neurobiology of mental illness*. New York: Oxford University Press.

Iwase, M., Ouchi, Y., Okada, H., Yokoyama, C., Nobezawa, S., Yoshikawa, E., et al. (2002). Neural substrates of human facial expression of pleasant emotion induced by comic films: A PET study. *NeuroImage, 17*, 758–768.

Jacob, S., McClintock, M. K., Zelano, B., & Ober, C. (2002). Paternally inherited HLA alleles are associated with women's choice of male odor. *Nature Genetics, 30*, 1 75–179.

Jacobs, B. (1994). Serotonin, motor activity and depression-related disorders. *American Scientist, 82*, 456–463.

Jacobs, B. L., van Praag, H., & Gage, F. H. (2000). Adult brain neurogenesis and psychiatry: A novel theory of depression. *Molecular Psychiatry, 5*, 262–269.

Jacobs, R., & Schmidt, R. E. (1999). Foundations in immunology. In M. Schedlowski & U. Tewes (Eds.), *Psychoneuroimmunology: An interdisciplinary introduction.* New York: Kluwer Academic/Plenum.

Jacobsen, L. K., Mencl, W. E., Pugh, K. R., Skudlarski, P., & Krystal, J. H. (2003). Preliminary evidence of hippocampal dysfunction in adolescent MDMA ("ecstasy") users: Possible relationship to neurotoxic effects. *Psychopharmacology, 173,* 383–390.

Jacobson, A. C., McKinley, P. A., Leroux, A., & Rainville, C. (2005). Argentine tango dancing as an effective means for improving cognition and complex task performance in at-risk elderly: A feasibility study. Program No. 757.7. Abstract viewer/itinerary planner. Washington, DC: Society for Neuroscience. Retrieved from http://sfn.scholarone.com/itin2005/

Jacobson, M. F., & Hurley, J. (2002). *Restaurant confidential.* New York: Workman.

Jain, K. K. (2008). Neuroprotection in traumatic brain injury. *Drug Discovery Today, 13,* 1082–1089.

James, W. (1890). *The principles of psychology.* New York: Holt.

Jamison, K. R. (1993). *Touched with fire: Manic depressive illness and the artistic temperament.* New York: Free Press.

Jamison, K. R. (1996). *An unquiet mind.* New York: Vintage Books.

Jamison, K. R. (1999). *Night falls fast: Understanding suicide.* Collingdale, PA: Diane Publishing.

Jamison, K. R. (2004). *Exuberance: The passion for life.* New York: Knopf.

Jamison, K. R. (2009). *Nothing was the same.* New York: Knopf.

Jarrett, R. B., Kraft, D., Doyle, J. L., Foster, B. M., Eaves, G. G., & Silver, P. C. (2001). Preventing recurrent depression using cognitive therapy with and without a continuation phase. *Archives of General Psychiatry, 58,* 381–388.

Jaycox, L. H., Stein, B. D., Paddock, S., Miles, J. N. V., Chandra, A., Meredith, L. S., et al. (2009). Impact of teen depression on academic, social, and physical functioning. *Pediatrics, 124,* 596–605.

Jeannotte, A. M., McCarthy, J. G., & Sidhu, A. (2009). Desipramine induced changes in the norepinephrine transporter, alpha- and gamma-synuclein in the hippocampus, amygdale and striatum. *Neuroscience Letters, 467,* 86–89.

Jenike, M. A., Baer, L., Ballantine, T., Martuza, R. L., Tynes, S., Giriunas, I., et al. (1991). Cingulotomy for refractory obsessive–compulsive disorder. *Archives of General Psychiatry, 48,* 548–555.

Jenike, M. A., Breiter, H. C., Baer, L., Kennedy, D. N., Savage, C. R., Olivares, M. J., et al. (1996). Cerebral structural abnormalities in obsessive–compulsive disorder. *Archives of General Psychiatry, 53,* 625–632.

Jenike, M. A., Rauch, S. L., Cummings, J. L., Savage, C. R., & Goodman, W. K. (1996). Recent developments in neurobiology of obsessive–compulsive disorder. *Journal of Clinical Psychiatry, 57*(10), 492–503.

Jenkins, L.W., Lyeth, B.G., Lewelt, W., Moszynski, K., DeWitt, D.S., Balster, R.L., et al. (1988). Combined pre-trauma scopolamine and phencyclidine attenuate posttraumatic increased sensitivity to delayed secondary ischemia. *Journal of Neurotrauma, 5,* 275–287.

Johannes, S., Wieringa, B. M., Nager, W., Rada, D., Muller-Vahl, K. R., Emrich, H. M., et al. (2003). Tourette syndrome and obsessive–compulsive disorder: Event-related brain potentials show similar mechanisms of frontal inhibition but dissimilar target evaluation processes. *Behavioral Neurology, 14,* 9–17.

Johnson, B. A., Roache, J. D., Javors, M. A., DiClemente, C. C., Cloninger, C. R., Prihoda, T. J., et al. (2000). Ondansetron for reduction of drinking among biologically predisposed alcoholic patients: A randomized controlled trial. *Journal of the American Medical Association, 284,* 963–971.

Jones, H. E., Johnson, R. E., Jasinski, D. R., & Milio, L. (2005). Randomized controlled study transitioning opioid-dependent pregnant women from short-acting morphine to buprenorphine or methadone. *Drug and Alcohol Dependence, 78,* 33–38.

Jones, K. L., Johnson, K. A., Dick, L. M., Felix, R. J., Kao, K. K., & Chambers, C. D. (2002). Pregnancy outcomes after first trimester exposure to phentermine/fenfluramine. *Teratology, 65,* 125–130.

Julien, R. (2004). *A primer of drug action* (10th ed.). New York: Worth.

Julien, R. M. (2007). *A primer of drug action: A concise, non-technical guide to the actions, uses, and side effects of psychoactive drugs* (11th ed.). New York: Worth.

Juster, R. P., McEwen, B. S., & Lupien, S. J. (2009). Allostatic load biomarkers of chronic stress and impact on health and cognition. *Neuroscience and Biobehavioral Reviews,* doi: 10.1016/j.neubiorev.2009.10.002.

Kadish, I., & Van Groen, T. (2002). Low levels of estrogen significantly diminish axonal sprouting after entorhinal cortex lesions in the mouse. *Journal of Neuroscience, 22,* 4095–4102.

Kaelin, D. L., Cifu, D. X., & Matthies, B. (1996). Methylphenidate effect on attention deficit in the acutely brain-injured adult. *Archives of Physical and Rehabilitative Medicine, 77,* 6–9.

Kalat, J. (2001). *Biological psychology.* New York: Wadsworth.

Kalivas, P. W., & Duffy, P. (1995). Selective activation of DA transmission in the shell of the nucleus accumbens by stress. *Brain Research, 675,* 325–328.

Kandel, E. R. (2006). *In search of memory: The emergence of a new science of mind.* New York: Norton.

Kandel, E. R., Schwartz, J. H., & Jessell, T. M. (1995). *Essentials of neural science and behavior.* Stamford, CT: Appleton & Lange.

Kandel, E. R., Schwartz, J. H., & Jessell, T. M. (2000). *Principles of neural science* (4th ed.). New York: McGraw-Hill.

Kandel, E. R., & Squire, L. R. (2000). Neuroscience: Breaking down scientific barriers to the study of brain and mind. *Science, 290,* 1113–1120.

Kant, R., Smith-Seemiller, L., & Zeiler, D. (1998). Treatment of aggression and irritability after head injury. *Brain Injury, 12,* 661–666.

Kapur, S., & Remington, G. (1996). Serotonin–dopamine interaction and its relevance to schizophrenia. *American Journal of Psychiatry, 153*(4), 466–476.

Karlsson, H., Bachmann, S., Schröder, J., McArthur, J., Torrey, E. F., & Yolken, R. H. (2001). Retroviral RNA identified in the cerebrospinal fluids and brains of individuals with schizophrenia. *Proceedings of the National Academy of Sciences, USA, 98,* 4634–4639.

Kasteleijn-Nolst Trenite, D. G., Martins da Silva, A., Ricci, S., Rubboli, G., Tassinari, C. A., Lopes, J., et al. (2002). Video games are exciting: A European study of video game–induced seizures and epilepsy. *Epileptic Disorders, 4,* 121–128.

Katayama, Y., Becker, D. P., Tamura, T., & Hovda, D. A. (1990). Massive increases in extracellular potassium and the indiscriminate release of glutamate following concussive brain injury. *Journal of Neurosurgery, 73,* 889–900.

Kato, T. (2001). The relationship between flexibility of coping to stress and depression. *Japanese Journal of Developmental Psychology, 72,* 57–63.

Katzman, D. K., Christensen, B., Young, A. R., & Zipursky, R. B. (2001). Starving the brain: Structural abnormalities and cognitive impairment in adolescents with anorexia nervosa. *Seminars in Clinical Neuropsychiatry, 6,* 146–152.

Kaufmann, J., Plotsky, P. M., Nemeroff, C. B., & Charney, D. S. (2000). Effects of early adverse experiences on brain structure and function: Clinical implications. *Biological Psychiatry, 48,* 778–790.

Kaye, W. H. (1992). Neuropeptide abnormalities. In K. A. Halmi (Ed.), *Psychobiology and treatment of anorexia and bulimia nervosa. American Psychopathological Association Series* (pp. 169–192). Washington, DC: American Psychiatric Press.

Kaye, W. H. (2001). *The neurobiology of anorexia and bulimia nervosa: Does dieting help people with eating disorders fit in their genes?* Retrieved March 19, 2001, from Ground Rounds at http://psychiatry.uchicago.edu/grounds010319

Kaye, W. H., Berrettini, W., Gwirtsman, H., & George, D. T. (1990). Altered cerebrospinal fluid neuropeptide Y and peptide YY immunoreactivity in anorexia and bulimia nervosa. *Archives of General Psychiatry, 47,* 548–556.

Kaye, W. H., Frank, G. K., Meltzer, C. C., Price, J. C., McConaha, C. W., Crossan, P. J., et al. (2001). Altered serotonin 2A receptor activity in women who have recovered from bulimia nervosa. *American Journal of Psychiatry, 158,* 1152–1155.

Kaye, W. H., & Strober, M. (2001). The neurobiology of eating disorders. In D. S. Charney, E. J. Nestler, & B. S. Bunney (Eds.), *Neurobiology of mental illness.* New York: Oxford University Press.

Kaye, W. H., Weltzin, T. E., Hsu, L. K., & Bulik, C. M. (1991). An open trial of fluoxetine in patients with anorexia nervosa. *Journal of Clinical Psychiatry, 52,* 464–471.

Kaye, W. H., Weltzin, T. E., Hsu, K. K. G., Sokol, M. S., McConaha, C. W., & Plotnicov, K. H. (1997). Relapse prevention with fluoxetine in anorexia nervosa: A double-blind placebo-controlled study, in 1997. In *Annual Meeting New Research Program and Abstracts.* Washington, DC: American Psychiatric Association.

Keck, M. E., Welt, T., Post, A., Muller, M. B., Toschi, N., Wigger, A., et al. (2001). Neuroendocrine and behavioral effects of repetitive transcranial magnetic stimulation in a psychopathological animal model are suggestive of antidepressant-like effects. *Neuropsychopharmacology, 24,* 337–349.

Kelley, W. M., Moran, J. M., Wig, G. S., Adams, R. B., Duval, M. G., & Magge, R. S. (2002). The neural funny bone: Dissociating cognitive and affective components of humor [Abstract]. *Society for Neuroscience Abstracts,* Program No. 517.6.

Kelly, D., Richardson, A., & Mitchell-Heggs, N. (1973). Stereotactic limbic leucotomy: Neurophysiological aspects and operative technique. *British Journal of Psychiatry, 123,* 133–140.

Kemeny, M. E. (2009). Psychobiological responses to social threat: Evolution of a psychological model in psychoneuroimmunology. *Brain, Behavior, and Immunity, 23,* 1–9.

Kemeny, M. E., & Laudenslager, M. L. (1999). Beyond stress: The role of individual difference factors in psychoneuroimmunology. *Brain, Behavior, and Immunity, 13,* 73–75.

Kemether, E. M., Buchsbaum, M. S., Byne, W., Hazlett, E. A., Hazndear, M., Brickman, A. M., et al. (2003). Magnetic resonance imaging of mediodorsal, pulvinar, and centromedian nuclei of the thalamus in patients with schizophrenia. *Archives of General Psychiatry, 60,* 983–991.

Kempermann, G. (2005). *Adult neurogenesis: Stem cells and neuronal development in the adult brain.* New York: Oxford University Press.

Kempermann, G., Kuhn, H. G., & Gage, F. H. (1997). More hippocampal neurons in adult mice living in an enriched environment. *Nature, 386,* 493–495.

Kendrick, K. M., Keverne, E. B., Hinton, M. R., & Goode, J. A. (1992). Oxytocin, amino acid and monoamine release in the region of the medial preoptic area and the bed nucleus of the stria terminalis of the sheep during parturition and suckling. *Brain Research, 569,* 199–209.

Kennedy, G. C. (1953). The role of depot fat in the hypothalamic control of food intake in the rat. *Proceedings of the Royal Society of London: Biological Sciences, 140,* 578–592.

Kennedy, S. H., Evans, K. R., Kruger, S., Mayberg, H. S., Meyer, J. H., McCann, S., et al. (2001). Changes in regional brain glucose metabolism measured with positron emission tomography after paroxetine treatment of major depression. *American Journal of Psychiatry, 158,* 899–905.

Kerr, D. A., Llado, J., Shamblott, M. J., Maragakis, N. J., Irani, D. N., Crawford, T. O., et al. (2003). Human embryonic germ cell derivatives facilitate motor recovery of rats with diffuse motor neuron injury. *Journal of Neuroscience, 23*(12), 5131–5140.

Kettlewell, C. (2000). *Skin game: A cutter's memoir.* New York: St. Martin's Griffin.

Keuker, J. I., de Biurrun, G., Luiten, P. G., & Fuchs, E. (2004). Preservation of hippocampal neuron numbers and hippocampal subfield volumes in behaviorally characterized aged tree shrews. *Journal of Comparative Neurology, 468*(4), 509–517.

Kiecolt-Glaser, J. K., & Glaser, R. (1991). Stress and immune function in humans. In R. Ader, D. L. Felten, & N. Cohen (Eds.), *Psychoneuroimmunology* (2nd ed.). New York: Academic Press.

Kiecolt-Glaser, J. K., & Glaser, R. (1999). Psychoneuroimmunology and cancer: Fact or fiction? *European Journal of Cancer, 35,* 1603–1607.

Kiecolt-Glaser, J. K., Glaser, R., Cacioppo, J. J., & Malarkey, W. B. (1998). Marital stress: Immunological, neuroendocrine and autonomic correlates. In S. M. McCann, E. M. Sternberg, J. M. Lipton, G. P. Chrousos, & C. C. Smith (Eds.), *Neuroimmunomodulation: Molecular aspects, integrative systems and clinical advances.* New York: New York Academy of Sciences.

Kiecolt-Glaser, J. K., Marucha, P. T., Malarkey, W. B., Mercado, A. M., & Glaser, R. (1995). Slowing of wound healing by psychological stress. *Lancet, 346,* 1194–1196.

Kim, J. H., Auerbach, J. M., Rodriguez-Gomez, J. A., Velasco, I., Gavin, D., Lumelsky, N., et al. (2002). Dopamine neurons derived from embryonic stem cells function in an animal model of Parkinson's disease. *Nature, 418,* 50–56.

Kinsley, C. H., & Lambert, K. G. (2006). The maternal brain. *Scientific American, 294,* 72–79.

Kinsley, C. H., & Lambert, K. G. (2008). Reproduction-induced neuroplasticity: Natural behavioral and neuronal alterations associated with the production and care of offspring. *Journal of Neuroendocrinology, 20,* 515–525.

Kinsley, C. H., Madonia, L., Gifford, G. W., Tureski, K., Griffin, G. R., Lowry, C., et al. (1999). Motherhood improves learning and memory: Neural activity in rats is enhanced by pregnancy and the demands of rearing offspring. *Nature, 402,* 137–138.

Kinsley, C. H., Trainer, R., Stafisso-Sandoz, G., Quadros, P., Marcus, L. K., Hearon, C., et al. (2006). Motherhood and the hormones of pregnancy modify concentrations of hippocampal neuronal dendritic spines. *Hormones and Behavior, 49,* 131–142.

Kirsch, I. (2010). *The emperor's new drugs: Exploding the antidepressant myth.* New York: Basic Books.

Kirsch, I., & Antonuccio, D. (2002) Antidepressants versus placebos: Meaningful advantages are lacking. *Psychiatric Times, 19.* Retrieved online January 4, 2010: http://www.psychiatrictimes.com/display/article/10168/47701?verify=0

Kirsch, I., & Sapirstein, G. (1998). Listening to Prozac but hearing placebo: A meta-analysis of antidepressant medication. *Prevention & Treatment, 1,* article 0002a. Retrieved August 2, 2002, from journals.apa.org/prevention/volume-1/toc-jun26-98.html

Kissebah, A. H., & Krakower, G. (1994). Regional adiposity and morbidity. *Physiological Review, 74,* 761–811.

Kleim, J. A., Swain, R. A., Armstrong, K. A., Napper, R. M., Jones, T. A., & Greenough, W. T. (1998). Selective synaptic plasticity within the cerebellar cortex following complex motor skill learning. *Neurobiology of Learning and Memory, 69,* 274–289.

Klein, S. L., Gamble, H. R., & Nelson, R. J. (1999). *Trichinella spiralis* infection in voles alters female odor preference but not partner preference. *Behavioral Ecology and Sociobiology, 45*, 323–329.

Klerman, G., Lavori, P., Rice, J., Reich, T., Endicott, N., Andreasen, N., et al. (1985). Birth cohort trends in rates of major depressive disorder among relatives of patients with affective disorder. *Archives of General Psychiatry, 42*, 689–693.

Klingberg, T. (2009). *The overflowing brain: information overload and the limits of working memory*. New York: Oxford University Press.

Kluger, J. (2001, April 2). Fighting phobias. *Time*, 52–62.

Knight, G. C. (1969). Stereotactic surgery for the relief of suicidal and severe depression and intractable psychoneurosis. *Postgraduate Medical Journal, 45*, 1–13.

Knivsberg, A. M., Reichelt, K. L., Hoien, T., & Nodland, M. (2002). A randomized, controlled study of dietary intervention in autistic syndromes. *Nutritional Neuroscience, 5*, 251–261.

Knivsberg, A. M., Reichelt, K. L., & Nodland, M. (2001). Reports on dietary intervention in autistic disorders. *Nutritional Neuroscience, 4*, 25–37.

Knott, A. B., Perkins, G., Schwarzenbacher, R. & Bossy-Wetzel, E. (2008). Mitochondrial fragmentation in neurodegeneration. *Nature Reviews Neuroscience, 9*, 505–515.

Kobak, K. A., Greist, J. H., Jefferson, J. W., Katzelnick, D. J., & Henk, H. J. (1998). Behavioral versus pharmacological treatments of obsessive disorder: A meta-analysis. *Psychopharmacology, 136*, 205–216.

Koenig, A. M., & Thase, M. E. (2009). First-line pharmacotherapies for depression—what is the best choice? *Polskie Archiwum Medycyny Wewnetrznej, 119*, 478–485.

Koenig, H. G., Cohen, H. J., George, L. K., Hays, J. C., Larson, D. B., & Blazer, D. G. (1997). Attendance at religious services, interleukin-6, and other biological parameters of immune function in older adults. *International Journal of Psychiatry in Medicine, 27*, 233–250.

Koenig, J. I., Kirkpatrick, B., & Lee, P. (2002). Glucocorticoid hormones and early brain development in schizophrenia. *Neuropsychopharmacology, 27*, 309–318.

Kolata, G. (1986). New drug counters alcohol intoxication. *Science, 234*, 1198–1199.

Kolb, B., & Whishaw, I. Q. (1996). *Fundamentals of human neuropsychology* (4th ed.). New York: Freeman.

Kolb, B., & Whishaw, I. Q. (2004). *Fundamentals of human neuropsychology* (5th ed.). New York: Worth.

Konopka, G., Bomar, J. M., Winden, K., Coppola, G., Jonsson, Z. O., Gao, F., et al. (2009). Human-specific transcriptional regulation of CNS development genes by FOXP2. *Nature, 462*, 213–218.

Koob, G. F., & Le Moal, M. (2008). Neurobiological mechanisms for opponent motivational processes in addiction. *Philosophical Transactions of the Royal Society, 363*, 3113–3123.

Koob, G. F., & Nestler, E. J. (1997a). The neurobiology of addiction. *Journal of Neuropsychiatry, 9*(3), 482–497.

Koob, G. F., & Nestler, E. (1997b). The neurobiology of drug addiction. In S. Salloway, P. Malloy, & J. L. Cummings (Eds.), *The neuropsychiatry of limbic and subcortical disorders*. Washington, DC: American Psychiatric Press.

Koob, G. F., & Volkow, N. D. (2010). Neurocircuitry of addiction. *Neuropsychopharmacology Reviews, 35*, 217–238.

Koolhaas, J. M. (2008). Coping style and immunity in animals: Making sense of individual variation. *Brain, Behavior, and Immunity, 22*, 662–667.

Koolhaas, J. M., de Boer, S. F., Buwalda, B., & van Reenen, K. (2007). Individual variation in coping with stress: A multidimensional approach of ultimate and proximate mechanisms. *Brain, Behavior, and Evolution, 70*, 218–226.

Koolhaas, J. M., Korte, S. M., De Boer, S. F., Van Der Vegt, B. J., Van Reenen, V., Hopster, H., et al. (1999). Coping styles in animals: Current status in behavior and stress-physiology. *Neuroscience and Behavioral Reviews, 23*, 925–935.

Korkotian, E., & Segal, M. (1999). Release of calcium from stores alters the morphology of dendritic spines in cultures hippocampal neurons. *Proceedings of the National Academy of Sciences, USA, 96*, 12068–12072.

Korte, S. M., Beuving, G., Ruesink, W., & Blokhuis, H. J. (1997). Plasma catecholamine and corticosterone levels during manual restraint in chicks from a high and low feather pecking line of laying hens. *Physiology and Behavior, 62*, 437–441.

Korte, S. M., Koolhaas, J. M., Wingfield, J. C., & McEwen, B. S. (2005). The Darwinian concept of stress: Benefits of allostasis and costs of allostatic load and the trade-offs in health and disease. *Neuroscience and Biobehavioral Reviews, 29*, 3–38.

Kovacs, G. L. (1987). The behavioral physiology of vasopressin and oxytocin. *Advances in Biochemical Psychopharmacology, 43*, 115–128.

Kovalev, V. A., Kruggel, F., & von Cramon, D. Y. (2003). Gender and age effects in structural brain asymmetry as revealed by MRI texture analysis. *NeuroImage, 19*(3), 895–905.

Kovelman, J. A., & Scheibel, A. B. (1984). A neurohistological correlate of schizophrenia. *Biological Psychiatry, 19*, 1601–1621.

Kramer, P. D. (1993). *Listening to Prozac.* New York: Viking Press.

Kraus, J. F., & Chu, L. D. (2005). Epidemiology. In J. M. Silver, T. W. McAllister, & S. C. Yudofsky (Eds.), *Textbook of traumatic brain injury.* Washington, DC: American Psychiatric Publishing.

Kraus, J. F., Morgenstern, H., Fife, D., Conroy, C., & Hourjah, P. (1989). Blood alcohol tests, prevalence of involvement, and outcomes following brain injury. *American Journal of Public Health, 79,* 294–299.

Krause, D., Matz, J., Weidinger, E., Wagner, J., Wildenauer, A., Obermeier, M., et al. (2010). Association between intracellular infectious agents and Tourette's syndrome. *European Archives of Psychiatry and Clinical Neuroscience, 260,* 359–363.

Krause, K. H., Dresel, S. H., Krause, J., la Fougere, C., & Ackenheil, M. (2003). The dopamine transporter and neuroimaging in attention deficit hyperactivity disorder. *Neuroscience and Biobehavioral Reviews, 27*(7), 605–613.

Kriegstein, A., & Alvarez-Buylla, A. (2009). The glial nature of embryonic and adult neural stem cells. *Annual Review of Neuroscience, 32,* 149–184.

Krishnan, K. R. R., McDonald, W. M., Escalona, P. R., Doraiswamy, P. M., Na, C., Husain, M. M., et al. (1992). Magnetic resonance imaging of the caudate nuclei in depression: Preliminary observations. *Archives of General Psychiatry, 49,* 553–557.

Krystal, A. D., West, M., Prado, R., Greenside, H., Zoldi, S., & Weiner, R. D. (2000). EEG effects of ECT: Implications for rTMS. *Depression and Anxiety, 12,* 157–165.

Krystal, J. H., Karper, L. P., Seibyl, J. P., Freeman, G. K., Delaney, R., Bremner, J. D., et al. (1994). Subanesthetic effects of the noncompetitive NMDA antagonist, ketamine, in humans: Psychotomimetic, perceptual, cognitive, and neuroendocrine responses. *Archives of General Psychiatry, 51*(3), 199–214.

Kuba, R., Brazdil, M., Novak, Z., Chrastina, J., & Rektor, I. (2003). Effect of vagal nerve stimulation on patients with bitemporal epilepsy. *European Journal of Neurology, 10,* 91–94.

Kulka, R. A., Schlenger, W. E., Fairbank, W. E., Hough, R. L., Jordan, B. K., Marmar, C. R., et al. (1990). *Trauma and the Vietnam War generation: Report of findings from the National Vietnam Veterans Readjustment Study.* New York: Brunner/Mazel.

Kupfer, D. J., & Frank, E. (2002). Effect of *Hypericum perforatum* (St. John's wort) in major depressive disorder: A randomized controlled trial. *Journal of the American Medical Association, 287,* 1853–1854.

Kurian, B. T., Ray, W. A., Arbogast, P. G., Fuchs, D. C., Dudley, J. A., & Cooper, W. O. (2007). Effect of regulatory warnings on antidepressant prescribing for children and adolescents. *Archives of Pediatrics & Adolescent Medicine, 161,* 690–696.

Kurlan, R. (1998). Tourette's syndrome and "PANDAS": Will the relation bear out? *Neurology, 50,* 1530–1534.

LaBar, K. S., & LeDoux, J. E. (2001). Coping with danger: The neural basis of defensive behaviors and fearful feelings. In B. S. McEwen (Ed.), *Handbook of physiology: Section 7. The endocrine system: Vol. IV. Coping with the environment: Neural and endocrine mechanisms* (pp. 139–154). New York: Oxford University Press.

Lacasse, J. R., & Leo, J. (2005). Serotonin and depression: A disconnect between the advertisements and the scientific literature. *PLoS Medicine, 2,* 1211–1216.

Ladd, C. O., Owens, M. J., & Nemeroff, C. B. (1996). Persistent changes in corticotropin-releasing factor neuronal systems induced by maternal deprivation. *Endocrinology, 137,* 1212–1218.

Lamarine, R. J. (1988). Alcohol abuse among Native Americans. *Journal of Community Health, 13,* 143–155.

Lambert, G., Hohansson, M., Agren, H., & Friberg, P. (2000). Reduced brain norepinephrine and dopamine release in treatment-refractory depressive illness. *Archives of General Psychiatry, 57,* 787–793.

Lambert, K. G. (1993). The activity-stress paradigm: Possible mechanisms and applications. *Journal of General Psychology, 120,* 21–32.

Lambert, K. G. (2006). Rising rates of depression in today's society: Consideration of the roles of effort-based rewards and enhanced resilience in day-to-day functioning. *Neuroscience and Biobehavioral Reviews, 30,* 497–510.

Lambert, K. G. (2008a). *Lifting Depression.* New York: Basic Books.

Lambert, K. G., (2008b, August/September). Depressingly easy. *Scientific American Mind,* 21–32.

Lambert, K. G., Buckelew, S. K., Staffiso-Sandoz, G., Gaffga, S., Carpenter, W., Fisher, J., et al. (1998). Activity-stress induces atrophy of apical dendrites of hippocampal pyramidal neurons in male rats. *Physiology and Behavior, 65*(1), 43–39.

Lambert, K. G., Meyer, M., Fischer-Stenger, K., Zanetti, D. J. C., DeVries, A. C., Glasper, E., et al. (2001). *Social contact during chronic unpredictable stress modulates stress responsivity and immunological functioning in* Peromyscus californicus. Poster presented at the annual meeting of the Society for Neuroscience, San Diego, CA.

Lambert, K. G., & Porter, J. H. (1992). Pimozide mitigates excessive running in activity-stress paradigm. *Physiology and Behavior, 52*, 299–304.

Landfield, P. W. (1987). Modulation of brain aging correlates by long-term alterations of adrenal steroids and neurally-active peptides. *Progress in Brain Research, 72*, 279–300.

Landfield, P. W., Baskin, R. K., & Pitler, T. A. (1981). Brain aging correlates: Retardation by hormonal–pharmacological treatments. *Science, 214*, 581–584.

Landgraf, R., Malkinson, T. J., Veale, W. L., Lederis, K., & Pittman, Q. J. (2003). Vasopressin and oxytocin in rat brain in response to prostaglandin fever. *American Journal of Physiology Regulatory, Integrative and Comparative Physiology, 259*, 1056–1062.

Langston, J. W., Ballard, P., Tetrud, J., & Irwin, I. (1983). Chronic parkinsonism in humans due to a product of meperidine-analog synthesis. *Science, 219*, 979–980.

Lanius, R. A., Williamson, P. C., Densmore, M., Boksman, K., Madhulika, A. G., Neufeld, R. W., et al. (2001). Neural correlates of traumatic memories in post-traumatic stress disorder: A functional MRI investigation. *American Journal of Psychiatry, 158*, 1920–1922.

Larsen, D. D., & Krubitzer, L. (2008). Genetic and epigenetic contributions to the cortical phenotype in mammals. *Brain Research Bulletin, 75*, 391–397.

Laugero, K. D. (2001). A new perspective on glucocorticoid feedback: Relation to stress, carbohydrate feeding and feeling better. *Journal of Neuroendocrinology, 13*, 827–835.

Le Bihan, D., Mangin, J. F., Poupon, C., Clark, C. A., Pappata, S., Molko, N., et al. (2001). Diffusion tensor imaging: Concepts and applications. *Journal of Magnetic Resonance Imaging, 13*, 534–546.

Leckman, J. F., Goodman, W. K., North, W. C., Chappell, P. B., Price, L. H., Pauls, D. L., et al. (1994). Elevated cerebrospinal fluid levels of oxytocin in obsessive–compulsive disorder: Comparison with Tourette's syndrome and healthy controls. *Archives of General Psychiatry, 51*, 782–792.

Leckman, J. F., Pauls, D. L., Zhang, H., Rosario-Campos, M. C., Katsovich, L., Kidd, K.K., et al. (2003). Obsessive–compulsive symptom dimensions in affected siblings pairs diagnosed with Gilles de la Tourette syndrome. *American Journal of Medical Genetics, 116*, 60–68.

Leckman, J. F., Price, R. A., Walkup, J. T., Ort S., Pauls, D. L., & Cohen, D. J. (1987). Nongenetic factors in Gilles de la Tourette's syndrome [Letter to the editor]. *Archives of General Psychiatry, 44*, 100.

Leckman, J. F., Riddle, M. A., Berrettini, W. H., Anderson, G. M., Hardin, M. T., Chappell, P.B., et al. (1988). Elevated CSF dynorphin A[1–8] in Tourette's syndrome. *Life Sciences, 43*, 2015–2023.

LeDoux, J. E. (1994). Emotion, memory and the brain. *Scientific American, 270*, 50–57.

LeDoux, J. E. (2002). *The synaptic self.* New York: Viking Press.

LeDoux, J. E., Cicchetti, P., Xagoraris, A., & Romanski, I. M. (1990). The lateral amygdaloid nucleus: Sensory interface of the amygdale in fear conditioning. *Journal of Neuroscience, 10*, 1062–1069.

LeGrange, D. (1999). Family therapy for adolescent anorexia nervosa. *Journal of Clinical Psychology, 55*, 727–739.

Leibowitz, S. F. (1992). Neurochemical neuroendocrine systems in the brain controlling macronutrient intake and metabolism. *Trends in Neuroscience, 15*, 491–497.

LeMagnen, J. (1981). The metabolic basis of dual periodicity of feeding in rats. *Behavioral and Brain Sciences, 4*, 561–607.

Lemke, G. (Ed.). (2009). *Developmental neurobiology.* New York: Academic Press.

Lenroot, R., Bustillo, J. R., Lauriello, J., & Keith, S. J. (2003). Integrated treatment of schizophrenia. *Psychiatric Services, 54*, 1499–1507.

Lenroot, R. K., Gogtay, N., Greenstein, D. K., Wells, E. M., Wallace, G. L., Clasen, L. S., et al. (2007). Sexual dimorphism of brain developmental trajectories during childhood and adolescence. *Neuroimage, 36*, 1065–1073.

Leonard, B. E., & Myint, A. M. (2009). The psychoneuroimmunology of depression. *Human Psychopharmacology, 24*, 165–175.

Leuner, B., & Gould, E. (2010). Structural plasticity and hippocampal function. *Annual Review of Psychology, 61*, 111–140.

LeVay, S. (1991). A difference in hypothalamic structure between heterosexual and homosexual men. *Science, 253*, 1034–1037.

Levin, H. S., Peters, B. H., Kalisky, S., High, W. M., von Laufen, A., Eisenberg, H. M., et al. (1986). Effects of oral physostigmine and lecithin on memory and attention in closed-head injured patients. *Central Nervous System Trauma, 3*, 333–342.

Levine, S. (2001). Primary social relationships influence the development of the hypothalamic–pituitary–adrenal axis in the rat. *Physiology and Behavior, 73*(3), 255–260.

Li, Z. M., Wang, L. X., Jiang, J. X., Geng, F. Y., & Qiang, F. (2010). Relationship between plasma cortisol levels and stress ulcer following acute and severe head injury. *Medical Principles and Practice, 19*, 17–21.

Lichtman, J. W., & Sanes, J. R. (2008). A technicolour approach to the connectome. *Nature Review Neuroscience, 9*, 417–422.

Lieberman, H. R., Tharion, W. J., Shukitt-Hale, B., Speckman, K. L., & Tulley, R. (2002). Effects of caffeine, sleep loss, and stress on cognitive performance and mood during U. S. Navy SEAL training. *Psychopharmacology, 164*, 250–261.

Life Magazine (August 8–16, 1945). *Quirk fowl play.*

Lilienfeld, S. O., Wood, J. M., & Garb, H. N. (2000). The scientific status of projective techniques. *Psychological Science in the Public Interest, 1*, 27–66.

Limosin, F., Rouillon, F., Payan, C., Cohen, J. M., & Strub, N. (2003). Prenatal exposure to influenza as a risk factor for adult schizophrenia. *Acta Psychiatrica Scandinavica, 107*, 331–335.

Lin, S., Glasper, E., Lambert, K. G., Madonia, L., Gatewood, J., & Kinsley, C. H. (2001, April). *Behavioral and neurobiological correlates of the addiction syndrome: Effects of maternal experience on withdrawal-induced changes in mesolimbic activity.* Poster presented at the annual meeting of the International Behavioral Neuroscience Society, Cancun, Mexico.

Liotti, M., & Mayberg, H. S. (2001). The role of functional neuroimaging in the neuropsychology of depression. *Journal of Clinical and Experimental Neuropsychology, 23*, 121–136.

Liotti, M., Mayberg, H. S., Brannan, S. K., McGinnis, S., Jerabek, P., & Fox, P. T. (2000). Differential cortico-limbic correlates of sadness and anxiety in healthy subjects: Implications for affective disorders. *Biological Psychiatry, 29*, 887–899.

Liotti, M., Woldorff, M. G., Perez, R., & Mayberg, H. S. (2000). An ERP study of the temporal course of the Stroop color-word interference effect. *Biological Psychiatry, 45*, 96.

Liu, B., & Hong, J. S. (2003). Role of microglia in inflammation-mediated neurodegenerative disease. *Journal of Pharmacology and Therapeutics, 304*, 1–7.

Lock, J., LeGrange, D., Agras, W. S., & Dare, C. (2001). *Treatment manual for anorexia nervosa: A family-based approach.* New York: Guilford Press.

Loewi, O. (1921). Uber humorale ubertragbartkeit der herzenvenwirkung. *Pfluegers Archiv, 189*, 239–242. (Reprinted as On the humoral propagation of cardiac nerve action. In I. Cooke & M. Lipkin, Jr. [Eds.], *Cellular neurophysiology: A source book* [pp. 460–466]. New York: Holt, Rhinehart, & Winston, 1972)

Loftus, E., & Ketcham, K. (1994). *The myth of repressed memory.* New York: St. Martin's Press.

Logue, A. W. (1991). *The psychology of eating and drinking* (2nd ed.). New York: Freeman.

Long, J. M., Mouton, P. R., Jucker, M., & Ingram, D. K. (1999). What counts in brain aging? Design-based stereological analysis of cell number. *Journal of Gerontology, Series A: Biological Sciences and Medical Sciences, 54*(10), B407–B417.

Lopez-Munoz, F., & Alamo, C. (2009). Depression at the frontier of the new century. *Frontiers in Neuroscience, 3*, 226–229.

LoPiccolo, P. (1996, October). Something snapped. *Technology Review*, 52–61.

Lovallo, W. R. (1997). *Stress and health: Biological and psychological interactions.* Thousand Oaks, CA: Sage Publications.

Lucarelli, S., Frediani, T., Zingoni, A. M., Feruzzi, F., Giardini, O., Quintieri, F., et al. (1995). Food allergy and infantile autism. *Panminerva Medica, 37*, 137–141.

Ludolph, A. G., Juengling, F. D., Gerhard, L., Ludolph, A. C., Fegert, J. M., & Kassubek, J. (2006). Grey-matter abnormalities in boys with Tourette syndrome: Magnetic resonance imaging study using optimized voxel-based morphometry. *British Journal of Psychiatry, 188*, 484–485.

Luhrmann, T. M. (2000). *Of two minds: The growing disorder in American psychiatry.* New York: Knopf.

Lund, I., Lundeberg, T., Kurosawa, M., & Uvnas-Moberg, K. (1999). Sensory stimulation (massage) reduces blood pressure in unanaesthetized rats. *Journal of the Autonomic Nervous System, 78*(1), 30–37.

Lupien, S. J., de Leon, M., de Santi, S., Convit, A., Tarshish, C., Nair, N. P. V., et al. (1998). Increase in cortisol during human aging predicts hippocampal atrophy and memory deficits. *Nature Neuroscience, 1*(1), 69–73.

Lupien, S. J., King, S., Meaney, M. J., & McEwen, B. S. (2000). Child's stress hormone levels correlate with mother's socioeconomic status and depressive state. *Society of Biological Psychiatry, 48*, 976–980.

Lupien, S. J., King, S., Meaney, M. J., & McEwen, B. S. (2001). Can poverty get under your skin? Basal cortisol levels and cognitive function in children from low and high socioeconomic status. *Development and Psychopathology, 13*, 653–676.

Luria, A. R. (1968). *The mind of a mnemonist.* Cambridge, MA: Harvard University Press.

Luria, A. R. (1972). *The man with a shattered world.* Cambridge, MA: Harvard University Press.

Luxenberg, J. S., Swedo, S. E., Flamant, M. F., Friedland, R. P., Rapoport, J., & Rapoport, S. I. (1988). Neuroanatomical abnormalities in obsessive–compulsive disorder detected with quantitative X-ray computed tomography. *American Journal of Psychiatry, 145,* 1089–1093.

Lykken, D. (1998). *A tremor in the blood: Uses and abuses of the lie detector.* New York: Perseus.

Mackenzie, J. N. (1896). The production of the so-called "rose cold" by means of an artificial rose. *American Journal of Medical Science, 91,* 45–57.

MacLean, P. D. (1949). Psychosomatic disease and the "visceral brain." *Psychosomatic Medicine, 11,* 338–353.

MacLean, P. D. (1954). Studies on limbic system ("visceral brain") and their bearing on psychosomatic problems. In E. D. Wittkower & R. A. Cleghorn (Eds.), *Recent developments in psychosomatic medicine* (pp. 101–125). Philadelphia: Lippincott.

MacLean, P. D. (1990). *The triune brain in evolution: Role in paleocerebral functions.* New York: Plenum Press.

MacLean, P. D. (1998). Paul D. MacLean. In L. R. Squire (Ed.), *The history of neuroscience in autobiography* (Vol. 2, pp. 244–275). New York: Academic Press.

MacLean, P. D., & Hakstian, A. R. (1990). Relative endurance of unipolar depression treatment effects: Longitudinal follow-up. *Journal of Consulting Clinical Psychology, 58,* 482–488.

Macmillan, M. (2000). *An odd kind of fame: Stories of Phineas Gage.* Cambridge, MA: MIT Press.

Madhav, T. R., Pei, Z., Grahame-Smith, D. G., & Zetterstrom, T. S. C. (2000). Repeated electroconvulsive shock promotes the sprouting of serotonergic axons in the lesioned rat hippocampus. *Neuroscience, 97,* 677–683.

Madsen, T. M., Treschow, A., Bengzon, J., Bolwig, T. G., Lindvall, O., & Tingstrom, A. (2000). Increased neurogenesis in a model of electroconvulsive therapy. *Biological Psychiatry, 47,* 1043–1049.

Magarinos, A. M., Deslandes, A., & McEwen, B. S. (1999). Effects of antidepressants and benzodiazepine treatments on the dendritic structure of CA3 pyramidal neurons after chronic stress. *European Journal of Pharmacology, 371,* 113–122.

Magarinos, A. M., & McEwen, B. S. (1995). Stress-induced atrophy of apical dendrites of hippocampal CA3c neurons: Involvement of glucocorticoid secretion and excitatory amino acid receptors. *Neuroscience, 69,* 89–98.

Maguire, E., Gadian, D., Johnsrude, E., Good, C., Ashburner, J., & Frackowiak, R. S. (2000). Navigation-related structural change in the hippocampi of taxi drivers. *Proceedings of the National Academy of Sciences, USA, 97,* 4398–4403.

Maguire, E., Spiers, H., Good, C., Hartley, T., Frackowiak, R., & Burgess, N. (2003). Navigation expertise and the human hippocampus: A structural brain imaging analysis. *Hippocampus, 13,* 250–259.

Maier, S. F., & Watkins, L. R. (1998). Cytokines for psychologists: Implications of bidirectional immune-to-brain communication for understanding behavior, mood, and cognition. *Psychological Review, 105*(1), 83–107.

Maletic-Savatic, M., Malinow, R., & Svoboda, K. (1999). Rapid dendritic morphogenesis in CA1 hippocampal dendrites induced by synaptic activity. *Science, 28,* 1860–1861.

Malhotra, A. K., Pinals, D. A., Weingartner, H., Sirocco, K., Missar, C. D., Pickar, D., et al. (1996). NMDA receptor function and human cognition: The effects of ketamine in healthy volunteers. *Neuropsychopharmacology, 14*(5), 301–307.

Mandel, H., & Young, J. (2009). *Here's the deal: Don't touch me.* New York: Bentam Press.

Manji, H. K., McNamara, R. K., & Lenox, R. H. (2000). Mechanisms of action of lithium in bipolar disorder. In U. Halbreich & S. A. Montgomery (Eds.), *Pharmacotherapy for mood, anxiety, and cognitive disorders* (pp. 111–142). Washington, DC: American Psychiatric Press.

Mann, P. E., Foltz, G., Rigero, B. A., & Bridges, R. S. (1999). The development of POMC gene expression in the medial basal hypothalamus of prepubertal rats. *Developmental Brain Research, 116,* 21–28.

Manning, J. S., & McElroy, S. L. (2009). Treating bipolar disorder in the primary care setting: The role of aripiprazole. *Primary Care Companion to the Journal of Clinical Psychiatry, 11,* 245–257.

Manolio, T. A., Collins, F. S., Cox, N. J., Goldstein, D. B., Hindorff, L. A., Hunter, D. J., et al. (2009). Finding the missing heritability of complex diseases. *Nature, 461,* 747–753.

Manuck, S., Marsland, A., Kaplan, J., & Williams, J. (1995). The pathogenicity of behavior and its neuroendocrine mediation: An example from coronary artery disease. *Psychosomatic Medicine, 57,* 275.

Marcus, S. (Ed.). (2002). *Neuroethics: Mapping the field.* New York: Dana Press.

Margolin, A., Kleber, H. D., Avants, S. K., Konefal, J., Gawin, F., Stark, E., et al. (2002). Acupuncture for the treatment of cocaine addiction: A randomized controlled trial. *Journal of the American Medical Association, 287,* 55–63.

Marino, R., & Cosgrove, G. R. (1997). Neurosurgical treatment of neuropsychiatric illness. *Neuropsychiatry of the Basal Ganglia, 20*(4), 933–943.

Marks, I. (1997). Behavior therapy for obsessive–compulsive disorder: A decade of progress. *Canadian Journal of Psychiatry, 42*, 1021–1027.

Maron, D. F. (2009). A devastating injury. *Newsweek.* Retrieved September 15, 2009, from http://www.newsweek.com/id/189848/output/print

Martell, B. A., Orson, F. M., Poling, J., Mitchell, E., Rossen, R. D., Gardner, T., et al. (2009). Cocaine vaccine for the treatment of cocaine dependence in methadone-maintained patients: A randomized, double-blind, placebo-controlled efficacy trial. *Archives of General Psychiatry, 66*, 1116–1123.

Martell, C. R., Addis, M. E., & Jacobson, N. S. (2001). *Depression in context.* New York: W.W. Norton.

Martin, M. (1992). *Hostage to the devil.* San Francisco: HarperCollins.

Martino, G., & Pluchino, S. (2006). The therapeutic potential of neural stem cells. *Nature Reviews Neuroscience, 7,* 395–406.

Masi, G., Mucci, M., & Pari, C. (2006). Children with schizophrenia: Clinical picture and pharmacological treatment. *CNS Drugs, 20,* 841–866.

Massou, J. M., Trichard, C., Attar-Levy, D., Feline, A., Corruble, E., Beaufils, B., et al. (1997). Frontal 5-HT 2A receptors studied in depressive patients during chronic treatment by selective serotonin reuptake inhibitors. *Psychopharmacology, 133,* 99–101.

Math, S. B., & Janardhan Reddy, Y. C. (2007). Issues in the pharamacological treatment of obsessive–compulsive disorder. *Clinical Practice, 61,* 1188–1197.

Matthews, K. A., Gump, B. B., & Owens, J. F. (2001). Chronic stress influences cardiovascular and neuroendocrine responses during acute stress and recovery, especially in men. *Health Psychology, 20*(6), 403–410.

Mattson, M. P., & Magnus, T. (2006). Ageing and neuronal vulnerability. *Nature Reviews Neuroscience, 7,* 278–294.

Mauss, I. G., Cook, C. L., Cheng, J. Y. J., & Gross, J. J. (2007). Individual differences in cognitive reappraisal: Experiential and physiological responses to an anger provocation. *International Journal of Psychophysiology, 66,* 116–124.

May, C. (1996, March 6). Moruya Hospital laughter room: An experiment. *The Lamp.*

Mayberg, H. S., Brannan, S. K., Tekell, J. L., Silva, A., Mahurin, R. K., McGinnis, S., et al. (2000). Regional metabolic effects of fluoxetine in major depression: Serial changes and relationship to clinical response. *Biological Psychiatry, 48,* 30–42.

Mayberg, H. S., Lozano, A. M., Voon, V., McNeely, H. E., Seminowicz, D., Hamani, C., et al. (2005). Deep brain stimulation for treatment-resistant depression. *Neuron, 45,* 651–660.

Mayer, J. (1953). Glucostatic mechanism of regulation of food intake. *New England Journal of Medicine, 249,* 13–16.

Mayer, J. (1955). Regulation of energy intake and the body weight: The glucostatic theory and the lipostatic hypothesis. *Annals of the New York Academy of Sciences, 63,* 15–43.

Mayo, W., George, O., Darbra, S., Bouyer, J. J., Vallee, M., Darnaudery, M., et al. (2003). Individual differences in cognitive aging: Implication of pregnenolone sulfate. *Progress in Neurobiology, 71,* 43–48.

Mazmanian, P. E., Kreutzer, J. S., Devany, C. W., & Martin, K. O. (1993). A survey of accredited and other rehabilitation facilities: Education, training, and cognitive rehabilitation in brain injury programmes. *Brain Injury, 7,* 319–331.

McAuley, E., White, S. M., Rogers, L. Q., Motl, R. W., & Courneya, K. S. (2010). Physical activity and fatigue in breast cancer and multiple sclerosis: Psychosocial mechanisms. *Psychosomatic Medicine,* doi:10.1097/PSY.0b013e3181c68157.

McClintock, M. K. (1998). On the nature of mammalian and human pheromones. *Annals of the New York Academy of Sciences, 855,* 390–392.

McConville, B. J., Fogelson, M. H., Norman, A. B., Klykylo, W. M., Manderscheid, P. Z., Parker, K. W., et al. (1991). Nicotine potentiation of haloperidol in reducing tic frequency in Tourette's disorder. *American Journal of Psychiatry, 148*(6), 793–794.

McDonald, C., & Murphy, K. C. (2003). The new genetics of schizophrenia. *Psychiatric Clinics of North America, 26*(1), 41–63.

McDougle, C. J. (1999). The neurobiology and treatment of obsessive–compulsive disorder. In D. S. Charney, E. J. Nestler, & B. Bunney (Eds.), *Neurobiology of mental illness* (pp. 518–533). New York: Oxford University Press.

McEvoy, J. P., & Allen, T. B. (2002). The importance of nicotinic acetylcholine receptors in schizophrenia, bipolar disorder and Tourette's syndrome. *Current Drug Targets CNS Neurological Disorders, 1,* 433–442.

McEwen, B. S. (1998). Protective and damaging effects of stress mediators. *New England Journal of Medicine, 338,* 171–179.

McEwen, B. S. (2000a). Allostasis and allostatic load. *Encyclopedia of Stress, 1,* 145–150.

McEwen, B. S. (2000b). Effects of adverse experiences for brain structure and function. *Biological Psychiatry, 18,* 721–731.

McEwen, B. S. (2000c). The neurobiology of stress: From serendipity to clinical relevance. *Brain Research Bulletin, 886,* 172–189.

McEwen, B. S. (2008). Central effects of stress hormones in health and disease: Understanding the protective and damaging effects of stress and stress mediators. *European Journal of Pharmacology, 538,* 174–185.

McEwen, B. S. (2010). The brain is the central organ of stress and adaptation. *Neuroimage, 47,* 911–913.

McEwen, B. S., deLeon, M. J., Lupien, S. J., & Meaney, M. J. (1999). Corticosteroids, the aging brain and cognition. *Trends in Endocrinology and Metabolism, 19,* 92–96.

McEwen, B. S., & Goodman, H. M. (2001). *Handbook of physiology: Section 7. The endocrine system: Vol. 4. Coping with the environment: Neural and endocrine mechanisms.* New York: Oxford University Press.

McEwen, B. S., & Lashley, E. A. (2002). *The end of stress as we know it.* Washington, DC: Joseph Henry Press.

McEwen, B. S., & Magarinos, A. M. (2001). Stress and hippocampal plasticity: Implications for the pathophysiology of affective disorders. *Human Psychopharmacology, 16,* S7–S19.

McEwen, B. S., & Sapolsky, R. M. (1995). Stress and cognitive function. *Current Opinion in Neurobiology, 5,* 205–216.

McEwen, B. S., & Schmeck, H. M. (1994). *The hostage brain.* New York: The Rockefeller Press.

McEwen, B. S., & Wingfield, J. C. (2009). What is in a name? Integrating homeostasis, allostastasis and stress. *Hormones and Behavior,* doi: 10.1016/j.yhbeh.2009.09.011.

McGowan, P. O., Sasaki, A., D'Alessio, A. C., Dymov, S., Labonté, B., Szyf, M., et al. (2009). Epigenetic regulation of the glucocorticoid receptor in human brain associates with childhood abuse. *Nature Neuroscience, 12,* 342–348.

McGraw, L. A., & Young, L. J. (2009). The prairie vole: an emerging model organism for understanding the social brain. *Trends in Neuroscience, 33,* 103–109.

McGuire, M., & Troisi, A. (1998). *Darwinian psychiatry.* New York: Oxford University Press.

McGuire, P. K., Bench, C. J., & Frith, C. D. (1994). Functional anatomy of obsessive–compulsive phenomena. *British Journal of Psychiatry, 51,* 62–70.

McHugh, P. R., Moran, K. T. H., & Killilea, M. (1989). The approaches to the study of human disorders in food ingestion and body weight maintenance. In L. H. Schenider, S. J. Cooper, & K. A. Halmi (Eds.), *The psychobiology of human eating disorders.* New York: New York Academy of Sciences.

McKee, A. C., Cantu, R. C., Nowinski, C. J., Hedley-Whyte, E. T., Gavett, B. E., Budson, A. E., et al. (2009). Chronic traumatic encephalopathy in athletes: Progressive tauopathy after repetitive head injury. *Journal of Neuropathology and Experimental Neurology, 68,* 709–735.

McKenzie, J. M., & Joyce, P. R. (1992). Hospitalization for anorexia nervosa. *International Journal of Eating Disorders, 11*(3), 235–241.

McLean, A., Temkin, N. R., Dikmen, S., & Wyler, A. R. (1983). The behavioral sequelae of head injury. *Journal of Clinical Neuropsychology, 5,* 361–376.

McMullan, S., & Fisher, L. (1992). Developmental progress of Romanian orphanage children in Canada. *Canadian Psychology, 33,* 504.

Meaney, M. J., Aitken, D. H., Bodnoff, S. R., Iny, L. J., Tatarewicz, J. E., & Sapolsky, R. M. (1985). Early, postnatal handling alters glucocorticoid receptor concentrations in selected brain regions. *Behavioral Neuroscience, 99,* 760–765.

Meaney, M. J., Aitken, D. H., & Sapolsky, R. M. (1991). Environmental regulation of the adrenocortical stress response in female rats and its implications for individual differences in aging. *Neurobiology of Aging, 12,* 31–38.

Medalia, A., Aluma, M., Tryon, W., & Merriam, A. (1998). Effectiveness of attention training in schizophrenia. *Schizophrenia Bulletin, 24,* 147–152.

Mednick, S. A., Machon, R. A., Huttunen, M. O., & Bonett, D. (1988). Adult schizophrenia following prenatal exposure to an influenza epidemic. *Archives of General Psychiatry, 45,* 189–192.

Melmed, R., & Gelpin, Y. (1996). Duodenal ulcer: The helicobacterization of a psychosomatic disease? *Israeli Journal of Medical Science, 32,* 211.

Mendoza, S. P., & Mason, W. A. (1986). Contrasting responses to intruders and to involuntary separation by monogamous and polygamous New World monkeys. *Physiology and Behavior, 38*(6), 795–801.

Menon, V., Rivera, S. M., White, C. D., Eliez, S., Glover, G. H., & Reiss, A. L. (2000). Functional optimization of arithmetic processing in perfect performers. *Brain Research and Cognitive Brain Research, 9,* 343–345.

Mermestein, P. G., & Becker, J. B. (1995). Increases in extracellular dopamine in the nucleus accumbens and the striatum of the female rat during paced copulatory behavior. *Behavioral Neuroscience, 109,* 345–365.

Mesulam, M. M. (2000). A plasticity-based theory of the pathogenesis of Alzheimer's disease [Abstract]. *Annals of the New York Academy of Sciences, 924,* 42–52.

Metal'nikov, S., & Chorine, V. (1926). Rôle des reflexes conditionnels dans l'immunité. *Annales de l'Institute Pasteur (Paris)*, *40*, 893–900.

Metal'nikov, S., & Chorine, V. (1928). Rôle des reflexes conditionnels dans la formation des anticorps. *Comptes Rendus des Séances de la Societé de Biologie et de ses Filiales*, *102*, 1333–1334.

Mets, B., Winger, G., Cabrera, C., Seo, S., Jamdar, S., Yang, G., et al. (1998). A catalytic antibody against cocaine prevents cocaine's reinforcing and toxic effects in rats. *Proceedings of the National Academy of Sciences, USA*, *95*, 10176–10181.

Metzger, L. J., Carson, M. A., Lasko, N. B., Paulus, L. A., Orr, S. P., Pitman, R. K., et al. (2008). Basal and suppressed salivary cortisol in female Vietnam nurse veterans with and without PTSD. *Psychiatry Research*, *15*, 330–335.

Mezey, G., & Robbins, I. (2001). Usefulness and validity of post-traumatic stress disorder as a psychiatric category. *British Medical Journal*, *323*, 561–563.

Michaelis, T., de Biurrun, G., Watanabe, T., Frahm, J., Ohl, F., & Fuchs, E. (2001). Gender-specific alterations of cerebral metabolites with aging and cortisol treatment. *Journal of Psychiatric Research*, *35*(4), 231–237.

Miguel, E. C., Rauch, S. L., & Jenike, M. A. (1997). Obsessive–compulsive disorder. *Neuropsychiatry of the Basal Ganglia*, *20*(4), 863–883.

Mihaly, E., Fekete, C., Lechan, R. M., & Liposits, Z. (2002). Corticotropin-releasing hormone-synthesizing neurons of the human hypothalamus receive neuropeptide Y-immunoreactive innervation from neurons residing primarily outside the infundibular nucleus. *Journal of Comparative Neurology*, *446*, 235–243.

Milen, B. (2009). Nitrous oxide (laughing gas) inhalation as an alternative to electroconvulsive therapy. *Medical Hypotheses*, *74*, 780–781.

Milewicz, A., Mikulski, E., & Bidzinska, B. (2000). Plasma insulin, cholecystokinin, galanin, neuropeptide Y and leptin levels in obese women with and without type 2 diabetes mellitus. *International Journal of Obesity-Related Metabolic Disorders*, *24*, 152–153.

Miller, S. D. (1989). Optical differences in cases of multiple personality disorder. *Journal of Nervous and Mental Disease*, *177*, 480–486.

Miller, S. D., Blackburn, T., Scholes, G., White, G. L., & Mamalis, N. (1991). Optical differences in multiple personality disorder. *Journal of Nervous and Mental Disease*, *179*, 132–135.

Milo, T. J., Kaufman, G. E., Barnes, W. E., Konopka, L. M., Crayton, J. W., Ringelstein, J. G., et al. (2001). Changes in regional cerebral blood flow after electroconvulsive therapy for depression. *Journal of ECT*, *17*, 15–21.

Mindus, P., & Jenike, M. A. (1992). Neurosurgical treatment of malignant obsessive–compulsive disorder. *Obsessional Disorders*, *15*(4), 921–937.

Mineka, S., & Suomi, S. J. (1978). Social separation in monkeys. *Psychological Bulletin*, *85*, 1376–1400.

Minor, R. K., Chang, J. W., & de Cabo, R. (2009). Hungry for life: How the arcuate nucleus and neuropeptide Y may play a critical role in mediating the benefits of calorie restriction. *Molecular and Cellular Endocrinology*, *299*, 779–788.

Mirsky, A. F., Bieliauskas, L. A., French, L. M., Van Kammen, D. P., Jonsson, E., & Sedvall, G. (2000). A 39-year followup of the Genain quadruplets. *Schizophrenia Bulletin*, *26*, 699–708.

Mirsky, A. F., DeLisi, L. E., Buchsbaum, M. S., Quinn, O. W., Schwerdt, P., Siever, L. J., et al. (1984). The Genain quadruplets: Psychological studies. *Psychiatry Research*, *13*, 77–93.

MIT News Office. (2004, February 20). *Carbs are essential for effective dieting and good mood, Wurtman says.* Retrieved March 2004 from http://web.mit.edu/newsoffice/2004/carbs.html

Modell, J. G., Mountz, J. M., Curtus, G. C., & Greden, J. F. (1989). Neurophysiologic dysfunction in basal ganglia/limbic striatal and thalamocortical circuits as a pathogenetic mechanism of obsessive–compulsive disorder. *Journal of Neuropsychiatry*, *1*(1), 27–36.

Moghaddam, B., Boliano, M. L., Stein-Behrens, B., & Sapolsky, R. (1994). Glucocorticoids mediate the stress-induced extracellular accumulation of glutamate. *Brain Research*, *655*, 251–254.

Montagu, A. (1965). *The human revolution.* Cleveland, OH: World Publishing.

Montgomery, S. A. (2000). Changing targets of antidepressant therapy: Serotonin and beyond. In U. Halbreich & S. A. Montgomery (Eds.), *Pharmacotherapy for mood, anxiety, and cognitive disorders* (pp. 199–212). Washington, DC: American Psychiatric Press.

Monti, B., Polazzi, E., & Contestabile, A. (2009). Biochemical, molecular and epigenetic mechanisms of valproic acid neuroprotection. *Current Molecular Pharmacology*, *2*, 95–109.

Morey, C. E., Cilom, M., Berry, J., & Cusick, C. (2003). The effect of Aricept in persons with persistent memory disorder following traumatic injury: A pilot study. *Brain Injury*, *17*, 809–816.

Morgan, C. M., Tanofsky-Kraff, M., Wilfley, D. E., & Yanovski, J. A. (2002). Childhood obesity. *Child and*

Adolescent Psychiatric Clinics of North America, 11, 257–278.

Moussavi, S., Chatterji, S., Verdes, E., Tandon, A., Patel, V., & Ustun, B. (2007). Depression, chronic diseases, and decrements in health: Results from the World Health Surveys. *Lancet, 370,* 851–858.

Move, G. (September 13, 2007). Happiness is a warm electrode. *Popular Mechanics.* Retrieved August 3, 2010, from http://www.popsci.com/scitech/article/2007-09/happiness-warm-electrode

Moyers, W. (1993). *Healing and the mind.* New York: Doubleday.

Mucke, L. (2009). Alzheimer's disease. *Nature, 461,* 895–897.

Mueser, K. T., & McGurk, S. R. (2004). Schizophrenia. *Lancet, 19,* 2063–2072.

Muller, S. V., Johannes, S., Wieringa, B., Weber, A., Muller-Vahl, K., Matzke, M., et al. (2003). Disturbed monitoring and response inhibition in patients with Gilles de la Tourette syndrome and comorbid obsessive–compulsive disorder. *Behavioral Neurology, 14,* 29–37.

Mullin, R. (2003). Drug development costs about 1.7 billion. *Chemical and Engineering News, 81,* 8.

Murray, M. (1998). *Boost your serotonin levels the natural way to overcome depression, obesity, and insomnia.* New York: Bantam Books.

Myers, A., & Hansen, C. (1997). *Experimental psychology.* New York: Brooks/Cole.

Myers, D. G. (2004). *Psychology* (7th ed.). New York: Worth.

Nagai, Y., Cavanna, A., & Critchley, H. D. (2009). Influence of sympathetic autonomic arousal on tics: Implications for a therapeutic behavioral intervention for Tourette syndrome. *Journal of Psychosomatic Research, 67,* 599–605.

Nakazato, M., Murakami, N., Date, Y., Kojima, M., Matsuo, H., Kangawa, K., et al. (2001). A role for ghrelin in the central regulation of feeding. *Nature, 409,* 194–198.

Naranjo, C. A., Tremblay, L. K., & Busto, U. E. (2001). The role of the brain reward system in depression. *Progress in Neuro-Psychopharmacological and Biological Psychiatry, 25,* 781–823.

Nardi, A. E., Valenca, A. M., Nascimento, I., & Zin, W. A. (2001). Hyperventilation challenge test in panic disorder and depression with panic attacks. *Psychiatry Research, 105,* 57–65.

Nasar, S. (2001). *A beautiful mind: A biography of John Forbes Nash, Jr., winner of the Nobel Prize in Economics, 1994.* New York: Simon & Schuster.

Nathan, P. J. (2001). *Hypericum perforatum* (St. John's wort). A nonselective reuptake inhibitor? A review of the recent advances in its pharmacology. *Journal of Psychopharmacology, 15*(1), 47–54.

National Center for Health Statistics. (1999). *Percentage of overweight and obese U. S. adults, age 20–70.* Retrieved June 2004 from http://www.cdc.gov/nchs/prducts/pubd/hestats/over99fig1.htm

National Institute on Drug Abuse (NIDA). (1996). Nationwide trends. http://archives.drugabuse.gov/NIDA_Notes/NNVol11N2/Immunize.html

National Institute on Drug Abuse (NIDA). (1996). Rats immunized against effects of cocaine. Retrieved from http://www.drugabuse.gov/NIDA_Notes/NNVol11N2/Immunize.html

National Institute on Drug Abuse. (2001, July 30). Ecstasy abuse and control. [Hearing before the Senate Subcommittee on Governmental Affairs. Testimony by Alan I. Leshner.]

National Institute of Mental Health. (2001). *Bipolar disorder.* Retrieved April 8 2004 from http://www.nimh.nih.gov/publicat/bipolar.cfm#intro

National Institute of Mental Health. (2004). *Autism spectrum disorders (pervasive development disorders).* Accessed June 2, 2004, from http://www.nimh.nih.gov/publicat/autism.cfm

National Institute of Neurological Disorders and Stroke. (1989). Interagency Head Injury Task Force report. Bethesda, MD: Author.

National Institutes of Health (NIH). (2009). *Stem cell information: The National Institutes of Health resource for stem cell research.* http://stemcells.nih.gov/info/basics/basics4.asp

National Library of Medicine. (2010). Color vision deficiency. Retrieved from http://ghr.nlm.nih.gov/condition=colorvisiondeficiency

Nature. (2010). A decade for psychiatric disorders. *Nature, 463,* 9.

Neese, R. M. (2000). Is depression an adaption? *Archives of General Psychiatry, 57,* 14–20.

Neese, R. M., & Williams, G. C. (1994a). *Darwinian medicine.* New York: Vintage Books.

Neese, R. M., & Williams, G. C. (1994b). *Why we get sick.* New York: Vintage Press.

Nemeroff, C. B. (1998). The neurobiology of depression. *Scientific American, 278,* 28–35.

Nemeroff, C. B., Owens, M. J., Bissette, G., Andorn, A. C., & Stanley, M. (1988). Reduced corticotropin-releasing factor binding sites in the frontal cortex of suicide victims. *Archives of General Psychiatry, 45,* 377–379.

Nemeroff, C. B., Widerlov, E., Bissette, B., Walleus, H., Karlsson, I., Eklund, K., et al. (1984). Elevated concentrations of CSF corticotropin-releasing factor-like immunoreactivity in depressed patients. *Science, 226,* 1342–1344.

Nestby, P., Schoffelmeer, A. N. M., Homberg, J. R., Warden, G., DeVries, T.J., Mulder, A.H., et al. (1999). Bremazocine reduces unrestricted free-choice ethanol self-administration in rats without affecting sucrose preference. *Psychopharmacology, 142,* 309–317.

Nestler, E. J. (1999). Cellular and molecular mechanisms of addiction. In D. S. Charney, E. J. Nestler, & B. S. Bunney (Eds.), *Neurobiology of mental illness.* New York: Oxford University Press.

Nestler, E. J. (2005). Is there a common molecular pathway for addiction. *Nature Neuroscience, 8,* 1445–1449.

Newlin, D. B. (1999). Evolutionary game theory and multiple chemical sensitivity. *Toxicology and Industrial Health, 15,* 313–322.

Newman, M. G., & Stone, A. A. (1996). Does humor moderate the effects of experimentally induced stress? *Annals of Behavioral Medicine, 18,* 101–109.

Nibuya, M., Morinobu, S., & Duman, R. S. (1995). Regulation of BDNF and trkB mRNA in rat brain by chronic elecftroconvulsive seizue and antidepressant drug treatments. *Journal of Neuroscience, 15,* 7539–7547.

NIH Consensus Development Panel on Rehabilitation of Persons with Traumatic Brain Injury. (1999). Consensus conference: Rehabilitation of persons with traumatic brain injury. *Journal of American Medical Association, 282,* 974–983.

Nobler, M. S., Oquendo, M. A., Kegeles, L. S., Malone, K. M., Campbell, C., Sackheim, H. A., et al. (2001). Decreased regional brain metabolism after ECT. *American Journal of Psychiatry, 158,* 305–308.

Nobler, M. S., Sackheim, H. A., & Devanand, D. P. (2000). Electroconvulsive therapy: Current practice and future directions. In U. Halbreich & S. A. Montgomery (Eds.), *Pharmacotherapy for mood, anxiety, and cognitive disorders* (pp. 167–187). Washington, DC: American Psychiatric Press.

Nocera, J. (2008, November 11). Taking science personally. *New York Times.* http://www.nytimes.com/2008/11/11/giving/11SICK.html

Norcross, J. I., & Newman, J. D. (1999). Effects of separation and novelty on distress vocalizations and cortisol in the common marmoset (*Callithrix jacchus*). *American Journal of Primatology, 47*(3), 209–222.

Norman, R. M., & Malla, A. K. (1993a). Stressful life events and schizophrenia: I. A review of the research. *British Journal of Psychiatry, 162,* 161–166.

Norman, R. M., & Malla, A. K. (1993b). Stressful life events and schizophrenia: II. Conceptual and methodological issues. *British Journal of Psychiatry, 162,* 166–174.

Nunn, R. G., Newton, K. S., & Faucher, P. (1992). 2.5 years follow-up of weight and body mass index values in the Weight Control for Life! program: A descriptive analysis. *Addictive Behaviors, 17,* 579–585.

Nuttin, B. J., & Cosyns, P. R. (1999). Electrical stimulation in anterior limbs of internal capsules in patients with obsessive–compulsive disorder. *Lancet, 354,* 1526.

Oades, R. D., Sadile, A. G., Sagvolden, T., Viggiano, D., Zuddas, A., Devoto, P., et al. (2005). The control of responsiveness in ADHD by catecholamines: Evidence for dopaminergic, noradrenergic and interactive roles. *Developmental Science, 8,* 122–131.

O'Brien, C. (1999). Principles of the pharmacotherapy of substance abuse disorders. In D. S. Charney, E. J. Nestler, & B. S. Bunney (Eds.), *Neurobiology of mental illness.* New York: Oxford University Press.

Ogden, C. L., Yanovski, S. Z., Carroll, M. D., & Flegal, K. M. (2007). The epidemiology of obesity. *Gastroenterology, 132,* 2087–2102.

Okugawa, G., Sedvall, G. C., & Agartz, I. (2003). Smaller cerebellar vermis but not hemisphere volumes in patients with chronic schizophrenia. *American Journal of Psychiatry, 160,* 1614–1617.

Olanow, C. W., Stern, M. B., & Sethi, K. (2009). The scientific and clinical basis for the treatment of Parkinson's disease. *Neurology, 72*(Suppl. 4), S1–S136.

Olds, J. (1958). Satiation effects in self-stimulation of the brain. *Journal of Comparative and Physiological Psychology, 51,* 675–678.

Olds, J., & Milner, P. (1954). Positive reinforcement produced by electrical stimulation of the septal area and other regions of the rat brain. *Journal of Comparative and Physiological Psychology, 47,* 419–428.

Omalu, B. I., DeKosky, S. T., Minster, R. L., Kamboh, M. I., Hamilton, R. L., & Wecht, C. H. (2006). Chronic traumatic encephalopathy in a National Footall League player. *Neurosurgery, 57,* 128–134.

Onion. (1998, June 27). Starbucks opens in restroom of existing Starbucks [Parody]. Retrieved from: http://www.theonion.com/articles/new-starbucks-opens-in-rest-room-of-existing-starb,560/

Onion. (2003, May 14). Pfizer launches "Zoloft for Everything" ad campaign [Parody]. Retrieved January 8, 2004, from http://www.theonion.com/articles/pfizer-launches-zoloft-for-everything-ad-campaign,297.htm

Orth, M., Amann, B., Robertson, M. M., & Rothwell, J. C. (2005). Excitability of motor cortex inhibitory circuits in Tourette syndrome before and after single dose nicotine. *Brain, 128,* 1292–1300.

Osborne, L. (2001, May 6). Regional disturbances. *New York Times Magazine,* pp. 8–102.

Padberg, J., Franca, J. G., Cooke, D. F., Soares, J. G. M., Rosa, M. G. P., Fiorani, M., et al. (2007). Parallel evolution of cortical areas involved in skilled hand use. *The Journal of Neuroscience, 27,* 10106–10115.

Pakkenberg, B., Pelvig, D., Marner, L., Bundgaard, M. J., Gundersen, H. J., Nyengaard, J. R., et al. (2003). Aging and the human neocortex. *Experimental Gerontology, 38*(1–2), 95–99.

Palanza, P., Gioiosa, I., & Parmigiani, S. (2001). Social stress in mice: Gender differences and effects of estrous cycle and social dominance. *Physiology and Behavior, 73*(3), 411–420.

Panksepp, J. (1998). *Affective neuroscience: The foundations of human and animal emotions.* New York: Oxford University Press.

Panksepp, J. (2000). The riddle of laughter: Neural and psychoevolutionary underpinnings of joy. *Current Directions in Psychological Science, 9,* 183–186.

Papez, J. W. (1937). A proposed mechanism of emotion. *Archives of Neurology and Psychiatry, 38,* 725–743.

Paquette, V., Levesque, J., Mensour, B., Leroux, J. M., Beaudoin, G., Bourgouin, P., et al. (2003). "Change the mind and you change the brain": Effects of cognitive-behavioral therapy on the neural correlates of spider phobia. *NeuroImage, 18,* 401–409.

Pardo, J. V., Pardo, P. J., Janer, K. W., & Raichle, M. E. (1990). The anterior cingulate cortex mediate processing selection in the Stroop attentional conflict paradigm. *Proceedings of the National Academy of Sciences, USA, 150,* 713–719.

Pare, W. P., Blair, G. R., Kluczynski, J., & Tejani-Butt, S. (1999). Gender differences in acute and chronic stress in Wistar Kyoto rats. *Integrative Physiological and Behavioral Science, 34,* 227–241.

Park, J. M., Matrix-Cols, D., Marks, I. M., Ngamthipwatthana, T., Marks, M., Araya, R., et al. (2001). Two-year follow-up after a randomized controlled trial of self-and clinician-accompanied exposure for phobia/panic disorders. *British Journal of Psychiatry, 178,* 543–548.

Parkinson, J. (1817). *An essay on the shaking palsy.* London: Whittingham and Rowland for Sherwood, Neely and Jones.

Parrott, A. C., Lees, A., Garnham, N. J., Jones, M., & Wesnes, K. (1998). Cognitive performance in recreational users of MDMA or "ectasy": Evidence for memory deficits. *Journal of Psychopharmacology, 12,* 79–83.

Parwani, A., Duncan, E. J., Bartlett, E., Madonick, S. H., Efferen, T. R., Rajan, R., et al. (2000). Impaired prepulse inhibition of acoustic startle in schizophrenia. *Biological Psychiatry, 47,* 662–669.

Pary, R., Lewis, S., Matuschka, P. R., & Lippmann, S. (2002). Attention-deficit/hyperactivity disorder: An update. *Southern Medical Journal, 95*(7), 743–749.

Pascual-Leone, A., Nguyet, D., Cohen, L., Brasil-Neto, J., Cammarota, A., & Hallet, M. (1995). Modulation of muscle responses evoked by transcranial magnetic stimulation during the acquisition of new fine motor skills. *Journal of Neurophysiology, 74,* 1037–1045.

Paulozzi, L. J., Logan, J. E., Hall, A. J., McKinstry, E., Kaplan, J. A., & Crosby, A. E. (2009). A comparison of drug overdose deaths involving methadone and other opioid analgesics in West Virginia. *Addiction, 104,* 1541–1548.

Paunovic, N., & Ost, I. G. (2001). Cognitive–behavior therapy vs exposure therapy in the treatment of PTSD in refugees. *Behavioral Research Therapy, 39*(10), 1183–1197.

Pavlov, I. P. (1927). *Conditioned reflexes.* London: Oxford University Press.

Payer, L. (1996). *Medicine and culture.* New York: Holt.

Paylor, R., & Crawley, J. N. (1997). Inbred strain differences in prepulse inhibition of the mouse startle response. *Psychopharmacology, 132,* 169–180.

Pendergrast, M. (1999). *Uncommon grounds.* New York: Basic Books.

Penfield, W. (1941). *Epilepsy and cerebral localization.* Baltimore: Thomas.

Peniston, E. G., & Kulsosky, P. J. (1989). Alpha–theta brain wave training and beta-endorphin levels in alcoholics. *Alcoholism: Clinical and Experimental Research, 13,* 271–279.

Pennebaker, J. W., Kiecolt-Glaser, J. K., & Glaser, R. (1988). Disclosure of traumas and immune function: Health implications for psychotherapy. *Journal of Consulting and Clinical Psychology, 56,* 239–245.

Perez-Cruz, C., Simon, M., Czeh, B., Flugge, G., & Fuchs, E. (2009). Hemispheric differences in basilar dendrites and spintes of pyramidal neurons in the rat prelimbic cortex: Activity- and stress-induced changes. *European Journal of Neuroscience, 29,* 738–747.

Perini, G. I., Tosin, C., Carraro, C., Bernasconi, G., Canevini, M. P., Canger, R., et al. (1996). Interictal mood and personality disorders in temporal lobe epilepsy and juvenile myoclonic epilepsy. *Journal of Neurological Psychiatry, 61,* 601–605.

Perse, T. (1988). Obsessive–compulsive disorder: A treatment review. *Journal of Clinical Psychiatry, 49,* 48.

Pert, C. (1999). *Molecules of emotion: The science behind mind-body medicine.* New York: Simon & Schuster.

Peters, A., Palay, S. L., & Webster, H. D. (1991). *The fine structure of the nervous system: Neurons and their supporting cells.* New York: Oxford University Press.

Peterson, B. S., Riddle, M. A., Cohen, D. J., Katz, L. D., Smith, J. C., Hardin, M. T., et al. (1993). Reduced basal ganglia volumes in Tourette's syndrome using 3-dimensional reconstruction techniques from magnetic resonance images. *Neurology, 43,* 941–949.

Pettit, H. O., Ettenberg, A., Bloom, F. E., & Koob, G. F. (1984). Destruction of dopamine in the nucleus accumbens selectively attenuates cocaine but not heroin self-administration in rats. *Psychopharmacology, 84,* 167–173.

Pettit, H. O., & Justice, J. G. (1991). Effect of dose of cocaine self-administration behavior and dopamine levels in the nucleus accumbens. *Brain Research, 539,* 94–102.

Phillips, A. G., Mora, F., & Rolls, E. T. (1979). Intracranial self-stimulation in orbitofrontal cortex and caudate nucleus of rhesus monkey: Effects of apomorphine, pimozide, and spiroperidol. *Psychopharmacology, 62,* 79–82.

Piazza, P. V., Deminiere, J. M., Maccare, S., Mormedi, P., LeMoal, M., & Simon, H. (1990). Individual reactivity to novelty predicts probability of amphetamine self-administration. *Behavioral Pharmacology, 1,* 339–345.

Pinel, J. P. J. (2000). *Biopsychology* (4th ed.). Needham Heights, MA: Allyn & Bacon.

Pinel, J. P. J. (2003). *Biopsychology* (5th ed.). Needham Heights, MA: Allyn & Bacon.

Pinel, J. P. J., Assanand, S., & Lehman, D. R. (2000). Hunger, eating, and ill health. *American Psychologist, 55,* 1105–1116.

Pinel, J. P. J., Mumby, D. G., Dastur, F. N., & Pinel, J. G. (1994). Rat (*Rattus norvegicus*) defensive behavior in total darkness: Risk-assessment function of defensive burying. *Journal of Comparative Psychology, 108*(2), 140–147.

Pirke, K. M. (1996). Central and peripheral noradrenalin regulation in eating disorders. *Psychiatry Research, 62,* 43–49.

Pizzagalli, D., Pascual-Marqui, R. D., Nitschke, J. G., Oakes, T. R., Larson, C. L., Abercrombie, H. C., et al. (2001). Anterior cingulate activity as a predictor of degree of treatment response in major depression: Evidence from brain electrical tomography analysis. *American Journal of Psychiatry, 1589,* 405–415.

Plotsky, P. M., & Meaney, M. J. (1993). Early, postnatal experience alters hypothalamic corticotropin-releasing factor (CRF) mRNA, median eminence CRF content and stress-induced release in adult rats. *Brain Research and Molecular Brain Research, 18,* 195–200.

Poling, J., Oliveto, A., Petry, N., Sofuoglu, M., Gonsai, K., Martell, B., et al. (2006). Six-month trial of bupropion with contingency management for cocaine dependence in a methadone-maintained population. *Archives of General Psychiatry, 63,* 219–228.

Porges, S. (2002). Polyvagal theory: Three neural circuits regulate behavioral reactivity. *Psychological Science Agenda, 15,* 9–11.

Porta, M., Brambilla, A., Cavanna, A. E., Servello, D., Sassi, M., Rickards, H., et al. (2009). Thalamic deep brain stimulation for treatment-refractory Tourette syndrome. *Neurology, 73,* 1375–1380.

Porter, N., Herman, J. P., & Landfield, P. W. (2001). Mechanisms of glucocorticoid actions in stress and brain aging. In B. S. McEwen (Ed.), *Handbook of physiology: Vol. 4. Coping with the environment* (pp. 293–309). Oxford, UK: Oxford University Press.

Post, R., & Weiss, S. R. B. (1999). Neurobiological models of recurrence in mood disorders. In D. S. Charney, E. J. Nestler, & B. S. Bunney (Eds.), *Neurobiology of mental illness.* New York: Oxford University Press.

Price, R. A., Kidd, K. K., Cohen, D. J., Pauls, D. L., & Leckman, J. F. (1985). A twin study of Tourette syndrome. *Archives of General Psychiatry, 42,* 815–820.

Proietto, J., Fam, B. C., Ainslie, D. A., & Thorburn, A. W. (2000). Novel anti-obesity drugs. *Expert Opinion on Investigating Drugs, 6,* 1317–1326.

Provine, R. R. (2000). *Laughter.* New York: Viking Press.

Psychosurgery: Operation to cure sick minds turns surgeon's blade into an instrument of mental therapy. (1947, March 3). *Life,* 93–116.

Puhl, R., & Brownell, K. D. (2001). Bias, discrimination, and obesity. *Obesity Research, 12,* 788–805.

Pulver, A. E. (2000). Search for schizophrenia susceptibility genes. *Biological Psychiatry, 47*(3), 221–230.

Purves, D. (1994). *Neural activity and the growth of the brain.* Cambridge, UK: Cambridge University Press.

Purves, D., & Lichtman, J. W. (1980). Elimination of synapses in the developing nervous system. *Science, 210,* 153–157.

Putignano, P., Dubini, A., Toja, P., Invitti, C., Bonfanti, S., Redaelli, G., et al. (2001). Salivary cortisol measurement in normal-weight, obese and anorexic women: Comparison with plasma cortisol. *European Journal of Endocrinology, 145,* 165–171.

Quallo, M. M., Price, C. J., Ueno, K., Asamizuya, T., Cheng, K., Lemon, R. N., et al. (2009). Gray and white matter changes associated with tool-use learning in macaque monkeys. *Proceedings of the National Academy of Sciences, 106,* 18379-18384.

Raadsheer, F. C., Hoogendijk, W. J. G., Stam, F. C., Tilders, F. H. J., & Swaab, D. F. (1994). Increased numbers of corticotropin-releasing hormone expressing neurons in the hypothalamic paraventricular nucleus of depressed patients. *Neuroendocrinology, 60,* 433-436.

Rabin, S. (1999). Stress, immune function, and health. In M. Schedlowski & U. Tewes (Eds.), *Psychoneuroimmunology: An interdisciplinary introduction.* New York: Kluwer Academic/Plenum.

Raedler, T. J., Knable, M. B., Jones, D. W., Urbina, R. A., Gorey, J. G., Lee, K. S., et al. (2003). In vivo determination of muscarinic acetylcholine receptor availability in schizophrenia. *American Journal of Psychiatry, 160,* 118-127.

Raisman, G., & Field, P. M. (1971). Sexual dimorphism in the preoptic area of the rat. *Science, 173,* 731-733.

Raison, C. I., & Miller, A. H. (2001). The neuroimmunology of stress and depression. *Seminars in Clinical Neuropsychiatry, 6*(4), 277-294.

Rajkowska, G. (2000). Postmortem studies in mood disorders indicate altered numbers of neurons and glial cells. *Biological Psychiatry, 48,* 766-777.

Rajkowska, G., & Miguel-Hidalgo, J. J. (2007). Gliogenesis and glial pathology in depression. *CNS and Neurological Disorders-Drug Targets, 6,* 219-233.

Raloff, J. (1997). Patients savor this brain disorder. *Science News, 151,* 348.

Ramachandran, V. S. (1998). The neurology and evolution of humor, laughter, and smiling: The false alarm theory. *Medical Hypotheses, 51,* 351-354.

Ramon y Cajal, S. (1928). *Degeneration and regeneration of the nervous system* (R. M. May, Trans.). London: Oxford University Press.

Ramon y Cajal, S. (1989). *Recollections of my life.* Cambridge: MIT press.

Rapoport, J. L. (1990). *The boy who couldn't stop washing: The experience and treatment of obsessive-compulsive disorder.* New York: Signet.

Rapoport, J. L., & Fiske, A. (1998). The new biology of obsessive-compulsive disorder: Implications for evolutionary psychology. *Perspectives in Biology and Medicine, 41*(2), 159-175.

Rasmussen, S. A. (1993). Genetic studies of obsessive-compulsive disorder. *Annals of Clinical Psychology, 5,* 241-248.

Rasmussen, S. A., & Eisen, J. L. (1990). Epidemiology of obsessive-compulsive disorder. *Journal of Clinical Psychiatry, 51*(2), 10-14.

Rastam, M., Bjure, J., Vestergren, E., Uvebrant, P., Billberg, I. C., Wentz, E., et al. (2001). Regional cerebral blood flow in weight-restored anorexia nervosa: A preliminary study. *Developmental Medicine and Child Neurology, 43,* 239-242.

Rauch, S. L., Jenike, M. A., Alpert, N. M., Baer, L., Breiter, H. C. R., Savage, C. R., et al. (1994). Regional cerebral blood flow measured during symptom provocation in obsessive-compulsive disorder using oxygen 15-labeled carbon dioxide and positron emission tomography. *Archives of General Psychiatry, 51,* 62-70.

Rauch, S. L., & Savage, C. R. (1997). Neuroimaging and neuropsychology of the striatum. *Neuropsychiatry of the Basal Ganglia, 20*(4), 741-768.

Read, J., Perry, B. D., Moskowitz, A., & Connolly, J. (2001). The contribution of early traumatic events to schizophrenia in some patients: A traumagenic neurodevelopmental model. *Psychiatry, 64,* 319-345.

Redei, E. E., Ahmadiyeh, N., Baum, A. E., Sasso, D. A., Slone, J. L., Solberg, L. C., et al. (2001). Novel animal models of affective disorders. *Seminars in Clinical Neuropsychiatry, 6,* 43-67.

Reeve, C. (2002). *Nothing is impossible.* New York: Random House.

Reeve, J. (1992). *Understanding motivation and emotion.* New York: Holt, Rinehart, & Winston.

Reichelt, K. L., & Knivsberg, A. M. (2003). Can the pathophysiology of autism be explained by the nature of the discovered urine peptides? *Nutritional Neuroscience, 6,* 19-28.

Reichelt, K. L., & Knivsberg, A. M. (2009). The possibility and probability of a gut-to-brain connection in autism. *Annals of Clinical Psychology, 21,* 205-211.

Regard, M., & Landis, T. (1997). "Gourmand syndrome": Eating passion associated with right anterior lesions. *Neurology, 48,* 1185-1190.

Ressler, K. J., & Nemeroff, C. B. (2000). Role of serotonergic and noradrenergic systems in the pathophysiology of depression and anxiety disorders. *Depression and Anxiety, 12,* 2-19.

Ressler, K. J., Rothbaum, B. O., Tannenbaum, L., Anderson, P., Graap, K., Zimand, E., et al. (2004). Cognitive enhancers as adjuncts to psychotherapy: Use of D-cycloserine in phobics to facilitate extinction of fear. *Archives of Psychiatry, 61,* 1136-1144.

Restak, R. M. (1994). *Receptors.* New York: Bantam Books.

Restak, R. M. (2001). *The secret life of the brain.* Washington, DC: Joseph Henry Press.

Restak, R. M. (2003). *The new brain: How the modern age is rewiring your mind.* Emmaus, PA: Rodale Press.

Richelson, E. (2001). Pharmacology of antidepressants. *Mayo Clinic Proceedings, 76,* 511–527.

Riley, B., & Kendler, K. S. (2006). Molecular genetic studies of schizophrenia. *European Journal of Human Genetics, 14,* 669–680.

Robbins, T. W., & Everitt, B. J. (1999). Drug addiction: Bad habits add up. *Nature, 398,* 567–570.

Robertson, M. M. (1996). D$_2$ be or not to be? *Nature Medicine, 2*(10), 1076–1077.

Robins, L. N., Davis, D. H., & Nurco, D. N. (1974). How permanent was Vietnam drug addiction? *American Journal of Public Health, 64,* 38–43.

Robinson, D., Wu, H., Munne, R. A., Ashtari, M., Alvir, J. M., Lerner, G., et al. (1995). Reduced caudate nucleus volume in obsessive–compulsive disorder. *Archives of General Psychiatry, 52,* 393–398.

Robinson, L. A., Berman, J. S., & Neimeyer, R. A. (1990). Psychotherapy for the treatment of depression: A comprehensive review of controlled outcome research. *Psychological Bulletin, 108,* 30–49.

Robinson, T. E., & Kolb, B. (1999). Alterations in the morphology of dendrites and dendritic spines in the nucleus accumbens and prefrontal cortex following repeated treatment with amphetamine or cocaine. *European Journal of Neuroscience, 11,* 1598–1604.

Rocha, B. A., Fumagalli, F., Gainetdinov, R. R., Jones, S. R., Ator, R., Giros, B., et al. (1998). Cocaine self-administration in dopamine-transporter knockout mice. *Nature Neuroscience, 1,* 132–137.

Roessner, V., Overlack, S., Baudewig, J., Dechent, P., Rothenberger, A., & Helms, G. (2009). No brain structure abnormalities in boys with Tourette's syndrome: A voxel-based morphometry study. *Movement Disorders, 24,* 2398–2403.

Rogers, M. A., Yamasue, H., Abe, O., Yamada, H., Ohtani, T., Iwanami, A., et al. (2009). Smaller amygdale volume and reduced anterior cingulated gray matter density associated with history of post-traumatic stress disorder. *Psychiatry Research: Neuroimaging, 174,* 210–216.

Rogers, P. J., & Blundell, J. E. (1980). Investigation of food selection and meal parameters during the development of dietary induced obesity [Abstract]. *Appetite, 1,* 85.

Rolls, B. J. (1986). Sensory-specific satiety. *Nutrition Reviews, 40,* 93–101.

Ronan, P. J., Steciuk, M., Kramer, G. L., Kram, M., & Petty, F. (2000). Increased septal 5-HIAA efflux in rats that do not develop learned helplessness after inescapable stress. *Journal of Neuroscience Research, 61,* 101–106.

Roozendaal, B., Koolhaas, J. M., & Bohus, B. (1990). Differential effect of lesioning of the central amygdala on the bradycardic and behavioral response of the rat in relation to conditioned social and solitary stress. *Behavioral Brain Research, 41,* 39–48.

Rosenberg, D. R., & Keshavan, M. S. (1998). Toward a neurodevelopmental model of obsessive–compulsive disorder. *Biological Psychiatry, 43,* 623–640.

Rosenman, R., Brand, R., Jenkins, C., Friedman, M., Straus, R., & Wurm, M. (1975). Coronary heart disease in the Western Collaborative Group Study: Final follow-up experience of 812 years. *Journal of the American Medical Association, 233,* 872.

Rosenstein, L. D. (1994). Potential neuropsychologic and neurophysiologic correlates of multiple personality disorder: Literature review and two case studies. *Neuropsychology, Neuropsychiatry and Behavioral Neurology, 7,* 215–229.

Rosenzweig, M. R., Breedlove, S. M., & Leiman, A. L. (1999). *Biological psychology* (2nd ed.). Sunderland, MA: Sinauer.

Rosenzweig, M. R., Breedlove, S. M., & Leiman, A. L. (2002). *Biological psychology* (3rd ed.). Sunderland, MA: Sinauer.

Ross, G. W., Abbott, R. D., Petrovitch, H., Morens, D. M., Grandinetti, A., Tung, K H., et al. (2000). Association of coffee and caffeine intake with the risk of Parkinson's disease. *Journal of the American Medical Association, 283,* 2674–2679.

Ross, G. W., & Petrovitch, H. (2001). Current evidence for neuroprotective effects of nicotine and caffeine against Parkinson's disease. *Drugs & Aging, 18,* 797–806.

Ross, P. (2003). Mind readers. *Scientific American, 289,* 74–77.

Rothschild, A. J. (2000). Sexual side effects of antidepressants. *Journal of Clinical Psychiatry, 61,* 28–36.

Rotter, J. B. (1993). Expectancies. In C. E. Walker (Ed.), *History of clinical psychology in autobiography* (Vol. 2, pp. 273–284). Pacific Grove, CA: Brooks/Cole.

Rozin, P., Dow, S., Moscovitch, M., & Rajaram, S. (1998). The role of memory for recent eating experiences in onset and cessation of meals. Evidence from the amnesic syndrome. *Psychological Science, 9,* 392–396.

Rubin, R. T., Poland, R. E., Lesser, I. M., Winston, R. A., & Blodgett, A. L. N. (1987). Neuroendocrine aspects of primary endogenous depression. *Archives of General Psychiatry, 44,* 328–336.

Ruden, R. A. (1997). *The craving brain: The biobalance approach to controlling addiction.* New York: HarperCollins.

Ruden, R. A. (2000). *The craving brain* (2nd ed.). New York: Perennial.

Ruff, M., & Pert, C. B. (1984). Small cell carcinoma of the lung: Macrophage-specific antigens suggest hemopoietic stem cell origin. *Science, 225,* 1034–1036.

Rush, A. J., Schlesser, M. A., Stokely, E. M., Bonte, F. R., & Altshuller, K. Z. (1982). Cerebral blood flow in depression and mania. *Psychopharmacological Bulletin, 18,* 6–8.

Russek, L. G., & Schwartz, G. (1997). Feelings of parental care predict health status in midlife: A 35-year follow-up of the Harvard Mastery of Stress Study. *Journal of Behavioral Medicine, 20,* 1–11.

Russell, G. F. M., & Treasure, J. (1989). The modern history of anorexia nervosa. In L. H. Schneider, S. J. Cooper, & K. A. Halmi (Eds.), *The psychobiology of human eating disorders.* New York: New York Academy of Sciences.

Russo-Neustadt, A. A., Beard, R. C., Huang, Y. M., & Cotman, C. W. (2000). Physical activity and antidepressant treatment potentiate the expression of specific brain-derived neurotrophic factor transcripts in the rat hippocampus. *Neuroscience, 101,* 305–312.

Russo-Neustadt, A. A., Ha, T., Ramirez, R., & Kesslak, J. P. (2001). Physical activity–antidepressant treatment combination: Impact on brain-derived neurotrophic factor and behavior in an animal model. *Behavioral Brain Research, 120,* 87–95.

Ryvlin, P. (2003). Beyond pharmacotherapy: Surgical management. *Epilepsia, 44,* 23–28.

Sacks, J. J., Holmgreen, P., Smith, S. M., & Sosin, D. M. (1988). Bicycle-associated head injuries and deaths in the United States from 1984 through 1988: How many are preventable? *Journal of American Medical Association, 266,* 3016–3018.

Sacks, J. J., Holmgreen, P., Smith, S. M., & Sosin, D. M. (1988). Bicycle-associated head injuries and deaths in the United States from 1984 through 1988. *Journal of the American Medical Association, 266,* 3016–3018.

Sacks, O. (1984). *A leg to stand on.* New York: Touchstone.

Sacks, O. (1985). *The man who mistook his wife for a hat.* New York: Touchstone.

Sacks, O. (1990). *Seeing voices.* New York: HarperCollins.

Sacks, O. (1995). *An anthropologist on Mars.* New York: Knopf.

Sacks, O. (1997). *The island of the colorblind.* New York: Vintage Press.

Sacks, O. (1999a). *Awakenings.* New York: Vintage Press. (Original work published 1973)

Sacks, O. (1999b). *Migraine.* Berkeley: University of California Press.

Sacks, O. (2001). *Uncle Tungsten: Memories of a chemical boyhood.* New York: Knopf.

Sacks, O. (2007). *Musicophilia.* New York: Knopf.

Sanes, D. H., Reh, T. A. & Harris, W. A. (2005). *Development of the Nervous System.* (2nd Ed.), New York: Academic Press.

Sahu, A. L, Sninsky, C. A., & Kalra, S. P. (1997). Evidence that hypothalamic neuropeptide Y gene expression and NPY levels in the paraventricular nucleus increase before the onset of hyperphagia in experimental diabetes. *Brain Research, 755,* 339–342.

Sajdyk, T. J., Johnson, P. L., Leitermann, R. J., Fitz, S. D., Dietrich, A., Morin, M., et al. (2008). Neuropeptide Y in the amygdala induces long-term resilience to stress-induced reductions in social responses but not hypothalamic–adrenal–pituitary axis activity or hypterthermia. *Journal of Neuroscience, 28,* 893–903.

Salazar, A. M., Warden, D. I., Schwab, K., Spector, J., Braverman, S., Walter, J., et al. (2000). Cognitive rehabilitation for traumatic brain injury: A randomized trial. *Journal of the American Medical Association, 283,* 3075–3081.

Sanberg, P. R., McConville, B. J., Fogelson, H. M., Manderscheid, P. Z., Parker, K. W., Blythe, M. M., et al. (1989). Nicotine potentiates the effects of haloperidol in animals and inpatients with Tourette's syndrome. *Biomedical Pharmacology, 43,* 19–23.

Sanchez, M. M., Hearn, E. F., Do, D., Rilling, J. K., & Herndon, J. G. (1998). Differential rearing affects corpus callosum size and cognitive function of rhesus monkeys. *Brain Research, 812*(1–2), 38–49.

Sanders, A. R., Detera-Wadleigh, S. D., & Gershon, E. S. (1999). Molecular genetics of mood disorders. In D. S. Charney, E. J. Nestler, & B. S. Bunney (Eds.), *Neurobiology of mental illness* (pp. 299–316). New York: Oxford University Press.

Sandfort, T. G., de Graaf, R., Bijl, R. V., & Schnabel, P. (2001). Same-sex sexual behavior and psychiatric disorders: Findings from the Netherlands Mental Health Survey and Incidence Study (NEMESIS). *Archives of General Psychiatry, 58,* 85–91.

Sanes, D. H., Reh, T. A. & Harris, W. A. (2005). *Development of the nervous system.* (2nd ed.), New York: Academic Press.

Sapolsky, R. M. (1996). Stress, glucocorticoids, and damage to the nervous system: The current state of confusion. *Stress, 1,* 1–19.

Sapolsky, R. M. (1997). *The trouble with testosterone.* New York: Touchstone.

Sapolsky, R. M. (1998). *Why zebras don't get ulcers.* New York: Freeman.

Sapolsky, R. M. (2000). Stress hormones: Good and bad. *Neurobiology of Disease, 7,* 540–542.

Sapolsky, R., Rivier, C., Yamamoto, G., Plotsky, P., & Vale, W. (1987). Interleukin-1 stimulates the secretion of hypothalamic corticotropin-releasing factor. *Science, 238,* 522–524.

Sasson, Y., Zohar, J., Chopra, M., Llustig, M., Iancu, I., & Hendler, T. (1997). Epidemiology of obsessive–compulsive disorder: A worldview. *Journal of Clinical Psychiatry, 58*(Suppl. 12), 7–10.

Satz, P., & Green, M. F. (1999). Atypical handedness in schizophrenia: Some methodological and theoretical issues. *Schizophrenia Bulletin, 25,* 533–542.

Saxby, E., & Peniston, E. G. (1995). Alpha–theta brainwave neurofeedback training: An effective treatment for male and female alcoholics with depressive symptoms. *Journal of Clinical Psychology, 51,* 685–693.

Scarone, S., Colombo, C., Livian, S., Abbruzzese, M., Ronchi, P., Locatelli, M., et al. (1992). Increased right caudate nucleus size in obsessive–compulsive disorder: Detection with magnetic resonance imaging. *Psychiatry Research, 45,* 115–121.

Schacter, D. L. (1996). *Searching for memory: The brain, the mind, and the past.* New York: Basic Books.

Schacter, D. L. (Ed.). (1997). *Memory distortion: How minds, brains, and societies construct the past.* Cambridge, MA: Harvard University Press.

Schedlowski, M., & Tewes, U. (Eds.). (1999). *Psychoneuroimmunology: An interdisciplinary introduction.* New York: Kluwer Academic/Plenum.

Schildkraut, J. J. (1965). The catecholamine hypothesis of affective disorders: A review of supporting evidence. *American Journal of Psychiatry, 122,* 509–522.

Schiller, D., Monfils, M. H., Raio, C. M., Johnson, D. C., Ledoux, J. E., et al. (2010). Preventing the return of fear in humans using reconsolidation update mechanisms. *Nature, 463,* 49–53.

Schlosser, E. (2002). *Fast food nation.* New York: HarperCollins.

Schoenbach, V. J., Kaplan, B. H., Friedman, J., & Kleinbaum, D. G. (1986). Social ties and mortality in Evans County, GA. *American Journal of Epidemiology, 123,* 577–591.

Scholz, G. H., Englaro, P., Thiele, I., Scholz, M., Klusman, T., Kellner, K., et al. (1996). Dissociation of serum leptin concentration and body fat content during long term dietary intervention in obese individuals. *Hormones and Metabolism Research, 28,* 718–723.

Schonknecht, P., Pantel, J., Klinga, K., Jensen, M., Hartmann, T., Salbach, B., et al. (2001). Reduced cerebrospinal fluid estradiol levels are associated with increased beta-amyloid levels in female patients with Alzheimer's disease. *Neuroscience Letters, 307,* 122–124.

Schouten, W. G. P., & Wiegant, V. M. (1997). Individual responses to acute and chronic stress in pigs. *Acta Physiologica Scandinavica, 640*(Suppl.), 188–191.

Schulkin, J. (2003). *Rethinking homeostasis: Allostatic regulation in physiology and pathophysiology.* Cambridge, MA: MIT Press.

Schulteis, G. (2000). Abolition of conditioned opiate withdrawal. *Nature, 405,* 1013–1014.

Schultz, D. P., & Schultz, S. E. (2000). *A history of modern psychology* (7th ed.). New York: Harcourt College Publishing.

Schumacher, M., Guennoun, R., Stein, D. G., & De Nicola, A. F. (2007). Progesterone: Therapeutic opportunities for neuroprotection and myelin repair. *Pharmacology & Therapeutics, 116,* 77–106.

Schwartz, J. M., & Begley, S. (2002). *The mind and the brain: Neuroplasticity and the power of mental force.* New York: HarperCollins.

Schwartz, J. M., & Beyette, B. (1996). *Brain lock: Free yourself from obsessive–compulsive behavior.* New York: HarperCollins.

Schwartz, J. M., Stoessel, P. W., Baxter, L. R., Martin, K. M., & Phelps, M. E. (1996). Systematic changes in cerebral glucose metabolic rate after successful behavior modification treatment of obsessive-compulsive disorder. *Archives of General Psychiatry, 53,* 109–111.

Schwartz, R., Gunzelmann, T., Hinz, A., & Brahler, E. (2001). Anxiety and depression in the general population over 60 years old. *Deutsche Medizinische Wochenschrift, 126,* 611–615.

Schwartz, S. (1964). Effect of neonatal cortical lesions and early environmental factors on adult rat behavior. *Journal of Comparative and Physiological Psychology, 57,* 72–77.

Schwarz, A. (2009, September 29). Dementia risk seen in players in N.F.L. study. *New York Times,* Retrieved November 6, 2009, from http://www.nytimes.com/2009/09/30/sports/football/30dementia.html

Schwarzschild, M. A., Chen, J. F., & Ascerio, A. (2002). Caffeinated clues and the promise of adenosine A (2A) antagonists in PD. *Neurology, 58,* 1154–1160.

Seeman, T. E., Singer, B., Wilkinson, C. W., & McEwen, B. S. (2001). Gender differences in age-related changes in HPA axis activity. *Psychoneuroendocrinology, 26*, 225–240.

Segal, M. (2005). Dendritic spines and long-term plasticity. *Nature Reviews Neuroscience, 6*, 277–284.

Segerstrom, S. C., Taylor, S. W., Kemeny, M., & Fahey, J. L. (1998). Optimism is associated with mood, coping, and immune change in response to stress. *Journal of Personality and Social Psychology, 74*, 1646–1655.

Seksel, K., & Lindeman, M. J. (1998). Use of clomipramine in the treatment of anxiety-related and obsessive–compulsive disorders in cats. *Australian Veterinarian Journal, 76*, 317–321.

Selemon, L. D., Rajkowska, G., & Goldman-Rakic, P. S. (1995). Abnormally high neuronal density in the schizophrenic cortex. A morphometric analysis of prefrontal area 9 and occipital area 17. *Archives of General Psychiatry, 52*(10), 805–820.

Seligman, M. E. P. (1990). *Learned optimism.* New York: Pocket Books.

Seligman, M. E. P., & Beagley, G. (1975). Learned helplessness in the rat. *Journal of Comparative and Physiological Psychology, 88*, 5166–5170.

Seligman, M. E. P., Schulman, P., & DeRubeis, R. J. (1999). The prevention of depression and anxiety. *Prevention and Treatment, 2*, 1–22.

Selye, H. (1936). A syndrome produced by diverse nocuous agents. *Nature, 138*, 32.

Selye, H. (1964). *From dream to discovery.* New York: McGraw-Hill.

Selye, H. (1976). *The stress of life.* New York: McGraw-Hill.

Serdula, M. K., Collins, M. E., Williamson, D. F., Anda, R. F., Pamuk, E. R., & Byers, T. E. (1993). Weight control practices of U.S. adolescents and adults. *Annals of International Medicine, 119*, 667–671.

Seroussi, K. (2002). *Unraveling the mystery of autism and pervasive developmental disorder.* New York: Broadway Books.

Shapiro, F. (1989). Eye movement desensitization: A new treatment for post-traumatic stress disorder. *Journal of Behavior Therapy and Experimental Psychiatry, 20*, 211–217.

Shavit, Y. (1991). Stress-induced immune modulation in animals: Opiates and endogenous opioid peptides. In R. Ader, D. L. Felten, & N. Cohen (Eds.), *Psychoneuroimmunology* (2nd ed.). New York: Academic Press.

Shaw, S. E., Morris, D. M., Usatte, G., McKay, S., Meythaler, J. M., & Taub, E. (2005). Constraint-induced movement therapy for recovery of upper-limb function following traumatic brain injury. *Journal of Rehabilitation Research and Development, 42*, 769–778.

Sheline, Y. I. (2000). 3D MRI studies of neuranatomic changes in unipolar major depression: The role of stress and medical comorbidity. *Biological Psychiatry, 48*, 791–800.

Sheline, Y. I., Wang, P., Gado, M., Csernansky, J., & Vannier, M. (1996). Hippocampal atrophy in recurrent major depression. *Proceedings of the National Academy of Sciences, USA, 93*, 3908–3913.

Shelton, R. C. (2009). St. John's wort (Hypericum perforatum) in major depression. *Journal of Clincial Psychiatry, 70*, 23–27.

Shepherd, J., Stein, K., & Milne, R. (2000). Eye movement desensitization and reprocessing in the treatment of post-traumatic stress disorder: A review of an emerging therapy. *Psychological Medicine, 30*, 863–871.

Sher, L., Matthews, J. R., Turner, E. H., Postolache, T. T., Katz, K. S., & Rosenthal, N. E. (2001). Early response to light therapy partially predicts long-term antidepressant effects in patients with seasonal affective disorder. *Journal of Psychiatry and Neuroscience, 26*(4), 336–338.

Shim, G., Jung, W. H., Choi, J. S., Jung, M. H., Jang, J. H., Park, J. Y., et al. (2009). Reduced cortical folding of the anterior cingulated cortex in obsessive–compulsive disorder. *Journal of Psychiatry and Neuroscience, 34*, 443–449.

Shorter, E. (1997). *A history of psychiatry.* New York: Wiley.

Shytle, R. D., Silver, A. A., & Sanberg, P. R. (2000). Comorbid bipolar disorder in Tourette's syndrome responds to the nicotinic receptor antagonist mecamylamine (Inversine). *Biological Psychiatry, 15*, 1028–1031.

Silbersweig, D. A., Stern, E., Frith, C., Cahill, C., Holmes, A., Grootoonk, S., et al. (1995). A functional neuroanatomy of hallucinations in schizophrenia. *Nature, 378*, 176–179.

Silva, I., Mor, G., & Naftolin, F. (2001). Estrogen and the aging brain. *Maturitas, 38*, 95–100.

Silver, A. A., Shytle, R. D., Philipp, M. K., & Sanberg, P. R. (1996). Case study: Long-term potentiation of neuroleptics with transdermal nicotine in Tourette's syndrome. *Journal of the American Academy of Child and Adolescent Psychiatry, 35*, 1631–1636.

Silver, A. A., Shytle, R. D., Sheehan, K. H., Sheehan, D. V., Ramos, A., & Sanberg, P. (2001). Multicenter, double-blind, placebo-controlled study of mecamylamine monotherapy for Tourette's disorder. *Journal of the American Academy of Child and Adolescent Psychiatry, 40*, 1103–1110.

Silver, J. M., Arciniegas, D. B., & Yudofsky, S. C. (2005). Psychopharmacology. In J. M. Silver, T. W. McAllister, & S. C. Yudofsky (Eds.), *Textbook of traumatic brain injury.* Washington, DC: American Psychiatric Publishing.

Silverstein, B., Peterson, B., & Perdue, L. (1986). Some correlates of the thin standard of bodily attractiveness for women. *International Journal of Eating Disorders, 5,* 895–905.

Simon, H. (1991). Exercise and human immune function. In R. Ader, D. L. Felten, & N. Cohen (Eds.), *Psychoneuroimmunology* (2nd ed.). New York: Academic Press.

Singer, H. S., Morris, C., & Grados, M. (2009). Glutamatergic modulatory therapy for Tourette syndrome. *Medical Hypotheses,* doi: 10.1016/j.mehy.2009.11.028.

Singer, H. S., & Walkup, J. T. (1991). Tourette syndrome and other tic disorders: Diagnosis, pathophysiology, and treatment. *Medicine, 70*(1), 15–32.

Singh, R., Bhalla, A., Lehl, S. S., & Sachdev, A. (2001). Video game epilepsy. *Epilepsia, 49,* 411–412.

Sinha, M. K., Caro, J. F. (1998). Clinical aspects of leptin. *Vitamins & Hormones, 54,* 1–30.

Sjogren, B., Widstrom, A. M., Edman, G., & Uvnas-Moberg, K. (2000). Changes in personality pattern during the first pregnancy and lactation. *Journal of Psychosomatic Obstetrics and Gynecology, 21,* 31–38.

Skinner, B. F. (1963). Behaviorism at fifty. *Science, 140,* 951–958.

Sloman, L., & Gilbert, P. (2000). *Subordination and defeat: An evolutionary approach to mood disorders and their therapy.* Mahwah, NJ: Erlbaum.

Smith, T. E., McGreer-Whitworth, B., & French, J. A. (1998). Close proximity of the heterosexual partner reduces the physiological and behavioral consequences of novel-cage housing in black tufted-ear marmosets (*Callithrix kuhli*). *Hormones and Behavior, 34*(3), 211–222.

Snowden, D. (2001). *Aging with grace.* New York: Bantam Books.

Soldatos, C. R., & Bergiannaki, J. D. (1999). Sleep in depression and the effects of antidepressants on sleep. In U. Halbreich & S. A. Montgomery (Eds.), *Pharmacotherapy for mood, anxiety, and cognitive disorders* (pp. 255–272). Washington, DC: American Psychiatric Press.

Solinas, M., Ferre, S., You, Z. B., Karcz-Kubicha, M., Popoli, P., & Goldberg, S. R. (2002). Caffeine induces dopamine and glutamate release in the shell of the nucleus accumbens. *Journal of Neuroscience, 22,* 6321–6324.

Solomon, A. (1994). *A stone boat.* Winchester, MA: Faber & Faber.

Solomon, A. (2001). *The noonday demon: An atlas of depression.* New York: Scribner's.

Sompayrac, L. (1999). *How the immune system works.* Malden, MA: Blackwell Science.

Song, C., & Leonard, B. E. (2000). *Fundamentals of psychoneuroimmunology.* New York: Wiley.

Sosin, D. M., Sniezek, J. E., & Thurman, D. J. (1996). Incidence of mild and moderate brain injury in the United States, 1991. *Brain Injury, 10,* 47–54.

Spiegel, D., Bloom, J., Kraemer, H., & Gottheil, E. (1989). Effect of psychosocial treatment on survival of patients with metastatic breast cancer. *Lancet, 2,* 888–891.

Spitz, R. A. (1946). Anaclitic depression. *Psychoanalytic Study of the Child, 2,* 313–347.

Spurlock, M. (Writer/Director). (2004). *Supersize Me* [Motion picture]. United States: Samuel Goldwyn Films.

Stafstrom, C. E., & Bough, K. J. (2003). The ketogenic diet for the treatment of epilepsy: A challenge for nutritional neuroscientists. *Nutritional Neuroscience, 6,* 67–79.

Stahl, S. M. (2000). Blue genes and the monoamine hypothesis of depression. *Journal of Clinical Psychiatry, 61,* 77–78.

Staley, J. K., & Mash, D. C. (1996). Adaptive increase in D_3 dopamine receptors in the brain reward circuits of human cocaine fatalities. *Journal of Neuroscience, 16,* 6100–6106.

Stanovich, K. E. (Ed.). (1998). *How to think straight about psychology* (5th ed.). New York: Addison-Wesley Longman.

Stein, D. G., Brailowsky, S., & Will, B. (1995). *Brain repair.* New York: Oxford University Press.

Stellar, E. (1954). The physiology of motivation. *Psychological Review, 61,* 5.

Sternberg, E. M. (2000). *The balance within: The science connecting health and emotions.* New York: Freeman.

Sternberg, E. M., & Gold, P. W. (1997). The mind–body interaction in disease. *Scientific American, 7*(1), 8–15.

Stewart, J. (1999). Pathways to relapse: The neurobiology of drug and stress-induced relapse to drug-taking. *Journal of Psychiatry and Neuroscience, 25,* 125–136.

Stice, E. (2002). The neglect of obesity. *American Psychological Association Monitor, 33,* 33.

Stoll, A. L., Renshaw, P. F., Yurgelun-Todd, D. A., & Cohen, B. M. (2000). Neuroimaging in bipolar disorder: What have we learned? *Biological Psychiatry, 48,* 505–517.

Strakowski, S. M., DelBello, M. P., Adler, C., Cecil, K. M., & Sax, K. W. (2000). Neuroimaging in bipolar disorder. *Bipolar Disorders, 2*, 148–164.

Straub, R. (2002). *Health psychology.* New York: Worth.

Strawbridge, W. J., Cohen, R. D., Shema, S. J., & Kaplan, G. A. (1997). Frequent attendance at religious services and mortality over 28 years. *American Journal of Public Health, 87*, 956–961.

Strober, M. (1980). Personality and symptomatological features in young, nonchronic anorexia nervosa patients. *Journal of Psychosomatic Research, 24*, 353–359.

Stuart, G., Spruston, N., & Hausser, M. (Eds.). (1999). *Dendrites.* New York: Oxford University Press.

Stunkard, A. J., & McLaren-Hume, M. (1959). The results of treatment of obesity: A review of the literature and report of a series. *Archives of Internal Medicine, 103*, 79–85.

Substance Abuse and Mental Health Services Administration, Office of Applied Statistics. (2008). *Results from the 2007 National Survey on Drug Use and Health: National Findings* (NSDUH Series H-34, DHHS Publication No. SMA 08-4343). Rockville, MD.

Suddath, R. L., Christison, G. W., Torrey, E. F., Casanova, M. F., & Weinberger, D. R. (1990). Anatomical abnormalities in the brains of monozygotic twins discordant for schizophrenia. *New England Journal of Medicine, 322*, 789–794.

Sugerman, H. J. (2001). Bariatric surgery for severe obesity. *Journal of the Associative Academy of Minor Physics, 12*, 129–136.

Suomi, S. (1983). Models of depression in primates. *Psychological Medicine, 13*, 465–468.

Suomi, S. (1997). Early determinants of behavior: Evidence from primate studies. *British Medical Bulletin, 53*, 170–184.

Sutton, M. A., Karanian, D. A., & Self, D. W. (2000). Factors that determine a propensity for cocaine-seeking behavior during abstinence in rats. *Neuropsychopharmacology, 22*, 625–641.

Suzuki, K., Awata, S., & Matsuoka, H. (2003). Short-term effect of ECT in middle-aged and elderly patients with intractable catatonic schizophrenia. *Journal of ECT, 19*, 73–80.

Swedo, S. E., Pietrini, P., Leonard, H. L., Schapiro, M. B., Rettew, D. C., Goldberger, E. L., et al. (1992). Cerebral glucose metabolism in childhood-onset obsessive-compulsive disorder. Revisualization during pharmacotherapy. *Archives of General Psychiatry, 49*, 690–694.

Swonguer, L., Lambert, K. G., & Klein, S. L. (2003, June). *Lipopolysaccharide-activated immune function influences affiliative behaviors and mating preferences in* Peromyscus californicus. Poster presented at the annual meeting of the Society for Behavioral Neuroendocrinology, University of Cincinnati, Cincinnati, OH.

Szesko, P. R., Christian, C., MacMaster, F., Lencz, T., Mirza, Y., Taormina, S. P., et al. (2008). Gray matter structural alterations in psychotropic drug-naive pediatric obsessive–compulsive disorder: An optimized voxel-based morphometry study. *American Journal of Psychiatry, 165*, 1299–1307.

Talairach, J., Bancaud, J., Geier, S., Bordas-Ferrer, M., Bonis, A., Szikla, G., et al. (1973). The cingulate gyrus and human behavior. *Electroencephalographic Clinical Neurophysiology, 34*, 45–52.

Tamminga, C. A. (1999). Principles of the pharmacotherapy of schizophrenia. In D. S. Charney, E. J. Nestler, & B. S. Bunney (Eds.), *Neurobiology of mental illness* (pp. 272–285). New York: Oxford University Press.

Tanskanen, A., & Hibbeln, J. R. (2001). Fish consumption, depression, and suicidality in a general population. *Archives of General Psychiatry, 58*, 512–513.

Taverni, J. P., Seliger, G., & Lichtman, S. W. (1998). Donepezil mediated memory improvement in traumatic brain injury during post actue rehabilitation. *Brain Injury, 12*, 77–80.

Taylor, K. M., Davidson, K., Mark, G. P., Rada, P., & Hoebel, B. G. (1992). Conditioned taste aversion induced by increased acetylcholine in the nucleus accumbens. *Society for Neuroscience Abstracts, 18*, 1066.

Taylor, S., Klein, L., Lewis, B., Gruenwald, T., Gurung, R., & Updegraff, J. (2000). Biobehavioral responses to stress in females: Tend-and-befriend, not fight-or-flight. *Psychological Review, 107*, 411–429.

Teff, K. L., Mattes, R. D., & Engelman, K. (1991). Cephalic phase insulin release in normal weight males: Verification and reliability. *American Journal of Physiology Endocrinology and Metabolism, 261*, E430–E436.

Temple, E., Deutsch, G., Poldrack, R., Miller, S., Tallal, P., Merzenich, M., et al. (2003). Neural deficits in children with dyslexia ameliorated by behavioral remediation: Evidence from functional MRI. *Proceedings of the National Academy of Sciences, USA, 100*, 2860–2865.

Tetrud, J. W. (1991). Preclinical Parkinson's disease: Detection of motor and nonmotor manifestations. *Neurology, 41*, 69S–71S.

Thapar, A. K., & Thapar, A. (2003). Attention-deficit hyperactivity disorder. *British Journal of General Practice, 53*, 225–30.

Thompson, P. M., Vidal, C., Giedd, J. N., Gochman, P., Blumenthal, J., Nicolson, R., et al. (2001). Mapping adolescent brain change reveals dynamic wave of accelerated gray matter loss in very early-onset schizophrenia. *Proceedings of the National Academy of Sciences, USA, 98,* 11650–11655.

Thompson, R. A. (2000). *The brain: A neuroscience primer.* New York: Worth.

Thurman, D. J., Alverson, C., Dunn, K. A., Guerrero, J., & Sniezek, J. E. (1999). Traumatic brain injury in the United States: A public health perspective. *Journal of Head Trauma Rehabilitation, 14,* 602–615.

Tiller, J. W. (1993). Clinical overview on moclobemide. *Progress in Neuro-Psychopharmacology and Biological Psychiatry, 17*(5), 703–712.

Tomizawa, K., Iga, N., Lu, Y.-F., Moriwaki, A., Matsushita, M., Li, S.-T., et al. (2003). Oxytocin improves long-lasting spatial memory during motherhood through MAP kinase cascade. *Nature Neuroscience, 6,* 384–390.

Torrey, E. F., Bowler, A. E., Taylor, E. H., & Gottesman, I. I. (1994). *Schizophrenia and manic-depressive disorder.* New York: Basic Books.

Toth, E., Gersner, R., Wilf-Yarkoni, A., Raizel, H., Dar, D. E., Richter-Levin, G., et al. (2008). Age-dependent effects of chronic stress on brain plasticity and depressive behavior. *Journal of Neurochemistry, 107,* 522–532.

Tramo, M. J. (2001). Music of the hemispheres. *Science, 291,* 54–56.

Trivedi, M. H. (1996). Functional neuroanatomy of obsessive–compulsive disorder. *Journal of Clinical Psychiatry, 57,* 26–36.

Tsai, G., Yang, P., Chung, L. C., Lange, N., & Coyle, J. T. (1998). D-Serine added to antipsychotics for the treatment of schizophrenia. *Biological Psychiatry, 44*(1), 1081–1089.

Tsien, J. Z. (2000, April). Building a brainier mouse. *Scientific American, 282,* 62–68.

Turbott, J. (1997). The meaning and function of ritual in psychiatric disorder, religion and everyday behavior. *Australian and New Zealand Journal of Psychiatry, 31*(6), 835–843.

Underwood, M. D., Khaibulina, A. A., Ellis, S. P., Moran, A., Rice, P. M., Mann, J. J., et al. (1999). Morphometry of the dorsal raphe nucleus serotonergic neurons in suicide victims. *Biological Psychiatry, 46,* 473–483.

Ungless, M. A., Whistler, J. L., Malenka, R. C., & Bonci, A. (2001). Single cocaine exposure in vivo induces long-term potentiation in dopamine neurons. *Nature, 411,* 583–587.

Uno, H., Tarrara, R., Else, J. G., Suleman, M. A., & Sapolsky, R. M. (1989). Hippocampal damage associated with prolonged and fatal stress in primates. *Journal of Neuroscience, 9,* 1705–1711.

U.S. Food and Drug Administration. (2001). *New device approval: LAP-BAND® adjustable gastric banding (LAGB®) system, June 6, 2001.* Retrieved June 15, 2004, from http://www.fda.gov/cdrh/mda/docs/p000008.html

Uvnas-Moberg, K. (1998). Antistress pattern induced by oxytocin. *News of the Physiological Sciences, 13,* 22–26.

Vakili, K., Srinivasan, S. P., Lafer, B., Fava, M., Renshaw, P. F., Bonello-Cintron, C.M., et al. (2000). Hippocampal volume in primary unipolar major depression: A magnetic resonance imaging study. *Biological Psychiatry, 47,* 1087–1090.

Valenstein, E. S. (1998). *Blaming the brain: The truth about drugs and mental health.* New York: Free Press.

Valentine, G. (2002). MDMA and Ecstasy. *Psychiatric Times, 19*(2). http://www.psychiatrictimes.com/depression/content/article/10168/47391

Van Bockstaele, E. J., Bajic, D., Proudfit, H., & Valentino, R. J. (2001). Topographic architecture of stress-related pathways targeting the noradrenergic locus coeruleus. *Physiology and Behavior, 73*(3), 273–283.

Van den Heuvel, O. A., Remijnse, P. L., Mataix-Cols, D., Vrenken, H., Groenewegen, H. J., Uylings, H. B. M., et al. (2009). The major symptom dimensions of obsessive–compulsive disorder are mediated by partially distinct neural systems. *Brain, 132,* 853–868.

Vance, A., Silk, T. J., Casey, M., Rinehart, N. J., Bradshaw, J. L., Bellgrove, M.A., et al. (2007). Right parietal dysfunction in children with attention deficit hyperactivity disorder, combined type: a functional MRI study. *Molecular Psychiatry, 12,* 826–83.

Vandereycken, W., & Pierloot, R. (1982). Pimozide combined with behavior therapy in the short-term treatment of anorexia nervosa. *Acta Psychiatrica et Neurologica Scandinavica, 66,* 445–450.

van Geel, B. M., Assies, J., Haverkort, E. B., Koelman, J. H., Berbeeten, B., Wanders, R. J., et al. (1999). Progression of abnormalities in adrenomyeloneuropathy and neurologically asymptomatic X-linked adrenoleukodystrophy despite treatment with Lorenzo's oil. *Journal of Neurology, Neurosurgery, and Psychiatry, 67,* 290–299.

van Voorhees, B. W., Paunesku, D., Gollan, J., Kuwabara, S., Reinecke, M., & Basu, A. (2008). Predicting future risk of depressive episode in adolescents: The Chicago adolescent depression risk assessment (CADRA). *Annals of Family Medicine, 6,* 503–511.

Verkerk, A. J., Pieretti, M., Sutcliffe, J. S., Fu, Y. H., Kuhl, D. P., Pizzuti, A., et al. (1991). Identification of a gene (FMR-1) containing a CGG repeat coincident with a breakpoint cluster region exhibiting length variation in fragile X syndrome. *Cell, 65*, 905–14.

Vogel, S. (1992). *Vital circuits*. New York: Oxford University Press.

Volkow, N. D., & Fowler, J. S. (2000). Addiction, a disease of compulsion and drive: Involvement of the orbitofrontal cortex. *Cerebral Cortex, 10*, 318–325.

Volkow, N. D., Fowler, J. S., & Wang, G. J. (1999). Imaging studies on the role of dopamine in cocaine reinforcement and addiction in humans. *Journal of Psychopharmacology, 13*(4), 337–345.

Volkow, N. D., Wang, G. J., Fowler, J. S., Logan, J., Gatley, S. J., Gifford, A., et al. (1999). Prediction of reinforcing responses to psychostimulants in humans by brain dopamine D_2 receptor levels. *American Journal of Psychiatry, 156*, 1440–1443.

Volkow, N. D., Wang, G. J., Newcorn, J., Telang, F., Solanto, M. V., Fowler, J. S. (2007). Depressed dopamine activity in caudate and preliminary evidence of limbic involvement in adults with attention-deficit/hyperactivity disorder. *Archives of Genral Psychiatry, 64*, 932–940.

Volmar, K. E., & Hutchins, G. M. (2001). Aortic and mitral fenfluramine-phentermine valvulopathy in 64 patients treated with anorectic agents. *Archives of Pathology and Laboratory Medicine, 125*, 1555–1561.

Vollmayr, B., Faust, H., Lewicka, S., & Henn, F. A. (2001). Brain-derived-neurotrophic-factor (BDNF) stress response in rats bred for learned helplessness. *Molecular Psychiatry, 6*, 471–474.

Wagner, A. K., Kline, A. E., Sokoloski, J., Zafonte, R. D., Capulong, E., & Dixon, C. E. (2002). Intervention with environmental enrichment after experimental brain trauma enhances cognitive recovery in male but not female rats. *Neuroscience Letters, 334*, 165–168.

Walker, E. F., & Diforio, D. (1997). Schizophrenia: A neural diathesis-stress mode. *Psychological Review, 4*, 1–19.

Walker, E. F., Grimes, K., Davis, D., & Smith, A. (1993). Childhood precursors of schizophrenia: Facial expressions of emotion. *American Journal of Psychiatry, 150*, 1654–1660.

Walker, E. F., Lewine, R. R. J., & Neumann, C. (1996). Childhood behavioral characteristics and adult brain morphology in schizophrenia. *Schizophrenia Research, 22*, 93–101.

Walker, E. F., Logan, C. B., & Walder, D. (1999). Indicators of neurodevelopmental abnormality in schizotypal personality disorder. *Psychiatric Annals, 29*, 132–136.

Walker, E. F., Savoie, T., & Davis, D. (1994). Neuromotor precursors of schizophrenia. *Schizophrenia Bulletin, 20*, 453–480.

Walkup, J. T., Leckman, J. F., Price, R. A., Hardin, M., Ort, S. I., & Cohen, D. J. (1988). The relationship between obsessive–compulsive disorder and Tourette's disorder and Tourette's syndrome: A twin study. *Psychopharmacological Bulletin, 24*, 375–379.

Walsh, T., McClellan, J. M., McCarthy, S. E., Addington, A. M., Pierce, S. B., Cooper, G. M., et al. (2008). Rare structural variants disrupt multiple genes in neurodevelopmental pathways in schizophrenia. *Science, 320*, 539–543.

Walters, E. E., & Kendler, K. S. (1995). Anorexia nervosa and anorexic-like syndromes in a population-based twin sample. *American Journal of Psychiatry, 52*, 34–38.

Wang, L., Ho, C.-L., Sun, D., Liem, R. K. H., & Brown, A. (2000). Rapid movement of axonal neurofilaments interrupted by prolonged pauses. *Nature Cell Biology, 2*, 137–141.

Warren, J., & Marshall, B. (1983). Unidentified curved bacilli on gastric epithelium in active chronic gastritis. *Lancet, 1*, 1273.

Wartella, J., Amory, E., Lomas, L. M., Macbeth, A., McNamara, I., Stevens, L., et al. (2003). Single or multiple reproductive experiences attenuate neurobehavioral stress and fear responses in the female rat. *Physiology and Behavior, 79*(3), 373–381.

Watanabe, Y., Gould, E., & McEwen, B. S. (1992). Stress induces atrophy of apical dendrites of hippocampal CA3 pyramidal neurons. *Brain Research, 588*, 341–345.

Watanabe, Y., Weiland, N. G., & McEwen, B. S. (1995). Effects of adrenal steroid manipulations and repeated restraint stress on dynorphin mRNA levels and excitatory amino acid receptor binding in hippocampus. *Brain Research, 680*, 217–225.

Watson, J. B. (1913). Psychology as the behaviorist views it. *Psychological Review, 20*, 158–177.

Watkins, L. R., Wiertelak, E. P., & Maier, S. F. (1993). The amygdale is necessary for the expression of conditioned but not unconditioned analgesia. *Behavioral Neuroscience, 107*, 402–405.

Wecker, L. (1986). Neurochemical effects of choline supplementation. *Canadian Journal of Physiological Pharmacology, 64*, 329–333.

Wedekind, C., & Penn, D. (2000). MHC genes, body odors, and odor preferences. *Nephrology Dialysis Transplantation, 15*, 1269–1271.

Weiss, D. W., Hirt, H., Tarcic, N., Berzon, Y., Ben-Zur, H., Breznitz, S., et al. (1996). Studies in psychoneuroimmunology: Psychological, immunological, and neuroendocrinological parameters in Israeli civilians during and after a period of Scud missile attacks. *Behavioral Medicine, 22*, 5–14.

Weiss, E. L., Longhurst, J. G., & Mazure, C. M. (1999). Childhood sexual abuse as a risk factor for depression in women: Psychosocial and neurobiological correlates. *American Journal of Psychiatry, 156*(6), 816–828.

Weiss, J. M. (1972). Influence of psychological variables on stress-induced pathology. In R. Porter & J. Knight (Eds.), *Physiology, emotion and psychosomatic illness.* Amsterdam: Associated Scientific Publishers.

Weiss, J. M. (1977). Psychological and behavioral influences on gastrointestinal lesions in animal models. In J. D. Maser & E. P. Seligman (Eds.), *Psychopathology: Experimental models.* San Francisco: Freeman.

Weiss, J. M., & Kilts, C. D. (1995). Animal models of depression and schizophrenia. In A. T. Schatzberg & C. B. Nemeroff (Eds.), *Textbook of psychopharmacology* (pp. 81–123). Washington, DC: American Psychiatric Press.

Weissman, I. L., & Cooper, M. D. (1993). How the immune system develops. In *Life, death, and the immune system: A* Scientific American *special issue* (pp. 14–25). New York: Freeman.

Weniger, G., Lange, C., Sachsse, U., & Irle, E. (2008). Amygdala and hippocampal volumes and cognition in adult survivors of childhood abuse with dissociative disorders. *Acta Psychiatrica Scandinavica, 118,* 281–290.

Werman, R., Davidoff, R. A., & Aprison, M. H. (1968). Inhibitors of glycine on spinal neurons in the cat. *Journal of Neurophysiology, 31,* 81–95.

Westermann, J., & Exton, M. S. (1999). Functional anatomy of the immune system. In M. Schedlowski & U. Tewes (Eds.), *Psychoneuroimmunology: An interdisciplinary approach.* New York: Kluwer Academic/Plenum.

Whale, R., Clifford, E. M., Bhagwagar, Z., & Cowan, P. J. (2001). Decreased sensitivity of 5-HT 1D receptors in melancholic depression. *British Journal of Psychiatry, 178,* 454–457.

Whelan, F. J., Walker, M. S., & Schultz, S. K. (2000). Donepezil in the treatment of cognitive dysfunction associated with traumatic brain injury. *Annals of Clinical Psychiatry, 42,* 120–122.

Whitcome, K., Shapiro, L. J., & Lieberman, D. E. (2007). Fetal load and the evolution of lumbar lordosis in bipedal hominins. *Nature, 405,* 1075–1078.

Whitten, W. (2000). Pheromones and regulation of ovulation. *Nature, 392,* 177–179.

Whitty, C. W. M., Duffield, J. E., & Tow, P. M. (1952). Anterior cingulectomy in the treatment of mental disease. *Lancet, 1,* 475–481.

Whyte, J., Hart, T., Schuster, K., Fleming, M., Polansky, M., & Coslett, M. B. (1997). Effects of methylphenidate on attentional function after traumatic brain injury: A randomized, placebo-controlled trial. *American Journal of Physical Medicine and Medical Rehabilitation, 76,* 440–450.

Wickelgren, I. (1998). Teaching the brain to take drugs. *Science, 280,* 2045–2047.

Widmaier, E. P. (1990). Glucose homeostasis and hypothalamic–pituitary–adrenocortical axis during development in rats. *American Journal of Physiology Endocrinology and Metabolism, 259,* E601–E613.

Wiertelak, E. P., Maier, S. F., & Watkins, L. R. (1992). Cholecystokinin antianalgesia: Safety cues abolish morphine analgesia. *Science, 256,* 830–833.

Wilens, T. E., Biederman, J., & Spencer, T. J. (2002). Attention deficit/hyperactivity disorder across the lifespan. *Annual Review of Medicine, 53,* 113–131.

Will, B., Galani, R., Kelche, C., & Rosenzweig, M. R. (2004). Recovery from brain injury in animals: Relative efficacy of environmental enrichment, physical exercise or formal training (1990–2002). *Progress in Neurobiology, 72,* 167–182.

Williams, G., Bing, C., Cai, X. J., Harrold, J. A., King, P. J., & Liu, X. H. (2001). The hypothalamus and the control of energy homeostasis: Different circuits, different purposes. *Physiology and Behavior, 74,* 683–701.

Willner, P., Muscat, R., & Papp, M. (1992). Chronic mild stress induced anhedonia: A realistic animal model of depression. *Neuroscience Biobehavior Review, 16,* 525–534.

Wilmut, I., Schnieke, A. E., McWhir, J., Kind, A. J., & Campbell, K. H. (1997). Viable offspring derived from fetal and adult mammalian cells. *Nature, 385,* 810–813 (erratum in *Nature, 386,* 200).

Wilsnack, R. W., Vogeltanz, N. D., Wilsnack, S. C., & Harris, T. R. (2000). Gender differences in alcohol consumption and adverse drinking consequences: Cross-cultural patterns. *Addiction, 95,* 251–265.

Wilson, M. A., & McNaughton, B. L. (1993). Dynamics of the hippocampal ensemble code for space. *Science, 261,* 1055–1058.

Wilson, M. A., & McNaughton, B. L. (1994). Reactivation of hippocampal ensemble memories during sleep. *Science, 265,* 676–679.

Winslow, J. T., Hastings, N., Carter, C. S., Harbaugh, C. R., & Insel, T. R. (1993). A role for central vasopressin in pair bonding in monogamous prairie voles. *Nature, 365,* 545–548.

Wise, R. A. (1982). Neuroleptics and operant behavior: The anhedonia hypothesis. *Behavioral Brain Science, 5,* 39–87.

Wise, R. A. (1999). Animal models of addiction. In D. S. Charney, E. J. Nestler, & B. S. Bunney (Eds.), *Neurobiology of mental illness*. New York: Oxford University Press.

Wise, R. A. (2000). Addiction becomes a brain disease. *Neuron, 26*, 27–33.

Woese, C. R. (2002). On the evolution of cells. *Proceedings of the National Academy of Sciences, USA, 99*, 8742–8747.

Wolf, O. T., Schommer, N. C., Hellhammer, D. H., McEwen, B. S., & Kirschbaum, C. (2001). The relationship between stress-induced cortisol levels and memory differs between men and women. *Psychoneuroendocrinology, 26*, 711–720.

Wolf, S. S., Jones, D. W., Knable, M. B., Gorey, J. G., Lee, K. S., Hyde, J. M., et al. (1996). Tourette syndrome: Prediction of phenotypic variation in monozygotic twins by caudate nucleus D_2 receptor binding. *Science, 273*, 1225–1227.

Woodruff, L. (2009, July 12). Can brains be saved? *Parade*. http://www.parade.com/health/2009/07/12-lee-woodruff-can-brains-be-saved.html

Woodruff, L., & Woodruff, R. (2007). *In an instant: A family's journey of love and healing*. New York: Random House.

Woods, S. C. (1991). The eating paradox: How we tolerate food. *Psychological Review, 98*, 488–505.

Woods, S. C., & Strubbe, J. H. (1994). The psychobiology of meals. *Psychonomic Bulletin and Review, 1*, 142–155.

Woolley, C. S., Gould, E., & McEwen, B. S. (1990). Exposure to excess glucocorticoids alters dendritic morphology of adult hippocampal pyramidal neurons. *Brain Research, 531*, 225–231.

World Health Organization. (2003). Retrieved August 2, 2010, from http://www.who.int/mental_health/management/schizophrenia/en/

Wright, T. J., & Huddart, H. (2002). The nature of the acetylcholine and 5-hydroxytryptamine receptors in buccal smooth muscle of the pest slug *Deroceras reticulatum*. *Journal of Comprehensive Physiology, 172*, 237–249.

Wroblewski, B. A., Guidos, A., Leary, J., & Joseph, A. B. (1992). Control of depression with fluoxetine and antiseizure medication in a brain injured patient. *American Journal of Psychiatry, 149*, 272–273.

Wu, C. W., & Kaas, J. H. (1999). Reorganization in primary motor cortex of primates with long-standing therapeutic amputations. *Journal of Neuroscience, 19*, 7679–7697.

Wu, C. W., & Kaas, J. H. (2002). The effects of long-standing limb loss on anatomical reorganization of the somatosensory afferents in the brainstem and spinal cord. *Somatosensory Motor Research, 19*, 153–163.

Wu, J. T., & Kral, J. G. (2004). Ghrelin: Integrative neuroendocrine peptide in health and disease. *Annals of Surgery, 239*(4), 464–474.

Wyles, J. S., Kunkel, J. G., & Wilson, A. C. (1983). Birds, behavior, and anatomical evolution. *Proceedings of the National Academy of Sciences, USA, 80*, 4394–4397.

Yamato, T., Yamasaki, S., Misumi, Y., Kino, M., Obata, T., & Aomine, M. (2002). Modulation of the stress response by coffee: An in vivo microdialysis study of hippocampal serotonin and dopamine levels in rat. *Neuroscience Letters, 332*, 87–90.

Yatham, L. N., Liddle, P. F., Dennie, J., Shiah, I. S., Adam, M. J., Lane, C. J., et al. (1999). Decrease in brain serotonin 2 receptor binding in patients with major depression following desipramine treatment: A positron emission tomography study with fluorine-18-labeled setoperone. *Archives of General Psychiatry, 56*, 705–711.

Yeragani, V. K., Srinivasan, K., Balon, R., Ramesh, C., & Berchou, R. (1994). Lactate sensitivity and cardiac cholinergic function in panic disorder. *American Journal of Psychiatry, 151*, 1226–1228.

Yonkers, K. A., Kando, J. C., Hamilton, J. A., & Halbreich, U. (2000). Gender differences in treatment of depression and anxiety. In U. Halbreich & S. A. Montgomery (Eds.), *Pharmacotherapy for mood, anxiety, and cognitive disorders* (pp. 59–72). Washington, DC: American Psychiatric Press.

Young, D., Lawlor, P., Leone, P., Dragunow, M., & During, M. (1999). Environmental enrichment inhibits spontaneous apoptosis, prevents seizures, and is neuroprotective. *Nature Medicine, 5*, 448–453.

Young, L. J. (2001). Oxytocin and vasopressin as candidate genes for psychiatric disorders: Lessons from animal models. *Neuropsychiatric Genetics, 105*, 53–54.

Yusim, A., Ajilore, O., Bliss, T., & Sapolsky, R. (2000). Glucocorticoids exacerbate insult-induced declines in metabolism in selectively vulnerable hippocampal cell fields. *Brain Research, 870*, 109–117.

Zachrisson, O. C. G., Balldin, J., Ekman, R., Naech, O., Rosengren, L., Agren, H., et al. (2000). No evident neuronal damage after electroconvulsive therapy. *Psychiatry Research, 96*, 157–165.

Zak, P. J., Stanton, A. A., & Ahmadi, S. (2007). Oxytocin increases generosity in humans. *PLoS ONE, 2*, e1128. doi: 10.1371/journal.pone.0001128.

Zald, D. H., & Kim, S. W. (1996a). Anatomy and function of the orbital frontal cortex: I. Anatomy, neurocircuitry, and obsessive–compulsive disorder. *Journal of Neuropsychiatry and Clinical Neurosciences, 8*, 125–138.

Zald, D. H., & Kim, S. W. (1996b). Anatomy and function of the orbital frontal cortex: II. Function and relevance to obsessive–compulsive disorder. *Journal of Neuropsychiatry and Clinical Neurosciences, 8,* 249–261.

Zec, R. F., & Travedi, M. A. (2002). The effects of estrogen replacement therapy on neuropsychological functioning in postmenopausal women with and without dementia: A critical and theoretical review. *Neuropsychology Review, 12,* 65–109.

Zelena, D. (2009). Yin-Yang neuropeptides in depression. *Frontiers in Neuroscience, 3,* 250–251.

Zhang, Q., Li, Y. & Tsien, R. W. (2009). The dynamic control of kiss-and-run and vesicular reuse probed with single nanoparticles. *Science, 323,* 1448–1453.

Zhang, X. F., Hu, X. T., & White, F. J. (1998). Whole cell plasticity in cocaine withdrawal: Reduced sodium currents in nucleus accumbens neurons. *Journal of Neuroscience, 18,* 488–498.

Zhou, J. N., Hofman, M. A., Gooren, L. J., & Swaab, D. F. (1995). A sex difference in the human brain and its relation to transsexuality. *Nature, 378,* 68–70.

Zigmond, M. J., Bloom, S. E., Landis, S. C., Roberts, J. L., Squire, L. R., & Woolley, R. S. (1999). *Fundamental neuroscience.* New York: Academic Press.

Zink, M., Englisch, S., & Meyer-Lindenberg, A. (2010). Polypharmacy in schizophrenia. *Current Opinion in Psychiatry, 23,* 103–111.

Zivin, J. A. (2000, April). Understanding clinical trials. *Scientific American, 282,* 69–75.

Zohar, J., Judge, R., & OCD Paroxetine Study Investigators. (1996). Paroxetine versus clomipramine in the treatment of obsessive–compulsive disorder. *British Journal of Psychiatry, 169,* 468–474.

Zoloft.com. (2003). *What is social anxiety disorder?* Accessed January 8, 2004, from http://www.zoloft.com/anxiety_types.aspx

Zoumakis, E., Rice, K. C., Gold, P. W., & Chrousos, G. P. (2006). Potential uses of corticotrophin-releasing hormone antagonists. *Annals of the New York Academy of Sciences, 1083,* 239–251.

Name Index

Subject Index